Fundamentals of Corporate Finance

Second Edition

Fundamentals of Corporate Finance

Second Edition

Richard A. Brealey
Bank of England and London Business School

Stewart C. Myers
Sloan School of Management
Massachusetts Institute of Technology

Alan J. Marcus
Wallace E. Carroll School of Management
Boston College

Boston   Burr Ridge, IL   Dubuque, IA   Madison, WI   New York   San Francisco   St. Louis
Bangkok   Bogotá   Caracas   Lisbon   London   Madrid
Mexico City   Milan   New Delhi   Seoul   Singapore   Sydney   Taipei   Toronto

Irwin/McGraw-Hill

A Division of The **McGraw·Hill** Companies

FUNDAMENTALS OF CORPORATE FINANCE

This book is printed on acid-free paper.

pbk 1 2 3 4 5 6 7 8 9 0 VNH/VNH 9 3 2 1 0 9 8
hc   1 2 3 4 5 6 7 8 9 0 VNH/VNH 9 3 2 1 0 9 8

ISBN 0-07-007486-0
ISBN 0-07-304009-6 (Wall Street Journal edition)

Vice president and editorial director: *Michael W. Junior*
Publisher: *Craig S. Beytien*
Associate sponsoring editor: *Shelley Kronzek*
Developmental editor: *Martin D. Quinn*
Senior marketing manager: *Katie Rose-Matthews*
Senior project manager: *Jean Lou Hess*
Production supervisor: *Melonie Salvati*
Cover designer: *Kiera Cunningham*
Interior design: *Ellen Pettengell*
Photo research coordinator: *Sharon Miller*
Compositor: *GTS Graphics, Inc.*
Typeface: *10.5/12 Times Roman*
Printer: *Von Hoffmann Press, Inc.*

Library of Congress Cataloging-in-Publication Data
Brealey, Richard A.
     Fundamentals of corporate finance/Richard A. Brealey, Stewart C. Myers,
Alan J. Marcus.—2nd ed.
     p. cm.
     ISBN 0-07-007486-0
     Includes index.
     1. Corporations—Finance. I. Myers, Stewart C. II. Marcus, Alan J.
III. Title.
HG4026.B6668   1998
658.15 dc—21   98-10507

INTERNATIONAL EDITION

http://www.mhhe.com

The Irwin/McGraw-Hill Series in Finance, Insurance, and Real Estate

Consulting Editor: Stephen A. Ross, Sterling Professor of Economics and Finance, Yale University

Financial Management

Benninga and Sarig
Corporate Finance: A Valuation Approach

Block and Hirt
Foundations of Financial Management
Eighth Edition

Brealey and Myers
Principles of Corporate Finance
Fifth Edition

Brealey, Myers and Marcus
Fundamentals of Corporate Finance
Second Edition

Brooks
PC FinGame: The Financial Management Decision Game Version 2.0–DOS and Windows

Bruner
Case Studies in Finance: Managing for Corporate Value Creation
Third Edition

Chew
The New Corporate Finance: Where Theory Meets Practice
Second Edition

Grinblatt and Titman
Financial Markets and Corporate Strategy

Helfert
Techniques of Financial Analysis: A Modern Approach
Ninth Edition

Higgins
Analysis for Financial Management
Fifth Edition

Hite
A Programmed Learning Guide to Finance

Kester, Fruhan, Piper and Ruback
Case Problems in Finance
Eleventh Edition

Nunnally and Plath
Cases in Finance
Second Edition

Parker and Beaver
Risk Management: Challenges and Solutions

Ross, Westerfield and Jaffe
Corporate Finance
Fifth Edition

Ross, Westerfield and Jordan
Essentials of Corporate Finance
Second Edition

Ross, Westerfield and Jordan
Fundamentals of Corporate Finance
Fourth Edition

Schall and Haley
Introduction to Financial Management
Sixth Edition

Smith
The Modern Theory of Corporate Finance
Second Edition

White
Financial Analysis with an Electronic Calculator
Third Edition

Investments

Ball and Kothari
Financial Statement Analysis

Bodie, Kane and Marcus
Essentials of Investments
Third Edition

Bodie, Kane and Marcus
Investments
Fourth Edition

Cohen, Zinbarg and Zeikel
Investment Analysis and Portfolio Management
Fifth Edition

Farrell
Portfolio Management: Theory and Applications
Second Edition

Hirt and Block
Fundamentals of Investment Management
Sixth Edition

Jarrow
Modelling Fixed Income Securities and Interest Rate Options

Morningstar, Inc. and Remaley
U.S. Equities OnFloppy Educational Version
Annual Edition

Shimko
The Innovative Investor
Version 2.0

Financial Institutions and Markets

Flannery and Flood
Flannery and Flood's ProBanker: A Financial Services Simulation

Johnson
Financial Institutions and Markets: A Global Perspective

Rose
Commercial Bank Management
Third Edition

Rose
Money and Capital Markets: Financial Institutions and Instruments in a Global Marketplace
Sixth Edition

Rose and Kolari
Financial Institutions: Understanding and Managing Financial Services
Fifth Edition

Santomero and Babbel
Financial Markets, Instruments, and Institutions

Saunders
Financial Institutions Management: A Modern Perspective
Second Edition

International Finance

Eun and Resnick
International Financial Management

Kester and Luehrman
Case Problems in International Finance
Second Edition

Levi
International Finance
Third Edition

Levich
International Financial Markets: Prices and Policies

Stonehill and Eiteman
Finance: An International Perspective

Real Estate

Berston
California Real Estate Principles
Seventh Edition

Brueggeman and Fisher
Real Estate Finance and Investments
Tenth Edition

Corgel, Smith and Ling
Real Estate Perspectives: An Introduction to Real Estate
Third Edition

Lusht
Real Estate Valuation: Principles and Applications

Sirmans
Real Estate Finance
Second Edition

Financial Planning and Insurance

Allen, Melone, Rosenbloom and VanDerhei
Pension Planning: Pension, Profit-Sharing, and Other Deferred Compensation Plans
Eighth Edition

Crawford
Life and Health Insurance Law
Eighth Edition (LOMA)

Harrington and Niehaus
Risk Management and Insurance

Hirsch
Casualty Claim Practice
Sixth Edition

Kapoor, Dlabay and Hughes
Personal Finance
Fifth Edition

Kellison
Theory of Interest
Second Edition

Lang
Strategy for Personal Finance
Fifth Edition

Skipper
International Risk and Insurance: An Environmental-Managerial Approach

Williams, Smith and Young
Risk Management and Insurance
Eighth Edition

About the Authors

Richard A. Brealey

Advisor to the Governors of the Bank of England and Visiting Professor of Finance at the London Business School. For many years Professor Brealey was the Tokai Bank Professor of Finance at the London Business School. He is a past President of the European Finance Association and Director of the American Finance Association. He is co-author (with Stewart Myers) of *Principles of Corporate Finance,* the leading graduate-level corporate finance textbook. Research interests include portfolio theory and international finance.

Stewart C. Myers

Gordon Y. Billard Professor of Finance at MIT's Sloan School of Management. Past President and Director of the American Finance Association. He is co-author (with Richard Brealey) of the leading graduate-level corporate finance textbook. His research is primarily concerned with the valuation of real and financial assets, corporate finance and financial aspects of government regulation of business. He is a Research Associate of the National Bureau of Economic Research and a Director of The Brattle Group, an economic and environmental consulting firm, and CAT Ltd., a reinsurance company. He is active as a financial consultant.

Alan J. Marcus

Chair and Professor of Finance at Boston College's Wallace E. Carroll School of Management. Professor Marcus's main research interests are in asset valuation, particularly in futures and options markets. Other books include *Investments* and *Essentials of Investments* (with co-authors Zvi Bodie and Alex Kane). He currently serves on the Advisory Council for the Currency Risk Management Alliance of State Street Bank and Windham Capital Management Boston. Formerly with the Financial Research department of the Federal Home Loan Mortgage Corporation (Freddie Mac).

To Our Wives

Preface

This book is about corporate finance. It focuses on how companies invest in real assets and how they raise the money to pay for these investments.

Financial management is important, interesting, and challenging. It is *important* because today's capital investment decisions may determine the businesses that the firm is in 10, 20, or more years ahead. Also, a firm's success or failure depends in large part on its ability to find the capital that it needs.

Finance is *interesting* for several reasons. Financial decisions often involve huge sums of money. Large investment projects or acquisitions may involve billions of dollars. Also, the financial community is international and fast moving, with colorful heroes and a sprinkling of unpleasant villains.

Finance is *challenging*. Financial decisions are rarely cut and dried, and the financial markets in which companies operate are changing rapidly. Good managers can cope with routine problems, but only the best managers can respond to change. To handle new problems, you need more than rules of thumb; you need to understand *why* companies and financial markets behave as they do and when common practice may not be best practice. Once you have a consistent framework for making financial decisions, complex problems become more manageable.

This book provides that framework. It is not an encyclopedia of finance. It focuses instead on setting out the basic *principles* of financial management and applying them to the main decisions faced by the financial manager. It explains why the firm's owners would like the manager to increase firm value and shows how managers value investments that may pay off at different points of time or have different degrees of risk. It also describes the main features of financial markets and discusses why companies may prefer a particular source of finance.

This text is intended for the first course in corporate finance. The typical reader will have little or no business or financial experience. Some texts written for this audience shy away from modern finance, and instead stick with more traditional, procedural, or institutional approaches. These are supposed to be easier or more practical.

We disagree emphatically. The concepts of modern finance, properly explained, make the subject simpler, not more difficult. They are *also* more practical. The tools of financial management are easier to grasp and use effectively when presented in a consistent conceptual framework. Modern finance provides that framework.

Modern financial management is not "rocket science." It is a set of ideas that can be made clear by words, graphs, and numerical examples. The ideas provide the "why" behind the tools that good financial managers use to make investment and financing decisions.

We wrote this book to make financial management clear, useful, interesting and fun for the beginning student. We set out to show that modern finance and good financial practice go together, even for the financial novice.

Fundamentals and Principles of Corporate Finance

This book is derived in part from its sister text *Principles of Corporate Finance*. The spirit of the two books is similar. Both apply modern finance to give students a working ability to make financial decisions. However, there are also substantial differences between the two books.

Fundamentals is geared toward the financial novice. We see the typical reader as an undergraduate with little or no business experience, and therefore we simplify the discussion in several ways. First, we provide much more detailed discussion of the principles and mechanics of the time value of money. This material underlies almost all of this text, and we spend a lengthy chapter providing extensive practice with this key concept.

Second, we use numerical examples in this text to a greater degree than in *Principles*. Each chapter presents several detailed numerical examples to help the reader become familiar and comfortable with the material.

Third, we have streamlined the treatment of most topics. Whereas *Principles* has 35 chapters, *Fundamentals* has only 25. The relative brevity of *Fundamentals* necessitates a broader-brush coverage of some topics, but we feel that this is an advantage for a beginning audience.

Fourth, we assume little in the way of background knowledge. While most users will have had an introductory accounting course, we review the concepts of accounting that are important to the financial manager in Chapter 2.

Principles is known for its relaxed and informal writing style, and we continue this tradition in *Fundamentals*. In addition, we use as little mathematical notation as possible. Even when we present an equation, we usually write it in words rather than symbols. This approach has two advantages. It is less intimidating, and it focuses attention on the underlying concept rather than the formula.

Organizational Design

Fundamentals is organized in nine parts.

Part I (Introduction) provides essential background material. In the first chapter we discuss how businesses are organized, the role of the financial manager and the financial markets in which the manager operates. We explain how shareholders want managers to take actions that increase the value of their investment and we describe some of the mechanisms that help to align the interests of managers and shareholders. Of course the task of increasing shareholder value does not justify corrupt and unscrupulous behavior. We therefore discuss some of the ethical issues that confront managers.

A large corporation is a team effort, and so companies produce financial statements to help the players monitor their progress. Chapter 2 provides a brief overview of these financial statements and introduces two key distinctions—between market and book values and between cash flows and profits. The chapter concludes with a summary of federal taxes.

Part II (Value) is concerned with valuation. In Chapter 3 we introduce the concept of the time value of money, and, since most readers will be more familiar with their own financial affairs than with the big leagues of finance, we motivate our discussion by looking first at some personal financial decisions. We show how to value long-lived streams of cash flows and work through the valuation of perpetuities and annuities. Chapter 3 also contains a short concluding section on inflation and the distinction between real and nominal returns.

Chapter 4 introduces the basic features of bonds and stocks and gives students a chance to apply the ideas of Chapter 3 to the valuation of these securities. We show how to find the value of a bond given its yield and we show how prices of bonds fluctuate as interest rates change. We look at what determines stock prices and how stock valuation formulas can be used to infer the return that investors expect. Finally, we see how investment opportunities are reflected in the stock price and why analysts focus on the price-earnings multiple.

The remaining chapters of Part II are concerned with the company's investment decision. In Chapter 5 we introduce the concept of net present value and show how to calculate the NPV of a simple investment project. We also look at other measures of an investment's attractiveness—the internal rate of return rule, payback, and the return on book. We then turn to more complex investment proposals, including choices between alternative projects, machine replacement decisions, and decisions of when to invest. Finally, we show how the profitability index can be used to choose between investment projects when capital is scarce.

The first step in any NPV calculation is to decide what to discount. Therefore, in Chapter 6 we work through a realistic example of a capital budgeting analysis, showing how the manager needs to recognize the investment in working capital and how taxes and depreciation affect cash flows.

We start Chapter 7 by looking at how companies organize the investment process and ensure everyone works toward a common goal. We then go on to look at various techniques to help managers identify the key assumptions in their estimates, such as sensitivity analysis, scenario analysis, and break-even analysis. We conclude the chapter by describing how managers try to build future flexibility into projects so that they can capitalize on good luck and modify the consequences of bad luck.

Part III (Risk) is concerned with the cost of capital. Chapter 8 starts with a historical survey of returns on bonds and stocks and goes on to distinguish between the unique risk and market risk of individual stocks. Chapter 9 shows how to measure market risk and discusses the relationship between risk and expected return. Chapter 10 introduces the weighted-average cost of capital and provides a practical illustration of how to estimate it.

Part IV (Financing) begins our discussion of the financing decision. In Chapter 11 we introduce the notion of market efficiency. Few other introductory texts include a chapter on this topic. We believe that without a solid understanding of market efficiency it is difficult to think through the issues that arise when firms issue securities or make capital structure and dividend decisions. Chapter 12 looks at the role of shareholders in large corporations and compares corporate governance in the USA and elsewhere. It also provides an overview of the securities that firms issue and their relative importance as sources of finance. In Chapter 13 we look at how firms issue securities and we follow a firm from its first need for venture capital, through its initial public offering to its continuing need to raise debt or equity.

Part V (Capital Structure and Dividend Policy) focuses on the two classic long-term financing decisions. How much the firm should borrow is addressed in Chapter 14, and how it should set its dividend policy is addressed in Chapter 15. In each case we start with Modigliani and Miller's (MM's) observation that in well-functioning markets the decision should not matter, but we use this observation to help the reader understand why financial managers in practice do pay attention to these decisions.

Part VI (Financial Planning) starts with financial statement analysis in Chapter 16 and shows how analysts summarize the large volume of accounting information by calculating some key financial ratios. Long-term financial planning is discussed in Chapter 17, where we look at how the financial manager considers the combined effects of investment and financing decisions on the firm as a whole. We also show how measures of internal and sustainable growth help managers check that the firm's planned growth is consistent with its financing plans. Chapter 18 is an introduction to working capital management. It also shows how managers ensure that the firm will have enough cash to pay its bills over the coming year and describes the principal sources of short-term borrowing.

Part VII (Short-Term Financial Decisions) is concerned with two important short-term problems. Chapter 19 explains the mechanics of cash collection and disbursement and shows how firms invest idle cash. It also looks at the general problem of managing inventories and shows how the decision to stock up on cash is similar to the decision to stock up on inventories of raw materials or finished goods. The parallel between the task of inventory management and cash management enables us to cover these topics with less repetition than in most other texts. In Chapter 20 we describe the basic steps of credit management and we summarize bankruptcy procedures when customers cannot pay their bills.

Part VIII (Special Topics) covers several important but somewhat more advanced topics—mergers (Chapter 21), international financial management (Chapter 22), options (Chapter 23), and risk management (Chapter 24). Some of these topics are touched on in earlier chapters. For example, we introduce the idea of options in Chapter 7, when we show how companies build flexibility into capital projects. However, Chapter 23 generalizes this material, explains at an elementary level how options are valued, and provides some examples of why the financial manager needs to be concerned about options. International finance is also not confined to Chapter 22. As one might expect from a book that is written by an international group of authors, examples from different countries and financial systems are scattered throughout the book. However, Chapter 22 tackles the specific problems that arise when a corporation is confronted by different currencies.

Part IX (Conclusion) contains a concluding chapter (Chapter 25), in which we review the most important ideas covered in the text. We also introduce some interesting questions that either were unanswered in the text or are still puzzles to the finance profession. Thus the last chapter is an introduction to future finance courses as well as a conclusion to this one.

Routes through the Book

There are about as many effective ways to organize a course in corporate finance as there are teachers. For this reason, we have ensured that the text is modular, so that topics can be introduced in different sequences.

We like to discuss the principles of valuation before plunging into detailed financial statement analysis or issues of financial planning. Nevertheless, we recognize that many instructors will prefer to move directly from Chapter 2 (Accounting and Finance) to Chapter 16 (Financial Statement Analysis) in order to provide a gentler transition from the typical prerequisite accounting course. We have made sure that Part VI (Financial Planning) can easily follow Part I.

Similarly, we like to discuss working capital after the student is familiar with the basic principles of valuation and financing, but we recognize that here also many instructors prefer to reverse our order. There should be no difficulty in taking Part VII out of order.

When we discuss project valuation in Part II, we stress that the opportunity cost of capital depends on project risk. But we do not discuss how to measure risk or how return and risk are linked until Part III. This ordering can easily be modified. For example, the chapters on risk and return can be introduced before, after, or midway through the material on project valuation.

Of course, there will also be occasions where instructors will wish to assign only part of a chapter. For example, we suspect that many instructors may prefer to assign the bond section of Chapter 4 and omit or postpone the stock valuation portion.

Changes in the Second Edition

This second edition of *Fundamentals* includes many changes. We have listened to the market and have rewritten and rearranged material to improve readability, and we have expanded the treatment of some topics and introduced others for the first time. Here are some examples of the changes that we have made.

Chapter 1 includes a wholly new section on financial institutions and the services that they provide. There is also an expanded discussion of ethical issues and, since there are rarely cut-and-dried answers to ethical problems, we give readers an opportunity to compare their responses to ethical dilemmas with those of the public.

Chapter 3 has an expanded coverage of annuities, including the value of annuities due and the future value of a stream of regular payments. The chapter includes additional explanations and examples on the use of financial calculators. There is also a new section on inflation and the distinction between real and nominal returns.

In Chapter 4 we have now combined bond and stock valuation in a single chapter. We have expanded the discussion of stock valuation to show how the same techniques that are used to value a single share can also be used to value the entire company.

Chapter 5 has been extensively reorganized to improve the flow. For example, we now discuss in the same chapter how NPV and IRR can be used to choose between mutually exclusive projects.

Rather than presenting the capital asset pricing model as an abstract theory, we outline in Chapter 9 how well the model explains actual returns on common stocks.

In the discussion of the cost of capital in Chapter 10 we include a new section on how to handle flotation costs.

The discussion of market efficiency in Chapter 11 has been considerably simplified and updated. For example, we refer to the performance of the *Forbes* honor roll of mutual funds to illustrate strong-form efficiency, and we use the example of Orange County when we list some of the lessons of market efficiency.

We have simplified and streamlined at many other points in the text. Examples include the simplified illustrations of the MM debt irrelevance propositions and the agency costs of excessive borrowing (Chapter 14); the discussion of inventory models and their implications for cash management (Chapter 19); a new and much simplified section on the measurement of the gains and costs of a merger or acquisition (Chapter 21), and a complete numerical example of how an international project is valued (Chapter 22).

Chapter 12 includes a new section comparing corporate governance in the United States with governance in Germany and Japan.

Chapter 16 includes new examples to help students understand the purposes for which financial ratios may be used, while a new section shows how common-size statements can help to make comparisons between companies.

Chapter 17 includes an expanded section on internal and sustainable rates of growth.

The discussion in Chapter 18 of sources of short-term borrowing includes a section on the ways that interest rates are quoted on these loans.

Chapter 24 has a new section, "Is Derivative a Four-Letter Word," that reviews recent events, including the collapse of Barings and discusses sensible and foolish uses of derivatives.

Chapter 25 ends with a challenging Trivial Pursuits quiz to pique students' curiosity to learn more about finance.

New and Enhanced Pedagogy

Other new or expanded features in the second edition include:

More Self-Test Questions   Each chapter includes self-test questions which enable students to check their understanding as they read. The second edition has over 150 of these questions. Answers are worked out at the end of each chapter.

More End-of-Chapter Problems   This edition provides students with even more hands-on problems. Each question is labeled by the topic it addresses. With nearly 600 questions, students have plenty of chances to learn by doing.

Mini-Cases   A new feature of the second edition is the inclusion of the following integrative cases, that allow students to apply their knowledge to relatively complex, practical situations.

Old Alfred Road (page 100): Time value of money.
Prairie Home Stores (page 144): Company valuation.
Sheetbend and Halyard (page 205): Capital investment decisions.
Peru Resources (page 233): Sensitivity, scenario, and break-even analysis.
Sea Shore Salt (page 317): The company cost of capital.

Information Management Resources (page 386): The cost and pricing of an IPO.
Londonderry Air (page 424): Capital structure.
Capstan Autos (page 538): Cash budgeting.
Miami Spice (page 590): Credit management.

Minicase

Old Alfred Road, who is well-known to drivers on the Maine Turnpike, has reached his seventieth birthday and is ready to retire. Mr. Road has no formal training in finance but has saved his money and invested carefully.

Mr. Road owns his home—the mortgage is paid off—and does not want to move. He is a widower, and he wants to bequeath the house and any remaining assets to his daughter.

He has accumulated savings of $180,000, conserva-

are indexed for inflation. That is, they will be automatically increased in proportion to changes in the Consumer Price Index.

Mr. Road's main concern is with inflation. The inflation rate has been below 3 percent recently, but a 3 percent rate is unusually low by historical standards. His social security payments will increase with inflation, but the interest on his investment portfolio will not.

What advice do you have for Mr. Road? Can he safely invest

Time Lines, Calculator Boxes, and Exercises In an effort to help students grasp the critical concept of Time Value of Money, many pedagogical tools have been added to Chapters 3, 4, and 5. Calculator Boxes provide examples for solving a variety of problems with directions for the three most popular financial calculators.

An Introduction to Financial Calculators

Financial calculators are designed with present value and future value formulas already programmed. Therefore, you can readily solve many problems simply by entering the inputs for the problem and punching a key for the solution.

The basic financial calculator uses five keys that correspond to the inputs for common problems involving the time value of money.

Each key represents the following input:

- *n* is the number of periods. (We have been using *t* to denote the length of time or number of periods. Most calculators use *n* for the same concept.)

Future Values

Recall Example 3.2, where we calculated the future value of your $100 credit card balance. Enter 100 into the *PV* register. (You enter the value by typing 100, and then pushing the *PV* key.) We assumed an interest rate of 1 percent per month, so enter 1 into the *i* register. Because the $100 had 12 months to compound, enter 12 into the *n* register. Enter 0 into the *PMT* register because there is no recurring payment involved in the calculation. Now ask the calculator to compute *FV*. On some calculators you simply press the *FV* key. On others you need to first press the "compute" key (which may be labeled *COMP* or *CPT*), and then press *FV*. The exact sequence of keystrokes for three popular financial calculators are as follows:[1]

| Hewlett-Packard | Sharpe | Texas Instruments |

Finance in Practice Almost every chapter includes at least one "Finance in Practice" box. These are excerpts, usually from the financial press, providing real-life illustrations of the chapter's topics. Examples are the initial public offering of Netscape stock, the misadventures of Metallgesellschaft, the story of Sealed Air's restructuring, and the debate over the cost of capital for a British nuclear power station.

Surfers Catch the Wave of a Rising Tide

"The Internet," commented the *Financial Times,* "is all the rage and where fashions go, investors follow, anxious to make money from any new trend. So this week's flotation of a company which makes products to help surfers find their way round the Net was bound to attract interest. But no one, not even the sponsors of the issue, was prepared for what happened when Netscape Communications went public on the Nasdaq stock market."

In mid-July, when the initial prospectus was published,

that profit and in frenzied trading the shares fell, ending their first day at $58 1/4. Even at that price the company as a whole was valued at over $2 billion. This was 45 times annualized sales and 37 times the shares' book value. It also made multimillionaires of several of the company's managers. At the end of the day the stock of the company's chairman was valued at $566 million, while the president held stock worth $245 million.

didn't ...... you would think that Netscape

Key Points   Summarized and located every few pages throughout the text, these Points underscore the importance of the material, as well as help students focus on the most relevant topics critical to their understanding.

Is a project that breaks even in accounting terms an acceptable investment? If you are not sure about the answer, here's a possibly easier question. Would you be happy about an investment in a stock that after 5 years gave you a total rate of return of zero? We hope not. You might break even on such a stock but a zero return does not compensate you for the time value of money or the risk that you have taken.

> **A project that simply breaks even on an accounting basis gives you your money back but does not cover the opportunity cost of the capital tied up in the project. A project that breaks even in accounting terms will surely have a negative NPV.**

Let's check this with the superstore project. Suppose that in each year the store has sales of $13.067 million—just enough to break even on an accounting basis. What would be the cash flow from operations?

New Design   The second edition's new design is not only visually engaging; it also helps understanding. For example, color is used to enhance essential equations and concepts and to highlight key terms. Each chapter has an opening photograph to alert the reader to an important issue.

Supplements

In addition to these many textual improvements, a major focus of this revision was to provide students and instructors with an extensive and valuable supplements package. The following supplements are available for use with this text:

PowerPoint Transparencies (0072909870)

Prepared by Richard A. Brealey, London Business School and Matthew Will, Johns Hopkins University. This visually stimulating software program provides the instructor with over 400 slides. With colorful graphs, charts, and lists from each text chapter, the instructor can edit or rearrange the transparencies to fit specific lectures.

F.A.S.T. Software (Financial Analysis Spreadsheet Templates) (0072909897)

These Excel-based spreadsheet templates are tied to specific end-of-chapter problems in the text. Providing students with over 100 problems, this software is available free with the purchase of *Fundamentals*.

Brealey, Myers, Marcus (BMM) Web Site

This Web site includes a variety of teaching and learning materials for both students and instructors. Visit this site at www.mhhe.com/business/finance/bmm.

Solutions Manual (0072909889)

Prepared by the authors. This critical teaching aid contains detailed solutions to all end-of-chapter problems in the text.

Instructor's Manual (0070074879)

Prepared by David R. Durst, University of Akron. This key teaching tool includes a "Chapter in Perspective" section that links each chapter's content to the remainder of the book, a topic outline highlighting key concepts and terms, teaching notes, suggestions for student career planning, an orientation to *The Wall Street Journal* and how it can be used to develop the concepts covered in the text, and a new section on financial calculators and spreadsheets, including examples and some basic commands using Excel and Lotus.

Test Bank (0070074887)

Prepared by William H. Sackley, University of Southern Mississippi and Assem Safieddine, Michigan State University, and Nathan Jithendaranathan of St. Thomas University (Minnesota). Improved for the Second Edition, the Test Bank now contains over 2,000 true/false, multiple-choice, and discussion questions and problems. The Test Bank is designed to test varying levels of comprehension, from purely definitional to problem-oriented applications. Complete answers are provided for all test questions and problems, and referenced to their location in the text.

Computerized Testing Software (0072909862)

This program makes test generation easy with a user-friendly menu system, keyword searching, password protection, and modification of the question database. Available for Windows, DOS, and Mac platforms.

TeleTest

Instructors can take advantage of Irwin/McGraw-Hill's free customized exam preparation service. Test and answer keys are printed according to the instructor's specifications and mailed at no charge.

Transparency Acetates (0070752893)

Prepared by the authors. These black and white acetates provide key exhibits from the text.

The Wall Street Journal *Edition (0073040096)*

Through a unique arrangement with Dow Jones, Irwin/McGraw-Hill is able to offer your students a 10-week subscription to *The Wall Street Journal* as part of the purchase price of the WSJ Edition text. The WSJ will keep students up to date on the world of finance.

Ready Notes (0073040088)

Prepared by Matthew Will, Johns Hopkins University. This innovative student supplement provides students with an inexpensive way to take notes. Featuring a reduced copy of every transparency included in the PowerPoint package, these notes allow students to listen and record notes during the lecture instead of simply trying to copy the transparency in their notebooks.

Essentials of Finance CD-ROM (0073039780)

Prepared by Robert F. Bruner, Kenneth Eades, and Robert Harris, all of the University of Virginia. Developed in conjunction with GMAC (General Management Admissions Council), this CD-ROM provides students with an interactive, self-paced walk-through of the tools of finance. Through the use of audio, graphics, and video, students learn concepts and reinforce their knowledge with fill-in exercises and instant feedback.

Student Study Guide (0072909870)

Prepared by David R. Durst, University of Akron, and Thomas E. Stitzel, Boise State University. The Study Guide highlights the key concepts within each chapter in a concise and understandable manner. Each chapter of the guide contains an introduction, learning checklist, references to data and articles for further information on various topics, a complete chapter outline highlighting key concepts and terms, self-test completion questions, and problems with solutions. The Study Guide is a valuable tool for students to use in mastering the concepts presented in the text.

Acknowledgments

We take this opportunity to thank all of those individuals who helped us prepare this Second Edition. We want to express our appreciation first to those instructors whose insightful comments and suggestions were invaluable to us during this revision. Many individuals helped us in our efforts early on:

Antonio Bernardo
University of California at Los Angeles

Genna Brown
University of Miami

James D. Harriss, Ph.D.
University of North Carolina

Gene C. Lai
University of Rhode Island

George H. Lentz
California State Polytechnic University

Richard A. Lord
Georgia College

Morgan J. Lynge, Jr.
University of Illinois at Urbana—Champaign

Herman Manakyan
Western Kentucky University

Surendra K. Mansinghka
San Francisco State University

Timothy G. Sullivan
Bentley College

Dr. Thomas S. Zorn
University of Nebraska

Other finance scholars and instructors have reviewed manuscript and provided us with invaluable suggestions and insights:

Ibrahim Affaneh
Indiana University of Pennsylvania

John Blease
University of Oregon

James D'Mello
Western Michigan University

Jeanette Diamond
University of Nebraska-Omaha

Scott Gibson
University of Minnesota

Raymond Gorman
Miami University of Ohio

Aptul Gupta
Bentley College

Gerald Hanweck
George Mason University

Marlin Jensen
Auburn University

James McNulty
Florida Atlantic University

Percy Poon
University of Nevada-Las Vegas

Assem Safieddine
Michigan State University

Ashtar Siddique
Georgetown University

Michael Weisbach
University of Arizona

In addition, we wish to thank our supplements authors, David Durst (*Study Guide* and *Instructor's Manual*), Thomas Stitzel (*Study Guide*), Matthew Will (*PowerPoint Presentations* and *Ready Notes*), and William Sackley (*Testbank*). Their efforts will help both instructors and students.

Finally, we are grateful to the talented staff at Burrston House and at Irwin/McGraw-Hill, especially Craig S. Beytien, Publisher; Shelley Kronzek, Associate Editor; Katie Rose-Matthews, Senior Marketing Manager; Martin Quinn, Developmental Editor; Jean Lou Hess, Senior Project Manager; Kiera Cunningham, Designer; Sharon Miller, Photo Researcher; Linda Hueneke, Supplement Coordinator, and Melonie Salvati, Production Supervisor. This was truly a team effort. A special debt goes to Shelley Kronzek, whose energy and enthusiasm were essential to this revision.

Finally, as was the case for the first edition, we cannot overstate the thanks due to our wives, Diana, Maureen, and Sheryl.

Richard A. Brealey
Stewart C. Myers
Alan J. Marcus

Contents in Brief

Contents

Part Four *Financing   319*

Chapter 11

Corporate Financing and the Lessons of Market Efficiency   321

Chapter 12

An Overview of Corporate Financing   341

Chapter 13

How Corporations Issue Securities   367

Part Five *Capital Structure and Dividend Policy* 393

Part Six *Financial Planning* 451

Part Seven   *Short-Term Financial Decisions   541*

Part Eight   *Special Topics   593*

Part One Introduction

1 The Firm and the Financial Manager

2 Accounting and Finance

A meeting of a corporation's directors.
Most large businesses are organized as corporations. Corporations are owned by
stockholders, who vote in a board of directors. The directors appoint the corporation's top
executives and approve major financial decisions.
© Comstock, Inc.

The Firm and the Financial Manager

Chapter 1

*T*his book is an introduction to corporate finance. In the following chapters we will discuss the various responsibilities of the corporation's financial managers and show you how to approach many of the problems that such managers are expected to solve. We begin in this chapter with a discussion of the corporation, the financial decisions it needs to make, and why they are important.

To survive and prosper, a company must satisfy its customers. It must also produce and sell products and services at a profit. In order to produce, it needs many assets—plant, equipment, offices, computers, technology, and so on. The company has to decide (1) which assets to buy and (2) how to pay for them. The financial manager plays a key role in both these decisions. The *investment decision,* that is, the decision to invest in assets like plant, equipment, and know-how, is in large part a responsibility of the financial manager. So is the *financing decision,* the choice of how to pay for such investments.

We start this chapter by explaining how businesses are organized. We then provide a brief introduction to the role of the financial manager and show you why corporate managers need a sophisticated understanding of financial markets. Next we turn to the goals of the firm and ask what makes for a good financial decision. Is the firm's aim to maximize profits? To avoid bankruptcy? To be a good citizen? We consider some conflicts of interest that arise in large organizations and review some mechanisms that align the interests of the firm's managers with the interests of its owners. Finally, we provide an overview of what is to come in the rest of the text.

After studying this chapter you should be able to

▶ Explain the advantages and disadvantages of the most common forms of business organization and determine which forms are most suitable to different types of businesses.

▶ Cite the major business functions and decisions that the firm's financial managers are responsible for.

▶ Explain why it makes sense for corporations to maximize their market values.

▶ Show why conflicts of interest may arise in large organizations and discuss how corporations can provide incentives for everyone to work toward a common end.

1.1 *Organizing a Business*

Sole Proprietorships

In 1901 pharmacist Charles Walgreen bought the drugstore in which he worked on the South Side of Chicago. Today Walgreen's is the largest drugstore chain in the United States. If like Charles Walgreen you start on your own, with no partners or

sole proprietor: Sole owner of a business which has no partners and no shareholders. The proprietor is personally liable for all the firm's obligations.

stockholders, you are said to be a **sole proprietor.** You bear all the costs and keep all the profits after the Internal Revenue Service has taken its cut.

As a sole proprietor, you are responsible for all the business's debts and other liabilities. If the business borrows from the bank and subsequently cannot repay the loan, the bank has a claim against your personal belongings. It could force you into personal bankruptcy if the business debts are big enough. Thus as sole proprietor you have *unlimited liability.*

Partnerships

partnership: Business owned by two or more persons who are personally responsible for all its liabilities.

Instead of starting on your own, you may wish to pool money and expertise with friends or business associates. If so, a sole proprietorship is obviously inappropriate. Instead, you can form a **partnership.** Your *partnership agreement* will set out how management decisions are to be made and the proportion of the profits to which each partner is entitled. The partners then pay personal income tax on their share of these profits.

Partners, like sole proprietors, have the disadvantage of unlimited liability. If the business runs into financial difficulties, each partner has unlimited liability for *all* the business's debts, not just his or her share.[1] The moral is clear and simple: "Know thy partner."

Many professional businesses are organized as partnerships. They include the large accounting, legal, and management consulting firms. Most large investment banks such as Morgan Stanley, Salomon Brothers, Merrill Lynch, First Boston, and Goldman Sachs started life as partnerships. So did many well-known companies, such as Microsoft and Apple Computer. But eventually these companies and their financing requirements grew too large for them to continue as partnerships.[2]

Corporations

corporation: Business owned by stockholders who are not personally liable for the business's liabilities.

As your firm grows, you may decide to *incorporate.* Unlike a proprietorship or partnership, a **corporation** is legally distinct from its owners. It is based on *articles of incorporation* that set out the purpose of the business, how many shares can be issued, the number of directors to be appointed, and so on. These articles must conform to the laws of the state in which the business is incorporated. For many legal purposes, the corporation is considered a resident of its state. For example, it can borrow or lend money, and it can sue or be sued. It pays its own taxes (but it cannot vote!).

limited liability: The owners of the corporation are not personally responsible for its obligations.

The corporation is owned by its stockholders and they get to vote on important matters. Unlike proprietorships or partnerships, corporations have **limited liability,** which means that the stockholders cannot be held personally responsible for the obligations of the firm. If, say, IBM were to fail, no one could demand that its shareholders put up more money to pay off the debts. The most a stockholder can lose is the amount invested in the stock.

While the stockholders of a corporation own the firm, they do not usually manage it. Instead, they elect a *board of directors,* which in turn appoints the top managers.

---

[1]Larger businesses can be set up as *limited partnerships.* In this case partners are classified as *general* or *limited.* General partners manage the business and have unlimited personal liability for the business's debts. Limited partners, however, are liable only for the money they contribute to the business. They can lose everything they put in, but no more. Limited partners usually have a restricted role in the management.

[2]Among the large investment banks, Goldman Sachs is the only firm still to be organized as a partnership.

Table 1.1

Characteristics of business organizations

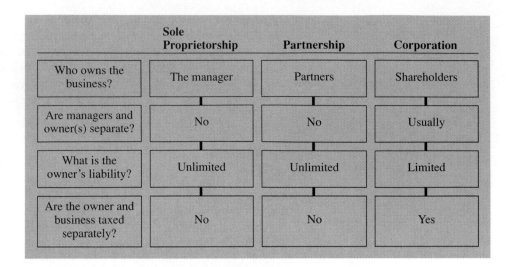

	Sole Proprietorship	Partnership	Corporation
Who owns the business?	The manager	Partners	Shareholders
Are managers and owner(s) separate?	No	No	Usually
What is the owner's liability?	Unlimited	Unlimited	Limited
Are the owner and business taxed separately?	No	No	Yes

The board is the representative of shareholders and is supposed to ensure that management is acting in their best interests.

This *separation of ownership and management* is one distinctive feature of corporations. In other forms of business organization, such as proprietorships and partnerships, the owners are the managers.

The separation between management and ownership gives a corporation more flexibility and permanence than a partnership. Even if managers of a corporation quit or are dismissed and replaced by others, the corporation can survive. Similarly, today's shareholders may sell all their shares to new investors without affecting the business. In contrast, ownership of a proprietorship cannot be transferred without selling out to another owner-manager.

By organizing as a corporation, a business may be able to attract a wide variety of investors. The shareholders may include individuals who hold only a single share worth a few dollars, receive only a single vote, and are entitled to only a tiny proportion of the profits. Shareholders may also include giant pension funds and insurance companies whose investment in the firm may run into the millions of shares and who are entitled to a correspondingly large number of votes and proportion of the profits.

Given these advantages, you might be wondering why all businesses are not organized as corporations. One reason is the time and cost required to manage a corporation's legal machinery. There is also an important tax drawback to corporations in the United States. Because the corporation is a separate legal entity, it is taxed separately. So corporations pay tax on their profits, and, in addition, shareholders pay tax on any dividends that they receive from the company.[3] By contrast, income received by partners and sole proprietors is taxed only once as personal income.

When you first establish a corporation, the shares may all be held by a small group, perhaps the company's managers and a small number of backers who believe the business will grow into a profitable investment. Your shares are not publicly traded and your company is *closely held*. Eventually, when the firm grows and new shares are

---

[3]The United States is unusual in its taxation of corporations. To avoid taxing the same income twice, most other countries give shareholders at least some credit for the taxes that their company has already paid.

issued to raise additional capital, the shares will be widely traded. Such corporations are known as *public companies*. Most well-known corporations are public companies.[4]

> To summarize, the corporation is a distinct, permanent legal entity. Its advantages are limited liability and the ease with which ownership and management can be separated. These advantages are especially important for large firms. The disadvantage of corporate organization is double taxation.

The financial managers of a corporation are responsible, by way of top management and the board of directors, to the corporation's shareholders. Financial managers are supposed to make financial decisions that serve shareholders' interests. Table 1.1 presents the distinctive features of the major forms of business organization.

▶ **Self-Test 1.1**

Which form of business organization might best suit the following?

a. A consulting firm with several senior consultants and support staff.
b. A house painting company owned and operated by a college student who hires some friends for occasional help.
c. A paper goods company with sales of $100 million and 2,000 employees.

1.2 *The Role of the Financial Manager*

real assets: Assets used to produce goods and services.

To carry on business, companies need an almost endless variety of **real assets.** Many of these assets are tangible, such as machinery, factories, and offices; others are intangible, such as technical expertise, trademarks, and patents. All of them must be paid for.

To obtain the necessary money, the company sells **financial assets,** or *securities*.[5] These pieces of paper have value because they are claims on the firm's real assets and the cash that those assets will produce. For example, if the company borrows money from the bank, the bank has a financial asset. That financial asset gives it a claim to a stream of interest payments and to repayment of the loan. The company's real assets need to produce enough cash to satisfy these claims.

financial assets: Claims to the income generated by real assets. Also called *securities*.

financial markets: Markets in which financial assets are traded.

Financial managers stand between the firm's real assets and the **financial markets** in which the firm raises cash. The financial manager's role is shown in Figure 1.1, which traces how cash flows from investors to the firm and back to investors again. The flow starts when financial assets are sold to raise cash (arrow 1 in the figure). The cash is employed to purchase the real assets used in the firm's operations (arrow 2). Later, if the firm does well, the real assets generate enough cash inflow to more than repay the initial investment (arrow 3). Finally, the cash is either reinvested (arrow 4*a*) or returned to the investors who contributed the money in the first place (arrow 4*b*). Of course the choice between arrows 4*a* and 4*b* is not a completely free one. For

---

[4]For example, when Microsoft was initially established as a corporation, its shares were closely held by a small number of employees and backers. Microsoft shares were issued to the public in 1986.

[5]For present purposes we are using *financial assets* and *securities* interchangeably, though "securities" usually refers to financial assets that are widely held, like the shares of IBM. An IOU ("I owe you") from your brother-in-law, which you might have trouble selling outside the family, is also a financial asset, but most people would not think of it as a security.

Figure 1.1

Flow of cash between capital markets and the firm's operations. Key: (1) Cash raised by selling financial assets to investors; (2) cash invested in the firm's operations; (3) cash generated by the firm's operations; (4a) cash reinvested; (4b) cash returned to investors.

capital budgeting decision: Decision as to which real assets the firm should acquire.

financing decision: Decision as to how to raise the money to pay for investments in real assets.

example, if a bank lends the firm money at stage 1, the bank has to be repaid this money plus interest at stage *4b*.

This flow chart suggests that the financial manager faces two basic problems. First, how much money should the firm invest, and what specific assets should the firm invest in? This is the firm's *investment,* or **capital budgeting, decision.** Second, how should the cash required for an investment be raised? This is the **financing decision.**

The Capital Budgeting Decision

Capital budgeting decisions are central to the company's success or failure. For example, in 1955 the Ford Motor Company decided to launch a new model, the Edsel. It was powerful, stylish, and packed with gadgets. By the time the new car was launched in September 1957, Ford had spent a quarter of a billion dollars, then a record capital investment for any consumer product. Yet the Edsel was dogged by problems. Not only did it have a tendency to rattle or stop, but its chrome, power, and gadgetry attracted more attention than customers. Just over 2 years after its introduction, the Edsel was withdrawn. It was one of the largest capital budgeting mistakes in history. On top of its initial investment, Ford lost a further $200 million during production—nearly $2,000 for each car sold.

Contrast that with Boeing's decision to "bet the company" by developing the 757 and 767 jets. Boeing's investment in these planes was $3 billion, more than double the total value of stockholders' investment as shown in the company's accounts at the time. By 1997, estimated cumulative profits from this investment were approaching $8 billion, and the planes were still selling well.

Ford's decision to invest in the Edsel and Boeing's decision to invest in a new generation of airliners are both examples of capital budgeting decisions. The success of such decisions is usually judged in terms of value. Good investment projects are worth more than they cost. Adopting such projects increases the value of the firm and therefore the wealth of its shareholders. For example, Boeing's investment produced a stream of cash flows that were worth much more than its $3 billion outlay.

Capital budgeting decisions are important to service as well as manufacturing firms. For example, America Online announced in 1997 that it would spend millions of dollars to add additional modems to facilitate access to its network. This investment will be crucial to the company's ability to service its existing customers and attract new ones.

Today's investments provide benefits in the future. Thus the financial manager is concerned not solely with the size of the benefits but also with how long the firm must wait for them. The sooner the profits come in, the better. In addition, these benefits are rarely certain; a new project may be a great success—but then again it could be a dismal failure. The financial manager needs a way to place a value on these uncertain future benefits.

We will spend considerable time in later chapters on project evaluation. While no one can guarantee that you will avoid disasters like the Edsel or that you will be blessed with successes like the 757 and 767, a disciplined, analytical approach to project proposals will weight the odds in your favor.

The Financing Decision

The financial manager's second responsibility is to raise the money to pay for the investment in real assets. This is the financing decision. When a company needs financing, it can invite investors to put up cash in return for a share of profits or it can promise investors a series of fixed payments. In the first case, the investor receives newly issued shares of stock and becomes a shareholder, a part-owner of the firm. In the second, the investor becomes a lender whom the corporation is obligated to repay. The choice of the long-term financing mix is often called the **capital structure** decision, since *capital* refers to the firm's sources of long-term financing, and the markets for long-term financing are called **capital markets.**[6]

capital structure: Firm's mix of long-term financing.

capital markets: Markets for long-term financing.

Within the basic distinction—issuing new shares of stock versus borrowing money—there are endless variations. Suppose the company decides to borrow. Should it go to capital markets for long-term debt financing or should it borrow from a bank? Should it borrow in Paris, receiving and promising to repay French francs, or should it borrow dollars in New York? Should it demand the right to pay off the debt early if future interest rates fall? We will look at these and other choices in later chapters.

The decision to invest in a new factory or to issue new shares of stock has long-term consequences. But the financial manager is also involved in some important short-term decisions. For example, she needs to make sure that the company has enough cash on hand to pay next week's bills and that any spare cash is put to work to earn interest. Such short-term financial decisions involve both investment (how to invest spare cash) and financing (how to raise cash to meet a short-term need).

▶ **Self-Test 1.2**   Are the following capital budgeting or financing decisions?

a. Intel decides to spend $500 million to develop a new microprocessor.
b. Volkswagen decides to raise 350 million deutschemarks through a bank loan.
c. Exxon constructs a pipeline to bring natural gas on shore from the Gulf of Mexico.
d. Pierre Lapin sells shares to finance expansion of his newly formed securities trading firm.
e. Glaxo buys a license to produce and sell a new drug developed by a biotech company.
f. Merck issues new shares to help pay for the purchase of Medco, a pharmaceutical distribution company.

---

[6]*Money markets* are used for short-term financing.

1.3 *Who Is the Financial Manager?*

In this book we will use the term *financial manager* to refer to anyone responsible for a significant corporate investment or financing decision. But except in the smallest firms, no *single* person is responsible for all the decisions discussed in this book. Responsibility is dispersed throughout the firm. Top management is of course constantly involved in financial decisions. But the engineer who designs a new production facility is also involved: the design determines the kind of asset the firm will invest in. Likewise the marketing manager who undertakes a major advertising campaign is making an investment decision: the campaign is an investment in an intangible asset that will pay off in future sales and earnings.

Nevertheless, there are managers who specialize in finance, and their functions are summarized in Figure 1.2. The **treasurer** is usually the person most directly responsible for looking after the firm's cash, raising new capital, and maintaining relationships with banks and other investors who hold the firm's securities.

For small firms, the treasurer is likely to be the only financial executive. Larger corporations usually also have a **controller**, who prepares the financial statements, manages the firm's internal accounting, and looks after its tax affairs. You can see that the treasurer and controller have different roles: the treasurer's main function is to obtain and manage the firm's capital, whereas the controller ensures that the money is used efficiently.

The largest firms usually appoint a **chief financial officer (CFO)** to oversee both the treasurer's and the controller's work. The CFO is deeply involved in financial policymaking and corporate planning. Often he or she will have general responsibilities beyond strictly financial issues.

Usually the treasurer, controller, or CFO is responsible for organizing and supervising the capital budgeting process. However, major capital investment projects are so closely tied to plans for product development, production, and marketing that managers from these other areas are inevitably drawn into planning and analyzing the projects. If the firm has staff members specializing in corporate planning, they are naturally involved in capital budgeting too.

Because of the importance of many financial issues, ultimate decisions often rest by law or by custom with the board of directors.[7] For example, only the board has

treasurer: Manager responsible for financing, cash management, and relationships with financial markets and institutions.

controller: Officer responsible for budgeting, accounting, and auditing.

chief financial officer (CFO): Officer who oversees the treasurer and controller and sets overall financial strategy.

Figure 1.2

The financial managers in large corporations.

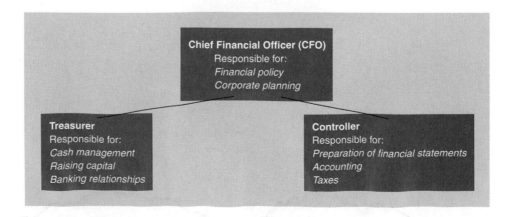

[7]Often the firm's chief financial officer is also a member of its board of directors.

the legal power to declare a dividend or to sanction a public issue of securities. Boards usually delegate decision-making authority for small- or medium-sized investment outlays, but the authority to approve large investments is almost never delegated.

▶ **Self-Test 1.3**   Sal and Sally went to business school together 10 years ago. They have just been hired by a midsized corporation that wants to bring in new financial managers. Sal studied finance, with an emphasis on financial markets and institutions. Sally majored in accounting and became a CPA 5 years ago. Who is more suited to be treasurer and who controller? Briefly explain.

1.4 *Understanding Financial Markets and Institutions*

Good capital budgeting and financing decisions both require an understanding of financial markets. For example, suppose a firm chooses to finance a major expansion program by borrowing money. The financial manager must have asked whether the value of the firm would be increased more by an issue of debt rather than an issue of shares. That required a theory of how the choice of financing affects value. Also, the financial manager must have considered the interest rate on the loan and concluded that it was not too high. That required a theory of how interest rates are set and loans are priced.

The investment decision cannot be separated from financial markets either. We have said that a successful investment is one that increases firm value. But how do investors value a firm? Answering this question requires a theory of how the firm's stock is priced.

Of course, theory is not the end of it. The financial manager is in day-by-day—sometimes hour-by-hour or minute-by-minute—contact with financial markets and must understand their institutions, regulations, and operating practices. We can't survey these things here, but a few definitions and observations will set the stage for later chapters.

Financial Markets

We have seen that financial markets allow companies to raise money by selling new financial assets. For example, if General Motors needs to raise funds to renovate an auto plant, it might hire an investment banking firm such as Goldman Sachs or Merrill Lynch to sell $500 million of General Motors stock to investors. Some of this stock may be bought directly by individuals; the remainder will be bought by financial institutions such as pension funds and insurance companies. In fact about a quarter of the shares of United States companies are owned by pension funds.

A new issue of securities increases both the amount of cash held by the company and the amount of stocks or bonds held by the public. Such an issue is known as a *primary issue* and it is sold in the **primary market.** But in addition to helping companies raise new cash, financial markets also allow investors to trade stocks or bonds between themselves. For example, Smith might decide to raise some cash by selling her AT&T stock at the same time that Jones invests his spare cash in AT&T. The result is simply a transfer of ownership from Smith to Jones, which has no effect on the

primary market: Market for the sale of new securities by corporations.

secondary market: Market in which already issued securities are traded among investors.

company itself. Such purchases and sales of existing securities are known as *secondary transactions* and they take place in the **secondary market.**

Some financial assets have no secondary market. For example, when a small company borrows money from the bank, it gives the bank an IOU promising to repay the money with interest. The bank will keep the IOU and will not sell it to another bank. Other financial assets are regularly traded. Thus when a large public company raises cash by selling new shares to investors, it knows that many of these investors may subsequently decide to sell their shares to others.

Most trading in the shares of large United States corporations takes place on stock exchanges such as the New York Stock Exchange (NYSE) or the American Stock Exchange (Amex). There is also a thriving *over-the-counter (OTC)* market in securities. The over-the-counter market is not a centralized exchange like the NYSE but a network of security dealers who use an electronic system known as NASDAQ[8] to quote prices at which they will buy and sell shares. While shares of stock may be traded either on exchanges or over-the-counter, almost all corporate debt is traded over-the-counter, if it is traded at all. United States government debt is also traded over-the-counter.

Many other things trade in financial markets, including foreign currencies; claims on commodities such as corn, crude oil, and silver; and options, which we dissect in Chapter 23.

Financial Institutions

financial intermediary: Firm that raises money from many small investors and provides financing to businesses or other organizations by investing in their securities.

Thus far we have pictured the financial manager as selling securities directly to, and thereby raising money directly from, investors. But often there is a **financial intermediary** in between. A financial intermediary invests primarily in financial assets. It provides financing to businesses, individuals, other organizations, and governments.

Suppose a company wishes to borrow $250 million for 9 months. It could issue a 9-month debt security to investors:

But given the debt's short duration, it might be easier to arrange a 9-month bank loan:

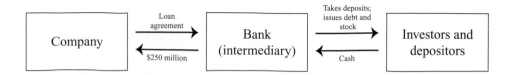

In this case the bank raises money by taking deposits or selling debt or stock to investors. It then lends the money on to the company. Of course the bank must charge interest sufficient to cover its costs and to compensate its debtholders and stockholders.

---

[8]National Association of Security Dealers Automatic Quotation system.

Banks and their immediate relatives, such as savings and loan companies, are the most familiar financial intermediaries. But there are many others, such as insurance companies.

In the United States, insurance companies are more important than banks for the *long-term* financing of business. They are massive investors in corporate stocks and bonds, and they often make long-term loans directly to corporations.

Suppose our company needs a loan for 9 years, not 9 months. It could issue a bond directly to investors, or it could negotiate a 9-year loan with an insurance company:

Notice how the insurance company raises the money to make the loan: it sells stock,[9] but most of its financing comes from sale of insurance policies. Say you buy a fire insurance policy on your home. You pay cash to the insurance company and get a financial asset (the policy) in exchange. You receive no interest payments on this financial asset, but if a fire does strike, the company is obliged to cover the damages up to the policy limit. This is the return on your investment.

Of course the company will issue not just one policy, but thousands. Normally the incidence of fires "averages out," leaving the company with a predictable obligation to its policyholders as a group. Of course the insurance company must charge enough for its policies to cover selling and administrative costs, pay policyholders' claims, and generate a profit for its stockholders.

Why is a financial intermediary different from a manufacturing corporation? First, it may raise money differently, for example, by taking deposits or selling insurance policies. Second, it invests that money in *financial* assets, for example, in stocks, bonds, or loans to businesses or individuals. The manufacturing company's main investments are in plant, equipment, and other *real* assets.

Functions of Financial Markets and Institutions

Financial markets and institutions provide financing for business. They also contribute in many other ways to our individual well-being and the smooth functioning of the economy. Here are some examples.[10]

The Payment Mechanism.   Think how inconvenient life would be if you had to pay for every purchase in cash or if General Motors had to ship truckloads of hundred-dollar bills round the country to pay its suppliers. Checking accounts, credit cards, and electronic transfers allow individuals and firms to send and receive payments quickly and safely over long distances. Banks are the obvious providers of payment services, but they are not alone. For example, if you buy shares in a money-market mutual fund, your money is pooled with that of other investors and used to buy safe,

---

[9]To ensure insurance companies' solvency, regulations strictly limit the amount and type of debt they can issue.

[10]Robert Merton gives an excellent overview of these functions in "A Functional Perspective of Financial Intermediation," *Financial Management* 24 (Summer 1995), pp. 23–41.

short-term securities. You can then write checks on this mutual fund investment, just as if you had a bank deposit.

Borrowing and Lending. Financial institutions allow individuals to transfer expenditures across time. If you have more money now than you need and you wish to save for a rainy day, you can (for example) put the money on deposit in a bank. If you wish to anticipate some of your future income to buy a car, you can borrow money from the bank. Both the lender and the borrower are happier than if they were forced to spend cash as it arrived. Of course, individuals are not alone in needing to raise cash from time to time. Firms with good investment opportunities raise cash by borrowing or selling new shares. The United States government runs at a deficit and issues more than $100 billion in new debt every year.

In principle, individuals or firms with cash surpluses could take out newspaper advertisements or surf the Net looking for counterparts with cash shortages. But it is usually cheaper and more convenient to use financial markets or institutions to link the borrower and the lender. For example, banks are equipped to check the borrower's creditworthiness and to monitor the use of the cash.

Almost all financial institutions are involved in channeling savings toward those who can best use them.

Pooling Risk. Financial markets and institutions allow individuals and firms to pool their risks. Insurance companies are an obvious example. Here is another. Suppose that you have only a small sum to invest. You could buy the stock of a single company, but then you could be wiped out if that company went belly-up. It's generally better to buy shares in a mutual fund that invests in a diversified portfolio of common stocks or other securities. In this case you are exposed only to the risk that security prices as a whole may fall.[11]

▶ **Self-Test 1.4**   Do you understand the following distinctions? Briefly explain in each case.

a. Real versus financial assets.
b. Investment versus financing decisions.
c. Capital budgeting versus capital structure decisions.
d. Primary versus secondary markets.
e. Financial intermediation versus direct financing from financial markets.

1.5 Goals of the Corporation

Shareholders Want Managers to Maximize Market Value

For small firms, shareholders and management may be one and the same. But for large companies, separation of ownership and management is a practical necessity. For example, AT&T has 2.2 million shareholders. There is no way that these share-

---

[11]Mutual funds provide other services. For example, they take care of much of the paperwork of holding shares. Investors also hope that the fund's professional managers will be able to outsmart the market and secure higher returns.

holders can be actively involved in management; it would be like trying to run New York City by town meetings. Authority has to be delegated.

How can shareholders decide how to delegate decision making when they all have different tastes, wealth, time horizons, and personal opportunities? Delegation can work only if the shareholders have a common objective. Fortunately there is a natural financial objective on which almost all shareholders can agree. This is to maximize the current value of their investment.

A smart and effective financial manager makes decisions which increase the current value of the company's shares and the wealth of its stockholders. That increased wealth can then be put to whatever purposes the shareholders want. They can give their money to charity or spend it in glitzy night clubs; they can save it or spend it now. Whatever their personal tastes or objectives, they can all do more when their shares are worth more.

Sometimes you hear managers speak as if the corporation has other goals. For example, they may say that their job is to "maximize profits." That sounds reasonable. After all, don't shareholders want their company to be profitable? But taken literally, profit maximization is not a well-defined corporate objective. Here are three reasons:

1. "Maximizing profits" leaves open the question of "which year's profits?" The company may be able to increase current profits by cutting back on maintenance or staff training, but shareholders may not welcome this if profits are damaged in future years.
2. A company may be able to increase future profits by cutting this year's dividend and investing the freed-up cash in the firm. That is not in the shareholders' best interest if the company earns only a very low rate of return on the extra investment.
3. Different accountants may calculate profits in different ways. So you may find that a decision that improves profits using one set of accounting rules may reduce them using another.

In a free economy a firm is unlikely to survive if it pursues other goals that reduce the firm's value. Suppose, for example, that a firm's only goal is to increase its market share. It aggressively reduces prices to capture new customers, even when the price discounts cause continuing losses. What would happen to such a firm? As losses mount, it will find it more and more difficult to borrow money, and it may not even have sufficient profits to repay existing debts. Sooner or later, however, outside investors would see an opportunity for easy money. They could offer to buy the firm from its current shareholders and, once they tossed out existing management, could increase the firm's value by changing its policies. They would profit by the difference between the price paid for the firm and the higher value it would have under new management. Managers who pursue goals that destroy value often land in early retirement.

> **We conclude that managers as a general rule will act to maximize the value of the firm to its stockholders. Management teams that deviate too far from this rule are likely to be replaced.**

Ethics and Management Objectives

We have suggested that managers should try to maximize market value. But some idealists say that managers should not be obliged to act in the selfish interests of their stockholders. Some realists argue that, regardless of what managers ought to do, they in fact look after themselves rather than their shareholders.

Let us respond to the idealists first. Does a focus on value mean that managers must act as greedy mercenaries riding roughshod over the weak and helpless? Most of this book is devoted to financial policies that increase firm value. None of these policies require gallops over the weak and helpless. In most instances there is little conflict between doing well (maximizing value) and doing good.

The first step in doing well is doing good by your customers. Here is how Adam Smith put the case in 1776:

> It is not from the benevolence of the butcher, the brewer, or the baker, that we expect our dinner, but from their regard to their own interest. We address ourselves, not to their humanity but to their self-love, and never talk to them of our own necessities but of their advantages.[12]

By striving to enrich themselves and their shareholders, businesspeople have to provide their customers with the products and services they truly desire.

Of course ethical issues do arise in business as in other walks of life. For example, the objective in football is to score points and win games, but that doesn't mean you should try to maim the opposition. Likewise, when we say that the objective of the firm is to maximize shareholder wealth, we do not mean that anything goes.

In football there are written rules that specify what players may and may not do. In the same way, the law limits what managers may do. Without doubt, there are financial managers who are out-and-out crooks, but most of us have no problem in recognizing and avoiding obvious crooked behavior. It is not the blatantly illegal action but the gray areas that pose the hardest dilemmas for the average manager. Should the firm be prepared to do business with a corrupt and repressive government? Should it employ child labor in countries where that is the norm? In the clarity of hindsight the answers to such questions may be obvious, but when the stakes are high, competition is intense, and a deadline is looming, it's easy to blunder. In such cases managers are tempted not to inquire as deeply as they should about the legality or morality of their actions.

Written rules and laws can help only so much. In addition to the written rules of football, there are also unwritten understandings about fair play. Players observe these unwritten rules partly because they know that it is in everybody's interests to abide by them and partly because they know that it is not in their selfish interests to get a reputation for dirty play.

In business there are also unwritten or implicit rules. These work because everyone knows that such rules are in the general interest. But they are reinforced because good managers know that their firm's reputation is one of its most important assets and therefore playing fair and keeping one's word are simply good business practices. Thus huge deals are regularly completed on a handshake and each side knows that the other will not renege later if things turn sour.[13]

Of course, it is not always easy to know where implicit agreements start and end, and there can be many gray areas of considerable disagreement about the obligations of one party to another. The nearby box presents several situations that call for an

See box p. 17

---

[12]Adam Smith, *An Inquiry into the Nature and Causes of the Wealth of Nations* (New York: Random House, 1937; first published 1776), p. 14.

[13]For example, the motto of the London Stock Exchange is "My word is my bond."

Things Are Not Always Fair in Love or Economics

What constitutes *fair* behavior by companies? One survey asked a number of individuals to state whether they regarded a particular action as acceptable or unfair. Before we tell you how they responded, think how *you* would rate each of the following actions:

1a. A small photocopying shop has one employee who has worked in the shop for 6 months and earns $9 per hour. Business continues to be satisfactory, but a factory in the area has closed and unemployment has increased. Other small shops in the area have now hired reliable workers at $7 an hour to perform jobs similar to those done by the photocopying shop employee. The owner of the photocopying shop reduces the employee's wage to $7.

1b. Now suppose that the shop does not reduce the employee's wage but he or she leaves. The owner decides to pay a replacement $7 an hour.

2. A house painter employs two assistants and pays them $9 per hour. The painter decides to quit house painting and go into the business of providing landscape services, where the going wage is lower. He reduces the workers' wages to $7 per hour for the landscaping work.

3a. A small company employs several workers and has been paying them average wages. There is severe unemployment in the area and the company could easily replace its current employees with good workers at a lower wage. The company has been making money. The owners reduce the current workers' wages by 5 percent.

3b. Now suppose instead that the company has been losing money and the owners reduce wages by 5 percent.

4. A grocery store has several months' supply of peanut butter in stock on shelves in the storeroom. The owner hears that the wholesale price of peanut butter has increased and immediately raises the price on the current stock of peanut butter.

5. A hardware store has been selling snow shovels for $15. The morning after a large snowstorm, the store raises the price to $20.

6. A store has been sold out of the popular Beanie Baby dolls for a month. A week before Christmas a single doll is discovered in a storeroom. The managers know that many customers would like to buy the doll. They announce over the store's public address system that the doll will be sold by auction to the customer who offers to pay the most.

Now compare your responses with the responses of a random sample of individuals:

Action	Percent Rating the Action As:	
	Acceptable	Unfair
1a	17	83
1b	73	27
2	63	37
3a	23	77
3b	68	32
4	21	79
5	18	82
6	26	74

Source: Adapted from D. Kahneman, J. L. Knetsch, and R. Thaler, "Fairness as a Constraint on Profit Seeking: Entitlements in the Market," *American Economic Review* 76 (September 1986), pp. 728–741.

ethically based decision, along with survey responses to the proper course of action in each circumstance. Compare your decisions with those of the general public.

If you buy a well-known brand in a store, you can be fairly sure what you are getting. But in financial transactions the other party often has more information than you and it is less easy to be sure of the quality of what you are buying. This opens up plenty of opportunities for sharp practice and outright fraud, and, because the activities of rogues are more entertaining than those of honest people, bookshelves are packed with accounts of financial fraudsters.

What is the reaction of honest financial firms? It is to build long-term relationships with their customers and establish a name for fair dealing and financial integrity. Major banks and securities firms know that their most valuable asset is their reputation and they emphasize their long history and their responsible behavior when seeking new customers. When something happens to undermine that reputation the costs can be enormous.

Consider the case of the Salomon Brothers bidding scandal in 1991.[14] A Salomon trader tried to evade rules limiting its participation in auctions of U.S. Treasury bonds by submitting bids in the names of the company's customers without the customers' knowledge. When this was discovered, Salomon settled the case by paying almost $200 million in fines and establishing a $100 million fund for payments of claims from civil lawsuits. Yet the value of Salomon Brothers stock fell by far more than $300 million. In fact, the price dropped by about a third, representing a $1.5 billion decline in market value.

Why did the value of the firm drop so dramatically? Largely because investors were worried that Salomon would lose business from customers that now distrusted the company. The damage to Salomon's reputation was far greater than the explicit costs of the scandal, and hundreds or thousands of times as costly as the potential gains it could have reaped from the illegal trades.

▶ **Self-Test 1.5**

Without knowing anything about the personal ethics of the owners, which company would you better trust to keep its word in a business deal?

a. Harry's Hardware has been in business for 50 years. Harry's grandchildren, now almost adults, plan to take over and operate the business. Hardware stores require considerable investment in customer relations to become established.
b. Victor's Videos just opened for business. It rents a storefront in a strip mall and has financed its inventory with a bank loan. Victor has little of his own money invested in the business. Video shops usually command little customer loyalty.

Do Managers Really Maximize Firm Value?

Owner-managers have no conflicts of interest in their management of the business. They work for themselves, reaping the rewards of good work and suffering the penalties of bad work. Their *personal* well-being is tied to the value of the firm.

In most large companies the managers are not the owners and they might be tempted to act in ways that are not in the best interests of the owners. For example, they might buy luxurious corporate jets for their travel, or overindulge in expense-account dinners. They might shy away from attractive but risky projects because they are worried more about the safety of their jobs than the potential for superior profits. They might engage in empire building, adding unnecessary capacity or employees. Such problems can arise because the managers of the firm, who are hired as *agents* of the owners, may have their own axes to grind. Therefore they are called **agency problems.**

agency problems: Conflict of interest between the firm's owners and managers.

Think of the company's net revenue as a pie that is divided among a number of claimants. These include the management and the work force as well as the lenders

---

[14]This discussion is based on Clifford W. Smith, Jr., "Economics and Ethics: The Case of Salomon Brothers," *Journal of Applied Corporate Finance* 5 (Summer 1992), pp. 23–28.

stakeholder: Anyone with a financial interest in the firm.

and shareholders who put up the money to establish and maintain the business. The government is a claimant, too, since it gets to tax the profits of the enterprise. It is common to hear these claimants called **stakeholders** in the firm. Each has a stake in the firm and their interests may not coincide.

All these stakeholders are bound together in a complex web of contracts and understandings. For example, when banks lend money to the firm, they insist on a formal contract stating the rate of interest and repayment dates, perhaps placing restrictions on dividends or additional borrowing. Similarly, large companies have carefully worked out personnel policies that establish employees' rights and responsibilities. But you can't devise written rules to cover every possible future event. So the written contracts are supplemented by understandings. For example, managers understand that in return for a fat salary they are expected to work hard and not spend the firm's money on unwarranted personal luxuries.

What enforces these understandings? Is it realistic to expect managers always to act on behalf of the shareholders? The shareholders can't spend their lives watching through binoculars to check that managers are not shirking or dissipating company funds on the latest executive jet.

A closer look reveals several arrangements that help to ensure that the shareholders and managers are working toward common goals.

Compensation Plans. Managers are spurred on by incentive schemes that provide big returns if shareholders gain but are valueless if they do not. For example, when Michael Eisner was hired as chief executive officer (CEO) by the Walt Disney Company his compensation package had three main components: a base annual salary of $750,000; an annual bonus of 2 percent of Disney's net income above a threshold of "normal" profitability; and a 10-year option that allowed him to purchase 2 million shares of stock for $14 per share, which was about the price of Disney stock at the time. Those options would be worthless if Disney's shares were selling for below $14 but highly valuable if the shares were worth more. This gave Eisner a huge personal stake in the success of the firm.

As it turned out, by the end of Eisner's 6-year contract the value of Disney shares had increased by $12 billion, more than sixfold. Eisner's compensation over the period was $190 million.[15] Was he overpaid? We don't know (and we suspect nobody else knows) how much Disney's success was due to Michael Eisner or how hard Eisner would have worked with a different compensation scheme. Our point is that managers often have a strong financial interest in increasing firm value.

The Board of Directors. Boards of directors are sometimes portrayed as passive supporters of top management. But when company performance starts to slide, and managers don't offer a credible recovery plan, boards do act. In recent years, the chief executives of IBM, Eastman Kodak, General Motors, and Apple Computer all were forced out.

If shareholders believe that the corporation is underperforming and that the board of directors is not sufficiently aggressive in holding the managers to task, they can try to replace the board in the next election. The dissident shareholders will attempt to convince other shareholders to vote for their slate of candidates to the board. If they succeed, a new board will be elected and it can replace the current management team.

[15]This discussion is based on Stephen F. O'Byrne, "What Pay for Performance Looks Like: The Case of Michael Eisner," *Journal of Applied Corporate Finance* 5 (Summer 1992), pp. 135–136.

Takeovers.   Poorly performing companies are also more likely to be taken over by another firm. After the takeover, the old management team may find itself out on the street. We discuss takeovers in Chapter 21.

Specialist Monitoring.   Finally, managers are subject to the scrutiny of specialists. Their actions are monitored by the security analysts who advise investors to buy, hold, or sell the company's shares. They are also reviewed by banks, which keep an eagle eye on the progress of firms receiving their loans.

Of course, this raises another question: Who monitors the directors, bankers, and security analysts to make sure that they are doing their jobs? The problem is rather like that faced by the citizens of Hawtch-Hawtch as described by Dr. Seuss:

> OH, THE JOBS people work at!
> Out west, near Hawtch-Hawtch,
> There's a Hawtch-Hawtch Bee Watcher,
> His job is to watch . . .
> Is to keep both his eyes on the lazy town bee,
> A bee that is watched will work harder, you see.
> Well . . . he watched and he watched.
> But in spite of his watch,
> that bee didn't work any harder. Not mawtch.
> So then somebody said,
> "Our old bee-watching man
> just isn't bee-watching as hard as he can.
> He ought to be watched by *another* Hawtch-Hawtcher.
> The thing that we need
> is a Bee-Watcher-Watcher."
>   WELL . . .
> The Bee-Watcher-Watcher watched the Bee Watcher.
> He didn't watch well. So another Hawtch-Hawtcher
> had to come in as a Watch-Watcher-Watcher.
> And today all the Hawtchers who live in Hawtch-Hawtch
> are watching on Watch-Watcher-Watchering-Watch,
> Watch-Watching the Watcher who's watching that bee.
> You're not a Hawtch-Hawtcher. You're lucky, you see.[16]

We do not want to leave the impression that corporate life is a series of squabbles and management-watcher-watching. It isn't, because practical corporate finance has evolved to reconcile personal and corporate interests—to keep everyone working together to increase the value of the whole pie, not merely the size of each person's slice.

> **The agency problem is mitigated in practice through several devices: compensation plans that tie the fortune of the manager to the fortunes of the firm; monitoring by lenders, stock market analysts, and investors; and ultimately the threat that poor performance will result in the removal of the manager.**

---

[16]From *Did I Ever Tell You How Lucky You Are?* by Dr. Seuss. TM and copyright © 1973 by Dr. Seuss Enterprises, L. P. Reprinted by permission of Random House, Inc.

▶ **Self-Test 1.6**   Corporations are now required to make public the amount and form of compensation (e.g., stock options versus salary versus performance bonuses) received by their top executives. Of what use would that information be to a potential investor in the firm?

1.6 Topics Covered in This Book

This book covers investment decisions first, then financing decisions, and then a variety of planning issues that require understanding of both investments and financing.

In Parts Two and Three we look at different aspects of the investment decision. The first is the problem of how to value assets, and the second is the link between risk and value. Our discussion of these topics occupies Chapters 3 through 10.

Eight chapters devoted to the simple problem of finding real assets that are worth more than they cost may seem excessive, but that problem is not so simple in practice. We will require a theory of how long-lived, risky assets are valued, and that requirement will lead us to basic questions about capital markets. For example:

- How are corporate bonds and stocks valued in capital markets?
- What risks are borne by investors in corporate securities? How can these risks be measured?
- What compensation do investors demand for bearing risk?
- What rate of return can investors in common stocks reasonably expect to receive?

Intelligent capital budgeting and financing decisions require answers to these and other questions about how capital markets work.

Financing decisions occupy Parts Four and Five. We begin in Chapter 11 with another basic question about capital markets: Do security prices reflect the fair value of the underlying assets? This question is crucially important because the financial manager must know whether securities can be issued at a fair price. The remaining chapters in Part Four describe the kinds of securities corporations use to raise money and explain how and when they are issued.

Part Five continues the analysis of the financing decision, covering dividend policy and debt policy. We will also describe what happens when firms find themselves in financial distress because of poor operating performance, excessive borrowing, or both.

Part Six covers financial planning. Decisions about investment, dividend policy, debt policy, and other financial issues cannot be reached independently. They have to add up to a sensible overall financial plan for the firm, one which increases the value of the shareholders' investment yet still retains enough flexibility for the firm to avoid financial distress and to pursue unexpected new opportunities.

Part Seven is devoted to decisions about the firm's short-term assets and liabilities. We discuss channels for short-term borrowing or investment, management of liquid assets (cash and marketable securities), and management of accounts receivable (money lent by the firm to its customers) and inventories.

Part Eight covers three important problems which require decisions about both investment and financing. First we look at mergers and acquisitions. Then we consider international financial management. All the financial problems of doing business at home are present overseas, but the international financial manager faces the

Finance through the Ages

Date unknown *Compound Growth.* Bacteria start to propagate by subdividing. They thereby demonstrate the power of compound growth. *(Chapter 3)*

c. 1800 B.C. *Interest Rates.* In Babylonia Hammurabi's Code established maximum interest rates on loans. Borrowers often mortgaged their property and sometimes their spouses but in these cases the lender was obliged to return the spouse in good condition within 3 years. *(Chapter 4)*

c. 1000 B.C. *Options.* One of the earliest recorded options is described by Aristotle. The philosopher Thales knew by the stars that there would be a great olive harvest, so, having a little money, he bought options for the use of olive presses. When the harvest came Thales was able to rent the presses at great profit. Today financial managers need to be able to evaluate options to buy or sell a wide variety of assets. *(Chapter 23)*

15th century *International Banking.* Modern international banking has its origins in the great Florentine banking houses. But the entire European network of the Medici empire employed only 57 people in eight offices. Today Citicorp has 81,000 employees and 3500 offices in 93 different countries. *(Chapter 12)*

1650 *Futures.* Futures markets allow companies to protect themselves against fluctuations in commodity prices. During the Tokugawa era in Japan feudal lords collected rents in the form of rice but often they wished to trade their future rice deliveries. Rice futures therefore came to be traded on what was later known as the Dojima Rice Market. Rice futures are still traded but now companies can also trade in futures on a range of items from pork bellies to stock market indexes. *(Chapter 24)*

17th century *Joint Stock Corporations.* Although investors have for a long time combined together as joint owners of an enterprise, the modern corporation with a large number of stockholders originates with the formation in England of the great trading firms like the East India Company (est. 1599). Another early trading firm, Hudson's Bay (est. 1670), still survives and is one of Canada's largest companies. *(Chapter 13)*

17th century *Money.* America has been in the forefront in the development of new types of money. Early settlers often used a shell known as wampum. For example, Peter Stuyvesant raised a loan in wampum and in Massachusetts it was legal tender. Unfortunately, the enterprising settlers found that with a little dye the relatively common white wampum shells could be converted profitably into the more valuable black ones, which simply demonstrated Gresham's law that bad money drives out good. The first issue of paper money in America (and almost in the world) was by the Massachusetts Bay Colony in 1690, and other colonies soon set their printing presses to producing money. In 1862 Congress agreed to an issue of paper money which would be legal tender. These notes, printed in green ink, immediately became known as greenbacks. *(Chapter 19)*

1720 *New Issue Speculation.* From time to time investors have been tempted by speculative new issues. During the South Sea Bubble in England one company was launched to develop perpetual motion. Another enterprising individual announced a company "for carrying on an undertaking of great advantage but nobody to know what it is." Within 5 hours he had raised £2000; within 6 hours he was on his way out of the country. *(Chapter 13)*

1792 *Formation of the New York Stock Exchange.* The New York Stock Exchange (NYSE) was founded in 1792 when a group of brokers met under a buttonwood tree and arranged to trade shares with one another at agreed rates of commission. Today the NYSE

additional complications created by multiple currencies, different tax systems, and special regulations imposed by foreign institutions and governments. Finally, we look at risk management and the specialized securities, including futures and options, that managers can use to hedge or lay off risks.

Part Nine is our conclusion. It also discusses some of the things that we *don't* know about finance. If you can be the first to solve any of these puzzles, you will be justifiably famous.

is the largest stock exchange in the world, trading on average 400 million shares a day. (*Chapter 4*)

1929 *Stock Market Crashes.* Common stocks are risky investments. In September 1929 stock prices in the United States reached an all-time high and the economist Irving Fisher forecast that they were at "a permanently high plateau." Some 3 years later stock prices were almost 90 percent lower and it was to be a quarter of a century before the prices of September 1929 were seen again. Contrary to popular impression, no Wall Street broker jumped out the window. (*Chapter 8*)

1960s *Eurodollar Market.* In the 1950s the Soviet Union transferred its dollar holdings from the United States to a Russian-owned bank in Paris. This bank was best known by its telex address, EUROBANK, and consequently dollars held outside the United States came to be known as eurodollars. In the 1960s U.S. taxes and regulation made it much cheaper to borrow and lend dollars in Europe rather than in the United States and a huge market in eurodollars arose. (*Chapter 12*)

1972 *Financial Futures.* Financial futures allow companies to protect themselves against fluctuations in interest rates, exchange rates, and so on. It is said that they originated from a remark by the economist Milton Friedman that he was unable to profit from his view that sterling was overpriced. The Chicago Mercantile Exchange founded the first financial futures market. Today futures exchanges in the United States trade 200 million contracts a year of financial futures. (*Chapter 24*)

1986 *Capital Investment Decisions.* The largest investment project undertaken by private companies was the construction of the tunnel under the English Channel. This started in 1986 and was completed in 1994 at a total cost of $15 billion. (*Chapter 5*)

1988 *Mergers.* The 1980s saw a wave of takeovers culminating in the $25 billion takeover of RJR Nabisco. Over a period of 6 weeks three groups battled for control of the company. As one of the contestants put it, "We were charging through the rice paddies, not stopping for anything and taking no prisoners." The takeover was the largest in history and generated almost $1 billion in fees for the banks and advisers. (*Chapter 22*)

1993 *Inflation.* Financial managers need to recognize the effect of inflation on interest rates and on the profitability of the firm's investments. In the United States inflation has been relatively modest, but some countries have suffered from hyperinflation. In Hungary after World War II the government issued banknotes worth 1000 trillion pengoes. In Yugoslavia in October 1993 prices rose by nearly 2000 percent and a dollar bought 105 million dinars. (*Chapter 3*)

1780 and 1997 *Inflation-Indexed Debt.* In 1780, Massachusetts paid Revolutionary War soldiers with interest-bearing notes rather than its rapidly eroding currency. Interest and principal payments on the notes were tied to the rate of subsequent inflation. After a 217-year hiatus, the United States Treasury issued 10-year inflation-indexed notes. Many other countries, including Britain and Israel, had done so previously. (*Chapter 3*)

1997 *Financial Swindles.* Bad financial deals are often difficult for the unsophisticated to spot, and this helps financial fraudsters. When Bre-X, a tiny Canadian mining company, announced that it had uncovered the world's largest gold deposit in the jungles of Borneo, investors rushed to share in the bonanza. In less than a year Bre-X's stock price rose almost a hundredfold. The first rumors of trouble began to circulate in February 1997 when the company's chief geologist was killed in a fall from a helicopter. An independent investigation revealed that the ore samples had been doctored and investors had been on the receiving end of an elaborate hoax. Bre-X shares, which had once been valued at $6 billion, were now bought by souvenir hunters for a few pennies each. (*Chapter 1*)

Snippets of History

See box pp. 22–23

Now let's lighten up a little. In this book we are going to describe how financial decisions are made today. But financial markets also have an interesting history. Look at the accompanying box, which lays out bits of this history, starting in prehistoric times, when the growth of bacteria anticipated the mathematics of compound interest, and continuing nearly to the present. We have keyed each of these episodes to the chapter of the book that discusses it.

1.7 Summary

1. Businesses may be organized as proprietorships, partnerships, or corporations. A corporation is legally distinct from its owners. Therefore, the shareholders who own a corporation enjoy limited liability for its obligations. Ownership and management of corporations are usually separate.

2. The overall task of financial management can be broken down into (1) the investment, or capital budgeting, decision and (2) the financing decision. In other words, the firm has to decide (1) how much to invest and what assets to invest in and (2) how to raise the necessary cash. The objective is to increase the value of the shareholders' stake in the firm.

3. The financial manager acts as the intermediary between the firm and financial markets. In small companies there is often only one financial executive. However, the larger corporation usually has both a treasurer and a controller. The treasurer's job is to obtain and manage the company's financing. By contrast, the controller's job is one of inspecting to see that the money is used correctly. Large firms may also appoint a chief financial officer, or CFO.

4. Value maximization is usually taken to be the goal of the firm. Such a strategy maximizes shareholders' wealth, thereby enabling them to pursue their personal goals. However, value maximization does not imply a disregard for ethical decision making, in part because the firm's reputation as an employer and business partner depends on its past actions.

5. Agency problems imply that managers may have interests that differ from those of the firm. These problems are kept in check by compensation plans that link the well-being of employees to that of the firm, by monitoring of management by the board of directors, securityholders, and creditors, and by the threat of takeover.

Key Terms

sole proprietor	financial intermediary	controller
partnership	capital budgeting	chief financial officer (CFO)
corporation	decision	primary market
limited liability	financing decision	secondary market
real assets	capital structure	agency problem
financial assets	capital markets	stakeholder
financial markets	treasurer	

Problems

1. **Financial Decisions.** Fit each of the following terms into the most appropriate space: *financing, real, stock, investment, executive airplanes, financial, capital budgeting, brand names.*

   Companies usually buy ___ assets. These include both tangible assets such as ___ and intangible assets such as ___. In order to pay for these assets, they sell ___ assets such as ___. The decision regarding which assets to buy is usually termed the ___ or ___ decision. The decision regarding how to raise the money is usually termed the ___ decision.

2. **Financial Managers.** Which of the following statements more accurately describes the treasurer than the controller?

   a. Likely to be the only financial executive in small firms
   b. Monitors capital expenditures to make sure that they are not misappropriated

    c. Responsible for investing the firm's spare cash

    d. Responsible for arranging any issue of common stock

    e. Responsible for the company's tax affairs

3. **Real versus Financial Assets.** Which of the following are real assets, and which are financial?

    a. A share of stock

    b. A personal IOU

    c. A trademark

    d. A truck

    e. Undeveloped land

    f. The balance in the firm's checking account

    g. An experienced and hardworking sales force

    h. A bank loan agreement

4. **Ethics.** Is there a conflict between "doing well" and "doing good"? In other words, are policies that increase the value of the firm (doing well) necessarily at odds with socially responsible policies (doing good)? When there are conflicts, how might government regulations or laws tilt the firm toward doing good? For example, how do taxes or fees charged on pollutants affect the firm's decision to pollute? Can you cite other examples of "incentives" used by governments to align private interests with public ones?

5. **Agency Issues.** Sometimes lawyers work on a contingency basis. They collect a percentage of their client's settlement instead of receiving a fixed fee. Why might clients prefer this arrangement? Would this sort of arrangement be more appropriate for clients that use lawyers regularly or infrequently?

6. **Reputation.** As you drive down a deserted highway you are overcome with a sudden desire for a hamburger. Fortunately, just ahead are two hamburger outlets; one is owned by a national brand, the other appears to be owned by "Joe." Which outlet has the greater incentive to serve you catmeat? Why?

7. **Ethics.** In some countries, such as Japan and Germany, corporations develop close long-term relationships with one bank and rely on that bank for a large part of their financing needs. In the United States companies are more likely to shop around for the best deal. Do you think that this practice is more or less likely to encourage ethical behavior on the part of the corporation?

8. **Agency.** Discuss which of the following forms of compensation is most likely to align the interests of managers and shareholders:

    a. A fixed salary

    b. A salary linked to company profits

    c. A salary that is paid partly in the form of the company's shares

    d. An option to buy the company's shares at an attractive price

9. **Corporate Control.** When a company's stock is widely held, it may not pay an individual shareholder to spend time monitoring the manager's performance and trying to replace poor management. Explain why. Do you think that a bank that has made a large loan to the company is in a different position?

10. **Goals of the Firm.** Explain why each of the following may not be appropriate corporate goals:

    a. Increase market share

    b. Minimize costs

    c. Underprice any competitors

    d. Expand profits

11. **Corporate Organization.** What are the advantages and disadvantages of setting up business as

    a. a sole proprietor
    b. a partnership
    c. a corporation

12. **Value Maximization.** Give an example of an action that might increase profits but at the same time reduce stock price.

13. **Agency Problems.** Many firms have devised defenses that make it much more costly or difficult for other firms to take them over. How might such takeover defenses affect the firm's agency problems? Are managers of firms with formidable takeover defenses more or less likely to act in the firm's interests rather than their own?

14. **The Financial Manager.** Give two examples of capital budgeting decisions and financing decisions.

15. **Agency Problems.** If agency problems can be mitigated by tying the manager's compensation to the fortunes of the firm, why don't firms compensate managers *exclusively* with shares in the firm?

16. **Financial Markets.** What is meant by over-the-counter trading? Is this trading mechanism used for stocks, bonds, or both?

17. **Financial Institutions.** We gave banks and insurance companies as two examples of financial institutions. What other types of financial institutions can you identify?

18. **Financial Markets.** In most years new issues of stock are a tiny fraction of total stock market trading. In other words, secondary market volume is much greater than primary market volume. Does this mean that most activity in the stock market is irrelevant to the financial manager? *Hint:* How is the price of the firm's stock determined, and why is it important to the financial manager?

Solutions to Self-Test Questions

1.1 a. The consulting firm is most suited to a partnership. Each senior consultant might be a partner, with partial responsibility for managing the firm and its clients

b. The college student would set up the business as a sole proprietorship. He or she is the only manager, and has little need for partners to contribute capital.

c. The large firm would be set up as a corporation. It requires great amounts of capital and with the budgetary, payroll, and management issues that arise with such a large number of employees, it probably needs a professional management team.

1.2 a. The development of a microprocessor is a capital budgeting decision. The investment of $500 million will purchase a real asset, the microprocessor.

b. The bank loan is a financing decision. This is how Volkswagen will raise money for its investment.

c. Capital budgeting.

d. Financing.

e. Capital budgeting. Though intangible, the license is a real asset that is expected to produce future sales and profits.

f. Financing.

1.3 Sal would more likely be the treasurer and Sally the controller. The treasurer raises money from the credit and financial markets and requires background in financial institutions. The controller is more of an overseer who requires background in accounting.

1.4 a. Real assets support the operations of the business. They are necessary to produce future profits and cash inflows. Financial assets or securities are claims on the profits and cash inflows generated by the firm's real assets and operations.

b. A company *invests* in real assets to support its operations. It *finances* the investment by raising money from banks, shareholders, or other investors.

c. Capital budgeting deals with investment decisions. Capital structure is the composition of the company's sources of financing.

d. When a company raises money from investors, it sells financial assets or securities in the primary market. Later trades among investors occur in the secondary market.

e. A company can raise money by selling securities directly to investors in financial markets, or it can deal with a financial intermediary. The intermediary raises money from investors and reinvests it in the company's securities. The intermediary invests primarily in financial assets.

1.5 Harry's has a far bigger stake in the reputation of the business than Victor's. The store has been in business for a long time. The owners have spent years establishing customer loyalty. In contrast, Victor's has just been established. The owner has little of his own money tied up in the firm, and so has little to lose if the business fails. In addition, the nature of the business results in little customer loyalty. Harry's is probably more reliable.

1.6 An investor would like top management to be compensated according to the fortunes of the firm. If management is willing to bet its own compensation on the success of the firm, that is good news, first because it shows management has confidence in the firm, and second because it gives managers greater incentives to work hard to make the firm succeed.

Accountants at work.

Accounting is not the same as finance, but if you don't understand at least the basics of accounting, you won't understand finance either.

Yale Center for British Art, Paul Mellow Collection

Accounting and Finance

*I*n Chapter 1 we pointed out that a large corporation is a team effort. All the players—the shareholders, lenders, directors, management, and employees—have a stake in the company's success and all therefore need to monitor its progress. For this reason the company prepares regular financial accounts and arranges for an independent firm of auditors to certify that these accounts present a "true and fair view."

Until the mid-nineteenth century most businesses were owner-managed and seldom required outside capital beyond personal loans to the proprietor. When businesses were small and there were few outside stakeholders in the firm, accounting could be less formal. But with the industrial revolution and the creation of large railroad and canal companies, the shareholders and bankers demanded information that would help them gauge a firm's financial strength. That was when the accounting profession began to come of age.

We don't want to discuss the details of accounting practice. But because we will be referring to financial statements throughout this book, it may be useful to review briefly their main features. In this chapter we introduce the major financial statements, the balance sheet, the income statement, and the statement of cash flow. We discuss the important differences between income and cash flow and between book values and market values. We also discuss the federal tax system.

After studying this chapter you should be able to

▶ Interpret the information contained in the balance sheet, income statement, and statement of cash flows.

▶ Distinguish between market and book value.

▶ Explain why income differs from cash flow.

▶ Understand the essential features of the taxation of corporate and personal income.

2.1 The Balance Sheet

balance sheet: Financial statement that shows the value of the firm's assets and liabilities at a particular time.

We will look first at the **balance sheet,** which presents a snapshot of the firm's assets and the source of the money that was used to buy those assets. The assets are listed on the left-hand side of the balance sheet. Some assets can be turned more easily into cash than others; these are known as *liquid* assets. The accountant puts the most liquid assets at the top of the list and works down to the least liquid.

Look, for example, at the left-hand column of Table 2.1, the balance sheet for Nike, Inc., at the end of 1995. You can see that Nike had $216 million of cash and marketable securities. In addition it had sold shoes worth $1,053 million but had not yet received payment. These payments are due soon and therefore the balance sheet shows the unpaid bills or *accounts receivable* (or simply *receivables*) as an asset. The next asset consists of inventories. These may be (1) raw materials and components that the firm bought from suppliers, (2) work in process such as shoes in process of manufacture, and (3) finished shoes waiting to be shipped from the warehouse. Of course

page 30 printed at bottom

Table 2.1

BALANCE SHEET FOR NIKE, INC. (Figures in millions of dollars)					
Assets	Dec. 30, 1995	Dec. 30, 1994	Liabilities and Shareholders' Equity	Dec. 30, 1995	Dec. 30, 1994
Current assets			Current liabilities		
Cash and marketable securities	216	519	Debt due for repayment	429	131
Accounts receivable	1,053	704	Accounts payable	298	211
Inventories	630	470	Other current liabilities	381	220
Other current assets	147	78	Total current liabilities	1,108	562
Total current assets	2,046	1,770			
Fixed assets			Long-term debt and other long-term liabilities	70	71
Property, plant, and equipment	891	639	Shareholders' equity		
Less accumulated depreciation	336	233	Common stock and other paid-in capital	127	96
Net fixed assets	555	406	Retained earnings	1,838	1,645
Other assets	542	197	Total shareholders' equity	1,965	1,741
Total assets	3,143	2,374	Total liabilities and shareholders' equity	3,143	2,374

Note: Columns may not add because of rounding.
Source: Nike, Inc., *1995 Annual Report.*

there are always some items that don't fit into neat categories. So the current assets category includes a fourth entry, *other current assets.*

Up to this point all the assets in Nike's balance sheet are likely to be used or turned into cash in the near future. They are therefore described as *current assets.* The other assets in the balance sheet are known as *fixed assets.* For Nike these consist of buildings, equipment, and vehicles. However, don't be misled by the balance sheet into thinking that these are its only fixed assets. Some of the most valuable assets may be intangible, such as patents, trademarks, reputation, a skilled management, and a well-trained labor force. Accountants are generally reluctant to record these intangible assets in the balance sheet unless they can be readily identified and valued.

The balance sheet shows that the gross value of Nike's fixed assets is $891 million. This is what the assets originally cost. But they are unlikely to be worth that now. For example, suppose it bought a delivery van 2 years ago; that van may be worth far less now than Nike paid for it. It might in principle be possible for the accountant to estimate separately the value today of the van, but this would be costly and somewhat subjective. Accountants rely instead on rules of thumb to estimate the depreciation in the value of assets and with rare exceptions they stick to these rules. For example, in the case of that delivery van the accountant may deduct a third of the original cost each year to reflect its declining value. So if Nike bought the van 2 years ago for $15,000, the balance sheet would show that accumulated depreciation is 2 × $5,000 = $10,000. Net of depreciation the value is only $5,000. Table 2.1 shows that Nike's total accumulated depreciation on fixed assets is $336 million. So while the assets cost $891 million, their net value in the accounts is only $891 − $336 = $555 million.

Now look at the right-hand portion of Nike's balance sheet, which shows where the money to buy the assets came from. The accountant starts by looking at the

Figure 2.1

THE MAIN BALANCE SHEET ITEMS

Current assets		Current liabilities
Cash & securities		Payables
Receivables		Short-term debt
Inventories		
+	=	+
Fixed assets		Long-term liabilities
Tangible assets		+
Intangible assets		Shareholders' equity

company's liabilities—that is, the money owed by the company. First come those liabilities that are likely to be paid off most rapidly. For example, Nike has borrowed $429 million, due to be repaid shortly. It also owes its suppliers $298 million for goods that have been delivered but not yet paid for. These unpaid bills are shown as *accounts payable* (or *payables*). Both the borrowings and the payables are debts that Nike must repay within the year. They are therefore classified as *current liabilities.*

Nike's current assets total $2,046 million; its current liabilities amount to $1,108 million. Therefore the difference between the value of Nike's current assets and its current liabilities is $2,046 − $1,108 = $938 million. This figure is known as Nike's *net current assets* or *net working capital*. It roughly measures the company's potential reservoir of cash.

Below the current liabilities Nike's accountants have listed the firm's long-term liabilities—that is, debts that come due after the end of a year. You can see that banks and other investors have made long-term loans to Nike of $70 million.

Nike's liabilities are financial obligations to various parties. For example, when Nike buys goods from its suppliers, it has a liability to pay for them; when it borrows from the bank, it has a liability to repay the loan. Thus the suppliers and the bank have first claim on the firm's assets. What is left over after the liabilities have been paid off belongs to the shareholders. This figure is known as the shareholders' *equity*. For Nike the total value of shareholders' equity amounts to $1,965 million. A small part of this sum ($127 million) has resulted from the sale of shares to investors. The remainder ($1,838 million) has come from earnings that Nike has retained and invested on shareholders' behalf.

Figure 2.1 shows how the separate items in the balance sheet link together. There are two classes of assets—current assets, which will soon be used or turned into cash, and long-term or "fixed" assets, which may be either tangible or intangible. There are also two classes of liability—current liabilities, which are due for payment shortly, and long-term liabilities. The difference between the assets and the liabilities represents the amount of the shareholders' equity.

▶ **Self-Test 2.1**

Suppose that Nike borrows $50 million by issuing new long-term bonds. It places $10 million of the proceeds in the bank and uses $40 million to buy new machinery. What items of the balance sheet would change? Would shareholders' equity change?

Book Values and Market Values

Throughout this book we will frequently make a distinction between the *book values* of the assets shown in the balance sheet and their market values.

Items in the balance sheet are valued according to **generally accepted accounting principles,** commonly called **GAAP.** These state that assets must be shown in the balance sheet at their *historical cost* adjusted for depreciation. These **book values** are therefore "backward-looking" measures of value. They are based on the past cost of the asset, not its current market price or value to the firm. For example, suppose that a printing press cost McGraw-Hill $1 million 2 years ago, but that in today's market such presses sell for $1.3 million. The book value of the press would be less than its market value and the balance sheet would understate the value of McGraw-Hill's assets.

Or consider a specialized plant that Intel develops for producing special-purpose computer chips at a cost of $100 million. The book value of the plant is $100 million less depreciation. But suppose that shortly after the plant is constructed, a new chip makes the existing one obsolete. The market value of Intel's new plant could fall by 50 percent. In this case market value would be less than book value.

The difference between book value and market value is greater for some assets than for others. It is zero in the case of cash but potentially very large for fixed assets where the accountant starts with the initial cost of the fixed assets and then depreciates that figure according to a prespecified schedule. The purpose of depreciation is to allocate the original cost of the asset over its life, and the rules governing the depreciation of asset values do not reflect actual loss of market value. As a result, the book value of fixed assets often is much higher than the market value, but often it is less.

The same goes for the right-hand side of the balance sheet. In the case of liabilities the accountant simply records the amount of money that you have promised to pay. For short-term liabilities this figure is generally close to the market value of that promise. For example, if you owe the bank $1 million tomorrow, the accounts show a book liability of $1 million. As long as you are not bankrupt, that $1 million is also roughly the value to the bank of your promise. But now suppose that $1 million is not due to be repaid for several years. The accounts still show a liability of $1 million, but how much your debt is worth depends on what happens to interest rates. If interest rates rise after you have issued the debt, lenders may not be prepared to pay as much as $1 million for your debt: if interest rates fall, they may be prepared to pay more than $1 million.[1] Thus the market value of a long-term liability may be higher or lower than the book value.

> To summarize, the market values of neither assets nor liabilities will generally equal their book values. Book values are based on historical or *original* values. Market values measure *current* values of assets and liabilities.

The difference between book value and market value is likely to be greatest for shareholders' equity. The book value of equity measures the cash that shareholders have contributed in the past plus the cash that the company has retained and reinvested in the business on their behalf. But this often bears little resemblance to the total market value that investors place on the shares.

If the market price of the firm's shares falls through the floor, don't try telling the shareholders that the book value is satisfactory—they won't want to hear. Share-

---

[1]We will show you how changing interest rates affect the market value of debt in Chapter 4.

holders are concerned with the market value of their shares; market value, not book value, is the price at which they can sell their shares. Managers who wish to keep their shareholders happy will focus on market values.

We will often find it useful to think about the firm in terms of a *market-value balance sheet*. Like a conventional balance sheet, a market-value balance sheet lists the firm's assets, but it records each asset at its current market value rather than at historical cost less depreciation. Similarly, each liability is shown at its market value.

> **The difference between the market values of assets and liabilities is the market value of the shareholders' equity claim. The stock price is simply the market value of shareholders' equity divided by the number of outstanding shares.**

▶ Example 2.1   *Market- versus Book-Value Balance Sheets*

Jupiter has developed a revolutionary auto production process that enables it to produce cars 20 percent more efficiently than any rival. It has invested $10 billion in producing its new plant. To finance the investment, Jupiter borrowed $4 billion and raised the remaining funds by selling new shares of stock in the firm. There are currently 100 million shares of stock outstanding. Investors are very excited about Jupiter's prospects. They believe that the flow of profits from the new plant justifies a stock price of $75.

If these are Jupiter's only assets, the book-value balance sheet immediately after it has made the investment is as follows:

BOOK-VALUE BALANCE SHEET FOR JUPITER MOTORS
(Figures in billions of dollars)

Assets		Liabilities and Shareholders' Equity	
Auto plant	$10	Debt	$4
		Shareholders' equity	6

Investors are placing a *market value* on Jupiter's equity of $7.5 billion ($75 per share times 100 million shares). We assume that the debt outstanding is worth $4 billion.[2] Therefore, if you owned all Jupiter's shares and all its debt, the value of your investment would be 7.5 + 4 = $11.5 billion. In this case you would own the company lock, stock, and barrel and would be entitled to all its cash flows. Because you can buy the entire company for $11.5 billion, the total value of Jupiter's assets must also be $11.5 billion. In other words, the market value of the assets must be equal to the market value of the liabilities plus the market value of the shareholders' equity.

We can now draw up the market-value balance sheet as follows:

MARKET-VALUE BALANCE SHEET FOR JUPITER MOTORS
(Figures in billions of dollars)

Assets		Liabilities and Shareholders' Equity	
Auto plant	$11.5	Debt	$4
		Shareholders' equity	7.5

---

[2]Jupiter has borrowed $4 billion to finance its investment, but if the interest rate has changed in the meantime, the debt could be worth more or less than $4 billion.

Notice that the market value of Jupiter's plant is $1.5 billion more than the plant cost to build. The difference is due to the superior profits that investors expect the plant to earn. Thus in contrast to the balance sheet shown in the company's books, the market-value balance sheet is forward-looking. It depends on the benefits that investors expect the assets to provide.

Is it surprising that market value exceeds book value? It shouldn't be. Firms find it attractive to raise money to invest in various projects because they believe the projects will be worth more than they cost. Otherwise, why bother? You will usually find that shares of stock sell for more than the value shown in the company's books.

▶ **Self-Test 2.2**

a. What would be Jupiter's price per share if the auto plant had a market value of $14 billion?
b. How would you reassess the value of the auto plant if the value of outstanding stock were $8 billion?

2.2 *The Income Statement*

income statement: Financial statement that shows the revenues, expenses, and net income of a firm over a period of time.

If Nike's balance sheet resembles a snapshot of the firm at a particular time, its **income statement** is like a video. It shows how profitable the firm has been during the past year.

Look at the summary income statement in Table 2.2. You can see that during 1995 Nike sold goods worth $4,761 million and that the total expenses of producing and

Table 2.2

INCOME STATEMENT FOR NIKE, INC., FOR YEAR ENDING DEC. 30, 1995 (All items in millions of dollars)		
Revenues	$4,761	
Cost of goods sold	2,794	
Administrative expenses	1,210	
Depreciation expense	71	
Other expenses	11	
Earnings before interest and taxes (EBIT)	675	
Interest expense	24	
Taxable income	651	
Income taxes	250	
Net income	400	
Allocation of net income		
Repurchase of outstanding stock		143
Addition to retained earnings		192
Dividends		65

Note: Numbers may not add because of rounding.
Source: Nike, Inc., *1995 Annual Report.*

selling goods was ($2,794 + $1,210 + $11) = $4,015 million. The bulk of the expenses, amounting to $2,794 million, consisted of the raw materials, labor, and so on, that were needed to produce the goods. Almost all the remaining expenses were administrative expenses such as head office costs, advertising, and distribution.

In addition to these out-of-pocket expenses, Nike also made a deduction for the value of the plant and equipment used up in producing the shoes. In 1995 this charge for depreciation was $71 million. Thus Nike's total *earnings before interest and taxes* (EBIT) were

$$\text{EBIT} = \text{total revenues} - \text{costs} - \text{depreciation}$$
$$= 4{,}761 - 4{,}015 - 71$$
$$= \$675 \text{ million}$$

The remainder of the income statement shows where these earnings went. As we saw earlier, Nike has partly financed its investment in plant and equipment by borrowing. In 1995 it paid $24 million of interest on this borrowing. A further slice of the profit went to the government in the form of taxes. This amounted in 1995 to $250 million. The $400 million that was left over after paying interest and taxes belonged to the shareholders. Of this sum Nike paid out $65 million in dividends, used $143 million to repurchase shares from existing Nike stockholders, and reinvested the remaining $192 million in the business. Presumably, these reinvested funds made the company more valuable.

Profits versus Cash Flow

It is important to distinguish between Nike's profits and the cash that the company generates. Here are three reasons why profits and cash are not the same:

1. When Nike's accountants prepare the income statement, they do not simply count the cash coming in and the cash going out. Instead the accountant starts with the cash payments but then divides these payments into two groups—current expenditures (such as wages) and capital expenditures (such as the purchase of new machinery). Current expenditures are deducted from current profits. However, rather than deducting the cost of machinery in the year it is purchased, the accountant makes an annual charge for depreciation. Thus the cost of machinery is spread over its forecast life.

   When calculating profits, the accountant does *not* deduct the expenditure on new equipment that year, even though cash is paid out. However, the accountant *does* deduct depreciation on assets previously purchased, even though no cash is currently paid out.

   To calculate the cash produced by the business it is necessary to *add back* the depreciation charge (which is not a cash payment) and to *subtract* the expenditure on new capital equipment (which is a cash payment).

2. Consider the following stages in a manufacturing business. In period 1 the firm produces the goods; it sells them in period 2 for $100; and it gets paid for them in period 3. Although the cash does not arrive until period 3, the sale shows up in the income statement for period 2. The figure for accounts receivable in the balance sheet for period 2 shows that the company's customers owe an extra $100 in unpaid bills. Next period, after the customers have paid their bills, the receivables decline by $100.

The cash that the company *receives* is equal to the sales shown in the income statement less the increase in unpaid bills:

Period:	2	3
Sales	100	0
− Change in receivables	100	(100)
= Cash received	0	+100

3. The accountant also tries to match the costs of producing the goods with the revenues from the sale. For example, suppose that it costs $60 in period 1 to produce the goods that are then sold in period 2 for $100. It would be misleading to say that the business made a loss in period 1 (when it produced the goods) and was very profitable in period 2 (when it sold them). Therefore, to provide a fairer measure of the firm's profitability, the income statement will not show the $60 as an expense of producing the goods until they are sold in period 2. This practice is known as *accrual accounting*. The accountant gathers together all expenses that are associated with a sale and deducts them from the revenues to calculate profit, even though the expenses may have occurred in an earlier period.

Of course the accountant cannot ignore the fact that the firm spent money on producing the goods in period 1. So the expenditure will be shown in period 1 as an *investment* in inventories. Subsequently in period 2, when the goods are sold, the inventories would decline again.

In our example, the cash is paid out when the goods are manufactured in period 1 but this expense is not recognized until period 2 when the goods are sold.

The cash *outflow* is equal to the cost of goods sold, which is shown in the income statement, plus the change in inventories:

Period:	1	2
Costs of goods sold	0	60
+ Change in inventories	60	(60)
= Cash paid out	+60	0

▶ **Self-Test 2.3**

A firm pays $100 in period 1 to produce some goods. It sells those goods for $150 in period 2 but does not collect payment from its customers until period 3. Calculate the cash flows to the firm in each period by completing the following table. Do the resulting values for net cash flow in each period make sense?

Period:	1	2	3
Sales			
Change in accounts receivable			
Cost of goods sold			
Change in inventories			
Net cash flow			

2.3 The Statement of Cash Flows

The firm requires *cash* when it buys new plant and machinery or when it pays interest to the bank and dividends to the shareholders. Therefore, the financial manager needs to keep track of the cash that is coming in and going out.

We have seen that the firm's cash flow can be quite different from its net income. These differences can arise for at least two reasons:

1. The income statement does not recognize capital expenditures as expenses in the year that the capital goods are paid for. Instead, it spreads those expenses over time in the form of an annual deduction for depreciation.
2. The income statement uses the accrual method of accounting, which means that revenues and expenses are recognized as they are incurred rather than when the cash is received or paid out.

Table 2.3

NIKE, INC., STATEMENT OF CASH FLOWS, FOR YEAR ENDING DEC. 30, 1995 (All figures in millions of dollars)	
Cash provided by operations	
Net income	$400
Noncash expenses	
Depreciation expense	71
Increase (decrease) in deferred income taxes	(25)
Other, including amortization	18
Changes in working capital	
Decrease (increase) in inventories	(70)
Decrease (increase) in accounts receivable	(302)
Decrease (increase) in other current assets	(10)
Increase (decrease) in accounts payable	173
Cash provided by operations	255
Cash provided (used) by investments	
Additions to property, plant, and equipment	(145)
Acquisitions of subsidiaries	(430)
Additions to other noncurrent assets	(6)
Cash provided (used) by investments	(581)
Cash provided (used) by financing activities	
Additions to (reductions in) debt	227
Repurchase of stock	(143)
Dividends	(65)
Other	5
Cash provided (used) by financing	25
Net increase in cash and marketable securities	(302)

Note: Numbers may not add because of rounding.
Source: Nike, Inc., *1995 Annual Report.*

statement of cash flows:
Financial statement that shows the firm's cash receipts and cash payments over a period of time.

The **statement of cash flows** shows the firm's cash inflows and outflows from operations as well as from its investments and financing activities. Table 2.3 is the cash-flow statement for Nike. It contains three sections. The first shows the cash flow from operations. This is the cash flow generated from Nike's normal business activity. Next comes the cash that Nike has invested in new plant and equipment. The final section reports cash flows from financing activities such as the sale of new debt or stocks. We will look at these three sections in turn.

The first section, cash flow from operations, starts with net income but adjusts that figure for those parts of the income statement that do not involve cash coming in or going out. For example, it *adds* back the allowance for depreciation because depreciation is not a cash flow even though it is treated as an expense in the income statement. It also adds back income tax that the firm deducted from profits but did not pay.

Any additions to current assets need to be *subtracted* from net income, since these absorb cash but do not show up in the income statement. Conversely, any additions to current liabilities need to be *added* to net income because these release cash. For example, you can see that the increase of $302 million in accounts receivable is *subtracted* from net income, because this represents sales that Nike shows in its income statement though it has not yet received payment. On the other hand, Nike increased accounts payable by $173 million. The accountant deducted this figure as part of the cost of the goods that Nike sold in 1995 though there was no cash payment involved. Thus the $173 million increase in accounts payable must be *added* back to calculate the cash flow from operations.

The second section of the cash-flow statement shows cash expenditures on fixed assets. We have pointed out that depreciation is not a cash payment; it is simply the accountant's allocation to the current year of the original cost of the capital equipment. Cash of course *does* flow out the door when the firm actually buys and pays for new capital equipment. This is therefore recorded in the cash-flow statement. You can see that Nike spent $145 million on new capital equipment, $430 million to purchase new subsidiaries, and $6 million on other noncurrent assets, for a total of $581 million.

Finally, the third section of the cash-flow statement shows the cash flow from financing activities. For example, Nike raised $227 million by issuing debt but used $143 million to repurchase stock and $65 million to pay dividends to its shareholders.[3]

To summarize, the cash flow statement tells us that Nike generated $255 million from operations, it spent $581 million on new investments, and it raised a net amount of $25 million on its various financing activities. Nike expended more cash than it raised; therefore, its cash balance fell by $302 million during the year. To calculate the change in cash balance, we subtract the uses of cash from the sources:

	In millions
Cash flow from operations	$ 255
− Cash flow for new investment	−581
+ Cash raised by new financing	+ 25
= Change in cash balance	−302

[3]You might think that interest payments also ought to be listed in this section. However, it is usual to include interest in the first section with cash flow from operations. This is because, unlike dividends, interest payments are not discretionary. The firm must pay interest when a payment comes due, so these payments are treated as a business expense rather than as a financing decision.

▶ **Self-Test 2.4**   Would the following activities increase or decrease the firm's cash balance?

a. Inventories are increased
b. The firm reduces its accounts payable
c. The firm issues additional common stock
d. The firm buys new equipment

2.4 *Accounting for Differences*

While generally accepted accounting principles go a long way to standardize accounting practice in the United States, accountants still have some leeway in reporting earnings and book values. Financial analysts have even more leeway in how to use those reports; for example, some analysts will include profits or losses from extraordinary or nonrecurring events when they report net income, but others will not. Similarly, accountants have discretion concerning the treatment of intangible assets such as patents, trademarks, or franchises. Some believe that including these intangibles on the balance sheet provides the best measure of the company's value as an ongoing concern. Others take a more conservative approach, and they exclude intangible assets. This approach is better suited for measuring the liquidation value of the firm.

Another source of imprecision arises from the fact that firms are not required to include all their liabilities on the balance sheet. For example, firms are not always required to include as liabilities on the balance sheet the value of their lease obligations.[4] They likewise are not required to include the value of several potential obligations such as warrants[5] sold to investors or issued to employees.

Even bigger differences can arise in international comparisons. Accounting practices can vary greatly from one country to another. For example, in the United States firms generally maintain one set of accounts that is sent to investors and a different set of accounts that is used to calculate their tax bill.[6] That would not be allowed in most countries. On the other hand, United States standards are more stringent in most other regards. For example, German firms have far greater leeway than United States firms to tuck money away in hidden reserve accounts.

When Daimler-Benz AG, producer of the Mercedes-Benz automobile, decided to list its shares on the New York Stock Exchange in 1993, it was required to revise its accounting practices to conform to United States standards. While it reported a modest profit in the first half of 1993 using German accounting rules, it reported a *loss*

---

[4]Some airlines at times actually have not had any aircraft on their balance sheets because their aircraft were all leased. In contrast, General Electric owns the world's largest private airfleet because of its leasing business.

[5]A warrant is the right to purchase a share of stock from the corporation for a specified price, called the *exercise price*.

[6]For example, in their published financial statements most firms in the United States use straight-line depreciation. In other words, they make the same deduction for depreciation in each year of the asset's life. However, when they calculate taxable income, the same companies usually use accelerated depreciation—that is, they make larger deductions for depreciation in the early years of the asset's life and smaller deductions in the later years.

of $592 million under the much more revealing United States rules, primarily because of differences in the treatment of reserves.

Such differences in international accounting standards pose a problem for financial analysts who attempt to compare firms using data from their financial statements. This is why foreign firms must restate their financial results using the generally accepted accounting principles (GAAP) of the United States before their shares can be listed on a U.S. stock exchange. Many firms have been reluctant to do this and have chosen to list their shares elsewhere.

Other countries allow foreign firms to be listed on stock exchanges if their financial statements are prepared according to International Accounting Standards (IAS) rules, which impose considerable uniformity in accounting practices and are nearly as revealing as U.S. standards. The nearby box reports on current negotiations for international accounting standards.

 See box p. 42

The lesson here is clear. While accounting values are often the starting point for the financial analyst, it is usually necessary to probe more deeply. The financial manager needs to know how the values on the statements were computed and whether there are important assets or liabilities missing altogether.

The trend today is toward greater recognition of the market values of various assets and liabilities. Firms are now required to acknowledge on the balance sheet the value of unfunded pension liabilities and other postemployment benefits, such as medical benefits.[7] In addition, a growing (although still controversial) trend toward "market-value accounting" would have them record many assets at market value rather than at historical book value.

2.5 Taxes

Taxes often have a major effect on financial decisions. Therefore, we should explain how corporations and investors are taxed.

Corporate Tax

Companies pay tax on their income. Table 2.4 shows that there are special low rates of corporate tax for small companies, but for large companies (those with income over $18.33 million) the corporate tax rate is 35 percent. Thus for every $100 that the firm earns it pays $35 in corporate tax.

Table 2.4
Corporate tax rates, 1996

Taxable Income, Dollars	Tax Rate, %
0–50,000	15
50,001–75,000	25
75,001–100,000	34
100,001–18,333,333	Varies between 39 and 34 percent
Over 18,333,333	35

[7]When General Motors recognized the value of its postemployment obligations to GM employees, it resulted in the largest quarterly loss in United States history.

Bean Counters, Unite!

Agreement on International Accounting Standards Is Closer than It Has Ever Been. But Can the Present Mood of Goodwill Last?

Not so many years ago, enthusiasts for international accounting standards seemed doomed to eternal frustration. Differences in the ways in which companies in different countries presented their financial results appeared so profound that no amount of compromise would result in meaningful international standards. Suddenly these differences appear smaller.

Helped by the globalization of capital markets, the International Accounting Standards Committee (IASC) has won wide support for its efforts to harmonize accounting rules. If it can clear a few remaining hurdles, the IASC should be able to produce a workable framework by the end of the decade. The greater ease with which companies' disclosures could then be compared would benefit investors and issuers alike.

The continuing globalization of capital markets has given firms a powerful incentive to abandon their resistance to change. Unless they can present their results in ways that foreign investors understand, companies may be unable to tap new sources of capital. They could, like Daimler-Benz, adopt the standards of the foreign market. But it would be much more convenient to agree on a single set of international rules that could be incorporated into, or sit alongside, the local ones. The greater the degree of incorporation, the closer firms would be to a single set of global accounts.

Momentum in this direction has never been so strong. The IASC has been working closely with the International Organization of Securities Commissions (IOSCO), a club of securities-market regulators which includes America's SEC, in an effort to ensure that its standards are accepted by financial markets.

The two bodies' efforts have already yielded fruit. In April 1994 the SEC allowed foreign companies that wish to raise capital in America to use an international standard on cash-flow statements. Recently, two further international standards were given the nod. More approvals are expected. "Our desire is for high-quality standards," says Linda Quinn, head of the SEC's corporate-finance division. "That does not mean that they have to be identical with existing American standards."

Softening

Compromise is in the air on the other side of the Atlantic too. Perhaps most remarkably, German officialdom has recently indicated that it is prepared to make concessions. Last month Herbert Biener, a Justice Ministry official who represents Germany on an IOSCO accounting-standards working party, proposed that Germany should "tolerate" the use of international standards for consolidated accounts by companies seeking listings abroad. This would ease the reporting burden on Daimler-Benz and others that may choose to follow its lead. Instead of publishing two sets of group accounts to satisfy both German and American authorities, such firms could publish a single, internationally accepted set.

Source: The Economist, June 10, 1995, pp. 67–68.

When firms calculate taxable income they are allowed to deduct expenses. These expenses include an allowance for depreciation. However, the Internal Revenue Service (IRS) specifies the rates of depreciation that the company can use for different types of equipment.[8] The rates of depreciation that are used to calculate taxes may differ from the rates that are used when the firm reports its profits to shareholders.

The company is also allowed to deduct interest paid to debtholders when calculating its taxable income, but dividends paid to shareholders are not deductible. These dividends are therefore paid out of after-tax income. Table 2.5 provides an example of how interest payments reduce corporate taxes.

---

[8]We will tell you more about these allowances in Chapter 6.

Table 2.5

Firms A and B both have earnings before interest and taxes (EBIT) of $100 million, but A pays out part of its profits as debt interest. This reduces the corporate tax paid by A.

	Firm A	Firm B
EBIT	100	100
Interest	40	0
Pretax income	60	100
Tax (35% of pretax income)	21	35
Net income	39	65

Note: Figures in millions of dollars.

The bad news about taxes is that each extra dollar of revenues increases taxable income by $1 and results in 35 cents of extra taxes. The good news is that each extra dollar of expense *reduces* taxable income by $1 and therefore reduces taxes by 35 cents. For example, if the firm borrows money, every dollar of interest it pays on the loan reduces taxes by 35 cents. Therefore, after-tax income is reduced by only 65 cents.

▶ **Self-Test 2.5**

Recalculate the figures in Table 2.5 assuming that Firm A now has to make interest payments of $60 million. What happens to taxes paid? Does net income fall by the additional $20 million interest payment compared to the case considered in Table 2.5, where interest expense was only $40 million?

When firms make profits, they pay 35 percent of the profits to the Internal Revenue Service. But the process doesn't work in reverse; if the firm takes a loss, the IRS does not send it a check for 35 percent of the loss. However, the firm can carry the losses back and deduct them from taxable income in earlier years, or it can carry them forward and deduct them from taxable income in the future.[9]

Personal Tax

Table 2.6 shows the U.S. rates of personal tax. Notice that as income increases the tax rate also increases. Notice also that the top personal tax rate is higher than the top corporate rate.

Table 2.6

Personal tax rates, 1996

TAXABLE INCOME DOLLARS		
Single Taxpayers	Married Taxpayers Filing Joint Returns	Tax Rate, %
0–24,000	0–40,100	15
24,001–58,150	40,101–96,900	28
58,151–121,300	96,901–147,700	31
121,301–263,750	147,701–263,750	36
Over 263,750	Over 263,750	39.6

[9]Losses can be carried back for a maximum of 3 years and forward for up to 15 years.

marginal tax rate: Additional taxes owed per dollar of additional income.

The tax rates presented in Table 2.6 are **marginal tax rates.** The marginal tax rate is the tax that the individual pays on each *extra* dollar of income. For example, as a single taxpayer, you would pay 15 cents of tax on each extra dollar you earn when your income is below $24,000, but once income exceeds $24,000, you would pay 28 cents of tax on each dollar of income up to an income of $58,150. For example, if your total income is $40,000, your tax bill is 15 percent of the first $24,000 of income and 28 percent of the remaining $16,000:

$$\text{Tax} = (.15 \times \$24,000) + (.28 \times \$16,000) = \$8,080$$

average tax rate: Total taxes owed divided by total income.

The **average tax rate** is simply the total tax bill divided by total income. In this example it is $8,080/$40,000 = .202 = 20.2 percent. Notice that the average rate is below the marginal rate. This is because of the lower rate on the first $24,000.

▶ **Self-Test 2.6**

What are the average and marginal tax rates for a single taxpayer with a taxable income of $70,000? What are the average and marginal tax rates for married taxpayers filing joint returns if their joint taxable income is also $70,000?

Financial managers need to worry about personal tax rates because the dividends and interest payments that companies make to individuals are both subject to tax at the rates shown in Table 2.6. If these payments are heavily taxed, individuals will be more reluctant to buy the company's shares or bonds. Remember that each dollar of income that the company earns is taxed at the corporate tax rate. If the company then pays a dividend out of this after-tax income, the shareholder also pays personal income tax on the dividend. Thus income that is paid out as dividends is taxed twice, once in the hands of the firm and once in the hands of the shareholder. Suppose instead that the company earns a dollar which is then paid out as interest. This dollar escapes corporate tax, but an individual who receives the interest must pay personal tax.

Capital gains are also taxed, but only when the capital gains are realized. For example, suppose that you bought Bio-technics stock when it was selling for 10 cents a share. Its market price is now $1 a share. As long as you hold onto your stock, there is no tax to pay on your gain. But if you sell, the 90 cents of capital gain is taxed with the rest of your income.

The tax rates in Table 2.6 apply to individuals. But financial institutions are major investors in shares and bonds. These institutions often have special rates of tax. For example, pension funds, which hold huge numbers of shares, are not taxed on either dividend income or capital gains.

Summary

1. Investors and other stakeholders in the firm need regular financial information to help them monitor the firm's progress. Accountants summarize this information in a balance sheet, income statement, and statement of cash flows.
2. The balance sheet provides a snapshot of the firm's assets and liabilities. The assets consist of current assets that can be rapidly turned into cash and fixed assets such as plant and machinery. The liabilities consist of current liabilities that are due for

payment shortly and long-term debts. The difference between the assets and the liabilities represents the amount of the shareholders' equity.

3. It is important to distinguish between the book values that are shown in the company accounts and the market values of the assets and liabilities. Book values are historical measures. For example, the assets in the balance sheet are shown at their historical cost less an allowance for depreciation. Similarly, the figure for shareholders' equity measures the cash that shareholders have contributed in the past or that the company has contributed on their behalf.

4. The income statement measures the profitability of the company during the year. Income is not the same as cash flow. There are two reasons for this: (a) investment in fixed assets is not deducted immediately from income but is instead spread over the expected life of the equipment, and (b) the accountant records revenues when the sale is made rather than when the customer actually pays the bill and at the same time deducts the production costs even though those costs may have been incurred earlier.

5. The statement of cash flows measures the sources and uses of cash. The change in the company's cash balance is the difference between sources and uses.

6. For large companies the rate of tax on income is 35 percent. In calculating taxable income the company deducts an allowance for depreciation and interest payments. It cannot deduct dividend payments to the shareholders.

7. Individuals are also taxed on their income, which includes dividends and interest on their investments. Capital gains are taxed, but only when the investment is sold and the gain realized.

Key Terms

balance sheet	book value	marginal tax rate
generally accepted accounting principles (GAAP)	income statement statement of cash flows	average tax rate

Problems

1. **Balance Sheet.** Construct a balance sheet for Sophie's Sofas given the following data. What is shareholders' equity?

   Cash balances = $10,000
   Inventory of sofas = $200,000
   Store and property = $100,000
   Accounts receivable = $22,000
   Accounts payable = $17,000
   Long-term debt = $170,000

2. **Cash Flow.** Can cash flow from operations be positive if net income is negative? Can operating cash flow be negative if net income is positive? Give examples.

3. **Income Statement.** Sheryl's Shingles had sales of $10,000 in 1997. The cost of goods sold was $6,500, general and administrative expenses were $1,000, interest expenses were $500, and depreciation was $1,000. The firm's tax rate is 35 percent.

   a. What is earnings before interest and taxes?
   b. What is net income?
   c. What is cash flow from operations?

4. **Cash Flows.** Ponzi Products produced 100 chain letter kits this quarter, resulting in a total cash outlay of $10 per unit. It will sell 50 of the kits next quarter at a price of $11, and the other 50 kits in two quarters at a price of $12. It takes a full quarter for it to collect its bills from its customers. (Ignore possible sales in earlier or later quarters.)

a. Prepare an income statement for Ponzi for today and for each of the next three quarters. Ignore taxes.

b. What are the cash flows for the company today and in each of the next three quarters?

c. What is Ponzi's net working capital in each quarter?

5. **Taxes.** You have set up your tax preparation firm as an incorporated business. You took $70,000 from the firm as your salary. The firm's taxable income for the year (net of your salary) was $30,000. How much taxes must be paid to the federal government, including both your personal taxes and the firm's taxes? Assume you pay personal taxes as an unmarried taxpayer. By how much will you reduce the total tax bill by reducing your salary to $50,000, thereby leaving the firm with taxable income of $50,000? Use the tax rates presented in Tables 2.4 and 2.6.

6. **Taxes.** This is harder. Reconsider the data in problem 5 which imply that you have $100,000 of total pretax income to allocate between your salary and your firm's profits. What allocation will minimize the total tax bill? *Hint:* Think about marginal tax rates and the ability to shift income from a higher marginal bracket to a lower one.

7. **Market versus Book Values.** The founder of Alchemy Products, Inc., discovered a way to turn lead into gold and patented this new technology. He then formed a corporation and invested $200,000 in setting up a production plant. He believes that he could sell his patent for $50 million.

a. What are the book value and market values of the firm?

b. If there are 2 million shares of stock in the new corporation, what would be the price per share and the book value per share?

8. **Cash Flows.** What impact will the following actions have on the firm's cash balance?

a. The firm sells some goods from inventory.

b. The firm sells some machinery to a bank, and leases it back for a period of 20 years.

c. The firm buys back 1 million shares of stock from existing shareholders.

9. **Tax Rates.** Using Table 2.6, calculate the marginal and average tax rates for a single taxpayer with the following incomes:

a. $20,000

b. $50,000

c. $270,000

d. $3,000,000

10. **Tax Rates.** What would be the marginal and average tax rates for a *corporation* with an income level of $100,000?

11. **Profits versus Cash Flow.** During the last year of operations, accounts receivable increased by $10,000, accounts payable increased by $5,000, and inventories decreased by $2,000. What is the total impact of these changes on the difference between profits and cash flow?

12. **Income Statement.** A firm's income statement included the following data. The firm's average tax rate was 20 percent.

Cost of goods sold	$8,000
Income taxes paid	2,000

Administrative expenses	3,000
Interest expense	1,000
Depreciation	1,000

a. What was the firm's net income?

b. What must have been the firm's revenues?

c. What was EBIT?

13. **Balance Sheet/Income Statement.** The year-end 1996 balance sheet of Brandex Inc. lists common stock and other paid-in capital at $1,100,000 and retained earnings at $3,400,000. The next year, retained earnings were listed at $3,700,000. The firm's net income in 1997 was $900,000. There were no stock repurchases during the year. What were dividends paid by the firm in 1997?

14. **Financial Statements.** Here are the 1996 and 1997 (incomplete) balance sheets for Nobel Oil Corp.

Nobel Oil Corp. Balance Sheet, as of end of year

Assets	1996	1997	Liabilities and Owners' Equity	1996	1997
Current assets	310	420	Current liabilities	210	240
Net fixed assets	1,200	1,420	Long-term debt	830	920

a. What was owner's equity at the end of 1996 and 1997?

b. If Nobel paid dividends of $100 in 1997, what must have been net income during the year?

c. If Nobel purchased $300 in fixed assets during the year, what must have been the depreciation charge on the income statement?

d. What was the change in net working capital between 1996 and 1997?

e. If Nobel issued $200 of new long-term debt, how much debt must have been paid off during the year?

15. **Financial Statements.** South Sea Baubles has the following (incomplete) balance sheet and income statement.

BALANCE SHEET, AS OF END OF YEAR
(Figures in millions of dollars)

Assets	1996	1997	Liabilities and Shareholders' Equity	1996	1997
Current assets	$90	$140	Current liabilities	$ 50	$ 60
Net fixed assets	800	900	Long-term debt	600	750

INCOME STATEMENT, 1997
(Figures in millions of dollars)

Revenue	$1,950
Cost of goods sold	1,030
Depreciation	350
Interest expense	240

a. What is shareholders' equity in 1996 and 1997?

b. What is net working capital in 1996 and 1997?

c. What is taxable income and taxes paid in 1997? Assume the firm pays taxes equal to 35 percent of taxable income.

d. What is cash provided by operations during 1997? Pay attention to changes in net working capital, using Table 2.3 as a guide.

e. Net fixed assets increased from $800 to $900 during 1997. What must have been South Sea's *gross* investment in fixed assets during 1997?

f. If South Sea reduced its outstanding accounts payable by $35 during the year, what must have happened to its other current liabilities?

Here are some data on Fincorp, Inc., that you should use for problems 16–23. The balance sheet items correspond to values at year-end of 1996 and 1997, while the income statement items correspond to revenues or expenses during the year ending in either 1996 or 1997. All values are in thousands of dollars.

	1996	1997
Revenue	4,000	4,100
Cost of goods sold	1,600	1,700
Depreciation	500	520
Inventories	300	350
Administrative expenses	500	550
Interest expense	150	150
Federal and state taxes[a]	400	420
Accounts payable	300	350
Accounts receivable	400	450
Net fixed assets[b]	5,000	5,800
Long-term debt	2,000	2,400
Notes payable	1,000	600
Dividends paid	410	410
Cash and marketable securities	800	300

[a] Taxes are paid in their entirety in the year that the tax obligation is incurred.

[b] Net fixed assets are fixed assets net of accumulated depreciation since the asset was installed.

16. **Balance Sheet.** Construct a balance sheet for Fincorp for 1996 and 1997. What is shareholders' equity?

17. **Working Capital.** What happened to net working capital during the year?

18. **Income Statement.** Construct an income statement for Fincorp for 1996 and 1997. What were retained earnings for 1997? How does that compare with the increase in shareholders' equity between the two years?

19. **Earnings per Share.** Suppose that Fincorp has 500,000 shares outstanding. What were earnings per share?

20. **Taxes.** What was the firm's average tax bracket for each year? Do you have enough information to determine the marginal tax bracket?

21. **Balance Sheet.** Examine the values for depreciation in 1997 and net fixed assets in 1996 and 1997. What was Fincorp's *gross* investment in plant and equipment during 1997?

22. **Cash Flows.** Construct a statement of cash flows for Fincorp for 1997.

23. **Book versus Market Value.** Now suppose that the *market value* (in thousands of dollars) of Fincorp's fixed assets in 1997 is $6,000, and that the value of its long-term debt is only $2,400. In addition, the consensus among investors is that Fincorp's past investments in developing the skills of its employees are worth $2,900. This investment of course does not show up on the balance sheet. What will be the price per share of Fincorp stock?

Solutions to Self-Test Questions

2.1 Cash and equivalents would increase by $10 million. Property, plant, and equipment would increase by $40 million. Long-term debt would increase by $50 million. Shareholders' equity would *not* increase: assets and liabilities have increased equally, leaving shareholders' equity unchanged.

2.2 a. If the auto plant were worth $14 billion, the equity in the firm would be worth $14 − $4 = $10 billion. With 100 million shares outstanding, each share would be worth $100.

b. If the outstanding stock were worth $8 billion, we would infer that the market values the auto plant at 8 + 4 = $12 billion.

2.3

Period:	1	2	3
Sales	0	150	0
− Change in accounts receivable	0	150	(150)
− Cost of goods sold	0	100	0
− Change in inventories	100	(100)	0
Net cash flow	−100	0	+150

The net cash flow pattern does make sense. The firm expends $100 in period 1 to produce the product, but it is not paid its $150 sales price until period 3. In period 2 no cash is exchanged.

2.4 a. An increase in inventories uses cash, reducing the firm's net cash balance.

b. A reduction in accounts payable uses cash, reducing the firm's net cash balance.

c. An issue of common stock is a source of cash.

d. The purchase of new equipment is a use of cash, and it reduces the firm's net cash balance.

2.5

	Firm A	Firm B
EBIT	100	100
Interest	60	0
Pretax income	40	100
Tax (35% of pretax income)	14	35
Net income	26	65

Note: Figures in millions of dollars.

Taxes owed by Firm A fall from $21 million to $14 million. The reduction in taxes is 35 percent of the extra $20 million of interest income. Net income does not fall by the full $20 million of extra interest expense. It instead falls by interest expense less the reduction in taxes, or $20 million − $7 million = $13 million.

2.6 For a single taxpayer with taxable income of $70,000, total taxes paid are

$$(.15 \times \$24,000) + [.28 \times (58,150 - 24,000)] + [.31 \times (70,000 - 58,150)]$$
$$= 3,600 + 9,562 + 3,673.50 = \$16,835.50$$

The marginal tax rate is 31 percent, but the average tax rate is only 16,835.50/70,000 = .241, or 24.1 percent.

For the married taxpayers filing jointly with taxable income of $70,000, total taxes paid are

$$(.15 \times \$40,100) + [.28 \times (70,000 - 40,100)] = 6,015 + 8,372 = \$14,387$$

The marginal tax rate is 28 percent, and the average tax rate is 14,387/70,000 = .206, or 20.6 percent.

Part Two
Value

Kangaroo Auto's view of the time value of money
Do you truly understand what these percentages mean? Do you realize that the dealership is not *quoting effective annual interest rates? If the dealership quotes a monthly payment on a four-year, $10,000 car loan, would you be able to double-check the dealership's calculations?*
© *Cameramann International, LTD.*

The Time Value of Money

ompanies invest in lots of things. Some are *tangible assets*—that is, assets you can kick, like factories, machinery, and offices. Others are *intangible assets*, such as patents or trademarks. In each case the company lays out some money now in the hope of receiving even more money later.

Individuals also make investments. For example, your college education may cost you $20,000 per year. That is an investment you hope will pay off in the form of a higher salary later in life. You are sowing now and expecting to reap later.

Companies pay for their investments by raising money and in the process assuming liabilities. For example, they may borrow money from a bank and promise to repay it with interest later. You also may have financed your investment in a college education by borrowing money which you plan to pay back out of that fat salary.

All these financial decisions require comparisons of cash payments at different dates. Will your future salary be sufficient to justify the current expenditure on college tuition? How much will you have to repay the bank if you borrow to finance your education?

In this chapter we take the first steps toward understanding the relationship between the value of dollars today and that of dollars in the future. We start by looking at how funds invested at a specific interest rate will grow over time. We then ask how much you would need to invest today to produce a specified future sum of money. Next we describe some shortcuts for working out the value of a series of cash payments. Finally, we consider how inflation affects these financial calculations.

After studying this chapter you should be able to

▶ Calculate the future value to which money invested at a given interest rate will grow.

▶ Compare interest rates quoted over different time intervals—for example, monthly versus annual rates.

▶ Calculate present and future values of streams of cash payments.

▶ Understand the difference between real and nominal cash flows and between real and nominal interest rates.

There is nothing complicated about these calculations, but if they are to become second nature, you should read the chapter thoroughly, work carefully through the examples (we have provided plenty), and make sure you tackle the self-test questions. We are asking you to make an investment now in return for a payoff later.

3.1 Future Values and Compound Interest

You have $100 invested in a bank account. Suppose banks are currently paying an interest rate of 6 percent per year on deposits. So after a year, your account will earn interest of $6:

$$\text{Interest} = \text{interest rate} \times \text{initial investment}$$
$$= .06 \times \$100 = \$6$$

You start the year with $100 and you earn interest of $6, so the value of your investment will grow to $106 by the end of the year.

$$\text{Value of investment after 1 year} = \$100 + \$6 = \$106$$

Notice that the $100 invested grows by the factor $(1 + .06) = 1.06$. In general, for any interest rate r, the value of the investment at the end of 1 year is $(1 + r)$ times the initial investment:

$$\text{Value after 1 year} = \text{initial investment} \times (1 + r)$$
$$= \$100 \times (1.06) = \$106$$

What if you leave your money in the bank for a second year? Your balance, now $106, will continue to earn interest of 6 percent. So

$$\text{Interest in Year 2} = .06 \times \$106 = \$6.36$$

You start the second year with $106 on which you earn interest of $6.36. So by the end of the year the value of your account will grow to $106 + $6.36 = $112.36.

In the first year your investment of $100 increases by a factor of 1.06 to $106; in the second year the $106 again increases by a factor of 1.06 to $112.36. Thus the initial $100 investment grows twice by a factor 1.06:

$$\text{Value of account after 2 years} = \$100 \times 1.06 \times 1.06$$
$$= \$100 \times (1.06)^2 = \$112.36$$

If you keep your money invested for a third year, your investment multiplies by 1.06 each year for 3 years. By the end of the third year it will total $100 $\times (1.06)^3$ = $119.10, scarcely enough to put you in the millionaire class, but even millionaires have to start somewhere.

Clearly for an investment horizon of t years, the original $100 investment will grow to $100 $\times (1.06)^t$. For an interest rate of r and a horizon of t years, the **future value** of your investment will be

future value: Amount to which an investment will grow after earning interest.

$$\textbf{Future value of \$100} = \textbf{\$100} \times (\textbf{1} + \textbf{\textit{r}})^t$$

Notice in our example that your interest income in the first year is $6 (6 percent of $100), and in the second year it is $6.36 (6 percent of $106). Your income in the second year is higher because you now earn interest on *both* the original $100 investment *and* the $6 of interest earned in the previous year. Earning interest on interest is called *compounding* or **compound interest.** In contrast, if the bank calculated the interest only on your original investment, you would be paid **simple interest.**

compound interest: Interest earned on interest.

Table 3.1 and Figure 3.1 illustrate the mechanics of compound interest. Table 3.1 shows that in each year, you start with a greater balance in your account—your savings have been increased by the previous year's interest. As a result, your interest income also is higher.

simple interest: Interest earned only on the original investment; no interest is earned on interest.

Obviously, the higher the rate of interest, the faster your savings will grow. Figure 3.2 shows that a few percentage points added to the (compound) interest rate can dramatically affect the future balance of your savings account. For example, after 10 years $1,000 invested at 10 percent will grow to $1,000 $\times (1.10)^{10}$ = $2,594. If invested at 5 percent, it will grow to only $1,000 $\times (1.05)^{10}$ = $1,629.

Table 3.1

Compound interest

Year	Balance at Start of Year	Interest Earned during Year	Balance at End of Year
1	$100.00	.06 × $100.00 = $6.00	$106.00
2	$106.00	.06 × $106.00 = $6.36	$112.36
3	$112.36	.06 × $112.36 = $6.74	$119.10
4	$119.10	.06 × $119.10 = $7.15	$126.25
5	$126.25	.06 × $126.25 = $7.57	$133.82

Calculating future values is easy using most any calculator. If you have the patience, you can multiply your initial investment by $1 + r$ (1.06 in our example) once for each year of your investment. A simpler procedure is to use the power key (the y^x key) on your calculator. For example, to compute $(1.06)^{10}$, enter 1.06, press the y^x key, enter 10, press = and discover that the answer is 1.791. (Try this!)

If you don't have a calculator, you can use a table of future values such as Table 3.2. Check that you can use it to work out the future value of a 10-year investment at 6 percent. First find the row corresponding to 10 years. Now work along that row until you reach the column for a 6 percent interest rate. The entry shows that $1 invested for 10 years at 6 percent grows to $1.791.

Now try one more example. If you invest $1 for 20 years at 10 percent, what will you have at the end? Your answer should be $6.727.

Table 3.2 gives futures values for only a small selection of years and interest rates. Table A.1 at the end of the book is a bigger version of Table 3.2. It presents the future value of a $1 investment for a wide range of time periods and interest rates.

Future value tables are tedious, and as Table 3.2 demonstrates, they show future values only for a limited set of interest rates and time periods. For example, suppose that you want to calculate future values using an interest rate of 7.835 percent. The power key on your calculator will be faster and easier than future value tables. A third alternative is to use a financial calculator. These are discussed in two boxes later in this chapter.

Figure 3.1

Compound interest

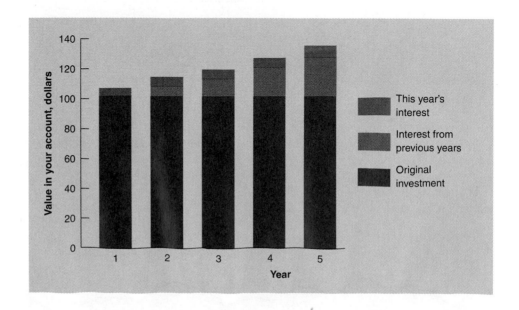

Figure 3.2

Future values with compound interest

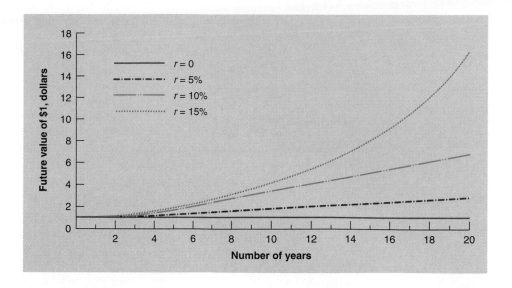

Table 3.2

Future value of $1

Number of Years	Interest Rate per Year					
	5%	**6%**	**7%**	**8%**	**9%**	**10%**
1	1.050	1.060	1.070	1.080	1.090	1.100
2	1.103	1.124	1.145	1.166	1.188	1.210
3	1.158	1.191	1.225	1.260	1.295	1.331
4	1.216	1.262	1.311	1.360	1.412	1.464
5	1.276	1.338	1.403	1.469	1.539	1.611
10	1.629	1.791	1.967	2.159	2.367	2.594
20	2.653	3.207	3.870	4.661	5.604	6.727
30	4.322	5.743	7.612	10.063	13.268	17.449

▶ **Example 3.1**   *Manhattan Island*

Almost everyone's favorite example of the power of compound interest is the sale of Manhattan Island for $24 in 1626 to Peter Minuit. Based on New York real estate prices today, it seems that Minuit got a great deal. But consider the future value of that $24 if it had been invested for 371 years (1997 minus 1626) at an interest rate of 8 percent per year:

$$\$24 \times (1.08)^{371} = \$60,315,000,000,000$$
$$= \$60,315 \text{ billion}$$

Perhaps the deal wasn't as good as it appeared. The total value of land on Manhattan today is probably a little less than $60 billion.

Though entertaining, this analysis is actually somewhat misleading. First, the 8 percent interest rate we've used to compute future values is quite high by historical standards. At a 3.5 percent interest rate, more consistent with historical experience, the future value of the $24 would be *dramatically* lower, only $24 \times (1.035)^{371} = $8,376,855! Second, we have understated the returns to Mr. Minuit and his successors:

we have ignored all the rental income that the island's land has generated over the last three or four centuries.

All things considered, if we had been around in 1626, we would have gladly paid $24 for the island.

The power of compounding is not restricted to money. Foresters try to forecast the compound growth rate of trees, demographers the compound growth rate of population. A social commentator once observed that the number of lawyers in the United States is increasing at a higher compound rate than the population as a whole (3.6 vs. .9 percent in the 1980s) and calculated that in about two centuries there will be more lawyers than people. In all these cases, the principle is the same:

> **Compound growth means that value increases each period by the factor (1 + growth rate). The value after t periods will equal the initial value times $(1 + \text{growth rate})^t$. When money is invested at compound interest, the growth rate is the interest rate.**

▶ **Self-Test 3.1**

Suppose that Peter Minuit did not become the first New York real estate tycoon, but instead had invested his $24 at a 5 percent interest rate in New Amsterdam Saving Bank. What would have been the balance in his account after 5 years? 50 years?

▶ **Example 3.2**   *Credit Cards*

As a saver, you may be understandably enthusiastic about compound interest. As a borrower, however, it works against you. Consider your credit card as an example. Suppose you have to pay interest on unpaid balances at the rate of 1 percent per *month*. What is it going to cost you if you don't pay off your unpaid balance for a year?

Don't be put off because the interest rate is quoted per month rather than per year. The important thing is to maintain consistency between the interest rate and the number of periods. If the interest rate is quoted as percent per month, then we must define the number of periods in our future value calculation as the number of months. So if you borrow $100 from the credit card company at 1 percent per month for 12 months, you will need to repay $100 \times (1.01)^{12} = \$112.68$.

Because the interest is calculated monthly and added to your unpaid balance, you are *paying* interest on interest. Thus your $100 debt grows after 1 year to $112.68. Using simple interest, you would pay interest only on the original $100 borrowed, and you would owe only $100 + $12 = $112 after 1 year.

▶ **Self-Test 3.2**

Start-up Enterprises had sales last year of only $.5 million. However, a stock market analyst is bullish on the company and predicts that sales will double each year for 4 years. What are projected sales at the end of this period?

3.2 An Application of Compounding: Effective Annual Interest Rates

effective annual interest rate: Interest rate that is annualized using compound interest.

Interest rates may be quoted for days, months, years, or any convenient interval. For example, when calculating your credit card payment, we used a monthly interest rate. When working out the value of Peter Minuit's investments, we used an annual rate. How should we compare rates when they are quoted for different periods, such as monthly versus annually?

Our analysis of the finance charges on your credit card in Example 3.2 suggests how to convert a monthly rate to an **effective annual interest rate.** We saw that a year's interest at 1 percent *per month* increases your unpaid balance after a year by a factor of $(1.01)^{12} = 1.1268$. The balance increases by 12.68 percent. Therefore, we say that the *effective* annual rate of interest, or, equivalently, the *annually compounded rate* on the loan, is 12.68 percent.

In general, the effective annual interest rate is defined as the annual growth rate allowing for the effects of compounding. Therefore.

$$(1 + \text{annual rate}) = (1 + \text{monthly rate})^{12}$$

When comparing interest rates, it is best to use effective annual rates. This compares interest paid or received over a common period (one year) and allows for possible compounding during the period. Unfortunately, common practice annualizes short-term rates using simple interest by multiplying the rate per period by the number of periods in a year. In fact, truth-in-lending laws in the United States *require* that rates be annualized in this manner. Such rates are called **annual percentage rates (APRs).**[1]

annual percentage rate (APR): Interest rate that is annualized using simple interest.

If rates are quoted on an APR basis, how can we find the effective annual rate? The solution is simple. First take the quoted APR and divide by the number of compounding periods in a year to recover the original rate per period actually charged on the loan. Then calculate the equivalent annually compounded interest rate. For example, interest on the credit card loan will be quoted as an APR of 12 percent. Because the interest is calculated monthly, there are 12 compounding periods in a year. So we first divide by 12 to obtain the rate of interest per month, 1 percent. Then we convert to an annually compounded rate:

$$(1 + \text{annual rate}) = (1 + \text{monthly rate})^{12} = (1 + .01)^{12} = 1.1268$$

The annual interest rate is $.1268 = 12.68$ percent.

In general, if an investment of \$1 is worth \$$(1 + r)$ after one period, and there are m periods in a year, the investment will grow after one year to \$$(1 + r)^m$ and the effective annual interest rate is $(1 + r)^m - 1$. For example, a credit card loan that charges a monthly interest rate of 1 percent has an APR of 12 percent but an effective annual interest rate of $(1.01)^{12} - 1 = .1268$, or 12.68 percent. To summarize:

> The effective annual rate is the rate at which invested funds will grow over the course of a year. It equals the rate of interest per period compounded for the number of periods in a year.

---

[1] The truth-in-lending laws apply to credit card loans, auto loans, home improvement loans, and some loans to small businesses. APRs are not commonly used or quoted in the big leagues of finance.

Table 3.3
Compounding frequency and effective annual interest rate (APR = 6%)

Compounding Period	Periods per Year	Per-Period Interest Rate	Growth Factor of Invested Funds	Effective Annual Rate
1 year	1	6%	1.06	6.0000%
Semiannually	2	3	$1.03^2 = 1.0609$	6.0900
Quarterly	4	1.5	$1.015^4 = 1.061364$	6.1364
Monthly	12	.5	$1.005^{12} = 1.061678$	6.1678
Weekly	52	.11538	$1.0011538^{52} = 1.061800$	6.1800
Daily	365	.01644	$1.0001644^{365} = 1.061831$	6.1831

▶ **Example 3.3**   *The Effective Interest Rates on Bank Accounts*

Back in the 1960s and 1970s federal regulation limited the (APR) interest rates banks could pay on savings accounts. Banks were hungry for depositors, and they searched for ways to increase the *effective* rate of interest that could be paid within the rules. Their solution was to keep the same APR but to calculate the interest on deposits more frequently. As interest is calculated at shorter and shorter intervals, less time passes before interest can be earned on interest. Therefore, the effective annually compounded rate of interest increases. Table 3.3 shows the calculations assuming that the maximum APR that banks could pay was 6 percent. (Actually, it was a bit less than this, but 6 percent is a nice round number to use for illustration.)

You can see from Table 3.3 how banks were able to increase the effective interest rate simply by calculating interest at more frequent intervals.

The ultimate step was to assume that interest was paid in a continuous stream rather than at fixed intervals. With one year's *continuous compounding,* $1 grows to e^{APR}, where $e = 2.718$ (a figure that may be familiar to you as the base for natural logarithms). Thus if you deposited $1 with a bank that offered a continuously compounded rate of 6 percent, your investment would grow by the end of the year to $2.718^{.06} = \$1.061837$, just a hair's breadth more than if interest were compounded daily.

▶ **Self-Test 3.3**   A car loan requiring quarterly payments carries an APR of 8 percent. What is the effective annual rate of interest?

Present Values

Money can be invested to earn interest. If you are offered the choice between $100,000 now and $100,000 at the end of the year, you naturally take the money now to get a year's interest. Financial managers make the same point when they say that money in hand today has a *time value* or when they quote perhaps the most basic financial principle:

A dollar today is worth more than a dollar tomorrow.

We have seen that $100 invested for 1 year at 6 percent will grow to a future value of $100 \times 1.06 = \$106$. Let's turn this around: How much do we need to invest now in order to produce $106 at the end of the year? Financial managers refer to this as the **present value (PV)** of the $106 payoff.

present value (PV): Value today of a future cash flow.

Future value is calculated by multiplying present investment by 1 plus the interest rate, .06, or 1.06. To calculate present value, we simply reverse the process and divide the future value by 1.06:

$$\text{Present value} = \text{PV} = \frac{\text{future value}}{1.06} = \frac{\$106}{1.06} = \$100$$

What is the present value of, say, $112.36 to be received 2 years from now? Again we ask, "How much would we need to invest now?" The answer is obviously $100; we've already calculated that at 6 percent $100 grows to $112.36:

$$\$100 \times (1.06)^2 = 112.36$$

However, if we don't know, or forgot the answer, we just divide future value by $(1.06)^2$:

$$\text{Present value} = \text{PV} = \frac{\$112.36}{(1.06)^2} = 100$$

In general, for a future value or payment t periods away, present value is

$$\textbf{Present value} = \frac{\textbf{future value after } t \textbf{ periods}}{(1 + r)^t}$$

discount rate: Interest rate used to compute present values of future cash flows.

In this context the interest rate r is known as the **discount rate** and the present value is often called the *discounted value* of the future payment. To calculate present value, we discounted the future value at the interest r.

▶ **Example 3.4**   *Saving to Buy a New Computer*

Suppose you need $3,000 next year to buy a new computer. The interest rate is 8 percent per year. How much money should you set aside now in order to pay for the purchase? Just calculate the present value at an 8 percent interest rate of a $3,000 payment at the end of one year. This value is

$$\text{PV} = \frac{\$3,000}{1.08} = \$2,777.77$$

Notice that $2,777.77 invested for 1 year at 8 percent will prove just enough to buy your computer:

$$\text{Future value} = \$2,777.77 \times 1.08 = \$3,000$$

The longer the time before you must make a payment, the less you need to invest today. For example, suppose that you can postpone buying that computer until the end of 2 years. In this case we calculate the present value of the future payment by dividing $3,000 by $(1.08)^2$:

$$\text{PV} = \frac{\$3,000}{(1.08)^2} = \$2,572.02$$

Thus you need to invest $2,777.77 today to provide $3,000 in 1 year but only $2,572.02 to provide the same $3,000 in 2 years.

We repeat the basic procedure.

> **To work out how much you will have in the future if you invest for *t* years at an interest rate *r*, *multiply* the initial investment by $(1 + r)^t$. To find the present value of a future payment, run the process in reverse and *divide* by $(1 + r)^t$.**

Present values are always calculated using compound interest. Whereas the ascending lines in Figure 3.2 showed the future value of $100 invested with compound interest, when we calculate present values we move back along the lines from future to present. Present values fall with longer horizons, as in Figure 3.3.

Thus present values decline, other things equal, when future cash payments are delayed. The longer you have to wait for money, the less it's worth today.

The present value formula is sometimes written differently. Instead of dividing the future payment by $(1 + r)^t$, we could equally well multiply it by $1/(1 + r)^t$:

$$PV = \frac{\text{future payment}}{(1 + r)^t}$$

$$= \text{future payment} \times \frac{1}{(1 + r)^t}$$

discount factor: Present value of a $1 future payment.

The expression $1/(1 + r)^t$ is called the **discount factor.** It measures the present value of $1 received in year *t*.

The simplest way to find the discount factor is to use a calculator, but financial managers sometimes find it convenient to use tables of discount factors. For example, Table 3.4 shows discount factors for a small range of years and interest rates.

Figure 3.3

Present value of a future cash flow of $1

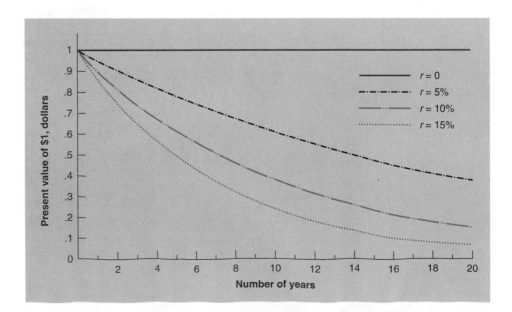

Table 3.4

Present value of $1

Number of Years	Interest Rate per Year					
	5%	6%	7%	8%	9%	10%
1	.952	.943	.935	.926	.917	.909
2	.907	.890	.873	.857	.842	.826
3	.864	.840	.816	.794	.772	.751
4	.823	.792	.763	.735	.708	.683
5	.784	.747	.713	.681	.650	.621
10	.614	.558	.508	.463	.422	.386
20	.377	.312	.258	.215	.178	.149
30	.231	.174	.131	.099	.075	.057

Table A.2 at the end of the book provides a set of discount factors for a wide range of years and interest rates.

Try using Table 3.4 to check our calculations of how much to put aside for that $3,000 computer purchase. If the interest rate is 8 percent, the present value of $1 paid at the end of 1 year is $.926. So the present value of $3,000 is

$$PV = \$3,000 \times \frac{1}{1.08} = \$3,000 \times .926 = \$2,778$$

which except for rounding error matches the value we obtained in Example 3.4.

What if the computer purchase is postponed until the end of 2 years? Table 3.4 shows that the present value of $1 paid at the end of 2 years is .857. So the present value of $3,000 is

$$PV = \$3,000 \times \frac{1}{(1.08)^2} = \$3,000 \times .857 = \$2,571$$

which again differs from the calculation in Example 3.4 only because of rounding error.

Notice that as you move along the rows in Table 3.4, moving to higher interest rates, present values decline. As you move down the columns, moving to longer discounting periods, present values again decline. (Why does this make sense?)

▶ **Example 3.5**   *Coca-Cola Enterprises Borrows Some Cash*

In 1995 Coca-Cola Enterprises needed to borrow about a quarter of a billion dollars for 25 years. It did so by selling IOUs, each of which simply promised to pay the holder $1000 at the end of 25 years.[2] The market interest rate at the time was 8.53 percent. How much would you have been prepared to pay for one of the company's IOUs?

---

[2]"IOU" means "I owe you." Coca-Cola's IOUs are called *bonds*. Usually, bond investors receive a regular *interest* or *coupon* payment. The Coca-Cola Enterprises bond will make only a single payment at the end of Year 25. It was therefore known as a *zero-coupon bond*. More on this in the next chapter.

To calculate present value we multiply the $1,000 future payment by the 25-year discount factor:

$$PV = \$1,000 \times \frac{1}{(1.0853)^{25}}$$
$$= \$1,000 \times .129 = \$129$$

Instead of using a calculator to find the discount factor, we could use Table A.2 at the end of the book. You can see that the 25-year discount factor is .146 if the interest rate is 8 percent and it is .116 if the rate is 9 percent. For an interest rate of 8.5 percent the discount factor is roughly halfway between at .131, a shade higher than the exact figure.

▶ **Self-Test 3.4**

Suppose that Coca-Cola had promised to pay $1,000 at the end of 10 years. If the market interest rate was 8.53 percent, how much would you have been prepared to pay for a 10-year IOU of $1,000?

▶ **Example 3.6**   *Finding the Value of Free Credit*

Kangaroo Autos is offering free credit on a $10,000 car. You pay $4,000 down and then the balance at the end of 2 years. Turtle Motors next door does not offer free credit but will give you $500 off the list price. If the interest rate is 10 percent,[3] which company is offering the better deal?

Notice that you pay more in total by buying through Kangaroo, but, since part of the payment is postponed, you can keep this money in the bank where it will continue to earn interest. To compare the two offers, you need to calculate the present value of the payments to Kangaroo. The *time line* in Figure 3.4 shows the cash

Figure 3.4
Present value of the cash flows to Kangaroo Autos

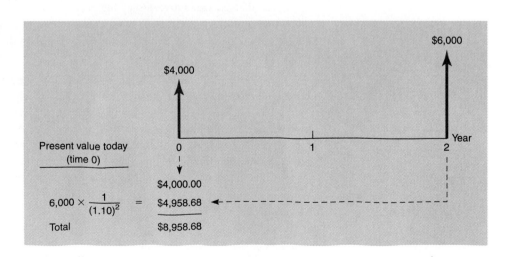

[3]We assume annual compounding, so there's no need to distinguish APRs from effective annual rates.

payments to Kangaroo. The first payment, $4,000, takes place today. The second payment, $6,000, takes place at the end of 2 years. To find its present value, we need to multiply by the 2-year discount factor. The total present value of the payments to Kangaroo is therefore

$$PV = \$4,000 + \$6,000 \times \frac{1}{(1.10)^2}$$

$$= \$4,000 + \$4,958.68 = \$8,958.68$$

If you pay $4,000 down and put aside $4,958.68 in a bank account, you will have just enough to pay Kangaroo Autos. The total cost of $8,958.68 is a better deal than the $9,500 charged by Turtle Motors.

These calculations illustrate how important it is to use present values when comparing alternative patterns of cash payment.

> **You should *never* compare cash flows occurring at different times without first discounting them to a common date. By calculating present values, we see how much cash must be set aside today to pay future bills.**

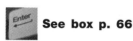 **See box p. 66**

The importance of discounting is highlighted in the nearby box, which examines the value of an extension of Eurotunnel's operating franchise from 65 to 999 years. While such an extension sounds like it would be extremely valuable, the article (and its accompanying diagram) points out that profits 65 years or more from now have negligible present value.

Finding the Interest Rate

When we looked at Coca-Cola's IOUs in the previous section, we used the interest rate to compute a fair market price for each IOU. Sometimes you are given the price and have to calculate the interest rate that is being offered.

For example, when Coca-Cola borrowed money, it did not announce an interest rate. It simply offered to sell each IOU for $129. Thus we know that

$$PV = \$1,000 \times \frac{1}{(1 + r)^{25}} = \$129$$

What is the interest rate?

There are several ways to approach this. First, you might use a table of discount factors. You need to find the interest rate for which the 25-year discount factor = .129. Look at Table A.2 at the end of the book and run your finger along the row corresponding to 25 years. You can see that an interest rate of 8 percent gives too high a discount factor and a rate of 9 percent gives too low a discount factor. The interest rate on the Coca-Cola loan was about halfway between at 8.5 percent.

Second, you can rearrange the equation and use your calculator.

$$\$129 \times (1 + r)^{25} = \$1,000$$

$$(1 + r)^{25} = \frac{\$1,000}{\$129} = 7.75$$

$$(1 + r) = (7.75)^{1/25} = 1.0853$$

$$r = .0853, \text{ or } 8.53\%$$

From Here to Eternity

Politicians, you may be aware, are fond of urging people to invest in the future. It would appear that some investors are taking them a bit too literally of late. The latest fad among emerging-market bond investors, eager to get a piece of the action, is to queue up for bonds with 100-year maturities, such as those issued by the Chinese government and Tenaga Nasional, a Malaysian electrical utility.

Not to be outdone by these century bonds, Eurotunnel, the beleaguered company that operates the railway beneath the English Channel, is trying to tempt investors with a millennium's worth of profits. Last week, in a bid to sweeten the pot for its shareholders and creditors, who must agree on an unpalatable financial restructuring, it asked the British and French governments to extend its operating franchise from a mere 65 years to 999 years. By offering investors some windfall profits, the firm hopes they will be more likely to ratify its plan. Has the distant future become the latest place to make a financial killing?

Alas, the future is not all that it is cracked up to be. Although at first glance 999 years of profits would seem far better than 65 years, those last nine centuries are really nothing to get excited about. The reason is that a dollar spent today, human nature being what it is, is worth more to people than a dollar spent tomorrow. So when comparing profits in the future with those in the present, the future profits must be "discounted" by a suitable interest rate.

Under the relentless pressures of compound interest, the value of future profits is ground to nothing as the years go by. Suppose, for example, that you had a choice between making the following two gifts to a university; you could write a cheque for $10,000 today, or give $1,000 a year for the next century. The latter donation might seem the more generous one, but at a 10% interest rate, they are worth the same amount. By the time compound discounting had finished with it, that final $1,000 payment would be worth only 7 cents today (see chart).

What does this mean for Eurotunnel's investors? Extending its franchise by 934 years should increase its value to today's investors by only 10-15%, after discounting. If they are feeling generous, perhaps the British and French governments should toss in another year and make the franchise an even 1,000.

Live for today
Present value of $1,000
discounted at 10%
received in year

Source: "From Here to Eternity" *The Economist,* May 3, 1997. © 1997 The Economist Newspaper Group Inc., Reprinted with permission. Further reproduction prohibited.

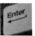 **see box pp. 70–71**   In general this is more accurate. You can also use a financial calculator (see the nearby box).

▶ **Example 3.7**   *Double Your Money*

How many times have you heard of an investment adviser who promises to double your money? Is this really an amazing feat? That depends on how long it will take for your money to double. With enough patience, your funds eventually will double even if they earn only a very modest interest rate. Suppose your investment adviser promises to double your money in 8 years. What interest rate is implicitly being promised?

The adviser is promising a future value of $2 for every $1 invested today. Therefore, we find the interest rate by solving for r as follows:

$$\text{Future value} = \text{PV} \times (1 + r)^t$$
$$\$2 = \$1 \times (1 + r)^8$$
$$1 + r = 2^{1/8} = 1.0905$$
$$r = .0905, \text{ or } 9.05\%$$

By the way, there is a convenient rule of thumb that one can use to approximate the answer to this problem. The *Rule of 72* states that the time it will take for an investment to double in value equals approximately 72/r, where r is expressed as a percentage. Therefore, if the doubling period is 8 years, the Rule of 72 implies an (approximate) interest rate of 9 percent (since 72/9 = 8 years). This is quite close to the exact solution of 9.05 percent.

---

 see box p. 72
see box p. 72

The nearby box discusses the Rule of 72 as well as other issues of compound interest. By now you easily should be able to explain why, as the box suggests, "10 + 10 = 21." In addition, the box considers the impact of inflation on the purchasing power of your investments. We will consider these issues at the end of the chapter.

▶ **Self-Test 3.5**

The Rule of 72 works best with relatively low interest rates. Suppose the time it will take for an investment to double in value is 12 years. Find the interest rate. What is the approximate rate implied by the Rule of 72? Now suppose that the doubling period is only 2 years. Is the approximation better or worse in this case?

3.4 Multiple Cash Flows

So far, we have considered problems involving only a single cash flow. This is obviously limiting. Most real-world investments, after all, will involve many cash flows over time. When there are many payments, you'll hear businesspeople refer to a *stream of cash flows*.

Future Value of Multiple Cash Flows

Recall the computer you hope to purchase in 2 years (see Example 3.4). Now suppose that instead of putting aside one sum in the bank to finance the purchase, you plan to save some amount of money each year. You might be able to put $1,200 in the bank now, and another $1,400 in 1 year. If you earn an 8 percent rate of interest, how much will you be able to spend on a computer in 2 years?

The time line in Figure 3.5 shows how your savings grow. There are two cash inflows into the savings plan. The first cash flow will have 2 years to earn interest and therefore will grow to $1,200 \times (1.08)^2 = \$1,399.68$ while the second deposit, which comes a year later, will be invested for only 1 year and will grow to $1,400 \times (1.08) = \$1,512$. After 2 years, then, your total savings will be the sum of these two amounts, or $2,911.68.

▶ **Example 3.8**   *Even More Saving*

Suppose that the computer purchase can be put off for an additional year and that you can make a third deposit of $1,000 at the end of the second year. How much will be available to spend 3 years from now?

Figure 3.5

Future value of two cash flows

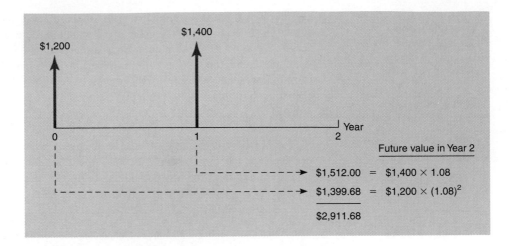

Again we organize our inputs using a time line as in Figure 3.6. The total cash available will be the sum of the future values of all three deposits. Notice that when we save for 3 years, the first two deposits each have an extra year for interest to compound:

$$\$1,200 \times (1.08)^3 = \$1,511.65$$
$$\$1,400 \times (1.08)^2 = 1,632.96$$
$$\$1,000 \times (1.08) = \underline{1,080.00}$$
$$\text{Total future value} = \$4,224.61$$

We conclude that problems involving multiple cash flows are simple extensions of single cash-flow analysis.

> **To find the value at some future date of a stream of cash flows, calculate what each cash flow will be worth at that future date, and then add up these future values.**

As we will now see, the same adding-up principle works for present value calculations.

Figure 3.6

Future value of a stream of cash flows

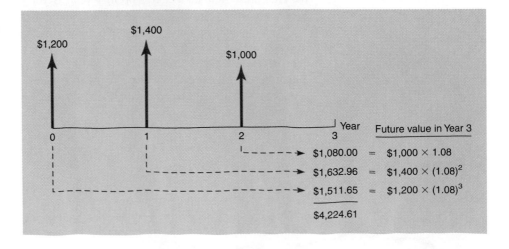

Present Value of Multiple Cash Flows

When we calculate the present value of a future cash flow, we are asking how much that cash flow would be worth today. If there is more than one future cash flow, we simply need to work out what each flow would be worth today and then add these present values.

▶ **Example 3.9**   *Cash Up Front versus an Installment Plan*

Suppose that your auto dealer gives you a choice between paying $15,500 for a new car or entering into an installment plan where you pay $8,000 down today and make payments of $4,000 in each of the next two years. Which is the better deal? Before reading this chapter, you might have compared the total payments under the two plans: $15,500 versus $16,000 in the installment plan. Now, however, you know that this comparison is wrong, because it ignores the time value of money. For example, the last installment of $4,000 is less costly to you than paying out $4,000 now. The true cost of that last payment is the present value of $4,000.

Assume that the interest rate you can earn on safe investments is 8 percent. Suppose you choose the installment plan. As the time line in Figure 3.7 illustrates, the present value of the plan's three cash flows is:

		Present Value
Immediate payment	$8,000	= $8,000.00
Second payment	$4,000/1.08	= 3,703.70
Third payment	$4,000/(1.08)^2	= 3,429.36
Total present value		= $15,133.06

Because the present value of the three payments is less than $15,500, the installment plan is in fact the cheaper alternative.

The installment plan's present value equals the amount that you would need to invest now to cover the three future payments. Let's check to see that this works. If you start with the present value of $15,133.06 in the bank, you could make the first

Figure 3.7
Present value of a stream of cash flows

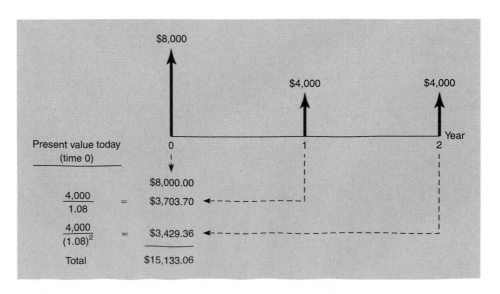

An Introduction to Financial Calculators

Financial calculators are designed with present value and future value formulas already programmed. Therefore, you can readily solve many problems simply by entering the inputs for the problem and punching a key for the solution.

The basic financial calculator uses five keys that correspond to the inputs for common problems involving the time value of money.

Each key represents the following input:

- n is the number of periods. (We have been using t to denote the length of time or number of periods. Most calculators use n for the same concept.)
- i is the interest rate per period, expressed as a percentage (not a decimal). For example, if the interest rate is 8 percent, you would enter 8, not .08. On some calculators this key is written I/Y or I/YR. (We have been using r to denote the interest rate or discount rate.)
- PV is the present value.
- FV is the future value.
- PMT is the amount of any recurring payment (called an annuity). In single cash-flow problems such as those we have considered so far, PMT is zero.

Given any four of these inputs, the calculator will solve for the fifth. We will illustrate with several examples.

Future Values

Recall Example 3.2, where we calculated the future value of your $100 credit card balance. Enter 100 into the PV register. (You enter the value by typing 100, and then pushing the PV key.) We assumed an interest rate of 1 percent per month, so enter 1 into the i register. Because the $100 had 12 months to compound, enter 12 into the n register. Enter 0 into the PMT register because there is no recurring payment involved in the calculation. Now ask the calculator to compute FV. On some calculators you simply press the FV key. On others you need to first press the "compute" key (which may be labeled *COMP* or *CPT*), and then press FV. The exact sequence of keystrokes for three popular financial calculators are as follows:[1]

Hewlett-Packard HP-10B		Sharpe EL-733A		Texas Instruments BA II Plus	
100	PV	100	PV	100	PV
12	n	12	n	12	n
1	I/YR	1	i	1	I/Y
0	PMT	0	PMT	0	PMT
FV		COMP	FV	CPT	FV

You should find after hitting the FV key that your calculator shows a value of -112.68, which, except for the minus sign, is the future value of the $100.

Why does the minus sign appear? Most calculators treat cash flows as either inflows (shown as positive numbers) or outflows (negative numbers). For example, if you borrow $100 using your credit card, you receive money

$8,000 payment and be left with $7,133.06. After 1 year, your savings would grow with interest to $7,133.06 $\times$ 1.08 = $7,703.70. You then would make the second $4,000 payment and be left with $3,703.70. This sum left in the bank would grow in the last year to $3,703.70 $\times$ 1.08 = $4,000, just enough to make the last payment.

> **The present value of a stream of future cash flows is the amount you would have to invest today to generate that stream.**

▶ **Self-Test 3.6** In order to avoid estate taxes, your rich aunt Frederica will pay you $10,000 per year for 4 years, starting 1 year from now. What is the present value of your benefactor's planned gifts? The interest rate is 7 percent. How much will you have 4 years from now if you invest each gift at 7 percent?

An Introduction to Financial Calculators (*Continued*)

now (a *positive* cash flow), but you will have to pay back $112.68 in a year, a *negative* cash flow at that time. Therefore, the calculator displays *FV* as a negative number. The following time line of cash flows shows the reasoning employed. The final negative cash flow of $112.68 has the same present value as the $100 borrowed today.

PV = $100

Month: 0--1--2--3--4--5--6--7--8--9--10--11--12

FV = $112.68

If, instead of borrowing, you were to *invest* $100 today to reap a future benefit, you would enter *PV* as a negative number (first press 100, then press the +/− key to make the value negative, and finally press *PV* to enter the value into the *PV* register). In this case, *FV* would appear as a positive number, indicating that you will reap a cash inflow when your investment comes to fruition.

Present Values

Suppose your savings goal is to accumulate $10,000 by the end of 30 years. If the interest rate is 8 percent, how much would you need to invest today to achieve your goal? Again, there is no recurring payment involved, so *PMT* is zero. We therefore enter the following: $n = 30$; $i = 8$; $FV = 1,000$; $PMT = 0$. Now compute *PV*, and you should get an answer of −993.77. The answer is displayed as a negative number because you need to make a cash outflow (an investment) of $993.77 now in order to enjoy a cash inflow of $10,000 in 30 years.

Finding the Interest Rate

The 25-year Coca-Cola Enterprises IOU in Example 3.5 sold at $129 and promised a final payment of $1,000. We may obtain the market interest rate by entering $n = 25$, $FV = 1,000$, $PV = -129$, and $PMT = 0$. Compute *i* and you will find that the interest rate is 8.53 percent. This is the value we computed directly (but with more work) in the example.

How Long an Investment?

In Example 3.7, we considered how long it would take for an investment to double in value. This sort of problem is easily solved using a calculator. If the investment is to double, we enter $FV = 2$ and $PV = -1$. If the interest rate is 9 percent, enter $i = 9$ and $PMT = 0$. Compute *n* and you will find that $n = 8.04$ years. If the interest rate is 9.05 percent, the doubling period falls to 8 years, as we found in the example.

[1]The BA II Plus requires a little extra work to initalize the calculator. When you buy the calculator, it is set to automatically interpret each period as a year but to assume that interest compounds monthly. In our experience, it is best to change the compounding frequency to once per period. To do so, press ⌷2nd⌷ {P/Y} 1 ⌷ENTER⌷, then press ⌷↓⌷ 1 ⌷ENTER⌷, and finally press ⌷2nd⌷ {QUIT} to return to standard calculator mode. You should need to do this only once, even if the calculator is shut off.

3.5 *Level Cash Flows: Perpetuities and Annuities*

annuity: Equally spaced level stream of cash flows.

perpetuity: Stream of level cash payments that never ends.

Frequently, you may need to value a stream of equal cash flows. For example, a home mortgage might require the homeowner to make equal monthly payments for the life of the loan. For a 30-year loan, this would result in 360 equal payments. A 4-year car loan might require 48 equal monthly payments. Any such sequence of equally spaced, level cash flows is called an **annuity.** If the payment stream lasts forever, it is called a **perpetuity.**

Confused by Investing? Maybe It's the New Math

If there's something about your investment portfolio that doesn't seem to add up, maybe you should check your math.

Lots of folks are perplexed by the mathematics of investing, so I thought a refresher course might help. Here's a look at some key concepts:

10 Plus 10 Is 21

Imagine you invest $100, which earns 10% this year and 10% next. How much have you made? If you answered 21%, go to the head of the class.

Here's how the math works. This year's 10% gain turns your $100 into $110. Next year, you also earn 10%, but you start the year with $110. Result? You earn $11, boosting your wealth to $121.

Thus, your portfolio has earned a *cumulative* 21% return over two years, but the *annualized* return is just 10%. The fact that 21% is more than double 10% can be attributed to the effect of investment compounding, the way that you earn money each year not only on your original investment, but also on earnings from prior years that you've reinvested.

The Rule of 72

To get a feel for compounding, try the rule of 72. What's that? If you divide a particular annual return into 72, you'll find out how many years it will take to double your money. Thus, at 10% a year, an investment will double in value in a tad over seven years.

What Goes Down Comes Back Slowly

In the investment world, winning is nice, but losses can really sting. Let's say you invest $100, which loses 10% in the first year, but bounces back 10% the next. Back to even? Not at all. In fact, you're down to $99.

Here's why. The initial 10% loss turns your $100 into $90. But the subsequent 10% gain earns you just $9, boosting your account's value to $99. The bottom line: To recoup any percentage loss, you need an even greater percentage gain. For instance, if you lose 25%, you need to make 33% to get back to even.

Not All Losses Are Equal

Which is less damaging, inflation of 50% or a 50% drop in your portfolio's value? If you said inflation, join that other bloke at the head of the class.

Confused? Consider the following example. If you have $100 to spend on cappuccino and your favorite cappuccino costs $1, you can buy 100 cups. What if your $100 then drops in value to $50? You can only buy 50 cups. And if the cappuccino's price instead rises 50% to $1.50? If you divide $100 by $1.50, you'll find you can still buy 66 cups, and even leave a tip.

Source: Jonathan Clements, "Getting Going: Confused by Investing?" *The Wall Street Journal*, February 20, 1996, p. C1. Reprinted by permission of *The Wall Street Journal*, © 1996 Dow Jones & Company, Inc. All Rights Reserved Worldwide.

How to Value Perpetuities

Some time ago the British government borrowed by issuing perpetuities. Instead of repaying these loans, the British government pays the investors holding these securities a fixed annual payment in perpetuity (forever).

The rate of interest on a perpetuity is equal to the promised annual payment C divided by the present value. For example, if a perpetuity pays $10 per year and you can buy it for $100, you will earn 10 percent interest each year on your investment. In general,

$$\text{Interest rate on a perpetuity} = \frac{\text{cash payment}}{\text{present value}}$$

$$r = \frac{C}{\text{PV}}$$

We can rearrange this relationship to derive the present value of a perpetuity, given the interest rate r and the cash payment C:

$$\text{PV of perpetuity} = \frac{C}{r} = \frac{\text{cash payment}}{\text{interest rate}}$$

Suppose some worthy person wishes to endow a chair in finance at your university. If the rate of interest is 10 percent and the aim is to provide $100,000 a year forever, the amount that must be set aside today is

$$\text{Present value of perpetuity} = \frac{C}{r} = \frac{\$100,000}{.10} = \$1,000,000$$

Two warnings about the perpetuity formula. First, at a quick glance you can easily confuse the formula with the present value of a single cash payment. A payment of $1 at the end of 1 year has a present value $1/(1+r)$. The perpetuity has a value of $1/r$. These are quite different.

Second, the perpetuity formula tells us the value of a regular stream of payments starting one period from now. Thus our endowment of $1 million would provide the university with its first payment of $100,000 one year hence. If the worthy donor wants to provide the university with an additional payment of $100,000 up front, he or she would need to put aside $1,100,000.

Sometimes you may need to calculate the value of a perpetuity that does not start to make payments for several years. For example, suppose that our philanthropist decides to provide $100,000 a year with the first payment 4 years from now. We know that in Year 3, this endowment will be an ordinary perpetuity with payments starting at the end of 1 year. So our perpetuity formula tells us that in Year 3 the endowment will be worth $100,000/r$. But it is not worth that much now. To find today's value we need to multiply by the 3-year discount factor. Thus, the "delayed" perpetuity is worth

$$\$100,000 \times \frac{1}{r} \times \frac{1}{(1+r)^3} = \$1,000,000 \times \frac{1}{(1.10)^3} = \$751,315$$

▶ **Self-Test 3.7**   A British government perpetuity pays £4 a year forever and is selling for £48. What is the interest rate?

How to Value Annuities

There are two ways to value an annuity that is, a limited number of cash flows. The slow way is to value each cash flow separately and add up the present values. The quick way is to take advantage of the following simplification. Figure 3.8 shows the cash payments and values of three investments.

Row 1.   The investment shown in the first row provides a perpetual stream of $1 payments starting in Year 1. We have already seen that this perpetuity has a present value of $1/r$.

Row 2.   Now look at the investment shown in the second row of Figure 3.8. It also provides a perpetual stream of $1 payments, but these payments don't start until

Figure 3.8

Valuing an annuity

	Cash Flow						Present Value
Year:	1	2	3	4	5	6...	
1. Perpetuity A	$1	$1	$1	$1	$1	$1...	$\dfrac{1}{r}$
2. Perpetuity B				$1	$1	$1...	$\dfrac{1}{r(1+r)^3}$
3. Three-year annuity	$1	$1	$1				$\dfrac{1}{r} - \dfrac{1}{r(1+r)^3}$

Year 4. This stream of payments is identical to the delayed perpetuity that we just valued. In Year 3, the investment will be an ordinary perpetuity with payments starting in 1 year and will therefore be worth $1/r$ in Year 3. To find the value today, we simply multiply this figure by the 3-year discount factor. Thus,

$$PV = \frac{1}{r} \times \frac{1}{(1+r)^3} = \frac{1}{r(1+r)^3}$$

Row 3. Finally, look at the investment shown in the third row of Figure 3.8. This provides a level payment of $1 a year for each of three years. In other words, it is a 3-year annuity. You can also see that, taken together, the investments in rows 2 and 3 provide exactly the same cash payments as the investment in row 1. Thus the value of our annuity (row 3) must be equal to the value of the row 1 perpetuity less the value of the delayed row 2 perpetuity:

$$\text{Present value of a 3-year \$1 annuity} = \frac{1}{r} - \frac{1}{r(1+r)^3}$$

The general formula for the value of an annuity that pays C dollars a year for each of t years is

$$\text{Present value of } t\text{-year annuity} = C\left[\frac{1}{r} - \frac{1}{r(1+r)^t}\right]$$

annuity factor: Present value of a $1 annuity.

The expression in square brackets shows the present value of a t-year annuity of $1 a year. It is generally known as the t-year **annuity factor.** Therefore, another way to write the value of an annuity is

Present value of t-year annuity = payment × annuity factor

Remembering formulas is about as difficult as remembering other people's birthdays. But as long as you bear in mind that an annuity is equivalent to the difference between an immediate and a delayed perpetuity, you shouldn't have any difficulty.

▶ **Example 3.10** *Back to Kangaroo Autos*

Let us return to Kangaroo Autos for the last time. Most installment plans call for level streams of payments. So let us suppose that this time Kangaroo offers an "easy

Figure for Example 3.10.
Time line for Kangaroo Auto

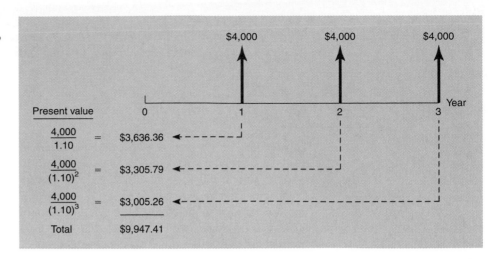

payment" scheme of $4,000 a year at the end of each of the next 3 years. First let's do the calculations the slow way, to show that if the interest rate is 10%, the present value of the three payments is $9,947.41. The time line in the figure for Example 3.10 shows these calculations. The present value of each cash flow is calculated and then the three present values are summed. The annuity formula, however, is much quicker:

$$\text{Present value} = \$4,000 \times \left[\frac{1}{.10} - \frac{1}{.10(1.10)^3} \right]$$
$$= \$4,000 \times 2.48685 = \$9,947.41$$

You can use a calculator to work out annuity factors or you can use a set of annuity tables. Table 3.5 is an abridged annuity table (an extended version is shown in Table A.3 at the end of the book). Check that you can find the 3-year annuity factor for an interest rate of 10 percent.

Table 3.5

Annuity table: present value of $1 a year for each of t years

Number of Years	Interest Rate per Year					
	5%	**6%**	**7%**	**8%**	**9%**	**10%**
1	.952	.943	.935	.926	.917	.909
2	1.859	1.833	1.808	1.783	1.759	1.736
3	2.723	2.673	2.624	2.577	2.531	2.487
4	3.546	3.465	3.387	3.312	3.240	3.170
5	4.329	4.212	4.100	3.993	3.890	3.791
10	7.722	7.360	7.024	6.710	6.418	6.145
20	12.462	11.470	10.594	9.818	9.129	8.514
30	15.372	13.765	12.409	11.258	10.274	9.427

▶ **Self-Test 3.8**   If the interest rate is 8 percent, what is the 4-year discount factor? What is the 4-year annuity factor? What is the relationship between these two numbers? Explain.

▶ **Example 3.11**   *Winning Big at a Slot Machine*

In May 1992, a 60-year-old nurse plunked down $12 in a Reno casino and walked away with the biggest jackpot in history—$9.3 million. We suspect she received unsolicited congratulations, good wishes, and requests for money from dozens of more or less worthy charities, relatives, and newly devoted friends. In response she could fairly point out that her prize wasn't really worth $9.3 million. That sum was to be paid in 20 annual installments of $465,000 each. What is the present value of the jackpot? The interest rate at the time was about 8 percent.

The present value of these payments is simply the sum of the present values of each payment. But rather than valuing each payment separately, it is much easier to treat the cash payments as a 20-year annuity. To value this annuity we simply multiply $465,000 by the 20-year annuity factor:

$$PV = \$465,000 \times \text{20-year annuity factor}$$
$$= \$465,000 \times \left[\frac{1}{r} - \frac{1}{r(1+r)^{20}} \right]$$

At an interest rate of 8 percent, the annuity factor is

$$\left[\frac{1}{.08} - \frac{1}{.08(1.08)^{20}} \right] = 9.818$$

(We also could look up the annuity factor in either Table 3.5 or Table A.3.) The present value of the $465,000 annuity is $465,000 × 9.818 = $4,565,000. That "$9.3 million prize" has a true value of about $4.6 million.

This present value is the price which investors would be prepared to offer for the series of cash flows. For example, the gambling casino might arrange for an insurance company to actually make the payments to the lucky winner. In this case, the company would charge a bit under $4.6 million to take over the obligation. With this amount in hand today, it could generate enough interest income to make the 20 payments before running its "account" down to zero.

Annuities Due

The perpetuity and annuity formulas assume that the first payment occurs at the end of the period. They tell you the value of a stream of cash payments starting one period hence.

However, streams of cash payments often start immediately. For example, Kangaroo Autos in Example 3.10 might have required three annual payments of $4,000 starting immediately. A level stream of payments starting immediately is known as an **annuity due**.

annuity due: Level stream of cash flows starting immediately.

If Kangaroo's loan were paid as an annuity due, you could think of the three payments as equivalent to an immediate payment of $4,000 plus an ordinary annuity of

$4,000 for the remaining 2 years. This is made clear in Figure 3.9, which compares the cash flow stream of the Kangaroo Auto loan treating the three payments as an annuity (panel *a*) and as an annuity due (panel *b*).

In general, the present value of an annuity due of *t* payments of $1 a year is the same as $1 plus the present value of an ordinary annuity comprised of the remaining *t* − 1 payments. The present value of an annuity due of $1 for *t* years is therefore

$$\text{PV annuity due} = 1 + \text{PV ordinary annuity of } t-1 \text{ payments}$$

$$= 1 + \left[\frac{1}{r} - \frac{1}{r(1 + r)^{t-1}} \right]$$

Figure 3.9

*Annuity versus annuity due.
(a) Three-year ordinary
annuity. (b) Three-year
annuity due.*

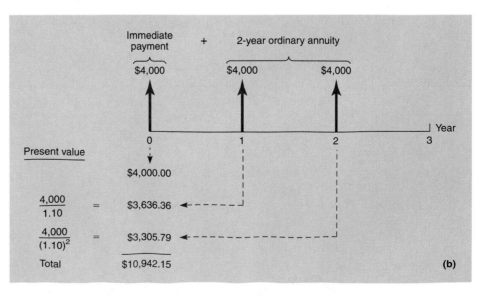

By comparing the two panels of Figure 3.9, you can see that each of the three cash flows in the annuity due comes one period earlier than the corresponding cash flow of the ordinary annuity. Therefore, the present value of an annuity due is $(1 + r)$ times the present value of an annuity.[4] Figure 3.9 shows that the effect of bringing the Kangaroo loan payments forward by 1 year was to increase their value from \$9,947.41 (as an annuity) to \$10,942.15 (as an annuity due). Notice that \$10,942.15 = \$9,947.41 × 1.10.

▶ **Self-Test 3.9**
When calculating the value of the slot machine winnings in Example 3.11, we assumed that the first of the 20 payments occurs at the end of 1 year. However, the payment was probably made immediately, with the remaining payments spread over the following 19 years. What is the present value of the \$9.3 million prize?

▶ **Example 3.12** *Home Mortgages*

Sometimes you may need to find the series of cash payments that would provide a given value today. For example, home purchasers typically borrow the bulk of the house price from a lender. The most common loan arrangement is a 30-year loan that is repaid in equal monthly installments. Suppose that a house costs \$125,000, and that the buyer puts down 20 percent of the purchase price, or \$25,000, in cash, borrowing the remaining \$100,000 from a mortgage lender such as the local savings bank. What is the appropriate monthly mortgage payment?

The borrower repays the loan by making monthly payments over the next 30 years (360 months). The savings bank needs to set these monthly payments so that they have a present value of \$100,000. Thus

$$\text{Present value} = \text{mortgage payment} \times \text{360-month annuity factor}$$
$$= \$100,000$$
$$\text{Mortgage payment} = \frac{\$100,000}{\text{360-month annuity factor}}$$

Suppose that the interest rate is 1 percent a month.[5] Then

$$\text{Mortgage payment} = \frac{\$100,000}{\dfrac{1}{.01} - \dfrac{1}{.01(1.01)^{360}}}$$
$$= \frac{\$100,000}{97.218}$$
$$= \$1,028.61$$

---

[4]Your financial calculator is equipped to handle annuities due. You simply need to put the calculator in "begin" mode, and the stream of cash flows will be interpreted as starting immediately. The begin key is labeled BGN or BEG/END. Each time you press the key, the calculator will toggle between ordinary annuity versus annuity due mode.

[5]This would be quoted as an APR of 12 percent. The effective annual rate is $(1.01)^{12} - 1 = .1268$, or 12.68 percent.

Figure 3.10

Mortgage amortization. This figure shows the breakdown of mortgage payments between interest and amortization. Monthly payments within each year are summed, so the figure shows the annual payment on the mortgage.

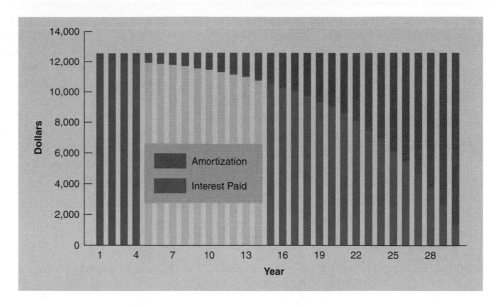

This type of loan, in which the monthly payment is fixed over the life of the mortgage, is called an *amortizing loan.* "Amortizing" means that part of the monthly payment is used to pay interest on the loan and part is used to reduce the amount of the loan. For example, the interest that accrues after 1 month on this loan will be 1 percent of $100,000, or $1,000. So $1,000 of your first monthly payment is used to pay interest on the loan and the balance of $28.61 is used to reduce the amount of the loan to $99,971.39. The $28.61 is called the *amortization* on the loan in that month.

Next month, there will be an interest charge of 1 percent of $99,971.39 = $999.71. So $999.71 of your second monthly payment is absorbed by the interest charge and the remaining $28.90 of your monthly payment ($1,028.61 − $999.71 = $28.90) is used to reduce the amount of your loan. Amortization in the second month is higher than in the first month because the amount of the loan has declined, and therefore less of the payment is taken up in interest. This procedure continues each month until the last month, when the amortization is just enough to reduce the outstanding amount on the loan to zero, and the loan is paid off.

Because the loan is progressively paid off, the fraction of the monthly payment devoted to interest steadily falls, while the fraction used to reduce the loan (the amortization) steadily increases. Thus the reduction in the size of the loan is much more rapid in the later years of the mortgage. Figure 3.10 illustrates how in the early years almost all of the mortgage payment is for interest. Even after 15 years, the bulk of the monthly payment is interest.

▶ **Self-Test 3.10**   What will the monthly payment be if you take out a $100,000 fifteen-year mortgage at an interest rate of 1 percent per month? How much of the first payment is interest and how much is amortization?

▶ **Example 3.13**   *How Much Luxury and Excitement Can $37 Billion Buy?*

The Sultan of Brunei is reputedly the world's richest person, with wealth estimated at $37 billion. We haven't yet met the Sultan, and so cannot fill you in on his plans for allocating the $37 billion between charitable good works and the cost of a life of luxury and excitement (L&E). So to keep things simple, we will just ask the following entirely hypothetical question: How much could the Sultan spend yearly on 40 more years of L&E if he were to devote the entire $37 billion to those purposes? Assume that his money is invested at 9 percent interest.

The 40-year, 9 percent annuity factor is 10.757. Thus

$$\text{Present value} = \text{annual spending} \times \text{annuity factor}$$
$$\$37,000,000,000 = \text{annual spending} \times 10.757$$
$$\text{Annual spending} = \$3,440,000,000$$

Warning to the Sultan: We haven't considered inflation. The cost of buying L&E will increase, so $3.4 billion won't buy as much L&E in 2020 as it will today. More on that later.

▶ **Self-Test 3.11**   Suppose you retire at age 70, with a life expectancy of 20 more years, and you expect to spend $55,000 a year during your retirement. How much money do you need to save by age 70 to support this consumption plan? Assume an interest rate of 7 percent.

Future Value of an Annuity

You are back in savings mode again. This time you are setting aside $3,000 at the end of every year in order to buy a car. If your savings earn interest of 8 percent a year, how much will they be worth at the end of 4 years? We can answer this question with the help of the time line in Figure 3.11. Your first year's savings will earn interest for 3 years, the second will earn interest for 2 years, the third will earn interest for 1 year, and the final saving in Year 4 will earn no interest. The sum of the future values of the four payments is

$$(\$3,000 \times 1.08^3) + (\$3,000 \times 1.08^2) + (\$3,000 \times 1.08) + \$3,000 = \$13,518$$

But wait a minute! We are looking here at a level stream of cash flows—an annuity. We have seen that there is a short-cut formula to calculate the *present* value of an annuity. So there ought to be a similar formula for calculating the *future* value of a level stream of cash flows.

Think first how much your stream of savings is worth today. You are setting aside $3,000 in each of the next 4 years. The *present* value of this 4-year annuity is therefore equal to

$$PV = \$3,000 \times \text{4-year annuity factor}$$

$$= \$3,000 \times \left[\frac{1}{.08} - \frac{1}{.08(1.08)^4}\right] = \$9,936$$

Figure 3.11

Future value of an annuity

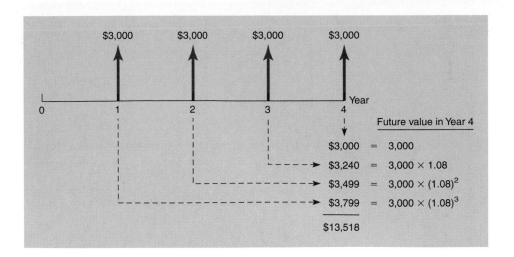

Now think how much you would have after 4 years if you invested $9,936 today. Simple! Just multiply by $(1.08)^4$:

$$\text{Value at end of Year 4} = \$9,936 \times 1.08^4 = \$13,518$$

We calculated the future value of the annuity by first calculating the present value and then multiplying by $(1 + r)^t$. The general formula for the future value of a stream of cash flows of $1 a year for each of t years is therefore.

Future value of annuity of $1 a year = present value of annuity

of $1 a year $\times$ $(1 + r)^t$

$$= \left[\frac{1}{r} - \frac{1}{r(1 + r)^t} \right] \times (1 + r)^t$$

$$= \frac{(1 + r)^t - 1}{r}$$

If you need to find the future value of just four cash flows as in our example, it is a toss up whether it is quicker to calculate the future value of each cash flow separately (as we did in Figure 3.11) or to use the annuity formula. If you are faced with a stream of 10 or 20 cash flows, there is no contest.

You can find a table of the future value of an annuity in Table 3.6, or the more extensive Table A.4 at the end of the book. You can see that in the row corresponding to $t = 4$ and the column corresponding to $r = 8\%$, the future value of an annuity of $1 a year is $4.506. Therefore, the future value of the $3,000 annuity is $3,000 $\times$ 4.506 = $13,518.

Remember that all our annuity formulas assume that the first cash flow does not occur until the end of the first period. If the first cash flow comes immediately, the future value of the cash-flow stream is greater, since each flow has an extra year to earn interest. For example, at an interest rate of 8 percent, the future value of an annuity starting with an immediate payment would be exactly 8 percent greater than the figure given by our formula.

Table 3.6
Future value of a $1 annuity

Number of Years	Interest Rate per Year					
	5%	**6%**	**7%**	**8%**	**9%**	**10%**
1	1.000	1.000	1.000	1.000	1.000	1.000
2	2.050	2.060	2.070	2.080	2.090	2.100
3	3.153	3.184	3.215	3.246	3.278	3.310
4	4.310	4.375	4.440	4.506	4.573	4.641
5	5.526	5.637	5.751	5.867	5.985	6.105
10	12.578	13.181	13.816	14.487	15.193	15.937
20	33.066	36.786	40.995	45.762	51.160	57.275
30	66.439	79.058	94.461	113.283	136.308	164.494

▶ **Example 3.14** *Saving for Retirement*

In only 50 more years, you will retire. (That's right—by the time you retire, the retirement age will be around 70 years. Longevity is not an unmixed blessing.) Have you started saving yet? Suppose you believe you will need to accumulate $500,000 by your retirement date in order to support your desired standard of living. How much must you save *each year* between now and your retirement to meet that future goal? Let's say that the interest rate is 10 percent per year. You need to find how large the annuity in the following figure must be to provide a future value of $500,000:

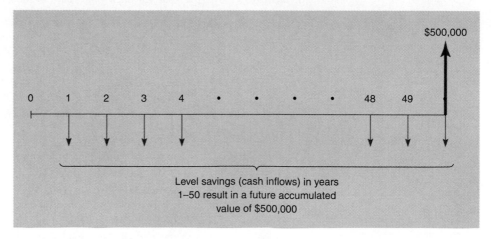

Level savings (cash inflows) in years
1–50 result in a future accumulated
value of $500,000

We know that if you were to save $1 each year your funds would accumulate to

$$\text{Future value of annuity of \$1 a year} = \frac{(1 + r)^t - 1}{r} = \frac{(1.10)^{50} - 1}{.10}$$
$$= \$1,163.91$$

(Rather than compute the future value formula directly, you could look up the future value annuity factor in Table 3.6 or Table A.4. Alternatively, you can use a financial calculator as we describe in the nearby box.) Therefore, if we save an amount of $C each year, we will accumulate $C \times 1,163.91$.

see box p. 83

Solving Annuity Problems Using a Financial Calculator

The formulas for both the present value and future value of an annuity are also built into your financial calculator. Again, we can input all but one of the five financial keys, and let the calculator solve for the remaining variable. In these applications, the *PMT* key is used to either enter or solve for the value of an annuity.

Solving for an Annuity

In Example 3.14, we determined the savings stream that would provide a retirement goal of $500,000 after 50 years of saving at an interest rate of 10 percent. To find the required savings each year, enter $n = 50$, $i = 10$, $FV = 500,000$, and $PV = 0$ (because your "savings account" currently is empty). Compute *PMT* and find that it is $429.59. Again, your calculator is likely to display the solution as −429.59, since the positive $500,000 cash value in 50 years will require 50 cash payments (outflows) of $429.59.

The sequence of key strokes on three popular calculators necessary to solve this problem is as follows:

Hewlett-Packard HP-10B		Sharpe EL-733A		Texas Instruments BA II Plus	
0	PV	0	PV	0	PV
50	n	50	n	50	n
10	I/YR	10	i	10	I/Y
500,000	FV	500,000	FV	500,000	FV
	PMT	COMP	PMT	CPT	PMT

Your calculator displays a negative number, as the 50 cash outflows of $429.59 are necessary to provide for the $500,000 cash value at retirement.

Present Value of an Annuity

In Example 3.12 we considered a 30-year mortgage with monthly payments of $1,028.61 and an interest rate of 1 percent. Suppose we didn't know the amount of the mortgage loan. Enter $n = 360$ (months), $i = 1$, $PMT = -1,028.61$ (we enter the annuity level paid by the borrower to the lender as a negative number since it is a cash outflow), and $FV = 0$ (the mortgage is wholly paid off after 30 years; there are no final future payments beyond the normal monthly payment). Compute *PV* to find that the value of the loan is $100,000.

What about the balance left on the mortgage after 10 years have passed? This is easy: the monthly payment is still $PMT = -1,028.61$, and we continue to use i = 1

and $FV = 0$. The only change is that the number of monthly payments remaining have fallen from 360 to 240 (20 years are left on the loan). So enter $n = 240$ and compute *PV* as 93,417.76. This is the principal balance remaining on the mortgage.

Future Value of an Annuity

In Figure 3.11, we showed that a 4-year annuity of $3,000 invested at 8 percent would accumulate to a future value of $13,518. To solve this on your calculator, enter $n = 4$, $i = 8$, $PMT = -3,000$ (we enter the annuity paid by the investor to her savings account as a negative number since it is a cash outflow), and $PV = 0$ (the account starts with no funds). Compute *FV* to find that the future value of the savings account after 3 years is 13,518.

Calculator Self-Test Review (answers follow)

1. Turn back to Kangaroo Autos in Example 3.10. Can you now solve for the present value of the three installment payments using you financial calculator? What key strokes must you use?
2. Now use your calculator to solve for the present value of the three installment payments if the first payment comes immediately, that is, as an annuity due.
3. Find the annual spending available to the Sultan of Brunei using the data in Example 3.13 and your financial calculator.

Solutions to Calculator Self-Test Review Questions

1. Inputs are $n = 3$, $i = 10$, $FV = 0$, and $PMT = 4,000$. Compute *PV* to find the present value of the cash flows as $9,947.41
2. If you put your calculator in BEGIN mode and recalculate *PV* using the same inputs, you will find that *PV* has increased by 10 percent to $10,942.15. Alternatively, as depicted in Figure 3.9, you can calculate the value of the $4,000 immediate payment plus the value of a 2-year annuity of $4,000. Inputs for the 2-year annuity are $n = 2$, $i = 10$, $FV = 0$, and $PMT = 4,000$. Compute *PV* to find the present value of the cash flows as $6,942.15. This amount plus the immediate $4,000 payment results in the same total present value: $10,942.15.
3. Inputs are $n = 40$, $i = 9$, $FV = 0$, $PV = -37,000$ million. Compute *PMT* to find that the 40-year annuity with present value of $37 billion is $3,440 million.

We need to choose C to ensure that $\$C \times 1{,}163.91 = \$500{,}000$. Thus $C = \$500{,}000/1{,}163.91 = \$429.59$. This appears to be surprisingly good news. Saving $\$429.59$ a year does not seem to be an extremely demanding savings program. Don't celebrate yet, however. The news will get worse (much worse) when we consider the impact of inflation.

▶ **Self-Test 3.12**   What is the required savings level if the interest rate is only 5 percent? Why has the amount increased?

3.6 *Inflation and the Time Value of Money*

When a bank offers to pay 6 percent on a savings account, it promises to pay interest of $60 for every $1,000 you deposit. The bank fixes the number of dollars that it pays, but it doesn't provide any assurance of how much those dollars will buy. If the value of your investment increases by 6 percent, while the prices of goods and services increase by 10 percent, you have actually lost ground in terms of the goods you can buy.

Real versus Nominal Cash Flows

Prices of goods and services continually change. Textbooks may become more expensive (sorry) while computers become cheaper. An overall general rise in prices is known as **inflation.** If the inflation rate is 5 percent per year, then goods that cost $1.00 a year ago typically cost $1.05 this year. The increase in the general level of prices means that the purchasing power of money has eroded. If a dollar bill bought one loaf of bread last year, the same dollar this year buys only part of a loaf.

inflation: Rate at which prices as a whole are increasing.

Economists track the general level of prices using several different price indexes. The best known of these is the *Consumer Price Index,* or *CPI.* This measures the number of dollars that it takes to buy a specified basket of goods and services that is supposed to represent the typical family's purchases.[6] Thus the percentage increase in the CPI from one year to the next measures the rate of inflation.

Figure 3.12 graphs the CPI since 1947. We have set the index for the end of 1947 to 100, so the graph shows the price level in each year as a percentage of 1947 prices. For example, the index in 1948 was 103. This means that on average $103 in 1948 would have bought the same quantity of goods and services as $100 in 1947. The inflation rate between 1947 and 1948 was therefore 3 percent. By the end of 1996, the index was 678, meaning that 1996 prices were 6.78 times as high as 1947 prices.[7]

real value of $1: Purchasing power-adjusted value of a dollar.

The purchasing power of money fell by a factor of 6.78 between 1947 and 1996. A dollar in 1996 would buy only 15 percent of the goods it could buy in 1947 ($1/6.78 = .15$). In this case, we would say that the **real value of $1** declined by $100 - 15 = 85$ percent from 1947 to 1996.

---

[6]Don't ask how you buy a "basket" of services.

[7]The choice of 100 for the index in 1947 is arbitrary. For example, we could have set the index at 50 in 1947. In this case the index in 1948 would have been 3 percent higher at 51.5 (that is, $50 in 1947 and $51.50 in 1948 would have bought the same basket of goods).

Figure 3.12
Consumer Price Index

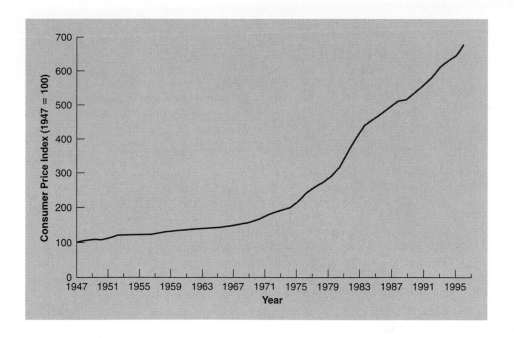

> ▶ **Example 3.15** *British Inflation*

Charles Dickens's character Mr. Micawber summed up his financial situation as follows: "Annual income twenty pounds, annual expenditure nineteen nineteen and six, result happiness. Annual income twenty pounds, annual expenditure twenty pounds ought and six, result misery."

How much did Mr. Micawber need to invest to escape misery? In 1850 the yield on perpetual British government loans was 3.1 percent. So if Mr. Micawber invested £645 in these loans, he would have just teetered on the edge:

$$\text{Annual income} = \text{yield on loan} \times \text{amount invested}$$
$$£20 = .031 \times £645$$

By investing in perpetual government loans Mr. Micawber and his heirs could have been assured of £20 a year forever.[8] Unfortunately, they could not have been assured of what that money would buy—the income on the loans is fixed in money but not in purchasing power. Between 1850 and 1996 retail prices in Britain increased by a factor of 55. So an annual income of £20 would nearly have bought happiness in 1850 but certainly not in 1996. In *real* terms (that is, measured in 1850 pounds), the income on the loans would have fallen from £20 in 1850 to £20/55 = £.36 in 1996.

---

[8]We oversimplify. Although the British government was not obliged ever to repay the loans, it had the *right* to do so. When interest rates fell in 1888 and again in 1902, it bought back the existing loans and replaced them with new perpetual loans offering a lower annual income.

> Economists sometimes talk about *current* or *nominal dollars* versus *constant* or *real dollars*. Current or nominal dollars refer to the actual number of dollars of the day; constant or real dollars refer to the amount of purchasing power.

Some expenditures are fixed in nominal terms, and therefore *decline* in real terms. Suppose you took out a 30-year house mortgage in 1986. The monthly payment was $800. It was still $800 in 1996, even though the CPI increased by a factor of 1.43 over those years.

What's the monthly payment for 1996 expressed in real 1986 dollars? The answer is $800/1.43, or $559.44 per month. The real burden of paying the mortgage was much less in 1996 than in 1986.

▶ **Self-Test 3.13**   The price index in 1980 was 370. If a family spent $250 a week on their typical purchases in 1947, how much would those purchases have cost in 1980? If your salary in 1980 was $30,000 a year, what would be the real value of that salary in terms of 1947 dollars?

Inflation and Interest Rates

Whenever you see an interest rate quoted in the United States, you can be fairly sure that it is a *nominal,* not a *real* rate. It sets the actual number of dollars you will be paid with no offset for future inflation.

nominal interest rate: Rate at which money invested grows.

If you deposit $1,000 in the bank at a **nominal interest rate** of 6 percent, you will have $1,060 at the end of the year. But this does not mean you are 6 percent better off. Suppose that the inflation rate during the year is also 6 percent. Then the goods that cost $1,000 last year will now cost $1,000 $\times$ 1.06 = $1,060, so you've gained nothing:

$$\text{Real future value of investment} = \frac{\$1,000 \times (1 + \text{nominal interest rate})}{(1 + \text{inflation rate})}$$

$$= \frac{\$1,000 \times 1.06}{1.06} = \$1,000$$

real interest rate: Rate at which the purchasing power of an investment increases.

In this example, the nominal rate of interest is 6 percent, but the **real interest rate** is zero.

The real rate of interest is calculated by

$$1 + \text{real interest rate} = \frac{1 + \text{nominal interest rate}}{1 + \text{inflation rate}}$$

In our example both the nominal interest rate and the inflation rate were 6 percent. So

$$1 + \text{real interest rate} = \frac{1.06}{1.06} = 1$$

$$\text{real interest rate} = 0$$

What if the nominal interest rate is 6 percent but the inflation rate is only 2 percent? In that case the real interest rate is 1.06/1.02 − 1 = .039, or 3.9 percent. Imagine that the price of a loaf of bread is $1, so that $1,000 would buy 1,000 loaves today. If you invest that $1,000 at a nominal interest rate of 6 percent, you will have $1,060 at the end of the year. However, if the price of loaves has risen in the meantime to $1.02, then your money will buy you only 1,060/1.02 = 1,039 loaves. The real rate of interest is 3.9 percent.

▶ **Self-Test 3.14**   a. Suppose that you invest your funds at an interest rate of 8 percent. What will be your real rate of interest if the inflation rate is zero? What if it is 5 percent?
b. Suppose that you demand a real rate of interest of 3 percent on your investments. What nominal interest rate do you need to earn if the inflation rate is zero? If it is 5 percent?

Here is a useful approximation. The real rate approximately equals the difference between the nominal rate and the inflation rate:[9]

Real interest rate ≈ nominal interest rate − inflation rate

Our example used a nominal interest rate of 6 percent, an inflation rate of 2 percent, and a real rate of 3.9 percent. If we round to 4 percent, the approximation gives the same answer:

$$\text{Real interest rate} \approx \text{nominal interest rate} - \text{inflation rate}$$
$$\approx 6 - 2 = 4\%$$

The approximation works best when both the inflation rate and the real rate are small.[10] When they are not small, throw the approximation away and do it right.

▶ **Example 3.16**   *Real and Nominal Rates*

In the United States in 1996, the interest rate on 1-year government borrowing was about 5.9 percent. The inflation rate was 3.3 percent. Therefore, the real rate can be found by computing

$$1 + \text{real interest rate} = \frac{1 + \text{nominal interest rate}}{1 + \text{inflation rate}}$$
$$= \frac{1.059}{1.033} = 1.025$$
$$\text{real interest rate} = .025, \text{ or } 2.5\%$$

The approximation rule gives a similar value of 5.9 − 3.3 = 2.6 percent. But the approximation would not have worked in the German hyperinflation of 1922–1923, when the inflation rate was well over 100 percent per *month* (at one point you needed 1 million marks to mail a letter) or in Peru in 1990, when prices increased by nearly 7500 percent.

---

[9]The squiggle (≈) means "approximately equal to."

[10]When the interest and inflation rates are expressed as decimals (rather than percentages), the approximation error equals the product (real interest rate × inflation rate).

What Fluctuates: Real or Nominal Rates?

Suppose that the expected inflation rate rises by one percentage point. What moves? Does the real interest rate go down or the nominal rate go up?

Investors are most concerned about the purchasing power of their money and the real rate of interest. We would therefore expect them to demand a higher nominal interest rate when the rate of inflation increases.

Suppose the real rate of interest is 5 percent, the inflation rate 10 percent, and the nominal interest rate 15.5 percent. If the rate of inflation goes to 11 percent, then the nominal rate should climb to roughly 16.5 percent. At this inflation rate, investors need 16.5 percent before inflation to maintain a 5 percent gain in actual purchasing power.

Real interest rates depend on the supply of savings and the demand for new investment. This supply–demand balance changes from year to year and country to country, so fluctuations in nominal interest rates cannot be due entirely to changes in expected inflation. Nevertheless, countries with high inflation almost always have high nominal interest rates. In the United States periods of high inflation and high nominal rates generally go together, as illustrated in Figure 3.13.

Valuing Real Cash Payments

Think again about how to value future cash payments. Earlier in the chapter you learned how to value payments in current dollars by discounting at the nominal interest rate. For example, suppose that the nominal interest rate is 10 percent. How much do you need to invest now to produce $100 in a year's time? Easy! Calculate the present value of $100 by discounting by 10 percent.

$$PV = \frac{\$100}{1.10} = \$90.91$$

Figure 3.13

Interest and inflation rates since 1953. Interest rates are those paid on U.S. Treasury bills.

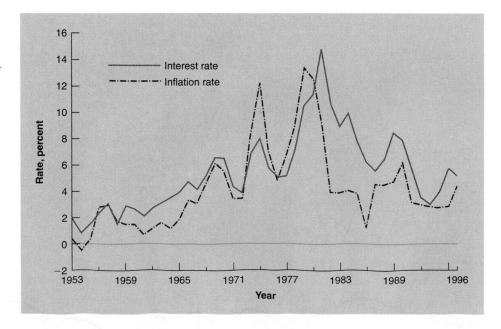

You get exactly the same result if you discount the *real* payment by the *real interest rate*. For example, assume that you expect inflation of 7 percent over the next year. The real value of that $100 is therefore only $100/1.07 = $93.46. In one year's time your $100 will buy only as much as $93.46 today. Also with a 7 percent inflation rate the real rate of interest is only about 3 percent. We can calculate it exactly from the formula

$$(1 + \text{real interest rate}) = \frac{1 + \text{nominal interest rate}}{1 + \text{inflation rate}}$$

$$= \frac{1.10}{1.07} = 1.028$$

$$\text{real interest rate} = .028, \text{ or } 2.8\%$$

If we now discount the $93.46 real payment by the 2.8 percent real interest rate, we have a present value of $90.91, just as before:

$$PV = \frac{\$93.46}{1.028} = \$90.91$$

The two methods should always give the same answer.[11]
Remember:

> **Current dollar cash flows must be discounted by the nominal interest rate; real cash flows must be discounted by the real interest rate.**

Mixing up nominal cash flows and real discount rates (or real rates and nominal flows) is an unforgivable sin. It is surprising how many sinners one finds.

▶ **Self-Test 3.15**   You are owed $5,000 by a relative who will pay back in 1 year. The nominal interest rate is 8 percent and the inflation rate is 5 percent. What is the present value of your relative's IOU? Show that you get the same answer (a) discounting the nominal payment at the nominal rate and (b) discounting the real payment at the real rate.

▶ **Example 3.17**   *How Inflation Might Affect the Sultan of Brunei*

We showed earlier (Example 3.13) that at an interest rate of 9 percent the Sultan of Brunei could, if he wished, turn his $37 billion wealth into a 40-year annuity of $3.4 billion per year of luxury and excitement (L&E). Unfortunately L&E expenses inflate just like gasoline and groceries. Thus the Sultan would find the purchasing power of that $3.4 billion steadily declining. If he wants the same luxuries in 2020 as in 1997

---

[11]If they don't there must be an error in your calculations. All we have done in the second calculation is to divide both the numerator (the cash payment) and the denominator (one plus the nominal interest rate) by the same number (one plus the inflation rate):

$$PV = \frac{\text{payment in current dollars}}{1 + \text{nominal interest rate}}$$

$$= \frac{(\text{payment in current dollars})/(1 + \text{inflation rate})}{(1 + \text{nominal interest rate})/(1 + \text{inflation rate})}$$

$$= \frac{\text{payment in constant dollars}}{1 + \text{real interest rate}}$$

he'll have to spend less in 1997, and then increase expenditures in line with inflation. How much should he spend in 1997? Assume the long-run inflation rate is 5 percent.

The Sultan needs to calculate a 40-year *real* annuity. The real interest rate is a little less than 4 percent:

$$1 + \text{real interest rate} = \frac{1 + \text{nominal interest rate}}{1 + \text{inflation rate}}$$

$$= \frac{1.09}{1.05} = 1.038$$

so the real rate is 3.8 percent. The 40-year annuity factor at 3.8 percent is 20.4. Therefore, annual spending (in 1997 dollars) should be chosen so that

$$\$37,000,000,000 = \text{annual spending} \times 20.4$$

$$\text{annual spending} = \$1,814,000,000$$

The Sultan could spend that amount on L&E in 1997 and 5 percent more (in line with inflation) in each subsequent year. This is only about half the value we calculated when we ignored inflation. Life has many disappointments, even for sultans.

▶ **Self-Test 3.16**   You have reached age 60 with a modest fortune of $3 million and are considering early retirement. How much can you spend each year for the next 30 years? Assume that spending is stable in real terms. The nominal interest rate is 10 percent and the inflation rate is 5 percent.

Real or Nominal?

Any present value calculation done in nominal terms can also be done in real terms, and vice versa. Most financial analysts forecast in nominal terms and discount at nominal rates. However, in some cases real cash flows are easier to deal with. In our example of the Sultan, the *real* expenditures were fixed. In this case, it was easiest to use real quantities. On the other hand, if the cash-flow stream is fixed in nominal terms (for example, the payments on a loan), it is easiest to use all nominal quantities.

Summary

1. An investment of $1 earning an interest rate of r will increase in value each period by the factor $(1 + r)$. After t periods its value will grow to $(1 + r)^t$. This is the future value of the $1 investment with compound interest.
2. Interest rates for short time periods are often quoted as annual rates by multiplying the per-period rate by the number of periods in a year. These annual percentage rates (APRs) do not recognize the effect of compound interest.
3. The present value of a future cash payment is the amount that you would need to invest today to match that future payment. To calculate present value we divide the cash payment by $(1 + r)^t$ or, equivalently, multiply by the discount factor $1/(1 + r)^t$. The discount factor measures the value today of $1 received in period t.

4. A level stream of cash payments that continues indefinitely is known as a perpetuity; one that continues for a limited number of years is called an annuity. Short-cut formulas make valuing perpetuities and annuities easy.
5. A dollar is a dollar but the amount of goods that a dollar can buy is eroded by inflation. If prices double, the real value of the dollar halves. Financial managers and economists often find it helpful to re-express future cash flows in terms of real dollars—that is, dollars of constant purchasing power.
6. Be careful to distinguish the promised nominal rate and the real interest rate—that is, the rate at which the real value of the investment grows.
7. Discount nominal cash flows (that is, cash flows measured in current dollars) at nominal interest rates. Discount real cash flows (cash flows measured in constant dollars) at real interest rates. *Never* mix and match nominal and real.

Key Terms

future value	discount rate	inflation
compound interest	discount factor	real value of $1
simple interest	perpetuity	nominal interest rate
effective annual interest rate	annuity	real interest rate
annual percentage rate (APR)	annuity factor	
present value (PV)	annuity due	

Problems

1. **Present Values.** Compute the present value of a $100 cash flow for the following combinations of discount rates and times:

   a. $r = 10$ percent. $t = 10$ years
   b. $r = 10$ percent. $t = 20$ years
   c. $r = 5$ percent. $t = 10$ years
   d. $r = 5$ percent. $t = 20$ years

2. **Future Values.** Compute the future value of a $100 cash flow for the same combinations of rates and times as in problem 1.

3. **Future Values.** In 1880 five aboriginal trackers were each promised the equivalent of 100 Australian dollars for helping to capture the notorious outlaw Ned Kelley. In 1993 the granddaughters of two of the trackers claimed that this reward had not been paid. The Victorian prime minister stated that if this was true, the government would be happy to pay the $100. However, the granddaughters also claimed that they were entitled to compound interest. How much was each entitled to if the interest rate was 5 percent? What if it was 10 percent?

4. **Future Values.** You deposit $1,000 in your bank account. If the bank pays 4 percent simple interest, how much will you accumulate in your account after 10 years? What if the bank pays compound interest? How much of your earnings will be interest on interest?

5. **Present Values.** You will require $700 in 5 years. If you earn 6 percent interest on your funds, how much will you need to invest today in order to reach your savings goal?

6. **Calculating Interest Rate.** Find the interest rate implied by the following combinations of present and future values:

Present Value	Years	Future Value
$400	11	$684
$183	4	$249
$300	7	$300

7. **Number of Periods.** How long will it take for $400 to grow to $1,000 at the interest rate specified?

    a. 4 percent
    b. 8 percent
    c. 16 percent

8. **Calculating Interest Rate.** Find the effective annual interest rate for each case:

(APR)	Compounding Period
12%	1 month
8%	3 months
10%	6 months

9. **Calculating Interest Rate.** Lenny Loanshark charges "one point" per week (that is, 1 percent per week) on his loans. What APR must he report to consumers? Assume exactly 52 weeks in a year. What is the effective annual rate?

10. **Calculating Interest Rate.** Find the APR (the stated interest rate) for each case:

Effective Annual Interest Rate	Compounding Period
10.00%	1 year
6.09%	6 months
8.24%	3 months

11. **Present Values.** Would you rather receive $1,000 a year for 10 years or $800 a year for 15 years if

    a. the interest rate is 5 percent
    b. the interest rate is 20 percent
    c. Why do your answers to (a) and (b) differ?

12. **Calculating Interest Rate.** Find the annual interest rate.

Present Value	Future Value	Time Period
100	115.76	3 years
200	262.16	4 years
100	110.41	5 years

13. **Growth of Funds.** If you earn 8 percent per year on your bank account, how long will it take an account with $100 to double to $200?

14. **Comparing Interest Rates.** Suppose you can borrow money at 8.6 percent per year (APR) compounded semiannually or 8.4 percent per year (APR) compounded monthly. Which is the better deal?

15. **Present Values.** What is the present value of the following cash-flow stream if the interest rate is 5 percent?

Year	Cash Flow
1	$200
2	$400
3	$300

16. **Annuity Values.**

    a. What is the present value of a 3-year annuity of $100 if the discount rate is 8 percent?
    b. What is the present value of the annuity in (a) if you have to wait 2 years instead of 1 year for the payment stream to start?

17. **Present Values.** A famous quarterback just signed a $15 million contract providing $3 million a year for 5 years. A less famous receiver signed a $14 million 5-year contract providing $4 million now and $2 million a year for 5 years. Who is better paid? The interest rate is 12 percent.

18. **Loan Payments.** If you take out an $8,000 car loan that calls for 48 monthly payments at an APR of 10 percent, what is your monthly payment? What is the effective annual interest rate on the loan?

19. **Rate on a Loan.** If you take out an $8,000 car loan that calls for 48 monthly payments of $225 each, what is the APR of the loan? What is the effective annual interest rate on the loan?

20. **Loan Payments.** Reconsider the car loan in the previous question. What if the payments are made in four annual year-end installments? What annual payment would have the same present value as the monthly payment you calculated? Use the same effective annual interest rate as in the previous question. Why is your answer not simply 12 times the monthly payment?

21. **Annuities and Interest Rates.** Professor's Annuity Corp. offers a lifetime annuity to retiring professors. For a payment of $80,000 at age 65, the firm will pay the retiring professor $600 a month until death.

    a. If the professor's remaining life expectancy is 20 years, what is the monthly rate on this annuity? What is the effective annual rate?
    b. If the monthly interest rate is .5 percent, what monthly annuity payment can the firm offer to the retiring professor?

22. **Annuity Values.** You want to buy a new car, but you can make an initial payment of only $2,000 and can afford monthly payments of at most $400.

    a. If the APR on auto loans is 12 percent and you finance the purchase over 48 months, what is the maximum price you can pay for the car?
    b. How much can you afford if you finance the purchase over 60 months?

23. **Calculating Interest Rate.** In a *discount interest loan,* you pay the interest payment up front. For example, if a 1-year loan is stated as $10,000 and the interest rate is 10 percent, the borrower "pays" .10 × $10,000 = $1,000 immediately, thereby receiving net funds of $9,000 and repaying $10,000 in a year.

    a. What is the effective interest rate on this loan?
    b. If you call the discount d (for example, $d = 10\%$ using our numbers), express the effective annual rate on the loan as a function of d.
    c. Why is the effective annual rate always greater than the stated rate d?

24. **Annuity Due.** Recall that an annuity due is like an ordinary annuity except that the first payment is made immediately instead of at the end of the first period.

    a. Why is the present value of an annuity due equal to $(1 + r)$ times the present value of an ordinary annuity?
    b. Why is the future value of an annuity due equal to $(1 + r)$ times the future value of an ordinary annuity?

25. **Valuing Delayed Annuities.** Suppose that you will receive annual payments of $10,000 for a period of 10 years. The first payment will be made 4 years from now. If the interest rate is 6 percent, what is the present value of this stream of payments?

26. **Perpetuities.** A local bank will pay you $100 a year for your lifetime if you deposit $2,500 in the bank today. If you plan to live forever, what interest rate is the bank paying?

27. **Perpetuities.** A local bank advertises the following deal: "Pay us $100 a year for 10 years and then we will pay you (or your beneficiaries) $100 a year *forever.*" Is this a good deal if the interest rate available on other deposits is 8 percent?

28. **Applying Time Value.** You can buy property today for $3 million and sell it in 5 years for $4 million. (You earn no rental income on the property.)

   a. If the interest rate is 8 percent, what is the present value of the sales price?
   b. Is the property investment attractive to you? Why or why not?
   c. Would your answer to (b) change if you also could earn $200,000 per year rent on the property?

29. **Perpetuities.** A property will provide $10,000 a year forever. If its value is $125,000, what must be the discount rate?

30. **EAR versus APR.** You invest $1,000 at a 6 percent annual interest rate, stated as an APR. Interest is compounded monthly. How much will you have in 1 year? In 1.5 years?

31. **Applying Time Value.** You invest $1,000 today and expect to sell your investment for $2,000 in 10 years.

   a. Is this a good deal if the discount rate is 5 percent?
   b. What if the discount rate is 10 percent?

32. **Calculating Interest Rate.** A store will give you a 3 percent discount on the cost of your purchase if you pay cash today. Otherwise, you will be billed the full price with payment due in 1 month. What is the implicit borrowing rate being paid by customers who choose to defer payment for the month?

33. **Growth of Funds.** Using the Rule of 72, if the interest rate is 8 percent per year, how long will it take for your money to *quadruple* in value?

34. **Annuity Value.** Your landscaping company can lease a truck for $8,000 a year (paid at year-end) for 6 years. It can instead buy the truck for $40,000. The truck will be valueless after 6 years. If the interest rate your company can earn on its funds is 7 percent, is it cheaper to buy or lease?

35. **Annuity Due Value.** Reconsider the previous problem. What if the lease payments are an annuity due, so that the first payment comes immediately? Is it cheaper to buy or lease?

36. **EAR.** If a bank pays 10 percent interest with continuous compounding, what is the effective annual rate?

37. **Annuity Due.** A store offers two payment plans. Under the installment plan, you pay 25 percent down and 25 percent of the purchase price in each of the next 3 years. If you pay the entire bill immediately, you can take a 10 percent discount from the purchase price. Which is a better deal if you can borrow or lend funds at a 6 percent interest rate?

38. **Annuity Value.** Reconsider the previous question. How will your answer change if the payments on the 4-year installment plan do not start for a full year?

39. **Annuity and Annuity Due Payments.**

   a. If you borrow $1,000 and agree to repay the loan in five equal annual payments at an interest rate of 12 percent, what will your payment be?
   b. What if you make the first payment on the loan immediately instead of at the end of the first year?

40. **Mortgage with Points.** Home loans typically involve "points," which are fees charged by the lender. Each point charged means that the borrower must pay 1 percent of the loan amount as a fee. For example, if the loan is for $100,000, and two points are charged, the loan repayment schedule is calculated on a $100,000 loan, but the net amount the borrower receives is only $98,000. What is the effective annual interest rate charged on such a loan assuming loan repayment occurs over 360 months? Assume the interest rate is 1 percent per month.

41. **Retirement Savings.** You believe you will need to have saved $500,000 by the time you retire in 40 years in order to live comfortably. If the interest rate is 5 percent per year, how much must you save each year to meet your retirement goal?

42. **Retirement Savings.** How much would you need in the previous problem if you believe that you will inherit $100,000 in 10 years?

43. **Retirement Savings.** You believe you will spend $40,000 a year for 20 years once you retire in 40 years. If the interest rate is 5 percent per year, how much must you save each year until retirement to meet your retirement goal?

44. **Calculating Interest Rate.** You borrow $10,000, and you repay the loan by making total payments of $12,000: $1,000 a month for 12 months. The lender argues that since the loan is for 1 year and the total amount of interest paid is $2,000, the interest rate on the loan is 20 percent. What is the APR and the effective annual rate on this loan? Is either rate as low as 20 percent? Why is the 20 percent rate quoted on this loan deceptive?

45. **Amortizing Loan.** You take out a 30-year $100,000 mortgage loan with an APR of 8 percent and monthly payments. In 12 years you decide to sell your house and pay off the mortgage. What is the principal balance on the loan?

46. **Amortizing Loan.** Consider a 4-year amortizing loan. You borrow $1,000 initially, and repay it in four equal annual year-end payments.

    a. If the interest rate is 10 percent, show that the annual payment is $315.47.
    b. Fill in the following table, which shows how much of each payment is comprised of interest versus principal repayment (that is, amortization), and the outstanding balance on the loan at each date.

Time	Loan Balance	Year-End Interest Due on Balance	Year-End Payment	Amortization of Loan
0	$1,000	$100	$315.47	$215.47
1	_____	_____	315.47	_____
2	_____	_____	315.47	_____
3	_____	_____	315.47	_____
4	0	0	—	—

    c. Show that the loan balance after 1 year is equal to the year-end payment of $315.47 times the 3-year annuity factor.

47. **Changing Interest Rates.** If the interest rate this year is 8 percent and the interest rate next year will be 10 percent, what is the future value of $1 after 2 years? What is the present value of a payment of $1 to be received in 2 years?

48. **Perpetuities.** British government 4 percent perpetuities pay £4 interest each year forever. Another bond, 2 ½ percent perpetuities, pays £2.50 a year forever. What is the value of 4 percent perpetuities, if the long-term interest rate is 6 percent? What is the value of 2 ½ percent perpetuities?

49. **Changing Interest Rates.** Your wealthy uncle established a $1,000 bank account for you when you were born. For the first 8 years of your life, the interest rate earned on the account

was 8 percent. Since then, rates have been only 6 percent. Now you are 21 years old and ready to cash in. How much is in your account?

50. **Applying Time Value.** A factory costs $400,000. You forecast that it will produce cash inflows of $120,000 in Year 1, $180,000 in Year 2, and $300,000 in Year 3. The discount rate is 12 percent. Is the factory a good investment? Explain.

51. **Future Values.** How much will $100 grow to if invested at a continuously compounded interest rate of 10 percent for 6 years? What if it is invested for 10 years at 6 percent?

52. **Annuity Values.** You can buy a car that is advertised for $12,000 on the following terms: (a) pay $12,000 and receive a $1,000 rebate from the manufacturer; (b) pay $250 a month for 4 years for total payments of $12,000, implying zero percent financing. Which is the better deal if the interest rate is 1 percent per month?

53. **Future Values.** I now have $20,000 in the bank earning interest of .5 percent per month. I need $30,000 to make a down payment on a house. I can save an additional $100 per month. How long will it take me to accumulate the $30,000?

54. **Real versus Nominal Dollars.** An engineer in 1950 was earning $6,000 a year. Today she earns $60,000 a year. However, on average, goods today cost 6 times what they did in 1950. What is her real income today in terms of constant 1950 dollars?

55. **Real versus Nominal Rates.** If investors are to earn a 4 percent real interest rate, what nominal interest rate must they earn if the inflation rate is:

a. zero
b. 4 percent
c. 6 percent

56. **Real Rates.** If investors receive an 8 percent interest rate on their bank deposits, what real interest rate will they earn if the inflation rate over the year is:

a. zero
b. 3 percent
c. 6 percent

57. **Real versus Nominal Rates.** You will receive $100 from a savings bond in 3 years. The nominal interest rate is 8 percent.

a. What is the present value of the proceeds from the bond?
b. If the inflation rate over the next few years is expected to be 3 percent, what will the real value of the $100 payoff be in terms of today's dollars?
c. What is the real interest rate?
d. Show that the real payoff from the bond (from part b) discounted at the real interest rate (from part c) gives the same present value for the bond as you found in part a.

58. **Real versus Nominal Dollars.** Your consulting firm will produce cash flows of $100,000 this year, and you expect cash flow to keep pace with any increase in the general level of prices. The interest rate currently is 8 percent, and you anticipate inflation of about 2 percent.

a. What is the present value of your firm's cash flows for Years 1 through 5?
b. How would your answer to (a) change if you anticipated no growth in cash flow?

59. **Real versus Nominal Annuities.** Good news: you will almost certainly be a millionaire by the time you retire in 50 years. Bad news: the inflation rate over your lifetime will average about 3 percent.

a. What will be the real value of $1 million by the time you retire in terms of today's dollars?
b. What real annuity (in today's dollars) will $1 million support if the real interest rate at retirement is 2 percent and the annuity must last for 20 years?

60. **Real Annuities.** A retiree wants level consumption in real terms over a 30-year retirement. If the inflation rate equals the interest rate she earns on her $450,000 of savings, how much can she spend in real terms each year over the rest of her life?

61. **Inflation.** Inflation in Brazil in 1992 averaged about 23 percent per month. What was the annual inflation rate?

62. **Real versus Nominal Annuities.**

   a. You plan to retire in 30 years and want to accumulate enough by then to provide yourself with $30,000 a year for 15 years. If the interest rate is 10 percent, how much must you accumulate by the time you retire?

   b. How much must you save each year until retirement in order to finance your retirement consumption?

   c. Now you remember that the annual inflation rate is 4 percent. If a loaf of bread costs $1.00 today, what will it cost by the time you retire?

   d. You really want to consume $30,000 a year in *real* dollars during retirement and wish to save an equal *real* amount each year until then. What is the real amount of savings that you need to accumulate by the time you retire?

   e. Calculate the required preretirement real annual savings necessary to meet your consumption goals. Compare to your answer to (b). Why is there a difference?

   f. What is the nominal value of the amount you need to save during the first year? (Assume the savings are put aside at the end of each year.) The thirtieth year?

Solutions to Self-Test Questions

3.1 Value after 5 years would have been $24 \times (1.05)^5 = \$30.63$; after 50 years, $24 \times (1.05)^{50} = \$275.22$.

3.2 Sales double each year. After 4 years, sales will increase by a factor of $2 \times 2 \times 2 \times 2 = 2^4 = 16$ to a value of $\$.5 \times 16 = \$8$ million.

3.3 The quarterly rate is $8/4 = 2$ percent. The effective annual rate is $(1.02)^4 - 1 = .0824$, or 8.24 percent.

3.4 Multiply the $1,000 payment by the 10-year discount factor:

$$PV = \$1,000 \times \frac{1}{(1.0853)^{10}} = \$441.06$$

3.5 If the doubling time is 12 years, then $(1 + r)^{12} = 2$, which implies that $1 + r = 2^{1/12} = 1.0595$, or $r = 5.95$ percent. The Rule of 72 would imply that a doubling time of 12 years is consistent with an interest rate of 6 percent: $72/6 = 12$. Thus, the Rule of 72 works quite well in this case. If the doubling period is only 2 years, then the interest rate is determined by $(1 + r)^2 = 2$, which implies that $1 + r = 2^{1/2} = 1.414$, or $r = 41.4$ percent. The Rule of 72 would imply that a doubling time of 2 years is consistent with an interest rate of 36 percent: $72/36 = 2$. Thus, the Rule of 72 is quite inaccurate when the interest rate is high.

3.6 **Gift at**

Year	Present Value	
1	$10,000/(1.07)$ =	$9,345.79
2	$10,000/(1.07)^2$ =	8,734.39
3	$10,000/(1.07)^3$ =	8,162.98
4	$10,000/(1.07)^4$ =	7,628.95
		$33,872.11

Gift at Year	Future Value at Year 4
1	$10,000(1.07)^3 = \$12,250.43$
2	$10,000(1.07)^2 = 11,449$
3	$10,000(1.07) = 10,700$
4	$10,000 = 10,000$
	$\$44,399.43$

3.7 The rate is $4/48 = .0833$, about 8.3 percent.

3.8 The 4-year discount factor is $1/(1.08)^4 = .735$. The 4-year annuity factor is $[1/.08 - 1/(.08 \times 1.08^4)] = 3.312$. This is the difference between the present value of a \$1 perpetuity starting next year and of a \$1 perpetuity starting in Year 5:

$$\text{PV (perpetuity starting next year)} = \frac{1}{.08} = 12.50$$

$$- \text{PV (perpetuity starting in Year 5)} = \frac{1}{.08} \times \frac{1}{(1.08)^4} = 12.50 \times .735 = 9.188$$

$$= \text{PV (4-year annuity)} \qquad = 12.50 - 9.188 = 3.312$$

3.9 Calculate the value of a 19-year annuity, then add the immediate \$465,000 payment:

$$\text{19-year annuity factor} = \frac{1}{r} - \frac{1}{r(1 + r)^{19}}$$

$$= \frac{1}{.08} - \frac{1}{.08(1.08)^{19}}$$

$$= 9.604$$

$$\text{PV} = \$465,000 \times 9.604 = \$4,466,000$$

$$\text{Total value} = \$4,466,000 + \$465,000$$

$$= \$4,931,000$$

Starting the 20-year cash flow stream immediately, rather than waiting 1 year, increases value by nearly \$400,000.

3.10 Fifteen years means 180 months. Then

$$\text{Mortgage payment} = \frac{100,000}{\text{180-month annuity factor}}$$

$$= \frac{100,000}{83.32}$$

$$= \$1,200.17 \text{ per month}$$

\$1,000 of the payment is interest. The remainder, \$200.17, is amortization.

3.11 You will need the present value at 7 percent of a 20-year annuity of \$55,000:
Present value = annual spending × annuity factor
The annuity factor is $[1/.07 - 1/(.07 \times 1.07^{20})] = 10.594$. Thus you need $55,000 \times 10.594 = \$582,670$.

3.12 If the interest rate is 5 percent, the future value of a 50-year, \$1 annuity will be

$$\frac{(1.05)^{50} - 1}{.05} = 209.348$$

Therefore, we need to choose the cash flow, C, so that $C \times 209.348 = \$500,000$. This requires that $C = \$500,000/209.348 = \$2,388.37$. This required savings level is much higher than we found in Example 3.14. At a 5 percent interest rate, current savings do not grow as rapidly as when the interest rate was 10 percent; with less of a boost from compound interest, we need to set aside greater amounts in order to reach the target of $500,000.

3.13 The weekly cost in 1980 is $250 \times (370/100) = \$925$. The real value of a 1980 salary of $30,000, expressed in real 1947 dollars, is $\$30,000 \times (100/370) = \$8,108$.

3.14 a. If there's no inflation, real and nominal rates are equal at 8 percent. With 5 percent inflation, the real rate is $(1.08/1.05) - 1 = .02857$, a bit less than 3 percent.

 b. If you want a 3 percent *real* interest rate, you need a 3 percent nominal rate if inflation is zero and an 8.15 percent rate if inflation is 5 percent. Note $1.03 \times 1.05 = 1.0815$.

3.15 The present value is

$$PV = \frac{\$5,000}{1.08} = \$4,629.63$$

The real interest rate is 2.857 percent (see Self-Test 3.14a). The real cash payment is $5,000/(1.05) = \$4,761.90$. Thus

$$PV = \frac{\$4,761.90}{1.02857} = \$4,629.63$$

3.16 Calculate the real annuity. The real interest rate is $1.10/1.05 - 1 = .0476$. We'll round to 4.8 percent. The real annuity is

$$\text{Annual payment} = \frac{\$3,000,000}{\text{30-year annuity factor}}$$

$$= \frac{\$3,000,000}{\dfrac{1}{.048} - \dfrac{1}{.048(1.048^{30})}}$$

$$= \frac{\$3,000,000}{15.73} = \$190,728$$

You can spend this much each year in dollars of constant purchasing power. The purchasing power of each dollar will decline at 5 percent per year so you'll need to spend more in nominal dollars: $\$190,728 \times 1.05 = \$200,264$ in the second year, $\$190,728 \times 1.05^2 = \$210,278$ in the third year, and so on.

Minicase

Old Alfred Road, who is well-known to drivers on the Maine Turnpike, has reached his seventieth birthday and is ready to retire. Mr. Road has no formal training in finance but has saved his money and invested carefully.

Mr. Road owns his home—the mortgage is paid off—and does not want to move. He is a widower, and he wants to bequeath the house and any remaining assets to his daughter.

He has accumulated savings of $180,000, conservatively invested. The investments are yielding 9 percent interest. Mr. Road also has $12,000 in a savings account at 5 percent interest. He wants to keep the savings account intact for unexpected expenses or emergencies.

Mr. Road's basic living expenses now average about $1,500 per month, and he plans to spend $500 per month on travel and hobbies. To maintain this planned standard of living, he will have to rely on his investment portfolio. The interest from the portfolio is $16,200 per year (9 percent of $180,000), or $1,350 per month.

Mr. Road will also receive $750 per month in social security payments for the rest of his life. These payments are indexed for inflation. That is, they will be automatically increased in proportion to changes in the Consumer Price Index.

Mr. Road's main concern is with inflation. The inflation rate has been below 3 percent recently, but a 3 percent rate is unusually low by historical standards. His social security payments will increase with inflation, but the interest on his investment portfolio will not.

What advice do you have for Mr. Road? Can he safely spend all the interest from his investment portfolio? How much could he withdraw at year-end from that portfolio if he wants to keep its real value intact?

Suppose Mr. Road will live for 20 more years and is willing to use up all of his investment portfolio over that period. He also wants his monthly spending to increase along with inflation over that period. In other words, he wants his monthly spending to stay the same in real terms. How much can he afford to spend per month?

Assume that the investment portfolio continues to yield a 9 percent rate of return and that the inflation rate is 4 percent.

The floor of the New York Stock Exchange.
Watching the hustle and bustle of a trading floor is fun but not informative. How do the buy and sell orders get to the floor? How are the trades actually executed? What underlying factors determine the values of traded stocks and bonds?
© *Jeremy Horner/Tony Stone Images*

Valuing Bonds and Stocks

Chapter 4

*I*nvestment in new plant and equipment requires money—often a lot of money. Sometimes firms may be able to save enough out of previous earnings to cover the cost of investments, but often they need to raise cash from investors. In broad terms, we can think of two ways to raise new money from investors: borrow the cash or sell additional shares of common stock.

If companies need the money only for a short while, they may borrow it from a bank; if they need it to make long-term investments, they generally issue bonds, which are simply long-term loans. When companies issue bonds, they promise to make a series of fixed interest payments and then to repay the debt. As long as the company generates sufficient cash, the payments on a bond are certain. Thus valuing creditworthy bonds involves straightforward time-value-of-money computations.

In the case of common stock, dividends fluctuate. Investors hope profits will expand, enabling the firm to increase dividends, but no one can forecast that with certainty. Also, unlike bonds, common stocks do not have a date at which they must be repaid; barring such corporate hazards as bankruptcy or acquisition, they are immortal.

Because the payments to the shareholder are more closely tied to the fortunes of the company, common stock investments are riskier than bond investments. To compensate for this risk, investors will demand higher expected rates of return to invest in stocks. We will have more to say about the *risk premium* on stocks in later chapters. For now, however, just remember that there is a difference in required returns.

We start this chapter with a look at how bonds are valued. Then we move on to common stocks. We look at what determines stock prices and how stock valuation formulas can be used to infer the return that investors are expecting. We will see how the firm's investment opportunities are reflected in the stock price, and why stock market analysts focus so much attention on the price-earnings or P/E ratio of the company.

In Chapter 13 we will look in more detail at the securities that companies issue and we will show that within our two broad classes of security there may be many variations on a theme. We will also describe in that chapter some hybrid securities, such as preferred stock and convertible bonds, that share some of the features of both bonds and stocks. But for now our focus is on the genus rather than the species.

After studying this chapter you should be able to

▶ Find the market price of a bond given its yield to maturity, find a bond's yield given its price, and demonstrate why prices and yields vary inversely.

▶ Calculate the present value of a stock given forecasts of future dividends and future stock price.

▶ Use stock valuation formulas to infer the expected rate of return on a common stock.

▶ Interpret price-earnings ratios.

4.1 Bond Prices and Yields

Bond Pricing

bond: Security that obligates the issuer to make specified payments to the bondholder.

coupon: The interest payments paid to the bondholder.

face value: Payment at the maturity of the bond. Also called *par value* or *maturity value.*

coupon rate: Annual interest payment as a percentage of face value.

A **bond** is simply a long-term loan. Governments and corporations borrow money by selling bonds to investors. The money they collect when the bond is *issued*, or sold to the public, is the amount of the loan. In return, they agree to make specified payments to the bondholders (the lenders). When you own a bond, you receive a fixed interest payment each year until the bond matures. This payment is known as the **coupon** because most bonds used to have coupons that the investors clipped off and mailed to the bond issuer to claim interest. At maturity the debt is repaid. The amount that is repaid is known as the bond's **face value,** *par value,* or *maturity value.*[1] In the United States most bonds have a face value of $1,000.

How do bonds work? Consider a U.S. Treasury bond as an example. Several years ago, the United States Treasury raised money by selling 6⅛ percent coupon, 2000 maturity Treasury bonds. Each bond has a face value of $1,000 and the **coupon rate** is 6⅛ percent of this face value. So each year until 2000 the government is obliged to make a coupon payment of 6⅛ percent of $1,000, or $61.25. Then in 2000 the government must also pay the face value of the bond, $1,000.

Suppose that in 1996 you decided to buy the 6⅛s of 2000, that is, the 6⅛ percent coupon bonds maturing in 2000. If you planned to hold the bond until maturity, you would then have looked forward to the cash flows depicted in Figure 4.1. The initial cash flow is negative and equal to the price you have to pay for the bond. Thereafter, the cash flows equal the annual coupon payment, until the maturity date in 2000, when you receive the face value of the bond, $1,000, in addition to the final coupon payment.

How much would you have to pay for this stream of cash flows? To answer, we need to look at the return provided by similar securities. In 1996, United States Treasury

FIGURE 4.1

Cash flows to an investor in the 6⅛ coupon bond maturing in the year 2000.

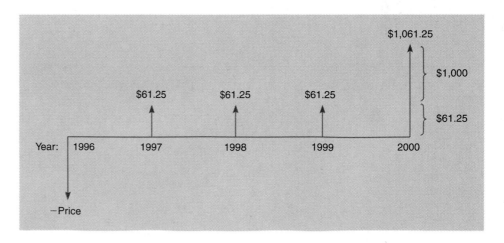

[1]Occasionally you come across zero-coupon bonds. In this case you receive the $1,000 face value at maturity but don't get any interest payments. In the last chapter you learned how to value a zero-coupon bond issued by Coca-Cola Enterprises. Sometimes you encounter bonds that *only* pay interest and never mature. The British government perpetuity that we valued in the last chapter is an example. But both these bonds are special cases.

bonds with similar maturities offered a return of about 6.6 percent. This interest rate is what investors could have earned on alternative investments of comparable risk. Therefore, to value the 6⅛s of 2000, we need to discount the prospective stream of cash flows at 6.6 percent:

$$\begin{aligned} PV &= \frac{\$61.25}{(1 + r)} + \frac{\$61.25}{(1 + r)^2} + \frac{\$61.25}{(1 + r)^3} + \frac{\$1,061.25}{(1 + r)^4} \\ &= \frac{\$61.25}{(1.066)} + \frac{\$61.25}{(1.066)^2} + \frac{\$61.25}{(1.066)^3} + \frac{\$1,061.25}{(1.066)^4} \\ &= \$983.76 \end{aligned}$$

Bond prices are usually expressed as a percentage of their face value. Thus we can say that our 6⅛ percent Treasury bond is worth 98.376 percent of face value, and its price commonly would be quoted simply as 98.376.

Why does this bond sell below its face value? Consider that the bond's coupon rate is 6⅛ = 6.125 percent, which is less than the 6.6 percent rate of return available on comparable-maturity Treasury bonds. Why would anyone pay face value for this bond, receiving an interest rate of 6.125 percent, when a 6.6 percent rate is available on other bonds? But if no one is willing to pay face value for the 6⅛ coupon bond, its price must fall below face value, in this case to only 98.376 percent of face value.

Conversely, if another bond had a coupon above 6.6 percent, it would sell above face value: if the bond could be purchased for face value, it would offer a better rate of return than is available on comparable investments. In this case, investors would bid up the price of the bond to a level above face value.

> We conclude that when the coupon rate is below the market interest rate, bonds sell below face value. When the coupon rate exceeds the market interest rate, bonds sell for more than face value.

The 6⅛ bond sells at a modest discount to face value when the market interest rate is 6.6 percent. The following example shows that when the rate available on alternative investments is even higher, the bond will sell at an even steeper discount to its face value.

▶ **Example 4.1**   *Bond Prices and Interest Rates*

Investors will pay $983.76 for a 6⅛ percent, 4-year Treasury bond, when the interest rate is 6.6 percent. Suppose that the interest rate is much higher—15 percent, say. Now what is the value of the bond? Simple! We just repeat our initial calculation with $r = .15$:

$$\begin{aligned} PV &= \frac{\$61.25}{1.15} + \frac{\$61.25}{(1.15)^2} + \frac{\$61.25}{(1.15)^3} + \frac{\$1,061.25}{(1.15)^4} \\ &= \$746.62 \end{aligned}$$

Did you notice that the coupon payments on the bond are an annuity? In other words, the bondholder receives a level stream of coupon payments of $61.25 a year for each of 4 years. At maturity the bondholder gets an additional payment of $1,000.

Therefore, you can use the annuity formula to value the coupon payments and the add on the present value of the final payment:

$$PV = PV(\text{coupons}) + PV(\text{final payment})$$
$$= (\text{coupon} \times \text{annuity factor}) + (\text{face value} \times \text{discount factor})$$
$$= \$61.25 \times \left[\frac{1}{.066} - \frac{1}{.066(1.066)^4}\right] + 1{,}000 \times \frac{1}{1.066^4}$$
$$= \$209.35 + \$774.41 = \$983.76$$

If you need to value a bond with many years to run before maturity, it is usually easiest to value the coupon payments as an annuity and then add on the present value of the final payment.

▶ **Self-Test 4.1**

Calculate the present value of a 6-year bond with a 9 percent coupon. The interest rate is 12 percent.

▶ **Example 4.2**   *Bond Prices and Semiannual Coupon Payments*

Thus far we've assumed that interest payments occur annually. This is the case for bonds in many European countries, but in the United States most bonds make coupon payments *semiannually*. So when you hear that a bond in the United States has a coupon rate of 6⅛ percent, you can generally assume that the bond makes a payment of $61.25/2 = $30.625 every 6 months. Similarly, when investors in the United States refer to the bond's interest rate, they usually mean the semiannually compounded interest rate. Thus an interest rate quoted at 6.6 percent really means that the 6-month rate is 6.6/2 = 3.3 percent.[2] Since our calculation of the present value of the Treasury bond assumed annual coupons and an annually compounded interest rate, our answer is a bit off. We should have discounted the series of semiannual payments by the semiannual rate of interest as follows:

$$PV = \frac{\$30.625}{1.033} + \frac{\$30.625}{1.033^2} + \frac{\$30.625}{1.033^3} + \cdots + \frac{\$30.625}{1.033^6} + \frac{\$30.625}{1.033^7} + \frac{\$1030.625}{1.033^8}$$
$$= \$983.54$$

which is a bit less than the value of $983.76 that we obtained when we treated the coupon payments as annual rather than semiannual. Since semiannual coupon payments just add to the arithmetic, we will stick to our approximation for the rest of the chapter and assume annual interest payments.

---

[2]You may have noticed that the semiannually compounded interest rate on the bond is also the bond's APR, although this term is not generally used by bond investors. To find the effective annual interest rate, we can use a formula that we presented in section 3.2:

$$\text{Effective annual interest rate} = \left(1 + \frac{APR}{m}\right)^m - 1$$

where m is the number of payments each year. In the case of our Treasury bond,

$$\text{Effective annual interest rate} = \left(1 + \frac{.066}{2}\right)^2 - 1 = 1.033^2 - 1 = .067, \text{ or } 6.7\%$$

The Yield to Maturity

Suppose you are considering the purchase of a 3-year bond with a coupon rate of 20 percent. Your investment adviser quotes a price for the bond. How do you calculate the rate of return the bond offers?

For bonds priced at face value the answer is easy. The rate of return is the coupon rate. We can check this by setting out the cash flows on your investment:

You Pay	Cash Paid to You in Year			Rate of Return
	1	**2**	**3**	
$1,000	$200	$200	$1,200	20%

Notice that in each year you earn 20 percent on your money ($200/$1,000). In the final year you also get your original investment of $1,000 back. Therefore, your total return is 20 percent, the same as the coupon rate

Now suppose that the market price of the 3-year bond is $1,248.69. Your cash flows are as follows:

You Pay	Cash Paid to You in Year			Rate of Return
	1	**2**	**3**	
$1,248.69	$200	$200	$1,200	?

What's the rate of return now? Notice that you are paying out $1,248.69 and receiving an annual income of $200. So your income as a proportion of the initial outlay is $200/$1,248.69 = .16, or 16 percent. This is termed the bond's **current yield**, because it focuses on the current cash income.

A current yield of 16 percent sounds attractive until you realize that the bond's price must fall. The price today is $1,248.69, but when the bond matures 3 years from now, the bond will sell for its face value, or $1,000. A price decline (i.e., a *capital loss*) of $248.69 is guaranteed, so the overall return over the next 3 years must be less than the 16 percent current yield.

Let us generalize. A bond that is priced above par value (i.e., face value) is said to sell at a *premium*. Investors who buy a bond at a premium face a capital loss over the life of the bond, so their return is always *less* than the bond's current yield. A bond priced below par value sells at a *discount*. Investors in discount bonds face a capital *gain* over the life of the bond; their return is *greater* than the current yield:

current yield: Annual coupon payments divided by bond price.

> **Because it focuses only on current income and ignores prospective price increases or decreases, the current yield mismeasures the bond's total rate of return. It overstates the return of premium bonds and understates that of discount bonds.**

We need a measure of return that takes account of both current yield and the change in a bond's value over its life. The standard measure is called **yield to maturity,** or *internal rate of return.* The yield to maturity is the answer to the following question: At what interest rate would the bond be correctly priced?

yield to maturity: Interest rate for which the present value of the bond's payments equals the price.

> **The yield to maturity is defined as the discount rate that makes the present value of the bond's payments equal to its price.**

If you can buy the 3-year bond at face value, the yield to maturity is the coupon rate, 20 percent. We can confirm this by noting that when we discount the cash flows at 20 percent, the present value of the bond is equal to its $1,000 face value:

$$PV \text{ at } 20\% = \frac{\$200}{1.20} + \frac{\$200}{1.20^2} + \frac{\$1,200}{1.20^3} = \$1,000$$

But if you have to buy the 3-year bond for $1,248.69, the yield to maturity is only 10 percent. At that discount rate, the bond's present value equals its actual market price, $1,248.69:

$$PV \text{ at } 10\% = \frac{\$200}{1.10} + \frac{\$200}{(1.10)^2} + \frac{\$1,200}{(1.10)^3} = \$1,248.69$$

▶ **Example 4.3**   *Calculating Yield to Maturity for the Treasury Bond*

We found the value of the 6⅛ percent coupon Treasury bond by discounting at a 6.6 percent interest rate. We could have phrased the question the other way around: If the price of the bond is $983.76, what return do investors expect? We need to find the yield to maturity, in other words, the discount rate r, that solves the following equation:

$$Price = \frac{\$61.25}{1 + r} + \frac{\$61.25}{(1 + r)^2} + \frac{\$61.25}{(1 + r)^3} + \frac{\$1,061.25}{(1 + r)^4}$$
$$= \$983.76$$

To find the yield to maturity, you can use a book of bond tables that shows values of r for different coupons and maturities. Today, most people use a financial calculator. For our Treasury bond you would enter a PV of $983.76. The bond provides a regular payment of $61.25, entered as PMT = 61.25. The bond has a future value of $1,000, so FV = 1,000. The bond life is 4 years, so $n = 4$. Now compute the interest rate, and you will find that the yield to maturity is 6.6 percent. The nearby

 See box p. 110

box reviews the use of the financial calculator in bond valuation problems.

The yield to maturity depends on the coupon payments that you receive each year ($61.25) and the final repayment of face value ($1,000). Thus it is a measure of the total return on this bond.

▶ **Self-Test 4.2**   A 4-year bond with a 14 percent coupon can be bought for $1,200. What is the yield to maturity? You will need a bit of trial and error (or a financial calculator) to answer this question.

The only *general* procedure for calculating yield to maturity is trial and error. In fact, when you use a financial calculator to compute yield to maturity, you will notice that it takes the calculator a few moments to compute the interest rate. This is because it must perform a series of trial-and-error calculations.

Figure 4.2 offers a graphical view of yield to maturity. It shows the present value of the bond for different interest rates. The actual bond price, $983.76, is marked on the vertical axis. A line is drawn from this price over to the present value curve and then down to the interest rate, 6.6 percent. If we picked a higher or lower figure for the interest rate, then we would not obtain a bond price of $983.76. Thus we know that the yield to maturity on the bond must be 6.6 percent.

Bond Valuation on a Financial Calculator

In Chapter 3 we saw that financial calculators can compute the present values of level annuities as well as the present values of one-time future cash flows. Coupon bonds present both of these characteristics: the coupon payments are level annuities and the final payment of par value is an additional one-time payment. Thus for the coupon bond we looked at in Example 4.3, you would treat the periodic payment as PMT = $61.25, the final or future one-time payment as FV = $1,000, the number of periods as n = 4 years, and the interest rate as the yield to maturity of the bond, i = 6.6 percent. You would thus compute the value of the bond using the following sequence of key strokes. By the way, the order in which the various inputs for the bond valuation problem are entered does not matter.

Hewlett-Packard HP-10B		Sharpe EL-733A		Texas Instruments BA II Plus	
61.25	PMT	61.25	PMT	61.25	PMT
1000	FV	1000	FV	1000	FV
4	N	4	n	4	N
6.6	I/YR	6.6	i	6.6	I/Y
PV		COMP	PV	CPT	PV

Your calculator should now display a value of −983.76. The minus sign reminds us that the initial cash flow is negative: you have to pay to buy the bond.

You can also use the calculator to find the yield to maturity of a bond. For example, if you buy this bond for $983.76, you should find that its yield to maturity is 6.6 percent. Let's check that this is so. You enter the PV as −983.76 because you buy the bond for this price. Thus to solve for the interest rate, use the following key strokes:

Hewlett-Packard HP-10B		Sharpe EL-733A		Texas Instruments BA II Plus	
61.25	PMT	61.25	PMT	61.25	PMT
1000	FV	1000	FV	1000	FV
4	N	4	n	4	N
−983.76	PV	−983.76	PV	−983.76	PV
I/YR		COMP	i	CPT	I/Y

Your calculator should now display 6.6 percent, the yield to maturity of the bond.

Figure 4.2 also illustrates a fundamental relationship between interest rates and bond prices:

> **When the interest rate rises, the present value of the payments to be received by the bondholders falls, and bond prices fall. Conversely, declines in the interest rate increase the present value of those payments and result in higher bond prices.**

A gentle warning! People sometimes confuse the *interest rate*—that is, the return that investors require—with the *interest*, or *coupon, payment* on the bond. Although interest rates change from day to day, the coupon payments on our Treasury bond are fixed at $61.25. Changes in interest rates affect the *present value* of the payments on the bond but not the payments themselves.

▶ **Self-Test 4.3**   Figure 4.2 illustrates another general point. If the interest rate (yield to maturity) is equal to the coupon payment— 6⅛ percent in our case—the bond is worth exactly $1,000. Show that this is true for the 6⅛ percent bond.

FIGURE 4.2

This figure shows how the value of the 4-year 6⅛ percent bond changes as the interest rate (yield to maturity) changes.

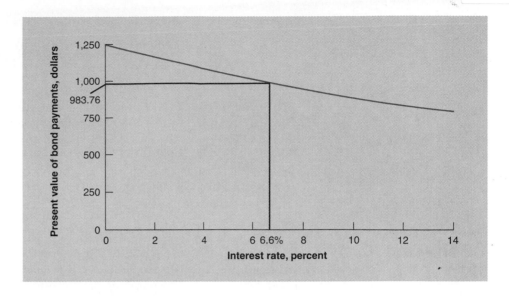

Rate of Return

rate of return: Total income per period per dollar invested.

The **rate of return** on an investment equals the dollars earned per period for every dollar invested. For investments in bonds, earnings come from the payment of coupons as well as from any price change in the bond. For example, if you buy the 6⅛ percent Treasury bond today for a price of $983.76 and sell it next year at a price of $995, your total income is the $61.25 coupon payment plus the price change of ($995 − $983.76) = $11.24. Your rate of return over the year therefore equals

$$\text{Rate of return} = \frac{\text{total income}}{\text{investment}} = \frac{\text{coupon income} + \text{price change}}{\text{investment}}$$

$$= \frac{\$61.25 + \$11.24}{\$983.76} = .074 = 7.4\%$$

Because bond prices fall when market interest rates rise and rise when market rates fall, the rate of return that you earn on a bond also will fluctuate with market interest rates. This is why we say bonds are subject to interest rate risk.

> Do not confuse the bond's rate of return over a particular investment period with its yield to maturity. The yield to maturity is defined as the discount rate that equates the bond's price to its present value. It is a measure of the average rate of return you will earn over the bond's life if you hold it to maturity. The rate of return, in contrast, can be calculated for any holding period and is based on the actual income, including price change, generated by the bond over that period.

▶ **Example 4.4**   *The Rate of Return on the U.S. Treasury Bond*

What will happen to the price of our 6⅛ percent Treasury bond if interest rates do *not* change? In 1997, the bond has only 3 years to maturity. If investors still demand an interest rate of 6.6 percent, the value of the bond will be

$$PV = \frac{\$61.25}{1.066} + \frac{\$61.25}{(1.066)^2} + \frac{\$1,061.25}{(1.066)^3}$$
$$= \$987.44$$

You invested $983.76. At the end of the year you receive a coupon payment of $61.25 and have a bond worth $987.44, slightly more than you paid for it. Your total profit is $61.25 + ($987.44 − $983.76) = $64.93. You have invested $983.76 for a profit of $64.93. The return on your investment is therefore $64.93/$983.76 = .066, or 6.6 percent. When interest rates do not change, the bond price changes with time so that the total return on the bond is equal to the yield to maturity.

▶ **Self-Test 4.4**   Suppose that you buy the 6⅛ percent Treasury bond for $987.44 in 1997 and sell it 1 year later (that is, 2 years before maturity). If the interest rate is still 6.6 percent when you sell, what return will you earn on your investment? Demonstrate your answer.

Interest Rate Risk

We have seen that bond prices fluctuate as interest rates change. If you buy a bond and the interest rate rises, the value of your investment will fall.

But all bonds are not equally affected by changing interest rates. Compare the two curves in Figure 4.3. The solid line shows how the value of the 4-year, 6⅛ percent coupon bond varies with the level of the interest rate. The broken line shows how the price of a 30-year, 6⅛ percent bond varies with the level of interest rates. You can see that it is more sensitive to interest rate fluctuations than the 4-year bond. This should not surprise you. If you buy a 4-year bond when the interest rate is 6.6 percent and rates then rise, you will be stuck with a bad deal—you have just loaned your money at a lower interest rate than if you had waited a little. However, think how much worse

FIGURE 4.3

Plot of bond prices versus interest rates for different maturities, illustrating greater exposure of long bonds.

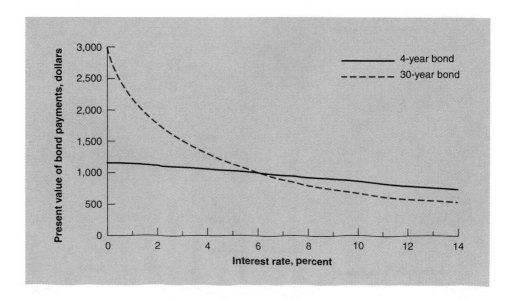

it would be if the loan had been for 30 years rather than 4 years. The longer the loan, the more income you have lost by accepting what turns out to be a low coupon rate. This shows up in a bigger decline in the price of the longer-term bond. Of course, there is a flip side to this effect, which you can also see from Figure 4.3. When interest rates fall, the longer-term bond responds with a greater increase in price.

▶ **Self-Test 4.5**   Suppose that the interest rate rises overnight from $6\frac{1}{8}$ percent to 12 percent. Calculate the present values of the $6\frac{1}{8}\%$ 4-year bond and of the $6\frac{1}{8}\%$ 30-year bond both before and after this change in interest rates. Confirm that your answers correspond with Figure 4.2. Use your financial calculator.

Reading the Financial Pages

The prices at which you can buy and sell bonds are shown each day in the financial press. Figure 4.4 is an excerpt from the bond quotation page of *The Wall Street Journal* and shows the prices of bonds and notes that have been issued by the United States Treasury. (A *note* is a bond with a maturity of less than 10 years at the time it is issued.) The entry for the $6\frac{1}{8}$ percent bond is highlighted. You can see that they are due to mature in July 2000; the letter *n* indicates that they are notes.

Prices are generally quoted in 32nds rather than decimals. Thus for the $6\frac{1}{8}$ percent bond the *asked price*—the price investors pay to *buy* the bond—is shown as 98:11. This means that the price is 98 and $^{11}\!/_{32}$, or 98.344 percent of par value, which is $983.44.[3]

FIGURE 4.4

Treasury bond quotes from The Wall Street Journal. *(Reprinted by permission of* The Wall Street Journal *© 1996 Dow Jones & Company, Inc. All Rights Reserved Worldwide.)*

TREASURY BONDS, NOTES & BILLS

Monday, July 15, 1996

Representative Over-the-Counter quotations based on transactions of $1 million or more.

Treasury bond, note and bill quotes are as of mid-afternoon. Colons in bid-and-asked quotes represent 32nds; 101:01 means 101 1/32. Net changes in 32nds. n-Treasury note. Treasury bill quotes in hundredths, quoted on terms of a rate of discount. Days to maturity calculated from settlement date. All yields are to maturity and based on the asked quote. Latest 13-week and 26-week bills are boldfaced. For bonds callable prior to maturity, yields are computed to the earliest call date for issues quoted above par and to the maturity date for issues below par. *-When issued.

Source: Federal Reserve Bank of New York.

U.S. Treasury strips as of 3 p.m. Eastern time, also based on transactions of $1 million or more. Colons in bid-and-asked quotes represent 32nds; 99:01 means 99 1/32. Net changes in 32nds. Yields calculated on the asked quotation. ci-stripped coupon interest. bp-Treasury bond, stripped principal. np-Treasury note, stripped principal. For bonds callable prior to maturity, yields are computed to the earliest call date for issues quoted above par and to the maturity date for issues below par.

Source: Bear, Stearns & Co. via Street Software Technology Inc.

GOVT. BONDS & NOTES				
Maturity				Ask
Rate Mo/Yr	Bid	Asked	Chg.	Yld.
$6\frac{1}{8}$ Jul 96n	100:01	100:03	....	3.58
$7\frac{7}{8}$ Jul 96n	100:04	100:06	....	2.89
$4\frac{3}{8}$ Aug 96n	99:29	99:31	....	4.68
8 Aug 96-01	100:05	100:09	+ 2	4.31
$6\frac{1}{4}$ Aug 96n	100:03	100:05	....	4.85
$7\frac{1}{4}$ Aug 96n	100:07	100:09	....	4.80
$6\frac{1}{2}$ Sep 96n	100:07	100:09	− 1	5.02
7 Sep 96n	100:11	100:13	....	4.90
$6\frac{3}{8}$ Jan 00n	99:14	99:16	− 1	6.54
$7\frac{3}{4}$ Jan 00n	103:20	103:22	− 3	6.57
$8\frac{1}{2}$ Feb 00n	106:01	106:03	− 1	6.56
$7\frac{1}{8}$ Feb 00n	101:22	101:24	− 3	6.57
$6\frac{7}{8}$ Mar 00n	100:28	100:30	− 4	6.59
$5\frac{1}{2}$ Apr 00n	96:13	96:15	− 2	6.58
$6\frac{3}{4}$ Apr 00n	100:14	100:16	− 4	6.60
$8\frac{7}{8}$ May 00n	107:19	107:21	+ 1	6.58
$6\frac{1}{4}$ May 00n	98:25	98:27	....	6.59
$5\frac{7}{8}$ Jun 00n	97:15	97:17	− 1	6.59
$6\frac{1}{8}$ Jul 00n	98:09	98:11	− 2	6.60
$8\frac{3}{4}$ Aug 00n	107:15	107:17	− 2	6.61
$6\frac{1}{4}$ Aug 00n	98:21	98:23	− 2	6.61
$6\frac{1}{8}$ Sep 00n	98:05	98:07	− 3	6.62
$5\frac{3}{4}$ Oct 00n	96:23	96:25	− 3	6.62
$8\frac{1}{2}$ Nov 00n	106:27	106:29	− 6	6.64
$5\frac{5}{8}$ Nov 00n	96:06	96:08	− 3	6.63

Maturity			Ask
Rate Mo/Yr	Bid Asked	Chg.	Yld.
$5\frac{1}{2}$ Dec 00n	95:22 95:24	− 3	6.62
$5\frac{1}{4}$ Jan 01n	94:25 94:27	− 4	6.58
$15\frac{3}{4}$ Nov 01	140:05 140:09	− 3	6.65
$14\frac{1}{4}$ Feb 02	134:23 134:27	− 5	6.67
$7\frac{1}{2}$ May 02n	103:25 103:27	− 4	6.69
$6\frac{3}{8}$ Aug 02n	98:08 98:10	− 5	6.72
$11\frac{3}{4}$ Feb 05-10	130:12 130:16	− 10	6.97
10 May 05-10	119:14 119:18	− 11	6.99
$12\frac{3}{4}$ Nov 05-10	138:28 139:00	− 10	6.99
$15\frac{3}{4}$ Nov 01	140:05 140:09	− 3	6.65
$14\frac{1}{4}$ Feb 02	134:23 134:27	− 5	6.67
$7\frac{1}{2}$ May 02n	103:25 103:27	− 4	6.69
$6\frac{3}{8}$ Aug 02n	98:08 98:10	− 5	6.72
$11\frac{3}{4}$ Feb 05-10	130:12 130:16	− 10	6.97
10 May 05-10	119:14 119:18	− 11	6.99
$12\frac{3}{4}$ Nov 05-10	138:28 139:00	− 10	6.99
$13\frac{7}{8}$ May 06-11	148:06 148:10	− 12	7.00
14 Nov 06-11	150:24 150:28	− 11	7.00
$10\frac{3}{8}$ Nov 07-12	125:09 125:13	− 10	7.08
12 Aug 08-13	139:10 139:14	− 12	7.09
$13\frac{1}{4}$ May 09-14	151:01 151:05	− 14	7.11
$12\frac{1}{2}$ Aug 09-14	145:10 145:14	− 14	7.11
$11\frac{3}{4}$ Nov 09-14	139:23 139:27	− 14	7.08
$11\frac{1}{4}$ Feb 15	141:28 141:30	− 14	7.14
$10\frac{5}{8}$ Aug 15	135:24 135:26	− 17	7.16
$9\frac{7}{8}$ Nov 15	128:02 128:04	− 15	7.16
$9\frac{1}{4}$ Feb 16	121:20 121:22	− 13	7.17
$7\frac{1}{4}$ May 16	100:23 100:25	− 10	7.18
$7\frac{1}{2}$ Nov 16	103:08 103:10	− 10	7.19
$8\frac{3}{4}$ May 17	116:22 116:24	− 13	7.19
$8\frac{7}{8}$ Aug 17	118:03 118:05	− 12	7.19
$9\frac{1}{8}$ May 18	121:01 121:03	− 15	7.19
9 Nov 18	119:27 119:29	− 14	7.20
$8\frac{7}{8}$ Feb 19	118:17 118:19	− 13	7.20
$8\frac{1}{8}$ Aug 19	110:09 110:11	− 14	7.20

[3]In our preceding examples we calculated the present value of the bond as $983.76. This small discrepancy from the actual price is due to rounding error in the discount rate we used to calculate present values. We also ignored the semiannual nature of the coupon payments.

The *bid price* is the price investors receive if they *sell* the bond. Just as the used car dealer earns his living by reselling cars at higher prices than he paid for them, so the bond dealer needs to charge a spread between the bid and asked price. Notice that the spread for the 6⅛ percent bonds is only 2/32, or about .06 percent of the bond's value. Don't you wish that used car dealers charged similar spreads?

The next column in the table shows the change in price since the previous day. The 6⅛ percent bonds have declined by 2/32. If you had bought the bond yesterday, you would have paid $984.06 and you would be showing a $0.62 loss. Finally, the column "Ask Yld." shows the yield to maturity for an investor buying the bond.

Other tables in *The Wall Street Journal* show the prices of bonds issued by government agencies, municipalities, and companies. Let us look briefly at Figure 4.5, which

FIGURE 4.5

Corporate bond quotes from The Wall Street Journal. *(Source: Reprinted by permission of* The Wall Street Journal *© 1996 Dow Jones & Company, Inc. All Rights Reserved Worldwide.)*

NEW YORK EXCHANGE BONDS

Quotations as of 4 p.m. Eastern Time
Monday, July 15, 1996

Volume $15,374,000

SALES SINCE JANUARY 1 (000 omitted)

1996	1995	1994
$3,181,824	$4,149,131	$4,267,980

	Domestic Mon.	Fri.	All Issues Mon.	Fri.
Issues traded	303	280	310	286
Advances	86	142	87	145
Declines	160	83	164	85
Unchanged	57	55	59	56
New highs	3	3	3	3
New lows	12	4	12	5

Dow Jones Bond Averages

-1995- High	Low	-1996- High	Low		Close	Chg.	%Yld	-1995- Close	Chg.
105.34	93.63	106.09	100.99	20 Bonds	100.99	-0.14	7.43	103.44	-0.16
102.30	89.08	102.43	97.46	10 Utilities	97.46	-0.12	7.58	99.60	-0.26
108.96	98.08	109.94	104.24	10 Industrials	104.53	-0.14	7.28	107.29	-0.05

CORPORATION BONDS
Volume, $15,066,000

Bonds	Cur Yld	Vol	Close	Net Chg.
ADT Op zr10	...	1	56½	- 1½
AMR 9s16	8.5	15	105⅜	- ⅝
ATT 4⅜99	4.6	12	94½	+ ⅛
ATT 5⅛01	5.5	46	92¾	- ⅛
ATT 7⅛02	7.1	40	100¼	- ¼
ATT 7s05	7.1	68	98⅞	- ⅛
ATT 7½06	7.3	1	103	+ 1⅝
ATT 8⅛22	8.0	203	101⅞	- ⅛
ATT 8½24	7.9	23	102½	+ ½
ATT 8.35s25	8.0	160	104⅜	+ ⅛
ATT 8⅝31	8.2	35	105	...
Advst 9s08	cv	10	103	...
AirbF 6¾01	cv	141	98¾	- 1
AlskAr 6⅞14	cv	38	94	- 1
AlldC zr97	...	40	93¾	+ ¼
AlldC zr01	...	30	69¼	+ ½
Allwst 7¼14	cv	30	82½	- 2½
Alza zr14	...	25	42	- ¼
Ametek 9¾04	9.4	29	104	...
Amoco 8⅝16	8.2	65	105⅜	- ⅛
AnnTaylr 8¾00	9.6	209	91½	- 1½
Argosy 12s01	cv	141	91	- ¾
ArmI 11⅜99	11.0	25	103	- 1
ArmI 9.2s00	9.4	7	98¼	- ¾
Arvin 7½14	cv	5	100	...
Ashlnd 6¾14	cv	34	100	- ¼
ARch 9⅞16	7.5	5	131	- 2⅞
BBN 6s12	cv	20	84½	- 4¼
BkrHgh zr03	...	41	71	- ½
Bally 10s06f	cv	105	101	- ⅛
BellPa 7⅛02	7.7	37	93⅛	- 1½
BellsoT 6½00	6.5	50	100⅜	+ 1⅝
BellsoT 6⅜04	6.8	1	94	- ½
BellsoT 8⅛32	8.0	25	103	+ ⅜
BellsoT 7⅞32	7.9	6	99½	- ⅞
BellsoT 7½33	7.7	10	96⅞	- ⅜
BellsoT 6¾33	7.6	10	89⅜	+ ½

Bonds	Cur Yld	Vol	Close	Net Chg.
LibPrp 8s01	cv	5	102	
LoneSfr 10s03	9.9	15	100¾	+ ⅜
LgIsLt 7.3s99	7.5	5	97¾	+ ⅛
LgIsLt 7.05s03	7.9	46	89	- ¼
LsIsLt 7s04	8.1	15	86¼	- ¾
LgIsLt 8.9s19	9.7	94	91⅜	- ⅜
LgIsLt 9¾21	9.8	10	99⅝	- ⅝
LgIsLt 9s22	9.7	20	92⅞	- ¼
LgIsLt 8.2s23	9.4	81	87⅜	- ⅝
LgIsLt 9⅝24	9.7	89	99	...
MGM Grd 11¾49	11.2	4	104¾	- 1⅞
MacNS 7⅞04	cv	2	85¾	- 1¼
Magntx 8s01	cv	18	96	+ ½
Malan 9½04	cv	15	92½	- ½
MarO 7s02	7.1	10	98	+ ⅝
Masco 5¼12	cv	3	88¼	- 2¾
Mascotch 03	cv	4	78¼	- ¼
Maxus 8½08	9.0	10	94¾	- ¼
McDnl 6¾03	6.8	23	98¾	+ 1¼
Medusa 6s03	cv	30	104½	+ ¾
MerLyStkMk 97	...	25	98½	- 1⅛
MerLyGlbI 98	...	20	95	+ ½
Metrom 9½298	9.7	40	98¼	- 1⅜
MichB 7s12	7.4	10	94½	- 1⅜
MPac 4¾20f	...	5	61	+ 1½
Mobil 8⅜01	7.8	53	106⅞	+ ⅞
Motrla zr13	...	23	72¼	- 2¼
Nabis 8s00	7.9	25	101½	- 1¼
NETelTel 6⅛06	6.8	8	90	+ 1⅜
NETelTel 6⅜08	7.2	6	88⅞	- ⅜
NJBTl 7¼11	7.5	26	96⅛	- ¾
NYTel 5⅞03	6.3	13	93½	+ ¾
NYTel 4⅝04	5.6	1	83	...
NYTel 6¼04	6.6	25	94	- ⅜
NYTel 7¾03	7.8	12	100	+ ¼
NYTel 7⅞17	7.9	10	100	+ 1
Noram 6s12	cv	53	81½	- ¼
Novacr 5½2000	cv	40	86¾	- ¼
Nynex rp9.55s10	...	15	89⅞	- 1¼

Bonds	Cur Yld	Vol	Close	Net Chg.
SptRec 4½00	cv	7	71	
StdCmcl 07	cv	22	78½	+
StdPac 10½00	10.3	10	101½	+
StoneCn 11⅞98	11.4	47	104½	-
StoneC 11½99	11.4	39	101⅜	
StoneCn 11s99	10.8	145	101½	+
StoneC 9⅞01	10.1	428	97½	-
StoneC 10¾402A	10.8	73	99⅜	-
StoneC 10¾420O	10.6	51	101⅜	-
StoneC 11½04	11.3	102	101⅝	-
StrTch 8s15	cv	62	107½	-
SwiftEn 6½cld	cv	35	160	+ 1
TVA 6⅛99	6.3	3	98⅞	-
TVA 7⅝99	7.6	29	100¼	
TVA 7⅞01	7.7	5	101¾	+
TVA 7⅞22	7.8	238	98	+
TVA 7¾22	7.8	46	99¼	+
TVA 8.05s24	8.1	26	100	-
TVA 8⅝29	8.2	184	105¼	-
TVA 7¼43	7.9	10	92	-
TVA 6⅞43	7.8	10	88⅛	-
TVA 7.85s44	8.0	110	98	+
Teledy 7s99	7.1	15	99¼	-
Teledy 10s04C	9.9	25	101¼	-
Tenet 10⅛05	9.6	10	105¼	-
Tenet 05	cv	7	98¼	-
Tenneco 7⅞02	7.7	10	102⅝	
TennGas 9s97	9.0	10	100	17/32 +
TennGas dc6s11	7.1	70	84	+
Tesor 13s00	12.6	20	103¼	
Texco 9s99D	8.5	5	106⅜	
Texfi 8¾99	9.7	10	90	
TmeWar 7.45s98	7.4	12	100½	-
TmeWar 7.98s04	8.1	7	98⅞	-
TmeWar 7¾405	8.0	8	97⅛	+
TmeWar 8.18s07	8.3	10	99	+
TmeWar 7.48s08	8.0	52	93⅜	+
TmeWE 7⅞08	7.9	20	92¼	+
TmeWar 9⅛13	8.8	80	104	+
TmeWar 9.15s23	8.9	71	102¼	+
TolEd 7½02	7.8	4	96	+
TolEd 8s03	8.2	42	97	+
Toll 9½03	9.2	70	102¾	
TollCp 4¾404	cv	3	97½	+
Trvlr 7⅞97	7.6	11	100¾	-
TucEP 8⅛01	8.1	10	100¾	-
Tyco 10⅛02	10.4	205	97	-
UNC 7½06	cv	11	87⅛	+
USX 5¾401	cv	110	90¾	+
USX zr05	cv	20	47	-
USX 7s17	cv	30	104½	-
Unisy na15s97	...	165	105⅛	-
Unisys 8¼00	cv	240	93¾	-
Unisys 8¼06	cv	40	112	-
WMS 5¾402	cv	3	95	-
WMX dc2s05	cv	36	87¼	-
Waban 6½02	cv	10	97	-
Watrhse 6s03	cv	10	157	
Webb 9¾03	10.0	85	97⅞	+
Webb 9s06	9.9	70	90½	+
WhlPit 9⅜03	10.1	57	92½	+
Whirl zr11	...	6	39¼	
WisBl 7¼07	7.3	15	99¾	+
XrxCr 10s99	9.3	10	107½	-
Zapt 10¼497f	...	10	102⅞	+
Zenith 6¼11	cv	37	74¾	+

FOREIGN BONDS
Volume, $308,000

Bonds	Cur Yld	Vol	Close	Net Chg.
Mexco 8⅛97	8.4	4	97¼	

is an extract from the corporate bond listings. Notice that AT&T has issued several different bonds. We have highlighted the 8⅛ bonds of 22. This means that the bonds pay a coupon of 8⅛ percent of $1,000, or $81.25, each year until 2022.[4] At that point the company repays the face value of $1,000.

Now skip to the next-to-last column, where the closing price of the bond on July 15, 1996, is given as 101⅞. This means that the bond traded at 101⅞ percent of face value, or $1018.75. The last column, "Net Chg.," shows that the price was down 1/8 of 1 percent of face value from the previous day's closing price. If you had bought the bond on the previous day, it would have cost you 102 percent of face value, or $1,020.

The column labeled "Cur Yld" reports the current yield of the bond, which is the annual interest income expressed as a percentage of the bond price. In this case, current yield is $81.25/$1,018.75 =.080, or 8.0 percent. As we've noted, the current yield tells only half the story. It measures only how much regular interest income you will receive for each dollar you invest, but it ignores the fact that you need to pay $1,018.75 for the 8⅛s while you get back only $1,000 at maturity. Investors will suffer an eventual loss of $1,018.75 − $1,000 = $18.75.

Sometimes investors speak loosely of the "yield" on a bond without specifying which measure of yield they are talking about; in the case of professional investors, it is a good bet that they mean *yield to maturity*. They are usually interested in total return, including both the regular income and any gain or loss in bond value.

Finally, the "Vol" column reports trading volume of 203, meaning that only 203 bonds traded on this day. This column reminds us that the bondholders may at any time sell to other investors. Of course, the price at which the bond can be sold depends on interest rates at the time of sale.

▶ **Self-Test 4.6**   Calculate the *current yield* on the 6⅛ percent Treasury bonds in 1996. Why is it less than the yield to maturity? Will current yield necessarily be less than yield to maturity for all bonds?

The Yield Curve

Look back for a moment to Figure 4.4. The U.S. Treasury bonds are arranged in order of their maturity. Notice that in general, the longer the maturity, the higher the yield. (Sometimes, however, long-term bonds offer *lower* yields.)

yield curve: Graph of the relationship between time to maturity and yield to maturity.

In addition to showing the yields on individual bonds, *The Wall Street Journal* also shows a daily plot of the relationship between bond yields and maturity. This is known as the **yield curve.** You can see from the yield curve in Figure 4.6 that bonds with 3 months to maturity offered a yield of about 5.25 percent; those with 30 years of maturity offered a yield of just over 7 percent.

Why didn't everyone buy long-maturity bonds and earn an extra 1.75 percentage points? Who were those (stupid?) investors who put their money into short-term Treasuries at only 5.25 percent?

Even when the yield curve is upward-sloping, investors might rationally stay away from long-term bonds for two reasons. First, the prices of long-term bonds fluctuate much more than prices of short-term bonds. Figure 4.3 illustrates that long-term bond

---

[4]To be more precise, they pay $81.25/2 = $40.625 every 6 months.

FIGURE 4.6
Yield curve from The Wall Street Journal. *(Source: Reprinted by permission of* The Wall Street Journal © *1996 Dow Jones & Company, Inc. All Rights Reserved Worldwide.)*

prices are more sensitive to shifting interest rates. A sharp increase in interest rates could easily knock 20 or 30 percent off long-term bond prices. If investors don't like price fluctuations, they will invest their funds in short-term bonds unless they receive a higher yield to maturity on long-term bonds.

Second, short-term investors can profit if interest rates rise. Suppose you hold a 1-year bond. A year from now when the bond matures you can reinvest the proceeds and enjoy whatever rates the bond market offers then. Rates then may be high enough to offset the first year's relatively low yield on the 1-year bond. Thus you often see an upward-sloping yield curve when future interest rates are expected to rise. We return to this issue in Chapter 11.

Credit Risk

National governments don't go bankrupt—they just print more money.[5] So investors don't worry that the United States Treasury will *default* on its bonds. But a corporation may not be able to find enough cash to pay the bondholders all that they have been promised. Thus payments promised to corporate bondholders represent a best-case scenario: the firm will never pay more than these payments, but it may pay less.

It should be no surprise that investors demand compensation for the risk that the debt may not be repaid. So we find that Chrysler needs to promise a higher rate of interest than, say, Exxon when it borrows money.

default premium: Difference in promised yields between a default-free bond and a riskier bond.

The difference between the promised yield on a corporate bond and the yield on a government bond with the same coupon and maturity is called the **default premium.** The higher the chance that the company will get into trouble, the higher the default premium demanded by investors.

[5]But they can't print money of other countries. Therefore, when a foreign government borrows dollars, investors worry that in some future crisis the government may not be able to come up with enough dollars to repay the debt. This worry shows up in the yield that investors demand on such debt. For example, after the 1994 Mexican currency crisis, yields on the dollar bonds issued by the Mexican government rose to 10 percentage points above the yields on comparable U.S. Treasury issues.

4.2 *Stocks and the Stock Market*

common stock: Ownership shares in a publicly held corporation.

Instead of borrowing cash to pay for its investments, a firm can sell new shares of **common stock** to investors.[6] Sales of new stock by the firm are said to occur in the primary market.

Shares of stock are risky investments. Even the biggest companies' stocks can lose half their value in a very short time. For example, in late 1991, Citicorp was hit by rumors of large losses on real estate loans and its stock price dropped 42 percent, from $14¾ to $8⅝. Of course there's upside potential too. By mid-1992 Citicorp stock was trading at about $21 (though by October it was back to $14).

You can understand why investors would be unhappy if forced to tie the knot with a particular company and hold its shares for better or worse, for richer or poorer. So large companies usually arrange for their stocks to be listed on a stock exchange. Stock exchanges allow investors to trade existing stocks among themselves. Exchanges are really markets for secondhand stocks, but they prefer to describe themselves as **secondary markets,** which sounds better.

secondary market: Market in which already-issued securities are traded among investors.

Reading the Stock Market Listings

When you read the stock market pages in the newspaper, you are looking at the secondary market. Figure 4.7 is an excerpt from *The Wall Street Journal* of NYSE trading on July 11, 1996. The colored bar in the figure highlights the listing for Dow Chemical.[7] The two numbers to the left of Dow are the highest and lowest prices at which the stock has traded in the last 52 weeks, $92½ and $65⅜ respectively. That's another reminder of just how much stock prices fluctuate.

Skip to the four columns on the right, and you will see the prices at which the stock traded on July 11. The highest price at which the stock traded that day was $78⅞ per share; the lowest was $77⅞, and the closing price was $78¾, which was ½ dollar higher than the previous day's close.

dividend: Periodic cash distribution from the firm to its shareholders.

The 3.00 value to the right of Dow is the annual **dividend** per share paid by the company.[8] In other words, investors in Dow Chemical shares currently receive an annual income of $3.00 on each share. Of course Dow is not bound to keep that level of dividend in the future. You hope earnings and dividends will rise, but it's possible that profits will slump and Dow will cut its dividend.

The dividend yield tells you how much dividend income you receive for each $100 that you invest in the stock. For Dow, the yield is $3.00/$78.75 = .038, or 3.8 percent. Therefore, for every $100 invested in the stock, you would receive annual dividend income of $3.80. The dividend yield on the stock is like the current yield on a bond. Both look at the current income as a percentage of price. Both ignore prospective capital gains or losses and therefore do not correspond to total rates of return.

---

[6]We use the terms "shares," "stock," and "common stock" interchangeably, as we do "shareholders" and "stockholders."

[7]The table shows not only the company's name, usually abbreviated, but also the symbol, or ticker, which is used to identify the company on the NYSE price screens. The symbol for Dow Chemical is "DOW"; other companies' symbols are not at first glance so obvious.

[8]Actually, it's the last quarterly dividend multiplied by 4.

FIGURE 4.7

Stock market listings from
The Wall Street Journal,
trading on July 19, 1996.
*(Reprinted by permission
of* The Wall Street Journal
© *1996 Dow Jones &
Company, Inc. All Rights
Reserved Worldwide.)*

NEW YORK STOCK EXCHANGE COMPOSITE TRANSACTIONS

52 Weeks Hi	52 Weeks Lo	Stock	Sym	Div	Yld %	PE	Vol 100s	Hi	Lo	Close	Net Chg
45⅞	20¼	DeVRY	DV		...	39	100	41¾	41⅜	41¾	+ ¼
29⅞	23	Dexter	DEX	.88	3.1	17	392	28½	28⅛	28¼	− ½
44⅞	33½	DiagnstPdt	DP	.48	1.3	21	262	38½	38	38¼	− ⅜
33¼	20⅞	DialCp	DL	.64	2.3	cc	2006	28¼	27⅞	28¼	
66¾	53½	DialCp pf		4.75	8.9	...	z260	55	53½	53½	...
n 58⅜	23⅜	DmndOffshr	DO		...	...	461	57⅜	57	57⅜	− ¼
34⅞	23⅜	DiaSham	DRM	.56	1.8	20	1333	30⅝	30¼	30⅝	+ ¼
120	5¼	DianaCp	DNA	stk	...	dd	2346	42½	39½	41⅞	+1⅛
s 48¼	28¾	Diebold	DBD	.68	1.5	27	528	46¾	46¼	46⅜	− ⅜
76½	35⅛	DigitalEqp	DEC		...	13	21529	38⅝	37⅜	37¾	− ⅛
26⅞	23¾	DigitalEqp pfA		2.22	9.3	...	558	24⅛	23⅞	23⅞	− ⅛
41¾	27⅛	DillardStrs	DDS	.12	.4	22	3015	34¾	33⅝	33⅞	− ½
14	10⅛	DimeBcp	DME		...	20	3627	12¾	12⅜	12⅝	...
20⅞	13¾ ♣	Dimon	DMN	.54	2.8	dd	759	19¼	19	19¼	+ ⅛
4⅜	1⅜	CG Dina	DIN		...	...	346	2⅜	2¼	2⅜	...
2¾	⅞	CG Dina L	DINL		...	...	106	1⅝	1⅝	1⅝	− ⅛
n 23⅜	14⅞	Disco	DXO		...	...	446	20⅞	20½	20⅞	+ ¼
33⅞	21¼	**DiscountAuto**	**DAP**		...	17	421	24½	22½	23⅛	−1¼
x 69⅞	50½	Disney	DIS	.44	.8	29	19840	58¼	57¼	58⅛	+ ¾
s 43¾	25⅛	DoleFood	DOL	.40	.9	cc	3650	43⅝	41¾	42⅞	+ ⅛
s 30	15²⅛₆₄ ♣	DlrGen	DG	.20	.7	26	2460	27¾	26⅝	26⅞	−1
20	17½	DominRes ubi	DOM	2.93e	14.8	...	485	20	19¾	19¾	− ¼
44⅛	34⅞	DominRes	D	2.58	6.7	14	1796	38¾	38⅜	38½	+ ⅛
10⅞	6⅝ ♣	Domtar g	DTC	.07e	...	...	167	7¼	7⅛	7⅛	...
28½	23⅞	Donaldson	DCI	.32	1.3	16	463	25½	25¼	25⅜	− ⅛
n 34¾	28	DonLufJen	DLJ	.50	1.6	9	952	30⅝	30	30⅝	+ ⅝
n 30⅛	23½	DonnaKrn	DK		...	...	5517	24¼	24	24	− ⅛
⏣ 41¼	33½	Donelley	DNY	.72	2.1	dd	2525	33⅝	33¼	33½	− ¼
s 53⅛	35⅛	Dover	DOV	.60	1.3	17	1377	45¼	44⅝	45⅛	+ ⅛
92½	65⅝	DowChem	DOW	3.00	3.8	10	9006	78⅞	77⅞	78¾	+ ½
41⅞	34⅛ ♣	DowJones	DJ	.96	2.3	22	1655	41¼	40¼	40⅞	− ¼
24⅜	17⅛	DowneyFnl	DSL	.48b	2.2	13	22	21⅝	21⅜	21⅜	− ¼
14⅞	11¼	Dravo	DRV		...	22	37	13½	13⅜	13½	...
32⅞	19⅛ ♣	DresserInd	DI	.68	2.2	24	3709	30¾	30	30¼	− ¼
9⅝	8¾	DreyfStrGvFd	DSI	.75	8.5	...	40	9	8⅞	8⅞	...
9¾	8½	DreyfStrMunBd	DSM	.62	6.6	...	378	9½	9¼	9⅜	...
10⅛	9¼	DreyfStrMuni	LEO	.67	6.7	...	598	10⅛	10	10	− ⅛
84⅞	60⅛	DuPont	DD	2.28f	2.9	14	8190	79¾	78⅛	79¾	+ ¾

If you scan Figure 4.7, you will see that dividend yields vary widely across companies. While Dow has a relatively high 3.8 percent yield, at the other extreme, Dravo doesn't even pay a dividend and therefore has zero yield. Investors are content with a low or zero current yield as long as they can look to higher future dividends and rising share prices.

price-earnings (P/E) multiple: Ratio of stock price to earnings per share.

The **price-earnings (P/E) multiple** for Dow is reported as 10. This is the ratio of the share price to earnings per share. The P/E ratio is a key tool of stock market analysts. For example, low P/E stocks are sometimes touted as good buys for investors. We will have more to say about P/E later in the chapter.

The column headed "Vol 100s" shows that the trading volume in Dow was 9,006 *round lots.* Each round lot is 100 shares, so 900,600 shares of Dow traded on this day. A trade of less than 100 shares is an *odd lot.*

▶ **Self-Test 4.7**   Explain the entries for Dow Jones in Figure 4.7.

4.3 Book Values, Liquidation Values, and Market Values

Why is Dow Chemical selling at 78¾ per share when the stock of Dow Jones, listed directly below Dow Chemical, is priced at $40⅞? And why does it cost $10 to buy one dollar of Dow Chemical earnings, while Dow Jones is selling at 22 times earnings? Do these numbers imply that one stock is a better buy than the other?

Finding the value of Dow Chemical stock may sound like a simple problem. Each year Dow publishes a balance sheet which shows the value of the firm's assets and liabilities. The simplified balance sheet in Table 4.1 shows that the book value of all Dow's assets—plant and machinery, inventories of materials, cash in the bank, and so on—was $23,582 million at end of 1995. Dow's liabilities—money that it owes the banks, taxes that are due to be paid, and the like—amounted to $16,221 million. The difference between the value of the assets and the liabilities was $7,361 million, about $7.4 billion. This was the **book value** of the firm's equity.[9] Book value records all the money that Dow has raised from its shareholders plus all the earnings that have been plowed back on their behalf.

book value: Net worth of the firm according to the balance sheet.

Book value is a reassuringly definite number. Deloitte and Touche, one of America's largest accounting firms, tells us:

> In our opinion, such consolidated financial statements . . . present fairly in all material respects, the financial position of The Dow Chemical Company and its subsidiaries at December 31, 1995 and 1994, and the results of their operations and their cash flows for each of the three years in the period ended December 31, 1996, in conformity with generally accepted accounting principles.

But does stock value equal book value? Let's see. Dow has issued 240 million shares, so the balance sheet suggests that each Dow share was worth $7,361/240 = $30.69.

But Dow shares actually were selling at $70⅜ on December 31, 1995. This and the other cases shown in Table 4.2 tell us that investors in the stock market do *not* just buy and sell at book value per share.

Investors know that accountants don't even try to estimate market values. The value of the assets reported on the firm's balance sheet is equal to their original (or "historical") cost less an allowance for depreciation. But that may not be a good guide to what the firm would need to pay to buy the same assets today. For example, in 1970

TABLE 4.1

BALANCE SHEET FOR DOW CHEMICAL, DECEMBER 31, 1995 (figures in millions of dollars)			
Assets		**Liabilities and Shareholders' Equity**	
Plant, equipment, and other assets	23,582	Liabilities	16,221
		Equity	7,361

Note: Shares of stock outstanding: 240 million. Book value of equity (per share): $30.69

[9]"Equity" is still another word for stock. Thus stockholders are often referred to as "equity investors."

TABLE 4.2

Market versus book values, December 1995

Firm	Stock Price	Book Value per Share	Ratio; Price/Book Value
Biogen	$61.50	$10.79	5.7
Boston Edison	29.50	20.61	1.4
Digital Equipment Corp.	64.13	24.95	2.6
Dow Chemical	70.38	30.69	2.4
McDonald's	45.13	10.71	4.2
Microsoft	87.38	10.47	8.4
Netscape	69.50	2.14	32.5
Pfizer	63.00	8.64	7.3

United Airlines bought four new Boeing 747s for $128 million each. By the end of 1986 they had been fully depreciated and were carried in the company accounts at residual book value of $200,000 each. But actual secondhand aircraft prices have often *appreciated,* not depreciated.[10] In fact, the planes could have been sold for upwards of $20 million each.

liquidation value: Net proceeds that would be realized by selling the firm's assets and paying off its creditors.

Well, maybe stock price equals **liquidation value** per share, that is, the amount of cash per share a company could raise if it sold off all its assets in secondhand markets and paid off all its debts. Wrong again. A successful company ought to be worth more than liquidation value. That's the goal of bringing all those assets together in the first place.

The difference between a company's actual value and its book or liquidation value is often attributed to *going-concern value.* We can trace going-concern value to three things.

1. *Extra earning power.* A company may have the ability to earn more than an adequate rate of return on assets. For example, if United can make better use of its planes than its competitors make of theirs, it will earn a higher rate of return. In this case the value of the planes to United will be higher than their book value or secondhand value.

2. *Intangible assets.* There are many assets that accountants don't put on the balance sheet. Some of these assets are extremely valuable to the companies owning or using them but would be difficult to sell intact to other firms. Take Pfizer, a pharmaceutical company. As you can see from Table 4.2, it sells at about 7.3 times book value per share. Where did all that extra value come from? Largely from the cash flow generated by the drugs it has developed, patented, and marketed. These drugs are the fruits of a research and development (R&D) program that since 1985 has averaged about $500 million annually. But United States accountants don't recognize R&D as an investment and don't put it on the company's balance sheet. Successful R&D does show up in stock prices, however.

3. *Value of future investments.* If investors believe a company will have the opportunity to make exceedingly profitable investments in the future, they will pay more for the company's stock today. When Netscape, the Internet software company, first

---

[10]This is partly due to inflation. Book values for United States corporations are not inflation-adjusted. Also, when the accountants set up the original depreciation schedule, nobody anticipated how long these aircraft would be able to remain in service.

sold its stock to investors on August 8, 1995, the book value of shareholders' equity was about $146 million. Yet the prices investors paid for the stock resulted in a market value of over $1 *billion.* By the close of trading on that day, the price of Netscape stock more than doubled, resulting in a stock market value of over $2 billion, nearly 15 times book value. In part, this reflected an intangible asset, the Internet browsing system for computers. In addition, Netscape was a *growth company.* Investors were betting that it had the know-how that would enable it to devise successful *follow-on* products.

> **Market price need not, and generally does not, equal either book value or liquidation value. Unlike market value, neither book value nor liquidation value treats the firm as a going concern.**

It is not surprising that stocks virtually never sell at book or liquidation values. Investors buy shares based on present and *future* earning power. Two key features determine the profits the firm will be able to produce: first, the earnings that can be generated by the firm's current tangible and intangible assets, and second, the opportunities the firm has to invest in lucrative projects that will increase future earnings.

▶ **Example 4.5**   *Boston Edison and Netscape*

Boston Edison isn't a growth company. Its market is limited and it is expanding capacity at a very deliberate pace. More important, it is a regulated utility, so its profits on present and future investments are limited. It is legally entitled only to a "fair and adequate" rate of return. It is no surprise that Boston Edison sells for only 40 percent above book value (see Table 4.2) and that investors value the company based mostly on current earnings and dividends.

In contrast, Netscape has little to show in the way of current earnings. By 1995, it had recorded accumulated *losses* of $16 million. Nevertheless, the total market value of Netscape stock at the end of 1995 was $5.6 billion. The value came from Netscape's market position, its highly regarded Internet browsing system, and the promise of new related products which presumably would lead to future earnings. Netscape was a pure growth firm, since its market value depended wholly on intangible assets and the profitability of future investments.

market-value balance sheet: Financial statement that uses the market value of all assets and liabilities.

Financial executives are not bound by generally accepted accounting principles, and they sometimes construct a **market-value balance sheet.** Take a look at Table 4.3. A market-value balance sheet contains two classes of assets: (1) assets already in place, (a) tangible and (b) intangible; and (2) opportunities to invest in attractive future ventures. Boston Edison's stock market value is dominated by tangible assets in place; Netscape's by the value of future investment opportunities.

TABLE 4.3

A MARKET-VALUE BALANCE SHEET	
Assets	**Liabilities and Shareholders' Equity**
Assets in place	Market value of debt and other obligations
Investment opportunities	Market value of shareholders' equity

Other firms, like Microsoft, have it all. Microsoft earns plenty from its current products. These earnings are part of what makes the stock attractive to investors. In addition, investors are willing to pay for the company's ability to invest profitably in new ventures that will increase future earnings.

Let's summarize. Just remember:

- *Book value* records what a company has paid for its assets, with a simple, and often unrealistic, deduction for depreciation and no adjustment for inflation. It does not capture the true value of a business.
- *Liquidation value* is what the company could net by selling its assets and repaying its debts. It does not capture the value of a successful going concern.
- *True Value* is market value, that is, the amount that investors are willing to pay for the shares of the firm. This depends on the earning power of *today's* assets and the profitability of *future* investments.

The next question is: What determines market value?

▶ **Self-Test 4.8**

In the 1970s, the computer industry was dominated by IBM and was growing rapidly. In the 1980s, many new competitors entered the market, and computer prices fell. Computer makers in the 1990s, including IBM, have struggled with thinning profit margins and intense competition. How has IBM's market-value balance sheet changed over time? Have assets in place become proportionately more or less important? Do you think this progression is unique to the computer industry?

4.4 *Valuing Common Stocks*

Today's Price and Tomorrow's Price

The cash payoff to owners of common stocks comes in two forms: (1) cash dividends and (2) capital gains or losses. Usually investors expect to get some of each. Suppose that the current price of a share is P_0, that the expected price a year from now is P_1, and that the expected dividend per share is DIV_1. The subscript on P_0 denotes time zero, which is today; the subscript on P_1 denotes time 1, which is 1 year hence. We simplify by assuming that dividends are paid only once a year and that the next dividend will come in 1 year. The rate of return that investors expect from this share over the next year is the expected dividend per share DIV_1 plus the expected increase in price $P_1 - P_0$, all divided by the price at the start of the year P_0:

$$\text{Expected return} = r = \frac{DIV_1 + P_1 - P_0}{P_0}$$

Let us now look at how our formula works. Suppose Blue Skies stock is selling for $75 a share ($P_0 = \$75$). Investors expect a $3 cash dividend over the next year ($DIV_1 = \$3$). They also expect the stock to sell for $81 a year hence ($P_1 = \$81$). Then the expected return to stockholders is 12 percent:

$$r = \frac{\$3 + \$81 - \$75}{\$75} = .12, \text{ or } 12\%$$

Notice that this expected return comes in two parts, the dividend yield and the capital appreciation:

$$\text{Expected return} = \begin{array}{c}\text{expected}\\\text{dividend}\\\text{yield}\end{array} + \begin{array}{c}\text{expected}\\\text{capital}\\\text{appreciation}\end{array}$$

$$= \frac{DIV_1}{P_0} + \frac{P_1 - P_0}{P_0}$$

$$= \frac{\$3}{\$75} + \frac{\$81 - \$75}{\$75}$$

$$= .04 \quad + .08 = .12, \text{ or } 12\%$$

Of course, the *actual* return for Blue Skies may turn out to be more or less than investors expect. For example, in 1996, the best performing stock on the New York Stock Exchange was Centennial Technologies. Its price at the end of the year was $52, up from $9⁷⁄₁₆ at the beginning of the year. Since the stock did not pay a dividend during the year, investors earned an actual return of ($0 + $52 − $9.4375)/ $9.4375 = 4.51, or 451 percent.

This figure was almost certainly well in excess of investor expectations. At the other extreme, the worst performing stock, Foxmyer Health, which declared bankruptcy during the year, provided an actual return of −92.5 percent, well below expectations. Never confuse the actual outcome with the expected outcome.

We saw how to work out the expected return on Blue Skies stock given today's stock price and forecasts of next year's stock price and dividends. You can also explain the market value of the stock in terms of investors' forecasts of dividends and price and the expected return offered by other equally risky stocks. This is just the present value of the cash flows the stock will provide to its owner:

$$\text{Price today} = P_0 = \frac{DIV_1 + P_1}{1 + r}$$

For Blue Skies $DIV_1 = \$3$ and $P_1 = \$81$. If stocks of similar risk offer an expected return of $r = 12$ percent, then today's price for Blue Skies should be $75:

$$P_0 = \frac{\$3 + \$81}{1.12} = \$75$$

How do we know that $75 is the right price? Because no other price could survive in competitive markets. What if P_0 were above $75? Then the expected rate of return on Blue Skies stock would be *lower* than on other securities of equivalent risk. (*Check this!*) Investors would bail out of Blue Skies stock and substitute the other securities. In the process they would force down the price of Blue Skies stock. If P_0 were less than $75, Blue Skies stock would offer a *higher* expected rate of return than equivalent-risk securities. (*Check this too.*) Everyone would rush to buy, forcing the price up to $75. When the stock is priced correctly (that is, price equals present value), the *expected* rate of return on Blue Skies stock is also the rate of return that investors *require* to hold the stock.

> At each point in time all securities of the same risk are priced to offer the same expected rate of return. This is a fundamental characteristic of prices in well-functioning markets. It is also common sense.

▶ **Self-Test 4.9**   Androscoggin Copper is increasing next year's dividend to $5.00 per share. The forecast stock price next year is $105. Equally risky stocks of other companies offer expected rates of return of 10 percent. What should Androscoggin common stock sell for?

The Dividend Discount Model

We have managed to explain today's stock price P_0 in terms of the dividend DIV_1 and the expected stock price next year P_1. But future stock prices are not easy to forecast directly, though you may encounter individuals who claim to be able to do so. A formula that requires tomorrow's stock price to explain today's stock price is not generally helpful.

dividend discount model: Computation of today's stock price which states that share value equals the present value of all expected future dividends.

As it turns out, we can express a stock's value as the present value of all the forecast future dividends paid by the company to its shareholders without referring to the future stock price. This is the **dividend discount model:**

$$P_0 = \text{present value of } (DIV_1, DIV_2, DIV_3, \ldots, DIV_t, \ldots)$$

$$= \frac{DIV_1}{1 + r} + \frac{DIV_2}{(1 + r)^2} + \frac{DIV_3}{(1 + r)^3} + \cdots + \frac{DIV_t}{(1 + r)^t} + \cdots$$

How far out in the future could we look? In principle, 40, 60, or 100 years or more—corporations are potentially immortal. However, far-distant dividends will not have significant present values. Most of the value of established companies comes from dividends to be paid within a person's working lifetime.

How do we get from the one-period formula $P_0 = (DIV_1 + P_1)/(1 + r)$ to the dividend discount model? We look at longer and longer investment horizons.

Let's start with a 1-year horizon:

$$P_0 = \frac{DIV_1 + P_1}{1 + r}$$

If this price formula holds now, it ought to hold next year as well:

$$\text{Price at year-end} = P_1 = \frac{DIV_2 + P_2}{1 + r}$$

That is, a year from now investors will be looking out at dividends in Year 2 and price at the end of Year 2. Thus we can forecast P_1 by forecasting DIV_2 and P_2. We can then substitute for P_1 and turn the one-period stock valuation model

$$P_0 = \frac{DIV_1 + P_1}{1 + r} \quad \text{and} \quad P_1 = \frac{DIV_2 + P_2}{1 + r}$$

into a two-period model

$$P_0 = \frac{DIV_1}{1 + r} + \frac{DIV_2 + P_2}{(1 + r)^2}$$

We have succeeded in relating today's price to the forecast dividends for the next 2 years (DIV_1 and DIV_2) plus the forecast price at the end of the *second* year (P_2). You will probably not be surprised to learn that we could go on to replace P_2 by ($DIV_3 + P_3$)/(1 + r) and relate today's price to the forecast dividends for 3 years (DIV_1, DIV_2, and DIV_3) plus the forecast price at the end of the *third* year (P_3). In fact we can look as far out into the future as we like, removing P's as we go. Suppose we call our horizon date H. This gives us a general formula for the value of the stock:

$$P_0 = \frac{\text{DIV}_1}{1 + r} + \frac{\text{DIV}_2}{(1 + r)^2} + \cdots + \frac{\text{DIV}_H + P_H}{(1 + r)^H}$$

> **In words, the intrinsic value of a stock is the present value of the dividends it will pay over the investor's horizon, plus the present value of the expected stock price at the end of that period.**

Regardless of the investment horizon, the stock value will be the same. This is because the stock price at the horizon date is determined by expectations of dividends from that date forward. Let's confirm this with an example.

▶ **Example 4.6**   *Valuing Blue Skies Stock*

Take Blue Skies. The firm is growing steadily and investors expect both the stock price and the dividend to increase at 8 percent per year. Now consider three investors, Erste, Zweiter, and Dritter. Erste plans to hold Blue Skies for 1 year, Zweiter for 2, and Dritter for 3. Compare their payoffs:

	Year 1	Year 2	Year 3
Erste	$\text{DIV}_1 = 3$ $P_1 = 81$		
Zweiter	$\text{DIV}_1 = 3$	$\text{DIV}_2 = 3.24$ $P_2 = 87.48$	
Dritter	$\text{DIV}_1 = 3$	$\text{DIV}_2 = 3.24$	$\text{DIV}_3 = 3.50$ $P_3 = 94.48$

Remember, we assumed that dividends and stock prices for Blue Skies are expected to grow at a steady 8 percent. Thus $\text{DIV}_2 = \$3 \times 1.08 = \$3.24$, $\text{DIV}_3 = \$3.24 \times 1.08 = \$3.50$, and so on.

Erste, Zweiter, and Dritter all require the same 12 percent expected return. So we can calculate present value over Erste's 1-year horizon:

$$\text{PV} = \frac{\text{DIV}_1 + P_1}{1 + r} = \frac{\$3 + \$81}{1.12} = \$75$$

or Zweiter's 2-year horizon:

$$\text{PV} = \frac{\text{DIV}_1}{1 + r} + \frac{\text{DIV}_2 + P_2}{(1 + r)^2}$$

$$= \frac{\$3.00}{1.12} + \frac{\$3.24 + \$87.48}{(1.12)^2}$$

$$= \$2.68 + \$72.32 = \$75$$

or Dritter's 3-year horizon:

$$\text{PV} = \frac{\text{DIV}_1}{1 + r} + \frac{\text{DIV}_2}{(1 + r)^2} + \frac{\text{DIV}_3 + P_3}{(1 + r)^3}$$

$$= \frac{\$3}{1.12} + \frac{\$3.24}{(1.12)^2} + \frac{\$3.50 + \$94.48}{(1.12)^3}$$

$$= \$2.68 + \$2.58 + \$69.74 = \$75$$

TABLE 4.4
Value of Blue Skies

Horizon, Years	PV (Dividends)	+	PV (Terminal Price)	+	Value per Share
1	$ 2.68		$72.32		$75.00
2	5.26		69.74		75.00
3	7.75		67.25		75.00
10	22.87		52.13		75.00
20	38.76		36.24		75.00
30	49.81		25.19		75.00
50	62.83		12.17		75.00
100	73.02		1.98		75.00

All agree the stock is worth $75 per share. This illustrates our basic principle: the value of a common stock equals the present value of dividends received out to the investment horizon, plus the present value of the forecast stock price at the horizon. Moreover, when you move the horizon date, the stock's present value should not change. The principle holds for horizons of 1, 3, 10, 20 and 50 years or more.

▶ **Self-Test 4.10**   Refer to Self-Test 4.9. Assume that Androscoggin Copper's dividend and share price are expected to grow at a constant 5 percent per year. Calculate the current value of Androscoggin stock with the dividend discount model using a 3-year horizon. You should get the same answer as in Self Test 4.9.

Look at Table 4.4, which continues the Blue Skies example for various time horizons, still assuming that the dividends are expected to increase at a steady 8 percent compound rate. The expected price increases at the same 8 percent rate. Each row in the table represents a present value calculation for a different horizon year. Note that present value does not depend on the investment horizon. Figure 4.8 presents the same data in a graph. Each column shows the present value of the dividends up to the horizon and the present value of the price at the horizon. As the horizon recedes, the dividend stream accounts for an increasing proportion of present value but the *total* present value of dividends plus terminal price always equals $75.

If the horizon is infinitely far away, then we can forget about the final horizon price—it has almost no present value—and simply say

Stock price = PV (all future dividends per share)

This is the dividend discount model.

4.5 *Simplifying the Dividend Discount Model*

The Dividend Discount Model with No Growth

Consider a company that pays out all its earnings to its common shareholders. Such a company could not grow because it could not reinvest.[11] Stockholders might enjoy a generous immediate dividend, but they could forecast no increase in future divi-

---
[11]We assume it does not raise money by issuing new shares.

FIGURE 4.8

Value of Blue Skies for different horizons.

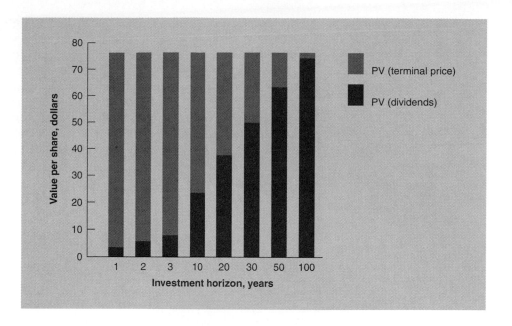

dends. The company's stock would offer a perpetual stream of equal cash payments, $DIV_1 = DIV_2 = \cdots = DIV_t = \cdots$.

The dividend discount model says that these no-growth shares should sell for the present value of a constant, perpetual stream of dividends. We learned how to do that calculation when we valued perpetuities in Chapter 3. Just divide the annual cash payment by the discount rate. The discount rate is the rate of return demanded by investors in other stocks of the same risk:

$$P_0 = \frac{DIV_1}{r}$$

Since our company pays out all its earnings as dividends, dividends and earnings are the same, and we could just as well calculate stock value by

$$\text{Value of a no-growth stock} = P_0 = \frac{EPS_1}{r}$$

where EPS_1 represents next year's earnings per share of stock. Thus some people loosely say, "Stock price is the present value of future earnings" and calculate value by this formula. Be careful—this is a special case. We'll return to the formula later in this chapter.

▶ **Self-Test 4.11**   Moonshine Industries has produced a barrel per week for the past 20 years but cannot grow because of certain legal hazards. It earns $25 per share per year and pays it all out to stockholders. The stockholders have alternative, equivalent-risk ventures yielding 20 percent per year on average. How much is one share of Moonshine worth? Assume the company can keep going indefinitely.

The Constant-Growth Dividend Discount Model

The dividend discount model requires a forecast of dividends for every year into the future, which poses a bit of a problem for stocks with potentially infinite lives. Unless we want to spend a lifetime forecasting dividends, we must use simplifying assumptions to reduce the number of estimates. The simplest simplification assumes a no-growth perpetuity which works for no-growth common shares.

Here's another simplification that finds a good deal of practical use. Suppose forecast dividends grow at a constant rate into the indefinite future. If dividends grow at a steady rate, then instead of forecasting an infinite number of dividends, we need to forecast only the next dividend and the dividend growth rate.

Recall Blue Skies Inc. It will pay a $3 dividend in 1 year. If the dividend grows at a constant rate of $g = .08$ (8 percent) thereafter, then dividends in future years will be

$$DIV_1 = \$3 \qquad\qquad\qquad = \$3.00$$
$$DIV_2 = \$3 \times (1 + g) = \$3 \times 1.08 \quad = \$3.24$$
$$DIV_3 = \$3 \times (1 + g)^2 = \$3 \times 1.08^2 = \$3.50$$

Plug these forecasts of future dividends into the dividend discount model:

$$P_0 = \frac{D_1}{1 + r} + \frac{D_1(1 + g)}{(1 + r)^2} + \frac{D_1(1 + g)^2}{(1 + r)^3} + \frac{D_1(1 + g)^3}{(1 + r)^4} + \cdots$$
$$= \frac{\$3}{1.12} + \frac{\$3.24}{1.12^2} + \frac{\$3.50}{1.12^3} + \frac{\$3.78}{1.12^4} + \cdots$$
$$= \$2.68 + \$2.58 + \$2.49 + \$2.40 + \cdots$$

Although there is an infinite number of terms, each term is proportionately smaller than the preceding one as long as the dividend growth rate g is less than the discount rate r. Because the present value of far-distant dividends will be ever-closer to zero, the sum of all of these terms is finite despite the fact that an infinite number of dividends will be paid. The sum can be shown to equal

$$P_0 = \frac{DIV_1}{r - g}$$

constant-growth dividend discount model: Version of the dividend discount model in which dividends grow at a constant rate.

This equation is called the **constant-growth dividend discount model,** or the *Gordon growth model* after Myron Gordon, who did much to popularize it.

Notice that the first dividend, DIV_1, is assumed to come at the *end* of the first period and is discounted for a full period. If there's an immediate dividend DIV_0, we have to add it in:

$$\text{Including immediate dividend:} \quad P_0 = DIV_0 + \frac{DIV_1}{r - g}$$

We could also base DIV_1 on the immediate dividend adjusted for a year's growth: $DIV_1 = DIV_0(1 + g)$, so

$$\text{Including immediate dividend:} \quad P_0 = DIV_0 + \frac{DIV_0(1 + g)}{r - g}$$

If DIV_0 has always been paid out, we obviously can't include its value in the stock price. However, we could still observe what it was and write

$$P_0 = \frac{DIV_1}{r - g} = \frac{DIV_0(1 + g)}{r - g}$$

▶ **Example 4.7**   *Blue Skies Valued by the Constant-Growth Model*

Let's apply the constant-growth model to Blue Skies. Assume a dividend has just been paid. The next dividend, to be paid in a year, is forecast at $DIV_1 = \$3$, the growth rate of dividends is $g = 8$ percent, and the discount rate is $r = 12$ percent. Therefore, we solve for the stock value as

$$P_0 = \frac{DIV_1}{r - g} = \frac{\$3}{.12 - .08} = \$75$$

The constant-growth formula is close to the formula for the present value of a perpetuity. Suppose you forecast no growth in dividends ($g = 0$). Then the dividend stream is a simple perpetuity, and the valuation formula is $P_0 = DIV_1/r$. This is precisely the formula you used in Self-Test 4.11 to value Moonshine, a no-growth common stock.

The constant-growth model generalizes the perpetuity formula to allow for constant growth in dividends. Notice that as g increases, the stock price also rises. However, the constant-growth formula is valid only when g is less than r. If someone forecasts perpetual dividend growth at a rate greater than investors' required return r, then two things happen:

1. The formula explodes. It gives nutty answers. (Try a numerical example.)
2. You know the forecast is wrong, because far-distant dividends would have incredibly high present values. (Again, try a numerical example. Calculate the present value of a dividend paid after 100 years, assuming $DIV_1 = \$3$, $r = .12$, but $g = .20$.)

Estimating Expected Rates of Return

We argued earlier that in competitive markets, common stocks with the same risk are priced to offer the same expected rate of return. But how do you figure out what that expected rate of return is?

It's not easy. Consensus estimates of future dividends, stock prices, or overall rates of return are not published in *The Wall Street Journal* or reported by TV newscasters. Economists argue about which statistical models give the best estimates. There are nevertheless some useful rules of thumb that can give sensible numbers.

One rule of thumb is based on the constant-growth dividend discount model. Remember that it forecasts a constant growth rate g in both future dividends and stock prices. That means forecast capital gains equal g per year.

We can calculate the expected rate of return by rearranging the constant-growth formula as

$$r = \frac{DIV_1}{P_0} + g$$

$$= \text{dividend yield} + \text{growth rate}$$

For Blue Skies, the expected first-year dividend is $3 and the growth rate 8 percent. With an initial stock price of $75, the expected rate of return is

$$r = \frac{DIV_1}{P_0} + g$$

$$= \frac{\$3}{\$75} + .08 = .04 + .08 = .12, \text{ or } 12\%$$

Suppose we found another stock with the same risk as Blue Skies. It ought to offer the same expected rate of return even if its immediate dividend or expected growth rate is very different. The required rate of return is not the unique property of Blue Skies or any other company; it is set in the worldwide market for common stocks. Blue Skies cannot change its value of r by paying higher or lower dividends or by growing faster or slower, unless these changes also affect the risk of the stock. When we use the rule of thumb formula, $r = DIV_1/P_0 + g$, we are *not* saying that r, the expected rate of return, is *determined by* DIV_1 or g. It is determined by the rate of return offered by other equally risky stocks. That return determines how much investors are willing to pay for Blue Skies's forecast future dividends:

$$\frac{DIV_1}{P_0} + g = r = \text{expected rate of return offered by other, equally risky stocks}$$

Given DIV_1 and g, investors set the stock price

so that Blue Skies offers an adequate expected rate of return r

▶ **Example 4.8**   *Blue Skies Gets a Windfall*

Blue Skies has won a lawsuit against its archrival, Nasty Manufacturing, which forces Nasty Manufacturing to withdraw as a competitor in a key market. As a result Blue Skies is able to generate 9 percent per year future growth without sacrificing immediate dividends. Will that increase r, the expected rate of return?

This is very good news for Blue Skies stockholders. The stock price will jump to

$$P_0 = \frac{DIV_1}{r - g} = \frac{\$3}{.12 - .09} = \$100$$

But at the new price Blue Skies will offer the same 12 percent expected return:

$$r = \frac{DIV_1}{P_0} + g$$
$$= \frac{\$3}{\$100} + .09 = .12, \text{ or } 12\%$$

Blue Skies's good news is reflected in a higher stock price today, not in a higher expected rate of return in the future. The unchanged expected rate of return corresponds to Blue Skies's unchanged risk.

▶ **Self-Test 4.12**   Androscoggin Copper can grow at 5 percent per year for the indefinite future. It's selling at $100 and next year's dividend is $5.00. What is the expected rate of return from investing in Carrabasset Mining common stock? Carrabasset and Androscoggin shares are equally risky.

Few real companies are expected to grow in such a regular and convenient way as Blue Skies or Androscoggin Copper. Nevertheless, in some mature industries, growth is reasonably stable and the constant-growth model approximately valid. In such cases the model can be turned around to infer the rate of return expected by investors.

Nonconstant Growth

Many companies grow at rapid or irregular rates for several years before finally settling down. Obviously we can't use the constant-growth dividend discount model in such cases. However, we have already looked at an alternative approach. Set the *investment horizon* (Year H) at the future year by which you expect the company's growth to settle down. Calculate the present value of dividends from now to the horizon year. Forecast the stock price in that year and discount it also to present value. Then add up to get the total present value of dividends plus the ending stock price. The formula is

$$P_0 = \frac{DIV_1}{1+r} + \frac{DIV_2}{(1+r)^2} + \cdots + \underbrace{\frac{DIV_H}{(1+r)^H}}_{\substack{\text{PV of dividends from} \\ \text{Year 1 to horizon}}} + \underbrace{\frac{P_H}{(1+r)^H}}_{\substack{\text{PV of stock price} \\ \text{at horizon}}}$$

The stock price in the horizon year is often called *terminal value*.

▶ **Example 4.9** *Estimating the Value of United Bird Seed's Stock*

Ms. Dawn Chorus, founder and president of United Bird Seed, is wondering whether the company should make its first public sale of common stock and if so at what price.

The company's financial plan envisages rapid growth over the next 3 years but only moderate growth afterwards. Forecast earnings and dividends are as follows:

Year:	1	2	3	4	5	6	7	8
Earnings per share	$2.45	3.11	3.78	5% growth thereafter				
Dividends per share	$1.00	1.20	1.44	5% growth thereafter				

Thus you have a forecast of the dividend stream for the next 3 years. The tricky part is to estimate the price in the horizon Year 3. Ms. Chorus could look at stock prices for mature pet food companies whose scale, risk, and growth prospects today roughly match those projected for United Bird Seed in Year 3. Suppose further that these companies tend to sell at price-earnings ratios of about 8. Then you could reasonably guess that the P/E ratio of United will likewise be 8. That implies

$$P_3 = 8 \times \$3.78 = \$30.24$$

You are now in a position to determine the value of shares in United. If investors demand a return of $r = 10$ percent, then price today should be

$$P_0 = \text{PV (dividends from Years 1 to 3)} + \text{PV (forecast stock price in Year 3)}$$

$$\text{PV (dividends)} = \frac{\$1.00}{1.10} + \frac{\$1.20}{1.10^2} + \frac{\$1.44}{1.10^3} = \$2.98$$

$$\text{PV}(P_H) = \frac{\$30.24}{(1.10)^3} = \$22.72$$

$$P_0 = \$2.98 + \$22.72 = \$25.70$$

Thus price today should be about $25.70 per share.

United Bird Seed is looking forward to several years of very rapid growth, so you could not use the constant-growth formula to value United's stock today. But the formula may help you check your estimate of the terminal price in Year 3 when the company has settled down to a steady rate of growth. Suppose that from then on dividends are forecast to grow at a constant rate of $g = .05$ (5 percent). Thus the expected dividend in Year 4 is

$$DIV_4 = 1.05 \times DIV_3 = 1.05 \times \$1.44 = \$1.512$$

and the expected terminal price in Year 3 is

$$P_3 = \frac{DIV_4}{r - g} = \frac{\$1.512}{.10 - .05} = \$30.24$$

the same value we found when we used the P/E ratio to predict P_3. In this case our two approaches give the same estimate of P_3, though you shouldn't bet on that always being the case in practice.

▶ **Self-Test 4.13**   Suppose that another stock market analyst predicts that United Bird Seed will not settle down to a constant 5 percent growth rate in dividends until after Year 4, and that dividends in Year 4 will be $1.73 per share. What is the fair price for the stock according to this analyst?

4.6 Growth Stocks and Income Stocks

We often hear investors speak of *growth stocks* and *income stocks*. They seem to buy growth stocks primarily in the expectation of capital gains, and they are interested in the future growth of earnings rather than in next year's dividends. On the other hand, they buy income stocks principally for the cash dividends. Let us see whether these distinctions make sense.

Think back once more to Blue Skies. It is expected to pay a dividend next year of $3 ($DIV_1 = 3$), and this dividend is expected to grow at a steady rate of 8 percent a year ($g = .08$). If investors require a return of 12 percent ($r = .12$), then the price of Blue Skies should be $DIV_1/(r - g) = \$3/(.12 - .08) = \$75$.

payout ratio: Fraction of earnings paid out as dividends.

Suppose that Blue Skies's existing assets generate earnings per share of $5.00. It pays out 60 percent of these earnings as a dividend. This **payout ratio** results in a dividend of $.60 \times \$5.00 = \$3.00$. The remaining 40 percent of earnings, the **plowback ratio,** is retained by the firm and plowed back into new plant and equipment. On this new equity investment Blue Skies earns a return of 20 percent.

plowback ratio: Fraction of earnings retained by the firm.

If *all* of these earnings were plowed back into the firm, Blue Skies would grow at 20 percent per year. Because a portion of earnings is not reinvested in the firm, the growth rate will be less than 20 percent. The higher the fraction of earnings plowed back into the company, the higher the growth rate. So assets, earnings, and dividends all grow by

$$g = \textbf{return on equity} \times \textbf{plowback ratio}$$
$$= 20\% \times .40 = 8\%$$

What if Blue Skies did not plow back any of its earnings into new plant and equipment? In that case it would pay out all its earnings as dividends but would forgo any growth in dividends. So we could recalculate value with $DIV_1 = \$5.00$ and $g = 0$:

$$P_0 = \frac{\$5.00}{.12 - 0} = \$41.67$$

Thus if Blue Skies did not reinvest any of its earnings, its stock price would not be $75 but $41.67. The $41.67 represents the value of earnings from the assets that are already in place. The rest of the stock price ($75 − $41.67 = $33.33) is the net present value of the future investments that Blue Skies is expected to make. This is reflected in the market-value balance sheet, Table 4.5.

What if Blue Skies kept to its policy of reinvesting 40 percent of its profits but the forecast return on this new investment was only 12 percent? In that case the expected growth in dividends would also be lower:

$$g = \text{return on equity} \times \text{plowback ratio}$$
$$= 12\% \times .40 = 4.8\%$$

If we plug this new value for g into our valuation formula, we come up again with a value of $41.67 for Blue Skies stock:

$$P_0 = \frac{DIV_1}{r - g} = \frac{\$3.00}{.12 - .048} = \$41.67$$

Plowing earnings back into new investments may result in growth in earnings and dividends but it does not add to the current stock price if that money is expected to earn only the return that investors require. Plowing earnings back *does* add to value if investors believe that the reinvested earnings will earn a higher rate of return. (Remember that investors expected Blue Skies to earn 20 percent on its new investments, well above the 12 percent expected return necessary to attract investors.)

present value of growth opportunities (PVGO): Net present value of a firm's future investments.

To repeat, if Blue Skies did not plow back earnings or if it earned only the return that investors required on the new investment, its stock price would be $41.67. The total value of Blue Skies stock is $75. Of this figure, $41.67 is the value of the assets already in place, and the remaining $33.33 is the present value of the superior returns on assets to be acquired in the future. The latter is called the **present value of growth opportunities,** or **PVGO.**

sustainable growth rate: Steady rate at which firm can grow; return on equity × plowback ratio.

By the way, growth rates calculated as

$$g = \text{return on equity} \times \text{plowback ratio}$$

are often referred to as **sustainable growth rates.**

TABLE 4.5

MARKET-VALUE BALANCE SHEET FOR BLUE SKIES (all quantities on a per-share basis)			
Assets		**Liabilities and Shareholders' Equity**	
Assets in place	$41.67	Shareholders' equity	$75
Investment opportunities	33.33		

▶ **Self-Test 4.14**   Suppose that instead of plowing money back into lucrative ventures, Blue Skies's management is investing at an expected return on equity of 10 percent, which is *below* the return of 12 percent that investors could expect to get from comparable securities.

a. Find the sustainable growth rate of dividends and earnings in these circumstances. Assume a 60 percent payout ratio.
b. Find the new value of its investment opportunities. Explain why this value is negative despite the positive growth rate of earnings and dividends.
c. If you were a corporate raider, would Blue Skies be a good candidate for an attempted takeover?

The Price-Earnings Ratio

The superior prospects of Blue Skies are reflected in its price-earnings ratio. With a stock price of $75.00 and earnings of $5.00, the P/E ratio is $75/$5 = 15. If Blue Skies had no growth opportunities, its stock price would be only $41.67 and its P/E would be $41.67/$5 = 8.33. The P/E ratio, therefore, is an indicator of the prospects of the firm. To justify a high P/E, one must believe the firm is endowed with ample growth opportunities.

What Do Earnings Mean?

Be careful when you look at price-earnings ratios. In our discussion, "expected future earnings" refers to expected cash flow less the true depreciation in the value of the assets. This is the amount a company could pay out if it did not reinvest earnings. But the earnings reported in the company's income statement are determined using arbitrary methods to measure the depreciation in the value of the firm's assets. A switch in the depreciation method can dramatically change reported earnings without affecting the true profitability of the firm. Other accounting choices that can affect reported earnings are the method for valuing inventories, the decision to treat research and development as a current expense rather than as an investment, and the way that tax liabilities are reported.

Valuing Entire Businesses

Investors routinely buy and sell shares of common stock. Companies frequently buy and sell entire businesses. So it is natural to ask whether the formulas that we have presented in this chapter can also be used to value these businesses.

Sure! Take the case of Blue Skies. Suppose that it has 2 million shares outstanding. It plans to pay a dividend of $DIV_1 = \$3$ a share. So the *total* dividend payment is 2 million × $3 = $6 million. Investors expect a steady dividend growth of 8 percent a year and require a return of 12 percent. So the total value of Blue Skies is

$$PV = \frac{\$6 \text{ million}}{.12 - .08} = \$150 \text{ million}$$

Alternatively, we could say that the total value of the company is the number of shares times the value per share:

$$PV = 2 \text{ million} \times \$75 = \$150 \text{ million}$$

A Small Spat about $1.6 Billion

Company valuation is not a precise science. When two companies dispute the price that one should pay for the other, a battle between their investment bankers can be guaranteed.

AT&T bought McCaw Cellular in 1994. As a result it acquired McCaw's 52 percent stake in the shares of a cellular communications company, LIN Broadcasting, and assumed an obligation to buy the remaining 48 percent of the shares at their fair value. The process for determining fair value was laid down when McCaw acquired its initial stake in LIN. AT&T and LIN had 30 days to come up with an initial valuation of the shares and then a further 15 days to consider their final numbers. If the two companies' valuations were less than 10 percent apart, AT&T would be obliged to buy at the average of the two prices. If they were more than 10 percent apart, an independent arbitrator would be appointed. If the arbitrator decided that the true value was about midway between the two companies' valuations, then the arbitrator's valuation would be used. If it was close to AT&T's valuation, then the arbitrator's price and AT&T's price would be averaged and LIN's valuation would be ignored. Conversely, if it was close to LIN's figure, then the arbitrator's price would be averaged in with LIN's valuation and AT&T's figure would be ignored.

Each company appointed an investment bank to prepare and argue its case. AT&T's case was presented by Morgan Stanley while LIN's case was prepared by Bear Stearns and Lehman Brothers. Each side faced a quandary. AT&T's advisers were tempted to go for a low figure, while LIN's advisers were tempted to come up with a high figure. But if the dispute went to arbitration, then an extreme valuation was more likely to be out of line with the arbitrator's figure and therefore was more likely to be ignored. It seemed to make sense to take an extreme posi-

tion only if each could be sure that the other side would do so also. Conversely, a more middle-of-the-road posture made sense if each could be confident that the other would provide a middle-of-the-road valuation.

When the two parties met at Morgan Stanley's offices to examine each other's valuations, there was a stunned silence, and then Bear Stearns's team began to laugh. Morgan Stanley's valuation was $100 a share, while Lehman Brothers and Bear Stearns came up with a figure of $162 a share. Since AT&T was proposing to buy 25 million LIN shares, the disagreement amounted to a thumping $1.6 billion.

Fifteen days later the two sides met again to exchange their final valuations. There was an air of shock in the room; despite hearing the other side's arguments, the difference in their valuations had barely narrowed. It seemed that an independent arbitrator was required and so another investment bank, Wasserstein Perella, was called in to provide an independent valuation.

Some weeks later a herd of about 50 investment bankers and lawyers crowded into the offices of Wasserstein Perella to defend their estimates of the value of LIN. Comparisons were made with the value of other cellular communications companies. Each side presented projections of LIN's future profits and dividends. There were also arguments about the rate at which these future dividends should be discounted. For example, each side argued that the other had failed to measure properly the risk of the stock.

The final upshot: After hearing the arguments from both sides, Wasserstein Perella placed a value of $127.50 on each share of LIN. This meant that the total cost of the shares to AT&T was about $3.3 billion.

Source: The story of the valuation of LIN Broadcasting is set out in S. Neish, "Wrong Number," *Global M&A* (Summer 1995).

Of course things are always harder in practice than in principle. Forecasting cash flows and settling on an appropriate discount rate require skill and judgment. As the nearby box shows, there can be plenty of room for disagreement.

 See box p. 135

4.7 *Summary*

1. A bond is a long-term debt of a government or corporation. When you own a bond, you receive a fixed interest payment each year until the bond matures. This payment

is known as the coupon. At maturity the bond's face value is repaid. In the United States most bonds have a face value of $1,000.

2. Bonds are valued by discounting the coupon payments and the final repayment by the rate of interest on comparable bonds. Bond prices are subject to interest rate risk, rising when market interest rates fall and falling when market rates rise. You may also start with the bond price and ask what interest rate the bond offers. This interest rate is known as the yield to maturity, the rate that equates the present value of bond payments to the bond price.

3. Long-term and short-term bond yields usually are different. The differences are commonly plotted on a graph called the yield curve. Investors also demand higher promised yields if there is a high probability that the borrower will run into trouble and default.

4. Firms that wish to raise new capital may either borrow money or bring new "partners" into the business by selling shares of common stock. Unlike the fixed interest payments that the firm promises to bondholders, the dividends that are paid to stockholders depend on the fortunes of the firm. That's why a company's common stock is riskier than its debt.

5. Large companies usually arrange for their stocks to be traded on a stock exchange.

6. Stockholders generally expect to receive (a) cash dividends and (b) capital gains or losses. The rate of return that they expect over the next year is defined as the expected dividend per share DIV_1 plus the expected increase in price $P_1 - P_0$, all divided by the price at the start of the year P_0:

$$\text{Expected return} = r = \frac{DIV_1 + P_1 - P_0}{P_0}$$

The return that investors expect on any one stock is also the return that they demand on all stocks subject to the same degree of risk.

7. The present value of a share is equal to the stream of expected dividends per share up to some horizon date plus the expected price at this date, all discounted at the return that investors require. If the horizon date is far away, we simply say that stock price equals the present value of all future dividends per share.

8. If dividends are expected to grow forever at a constant rate g, then the expected return on the stock is equal to the dividend yield (DIV_1/P_0) plus the expected rate of dividend growth. The value of the stock is equal to $P_0 = DIV_1/(r - g)$.

9. You can think of a share's value as the sum of two parts—the value of the assets in place and the value of the future opportunities for the firm to invest in high-return projects. The price-earnings (P/E) ratio reflects the market's assessment of the firm's growth opportunities. Firms with no growth opportunities should have a P/E ratio that is just the reciprocal of the return that investors demand, r. As growth opportunities become more important, the price-earnings ratio increases and the earnings-price ratio falls below r.

Key Terms

bond	current yield	common stock
coupon	yield to maturity	secondary market
face value, par value,	rate of return	dividend
maturity value	yield curve	price-earnings (P/E)
coupon rate	default premium	multiple

book value	constant-growth dividend	present value of growth
liquidation value	discount model	opportunities (PVGO)
market-value balance sheet	payout ratio	sustainable growth rate
dividend discount model	plowback ratio	

Problems

1. **Bond Yields.** A 30-year Treasury bond is issued with par value of $1,000, paying interest of $80 per year. If market yields increase shortly after the T-bond is issued, what happens to the bond's:

   a. coupon rate
   b. price
   c. yield to maturity
   d. current yield

2. **Bond Yields.** If a bond with par value of $1,000 and a coupon rate of 8 percent is selling at a price of $970, is the bond's yield to maturity more or less than 8 percent? What about the current yield?

3. **Bond Yields.** A bond with par value $1,000 has a current yield of 7.5 percent and a coupon rate of 8 percent. What is the bond's price?

4. **Coupon Rate.** General Matter's outstanding bond issue has a coupon rate of 10 percent and a current yield of 9.6 percent, and it sells at a yield to maturity of 9.25 percent. The firm wishes to issue additional bonds to the public at par value. What coupon rate must the new bonds offer in order to sell at par?

5. **Bond Prices and Returns.** One bond has a coupon rate of 8 percent, another a coupon rate of 12 percent. Both bonds have 10-year maturities and sell at a yield to maturity of 10 percent. If their yields to maturity next year are still 10 percent, what is the rate of return on each bond? Does the higher coupon bond give a higher rate of return?

6. **Consol Bonds.** Perpetual Life Corp. has issued consol bonds with coupon payments of $80. (Consols pay interest forever, and never mature. They are perpetuities.) If the required rate of return on these bonds at the time they were issued was 8 percent, at what price were they sold to the public? If the required return today is 12 percent, at what price do the consols sell?

7. **Bond Pricing.** A 6-year Circular File bond pays interest of $80 annually and sells for $950. What is its coupon rate, current yield, and yield to maturity?

8. **Bond Pricing.** If Circular File (see question 7) wants to issue a new 6-year bond at face value, what coupon rate must the bond offer?

9. **Bond Pricing.** A General Motors bond carries a coupon rate of 8 percent, has 9 years until maturity, and sells at a yield to maturity of 9 percent.

   a. What interest payments do bondholders receive each year?
   b. At what price does the bond sell? (Assume annual interest payments.)
   c. What will happen to the bond price if the yield to maturity falls to 7 percent?

10. **Bond Yields.** An AT&T bond has 10 years until maturity, a coupon rate of 8 percent, and sells for $1,050.

    a. What is the current yield on the bond?
    b. What is the yield to maturity?

11. **Bond Returns.**

    a. If the AT&T bond in problem 10 has a yield to maturity of 8 percent 1 year from now, what will its price be?

b. What will be the rate of return on the bond?

c. If the inflation rate during the year is 3 percent, what is the real rate of return on the bond?

12. **Bond Pricing.** Large Industries bonds sell for $1,065.15. The bond life is 9 years, and the yield to maturity is 7 percent. What must be the coupon rate on the bonds?

13. **Bond Prices and Yields.**

a. Several years ago, Castles in the Sand, Inc., issued bonds at face value at a yield to maturity of 8 percent. Now, with 8 years left until the maturity of the bonds, the company has run into hard times and the yield to maturity on the bonds has increased to 14 percent. What has happened to the price of the bond?

b. Suppose that investors believe that Castles can make good on the promised coupon payments, but that the company will go bankrupt when the bond matures and the principal comes due. The expectation is that investors will receive only 80 percent of face value at maturity. If they buy the bond today, what yield to maturity do they expect to receive?

 14. **Interest Rate Risk.** Consider three bonds with 8 percent coupon rates, all selling at face value. The short-term bond has a maturity of 4 years, the intermediate-term bond has maturity 8 years, and the long-term bond has maturity 30 years.

a. What will happen to the price of each bond if their yields increase to 9 percent?

b. What will happen to the price of each bond if their yields decrease to 7 percent?

c. What do you conclude about the relationship between time to maturity and the sensitivity of bond prices to interest rates?

15. **Bond Returns.** You buy an 8 percent coupon, 10-year maturity bond for $980. A year later, the bond price is $1,050.

a. What is the new yield to maturity on the bond?

b. What is your rate of return over the year?

16. **Bond Returns.** You buy an 8 percent coupon, 10-year maturity bond when its yield to maturity is 9 percent. A year later, the yield to maturity is 10 percent. What is your rate of return over the year?

17. **Bond Risk.** A bond's credit rating provides a guide to its risk. Long-term bonds rated Aa currently offer yields to maturity of 8.5 percent. A-rated bonds sell at yields of 8.8 percent. If a 10-year bond with a coupon rate of 8 percent is downgraded by Moody's from Aa to A rating, what is the likely effect on the bond price?

18. **Dividend Yield.** Favored stock will pay a dividend this year of $2.40 per share. Its dividend yield is 8 percent. At what price is the stock selling?

19. **Rate of Return.** Steady As She Goes, Inc., will pay a year-end dividend of $2.50 per share. Investors expect the dividend to grow at a rate of 4 percent indefinitely.

a. If the stock currently sells for $25 per share, what is the expected rate of return on the stock?

b. If the expected rate of return on the stock is 16.5 percent, what is the stock price?

20. **Dividend Discount Model.** How can we say that price equals the present value of all future dividends when many actual investors may be seeking capital gains and planning to hold their shares for only a year or two? Explain.

 21. **Stock Values.** Integrated Potato Chips paid a $1 per share dividend *yesterday*. You expect the dividend to grow steadily at a rate of 4 percent per year.

a. What is the expected dividend in each of the next 3 years?

b. If the discount rate for the stock is 12 percent, at what price will the stock sell?

   c. What is the expected stock price 3 years from now?

   d. If you buy the stock and plan to hold it for 3 years, what payments will you receive? What is the present value of those payments? Compare your answer to (b).

22. **Dividend Growth.** Grandiose Growth has a dividend growth rate of 20 percent. The discount rate is 10 percent. The end-of-year dividend will be $2 per share.

   a. What is the present value of the dividend to be paid in Year 1? Year 2? Year 3?

   b. Could anyone rationally expect this growth rate to continue indefinitely?

23. **Constant-Growth Model.** Gentleman Gym just paid its annual dividend of $2 per share, and it is widely expected that the dividend will increase by 5 percent per year indefinitely.

   a. What price should the stock sell at? The discount rate is 15 percent.

   b. How would your answer change if the discount rate were only 12 percent? Why does the answer change?

24. **Constant-Growth Model.** Arts and Crafts, Inc., will pay a dividend of $5 per share in 1 year. It sells at $50 a share, and firms in the same industry provide an expected rate of return of 14 percent. What must be the expected growth rate of the company's dividends?

25. **Preferred Stock Valuation.** Unlike common stocks, preferred stocks pay a fixed dividend. Suppose a share of preferred stock pays a fixed dividend of $4 a year forever. If it sells for $80, what must be the discount rate?

26. **Constant-Growth Model.** Eastern Electric currently pays a dividend of about $1.64 per share and sells for $27 a share.

   a. If investors believe the growth rate of dividends is 3 percent per year, what rate of return do they expect to earn on the stock?

   b. If investors' required rate of return is 10 percent, what must be the growth rate they expect of the firm?

   c. If the sustainable growth rate is 5 percent, and the plowback ratio is .4, what must be the rate of return earned by the firm on its new investments?

27. **Constant-Growth Model.** You believe that the Non-stick Gum Factory will pay a dividend of $2 on its common stock next year. Thereafter, you expect dividends to grow at a rate of 6 percent a year in perpetuity. If you require a return of 12 percent on your investment, how much should you be prepared to pay for the stock?

28. **Negative Growth.** Horse and Buggy Inc. is in a declining industry. Sales, earnings, and dividends are all shrinking at a rate of 10 percent per year.

   a. If $r = 15$ percent and $DIV_1 = \$3$, what is the value of a share?

   b. What price do you forecast for the stock next year?

   c. What is the expected rate of return on the stock?

   d. Can you distinguish between "bad stocks" and "bad companies"? Does the fact that the industry is declining mean that the stock is a bad buy?

29. **Nonconstant Growth.** You expect a share of stock to pay dividends of $1.00, $1.25, and $1.50 in each of the next 3 years. You believe the stock will sell for $20 at the end of the third year.

   a. What is the stock price if the discount rate for the stock is 10 percent?

   b. What is the dividend yield?

30. **Sustainable Growth.** Computer Corp. reinvests 60 percent of its earnings in the firm. The stock sells for $50, and the next dividend will be $2.50 per share. The discount rate is 15 percent. What is the rate of return on the company's reinvested funds?

31. **P/E Ratios.** No-Growth Industries pays out all of its earnings as dividends. It will pay its next $4 per share dividend in a year. The discount rate is 12 percent.

    a. What is the price-earnings ratio of the company?
    b. What would the P/E ratio be if the discount rate were 10 percent?

32. **Constant-Growth Model.** A stock sells for $40. The next dividend will be $4 per share. If the rate of return earned on reinvested funds is 15 percent and the company reinvests 40 percent of earnings in the firm, what must be the discount rate?

33. **Stock Valuation.** Start-up Industries is a new firm which has raised $100 million by selling shares of stock. Management plans to earn a 24 percent rate of return on equity, which is more than the 15 percent rate of return available on comparable-risk investments. Half of all earnings will be reinvested in the firm.

    a. What will be Start-up's ratio of market value to book value?
    b. How would that ratio change if the firm can earn only a 10 percent rate of return on its investments?

34. **Growth Opportunities.** Stormy Weather has no attractive investment opportunities. Its return on equity equals the discount rate, which is 10 percent. Its expected earnings this year are $3 per share. Find the stock price, P/E ratio, and growth rate of dividends for plowback ratios of

    a. zero
    b. .40
    c. .80

35. **Growth Opportunities.** Trend-line Inc. has been growing at a rate of 6 percent per year and is expected to continue to do so indefinitely. The next dividend is expected to be $5 per share.

    a. If the market expects a 10 percent rate of return on Trend-line, at what price must it be selling?
    b. If Trend-line's earnings per share will be $8, what part of Trend-line's value is due to assets in place, and what part to growth opportunities?

36. **P/E Ratios.** Castles in the Sand generates a rate of return of 20 percent on its investments and maintains a plowback ratio of .30. Its earnings this year will be $2 per share. Investors expect a 12 percent rate of return on the stock.

    a. Find the price and P/E ratio of the firm.
    b. What happens to the P/E ratio if the plowback ratio is reduced to .20? Why?
    c. Show that if plowback equals zero, the earnings-price ratio E/P falls to the expected rate of return on the stock.

37. **Constant-Growth Model.** Metatrend's stock will generate earnings of $5 per share this year. The discount rate for the stock is 15 percent and the rate of return on reinvested earnings also is 15 percent.

    a. Find both the growth rate of dividends and the price of the stock if the company reinvests the following fraction of its earnings in the firm: (i) 0 percent; (ii) 40 percent; (iii) 60 percent.
    b. Redo part (a) now assuming that the rate of return on reinvested earnings is 20 percent. What is the present value of growth opportunities for each reinvestment rate?
    c. Considering your answers to parts (a) and (b), can you briefly state the difference between companies experiencing growth versus companies with growth opportunities?

38. **Nonconstant Growth.** Better Mousetraps has come out with an improved product, and the world is beating a path to its door. As a result, the firm projects growth of 20 percent per year for 4 years. By then, other firms will have copycat technology, competition will drive down profit margins, and the sustainable growth rate will fall to 5 percent. The most recent annual dividend was $DIV_0 = \$1.00$ per share.

a. What are the expected values of DIV_1, DIV_2, DIV_3, and DIV_4?

b. What is the expected stock price 4 years from now? The discount rate is 10 percent.

c. What is the stock price today?

d. Find the dividend yield, DIV_1/P_0.

e. What will next year's stock price, P_1, be?

f. What is the expected rate of return to an investor who buys the stock now and sells it in 1 year?

39. **Nonconstant Growth.** A company will pay a $1 per share dividend in 1 year. The dividend in 2 years will be $2 per share, and it is expected that dividends will grow at 5 percent per year thereafter. The expected rate of return on the stock is 12 percent.

a. What is the current price of the stock?

b. What is the expected price of the stock in a year?

c. Show that the expected return, 12 percent, equals dividend yield plus capital appreciation.

40. **Nonconstant Growth.** Phoenix Industries has pulled off a miraculous recovery. Four years ago it was near bankruptcy. Today, it announced a $1 per share dividend to be paid a year from now, the first dividend since the crisis. Analysts expect dividends to increase by $1 a year for another 2 years. After the third year (in which dividends are $3 per share) dividend growth is expected to settle down to a more moderate long-term growth rate of 6 percent. If the firm's investors expect to earn a return of 14 percent on this stock, what must be its price?

41. **Nonconstant Growth.** Compost Science, Inc. (CSI), is in the business of converting Boston's sewage sludge into fertilizer. The business is not in itself very profitable. However, to induce CSI to remain in business, the Metropolitan District Commission (MDC) has agreed to pay whatever amount is necessary to yield CSI a 10 percent return on investment. At the end of the year, CSI is expected to pay a $4 dividend. It has been reinvesting 40 percent of earnings and growing at 4 percent a year.

a. Suppose CSI continues on this growth trend. What is the expected rate of return from purchasing the stock at $100?

b. What part of the $100 price is attributable to the present value of growth opportunities?

c. Now the MDC announces a plan for CSI to treat Cambridge sewage. CSI's plant will therefore be expanded gradually over 5 years. This means that CSI will have to reinvest 80 percent of its earnings for 5 years. Starting in Year 6, however, it will again be able to pay out 60 percent of earnings. What will be CSI's stock price once this announcement is made and its consequences for CSI are known?

Solutions to Self-Test Questions

4.1 The coupon is 9 percent of $1,000, or $90 a year. First value the 6-year annuity of coupons:

$$PV = \$90 \times (\text{6-year annuity factor})$$

$$= \$90 \times \left[\frac{1}{.12} - \frac{1}{.12(1.12^6)} \right]$$

$$= \$90 \times 4.11 = \$370.03$$

Then value the final payment and add up:

$$PV = \frac{\$1,000}{(1.12)^6} = \$506.63$$

$$PV \text{ of bond} = \$370.03 + \$506.63 = \$876.66$$

4.2 The yield to maturity is about 8 percent, because the present value of the bond's cash returns is $1,199 when discounted at 8 percent:

$$PV = PV \text{ (coupons)} + PV \text{ (final payment)}$$

$$= (\text{coupon} \times \text{annuity factor}) + (\text{face value} \times \text{discount factor})$$

$$= \$140 \times \left[\frac{1}{.08} - \frac{1}{.08(1.08^4)} \right] + \$1,000 \times \frac{1}{1.08^4}$$

$$= \$463.70 + \$735.03 = \$1,199$$

4.3 Calculate PV with a discount rate of $6\frac{1}{8}$ percent:

$$PV = \$61.25 \times \left[\frac{1}{.06125} - \frac{1}{.06125(1.06125^4)} \right] + \$1,000 \times \frac{1}{1.06125^4}$$

$$= \$211.63 + \$788.37 = \$1,000$$

4.4 You'll earn 6.6 percent. To show this, calculate the value of the bond 1 year hence, when maturity is 2 years:

$$PV = \$61.25 \times \left[\frac{1}{.066} - \frac{1}{.066(1.066^2)} \right] + \$1,000 \times \frac{1}{1.066^2}$$

$$= \$111.36 + \$880.00 = \$991.36$$

Your total return is the coupon, $61.25, plus a gain of $991.36 − $987.44 = $3.92, for a total of $65.17. The rate of return is $65.17/$987.44 = .066, exactly 6.6 percent.

4.5 The 4-year bond price falls from $1,000 to $821.56. You can confirm this on your calculator using the following inputs: $n = 4$; PMT = 61.25; FV = 1,000; $i = 12$; compute PV. The 30-year bond price falls from $1,000 to $526.76. You can confirm this on your calculator using the following inputs: $n = 30$; PMT = 61.25; FV = 1,000; $i = 12$; compute PV.

4.6 Current yield = $61.25/$983.76 = .062, or 6.2 percent. The current yield is lower than the 6.6 percent interest rate and overall return. Current yield need not always be less than yield to maturity. For bonds selling above face value, yield to maturity will be less than current yield, since yield to maturity accounts for the built-in price decline of the bond, which is bought for more than face value and eventually will be redeemed for face value.

4.7 Dow Jones's high and low prices over the past 52 weeks have been $41\frac{7}{8}$ and $34\frac{1}{8}$ per share. Its annual dividend was $.96 per share and its dividend yield (annual dividend as a percentage of stock price) 2.3 percent. The ratio of stock price to earnings per share, the P/E ratio, is 22. Trading volume was 165,500 shares. The highest price at which the shares traded during the day was $41\frac{1}{4}$, the lowest price was $40\frac{1}{4}$, and the closing price was $40\frac{7}{8}$, which was $1/4 lower than the previous day's closing price.

4.8 IBM's forecast future profitability has fallen. Thus the value of future investment opportunities has fallen relative to the value of assets in place. This happens in all growth industries sooner or later, as competition increases and profitable new investment opportunities shrink.

4.9
$$P_0 = \frac{DIV_1 + P_1}{1 + r} = \frac{\$5 + \$105}{1.10} = \$100$$

4.10 Since dividends and share price grow at 5 percent,

$$DIV_2 = \$5 \times 1.05 = \$5.25, \quad DIV_3 = \$5 \times 1.05^2 = \$5.51$$

$$P_3 = \$100 \times 1.05^3 = \$115.76$$

$$P_0 = \frac{DIV_1}{1+r} + \frac{DIV_2}{(1+r)^2} + \frac{DIV_3 + P_3}{(1+r)^3}$$

$$= \frac{\$5.00}{1.10} + \frac{\$5.25}{1.10^2} + \frac{\$5.51 + \$115.76}{1.10^3} = \$100$$

4.11

$$P_0 = \frac{DIV}{r} = \frac{\$25}{.20} = \$125$$

4.12 The two firms have equal risk, so we can use the data for Androscoggin to find the expected return on either stock:

$$r = \frac{DIV_1}{P_0} + g = \frac{\$5}{\$100} + .05 = .10, \text{ or } 10\%$$

4.13 We've already calculated the present value of dividends through Year 3 as $2.98. We can also forecast stock price in Year 4 as

$$P_4 = \frac{\$1.73 \times 1.05}{.10 - .05} = \$36.33$$

$$P_0 = PV(\text{dividends through Year 3}) + PV(DIV_4) + PV(P_4)$$

$$= \$2.98 + \frac{\$1.73}{1.10^4} + \frac{\$36.33}{1.10^4}$$

$$= \$2.98 + \$1.18 + \$24.81 = \$28.97$$

4.14 a. The sustainable growth rate is

$$g = \text{return on equity} \times \text{plowback ratio}$$

$$= 10\% \times .40 = 4\%$$

b. First value the company. At a 60 percent payout ratio, $DIV_1 = \$3.00$ as before. Using the constant-growth model,

$$P_0 = \frac{\$3}{.12 - .04} = \$37.50$$

which is $4.17 per share less than the company's no-growth value of $41.67. In this example Blue Skies is throwing away $4.17 of potential value by investing in projects with unattractive rates of return.

c. Sure. A raider could take over the company and generate a profit of $4.17 per share just by halting all investments offering less than the 12 percent rate of return demanded by investors. This assumes the raider could buy the shares for $37.50.

Minicase

Terence Breezeway, the CEO of Prairie Home Stores, wondered what retirement would be like. It was almost 20 years to the day since his uncle Jacob Breezeway, Prairie Home's founder, had asked him to take responsibility for managing the company. Now it was time to spend more time riding and fishing on the old Lazy Beta Ranch.

Under Mr. Breezeway's leadership Prairie Home had grown slowly but steadily and was solidly profitable. (Table 4.6 shows earnings, dividends, and book asset values for the last 5 years.) Most of the company's supermarkets had been modernized and its brand name was well-known.

Mr. Breezeway was proud of this record, although he wished that Prairie Home could have grown more rapidly. He had passed up several opportunities to build new stores in adjacent counties. Prairie Home was still just a family company. Its common stock was distributed among 15 grandchildren and nephews of Jacob Breezeway, most of whom had come to depend on generous regular dividends. The commitment to high dividend payout[1] had reduced the earnings available for reinvestment and thereby constrained growth.

Mr. Breezeway believed the time had come to take Prairie Home public. Once its shares were traded in the

public market, the Breezeway descendants who needed (or just wanted) more cash to spend could sell off part of their holdings. Others with more interest in the business could hold on to their shares and be rewarded by higher future earnings and stock prices.

But if Prairie Home did go public, what should its shares sell for? Mr. Breezeway worried that shares would be sold, either by Breezeway family members or by the company itself, at too low a price. One relative was about to accept a private offer for $200, the current book value per share, but Mr. Breezeway had intervened and convinced the would-be seller to wait.

Prairie Home's value did not just depend on its current book value or earnings, but on its future prospects, which were good. One financial projection (shown in the top panel of Table 4.7) called for growth in earnings of over 100 percent by 2006. Unfortunately this plan would require reinvestment of all of Prairie Home's earnings from 2001 to 2005. After that the company could resume its normal dividend payout and growth rate. Mr. Breezeway believed this plan was feasible.

He was determined to step aside for the next generation of top management. But before retiring he had to decide whether to recommend that Prairie Home Stores "go

TABLE 4.6

Financial data for Prairie Home Stores, 1996–2000 (figures in millions)

	1996	1997	1998	1999	2000
Book value, start of year	$62.7	66.1	69.0	73.9	76.5
Earnings	$9.7	9.5	11.8	11.0	11.2
Dividends	$6.3	6.6	6.9	7.4	7.7
Retained earnings	$3.4	2.9	4.9	2.6	3.5
Book value, end of year	$66.1	69.0	73.9	76.5	80.0

Notes:
  1. Prairie Home Stores has 400,000 common shares.
  2. The company's policy is to pay cash dividends equal to 10 percent of start-of-year book value.

TABLE 4.7

Financial projections for Prairie Home Stores, 2001–2006 (figures in millions)

	2001	2002	2003	2004	2005	2006
Rapid-Growth Scenario						
Book value, start of year	80	92	105.8	121.7	139.9	146.9
Earnings	12	13.8	15.9	18.3	21.0	22.0
Dividends	0	0	0	0	14	14.7
Retained earnings	12	13.8	15.9	18.3	7.0	7.4
Book value, end of year	92	105.8	121.7	140.0	146.9	154.3
Constant-Growth Scenario						
Book value, start of year	80	84	88.2	92.6	97.2	102.1
Earnings	12	12.6	13.2	13.9	14.6	15.3
Dividends	8	8.4	8.8	9.3	9.7	10.2
Retained earnings	4	4.2	4.4	4.6	4.9	5.1
Book value, end of year	84	88.2	92.6	97.2	102.1	107.2

Notes:

1. Both panels assume earnings equal to 15 percent of start-of-year book value. This profitability rate is constant.
2. The top panel assumes all earnings are reinvested from 2001 to 2004. In 2005 and later years, two-thirds of earnings are paid out as dividends and one-third reinvested.
3. The bottom panel assumes two-thirds of earnings are paid out as dividends in all years.
4. Columns may not add up because of rounding.

public"—and before that decision he had to know what the company was worth.

The next morning he rode thoughtfully to work. He left his horse at the south corral and ambled down the dusty street to Mike Gordon's Saloon, where Francine Firewater, the company's CFO, was having her usual steak-and-beans breakfast. He asked Ms. Firewater to prepare a formal report to Prairie Home stockholders, valuing the company on the assumption that its shares were publicly traded.

Ms. Firewater asked two questions immediately. First, what should she assume about investment and growth? Mr. Breezeway suggested two valuations, one assuming more rapid expansion (as in the top panel of Table 4.7)

and another just projecting past growth (as in the bottom panel of Table 4.7).

Second, what rate of return should she use? Mr. Breezeway said that 15 percent, Prairie Home's usual return on book equity, sounded right to him, but he referred her to an article in the *Journal of Finance* indicating that investors in rural supermarket chains, with risks similar to Prairie Home Stores, expected to earn about 11 percent on average.

[1]The company traditionally paid out cash dividends equal to 10 percent of start-of-period book value. See Table 4.6.

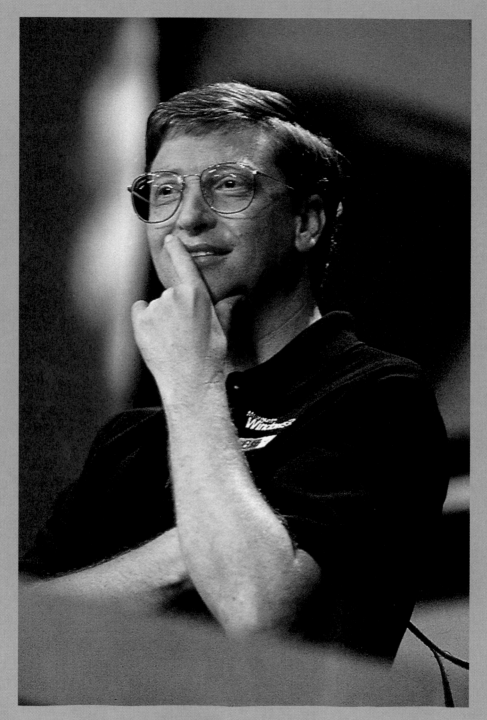

A positive NPV always inspires confidence
This man is not worrying about the payback period or the book rate of return.
© *Jim Levitt/Impact Visuals*

Net Present Value and Other Investment Criteria

Chapter 5

T he investment decision, also known as *capital budgeting,* is central to the success of the company. We have already seen that capital investments sometimes absorb substantial amounts of cash; they also have very long-term consequences. The assets you buy today may determine the business you are in many years hence.

For some investment projects "substantial" is an understatement. Consider the following examples:

▶ Construction of the Channel Tunnel linking England and France cost about $15 billion from 1986 to 1994.

▶ The cost of bringing one new prescription drug to market was estimated to be at least $300 million in 1996.

▶ The development cost of Ford's "world car," the Mondeo, was about $6 billion.

▶ Production and merchandising costs for three new *Star Wars* movies will amount to about $3 billion.

▶ The future development cost of a super-jumbo jet airliner, seating 600 to 800 passengers, has been estimated at over $10 billion.

▶ TAPS, The Alaska Pipeline System, which brings crude oil from Prudhoe Bay to Valdez on the southern coast of Alaska, cost $9 billion.

Notice from these examples of big capital projects that many projects require heavy investment in intangible assets. The costs of drug development are almost all research and testing, for example, and much of the development of Ford's Mondeo went into design and testing. Any expenditure made in the hope of generating more cash later can be called a *capital investment project*, regardless of whether the cash outlay goes to tangible or intangible assets.

A company's shareholders prefer to be rich rather than poor. Therefore, they want the firm to invest in every project that is worth more than it costs. The difference between a project's value and its cost is termed the *net present value.* Companies can best help their shareholders by investing in projects with a *positive* net present value.

We start this chapter by showing how to calculate the net present value of a simple investment project. We also examine other criteria that companies sometimes consider when evaluating investments, such as the project's payback period or book rate of return. We will see that these are little better than rules of thumb. Although there is a place for rules of thumb in this world, an engineer needs something more accurate when designing a 100-story building, and a financial manager needs more than a rule of thumb when making a substantial capital investment decision.

Instead of calculating a project's net present value, companies sometimes compare the expected rate of return from investing in a project with the return that shareholders could earn on equivalent-risk investments in the capital market. Companies accept only those projects that provide a higher return than shareholders could earn for themselves. This rate of return rule generally gives the same answers as the net present value rule but, as we shall see, it has some pitfalls.

We then turn to more complex issues such as project interactions. These occur when a company is obliged to *choose* between two or more competing proposals; if it accepts one proposal, it cannot take the other. For example, a company may need to choose between buying an expensive, durable machine or a cheap and short-lived one. We will show how the net present value criterion can be used to make such choices.

Sometimes the firm may be forced to make choices because it does not have enough money to take on every project that it would like. We will explain how to maximize shareholder wealth when capital is rationed. It turns out that the solution is to pick the projects that have the highest net present value per dollar invested. This measure is known as the *profitability index*.

After studying this chapter you should be able to

▶ Calculate the net present value of an investment.

▶ Calculate the internal rate of return of a project and know what to look out for when using the internal rate of return rule.

▶ Explain why the payback rule and book rate of return rule *don't* always make shareholders better off.

▶ Use the net present value rule to analyze three common problems that involve competing projects: (a) when to postpone an investment expenditure, (b) how to choose between projects with equal lives, and (c) when to replace equipment.

▶ Calculate the profitability index and use it to choose between projects when funds are limited.

5.1 Net Present Value

In Chapter 3 you learned how to discount future cash payments to find their present value. We now apply these ideas to evaluate a simple investment proposal.

Suppose that you are in the real estate business. You are considering construction of an office block. The land would cost $50,000 and construction would cost a further $300,000. You foresee a shortage of office space and predict that a year from now you will be able to sell the building for $400,000. Thus you would be investing $350,000 now in the expectation of realizing $400,000 at the end of the year. You should go ahead if the present value of the $400,000 payoff is greater than the investment of $350,000.

Assume for the moment that the $400,000 payoff is a sure thing. The office building is not the only way to obtain $400,000 a year from now. You could invest in a 1-year U.S. government loan. Suppose the loan offers interest of 7 percent. How much would you have to invest in it in order to receive $400,000 at the end of the year? That's easy: you would have to invest

$$\$400,000 \times \frac{1}{1.07} = \$400,000 \times .935 = \$373,832$$

Therefore, at an interest rate of 7 percent, the present value of $400,000 is $373,832.

Let's assume that as soon as you have purchased the land and laid out the money for construction, you decide to cash in on your project. How much could you sell it for? Since the property will be worth $400,000 in a year, investors would be willing to pay at most $373,832 for it now. That's all it would cost them to get the same $400,000 payoff by investing in a government security. Of course you could always sell your property for less, but why sell for less than the market will bear?

The $373,832 present value is the only price that satisfies both buyer and seller. In general, the present value is the only feasible price, and the present value of the property is also its *market price* or *market value*.

To calculate present value, we discounted the expected future payoff by the rate of return offered by comparable investment alternatives. The discount rate—7 percent in our example—is often known as the **opportunity cost of capital**. It is called the opportunity cost because it is the return that is being given up by investing in the project.

opportunity cost of capital: Expected rate of return given up by investing in a project.

net present value (NPV): Present value of cash flows minus initial investment.

The building is worth $373,832, but this does not mean that you are $373,832 better off. You committed $350,000, and therefore your **net present value (NPV)** is $23,832. Net present value is found by subtracting the required initial investment from the present value of the project cash flows:

$$\textbf{NPV} = \textbf{PV} - \textbf{required investment}$$
$$= \$373,832 - \$350,000 = \$23,832$$

In other words, your office development is worth more than it costs—it makes a *net* contribution to value.

> The net present value *rule* states that managers increase shareholders' wealth by accepting all projects that are worth more than they cost. Therefore, they should accept all projects with a positive net present value.

A Comment on Risk and Present Value

In our discussion of the office development we assumed we knew the value of the completed project. Of course, you will never be *certain* about the future values of office buildings. The $400,000 represents the best *forecast*, but it is not a sure thing.

Therefore, our initial conclusion about how much investors would pay for the building is wrong. Since they could achieve $400,000 risklessly by investing in $373,832 worth of U.S. government loans, they would not buy your building for that amount. You would have to cut your asking price to attract investors' interest.

Here we can invoke a basic financial principle:

> A risky dollar is worth less than a safe one.

Most investors avoid risk when they can do so without sacrificing return. However, the concepts of present value and the opportunity cost of capital still apply to risky investments. It is still proper to discount the payoff by the rate of return offered by a comparable investment. But we have to think of *expected* payoffs and the *expected* rates of return on other investments.

Not all investments are equally risky. The office development is riskier than a government loan but is probably less risky than investing in a start-up biotech company. Suppose you believe the office development is as risky as an investment in the stock market and that you forecast a 12 percent rate of return for stock market investments.

Then 12 percent would be the appropriate opportunity cost of capital. That is what you are giving up by not investing in comparable securities. You can now recompute NPV:

$$PV = \$400,000 \times \frac{1}{1.12} = \$400,000 \times .893 = \$357,143$$
$$NPV = PV - \$350,000 = \$7,143$$

If other investors agree with your forecast of a \$400,000 payoff and with your assessment of a 12 percent opportunity cost of capital, then the property ought to be worth \$357,143 once construction is under way. If you tried to sell for more than that, there would be no takers, because the property would then offer a lower expected rate of return than the 12 percent available in the stock market. The office building still makes a net contribution to value, but it is much smaller than our earlier calculations indicated.

▶ Self-Test 5.1

What is the office development's NPV if construction costs increase to \$355,000? Assume the opportunity cost of capital is 12 percent. Is the development still a worthwhile investment? How high can development costs be before the project is no longer attractive? Now suppose that the opportunity cost of capital is 20 percent with construction costs of \$355,000. Why is the office development no longer an attractive investment?

Valuing Long-Lived Projects

The net present value rule works for projects of any length. For example, suppose that you have identified a possible tenant who would be prepared to rent your office block for 3 years at a fixed annual rent of \$16,000. You forecast that after you have collected the third year's rent the building could be sold for \$450,000. Thus the cash flow in the first year is $C_1 = \$16,000$, in the second year it is $C_2 = \$16,000$, and in the third year it is $C_3 = \$466,000$. For simplicity, we will again assume that these cash flows are certain and that the opportunity cost of capital is $r = 7$ percent.

Figure 5.1 shows a time line of these cash flows and their present values. To find the present values, we discount the future cash flows at the 7 percent opportunity cost of capital:

$$PV = \frac{C_1}{1 + r} + \frac{C_2}{(1 + r)^2} + \frac{C_3}{(1 + r)^3}$$
$$= \frac{\$16,000}{1.07} + \frac{\$16,000}{(1.07)^2} + \frac{\$466,000}{(1.07)^3} = \$409,323$$

The net present value of the revised project is NPV = \$409,323 − \$350,000 = \$59,323. Constructing the office block and renting it for 3 years makes a greater addition to your wealth than selling the office block at the end of the first year.

Of course, rather than subtracting the initial investment from the project's present value, you could calculate NPV directly, as in the following equation, where C_0 denotes the initial cash outflow required to build the office block. (Notice that C_0 is negative, reflecting the fact that it is a cash outflow.)

FIGURE 5.1

Cash flows and their present values for office block project. Final cash flow of $466,000 is the sum of the rental income in Year 3 plus the forecasted sales price for the building.

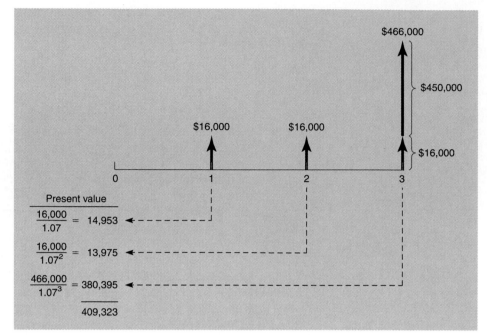

$$\text{NPV} = \quad C_0 \quad + \frac{C_1}{1 + r} + \frac{C_2}{(1 + r)^2} + \frac{C_3}{(1 + r)^3}$$

$$= -\$350,000 + \frac{\$16,000}{1.07} + \frac{\$16,000}{(1.07)^2} + \frac{\$466,000}{(1.07)^3} = \$59,323$$

Let's check that the owners of this project really are better off. Suppose you put up $350,000 of your own money, commit to build the office building, and sign a lease that will bring $16,000 a year for 3 years. Now you can cash in by selling the project to someone else.

Suppose you sell 1,000 shares in the project. Each share represents a claim to 1/1000 of the future cash flows. Since the cash flows are sure things, and the interest rate offered by other sure things is 7 percent, investors will value the shares for

$$\text{Price per share} = P = \frac{\$16}{1.07} + \frac{\$16}{(1.07)^2} + \frac{\$466}{(1.07)^3} = \$40.93$$

Thus you can sell the project to outside investors for 1,000 × $40.93 = $409,300, which, save for rounding, is exactly the present value we calculated earlier. Your net gain is

$$\text{Net gain} = \$409,300 - \$350,000 = \$59,300$$

which is the project's NPV. This equivalence should be no surprise, since the present value calculation is *designed* to calculate the value of future cash flows to investors in the capital markets.

Notice that in principle there could be a different opportunity cost of capital for each period's cash flow. In that case we would discount C_1 by r_1, the discount rate for 1-year cash flows; C_2 would be discounted by r_2; and so on. Here we assume that the cost of capital is the same regardless of the date of the cash flow. We do this for one reason only—simplicity. But we are in good company: with only rare exceptions firms decide on an appropriate discount rate and then use it to discount all project cash flows.

▶ **Example 5.1**   *Valuing a New Computer System*

Obsolete Technologies is considering purchase of a new computer system to help handle its warehouse inventories. The system costs $50,000, is expected to last 4 years, and should reduce the cost of managing inventories by $22,000 a year. The opportunity cost of capital is 10 percent. Should Obsolete go ahead?

Don't be put off by the fact that the computer system does not generate any sales. If the expected cost savings are realized, the company's cash flows will be $22,000 a year higher as a result of buying the computer. Thus we can say that the computer increases cash flows by $22,000 a year for each of 4 years. To calculate present value, you can discount each of these cash flows by 10 percent. However, it is smarter to recognize that the cash flows are level and therefore you can use the annuity formula to calculate the present value:

$$\text{PV} = \text{cash flow} \times \text{annuity factor} = \$22,000 \times \left[\frac{1}{.10} - \frac{1}{.10(1.10)^4}\right]$$
$$= \$22,000 \times 3.170 = \$69,740$$

The net present value is

$$\text{NPV} = -\$50,000 + \$69,740 = \$19,740$$

The project has a positive NPV of $19,740. Undertaking it would *increase* the value of the firm by that amount.

The first two steps in calculating NPVs—forecasting the cash flows and estimating the opportunity cost of capital—are tricky, and we will have a lot more to say about them in later chapters. But once you have assembled the data, the calculation of present value and net present value should be routine. Here are two more examples.

▶ **Example 5.2**   *Calculating Eurotunnel's NPV*

One of the world's largest commercial investment projects was construction of the Channel Tunnel by the Anglo-French company Eurotunnel. Here is a chance to put yourself in the shoes of Eurotunnel's financial manager and find out whether the project looked like a good deal for shareholders. The figures in the column headed *cash flow* in Table 5.1 are based on the forecasts of construction costs and revenues that the company provided to investors in 1986.

The Channel Tunnel project was not a safe investment. Indeed the prospectus to the Channel Tunnel share issue cautioned investors that the project "involves significant risk and should be regarded at this stage as speculative. If for any reason the Project is abandoned or Eurotunnel is unable to raise the necessary finance, it is likely that equity investors will lose some or all of their money."

To induce them to invest in the project, investors needed a higher prospective rate of return than they could get on safe government bonds. Suppose investors expected a return of 13 percent from investments in the capital market that had a degree of risk similar to that of the Channel Tunnel. That was what investors were giving up when they provided the capital for the tunnel. To find the project's NPV we therefore discount the cash flows in Table 5.1 at 13 percent.

TABLE 5.1

Forecast cash flows and present values in 1986 for the Channel Tunnel. The investment apparently had a small positive NPV of £251 million (figures in millions of pounds).

Year	Cash Flow	PV at 13 Percent
1986	−£457	−£457
1987	−476	−421
1988	−497	−389
1989	−522	−362
1990	−551	−338
1991	−584	−317
1992	−619	−297
1993	211	90
1994	489	184
1995	455	152
1996	502	148
1997	530	138
1998	544	126
1999	636	130
2000	594	107
2001	689	110
2002	729	103
2003	796	100
2004	859	95
2005	923	90
2006	983	86
2007	1,050	81
2008	1,113	76
2009	1,177	71
2010	17,781	946
Total		+£251
NPV = total = £251 million		

Note: Cash flow for 2010 includes the value in 2010 of forecast cash flows in all subsequent years.
Source: Eurotunnel Equity II Prospectus, October 1986. Used by permission. Some of these figures involve guesswork because the prospectus reported accumulated construction costs including interest expenses.

Since the tunnel was expected to take about 7 years to build, there are 7 years of negative cash flows in Table 5.1. To calculate NPV you just discount all the cash flows, positive and negative, at 13 percent and sum the results. Call 1986 Year 0, call 1987 Year 1, and so on. Then

$$\text{NPV} = C_0 + \frac{C_1}{1 + r} + \frac{C_2}{(1 + r)^2} + \cdots$$

$$= -£457 + \frac{-£476}{1.13} + \frac{-£497}{(1.13)^2} + \cdots = £251 \text{ million}$$

Net present value of the forecast cash flows is £251 million, making the tunnel a worthwhile project, though not by a wide margin, considering the planned investment of nearly £4 billion.

Of course, NPV calculations are only as good as the underlying cash-flow forecasts. The well-known Pentagon Law of Large Projects states that anything big takes longer and costs more than you're originally led to believe. As the law predicted, the tunnel proved much more expensive to build than anticipated in 1986, and the opening was delayed by more than a year. Revenues also have been below forecast, and Eurotunnel has not even generated enough profits to pay the interest on its debt. Thus with hindsight, the tunnel was a negative-NPV venture.

5.2 Other Investment Criteria

Use of the net present value rule as a criterion for accepting or rejecting investment projects will maximize the value of the firm's shares. However, other criteria are sometimes also considered by firms when evaluating investment opportunities. Some of these rules are liable to give wrong answers; others simply need to be used with care. In this section, we introduce three of these alternative investment criteria: internal rate of return, payback period, and book rate of return.

Internal Rate of Return

Instead of calculating a project's net present value, companies often prefer to ask whether the project's return is higher or lower than the opportunity cost of capital. For example, think back to the original proposal to build the office block. You planned to invest \$350,000 to get back a cash flow of $C_1 = \$400,000$ in 1 year. Therefore, you forecasted a profit on the venture of \$400,000 − \$350,000 = \$50,000, and a rate of return of

$$\text{Rate of return} = \frac{\text{profit}}{\text{investment}} = \frac{C_1 - \text{investment}}{\text{investment}} = \frac{\$400,000 - \$350,000}{\$350,000}$$

$$= .1429, \text{ or about } 14.3\%$$

The alternative of investing in a government loan would provide a return of only 7 percent. Thus the return on your office building is higher than the opportunity cost of capital.[1]

This suggests two rules for deciding whether to go ahead with an investment project:

1. *The NPV rule.* Invest in any project that has a positive NPV when its cash flows are discounted at the opportunity cost of capital.
2. *The rate of return rule.* Invest in any project offering a rate of return that is higher than the opportunity cost of capital.

Both rules set the same cutoff point. An investment that is on the knife edge with an NPV of zero will also have a rate of return that is just equal to the cost of capital.

Suppose that the rate of interest on Treasury bills is not 7 percent but 14.3 percent. Since your office project also offers a return of 14.3 percent, the rate of return rule suggests that there is now nothing to choose between taking the project and leaving your money in Treasury bills.

---

[1]Recall that we are assuming the profit on the office building is risk-free. Therefore, the opportunity cost of capital is the rate of return on other risk-free investments.

The NPV rule also tells you that if the interest rate is 14.3 percent, the project is evenly balanced with an NPV of zero:[2]

$$\text{NPV} = C_0 + \frac{C_1}{1+r} = -\$350,000 + \frac{\$400,000}{1.143} = 0$$

The project would make you neither richer nor poorer; it is worth what it costs. Thus the NPV rule and the rate of return rule both give the same decision on accepting the project.

A Closer Look at the Rate of Return Rule

We know that if the office project's cash flows are discounted at a rate of 7 percent the project has a net present value of $23,832. If they are discounted at a rate of 14.3 percent, it has an NPV of zero. In Figure 5.2 the project's NPV for a variety of discount rates is plotted. Notice two important things about Figure 5.2:

1. The project rate of return (in our example, 14.3 percent) is also the discount rate which would give the project a zero NPV. This gives us a useful definition: *the rate of return is the discount rate at which NPV equals zero.*[3]
2. If the opportunity cost of capital is less than the project rate of return, then the NPV of your project is positive. If the cost of capital is greater than the project rate of return, then NPV is negative. Thus the rate of return rule and the NPV rule are equivalent.

Calculating the Rate of Return for Long-Lived Projects

There is no ambiguity in calculating the rate of return for an investment that generates a single payoff after one period. Remember that C_0, the time 0 cash flow corre-

FIGURE 5.2

The value of the office project is lower when the discount rate is higher. The project has positive NPV if the discount rate is less than 14.3 percent.

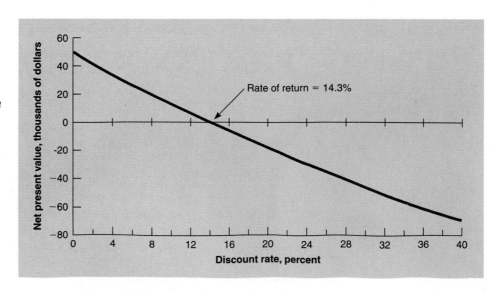

[2]Notice that the initial cash flow C_0 is negative. The *investment* in the project is therefore $-C_0 = -(-\$350,000)$, or $350,000.
[3]Check it for yourself. If NPV $= C_0 + C_1/(1+r) = 0$, then rate of return $= (C_1 + C_0)/-C_0 = r$.

sponding to the initial investment, is negative. Thus

$$\text{Rate of return} = \frac{\text{profit}}{\text{investment}} = \frac{C_1 - \text{investment}}{\text{investment}} = \frac{C_1 + C_0}{-C_0}$$

internal rate of return (IRR): Discount rate at which project NPV = 0.

But how do we calculate return when the project generates cash flows in several periods? Go back to the definition that we just introduced—*the project rate of return is also the discount rate which gives the project a zero NPV.* Managers usually refer to this figure as the project's **internal rate of return,** or **IRR.**[4] It is also known as the *discounted cash flow (DCF) rate of return.*

Let's calculate the IRR for the revised office project. If you rent out the office block for 3 years, the cash flows are as follows:

Year	0	1	2	3
Cash flows	−$350,000	+16,000	+16,000	+466,000

The IRR is the discount rate at which these cash flows would have zero NPV. Thus

$$\text{NPV} = -\$350,000 + \frac{\$16,000}{1 + \text{IRR}} + \frac{\$16,000}{(1 + \text{IRR})^2} + \frac{\$466,000}{(1 + \text{IRR})^3} = 0$$

There is no simple general method for solving this equation. You have to rely on a little trial and error. Let us arbitrarily try a zero discount rate. This gives an NPV of $148,000:

$$\text{NPV} = -\$350,000 + \frac{\$16,000}{1.0} + \frac{\$16,000}{(1.0)^2} + \frac{\$466,000}{(1.0)^3} = \$148,000$$

With a zero discount rate the NPV is positive. So the IRR must be greater than zero.

FIGURE 5.3

The internal rate of return is the discount rate for which NPV equals zero.

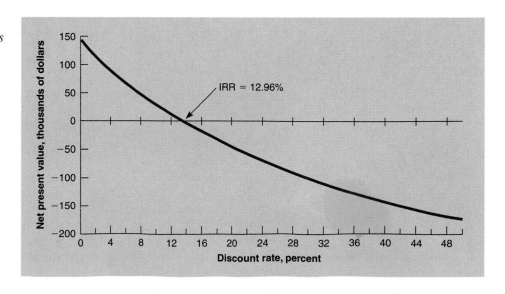

[4]In Chapter 4 you learned how to calculate the yield to maturity on a bond. A bond's yield to maturity is just its internal rate of return.

Using Financial Calculators to Find NPV and IRR

We saw in Chapter 3 that the formulas for the present and future values of level annuities and one-time cash flows are built into financial calculators. However, as the example of the office block illustrates, most investment projects entail multiple cash flows that cannot be expected to remain level over time. Fortunately, many calculators are equipped to handle problems involving a sequence of uneven cash flows. In general, the procedure is quite simple. You enter the cash flows one by one into the calculator, and then you press the IRR key to find the project's internal rate of return. The first cash flow you enter is interpreted as coming immediately, the next cash flow is interpreted as coming at the end of one period, and so on. We can illustrate using the office block as an example. To find the project IRR, you would use the following sequence of keystrokes:

Hewlett-Packard HP-10B		Sharpe EL-733A		Texas Instruments BA II Plus		
−350,000	CFj	−350,000	CFi		CF	
16,000	CFj	16,000	CFi		2nd	CLR Work
16,000	CFj	16,000	CFi	−350,000	ENTER	↓
466,000	CFj	466,000	CFi	16,000	ENTER	↓
				16,000	ENTER	↓
				466,000	ENTER	↓
	IRR/YR		IRR		IRR	
					CPT	

The calculator should display the value 12.96, the project's internal rate of return.

To calculate project NPV, the procedure is similar. You need to enter the discount rate in addition to the project cash flows, and then simply press the NPV key. Here is the specific sequence of keystrokes, assuming that the opportunity cost of capital is 7 percent:

Hewlett-Packard HP-10B		Sharpe EL-733A		Texas Instruments BA II Plus		
−350,000	CFj	−350,000	CFi		CF	
16,000	CFj	16,000	CFi		2nd	CLR Work
16,000	CFj	16,000	CFi	−350,000	ENTER	↓
466,000	CFj	466,000	CFi	16,000	ENTER	↓
7	I/YR	7	i	16,000	ENTER	↓
				466,000	ENTER	↓
	NPV		NPV		NPV	
				10	ENTER	
				↓	CPT	

The calculator should display the value 59,323, the project's NPV when the discount rate is 7 percent.

By the way, you can check the accuracy of our earlier calculations using your calculator. Enter 50 percent for the discount rate (press 50, then press i) and then press the NPV key to find that NPV = −194,148. Enter 12.96 (the project's IRR) as the discount rate and you will find that NPV is just about zero (it is not exactly zero, because we are rounding off the IRR to only two decimal places).

See box p. 158

The next step might be to try a discount rate of 50 percent. In this case NPV is −$194,000:

$$\text{NPV} = -\$350,000 + \frac{\$16,000}{1.50} + \frac{\$16,000}{(1.50)^2} + \frac{\$466,000}{(1.50)^3} = -\$194,000$$

NPV is now negative. So the IRR must lie somewhere between zero and 50 percent. In Figure 5.3 we have plotted the net present values for a range of discount rates. You can see that a discount rate of 12.96 percent gives an NPV of zero. Therefore, the IRR is 12.96 percent. You can always find the IRR by plotting a graph like Figure 5.3, but it is quicker and more accurate to let a computer or specially programmed financial calculator do the trial and error for you. The nearby box illustrates how to do so.

The rate of return rule tells you to accept a project if the rate of return exceeds the opportunity cost of capital. You can see from Figure 5.3 why this makes sense.

As long as the opportunity cost of capital is less than the project's 12.96 percent IRR, the project has a positive NPV. If the opportunity cost of capital is higher than the 12.96 percent IRR, NPV is negative. Therefore, when we compare the project IRR with the opportunity cost of capital, we are effectively asking whether the project has a positive NPV. This was true for our one-period office project. It is also true for our three-period office project.

> In fact the rate of return rule will give the same answer as the NPV rule *as long as the NPV of a project declines smoothly as the discount rate increases.*

The usual agreement between the net present value and internal rate of return rules should not be a surprise. Both are *discounted cash flow* methods of choosing between projects. Both are concerned with identifying those projects that make shareholders better off and both recognize that companies always have a choice: they can invest in a project or, if the project is not sufficiently attractive, they can give the money back to shareholders and let them invest it for themselves in the capital market.

▶ **Self-Test 5.2**

Suppose the cash flow in Year 3 is only $416,000. Redraw Figure 5.3. How would the IRR change?

A Word of Caution

Some people confuse the internal rate of return on a project with the opportunity cost of capital. Remember that the project IRR measures the profitability of the project. It is an *internal* rate of return in the sense that it depends only on the project's own cash flows. The opportunity cost of capital is the standard for deciding whether to accept the project. It is equal to the return offered by equivalent-risk investments in the capital market.

Payback

These days almost all large companies use discounted cash flow in some form, but sometimes they use it in combination with other theoretically inappropriate measures of performance. We next examine two of these measures, the payback period and the book rate of return.

We suspect that you have often heard conversations that go something like this: "A washing machine costs about $400. But we are currently spending $3 a week, or around $150 a year, at the laundromat. So the washing machine should pay for itself in less than 3 years." You have just encountered the payback rule.

payback period: Time until cash flows recover the initial investment of the project.

A project's **payback period** is the length of time before you recover your initial investment. For the washing machine the payback period was just under 3 years. The *payback rule* states that a project should be accepted if its payback period is less than a specified cutoff period. For example, if the cutoff period is 4 years, the washing machine makes the grade; if the cutoff is 2 years, it doesn't.

As a rough rule of thumb the payback rule may be adequate, but it is easy to see that it can lead to nonsensical decisions. For example, compare projects A and B. Project A has a 2-year payback and a large positive NPV. Project B also has a 2-year payback but a negative NPV. Project A is clearly superior, but the payback rule ranks both equally.

This is because payback does not consider any cash flows that arrive after the payback period. A firm that uses the payback criterion with a cutoff of two or more years would accept both A and B despite the fact that only A would increase shareholder wealth.

Cash Flows, Dollars

Project	C_0	C_1	C_2	C_3	Payback Period, Years	NPV at 10%
A	−2,000	+1,000	+1,000	+10,000	2	$7,249
B	−2,000	+1,000	+1,000	0	2	−264
C	−2,000	0	+2,000	0	2	−347

A second problem with payback is that it gives equal weight to all cash flows arriving *before* the cutoff period, despite the fact that the more distant flows are less valuable. For example, look at project C. It also has a payback period of 2 years but it has an even lower NPV than project B. Why? Because its cash flows arrive later within the payback period.

To use the payback rule a firm has to decide on an appropriate cutoff period. If it uses the same cutoff regardless of project life, it will tend to accept too many short-lived projects and reject too many long-lived ones. The payback rule will bias the firm against accepting long-term projects because cash flows that arrive after the payback period are ignored.

Earlier in the chapter we evaluated the Channel Tunnel project. Large construction projects of this kind inevitably have long payback periods. The cash flows that we presented in Table 5.1 implied a payback period of just over 14 years. But most firms that employ the payback rule use a much shorter cutoff period than this. If they used the payback rule mechanically, long-lived projects like the Channel Tunnel wouldn't have a chance.

The primary attraction of the payback criterion is its simplicity. But remember that the hard part of project evaluation is forecasting the cash flows, not doing the arithmetic. Today's spreadsheets make discounting a trivial exercise. Therefore, the payback rule saves you only the easy part of the analysis.[5]

We have had little good to say about payback. So why do many large companies continue to use it? Senior managers don't truly believe that all cash flows after the

---

[5]Sometimes managers calculate the *discounted payback period*. This is the number of periods before the present value of prospective cash flows equals or exceeds the initial investment. Therefore, this rule asks, "How long must the project last in order to offer a positive net present value?" This surmounts the objection that equal weight is given to all cash flows before the cutoff date. However, the discounted payback rule still takes no account of any cash flows after the cutoff date.

The discounted payback does offer one important advantage over the normal payback criterion. If a project meets a discounted payback cutoff, it must have a positive NPV, because the cash flows that accrue up to the discounted payback period are (by definition) just sufficient to provide a present value equal to the initial investment. Any cash flows that come after that date tip the balance and ensure positive NPV.

Despite this advantage, the discounted payback has little to recommend it. It still ignores all cash flows occurring after the arbitrary cutoff date and therefore will incorrectly reject some positive NPV opportunities. It is no easier to use than the NPV rule, because it requires determination of both project cash flows and an appropriate discount rate. The best that can be said about it is that it is a better criterion than the even more unsatisfactory ordinary payback rule.

payback period are irrelevant. It seems more likely (and more charitable to those managers) that payback survives because the deficiencies are relatively unimportant or because there are some offsetting benefits. Thus managers may point out that payback is the simplest way to *communicate* an idea of project desirability. Investment decisions require discussion and negotiation between people from all parts of the firm and it is important to have a measure that everyone can understand. Perhaps also managers favor quick payback projects even when they have lower NPVs, because they believe that quicker profits mean quicker promotion. That takes us back to Chapter 1 where we discussed the need to align the objectives of managers with those of the shareholders.

In practice payback is most commonly used when the capital investment is small or when the merits of the project are so obvious that more formal analysis is unnecessary. For example, if a project is expected to produce constant cash flows for 10 years and the payback period is only 2 years, the project in all likelihood has a positive NPV.

▶ **Self-Test 5.3**

A project costs $5,000 and will generate cash flows of $55 per *month* for 20 years. What is the payback period? If the interest rate is .5 percent per month, what is the project NPV? Should the project be accepted?

Book Rate of Return

We pointed out that net present value and internal rate of return are both discounted cash-flow measures. In other words, each measure depends only on the project's cash flows and the opportunity cost of capital. But when companies report to shareholders on their performance, they do not show simply the cash flows. Instead they report the firm's book income and book assets.

book rate of return:
Accounting income divided by book value. Also called *accounting rate of return.*

Shareholders and financial managers sometimes use these accounting numbers to calculate a **book rate of return** (also called the *accounting rate of return*). In other words, they look at the company's book income (i.e., accounting profits) as a proportion of the book value of the assets:

$$\text{Book rate of return} = \frac{\text{book income}}{\text{book assets}}$$

We have already seen that cash flows and accounting income may be very different. For example, the accountant labels some cash outflows as *capital investments* and others as *operating expenses*. The operating expenses are deducted immediately from each year's income, while the capital investment is depreciated over a number of years. Thus the book rate of return depends on which items the accountant chooses to treat as capital investments and how rapidly they are depreciated. Book rate of return is not generally the same as the internal rate of return and, as you can see in Self-Test 5.4, the difference between the two can be considerable. Book rate of return therefore can easily give a misleading impression of the attractiveness of a project.

Managers seldom make investment decisions nowadays on the basis of accounting numbers. But they know that the company's shareholders pay considerable attention to book measures of profitability and naturally, therefore, they look at how major projects would affect the company's book rate of return.

▶ **Self-Test 5.4**

Suppose that a company invests $60,000 in a project. The project generates a cash inflow of $30,000 a year for each of 3 years and nothing thereafter. Book income in each year is equal to this cash flow *less* an allowance for depreciation of $20,000 a year. For simplicity, we assume there are no taxes.

a. Calculate the project's internal rate of return. (If you do not have a financial calculator or spreadsheet program, this will require a little trial-and-error.)

b. Now calculate the book rate of return in each year by dividing the book income for that year by the book value of the assets at the start of the year.

5.3 Project Interactions

Mutually Exclusive Projects

Most of the projects we have considered so far involve take-it-or-leave-it decisions. But almost all real-world decisions about capital expenditures involve either–or choices. You could build an apartment block on that vacant site rather than build an office block. You could build a 5-story office block or a 50-story one. You could heat it with oil or with natural gas. You could build it today, or wait a year to start construction. Such choices are said to be **mutually exclusive.**

mutually exclusive projects: Two or more projects that cannot be pursued simultaneously.

> **When you need to choose between mutually exclusive projects, the decision rule is simple. Calculate the NPV of each project and, from those options that have a positive NPV, choose the one whose NPV is highest.**

▶ **Example 5.3**   *Choosing the Best Office Block Project*

Think back to your initial proposal to build an office block. At that point you envisaged investing $350,000 in the building and then selling it at the end of the year for $400,000. Under the revised proposal, you planned to rent out the offices for 3 years at a fixed annual rent of $16,000 and then sell the building for $450,000. If the cost of capital is 7 percent, which is the better option?

The following table summarizes the cash flows and NPVs of the two proposals:

	Cash Flows, Thousands of Dollars				
	C_0	C_1	C_2	C_3	NPV at 7%
Initial proposal	−350	+400			24
Revised proposal	−350	+16	+16	+466	59

In both cases the proposed office block is worth more than it costs, but renting out the building for 3 years would make the greater contribution to value and should therefore be your preferred choice.

Mutually exclusive projects, such as our two proposals to develop an office block, involve a *project interaction*, since taking one project forecloses the other.

Unfortunately, not every project interaction is so simple to evaluate as the choice between the two office projects, but we will explain how to tackle three important decisions:

- *The investment timing decision.* Should you buy a computer now or wait and think again next year? (Here today's investment is competing with possible future investments.)
- *The choice between long- and short-lived equipment.* Should the company save money today by installing cheaper machinery that will not last as long? (Here today's decision would accelerate a later investment in machine replacement.)
- *The replacement decision.* When should existing machinery be replaced? (Using it another year could delay investment in machine replacement.)

Investment Timing

Let us return to Example 5.1, where Obsolete Technologies was contemplating a new computer system. The proposed investment has a net present value of $20,000, so it appears that the cost savings would easily justify the expense of the system. However, the financial manager is not persuaded. She reasons that the price of computers is continually falling and therefore proposes postponing the purchase, arguing that the NPV of the system will be even higher if the firm waits until the following year. Unfortunately, she has been making the same argument for 20 years and the company is steadily losing business to competitors with more efficient systems. Is there a flaw in her reasoning?

This is a problem in investment timing. When is it best to commit to a positive-NPV investment?

Table 5.2 lays out the basic data for Obsolete. You can see that the cost of the computer is expected to decline from $50,000 today to $45,000 next year, and so on. The present value of the savings from the computer system is expected to stay at $70,000. Thus if Obsolete invests today, it achieves an NPV of $70,000 − $50,000 = $20,000; if it invests next year, it will have an NPV of $70,000 −$45,000 = $25,000.

Isn't a gain of $25,000 better than one of $20,000? Well, not necessarily—you may prefer to be $20,000 richer *today* rather than $25,000 richer *next year.* The better choice depends on the cost of capital. The fourth column of Table 5.2 shows the value today (Year 0) of those net present values at a 10 percent cost of capital. For example, you can see that the discounted value of that $25,000 gain is $25,000/1.10 = $22,700. The financial manager has a point. It is worth postponing investment in the computer, but

TABLE 5.2

Obsolete Technologies: the gain from purchase of a computer is rising, but the NPV today *is highest if the computer is purchased in Year 3 (figures in thousands of dollars).*

Year of Purchase	Cost of Computer	PV Savings	NPV at Year of Purchase $(r=10\%)$	NPV Today	
0	$50	$70	$20	$20.0	
1	45	70	25	22.7	
2	40	70	30	24.8	
3	36	70	34	25.5	← optimal
4	33	70	37	25.3	purchase
5	31	70	39	24.2	date

it should not be postponed indefinitely. You maximize net present value today by buying the computer in Year 3.

Notice that you are involved in a trade-off. The sooner you can capture the $70,000 savings the better, but if it costs you less to realize those savings by postponing the investment, it may pay you to do so. If you postpone purchase by 1 year, the gain from buying a computer rises from $20,000 to $25,000, an increase of 25 percent. Since the cost of capital is only 10 percent, it pays to postpone at least until Year 1. If you postpone from Year 3 to Year 4, the gain rises from $34,000 to $37,000, a rise of just under 9 percent. Since this is less than the cost of capital, it is not worth waiting any longer.

> **The decision rule for investment timing is to choose the investment date that results in the highest net present value *today*.**

▶ **Self-Test 5.5**

Unfortunately Obsolete Technology's business is shrinking as the company dithers and dawdles. Its chief financial officer realizes that the savings from installing the new computer will likewise shrink by $4,000 per year, from a present value of $70,000 now, to $66,000 next year, then to $62,000, and so on. Redo Table 5.2 with this new information. When should Obsolete buy the new computer?

Long- versus Short-Lived Equipment

Suppose the firm is forced to choose between two machines, D and E. The two machines are designed differently but have identical capacity and do exactly the same job. Machine D costs $15,000 and will last 3 years. It costs $4,000 per year to run. Machine E is an "economy" model, costing only $10,000, but it will last only 2 years and costs $6,000 per year to run.

Because the two machines produce exactly the same product, the only way to choose between them is on the basis of cost. Suppose we compute the present value of the costs:

Costs, Thousands of Dollars

Year:	0	1	2	3	PV at 6%
Machine D	15	4	4	4	25.69
Machine E	10	6	6	—	21.00

Should we take machine E, the one with the lower present value of costs? Not necessarily. All we have shown is that machine E offers 2 years of service for a lower cost than 3 years of service from machine D. But is the *annual* cost of using E lower than that of D?

Suppose the financial manager agrees to buy machine D and pay for its operating costs out of her budget. She then charges the plant manager an annual amount for use of the machine. There will be three equal payments starting in Year 1. Obviously, the financial manager has to make sure that the present value of these payments equals the present value of the costs of machine D, $25,690. The payment stream with such a present value when the discount rate is 6 percent turns out to be $9,610 a year. In other words, the cost of buying and operating machine A is equivalent to an annual charge of $9,610 a year for 3 years. This figure is therefore termed the **equivalent annual cost** of machine D.

equivalent annual cost:
The cost per period with the same present value as the cost of buying and operating a machine.

	Costs, Thousands of Dollars				
Year:	0	1	2	3	PV at 6%
Machine D	15	4	4	4	25.69
Equivalent annual cost		9.61	9.61	9.61	25.69

How did we know that an annual charge of $9,610 has a present value of $25,690? The annual charge is a 3-year annuity. So we calculate the value of this annuity and set it equal to $25,690:

Equivalent annual cost $\times$ 3-year annuity factor = PV costs of D = $25,690

If the cost of capital is 6 percent, the 3-year annuity factor is 2.673. So

$$\textbf{Equivalent annual cost} = \frac{\textbf{present value of costs}}{\textbf{annuity factor}}$$

$$= \frac{\$25,690}{\text{3-year annuity factor}} = \frac{\$25,690}{2.673} = \$9,610$$

If we make a similar calculation of costs for machine E, we get:

	Costs, Thousands of Dollars			
Year:	0	1	2	PV at 6%
Machine E	10	6	6	21.00
Equivalent 2-year annuity		11.45	11.45	21.00

We see now that machine D is better, because its equivalent annual cost is less ($9,610 for D versus $11,450 for E). In other words, the financial manager could afford to set a lower *annual* charge for the use of D.

> **We thus have a rule for comparing assets of different lives: *Select the machine that has the lowest equivalent annual cost.***

Think of the equivalent annual cost as the level annual charge[6] necessary to recover the present value of investment outlays and operating costs. The annual charge continues for the life of the equipment. Calculate equivalent annual cost by dividing the appropriate present value by the annuity factor.

▶ **Example 5.4**   *Equivalent Annual Cost*

You need a new car. You can either purchase one outright for $15,000 or lease one for 7 years for $3,000 a year. If you buy the car, it will be worth $500 to you in 7 years. The discount rate is 10 percent. Should you buy or lease? What is the maximum lease you would be willing to pay?

---

[6]This introduction to equivalent annual cost is somewhat simplified. For example, equivalent annual costs should be escalated with inflation when inflation is significant and the equipment long-lived. This would require us to equate equipment cost to the present value of a *growing* annuity.

The present value of the cost of purchasing is

$$PV = \$15,000 - \frac{\$500}{(1.10)^7} = \$14,743$$

The equivalent annual cost of purchasing the car is therefore the annuity with this present value:

$$\text{Equivalent annual cost} \times \frac{\textbf{7-year annuity}}{\textbf{factor at 10\%}} = \frac{\textbf{PV costs}}{\textbf{of buying}} = \$14,743$$

$$\text{Equivalent annual cost} = \frac{\$14,743}{\text{7-year annuity factor}} = \frac{\$14,743}{4.8684} = \$3,028$$

Therefore, the annual lease payment of $3,000 is less than the equivalent annual cost of buying the car. You should be willing to pay up to $3,028 annually to lease.

Replacing an Old Machine

The previous example took the life of each machine as fixed. In practice, the point at which equipment is replaced reflects economics, not physical collapse. *We* usually decide when to replace. The machine will rarely decide for us.

Here is a common problem. You are operating an old machine that will last 2 more years before it gives up the ghost. It costs $12,000 per year to operate. You can replace it now with a new machine, which costs $25,000 but is much more efficient ($8,000 per year in operating costs) and will last for 5 years. Should you replace now or wait a year? The opportunity cost of capital is 6 percent.

We can calculate the NPV of the new machine and its equivalent annual cost, that is, the 5-year annuity that has the same present value.

	Costs, Thousands of Dollars						
Year:	0	1	2	3	4	5	PV at 6%
New machine	25	8	8	8	8	8	58.70
Equivalent 5-year annuity		13.93	13.93	13.93	13.93	13.93	58.70

The cash flows of the new machine are equivalent to an annuity of $13,930 per year. So we can equally well ask at what point we would want to replace our old machine, which costs $12,000 a year to run, with a new one costing $13,930 a year. When the question is posed this way, the answer is obvious. As long as your old machine costs only $12,000 a year, why replace it with a new machine that costs $1,930 more?

▶ **Self-Test 5.6**

Machines F and G are mutually exclusive and have the following investment and operating costs. Note that machine F lasts for only 2 years:

Year:	0	1	2	3
F	10,000	1,100	1,200	—
G	12,000	1,100	1,200	1,300

Calculate the equivalent annual cost of each investment using a discount rate of 10 percent. Which machine is the better buy?

Now suppose you have an existing machine. You can keep it going for 1 more year only, but it will cost $2,500 in repairs and $1,800 in operating costs. Is it worth replacing now with either F or G?

Mutually Exclusive Projects and the IRR Rule

Whereas the NPV rule deals easily with mutually exclusive projects, the IRR rule does not. Because of the potential pitfalls in the use of the IRR rule, our advice is always to base your final decision on the project's net present value.[7]

Pitfall 1: Mutually Exclusive Projects. We have seen that firms are seldom faced with take-it-or-leave-it projects. Usually they need to choose from a number of mutually exclusive alternatives. Given a choice between competing projects, you should accept the one that adds most to shareholder wealth. This is the one with the higher NPV. However, it won't necessarily be the project with the higher internal rate of return. So the IRR rule can lead you astray when choosing between projects.

Think once more about the two office-block proposals. Here are the cash flows, their IRRs, and their NPVs (ignore for a moment the bottom row of the table):

Cash Flows, Thousands of Dollars

Project	C_0	C_1	C_2	C_3	IRR	NPV at 7%
H: Initial proposal	−350	+400			+14.29	+$24,000
I: Revised proposal	−350	+16	+16	+466	+12.96	+$59,000
Difference, I − H	0	−384	+16	+466	+12.26	+$35,000

Both projects are good investments; both offer a positive NPV. But the revised proposal has the higher net present value and therefore is the better choice. Unfortunately, the superiority of the revised proposal doesn't show up as a higher rate of return. The IRR rule seems to say you should go for the initial proposal because it has the higher IRR. If you follow the IRR rule, you have the satisfaction of earning a 14.29 percent rate of return; if you use NPV, you are $59,000 richer.

Figure 5.4 shows why the IRR rule gives the wrong signal. If the opportunity cost of capital is higher than 12.26 percent, the initial proposal with its rapid cash inflow is the superior investment. If the cost of capital is lower than 12.26 percent (we assume that it is 7 percent), then the revised proposal dominates. The higher IRR of the initial proposal has no bearing on the relative merits of the two projects.

You can salvage the IRR rule in these cases by looking at the IRR on the incremental cash flows. Here is how to do it. First consider the initial proposal. It has an IRR of 14.29 percent, well in excess of the 7 percent opportunity cost of capital. You know therefore that it is acceptable. Now consider the extra cash flows from switching to the revised proposal. You can see from the bottom row of the preceding table that the cash flow in Year 1 is *reduced* by $384,000, but in each of the next 2 years you get a cash *increase* from the switch. Thus by switching to the revised proposal you are making an investment in Year 1 but you reap the benefits in Years 2 and 3. The rate of return on this extra investment is 12.26 percent, also well in excess of the cost of capital. Thus the switch to the revised proposal is worthwhile.

[7]The other rules we've considered, such as payback or book rate of return, give poor guidance even in the much simpler case of the accept/reject decision of a project considered in isolation. They are of no help in choosing among mutually exclusive projects.

FIGURE 5.4

The initial proposal to build an office block offers a higher internal rate of return than the revised proposal, but its NPV is lower if the discount rate is less than 12.26 percent.

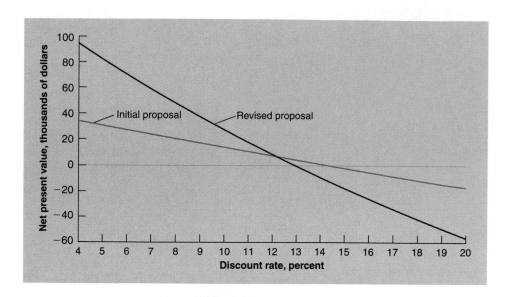

Whenever you are using the rate of return rule to choose between mutually exclusive projects, you need to calculate the IRR on the incremental cash flows. It is easy to do; it is also easy to forget.

In our example both projects involved the same outlay, but the revised proposal had the longer life. The IRR rule mistakenly favored the quick payback project with the high percentage return but the lower NPV.

> **Remember, a high IRR is not an end in itself. You want projects that increase the value of the firm. Projects that earn a good rate of return for a long time often have higher NPVs than those that offer high percentage rates of return but die young.**

▶ **Self Test 5.7**

A rich, friendly, and probably slightly unbalanced benefactor offers you the opportunity to invest $1 million in two mutually exclusive ways. The payoffs are:

a. $2 million after 1 year, a 100 percent return.
b. $300,000 a year forever.

Neither investment is risky, and safe securities are yielding 7.5 percent. Which investment will you take? You can't take both, so the choices are mutually exclusive. Do you want to earn a high percentage return or do you want to be rich? By the way, if you really had this investment opportunity, you'd have no trouble borrowing the money to undertake it.

Pitfall 1a: Mutually Exclusive Projects Involving Different Outlays.   A similar misranking also may occur when comparing projects with the same lives but different outlays. In this case the IRR may mistakenly favor small projects with high rates of return but low NPVs.

▶ **Self-Test 5.8**   Your wacky benefactor now offers you the choice of two opportunities:

a. Invest $1,000 today and quadruple your money—a 300 percent return—in 1 year with no risk.
b. Invest $1 million for 1 year at a guaranteed 50 percent return.

Which will you take? Do you want to earn a wonderful rate of return (300 percent) or do you want to be rich?

Other Pitfalls of the IRR Rule

The IRR rule is subject to problems beyond those associated with mutually exclusive investments. Here are a few more pitfalls to avoid.

Pitfall 2: Lending or Borrowing?   Remember our condition for the IRR rule to work: the project's NPV must fall as the discount rate increases. Now consider the following projects:

| | **Cash Flows, Dollars** | | | |
Project	C_0	C_1	IRR, %	NPV at 10%
J	−100	+150	+50	+$36.4
K	+100	−150	+50	−$36.4

Each project has an IRR of 50 percent. In other words, if you discount the cash flows at 50 percent, both of them would have zero NPV.

Does this mean that the two projects are equally attractive? Clearly not. In the case of J we are paying out $100 now and getting $150 back at the end of the year. That is better than any bank account. But what about K? Here we are getting paid $100 now but we have to pay out $150 at the end of the year. That is equivalent to borrowing money at 50 percent.

If someone asked you whether 50 percent was a good rate of interest, you could not answer unless you also knew whether that person was proposing to lend or borrow at that rate. Lending money at 50 percent is great (as long as the borrower does not flee the country), but borrowing at 50 percent is not usually a good deal (unless of course you plan to flee the country). When you lend money, you want a *high* rate of return; when you borrow, you want a *low* rate of return.

If you plot a graph like Figure 5.2 for project K, you will find the NPV increases as the discount rate increases. *(Try it!)* Obviously, the rate of return rule will not work in this case.

Project K is a fairly obvious trap, but if you want to make sure you don't fall into it, calculate the project's NPV. For example, suppose that the cost of capital is 10 percent. Then the NPV of project J is + $36.4 and the NPV of project K is −$36.4. The NPV rule correctly warns us away from a project that is equivalent to borrowing money at 50 percent.

When NPV rises as the interest rate rises, the rate of return rule is reversed:

> **When NPV is higher as the discount rate increases, a project is acceptable only if its internal rate of return is *less* than the opportunity cost of capital.**

Pitfall 3: Multiple Rates of Return. Here is a trickier problem. King Coal Corporation is considering a project to strip mine coal. The project requires an investment of $22 million and is expected to produce a cash inflow of $15 million in each of Years 1 through 4. However, the company is obliged in Year 5 to reclaim the land at a cost of $40 million. At a 10 percent opportunity cost of capital the project has an NPV of $.7 million.

To find the IRR, we have calculated the NPV for various discount rates and plotted the results in Figure 5.5. You can see that there are *two* discount rates at which NPV = 0. That is, *each* of the following statements holds:

$$NPV = -22 + \frac{15}{1.06} + \frac{15}{1.06^2} + \frac{15}{1.06^3} + \frac{15}{1.06^4} - \frac{40}{1.06^5} = 0$$

and

$$NPV = -22 + \frac{15}{1.28} + \frac{15}{1.28^2} + \frac{15}{1.28^3} + \frac{15}{1.28^4} - \frac{40}{1.28^5} = 0$$

In other words, the investment has an IRR of both 6 *and* 28 percent. The reason for this is the double change in the sign of the cash flows. There can be as many different internal rates of return as there are changes in the sign of the cash-flow stream.[8]

Is the coal mine worth developing? The simple IRR rule—accept if the IRR is greater than the cost of capital—won't help. For example, you can see from Figure 5.5 that with a low cost of capital (less than 6 percent) the project has a negative NPV. It has a positive NPV only if the cost of capital is between 6 percent and 28 percent.

> **When there are multiple changes in the sign of the cash flows, the IRR rule does not work. But the NPV rule always does.**

FIGURE 5.5

King Coal's project has two internal rates of return. NPV = 0 when the discount rate is either 6 percent or 28 percent.

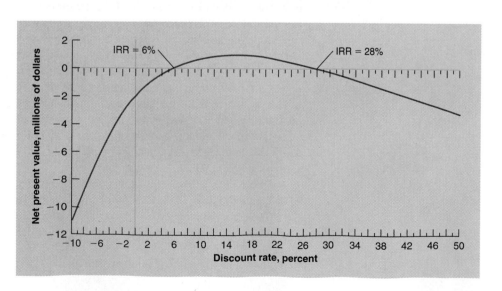

[8]There may be *fewer* IRRs than the number of sign changes. You may even encounter projects for which there is *no* IRR. For example, there is no IRR for a project that has cash flows of +$1,000 in Year 0, −$3,000 in Year 1, and +$2,500 in Year 2. If you don't believe us, try plotting NPV for different discount rates. Can such a project ever have a negative NPV?

5.4 Capital Rationing

A firm maximizes its shareholders' wealth by accepting every project that has a positive net present value. But this assumes that the firm can raise the funds needed to pay for these investments. This is usually a good assumption, particularly for major firms which can raise very large sums of money on fair terms and short notice. Why then does top management sometimes tell subordinates that capital is limited and that they may not exceed a specified amount of capital spending? There are two reasons.

Soft Rationing

capital rationing: Limit set on the amount of funds available for investment.

For many firms the limits on capital funds are "soft." By this we mean that the **capital rationing** is not imposed by investors. Instead the limits are imposed by top management. For example, suppose that you are an ambitious, upwardly mobile junior manager. You are keen to expand your part of the business and as a result you tend to overstate the investment opportunities. Rather than trying to determine which of your many bright ideas really are worthwhile, upper management may find it simpler to impose a limit on the amount that you and other junior managers can spend. This limit forces you to set your own priorities.

Even if capital is not rationed, other resources may be. For example, very rapid growth can place considerable strains on management and the organization. A somewhat rough-and-ready response to this problem is to ration the amount of capital that the firm spends.

Hard Rationing

Soft rationing should never cost the firm anything. If the limits on investment become so tight that truly good projects are being passed up, then upper management should raise more money and relax the limits it has imposed on capital spending.

But what if there is "hard rationing," meaning that the firm actually cannot raise the money it needs? In that case, it may be forced to pass up positive-NPV projects.

With hard rationing you may still be interested in net present value, but you now need to select the package of projects which is within the company's resources and yet gives the highest net present value.

Let us illustrate. Suppose that the opportunity cost of capital is 10 percent, that the company has total resources of $20 million, and that it is presented with the following project proposals:

	Cash Flows, Millions of Dollars				
Project	C_0	C_1	C_2	PV at 10%	NPV
L	−3	+2.2	+2.42	$ 4	$1
M	−5	+2.2	+4.84	6	1
N	−7	+6.6	+4.84	10	3
O	−6	+3.3	+6.05	8	2
P	−4	+1.1	+4.84	5	1

All five projects have a positive NPV. Therefore, if there were no shortage of capital, the firm would like to accept all five proposals. But with only $20 million available, the firm needs to find the package that gives the highest possible NPV within the budget.

The solution is to pick the projects that give the highest net present value *per dollar of investment*. The ratio of net present value to initial investment is known as the **profitability index.**[9]

profitability index: Ratio of present value to initial investment.

$$\text{Profitability index} = \frac{\text{net present value}}{\text{initial investment}}$$

For our five projects the profitability index is calculated as follows:

Project	PV	Investment	NPV	Profitability Index
L	$ 4	$3	1	1/3 = 0.33
M	6	5	1	1/5 = 0.20
N	10	7	3	3/7 = 0.43
O	8	6	2	2/6 = 0.33
P	5	4	1	1/4 = 0.25

Project N offers the highest ratio of net present value to investment (0.43) and therefore N is picked first. Next come projects L and O, which tie with a ratio of 0.33, and after them comes P. These four projects exactly use up the $20 million budget. Between them they offer shareholders the highest attainable gain in wealth.[10]

▶ Self-Test 5.9

Which projects should the firm accept if its capital budget is only $10 million?

Pitfalls of the Profitability Index

The profitability index is sometimes used to rank projects even when there is no soft or hard capital rationing. In this case the unwary user may be led to favor small projects over larger projects with higher NPVs. The profitability index was designed to select the projects with the most bang per buck—the greatest NPV per dollar spent. That's the right objective when bucks are limited. When they are not, a bigger bang is always better than a smaller one, even when more bucks are spent. Self-Test 5.10 is a numerical example.

▶ Self-Test 5.10

Calculate the profitability indexes of the two pairs of mutually exclusive investments in Self-Tests 5.7 and 5.8. Use a 7.5 percent discount rate. Does the profitability index give the right ranking in each case?

[9]Sometimes the profitability index is defined as the ratio of present value to required investment. By this definition, all the profitability indexes calculated below are increased by 1.0. For example, project L's index would be PV/investment = 4/3 = 1.33. Note that project rankings under either definition are identical.

[10]Unfortunately, when capital is rationed in more than one period, or when personnel, production capacity, or other resources are rationed in addition to capital, it isn't always possible to get the NPV-maximizing package just by ranking projects on their profitability index. Tedious trial and error may be called for, or linear programming methods may be used.

Summary

1. The net present value of a project measures the difference between its value and cost. NPV is therefore the amount that the project will add to shareholder wealth. A company maximizes shareholder wealth by accepting all projects that have a positive NPV.

2. Investment decisions are rarely take-it-or-leave-it decisions. Usually they involve a choice. We looked at three common cases:
   - Sometimes a project may have a positive NPV if undertaken today but an even higher NPV if the investment is delayed. Choose between these alternatives by comparing their NPVs *today.*
   - When you have to choose between projects with different lives, you should put them on an equal footing by comparing the equivalent annual cost or benefit of the two projects.
   - When you are considering whether to replace an aging machine with a new one, you should compare the cost of operating the old one with the equivalent annual cost of the new one.

3. Instead of asking whether projects have a positive NPV, many businesses prefer to ask whether they offer a higher return than shareholders could expect to get by investing in the capital market. Return is usually defined as the discount rate that would result in a zero NPV. This is known as the internal rate of return, or IRR. There are some pitfalls in using the internal rate of return rule. Be careful about using the IRR when (a) the early cash flows are positive, (b) there is more than one change in the sign of the cash flows, or (c) you need to choose between two mutually exclusive projects.

4. The net present value rule and the rate of return rule both properly reflect the time value of money. But companies also use rules of thumb to judge projects. One is the payback rule, which states that a project is acceptable if you get your money back within a specified period. The payback rule takes no account of any cash flows that arrive after the payback period and fails to discount cash flows within the payback period.

5. Book (or accounting) rate of return is the income of a project divided by the book value. Unlike the internal rate of return, book rate of return does not depend just on the project's cash flows. It also depends on which cash flows are classified as capital investments and which as operating expenses. Managers often look at how projects would affect book return.

6. If there is a shortage of capital, companies need to choose projects that offer the highest net present value per dollar of investment. This measure is known as the *profitability index.*

Key Terms

capital budgeting decision	mutually exclusive projects	book rate of return
opportunity cost of capital	capital rationing	(accounting rate of return)
net present value (NPV)	profitability index	
internal rate of return (IRR)	payback period	

Problems

Problems 1–9 refer to two projects with the following cash flows:

Year	Project A	Project B
0	−$100	−$100
1	40	50
2	40	50
3	40	50
4	40	

1. **IRR/NPV.** If the opportunity cost of capital is 11 percent, which of these projects is worth pursuing?
2. **Mutually Exclusive Investments.** Suppose that you can choose only one of these projects. Which would you choose? The discount rate is still 11 percent.
3. **IRR/NPV.** Which project would you choose if the opportunity cost of capital were 16 percent?
4. **IRR.** What are the internal rates of return on projects A and B?
5. **Investment Criteria.** In light of your answers to problems 2–4, is there any reason to believe that the project with the higher IRR is the better project?
6. **Profitability Index.** If the opportunity cost of capital is 11 percent, what is the profitability index for each project? Does the profitability index rank the projects correctly?
7. **Payback.** What is the payback period of each project?
8. **Investment Criteria.** Considering your answers to problems 2, 3, and 7, is there any reason to believe that the project with the lower payback period is the better project?

9. **Book Rate of Return.** Accountants have set up the following depreciation schedules for the two projects:

Year:	1	2	3	4
Project A	$25	$25	$25	$25
Project B	33.33	33.33	33.34	

Calculate book rates of return for each year. Are these book returns the same as the IRR?

10. **Replacement Decision.** You are operating an old machine that is expected to produce a cash inflow of $5,000 in each of the next 3 years before it fails. You can replace it now with a new machine that costs $20,000 but is much more efficient and will provide a cash flow of $10,000 a year for 4 years. Should you replace your equipment now? The discount rate is 15 percent.

11. **Equivalent Annual Cost.** Econo-cool air conditioners cost $300 to purchase, result in electricity bills of $150 per year, and last for 5 years. Luxury Air models cost $500, result in electricity bills of $100 per year, and last for 8 years. The discount rate is 21 percent.

  a. What are the equivalent annual costs of the Econo-cool and Luxury Air models?
  b. Which model is more cost effective?
  c. Now you remember that the inflation rate is expected to be 10 percent per year for the foreseeable future. Redo parts (a) and (b).

12. **Investment Timing.** You can purchase an optical scanner today for $400. The scanner provides benefits worth $60 a year. The expected life of the scanner is 10 years. Scanners are expected to decrease in price by 20 percent per year. Suppose the discount rate is 10 percent. Should you purchase the scanner today or wait to purchase? When is the best purchase time?

13. **Replacement Decision.** A forklift will last for only 2 more years. It costs $5,000 a year to maintain. For $20,000 you can buy a new lift which can last for 10 years and should require maintenance costs of only $2,000 a year.

    a. If the discount rate is 5 percent per year, should you replace the forklift?
    b. What if the discount rate is 10 percent per year? Why does your answer change?

14. **IRR.** Marielle Machinery Works forecasts the following cash flows on a project under consideration. It uses the internal rate of return rule to accept or reject projects. Should this project be accepted if the required return is 12 percent?

C_0	C_1	C_2	C_3
−$10,000	0	+$7,500	+$8,500

15. **NPV/IRR.** A new computer system will require an initial outlay of $20,000 but it will increase the firm's cash flows by $4,000 a year for each of the next 8 years. Is the system worth installing if the required rate of return is 9 percent? What if it is 14 percent? How high can the discount rate be before you would reject the project?

16. **Investment Criteria.** If you insulate your office for $1,000, you will save $100 a year in heating expenses. These savings will last forever.

    a. What is the NPV of the investment when the cost of capital is 8 percent? 10 percent?
    b. What is the IRR of the investment?
    c. What is the payback period on this investment?

17. **Book Rate of Return.** A project requires an initial investment of $10,000, and over its 5-year life it will generate annual cash revenues of $5,000 and cash expenses of $2,000. The firm will use straight-line depreciation, but it does not pay taxes.

    a. Find the book rates of return on the project for each year.
    b. Is the project worth pursuing if the opportunity cost of capital is 8 percent?
    c. What would happen to the book rates of return if half the initial $10,000 outlay were treated as an expense instead of a capital investment? *Hint:* Instead of depreciating all of the $10,000, treat $5,000 as an expense in the first year.
    d. Does NPV change as a result of the different accounting treatment proposed in (c)?

18. **NPV versus IRR.** Here are the cash flows for two mutually exclusive projects:

Project	C_0	C_1	C_2	C_3
A	−$20,000	+$8,000	+$8,000	+$ 8,000
B	−$20,000	0	0	+$25,000

    a. At what interest rates would you prefer project A to B? *Hint:* Try drawing the NPV profile of each project.
    b. What is the IRR of each project?

19. **Multiple IRR.** Consider the following cash flows:

C_0	C_1	C_2	C_3	C_4
−22	+20	+20	+20	−40

    a. Confirm that one internal rate of return on this project is (a shade above) 7 percent, and that the other is (a shade below) 34 percent.
    b. Is the project attractive if the discount rate is 5 percent?

  c. What if it is 20 percent? 40 percent?

  d. Why is the project attractive at midrange discount rates but not at very high or very low rates?

20. **Profitability Index versus NPV.** Consider these two projects:

Project	C_0	C_1	C_2	C_3
A	−$18	+$10	+$10	+$10
B	−$50	+$25	+$25	+$25

  a. Which project has the higher NPV if the discount rate is 10 percent?

  b. Which has the higher profitability index?

  c. Which project is most attractive to a firm that can raise an unlimited amount of funds to pay for its investment projects? Which project is most attractive to a firm that is limited in the funds it can raise?

21. **NPV/IRR.** Consider projects A and B:

Project	Cash Flows, Dollars			
	C_0	C_1	C_2	NPV at 10%
A	−30,000	21,000	21,000	+$6,446
B	−50,000	33,000	33,000	+$7,273

Calculate IRRs for A and B. Which project does the IRR rule suggest is best? Calculate the NPV of the incremental investment in B over A. Which project is really best?

22. **Capital Rationing.** You are a manager with an investment budget of $8 million. You may invest in the following projects. Investment and cash-flow figures are in millions of dollars.

Project	Discount Rate, %	Investment	Annual Cash Flow	Project Life, Years
A	10	3	1	5
B	12	4	1	8
C	8	5	2	4
D	8	3	1.5	3
E	12	3	1	6

  a. Why might these projects have different discount rates?

  b. Which projects should the manager choose?

  c. Which projects will be chosen if there is no capital rationing?

23. **IRR.** You have the chance to participate in a project that produces the following cash flows:

C_0	C_1	C_2
+$5,000	+$4,000	−$11,000

The internal rate of return is 13.6 percent. If the opportunity cost of capital is 12 percent, would you accept the offer?

24. **Book Rate of Return.** A machine costs $8,000 and is expected to produce profit before depreciation of $2,500 in each of Years 1 and 2 and $3,500 in each of Years 3 and 4. Assuming that the machine is depreciated at a constant rate of $2,000 a year and that there are no taxes, what is the average return on book?

25. **NPV/IRR.**

    a. Calculate the net present value of the following project for discount rates of 0, 50, and 100 percent:

C_0	C_1	C_2
−$6,750	+$4,500	+$18,000

    b. What is the IRR of the project?

26. **Profitability Index.** Consider the following projects:

Project	C_0	C_1	C_2
A	−$2,100	+$2,000	+$1,200
B	− 2,100	+ 1,440	+ 1,728

    a. Calculate the profitability index for A and B assuming a 20 percent opportunity cost of capital.
    b. Use the profitability index rule to determine which project(s) you should accept (i) if you could undertake both and (ii) if you could undertake only one.

27. **Payback and NPV.** A project has a life of 10 years and a payback period of 10 years. What must be true of project NPV?

28. **Book Rate of Return.** Consider these data on a proposed project:
    Original investment = $200
    Straight-line depreciation of $50 a year for 4 years
    Project life = 4 years

Year:	0	1	2	3	4
Book Value	$200	—	—	—	—
Sales		100	110	120	130
Costs		30	35	40	45
Depreciation		—	—	—	—
Net income		—	—	—	—

    a. Fill in the blanks in the table.
    b. Find the book rate of return of this project in each year.
    c. Find project NPV if the discount rate is 20 percent.

29. **Mutually Exclusive Investments.** Here are the cash flow forecasts for two *mutually exclusive* projects:

Year	Project A	Project B
0	−$100	−$100
1	30	49
2	50	49
3	70	49

    Cash Flows, Dollars

    a. Which project would you choose if the opportunity cost of capital is 2 percent?
    b. Which would you choose if the opportunity cost of capital is 12 percent?
    c. Why does your answer change?

30. **IRR/NPV.** Consider this project with an internal rate of return of 13.1 percent. Should you accept or reject the project if the discount rate is 12 percent?

Year	Cash Flow
0	+$100
1	−60
2	−60

31. **Payback and NPV.**

a. What is the payback period on each of the following projects?

	Cash Flows, Dollars				
Project	Time: 0	1	2	3	4
A	−5,000	+1,000	+1,000	+3,000	0
B	−1,000	0	+1,000	+2,000	+3,000
C	−5,000	+1,000	+1,000	+3,000	+5,000

b. Given that you wish to use the payback rule with a cutoff period of 2 years, which projects would you accept?

c. If you use a cutoff period of 3 years, which projects would you accept?

d. If the opportunity cost of capital is 10 percent, which projects have positive NPVs?

e. "Payback gives too much weight to cash flows that occur after the cutoff date." True or false?

 32. **NPV/IRR.** Growth Enterprises believes its latest project, which will cost $80,000 to install, will generate a perpetual growing stream of cash flows. Cash flow at the end of this year will be $5,000, and cash flows in future years are expected to grow indefinitely at an annual rate of 5 percent.

a. If the discount rate for this project is 10 percent, what is the project NPV?

b. What is the project IRR?

Solutions to Self-Test Questions

5.1 Even if construction costs are $355,000, NPV is still positive:

$$NPV = PV - \$355,000 = \$357,143 - \$355,000 = \$2,143$$

Therefore, the project is still worth pursuing. The project is viable as long as construction costs are less than the PV of the future cash flow, that is, as long as construction costs are less than $357,143. However, if the opportunity cost of capital is 20 percent, the PV of the $400,000 sales price is lower and NPV is negative:

$$PV = \$400,000 \times \frac{1}{1.20} = \$333,333$$

$$NPV = PV - \$355,000 = -\$21,667$$

The present value of the future cash flow is not as high when the opportunity cost of capital is higher. The project would need to provide a higher payoff in order to be viable in the face of the higher opportunity cost of capital.

5.2 The IRR is now about 8.9 percent because

$$NPV = -\$350,000 + \frac{\$16,000}{1.089} + \frac{\$16,000}{(1.089)^2} + \frac{\$416,000}{(1.089)^3} = 0$$

FIGURE 5.6

NPV falls to zero at an interest rate of 8.9 percent.

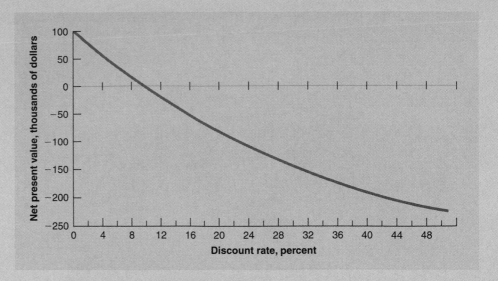

Note in Figure 5.6 that NPV falls to zero as the discount rate reaches 8.9 percent.

5.3 The payback period is about 91 months, or 7.6 years. Calculate NPV as follows. The present value of a $55 annuity for 240 months at .5 percent per month is

$$PV \text{ annuity} = \$7,677$$

$$NPV = -\$5,000 + \$7,677 = +\$2,677$$

The project should be accepted.

5.4 a. IRR = 23% (i.e., $-60 + 30/1.23 + 30/1.23^2 + 30/1.23^3 = 0$).

b. Year 1: Income/book value at start of Year 1 = $(30 - 20)/60 = .17$, or 17%.
Year 2: Income/book value at start of Year 2 = $(30 - 20)/40 = .25$, or 25%.
Year 3: Income/book value at start of Year 3 = $(30 - 20)/20 = .50$, or 50%.

5.5

Year of Purchase	Cost of Computer	PV Savings	NPV at Year of Purchase	NPV Today
0	50	70	20	20
1	45	66	21	19.1
2	40	62	22	18.2
3	36	58	22	16.5
4	33	54	21	14.3
5	31	50	19	11.8

Purchase the new computer now.

5.6

Year:	0	1	2	3	PV of Costs
F. Cash flows	10,000	1,100	1,200		11,992
Equivalent annual cost		6,910	6,910		11,992
G. Cash flows	12,000	1,100	1,200	1,300	14,968
Equivalent annual cost		6,019	6,019	6,019	14,968

Machine G is the better buy. However, it's still better to keep the old machine going one more year. That costs $4,300, which is less than G's equivalent annual cost, $6,019.

5.7 You want to be rich. The NPV of the long-lived investment is much larger.

$$\text{Short:} \quad \text{NPV} = -\$1 + \frac{\$2}{1.075} = +\$.8605 \text{ million}$$

$$\text{Long:} \quad \text{NPV} = -\$1 + \frac{\$.3}{.075} = +\$3 \text{ million}$$

5.8 You want to be richer. The second alternative generates greater value at any reasonable discount rate. For example, suppose other risk-free investments offer 8 percent. Then

$$\text{NPV} = -\$1,000 + \frac{\$4,000}{1.08} = +\$2,703$$

$$\text{NPV} = -\$1,000,000 + \frac{\$1,500,000}{1.08} = +\$388,888$$

5.9 Rank each project in order of profitability index as in the following table:

Project	Profitability Index	Investment
N	0.43	$7
L	0.33	3
O	0.33	6
P	0.25	4
M	0.20	5

Starting from the top, we run out of funds after accepting projects N and L. While L and O have equal profitability indexes, project O could not be chosen because it would force total investment above the limit of $10 million.

5.10 The profitability index gives the wrong ranking for the first pair, correct ranking for the second:

Project	PV	Investment	NPV	Profitability Index (NPV/Investment)
Short	1,860,000	1,000,000	860,000	0.86
Long	4,000,000	1,000,000	3,000,000	3.0
Small	$ 3,703	$ 1,000	2,703	2.7
Large	1,388,888	1,000,000	388,888	0.39

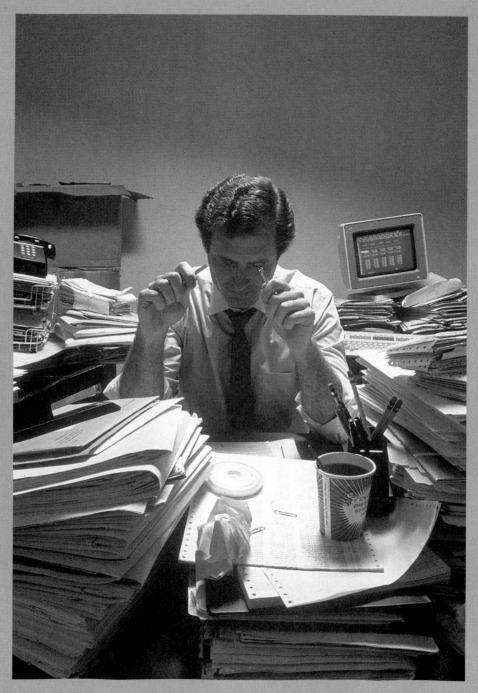

Calculating NPV can be hard work
But you've got to sweat the details and learn to do it right.
© Comstock, Inc.

Chapter 6

Using Discounted Cash-Flow Analysis to Make Investment Decisions

I n Chapter 5 we used the net present value rule to make a simple capital budgeting decision. You tackled the problem in four steps:

Step 1: Forecast the project cash flows.

Step 2: Estimate the opportunity cost of capital—that is, the rate of return that your shareholders could expect to earn if they invested their money in the capital market.

Step 3: Use the opportunity cost of capital to discount the future cash flows. The project's present value (PV) is equal to the sum of the discounted future cash flows.

Step 4: Net present value (NPV) measures whether the project is worth more than it costs. To calculate NPV you need to subtract the required investment from the present value of the future payoffs:

$$NPV = PV - \text{required investment}$$

You should go ahead with the project if it has a positive NPV.

We now need to consider how to apply the net present value rule to practical investment problems. The first step is to decide what to discount. We know the answer in principle: discount cash flows. This is why capital budgeting is often referred to as *discounted cash flow,* or *DCF,* analysis. But useful forecasts of cash flows do not arrive on a silver platter. Often the financial manager has to make do with raw data supplied by specialists in product design, production, marketing, and so on, and must adjust such data before they are useful. In addition, most financial forecasts are prepared in accordance with accounting principles that do not necessarily recognize cash flows when they occur. These data must also be adjusted.

We start this chapter with a discussion of the principles governing the cash flows that are relevant for discounting. We then present an example designed to show how standard accounting information can be used to compute those cash flows and why cash flows and accounting income usually differ. The example will lead us to various further points, including the links between depreciation and taxes and the importance of tracking investments in working capital.

After studying this chapter you should be able to

▸ Identify the cash flows properly attributable to a proposed new project.

▸ Calculate the cash flows of a project from standard financial statements.

▸ Understand how the company's tax bill is affected by depreciation and how this affects project value.

▸ Understand how changes in working capital affect project cash flows.

6.1 Discount Cash Flows, Not Profits

Up to this point we have been concerned mainly with the mechanics of discounting and with the various methods of project appraisal. We have had almost nothing to say about the problem of *what* you should discount. The first and most important point is this: to calculate net present value you need to discount cash flows, *not* accounting profits.

We stressed the difference between cash flows and profits in Chapter 2. Here we stress it again. Income statements are intended to show how well the firm has performed. They do not track cash flows.

If the firm lays out a large amount of money on a big capital project, you would not conclude that the firm performed poorly that year, even though a lot of cash is going out the door. Therefore, the accountant does not deduct capital expenditure when calculating the year's income but instead depreciates it over several years.

That is fine for computing year-by-year profits, but it could get you into trouble when working out net present value. For example, suppose that you are analyzing an investment proposal. If costs $2,000 and is expected to bring in a cash flow of $1,500 in the first year and $500 in the second. You think that the opportunity cost of capital is 10 percent and so calculate the present value of the cash flows as follows:

$$PV = \frac{\$1,500}{1.10} + \frac{\$500}{(1.10)^2} = \$1,776.86$$

The project is worth less than it costs; it has a negative NPV:

$$NPV = \$1,776.86 - \$2,000 = -\$223.14$$

The project costs $2,000 today, but an accountant would not treat that outlay as an immediate expense. He or she would depreciate that $2,000 over 2 years and deduct the depreciation from the cash flow to obtain accounting income:

	Year 1	Year 2
Cash inflow	+$1,500	+ $500
Less depreciation	− 1,000	−1,000
Accounting income	+ 500	− 500

Thus an accountant would forecast income of $500 in Year 1 and an accounting loss of $500 in Year 2.

Suppose you were given this forecast income and loss and naively discounted them. Now NPV *looks* positive:

$$\text{Apparent NPV} = \frac{\$500}{1.10} + \frac{-\$500}{(1.10)^2} = \$41.32$$

Of course we know that this is nonsense. The project is obviously a loser; we are spending money today ($2,000 cash outflow) and we are simply getting our money back ($1,500 in Year 1 and $500 in Year 2). We are earning a zero return when we could get a 10 percent return by investing our money in the capital market.

The message of the example is this:

> **When calculating NPV, recognize investment expenditures when they occur, not later when they show up as depreciation. Projects are financially attractive because of the cash they generate, either for distribution to shareholders or for reinvestment in the firm. Therefore, the focus of capital budgeting must be on cash flow, not profits.**

Here is another example of the distinction between cash flow and accounting profits. Accountants try to show profit as it is earned, rather than when the company and the customer get around to paying their bills. For example, an income statement will recognize revenue when the sale is made, even if the bill is not paid for months. This practice also results in a difference between accounting profits and cash flow. The sale generates immediate profits, but the cash flow comes later.

▶ **Example 6.1**   *Sales before Cash*

Reggie Hotspur, ace computer salesman, closed a $500,000 sale on December 15, just in time to count it toward his annual bonus. How did he do it? Well, for one thing he gave the customer 180 days to pay. The income statement will recognize Hotspur's sale in December, even though cash will not arrive until June. But a financial analyst tracking cash flows would concentrate on the latter event.

The accountant takes care of the timing difference by adding $500,000 to accounts receivable in December, then reducing accounts receivable when the money arrives in June. (The total of accounts receivable is just the sum of all cash due from customers.)

You can think of the increase in accounts receivable as an investment—it's effectively a 180-day loan to the customer—and a cash outflow. That investment is recovered when the customer pays. Thus financial analysts often find it convenient to calculate cash flow as follows:

December		**June**	
Sales	$500,000	Sales	0
Less investment in accounts receivable	− 500,000	Plus recovery of accounts receivable	+$500,000
Cash flow	0	Cash flow	$500,000

Note that this procedure gives the correct cash flow of $500,000 in June.

It is not always easy to translate accounting data back into actual dollars. If you are in doubt about what is a cash flow, simply count the dollars coming in and take away the dollars going out.

▶ **Self-Test 6.1**   A regional supermarket chain is deciding whether to install a tewgit machine in each of its stores. Each machine costs $250,000. Projected income per machine is as follows:

Year:	1	2	3	4	5
Sales	$250,000	$300,000	$300,000	$250,000	$250,000
Operating expenses	200,000	200,000	200,000	200,000	200,000
Depreciation	50,000	50,000	50,000	50,000	50,000
Accounting income	0	50,000	50,000	0	0

Why would the stores continue to operate a machine in Years 4 and 5 if it produces no profits? What are the cash flows from investing in a machine? Assume each tewgit machine is completely depreciated and has no salvage value at the end of its 5-year life.

6.2 *Discount* Incremental *Cash Flows*

A project's present value depends on the *extra* cash flows that it produces. Forecast first the firm's cash flows if you go ahead with the project. Then forecast the cash flows if you *don't* accept the project. Take the difference and you have the extra (or *incremental*) cash flows produced by the project:

$$\text{Incremental cash flow} = \text{cash flow with project} - \text{cash flow without project}$$

▶ **Example 6.2**   *Launching a New Product*

Consider the decision by Intel to launch its Pentium microprocessor in 1993. A successful launch could mean sales of 50 million processors a year and several billion dollars in profits.

But are these profits all incremental cash flows? Certainly not. Our with-versus-without principle reminds us that we need also to think about what the cash flows would be *without* the new processor. Intel recognized that if it went ahead with the Pentium, demand for its older 486 processors would be reduced. The incremental cash flows therefore are

$$\text{Cash flow with Pentium (including lower cash flow from 486 processors)} - \text{cash flow without Pentium (with higher cash flow from 486 processors)}$$

The trick in capital budgeting is to trace all the incremental flows from a proposed project. Here are some things to look out for.

Include All Indirect Effects

Intel's new processor illustrates a common indirect effect. New products often damage sales of an existing product. Of course, companies frequently introduce new products anyway, usually because they believe that their existing product line is under threat from competition. Even if you don't go ahead with a new product, there is no guarantee that sales of the existing product line will continue at their present level. Sooner or later they will decline.

Sometimes a new project will *help* the firm's existing business. Suppose that you are the financial manager of an airline that is considering opening a new short-haul route from Peoria, Illinois, to Chicago's O'Hare Airport. When considered in isolation, the new route may have a negative NPV. But once you allow for the additional business that the new route brings to your other traffic out of O'Hare, it may be a very worthwhile investment.

> To forecast incremental cash flow, you must trace out all indirect effects of accepting the project.

Some capital investments have very long lives once all indirect effects are recognized. Consider the introduction of a new jet engine. Engine manufacturers often offer attractive pricing to achieve early sales, because once an engine is installed, 15 years' sales of replacement parts are almost assured. Also, since airlines prefer to reduce the number of different engines in their fleet, selling jet engines today improves sales tomorrow as well. Later sales will generate further demands for replacement parts. Thus the string of incremental effects from the first sales of a new model engine can run out 20 years or more.

Forget Sunk Costs

Sunk costs are like spilled milk: they are past and irreversible outflows.

> **Sunk costs remain the same whether or not you accept the project. Therefore, they do not affect project NPV.**

Unfortunately, managers often are influenced by sunk costs. For example, in 1971 Lockheed sought a federal guarantee for a bank loan to continue development of the Tristar airplane. Lockheed and its supporters argued that it would be foolish to abandon a project on which nearly $1 billion had already been spent. This was a poor argument, however, because the $1 billion was sunk. The relevant questions were how much more needed to be invested and whether the finished product warranted the *incremental* investment.

Lockheed's supporters were not the only ones to appeal to sunk costs. Some of its critics claimed that it would be foolish to continue with a project that offered no prospect of a satisfactory return on that $1 billion. This argument too was faulty. The $1 billion was gone, and the decision to continue with the project should have depended only on the return on the incremental investment.

Include Opportunity Costs

opportunity cost: Benefit or cash flow forgone as a result of an action.

Resources are almost never free, even when no cash changes hands. For example, suppose a new manufacturing operation uses land that could otherwise be sold for $100,000. This resource is costly; by using the land you pass up the opportunity to sell it. There is no out-of-pocket cost but there is an **opportunity cost,** that is, the value of the forgone alternative use of the land.

This example prompts us to warn you against judging projects "before versus after" rather than "with versus without." A manager comparing before versus after might not assign any value to the land because the firm owns it both before and after:

Before	Take Project	After	Cash Flow, Before versus After
Firm owns land	⟶	Firm still owns land	0

The proper comparison, with versus without, is as follows:

Before	Take Project	After	Cash Flow, with Project
Firm owns land	⟶	Firm still owns land	0

Before	Do Not Take Project	After	Cash Flow, without Project
Firm owns land	⟶	Firm sells land for $100,000	$100,000

Comparing the cash flows with and without the project, we see that $100,000 is given up by undertaking the project. The original cost of purchasing the land is irrelevant—that cost is sunk.

> **The opportunity cost equals the cash that could be realized from selling the land now, and therefore is a relevant cash flow for project evaluation.**

When the resource can be freely traded, its opportunity cost is simply the market price.[1] However, sometimes opportunity costs are difficult to estimate. Suppose that you go ahead with a project to develop Computer Nouveau, pulling your software team off their work on a new operating system that some existing customers are not-so-patiently awaiting. The exact cost of infuriating those customers may be impossible to calculate, but you'll think twice about the opportunity cost of moving the software team to Computer Nouveau.

Recognize the Investment in Working Capital

net working capital: Current assets minus current liabilities.

Net working capital (often referred to simply as *working capital*) is the difference between a company's short-term assets and liabilities. The principal short-term assets are cash, accounts receivable (customers' unpaid bills), and inventories of raw materials and finished goods. The principal short-term liabilities are accounts payable (bills that *you* have not paid), notes payable, and accruals (liabilities for items such as wages or taxes that have recently been incurred but have not yet been paid).

Most projects entail an additional investment in working capital. For example, before you can start production, you need to invest in inventories of raw materials. Then, when you deliver the finished product, customers may be slow to pay and accounts receivable will increase. (Remember Reggie Hotspur's computer sale, described in Example 6.1. It required a $500,000, six-month investment in accounts receivable.) Next year, as business builds up, you may need a larger stock of raw materials and you may have even more unpaid bills.

> **Investments in working capital, just like investments in plant and equipment, result in cash outflows.**

We find that working capital is one of the most common sources of confusion in forecasting project cash flows.[2] Here are the most common mistakes:

1. *Forgetting about working capital entirely.* We hope that you never fall into that trap.
2. *Forgetting that working capital may change during the life of the project.* Imagine that you sell $100,000 of goods per year and customers pay on average 6 months late. You will therefore have $50,000 of unpaid bills. Now you increase prices by 10 percent, so that revenues increase to $110,000. If customers continue to pay 6 months late, unpaid bills increase to $55,000, and therefore you need to make an *additional* investment in working capital of $5,000.
3. *Forgetting that working capital is recovered at the end of the project.* When the project comes to an end, inventories are run down, any unpaid bills are (you hope) paid off, and you can recover your investment in working capital. This generates a cash *inflow*.

---

[1] If the value of the land to the firm were less than the market price, the firm would sell it. On the other hand, the opportunity cost of using land in a particular project cannot exceed the cost of buying an equivalent parcel to replace it.

[2] If you are not clear *why* working capital affects cash flow, look back to Chapter 2, where we gave a primer on working capital and a couple of simple examples.

Beware of Allocated Overhead Costs

We have already mentioned that the accountant's objective in gathering data is not always the same as the investment analyst's. A case in point is the allocation of overhead costs such as rent, heat, or electricity. These overhead costs may not be related to a particular project, but they must be paid for nevertheless. Therefore, when the accountant assigns costs to the firm's projects, a charge for overhead is usually made. But our principle of incremental cash flows says that in investment appraisal we should include only the *extra* expenses that would result from the project.

> A project may generate extra overhead costs, but then again, it may not. We should be cautious about assuming that the accountant's allocation of overhead costs represents the *incremental* cash flow that would be incurred by accepting the project.

▶ **Self-Test 6.2**

A firm is considering an investment in a new manufacturing plant. The site already is owned by the company, but existing buildings would need to be demolished. Which of the following should be treated as incremental cash flows?

a. The market value of the site.
b. The market value of the existing buildings.
c. Demolition costs and site clearance.
d. The cost of a new access road put in last year.
e. Lost cash flows on other projects due to executive time spent on the new facility.
f. Future depreciation of the new plant.

6.3 Discount Nominal Cash Flows by the Nominal Cost of Capital

The distinction between nominal and real cash flows and interest rates is crucial in capital budgeting. Interest rates are usually quoted in *nominal* terms. If you invest $100 in a bank deposit offering 6 percent interest, then the bank promises to pay you $106 at the end of the year. It makes no promises about what that $106 will buy. The real rate of interest on the bank deposit depends on inflation. If inflation is 2 percent, that $106 will buy you only 4 percent more goods at the end of the year than your $100 could buy today. The *real* rate of interest is therefore about 4 percent.[3]

If the discount rate is nominal, consistency requires that cash flows be estimated in nominal terms as well, taking account of trends in selling price, labor and materi-

---

[3]Remember from Chapter 3,

$$\text{Real rate of interest} \approx \text{nominal rate of interest} - \text{inflation rate}$$

The exact formula is

$$1 + \text{real rate of interest} = \frac{1 + \text{nominal rate of interest}}{1 + \text{inflation rate}}$$

$$= \frac{1.06}{1.02} = 1.0392$$

Therefore, the real interest rate is .039, or 3.9 percent.

als costs, and so on. This calls for more than simply applying a single assumed inflation rate to all components of cash flow. Some costs or prices increase faster than inflation, some slower. For example, perhaps you have entered into a 5-year fixed-price contract with a supplier. No matter what happens to inflation over this period, this part of your costs is fixed in nominal terms.

Of course, there is nothing wrong with discounting real cash flows at the real interest rate, although this is not commonly done. We saw in Chapter 3 that real cash flows discounted at the real discount rate give exactly the same present values as nominal cash flows discounted at the nominal rate.

> **It should go without saying that you cannot mix and match real and nominal quantities. Real cash flows must be discounted at a real discount rate, nominal cash flows at a nominal rate. Discounting real cash flows at a nominal rate is a *big* mistake.**

While the need to maintain consistency may seem like an obvious point, analysts sometimes forget to account for the effects of inflation when forecasting future cash flows. As a result, they end up discounting real cash flows at a nominal interest rate. This can grossly understate project values.

▶ **Example 6.3**   *Cash Flows and Inflation*

City Consulting Services is considering moving into a new office building. The cost of a 1-year lease is $8,000, but this cost will increase in future years at the annual inflation rate of 3 percent. The firm believes that it will remain in the building for 4 years. What is the present value of its rental costs if the discount rate is 10 percent?

The present value can be obtained by discounting the nominal cash flows at the 10 percent discount rate as follows:

Year	Cash Flow	Present Value at 10% Discount Rate	
1	8,000	$8,000/1.10$	$= 7,272.73$
2	$8,000 \times 1.03 = 8,240$	$8,240/1.10^2$	$= 6,809.92$
3	$8,000 \times 1.03^2 = 8,487.20$	$8,487.20/1.10^3$	$= 6,376.56$
4	$8,000 \times 1.03^3 = 8,741.82$	$8,741.82/1.10^4$	$= \underline{5,970.78}$
			$\$26,429.99$

Alternatively, the real discount rate can be calculated as $1.10/1.03 - 1 = .067961 = 6.7961\%$. The present value of the cash flows can also be computed by discounting the real cash flows at the real discount rate as follows:

Year	Real Cash Flow	Present Value at 6.7961% Discount Rate	
1	$8,000/1.03 = 7,766.99$	$7,766.99/1.067961$	$= 7,272.73$
2	$8,240/1.03^2 = 7,766.99$	$7,766.99/1.067961^2$	$= 6,809.92$
3	$8,487.20/1.03^3 = 7,766.99$	$7,766.99/1.067961^3$	$= 6,376.56$
4	$8,741.82/1.03^4 = 7,766.99$	$7,766.99/1.067961^4$	$= \underline{5,970.78}$
			$\$26,429.99$

Notice the real cash flow is a constant, since the lease payment increases at the rate of inflation. The present value of *each* cash flow is the same regardless of the method used to discount. The sum of the present values is, of course, also identical.

▶ **Self-Test 6.3**Nasty Industries is closing down an outmoded factory and throwing all of its workers out on the street. Nasty's CEO, Cruella DeLuxe, is enraged to learn that it must continue to pay for workers' health insurance for 4 years. The cost per worker next year will be $2,400 per year, but the inflation rate is 4 percent, and health costs have been increasing at three percentage points faster than inflation. What is the present value of this obligation? The (nominal) discount rate is 10 percent.

6.4 Separate Investment and Financing Decisions

When we calculate the cash flows from a project, we ignore how that project is financed. The company may decide to finance partly by debt but, even if it did, we would *neither* subtract the debt proceeds from the required investment *nor* recognize the interest and principal payments as cash outflows. Regardless of the actual financing, we should view the project as if it were all equity-financed, treating all cash outflows required for the project as coming from stockholders and all cash inflows as going to them.

We do this to separate the analysis of the investment decision from the financing decision. We first measure whether the project has a positive net present value, assuming all-equity financing. Then we can undertake a separate analysis of the financing decision. We discuss financing decisions later in the book.

6.5 Example: Blooper Industries

The best way to understand how to track a project's cash flows is to work through an example. As the newly appointed financial manager of Blooper Industries, you are about to analyze a proposal for mining and selling a small deposit of high-grade magnoosium ore.[4] You are given the forecasts shown in Table 6.1. We will walk through the lines in the table.

Capital Investment (line 1).   The project requires an investment of $10 million in mining machinery. At the end of 5 years the machinery has no further value.

Working Capital (lines 2 and 3).   Line 2 shows the level of working capital. This increases in the initial years, but the working capital is recovered at the end of the

[4]Readers have inquired whether magnoosium is a real substance. Here, now, for the first time, are the facts. Magnoosium was created in the early days of TV, when a splendid-sounding announcer closed a variety show by saying, "This program has been brought to you by Blooper Industries, proud producer of aleemium, magnoosium, and stool." We forget the company, but the blooper really happened.

TABLE 6.1

Profit projections for Blooper's magnoosium mine (figures in thousands of dollars)

	Year: 0	1	2	3	4	5	6
1. Capital investment	10,000						
2. Working capital	1,500	4,075	4,279	4,493	4,717	3,039	0
3. Change in working capital	1,500	2,575	204	214	225	−1,678	−3,039
4. Revenues		15,000	15,750	16,538	17,364	18,233	
5. Expenses		10,000	10,500	11,025	11,576	12,155	
6. Depreciation of mining equipment		2,000	2,000	2,000	2,000	2,000	
7. Pretax profit		3,000	3,250	3,513	3,788	4,078	
8. Tax (35 percent)		1,050	1,137	1,230	1,326	1,427	
9. Profit after tax		1,950	2,113	2,283	2,462	2,651	

project's life. We will look soon at where these figures came from, but for now you can take them on trust.

Line 3 shows the *change* in working capital from year to year. Notice that in Years 1–4 the change is positive; in these years the project requires a continuing investment in working capital. Starting in Year 5 the change is negative; there is a *disinvestment* as working capital is recovered.

Revenues (line 4). The company expects to be able to sell 750,000 pounds of magnoosium a year at a price of $20 a pound in Year 1. That points to initial revenues of 750,000 × 20 = $15,000,000. But be careful; inflation is running at about 5 percent a year. If magnoosium prices keep pace with inflation, you should up your forecast of the second-year revenues by 5 percent. Third-year revenues should increase by a further 5 percent, and so on. Line 4 in Table 6.1 shows revenues rising in line with inflation.

The sales forecasts in Table 6.1 are cut off after 5 years. That makes sense if the ore deposit will run out at that time. But if Blooper could make sales for Year 6, you should include them in your forecasts. We have sometimes encountered financial managers who assume a project life of (say) 5 years, even when they confidently expect revenues for 10 years or more. When asked the reason, they explain that forecasting beyond 5 years is just too hazardous. We sympathize, but you can't *avoid* making a forecast. If you value a long-lived project using cash flows for only 5 years, you have implicitly made a forecast of zero cash flows thereafter. Do not arbitrarily truncate a project's life.

Expenses (line 5). We assume that the expenses of mining and refining also increase in line with inflation at 5 percent a year.

straight-line depreciation: Constant depreciation for each year of the asset's accounting life.

Depreciation (line 6). The company applies **straight-line depreciation** to the mining equipment over 5 years. This means that it deducts one-fifth of the initial $10 million investment from profits. Thus line 6 shows that the annual depreciation deduction is $2 million.

Pretax Profit (line 7). Profit after depreciation is equal to (revenues − expenses − depreciation).

Tax (line 8).   Company taxes are 35 percent of pretax profits. For example, in Year 1,

$$\text{Tax} = .35 \times 3,000 = 1,050, \text{ or } \$1,050,000$$

Profit after Tax (line 9).   Profit after tax is simply equal to pretax profit less taxes.

Calculating Blooper's Project Cash Flows

Table 6.1 provides all the information you need to figure out the cash flows on the magnoosium project. Project cash flows are the sum of three components: investment in plant and equipment, investment in working capital, and cash flow from operations:

Cash flow from investments in plant and equipment
+ Cash flow from investments in working capital
+ Cash flow from operations
= Total project cash flow

In Table 6.2 we have set out the project cash flows. Now let's see where these figures came from.

Capital Investment.   Investment in plant and equipment is taken from line 1 of Table 6.1. Blooper's initial investment is a negative cash flow of −$10 million.

Investment in Working Capital.   When the company builds up inventories of refined magnoosium, the company's cash is reduced; when customers are slow to pay their bills, cash is reduced. Thus investment in working capital, just like investment in plant and equipment, produces a negative cash flow. The numbers required for these calculations come from lines 1 and 2 of Table 6.1.

Suppose that Blooper makes an initial (Year 0) investment of $1,500,000 in inventories of magnoosium. Then in Year 1 it accumulates an additional $2,575,000. The *total* level of inventories is now $1,500,000 + $2,575,000 = $4,075,000, but the cash expenditure in Year 1 is simply the $2,575,000 addition to inventory. Thus the $2,575,000 investment in additional inventory results in a cash flow of −$2,575,000.

The investment in working capital shown in Table 6.2 is simply taken from line 3 of Table 6.1. Notice:

- **The cash flow is measured by the *change* in working capital, not the *level* of working capital.**
- **An increase in working capital implies a negative cash flow; a decrease implies a positive cash flow.**

Cash Flow from Operations.   The third component of project cash flow is cash flow from operations. The necessary data for these calculations come from lines 4–9 of Table 6.1. There are at least two ways to work this out:

1. Take the items from the income statement that represent cash flows. These include revenues, cash expenses, and taxes paid, but not depreciation (remember, depreciation is *not* a cash outflow but just an accounting entry). Thus for Year 1,

$$\text{Cash flow from operations} = \text{revenues} - \text{cash expenses} - \text{taxes}$$
$$= 15,000 - 10,000 - 1,050$$
$$= 3,950, \text{ or } \$3,950,000$$

TABLE 6.2

Cash flows for Blooper's magnoosium project (figures in thousands of dollars)

Year:	0	1	2	3	4	5	6
1. Capital investment	−10,000						
2. Investment in working capital	− 1,500	−2,575	− 204	− 214	− 225	+1,678	+3,039
3. Cash flow from operations		+3,950	+4,113	+4,283	+4,462	+4,651	
Total cash flow	−11,500	+1,375	+3,909	+4,069	+4,237	+6,329	+3,039

2. Take the net after-tax profit and add back depreciation or other noncash expenses. For Year 1, we proceed as follows:

	Revenues	15,000
−	Expenses	10,000
−	Depreciation	2,000
=	Profit before tax	3,000
−	Tax at 35%	1,050
=	Net profit	1,950
+	Depreciation	2,000
=	Cash flow from operations	3,950 or $3,950,000

To summarize this approach,

$$\text{Cash flow from operations} = \text{net profit} + \text{depreciation}$$
$$= 1,950 + 2,000$$
$$= 3,950, \text{ or } \$3,950,000$$

▶ **Self-Test 6.4**

A project generates revenues of $600, expenses of $300, and depreciation charges of $200 in a particular year. The firm's tax bracket is 35 percent. Find the operating cash flow of the project using both approaches.

Calculating the NPV of Blooper's Project

You have now derived (in Table 6.2) the forecast cash flows from Blooper's magnoosium mine. Assume that investors expect a return of 12 percent from investments in the capital market with the same risk as the magnoosium project. This is the opportunity cost of the shareholders' money that Blooper is proposing to invest in the project. Therefore, to calculate NPV you need to discount the cash flows at 12 percent.

Table 6.3 sets out the calculations. Remember that to calculate the present value of a cash flow in Year t you can divide the cash flow by $(1 + r)^t$ or you can multiply by a discount factor which is equal to $1/(1 + r)^t$. When all cash flows are discounted and added up, the magnoosium project is seen to offer a positive net present value of about $3.6 million.

Now here is a small point that often causes confusion. To calculate the present value of the first year's cash flow, we divide by $(1 + r) = 1.12$. But this makes sense only if all the sales and all the costs occur exactly 365 days, zero hours, and zero

TABLE 6.3

Cash flows and net present value of Blooper's project (figures in thousands of dollars)

Year:	0	1	2	3	4	5	6
Total cash flow	−11,500	+1,375	+3,909	+4,069	+4,237	+6,329	+3,039
Discount factor	1.0	.8929	.7972	.7118	.6355	.5674	.5066
Present value	−11,500	+1,228	+3,116	+2,896	+2,693	+3,591	+1,540
Net present value	3,564, or $3,564,000						

minutes from now. But of course the year's sales don't all take place on the stroke of midnight on December 31. However, when making capital budgeting decisions, companies are usually happy to pretend that all cash flows occur at 1-year intervals. They pretend this for one reason only—simplicity. When sales forecasts are sometimes little more than intelligent guesses, it may be pointless to inquire how the sales are likely to be spread out during the year.[5]

Further Notes and Wrinkles Arising from Blooper's Project

Before we leave Blooper and its magnoosium project, we should cover a few extra wrinkles.

depreciation tax shield:
Reduction in taxes attributable to the depreciation allowance.

A Further Note on Depreciation.   We have seen that firms can deduct depreciation when calculating their tax bill. Consequently, the depreciation deduction reduces taxable income. For example, if the firm's tax bracket is 35 percent, each additional dollar of depreciation reduces taxable income by $1 and taxes owed by 35 cents. The total **depreciation tax shield** equals the product of depreciation and the tax rate:

Depreciation tax shield = depreciation × tax rate

For Blooper, the depreciation is $2 million annually, so the annual depreciation tax shield is .35 × $2 million = $700,000.

This suggests a third way to calculate cash flow from operations. First calculate net profit assuming zero depreciation, that is, based only on *cash* revenues and expenses, and then add back the tax shield created by depreciation. For example, with no depreciation, cash flow from operations in Year 1 would be calculated as follows:

	Revenues	15,000
−	Expenses	10,000
=	Profit before tax	5,000
−	Tax at 35%	1,750
=	Net profit (with no depreciation)	3,250
+	Depreciation tax shield (2,000 × .35)	700
=	Cash flow from operations	3,950 or $3,950,000

[5]Financial managers sometimes assume cash flows arrive in the middle of the calendar year, that is, at the end of June. This makes NPV also a midyear number. If you are standing at the *start* of the year, the NPV must be discounted for a further half year. To do this, divide the midyear NPV by the square root of $(1 + r)$.

This midyear convention is roughly equivalent to assuming cash flows are distributed evenly throughout the year. This is a bad assumption for some industries. In retailing, for example, most of the cash flow comes late in the year, as the holiday season approaches.

We warned you earlier not to assume that all cash flows are likely to increase with inflation. The depreciation tax shield is a case in point, because the Internal Revenue Service lets companies depreciate only the amount of the original investment. It is no good, for example, going back to the IRS and saying that there has been a lot of inflation since you made the investment and that you should be allowed to depreciate more. The IRS won't listen. The *nominal* amount of depreciation is fixed, and therefore the higher the rate of inflation, the lower the *real* value of the depreciation that you can claim.

We assumed in our calculations that Blooper could depreciate its investment in mining equipment by $2 million a year. That produced an annual tax shield of $2 million $\times$ .35 = $.70 million per year for 5 years. These tax shields increase cash flows from operations and therefore increase present value. So, if Blooper could get those tax shields sooner, they would be worth more, right? Fortunately tax law allows corporations to do just that. It allows *accelerated depreciation*.

Accelerated Cost Recovery System (ACRS): Depreciation method that allows higher tax deductions in early years and lower deductions later.

The rate at which firms are permitted to depreciate equipment is known as the **Accelerated Cost Recovery System,** or **ACRS.** ACRS places assets into one of six classes, each of which has an assumed life. Table 6.4 shows the rate of depreciation that the company can use for each of these classes. Most industrial equipment falls into the 5- and 7-year classes. To keep life simple, we will assume that all of Blooper's mining equipment goes into 5-year assets. Thus Blooper can depreciate 20 percent of

TABLE 6.4

Tax depreciation allowed under the Accelerated Cost Recovery System (figures in percent of depreciable investment)

Year(s)	Recovery Period Class					
	3-Year	5-Year	7-Year	10-Year	15-Year	20-Year
1	33.33	20.00	14.29	10.00	5.00	3.75
2	44.45	32.00	24.49	18.00	9.50	7.22
3	14.81	19.20	17.49	14.40	8.55	6.68
4	7.41	11.52	12.49	11.52	7.70	6.18
5		11.52	8.93	9.22	6.93	5.71
6		5.76	8.93	7.37	6.23	5.28
7			8.93	6.55	5.90	4.89
8			4.45	6.55	5.90	4.52
9				6.55	5.90	4.46
10				6.55	5.90	4.46
11				3.29	5.90	4.46
12					5.90	4.46
13					5.90	4.46
14					5.90	4.46
15					5.90	4.46
16					2.99	4.46
17–20						4.46
21						2.25

Notes:
1. Tax depreciation is lower in the first year because assets are assumed to be in service for 6 months.
2. Real property is depreciated straight-line over 27.5 years for residential property and 39 years for nonresidential property.

TABLE 6.5

The switch from straight-line to ACRS depreciation increases the value of Blooper's depreciation tax shield from $2,523,000 to $2,583,000 (figures in thousands of dollars)

| | Straight-Line Depreciation | | | | ACRS Depreciation | | |
Year	Depreciation	Tax Shield	PV Tax Shield at 12%		Depreciation	Tax Shield	PV Tax Shield at 12%
1	2,000	700	625		2,000	700	625
2	2,000	700	558		3,200	1,120	893
3	2,000	700	498		1,920	672	478
4	2,000	700	445		1,152	403	256
5	2,000	700	397		1,152	403	229
6	0	0	0		576	202	102
Totals	10,000	3,500	2,523		10,000	3,500	2,583

Note: Column sums subject to rounding error.

its $10 million investment in Year 1. In the second year it could deduct depreciation of .32 × 10 = $3.2 million, and so on.[6]

How does use of ACRS depreciation affect the value of the depreciation tax shield for the magnoosium project? Table 6.5 gives the answer. Notice that it does not affect the total amount of depreciation that is claimed. This remains at $10 million just as before. But ACRS allows companies to get the depreciation deduction earlier and that increases the present value of the depreciation tax shield from $2,523,000 to $2,583,000, an increase of $60,000. Before we recognized ACRS depreciation, we calculated project NPV as $3,564,000. When we recognize ACRS, we should increase that figure by $60,000.

All large corporations keep two sets of books, one for stockholders and one for the Internal Revenue Service. It is common to use straight-line depreciation on the stockholder books and ACRS depreciation on the tax books. Only the tax books are relevant in capital budgeting.

▶ **Self-Test 6.5**   Suppose that Blooper's mining equipment could be put in the 3-year recovery period class. What is the present value of the depreciation tax shield?

What to Do about Salvage Value.   We assumed earlier that the mining equipment would be worthless when the magnoosium mine closed. But suppose that it can be sold for $2 million in Year 6. (The $2 million forecast salvage value recognizes inflation.)

You recorded the initial $10 million investment as a negative cash flow. Now in Year 6 you have a forecast return of $2 million of that investment. That is a positive cash flow.

[6]You might wonder why the 5-year asset class provides a depreciation deduction in Years 1 through 6. This is because the tax authorities assume that the assets are in service for only 6 months of the first year and 6 months of the last year. The total project life is 5 years, but that 5-year life spans parts of 6 calendar years. This assumption also explains why the depreciation is lower in the first year than it is in the second.

When you sell the equipment, the IRS will check its books and see that you have already claimed depreciation of $10 million.[7] So the value of your investment in Blooper's tax books will be zero. Any difference between the sale price ($2 million) and the value in the tax books (zero) is treated as a taxable gain. So your sale of the equipment will also land you with an additional tax bill in Year 6 of .35 × ($2 million − 0) = $.70 million. The extra cash flow in Year 6 is

$$\text{Salvage value} - \text{tax on gain} = \$2 \text{ million} - \$.70 \text{ million}$$
$$= \$1.30 \text{ million}$$

When discounted back to Year 0, this adds $.659 million, or $659,000, to the value of the project.

A Further Note on Working Capital. The figures for Blooper's working capital appeared to come out of the air. Table 6.6 shows where they in fact came from.

An important component of working capital is inventories of raw materials, work in process, and finished goods awaiting sale. In this example, we will just look at inventories of refined magnoosium. You estimate that Blooper needs to keep an 8-week supply of refined magnoosium ready for shipment. So each year inventories are about 15 percent of next year's cost of goods sold, reported on the expenses line of Table 6.1 (since 8 weeks is about 15 percent of a year). For example, the initial inventory is .15 × 10,000 = 1,500, or $1.5 million, and by Year 1 you need an inventory of .15 × 10,500 = 1,575, or $1.575 million. This is inserted in the second line of Table 6.6.

The other component of Blooper's working capital is accounts receivable. You estimate that customers will on average pay with a delay of 2 months.[8] Thus you can see from Table 6.6 that at the end of Year 1 you will have accumulated unpaid bills of 2/12 × 15,000 = $2,500. Accounts receivable will equal 2/12 of sales in each year.

Further advances on the working capital front are put off until Chapter 18.

TABLE 6.6
Working capital for Blooper's project (figures in thousands of dollars)

	Year: 0	1	2	3	4	5
1. Revenues		15,000	15,750	16,538	17,364	18,233
2. Inventory of refined magnoosium (15% of *next year's* cost of goods sold)	1,500	1,575	1,654	1,736	1,823	0
3. Accounts receivable (2/12 of this year's revenues)		2,500	2,625	2,756	2,894	3,039
4. Working capital (lines 2 and 3)	1,500	4,075	4,279	4,493	4,717	3,039

[7]The ACRS tax depreciation schedules assume zero salvage value at the end of assets' depreciable lives. For reports to shareholders, however, positive expected salvage values are often recognized. For example, Blooper's financial statements might assume that its $10 million investment in mining equipment would be worth $2 million in Year 6. In this case, depreciation would be based on the *difference* between investment and salvage value, that is, $8 million. Straight-line depreciation would be $1.6 million per year.

[8]For convenience we assume that Blooper pays all its bills immediately and therefore accounts payable equals zero. If it didn't, working capital would be reduced by the amount of the payables.

Summary

1. Here is a checklist to bear in mind when forecasting a project's cash flows:
   * Discount cash flows, not profits.
   * Estimate the project's incremental cash flows—that is, the difference between the cash flows with the project and those without the project.
   * Include all indirect effects of the project, such as its impact on the sales of the firm's other products.
   * Forget sunk costs.
   * Include opportunity costs, such as the value of land which you could otherwise sell.
   * Beware of allocated overhead charges for heat, light, and so on. These may not reflect the incremental effects of the project on these costs.
   * Remember the investment in working capital. As sales increase, the firm may need to make additional investments in working capital and, as the project finally comes to an end, it will recover these investments.
   * Do not include debt interest or the cost of repaying a loan. When calculating NPV, assume that the project is financed entirely by the shareholders and that they receive all the cash flows. This isolates the investment decision from the financing decision.
2. If you use a nominal cost of capital, consistency requires that you forecast nominal cash flows—that is, cash flows that recognize the effect of inflation.
3. Depreciation is not a cash flow. However, because depreciation reduces taxable income, it reduces taxes. This tax reduction is called the depreciation tax shield.

Key Terms

opportunity cost	Accelerated Cost	straight-line depreciation
net working capital	Recovery System (ACRS)	
depreciation tax shield		

Problems

1. **Proper Cash Flows.** Conference Services Inc. has leased a large office building for $4 million per year. The building is larger than the company needs: two of the building's eight stories are almost empty. A manager wants to expand one of her projects, but this will require using one of the empty floors. In calculating the net present value of the proposed expansion, upper management allocates one-eighth of $4 million = $.5 million of building rental costs to the project expansion, reasoning that the project will use one-eighth of the building's capacity.

   a. Is this a reasonable procedure for purposes of calculating NPV?
   b. Can you suggest a better way to assess a cost of the office space used by the project?

2. **Cash Flows.** We've emphasized that the firm should pay attention only to cash flows when assessing the net present value of proposed projects. Depreciation is a noncash expense. Why then does it matter whether we assume straight-line or ACRS depreciation when we assess project NPV?

3. **Proper Cash Flows.** Quick Computing currently sells 10 million computer chips each year at a price of $20 per chip. It is about to introduce a new chip, and it forecasts annual sales of 12 million of these improved chips at a price of $25 each. However, demand for

the old chip will decrease, and sales of the old chip are expected to fall to 3 million per year. The old chip costs $6 each to manufacture, and the new ones will cost $8 each. What is the proper cash flow to use to evaluate the present value of the introduction of the new chip?

4. **Salvage Value.** Quick Computing (from the previous problem) installed its previous generation of computer chip manufacturing equipment 3 years ago. Some of that older equipment will become unnecessary when the company goes into production of its new product. The obsolete equipment, which originally cost $40 million, has been depreciated straight line over an assumed tax life of 5 years, but it can be sold now for $18 million. The firm's tax rate is 35 percent. What is the after-tax cash flow from the sale of the equipment?

5. **Salvage Value.** Your firm purchased machinery with a 7-year ACRS life for $10 million. The project, however, will end after 5 years. If the equipment can be sold for $4 million at the completion of the project, and your firm's tax rate is 35 percent, what is the after-tax cash flow from the sale of the machinery?

6. **Cash Flows and Working Capital.** The only capital investment required for a small project is investment in inventory. Profits this year were $10,000, and inventory increased from $4,000 to $5,000. What was the cash flow from the project?

7. **Calculating Net Income.** The owner of a bicycle repair shop forecasts revenues of $160,000 a year. Variable costs will be $45,000, and rental costs for the shop are $35,000 a year. Depreciation on the repair tools will be $10,000. Prepare an income statement for the shop based on these estimates. The tax rate is 35 percent.

8. **Cash Flows.** Calculate the operating cash flow for the repair shop in the previous problem using all three methods suggested in the chapter: (a) net income plus depreciation; (b) cash inflow/cash outflow analysis; and (c) the depreciation tax shield approach. Confirm that all three approaches result in the same value for cash flow.

9. **Cash Flows and Working Capital.** A house painting business had revenues of $16,000 and expenses of $9,000. There were no depreciation expenses. However, the business reported the following changes in various components of working capital:

	Beginning	End
Accounts receivable	$1,200	$4,500
Accounts payable	600	200

Calculate net cash flow for the business for this period.

10. **Incremental Cash Flows.** A corporation donates a valuable painting from its private collection to an art museum. Which of the following are incremental cash flows associated with the donation?

   a. The price the firm paid for the painting.
   b. The current market value of the painting.
   c. The deduction from income that it declares for its charitable gift.
   d. The reduction in taxes due to its declared tax deduction.

11. **Operating Cash Flows.** Laurel's Lawn Care, Ltd., has a new mower line that can generate revenues of $120,000 per year. Direct production costs are $40,000 and the fixed costs of maintaining the lawn mower factory are $15,000 a year. The factory originally cost $1 million and is being depreciated for tax purposes over 25 years using straight-line depreciation. Calculate the operating cash flows of the project if the firm's tax bracket is 35 percent.

12. **Cash Flows and Working Capital.** A firm had net income last year of $1.2 million. Its depreciation expenses were $.5 million, and its total cash flow was $1.2 million. What happened to net working capital during the year?

13. **Operating Cash Flows.** Talia's Tutus bought a new sewing machine for $40,000 that will be depreciated using the ACRS depreciation schedule for a 5-year recovery period.

    a. Find the depreciation charge each year.
    b. If the sewing machine is sold after 3 years for $20,000, what will be the after-tax proceeds on the sale if the firm's tax bracket is 35 percent?

14. **Cash Flows and Working Capital.** A firm's balance sheets for year-end 1997 and 1998 contain the following data. What happened to investment in net working capital during 1998? All items are in millions of dollars.

	Dec. 31, 1997	Dec. 31, 1998
Accounts receivable	32	35
Inventories	25	30
Accounts payable	12	25

15. **Depreciation and Cash Flow.** Bottoms Up Diaper Service is considering the purchase of a new industrial washer. It can purchase the washer for $6,000 and sell its old washer for $2,000. The new washer will last for 6 years and save $1,500 a year in expenses. The opportunity cost of capital is 15 percent, and the firm's tax rate is 40 percent.

    a. If the firm uses straight-line depreciation to an assumed salvage value of zero over a 6-year life, what are the cash flows of the project in Years 0–6? The new washer will in fact have zero salvage value after 6 years, and the old washer is fully depreciated.
    b. What is project NPV?
    c. What will NPV be if the firm uses ACRS depreciation with a 5-year tax life?

16. **Equivalent Annual Cost.** What is the equivalent annual cost of the washer in the previous problem if the firm uses straight-line depreciation?

17. **Project Evaluation.** Revenues generated by a new fad product in each of the next 5 years are forecast as follows:

Year	Revenues
1	$40,000
2	30,000
3	20,000
4	10,000
Thereafter	0

Expenses are expected to be 40 percent of revenues, and working capital required in each year is expected to be 20 percent of revenues in the following year. The product requires an immediate investment of $50,000 in plant and equipment.

    a. What is the initial investment in the product? Remember working capital.
    b. If the plant and equipment are depreciated over 4 years to a salvage value of zero using straight-line depreciation, and the firm's tax rate is 40 percent, what are the project cash flows in each year?
    c. If the opportunity cost of capital is 10 percent, what is project NPV?
    d. What is project IRR?

18. **Buy versus Lease.** You can buy a car for $25,000 and sell it in 5 years for $5,000. Or you can lease the car for 5 years for $5,000 a year. The discount rate is 10 percent per year.

    a. Which option do you prefer?
    b. What is the maximum amount you should be willing to pay to lease rather than buy the car?

19. **Project Evaluation.** Blooper Industries must replace its magnoosium purification system. Quick & Dirty Systems sells a relatively cheap purification system for $10 million. The system will last 5 years. Do-It-Right sells a sturdier but more expensive system for $12 million; it will last for 8 years. Both systems entail $1 million in operating costs; both will be depreciated straight line to a final value of zero over their useful lives; neither will have any salvage value at the end of its life. The firm's tax rate is 35 percent, and the discount rate is 12 percent. Which system should Blooper install?

20. **Project Evaluation.** The following table presents sales forecasts for Golden Gelt Giftware. The unit price is $40. The unit cost of the giftware is $25.

Year	Unit Sales
1	22,000
2	30,000
3	14,000
4	5,000
Thereafter	0

It is expected that net working capital will amount to 25 percent of sales in the following year. For example, the store will need an initial (Year 0) investment in working capital of .25 × 22,000 × $40 = $220,000. Plant and equipment necessary to establish the Giftware business will require an additional investment of $200,000. This investment will be depreciated using ACRS and a 3-year life. After 4 years, the equipment will have an economic and book value of zero. The firm's tax rate is 35 percent. What is the net present value of the project? The discount rate is 20 percent.

21. **Project Evaluation.** Ilana Industries, Inc., needs a new lathe. It can buy a new high-speed lathe for $1 million. The lathe will cost $35,000 to run, will save the firm $125,000 in labor costs, and will be useful for 10 years. Suppose that for tax purposes, the lathe will be depreciated on a straight-line basis over its 10-year life to a salvage value of $100,000. The actual market value of the lathe at that time also will be $100,000. The discount rate is 10 percent and the corporate tax rate is 35 percent. What is the NPV of buying the new lathe?

22. **Project Evaluation.** The efficiency gains resulting from a just-in-time inventory management system will allow a firm to reduce its level of inventories permanently by $250,000. What is the most the firm should be willing to pay for installing the system?

23. **Project Evaluation.** Better Mousetraps has developed a new trap. It can go into production for an initial investment in equipment of $6 million. The equipment will be depreciated straight line over 5 years to a value of zero, but in fact it can be sold after 5 years for $500,000. The firm believes that working capital at each date must be maintained at a level of 10 percent of next year's forecast sales. The firm estimates production costs equal to $1.50 per trap and believes that the traps can be sold for $4 each. Sales forecasts are given in the following table. The project will come to an end in 5 years, when the trap becomes technologically obsolete. The firm's tax bracket is 35 percent, and the required rate of return on the project is 12 percent. What is project NPV?

Year:	0	1	2	3	4	5	Thereafter
Sales (millions of traps)	0	.5	.6	1.0	1.0	.6	0

24. **Working Capital Management.** Return to the previous problem. Suppose the firm can cut its requirements for working capital in half by using better inventory control systems. By how much will this increase project NPV?

Solutions to Self-Test Questions

6.1 Remember, discount cash flows, not profits. Each tewgit machine costs $250,000 right away. Recognize that outlay, but forget accounting depreciation. Cash flows per machine are:

Year:	0	1	2	3	4	5
Investment (outflow)	−250,000					
Sales		250,000	300,000	300,000	250,000	250,000
Operating expenses		−200,000	−200,000	−200,000	−200,000	−200,000
Cash flow	−250,000	+ 50,000	+100,000	+100,000	+ 50,000	+ 50,000

Each machine is forecast to generate $50,000 of cash flow in Years 4 and 5. Thus it makes sense to keep operating for 5 years.

6.2 a,b. The site and buildings could have been sold or put to another use. Their values are opportunity costs, which should be treated as incremental cash outflows.

   c. Demolition costs are incremental cash outflows.

   d. The cost of the access road is sunk and not incremental.

   e. Lost cash flows from other projects are incremental cash outflows.

   f. Depreciation is not a cash expense and should not be included, except as it affects taxes. (Taxes are discussed later in this chapter.)

6.3 Actual health costs will be increasing at about 7 percent a year.

Year	1	2	3	4
Cost per worker	$2,400	$2,568	$2,748	$2,940

The present value at 10 percent is $9,214 if the first payment is made immediately. If it is delayed a year, present value falls to $8,377.

6.4 The tax rate is $T = 35$ percent. Taxes paid will be

$$T \times (\text{revenue} - \text{expenses} - \text{depreciation}) = .35 \times (600 - 300 - 200) = \$35$$

Operating cash flow can be calculated as follows.

   a.   Revenue − expenses − taxes = 600 − 300 − 35 = $265

   b. Net after-tax income + depreciation = (600 − 300 − 200 − 35) + 200
   $$= 65 + 200 = 265$$

6.5

Year	ACRS 3-Year Depreciation	Tax Shield	PV Tax Shield at 12%
1	3,333	1,167	1,042
2	4,445	1,556	1,240
3	1,481	518	369
4	741	259	165
Totals	10,000	3,500	2,816

The present value increases to 2,816, or $2,816,000.

Minicase

Jack Tar, CFO of Sheetbend & Halyard, Inc., opened the company-confidential envelope. It contained a draft of a competitive bid for a contract to supply duffel canvas to the U.S. Navy. The cover memo from Sheetbend's CEO asked Mr. Tar to review the bid before it was submitted.

The bid and its supporting documents had been prepared by Sheetbend's sales staff. It called for Sheetbend to supply 100,000 yards of duffel canvas per year for 5 years. The proposed selling price was fixed at $30 per yard.

Mr. Tar was not usually involved in sales, but this bid was unusual in at least two respects. First, if accepted by the navy, it would commit Sheetbend to a fixed price, long-term contract. Second, producing the duffel canvas would require an investment of $1.5 million to purchase machinery and to refurbish Sheetbend's plant in Pleasantboro, Maine.

Mr. Tar set to work and by the end of the week had collected the following facts and assumptions:

- The plant in Pleasantboro had been built in the early 1900s and is now idle. The plant was fully depreciated on Sheetbend's books, except for the purchase cost of the land (in 1947) of $10,000.
- Now that the land was valuable shorefront property, Mr. Tar thought the land and the idle plant could be sold, immediately or in the future, for $600,000.
- Refurbishing the plant would cost $500,000. This investment would be depreciated for tax purposes on the 10-year ACRS schedule.

- The new machinery would cost $1 million. This investment could be depreciated on the 5-year ACRS schedule.
- The refurbished plant and new machinery would last for many years. However, the remaining market for duffel canvas was small, and it was not clear that additional orders could be obtained once the navy contract was finished. The machinery was custom built and could be used only for duffel canvas. Its second-hand value at the end of 5 years was probably zero.
- Table 6.7 shows the sales staff's forecasts of income from the navy contract. Mr. Tar reviewed this forecast and decided that its assumptions were reasonable, except that the forecast used book, not tax, depreciation.
- But the forecast income statement contained no mention of working capital. Mr. Tar thought that working capital would average about 10 percent of sales.

Armed with this information, Mr. Tar constructed a spreadsheet to calculate the NPV of the duffel canvas project, assuming that Sheetbend's bid would be accepted by the navy.

He had just finished debugging the spreadsheet when another confidential envelope arrived from Sheetbend's CEO. It contained a firm offer from a Maine real estate developer to purchase Sheetbend's Pleasantboro land and plant for $1.5 million in cash.

Should Mr. Tar recommend submitting the bid to the navy at the proposed price of $30 per yard? The discount rate for this project is 12 percent.

Table 6.7

Forecasted income statement for the navy duffel canvas project (dollar figures in thousands, except price per yard)

Year	1	2	3	4	5
1. Yards sold	100.00	100.00	100.00	100.00	100.00
2. Price per yard	30.00	30.00	30.00	30.00	30.00
3. Revenue (1 × 2)	3,000.00	3,000.00	3,000.00	3,000.00	3,000.00
4. Cost of goods sold	2,100.00	2,184.00	2,271.36	2,362.21	2,456.70
5. Operating cash flow (3 − 4)	900.00	816.00	728.64	637.79	543.30
6. Depreciation	250.00	250.00	250.00	250.00	250.00
7. Income (5 − 6)	650.00	566.00	478.64	387.79	293.30
8. Tax at 35%	227.50	198.10	167.52	135.72	102.65
9. Net income (7 − 8)	$422.50	$367.90	$311.12	$252.06	$190.64

Notes:

1. Yards sold and price per yard would be fixed by contract.
2. Cost of goods includes fixed cost of $300,000 per year plus variable costs of $18 per yard. Costs are expected to increase at the inflation rate of 4 percent per year.
3. Depreciation: A $1 million investment in machinery is depreciated straight-line over 5 years ($200,000 per year). The $500,000 cost of refurbishing the Pleasantboro plant is depreciated straight-line over 10 years ($50,000 per year).

"But Mr. Mitterand, have you thought of sensitivity analysis?"
Prime Minister Margaret Thatcher and President Francois Mitterand meet to sign the treaty leading to construction of a railway tunnel under the English Channel between England and France.
AP/Wide World.

Chapter 7

Project Analysis

*I*t helps to use discounted cash-flow techniques to value new projects but good investment decisions also require good data. Therefore, we start this chapter by thinking about how firms organize the capital budgeting operation to get the kind of information they need. In addition, we look at how they try to ensure that everyone involved works together toward a common goal.

Project evaluation should never be a mechanical exercise in which the financial manager takes a set of cash-flow forecasts and cranks out a net present value. Cash-flow estimates are just that—estimates. Financial managers need to look behind the forecasts to try to understand what makes the project tick and what could go wrong with it. A number of techniques have been developed to help managers identify the key assumptions in their analysis. These techniques involve asking a number of "what-if" questions. What if your market share turns out to be higher or lower than you forecast? What if interest rates rise during the life of the project? In the second part of this chapter we show how managers use the techniques of sensitivity analysis, scenario analysis, and break-even analysis to help answer these what-if questions.

Books about capital budgeting sometimes create the impression that once the manager has made an investment decision, there is nothing to do but sit back and watch the cash flows develop. But since cash flows rarely proceed as anticipated, companies constantly need to modify their operations. If cash flows are better than anticipated, the project may be expanded; if they are worse, it may be scaled back or abandoned altogether. In the third section of this chapter we describe how good managers take account of these options when they analyze a project and why they are willing to pay money today to build in future flexibility.

After studying this chapter you should be able to

▶ Appreciate the practical problems of capital budgeting in large corporations.

▶ Use sensitivity, scenario, and break-even analysis to see how project profitability would be affected by an error in your forecasts and understand why an overestimate of sales is more serious for projects with high operating leverage.

▶ Recognize the importance of managerial flexibility in capital budgeting.

7.1 How Firms Organize the Investment Process

For most sizable firms, investments are evaluated in two separate stages.

Stage 1: The Capital Budget

capital budget: List of planned investment projects.

Once a year, the head office generally asks each of its divisions and plants to provide a list of the investments that they would like to make.[1] These are gathered together into a proposed **capital budget.**

---

[1]Large firms may be divided into several divisions. For example, International Paper has divisions that specialize in printing paper, packaging, specialty products, and forest products. Each of these divisions may be responsible for a number of plants.

This budget is then reviewed and pruned by senior management and staff specializing in planning and financial analysis. Usually there are negotiations between the firm's senior management and its divisional management, and there may also be special analyses of major outlays or ventures into new areas. Once the budget has been approved, it generally remains the basis for planning over the ensuing year.

Many investment proposals bubble up from the bottom of the organization. But sometimes the ideas are likely to come from higher up. For example, the managers of plants A and B cannot be expected to see the potential benefits of closing their plants and consolidating production at a new plant C. We expect divisional management to propose plant C. Similarly, divisions 1 and 2 may not be eager to give up their own data processing operations to a large central computer. That proposal would come from senior management.

Senior management's concern is to see that the capital budget matches the firm's strategic plans. It needs to ensure that the firm is concentrating its efforts in areas where it has a real competitive advantage. As part of this effort, management must also identify declining businesses that should be sold or allowed to run down.

The firm's capital investment choices should reflect both "bottom-up" and "top-down" processes—capital budgeting and strategic planning, respectively. The two processes should complement each other. Plant and division managers, who do most of the work in bottom-up capital budgeting, may not see the forest for the trees. Strategic planners may have a mistaken view of the forest because they do not look at the trees.

Stage 2: Project Authorizations

The annual budget is important because it allows everybody to exchange ideas before attitudes have hardened and personal commitments have been made. However, the fact that your pet project has been included in the annual budget doesn't mean you have permission to go ahead with it. At a later stage you will need to draw up a detailed proposal describing particulars of the project, engineering analyses, cash-flow forecasts, and present value calculations. If your project is large, this proposal may have to pass a number of hurdles before it is finally approved.

The type of backup information that you need to provide depends on the project category. For example, some firms use a fourfold breakdown:

1. Outlays required by law or company policy, for example, for pollution control equipment. These outlays do not need to be justified on financial grounds. The main issue is whether requirements are satisfied at the lowest possible cost. The decision is therefore likely to hinge on engineering analyses of alternative technologies.
2. Maintenance or cost reduction, such as machine replacement. Engineering analysis is also important in machine replacement, but new machines have to pay their own way. In this category of proposal the firm faces the classical capital budgeting problems described in Chapters 5 and 6.
3. Capacity expansion in existing businesses. Projects in this category are less straightforward; these decisions may hinge on forecasts of demand, possible shifts in technology, and the reactions of competitors.
4. Investment for new products. Projects in this category are most likely to depend on strategic decisions. The first projects in a new area may not have positive NPVs if considered in isolation, but they may give the firm a valuable option to undertake follow-up projects. More about this later in the chapter.

Problems and Some Solutions

Valuing capital investment opportunities is hard enough when you can do the entire job yourself. In most firms, however, capital budgeting is a cooperative effort, and this brings with it some challenges.

Ensuring that Forecasts Are Consistent.   Inconsistent assumptions often creep into investment proposals. For example, suppose that the manager of the furniture division is bullish (optimistic) on housing starts but the manager of the appliance division is bearish (pessimistic). This inconsistency makes the projects proposed by the furniture division look more attractive than those of the appliance division.

To ensure consistency, many firms begin the capital budgeting process by establishing forecasts of economic indicators, such as inflation and the growth in national income, as well as forecasts of particular items that are important to the firm's business, such as housing starts or the price of raw materials. These forecasts can then be used as the basis for all project analyses.

Eliminating Conflicts of Interest.   In Chapter 1 we pointed out that while managers want to do a good job, they are also concerned about their own futures. If the interests of managers conflict with those of stockholders, the result is likely to be poor investment decisions. For example, new plant managers naturally want to demonstrate good performance right away. To this end, they might propose quick-payback projects even if NPV is sacrificed. Unfortunately, many firms measure performance and reward managers in ways that encourage such behavior. If the firm always demands quick results, it is unlikely that plant managers will concentrate only on NPV.

Reducing Forecast Bias.   Someone who is keen to get a project proposal accepted is also likely to look on the bright side when forecasting the project's cash flows. Such overoptimism is a common feature in financial forecasts. For example, think of large public expenditure proposals. How often have you heard of a new missile, dam, or highway that actually cost *less* than was originally forecast? Think back to the Eurotunnel project introduced in Chapter 5. The final cost of the project was about 50 percent higher than initial forecasts. It is probably impossible to ever eliminate bias completely, but if senior management is aware of why bias occurs, it is at least partway to solving the problem.

Project sponsors are likely to overstate their case deliberately only if the head office encourages them to do so. For example, if middle managers believe that success depends on having the largest division rather than the most profitable one, they will propose large expansion projects that they do not believe have the largest possible net present value. Or if divisions must compete for limited resources, they will try to outbid each other for those resources. The fault in such cases is top management's—if lower level managers are not rewarded based on net present value and contribution to firm value, it should not be surprising that they focus their efforts elsewhere.

Other problems stem from sponsors' eagerness to obtain approval for their favorite projects. As the proposal travels up the organization, alliances are formed. Thus once a division has screened its own plants' proposals, the plants in that division unite in competing against outsiders. The result is that the head office may receive several thousand investment proposals each year, all essentially sales documents presented by united fronts and designed to persuade. The forecasts have been doctored to ensure that NPV appears positive.

Since it is difficult for senior management to evaluate each specific assumption in an investment proposal, capital investment decisions are effectively decentralized whatever the rules say. Some firms accept this; others rely on head office staff to check capital investment proposals.

Sorting the Wheat from the Chaff. Senior managers are continually bombarded with requests for funds for capital expenditures. All these requests are supported with detailed analyses showing that the projects have positive NPVs. How then can managers ensure that only worthwhile projects make the grade? One response of senior managers to this problem of poor information is to impose rigid expenditure limits on individual plants or divisions. These limits force the subunits to choose among projects. The firm ends up using capital rationing not because capital is unobtainable but as a way of decentralizing decisions.[2]

Senior managers might also ask some searching questions about why the project has a positive NPV. After all, if the project is so attractive, why hasn't someone already undertaken it? Will others copy your idea if it is so profitable? Positive NPVs are plausible only if your company has some competitive advantage.

Such an advantage can arise in several ways. You may be smart or lucky enough to be the first to the market with a new or improved product for which customers will pay premium prices. Your competitors eventually will enter the market and squeeze out excess profits, but it may take them several years to do so. Or you may have a proprietary technology or production cost advantage that competitors cannot easily match. You may have a contractual advantage such as the distributorship for a particular region. Or your advantage may be as simple as a good reputation and an established customer list.

Analyzing competitive advantage can also help ferret out projects that incorrectly appear to have a negative NPV. If you are the lowest cost producer of a profitable product in a growing market, then you should invest to expand along with the market. If your calculations show a negative NPV for such an expansion, then you probably have made a mistake.

7.2 Some "What-If" Questions

Sensitivity Analysis

sensitivity analysis:
Analysis of the effects of changes in sales, costs, and so on, on project profitability.

Uncertainty means that more things *can* happen than *will* happen. Therefore, whenever managers are given a cash-flow forecast, they try to determine what else might happen and the implications of those possible events. This is called **sensitivity analysis.**

Put yourself in the well-heeled shoes of the financial manager of the Finefodder supermarket chain. Finefodder is considering opening a new superstore in Gravenstein and your staff members have prepared the figures shown in Table 7.1. The figures are fairly typical for a new supermarket, except that to keep the example simple we have assumed no inflation. We have also assumed that the entire investment can be depreciated straight-line for tax purposes, we have neglected the working capital

[2]We discussed capital rationing in Chapter 5.

Table 7.1

Cash-flow forecasts for Finefodder's new superstore

	Year 0	Years 1–12
Investment	−$5,400,000	
1. Sales		$16,000,000
2. Variable costs		13,000,000
3. Fixed costs		2,000,000
4. Depreciation		450,000
5. Pretax profit $(1 - 2 - 3 - 4)$		550,000
6. Taxes (at 40%)		220,000
7. Profit after tax		330,000
8. Cash flow from operations $(4 + 7)$		780,000
Net cash flow	−$5,400,000	$ 780,000

requirement, and we have ignored the fact that at the end of the 12 years you could sell off the land and buildings.

As an experienced financial manager, you recognize immediately that these cash flows constitute an annuity and therefore you calculate present value by multiplying the $780,000 cash flow by the 12-year annuity factor. If the cost of capital is 8 percent, present value is

$$PV = \$780,000 \times \text{12-year annuity factor}$$
$$= \$780,000 \times 7.536 = \$5.878 \text{ million}$$

Subtract the initial investment of $5.4 million and you obtain a net present value of $478,000:

$$NPV = PV - \text{investment}$$
$$= \$5.878 \text{ million} - \$5.4 \text{ million} = \$478,000$$

Before you agree to accept the project, however, you want to delve behind these forecasts and identify the key variables that will determine whether the project succeeds or fails.

Some of the costs of running a supermarket are fixed. For example, regardless of the level of output, you still have to heat and light the store and pay the store manager. These **fixed costs** are forecast to be $2 million per year.

Other costs vary with the level of sales. In particular, the lower the sales, the less food you need to buy. Also, if sales are lower than forecast, you can operate a lower number of checkouts and reduce the staff needed to restock the shelves. The new superstore's variable costs are estimated at 81.25 percent of sales. Thus **variable costs** = .8125 × $16 million = $13 million.

The initial investment of $5.4 million will be depreciated on a straight-line basis over the 12-year period, resulting in annual depreciation of $450,000. Profits are taxed at a rate of 40 percent.

These seem to be the important things you need to know, but look out for things that may have been forgotten. Perhaps there will be delays in obtaining planning permission, or perhaps you will need to undertake costly landscaping. The greatest dangers often lie in these *unknown* unknowns, or "unk-unks," as scientists call them.

fixed costs: Costs that do not depend on the level of output.

variable costs: Costs that change as the level of output changes.

Table 7.2
Sensitivity analysis for superstore project

Variable	Range			NPV		
	Pessimistic	**Expected**	**Optimistic**	**Pessimistic**	**Expected**	**Optimistic**
Investment	6,200,000	5,400,000	5,000,000	−121,000	+478,000	+778,000
Sales	14,000,000	16,000,000	18,000,000	−1,218,000	+478,000	+2,174,000
Variable cost as percent of sales	83	81.25	80	−788,000	+478,000	+1,382,000
Fixed cost	2,100,000	2,000,000	1,900,000	+26,000	+478,000	+930,000

Having found no unk-unks (no doubt you'll find them later), you look at how NPV may be affected if you have made a wrong forecast of sales, costs, and so on. To do this, you first obtain optimistic and pessimistic estimates for the underlying variables. These are set out in the left-hand columns of Table 7.2.

Next you see what happens to NPV under the optimistic or pessimistic forecasts for each of these variables. You recalculate project NPV under these various forecasts to determine which variables are most critical to NPV.

▶ **Example 7.1**   *Sensitivity Analysis*

The right-hand side of Table 7.2 shows the project's net present value if the variables are set *one at a time* to their optimistic and pessimistic values. For example, if fixed costs are $1.9 million rather than the forecast $2.0 million, annual cash flows are increased by (1 − tax rate) × ($2.0 million − $1.9 million) = .6 × $100,000 = $60,000. If the cash flow increases by $60,000 a year for 12 years, then the project's present value increases by $60,000 times the 12-year annuity factor, or $60,000 × 7.536 = $452,000. Therefore, NPV increases from the expected value of $478,000 to $478,000 + $452,000 = $930,000, as shown in the bottom right corner of the table. The other entries in the three columns on the right in Table 7.2 similarly show how the NPV of the project changes when each input is changed.

Your project is by no means a sure thing. The principal uncertainties appear to be sales and variable costs. For example, if sales are only $14 million rather than the forecast $16 million (and all other forecasts are unchanged), then the project has an NPV of −$1.218 million. If variable costs are 83 percent of sales (and all other forecasts are unchanged), then the project has an NPV of −$788,000.

▶ **Self-Test 7.1**   Recalculate cash flow as in Table 7.1 if variable costs are 83 percent of sales. Confirm that NPV will be −$788,000.

Value of Information.   Now that you know the project could be thrown badly off course by a poor estimate of sales, you might like to see whether it is possible to resolve some of this uncertainty. Perhaps your worry is that the store will fail to attract sufficient shoppers from neighboring towns. In that case, additional survey data and more careful analysis of travel times may be worthwhile.

On the other hand, there is less value to gathering additional information about fixed costs. Because the project is marginally profitable even under pessimistic assumptions about fixed costs, you are unlikely to be in trouble if you have misestimated that variable.

Limits to Sensitivity Analysis.   Your analysis of the forecasts for Finefodder's new superstore is known as a *sensitivity analysis*. Sensitivity analysis expresses cash flows in terms of unknown variables and then calculates the consequences of misestimating those variables. It forces the manager to identify the underlying factors, indicates where additional information would be most useful, and helps to expose confused or inappropriate forecasts.

Of course, there is no law stating which variables you should consider in your sensitivity analysis. For example, you may wish to look separately at labor costs and the costs of the goods sold. Or, if you are concerned about a possible change in the corporate tax rate, you may wish to look at the effect of such a change on the project's NPV.

One drawback to sensitivity analysis is that it gives somewhat ambiguous results. For example, what exactly does *optimistic* or *pessimistic* mean? One department may be interpreting the terms in a different way from another. Ten years from now, after hundreds of projects, hindsight may show that one department's pessimistic limit was exceeded twice as often as the other's; but hindsight won't help you now while you're making the investment decision.

Another problem with sensitivity analysis is that the underlying variables are likely to be interrelated. For example, if sales exceed expectations, demand will likely be stronger than you anticipated and your profit margins will be wider. Or, if wages are higher than your forecast, both variable costs and fixed costs are likely to be at the upper end of your range.

Because of these connections, you cannot push *one-at-a-time* sensitivity analysis too far. It is impossible to obtain expected, optimistic, and pessimistic values for total *project* cash flows from the information in Table 7.2. Still, it does give a sense of which variables should be most closely monitored.

Scenario Analysis

scenario analysis: Project analysis given a particular combination of assumptions.

When variables are interrelated, managers often find it helpful to look at how their project would fare under different scenarios. **Scenario analysis** allows them to look at different but *consistent* combinations of variables. Forecasters generally prefer to give an estimate of revenues or costs under a particular scenario rather than giving some absolute optimistic or pessimistic value.

▶ **Example 7.2**   *Scenario Analysis*

You are worried that Stop and Scoff may decide to build a new store in nearby Salome. That would reduce sales in your Gravenstein store by 15 percent and you might be forced into a price war to keep the remaining business. Prices might be reduced to the point that variable costs equal 82 percent of revenue. Table 7.3 shows

Table 7.3
Scenario analysis, NPV of Finefodder's Gravenstein superstore with scenario of new competing store in nearby Salome

	Cash Flows Years 1–12	
	Base Case	**Competing Store Scenario[a]**
1. Sales	$16,000,000	$13,600,000
2. Variable costs	13,000,000	11,152,000
3. Fixed costs	2,000,000	2,000,000
4. Depreciation	450,000	450,000
5. Pretax profit (1 − 2 − 3 − 4)	550,000	−2,000
6. Taxes (40%)	220,000	−800
7. Profit after tax	330,000	−1,200
8. Cash flow from operations (4 + 7)	780,000	448,800
Present value of cash flows	5,878,000	3,382,000
NPV	478,000	−2,018,000

[a]*Assumptions:* Competing store causes (1) a 15 percent reduction in sales, and (2) variable costs to increase to 82 percent of sales.

that under this scenario of lower sales and smaller margins your new venture would no longer be worthwhile.

simulation analysis: Estimation of the probabilities of different possible outcomes, e.g., from an investment project.

An extension of scenario analysis is called **simulation analysis**. Here, instead of specifying a relatively small number of scenarios, a computer generates several hundred or thousand possible combinations of variables according to probability distributions specified by the analyst. Each combination of variables corresponds to one scenario. Project NPV and other outcomes of interest can be calculated for each combination of variables, and the entire probability distribution of outcomes can be constructed from the simulation results.

▶ **Self-Test 7.2**   What is the basic difference between sensitivity analysis and scenario analysis?

Break-Even Analysis

When we undertake a sensitivity analysis of a project or when we look at alternative scenarios, we are asking how serious it would be if we have misestimated sales or costs. Managers sometimes prefer to rephrase this question and ask how far off the estimates could be before the project begins to lose money. This exercise is known as **break-even analysis.**

break-even analysis: Analysis of the level of sales at which the company breaks even.

For many projects, the make-or-break variable is sales volume. Therefore, managers most often focus on the break-even level of sales. However, you might also look at other variables, for example, at how high costs could be before the project goes into the red.

As it turns out, "losing money" can be defined in more than one way. Most often, the break-even condition is defined in terms of accounting profits. More properly, however, it should be defined in terms of net present value. We will start with accounting break-even, show that it can lead you astray, and then show how NPV break-even can be used as an alternative.

Accounting Break-Even Analysis

The *accounting break-even* point is the level of sales at which profits are zero or, equivalently, at which total revenues equal total costs. As we have seen, some costs are fixed regardless of the level of output. Other costs vary with the level of output.

When you first analyzed the superstore project, you came up with the following estimates:

Sales	$16	million
Variable cost	13	million
Fixed costs	2	million
Depreciation	0.45	million

Notice that variable costs are 81.25 percent of sales. So, for each additional dollar of sales, costs increase by only $.8125. We can easily determine how much business the superstore needs to attract to avoid losses. If the store sells nothing, the income statement will show fixed costs of $2 million and depreciation of $450,000. Thus there will be a *loss* of $2.45 million. Each dollar of sales reduces this loss by $1.00 − $.8125 =$.1875. Therefore, to cover fixed costs plus depreciation, you need sales of 2.45 million/.1875 = $13.067 million. At this sales level, the firm will break even. More generally,

$$\textbf{Break-even level of revenues} = \frac{\textbf{fixed costs including depreciation}}{\textbf{additional profit from each additional dollar of sales}}$$

Table 7.4 shows how the income statement looks with only $13.067 million of sales.

Figure 7.1 shows how the break-even point is determined. The 45-degree line shows accounting revenues. The cost line shows how costs vary with sales. If the store doesn't sell a cent, it still incurs fixed costs and depreciation amounting to $2.45 million. Each extra dollar of sales adds $.8125 to these costs. When sales are $13.067 million, the two lines cross, indicating that costs equal revenues. For lower sales, revenues are less than costs and the project is in the red; for higher sales, revenues exceed costs and the project moves into the black.

Table 7.4

Income statement, break-even sales volume

Item	$ Thousands	
Revenues	13,067	
Variable costs	10,617	(81.25 percent of sales)
Fixed costs	2,000	
Depreciation	450	
Pretax profit	0	
Taxes	0	
Profit after tax	0	

FIGURE 7.1

Accounting break-even analysis

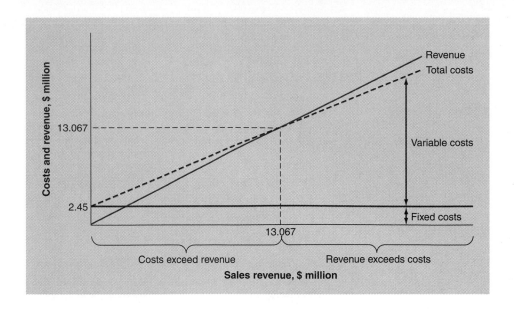

Is a project that breaks even in accounting terms an acceptable investment? If you are not sure about the answer, here's a possibly easier question. Would you be happy about an investment in a stock that after 5 years gave you a total rate of return of zero? We hope not. You might break even on such a stock but a zero return does not compensate you for the time value of money or the risk that you have taken.

> **A project that simply breaks even on an accounting basis gives you your money back but does not cover the opportunity cost of the capital tied up in the project. A project that breaks even in accounting terms will surely have a negative NPV.**

Let's check this with the superstore project. Suppose that in each year the store has sales of $13.067 million—just enough to break even on an accounting basis. What would be the cash flow from operations?

$$\text{Cash flow from operations} = \text{profit after tax} + \text{depreciation}$$
$$= 0 + \$450{,}000 = \$450{,}000$$

The initial investment is $5.4 million. In each of the next 12 years, the firm receives a cash flow of $450,000. So the firm gets its money back:

$$\text{Total cash flow from operations} = \text{initial investment}$$
$$12 \times \$450{,}000 = \$5.4 \text{ million}$$

But revenues are *not* sufficient to repay the *opportunity cost* of that $5.4 million investment. NPV is negative.

NPV Break-Even Analysis

Instead of asking how bad sales can get before the project makes an accounting loss, it is more useful to focus on the point at which NPV switches from positive to negative.

The cash flows of the project in each year will depend on sales as follows:

1. Variable costs	81.25 percent of sales
2. Fixed costs	$2 million
3. Depreciation	$450,000
4. Pretax profit	$(.1875 \times \text{sales}) - \$2.45$ million
5. Tax (at 40%)	$.40 \times (.1875 \times \text{sales} - \$2.45$ million)
6. Profit after tax	$.60 \times (.1875 \times \text{sales} - \$2.45$ million)
7. Cash flow (3 + 6)	$\$450,000 + .60 \times (.1875 \times \text{sales} + \$2.45$ million)
	$= .1125 \times \text{sales} - \$1.02$ million

This cash flow will last for 12 years. So to find its present value we multiply by the 12-year annuity factor. With a discount rate of 8 percent, the present value of $1 a year for each of 12 years is $7.536. Thus the present value of the cash flows is

$$\text{PV (cash flows)} = 7.536 \times (.1125 \times \text{sales} - \$1.02 \text{ million})$$

The project breaks even in present value terms (that is, has a zero NPV) if the present value of these cash flows is equal to the initial $5.4 million investment. Therefore, break-even occurs when

$$\text{PV (cash flows)} = \text{investment}$$
$$7.536 \times (.1125 \times \text{sales} - \$1.02 \text{ million}) = \$5.4 \text{ million}$$
$$-\$7.69 \text{ million} + .8478 \times \text{sales} = \$5.4 \text{ million}$$
$$\text{sales} = \frac{5.4 + 7.69}{.8478} = \$15.4 \text{ million}$$

This implies that the store needs sales of $15.4 million a year for the investment to have a zero NPV. This is more than 18 percent higher than the point at which the project has zero profit.

Figure 7.2 is a plot of the present value of the inflows and outflows from the super-store as a function of annual sales. The two lines cross when sales are $15.4 million.

FIGURE 7.2
NPV break-even analysis

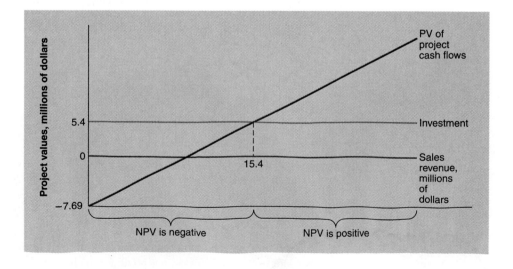

This is the point at which the project has zero NPV. As long as sales are greater than this, the present value of the inflows exceeds the present value of the outflows and the project has a positive NPV.

▶ **Self-Test 7.3**   What would be the NPV break-even level of sales if the capital investment was only $5 million?

▶ **Example 7.3**   *Break-Even Analysis*

We have said that projects that break even on an accounting basis are really making a loss—they are losing the opportunity cost of their investment. Here is a dramatic example. Lophead Aviation is contemplating investment in a new passenger aircraft, code-named the Trinova. Lophead's financial staff has gathered together the following estimates:

1. The cost of developing the Trinova is forecast at $900 million, and this investment can be depreciated in six equal annual amounts.
2. Production of the plane is expected to take place at a steady annual rate over the following 6 years.
3. The average price of the Trinova is expected to be $15.5 million.
4. Fixed costs are forecast at $175 million a year.
5. Variable costs are forecast at $8.5 million a plane.
6. The tax rate is 50 percent.
7. The cost of capital is 10 percent.

How many aircraft does Lophead need to sell to break even in accounting terms? And how many does it need to sell to break even on the basis of NPV? (Notice that the break-even point is defined here in terms of number of aircraft, rather than revenue. But since revenue is proportional to planes sold, these two break-even concepts are interchangeable.)

To answer the first question we set out the profits from the Trinova program in rows 1 to 7 of Table 7.5 (ignore row 8 for a moment).

Table 7.5

Forecast profitability for production of the Trinova airliner (figures in millions of dollars)

	Year 0	Years 1–6
Investment	$900	
1. Sales		15.5 × planes sold
2. Variable costs		8.5 × planes sold
3. Fixed costs		175
4. Depreciation		900/6 = 150
5. Pretax profit (1 − 2 − 3 − 4)		(7 × planes sold) − 325
6. Taxes (at 50%)		(3.5 × planes sold) − 162.5
7. Net profit (5 − 6)		(3.5 × planes sold) − 162.5
8. Net cash flow (4 + 7)	−$900	(3.5 × planes sold) − 12.5

In accounting terms the venture breaks even when pretax profit (and therefore net profit) is zero. In this case

$$(7 \times \text{planes sold}) - 325 = 0$$

$$\text{Planes sold} = \frac{325}{7} = 46$$

Thus Lophead needs to sell about 46 planes a year, or a total of about 280 planes over the 6 years to show a profit.

Notice that we obtain the same result if we attack the problem in terms of the break-even level of revenue. The variable cost of each plane is $8.5 million, which is 54.8 percent of the $15.5 million price. Therefore, each dollar of sales increases pretax profits by $1 - \$.548 = \$.452$. So

$$\text{Break-even revenue} = \frac{\text{fixed costs including depreciation}}{\text{additional profit from each additional dollar of sales}}$$

$$= \frac{\$325 \text{ million}}{.452} = \$719 \text{ million}$$

Since each plane cost $15.5 million, this revenue level implies sales of $719/15.5 = 46$ planes per year.

Now let us look at what sales are needed before the project has a zero NPV. Development of the Trinova costs $900 million. For each of the next 6 years the company expects a cash flow of $3.5 million \times \text{planes sold} - \$12.5$ million (see row 8 of Table 7.5). If the cost of capital is 10 percent, the 6-year annuity factor is 4.355. So

$$\text{NPV} = -900 + 4.355(3.5 \times \text{planes sold} - 12.5)$$

$$= 15.24 \times \text{planes sold} - 954.44$$

If the project has a zero NPV,

$$0 = 15.24 \text{ planes sold} - 954.44$$

$$\text{planes sold} = 63$$

Thus Lophead can recover its initial investment with sales of 46 planes a year (about 280 in total), but it needs to sell 63 a year (or about 375 in total) to earn a return on this investment equal to the opportunity cost of capital.

Our example may seem fanciful but it is based loosely on reality. In 1971 Lockheed was in the middle of a major program to bring out the L-1011 TriStar airliner. This program was to bring Lockheed to the brink of failure and it tipped Rolls-Royce (supplier of the TriStar engine) over the brink. In giving evidence to Congress, Lockheed argued that the TriStar program was commercially attractive and that sales would eventually exceed the break-even point of about 200 aircraft. But in calculating this break-even point Lockheed appears to have ignored the opportunity cost of the huge capital investment in the project. Lockheed probably needed to sell about 500 aircraft to reach a zero net present value.[3]

---

[3]The true break-even point for the TriStar program is estimated in U. E. Reinhardt, "Break-Even Analysis for Lockheed's TriStar: An Application of Financial Theory," *Journal of Finance* 28 (September 1973), pp. 821–838.

▶ **Self-Test 7.4**   What is the basic difference between sensitivity analysis and break-even analysis?

Operating Leverage

A project's break-even point depends on both its *fixed costs* that do not vary with sales, and the profit on each extra sale. Managers often face a trade-off between these variables. For example, we typically think of rental expenses as fixed costs. But supermarket companies sometimes rent stores with contingent rent agreements. This means that the amount of rent the company pays is tied to the level of sales from the store. Rent rises and falls along with sales. The store thus replaces a fixed cost with a *variable cost* that rises along with sales. Because a greater proportion of the company's expenses will fall when its sales fall, its break-even point is reduced.

Of course, a high proportion of fixed costs is not all bad. The firm whose costs are largely fixed fares poorly when demand is low, but it may make a killing during a boom. Let us illustrate.

Finefodder has a policy of hiring long-term employees who will not be laid off except in the most dire circumstances. For all intents and purposes, these salaries are fixed costs. Its rival, Stop and Scoff, has a much smaller permanent labor force and uses expensive temporary help whenever demand for its product requires extra staff. A greater proportion of its labor expenses are therefore variable costs.

Suppose that if Finefodder adopted its rival's policy, fixed costs in its new superstore would fall from $2 million to $1.56 million but variable costs would rise from 81.25 to 84 percent of sales. Table 7.6 shows that with the normal level of sales, the two policies fare equally. In a slump a store that relies on temporary labor does better since its costs fall along with revenue. In a boom the reverse is true and the store with the higher proportion of fixed costs has the advantage.

If Finefodder follows its normal policy of hiring long-term employees, each extra dollar of sales results in a change of $1.00 − $.8125 = $.1875 in pretax profits. If it uses temporary labor, an extra dollar of sales leads to a change of only $1.00 − $.84 = $.16 in profits. As a result, a store with high fixed costs is said to have high **operating leverage.** High operating leverage magnifies the effect on profits of a fluctuation in sales.

operating leverage:
Degree to which costs are fixed.

Table 7.6
A store with high operating leverage performs relatively badly in a slump but flourishes in a boom (figures in thousands of dollars)

	High Fixed Costs			High Variable Costs		
	Slump	**Normal**	**Boom**	**Slump**	**Normal**	**Boom**
Sales	13,000	16,000	19,000	13,000	16,000	19,000
− Variable costs	10,563	13,000	15,438	10,920	13,440	15,960
− Fixed costs	2,000	2,000	2,000	1,560	1,560	1,560
− Depreciation	450	450	450	450	450	450
= Pretax profit	−13	550	1,112	70	550	1,030

degree of operating leverage (DOL): Percentage change in profits given a 1 percent change in sales.

We can measure a business's operating leverage by asking how much profits change for each 1 percent change in sales. The **degree of operating leverage,** often abbreviated as **DOL,** is this measure.

$$DOL = \frac{\text{percentage change in profits}}{\text{percentage change in sales}}$$

For example, Table 7.6 shows that as the store moves from normal conditions to boom, sales increase from $16 million to $19 million, a rise of 18.75 percent. For the policy with high fixed costs, profits increase from $550,000 to $1,112,000, a rise of 102.2 percent. Therefore,

$$DOL = \frac{102.2}{18.75} = 5.45$$

The percentage change in sales is magnified more than fivefold in terms of the percentage impact on profits.

Now look at the operating leverage of the store if it uses the policy with low fixed costs but high variable costs. As the store moves from normal times to boom, profits increase from $550,000 to $1,030,000, a rise of 87.3 percent. Therefore,

$$DOL = \frac{87.3}{18.75} = 4.65$$

Because some costs remain fixed, a change in sales continues to have a magnified effect on profits but the degree of operating leverage is lower.

In fact, one can show that degree of operating leverage depends on fixed charges (including depreciation) in the following manner:[4]

$$DOL = 1 + \frac{\text{fixed costs}}{\text{profits}}$$

This relationship makes it clear that operating leverage increases with fixed costs.

▶ **Example 7.4**   *Operating Leverage*

Suppose the firm adopts the high-fixed-cost policy. Then fixed costs including depreciation will be 2.00 + .45 = $2.45 million. Since the store produces profits of $.55 million at a normal level of sales, DOL should be

$$DOL = 1 + \frac{\text{fixed costs}}{\text{profits}} = 1 + \frac{2.00 + .45}{.55} = 5.45$$

[4]This formula for DOL can be derived as follows. If sales increase by 1 percent, the variable costs also should increase by 1 percent, and profits will increase by .01 × (sales − variable costs) = .01 × (profits + fixed costs). Now recall the definition of DOL:

$$DOL = \frac{\text{percentage change in profits}}{\text{percentage change in sales}} = \frac{\text{change in profits/level of profits}}{.01}$$

$$= 100 \times \frac{\text{change in profits}}{\text{level of profits}} = 100 \times \frac{.01 \times (\text{profits + fixed costs})}{\text{level of profits}}$$

$$= 1 + \frac{\text{fixed costs}}{\text{profits}}$$

This value matches the one we obtained by comparing the actual percentage changes in sales and profits.

> You can see from this example that the risk of a project is affected by the degree of operating leverage. If a large proportion of costs is fixed, a shortfall in sales has a magnified effect on profits.

We will have more to say about risk in the next three chapters.

▶ **Self-Test 7.5** Suppose that sales increase by 10 percent from the values in the normal scenario. Compute the percentage change in pretax profits from the normal level for both policies in Table 7.6. Compare your answers to the values predicted by the DOL formula.

7.3 *Flexibility in Capital Budgeting*

Sensitivity analysis and break-even analysis help managers understand why a venture might fail. Once you know this you can decide whether it is worth investing more time and effort in trying to resolve the uncertainty.

Of course it is impossible to clear up all doubts about the future. Therefore, managers also try to build flexibility into the project and they value more highly a project that allows them to mitigate the effect of unpleasant surprises and to capitalize on pleasant ones.

Decision Trees

The scientists of MacCaugh have developed a diet whiskey and the firm is ready to go ahead with pilot production and test marketing. The preliminary phase will take a year and cost $200,000. Management feels that there is only a 50-50 chance that the pilot production and market tests will be successful. If they are, then MacCaugh will build a $2 million plant which will generate an expected annual cash flow in perpetuity of $480,000 a year after taxes. Given an opportunity cost of capital of 12 percent, project NPV in this case will be −$2 million + $480,000/.12 = $2 million. If the tests are not successful, MacCaugh will discontinue the project and the cost of the pilot production will be wasted. How can MacCaugh decide whether to spend the money on the pilot program?

Notice that the only decision MacCaugh needs to make now is whether to go ahead with the preliminary phase. Depending on how that works out, it may choose to go ahead with full-scale production.

decision tree: Diagram of sequential decisions and possible outcomes.

When faced with projects like this that involve sequential decisions, it is often helpful to draw a **decision tree,** as in Figure 7.3. You can think of the problem as a game between MacCaugh and fate. The square represents a decision point for MacCaugh and the circle represents a decision point for fate. MacCaugh starts the play at the left-hand box. If MacCaugh decides to test, then fate will cast the enchanted dice and decide the result of the tests. Given the test results, the firm faces a second decision: Should it invest $2 million and start full-scale production?

FIGURE 7.3
Decision tree

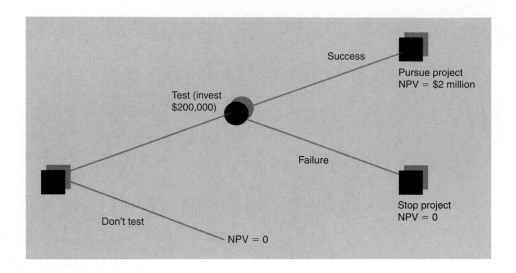

The second-stage decision is obvious: *Invest if the tests indicate that NPV is positive, and stop if they indicate that NPV would be negative.* Now the firm can easily decide between paying for the test program or stopping immediately. The net present value of stopping is zero, so the first-stage decision boils down to a simple problem: Should MacCaugh invest $200,000 now to obtain a 50 percent chance of a project with an NPV of $2 million a year later? If payoffs of zero and $2 million are equally likely, the *expected* payoff is $(.5 \times 0) + (.5 \times 2 \text{ million}) = \$1$ million. Thus the pilot project offers an expected payoff of $1 million on an investment of $200,000. At any reasonable cost of capital this is a good deal.

The Option to Expand

Notice that MacCaugh's expenditure on the pilot program buys a valuable managerial option. The firm has the *option* to produce the new product depending on the outcome of the tests. If the pilot program turns up disappointing results, the firm can walk away from the project without incurring additional costs.

> **The option to walk away once the results are revealed introduces a valuable asymmetry. Good outcomes can be exploited, while bad outcomes can be limited by canceling the project.**

MacCaugh was not obliged to have a pilot program. Instead, it could have gone directly into full-scale whiskey production. After all, if diet whiskey is a success, the sooner MacCaugh can clean up the market the better. But it is possible that the product will *not* take off; in that case the expenditure on the pilot operation may help the firm avoid a costly mistake. When it proposed a pilot project, MacCaugh's management was simply following the fundamental rule of swimmers: If you know the water temperature (and depth), dive in; if you don't, try putting a toe in first.

Here is another example of an apparently unprofitable investment that has value because of the flexibility it gives to make further follow-on investments. Some of the world's largest oil reserves are found in the tar sands of Athabasca, Canada. Unfortunately, the cost of extracting oil from the sands is substantially higher than the current market price and almost certainly higher than most people's estimate of the likely price in the future. Yet oil companies have been prepared to pay considerable sums for these tracts of barren land. Why?

The answer is that ownership of these tracts gives the companies an option. They are not obliged to extract the oil. If oil prices remain below the cost of extraction, the Athabasca sands will remain undeveloped. But if prices do rise above the cost of extraction, those land purchases could prove very profitable.

Notice that the option to develop the tar sands is valuable because the future price of oil is uncertain. If we *knew* that oil prices would remain at their current level, nobody would pay a cent for the tar sands. It is the possibility that oil prices may fluctuate sharply above or below their present level that gives the option value.[5]

> As a general rule, flexibility is most valuable when the future is most uncertain. The ability to change course as events develop and new information becomes available is most valuable when it is hard to predict with confidence what the best action ultimately will turn out to be.

You can probably think of many other investments that take on added value because of the further opportunities that they may open up. For example, when designing a factory, it may make sense to provide for the possibility in the future of an additional production line; when building a four-lane highway, it may pay to build six-lane bridges so that the road can be converted later to six lanes if traffic volume turns out to be higher than expected.

Abandonment Options

If the option to expand has value, what about the option to bail out? Projects don't just go on until the equipment disintegrates. The decision to terminate a project is usually taken by management, not by nature. Once the project is no longer profitable, the company will cut its losses and exercise its option to abandon the project.

Some assets are easier to bail out of than others. Tangible assets are usually easier to sell than intangible ones. It helps to have active secondhand markets, which really exist only for standardized, widely used items. Real estate, airplanes, trucks, and certain machine tools are likely to be relatively easy to sell. On the other hand, the knowledge accumulated by a drug company's research and development program is a specialized intangible asset and probably would not have significant abandonment value. Some assets, such as old mattresses, even have negative abandonment value; you have to pay to get rid of them. It is very costly to decommission nuclear power plants or to reclaim land that has been strip-mined. Managers recognize the option to abandon when they make the initial investment.

▶ **Example 7.5**

Abandonment Option

Suppose that the Wigeon Company must choose between two technologies for the manufacture of a new product, a Wankel engine outboard motor:

1. Technology A uses custom-designed machinery to produce the complex shapes required for Wankel engines at low cost. But if the Wankel engine doesn't sell, this equipment will be worthless.
2. Technology B uses standard machine tools. Labor costs are much higher, but the tools can easily be sold if the motor doesn't sell.

---

[5]Oil prices sometimes move very sharply. They roughly doubled in 1979; in 1986 they fell by more than 40 percent.

Technology A looks better in an NPV analysis of the new product, because it was designed to have the lowest possible cost at the planned production volume. Yet you can sense the advantage of technology B's flexibility if you are unsure whether the new outboard will sink or swim in the marketplace. ◄

> **When you are unsure about the success of a venture, you may wish to choose a flexible technology with a good resale market to preserve the option to abandon the project at low cost.**

▶ **Self-Test 7.6** Consider a firm operating a copper mine that incurs both variable and fixed costs of production. Suppose the mine can be shut down temporarily if copper prices fall below the variable cost of mining copper. Why is this a valuable operating option? How does it increase the NPV of the mine to the operator?

Flexible Production Facilities

Companies try to avoid becoming dependent on a single source of raw materials, building flexibility into their production facilities whenever possible. For example, at current prices gas-fired industrial boilers are cheaper to operate than oil-fired ones. Yet most companies prefer to buy boilers that can use *either* oil *or* natural gas, even though these dual-fired boilers cost about 10 percent more than a gas-fired boiler.[6] The reason is obvious. If gas prices rise relative to oil prices, the dual-fired boiler gives the company a valuable option to switch to low-cost oil. In effect the company has the option to exchange one asset (an oil-fired boiler) for another (a gas-fired boiler).

If the firm is uncertain about the future demand for its products, it may also build in the option to vary the output mix. For example, in recent years automobile manufacturers have made major investments in flexible production facilities that allow them to change their output rapidly in response to consumer demand.

Investment Timing Options

Suppose that you have a project that might be a big winner or a big loser. The project's upside potential outweighs its downside potential, and it has a positive NPV if undertaken today. However, the project is not "now-or-never." Should you invest right away or wait? It's hard to say. If the project truly is a winner, waiting means loss or deferral of its early cash flows. But if it turns out to be a loser, it may pay to wait and get a better fix on the likely demand.

You can think of any project proposal as giving you the *option* to invest today. You don't have to exercise that option immediately. Instead you need to weigh the value of the cash flows lost by delaying against the possibility that you will pick up some valuable information.

Think again of those tar sands in Athabasca. Suppose that the price of oil rises to 10 cents a barrel above your cost of production. You can extract the oil profitably at

[6]See N. Kulatilaka, "The Value of Flexibility: The Case of a Dual-Fuel Industrial Steam Boiler," *Financial Management* 22 (Autumn 1993), pp. 271–280.

this price, and the required investment has a small positive NPV if the price stays where it is. But it still might be worth delaying production. After all, if the price plummets, you will by waiting avoid a costly mistake. If it rises further, however, you can invest and make a killing.

We repeat, it is because the future is so uncertain that managers value flexibility. Ideally, a project will give the firm an option to expand if things go well and to bail out or switch production if they don't. In addition, it may pay the firm to postpone the project.

Some managers treat capital investment decisions as black boxes; they are handed cash-flow forecasts and they churn out present values without looking inside the black box. But successful firms ask not only what could be wrong with the forecasts but whether there are opportunities to respond to surprises. In other words, they recognize the value of flexibility.

▶ **Self-Test 7.7**   Investments in new products or production capacity often include an option to expand. What are the other major types of options encountered in capital investment decisions?

7.4 *Summary*

1. For most large corporations there are two stages in the investment process: the preparation of the capital budget, which is a list of planned investments, and the authorization process for individual projects. This process is usually a cooperative effort.
2. The choice of investment projects should never be a purely mechanical process. Managers need to ask why a project should have a positive NPV. A positive NPV is plausible only if the company has some competitive advantage that prevents its rivals from stealing most of the gains.
3. Good managers realize that the forecasts behind NPV calculations are imperfect. Therefore they explore the consequences of a poor forecast and check whether it is worth doing some more homework. They use two principal tools to answer these what-if questions:
   • Sensitivity analysis, where one variable at a time is changed.
   • Scenario analysis, where the manager looks at the project under alternative scenarios.
4. In break-even analysis the focus is on how far sales could fall before the project begins to lose money. Often the phrase "lose money" is defined in terms of accounting losses, but it makes more sense to define it as "failing to cover the opportunity cost of capital"—in other words, as a negative NPV.
5. A project's break-even point will be affected by the extent to which costs can be reduced as sales decline. If costs are largely fixed, the project is said to have high *operating leverage.*
6. Some projects may take on added value because they give the firm the option to bail out if things go wrong or to capitalize on success by expanding. We showed how decision trees may be used to analyze such flexibility.

Key Terms

capital budget	scenario analysis	degree of operating leverage (DOL)
sensitivity analysis	break-even analysis	decision tree
fixed costs	operating leverage	
variable costs	simulation analysis	

Problems

1. **Fixed and Variable Costs.** In a slow year, Wimpy's Burgers will produce 1 million hamburgers at a total cost of $1.75 million. In a good year, it can produce 2 million hamburgers at a total cost of $2.25 million. What are the fixed and variable costs of hamburger production?

2. **Average Cost.** Reconsider Wimpy's Burgers from problem 1.

   a. What is the average cost per burger when the firm produces 1 million hamburgers?
   b. What is average cost when the firm produces 2 million hamburgers?
   c. Why is average cost lower when more burgers are produced?

3. **Break-Even.** Dime a Dozen Diamonds makes synthetic diamonds by treating carbon. Each diamond can be sold for $100. The materials cost for a standard diamond is $30. The fixed costs incurred each year for factory upkeep and administrative expenses are $200,000. The machinery costs $1 million a year and is depreciated straight-line over 10 years to a salvage value of zero.

   a. What is the accounting break-even level of sales in terms of number of diamonds sold?
   b. What is NPV break-even sales assuming a tax rate of 35 percent, a 10-year project life, and a discount rate of 12 percent?

4. **Break-Even.** Turn back to problem 3.

   a. Would the accounting break-even point in the first year of operation increase or decrease if the machinery were depreciated over a 5-year period?
   b. Would the NPV break-even point increase or decrease if the machinery were depreciated over a 5-year period?

5. **Break-Even.** You are evaluating a project that will require an investment of $10 million that will be depreciated over a period of 7 years. You are concerned that the corporate tax rate will increase during the life of the project. Would such an increase affect the accounting break-even point? Would it affect the NPV break-even point?

6. **Operating Leverage.** You estimate that your cattle farm will generate $1 million of profits on sales of $4 million under normal economic conditions, and that the degree of operating leverage is 7.5. What will profits be if sales turn out to be $3.5 million? What if they are $4.5 million?

7. **Break-Even.** Define the *cash-flow break-even point* as the sales volume (in dollars) at which cash flow equals zero. Is the cash-flow break-even level of sales higher or lower than the zero-profit break-even point?

8. **Break-Even and NPV.** If a project operates at cash-flow break-even (see problem 7) for its entire life, what must be true of the project's NPV?

9. **Break-Even.** Modern Artifacts can produce keepsakes that will be sold for $80 each. Non-depreciation fixed costs are $1,000 per year and variable costs are $60 per unit.

   a. If the project requires an initial investment of $3,000 and is expected to last for 5 years and the firm pays no taxes, what are the accounting and NPV break-even levels of sales? The initial investment will be depreciated straight-line over 5 years to a final value of zero, and the discount rate is 10 percent.
   b. How do your answers change if the firm's tax rate is 40 percent?

10. **Operating Leverage.**

    a. What is the degree of operating leverage of Modern Artifacts (in the preceding problem) when sales are $8,000?
    b. What is the degree of operating leverage when sales are $10,000?
    c. Why is operating leverage different at these two levels of sales?

11. **Operating Leverage.** What is the lowest possible value for the degree of operating leverage for a profitable firm? Show with a numerical example that if Modern Artifacts (see problem 9a) has zero fixed costs, then DOL = 1 and in fact sales and profits are directly proportional so that a 1 percent change in sales results in a 1 percent change in profits.

12. **Sensitivity Analysis.** A project currently generates sales of $10 million, variable costs equal to 50 percent of sales, and fixed costs of $2 million. The firm's tax rate is 35 percent. What are the effects of the following changes on after-tax profits and cash flow?

    a. Sales increase from $10 million to $11 million.
    b. Variable costs increase to 60 percent of sales.

13. **Sensitivity Analysis.** The project in the preceding problem will last for 10 years. The discount rate is 12 percent.

    a. What is the effect on project NPV of each of the changes considered in the problem?
    b. If project NPV under the base-case scenario is $2 million, how much can fixed costs increase before NPV turns negative?
    c. How much can fixed costs increase before accounting profits turn negative?

14. **Break-Even.** The following estimates have been prepared for a project under consideration:

Fixed costs:	$20,000
Depreciation:	$10,000
Price:	$2
Accounting break-even:	60,000 units

    What must be the variable cost per unit?

15. **Break-Even.** A financial analyst has computed both accounting and NPV break-even sales levels for a project under consideration using straight-line depreciation over a 6-year period. The project manager wants to know what will happen to these estimates if the firm uses ACRS depreciation instead. The capital investment will be in a 5-year recovery period class under ACRS rules (see Table 6.4). The firm is in a 35 percent tax bracket.

    a. What (qualitatively) will happen to the accounting break-even level of sales in the first years of the project?
    b. What (qualitatively) will happen to NPV break-even level of sales?
    c. If you were advising the analyst, would the answer to (a) or (b) be important to you? Specifically, would you say that the switch to ACRS makes the project more or less attractive?

16. **Scenario Analysis.** The most likely outcomes for a particular project are estimated as follows:

Unit price:	$50
Variable cost:	$30
Fixed cost	$300,000
Expected Sales:	30,000 units per year

However, you recognize that some of these estimates are subject to error. Suppose that each variable may turn out to be either 10 percent higher or 10 percent lower than the initial estimate. The project will last for 10 years and requires an initial investment of $1 million, which will be depreciated straight-line over the project life to a final value of zero. The firm's tax rate is 35 percent and the required rate of return is 14 percent. What is project NPV in the "best-case scenario," that is, assuming all variables take on the best possible value? What about the worst-case scenario?

17. **Scenario Analysis.** Reconsider the best- and worst-case scenarios in the previous problem. Do the best- and worst-case outcomes when each variable is treated independently seem to be reasonable scenarios in terms of the combinations of variables? For example, if price is higher than predicted, is it more or less likely that cost is higher than predicted? What other relationships may exist among the variables?

18. **Operating Leverage.** A project has fixed costs of $1,000 per year, depreciation charges of $500 a year, revenue of $6,000 a year, and variable costs equal to two-thirds of revenues.

    a. If sales increase by 5 percent, what will be the increase in pretax profits?
    b. What is the degree of operating leverage of this project?
    c. Confirm that the percentage change in profits equals DOL times the percentage change in sales.

19. **Sensitivity Analysis.** Emperor's Clothes Fashions can invest $5 million in a new plant for producing invisible makeup. The plant has an expected life of 5 years, and expected sales are 6 million jars of makeup a year. Fixed costs are $2 million a year, and variable costs are $1 per jar. The product will be priced at $2 per jar. The plant will be depreciated straight-line over 5 years to a salvage value of zero. The opportunity cost of capital is 12 percent, and the tax rate is 40 percent.

    a. What is project NPV under these base-case assumptions?
    b. What is NPV if variable costs turn out to be $1.20 per jar?
    c. What is NPV if fixed costs turn out to be $1.5 million per year?
    d. At what price per jar would project NPV equal zero?

20. **Break-Even.** Reconsider Finefodder's new superstore. Suppose that by investing an additional $600,000 initially in more efficient checkout equipment, Finefodder could reduce variable costs to 80 percent of sales.

    a. Using the base-case assumptions (Table 7.1), find the NPV of this alternative scheme. *Hint:* Remember to focus on the *incremental* cash flows from the project.
    b. At what level of sales will accounting profits be unchanged if the firm invests in the new equipment? Assume the equipment receives the same 12-year straight-line depreciation treatment as in the original example. *Hint:* Focus on the project's incremental effects on fixed and variable costs.
    c. What is the NPV break-even point?

21. **Break-Even and NPV.** If the superstore project (see the previous problem) operates at accounting break-even, will net present value be positive or negative?

22. **Project Options.** Your midrange guess as to the amount of oil in a prospective field is 10 million barrels, but in fact there is a 50 percent chance that the amount of oil is 15 million barrels, and a 50 percent chance of 5 million barrels. If the actual amount of oil is 15 million barrels, the present value of the cash flows from drilling will be $8 million. If the amount is only 5 million barrels, the present value will be only $2 million. It costs $3 mil-

lion to drill the well. Suppose that a seismic test that costs $100,000 can verify the amount of oil under the ground. Is it worth paying for the test? Use a decision tree to justify your answer.

23. **Project Options.** A silver mine can yield 10,000 ounces of copper at a variable cost of $8 per ounce. The fixed costs of operating the mine are $10,000 per year. In half the years, silver can be sold for $12 per ounce; in the other years, silver can be sold for only $6 per ounce. Ignore taxes.

    a. What is the average cash flow you will receive from the mine if it is always kept in operation and the silver always is sold in the year it is mined?
    b. Now suppose you can shut down the mine in years of low silver prices. What happens to the average cash flow from the mine?

24. **Project Options.** An auto plant that costs $1 million to build can produce a new line of cars that will produce cash flows with a present value of $1.4 million if the line is successful, but only $500,000 if it is unsuccessful. You believe that the probability of success is only about 50 percent.

    a. Would you build the plant?
    b. Suppose that the plant can be sold for $900,000 to another automaker if the auto line is not successful. Now would you build the plant?
    c. Illustrate the option to abandon in (b) using a decision tree.

25. **Abandonment Option.** Hit or Miss Sports is introducing a new product this year. If its see-at-night soccer balls are a hit, the firm expects to be able to sell 50,000 units a year at a price of $60 each. If the new product is a bust, only 30,000 units can be sold at a price of $55. The variable cost of each ball is $30, and fixed costs are zero. The cost of the manufacturing equipment is $6 million, and the project life is estimated at 10 years. The firm will use straight-line depreciation over the 10-year life of the project. The firm's tax rate is 35 percent and the discount rate is 12 percent.

    a. If each outcome is equally likely, what is expected NPV? Will the firm accept the project?
    b. Suppose now that the firm can abandon the project and sell off the manufacturing equipment for $5.4 million if demand for the balls turns out to be weak. The firm will make the decision to continue or abandon after the first year of sales. Does the option to abandon change the firm's decision to accept the project?

26. **Expansion Option.** Now suppose that Hit or Miss Sports from the previous problem can expand production if the project is successful. By paying its workers overtime, it can increase production by 20,000 units; the variable cost of each ball will be higher, however, equal to $35 per unit. By how much does this option to expand production increase the NPV of the project?

27. **Production Options.** Explain why options to expand or contract production are most valuable when forecasts about future business conditions are most uncertain.

Solutions to Self-Test Questions

7.1 Cash flow forecasts for Finefodder's new superstore:

	Year 0	Years 1–12
Investment	−5,400,000	
1. Sales		16,000,000
2. Variable costs		13,280,000
3. Fixed costs		2,000,000
4. Depreciation		450,000
5. Pretax profit (1 − 2 − 3 − 4)		270,000
6. Taxes (at 40%)		108,000
7. Profit after tax		162,000
8. Cash flow from operations (4 + 7)		612,000
Net cash flow	−5,400,000	612,000

$$\text{NPV} = -\$5.4 \text{ million} + (7.536 \times \$612,000) = -\$788,000$$

7.2 Both calculate how NPV depends on input assumptions. Sensitivity analysis changes inputs one at a time, whereas scenario analysis changes several variables at once. The changes should add up to a consistent scenario for the project as a whole.

7.3 With the lower initial investment, depreciation is also lower; it now equals $417,000 per year. Cash flow is now as follows:

1. Variable costs	81.25 percent of sales
2. Fixed costs	$2 million
3. Depreciation	$417,000
4. Pretax profit	(.1875 × sales) − $2.417 million
5. Tax (at 40%)	.4 × (.1875 × sales − $2.417 million)
6. Profit after tax	.6 × (.1875 × sales − $2.417 million)
7. Cash flow (3 + 6)	.6 × (.1875 × sales − $2.417 million) + $417,000 = .1125 × sales − $1.033 million

Break-even occurs when

$$\text{PV (cash inflows)} = \text{investment}$$
$$7.536 \times (.1125 \times \text{sales} - \$1.033 \text{ million}) = \$5.0 \text{ million}$$

and sales = $15.08 million.

7.4 Break-even analysis finds the level of sales or revenue at which NPV = 0. Sensitivity analysis changes these and other input variables to optimistic and pessimistic values and recalculates NPV.

7.5 Reworking Table 7.6 for the normal level of sales and 10 percent higher sales gives the following:

	High Fixed Costs		High Variable Costs	
	Normal	10% Higher Sales	Normal	10% Higher Sales
Sales	16,000	17,600	16,000	17,600
− Variable costs	13,000	14,300	13,440	14,784
− Fixed costs	2,000	2,000	1,560	1,560
− Depreciation	450	450	450	450
= Pretax profit	550	850	550	806

For the high-fixed-cost policy, profits increase by 54.5 percent, from $550,000 to $850,000. For the low-fixed-cost policy, profits increase by 46.5 percent. In both cases the percentage increase in profits equals DOL times the percentage increase in sales. This illustrates that DOL measures the sensitivity of profits to changes in sales.

7.6 The option to shut down is valuable because the mine operator can avoid incurring losses when copper prices are low. If the shut-down option were not available, cash flow in the low-price periods would be negative. With the option, the worst cash flow is zero. By allowing managers to respond to market conditions, the option makes the worst-case cash flow better than it would be otherwise. The average cash flow (that is, averaging over all possible scenarios) therefore must improve, which increases project NPV.

7.7 Abandonment options, options due to flexible production facilities, investment timing options.

Minicase

Maxine Peru, the CEO of Peru Resources, hardly noticed the plate of savory quenelles de brochet and the glass of Corton Charlemagne '94 on the table before her. She was absorbed by the engineering report handed to her just as she entered the executive dining room.

The report described a proposed new mine on the North Ridge of Mt. Zircon. A vein of transcendental zirconium ore had been discovered there on land owned by Ms. Peru's company. Test borings indicated sufficient reserves to produce 340 tons per year of transcendental zirconium over a 7-year period.

The vein probably also contained hydrated zircon gemstones. The amount and quality of these zircons were hard to predict, since they tended to occur in "pockets." The new mine might come across one, two, or dozens of pockets. The mining engineer guessed that 150 pounds per year might be found. The current price for high-quality hydrated zircon gemstones was $3,300 per pound.

Peru Resources was a family-owned business with total assets of $45 million, including cash reserves of $4 million. The outlay required for the new mine would be a major commitment. Fortunately, Peru Resources was conservatively financed, and Ms. Peru believed that the company could borrow up to $9 million at an interest rate of about 8 percent.

The mine's operating costs were projected at $900,000 per year, including $400,000 of fixed costs and $500,000 of variable costs. Ms. Peru thought these forecasts were accurate. The big question marks seemed to be the initial cost of the mine and the selling price of transcendental zirconium.

Opening the mine, and providing the necessary machinery and ore-crunching facilities, was supposed to cost $10 million, but cost overruns of 10 percent or 15 percent were common in the mining business. In addi-

tion, new environmental regulations, if enacted, could increase the cost of the mine by $1.5 million.

There was a cheaper design for the mine, which would reduce its cost by $1.7 million and eliminate much of the uncertainty about cost overruns. Unfortunately, this design would require much higher fixed operating costs. Fixed costs would increase to $850,000 per year at planned production levels.

The current price of transcendental zirconium was $10,000 per ton, but there was no consensus about future prices.[1] Some experts were projecting rapid price increases to as much as $14,000 per ton. On the other hand, there were pessimists saying that prices could be as low as $7,500 per ton. Ms. Peru did not have strong views either way: her best guess was that price would just increase with inflation at about 3.5 percent per year. (Mine operating costs would also increase with inflation.)

Ms. Peru had wide experience in the mining business, and she knew that investors in similar projects usually wanted a forecasted nominal rate of return of at least 14 percent.

You have been asked to assist Ms. Peru in evaluating this project. Lay out the base-case NPV analysis and undertake sensitivity, scenario, or break-even analyses as appropriate. Assume that Peru Resources pays tax at a 35 percent rate. For simplicity, also assume that the investment in the mine could be depreciated for tax purposes straight-line over 7 years.

What forecasts or scenarios should worry Ms. Peru the most? Where would additional information be most helpful? Is there a case for delaying construction of the new mine?

---

[1] There were no traded forward or futures contracts on transcendental zirconium. See Chapter 24.

Part Three *Risk*

Risk is now. The return comes later.
Mark Andriessen, founder of Netscape, wasn't afraid to bear risk. How much future return
can an investor rationally expect?
Netscape/Reuters/Archive Photos.

Chapter 8

Introduction to Risk, Return, and the Opportunity Cost of Capital

W e have thus far skirted the issue of project risk; now it is time to confront it head-on. We can no longer be satisfied with vague statements like "The opportunity cost of capital depends on the risk of the project." We need to know how to measure risk and we need to understand the relationship between risk and the cost of capital. These are the topics of the next two chapters.

Think for a moment what the cost of capital for a project means. It is the rate of return that shareholders could expect to earn if they invested in equally risky securities. So one way to estimate the cost of capital is to find securities that have the same risk as the project and then estimate the expected rate of return on these securities.

We start our analysis by looking at the rates of return earned in the past from different investments, concentrating on the *extra* return that investors have received for investing in risky rather than safe securities. We then show how to measure the risk of a portfolio by calculating its standard deviation and we look again at past history to find out how risky it is to invest in the stock market.

Finally, we explore the concept of diversification. Most investors do not put all their eggs into one basket—they diversify. Thus investors are not concerned with the risk of each security in isolation; instead they are concerned with how much it contributes to the risk of a diversified portfolio. We therefore need to distinguish between the risk that can be eliminated by diversification and the risk that cannot be eliminated.

After studying this chapter you should be able to

▶ Estimate the opportunity cost of capital for an "average-risk" project.

▶ Calculate the standard deviation of returns for individual common stocks or for a stock portfolio.

▶ Understand why diversification reduces risk.

▶ Distinguish between unique risk, which can be diversified away, and market risk, which cannot.

8.1 Rates of Return: A Review

In Chapter 4 we saw that if you buy a stock or a bond, your return comes in two forms: (1) a dividend or interest payment, and (2) a *capital gain* or *capital loss*. For example, suppose you were lucky enough to buy the stock of Nike at the beginning of 1996 when its price was $71.125 a share. By the end of the year the value of that investment had appreciated to $120, giving a capital gain of $120 − $71.125 = $48.875 a share. In addition, in 1996 Nike paid a dividend of $.65 a share.

The *percentage* return on your investment was therefore

$$\text{Percentage return} = \frac{\text{capital gain} + \text{dividend}}{\text{initial share price}}$$
$$= \frac{\$48.875 + \$.65}{71.125} = .6963, \text{ or } 69.63\%$$

The percentage return also can be expressed as the sum of the *dividend yield* and *capital gains yield*. The dividend yield is the dividend expressed as a percentage of the stock price at the beginning of the year:

$$\text{Dividend yield} = \frac{\text{dividend}}{\text{initial share price}} = \frac{\$.65}{\$71.125} = .0091, \text{ or } .91\%$$

Similarly, the capital gains yield is the capital gain expressed as a percentage of the stock price at the beginning of the year:

$$\text{Capital gains yield} = \frac{\text{capital gain}}{\text{initial share price}} = \frac{\$48.875}{\$71.125} = .6872, \text{ or } 68.72\%$$

Thus the total return is the sum of 0.91% + 68.72% = 69.63%.

Remember that in Chapter 3 we made a distinction between the *nominal* rate of return and the *real* rate of return. The nominal return measures how much more money you will have at the end of the year if you invest today. The return that we just calculated for Nike stock is therefore a nominal return. The real rate of return tells you how much more you will be able to *buy* with your money at the end of the year. To convert from a nominal to a real rate of return, we use the following relationship:

$$1 + \text{real rate of return} = \frac{1 + \text{nominal rate of return}}{1 + \text{inflation rate}}$$

In 1996 inflation was 3.3 percent. So we calculate the real return for Nike stock as follows:

$$1 + \text{real rate of return} = \frac{1 + .6963}{1 + .033} = 1.6421$$

Therefore the real rate of return equals .6421, or 64.21 percent.

▶ **Self-Test 8.1**   Suppose you buy a bond for $1,020 with a 15-year maturity paying an annual coupon of $80. A year later interest rates have dropped and the bond's price has increased to $1,050. What are your nominal and real rates of return? Assume the inflation rate is 4 percent.

8.2 Seventy-One Years of Capital Market History

When you invest in a stock, you can't be sure that your return is going to be as high as Nike's in 1996. But by looking back at the history of security returns, you can get some idea of the return that investors might reasonably expect from investments in different types of securities and of the risks that they face. Therefore, we begin with a brief review of the risk–return trade-off investors have experienced in the past.

Market Indexes

Investors can choose from an enormous number of different securities. Currently, about 2,700 common stocks trade on the New York Stock Exchange, about 1,000 are

market index: Measure of the investment performance of the overall market.

traded on the American Stock Exchange and the regional exchanges, and well over 4,000 are traded by a network of dealers linked by computer terminals and telephones.[1] Financial analysts can't track every stock, so they rely on **market indexes** to summarize the return on different classes of securities.

The best-known stock market index in the United States is the **Dow Jones Industrial Average,** generally known as the *Dow.* The Dow tracks the performance of a portfolio that invests one share in each of 30 large firms. For example, suppose that the Dow starts the day at a value of 7,700 and then rises by 77 points to a new value of 7,777. Investors who own one share in each of the 30 companies make a capital gain on their portfolios of $77/7,700 = .01$ or 1 percent.[2]

Dow Jones Industrial Average: Index of the investment performance of a portfolio of 30 "blue-chip" stocks.

The Dow Jones Industrial Average was first computed in 1896. Most people are used to it and expect to hear about it on the 6 o'clock news. However, it is far from the best measure of the performance of the stock market. First, with only 30 large industrial stocks, it is not representative of stocks generally. Second, investors don't usually hold an equal number of shares in each company. For example, in 1996 there were 681 million shares in Du Pont and only 159 million shares in Union Carbide. So on average investors did *not* hold the same number of shares in the two firms. Instead, they held over four times as many shares in Du Pont as in Union Carbide. It doesn't make sense, therefore, to look at an index that measures the performance of a portfolio with an equal number of shares in the two firms.

Standard & Poor's Composite Index: Index of the investment performance of a portfolio of 500 large stocks. Also called the *S&P 500.*

The **Standard & Poor's Composite Index,** better known as the *S&P 500,* includes the stocks of 500 major companies and is therefore a more comprehensive index than the Dow. Also, it measures the performance of a portfolio that holds shares in each firm in proportion to the number of shares that have been issued. For example, the S&P portfolio would hold just over four times as many shares in Du Pont as Union Carbide. Thus the S&P 500 shows the *average* performance of investors in the 500 firms.

Only a small proportion of the 7,000 or so publicly traded companies are represented in the S&P 500. However, these firms are among the largest in the country and they account for roughly 70 percent of the *value* of stocks traded. Therefore, success for professional and institutional investors usually means "beating the S&P."

Some stock market indexes, such as the Wilshire 5000, include an even larger number of stocks, while others focus on special groups of stocks such as the stocks of small companies. There are also stock market indexes for other countries, such as the Nikkei Index for Tokyo and the Financial Times Index for London. Morgan Stanley Capital International (MSCI) even computes a world stock market index. Dow Jones, Inc., which publishes the Dow, has responded with its own World Stock Index.

The Historical Record

The historical returns of stock or bond market indexes can give us an idea of the typical performance of different investments. One popular source of such information is the Center for Research in Security Prices (CRSP) at the University of Chicago, which

---

[1]This network of traders comprises the *over-the-counter market.* The computer network and price quotation system is called the NASDAQ system. NASDAQ stands for the National Association of Security Dealers Automated Quotation system.

[2]Stock market indexes record the market value of the portfolio. To calculate the total return on the portfolio we would also need to add in any dividends that are paid.

reports the performance of several portfolios of securities since 1926. The CRSP tape includes:

1. A portfolio of 3-month loans issued each week by the United States government. These loans are known as *Treasury bills*.
2. A portfolio of long-term *Treasury bonds* issued by the United States government and maturing in about 20 years.
3. A portfolio of stocks of the 500 large firms that make up the Standard & Poor's Composite Index.

These portfolios are not equally risky. Treasury bills are about as safe an investment as you can make. Because they are issued by the United States government, you can be sure that you will get your money back. Their short-term maturity means that their prices are relatively stable. In fact, investors who wish to lend money for 3 months can achieve a certain payoff by buying 3-month Treasury bills. Of course, they can't be sure what that money will buy: there is still some uncertainty about inflation.

Long-term Treasury bonds are also certain to be repaid when they mature, but the prices of these bonds fluctuate more as interest rates vary. When interest rates fall, the value of a long-term bond portfolio rises; when rates rise, the value of the bond portfolio falls.

Common stocks are the riskiest of the three groups of securities. When you invest in common stocks, there is no promise that you will get your money back. As a part-owner of the corporation, you receive whatever is left over after the bonds and any other debts have been repaid.

Figure 8.1 illustrates the investment performance for stocks, bonds, and bills since 1926. The figure shows how much one dollar invested at the start of 1926 would have grown to by the end of 1996 assuming that all dividend or interest income had been reinvested in the portfolio.

You can see that the performance of the portfolios fits our intuitive risk ranking. Common stocks were the riskiest investment but they also offered the greatest gains.

FIGURE 8.1

The value to which a $1 investment in 1926 would have grown by the end of 1996. Prepared from data provided by the Center for Research in Security Prices.

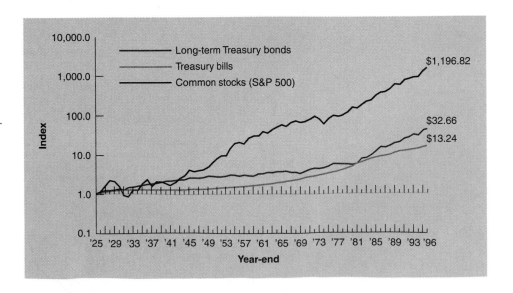

One dollar invested in 1926 in a portfolio of the S&P 500 stocks would have grown to $1197 by 1996. At the other end of the spectrum, an investment of $1 in Treasury bills would have accumulated to only $13.24.

The Center for Research in Security Prices has compiled rates of return for each of these portfolios for each year from 1926 to 1996. These rates of return are comparable to the figure that we calculated for Nike. In other words, they include (1) dividends or interest and (2) any capital gains or losses. The averages of the 71 annual rates of return are shown in Table 8.1.

The safest investment, Treasury bills, had the lowest rate of return—3.8 percent a year in *nominal* terms and .6 percent in *real* terms. In other words, the average rate of inflation over this period was about 3.2 percent a year. Long-term government bonds gave slightly higher returns than Treasury bills. This difference is called the **maturity premium.** Common stocks were in a class by themselves. Investors who accepted the risk of common stocks received on average an extra return of 8.7 percent a year over the return on Treasury bills. This compensation for taking on the risk of common stock ownership is known as the **risk premium.**

maturity premium: Extra average return from investing in long- versus short-term Treasury securities.

risk premium: Expected return in excess of risk-free return as compensation for risk.

> The historical record shows that investors demand and receive a risk premium for holding risky assets. Average returns on high-risk assets are higher than those on low-risk assets.

You may ask why we look back over such a long period to measure average rates of return. The reason is that annual rates of return for common stocks fluctuate so much that averages taken over short periods are extremely unreliable. In some years investors in common stocks had a disagreeable shock and received a substantially lower return than they expected. In other years they had a pleasant surprise and received a higher return. Our only hope of gaining insights from historical rates of return is to look at a very long period. By averaging the returns across both the rough years and the smooth, we should get a fair idea of the typical return that investors might justifiably expect.

While common stocks have offered the highest average returns, they have also been riskier investments. Figure 8.2 shows the 71 annual rates of return for the three portfolios. The fluctuations in year-to-year stock returns are remarkably wide. There were two years (1933 and 1954) when investors earned a return of more than 50 percent. However, Figure 8.2 shows that you can also lose money by investing in the stock market. The most dramatic case was the stock market crash of 1929–1932. Shortly after President Coolidge joyfully observed that stocks were "cheap at current prices," stocks rapidly became even cheaper. By July 1932 the Dow Jones Industrial Average had fallen in a series of agonizing slides by 89 percent.

TABLE 8.1

Average rates of return on Treasury bills, government bonds, and common stocks, 1926–1996 (figures in percent per year)

Portfolio	Average Annual Rate of Return (Nominal)	Average Annual Rate of Return (Real)	Average Risk Premium (Extra Return versus Treasury Bills)
Treasury bills	3.8	0.6	
Treasury bonds	5.3	2.1	1.5
Common stocks	12.5	9.3	8.7

Source: Based on data compiled by the Center for Research in Security Prices.

FIGURE 8.2

Rates of return, 1926–1996. Prepared from data provided by the Center for Research in Security Prices.

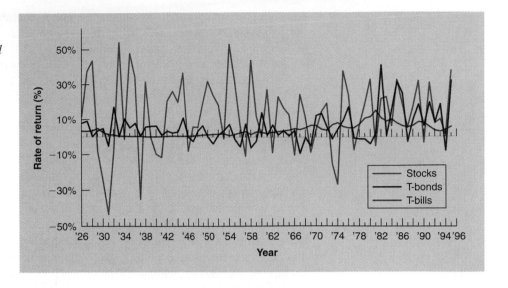

Another major market crash, that of Monday, October 19, 1987, does not show up in Figure 8.2. On that day stock prices fell by 23 percent, their largest one-day fall in history. However, Black Monday came after a prolonged rise in stock prices, so that over 1987 as a whole investors in common stocks earned a return of 5.2 percent. This was not a terrible return, but many investors who rode the 1987 roller coaster feel that it is not a year they would care to repeat.

▶ **Self-Test 8.2**

Here are the average rates of return for the postwar period 1950–1996:

Stocks	14.1%
Treasury bonds	5.9
Treasury bills	5.2

What were the risk premium on stocks and the maturity premium on Treasury bonds for this period?

Using Historical Evidence to Estimate Today's Cost of Capital

Think back now to Chapter 5, where we showed how firms calculate the present value of a new project by discounting the expected cash flows by the opportunity cost of capital. The opportunity cost of capital is the return that the firm's shareholders are giving up by investing in the project rather than in comparable risk alternatives.

Measuring the cost of capital is easy if the project is a sure thing. Since shareholders can obtain a sure-fire payoff by investing in a U.S. Treasury bill, the firm should invest in a risk-free project only if it can at least match the rate of interest on such a loan. If the project is risky—and most projects are—then the firm needs to at least match the return that shareholders could expect to earn if they invested in securities of similar risk. It is not easy to put a precise figure on this, but our skim through history provides an idea of the average return an investor might expect to earn from an investment in risky common stocks.

Suppose there is an investment project which you *know*—don't ask how—has the same risk as an investment in the portfolio of stocks in Standard & Poor's Composite Index. We will say that it has the same degree of risk as the *market portfolio* of common stocks.[3]

Instead of investing in the project, your shareholders could invest directly in this market portfolio of common stocks. Therefore, the opportunity cost of capital for your project is the return that the shareholders could expect to earn on the market portfolio. This is what they are giving up by investing money in your project.

The problem of estimating the project cost of capital boils down to estimating the currently expected rate of return on the market portfolio. One way to estimate the expected market return is to assume that the future will be like the past and that today's investors expect to receive the average rates of return shown in Table 8.1. In this case, you would judge that the expected market return today is 12.5 percent, the average of past market returns.

Unfortunately, this is *not* the way to do it. Investors are not likely to demand the same return each year on an investment in common stocks. For example, we know that the interest rate on safe Treasury bills varies over time. At their peak in 1981, Treasury bills offered a return of 14 percent, more than 10 percentage points above the 3.8 percent average return on bills shown in Table 8.1.

What if you were called upon to estimate the expected return on common stocks in 1981? Would you have said 12.5 percent? That doesn't make sense. Who would invest in the risky stock market for an expected return of 12.5 percent when you could get a safe 14 percent from Treasury bills?

A better procedure is to take the *current* interest rate on Treasury bills plus 8.7 percent, the average *risk premium* shown in Table 8.1. In 1981, when the rate on Treasury bills was 14 percent, that would have given

$$\text{Expected market} \atop \text{return (1981)} = {\text{interest rate on} \atop \text{Treasury bills (1981)}} + {\text{normal risk} \atop \text{premium}}$$
$$= 14\% + 8.7\% = 22.7\%$$

The first term on the right-hand side tells us the time value of money in 1981; the second term measures the compensation for risk.

> **The expected return on an investment provides compensation to investors both for waiting (the time value of money) and for worrying (the risk of the particular asset).**

This calculation assumes that there is a normal, stable risk premium on the market portfolio, so that the expected *future* risk premium can be measured by the average past risk premium. One could quarrel with this assumption, but it does yield estimates of the expected market return that are reasonable.

What about today? As we write this in mid-1997, inflation has fallen from its 1981 figure of 8.9 percent to about 3 percent. As a result interest rates are also much lower and Treasury bills offer a return of only 5.5 percent. This suggests investors in common

---

[3]This is speaking a bit loosely, because the S&P 500 does not include all stocks traded in the United States, much less in world markets.

stocks are looking for a return of just over 14 percent:[4]

$$\begin{array}{c}\text{Expected market}\\\text{return (1997)}\end{array} = \begin{array}{c}\text{interest rate on}\\\text{Treasury bills (1997)}\end{array} + \begin{array}{c}\text{normal risk}\\\text{premium}\end{array}$$
$$= 5.5\% + 8.7\% = 14.2\%$$

You now have a couple of benchmarks. You know that the opportunity cost of capital for safe projects must be the rate of return offered by safe Treasury bills and you know that the opportunity cost of capital for "average-risk" projects must be the expected rate of return on the market portfolio. But you *don't* know how to estimate the cost of capital for projects that do not fit these two simple cases. Before you can do this, you need to understand more about investment risk.

8.3 *Measuring Risk*

The average fuse time for army hand grenades is 7.0 seconds, but that average hides a lot of potentially relevant information. If you are in the business of throwing grenades, you need some measure of the variation around the average fuse time.[5] Similarly, if you are in the business of investing in securities, you need some measure of how far the returns may differ from the average.

Figure 8.2 showed the year-by-year returns for several investments from 1926 to 1996. Another way of presenting these data is by histograms such as Figure 8.3. Each bar shows the number of years that the market return fell within a specific range. For example, you can see that in 8 of the 71 years the return on common stocks was between +15 percent and +20 percent. The risk shows up in the wide spread of outcomes. In 2 years the return was between +50 percent and +55 percent but there was also 1 year in which it was between −40 percent and −45 percent.

Variance and Standard Deviation

The third histogram in Figure 8.3 shows the variation in common stock returns. The returns on common stock have been more variable than returns on bonds and Treasury bills. Common stocks have been risky investments. They will almost certainly continue to be risky investments.

Investment risk depends on the dispersion or spread of possible outcomes. Sometimes a picture like Figure 8.3 tells you all you need to know about (past) dispersion. But in general, pictures do not suffice. The financial manager needs a numerical measure of dispersion. The standard measures are **variance** and **standard deviation.** More variable returns imply greater investment risk. This suggests that some measure of dispersion will provide a reasonable measure of risk, and dispersion is precisely what is measured by variance and standard deviation.

variance: Average value of squared deviations from mean. A measure of volatility.

standard deviation: Square root of variance. Another measure of volatility.

---

[4]In practice, things might be a bit more complicated. We've mentioned the yield curve, the relationship between bond maturity and yield. When firms consider investments in long-lived projects, they usually think about risk premiums relative to long-term bonds. In this case, the risk-free rate would be taken as the current long-term bond yield less the average maturity premium on such bonds.

[5]We can reassure you; the variation around the standard fuse time is very small.

FIGURE 8.3

Historical returns on major asset classes, 1926–1996. Prepared from data provided by the Center for Research in Security Prices.

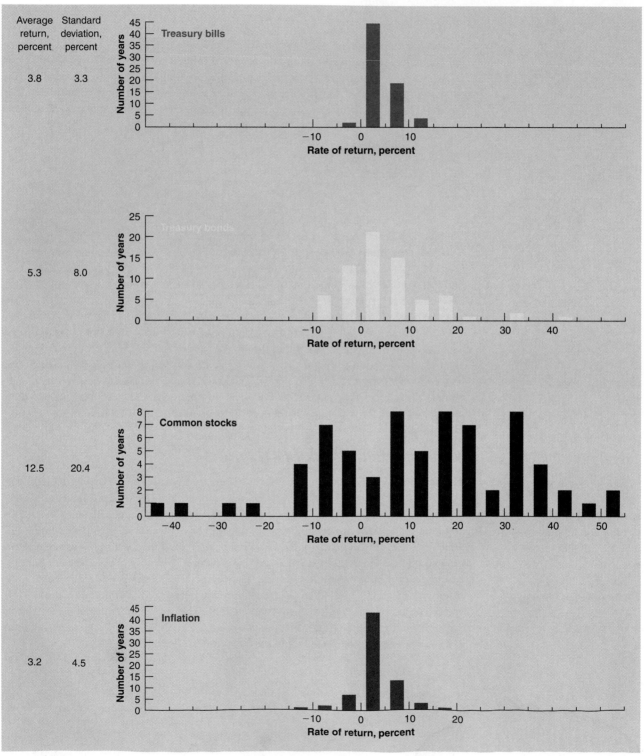

Here is a very simple example showing how variance and standard deviation are calculated. Suppose that you are offered the chance to play the following game. You start by investing $100. Then two coins are flipped. For each head that comes up your starting balance will be *increased* by 20 percent, and for each tail that comes up your starting balance will be *reduced* by 10 percent. Clearly there are four equally likely outcomes:

- Head + head: You make 20 + 20 = 40%
- Head + tail: You make 20 − 10 = 10%
- Tail + head: You make −10 + 20 = 10%
- Tail + tail: You make −10 − 10 = −20%

There is a chance of 1 in 4, or .25, that you will make 40 percent; a chance of 2 in 4, or .5, that you will make 10 percent; and a chance of 1 in 4, or .25, that you will lose 20 percent. The game's expected return is therefore a weighted average of the possible outcomes:

$$\text{Expected return} = \text{Probability-weighted average of possible outcomes}$$
$$= (.25 \times 40) + (.5 + 10) + (.25 \times -20) = +10\%$$

If you play the game a very large number of times, your average return should be 10 percent.

Table 8.2 shows how to calculate the variance and standard deviation of the returns on your game. Column 1 shows the four equally likely outcomes. In column 2 we calculate the difference between each possible outcome and the expected outcome. You can see that at best the return could be 30 percent higher than expected; at worst it could be 30 percent lower.

These deviations in column 2 illustrate the spread of possible returns. But if we want a measure of this spread, it is no use just averaging the deviations in column 2—the average is always going to be zero. To get around this problem, we *square* the deviations in column 2 before averaging them. These squared deviations are shown in column 3.[6] The variance is the average of these squared deviations and therefore is a natural measure of dispersion:

$$\textbf{Variance = average of squared deviations around the average}$$
$$= \frac{1,800}{4} = 450$$

When we squared the deviations from the expected return, we changed the units of measurement from *percentages* to *percentages squared*. Our last step is to get back to percentages by taking the square root of the variance. This is the standard deviation:

$$\textbf{Standard deviation = square root of variance}$$
$$= \sqrt{450} = 21\%$$

---

[6]Notice that in Table 8.2 we itemized the four equally likely outcomes. An alternative is to recognize that a 10 percent return is more likely than the other two possibilities. There is a .5 chance of a 10 percent return, a .25 chance of a 40 percent return, and a .25 chance of a −20 percent return. When the probabilities of different outcomes are not all equal, you can calculate variance by weighting the squared deviations by the probabilities and adding up these probability-weighted squared deviations. Thus, in our example,

$$\text{Variance} = (.25 \times 30^2) + (.5 \times 0^2) + [.25 \times (-30)^2] = 450$$

Notice that this probability-weighted average of squared deviations is similar in spirit to the probability-weighted average of possible outcomes used to calculate the expected return.

TABLE 8.2

The coin-toss game; calculating variance and standard deviation

(1) Percent Rate of Return	(2) Deviation from Expected Return	(3) Squared Deviation
+40	+30	900
+10	0	0
+10	0	0
−20	−30	900

Variance = average of squared deviations = 1,800/4 = 450
Standard deviation = square root of variance = $\sqrt{450}$ = 21.2, about 21%

Because standard deviation is simply the square root of variance, it too is a natural measure of risk. If the outcome of the game had been certain, the standard deviation would have been zero because there would then be no deviations from the expected outcome. The actual standard deviation is positive because we *don't* know what will happen.

Now think of a second game. It is the same as the first except that each head means a 35 percent gain and each tail means a 25 percent loss. Again there are four equally likely outcomes:

- Head + head: You gain 70%
- Head + tail: You gain 10%
- Tail + head: You gain 10%
- Tail + tail: You lose 50%

For this game, the expected return is 10 percent, the same as that of the first game, but it is more risky. For example, in the first game, the worst possible outcome is a loss of 20 percent, which is 30 percent worse than the expected outcome. In the second game the downside is a loss of 50 percent, or 60 percent below the expected return. This increased spread of outcomes shows up in the standard deviation, which is double that of the first game, 42 percent versus 21 percent. By this measure the second game is twice as risky as the first.

▶ **Self-Test 8.3**   Calculate the variance and standard deviation of this second coin-tossing game in the same format as Table 8.2.

Measuring the Variation in Stock Returns

When estimating the spread of possible outcomes from investing in the stock market, most financial analysts start by assuming that the spread of returns in the past is a reasonable indication of what could happen in the future. Therefore, they calculate the standard deviation of past returns. To illustrate, suppose that you were presented with the data for stock market returns shown in Table 8.3. The average return over the 5 years from 1992 to 1996 was 15.92 percent. This is just the sum of the returns over the 5 years divided by 5 (79.58 = 15.92 percent).

Column 2 in Table 8.3 shows the difference between each year's return and the average return. For example, in 1992 the return of 7.71 percent on common stocks

TABLE 8.3

The average return and standard deviation of stock market returns, 1992–1996

Year	Rate of Return	Deviation from Average Return	Squared Deviation
1992	7.71	−8.21	67.34
1993	9.87	−6.05	36.55
1994	1.29	−14.63	213.92
1995	37.71	21.79	474.98
1996	23.00	7.08	50.18
Total	79.58		842.97

Average rate of return = 79.58/5 = 15.92
Variance = average of squared deviations = 842.97/5 = 168.59
Standard deviation = square root of variance = 12.98%
Source for rates of return: Center for Research in Security Prices.

was below the 5-year average by 8.21 percent ($7.71 - 15.92 = -8.21$ percent). In column 3 we square these deviations from the average. The variance is then the average of these squared deviations.[7]

$$\text{Variance} = \text{average of squared deviations}$$
$$= \frac{842.97}{5} = 168.59$$

Since standard deviation is the square root of the variance,

$$\text{Standard deviation} = \text{square root of variance}$$
$$= \sqrt{168.59} = 12.98\%$$

It is difficult to measure the risk of securities on the basis of just five past outcomes. Therefore, Table 8.4 lists the annual standard deviations for our three portfolios of securities over the period 1926–1996. As expected, Treasury bills were the least variable security, and common stocks were the most variable. Treasury bonds hold the middle ground.

Of course, there is no reason to believe that the market's variability should stay the same over many years. Indeed many people believe that in recent years the stock market has become more volatile due to irresponsible speculation by . . . (fill in here

TABLE 8.4

Standard deviation of rates of return, 1926–1996

Portfolio	Standard Deviation, %
Treasury bills	3.3
Long-term government bonds	8.0
Common stocks	20.4

Source: Computed from data on the CRSP tapes.

[7]Consider this technical point. When we use a series of past returns to predict the variability of returns, the sum of the squared deviations should be divided by the number of observations *minus one*. This corrects for what statisticians call the *loss of a degree of freedom.* The corrected variance is 842.97/4 = 210.74 and the corrected standard deviation is 14.52 percent.

FIGURE 8.4
*Stock market volatility,
1926–1996.*

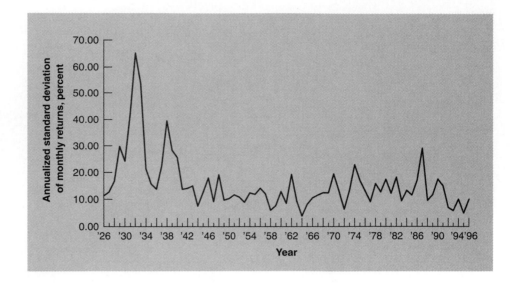

the name of your preferred guilty party). Figure 8.4 provides a chart of the volatility of the United States stock market for each year from 1926 to 1996.[8] You can see that there are periods of unusually high variability, but there is no long-term upward trend.

8.4 Risk and Diversification

Diversification

We can calculate our measures of variability equally well for individual securities and portfolios of securities. Of course, the level of variability over 71 years is less interesting for specific companies than for the market portfolio because it is a rare company that faces the same business risks today as it did in 1926.

Table 8.5 presents estimated standard deviations for 10 well-known common stocks for a recent 5-year period.[9] Do these standard deviations look high to you? They should. Remember that the market portfolio's standard deviation was about 20 percent over the entire 1926–1996 period. Of our individual stocks only AT&T, Coca-Cola, and Exxon had standard deviations of less than 20 percent. Most stocks are substantially more variable than the market portfolio; only a handful are less variable.

diversification: Strategy designed to reduce risk by spreading the portfolio across many investments.

This raises an important question: The market portfolio is made up of individual stocks, so why isn't its variability equal to the average variability of its components? The answer is that **diversification** *reduces variability.*

---

[8]We converted the monthly variance to an annual variance by multiplying by 12. In other words, the variance of annual returns is 12 times that of monthly returns. The longer you hold a security, the more risk you have to bear.

[9]We pointed out earlier that five annual observations are insufficient to give a reliable estimate of variability. Therefore, these estimates are derived from 60 monthly rates of return and then the monthly variance is multiplied by 12.

TABLE 8.5

Standard deviations for selected common stocks, 1991–1996

Stock	Standard Deviation, %
AT&T	18.1
Biogen	53.0
Coca-Cola	16.3
Compaq	39.4
Delta Airlines	27.2
Exxon	12.0
Ford Motor Co.	25.5
Microsoft	24.9
Nike	40.0
Polaroid	22.0

Selling umbrellas is a risky business; you may make a killing when it rains but you are likely to lose your shirt in a heat wave. Selling ice cream is no safer; you do well in the heat wave but business is poor in the rain. Suppose, however, that you invest in both an umbrella shop and an ice cream shop. By diversifying your investment across the two businesses you make an average level of profit come rain or shine.

Portfolio diversification works because prices of different stocks do not move exactly together. Statisticians make the same point when they say that stock price changes are less than perfectly correlated. Diversification works best when the returns are negatively correlated, as is the case for our umbrella and ice cream businesses. When one business does well, the other does badly. Unfortunately, in practice, stocks that are negatively correlated are as rare as pecan pie in Budapest.

Asset versus Portfolio Risk

The history of returns on different asset classes provides compelling evidence of a risk–return trade-off and suggests that the variability of the rates of return on each asset class is a useful measure of risk. However, volatility of returns can be a misleading measure of risk for an individual asset held as part of a portfolio. To see why, consider the following example.

Suppose there are three equally likely outcomes, or *scenarios,* for the economy: a recession, normal growth, and a boom. An investment in an auto stock will have a rate of return of −8 percent in a recession, 5 percent in a normal period, and 18 percent in a boom. Auto firms are *cyclical:* They do well when the economy does well. In contrast, gold firms are often said to be *countercyclical,* meaning that they do well when other firms do poorly. Suppose that stock in a gold mining firm will provide a rate of return of 20 percent in a recession, 3 percent in a normal period, and −20 percent in a boom. These assumptions are summarized in Table 8.6.

It appears that gold is the more volatile investment. The difference in return across the boom and bust scenarios is 40 percent (−20 percent in a boom versus +20 percent in a recession), compared to a spread of only 26 percent for the auto stock. In fact, we can confirm the higher volatility by measuring the variance or standard deviation of returns of the two assets. The calculations are set out in Table 8.7.

TABLE 8.6

Rate of return assumptions for two stocks

Scenario	Probability	Rate of Return, % Auto Stock	Gold Stock
Recession	1/3	− 8	+20
Normal	1/3	+ 5	+ 3
Boom	1/3	+18	−20

Since all three scenarios are equally likely, the expected return on each stock is simply the average of the three possible outcomes.[10] For the auto stock the expected return is 5 percent; for the gold stock it is 1 percent. The variance is the average of the squared deviations from the expected return, and the standard deviation is the square root of the variance.

▶ **Self-Test 8.4**

Suppose the probabilities of the recession or boom are .30, while the probability of a normal period is .40. Would you expect the variance of returns on these two investments to be higher or lower? Why? Confirm by calculating the standard deviation of the auto stock. (Refer back to the coin-toss example if you are unsure of how to do this.)

The gold mining stock offers a lower expected rate of return than the auto stock, and *more* volatility—a loser on both counts, right? Would anyone be willing to hold gold mining stocks in an investment portfolio? The answer is a resounding yes.

TABLE 8.7

Expected return and volatility for two stocks

Scenario	Auto Stock Rate of Return, %	Deviation from Expected Return, %	Squared Deviation	Gold Stock Rate of Return, %	Deviation from Expected Return, %	Squared Deviation
Recession	−8	−13	169	+20	+19	361
Normal	+5	0	0	+3	+2	4
Boom	+18	+13	169	−20	−21	441
Expected return	$\frac{1}{3}(-8 + 5 + 18) = 5\%$			$\frac{1}{3}(+20 + 3 - 20) = 1\%$		
Variance[a]	$\frac{1}{3}(169 + 0 + 169) = 112.7$			$\frac{1}{3}(361 + 4 + 441) = 268.7$		
Standard deviation ($=\sqrt{\text{variance}}$)	$\sqrt{112.7} = 10.6\%$			$\sqrt{268.7} = 16.4\%$		

[a]Variance = average of squared deviations from the expected value.

[10]If the probabilities were not equal, we would need to weight each outcome by its probability in calculating the expected outcome and the variance.

To see why, suppose you do believe that gold is a lousy asset, and therefore hold your entire portfolio in the auto stock. Your expected return is 5 percent and your standard deviation is 10.6 percent. We'll compare that portfolio to a partially diversified one, invested 75 percent in autos and 25 percent in gold. For example, if you have a $10,000 portfolio, you could put $7,500 in autos and $2,500 in gold.

First, we need to calculate the return on this portfolio in each scenario. The portfolio return is the weighted average of returns on the individual assets with weights equal to the proportion of the portfolio invested in each asset. For a portfolio formed from only two assets,

$$
\begin{aligned}
\text{Portfolio rate} \atop \text{of return} =\ &\left(\begin{array}{cc} \text{fraction of portfolio} & \text{rate of return} \\ \text{in first asset} & \times\ \text{on first asset} \end{array} \right) \\
+\ &\left(\begin{array}{cc} \text{fraction of portfolio} & \text{rate of return} \\ \text{in second asset} & \times\ \text{on second asset} \end{array} \right)
\end{aligned}
$$

For example, autos have a weight of .75 and a rate of return of −8 percent in the recession, and gold has a weight of .25 and a return of 20 percent in a recession. Therefore, the portfolio return in the recession is the following weighted average:[11]

$$\text{Portfolio return in recession} = [.75 \times (-8\%)] + [.25 \times 20\%]$$
$$= -1\%$$

Table 8.8 expands Table 8.6 to include the portfolio of the auto stock and the gold mining stock. The expected returns and volatility measures are summarized at the bottom of the table. The surprising finding is this: When you shift funds from the auto stock to the more volatile gold mining stock, your portfolio variability actually *decreases*. In fact, the volatility of the auto-plus-gold stock portfolio is considerably less than the volatility of *either* stock separately. This is the payoff to diversification.

We can understand this more clearly by focusing on asset returns in the two extreme scenarios, boom and recession. In the boom, when auto stocks do best, the

TABLE 8.8

Rates of return for two stocks and a portfolio

Scenario	Probability	Auto Stock	Gold Stock	Portfolio Return, %[a]
		Rate of Return, %		
Recession	1/3	−8	+20	−1.0%
Normal	1/3	+5	+3	+4.5
Boom	1/3	+18	−20	+8.5
Expected return		5%	1%	4%
Variance		112.7	268.7	15.2
Standard deviation		10.6%	16.4%	3.9%

[a] Portfolio return = (.75 × auto stock return) + (.25 × gold stock return).

[11] Let's confirm this. Suppose you invest $7,500 in autos and $2,500 in gold. If the recession hits, the rate of return on autos will be −8 percent, and the value of the auto investment will fall by 8 percent to $6,900. The rate of return on gold will be 20 percent, and the value of the gold investment will rise 20 percent to $3,000. The value of the total portfolio falls from its original value of $10,000 to $6,900 + $3,000 = $9,900, which is a rate of return of −1 percent. This matches the rate of return given by the formula for the weighted average.

poor return on gold reduces the performance of the overall portfolio. However, when auto stocks are stalling in a recession, gold shines, providing a substantial positive return that boosts portfolio performance. The gold stock offsets the swings in the performance of the auto stock, reducing the best-case return but improving the worst-case return. The inverse relationship between the returns on the two stocks means that the addition of the gold mining stock to an all-auto portfolio stabilizes returns.

A gold stock is really a *negative risk* asset to an investor starting with an all-auto portfolio. Adding it to the portfolio reduces the volatility of returns. The *incremental* risk of the gold stock (that is, the *change* in overall risk when gold is added to the portfolio) is *negative* despite the fact that gold returns are highly volatile.

In general, the incremental risk of a stock depends on whether its returns tend to vary with or against the returns of the other assets in the portfolio. Incremental risk does not just depend on a stock's volatility. If returns do not move closely with those of the rest of the portfolio, the stock will reduce the volatility of portfolio returns.

We can summarize as follows:

> 1. **Investors care about the expected return and risk of their *portfolio* of assets. The risk of the overall portfolio can be measured by the volatility of returns, that is, the variance or standard deviation.**
> 2. **The standard deviation of the returns of an individual security measures how risky that security would be if held in isolation. But an investor who holds a portfolio of securities is interested only in how each security affects the risk of the entire portfolio. The contribution of a security to the risk of the portfolio depends on how the security's returns vary with the investor's other holdings. Thus a security that is risky if held in isolation may nevertheless serve to reduce the variability of the portfolio, as long as its returns vary inversely with those of the rest of the portfolio.**

▶ **Example 8.1** *Microsoft and Newmont Mining*

Let's look at a more realistic example of the effect of diversification. Figure 8.5*a* shows the monthly returns of Microsoft stock from 1991 to 1996. The average *monthly* return was .85 percent but you can see that there was considerable variation around that average. The standard deviation of *monthly* returns was 8.0 percent. As a rule of thumb, in roughly one-third of the months the return is likely to be more than one standard deviation above or below the average return.[12] The figure shows that the return did indeed differ by more than 8.0 percent from the average on about a third of the occasions.

Figure 8.5*b* shows the monthly returns of Newmont Mining. The average *monthly* return on Newmont Mining was 3.1 percent and the standard deviation was 8.3 percent, about the same as that of Microsoft. Again you can see that in about a third of the cases the return differed from the average by more than one standard deviation.

An investment in *either* Microsoft or Newmont Mining would have been very variable. But the fortunes of the two stocks were not perfectly related. There were many occasions when a decline in the value of one stock was canceled by a rise in the price of the other. Because the two stocks did not move in exact lockstep, there was an

---

[12]For any normal distribution, approximately one-third of the observations lie more than one standard deviation above or below the average. Over short intervals stock returns are roughly normally distributed.

FIGURE 8.5

The variability of a portfolio with equal holdings in Microsoft and Newmont Mining would have been only 60 percent of the variability of the individual stocks.

opportunity to reduce variability by spreading one's investment between them. For example, Figure 8.5*c* shows the returns on a portfolio that was equally divided between the stocks. The monthly standard deviation of this portfolio would have been only 5.0 percent—that is, less than 60 percent of the variability of the individual stocks.

▶ **Self-Test 8.5**   An investor is currently fully invested in gold mining stocks. Which action would do more to reduce portfolio risk: diversification into silver mining stocks or into automotive stocks? Why?

Market Risk versus Unique Risk

Our examples illustrate that even a little diversification can provide a substantial reduction in variability. Suppose you calculate and compare the standard deviations of randomly chosen one-stock portfolios, two-stock portfolios, five-stock portfolios, and so on. You can see from Figure 8.6 that diversification can cut the variability of returns by about half. But you can get most of this benefit with relatively few stocks: the improvement is slight when the number of stocks is increased beyond, say, 15.

Figure 8.6 also illustrates that no matter how many securities you hold, you cannot eliminate all risk. There remains the danger that the market—every share, including your portfolio—will plummet.

unique risk: Risk factors affecting only that firm. Also called *diversifiable risk.*

The risk that can be eliminated by diversification is called **unique risk**. The risk that you can't avoid regardless of how much you diversify is generally known as **market risk** or *systematic risk.*

market risk: Economy-wide (macroeconomic) sources of risk that affect the overall stock market. Also called *systematic risk.*

> *Unique risk* arises because many of the perils that surround an individual company are peculiar to that company and perhaps its direct competitors. *Market risk* stems from economy-wide perils that threaten all businesses. Market risk explains why stocks have a tendency to move together, so that even well-diversified portfolios are exposed to market movements.

Figure 8.7 divides risk into its two parts—unique risk and market risk. If you have only a single stock, unique risk is very important; but once you have a portfolio of 15 or more stocks, diversification has done most of what it can to eliminate risk.

> **For a reasonably well-diversified portfolio, only market risk matters.**

FIGURE 8.6

Diversification reduces risk (standard deviation) rapidly at first, then more slowly.

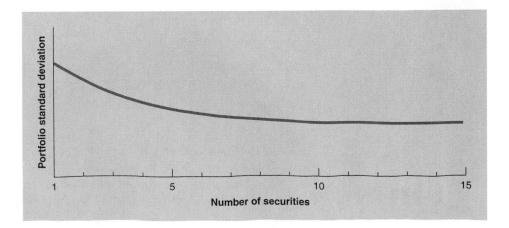

FIGURE 8.7

Diversification eliminates unique risk. But there is some risk that diversification cannot *eliminate. This is* called *market* risk.

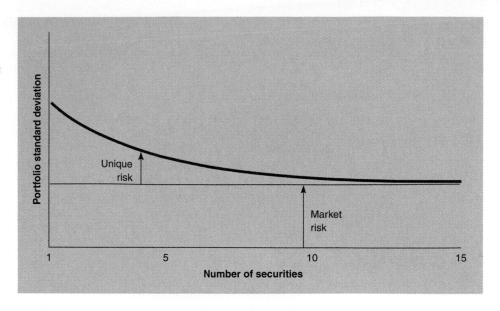

8.5 *Thinking about Risk*

How can you tell which risks are unique and diversifiable? Where do market risks come from? Here are three messages to help you think clearly about risk.

Message 1: Some Risks Look Big and Dangerous but Really Are Diversifiable

Managers confront risks "up close and personal." They must make decisions about particular investments. The failure of such an investment could cost a promotion, bonus, or otherwise steady job. Yet that same investment may not seem risky to an investor who can stand back and combine it in a diversified portfolio with many other assets or securities.

▶ **Example 8.2**   *Wildcat Oil Wells*

You have just been promoted to director of exploration, Western Hemisphere, of MPS Oil. The manager of your exploration team in far-off Costaguana has appealed for $20 million extra to drill in an even steamier part of the Costaguanan jungle. The manager thinks there may be an "elephant" field worth $500 million or more hidden there. But the chance of finding it is at best one in ten, and yesterday MPS's CEO sourly commented on the $100 million already "wasted" on Costaguanan exploration.

Is this a risky investment? For you it probably is; you may be a hero if oil is found and a goat otherwise. But MPS drills hundreds of wells worldwide; for the company as a whole, it's the *average* success rate that matters. Geologic risks (is there oil or not?) should average out. The risk of a worldwide drilling program is much less than the apparent risk of any single wildcat well.

Back up one step, and think of the investors who buy MPS stock. The investors may hold other oil companies too, as well as companies producing steel, computers, clothing, cement, and breakfast cereal. They naturally—and realistically—assume that your successes and failures in drilling oil wells will average out with the thousands of independent bets made by the companies in their portfolio.

Therefore, the risks you face in Costaguana do not affect the rate of return they demand for investing in MPS Oil. Diversified investors in MPS stock will be happy if you find that elephant field, but they probably will not notice if you fail and lose your job. In any case, they will not demand a higher *average* rate of return for worrying about geologic risks in Costaguana.

▶ **Example 8.3**   *Fire Insurance*

Would you be willing to write a $100,000 fire insurance policy on your neighbor's house? The neighbor is willing to pay you $1,000 for a year's protection, and experience shows that the chance of fire damage in a given year is substantially less than one in a thousand. But if your neighbor's house is damaged by fire, you would have to pay up.

Few of us have deep enough pockets to insure our neighbors, even if the odds of fire damage are very low. Insurance seems a risky business if you think policy by policy. But a large insurance company, which may issue a million policies, is concerned only with average losses, which can be predicted with excellent accuracy. The risk of fire on your neighbor's house is not in itself a big deal to the insurance company, providing that the fire insurance premium covers expected losses.

▶ **Self-Test 8.6**   Imagine a laboratory at IBM, late at night. One scientist speaks to another.

"You're right, Watson, I admit this experiment will consume all the rest of this year's budget. I don't know what we'll do if it fails. But if this yttrium–magnoosium alloy superconducts, the patents will be worth millions."

Would this be a good or bad investment for IBM? Can't say. But from the ultimate investors' viewpoint this is *not* a risky investment. Explain why.

Message 2: Market Risks Are Macro Risks

We have seen that diversified portfolios are not exposed to the unique risks of individual stocks but are exposed to the uncertain events that affect the entire securities market and the entire economy. These are macroeconomic, or "macro," factors such as changes in interest rates, industrial production, inflation, foreign exchange rates, and energy costs. These factors affect most all firms' earnings and stock prices. When the relevant macro risks turn generally favorable, stock prices rise and investors do well; when the same variables go the other way, investors suffer.

You can often assess relative market risks just by thinking through exposures to the business cycle and other macro variables. The following businesses have substantial macro and market risks:

- *Airlines.* Because business travel falls during a recession, and individuals postpone vacations and other discretionary travel, the airline industry is subject to the swings of the business cycle. On the positive side, airline profits really take off when business is booming and personal incomes are rising.
- *Machine tool manufacturers.* These businesses are especially exposed to the business cycle. Manufacturing companies that have excess capacity rarely buy new machine tools to expand. During recessions, excess capacity can be quite high.

Here, on the other hand, are two industries with less than average macro exposures:

- *Food companies.* Companies selling staples, such as breakfast cereal, flour, and dog food, find that demand for their products is relatively stable in good times and bad.
- *Electric utilities.* Business demand for electric power varies somewhat across the business cycle, but by much less than demand for air travel or machine tools. Also, many electric utilities' profits are regulated. Regulation cuts off upside profit potential but also gives the utilities the opportunity to increase prices when demand is slack.

> **Remember, investors holding diversified portfolios are mostly concerned with macroeconomic risks. They do not worry about microeconomic risks peculiar to a particular company or investment project. Micro risks wash out in diversified portfolios.** *Managers* **worry about both macro and micro risks, but only the former affect the cost of capital.**

▶ **Self-Test 8.7**   Which company of each of the following pairs would you expect to be more exposed to macro risks?

a. A luxury Manhattan restaurant or an established Burger Queen franchise?

b. A paint company that sells through small paint and hardware stores to do-it-yourselfers, or a paint company that sells in large volumes to Ford, GM, and Chrysler?

Message 3: Risk Can Be Measured

United Airlines clearly has more exposure to macro risks than food companies such as Kellogg or General Mills. These are easy cases. But is IBM stock a riskier investment than Exxon? That's not an easy question to reason through. We can, however, *measure* the risk of IBM and Exxon by looking at how their stock prices fluctuate.

We've already hinted at how to do this. Remember that diversified investors are concerned with market risks. The movements of the stock market sum up the net effects of all relevant macroeconomic uncertainties. If the market portfolio of all traded stocks is up in a particular month, we conclude that the net effect of macroeconomic news is positive. Remember, the performance of the market is barely affected by a firm-specific event. These cancel out across thousands of stocks in the market.

How do we measure the risk of a single stock, like IBM or Exxon? We do not look at the stocks in isolation, because the risks that loom when you're up close to a single company are often diversifiable. Instead we measure the individual stock's sensitivity to the fluctuations of the overall stock market. We will show you how this works in the next chapter.

Summary

1. The payoff from an investment in stocks or bonds consists of both the dividend or interest payment and any capital gain. The rate of return is equal to the payoff divided by the amount of the initial investment.
2. Over the past 71 years the return on common stocks has averaged 8.7 percent a year higher than the return on safe Treasury bills. This is the premium that investors have received for taking on the risk of investing in stocks. Long-term bonds have offered a higher return than Treasury bills but less than stocks.
3. If the risk premium in the past is a guide to the future, we can estimate the expected return on the market today by adding that 8.7 percent expected risk premium to today's interest rate on Treasury bills.
4. The spread of outcomes on different investments is commonly measured by the standard deviation. The standard deviation of the returns on a market portfolio of common stocks has averaged about 20 percent a year.
5. The standard deviation of returns is generally higher on individual stocks than it is on the market. Because individual stocks do not move in exact lockstep, much of their risk can be diversified away. This diversifiable risk is known as unique risk.
6. Even if you hold a well-diversified portfolio, you will not eliminate all risk. You will still be exposed to macroeconomic changes that affect most stocks and the overall stock market. These macro risks combine to create market risk—that is, the risk that the market as a whole will slump.
7. Stocks are not all equally risky. But what do we mean by a "high-risk stock"? We don't mean a stock that is risky if held in isolation; we mean a stock that makes an above-average contribution to the risk of a diversified portfolio. In other words, investors don't need to worry much about the risk that they can diversify away; they *do* need to worry about risk that can't be diversified. This depends on the stock's sensitivity to macroeconomic conditions.

Key Terms

market index	risk premium	diversification
Dow Jones Industrial Average	variance	unique risk
Standard & Poor's Composite Index	standard deviation	market risk
maturity premium		

Problems

1. **Rate of Return.** A stock is selling today for $40 per share. At the end of the year, it pays a dividend of $2 per share and sells for $44. What is the total rate of return on the stock? What are the dividend yield and capital gains yield?
2. **Rate of Return.** Return to problem 1. Suppose the year-end stock price after the dividend is paid is $36. What are the dividend yield and capital gains yield in this case? Why is the dividend yield unaffected?

3. **Real versus Nominal Returns.** You purchase 100 shares of stock for $40 a share. The stock pays a $2 per share dividend at year-end. What is the rate of return on your investment for these end-of-year stock prices? What is your real (inflation-adjusted) rate of return? Assume an inflation rate of 5 percent.

   a. $38
   b. $40
   c. $42

4. **Real versus Nominal Returns.** The Costaguanan stock market provided a rate of return of 95 percent. The inflation rate in Costaguana during the year was 80 percent. In the United States, in contrast, the stock market return was only 14 percent, but the inflation rate was only 3 percent. Which country's stock market provided the higher real rate of return?

5. **Real versus Nominal Returns.** The inflation rate in the United States between 1950 and 1996 averaged 4.2 percent. What was the average real rate of return on Treasury bills, Treasury bonds, and common stocks in that period? Use the data in Self-Test 8.2.

6. **Real versus Nominal Returns.** Do you think it is possible for risk-free Treasury bills to offer a negative nominal interest rate? Might they offer a negative *real* expected rate of return?

7. **Market Indexes.** The accompanying table shows the complete history of stock prices on the Polish stock exchange for 9 weeks in 1991. At that time only 5 stocks were traded. Construct two stock market indexes, one using weights as calculated in the Dow Jones Industrial Average, the other using weights as calculated in the Standard & Poor's Composite Index.

Prices (in zlotys) for the first 9 weeks' trading on the Warsaw Stock Exchange, beginning in April 1991. There was one trading session per week. Only five stocks were listed in the first 9 weeks.

	Stock				
Week	Tonsil (Electronics) 1500*	Prochnik (Garments) 1500*	Krosno (Glass) 2200*	Exbud (Construction) 1000*	Kable (Electronics) 1000*
1	85	56	59.5	149	80
2	76.5	51	53.5	164	80
3	69	46	49	180	80
4	62.5	41.5	47	198	79.5
5	56.5	38	51.5	217	80
6	56	41.5	56.5	196	80
7	61.5	45.5	62	177	80
8	67.5	50	60	160	80.5
9	61	45.5	54	160	72.5

*Number of shares outstanding.
Source: We are indebted to Professor Mary M. Cutler for providing these data.

8. **Stock Market History.**

   a. What was the average rate of return on large U.S. common stocks from 1926 to 1996?
   b. What was the average risk premium on large stocks?
   c. What was the standard deviation of returns on the S&P 500 portfolio?

9. **Risk Premiums.** Here are stock market and Treasury bill returns between 1992 and 1996:

Year	S&P Return	T-Bill Return
1992	7.71	3.54
1993	9.87	2.97
1994	1.29	3.91
1995	37.71	5.58
1996	23.00	5.20

a. What was the risk premium on the S&P 500 in each year?

b. What was the average risk premium?

c. What was the standard deviation of the risk premium?

10. **Market Indexes.** In 1990, the Dow Jones Industrial Average was at a level of about 2,600. In mid-1997, it was about 7,700. Would you expect the Dow in 1997 to be more or less likely to move up or down by more than 40 points in a day than in 1990? Does this mean the market was riskier in 1997 than it was in 1990?

11. **Maturity Premiums.** Investments in long-term government bonds produced a negative average return during the period 1977–1981. How should we interpret this? Did bond investors in 1977 expect to earn a negative maturity premium? What do these 5 years' bond returns tell us about the normal future maturity premium?

12. **Risk Premiums.** What will happen to the opportunity cost of capital if investors suddenly become especially conservative and less willing to bear investment risk?

13. **Risk Premiums and Discount Rates.** You believe that a stock with the same market risk as the S&P 500 will sell at year-end at a price of $50. The stock will pay a dividend at year-end of $2. What price will you be willing to pay for the stock today? *Hint:* Start by checking today's 1-year Treasury rates.

14. **Scenario Analysis.** The common stock of Leaning Tower of Pita, Inc., a restaurant chain, will generate the following payoffs to investors next year:

	Dividend	Stock Price
Boom	$5.00	$195
Normal economy	2.00	100
Recession	0	0

The company goes out of business if a recession hits. Calculate the expected rate of return and standard deviation of return to Leaning Tower of Pita shareholders. Assume for simplicity that the three possible states of the economy are equally likely. The stock is selling today for $90.

15. **Portfolio Risk.** Who would view the stock of Leaning Tower of Pita (see problem 14) as a risk-reducing investment—the owner of a gambling casino or a successful bankruptcy lawyer? Explain.

16. **Scenario Analysis.** The common stock of Escapist Films sells for $25 a share and offers the following payoffs next year:

	Dividend	Stock Price
Boom	0	$18
Normal economy	$1.00	26
Recession	3.00	34

Calculate the expected return and standard deviation of Escapist. All three scenarios are equally likely. Then calculate the expected return and standard deviation of a portfolio half-invested in Escapist and half in Leaning Tower of Pita (from problem 14). Show that the portfolio standard deviation is lower than either stock's. Explain why this happens.

17. **Scenario Analysis.** Consider the following scenario analysis:

Scenario	Probability	Rate of Return	
		Stocks	Bonds
Recession	.20	−5%	+14%
Normal economy	.60	+15	+8
Boom	.20	+25	+4

a. Is it reasonable to assume that Treasury bonds will provide higher returns in recessions than in booms?
b. Calculate the expected rate of return and standard deviation for each investment.
c. Which investment would *you* prefer?

18. **Portfolio Analysis.** Use the data in the previous problem and consider a portfolio with weights of .60 in stocks and .40 in bonds.

a. What is the rate of return on the portfolio in each scenario?
b. What is the expected rate of return and standard deviation of the portfolio?
c. Would you prefer to invest in the portfolio, in stocks only, or in bonds only?

19. **Risk Premium.** If the stock market return in 2002 turns out to be −20 percent, what will happen to our estimate of the "normal" risk premium? Does this make sense?

20. **Diversification.** In which of the following situations would you get the largest reduction in risk by spreading your portfolio across two stocks?

a. The stock returns vary with each other.
b. The stock returns are independent.
c. The stock returns vary against each other.

21. **Market Risk.** Which firms of each pair would you expect to have greater market risk:

a. General Steel or General Food Supplies.
b. Club Med or General Cinemas.

22. **Risk and Return.** A stock will provide a rate of return of either −20 percent or +30 percent.

a. If both possibilities are equally likely, calculate the expected return and standard deviation.
b. If Treasury bills yield 5 percent, and investors believe that the stock offers a satisfactory expected return, what must the market risk of the stock be?

23. **Unique versus Market Risk.** Sassafras Oil is staking all its remaining capital on wildcat exploration off the Côte d'Huile. There is a 10 percent chance of discovering a field with reserves of 50 million barrels. If it finds oil, it will immediately sell the reserves to Big Oil, at a price depending on the state of the economy. Thus the possible payoffs are as follows:

	Value of Reserves, per Barrel	Value of Reserves 50 Million Barrels	Value of Dryholes
Boom	$4.00	$200,000,000	0
Normal economy	$5.00	$250,000,000	0
Recession	$6.00	$300,000,000	0

Is Sassafras Oil a risky investment for a diversified investor in the stock market—compared, say, to the stock of Leaning Tower of Pita, described in problem 14? Explain.

Solutions to Self-Test Questions

8.1 The bond price at the end of the year is $1,050. Therefore, the capital gain on each bond is $1,050 − 1,020 = $30. Your dollar return is the sum of the income from the bond, $80, plus the capital gain, $30, or $110. The rate of return is

$$\frac{\text{Income plus capital gain}}{\text{Original price}} = \frac{80 + 30}{1,020} = .108, \text{ or } 10.8\%$$

Real rate of return is

$$\frac{1 + \text{nominal return}}{1 + \text{inflation rate}} - 1 = \frac{1.108}{1.04} - 1 = .065, \text{ or } 6.5\%$$

8.2 The risk premium on stocks is the average return in excess of Treasury bills. This was $14.1 − 5.2 = 8.9\%$. The maturity premium is the average return on Treasury bonds minus the return on Treasury bills. It was $5.9 − 5.2 = 0.7\%$.

8.3

Rate of Return	Deviation	Squared Deviation
+70%	+60%	3,600
+10	0	0
+10	0	0
−50	−60	3,600

Variance = average of squared deviations = 7,200/4 = 1,800
Standard deviation = square root of variance = $\sqrt{1,800}$ = 42.4, or about 42%

8.4 The standard deviation should decrease because there is now a lower probability of the more extreme outcomes. The expected rate of return on the auto stock is now

$$[.3 \times (-8\%)] + [.4 \times 5\%] + [.3 \times 18\%] = 5\%$$

The variance is

$$[.3 \times (-8 - 5)^2] + [.4 \times (5 - 5)^2] + [.3 \times (18 - 5)^2] = 101.4$$

The standard deviation is $\sqrt{101.4} = 10.07$ percent, which is lower than the value assuming equal probabilities of each scenario.

8.5 The gold mining stock's returns are more highly correlated with the silver mining company than with a car company. As a result, the automotive firm will offer a greater diversification benefit. The power of diversification is lowest when rates of return are highly correlated, performing well or poorly in tandem. Shifting the portfolio from one such firm to another has little impact on overall risk.

8.6 The success of this project depends on the experiment. Success does *not* depend on the performance of the overall economy. The experiment creates a diversifiable risk. A portfolio of many stocks will embody "bets" on many such unique risks. Some bets will work out and some will fail. Because the outcomes of these risks do not depend on common factors, such as the overall state of the economy, the risks will tend to cancel out in a well-diversified portfolio.

8.7 a. The luxury restaurant will be more sensitive to the state of the economy because expense account meals will be curtailed in a recession. Burger Queen meals should be relatively recession-proof.

b. The paint company that sells to the auto producers will be more sensitive to the state of the economy. In a downturn, auto sales fall dramatically as consumers stretch the lives of their cars. In contrast, in a recession, more people "do it themselves," which makes paint sales through small stores more stable and less sensitive to the economy.

Professor William F. Sharpe receiving the Nobel Prize in Economics
The prize was for Sharpe's development of the capital asset pricing model. This model shows how risk should be measured and provides a formula relating risk to the opportunity cost of capital.
Leif Jansson/Pica Pressfoto

Chapter 9

Risk, Return, and Capital Budgeting

*I*n Chapter 8 we distinguished *unique* risk from macro, or *market,* risk. Unique risk arises from events that affect only the individual firm or its immediate competitors; it can be eliminated by diversification. But regardless of how much you diversify, you cannot avoid the macroeconomic events that create market risk. This is why investors do not require a higher rate of return to compensate for unique risk but do need a higher return to persuade them to take on market risk.

How can you measure the market risk of a security or a project? We will see that market risk is usually measured by the sensitivity of the investment's returns to fluctuations in the market. We will also see that the risk premium investors demand should be proportional to this sensitivity. This relationship between risk and return is a useful way to estimate the return that investors expect from investing in common stocks.

Finally, we will distinguish between the risk of the company's securities and the risk of an individual project. We will also consider what managers should do when the risk of the project is different from that of the company's existing business.

After studying this chapter you should be able to

▶ Measure and interpret the market risk, or beta, of a security.

▶ Relate the market risk of a security to the rate of return that investors demand.

▶ Calculate the opportunity cost of capital for a project.

9.1 *Measuring Market Risk*

market portfolio: Portfolio of all assets in the economy. In practice a broad stock market index, such as the Standard & Poor's Composite, is used to represent the market.

Changes in interest rates, government spending, monetary policy, oil prices, foreign exchange rates, and other macroeconomic events affect almost all companies and the returns on almost all stocks. We can therefore assess the impact of "macro" news by tracking the rate of return on a **market portfolio** of all securities. If the market is up on a particular day, then the net impact of macroeconomic changes must be positive. We know the performance of the market reflects only macro events, because firm-specific events—that is, unique risks—average out when we look at the combined performance of thousands of companies and securities.

In principle the market portfolio should contain all assets in the world economy—not just stocks, but bonds, foreign securities, real estate, and so on. In practice, however, financial analysts make do with indexes of the stock market, usually the Standard & Poor's Composite Index (the S&P 500).[1]

Our task here is to define and measure the risk of *individual* common stocks. You can probably see where we are headed. Risk depends on exposure to macroeconomic events and can be measured as the sensitivity of a stock's returns to fluctuations in returns on the market portfolio. This sensitivity is called the stock's **beta.** Beta is often written as the Greek letter β.

beta: Sensitivity of a stock's return to the return on the market portfolio.

[1]We discussed the most popular stock market indexes in Section 8.2.

Measuring Beta

In the last chapter we looked at the variability of individual securities. Biogen had the highest standard deviation and Exxon the lowest. If you had held Biogen on its own, your returns would have varied four times as much as if you had held Exxon. But wise investors don't put all their eggs in just one basket: they reduce their risk by diversification. An investor with a diversified portfolio will be interested in the effect each stock has on the risk of the entire portfolio.

Diversification can eliminate the risk that is unique to individual stocks, but not the risk that the market as a whole may decline, carrying your stocks with it.

Some stocks are less affected than others by market fluctuations. Investment managers talk about "defensive" and "aggressive" stocks. Defensive stocks are not very sensitive to market fluctuations. In contrast, aggressive stocks amplify any market movements. If the market goes up, it is good to be in aggressive stocks; if it goes down, it is better to be in defensive stocks (and better still to have your money in the bank).

> Aggressive stocks have high betas, betas greater than 1.0, meaning that their returns tend to respond more than one-for-one to changes in the return of the overall market. The betas of defensive stocks are less than 1.0. The returns of these stocks vary less than one-for-one with market returns. The average beta of all stocks is—no surprises here—1.0 exactly.

Now we'll show you how betas are measured.

▶ Example 9.1 — *Measuring Beta for Turbot-Charged Seafoods*

Suppose we look back at the trading history of Turbot-Charged Seafoods and pick out 6 months when the return on the market portfolio was plus or minus 1 percent.

Month	Market Return, %	Turbot-Charged Seafood's Return, %	
1	+1	+ .8	
2	+1	+1.8	Average = .8%
3	+1	− .2	
4	−1	−1.8	
5	−1	+ .2	Average = −.8%
6	−1	− .8	

Look at Figure 9.1, where these observations are plotted. We've drawn a line through the average performance of Turbot when the market is up or down by 1 percent. *The slope of this line is Turbot's beta.* You can see right away that the beta is .8, because on average Turbot stock gains or loses .8 percent when the market is up or down by 1 percent. Notice that a 2-percentage-point difference in the market return (−1 to +1) generates on average a 1.6-percentage-point difference for Turbot shareholders (−.8 to +.8). The ratio, 1.6/2 = .8, is beta.

In 4 months, Turbot's returns lie above or below the line in Figure 9.1. The distance from the line shows the response of Turbot's stock returns to news or events that affected Turbot but did *not* affect the overall market. For example, in Month 2, investors in Turbot stock benefited from good macroeconomic news (the market was

Figure 9.1

This figure is a plot of the data presented in the table from Example 9.1. Each point shows the performance of Turbot-Charged Seafoods stock when the overall market is either up or down by 1 percent. On average, Turbot-Charged moves in the same direction as the market, but not as far. Therefore, Turbot-Charged's beta is less than 1.0. We can measure beta by the slope of a line fitted to the points in the figure. In this case it is .8.

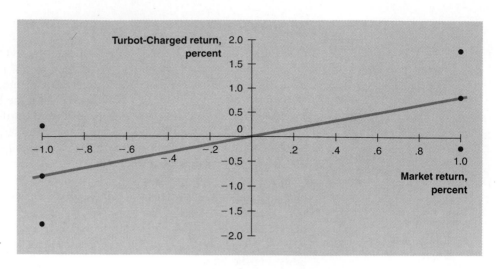

up 1 percent) and also from some favorable news specific to Turbot. The market rise gave a boost of .8 percent to Turbot stock (beta of .8 times the 1 percent market return). Then firm-specific news gave Turbot stockholders an extra 1 percent return, for a total return that month of 1.8 percent.

> As this example illustrates, we can break down common stock returns into two parts: the part explained by market returns and the firm's beta, and the part due to news that is specific to the firm. Fluctuations in the first part reflect market risk; fluctuations in the second part reflect unique risk.

Of course diversification can get rid of the unique risks. That's why wise investors, who don't put all their eggs in one basket, will look to Turbot's less-than-average beta and call its stock "defensive."

▶ **Self-Test 9.1**

Here are 6 months' returns to stockholders in the Anchovy Queen restaurant chain:

Month	Market Return, %	Anchovy Queen Return, %
1	+1	+2.0
2	+1	+ 0
3	+1	+1.0
4	−1	−1.0
5	−1	+ 0
6	−1	−2.0

Draw a figure like Figure 9.1 and check the slope of the fitted line. What is Anchovy Queen's beta?

Real life doesn't serve up numbers quite as convenient as those in our examples so far. However, the procedure for measuring real companies' betas is exactly the same:

1. Observe rates of return, usually monthly, for the stock and the market.
2. Plot the observations as in Figure 9.1.
3. Fit a line showing the average return to the stock at different market returns.

Beta is the slope of the fitted line.

   This may sound like a lot of work but in practice computers do it for you. Here are two real examples.

Betas for Delta Air Lines and Duke Power

Each point in Figure 9.2a shows the return on Delta Air Lines stock and the return on the market index in a different month. For example, the circled point shows that in the month of September 1995 Delta stock price fell by 6.9 percent, whereas the

Figure 9.2

(a) Each point in this figure shows the returns on Delta common stock and the overall market in a particular month. Sixty months are plotted in all. Delta's beta is the slope of the line fitted to these points. Delta has a relatively high beta of 1.5. (b) In this plot of 60 months' returns for Duke Power and the overall market the slope of the fitted line is much less than Delta's beta in (a). Duke Power has a relatively low beta of .70.

(a)

(b)

market index rose by 4.2 percent. Notice that more often than not Delta <u>outperformed</u> the market when the index rose and underperformed the market when the index fell. Thus Delta was a relatively aggressive, high-beta stock.

We have drawn a line of best fit through the points in the figure.[2] The slope of this line is 1.5. For each extra 1 percent rise in the market Delta stock price moved on average an extra 1.5 percent. For each extra 1 percent fall Delta stock price fell an extra 1.5 percent. Thus Delta's beta was 1.5.

Of course, Delta's stock returns are not perfectly related to market returns. The company was also subject to unique risk, which shows up in the scatter of points about the line. Sometimes Delta flew south while the market went north (for example, in September 1995), or vice versa.

Figure 9.2*b* shows a similar plot of the monthly returns for Duke Power. In contrast to Delta, Duke Power was a defensive, low-beta stock. It was not highly sensitive to market movements, usually lagging when the market rose and yet doing better (or less badly) when the market fell. The slope of the line of best fit shows that on average an extra 1 percent change in the index resulted in an extra .70 percent change in the price of Duke Power stock. Thus Duke Power's beta was .70.

You may find it interesting to look at Table 9.1, which shows how past market movements have affected several well-known stocks. Polaroid had the lowest beta: its stock return was less than half as sensitive as the average stock to market movements. Biogen was at the other extreme: its return was 2.01 times as sensitive as the average stock to market movements.

Portfolio Betas

Diversification decreases variability from unique risk but not from market risk. The beta of a portfolio is just an average of the betas of the securities in the portfolio, weighted by the investment in each security. For example, a portfolio comprised of only two stocks would have a beta as follows:

> **Beta of portfolio = (fraction of portfolio in first stock × beta of first stock)**
> **+ (fraction of portfolio in second stock × beta of**
> **second stock)**

Thus a portfolio invested 50-50 in Delta and Duke Power would have a beta of (.5 × 1.5) + (.5 × .70) = 1.10.

Table 9.1

Betas of selected common stocks

Stock	Beta	Stock	Beta
AT&T	1.09	Exxon	.69
Bethlehem Steel	1.69	Ford Motor Co.	.99
Biogen	2.01	Home Depot	.89
Coca-Cola	.84	McDonald's	.99
Compaq	.99	Merck	1.22
Delta Air Lines	1.50	Nike	1.20
Duke Power	.70	Polaroid	.53

Note: Betas are calculated from 5 years of monthly returns.

[2]The line of best fit is usually known as a *regression* line. The slope of the line can be calculated using *ordinary least squares* regression. The dependent variable is the return on the stock (Delta). The independent variable is the return on the market index, in this case the S&P 500.

A well-diversified portfolio of stocks all with betas of 1.5, like Delta, would still have a portfolio beta of 1.5. However, most of the individual stocks' unique risk would be diversified away. The market risk would remain, and such a portfolio would end up 1.5 times as variable as the market. For example, if the market has an annual standard deviation of 20 percent (about the historical average reported in Chapter 8), a fully diversified portfolio with beta of 1.5 has a standard deviation of $1.5 \times 20 = 30$ percent.

Portfolios with betas between 0 and 1.0 tend to move in the same direction as the market but not as far. A well-diversified portfolio of low-beta stocks like Duke Power, all with betas of .70, has almost no unique risk and is relatively unaffected by market movements. Such a portfolio is .70 times as variable as the market.

Of course, on average stocks have a beta of 1.0. A well-diversified portfolio including all kinds of stocks, with an average beta of 1, has the same variability as the market index.

▶ **Self-Test 9.2** Say you invested an equal amount in each of the stocks shown in Table 9.1. Calculate the beta of your portfolio.

▶ **Example 9.2** *How Risky Are Mutual Funds?*

You don't have to be wealthy to own a diversified portfolio. You can buy shares in one of the more than 6,000 mutual funds in the United States.

Investors buy shares of the funds, and the funds use the money to buy portfolios of securities. The returns on the portfolios are passed back to the funds' owners in proportion to their shareholdings. Therefore, the funds act like investment cooperatives, offering even the smallest investors diversification and professional management at low cost.

Let's look at the betas of two mutual funds that invest in stocks. Figure 9.3a shows how market movements have affected the returns of Vanguard's Windsor II mutual fund in a recent 5-year period. You can see that the stocks in the Windsor II fund had nearly average sensitivity to market changes: they had on average a beta of .9.

If the Windsor II fund had no unique risk, its portfolio would have been .9 times as variable as the market portfolio. But the fund had not diversified away quite all the unique risk; there is still some scatter about the line in Figure 9.3a. As a result, the variability of the fund was somewhat more than .9 times that of the market.

Figure 9.3b shows the same sort of plot for Vanguard's Index Trust 500 Portfolio mutual fund. Notice that this fund has a beta of 1.0 and only a tiny residual of unique risk—the fitted line fits almost exactly because an *index fund* is designed to track the market as closely as possible. The managers of the fund do not attempt to pick good stocks but just work to achieve full diversification at very low cost. (The Vanguard index fund takes investments of as little as $3,000 and manages the fund for an annual fee of less than .20 percent of the fund's assets.) The index fund is *fully diversified*. Investors in this fund buy the market as a whole and don't have to worry at all about unique risk.

▶ **Self-Test 9.3** Suppose you could achieve full diversification in a portfolio constructed from stocks with an average beta of .5. If the standard deviation of the market is 20 percent per year, what is the standard deviation of the portfolio return?

Figure 9.3

(a) The slope of the fitted line shows that investors in the Windsor II mutual fund bore market risk slightly below that of the S&P 500 portfolio. Windsor II's beta was .9. This was the average beta of the individual common stocks held by the fund. They also bore some unique risk, however; note the scatter of Windsor II's returns above and below the fitted line.

(b) The Vanguard 500 Portfolio is a fully diversified index fund designed to track the performance of the market. Note the fund's beta (1.0 and the absence of unique risk. The fund's returns lie almost precisely on the fitted line relating its returns to those of the S&P 500 portfolio.

(a)

(b)

 Risk and Return

In Chapter 8 we looked at past returns on selected investments. The least risky investment was U.S. Treasury bills. Since the return on Treasury bills is fixed, it is unaffected by what happens to the market. Thus the beta of Treasury bills is zero. The *most* risky investment that we considered was the market portfolio of common stocks. This has average market risk: its beta is 1.0.

Wise investors don't run risks just for fun. They are playing with real money, and therefore require a higher return from the market portfolio than from Treasury bills. The difference between the return on the market and the interest rate on bills is termed the **market risk premium.** Over the past 71 years the average market risk premium has been 8.7 percent a year. Of course, there is plenty of scope for argument as to whether the past 71 years constitute a typical period, but we will just assume here that 8.7 percent is the normal risk premium, that is, the additional return that an investor could reasonably expect from investing in the stock market rather than Treasury bills.

In Figure 9.4*a* we plotted the risk and expected return from Treasury bills and the market portfolio. You can see that Treasury bills have a beta of zero and a risk-free

market risk premium:
Risk premium of market portfolio. Difference between market return and return on risk-free Treasury bills.

Figure 9.4
(a) Here we begin the plot of expected rate of return against beta. The first benchmarks are Treasury bills (beta = 0) and the market portfolio (beta = 1.0). We assume a Treasury bill rate of 4 percent and a market return of 12.7 percent. The market risk premium is 12.7 − 4 = 8.7 percent.
(b) A portfolio split evenly between Treasury bills and the market will have beta = .5 and an expected return of 8.35 percent (point X). A portfolio invested 80 percent in the market and 20 percent in Treasury bills has beta = .8 and an expected rate of return of 10.96 percent (point Y). Note that the expected rate of return on any portfolio mixing Treasury bills and the market lies on a straight line. The risk premium is proportional to the portfolio beta.

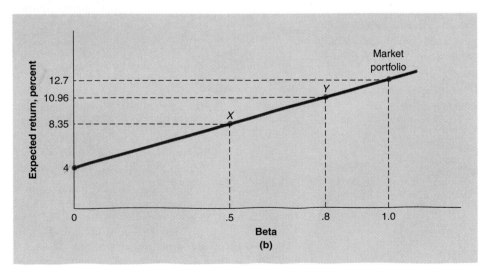

return; we'll assume that return is 4 percent. The market portfolio has a beta of 1.0 and an assumed expected return of 12.7 percent.[3]

Now, given these two benchmarks, what expected rate of return should an investor require from a stock or portfolio with a beta of .5? Halfway between, of course. Thus in Figure 9.4b we drew a straight line through the Treasury bill return and the expected market return and marked with an X the expected return for a beta of .5, that is, 8.35 percent.[4] This includes a risk premium of 4.35 percent above the Treasury bill return of 4 percent.

You can calculate this return as follows: start with the difference between the expected market return r_m and the Treasury bill rate r_f. This is the expected market risk premium.

$$\text{Market risk premium} = r_m - r_f = 12.7\% - 4\% = 8.7\%$$

Beta measures risk relative to the market. Therefore, the expected risk premium on any asset equals beta times the market risk premium:

$$\textbf{Risk premium on any asset} = r - r_f = \beta(r_m - r_f)$$

With a beta of .5 and a market risk premium of 8.7 percent,

$$\text{Risk premium} = \beta(r_m - r_f) = .5 \times 8.7 = 4.35\%$$

The total expected rate of return is the sum of the risk-free rate and the risk premium:

$$\textbf{Expected return = risk-free rate + risk premium}$$
$$r = r_f \qquad\qquad + \beta(r_m - r_f)$$
$$= 4\% + 4.35\% = 8.35\%$$

You could have calculated the expected rate of return in one step from this formula:

$$\text{Expected return} = r = r_f + \beta(r_m - r_f)$$
$$= 4\% + (.5 \times 8.7\%) = 8.35\%$$

capital asset pricing model (CAPM): Theory of the relationship between risk and return which states that the expected risk premium on any security equals its beta times the market risk premium.

This formula states the basic risk–return relationship called the **capital asset pricing model,** or **CAPM.** The CAPM has a simple interpretation.

> The expected rates of return demanded by investors depend on two things: (1) compensation for the time value of money (the risk-free rate r_f), and (2) a risk premium, which depends on beta and the market risk premium.

Note that the expected rate of return on an asset with $\beta = 1$ is just the market return. With a risk-free rate of 4 percent and market risk premium of 8.7 percent,

$$r = r_f + \beta(r_m - r_f)$$
$$= 4\% + (1 \times 8.7\%) = 12.7\%$$

[3]On past evidence the risk premium on the market is 8.7 percent. With a 4 percent Treasury bill rate, the expected market return would be $4 + 8.7 = 12.7$ percent.

[4]We report returns to two decimal places only so that you can follow through the calculations. No right-minded financial manager would pretend to be able to estimate the expected return on a stock with such precision.

▶ **Self-Test 9.4**   What are the risk premium and expected rate of return on a stock with $\beta = 1.5$? Assume a Treasury bill rate of 6 percent and a market risk premium of 8.7 percent.

Why the CAPM Works

The CAPM assumes that the stock market is dominated by well-diversified investors who are concerned only with market risk. That makes sense in a stock market where trading is dominated by large institutions and even small fry can diversify at very low cost.

▶ **Example 9.3**   *How Would You Invest $1 Million?*

Have you ever daydreamed about receiving a $1 million check, no strings attached, from an unknown benefactor? Let's daydream about how you would invest it.

We have two good candidates: Treasury bills, which offer an absolutely safe return, and the market portfolio (possibly via the Vanguard index fund discussed earlier in this chapter). The market has generated superior returns on average, but those returns have fluctuated a lot. (Look back to Figure 8.3.) So your investment policy is going to depend on your tolerance for risk.

If you're a cautious soul, you may invest only part of your money in the market portfolio and lend the remainder to the government by buying Treasury bills. Suppose that you invest 80 percent of your money in the market portfolio and lend out the other 20 percent to the government by buying U.S. Treasury bills. Then the beta of your portfolio will be a mixture of the beta of the market ($\beta_{\text{market}} = 1.0$) and the beta of the T-bills ($\beta_{\text{T-bills}} = 0$):

$$\text{Beta of portfolio} = \left(\begin{array}{c}\text{proportion} \\ \text{in market}\end{array} \times \begin{array}{c}\text{beta of} \\ \text{market}\end{array}\right) + \left(\begin{array}{c}\text{proportion} \\ \text{in T-bills}\end{array} \times \begin{array}{c}\text{beta of} \\ \text{T-bills}\end{array}\right)$$

$$\beta = (.8 \times \beta_{\text{market}}) \qquad + (.2 \times \beta_{\text{T-bills}})$$
$$= (.8 \times 1.0) \qquad + (.2 \times 0) = .80$$

The fraction of funds that you invest in the market also affects your return. If you invest your entire million in the market portfolio, you earn the full market risk premium. But if you invest only 80 percent of your money in the market, you earn only 80 percent of the risk premium.

$$\begin{array}{c}\text{Expected} \\ \text{risk premium} \\ \text{on portfolio}\end{array} = \left(\begin{array}{c}\text{proportion in} \\ \text{T-bills}\end{array} \times \begin{array}{c}\text{risk premium} \\ \text{on T-bills}\end{array}\right) + \left(\begin{array}{c}\text{proportion in} \\ \text{market}\end{array} \times \begin{array}{c}\text{market risk} \\ \text{premium}\end{array}\right)$$

$$= (.2 \times 0) + (.8 \times \text{expected market risk premium})$$
$$= .8 \times \text{expected market risk premium}$$
$$= .8 \times 8.7 = 6.96\%$$

The expected return on your portfolio is equal to the risk-free interest rate plus the expected risk premium:

Expected portfolio return = $r_{\text{portfolio}}$ = 4 + 6.96 = 10.96%

In Figure 9.4*b* we show the beta and expected return on this portfolio by the letter *Y*.

The Security Market Line

security market line:
Relationship between
expected return and beta.

Example 9.3 illustrates a general point: by investing some proportion of your money in the market portfolio and lending (or borrowing)[5] the balance, you can obtain any combination of risk and expected return along the sloping line in Figure 9.5. This line is generally known as the **security market line.**

▶ **Self-Test 9.5**

How would you construct a portfolio with a beta of .25? What is the expected return to this strategy? Assume Treasury bills yield 6 percent and the market risk premium is 8.7 percent.

Figure 9.5

The security market line shows how expected rate of return depends on beta. According to the capital asset pricing model, expected rates of return for all securities and all portfolios lie on this line.

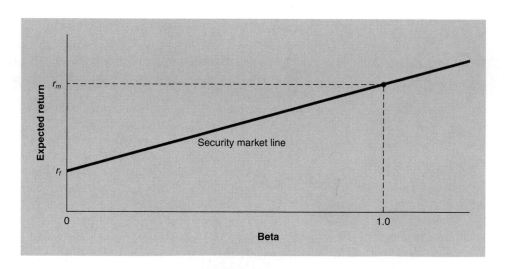

[5]Notice that the security market line extends above the market return at $\beta = 1$. How would you generate a portfolio with, say, $\beta = 2$? It's easy, but it's risky. Suppose you borrow $1 million and invest the loan plus $1 million in the market portfolio. That gives you $2 million invested and a $1 million liability. Your portfolio now has a beta of 2.0:

Beta$_{\text{portfolio}}$ = (proportion in market × beta of market) + (proportion in loan × beta of loan)

β = (2 × β_{market}) + (−1 × β_{loan})

= (2 × 1.0) + (−1 × 0) = 2

Notice that the proportion in the loan is negative because you are borrowing, not lending money.

By the way, borrowing from a bank or stockbroker would not be difficult or unduly expensive as long as you put up your $2 million stock portfolio as security for the loan.

Can you calculate the risk premium and the expected rate of return on this borrow-and-invest strategy?

> The security market line describes the expected returns and risks from investing different fractions of your funds in the market. It also sets a standard for other investments. Investors will be willing to hold other investments only if they offer equally good prospects. Thus the required risk premium for *any* investment is given by the security market line:
>
> **Risk premium on investment = beta × expected market risk premium**

Look back to Figure 9.4*b*, which asserts that an individual common stock with β = .5 must offer an 8.35 percent expected rate of return when Treasury bills yield 4 percent and the market risk premium is 8.7 percent. You can now see why this has to be so. If that stock offered a lower rate of return, nobody would buy even a little of it—they could get 8.35 percent just by investing 50-50 in Treasury bills and the market. And if nobody wants to hold the stock, its price has to drop. A lower price means a better buy for investors, that is, a higher rate of return. The price will fall until the stock's expected rate of return is pushed up to 8.35 percent. At that price and expected return the CAPM holds.

If, on the other hand, our favorite stock offered more than 8.35 percent, diversified investors would want to buy more of it. That would push the price up and the expected return down to the levels predicted by the CAPM.

This reasoning holds for stocks with any beta. That's why the CAPM makes sense, and why the expected risk premium on an investment should be proportional to its beta.

▶ **Self-Test 9.6**

Suppose you invest $400,000 in Treasury bills and $600,000 in the market portfolio. What is the return on your portfolio if bills yield 6 percent and the expected return on the market is 14.7 percent? What does the return on this portfolio imply for the expected return on individual stocks with betas of .6?

The basic idea behind the capital asset pricing model is that investors expect a reward for both waiting and worrying. The greater the worry, the greater the expected return. If you invest in a risk-free Treasury bill, you just receive the rate of interest. That's the reward for waiting. When you invest in risky stocks, you can expect an extra return or risk premium for worrying. The capital asset pricing model states that this risk premium is equal to the stock's beta times the market risk premium. Therefore,

Expected return on stock = risk-free interest rate + (beta × market risk premium)

$$r = r_f + \beta(r_m - r_f)$$

How well does the CAPM work in practice? Do the returns on stocks with betas of .5 on average lie halfway between the return on the market portfolio and the interest rate on Treasury bills? Unfortunately, the evidence is conflicting. Let's look back to the actual returns earned by investors in low-beta stocks and in high-beta stocks.

Imagine that in 1931 ten investors gathered in a Wall Street bar to discuss their portfolios. Each agreed to follow a different strategy. Investor 1 opted to buy each year the 10 percent of New York Stock Exchange stocks with the lowest betas; investor 2 chose the 10 percent with the next-lowest betas; and so on, up to investor 10, who agreed to buy the stocks with the highest betas. They also agreed that they would return 60 years later to compare results, and so they parted with much cordiality and good wishes.

Figure 9.6

The capital asset pricing model states that the expected risk premium from any investment should lie on the market line. The dots show the actual average risk premiums from portfolios with different betas. The high-beta portfolios generated higher average returns, just as predicted by the CAPM. But the high-beta portfolios plotted below the security market line, and four of the five low-beta portfolios plotted above. A line fitted to the 10 portfolio returns would be flatter than the market line. (Source: F. Black, "Beta and Return," Journal of Portfolio Management *20 (Fall 1993, pp. 8–18.) The copyrighted material is reprinted with permission from the* Journal of Portfolio Management, *a publication of Institutional Investor, Inc., 488 Madison Avenue, New York, New York 10022.*

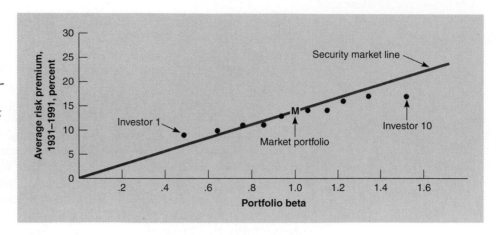

In 1991 the same 10 investors, now much older and wealthier, met again in the same bar. Figure 9.6 shows how they fared. Investor 1's portfolio turned out to be much less risky than the market; its beta was only .49. However, investor 1 also realized the lowest return, 9 percent above the risk-free rate of interest. At the other extreme, the beta of investor 10's portfolio was 1.52, about three times that of investor 1's portfolio. But investor 10 was rewarded with the highest return, averaging 17 percent above the interest rate. So over this 60-year period returns did indeed increase with beta.

As you can see from Figure 9.6, the market portfolio over the same 60-year period provides an average return of 14 percent above the interest rate[6] and (of course) had a beta of 1.0. The CAPM predicts that the risk premium should lie on the upward-sloping security market line in Figure 9.6. Since the market provided a risk premium of 14 percent, investor 1's portfolio, with a beta of .49, should have provided a risk premium of a shade under 7 percent and investor 10's portfolio, with a beta of 1.52, should have given a premium of a shade over 21 percent. You can see that while high-beta stocks performed better than low-beta stocks, the difference was not as great as the CAPM predicts.

Figure 9.6 provides broad support for the CAPM, though it suggests that the line relating return to beta has been too flat. But recent years have been less kind to the CAPM. For example, if the 10 friends had invested their cash in 1966 rather than 1931, there would have been very little relation between their portfolio returns and beta. Does this imply that there has been a fundamental change in the relation between risk and return in the last 30 years or did high-beta stocks just happen to perform worse during these years than investors expected? It is hard to be sure.

There is little doubt that the CAPM is too simple to capture everything that is going on in the stock market. For example, it appears that stocks of small companies or stocks with low price-earnings ratios have offered higher rates of return than the CAPM predicts. This has prompted headlines like "Is Beta Dead?" in the business press.[7] It is not the first time that beta has been declared dead, but the CAPM is still being used. Only strong theories can have more than one funeral.

---

[6]In Figure 9.6 the stocks in the "market portfolio" are weighted equally. Since the stocks of small firms have provided higher average returns than those of large firms, the risk premium on an equally weighted index is higher than on a value-weighted index. This is one reason for the difference between the 14 percent market risk premium in Figure 9.6 and the 8.7 percent premium reported in Table 8.1.

[7]A. Wallace, "Is Beta Dead?" *Institutional Investor* 14 (July 1980), pp. 22–30.

This CAPM is not the only model of risk and return. It has several brothers and sisters as well as second cousins. However, the CAPM captures in a simple way two fundamental ideas. First, almost everyone agrees that investors require some extra return for taking on risk. Second, investors appear to be concerned principally with the market risk that they cannot eliminate by diversification. That is why financial managers rely on the capital asset pricing model as a good rule of thumb.

Using the CAPM to Estimate Expected Returns

To calculate the returns that investors are expecting from particular stocks, we need three numbers—the risk-free interest rate, the expected market risk premium, and beta. In mid-1997, the interest rate on Treasury bills was about 5.3 percent. Assume as before that the market risk premium is 8.7 percent. Finally, look back to Table 9.1, where we gave you betas of several stocks. Table 9.2 puts these numbers together to give an estimate of the expected return from each stock. Let's take Duke Power as an example:

$$\text{Expected return on Duke Power} = \text{risk-free interest rate} + \left(\text{beta} \times \text{expected market risk premium} \right)$$

$$r = 5.3\% + (.70 \times 8.7\%)$$

$$= 11.39\%$$

You can also use the capital asset pricing model to find the discount rate for a new capital investment. For example, suppose you are asked to analyze a proposal by Merck to expand its operations.[8] At what rate should you discount the forecast cash flows? According to Table 9.2 investors are looking for a return of 15.9 percent from investments with the risk of Merck stock. That is the opportunity cost of capital for Merck's expansion project.

In practice, choosing a discount rate is seldom this easy. (After all, you can't expect to become a captain of finance simply by plugging numbers into a formula.) For example, you must learn how to adjust for the extra risk caused by company borrowing and how to estimate the discount rate for projects that do not have the same risk as the company's existing business. We will come to these refinements later.

Table 9.2

Expected rates of return

Stock	Expected Return, %	Stock	Expected Return, %
AT&T	14.8	Exxon	11.3
Bethlehem Steel	20.0	Ford Motor Co.	13.9
Biogen	22.8	Home Depot	13.0
Coca-Cola	12.6	McDonald's	13.9
Compaq	13.9	Merck	15.9
Delta Air Lines	18.4	Nike	15.7
Duke Power	11.4	Polaroid	9.9

Note: Expected return $= r = r_f + \beta(r_m - r_f) = 5.3\% + (\beta \times 8.7\%)$.

[8]We've chosen a company with hardly any debt, so the risk of its assets equals the risk of its stock. This is not true when the company's assets are partly debt-financed. We'll explain how to handle this more general case in Chapter 10.

▶ **Example 9.4**   *Comparing Project Returns and the Opportunity Cost of Capital*

You have forecast the cash flows on a project and calculated that its internal rate of return is 15.0 percent. Suppose that Treasury bills offer a return of 4 percent and the expected market risk premium is 8.7 percent. Should you go ahead with the project?

To answer this question you need to figure out the opportunity cost of capital r. This depends on the project's beta. For example, if the project is a sure thing, the beta is zero and the cost of capital equals the interest rate on Treasury bills:

$$r = 4 + (0 \times 8.7) = 4\%$$

If your project offers a return of 15.0 percent when the cost of capital is 4 percent, you should obviously go ahead.[9]

Sure-fire projects rarely occur outside finance texts. So let's think about the cost of capital if the project has the same risk as the market portfolio. In this case beta is 1.0 and the cost of capital is the expected return on the market:

$$r = 4 + (1.0 \times 8.7) = 12.7\%$$

The project appears less attractive than before but still worth doing.

But what if the project has even higher risk? Suppose, for example, that it has a beta of 1.5. What is the cost of capital in this case? To find the answer, we plug a beta of 1.5 into our formula for r:

$$r = 4 + (1.5 \times 8.7) = 17.05\%$$

A project this risky would need a return of at least 17.05 percent to justify going ahead. The 15 percent project should be rejected.

This rejection occurs because, as Figure 9.7 shows, the project's expected rate of return plots below the security market line. The project offers a lower return than investors can get elsewhere, so it is a negative-NPV investment.

Figure 9.7

The expected return of this project is less than the expected return one could earn on stock market invest-ments with the same market risk (beta). Therefore, the project's expected return–risk combination lies below the security market line, and the project should be rejected.

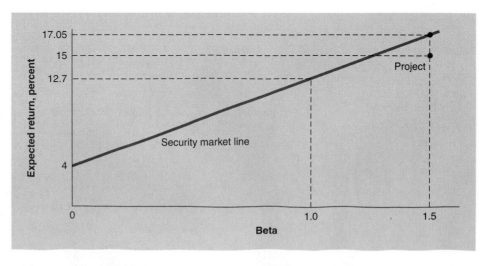

[9]In Chapter 5 we described some special cases where you should prefer projects that offer a *lower* inter-nal rate of return than the cost of capital. We assume here that your project is a "normal" one, and that you prefer high IRRs to low ones..

> The security market line provides a standard for project acceptance. If the project's return lies above the security market line, then the return is higher than investors could expect to get by investing their funds in the capital market and therefore is an attractive investment opportunity.

▶ **Self-Test 9.7**   Suppose that Merck's expansion project is forecast to produce cash flows of $50 million a year for each of 10 years. What is its present value? Use data from Table 9.2. What would the present value be if the beta of the investment were .7?

9.3 *Capital Budgeting and Project Risk*

Company versus Project Risk

Long before the development of modern theories linking risk and return, smart financial managers adjusted for risk in capital budgeting. They realized intuitively that, other things equal, risky projects are less desirable than safe ones and must provide higher rates of return.

company cost of capital: Expected rate of return demanded by investors in a company, determined by the average risk of the company's assets and operations.

Many companies estimate the rate of return required by investors in their securities and use this **company cost of capital** to discount the cash flows on all new projects. Since investors require a higher rate of return from a risky company, risky firms will have a higher company cost of capital and will set a higher discount rate for their new investment opportunities. For example, we showed in Table 9.1 that on past evidence Merck has a beta of 1.22 and the corresponding expected rate of return (see Table 9.2) is 15.9 percent. According to the company cost of capital rule, Merck should use a 15.9 percent cost of capital to calculate project NPVs.

This is a step in the right direction, but this approach can get a firm in trouble if its new projects do not have the same risk as its existing business. Merck's beta reflects investors' estimate of the risk of the pharmaceutical business and its company cost of capital is the return that investors require for taking on this risk. If Merck is considering an expansion of its regular business, it makes sense to discount the forecast cash flows by the company cost of capital. But suppose that Merck is wondering whether to branch out into production of computer hardware. Its beta tells us nothing about the **project cost of capital.** That depends on the risk of the hardware business and the return that shareholders require from investing in such a business.

project cost of capital: Minimum acceptable expected rate of return on a project given its risk.

> The project cost of capital depends on the use to which that capital is put. Therefore, it depends on the risk of the project and not on the risk of the company. If a company invests in a low-risk project, it should discount the cash flows at a correspondingly low cost of capital. If it invests in a high-risk project, those cash flows should be discounted at a high cost of capital.

▶ **Self-Test 9.8**   The company cost of capital for Merck is about 16 percent (see Table 9.2); for Compaq Computer it is about 14 percent. What would be the more reasonable discount rate for Merck to use for its proposed computer hardware division? Why?

Determinants of Project Risk

We have seen that the company cost of capital is the correct discount rate for projects that have the same risk as the company's existing business, but *not* for those projects that are safer or riskier than the company's average. How do we know whether a project is unusually risky? Estimating project risk is never going to be an exact science, but here are two things to bear in mind.

First, we saw in Chapter 7 that operating leverage increases the risk of a project. When a large fraction of your costs is fixed, any change in revenues can have a dramatic effect on earnings. Therefore, projects that involve high fixed costs tend to have higher betas.

Second, many people intuitively associate risk with the variability of earnings. But much of this variability reflects diversifiable risk. Lone prospectors in search of gold look forward to extremely uncertain future earnings, but whether they strike it rich is not likely to depend on the performance of the rest of the economy. These investments have a high standard deviation but a low beta.

> **What matters is the strength of the relationship between the firm's earnings and the aggregate earnings of all firms. Thus cyclical businesses, whose revenues and earnings are strongly dependent on the state of the economy, tend to have high betas and a high cost of capital. By contrast, businesses that produce essentials, such as food, beer, and cosmetics, are less affected by the state of the economy. They tend to have low betas and a low cost of capital.**

Don't Add Fudge Factors to Discount Rates

Risk to an investor arises because an investment adds to the spread of possible portfolio returns. To a diversified investor, risk is predominantly market risk. But in everyday usage *risk* simply means "bad outcome." People think of the "risks" of a project as the things that can go wrong. For example,

- A geologist looking for oil worries about the risk of a dry hole.
- A pharmaceutical manufacturer worries about the risk that a new drug which reverses balding may not be approved by the Food and Drug Administration.
- The owner of a hotel in a politically unstable part of the world worries about the political risk of expropriation.

Managers sometimes add fudge factors to discount rates to account for worries such as these.

This sort of adjustment makes us nervous. First, the bad outcomes we cited appear to reflect diversifiable risks which would not affect the expected rate of return demanded by investors. Second, the need for an adjustment in the discount rate usually arises because managers fail to give bad outcomes their due weight in cash-flow forecasts. They then try to offset that mistake by adding a fudge factor to the discount rate. For example, if a manager is worried about the possibility of a bad outcome such as a dry hole in oil exploration, he or she may reduce the value of the project by using a higher discount rate. This approach is unsound, however. Instead, the possibility of the dry hole should be included in the calculation of the expected cash flows to be derived from the well. Suppose that there is a 50 percent chance of a dry hole and a 50 percent chance that the well will produce oil worth $20 million. Then the *expected* cash flow is not $20 million but $(.5 \times 0) + (.5 \times 20) = $10 million. You should discount the $10 million expected cash flow at the opportunity cost of capital: it does not make sense to discount the $20 million using a fudged discount rate.

> Expected cash-flow forecasts should already reflect the probabilities of *all* possible outcomes, good and bad. If the cash-flow forecasts are prepared properly, the discount rate should reflect only the market risk of the project. It should not have to be fudged to offset errors or biases in the cash-flow forecast.

Summary

1. The contribution of a security to the risk of a diversified portfolio depends on its market risk. But not all securities are equally affected by fluctuations in the market. The sensitivity of a stock to market movements is known as beta. Stocks with a beta greater than 1.0 are particularly sensitive to market fluctuations. Those with a beta of less than 1.0 are not so sensitive to such movements. The average beta of all stocks is 1.0.

2. The extra return that investors require for taking risk is known as the risk premium. The capital asset pricing model states that the expected risk premium of an investment should be proportional to its beta. The expected rate of return from any investment is equal to the risk-free interest rate plus the risk premium, so the CAPM boils down to

$$r = r_f + \beta(r_m - r_f)$$

3. The opportunity cost of capital is the return that investors give up by investing in the project rather than in securities of equivalent risk. Financial managers use the capital asset pricing model to estimate the opportunity cost of capital.

4. The opportunity cost of capital depends on the use to which the capital is put. Therefore, required rates of return are determined by the risk of the project, not by the risk of the firm's existing business.

5. Your cash-flow forecasts should already factor in the chances of pleasant and unpleasant surprises. Potential bad outcomes should be reflected in the discount rate only to the extent that they affect beta.

Key Terms

market portfolio	capital asset pricing	company cost of capital
beta	model (CAPM)	project cost of capital
market risk premium	security market line	

Problems

1. **Risk and Return.** True or false? Explain or qualify as necessary.

   a. Investors demand higher expected rates of return on stocks with more variable rates of return.

   b. The capital asset pricing model predicts that a security with a beta of zero will provide an expected return of zero.

   c. An investor who puts $10,000 in Treasury bills and $20,000 in the market portfolio will have a portfolio beta of 2.0.

   d. Investors demand higher expected rates of return from stocks with returns that are highly exposed to macroeconomic changes.

e. Investors demand higher expected rates of return from stocks with returns that are very sensitive to fluctuations in the stock market.

2. **Diversifiable Risk.** In light of what you've learned about market versus diversifiable (unique) risks, explain why an insurance company has no problem in selling life insurance to individuals but is reluctant to issue policies insuring against flood damage to residents of coastal areas. Why don't the insurance companies simply charge coastal residents a premium that reflects the actuarial probability of damage from hurricanes and other storms?

3. **Risk and Return.** Suppose that the risk premium on stocks and other securities did in fact rise with total risk (that is, the variability of returns) rather than just market risk. Explain how investors could exploit the situation to create portfolios with high expected rates of return but low levels of risk.

4. **CAPM and Hurdle Rates.** A project under consideration has an internal rate of return of 14 percent and a beta of .6. The risk-free rate is 5 percent and the expected rate of return on the market portfolio is 14 percent.

a. Should the project be accepted?
b. Should the project be accepted if its beta is 1.6?
c. Why does your answer change?

5. **CAPM and Expected Return.** If the risk-free rate is 6 percent and the expected rate of return on the market portfolio is 14 percent, is a security with a beta of 1.25 and an expected rate of return of 16 percent overpriced or underpriced?

6. **CAPM and Valuation.** You are considering acquiring a firm that you believe can generate expected cash flows of $10,000 a year forever. However, you recognize that those cash flows are uncertain.

a. Suppose you believe that the beta of the firm is .4. How much is the firm worth if the risk-free rate is 5 percent and the expected rate of return on the market portfolio is 15 percent?
b. By how much will you overvalue the firm if its beta is actually .6?

7. **CAPM.** Consider the following two scenarios for the economy, and the returns in each scenario for the market portfolio, an aggressive stock A, and a defensive stock D.

		Rate of Return	
Scenario	Market	Aggressive Stock A	Defensive Stock D
Bust	−8%	−10%	−6%
Boom	32	38	24

a. Find the beta of each stock. In what way is stock D defensive?
b. If each scenario is equally likely, find the expected rate of return on the market portfolio and on each stock.
c. If the T-bill rate is 4 percent, what does the CAPM say about the fair expected rate of return on the two stocks?
d. Which stock seems to be a better buy based on your answers to (a) through (c)?

8. **Using Beta.** Investors expect the market rate of return this year to be 14 percent. A stock with a beta of .8 has an expected rate of return of 12 percent. If the market return this year turns out to be 10 percent, what is your best guess as to the rate of return on the stock?

9. **Unique vs. Market Risk.** Figure 9.8 shows plots of monthly rates of return on three stocks versus the stock market index. The beta and standard deviation of each stock is given beside its plot.

a. Which stock is riskiest to a diversified investor?

b. Which stock is riskiest to an undiversified investor who puts all her funds in one of these stocks?

c. Consider a portfolio with equal investments in each stock. What would this portfolio's beta have been?

d. Consider a well-diversified portfolio made up of stocks with the same beta as Exxon. What are the beta and standard deviation of this portfolio's return? The standard deviation of the market portfolio's return is 20 percent.

e. What is the expected rate of return on each stock? Use the capital asset pricing model with a market risk premium of 8 percent. The risk-free rate of interest is 4 percent.

Figure 9.8

These plots show monthly rates of return for (a) Exxon, (b) Polaroid, (c) Nike, and the market portfolio. See problem 9.

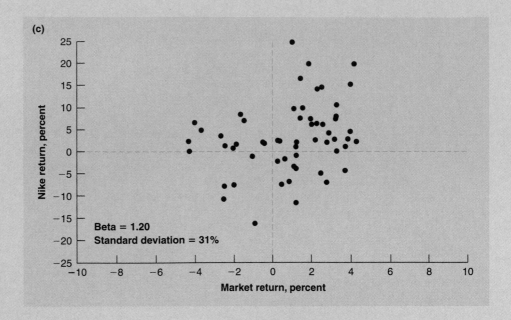

(c)

Beta = 1.20
Standard deviation = 31%

Nike return, percent (y-axis)
Market return, percent (x-axis)

10. **Calculating Beta.** Following are several months' rates of return for Tumblehome Canoe Company. Prepare a plot like Figure 9.1. What is Tumblehome's beta?

Month	Market Return, %	Tumblehome Return, %
1	0	+1
2	0	−1
3	−1	−2.5
4	−1	−0.5
5	+1	+2
6	+1	+1
7	+2	+4
8	+2	+2
9	−2	−2
10	−2	−4

11. **Unique vs. Market Risk.** Figure 9.9 plots monthly rates of return from 1992 to 1996 for the Snake Oil mutual fund. Was this fund well-diversified? Explain.

12. **CAPM and Cost of Capital.** Draw the security market line when the Treasury bill rate is 10 percent and the market risk premium is 8 percent. What are the project costs of capital for new ventures with betas of .75 and 1.75? Which of the following capital investments have positive NPVs?

Project	Beta	Internal Rate of Return, %
P	1.0	20
Q	0	10
R	2.0	25
S	0.4	16
T	1.6	25

13. **CAPM and Valuation.** You are a consultant to a firm evaluating an expansion of its current business. The cash-flow forecasts (in millions of dollars) for the project are:

Figure 9.9

Monthly rates of return for the Snake Oil mutual fund and the Standard & Poor's Composite Index. See problem 11.

Years	Cash Flow
0	−100
1–10	+ 15

Based on the behavior of the firm's stock, you believe that the beta of the firm is 1.4. Assuming that the rate of return available on risk-free investments is 5 percent and that the expected rate of return on the market portfolio is 15 percent, what is the net present value of the project?

14. **CAPM and Cost of Capital.** Reconsider the project in the preceding problem. What is the project IRR? What is the cost of capital for the project? Does the accept–reject decision using IRR agree with the decision using NPV?

15. **CAPM and Valuation.** A share of stock with a beta of .75 now sells for $50. Investors expect the stock to pay a year-end dividend of $2. The T-bill rate is 4 percent, and the market risk premium is 8 percent. If the stock is perceived to be fairly priced today, what must be investors' expectation of the price of the stock at the end of the year?

16. **CAPM and Expected Return.** Reconsider the stock in the preceding problem. Suppose investors actually believe the stock will sell for $54 at year-end. Is the stock a good or bad buy? What will investors do? At what point will the stock reach an "equilibrium" at which it again is perceived as fairly priced?

17. **CAPM and Valuation.** You are considering the purchase of real estate which will provide perpetual income that should average $50,000 per year. How much will you pay for the property if you believe its market risk is the same as the market portfolio's? The T-bill rate is 5 percent, and the expected market return is 12.5 percent.

18. **Risk and Return.** According to the CAPM, would the expected rate of return on a security with a beta less than zero be more or less than the risk-free interest rate? Why would investors be willing to invest in such a security? *Hint:* Look back to the auto and gold example in Chapter 8.

19. **CAPM and Expected Return.** The table on the next page shows betas for several companies. Calculate each stock's expected rate of return using the CAPM. Assume the risk-free rate of interest is 5 percent. Use the historical risk premium on the market portfolio.

Company	Beta
Bristol-Myers Squibb	1.13
Digital Equipment Corp.	0.86
General Mills	0.70
McGraw-Hill	0.92
Microsoft	0.82

20. **Project Cost of Capital.** Suppose General Mills is considering a new investment in the common stock of a publishing company. Which of the betas shown in the table in problem 19 is most relevant in determining the required rate of return for this venture? Explain why the expected return to General Mills stock is *not* the appropriate required return.

21. **Risk and Return.** True or false? Explain or qualify as necessary.

   a. The expected rate of return on an investment with a beta of 2 is twice as high as the expected rate of return of the market portfolio.

   b. The contribution of a stock to the risk of a diversified portfolio depends on the market risk of the stock.

   c. If a stock's expected rate of return plots below the security market line, it is underpriced.

   d. A diversified portfolio with beta of 2 is twice as volatile as the market portfolio.

   e. An undiversified portfolio with beta of 2 is twice as volatile as the market portfolio.

22. **CAPM and Expected Return.** Stock A has a beta of .5 and investors expect it to return 5 percent. Stock B has a beta of 1.5 and investors expect it to return 13 percent. Use the CAPM to find the market risk premium and the expected rate of return on the market.

23. **CAPM and Expected Return.** A mutual fund manager expects her portfolio to earn a rate of return of 12 percent this year. The beta of her portfolio is .8. If the rate of return available on risk-free assets is 5 percent and you expect the rate of return on the market portfolio to be 15 percent, should you invest in this mutual fund?

24. **Required Rate of Return.** Reconsider the mutual fund manager in the previous problem. Explain how you would use a stock index mutual fund and a risk-free position in Treasury bills (or a money market mutual fund) to create a portfolio with the same risk as the manager's but with a higher expected rate of return. What is the rate of return on that portfolio?

25. **Required Rate of Return.** In view of your answer to the preceding problem, explain why a mutual fund must be able to provide an expected rate of return in excess of that predicted by the security market line for investors to consider the fund an attractive investment opportunity.

26. **Leverage and Portfolio Risk.** Footnote 5 in the chapter asks you to consider a borrow-and-invest strategy in which you use $1 million of your own money and borrow another $1 million to invest $2 million in a market index fund. If the risk-free interest rate is 4 percent and the expected rate of return on the market index fund is 12 percent, what is the risk premium and expected rate of return on the borrow-and-invest strategy? Why is the risk of this strategy twice that of simply investing your $1 million in the market index fund?

27. **CAPM and Expected Return.** If the expected rate of return on the market portfolio is 14 percent and T-bills yield 6 percent, what must be the beta of a stock that investors expect to return 10 percent?

28. **CAPM.** We Do Bankruptcies is a law firm that specializes in providing advice to firms in financial distress. It prospers in recessions when other firms are struggling. Consequently, its beta is negative, −.2.

   a. If the interest rate on Treasury bills is 5 percent and the expected return on the market portfolio is 15 percent, what is the expected return on the shares of the law firm according to the CAPM?

   b. Suppose you invested 90 percent of your wealth in the market portfolio and the remainder of your wealth in the shares in the law firm. What would be the beta of your portfolio?

Solutions to Self-Test Questions

9.1 See Figure 9.10. Anchovy Queen's beta is 1.0.

9.2 A portfolio's beta is just a weighted average of the betas of the securities in the portfolio. In this case the weights are equal, since an equal amount is assumed invested in each of the stocks in Table 9.1. The average beta of these stocks is $(1.09 + 1.69 + 2.01 + .84 + .99 + 1.50 + .70 + .69 + .99 + .89 + .99 + 1.22 + 1.20 + .53)/14 = 1.10$.

9.3 The standard deviation of a fully diversified portfolio's return is proportional to its beta. The standard deviation in this case is $.5 \times 20 = 10$ percent.

9.4 $r = r_f + \beta(r_m - r_f)$

$= 6 + (1.5 \times 8.7) = 19.05\%$

9.5 Put 25 percent of your money in the market portfolio and the rest in Treasury bills. The portfolio's beta is .25 and its expected return is

$$r_{\text{portfolio}} = (.75 \times 6) + (.25 \times 14.7) = 8.175\%$$

9.6 $r_{\text{portfolio}} = (.4 \times 6) + (.6 \times 14.7) = 11.22\%$

This portfolio's beta is .6, since \$600,000, which is 60 percent of the investment, is in the market portfolio. Investors in a stock with a beta of .6 would not buy it unless it also offered a rate of return of 11.22 percent and would rush to buy if it offered more. The stock price would adjust until the stock's expected rate of return was 11.22 percent.

9.7 Present value = \$50 million $\times$ 10-year annuity factor at 15.9%

$= \$242.6$ million

If $\beta = .7$, then the cost of capital falls to

$$r = 5.3\% + (.7 \times 8.7\%) = 11.4\%$$

and the value of the 10-year annuity increases to \$289.6 million.

9.8 Merck should use Compaq's cost of capital. Merck's company cost of capital tells us what expected rate of return investors demand from the pharmaceutical business. This is not the appropriate project cost of capital for Merck's venture into computer hardware.

Figure 9.10

Each point shows the performance of Anchovy Queen stock when the market is up or down by 1 percent. On average, Anchovy Queen stock follows the market; it has a beta of 1.0.

Jo Ann Cox needs to calculate the required rate of return on this geothermal plant.
How should she do it?
© *Cameramann International, Ltd.*

Chapter 10
The Cost of Capital

The company cost of capital is defined as the return that the firm's investors could expect to earn if they invested in securities with a comparable degree of risk. It is, therefore, the return that investors are giving up when they invest in the firm.[1] We *use* the company cost of capital to discount the cash flows from projects that have the same degree of risk as the firm's existing business.

In the last chapter you learned how to use the capital asset pricing model to estimate the expected return on a company's common stock. If the firm is financed wholly by common stock, then the stockholders own all the firm's assets and are entitled to all the cash flows. In this case, the expected return on the common stock and the company cost of capital are identical.

Most companies, however, are financed by a mixture of securities, including common stock, bonds, and often preferred stock or other securities. Each of these securities has different risks and therefore investors in them look for different rates of return. In these circumstances, the company cost of capital is no longer the same as the expected return on the common stock. It depends on the expected return from all the securities that the company has issued.

In this chapter we will show you how to calculate the company cost of capital when the firm is financed by a mixture of debt and equity and how to use this figure to judge the appropriate discount rate for a new project. This chapter will also explain how financial managers translate the risks and returns on *securities* issued by the company into required rates of return for capital investment projects.

After studying this chapter you should be able to

▶ Calculate a firm's capital structure.

▶ Estimate the required rates of return on the securities issued by the firm.

▶ Calculate the weighted average cost of capital.

▶ Understand when the weighted-average cost of capital is—or isn't—the appropriate discount rate for a new project.

The Cost of Capital

Jo Ann Cox, a recent graduate of a prestigious eastern business school, poured a third cup of black coffee and tried again to remember what she once knew about project hurdle rates. Why hadn't she paid more attention in Finance 101? Why had she sold her finance text the day after passing the finance final?

Costas Thermopolis, her boss and CEO of Geothermal Corporation, had told her to prepare a financial evaluation of a proposed expansion of Geothermal's production. She was to report at 9:00 Monday morning. Thermopolis, whose background was

---

[1]Investors will invest in the firm's securities only if they offer the same expected return as that of other equally risky securities. When securities are properly priced, the return that investors can *expect* from their investments is therefore also the return that they *require*.

geophysics, not finance, not only expected a numerical analysis; he expected her to explain it to him.[2]

Thermopolis had founded Geothermal in 1993 to produce electricity from geothermal energy trapped deep under Nevada. The company had pioneered this business and had been able to obtain perpetual production rights for a large tract on favorable terms from the United States government. When the 1999 oil shock drove up energy prices worldwide, Geothermal became an exceptionally profitable company. It was currently reporting a rate of return on book assets of 25 percent per year.

Now, in 2001, production rights were no longer cheap. The proposed expansion would cost $30 million and should generate a perpetual after-tax cash flow of $4.5 million annually. The projected rate of return was 4.5/30 = .15, or 15 percent, much less than the profitability of Geothermal's existing assets. However, once the new project was up and running, it would be no riskier than Geothermal's existing business.

Jo Ann realized that 15 percent was not necessarily a bad return—though of course 25 percent would have been better. Fifteen percent might still exceed Geothermal's cost of capital, that is, exceed the expected rate of return that outside investors would demand to invest money in the project. If the cost of capital was less than the 15 percent expected return, expansion would be a good deal and would generate net value for Geothermal and its stockholders.

Jo Ann remembered how to calculate the cost of capital for companies which used only common stock financing. Briefly she sketched the argument.

"I need the expected rate of return investors would require from Geothermal's real assets—the wells, pumps, generators, etc. That rate of return depends on the assets' risk. However, the assets aren't traded in the stock market, so I can't observe how risky they have been. I can only observe the risk of Geothermal's common stock.

"But if Geothermal issues only stock—no debt—then owning the stock means owning the assets, and the expected return demanded by investors in the stock must also be the cost of capital for the assets." She jotted down the following identities:

Value of business   = value of stock
Risk of business   = risk of stock
Rate of return on business   = rate of return on stock
Investors' required return from business = investors' required return from stock

Unfortunately, Geothermal had borrowed a substantial amount of money; its stockholders did *not* have unencumbered ownership of Geothermal's assets. The expansion project would also justify some extra debt finance. Jo Ann realized that she would have to look at Geothermal's **capital structure**—its mix of debt and equity financing—and consider the required rates of return of debt as well as equity investors.

capital structure: Firm's mix of long-term financing.

Geothermal had issued 22.65 million shares, now trading at $20 each. Thus shareholders valued Geothermal's equity at $20 × 22.65 million = $453 million. In addition, the company had issued bonds with a market value of $194 million. The market value of the company's capital was therefore

Debt	$194	(30%)
Equity	453	(70%)
Total value	$647 million	(100%)

[2]This case is not prepared for class discussion, but to illustrate the proper analysis of a financial problem. It was prepared by Prof. Tony Blair with research assistance from Charles DeGaulle.

"Geothermal's worth more to investors than either its debt or its equity," Jo Ann mused. "But I ought to be able to find the overall value of Geothermal's business by adding up the debt and equity." She sketched a rough balance sheet:

Assets		Liabilities and Shareholders' Equity		
Market value of assets = value of Geothermal's existing business	$647	Market value of debt	$194	(30%)
		Market value of equity	$453	(70%)
Total value	$647	Total value	$647	(100%)

"Holy Toledo, I've got it!" Jo Ann exclaimed. "If I bought *all* the securities issued by Geothermal, debt as well as equity, I'd own the entire business. That means. . . ." She jotted again:

$$\text{Value of business} = \text{value of portfolio of all the firm's debt and equity securities}$$

$$\text{Risk of business} = \text{risk of portfolio}$$

$$\text{Rate of return on business} = \text{rate of return on portfolio}$$

$$\text{Investors' required return on business (company cost of capital)} = \text{investors' required return on portfolio}$$

"All I have to do is calculate the expected rate of return on a portfolio of all the firm's securities. That's easy. The debt's yielding 8 percent, and Fred, that skinny banker, says that equity investors want 14 percent. The portfolio would contain 30 percent debt and 70 percent equity, so. . . ."

$$\text{Portfolio return} = (.3 \times 8\%) + (.7 \times 14\%) = 12.2\%$$

$$\text{Company cost of capital} = 12.2\%$$

It was all coming back to her now. The company cost of capital is just a weighted average of returns on debt and equity, with weights depending on relative market values of the two securities. The result, in this case 12.2 percent, is also the cost of capital for new investments with the same risk and financing.

"Looks like the expansion's a good deal. Fifteen's better than 12.2. But I need a break."

10.2 *The Company Cost of Capital and the Weighted-Average Cost of Capital*

See box p. 297

Jo Ann Cox was engaged in an important project for Geothermal. It should be obvious by now that the choice of the discount rate can be crucial, especially when the project involves large capital expenditures or is long-lived. The nearby box describes how a major investment in a power station—an investment with both a large capital expenditure and very long life—turned on the choice of the discount rate.

Think again what the *company* cost of capital is, and what it is used for. We *define* it as the opportunity cost of capital for the firm's existing assets; we *use* it to value new assets that have the same risk as the old ones.

Choosing the Discount Rate

Shortly before the British government began to sell off the electricity industry to private investors, controversy erupted over the industry's proposal to build a 1,200-megawatt nuclear power station known as Hinkley Point C. The government argued that a nuclear station would both diversify the sources of electricity generation and reduce sulfur dioxide and carbon dioxide emissions. Protesters emphasized the dangers of nuclear accidents and attacked the proposal as "bizarre, dated and irrelevant."

At the public inquiry held to consider the proposal, opponents produced some powerful evidence that the nuclear station was also a very high cost option. Their principal witness, Professor Elroy Dimson, argued that the government-owned power company had employed an unrealistically low figure for the opportunity cost of capital. Had the government-owned industry used a more plausible figure, the cost of building and operating the nuclear station would have been higher than that of a comparable station based on fossil fuels.

The reason why the choice of discount rate was so important was that nuclear stations are expensive to build but cheap to operate. If capital is cheap (i.e., the discount rate is low), then the high up-front cost is less serious. But if the cost of capital is high, then the high initial cost of nuclear stations made them uneconomic.

Evidence produced at the inquiry suggested that the construction cost of a nuclear station was £1,527 million (or about $2.3 billion), while the cost of a comparable nonnuclear station was only £895 million. However, power stations last about 40 years and, once built, nuclear stations cost much less to operate than nonnuclear stations. If operated at 75 percent of theoretical capacity, the running costs of the nuclear station would be about £63 million a year, compared with running costs of £168 million a year for the nonnuclear station.

The following table shows the cost advantage of the nuclear power station at different (real) discount rates. At a 5 percent discount rate, which was the figure used by

the government, the present value of the costs of the nuclear option was nearly £1 billion lower than that of a station based on fossil fuels. But with a discount rate of 16 percent, which was the figure favored by Professor Dimson, the position was almost exactly reversed, so that the government could save nearly £1 billion by refusing the power company permission to build Hinkley Point C and relying instead on new fossil-fuel power stations.

Eight years after the inquiry, the proposal to construct Hinkley Point C continues to gather dust, and British Energy, the privatized electric utility, has declared that it has no plans to build a new nuclear power station in the near future.

Present value of the cost advantage to a nuclear rather than a fossil-fuel station (figures in billions of pounds)

Real Discount Rate	Present Value of the Cost Advantage of the Nuclear Station
5%	0.9
8	0.2
10	−0.1
12	−0.4
14	−0.7
16	−0.9
18	−1.2

Technical Notes:
1. Present values are measured at the date that the power station comes into operation.
2. The above table assumes for simplicity that construction costs for nuclear stations are spread evenly over the 8 years before the station comes into operation, while the costs for fossil-fuel stations are assumed to be spread evenly over the 4 years before operation. As a result the present value of the costs of the two stations may differ slightly from the more precise estimates produced by Professor Dimson.

Source: Adapted with permission from *Energy Economics*, July 1989, E. Dimson, "The Discount Rate for a Power Station," 1989, Elsevier Science Ltd., Oxford, England.

In this section we will start with the company cost of capital and then move on to its close relative, the weighted-average cost of capital, or WACC. WACC is a way of *estimating* the company cost of capital; it also incorporates an adjustment for the taxes a company saves when it borrows.

Calculating Company Cost of Capital as a Weighted Average

Calculating the company cost of capital is straightforward, though not always easy, when only common stock is outstanding. For example, a financial manager could estimate beta and calculate shareholders' required rate of return using the capital asset pricing model (CAPM). This would be the expected rate of return investors require on the company's existing assets and operations and also the expected return they will require on new investments that do not change the company's market risk.

But most companies issue debt as well as equity.

> The company cost of capital is a *weighted average* of the returns demanded by debt and equity investors. It is the expected rate of return investors would demand on a portfolio of all the firm's outstanding securities.

Let's review Jo Ann Cox's calculations for Geothermal. The total market value of that firm, which we denote as V, is the sum of the values of the outstanding debt D and the equity E. Thus firm value is $V = D + E = \$194$ million $+ \$453$ million $= \$647$ million. Debt accounts for 30 percent of the value and equity accounts for the remaining 70 percent. If you held all the shares and all the debt, your investment in Geothermal would be $V = \$647$ million. Between them, the debt and equity holders own *all* the firm's assets. So V is also the value of these assets—the value of Geothermal's existing business.

Suppose that Geothermal's equity investors require a 14 percent rate of return on their investment in the stock. What rate of return must a new project provide in order that all investors—both debtholders and stockholders—earn a fair rate of return? The debtholders require a rate of return of $r_{debt} = 8$ percent. So each year the firm will need to pay interest of $r_{debt} \times D = .08 \times \$194$ million $= \$15.52$ million. The shareholders, who have invested in a riskier security, require a return of $r_{equity} = 14$ percent on their investment of $\$453$ million. Thus in order to keep shareholders happy, the company needs additional income of $r_{equity} \times E = .14 \times \$453$ million $= \$63.42$ million. To satisfy both the debtholders and the shareholders, Geothermal needs to earn $\$15.52$ million $+ \$63.42$ million $= \$78.94$ million. This is equivalent to earning a return of $r_{assets} = 78.94/647 = .122$, or 12.2 percent.

Figure 10.1 illustrates the reasoning behind our calculations. The figure shows the amount of income needed to satisfy the debt and equity investors. Notice that debtholders account for 30 percent of Geothermal's capital structure but receive less than 30 percent of its expected income. On the other hand, they bear less than a 30 percent share of risk, since they have first cut at the company's income, and also first claim on its assets if the company gets in trouble. Shareholders expect a return of more than 70 percent of Geothermal's income because they bear correspondingly more risk.

However, if you buy *all* Geothermal's debt and equity, you own its assets lock, stock, and barrel. You receive all the income and bear all the risks. The expected rate of return you'd require on this portfolio of securities is the same return you'd require from unencumbered ownership of the business. This rate of return—12.2 percent in our example—is therefore the company cost of capital and the required rate of return from an equal-risk expansion of the business.

The bottom line is

Company cost of capital = weighted average of debt and equity returns

Figure 10.1

Geothermal's debtholders account for 30 percent of the company's capital structure, but they get a smaller share of income because their return is guaranteed by the company. Geothermal's stockholders bear more risk and receive, on average, greater return. Of course if you buy all the debt and all the equity, you get all the income.

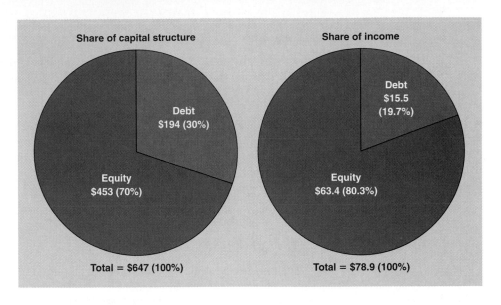

The underlying algebra is simple. Debtholders need income of ($r_{debt} \times D$) and the equity investors need income of ($r_{equity} \times E$). The *total* income that is needed is ($r_{debt} \times D$) + ($r_{equity} \times E$). The amount of their combined existing investment in the company is V. So to calculate the return that is needed on the assets, we simply divide the income by the investment:

$$r_{assets} = \frac{\text{total income}}{\text{value of investment}}$$

$$= \frac{(D \times r_{debt}) + (E \times r_{equity})}{V}$$

$$= \left(\frac{D}{V} \times r_{debt}\right) + \left(\frac{E}{V} \times r_{equity}\right)$$

For Geothermal,

$$r_{assets} = (.30 \times 8\%) + (.70 \times 14\%) = 12.2\%$$

This figure is the expected return demanded by investors in the firm's assets.

Three Steps in Calculating Cost of Capital

There are three steps in calculating the weighted average:

Step 1. Calculate the value of each security as a proportion of the firm's market value. For Geothermal, debt accounted for 30 percent of the value ($D/V = .30$) and equity for 70 percent ($E/V = .70$).

Step 2. Determine the required rate of return on each security. For Geothermal, debtholders required a return of 8 percent ($r_{debt} = 8\%$) and the equity holders required a return of 14 percent ($r_{equity} = 14\%$).

Step 3. Calculate a weighted average of these required returns. For Geothermal, the company cost of capital is $(.3 \times 8\%) + (.7 \times 14\%) = 12.2\%$.

Geothermal can use this cost of capital to value new projects that have the same risk as its existing business and that also support a 30 percent debt ratio.

▶ **Self-Test 10.1**

Hot Rocks Corp., one of Geothermal's competitors, has issued long-term bonds with a market value of $50 million and an expected return of 9.0 percent. It has 4 million shares outstanding trading for $10 each. At this price the shares offer an expected return of 17 percent. What is the company cost of capital for Hot Rocks's assets and operations?

Market versus Book Weights

The company cost of capital is the expected rate of return that investors demand from the company's assets and operations.

> **Therefore, the cost of capital must be based on what investors are actually willing to pay for the company's outstanding securities—that is, based on the securities' *market* values.**

Market values usually differ from the values recorded by accountants in the company's books. The book value of Geothermal's equity reflects money raised in the past from shareholders or reinvested by the firm on their behalf. If investors recognize Geothermal's excellent prospects, the market value of equity may be much higher than book, and the debt ratio will be lower when measured in terms of market values rather than book values.

Financial managers use book debt-to-value ratios for various other purposes, and sometimes they unthinkingly look to the book ratios when calculating weights for the company cost of capital. That's a mistake, because the company cost of capital measures what investors want from the company, and it depends on how *they* value the company's securities. That value depends on future profits and cash flows, not on accounting history. Book values, while useful for many other purposes, only measure net cumulative historical outlays; they don't generally measure market values accurately.

▶ **Self-Test 10.2**

Here is a book balance sheet for Duane S. Burg Associates. Figures are in millions.

Assets		Liabilities and Shareholders' Equity	
Assets (book value)	$75	Debt	$25
		Equity	50
	$75		$75

Unfortunately, the company has fallen on hard times. The 6 million shares are trading for only $4 apiece, and the market value of its debt securities is 20 percent below the face (book) value.

Suppose shareholders now demand a 20 percent expected rate of return. The bonds are now yielding 14 percent. What is the company cost of capital?

Taxes and the Weighted-Average Cost of Capital

Our formula for the company cost of capital ignored taxes. Taxes are important because interest payments are deducted from income before tax is calculated. Therefore, the cost to the company of an interest payment is reduced by the amount of this tax saving.

The interest rate on Geothermal's debt is $r_{debt} = 8$ percent. However, with a corporate tax rate of $T_c = .35$, the government bears 35 percent of the cost of the interest payments. The government doesn't send the firm a check for this amount, but the income tax that the firm pays is reduced by 35 percent of its interest expense.

Therefore, Geothermal's after-tax cost of debt is only $100 - 35 = 65$ percent of the 8 percent pretax cost:

$$\text{After-tax cost of debt} = \text{pretax cost} \times (1 - \text{tax rate})$$
$$= r_{debt} \times (1 - T_c)$$
$$= 8\% \times (1 - .35) = 5.2\%$$

We can now adjust our calculation of Geothermal's cost of capital to recognize the tax saving associated with interest payments:

$$\text{Company cost of capital, after-tax} = (.3 \times 5.2\%) + (.7 \times 14\%) = 11.4\%$$

▶ **Self-Test 10.3**

Criss-cross Industries has earnings before interest and taxes (EBIT) of $10 million. Interest payments are $2 million and the corporate tax rate is 35 percent. Construct a simple income statement to show that the debt interest reduces the taxes the firm owes to the government. How much more tax would Criss-cross pay if it were financed solely by equity?

---

weighted-average cost of capital (WACC): Expected rate of return on a portfolio of all the firm's securities.

The after-tax version of the company cost of capital is called the **weighted-average cost of capital,** or **WACC.** The general formula is

$$\textbf{Weighted-average cost of capital} = \left[\frac{D}{V} \times (1 - T_c)r_{debt}\right] + \left(\frac{E}{V} \times r_{equity}\right)$$

Geothermal's proposed expansion is actually better than Jo Ann Cox thought. The project's 15 percent rate of return is well in excess of 11.4 percent.

We have simplified our discussion of the cost of capital by assuming the firm has outstanding only two classes of securities: debt and equity. Even if the firm has issued other classes of securities, our general approach to calculating WACC remains unchanged. You simply calculate the weighted-average after-tax return of each security type.

For example, suppose the firm also has outstanding preferred stock. Preferred stock has some of the characteristics of both common stock and fixed-income securities. Like bonds, preferred stock promises to pay a given, usually level, stream of dividends. Unlike bonds, however, there is no maturity date for the preferred stock. The promised dividends constitute a perpetuity as long as the firm stays in business. Moreover, a failure to come up with the cash to pay the dividends does not push the firm into bankruptcy. Instead, dividends owed simply cumulate; the common stockholders do not receive dividends until the accumulated preferred dividends have been paid. Finally, unlike interest payments, preferred stock dividends are not considered tax-deductible expenses.

How would we calculate WACC for a firm with preferred stock as well as common stock and bonds outstanding? Using P to denote preferred stock, we simply generalize the formula for WACC as follows:

$$\text{WACC} = \left[\frac{D}{V} \times (1 - T_c)r_{\text{debt}}\right] + \left(\frac{P}{V} \times r_{\text{preferred}}\right) + \left(\frac{E}{V} \times r_{\text{equity}}\right)$$

Let's try an example to make this concrete.

▶ Example 10.1   *Weighted-Average Cost of Capital for Executive Fruit*

Unlike Geothermal, Executive Fruit has issued three types of securities—debt, preferred stock, and common stock. The debtholders require a return of 6 percent, the preferred stockholders require an expected return of 12 percent, and the common stockholders require 18 percent. The debt is valued at $4 million ($D = 4$), the preferred stock at $2 million ($P = 2$), and the common stock at $6 million ($E = 6$). The corporate tax rate is 35 percent. What is Executive's weighted-average cost of capital?

Don't be put off by the third security, preferred stock. We simply work through the same three steps.

Step 1. Calculate the value of each security as a proportion of the firm's value. Firm value is $V = D + P + E = 4 + 2 + 6 = \$12$ million. So $D/V = 4/12 = .33$; $P/V = 2/12 = .17$; and $E/V = 6/12 = .5$.

Step 2. Determine the required rate of return on each security. We have already given you the answers: $r_{\text{debt}} = 6\%$, $r_{\text{preferred}} = 12\%$, and $r_{\text{equity}} = 18\%$.[3]

Step 3. Calculate a weighted average of the cost of the after-tax return on debt and the return on the preferred and common stock:

$$
\begin{aligned}
\text{Weighted-average} \atop \text{cost of capital} &= \left[\frac{D}{V} \times (1 - T_c)r_{\text{debt}}\right] + \left(\frac{P}{V} \times r_{\text{preferred}}\right) + \left(\frac{E}{V} \times r_{\text{equity}}\right) \\
&= [.33 \times (1 - .35)\ 6\%] + (.17 \times 12\%) + (.5 \times 18\%) \\
&= 12.3\%
\end{aligned}
$$

Wrapping Up Geothermal

We now turn one last time to Jo Ann Cox and Geothermal's proposed expansion. We want to make sure that she—and you—know how to *use* the weighted-average cost of capital.

Remember that the proposed expansion cost $30 million and should generate a perpetual cash flow of $4.5 million per year. A simple cash-flow worksheet might look like this:[4]

---

[3]Financial managers often use "equity" to refer to *common* stock, even though a firm's equity strictly includes both common and preferred stock. We continue to use r_{equity} to refer specifically to the expected return on the common stock.

[4]For this example we ignore depreciation, a noncash but tax-deductible expense. (If the project were really perpetual, why depreciate?)

Revenue	$10.00 million
Operating expenses	3.08
Pretax operating cash flow	6.92
Tax at 35%	2.42
After-tax cash flow	$ 4.50 million

Note that these cash flows ignore the tax benefits of using debt.

Geothermal's managers and engineers forecast revenues, costs, and taxes as if the project was to be all-equity financed. The interest tax shields generated by the project's actual debt financing are not forgotten, however. They are accounted for by using the *after-tax* cost of debt in the weighted-average cost of capital.

Project net present value is calculated by discounting the cash flow (which is a perpetuity) at Geothermal's 11.4 percent weighted-average cost of capital:

$$\text{NPV} = -30 + \frac{4.5}{.114} = + \$9.5 \text{ million}$$

Expansion will thus add $9.5 million to the net wealth of Geothermal's owners.

Checking Our Logic

Any project offering a rate of return more than 11.4 percent will have a positive NPV, assuming that the project has the same risk and financing as Geothermal's business. A project offering exactly 11.4 percent would be just break-even; it would generate just enough cash to satisfy both debtholders and stockholders.

Let's check that out. Suppose the proposed expansion had revenues of only $8.34 million and after-tax cash flows of $3.42 million:

Revenue	$8.34 million
Operating costs	3.08
Pretax operating cash flow	5.26
Tax at 35%	1.84
After-tax cash flow	$3.42 million

With an investment of $30 million, the internal rate of return on this perpetuity is exactly 11.4 percent:

$$\text{Rate of return} = \frac{3.42}{30} = .114, \text{ or } 11.4\%$$

NPV is exactly zero:

$$\text{NPV} = -30 + \frac{3.42}{.114} = 0$$

When we calculated Geothermal's weighted-average cost of capital, we recognized that the company's debt ratio was 30 percent. When Geothermal's analysts use the weighted-average cost of capital to evaluate the new project, they are *assuming* that the $30 million additional investment would support the issue of additional debt equal to 30 percent of the investment, or $9 million. The remaining $21 million is provided by the shareholders.

The following table shows how the cash flows would be shared between the debtholders and shareholders. We start with the pretax operating cash flow of $5.26 million:

Cash flow before tax and interest	$5.26 million
Interest payment (.08 × $9 million)	.72
Pretax cash flow	4.54
Tax at 35%	1.59
Cash flow after tax	$2.95 million

Project cash flows before tax and interest are forecast to be $5.26 million. Out of this figure, Geothermal needs to pay interest of 8 percent of $9 million, which comes to $.72 million. This leaves a pretax cash flow of $4.54 million, on which the company must pay tax. Taxes equal .35 × 4.54 = $1.59 million. Shareholders are left with $2.95 million, just enough to give them the 14 percent return that they need on their $21 million investment. (Note that 2.95/21 = .14, or 14 percent.) Therefore, everything checks out.

> **If a project has zero NPV when the expected cash flows are discounted at the weighted-average cost of capital, then the project's cash flows are just sufficient to give debtholders and shareholders the return they require.**

▶ **Self-Test 10.4**   Calculate the weighted-average cost of capital for Duane S. Burg Associates. (See Self-Test 10.2.) The corporate tax rate is 35 percent.

10.3 *Measuring Capital Structure*

You now know the formula for calculating the weighted-average cost of capital. We will now look at some of the practical problems in applying that formula. Suppose that the financial manager of Big Oil has asked you to estimate the firm's weighted-average cost of capital. Your first step is to work out Big Oil's capital structure. But where do you get the data?

> **Financial managers usually start with the company's accounts, which show the *book* value of debt and equity, whereas the weighted-average cost of capital formula calls for their *market* values. A little work and a dash of judgment are needed to go from one to the other.**

Table 10.1 shows the debt and equity issued by Big Oil. The firm has borrowed $200 million from banks and has issued a further $200 million of long-term bonds. These bonds have a coupon rate of 8 percent and mature at the end of 12 years. Finally, there are 100 million shares of common stock outstanding, each with a par value of $1.00. But the accounts also recognize that Big Oil has in past years plowed back into the firm $300 million of retained earnings. The total book value of the equity shown in the accounts is $100 million + $300 million = $400 million.

The figures shown in Table 10.1 are taken from Big Oil's annual accounts and are therefore book values. Sometimes the differences between book values and market values are negligible. For example, consider the $200 million that Big Oil owes the bank. The interest rate on bank loans is usually linked to the general level of interest rates.

Table 10.1

The book *value of Big Oil's debt and equity (dollar figures in millions)*

Bank debt	$200	25.0%
Long-term bonds (12-year maturity, 8% coupon)	200	25.0
Common stock (100 million shares, par value $1)	100	12.5
Retained earnings	300	37.5
Total	$800	100.0%

Thus if interest rates rise, the rate charged on Big Oil's loan also rises to maintain the loan's value. As long as Big Oil is reasonably sure to repay the loan, the loan is worth close to $200 million. Most financial managers most of the time are willing to accept the book value of bank debt as a fair approximation of its market value.

What about Big Oil's long-term bonds? Since the bonds were originally issued, long-term interest rates have risen to 9 percent.[5] We can calculate the value today of each bond as follows.[6] There are 12 coupon payments of .08 × 200 = $16 million, and then repayment of principal 12 years out. Thus the final cash payment to the bondholders is $216 million. All the bond's cash flows are discounted back at the *current* interest rate of 9 percent.

$$ PV = \frac{16}{1.09} + \frac{16}{(1.09)^2} + \frac{16}{(1.09)^3} + \cdots + \frac{216}{(1.09)^{12}} = \$185.7 $$

Therefore, the bonds are worth only $185.7 million, 92.8 percent of their face value. If you used the book value of Big Oil's long-term debt rather than its market value, you would be a little bit off in your calculation of the weighted-average cost of capital, but probably not seriously so.

The really big errors are likely to arise if you use the book value of equity rather than its market value. The $400 million book value of Big Oil's equity measures the total amount of cash that the firm has raised from shareholders in the past or has retained and invested on their behalf. But perhaps Big Oil has been able to find projects that were worth more than they originally cost or perhaps the value of the assets has increased with inflation. Perhaps investors see great future investment opportunities for the company. All these considerations determine what investors are willing to pay for Big Oil's common stock.

In September 2001 Big Oil stock was $12 a share. Thus the total *market value* of the stock was

Number of shares × share price = 100 million × $12 = $1,200 million

In Table 10.2 we show the market value of Big Oil's debt and equity. You can see that debt accounts for 24.3 percent of company value (D/V = .243) and equity accounts for 75.7 percent (E/V = .757). These are the proportions to use when calculating the weighted-average cost of capital. Notice that if you looked only at the book values shown in the company accounts, you would mistakenly conclude that debt and equity each accounted for 50 percent of value.

[5]If Big Oil's bonds are traded, you can simply look up their price. But many bonds are not regularly traded, and in such cases you need to infer their price by calculating the bond's value using the rate of interest offered by similar bonds.

[6]We assume that coupon payments are annual. Most bonds in the United States actually pay interest twice a year.

Table 10.2

The market *values of Big Oil's debt and equity (dollar figures in millions)*

Bank debt	$200.0	12.6%
Long-term bonds	185.7	11.7
Total debt	385.7	24.3
Common stock, 100 million shares at $12	1,200.0	75.7
Total	$1,585.7	100.0%

10.4 Calculating Required Rates of Return

To calculate Big Oil's weighted-average cost of capital, you also need the rate of return that investors require from each security.

The Expected Return on Bonds

We know that Big Oil's bonds offer a yield to maturity of 9 percent. As long as the company does not go belly-up, that is the rate of return investors can expect to earn from holding Big Oil's bonds. If there is any chance that the firm may be unable to repay the debt, however, the yield to maturity of 9 percent represents the most favorable outcome and the *expected* return is lower than 9 percent.

For most large and healthy firms, the probability of bankruptcy is sufficiently low that financial managers are content to take the promised yield to maturity on the bonds as a measure of the expected return. But beware of assuming that the yield offered on the bonds of Fly-by-Night Corporation is the return that investors could *expect* to receive.

The Expected Return on Common Stock

Estimates Based on the Capital Asset Pricing Model. In the last chapter we showed you how to use the capital asset pricing model to estimate the expected rate of return on common stock. The capital asset pricing model tells us that investors demand a higher rate of return from stocks with high betas. The formula is

$$\begin{array}{c}\text{Expected return} \\ \text{on stock}\end{array} = \begin{array}{c}\text{risk-free} \\ \text{interest rate}\end{array} + \left(\begin{array}{c}\text{stock's} \\ \text{beta}\end{array} \times \begin{array}{c}\text{expected market} \\ \text{risk premium}\end{array}\right)$$

Financial managers and economists measure the risk-free rate of interest by the yield on Treasury bills. To measure the expected market risk premium, they usually look back at capital market history, which suggests that investors have received an extra 8 to 9 percent a year from investing in common stocks rather than Treasury bills. Yet wise financial managers use this evidence with considerable humility, for who is to say whether investors in the past received more or less than they expected, or whether investors today require a higher or lower reward for risk than their parents did?

Let's suppose Big Oil's common stock beta is estimated at .85, the risk-free interest rate of r_f is 6 percent, and the expected market risk premium ($r_m - r_f$) is 9 percent. Then the CAPM would put Big Oil's cost of equity at

$$\text{Cost of equity} = r_{\text{equity}} = r_f + \beta(r_m - r_f)$$
$$= 6\% + .85(9\%) = 13.65\%$$

Of course no one can estimate expected rates of return to two decimal places, so we'll just round to 13.5 percent.

▶ **Self-Test 10.5** Jo Ann Cox decides to check whether Fred, the skinny banker, was correct in claiming that Geothermal's cost of equity is 14 percent. She estimates Geothermal's beta at 1.20. The risk-free interest rate in 2001 is 6 percent, and the long-run average market risk premium is 9 percent. What is the expected rate of return on Geothermal's common stock, assuming of course that the CAPM is true? Recalculate Geothermal's weighted-average cost of capital.

Dividend Discount Model Cost of Equity Estimates. Whenever you are given an estimate of the expected return on a common stock, always look for ways to check whether it is reasonable. One check on the estimates provided by the CAPM can be obtained from the dividend discount model (DDM). In Chapter 4 we showed you how to use the constant-growth DDM formula to estimate the return that investors expect from different common stocks. Remember the formula: if dividends are expected to grow indefinitely at a constant rate g, then the price of the stock is equal to

$$P_0 = \frac{\text{DIV}_1}{r_{\text{equity}} - g}$$

where P_0 is the current stock price, DIV_1 is the forecast dividend at the end of the year, and r_{equity} is the expected return from the stock. We can rearrange this formula to provide an estimate of r_{equity}:

$$r_{\text{equity}} = \frac{\text{DIV}_1}{P_0} + g$$

In other words, the expected return on equity is equal to the dividend yield (DIV_1/P_0) plus the expected growth rate in dividends (g).

This constant-growth dividend discount model is widely used in estimating expected rates of return on common stocks of public utilities. Utility stocks have a fairly stable growth pattern and are therefore tailor-made for the constant-growth formula.

> **Remember that the constant-growth formula will get you into trouble if you apply it to firms with very high current rates of growth. Such growth can rarely be sustained indefinitely as the constant-growth DDM assumes.**

Using the formula in these circumstances will lead to an overestimate of the expected return.

Beware of False Precision. Do not expect estimates of the cost of equity to be precise. In practice you can't know whether the capital asset pricing model fully explains expected returns or whether the assumptions of the dividend discount model hold exactly. Even if your formulas were right, the required inputs would be noisy and subject to error. Thus a financial analyst who can confidently locate the cost of equity in a band of two or three percentage points is doing pretty well. In this endeavor it is perfectly OK to conclude that the cost of equity is, say, "about 15 percent" or "somewhere between 14 and 16 percent."[7]

[7]The calculations in this chapter have been done to one or two decimal places only to avoid confusion from rounding.

Sometimes accuracy can be improved by estimating the cost of equity or WACC for an industry or a group of comparable companies. This cuts down the "noise" that plagues single-company estimates. Suppose, for example, that Jo Ann Cox is able to identify three companies with investments and operations similar to Geothermal's. The average WACC for these three companies would be a valuable check on her estimate of WACC for Geothermal alone.

Or suppose that Geothermal is contemplating investment in oil refining. For this venture Geothermal's existing WACC is probably not right; it needs a discount rate reflecting the risks of the refining business. It could therefore try to estimate WACC for a sample of oil refining companies. If too few "pure-play" refining companies were available—most oil companies invest in production and marketing as well as refining—an industry WACC for a sample of large oil companies could be a useful check or benchmark. (We report estimates of oil industry WACCs at the end of the next section.)

The Expected Return on Preferred Stock

Preferred stock that pays a fixed annual dividend can be valued from the perpetuity formula:

$$\text{Price of preferred} = \frac{\text{dividend}}{r_{\text{preferred}}}$$

where $r_{\text{preferred}}$ is the appropriate discount rate for the preferred stock. Therefore, we can infer the required rate of return on preferred stock by rearranging the valuation formula to

$$r_{\text{preferred}} = \frac{\textbf{dividend}}{\textbf{price of preferred}}$$

For example, if a share of preferred stock sells for $20 and pays a dividend of $2 per share, the expected return on preferred stock is $r_{\text{preferred}} = \$2/\$20 = 10$ percent, which is simply the dividend yield.

10.5 *Calculating the Weighted-Average Cost of Capital*

Now that you have worked out Big Oil's capital structure and estimated the expected return on its securities, you need only simple arithmetic to calculate the weighted-average cost of capital. Table 10.3 summarizes the necessary data. Now all you need to do is plug the data in Table 10.3 into the weighted-average cost of capital formula:

$$\begin{aligned}
\text{Weighted-average} \atop \text{cost of capital} &= \left[\frac{D}{V} \times (1 - T_c)r_{\text{debt}}\right] + \left(\frac{E}{V} \times r_{\text{equity}}\right) \\
&= [.243 \times (1 - .35)\,9\%] + (.757 \times 13.5\%) = 11.6\%
\end{aligned}$$

Suppose that Big Oil needed to evaluate a project with the same risk as its existing business that would also support a 24.3 percent debt ratio. The 11.6 percent

Table 10.3
Data needed to calculate Big Oil's weighted-average cost of capital (dollar figures in millions)

Security Type	Capital Structure		Required Rate of Return
Debt	$D = \$385.7$	$D/V = .243$	$r_{debt} = .09$, or 9%
Common stock	$E = \$1,200.0$	$E/V = .757$	$r_{equity} = .135$, or 13.5%
Total	$V = \$1,585.7$		

Note: Corporate tax rate $= T_c = .35$.

weighted-average cost of capital is the appropriate discount rate for the cash flows.

Real Oil Company WACCs

Big Oil is entirely hypothetical—and not even very big compared to actual oil companies. Figure 10.2 shows estimated average costs of equity (r_{equity}) and WACCs for a sample of 10 to 12 large oil companies from 1965 to 1992. The latest estimates seem to be around 10 percent, less than our hypothetical figure for Big Oil.

The WACC estimates in Figure 10.2 decline steadily since the early 1980s. Some of that decline can be attributed to a decline in interest rates over the 1980s and early 1990s. We have included a plot of the risk-free rate (r_f) in Figure 10.2 as a reference point. However, the spread between the WACC estimates and these interest rates has also narrowed, suggesting that investors viewed the oil business as less risky in the early 1990s than a decade earlier.

Remember, the WACCs shown in Figure 10.2 are industry averages and therefore cover a wide range of activities. The large oil companies sampled are involved in some risky activities, such as exploration, and some relatively safe activities, such as franchising retail gas stations. The industry average will not be right for everything the industry does.

Figure 10.2
The middle line represents average weighted-average costs of capital for a sample of large oil companies. Average costs of equity (for the same sample) and the risk-free rate of interest are also plotted for comparison.

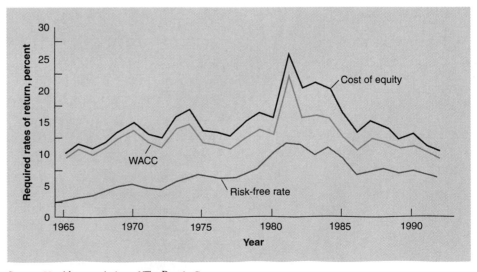

Source: Used by permission of The Brattle Group.

10.6 *Interpreting the Weighted-Average Cost of Capital*

When You Can and Can't Use WACC

We first discussed the company cost of capital in Chapter 9, but at that stage we did not know how to measure the company cost of capital when the firm has issued different types of securities or how to adjust for the tax-deductibility of interest payments. The weighted-average cost of capital formula solves those problems.

> **The weighted-average cost of capital is the rate of return that the firm must expect to earn on its average-risk investments in order to provide a fair expected return to all its security holders. We use it to value new assets that have the same risk as the old ones and that support the same ratio of debt. Strictly speaking, the weighted-average cost of capital is an appropriate discount rate only for a project that is a carbon copy of the firm's existing business. But often it is used as a company-wide benchmark discount rate; the benchmark is adjusted upward for unusually risky projects and downward for unusually safe ones.**

There is a good musical analogy here. Most of us, lacking perfect pitch, need a well-defined reference point, like middle C, before we can sing on key. But anyone who can carry a tune gets *relative* pitches right. Businesspeople have good intuition about *relative* risks, at least in industries they are used to, but not about absolute risk or required rates of return. Therefore, they set a company- or industry-wide cost of capital as a benchmark. This is not the right hurdle rate for everything the company does, but judgmental adjustments can be made for more risky or less risky ventures.

Some Mistakes People Make Using the WACC

One danger with the weighted-average formula is that it tempts people to make logical errors. Think back to your estimate of the cost of capital for Big Oil:

$$\text{WACC} = \left[\frac{D}{V} \times (1 - T_c)r_{\text{debt}}\right] + \left(\frac{E}{V} \times r_{\text{equity}}\right)$$
$$= [.243 \times (1 - .35) \, 9\%] + (.757 \times 13.5\%) = 11.6\%$$

Now you might be tempted to say to yourself, "Aha! Big Oil has a good credit rating. It could easily push up its debt ratio to 50 percent. If the interest rate is 9 percent and the required return on equity is 13.5 percent, the weighted-average cost of capital would be

$$\text{WACC} = [.50 \times (1 - .35) \, 9\%] + (.50 \times 13.5\%) = 9.7\%$$

At a discount rate of 9.7 percent, we can justify a lot more investment."

That reasoning will get you into trouble. First, if Big Oil increased its borrowing, the lenders would almost certainly demand a higher rate of interest on the debt. Second, as the borrowing increased, the risk of the common stock would also increase and therefore the stockholders would demand a higher return.

> **There are actually two costs of debt finance. The explicit cost of debt is the rate of interest that bondholders demand. But there is also an implicit cost, because borrowing increases the required return to equity.**

When you jumped to the conclusion that Big Oil could lower its weighted-average cost of capital to 9.7 percent by borrowing more, you were recognizing only the explicit cost of debt and not the implicit cost.

▶ **Self-Test 10.6**   Jo Ann Cox's boss has pointed out that Geothermal proposes to finance its expansion entirely by borrowing at an interest rate of 8 percent. He argues that this is therefore the appropriate discount rate for the project's cash flows. Is he right?

How Changing Capital Structure Affects Expected Returns

We will illustrate how changes in capital structure affect expected returns by focusing on the simplest possible case, where the corporate tax rate T_c is zero.

Think back to our earlier example of Geothermal. Geothermal, you may remember, has the following market-value balance sheet:

Assets		Liabilities and Shareholders' Equity		
Assets = value of Geothermal's existing business	$647	Debt	$194	(30%)
		Equity	$453	(70%)
Value	$647	Value	$647	(100%)

Geothermal's debtholders require a return of 8 percent and the shareholders require a return of 14 percent. Since we assume here that Geothermal pays no corporate tax, its weighted-average cost of capital is simply the expected return on the firm's assets:

$$\text{WACC} = r_{\text{assets}} = (.3 \times 8\%) + (.7 \times 14\%) = 12.2\%$$

This is the return you would expect if you held all Geothermal's securities and therefore owned all its assets.

Now think what will happen if Geothermal borrows an additional $97 million and uses the cash to buy back and retire $97 million of its common stock. The revised market-value balance sheet is

Assets		Liabilities and Shareholders' Equity		
Assets = value of Geothermal's existing business	$647	Debt	$291	(45%)
		Equity	356	(55%)
Value	$647	Value	$647	(100%)

If there are no corporate taxes, the change in capital structure does not affect the total cash that Geothermal pays out to its security holders and it does not affect the risk of those cash flows. Therefore, if investors require a return of 12.2 percent on the total package of debt and equity before the financing, they must require the same 12.2 percent return on the package afterward. The weighted-average cost of capital is therefore unaffected by the change in the capital structure.

Although the required return on the *package* of the debt and equity is unaffected, the change in capital structure does affect the required return on the individual securities. Since the company has more debt than before, the debt is riskier and debtholders are likely to demand a higher return. Increasing the amount of debt also makes the equity riskier and increases the return that shareholders require.

What Happens When the Corporate Tax Rate Is Not Zero

We have shown that when there are no corporate taxes the weighted-average cost of capital is unaffected by a change in capital structure. Unfortunately, taxes can complicate the picture.[8] For the moment, just remember

- **It is the weighted-average cost of capital that is relevant to capital budgeting decisions, *not* the expected return on the common stock.**
- **The weighted-average cost of capital is the return the company needs to earn after tax in order to satisfy its security holders.**
- **If the firm increases its debt ratio, both the debt and the equity will become more risky. The debtholders and equity holders require a higher return to compensate for the increased risk.**

The weighted-average cost of capital (WACC), which incorporates the *after-tax* cost of debt financing, is the right choice for average-risk projects.

10.7 Flotation Costs and the Cost of Capital

To raise the necessary cash for a new project, the firm may need to issue stocks, bonds, or other securities. The costs of issuing these securities to the public can easily amount to 5 percent of funds raised. For example, a firm issuing $100 million in new equity may net only $95 million after incurring the costs of the issue. We will examine *flotation costs,* that is, the costs of "floating" new securities to the public, in Chapter 13.

Flotation costs involve real money. A new project is less attractive if the firm must spend large sums on issuing new securities. To illustrate, consider a project that will cost $900,000 to install and is expected to generate a level perpetual cash-flow stream of $90,000 a year. At a required rate of return of 10 percent, the project is just barely viable, with an NPV of zero: $-\$900,000 + \$90,000/.10 = 0$.

Now suppose that the firm needs to raise equity to pay for the project, and that flotation costs are 10 percent of funds raised. To raise $900,000, the firm actually must sell $1 million of equity. Since the installed project will be worth only $\$90,000/.10 = \$900,000$, NPV including flotation costs is actually $-\$1$ million $+ \$900,000 = -\$100,000$.

In our example, we recognized flotation costs as one of the incremental costs of undertaking the project. But instead of recognizing these costs explicitly, some companies attempt to cope with flotation costs by increasing the cost of capital used to discount project cash flows. By using a higher discount rate, project present value is reduced.

---

[8]There's nothing wrong with our formulas and examples, *provided* that the tax deductibility of interest payments doesn't change the aggregate risk of the debt and equity investors. However, if the tax savings from deducting interest are treated as safe cash flows, the formulas get more complicated.

This procedure is flawed on practical as well as theoretical grounds. First, on a purely practical level, it is far easier to account for flotation costs as a negative cash flow than to search for an adjustment to the discount rate that will give the right NPV. Finding the necessary adjustment is easy only when cash flows are level or will grow indefinitely at a constant trend rate. This is almost never the case in practice, however. Of course, there always exists some discount rate that will give the right measure of the project's NPV, but this rate could no longer be interpreted as the rate of return available in the capital market for investments with the same risk as the project.

> **The cost of capital depends only on interest rates and the risk of the project. Flotation costs should be treated as incremental (negative) cash flows; they do not increase the required rate of return.**

Summary

1. The weighted-average cost of capital (WACC) is an average of the required rates of return on all the securities issued by the firm.
2. Since interest payments can be used to reduce the firm's tax bill, the required return on debt is measured on an after-tax basis.
3. In calculating the weighted-average cost of capital, the required return on each security is weighted by its proportion of the firm's value. The proportions should be based on the market values of the securities, not their book values.
4. When you estimate the weighted-average cost of capital, the tricky part is to figure out the expected return on the firm's shares. Financial managers commonly use the capital asset pricing model to estimate expected return. But for steady-growth companies, it may also make sense to use the constant-growth discounted cash-flow model. Remember, estimates of the expected return are less reliable for a single firm than for a sample of comparable-risk firms.
5. Do *not* assume that the expected return on each of the firm's securities will remain the same if the firm changes the proportions of debt and equity. For example, increasing the debt proportion will increase the risk of both debtholders and equity holders and cause them to demand a higher return.
6. The weighted-average cost of capital can be used to discount the after-tax cash flows on new projects that are carbon copies of the firm's existing business.

Key Terms

capital structure   weighted-average cost of capital (WACC)

Problems

1. **Cost of Debt.** Advanced Spinoffs, Inc., issued 20-year debt last year at par value with a coupon rate of 9 percent, paid annually. Today, the debt is selling at $1,050. If the firm's tax bracket is 35 percent, what is its after-tax cost of debt?
2. **Cost of Preferred Stock.** Advanced Spinoffs also has preferred stock outstanding. The stock pays a dividend of $4 per share, and the stock sells for $40. What is the cost of preferred stock?
3. **Cost of Equity.** Reliable Electric is a regulated public utility, and it is expected to provide steady growth of dividends of 5 percent per year for the indefinite future. Its last

dividend was $5 per share; the stock sold for $60 per share just after the dividend was paid. What is the company's cost of equity?

4. **Cost of Equity.** Bunkhouse Electronics is a recently incorporated firm that makes electronic entertainment systems. Its earnings and dividends have been growing at a rate of 30 percent, and the current dividend yield is 2 percent. Its beta is 1.2, the market risk premium is 8 percent, and the risk-free rate is 4 percent.

   a. Calculate two estimates of the firm's cost of equity.
   b. Which estimate seems more reasonable to you? Why?

5. **Cost of Debt.** Olympic Sports has two issues of debt outstanding. One is a 9 percent coupon bond with a face value of $20 million, a maturity of 10 years, and a yield to maturity of 10 percent. The coupons are paid annually. The other bond issue has a maturity of 15 years, with coupons also paid annually, and a coupon rate of 10 percent. The face value of the issue is $25 million, and the issue sells for 92.8 percent of par value. The firm's tax rate is 35 percent.

   a. What is the before-tax cost of debt for Olympic?
   b. What is Olympic's after-tax cost of debt?

6. **WACC and Taxes.** "The after-tax cost of debt is lower when the firm's tax rate is higher; therefore, the WACC falls when the tax rate rises. Thus, with a lower discount rate, the firm must be worth more if its tax rate is higher." Comment.

7. **Capital Structure.** Passive Footwear has a WACC of 12 percent. Its debt sells at a yield to maturity of 9 percent, and its tax rate is 40 percent. Its cost of equity is 15 percent. What is the fraction of the firm financed with debt versus equity?

8. **Calculating WACC.** Reactive Industries has the following capital structure. Its corporate tax rate is 35 percent. What is its WACC?

Security	Market Value	Required Rate of Return
Debt	$20 million	8%
Preferred stock	$10 million	10%
Common stock	$50 million	15%

9. **WACC.** The common stock of Buildwell Conservation & Construction, Inc. has a beta of .80. The Treasury bill rate is 4 percent and the market risk premium is estimated at 8 percent. BCCI's capital structure is 30 percent debt paying a 5 percent interest rate, and 70 percent equity. What is BCCI's cost of equity capital? Its WACC? Buildwell pays no taxes.

10. **WACC and NPV.** BCCI (see the previous problem) is evaluating a project with an internal rate of return of 12 percent. Should it accept the project? If the project will generate a cash flow of $100,000 a year for 7 years, what is the most BCCI should be willing to pay to initiate the project?

11. **Calculating WACC.** Find the WACC of William Tell Computers. The total book value of the firm's equity is $10 million; book value per share is $20. The stock sells for a price of $30 per share, and the cost of equity is 15 percent. The firm's bonds have a par value of $5 million and sell at a price of 110 percent of par. The yield to maturity on the bonds is 9 percent, and the firm's tax rate is 40 percent.

12. **Cost of Preferred Stock.** In September, 1996, Ford Motor preferred stock sold at a price of $108. The annual dividend on the preferred is $4.20 per share. What is the cost of Ford Motor's preferred stock?

13. **Capital Structure.** Examine the following book-value balance sheet for University Products, Inc. What is the capital structure of the firm based on market values? The preferred

stock currently sells for $15 per share and the common stock for $20 per share. There are one million common shares outstanding.

BOOK VALUE BALANCE SHEET
(all values in millions)

Assets		Liabilities and Net Worth	
Cash and short-term securities	$ 1	Bonds, coupon = 8%, paid annually (maturity = 10 years, current yield to maturity = 9%)	$10.0
Accounts receivable	3	Preferred stock (par value $20 per share)	2.0
Inventories	7	Common stock (par value $.10)	.1
Plant and equipment	21	Additional paid in stockholders' capital	9.9
		Retained earnings	10.0
Total	$32	Total	$32.0

14. **Calculating WACC.** Turn back to University Products' balance sheet from the previous problem. If the preferred stock pays a dividend of $2 per share, the beta of the stock is .8, the market risk premium is 10 percent, the risk-free rate is 6 percent, and the firm's tax rate is 40 percent, what is University's weighted-average cost of capital?

15. **Project Discount Rate.** University Products from the previous problems is evaluating a new venture into home computer systems. The internal rate of return on the new venture is estimated at 13.4 percent. WACCs of firms in the personal computer industry tend to average around 14 percent. Should the new project be pursued? Will University Products make the correct decision if it discounts cash flows on the proposed venture at the firm's WACC?

16. **WACC.** Nodebt, Inc., is a firm with all-equity financing. Its equity beta is .80. The Treasury bill rate is 5 percent and the market risk premium is expected to be 10 percent. What is Nodebt's asset beta? What is Nodebt's weighted-average cost of capital? The firm is exempt from paying taxes.

17. **Cost of Capital.** The total market value of Okefenokee Real Estate Company is $6 million, and the total value of its debt is $4 million. The treasurer estimates that the beta of the stock currently is 1.5 and that the expected risk premium on the market is 10 percent. The Treasury bill rate is 4 percent.

    a. What is the required rate of return on Okefenokee stock?
    b. What is the beta of the company's existing portfolio of assets? The debt is perceived to be virtually risk-free.
    c. Estimate the weighted-average cost of capital assuming a tax rate of 40 percent.
    d. Estimate the discount rate for an expansion of the company's present business.
    e. Suppose the company wants to diversify into the manufacture of rose-colored glasses. The beta of optical manufacturers with no debt outstanding is 1.2. What is the required rate of return on Okefenokee's new venture?

18. **Project Cost of Capital.** A firm with an asset beta of .9 engages in two lines of business. Aircraft production accounts for 70 percent of the value of the firm and sporting goods manufacturing accounts for the rest. If the asset beta of Consolidated Jets, which is exclusively engaged in aircraft production, is 1.0, what must be the beta of the sporting goods project?

19. **Cost of Capital.** A financial analyst at Dawn Chemical notes that the firm's total interest payments this year were $10 million while total debt outstanding was $80 million, and he concludes that the cost of debt was 12.5 percent. What is wrong with this conclusion?

20. **Cost of Capital.** The analyst at Dawn Chemical now notes that its cost of debt is far below that of equity. He concludes that it is important for the firm to maintain the ability to increase its borrowing because if it cannot borrow, it will be forced to use more expensive equity to finance some projects. This might lead it to reject some projects that would have seemed attractive if evaluated at the lower cost of debt. Comment on this reasoning.

Solutions to Self-Test Questions

10.1 Hot Rocks's 4 million common shares are worth $40 million. Its market value balance sheet is:

Assets		Liabilities and Shareholders' Equity		
Assets	$90	Debt	$50	(56%)
		Equity	40	(44%)
Value	$90	Value	$90	

Company cost of capital = (.56 × 9%) + (.44 × 17%) = 12.5%

Note that this question ignores taxes.

10.2 Burg's 6 million shares are now worth only 6 million × $4 = $24 million. The debt is selling for 80 percent of book, or $20 million. The market value balance sheet is:

Assets		Liabilities and Shareholders' Equity		
Assets	$44	Debt	$20	(45%)
		Equity	24	(55%)
Value	$44	Value	$44	

Company cost of capital = (.45 × 14%) + (.55 × 20%) = 17.3%

10.3 Compare the two income statements, one for Criss-cross Industries and the other for a firm with identical EBIT but no debt in its capital structure. (All figures in millions.)

	Criss-cross	Unleveraged Firm
EBIT	$10.0	$10.0
Interest expense	2.0	0.0
Taxable income	8.0	10.0
Taxes owed	2.8	3.5
Net income	5.2	6.5
Total income accruing to debt & equity holders	7.2	6.5

Notice that Criss-cross pays $.7 million less in taxes than its unleveraged counterpart. Accordingly, the total income available to debt plus equity holders is $.7 million higher.

10.4 WACC = .45 (1 − .35)14% + .55(20%) = 15.1%

10.5 From the CAPM:

$$r_{equity} = r_f + \beta_{equity} (r_m - r_f)$$
$$= 6\% + 1.20(9\%) = 16.8\%$$
$$WACC = .3(1 - .35) 8\% + .7(16.8\%) = 13.3\%$$

10.6 Jo Ann's boss is wrong. The ability to borrow at 8 percent does not mean that the cost of capital is 8 percent. This analysis ignores the side effects of the borrowing, for example, that at the higher indebtedness of the firm the equity will be riskier, and therefore the equityholders will demand a higher rate of return on their investment.

Minicase

Bernice Mountaindog was glad to be back at Sea Shore Salt. Employees were treated well. When she had asked a year ago for a leave of absence to complete her degree in finance, top management promptly agreed. When she returned with an honors degree, she was promoted from administrative assistant (she had been secretary to Joe-Bob Brinepool, the president) to treasury analyst.

Bernice thought the company's prospects were good. Sure, table salt was a mature business, but Sea Shore Salt had grown steadily at the expense of its less well-known competitors. The company's brand name was an important advantage, despite the difficulty most customers had in pronouncing it rapidly.

Bernice started work on January 2, 2000. The first two weeks went smoothly. Then Mr. Brinepool's cost of capital memo (shown on the next page) assigned her to explain Sea Shore Salt's weighted-average cost of capital to other managers. The memo came as a surprise to Bernice, so she stayed late to prepare for the questions that would surely come the next day.

Bernice first examined Sea Shore Salt's most recent balance sheet, summarized in Table 10.4. Then she jotted down the following additional points:

- The company's bank charged interest at current market rates, and the long-term debt had just been issued. Book and market values could not differ by much.
- But the preferred stock had been issued 35 years ago, when interest rates were much lower. The preferred stock was now trading for only $70 per share.
- The common stock traded for $40 per share. Next year's earnings per share would be about $4.00 and dividends per share probably $2.00. Sea Shore Salt

had traditionally paid out 50 percent of earnings as dividends and plowed back the rest.
- Earnings and dividends had grown steadily at 6 to 7 percent per year, in line with the company's sustainable growth rate:

$$\text{Sustainable growth rate} = \frac{\text{return}}{\text{on equity}} \times \frac{\text{plowback}}{\text{ratio}}$$
$$= 4.00/30 \times .5$$
$$= .067, \text{ or } 6.7\%$$

- Sea Shore Salt's beta had averaged about .5, which made sense, Bernice thought, for a stable, steady-growth business. She made a quick cost of equity calculation using the capital asset pricing model (CAPM). With current interest rates of about 7 percent, and a market risk premium of 8 percent,

$$\text{CAPM cost of equity} = r_E = r_f + \beta(r_m - r_f)$$
$$= 7\% + .5(8\%) = 11\%$$

This cost of equity was significantly less than the 16 percent decreed in Mr. Brinepool's memo. Bernice scanned her notes apprehensively. What if Mr. Brinepool's cost of equity was wrong? Was there some other way to estimate the cost of equity as a check on the CAPM calculation? Could there be other errors in his calculations?

Bernice resolved to complete her analysis that night. If necessary, she would try to speak with Mr. Brinepool when he arrived at his office the next morning. Her job was not just finding the right number. She also had to figure out how to explain it all to Mr. Brinepool.

Table 10.4

Sea Shore Salt's balance sheet, taken from the company's 1999 balance sheet (figures in millions)

Assets		Liabilities and Net Worth	
Working capital	$200	Bank loan	$120
Plant and equipment	360	Long-term debt	80
Other assets	40	Preferred stock	100
		Common stock, including retained earnings	300
Total	$600	Total	$600

Notes:
1. At year-end 1999, Sea Shore Salt had 10 million common shares outstanding.
2. The company had also issued 1 million preferred shares with book value of $100 per share. Each share receives an annual dividend of $6.00.

Sea Shore Salt Company
Spring Vacation Beach, Florida

CONFIDENTIAL MEMORANDUM

```
DATE:     January 15, 2000
TO:       S.S.S. Management
FROM:     Joe-Bob Brinepool, President
SUBJECT:  Cost of Capital
```

This memo states and clarifies our company's long-standing policy regarding hurdle rates for capital investment decisions. There have been many recent questions, and some evident confusion, on this matter.

Sea Shore Salt evaluates replacement and expansion investments by discounted cash flow. The discount or hurdle rate is the company's after-tax weighted-average cost of capital.

The weighted-average cost of capital is simply a blend of the rates of return expected by investors in our company. These investors include banks, bond holders, and preferred stock investors in addition to common stockholders. Of course many of you are, or soon will be, stockholders of our company.

The following table summarizes the composition of Sea Shore Salt's financing.

	Amount (in millions)	Percent of Total	Rate of Return
Bank loan	$120	20%	8%
Bond issue	80	13.3	7.75
Preferred stock	100	16.7	6
Common stock	300	50	16
	$600	100%	

The rates of return on the bank loan and bond issue are of course just the interest rates we pay. However, interest is tax-deductible, so the after-tax interest rates are lower than shown above. For example, the after-tax cost of our bank financing, given our 35% tax rate, is 8(1 − .35) = 5.2%.

The rate of return on preferred stock is 6%. Sea Shore Salt pays a $6 dividend on each $100 preferred share.

Our target rate of return on equity has been 16% for many years. I know that some newcomers think this target is too high for the safe and mature salt business. But we must all aspire to superior profitability.

Once this background is absorbed, the calculation of Sea Shore Salt's weighted-average cost of capital (WACC) is elementary:

$$WACC = 8(1 - .35)(.2) + 7.75(1 - .35)(.133) + 6(.167) + 16(.50) = 10.7\%$$

The official corporate hurdle rate is therefore 10.7%.

If you have further questions about these calculations, please direct them to our new Treasury Analyst, Ms. Bernice Mountaindog. It is a pleasure to have Bernice back at Sea Shore Salt after a year's leave of absence to complete her degree in finance.

Part Four

Financing

Some stock market analysts use computer applications like these to identify stocks that are "going up."
But if the stock market is efficient, such methods are worthless.
SuperStock

Chapter 11

Corporate Financing and the Lessons of Market Efficiency

U p to this point we have concentrated almost exclusively on the firm's capital expenditure decision. Now we move to the other side of the balance sheet to look at how the firm can finance those capital expenditures. To put it crudely, you've learned how to spend money—now learn how to raise it.

In the next few chapters, therefore, we assume that the firm has already decided on which investment projects to accept and we focus on the best way to finance these projects. We begin in this chapter with some general lessons about the capital markets, where firms raise new capital.

Economists often talk about "efficient capital markets." By this they don't mean that the filing is up-to-date and desktops are tidy. They mean that information is widely and cheaply available to investors and that all relevant and ascertainable information is already reflected in security prices. All stocks, bonds, and other securities are fairly priced in efficient markets and offer expected returns just sufficient to compensate for the securities' risks.

Why should a hard-nosed financial manager care about market efficiency? He or she just wants to raise financing at the lowest possible cost, right?

Right—but finding financing that's *truly* low-cost is not as easy as it sounds. You've got to know where to look—and where not to look. Capital markets are full of traps and mirages for the unwary or naive manager who believes that it is easy to spot mispriced securities. The wary and sophisticated financial manager, who understands the implications of capital market efficiency, is much less likely to make an expensive financing mistake.

Of course no human institution is perfect, and no financial market is perfectly efficient. But we always advise financial managers to start by assuming efficient capital markets. From that vantage point they can look out for the specific inefficiencies or imperfections (possibly due to taxes or government regulations) that can be used to create advantageous financing strategies.

After studying this chapter you should be able to

▶ Show how competition among investors leads to efficient markets.

▶ Cite evidence that supports the hypothesis that security markets are efficient—as well as some that contradicts it.

▶ Understand the implications of market efficiency for a firm's financial decisions.

11.1 Differences between Investment and Financing Decisions

In some ways financing decisions are more complicated than investment decisions. You need to be aware of the major financial institutions that provide financing and of the wide variety of securities that can be issued.

There are also ways in which financing decisions are easier than investment decisions. First, financing decisions do not have the same degree of finality as investment decisions. They are easier to reverse. For example, Ford Motor Company can issue a bond and buy it back later if second thoughts arise. It would be far more difficult for Ford to dismantle or sell an auto factory that is no longer needed.

Second, it's harder to make or lose money by smart or stupid financing strategies. It is difficult to make money—that is, to find cheap financing—because the investors who supply the financing demand fair terms. At the same time, it's harder to lose money because competition among investors prevents any one of them from demanding *more* than fair terms.

Competition in financial markets is more intense than in most product markets. In product markets, companies regularly find competitive advantages that allow positive-NPV investments. For example, a company may have only a few competitors that specialize in the same line of business in the same geographical area. Or it may be able to capitalize on patents or technology, or on customer recognition and loyalty. All this opens up the opportunity to make superior profits and find projects with positive NPVs.

But there are few protected niches in *financial* markets. You can't patent the design of a new security. Moreover, in these markets you always face fast-moving competition, including all the other corporations seeking funds, to say nothing of the state, local, and federal governments, financial institutions, individuals, and foreign firms and governments that also come to New York, London, or Tokyo for financing. The investors who supply financing are numerous, and they are smart—money attracts brains. Most likely, these investors can assess values of securities at least as well as you can.

A smart financing decision generates a positive NPV. For example, the firm might hope to sell a security for more than the present value of the cash flows it must pay the security holder. But if selling a security generates a positive NPV for you, it must generate a negative NPV for the buyer. What are the chances that your firm could consistently trick investors into buying securities with negative NPVs to them? Pretty low. In general, firms should assume that the securities they issue sell for their true values.

But what do we mean by *true value*? It is a potentially slippery phrase. True value does not mean ultimate *future* value—we do not expect investors to be fortunetellers. It means a price that incorporates all the information *currently* available to investors. That is our definition of **efficient capital markets.**

efficient capital markets: Financial markets in which security prices rapidly reflect all relevant information about asset values.

> If capital markets are efficient, all securities are fairly priced in light of the information available to investors. If securities are fairly priced, then financing at prevailing market terms is never a positive-NPV transaction.

Does that sound like a sweeping statement? It is. That is why we devote the rest of this chapter to the history, logic, and tests of market efficiency.

You may ask why we start our discussion of financing issues with this conceptual point, before you have even the most basic knowledge about securities, issue procedures, and financial institutions. We do it this way because financing decisions seem overwhelmingly complex if you don't learn to ask the right questions. You need to understand the efficient-market hypothesis, not because it is *universally* true but because it leads you to ask the right questions.

What Is an Efficient Market?

A Startling Discovery: Price Changes Are Random

As is so often the case with important ideas, the concept of efficient markets was a byproduct of a chance discovery. In 1953 the Royal Statistical Society met in London to discuss a rather unusual paper.[1] Its author, Maurice Kendall, was a distinguished statistician, and the subject was the behavior of stock and commodity prices. Kendall had been looking for regular price cycles, but to his surprise he could not find them. Prices seemed to wander randomly, virtually equally likely to go up or go down on any particular day, *regardless of what had occurred on previous days.* In other words, prices seemed to follow a **random walk.**

random walk: Security prices change randomly, with no predictable trends or patterns.

If you are not sure what we mean by "random walk," consider the following example. You are given $100 to play a game. At the end of each week a coin is tossed. If it comes up heads, you win 3 percent of your investment; if it is tails, you lose 2.5 percent. Therefore, your capital at the end of the first week is either $103.00 or $97.50. At the end of the second week the coin is tossed again. Now the possible outcomes are as follows:

```
                                        ___ Heads  $106.09
              ___ Heads   $103.00 <____ 
                                        ‾‾‾ Tails   $100.43
$100 <____
                                        ___ Heads   $100.43
              ‾‾‾ Tails   $ 97.50 <____
                                        ‾‾‾ Tails   $ 95.06
```

This process is a random walk because successive changes in the value of your stake are independent. That is, the odds of making money each week are 50 percent, regardless of the value at the start of the week or the pattern of heads or tails in the previous weeks.

If a stock's price follows a random walk, the odds of an increase or decrease during any day, month, or year do not depend *at all* on the stock's previous price moves. The historical path of prices gives no useful information about the future—just as a long series of recorded heads and tails gives no information about the next coin toss.

Some people find it difficult to believe that stock prices follow a random walk. If you are one of them, look at the two charts in Figure 11.1. One of these charts shows the outcome from playing our game for 5 years; the other shows the actual performance of the Standard & Poor's Index for a 5-year period. Can you tell which one is which?

Of course, you would need much more evidence than Figure 11.1 before you could be confident that stock prices do indeed follow a random walk. Researchers have therefore employed a battery of sophisticated statistical tests and have looked at the behavior of many individual stocks as well as market indexes over many periods. With remarkable unanimity these researchers have concluded that there is little useful information in the sequence of past stock price changes. As a result, many of the researchers have become famous. Few, if any, have become rich.

▶ **Self-Test 11.1**

True or false: If stock prices follow a random walk,

a. Successive stock price changes are not related.
b. Stock prices fluctuate randomly above and below a normal, long-run price.

---

[1]See M. G. Kendall, "The Analysis of Economic Time-Series, Part I. Prices," *Journal of the Royal Statistical Society* 96 (1953), pp. 11–25.

Figure 11.1

One of these charts shows the Standard & Poor's Index for a 5-year period. The other shows the results of playing our coin-toss game for 5 years. Can you tell which is which? (The answer is given in problem 12 at the end of the chapter.)

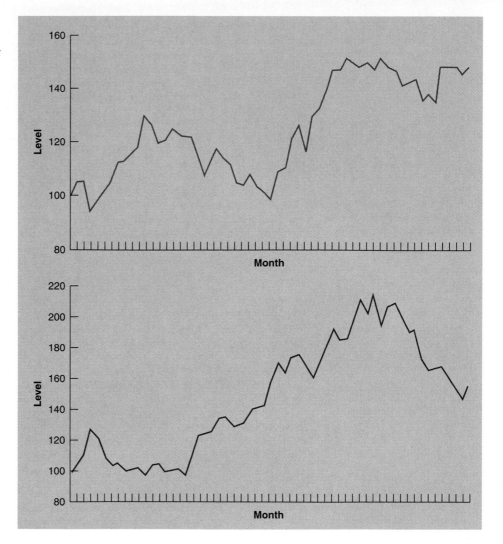

c. The history of stock prices cannot be used to predict future returns to investors.

d. A historical plot of a stock's trading prices will show no apparent "peaks and valleys."

---

technical analysts:
Investors who attempt to identify over- or undervalued stocks by searching for patterns in past prices.

Some investors *try* to get rich by looking for patterns in stock prices. These investors are known as **technical analysts.** Some technical analysts are very successful investors, but we credit this to luck and good judgment, not to technical trading rules, because technical trading rules are useless when stock prices follow a random walk.

Technical analysts can help keep the market efficient, however. Their trading would extinguish any predictable patterns in stock prices. Suppose that there were a trend in some company's stock price. Then technical analysts could make superior profits, at least temporarily. For example, Figure 11.2 shows a hypothetical 2-month upswing for Establishment Industries (EI). The upswing started last month, when EI's stock price was $40, and it is expected to carry the stock price to $60 next month. What will happen when technicians perceive this bonanza? It will self-destruct. Since EI

Figure 11.2

Cycles self-destruct as soon as they are recognized by investors. The stock price instantaneously jumps to the present value of the expected future price.

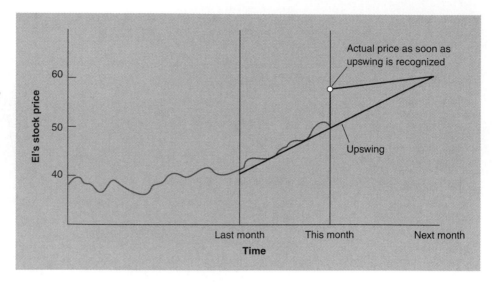

stock is a bargain at $50, investors will rush to buy. They will stop buying only when the stock offers a normal rate of return. Therefore, as soon as a price pattern becomes apparent to technical analysts, they immediately eliminate it by their trading.

Three Forms of the Efficient-Market Theory

If stock prices follow a random walk, you can't make superior profits just by studying past stock prices. Any information in those stock prices is already reflected in today's price. So the market is at least efficient in this sense. Such a market is called **weak-form efficient.**

weak-form efficiency:
Market prices rapidly reflect all information contained in the history of past prices.

But what about other kinds of publicly available information? Are they also immediately reflected in stock prices? After all, most investors don't just look at past stock prices. Instead they try to gauge a firm's business prospects by studying the financial and trade press, the company's financial accounts, the president's annual statement, the recommendations made by stockbrokers, and so on. These investors are **fundamental analysts,** in contrast to technical analysts, who examine past stock price movements.

fundamental analysts:
Analysts who attempt to find under- or overvalued securities by analyzing fundamental information, such as earnings, asset values, and business prospects.

Figure 11.3 illustrates how the release of relevant news is immediately reflected in security prices. The graph shows the price run-up of a sample of 194 firms that were targets of takeover attempts. In most takeovers, the acquiring firm is willing to pay a large premium over the current market price of the acquired firm; therefore, when a firm becomes a target of a takeover attempt, its stock price increases in anticipation of the takeover premium. Figure 11.3 shows that on the day the public become aware of a takeover attempt (Day 0 in the graph), the stock price of the typical target takes a big upward jump. The adjustment in stock price is immediate: after the big price move on the public announcement day, the run-up is over, and there is no further drift in the stock price, either upward or downward.[2] Within the day, the new stock prices apparently reflect (at least on average) the magnitude of the eventual takeover premium.

[2]However, prices on the days *before* the public announcement do show evidence of a sustained upward drift. This is evidence of a gradual "leakage" of information concerning the takeover attempt to insiders and their associates, who begin to purchase the target firm in anticipation of the public announcement. Consistent with efficient markets, however, once the information becomes public, it is reflected fully and immediately in stock prices.

Figure 11.3

The performance of the stocks of target companies compared with that of the market. The prices of target stocks jump up on the announcement day, but from then on, there are no unusual price movements. The announcement of the takeover attempt seems to be fully reflected in the stock price on the announcement day.

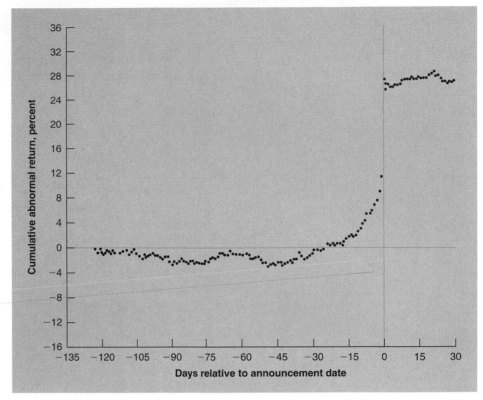

Source: Arthur Keown and John Pinkerton, "Merger Announcements and Insider Trading Activity," *Journal of Finance* 36 (September 1981).

Researchers have looked at the stock price reaction to many other types of news, for example, earnings and dividend announcements, plans to issue additional stock or to merge with another firm, or various sorts of macroeconomic news. Most of the information was rapidly and accurately reflected in the price of the stock; therefore, investors were not able to earn superior returns by buying or selling after the announcement. Such a market in which it is impossible to make superior returns from publicly available information is said to be **semi-strong-form efficient.**

Finally, there's **strong-form efficiency,** in which prices reflect not just public information but *all* the information that can be acquired by painstaking analysis of the company and the economy. In such a market, prices would *always* be fair and *no* investor would be able to make consistently superior forecasts of stock prices.

Most tests of strong-form efficiency have analyzed the performance of professionally managed portfolios. Managers of such portfolios have every kind of published and unpublished information at their fingertips. If the market were not strong-form efficient, these managers ought to generate higher returns than ordinary investors. Yet no group of portfolio managers has been able to outperform the market consistently, after taking account of differences in risk.

Of course, it would be surprising if some managers were not smarter than others and could earn superior returns. But it seems to be difficult to spot the smart ones, and the top-performing manager one year has about an average chance of falling on his face the next year.

semi-strong-form efficiency: Market prices reflect all publicly available information.

strong-form efficiency: Market prices rapidly reflect all information that could in principle be used to determine true value.

▶ Example 11.1

*Performance of
Money Managers*

Forbes Magazine, a widely read investment magazine, has published annually since 1975 an "honor roll" of the most consistently successful mutual funds. Suppose that each year, when *Forbes* announced its honor roll, you invested an equal sum in each of these exceptional funds. You would have outperformed the market in only 5 of the following 16 years and your average annual return before paying any initial fees would have been more than 1 percent below the return on the market.[3]

When evidence of the only-average performance of professional investment managers first appeared, it was also greeted with skepticism—especially by the managers! But many investment managers are now convinced and indeed have given up the pursuit of superior performance. They simply "buy the index," which maximizes diversification and minimizes the costs of managing their portfolios. Corporate pension plans now invest over a quarter of their United States equity holdings in index funds.[4]

Indexing of professionally managed money makes sense if no manager can get useful information consistently ahead of the rest of the pack. When information does arrive, managers trade on it immediately, and stock prices respond right away. Such a market ends up strong-form efficient, even though the information moving stock prices is not readily available to the amateur investor.

The difficulty of "beating the market" has led some to suggest, only partially in jest, that one might as well choose stocks by throwing darts at *The Wall Street Journal* as by "rational" selection. Actually, this view is far too simplistic *even if* markets are fully efficient, for it overlooks the importance of efficient diversification and the choice of an appropriate level of portfolio risk. Nevertheless, also only partially in jest, *The Wall Street Journal* has initiated a series of overlapping 6-month investment contests between well-known stock market analysts and randomly selected stocks. The *Journal* publishes the results of the contest every month. The nearby box reports on the European version of this contest.

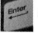
See box p. 329

▶ Self-Test 11.2

Technical analysts, fundamental analysts, and professional portfolio managers all try to earn superior returns in the stock market. Explain how each group's efforts help keep the market efficient.

No Theory Is Perfect

We have seen that there are three forms of the efficient-market theory:

Weak form (the random walk theory)	Market prices reflect all information contained in past market prices
Semi-strong form	Market prices reflect all publicly available information
Strong form	Market prices reflect all known information

[3]The classic study of fund performance is M. C. Jensen, "The Performance of Mutual Funds in the Period 1945–64," *Journal of Finance* 23 (May 1968), pp. 389–416. Recent studies include M. J. Gruber, "Another Puzzle: The Growth in Actively Managed Mutual Funds," *Journal of Finance* 51 (July 1996), pp. 783–810, and B. G. Malkiel, "Returns from Investing in Equity Mutual Funds 1971 to 1991," *Journal of Finance* 50 (June 1995), pp. 549–572. The performance of the *Forbes* "Honor Roll" funds was analyzed in Burton Malkiel's paper.

[4]Greenwich Associates, *Seismic Shift in Pension Planning,* 1994. An index fund is designed to replicate the investment performance of a particular stock market index. The portfolio is invested in each stock in proportion to the stock's weight in the index. Individual investors can index, too. See Example 9.2 in Chapter 9.

Monkey Business

What makes a good investor? A good ear for the news, agility, above-average intelligence and, perhaps, a modicum of luck?

By that definition, at least, any chimpanzee—a primate noted for its large ears, long arms and high IQ (relatively speaking, of course)—has a chance of ranking up there with the greats.

Certainly, the investment performance by *The Wall Street Journal Europe*'s chimp over the last six months is impressive—thanks mainly to a lucky call on French sporting-goods manufacturer Salomon SA, whose new golf club has powered the company's stock up more than 50% since February.

However, the chimp's longer-term returns have proved disappointing compared with the gains by professional stockpickers.

The idea behind the contest is to determine whether stock markets are truly efficient. If they were so, then all available information would be immediately taken into account by stock prices and investment professionals wouldn't be able to predict today, based on what they know, what will happen to tomorrow's stock prices.

In his book *A Random Walk Down Wall Street,* Burton Malkiel took the idea to its logical conclusion. He suggested that in order to save on hefty broker and management fees, investors should entrust their stock-market portfolio to a blindfolded monkey tossing darts at the financial pages of a newspaper.

Since January 1992 *The Wall Street Journal Europe*'s reporters have been testing the theory every month by tossing darts for the imaginary monkey. The portfolio then competes over six months against four stocks picked more scientifically by four investment professionals. Returns are calculated at the end of the six months, measuring a stock's gains or losses in local currency and including net dividends paid.

[In the latest round of the competition] the four investment professionals taking part in the competition are up against a rival who is back in peak condition after a disappointing start to the year. The newspaper's dart-wielding monkey . . . scored an impressive 27% average return on his portfolio over the previous six months.

Since the contest began, the pros have beaten the monkey 26 times, while the monkey has won 23 times. However, when the returns of each round are cumulated, the monkey is trailing well behind, with an aggregate 251.2% gain, compared with the professionals' overall 446.6% gain.

Few simple economic ideas are as well supported by the evidence as the efficient-market theory. But it would be wrong to pretend that there are no puzzles or apparent exceptions. For instance, company managers have made consistently superior profits when they deal in their own company's stock.[5] This does not square well with the strong form of the efficient-market theory. It implies that managers know more about their companies' prospects than even professional portfolio managers do.

It is not so surprising that insiders make superior profits, but there are other phenomena that take more explaining. For example, look at Figure 11.4, which shows the results of investing $1 in 1926 in the stocks of either small or large firms. By 1996 the $1 invested in small-firm stocks had appreciated to $4,413, while the investment in large firms was worth only $1,197. This superior performance of small-firm stocks took place over a relatively short period. Until the early 1960s small-firm and large-firm stocks were neck and neck. A wide gap then opened in the next two decades but narrowed again in the 1980s.

Now the superior performance of small-firm stocks could mean one of three things. First, it could be that investors have demanded a higher return from small firms to

[5]See H. N. Seyhun, "Insiders' Profits, Costs of Trading, and Market Efficiency," *Journal of Financial Economics* 16 (June 1986), pp. 189–212.

Figure 11.4

One dollar invested in a portfolio of small firms in 1926 would have grown to $4,413 by 1996. A $1 investment in large-firm stocks would have grown to $1,197.

Source: Authors' calculations, based on data from the Center for Research in Security Prices.

compensate for their extra risk. The difference in the betas of small and large firms is not nearly large enough to explain the difference in returns, but maybe small firms have some extra risk that is not captured in their betas. Second, the higher returns of small firms could simply be a coincidence, a finding that stems from the efforts of many researchers to find interesting patterns in the data. The third possibility is that we have here an important exception to the efficient-market theory, one that provided investors with the opportunity to make predictably superior profits over two decades.

But this is not the end of the puzzle, for look now at Figure 11.5, which shows the difference between the performance of small- and large-firm stocks in January and the remaining months. Notice that almost all the gains from investing in small firms came in the month of January. This seems to violate even weak-form efficiency, since a mechanical trading rule ("Buy small stocks in December, sell in February") would apparently have generated superior returns. What is going on here? We don't really know whether Figure 11.5 is an example of an irrational and inefficient market, or just another coincidence.

We believe that there is now widespread agreement that capital markets function well. So nowadays when economists come across instances where this apparently isn't true, they don't throw the efficient-market hypothesis onto the economic garbage heap. Instead they ask whether there is some missing ingredient that their theories ignore. Thus, despite the apparent superior performance of small-company stocks in January, few economists have to our knowledge been tempted to make a king-size investment in such stocks. Instead economists have assumed that investors aren't stupid and have looked at whether small-firm stocks suffer from some other defect, such as a lack of easy marketability, that is not allowed for in our theories or tests.

Figure 11.5

*The size premium—difference between the average return on small firms and that on large firms— between April 1962 and December 1989, by month. Notice that the small-firm effect occurs entirely in January. (*Source: *G. Hawawini and D. B. Keim, "On the Predictability of Common Stock Returns: World-Wide Evidence," in R. A. Jarrow, V. Maksimovic, and W. T. Ziemba (eds.),* Finance, *Amsterdam: North Holland, 1994.)*

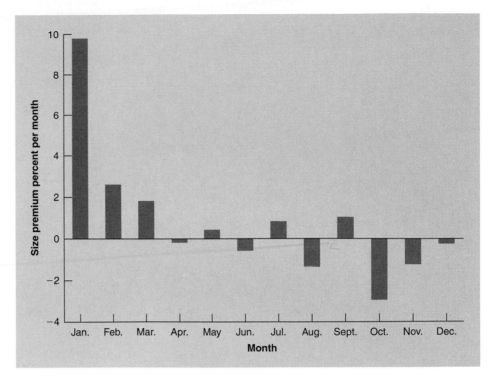

The Crash of 1987

On Monday, October 19, 1987, the Standard & Poor's Composite Index of stock prices (the S&P 500) fell 20 percent in *1 day.* This crash fell in the midst of 2 weeks of incredible volatility, as you can see in Figure 11.6. As we write this chapter 10 years after Black Monday, markets around the world are once again in a period of unusual turmoil.

In the wake of the crash, investors asked why prices fell so sharply. There was no obvious *new* information to justify such a sharp decline. The idea that market prices accurately reflect all information available to investors, and thus are the best estimates of true values, seemed less compelling than before. It appears that prices were either irrationally high before Black Monday or irrationally low afterward. Could the theory of efficient markets be another casualty of the crash?

The crash reminds us of how exceptionally difficult it is to value common stocks from scratch. For example, suppose that in September 1996 you wanted to check whether common stocks were fairly valued. At least as a first stab, you might use the constant-growth formula that we introduced in Chapter 4. The annual dividend on the Standard & Poor's Composite Index was about $13.60.[6] If this dividend was expected to grow at a steady rate of 10 percent a year and investors required an annual return of 12 percent a year from common stocks,[7] the constant-growth formula gives a value

---

[6]The level of the index was about 667. If you had invested $667, spread out across all the stocks in the index, you would have received dividends of about $13.60 per year.

[7]The Treasury bill rate was about 3.2 percent at the time. If we assume investors expected an 8.7 percent risk premium from investing in the stock market—the same as the historical average risk premium—then the total expected market return was 3.2 + 8.7 = 11.9, or about 12 percent.

Figure 11.6

Daily rates of return on S&P 500 Index in 1987.

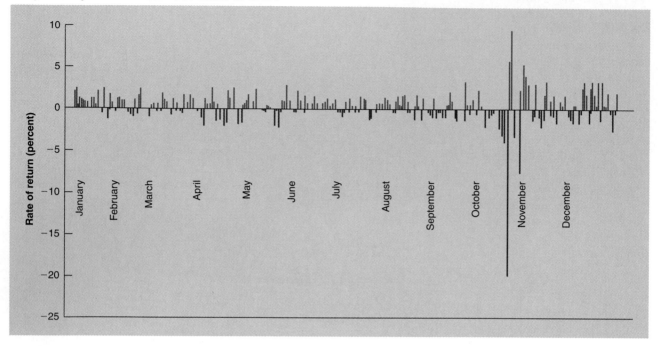

for the index of

$$PV \text{ (index)} = \frac{DIV}{r - g} = \frac{13.60}{.12 - .10} = 680$$

which is close to the actual level of the index in September 1996. But how confident would you be about any of these figures? Suppose investors revised their assessment of the likely dividend growth rate to only 9.5 percent per year. This would produce a downward revision of 20 percent in your estimate of the correct level for the index, from 680 to 544.

$$PV \text{ (index)} = \frac{DIV}{r - g} = \frac{13.60}{.12 - .095} = 544$$

In other words, a price drop like Black Monday's could have occurred in September 1996 if investors had suddenly become .5 percentage point less optimistic about future dividend growth.

The extreme difficulty of valuing common stocks from scratch has two important consequences. First, investors almost always price a common stock relative to yesterday's price or relative to today's price of comparable securities. In other words, they generally take yesterday's price as correct, and then adjust it upward or downward according to today's information. If information arrives smoothly, then as time passes investors become more and more confident that today's market level is correct. However, when investors lose confidence in the benchmark of yesterday's price, there may be a period of confused trading and volatile prices before a new benchmark is established.

Second, the idea that stock price *always* equals true value is nearly impossible to test, precisely because it's so difficult to calculate value without referring to prices. Thus the crash didn't conclusively disprove the hypothesis. But many people now find it less plausible.

However, the crash does not undermine the evidence for market efficiency with respect to *relative* prices. Take, for example, Exxon, which sold for about $80 per share in September 1996. Could we *prove* that true value is $80? No, but we could be confident that Exxon's price should be substantially greater than that of Phillips Petroleum (about $40 at the same time), since the two companies were leaders in the same industry, but Exxon paid a higher dividend and had much higher forecast earnings per share. Moreover, if Exxon announced unexpectedly higher earnings, we could be quite confident that its share price would respond instantly and without bias. In other words, the subsequent price would be set correctly relative to the prior price.

Most of the corporate finance lessons of the efficient-markets hypothesis depend on these kinds of relative efficiency. Let us turn now to consider some of these lessons and at the same time introduce briefly some of the issues discussed in subsequent chapters.

▶ **Self-Test 11.3**

Which of the following hypothetical "facts" would be violations of the efficient-market hypothesis? If inconsistent with market efficiency, which version of efficiency would be violated?

a. Stock returns tend to be more volatile in January than in other months.
b. Stocks that perform poorly in one week tend to outperform the rest of the market in the following week.
c. Roughly half of a group of professional portfolio managers "beat the market" in 1998.
d. Consistently superior returns are earned by buying a company's stock *the day after* announcement of good news, for example, after an increase in earnings.

11.3 *Lessons of Market Efficiency*

Markets Have No Memory

The weak form of the efficient-market theory states that the sequence of past price changes contains no information about future changes. Economists express the same idea more concisely when they say that "stock prices follow a random walk" or "the market has no memory." Sometimes financial managers seem to act as if this were not the case. For example, they are often reluctant to issue stock after a fall in price. They are inclined to wait for a rebound. Similarly, managers favor equity rather than debt financing after an abnormal price rise. The idea is to "catch the market while it's high." But we know that the market has no memory and the cycles that financial managers seem to rely on do not exist.

Sometimes a financial manager will have inside information indicating that the firm's stock is overpriced or underpriced. Suppose, for example, that there is some good news which the market does not know but managers do. The stock price will rise sharply when the news is revealed. Therefore, if the company sold shares at the current price, instead of waiting until the good news got out, it would be offering a bargain to new investors at the expense of present stockholders.

Naturally managers are reluctant to sell new shares when they have favorable inside information. But such inside information has nothing to do with the history of the stock price. Your firm's stock could be selling now at half its price of a year ago and yet you could have special information suggesting that it is *still* grossly overvalued. Or it may still be undervalued at twice last year's price.

There Are No Financial Illusions

In an efficient market there are no financial illusions. Investors are unromantically concerned with the firm's cash flows and the portion of those cash flows to which they are entitled.

There are occasions, however, on which managers seem to assume that investors suffer from financial illusions. For example, some firms devote enormous ingenuity to the task of manipulating earnings reported to stockholders. This is done by "creative accounting"—that is, by choosing accounting methods which stabilize and increase *reported* earnings without affecting the firm's cash flow. Presumably firms go to this trouble because management believes that stockholders take the earnings figures at face value. Some years ago, a leading accountant echoed this belief in the following complaint:

> Let us assume that you sincerely want to report the profits in the way you feel fairly
> presents the true results of your company's business. This is an admirable and
> objective motive; but when you do this, you find that your competitor shows a
> relatively more favorable profit result than you do. This creates a demand for the
> competitor's stock, while yours lags behind. You put your analyst to work, and you
> find that if your competitor followed the same accounting practices you do, your
> results would be better than his. You show this analysis to your complaining
> stockholders. Naturally, they ask, "If this is true, and if your competitor's accounting
> practices are generally accepted, too, why not change your accounting practices and
> thus improve your profits?" At that point you try to explain why your accounting is
> much more factual and reliable than your competitor's. Your stockholders listen, but
> nothing you can say will convince them that they should give up a 20 percent, 50
> percent, or 100 percent possible increase in the market value just because you like
> certain accounting practices better than others.[8]

Was he right? Can the firm increase its market value by creative accounting? Researchers have tried to resolve this question by looking at how the market reacts when companies change their accounting methods in order to boost their earnings. The results have suggested that investors are not easily fooled by such shenanigans and that the firm's shares are traded in an efficient, well-functioning market, where investors look to the face behind the mask.[9]

---

[8]L. Spacek, "Business Success Requires an Understanding of Unsolved Problems of Accounting and Financial Reporting," address to the financial accounting class, Graduate School of Business Administration, Harvard University, September 25, 1959.

[9]See, for example, R. S. Kaplan and R. Roll, "Investor Evaluation of Accounting Information: Some Empirical Evidence," *Journal of Business* 45 (April 1972), pp. 225–257, and R. W. Holthausen, "Evidence on the Effect of Bond Covenants and Management Compensation Contracts on the Choice of Accounting Technique: The Case of the Depreciation Switch-Back," *Journal of Accounting and Economics* 3 (1981), pp. 73–109.

There Are No Free Lunches on Wall Street

In an efficient market you can trust market prices. To put it another way, there are no free lunches on Wall Street. Here is an example.

Short-term interest rates are often different from long-term rates. For example, suppose that the interest rate on 1-year bonds is 4 percent and the rate on 2-year bonds is 6 percent. Does this mean that investors should sell all their 1-year bonds and rush to take advantage of the high interest rates on the 2-year bonds? Could firms reduce the cost of their borrowing by issuing 1-year rather than 2-year bonds?

If you believe that markets are efficient, you should be suspicious of any simple rule that says one type of bond is cheap and another expensive. So what's the explanation? One possibility is that investors expect short-term interest rates to rise over the coming year. For example, suppose that the 1-year interest rate is expected to rise to 8 percent. Then investors who buy a 1-year bond now and reinvest the proceeds in another 1-year bond at the end of the year can expect to earn a total return over the 2 years of just over 12 percent—almost identical to the total return that you would get from buying the 2-year bond.[10] Conversely, companies could not expect to borrow any more cheaply by issuing two 1-year bonds in succession than by issuing a 2-year bond.

Thus when you see that short-term rates are different from long-term rates, there is probably a good reason for it—the market may be telling you that interest rates are expected to change.[11]

▶ **Self-Test 11.4**   By 1997 average dividend yields on stocks had fallen to about 2 percent. Some investors in the stock market were upset at the meager immediate cash return on their money and therefore switched into high-dividend stocks. For example, they might sell a diversified mutual fund and buy stocks of electric and gas utilities, many of which offered dividend yields of over 5 percent. Such a shift could double the dividends received per dollar invested. But were these investors really better off? Would you expect their total returns (dividends plus capital gains) to increase?

 Summary

1. Sophisticated investors do not assume that superior returns come easy. Sophisticated financial managers do not assume that investors will willingly give them cheap financing. Both know that modern capital markets are highly competitive and efficient—and in particular that prices of stocks, bonds, and other securities react quickly and accurately when new information arrives.

2. Although capital markets are not always 100 percent efficient, smart financial managers generally start by assuming efficient capital markets. Financial traps and mirages are most easily seen from that vantage point. Of course financial managers sometimes find opportunities in the wake of inefficiencies and imperfections.

---

[10]The total expected return on two 1-year bonds is $1.04 \times 1.08 - 1 = .1232$, or 12.32 percent. The total return on a 2-year bond is $1.06 \times 1.06 - 1 = .1236$, or 12.36 percent.

[11]Another explanation may be that the prices of long-term bonds fluctuate more than those of short-term bonds. A higher interest rate on long-term bonds is needed to compensate investors for this extra risk.

In that case they abandon the efficient-markets vantage point and adapt financing strategy accordingly.

3. Competition between investors will tend to produce an efficient market. In such a market, prices will rapidly digest any new information, and it will be very difficult for investors to make consistently superior returns. We may indeed *hope* to beat the market, but in an efficient market all we can rationally *expect* is a return that is just sufficient on average to compensate for the time value of money and for the risks we bear.

4. The efficient-market hypothesis comes in three different flavors. The weak form states that prices efficiently reflect all the information contained in the past series of stock prices. In this case it is impossible to earn superior returns simply by looking for patterns in stock prices; in other words, price changes are a random walk. The semi-strong form states that prices reflect all published information. That means it is impossible to make consistently superior returns just by reading the newspaper, looking at the company's annual accounts, and so on. The strong form states that stock prices effectively impound all available information. This form tells us that useful private information is hard to find, because in pursuing it you are in competition with thousands—perhaps millions—of active, intelligent, and greedy investors. The best you can do in this case is to assume that securities are fairly priced.

5. The concept of an efficient market is astonishingly simple and remarkably well-supported by the facts. Less than 30 years ago any suggestion that security investment is a fair game was generally regarded as bizarre. Today it is not only widely accepted in business schools, but it also permeates investment practice and government policy toward the security markets. And because security prices are set fairly, it is easier to add value by smart investment decisions than by smart financing decisions.

6. An efficient market has no memory, financial illusions, or free lunches. Stock prices follow a random walk, in which the odds of a gain or loss tomorrow do not depend on past changes, so that managers cannot time security issues advantageously unless they have information the rest of the market does not. Moreover, because there are no financial illusions, managers cannot fool the market simply by manipulating accounting data.

Key Terms

efficient capital markets	weak-form efficiency	semi-strong-form efficiency
random walk	fundamental analysts	strong-form efficiency
technical analysts		

Problems

1. **Forms of EMH.** Supply the missing words from the following list: *fundamental, semi-strong, strong, technical, weak.*

There are three forms of the efficient-market hypothesis. Tests of randomness in stock prices provide evidence for the _____ form of the hypothesis. Tests of stock price reaction to well-publicized news provide evidence for the _____ form and tests of the performance of professionally managed funds provide evidence for the _____ form. Market efficiency results from competition between investors. Many investors search for new information about the company's business that would help them to value the stock more accurately. This is known as _____ research. Such research helps to ensure that prices reflect all available information; in other words, it helps to keep the market efficient in the _____ form. Other investors study past stock prices for recurrent patterns that would allow them to make superior profits. This is known as _____ research. Such research helps to ensure that prices reflect all the information contained in past stock prices; in other words, it helps to keep the market efficient in the _____ form.

2. **Interpreting EMH.** True or false?

   a. The efficient-market hypothesis asserts that investors have perfect forecasting ability.
   b. The semi-strong form of the efficient-market hypothesis states that prices reflect all publicly available information.
   c. In efficient markets the expected return on each stock is the same.
   d. Fundamental analysis by security analysts and investors helps keep markets efficient.
   e. If the efficient-market hypothesis is correct, managers will not be able to increase stock prices by "creative accounting," which boosts reported earnings.

3. **Interpreting EMH.** How would you respond to the following comments?

   a. "Efficient market, my eye! I know of lots of investors who do crazy things."
   b. "Efficient market? Balderdash! I know at least a dozen people who have made a bundle in the stock market."
   c. "The trouble with the efficient-market theory is that it ignores investors' psychology."
   d. "The business cycle is at least somewhat predictable and stocks with positive betas respond to the state of the economy. Therefore, stock prices must be predictable."

4. **Forms of EMH.** Which of the following observations *appear* to violate market efficiency? Explain whether the inefficiency is weak, semistrong, or strong.

   a. Managers make superior returns on their purchases of their company's stock.
   b. There is a positive relationship between the return on the market in one quarter and the change in aggregate corporate profits in the next quarter.
   c. Stocks of companies with unexpectedly high earnings appear to offer high returns for several months after the earnings announcement.
   d. Very risky stocks on the average give higher returns than safe stocks.

 5. **Random Walks.** Here are actual rates of return for the Standard & Poor's 500 Index for a 60-month period. Figures are in percent per month.

   +2.0, +1.0, −.3, +4.0, +.6, +8.4, +6.2, −.3, +1.3, −2.8, +8.3, +1.5, −3.5, +4.1, +7.1, −.04, −5.9, +4.1, +5.3, −3.3, −4.4, +6.6, −.5, +3.7, −4.0, −2.6, +2.2, +3.9, +4.4, +.04, +1.3, −5.1, −6.0, −3.0, +2.3, −4.0, +4.5, −1.4, +3.3, +3.4, +2.1, +2.8, +4.5, +1.8, +5.0, +2.7, +2.8, +5.4, +.5, +.5, +.2, +4.0, +2.4, −.2, +3.6, −1.0, −4.4, +1.3, +1.9, +2.9

   Now flip a coin 60 times and write down the returns that would be generated by the coin-toss game described at the start of Section 11.2. Calculate and plot the value of a $100 investment in the coin-toss game. Do the same calculation and plot for the actual market returns given above. See if your friends can tell which series is the real market.

6. **Information and EMH.** "It's competition for information that makes securities markets efficient." Is this statement correct? Explain.

7. **Real vs. Financial Investments.** Why do investments in financial markets almost always have zero NPVs, whereas firms can find many investments in their product markets with positive NPVs?

8. **Indexing.** In an efficient market, it is hard to beat a simple indexing strategy. Does this mean that it is just as difficult to underperform that strategy, and therefore that there is no harm in trying? Explain why or why not.

9. **Portfolio Management in Efficient Markets.** Even if markets are efficient there still are important roles for professional money managers. What are some of these roles?

10. **Investment Performance.** It seems that every month we read an article in *The Wall Street Journal* about a stockpicker with a marvelous track record. Do these examples mean that financial markets really are not efficient?

11. **Implications of EMH.** The president of Good Fortunes, Inc., states at a press conference that the company has a 30-year history of ever-increasing dividend payments. Good Fortunes is widely regarded as one of the best run firms in its industry. Does this make the stock of the firm a good buy? Explain.

12. **Trend Analysis.** The top graph in Figure 11.1 shows the actual performance of the Standard & Poor's 500 Index for a 5-year period. Two financial managers, Alpha and Beta, are contemplating this chart. Each manager's company needs to issue new shares of common stock sometime in the next year.

    Alpha: "My company's going to issue right away. The stock market cycle has obviously topped out, and the next move is almost surely down. Better to issue now and get a decent price for the shares."

    Beta: "You're too nervous—we're waiting. It's true that the market's been going nowhere for the past year or so, but the figure clearly shows a basic upward trend. The market's on the way up to a new plateau."

    What would you say to Alpha and Beta?

13. **Implications of EMH.** "Long-term interest rates are at record highs. Most companies, therefore, find it cheaper to finance with common stock or relatively inexpensive short-term bank loans." Discuss.

14. **Interpreting Price Changes.** In May 1987 Citicorp announced that it was bolstering its loan loss reserves by $3 billion in order to reflect its exposure to Third World borrowers. Consequently, second-quarter earnings were transformed from a $.5 billion profit to a $2.5 billion loss.

    In after-hours trading the price of Citicorp stock fell sharply from its closing level of $50, but the next day when the market had had a chance to digest the news, the price recovered to $53. Other bank stocks fared less well and *The Wall Street Journal* reported that Citicorp's decision "triggered a big sell-off of international banking stocks that roiled stock markets around the world."

    Response to the Citicorp action varied. The bank's chairman claimed that "it significantly strengthens the institution," and analysts and bankers suggested that it was a notable step toward realism. For example, one argued that it was the recognition of the problem that made the difference, while another observed that the action "is merely recognizing what the stock market has been saying for several months: that the value of the sovereign debt of the big U.S. money center banks is between 25% and 50% less than is carried in their books." The London *Financial Times* made the more cautionary comment that Citicorp had "simply rearranged its balance sheet, not strengthened its capital base" and the Lex column described the move as an "outsize piece of cosmetic self-indulgence rather than a great stride towards the reconstruction of Third World debt." A lead article in the same paper stated that "even if all this means that Citicorp shareholders are $3 billion poorer today, the group as a whole is better placed to absorb whatever shocks lie ahead."

    There was also considerable discussion of the implications for other banks. As one analyst summed up, "There's no question that the market will put higher confidence in those institutions that can reserve more fully."

    Discuss the general reaction to the Citicorp announcement. It is not often that a company announces a $2.5 billion loss in one quarter and its stock price rises. Do you think that the share price reaction was consistent with an efficient market?

15. **Implications of EMH.** Suppose that a company *splits* its stock two for one, meaning that it doubles the number of shares outstanding. Each shareholder is given a new share for

each one previously held, so that the number of shares held doubles. The split is not associated with any change in the firm's investment policy.

a. Has the firm acquired any new assets as a result of the split?
b. Has anything happened to the value of the firm's real assets (its projects)?
c. What will happen to earnings per share?
d. What should happen to the firm's stock price?
e. What should happen to the dollar value of the shareholder's stock? Has investor wealth changed?

16. **Expectations and EMH.** Geothermal Corp. just announced good news: its earnings increased by 20 percent from last year's value. Most investors had anticipated an increase of 25 percent. Will Geothermal's stock price increase or decrease when the announcement is made?

17. **Yield Curve and EMH.** If the yield curve is downward-sloping, meaning that long-term interest rates are lower than current short-term rates, what might investors believe about *future* short-term interest rates?

Solutions to Self-Test Questions

11.1 a. True
  b. False. There cannot be a long-run stock price. If there were, investors could make easy profits by investing in stocks when they are below the long-run price. This would be inconsistent with the notion that prices reflect all useful information about the firm.
  c. True
  d. False. Note the *apparent* peaks and valleys in Figure 11.1.

11.2 Each looks for information about over- or undervalued securities. Technical analysts look for patterns in past prices, and fundamental analysts focus on published information. Portfolio managers may use both technical and fundamental information and also have in-house analysts who try to uncover hidden or superior information. When any of them find useful information, indicating, say, an undervalued stock, they buy aggressively, trying to beat other investors to the bargain. This trading moves the stock price up until the bargain disappears. Then the favorable information is fully incorporated in the stock price.

  Of course the process works in reverse if unfavorable information is discovered. In either case, trading by informed investors moves the price until the information is fully reflected in it. This is the efficient-market outcome.

11.3 a. No violation. Even if volatility is predictable, this offers no way for investors to make excessive profits. It could simply be that more information is released in January. More news would generate higher volatility, but that does not imply that prices are incorrect.
  b. Violation of weak-form efficiency. If stocks tended to reverse their performance from one week to the next, it would be easy for investors to make easy money: simply buy stocks of firms that performed poorly last week. The knowledge of a stock's price history would provide a route to easy profits.
  c. No violation. This outcome is normal in a strong-form efficient market where portfolio managers cannot beat the market average. We expect roughly one-half of these managers to get lucky in any particular year.
  d. Violation of semi-strong efficiency. The good news ought to be fully incorporated in the stock price on the announcement day, leaving no superior profits for late buyers.

11.4 No and no. In an efficient market, investors are concerned with total return, including capital gains as well as dividends. Investors pursuing immediate dividend yield generally move into mature, low-growth companies and sacrifice the chance for substantial capital gains. Total return should depend on risk but not on the fraction of return received as dividends.

Financial managers and investors must understand well the different securities that firms issue. Marriott's bondholders got into trouble because they did not look carefully at the details of their loan.

© Cameramann International, Ltd.

Chapter 12
An Overview of Corporate Financing

This chapter begins our analysis of long-term financing decisions. In later chapters this will involve a careful look at some classic finance problems, such as how much firms should borrow and what dividends they should pay their shareholders. But before getting down to specifics, we will provide a brief overview of types of long-term finance.

It is customary to classify sources of finance as debt or equity. When the firm borrows, it promises to repay the debt with interest. If it doesn't keep its promise, the debtholders may force the firm into bankruptcy. However, no such commitments are made to the equityholders. They are entitled to whatever is left over after the debtholders have been paid off. For this reason, equity is called a *residual claim* on the firm.

However, a simple division of sources of finance into debt and equity would miss the enormous *variety* of financing instruments that companies use today. For example, Table 12.1 shows the many long-term securities issued by Mobil. Yet Mobil has not come close to exhausting the menu of possible securities.

This chapter introduces you to the principal families of securities and explains how they are used by corporations. We also draw attention to some of the interesting aspects of firms issuing these securities.

After studying this chapter you should be able to

▶ Describe the major classes of securities issued by firms to raise capital.

▶ Summarize recent trends in the use made by firms of different sources of finance.

Common Stock

treasury stock: Stock that has been repurchased by the company and held in its treasury.

issued shares: Shares that have been issued by the company.

outstanding shares: Shares that have been issued by the company and are held by investors.

authorized share capital: Maximum number of shares that the company is permitted to issue, as specified in the firm's articles of incorporation.

Most major corporations are far too large to be owned by one investor. For example, you would need to lay your hands on about $48 billion if you wanted to own the whole of Mobil.

Mobil is owned by about 185,000 different investors, each of whom holds a number of shares of common stock. These investors are therefore known as *shareholders* or *stockholders*. Altogether Mobil has outstanding 394 million shares of common stock. So if you were to buy one Mobil share, you would own 1/394,000,000, or about .00000025 percent, of the company. Of course, a large pension fund might hold many thousands of Mobil shares.

The 394 million shares held by investors are not the only shares that have been issued by Mobil. Mobil also issued a further 52 million shares, which it later bought back from investors. These shares are held in the company's treasury and are known as **treasury stock.** The shares held by investors are said to be **issued** and **outstanding shares.** By contrast, the 52 million treasury shares are said to be *issued but not outstanding.*

If Mobil wishes to raise more money, it can sell more shares. However, there is a limit to the number that it can issue without getting the approval of the current shareholders. The maximum number of shares that can be issued is known as the **authorized share capital**—for Mobil, this is 600 million shares. Since Mobil has already issued 446 million shares, it can issue 154 million more without shareholders' approval.

Table 12.1

Large firms often use many different kinds of securities. Look at the variety of long-term securities issued by Mobil:

Equity
   Common Stock
   Preferred Stock
Long-term debt
   Debentures
   Industrial revenue bonds
   Notes
   Floating-rate notes
   Japanese yen loans
   Sterling eurobonds
   Canadian dollar eurobonds
   ECU eurobonds
   Swiss franc notes

par value: Value of security shown on certificate.

additional paid-in capital: Difference between issue price and par value of stock. Also called *capital surplus.*

retained earnings: Earnings not paid out as dividends.

Table 12.2 shows how the investment by Mobil's common stockholders is recorded in the company's books. The price at which each share is recorded is known as its **par value.** In Mobil's case each share has a par value of $2.00. Thus the total par value of the issued shares is 446 million shares × $2 per share = $892 million. Par value has little economic significance.[1]

The price at which new shares are sold to investors almost always exceeds the par value. The difference is entered into the company's accounts as **additional paid-in capital** or *capital surplus.* For example, if Mobil sold an additional 100,000 shares at $122 a share, the par value of the common stock would increase by 100,000 × $2 = $200,000 and additional paid-in capital would increase by 100,000 × ($122 − $2) = $12,000,000. You can see from this example that the funds raised from the stock issue are divided between par value and additional paid-in capital. Since the choice of par value in the first place was immaterial, so is the allocation between par value and additional paid-in capital.

Besides buying new stock, shareholders also indirectly contribute new capital to the firm whenever profits that could be paid out as dividends are instead plowed back into the company. Table 12.2 shows that the cumulative amount of such **retained earnings** is $19,108 million.

Mobil's books also show the amount that the company has spent in the past on repurchasing its own stock. The repurchase of the 52 million shares cost Mobil $2,643 million. This is money that has in effect been returned to shareholders.

Finally, the common stock account shows a minor adjustment for currency translation losses resulting from Mobil's foreign operations. We'd rather not get into foreign exchange accounting here.

The sum of the par value, additional paid-in capital, and total retained earnings less repurchased stock and currency translation losses is known as the net common equity of the firm. It equals the total amount contributed directly by shareholders

[1]Because some states do not allow companies to sell new shares below par value, par value is generally set at a low figure. Some companies even issue shares with no par value, in which case the stock is listed in the accounts at an arbitrarily determined figure.

Table 12.2

Book value of common stockholders' equity of Mobil, December 31,1996 (figures in millions)

Common shares ($2.00 par value per share)	$891
Additional paid-in capital	1,468
Retained earnings	19,108
Currency translation adjustment	(73)
Treasury shares at cost	(2,643)
Net common equity	18,751

Note:

Authorized shares	600
Issued shares, of which	446
Outstanding shares	394
Treasury shares	52

when the firm issued new stock and indirectly when it plowed back part of its earnings.

▶ **Self-Test 12.1**

Generic Products has had one stock issue in which it sold 100,000 shares to the public at $15 per share. Can you fill in the following table?

Common shares ($1.00 par value per share)	_____
Additional paid-in capital	_____
Retained earnings	_____
Net common equity	$4,500,000

Book Value versus Market Value

We discussed the distinction between book and market value in Chapters 2 and 4, but it bears repeating.

> **Book value is a backward-looking measure. It tells us how much capital the firm has raised from shareholders in the past. It does not measure the value that investors place on those shares today. The market value of the firm is forward-looking; it depends on the future dividends that shareholders expect to receive.**

Mobil's common equity has a book value of $18,751 million. With 394 million shares outstanding, this translates to a book value of $18,751/394 = $47.59 per share. But in December 1996, when the firm issued stock, Mobil shares were priced at $122 each. So the total *market* value of the common stock was 394 million shares × $122 per share = $48.1 billion, more than double the book value.

Market value is usually greater than book value. This is partly because inflation has driven the value of many assets above what they originally cost. Also, firms raise capital to invest in projects with present values that exceed initial cost. These positive-NPV projects made the shareholders better off. So we would expect the market value of the firm to be higher than the amount of money put up by the shareholders.

However, sometimes projects do go awry and companies fall on hard times. In this case, market value can fall below book value.

> ▶ **Self-Test 12.2**

No-name News can be established by investing $10 million in a printing press. The newspaper is expected to generate a cash flow of $2 million a year for 20 years. If the cost of capital is 10 percent, is the firm's market or book value greater? What if the cost of capital is 20 percent?

Dividends

Shareholders hope to receive a series of dividends on their investment. However, the company is not obliged to pay any dividend and the decision is up to the board of directors. In Chapter 15, we will discuss how that decision affects the value of the stock.

Because dividends are discretionary, they are not considered to be a business expense. Therefore, companies are not allowed to deduct dividend payments when they calculate their taxable income.

Stockholders' Rights

Stockholders have the ultimate control of the company's affairs. Occasionally companies need shareholder approval before they can take certain actions. For example, they need approval to increase the authorized capital or to merge with another company.

> **On most other matters, shareholder control boils down to the right to vote on appointments to the board of directors.**

The board usually consists of the company's top management as well as *outside directors,* who are not employed by the firm. In principle, the board is elected as an agent of the shareholders. It appoints and oversees the management of the firm and meets to vote on such matters as new share issues. Most of the time the board will go along with the management, but in crisis situations it can be very independent. For example, when the management of RJR Nabisco announced that it wanted to take over the company, the outside directors stepped in to make sure that the company was sold to the highest bidder.

Voting Procedures

majority voting: Voting system in which each director is voted on separately.

cumulative voting: Voting system in which all the votes one shareholder is allowed to cast can be cast for one candidate for the board of directors.

In most companies stockholders elect directors by a system of **majority voting.** In this case each director is voted on separately and stockholders can cast one vote for each share they own. In some companies directors are elected by **cumulative voting.** The directors are then voted on jointly and the stockholders can, if they choose, cast all their votes for just one candidate. For example, suppose there are five directors to be elected and you own 100 shares. You therefore have a total of $5 \times 100 = 500$ votes. Under majority voting you can cast a maximum of 100 votes for any one candidate. With a cumulative voting system you can cast all 500 votes for your favorite candidate. Cumulative voting makes it easier for a minority group of the stockholders to elect a director to represent their interests. That is why minority groups devote so much effort to campaigning for cumulative voting.

On many issues a simple majority of the votes cast is enough to carry the day, but there are some decisions that require a "supermajority" of, say, 75 percent of those eligible to vote. For example, a supermajority vote is sometimes needed to approve a merger. This requirement makes it difficult for the firm to be taken over and therefore helps to protect the incumbent management.

Shareholders can either vote in person or appoint a proxy to vote. The issues on which they are asked to vote are rarely contested, particularly in the case of large, publicly traded firms. Occasionally, however, there are **proxy contests** in which outsiders compete with the firm's existing management and directors for control of the corporation. But the odds are stacked against the outsiders, for the insiders can get the firm to pay all the costs of presenting their case and obtaining votes.

proxy contest: Takeover attempt in which outsiders compete with management for shareholders' votes.

Classes of Stock

Most companies issue just one class of common stock. Sometimes, however, a firm may have two or more classes outstanding, which differ in their right to vote or receive dividends. Suppose that a firm needs fresh capital but its present stockholders do not want to give up control of the firm. The existing shares could be labeled class A, and then class B shares could be issued to outside investors. The class B shares could have limited voting rights, although they would probably sell for less as a result.

Corporate Governance in the United States and Elsewhere

Mobil's shareholders own the company but they don't manage it. Management is delegated to a team of professional managers. Each shareholder owns only a small fraction of Mobil's shares and can exert little influence on the way the company is run. If shareholders do not like the policies the management team pursues, they can try to vote in another board of directors who will bring about a change in policy. But such attempts are rarely successful, and the shareholders' simplest solution is to sell the shares.

The separation between ownership and management in major United States corporations creates a potential conflict between shareholders (the principals who own the company) and managers (their agents who make the decisions). We noted in Chapter 2 several mechanisms that have evolved to mitigate this conflict:

- Shareholders elect a board of directors, which then appoints the managers, oversees them, and on occasion fires them.
- Managers' remuneration is tied to their performance.
- Poorly performing companies are taken over and the management is replaced by a new team.

These principles of corporate governance do not apply worldwide. The United States, Canada, Britain, Australia, and other English-speaking countries all have broadly similar systems, but other countries do not. In Japan industrial and financial companies are often linked together in a group, called a *keiretsu*. For example, the Mitsubishi keiretsu contains 29 core companies, including two banks, two insurance companies, an automobile manufacturer, a steel producer, and a cement company. Members of the keiretsu are tied together in several ways. First, managers may sit on the boards of directors of other group companies, and a "president's council" of chief executives meets regularly. Second, each company in the group holds shares in many of the other companies. And third, companies generally borrow from the keiretsu's bank or from elsewhere within the group. These links may have several advantages. Companies can obtain funds from other members of the group without the need to reveal confidential information to the public, and if a member of the group runs into financial heavy weather, its problems can be worked out with other members of the group rather than in the bankruptcy court.

The more stable and concentrated shareholder base of large Japanese corporations may make it easier for them to resist pressures for short-term performance and allow them to focus on securing long-term advantage. But the Japanese system of corporate governance also has its disadvantages, for the lack of market discipline may promote a too-cozy life and allow lagging or inefficient Japanese corporations to put off painful surgery.

Keiretsus are found only in Japan. But large companies in continental Europe are linked in some similar ways. For example, banks and other companies often own or control large blocks of shares and can push hard for changes in the management or strategy of poorly performing firms. (Banks in the United States are prohibited from large or permanent holdings of the stock of nonfinancial corporations.) Thus oversight and control are entrusted largely to banks and other corporations. Hostile takeovers of poorly performing companies are very rare in Germany and virtually impossible in Japan.

> For large corporations, separation of ownership and control is seen the world over. In the United States, control of large public companies is exercised through the board of directors and pressure from the stock market. In other countries the stock market is less important, and control shifts to major stockholders, typically banks and other companies.

Preferred Stock

preferred stock: Stock that takes priority over common stock in regard to dividends.

net worth: Book value of common stockholders' equity plus preferred stock.

Usually when investors talk about equity or stock, they are referring to common stock. You might have noticed in Table 12.1 that Mobil also has issued **preferred stock.** When we add in the $686 million of preferred stock issued by Mobil, book equity increases to $18,751 + $686 = $19,437 million. This figure is Mobil's **net worth.**

For most companies preferred stock is much less important than common stock. However, it can be a useful method of financing in mergers and certain other special situations.

Like debt, preferred stock promises a series of fixed payments to the investor and with relatively rare exceptions preferred dividends are paid in full and on time. Nevertheless, preferred stock is legally an equity security. This is because payment of a preferred dividend is almost invariably within the discretion of the directors. The only obligation is that no dividends can be paid on the common stock until the preferred dividend has been paid.[2] If the company goes out of business, the preferred stockholders get in the queue after the debtholders but before the common stockholders.

Preferred stock rarely confers full voting privileges. This is an advantage to firms that want to raise new money without sharing control of the firm with the new shareholders. However, if there is any matter that affects their place in the queue, preferred stockholders usually get to vote on it. Most issues also provide the holder with some voting power if the preferred dividend is skipped.

Companies cannot deduct preferred dividends when they calculate taxable income. Like common stock dividends, preferred dividends are paid from after-tax income. For most industrial firms this is a serious deterrent to issuing preferred. However, reg-

---

[2]These days this obligation is usually cumulative. In other words, before the common stockholders get a cent, the firm must pay any preferred dividends that have been missed in the past.

ulated public utilities can take tax payments into account when they negotiate with regulators the rates they charge customers. So they can effectively pass the tax disadvantage of preferred on to the consumer. A large fraction of the dollar value of new offerings of ordinary preferred stock consists of issues by utilities.

Preferred stock does have one tax advantage. If one corporation buys another's stock, only 30 percent of the dividends it receives is taxed. This rule applies to dividends on both common and preferred stock, but it is most important for preferred, for which returns are dominated by dividends rather than capital gains.

Suppose that your firm has surplus cash to invest. If it buys a bond, the interest will be taxed at the company's tax rate of 35 percent. If it buys a preferred share, it owns an asset like a bond (the preferred dividends can be viewed as "interest"), but the effective tax rate is only 30 percent of 35 percent, $.30 \times .35 = .105$, or 10.5 percent. It is no surprise that most preferred shares are held by corporations.

If you invest your firm's spare cash in a preferred stock, you will want to make sure that when it is time to sell the stock, it won't have plummeted in value. One problem with garden-variety preferred stock that pays a fixed dividend is that the preferreds' market prices go up and down as interest rates change (because present values fall when rates rise). So one ingenious banker thought up a wrinkle: Why not link the dividend on the preferred stock to interest rates so that it goes up when interest rates rise and vice versa? The result is known as **floating-rate preferred**. If you own floating-rate preferred, you know that any change in interest rates will be counterbalanced by a change in the dividend payment, so the value of your investment is protected.

floating-rate preferred:
Preferred stock paying dividends that vary with short-term interest rates.

▶ **Self-Test 12.3**

A company in a 35 percent tax bracket can buy a bond yielding 10 percent or a preferred stock of the same firm that is priced to yield 8 percent. Which will provide the higher after-tax yield? What if the purchaser is a private individual in a 35 percent tax bracket?

Corporate Debt

When they borrow money, companies promise to make regular interest payments and to repay the principal (that is, the original amount borrowed).

> **However, corporations have limited liability. By this we mean that the promise to repay the debt is not always kept. If the company gets into deep water, the company has the right to default on the debt and to hand over the company's assets to the lenders.**

Clearly it will choose bankruptcy only if the value of the assets is less than the amount of the debt. In practice, when companies go bankrupt, this handover of assets is far from straightforward. For example, when the furniture company Wickes went into bankruptcy, there were 250,000 creditors all jostling for a better place in the queue. Sorting out these problems is left to the bankruptcy court.

Because lenders are not regarded as owners of the firm, they don't normally have any voting power. Also, the company's payments of interest are regarded as a cost and are therefore deducted from taxable income. Thus interest is paid out of *before-tax* income, whereas dividends on common and preferred stock are paid out of *after-*

tax income. This means that the government provides a tax subsidy on the use of debt, which it does not provide on stock.

Debt Comes in Many Forms

Some orderly scheme of classification is essential to cope with the almost endless variety of debt issues. We will walk you through the major distinguishing characteristics.

Interest Rate. The interest payment, or *coupon,* on most long-term loans is fixed at the time of issue. If a $1000 bond is issued with a coupon of 10 percent, the firm continues to pay $100 a year regardless of how interest rates change. As we pointed out in Chapter 3, you sometimes encounter zero-coupon bonds. In this case the firm does not make a regular interest payment. It just makes a single payment at maturity. Obviously, investors pay less for zero-coupon bonds.

prime rate: Benchmark interest rate charged by banks.

Most loans from a bank and some long-term loans carry a *floating interest rate.* For example, your firm may be offered a loan at "1 percent over prime." The **prime rate** is the benchmark interest rate charged by banks to large customers with good to excellent credit. (But the largest and most creditworthy corporations can, and do, borrow at *less* than prime.) The prime rate is adjusted up and down with the general level of interest rates. When the prime rate changes, the interest on your floating-rate loan also changes.

Floating-rate loans are not always tied to the prime rate. Often they are tied to the rate at which international banks lend to one another. This is known as the *London Interbank Offered Rate,* or *LIBOR.*

▶ **Self-Test 12.4**

Would you expect the price of a 10-year floating-rate bond to be more or less sensitive to changes in interest rates than the price of a 10-year maturity fixed-rate bond?

---

funded debt: Debt with more than 1 year remaining to maturity.

Maturity. **Funded debt** is any debt repayable more than 1 year from the date of issue. Debt due in less than a year is termed *unfunded* and is carried on the balance sheet as a current liability. Unfunded debt is often described as short-term debt and funded debt is described as long-term, although it is clearly artificial to call a 364-day debt short-term and a 366-day debt long-term (except in leap years).

There are corporate bonds of nearly every conceivable maturity. For example, Walt Disney Co. issued bonds in 1993 with a 100-year maturity. Some British banks have issued perpetuities—that is, bonds which may survive forever. At the other extreme we find firms borrowing literally overnight.

sinking fund: Fund established to retire debt before maturity.

Repayment Provisions. Long-term loans are commonly repaid in a steady regular way, perhaps after an initial grace period. For bonds that are publicly traded, this is done by means of a **sinking fund.** Each year the firm puts aside a sum of cash into a sinking fund that is then used to buy back the bonds. When there is a sinking fund, investors are prepared to lend at a lower rate of interest. They know that they are more likely to be repaid if the company sets aside some cash each year than if the entire loan has to be repaid on one specified day.

callable bond: Bond that may be repurchased by firm before maturity at specified call price.

Most firms issuing debt to the public also reserve the right to *call* the debt—that is, issuers of **callable bonds** may buy back the bonds before the final maturity date. The price at which the firm can call the bonds is set at the time that the bonds are issued.

This option to call the bond is attractive to the issuer. If interest rates decline and bond prices rise, the issuer may repay the bonds at the specified call price and borrow the money back at a lower rate of interest.[3]

The call provision comes at the expense of bondholders, for it limits investors' capital gain potential. If interest rates fall and bond prices rise, holders of callable bonds may find their bonds bought back by the firm for the call price.

▶ **Self-Test 12.5**

Suppose Mobil is considering two issues of 20-year maturity coupon bonds; one issue will be callable, the other not. For a given coupon rate, will the callable or noncallable bond sell at the higher price? If the bonds are both to be sold to the public at par value, which bond must have the higher coupon rate?

---

subordinated debt: Debt that may be repaid in bankruptcy only after senior debt is paid.

Seniority.   Some debts are **subordinated.** In the event of default the subordinated lender gets in line behind the firm's general creditors. The subordinated lender holds a junior claim and is paid only after all senior creditors are satisfied.

When you lend money to a firm, you can assume that you hold a senior claim unless the debt agreement says otherwise. However, this does not always put you at the front of the line, for the firm may have set aside some of its assets specifically for the protection of other lenders. That brings us to our next classification.

Security.   When you borrow to buy your home, the savings and loan company will take out a mortgage on the house. The mortgage acts as security for the loan. If you default on the loan payments, the S&L can seize your home.

secured debt: Debt that has first claim on specified collateral in the event of default.

When companies borrow, they also may set aside certain assets as security for the loan. These assets are termed *collateral* and the debt is said to be **secured.** In the event of default, the secured lender has first claim on the collateral; unsecured lenders have a general claim on the rest of the firm's assets but only a junior claim on the collateral.

Default Risk.   Seniority and security do not guarantee payment. A debt can be senior and secured but still as risky as a dizzy tightrope walker—it depends on the value and risk of the firm's assets.

The safety of most corporate bonds can be judged from *bond ratings* provided by Moody's and Standard & Poor's. For example, the bonds that receive the highest Moody's rating are known as Aaa (or "triple A") bonds. Then come Aa ("double A"), A, Baa bonds, and so on.[4] Bonds rated Baa and above are called **investment grade,** while those with a rating of Ba or below are known as *speculative grade,* or **junk bonds.** Table 12.3 describes the criteria in more detail.

investment grade: Bonds rated Baa or above by Moody's or BBB or above by Standard & Poor's.

junk bond: Bond with a rating below Baa or BBB.

Some junk issues are "fallen angels," securities that were investment grade when issued but that subsequently fell from grace. But in the late 1970s a *new-issue* junk bond market was created. Companies discovered a pool of investors willing to accept unusually high default risks in exchange for high promised yields. Junk bonds were

---

[3]Sometimes callable bonds specify a period during which the firm is not allowed to call the bond if the purpose is simply to issue another bond at a lower interest rate.

[4]Standard & Poor's categories are similar. A Standard & Poor's rating of BBB, for example, closely corresponds to a Moody's rating of Baa. Similarly, a Standard & Poor's rating of BB corresponds to a Moody's rating of Ba.

Table 12.3

Key to Moody's bond ratings

Aaa

Bonds which are rated **Aaa** are judged to be of the best quality. They carry the smallest degree of investment risk and are generally referred to as "gilt edge." Interest payments are protected by a large or by an exceptionally stable margin, and principal is secure. While the various protective elements are likely to change, such changes as can be visualized are most unlikely to impair the fundamentally strong position of such issues.

Aa

Bonds which are rated **Aa** are judged to be of high quality by all standards. Together with the Aaa group they comprise what are generally known as high-grade bonds. They are rated lower than the best bonds because margins of protection may not be as large as in Aaa securities, or fluctuation of protective elements may be of greater amplitude, or there may be other elements present which make the long-term risks appear somewhat larger than in Aaa securities.

A

Bonds which are rated **A** possess many favorable investment attributes and are to be considered as upper-medium-grade obligations. Factors giving security to principal and interest are considered adequate but elements may be present which suggest a susceptibility to impairments sometime in the future.

Baa

Bonds which are rated **Baa** are considered as medium-grade obligations; i.e., they are neither highly protected nor poorly secured. Interest payments and principal security appear adequate for the present but certain protective elements may be lacking or may be characteristically unreliable over any great length of time. Such bonds lack outstanding investment characteristics and in fact have speculative characteristics as well.

Ba

Bonds which are rated **Ba** are judged to have speculative elements; their future cannot be considered as well assured. Often the protection of interest and principal payments may be very moderate and thereby not well safeguarded during both good and bad times over the future. Uncertainty of position characterizes bonds in this class.

B

Bonds which are rated **B** generally lack characteristics of the desirable investment. Assurance of interest and principal payments or of maintenance of other terms of the contract over any long period of time may be small.

Caa

Bonds which are rated **Caa** are of poor standing. Such issues may be in default or there may be present elements of danger with respect to principal or interest.

Ca

Bonds which are rated **Ca** represent obligations which are speculative in a high degree. Such issues are often in default or have other marked shortcomings.

C

Bonds which are rated **C** are the lowest-rated class of bonds, and issues so rated can be regarded as having extremely poor prospects of ever attaining any real investment standing.

Source: Moody's Investors Services.

often issued at short notice to finance acquisitions and minnows found that by issuing junk bonds they could get enough cash to bag whales.

New issues of junk bonds took a hit in the mid-1980s when it emerged that a number of savings and loan companies had speculated heavily in these bonds. The investment bank that had popularized junk bonds (Drexel Burnham Lambert) went into bankruptcy and the head of its junk bond operation (Michael Milken) went to prison.

As you would expect, investors demand a high return from low-rated bonds. Figure 12.1 presents the yields on default-free long-term U.S. Treasury bonds, Aaa-rated corporate bonds, and Baa-rated bonds since 1954. It also shows junk bond yields starting in November 1984. You can see that yields on the four groups of bonds track each other closely. However, promised yields go up as safety falls off.

Country and Currency. These days capital markets know few national boundaries and many large firms in the United States borrow abroad. For example, an American company may choose to finance a new plant in Spain by borrowing pesetas from a Spanish bank, or it may expand its Dutch operation by issuing a bond in Holland.

In addition to these national capital markets, there is also an international capital market centered mainly in London. There are some 500 banks in London from over 70 different countries; they include such giants as Citicorp, Union Bank of Switzerland, Deutsche Bank, Dai-ichi Kangyo Bank, Banque Nationale de Paris, and Barclays Bank. One reason they are there is to collect deposits in the major currencies. For example, suppose an Arab sheikh has just received payment in dollars for a large sale of oil to the United States. Rather than depositing the check in the United States, he may choose to open a dollar account with a bank in London. Dollars held in a bank outside the United States are known as **eurodollars** (similarly, francs held outside France are known as eurofrancs, deutschemarks held outside Germany are known as eurodeutschemarks, and so on).

eurodollars: Dollars held on deposit in a bank outside the United States.

The London bank branch that is holding the sheikh's dollar deposit may temporarily lend those dollars to a company, in the same way that a bank in the United States may relend dollars that have been deposited with it. Thus a company can either borrow dollars from a bank in the United States or borrow eurodollars from a bank in London.[5]

Figure 12.1

Yields on long-term bonds.

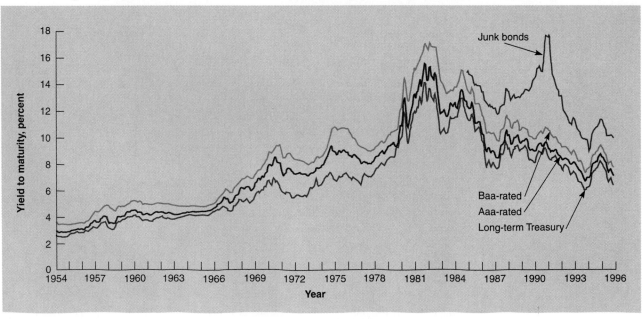

[5]Because the Federal Reserve requires banks in the United States to keep interest-free reserves, there is in effect a tax on dollar deposits in the United States. Eurodollar deposits are free of this tax and therefore banks can offer the borrower slightly lower interest rates on eurodollars.

eurobond: Bond that is marketed internationally.

If a firm wants to make an issue of long-term bonds, it can choose to do so in the United States. Alternatively, it can sell the bonds to investors in several countries. Such bonds are known as **eurobonds.** Eurobonds are usually sold to the London branches of the major international banks, which then resell them to investors throughout the world.

Public versus Private Placements. Publicly issued bonds are sold to anyone who wishes to buy and, once they have been issued, they can be freely traded in the securities markets. In a **private placement,** the issue is sold directly to a small number of banks, insurance companies, or other investment institutions. Privately placed bonds cannot be resold to individuals in the United States but only to other qualified institutional investors. However, there is increasingly active trading *among* these investors.

private placement: Sale of securities to a limited number of investors without a public offering.

We will have more to say about the difference between public issues and private placements in the next chapter.

Protective Covenants. When investors lend to a company, they know that they might not get their money back. But they expect that the company will use their money well and not take unreasonable risks. To help ensure this, lenders usually impose a number of conditions, or **protective covenants,** on companies that borrow from them. An honest firm is willing to accept these conditions because it knows that they enable the firm to borrow at a reasonable rate of interest.

protective covenant: Restriction on a firm to protect bondholders.

Companies that borrow in moderation are less likely to get into difficulties than those that are up to the gunwales in debt. So lenders usually restrict the amount of extra debt that the firm can issue. Lenders are also eager to prevent others from pushing ahead of them in the queue if trouble occurs. So they will not allow the company to create new debt that is senior to them or to put aside assets for other lenders.

Another possible hazard for lenders is that the company will pay a bumper dividend to the shareholders, leaving no cash for the debtholders. Therefore, lenders sometimes limit the size of the dividends that can be paid.

See box p. 354

The story of Marriott in the nearby box shows what can happen when bondholders are not sufficiently careful about the conditions they impose. In the wake of the large losses suffered by Marriott bondholders, several observers predicted that investors would demand more restrictive bond covenants in future transactions.

> ▶ **Self-Test 12.6**

In 1988 RJR Nabisco, the food and tobacco giant, had $5 billion of A-rated debt outstanding. In that year the company was taken over, and $19 billion of debt was issued and used to buy back equity. The debt ratio skyrocketed, and the debt was downgraded to BB. The holders of the previously issued debt were furious, and one filed a lawsuit claiming that RJR had violated an *implicit* obligation not to undertake major financing changes at the expense of existing bondholders. Why did these bondholders believe they had been harmed by the massive issue of new debt? What type of *explicit* restriction would you have wanted if you had been one of the original bondholders?

A Debt by Any Other Name. The word *debt* sounds straightforward, but companies enter into a number of financial arrangements that look suspiciously like debt yet are treated differently in the accounts. Some of these obligations are easily identifiable. For example, accounts payable are simply obligations to pay for goods that have already been delivered and are therefore like a short-term debt.

Marriott Plan Enrages Holders of Its Bonds

Marriott Corp. has infuriated bond investors with a restructuring plan that may be a new way for companies to pull the rug out from under bondholders.

Prices of Marriott's existing bonds have plunged as much as 30% in the past two days in the wake of the hotel and food-services company's announcement that it plans to separate into two companies, one burdened with virtually all of Marriott's debt.

On Monday, Marriott said that it will divide its operations into two separate businesses. One, Marriott International Inc., is a healthy company that will manage Marriott's vast hotel chain; it will get most of the old company's revenue, a larger share of the cash flow and will be nearly debt-free.

The second business, called Host Marriott Corp., is a debt-laden company that will own Marriott hotels along with other real estate and retain essentially all of the old Marriott's $3 billion of debt.

The announcement stunned and infuriated bondholders, who watched nervously as the value of their Marriott bonds tumbled and as Moody's Investors Service Inc. downgraded the bond to the junk-bond category from investment-grade.

Price Plunge

In trading, Marriott's 10% bonds that mature in 2012, which Marriott sold to investors just six months ago, were quoted yesterday at about 80 cents on the dollar, down from 110 Friday. The price decline translates into a stunning loss of $300 for a bond with a $1,000 face amount.

Marriott officials concede that the company's spinoff plan penalizes bondholders. However, the company notes that, like all public corporations, its fiduciary duty is to stockholders, not bondholders. Indeed, Marriott's stock jumped 12% Monday. (It fell a bit yesterday.)

Bond investors and analysts worry that if the Marriott spinoff goes through, other companies will soon follow suit by separating debt-laden units from the rest of the company. "Any company that fears it has underperforming divisions that are dragging down its stock price is a possible candidate" for such a restructuring, says Dorothy K. Lee, an assistant vice president at Moody's.

If the trend heats up, investors said, the Marriott restructuring could be the worst news for corporate bondholders since RJR Nabisco Inc.'s managers shocked investors in 1987 by announcing they were taking the company private in a record $25 billion leveraged buyout. The move, which loaded RJR with debt and tanked the value of RJR bonds, triggered a deep slump in prices of many investment-grade corporate bonds as investors backed away from the market.

Strong Covenants May Re-Emerge

Some analysts say the move by Marriott may trigger the re-emergence of strong covenants, or written protections, in future corporate bond issues to protect bondholders against such restructurings as the one being engineered by Marriott. In the wake of the RJR buy-out, many investors demanded stronger covenants in new corporate bond issues.

Some investors blame themselves for not demanding stronger covenants. "It's our own fault," said Robert Hickey, a bond fund manager at Van Kampen Merritt. In their rush to buy bonds in an effort to lock in yields, many investors have allowed companies to sell bonds with covenants that have been "slim to none," Mr. Hickey said.

lease: Long-term rental agreement.

Other arrangements are not so easy to spot. For example, instead of borrowing money to buy equipment, many companies **lease** or rent it on a long-term basis. In this case the firm promises to make a series of payments to the lessor (the owner of the equipment). This is just like the obligation to make payments on an outstanding loan. What if the firm can't make the payments? The lessor can then take back the equipment, which is precisely what would happen if the firm had *borrowed* money from the lessor, using the equipment as collateral for the loan.

▶ **Example 12.1**　*The Terms of Mobil's Bond Issue*

Now that you are familiar with some of the jargon, you might like to look at an example of a bond issue. Table 12.4 is a summary of the terms of a bond issue by Mobil taken from *Moody's Industrial Manual*. We have added some explanatory notes.

Innovation in the Debt Market

We have discussed domestic bonds and eurobonds, fixed-rate and floating-rate loans, secured and unsecured loans, senior and junior loans, and much more. You might think that this gives you all the choice you need. Yet almost every day companies and their advisers dream up a new type of debt. Here are some examples of unusual bonds.

Indexed bonds make payments tied to some price index. For example, in high-inflation countries such as Brazil, payments on most debt are indexed to the rate of inflation. Although the United States has a low rate of inflation, the Treasury Department decided to sell inflation-indexed bonds in 1997. A few firms in the United States have tied payments to the price of a particular commodity. For instance, in 1986 Standard Oil issued a zero-coupon note maturing in 1992. At maturity the lenders were promised at least the $1000 face value, and, in addition, they were entitled to a bonus of 200 times the amount by which the oil price exceeded $25 a barrel. The bond gave Standard Oil protection against the vagaries of oil prices. If oil prices were depressed in 1992, it was likely that the firm's income would be low. But in this case, the cost of debt would be low also. Likewise, Mexico, which is a large oil producer, has issued billions of dollars worth of bonds that provide an extra payoff if oil prices remain above $20 a barrel. Like Standard Oil, Mexico reasons that the oil-linked bonds hedge its income risk. If the price of oil is high, it can afford the higher payments on the bond. If oil prices are low, its interest payments also will be lower.

Reverse floaters are floating-rate bonds that pay a higher rate of interest when other interest rates fall and a lower rate when other rates rise. Reverse floaters are riskier than normal bonds. When interest rates rise, the prices of all bonds fall, but the prices of reverse floaters suffer a double whammy because the coupon payments on the bonds fall as the discount rate rises. In 1994 Orange County, California, learned this the hard way, when it invested heavily in reverse floaters. Robert Citron, the treasurer, was betting that interest rates would fall. He was wrong; interest rates rose sharply and partly as a result of its investment in reverse floaters, the county lost $1.7 billion.

Pay in kind bonds (PIKs) make regular interest payments, but in the early years of the bonds' life, the issuer can choose to pay interest in the form of either cash or more bonds with the equivalent face value. This gives the firm a valuable option. If it falls on hard times and is strapped for cash, it can hand over more bonds to the investor rather than hard cash. Of course, the last thing that the investor wants is more bonds in a cash-starved firm.

These three examples illustrate the great variety of potential security designs. As long as you can convince investors of its attractions, you can issue a callable, subordinated, floating-rate bond denominated in deutschemarks. Rather than combining features of existing securities, you may be able to create an entirely new one. We can imagine a copper mining company issuing preferred shares on which the

Table 12.4

Mobil's bond issue

Comment	Description of Bond
1. A debenture is an unsecured bond.	**Mobil Corp. debentures 8s, due 2032:**
2. Coupon is 8 percent. Thus each bond makes an annual interest payment of .08 × $1000 = $80.	
3. Moody's bond rating is Aa, the second highest quality rating.	**Rating—Aa**
4. Mobil is authorized to issue (and has outstanding) $250 million of the bonds.	AUTH. $250,000,000: outstg. $250,000,000.
5. The bond was issued in October 1991 and is to be repaid in August 2032.	DATED October 30, 1991. DUE Aug. 12, 2032.
6. Interest is payable at 6-month intervals on February and August 12.	INTEREST F&A 12.
7. A trustee is appointed to look after the bondholders' interest.	TRUSTEE Chemical Bank.
8. The bonds are registered. The registrar keeps a record of who owns the bonds, so you don't need to worry about losing the bond certificate.	DENOMINATION Fully registered. $1,000 and integral multiples thereof. Transferable and exchangable without service charge.
9. The bond can be held in multiples of $1,000.	
10. From 2003 Mobil can call (buy back) the bond at prespecified prices.	CALLABLE As a whole or in part at any time on or after Aug. 2002 at the option of the Company on at least 30 but not more that 60 days' notice to each Aug. 11 as follows:

2003	105.007	2004	104.756
2005	104.566	2006	104.256
2007	104.005	2008	103.755
2009	103.505	2010	103.254
2011	103.004	2012	102.754
2013	102.503	2014	102.253
2015	102.003	2016	101.752
2017	101.502	2018	101.252
2019	101.001	2020	100.751
2021	100.501	2022	100.250

and thereafter at 100 plus accrued interest.

Comment	Description of Bond
11. The bonds are not secured, that is, no assets have been set aside to protect the bondholders in the event of default.	SECURITY Not secured. Ranks equally with all other unsecured and unsubordinated indebtedness of the Company. Company or any affiliate will not create as security for any indebtedness for borrowed money, any mortgage, pledge, security interest or lien on any stock or indebtedness of any affiliate . . . without effectively providing that the debentures shall be secured equally and ratably with such indebtedness.
12. However, if Mobil sets aside assets to protect any *other* bondholders, the debenture will also be secured on these assets.	
	LISTED On New York Stock Exchange.
13. The bonds were sold at a price of 99.51 percent of face value. After deducting the cost of the issue, the company received $991.10 per bond. The bonds could be bought from the listed investment banks.	OFFERED: $250,000,000 at 99.51 plus accrued interest (proceeds to Co. 99.11) on Aug. 5, 1992 thru Merrill Lynch & Co., Donaldson, Lufkin & Jenrette Securities Corp., Paine Webber, Inc., Prudential Securities, Inc., Smith Barney, Harris Upham & Co., Inc. and associates.

dividend fluctuates with the world copper price. We know of no such security, but it is perfectly legal to issue it and—who knows?—it might generate considerable interest among investors.[6]

Variety is intrinsically good. People have different tastes, levels of wealth, rates of tax, and so on. Why not offer them a choice? Of course the problem is the expense of designing and marketing new securities. But if you can think of a new security that will appeal to investors, you may be able to issue it on especially favorable terms and thus increase the value of your company.

12.4 Convertible Securities

warrant: Right to buy shares from a company at a stipulated price before a set date.

We have seen that companies sometimes have the option to repay an issue of bonds before maturity. There are also cases in which *investors* have an option. The most dramatic case is provided by a **warrant,** which is *nothing but* an option. Companies often issue warrants and bonds in a package.

▶ **Example 12.2**

Warrants

Macaw Bill wishes to make a bond issue, it could include some warrants as a "sweetener." Each warrant might allow you to purchase one share of Macaw stock at a price of $50 any time during the next 5 years. If Macaw's stock performs well, that option could turn out to be very valuable. For instance, if the stock price at the end of the 5 years is $80, then you pay the company $50 and receive in exchange a share worth $80. Of course, an investment in warrants also has its perils. If the price of Macaw stock fails to rise above $50, then the warrants expire worthless. ◀

convertible bond: Bond that the holder may exchange for a specified amount of another security.

A **convertible bond** gives its owner the option to exchange the bond for a predetermined number of common shares. The convertible bondholder hopes that the company's share price will zoom up so that the bond can be converted at a big profit. But if the shares zoom down, there is no obligation to convert; the bondholder remains just that. Not surprisingly, investors value this option to keep the bond or exchange it for shares, and therefore a convertible bond sells at a higher price than a comparable bond that is not convertible.

The convertible is rather like a package of a bond and a warrant. But there is an important difference: when the owners of a convertible wish to exercise their options to buy shares, they do not pay cash—they just exchange the bond for shares of the stock.

Companies may also issue convertible preferred stock. In this case the investor receives preferred stock with fixed dividend payments but has the option to exchange this preferred stock for the company's common stock. The preferred stock issued by Mobil is convertible into common stock.

These examples do not exhaust the options encountered by the financial manager. In fact once you read Chapter 23 and learn how to analyze options, you will find that they are all around you.

---

[6]However, our copper bond seems humdrum compared with some bonds that have been issued. For example, in 1990 the Swedish company Electrolux issued a bond whose final payment depends on whether there has been an earthquake in Japan.

12.5 *Patterns of Corporate Financing*

That completes our tour of corporate securities. You may feel like the tourist who has just gone through 12 cathedrals in 5 days. But there will be plenty of time in later chapters for reflection and analysis. For now, let's look at how firms use these sources of finance.

> **Firms have two broad sources of cash. They can raise money from external sources by an issue of debt or equity. Or they can plow back part of their profits. When the firm retains cash rather than paying the money out as dividends, it is increasing shareholders' investment in the firm.**

internally generated funds: Cash reinvested in the firm: depreciation plus earnings not paid out as dividends.

Figure 12.2 summarizes the sources of capital for United States corporations. The most striking aspect of this figure is the dominance of **internally generated funds,** defined as depreciation plus earnings that are not paid out as dividends.[7] During the 1980s internally generated cash covered approximately three-quarters of firms' capital requirements.

Do Firms Rely Too Heavily on Internal Funds?

Gordon Donaldson, in a survey of corporate debt policies, encountered several firms which acknowledged "that it was their long-term object to hold to a rate of growth which was consistent with their capacity to generate funds internally." A number of other firms appeared to think less hard about expenditure proposals that could be financed internally.[8]

At first glance, this behavior doesn't make sense. As we have already noted, retained profits are additional capital invested by shareholders and represent, in effect, a compulsory issue of shares. A firm that retains $1 million could have paid out the cash as dividends and then sold new common shares to raise the same amount of additional

Figure 12.2

Sources of funds, nonfinancial corporate sector.

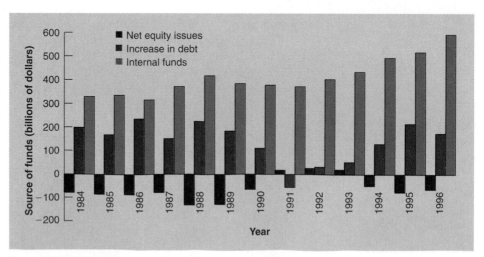

Source: *Flow of Funds Accounts of the United States,* Board of Governors of the Federal Reserve System, 1997.

[7]Remember that depreciation is a noncash expense.

[8]See G. Donaldson, *Corporate Debt Capacity,* Division of Research, Graduate School of Business Administration, Harvard University, Boston, 1961, Chapter 3, especially pp. 51–56.

capital. The opportunity cost of capital ought not to depend on whether the project is financed by retained profits or a new stock issue.

Why then do managers have an apparent preference for financing by retained earnings? Perhaps managers are simply taking the line of least resistance, dodging the discipline of the securities markets.

Think back to Chapter 1, where we pointed out that a firm is a team effort involving managers, shareholders, debtholders, and so on. The shareholders and debtholders would like to monitor management to make sure that it is pulling its weight and truly maximizing market value. It is costly for individual investors to keep checks on management. However, large financial institutions are specialists in monitoring, so when the firm goes to the bank for a large loan or makes a public issue of stocks or bonds, managers know that they had better have all the answers. If they want a quiet life, they will avoid going to the capital market to raise money and they will retain sufficient earnings to be able to meet unanticipated demands for cash.

We do not mean to paint managers in general as loafers. There are also rational reasons for relying on internally generated funds. The costs of new securities are avoided, for example. Moreover, the announcement of a new equity issue is usually bad news for investors, who worry that the decision signals lower profits.[9] Raising equity capital from internal sources avoids the costs and the bad omens associated with equity issues.

▶ **Self-Test 12.7**   "Since internal funds provide the bulk of industry's needs for capital, the securities markets serve little function." Does the speaker have a point?

External Sources of Capital

Of course firms don't rely exclusively on internal funds. They also issue securities and retire them, sometimes in big volume. For example, in the early 1980s Mobil dramatically increased its reliance on debt by issuing considerable amounts of bonds. In 1983 alone, the amount of its outstanding debt more than doubled. After 1984, however, Mobil gradually reduced its borrowing by buying back portions of outstanding debt issues.

During the early 1980s, Mobil actually bought back shares from the public. Between 1981 and 1982, for example, the number of shares outstanding fell by a bit more than 6 percent. So over this period, Mobil had *negative* net stock issues.

Figure 12.3 shows the ratio of the book value of Mobil's long-term debt to both the book value and market value of equity. The ratios peaked in 1984 when Mobil had nearly as much long-term debt as equity outstanding. However, as debt was paid off and equity slowly increased, the firm came full circle, reestablishing the debt ratios of the early part of the decade.

If you look back at Figure 12.2, you will see that Mobil was not alone in its buildup of debt in the early 1980s. The figure shows that for most of the decade corporate

---

[9]Managers do have insiders' insights and naturally are tempted to issue stock when the stock price looks good to them, that is, when they are less optimistic than outside investors. The outside investors realize all this and will buy a new issue only at a discount from the preannouncement price. Stock issues are discussed further in the next chapter.

Figure 12.3

Debt-equity ratios for Mobil Corporation.

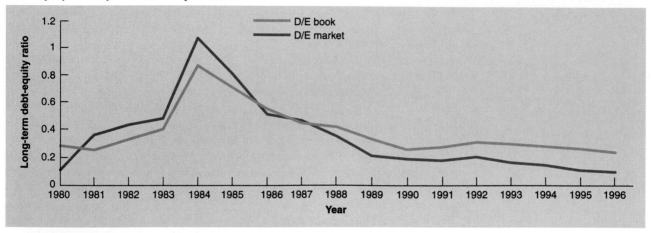

America was making large issues of debt and using part of the money to buy back common stock.

The net effect of these financing policies is shown in Figure 12.4, which confirms that debt-to-asset ratios for United States firms rose noticeably in the 1980s after declining for much of the 1970s.

United States corporations are carrying a lot more debt than they used to. Should we be worried? It is true that higher debt ratios mean that more companies are likely to fall into financial distress when a serious recession hits the economy. But all companies live with this risk to some degree, and it does not follow that less risk is better. Finding the optimal debt ratio is like finding the optimal speed limit: we can agree that accidents at 30 miles per hour are less dangerous, other things being equal, than accidents at 60 miles per hour, but we do not therefore set the national speed limit at 30. Speed has benefits as well as risks. So does debt, as we will see in Chapter 14.

Figure 12.4

Debt-asset ratio, nonfinancial corporate sector.

Summary

1. As owners of the corporation, the common stockholders elect the board of directors and vote on major issues. Companies may raise money from shareholders by issuing more shares. They also raise money indirectly by plowing back money that could otherwise have been paid out as dividends.
2. Preferred stock offers a fixed dividend but the company has the discretion not to pay it. It can't, however, then pay a dividend on the common stock. Despite its name, preferred stock is not a popular source of finance, but it is useful in special situations.
3. When companies issue debt, they promise to make a series of interest payments and to repay the principal. However, this liability is limited. Stockholders have the right to default on their obligation and to hand over the assets to the debtholders. Unlike dividends on common stock and preferred stock, the interest payments on debt are regarded as a cost and therefore they are paid out of before-tax income. Here are some of the various forms of debt:
   - *Fixed-rate* and *floating-rate* debt
   - *Funded* (long-term) and *unfunded* (short-term) debt
   - *Callable* and *sinking-fund* debt
   - *Senior* and *subordinated* debt
   - *Secured* and *unsecured* debt
   - *Investment grade* and *junk* debt
   - *Domestic* debt and *eurobonds*
   - *Publicly traded* debt and *private placements*
4. The fourth source of finance consists of options and optionlike securities. The simplest option is a warrant, which gives its holder the right to buy a share from the firm at a set price by a set date. Warrants are often sold in combination with other securities. Convertible bonds give their holder the right to convert the bond to shares. They therefore resemble a package of straight debt and a warrant.
5. Internally generated cash is the principal source of company funds. Some people worry about that; they think that if management does not go to the trouble of raising money, it may be profligate in spending it.
6. For a large part of the 1980s, net equity issues were *negative;* that is, companies repurchased more equity than they issued. At the same time companies issued large quantities of debt. The result is that debt ratios increased during the 1980s. Some find this a cause for concern, though it so far appears that reliance on debt financing has moderated in the 1990s.

Key Terms

treasury stock	cumulative voting	callable bond
issued shares	proxy contest	subordinated debt
outstanding shares	preferred stock	secured debt
authorized share capital	net worth	investment grade
par value	floating-rate preferred	junk bond
additional paid-in capital	prime rate	eurodollars
retained earnings	funded debt	eurobond
majority voting	sinking fund	private placement
protective covenant	warrant	internally generated funds
lease		convertible bond

Problems

1. **Equity Accounts.** The authorized share capital of the Alfred Cake Company is 100,000 shares. The equity is currently shown in the company's books as follows:

Common stock ($1.00 par value)	$ 60,000
Additional paid-in capital	10,000
Retained earnings	30,000
Common equity	100,000
Treasury stock (2000 shares)	5,000
Not common equity	95,000

   a. How many shares are issued?

   b. How many are outstanding?

   c. How many more shares can be issued without the approval of shareholders?

2. **Equity Accounts.**

   a. Look back at problem 1. Suppose that the company issues 10,000 shares at $5 a share. Which of the above figures would change?

   b. What would happen to the company's books if instead it bought back 1,000 shares at $5 per share?

3. **Equity Accounts.** Common Products has just made its first issue of stock. It raised $2 million by selling 200,000 shares of stock to the public. These are the only shares outstanding. The par value of each share was $1.50. Fill in the following table:

Common shares (par value)	_____
Additional paid-in capital	_____
Retained earnings	_____
Net common equity	$2,500,000

4. **Preferred Stock.** In what ways is preferred stock like long-term debt? In what ways is it like common stock?

5. **Voting for Directors.** If there are 10 directors to be elected and a shareholder owns 90 shares, indicate the maximum number of votes that he or she can cast for a favorite candidate under

   a. majority voting

   b. cumulative voting

6. **Voting for Directors.** The shareholders of the Pickwick Paper Company need to elect five directors. There are 400,000 shares outstanding. How many shares do you need to own to *ensure* that you can elect at least one director if the company has

   a. majority voting

   b. cumulative voting

   Hint: How many votes in total will be cast? How many votes are required to ensure that at least one-fifth of votes are cast for your choice?

7. **Financing Terms.** Fill in the blanks by choosing the appropriate term from the following list: *lease, funded, floating-rate, eurobond, convertible, subordinated, call, sinking fund, prime rate, private placement, public issue, senior, unfunded, eurodollar rate, warrant, debentures, term loan.*

   a. Debt maturing in more than 1 year is often called _____ debt.

   b. An issue of bonds that is sold simultaneously in several countries is called a(n) _____.

 c. If a lender ranks behind the firm's general creditors in the event of default, the loan is said to be _____.

 d. In many cases a firm is obliged to make regular contributions to a(n) _____, which is then used to repurchase bonds.

 e. Most bonds give the firm the right to repurchase or _____ the bonds at specified prices.

 f. The benchmark interest rate that banks charge to their customers with good to excellent credit is generally termed the _____.

 g. The interest rate on bank loans is often tied to short-term interest rates. These loans are usually called _____ loans.

 h. Where there is a(n) _____, securities are sold directly to a small group of institutional investors. These securities cannot be resold to individual investors. In the case of a(n) _____, debt can be freely bought and sold by individual investors.

 i. A long-term rental agreement is called a(n) _____.

 j. A(n) _____ bond can be exchanged for shares of the issuing corporation.

 k. A(n) _____ gives its owner the right to buy shares in the issuing company at a predetermined price.

8. **Financing Trends.** True or false? Explain

 a. In several recent years, nonfinancial corporations in the United States have repurchased more stock than they have issued.

 b. A corporation pays tax on only 30 percent of the common or prefered dividends it receives from other corporations.

 c. Because of the tax advantage, a large fraction of preferred shares is held by corporations.

9. **Equity Accounts.** Look back at Table 12.2.

 a. Suppose that Mobil issues 10 million shares at $110 a share. Rework Table 12.2 to show the company's equity after the issue.

 b. Suppose that Mobil *subsequently* repurchased 500,000 shares at $120 a share. Rework part (a) to show the effect of the further change.

10. **Preferred Stock.** Preferred stock of financially strong firms sometimes sells at lower yields than the bonds of those firms. For weaker firms, the preferred stock has a higher yield. What might explain this pattern?

11. **Income Bonds.** *Income bonds* are unusual. Interest payments on such bonds may be skipped or deferred if the firm's income is insufficient to make the payment. In what way are these bonds like preferred stock? Why might a firm choose to issue an income bond instead of preferred stock?

12. **Bond Yields.** Other things equal, will the following provisions increase or decrease the yield to maturity at which a firm can issue a bond?

 a. A call provision

 b. A restriction on further borrowing

 c. A provision of specific collateral for the bond

 d. An option to convert the bonds into shares

13. **Protective Covenants.** Why might a bond agreement limit the amount of assets that the firm can lease?

Solutions to Self-Test Questions

12.1 Par value of common shares must be $1 × 100,000 shares = $100,000. Additional paid-in capital is ($15 − $1) × 100,000 = $1,400,000. Since book value is $4,500,000, retained earnings must be $3,000,000. Therefore, the accounts look like this:

Common shares ($1.00 par value per share)	100,000
Additional paid-in capital	1,400,000
Retained earnings	3,000,000
Net common equity	$4,500,000

12.2 Book value is $10 million. At a discount rate of 10 percent, the market value of the firm ought to be $2 million × 20-year annuity factor at 10% = $17 million, which exceeds book value. At a discount rate of 20 percent, market value falls to $9.7 million, which is below book value.

12.3 The corporation's after-tax yield on the bonds is 10% − (.35 × 10%) = 6.5%. The after-tax yield on the preferred is 8% − [.35 × (.30 × 8%)] = 7.16%. The preferred stock provides the higher after-tax rate despite its lower before-tax rate. For the individual, the tax rate on both the preferred and the bond is equal to 35 percent, so the investment with the higher before-tax rate also provides the higher after-tax rate.

12.4 Because the coupon on floating-rate debt adjusts periodically to current market conditions, the bondholder is less vulnerable to changes in market yields. The coupon rate paid by the bond is not locked in for as long a period of time. Therefore, prices of floaters should be less sensitive to changes in market interest rates.

12.5 The callable bond will sell at a lower price. Investors will not pay as much for the callable bond since they know that the firm may call it away from them if interest rates fall. Thus they know that their capital gains potential is limited, which makes the bond less valuable. If both bonds are to sell at par value, the callable bond must pay a higher coupon rate as compensation to the investor for the firm's right to call the bond.

12.6 The extra debt makes it more likely that the firm will not be able to make good on its promised payments to its creditors. If the new debt is not junior to the already-issued debt, then the original bondholders suffer a loss when their bonds become more susceptible to default risk. A protective covenant limiting the amount of new debt that the firm can issue would have prevented this problem. Investors, having witnessed the problems of the RJR bondholders, generally demanded the covenant on future debt issues.

12.7 Capital markets provide liquidity for investors. Because individual stockholders can always lay their hands on cash by selling shares, they are prepared to invest in companies that retain earnings rather than pay them out as dividends. Well-functioning capital markets allow the firm to serve all its stockholders simply by maximizing value. Capital markets also provide managers with information. Without this information, it would be very difficult to determine opportunity costs of capital or to assess financial performance.

Planet Hollywood shares are offered to investors
Ethan Miller/Reuters/Archive Photos

How Corporations Issue Securities

Chapter 13

Bill Gates and Paul Allen founded Microsoft in 1975, when both were around 20 years old. Eleven years later Microsoft shares were sold to the public for $21 a share and immediately zoomed to $35. The largest shareholder was Bill Gates, whose shares in Microsoft then were worth $350 million.

In 1976 two college dropouts, Steve Jobs and Steve Wozniak, sold their most valuable possessions, a van and a couple of calculators, and used the cash to start manufacturing computers in a garage. In 1980, when Apple Computer went public, the shares were offered to investors at $22 and jumped to $36. At that point, the shares owned by the company's two founders were worth $414 million.

Such stories illustrate that the most important asset of a new firm may be a good idea. But that is not all you need. To take an idea from the drawing board to a prototype and through to large-scale production requires ever greater amounts of capital.

To get a new company off the ground, entrepreneurs may rely on their own savings and personal bank loans. But this is unlikely to be sufficient to build a successful enterprise. *Venture capital* firms specialize in providing new equity capital to help firms over the awkward adolescent period before they are large enough to "go public." In the first part of this chapter we will explain how venture capital firms do this.

If the firm continues to be successful, there is likely to come a time when it needs to tap a wider source of capital. At this point it will make its first public issue of common stock. This is known as an *initial public offering,* or *IPO.* In the second section of the chapter we will describe what is involved in an IPO.

A company's initial public offering is seldom its last. In Chapter 12 we saw that internally generated cash is not usually sufficient to satisfy the firm's needs. Established companies make up the deficit by issuing more equity or debt. The remainder of this chapter looks at this process.

After studying this chapter you should be able to

▶ Understand how venture capital firms design successful deals.

▶ Understand how firms make initial public offerings and the costs of such offerings.

▶ Know what is involved when established firms make a general cash offer or a private placement of securities.

▶ Explain the role of the underwriter in an issue of securities.

13.1 Venture Capital

You have taken a big step. With a couple of friends, you have formed a corporation to open a number of fast-food outlets, offering innovative combinations of national dishes such as sushi with sauerkraut, curry Bolognese, and chow mein with Yorkshire pudding. Breaking into the fast-food business costs money, but, after pooling your savings and borrowing to the hilt from the bank, you have raised $100,000 and purchased 1 million shares in the new company. At this *zero-stage* investment, your company's assets are $100,000 plus the *idea* for your new product.

That $100,000 is enough to get the business off the ground, but if the idea takes off, you will need more capital to pay for new restaurants. You therefore decide to look for an investor who is prepared to back an untried company in return for part of the profits. Equity capital in young businesses is known as **venture capital** and it is provided by specialist venture capital firms, wealthy individuals, and investment institutions such as pension funds.

venture capital: Money invested to finance a new firm.

Most entrepreneurs are able to spin a plausible yarn about their company. But it is as hard to convince a venture capitalist to invest in your business as it is to get a first novel published. Your first step is to prepare a *business plan*. This describes your product, the potential market, the production method, and the resources—time, money, employees, plant, and equipment—needed for success. It helps if you can point to the fact that you are prepared to put your money where your mouth is. By staking all your savings in the company, you *signal* your faith in the business.

The venture capital company knows that the success of a new business depends on the effort its managers put in. Therefore, it will try to structure any deal so that you have a strong incentive to work hard. For example, if you agree to accept a modest salary (and look forward instead to increasing the value of your investment in the company's stock), the venture capital company knows you will be committed to working hard. However, if you insist on a watertight employment contract and a fat salary, you won't find it easy to raise venture capital.

You are unlikely to persuade a venture capitalist to give you as much money as you need all at once. Rather, the firm will probably give you enough to reach the next major checkpoint. Suppose you can convince the venture capital company to buy 1 million new shares for $.50 each. This will give it one-half ownership of the firm: it owns 1 million shares and you and your friends also own 1 million shares. Because the venture capitalist is paying $500,000 for a claim to half your firm, it is placing a $1 million value on the business. After this *first-stage* financing, your company's balance sheet looks like this:

FIRST-STAGE MARKET VALUE BALANCE SHEET
(figures in millions)

Assets		Liabilities and Shareholders' Equity	
Cash from new equity	$ .5	New equity from venture capital	$ .5
Other assets	.5	Your original equity	.5
Value	$1.0	Value	$1.0

▶ Self-Test 13.1

Why might the venture capital company prefer to put up only part of the funds up-front? Would this affect the amount of effort put in by you, the entrepreneur? Is your willingness to accept only part of the venture capital that will eventually be needed a good signal of the likely success of the venture?

Suppose that 2 years later your business has grown to the point at which it needs a further injection of equity. This *second-stage* financing might involve the issue of a further 1 million shares at $1 each. Some of these shares might be bought by the original backers and some by other venture capital firms. The balance sheet after the new financing would then be as follows:

SECOND-STAGE MARKET VALUE BALANCE SHEET
(figures in millions)

Assets		Liabilities and Shareholders' Equity	
Cash from new equity	$1.0	New equity from second-stage financing	$1.0
Other assets	2.0	Equity from first stage	1.0
		Your original equity	1.0
Value	$3.0	Value	$3.0

Notice that the value of the initial 1 million shares owned by you and your friends has now been marked up to $1 million. Does this begin to sound like a money machine? It was so only because you have made a success of the business and new investors are prepared to pay $1 to buy a share in the business. When you started out, it wasn't clear that sushi and sauerkraut would catch on. If it hadn't caught on, the venture capital firm could have refused to put up more funds.

You are not yet in a position to cash in on your investment, but your gain is real. The second-stage investors have paid $1 million for a one-third share in the company. (There are now 3 million shares outstanding, and the second-stage investors hold 1 million shares.) Therefore, at least these impartial observers—who are willing to back up their opinions with a large investment—must have decided that the company was worth at least $3 million. Your one-third share is therefore also worth $1 million.

For every 10 first-stage venture capital investments, only two or three may survive as successful, self-sufficient businesses, and only one may pay off big.[1] From these statistics come two rules of success in venture capital investment. First, don't shy away from uncertainty; accept a low probability of success. But don't buy into a business unless you can see the *chance* of a big, public company in a profitable market. There's no sense taking a big risk unless the reward is big if you win. Second, cut your losses; identify losers early, and, if you can't fix the problem—by replacing management, for example—don't throw good money after bad.

The same advice holds for any backer of a risky startup business—after all, only a fraction of new businesses are funded by card-carrying venture capitalists. Some startups are funded directly by managers or by their friends and families. Some grow using bank loans and reinvested earnings. But if your startup combines high risk, sophisticated technology, and substantial investment, you will probably try to find venture-capital financing.

13.2 The Initial Public Offering

Very few new businesses make it big, but venture capitalists keep sane by reminding themselves of the success stories—the investors who got in on the ground floor of firms like Federal Express, Intel, and Lotus Development Corporation.[2]

If a startup is successful, the firm may need to raise a considerable amount of capital to gear up its production capacity. At this point, it needs more capital than can

---

[1] One study of venture capital investments between 1960 and 1975 found that about one in six were total failures. On the other hand, thanks to a few outstanding successes, the average return was about 19 percent a year. See B. Huntsman and J. P. Hoban, Jr., "Investment in New Enterprise: Some Empirical Observations on Risk, Return, and Market Structure," *Financial Management* 9 (Summer 1980), pp. 44–51.

[2] The founder of Lotus took a class from one of the authors. Within 5 years the student had become a multimillionaire. Perhaps that will make you feel better about the cost of this book.

comfortably be provided by a small number of individuals or venture capitalists. The firm decides to sell shares to the public to raise the necessary funds.

> A firm is said to *go public* when it sells its first issue of shares in a general offering to investors. This first sale of stock is called an *initial public offering,* or *IPO.*

initial public offering (IPO): First offering of stock to the general public.

An IPO is called a *primary* offering when new shares are sold to raise additional cash for the company. It is a *secondary* offering when the company's founders and the venture capitalist cash in on some of their gains by selling shares. A secondary offer therefore is no more than a sale of shares from the early investors in the firm to new investors, and the cash raised in a secondary offer does not flow to the company. Of course, IPOs can be and commonly are both primary and secondary: the firm raises new cash at the same time that some of the already-existing shares in the firm are sold to the public. Some of the biggest secondary offerings have involved governments selling off stock in nationalized enterprises. For example, the Japanese government raised $12.6 billion by selling its stock in Nippon Telegraph and Telephone and the British government took in $9 billion from its sale of British Gas.

Arranging a Public Issue

Once a firm decides to go public, the first task is to select the underwriters.

underwriter: Firm that buys an issue of securities from a company and resells it to the public.

> *Underwriters* are investment banking firms that act as financial midwives to a new issue. Usually they play a triple role—first providing the company with procedural and financial advice, then buying the stock, and finally reselling it to the public.

A small IPO may have only one underwriter, but larger issues usually require a syndicate of underwriters who buy the issue and resell it. For example, the initial public offering by Microsoft involved a total of 114 underwriters.

In the typical underwriting arrangement, called a *firm commitment,* the underwriters buy the securities from the firm and then resell them to the public. The underwriters receive payment in the form of a **spread**—that is, they are allowed to sell the shares at a slightly higher price than they paid for them. But the underwriters also accept the risk that they won't be able to sell the stock at the agreed offering price. If that happens, they will be stuck with unsold shares and must get the best price they can for them. In the more risky cases, the underwriter may not be willing to enter into a firm commitment and handles the issue on a *best efforts* basis. In this case the underwriter agrees to sell as much of the issue as possible but does not guarantee the sale of the entire issue.

spread: Difference between public offer price and price paid by underwriter.

Before any stock can be sold to the public, the company must register the stock with the Securities and Exchange Commission (SEC). This involves preparation of a detailed and sometimes cumbersome registration statement, which contains information about the proposed financing and the firm's history, existing business, and plans for the future. The SEC does not evaluate the wisdom of an investment in the firm but it does check the registration statement for accuracy and completeness. The firm must also comply with the "blue-sky" laws of each state, so named because they seek to protect the public against firms that fraudulently promise the blue sky to investors.[3]

[3]Sometimes states go beyond blue-sky laws in their efforts to protect their residents. In 1980 when Apple Computer Inc. made its first public issue, the Massachusetts state government decided the offering was too risky for its residents and therefore banned the sale of the shares to investors in the state. The state relented later, after the issue was out and the price had risen. Massachusetts investors obviously did not appreciate this "protection."

prospectus: Formal summary that provides information on an issue of securities.

The first part of the registration statement is distributed to the public in the form of a preliminary **prospectus.** Such a prospectus is generally known as a *red herring* because of the statement printed in red ink, denying that the firm is trying to sell securities before the SEC has approved the registration statement. A final copy of the prospectus is sent to all investors in the issue.

One function of the prospectus is to warn investors about the risks involved in any investment in the firm. Some investors have joked that if they read prospectuses carefully, they would never dare buy any new issue. The appendix to this chapter is a possible prospectus for your fast-food business.

The company and its underwriters also need to set the issue price. To gauge how much the stock is worth, they may undertake discounted cash-flow calculations like those described in Chapter 4. They also look at the price-earnings ratios of the shares of the firm's principal competitors.

The managers of the firm are eager to secure the highest possible price for their stock, but the underwriters are likely to be cautious because they will be left with any unsold stock if they overestimate investor demand. As a result, underwriters typically try to underprice the initial public offering. **Underpricing,** they argue, is needed to tempt investors to buy stock and to reduce the cost of marketing the issue to customers.

underpricing: Issuing securities at an offering price set below the true value of the security.

> **Underpricing represents a cost to the existing owners since the new investors are allowed to buy shares in the firm at a favorable price. The cost of underpricing may be very large.**

 See box p. 373

It is common to see the stock price increase substantially from the issue price in the days following an issue. Such immediate price jumps indicate the amount by which the shares were underpriced compared to what investors were willing to pay for them. A study by Ibbotson, Sindelar, and Ritter of approximately 9,000 new issues from 1960 to 1987 found average underpricing of 16 percent.[4] Sometimes new issues are dramatically underpriced. For example, in April 1996, stock in Optical Cable Corporation was sold in an IPO at a price of $10 a share. After 1 month, the stock hit a high of $136 before plummeting 3 days later to $57, still nearly six times the initial offer price. The nearby box describes a better known new issue, that for Netscape Communications.

Unfortunately, underpricing does not mean that anyone can become wealthy by buying stock in IPOs. If an issue is underpriced, everybody will want to buy it and the underwriters will not have enough stock to go around. You are therefore likely to get only a small share of these hot issues. If it is overpriced, other investors are unlikely to want it and the underwriter will be only too delighted to sell it to you. This phenomenon is known as the *winner's curse*.[5] It implies that, unless you can spot which issues are underpriced, you are likely to receive a small proportion of the cheap issues and a large proportion of the expensive ones. Since the dice are loaded against uninformed investors, they will play the game only if there is substantial underpricing on average.

[4]R. G. Ibbotson, J. L. Sindelar, and J. R. Ritter, "Initial Public Offerings," *Journal of Applied Corporate Finance* 1 (Summer 1988), pp. 37–45. Note, however, that initial underpricing does not mean that IPOs are superior long-run investments. In fact, IPO returns over the first 3 years of trading have been *less* than a control sample of matching firms. See J. R. Ritter, "The Long-run Performance of Initial Public Offerings," *Journal of Finance* 46 (March 1991), pp. 3–27.

[5]The highest bidder in an auction is the participant who places the highest value on the auctioned object. Therefore, it is likely that the winning bidder has an overly optimistic assessment of true value. Winning the auction suggests that you have overpaid for the object—this is the winner's curse. In the case of IPOs, your ability to "win" an allotment of shares may signal that the stock is overpriced.

Surfers Catch the Wave of a Rising Tide

"The Internet," commented the *Financial Times,* "is all the rage and where fashions go, investors follow, anxious to make money from any new trend. So this week's flotation of a company which makes products to help surfers find their way round the Net was bound to attract interest. But no one, not even the sponsors of the issue, was prepared for what happened when Netscape Communications went public on the Nasdaq stock market."

In mid-July, when the initial prospectus was published, the underwriters indicated that the company would sell 3.5 million shares at a price between $12 and $14 each. That would have raised less than $50 million and valued the company at around $500 million. Enthusiasm was sufficiently strong that a few days later the underwriters increased the shares available to 5 million and upped the price range to $21 to $24. Even that did not choke off demand, and so, when they came to set the final price that evening, the underwriters lifted the price to $28. Next morning the huge volume of orders delayed the start of trading by an hour and a half. When trading finally began, the shares were quoted at $71 and even made it to $75 for a moment. That gave any investors lucky enough to be allocated stock an instant 150 percent profit. Many took

that profit and in frenzied trading the shares fell, ending their first day at $58 1/4. Even at that price the company as a whole was valued at over $2 billion. This was 45 times annualized sales and 37 times the shares' book value. It also made multimillionaires of several of the company's managers. At the end of the day the stock of the company's chairman was valued at $566 million, while the president held stock worth $245 million.

If you didn't know better, you would think that Netscape was a substantial company with a strong earnings record. In fact it had been founded only 16 months earlier. It had never made a profit. Its market was in its infancy and its sales in the latest quarter were only $12 million.

On the front page of the Netscape prospectus, in large letters, was the customary warning, "This offering involves a high degree of risk." It certainly did. Yet the underwriters said there were buyers for 100 million shares even after it had doubled the number it first thought of to $28.

Source: Adapted from M. Urry, "Surfers Catch the Wave of a Rising Tide," *Financial Times,* August 12, 1995. p. 11. From *Financial Times,* August 12, 1995. Copyright © 1995. Used by permission of the *Financial Times.*

▶ **Example 13.1**   *Underpricing of IPOs and Investor Returns*

Suppose that an investor will earn an immediate 10 percent return on underpriced IPOs and lose 5 percent on overpriced IPOs. But because of high demand, you may get only half the shares you bid for when the issue is underpriced. Suppose you bid for $1,000 of shares in two issues, one overpriced and the other underpriced. You are awarded the full $1,000 of the overpriced issue, but only $500 worth of shares in the underpriced issue. The net gain on your two investments $(.10 \times \$500) - (.05 \times \$1,000) = 0$. Your net profit is zero, despite the fact that on average, IPOs are underpriced. You have suffered the winner's curse: you "win" a larger allotment of shares when they are overpriced.

▶ **Self-Test 13.2**   What is the percentage profit earned by an investor who can identify the underpriced issues in Example 13.1? Who are such investors likely to be?

Underpricing is not the only cost to a new issue. There is also the underwriting spread. (Remember, underwriters make their profit by selling the issue at a higher price than they paid for it.) In addition, there are substantial administrative costs. For example, preparation of the registration statement and prospectus involves management, legal counsel, and accountants, as well as the underwriters and their advisers. These are called the *direct costs* of the issue.

Table 13.1

Average expenses of 1,767 initial public offerings, 1990–1994[a]

Value of Issue (millions of dollars)	Direct Costs, %[b]	Average First-Day Return, %[b]	Total Costs, %[c]
2–9.99	16.96	16.36	25.16
10–19.99	11.63	9.65	18.15
20–39.99	9.70	12.48	18.18
40–59.99	8.72	13.65	17.95
60–79.99	8.20	11.31	16.35
80–99.99	7.91	8.91	14.14
100–199.99	7.06	7.16	12.78
200–499.99	6.53	5.70	11.10
500 and up	5.72	7.53	10.36
All issues	11.00	12.05	18.69

[a] The table includes only issues where there was a firm underwriting commitment.
[b] Direct costs (i. e., underwriting spread plus administrative costs) and average initial return are expressed as a percentage of the issue price.
[c] Total costs (i. e., direct costs plus underpricing) are expressed as a percentage of the market price of the share.
Source: J. R. Ritter et al., "The Costs of Raising Capital," *Journal of Financial Research* Vol. XIX, No. 1, Spring 1996. Reprinted by permission.

Table 13.1 summarizes the costs of going public. The table includes the underwriting spread and administrative costs as well as the cost of underpricing, as measured by the initial return on the stock. For a small IPO of no more than $10 million, the underwriting spread and administrative costs are likely to absorb 15 to 20 percent of the proceeds from the issue. For the very largest IPOs, these direct costs may amount to only 5 percent of the proceeds.

▶ **Example 13.2** *Costs of an IPO*

When Microsoft went public in 1986, the sale was partly a primary issue (the company sold new shares to raise cash) and partly a secondary one (the company's original founders and backers cashed in some of their shares). The underwriters acquired a total of 2.8 million Microsoft shares for $19.69 each and sold them to the public at an offering price of $21. The underwriters' spread was therefore $21 − $19.69 = $1.31. The firm also paid $.5 million in legal fees and other costs. Within hours of public trading the stock price rose to $35.

Here are the direct costs of the Microsoft issue:

Direct Expenses

Underwriting Spread	2.8 million × $1.31 = $3.7 million
Other expenses	.5
Total direct expenses	$4.2 million

The firm and selling shareholders received 2.8 million × $19.69 − $.5 million = $54.6 million. Thus direct expenses absorbed 7.1 percent of the gross proceeds of the issue (that is, 4.2/(4.2 + 54.6) = .071).

In addition to these direct costs, there was underpricing. The market valued each share of Microsoft at $35, so the cost of underpricing was ($35 − $21) × 2.8 million = $39.2 million, resulting in total costs of $4.2 + $39.2 = $43.4 million. Therefore, while the total market value of the issued shares was 2.8 million × $35 = $98 million, direct costs and the costs of underpricing absorbed 44 percent of the market value of the shares.

▶ **Self-Test 13.3**   Suppose that the underwriters acquired Microsoft shares for $25 each and sold them to the public at an offering price of $27. If all other features of the offer were unchanged (and the stock still sold for $35 a share), what would have been the direct costs of the issue and the costs of underpricing? What would have been the total costs as a proportion of the market value of the shares?

13.3 *The Underwriters*

We have described underwriters as playing a triple role—providing advice, buying a new issue from the company, and reselling it to investors. Underwriters don't just help the company to make its initial public offering; they are called in whenever a company wishes to raise cash by selling securities to the public.

> **Most companies raise capital only occasionally, but underwriters are in the business all the time. Established underwriters are careful of their reputation and will not handle a new issue unless they believe the facts have been presented fairly to investors. Thus, in addition to handling the sale of an issue, the underwriters in effect give it their seal of approval. This implied endorsement may be worth quite a bit to a company that is coming to the market for the first time.**

Underwriting is not always fun. On October 15, 1987, the British government finalized arrangements to sell its holding of British Petroleum (BP) shares at £3.30 a share. This huge issue involving more than $12 billion was the largest stock offering in history. It was underwritten by an international group of underwriters and simultaneously marketed in a number of countries. Four days after the underwriting arrangement was finalized, the October stock market crash occurred and stock prices nosedived. The underwriters appealed to the British government to cancel the issue but the government hardened its heart and pointed out that the underwriters knew the risks when they agreed to handle the sale.[6] By the closing date of the offer, the price of BP stock had fallen to £2.96 and the underwriters had lost more than $1 billion.

Who Are the Underwriters?

Since underwriters play such a crucial role in new issues, we should look at who they are. Several thousand investment banks, security dealers, and brokers are at least

---

[6]The government's only concession was to put a floor on the underwriters' losses by giving them the option to resell their stock to the government at £2.80 a share. The BP offering is described and analyzed in C. Muscarella and M. Vetsuypens, "The British Petroleum Stock Offering: An Application of Option Pricing," *Journal of Applied Corporate Finance* 1 (1989), pp. 74–80.

Table 13.2

Top underwriters of security issues in the United States in order of total issues underwritten, 1996 (figures in billions)

Merrill Lynch	$155.9
Lehman Brothers	100.7
Goldman Sachs	98.5
Salomon Brothers	96.2
Morgan Stanley	83.7
J. P. Morgan	68.7
CS First Boston	60.0
Bear Stearns	41.7
Donaldson Lufkin & Jenrette	34.8
Smith Barney	29.9

Source: Reprinted by permission of *The Wall Street Journal,* © 1997 Dow Jones & Company, Inc. All Rights Reserved Worldwide.

sporadically involved in underwriting. However, the market for the larger issues is dominated by the major investment banking firms, which specialize in underwriting new issues, dealing in securities, and arranging mergers. These firms enjoy great prestige, experience, and financial muscle. Table 13.2 lists some of the largest firms, ranked by total volume of issues in 1996. Merrill Lynch, the winner, raised a total of $155.9 billion. Of course, only a small proportion of these issues was for companies that were coming to the market for the first time.

In Chapter 12 we pointed out that instead of issuing bonds in the United States, many corporations issue eurobonds in London, which are then sold to investors outside the United States. In addition, new equity issues by large multinational companies are increasingly marketed to investors throughout the world. Since these securities are sold in a number of countries, many of the major international banks are involved in underwriting the issues. For example, look at Table 13.3 which shows the names of the principal underwriters of non-U.S. securities in 1996. Notice that the list includes J. P. Morgan, which is a United States commercial bank. These banks are limited by law in the extent to which they can underwrite in the United States, but their London branches are free to join in underwriting eurobonds.

Table 13.3

Top underwriters of non-U.S. securities

Manager	Amount (in billions)	1996 Market Share	1995 Market Share
Merrill Lynch	$30.3	6.5%	5.9%
SBC Warburg	28.2	6.1	6.4
Goldman Sachs	26.0	5.6	4.6
Deutsche Morgan Grenfell	23.6	5.1	5.2
Morgan Stanley	21.7	4.7	4.5
ABN AMRO Hoare Govett	20.4	4.4	4.7
J. P. Morgan	18.4	4.0	4.5
CS First Boston	17.9	3.9	4.4
BZW/Barclays PLC	17.9	3.9	3.0
UBS	16.2	3.5	3.5
Top 10	$220.6	47.6%	46.6%
Industry Total	$463.5	100%	100%

Source: Reprinted by permission of *The Wall Street Journal,* © 1997 Dow Jones & Company, Inc. All Rights Reserved Worldwide.

13.4 *General Cash Offers by Public Companies*

seasoned offering: Sale of securities by a firm that is already publicly traded.

After the initial public offering a successful firm will continue to grow and from time to time it will need to raise more money by issuing stock or bonds. An issue of additional stock by a company whose stock already is publicly traded is called a **seasoned offering.** Any issue of securities needs to be formally approved by the firm's board of directors. If a stock issue requires an increase in the company's authorized capital, it also needs the consent of the stockholders.

rights issue: Issue of securities offered only to current stockholders.

Public companies can issue securities either by making a general cash offer to investors at large or by making a **rights issue,** which is limited to existing shareholders. In the latter case, the company offers the shareholders the opportunity, or *right,* to buy more shares at an "attractive" price. For example, if the current stock price is $100, the company might offer investors an additional share at $50 for each share they hold. Suppose that before the issue an investor has one share worth $100 and $50 in the bank. If the investor takes up the offer of a new share, that $50 of cash is transferred from the investor's bank account to the company's. The investor now has two shares that are a claim on the original assets worth $100 and on the $50 cash that the company has raised. So the two shares are worth a total of $150, or $75 each.

▶ **Example 13.3** *Rights Issues*

Easy Writer Word Processing Company has 1 million shares outstanding, selling at $20 a share. To finance the development of a new software package, it plans a rights issue, allowing one new share to be purchased for each 10 shares currently held. The purchase price will be $10 a share. How many shares will be issued? How much money will be raised? What will be the stock price after the rights issue?

The firm will issue one new share for every 10 old ones, or 100,000 shares. So shares outstanding will rise to 1.1 million. The firm will raise $10 × 100,000 = $1 million. Therefore, the total value of the firm will increase from $20 million to $21 million, and the stock price will fall to $21 million/1.1 million shares = $19.09 per share.

In some countries the rights issue is the most common or only method for issuing stock, but in the United States they are now very rare. We therefore will concentrate on the mechanics of the general cash offer.

General Cash Offers and Shelf Registration

general cash offer: Sale of securities open to all investors by an already-public company.

When a public company makes a **general cash offer** of debt or equity, it goes through much the same procedure as when it first went public. In other words, it registers the issue with the SEC and then sells it to an underwriter (or a syndicate of underwriters), which in turn offers the securities to the public.[7]

---

[7]The procedure is similar when a company issues a eurobond but, since the bond is not sold publicly in the United States, it is not registered with the SEC.

shelf registration: A procedure that allows firms to file one registration statement for several issues of the same security.

In 1982 the SEC issued its *Rule 415,* which allows companies to file a single registration statement covering financing plans for up to 2 years into the future. The actual issues can then be sold to the public with scant additional paperwork, whenever the firm needs cash or thinks it can issue securities at an attractive price. This is called **shelf registration**—the registration is put "on the shelf," to be taken down, dusted off, and used as needed.

Think of how you might use shelf registration when you are a financial manager. Suppose that your company is likely to need up to $200 million of new long-term debt over the next year or so. It can file a registration statement for that amount. It now has approval to issue up to $200 million of debt, but it isn't obliged to issue any. Nor is it required to work through any *particular* underwriters—the registration statement may name the underwriters the firm thinks it may work with, but others can be substituted later.

Now you can sit back and issue debt as needed, in bits and pieces if you like. Suppose Merrill Lynch comes across an insurance company with $10 million ready to invest in corporate bonds, priced to yield, say, 7.3 percent. If you think that's a good deal, you say "OK" and the deal is done, subject to only a little additional paperwork. Merrill Lynch then resells the bonds to the insurance company, hoping for a higher price than it paid for them.

Here is another possible deal. Suppose you think you see a window of opportunity in which interest rates are "temporarily low." You invite bids for $100 million of bonds. Some bids may come from large investment bankers acting alone, others from ad hoc syndicates. But that's not your problem; if the price is right, you just take the best deal offered.

Thus shelf registration gives firms several different things that they did not have previously:

1. Securities can be issued in dribs and drabs without incurring excessive costs.
2. Securities can be issued on short notice.
3. Security issues can be timed to take advantage of "market conditions" (although any financial manager who can *reliably* identify favorable market conditions could make a lot more money by quitting and becoming a bond or stock trader instead).
4. The issuing firm can make sure that underwriters compete for its business.

Underwriters *do* compete. Although several large investment banks lobbied hard against Rule 415 when it was first proposed, once it had been approved, the same banks played the new game with gusto. As an attorney who works with them observed, "If the SEC passed a rule saying you had to do underwriting in Watertown, NY, in the snow stark naked, these guys would take the first plane up."[8]

Not all companies eligible for shelf registration actually use it for all their public issues. Sometimes they believe they can get a better deal by making one large issue through traditional channels, especially when the security to be issued has some unusual feature or when the firm believes it needs the investment banker's counsel or stamp of approval on the issue. Thus shelf registration is less often used for issues of common stock than for garden-variety corporate bonds.

---

[8]Quoted in Tim Carrington, "New Ball Game: Investment Bankers Enter a New Era," *The Wall Street Journal,* June 21, 1982, p. 10.

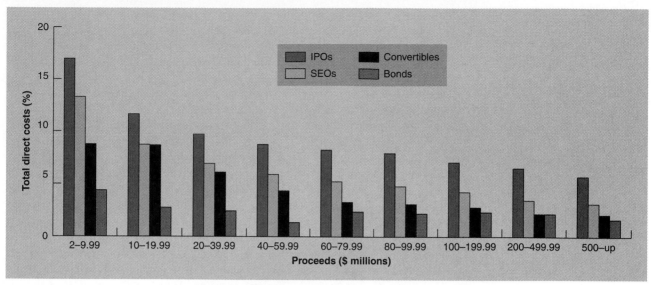

Source: Immoo Lee, Scott Lochhead, Jay Ritter, and Quanshui Zhao, "The Costs of Raising Capital," *Journal of Financial Research* 19 (Spring 1996), 59–74.

Figure 13.1

Total Direct Costs as a Percentage of Gross Proceeds. The total direct costs for initial public offerings (IPOs), seasoned equity offerings (SEOs), convertible bonds, and straight bonds are composed of underwriter spreads and other direct expenses.

Costs of the General Cash Offer

Whenever a firm makes a cash offer, it incurs substantial administrative costs. Also, the firm needs to compensate the underwriters by selling them securities below the price that they expect to receive from investors. Figure 13.1 shows the average underwriting spread and administrative costs for several types of security issues in the United States.[9]

The figure clearly shows the economies of scale in issuing securities. Costs may absorb 15 percent of a $1 million seasoned equity issue but less than 4 percent of a $500 million issue. This occurs because a large part of the issue cost is fixed.

Figure 13.1 shows that issue costs are higher for equity than for debt securities—the costs for both types of securities, however, show the same economies of scale. Issue costs are higher for equity than for debt because administrative costs are somewhat higher, and also because underwriting stock is riskier than underwriting bonds. The underwriters demand additional compensation for the greater risk they take in buying and reselling equity.

▶ **Self-Test 13.4**

Use Figure 13.1 to compare the costs of 10 issues of $15 million of stock in a seasoned offering versus one issue of $150 million.

Market Reaction to Stock Issues

Because stock issues usually throw a sizable number of new shares onto the market, it is widely believed that they must temporarily depress the stock price. If the proposed issue is very large, this price pressure may, it is thought, be so severe as to make it almost impossible to raise money.

[9]These figures do not capture *all* administrative costs. For example, they do not include management time spent on the issue.

This belief in price pressure implies that a new issue depresses the stock price temporarily below its true value. However, that view doesn't appear to fit very well with the notion of market efficiency. If the stock price falls solely because of increased supply, then that stock would offer a higher return than comparable stocks and investors would be attracted to it as ants to a picnic.

Economists who have studied new issues of common stock have generally found that the announcement of the issue *does* result in a decline in the stock price. For industrial issues in the United States this decline amounts to about 3 percent.[10] While this may not sound overwhelming, such a price drop can be a large fraction of the money raised. Suppose that a company with a market value of equity of $5 billion announces its intention to issue $500 million of additional equity and thereby causes the stock price to drop by 3 percent. The loss in value is .03 × $5 billion, or $150 million. That's 30 percent of the amount of money raised (.30 × $500 million = $150 million).

What's going on here? Is the price of the stock simply depressed by the prospect of the additional supply? Possibly, but here is an alternative explanation.

Suppose managers (who have better information about the firm than outside investors) know that their stock is undervalued. If the company sells new stock at this low price, it will give the new shareholders a good deal at the expense of the old shareholders. In these circumstances managers might be prepared to forgo the new investment rather than sell shares at too low a price.

If managers know that the stock is *overvalued,* the position is reversed. If the company sells new shares at the high price, it will help its existing shareholders at the expense of the new ones. Managers might be prepared to issue stock even if the new cash were just put in the bank.

Of course investors are not stupid. They can predict that managers are more likely to issue stock when they think it is overvalued and therefore they mark the price of the stock down accordingly.

> **The tendency for stock prices to decline at the time of an issue may have nothing to do with increased supply. Instead, the stock issue may simply be a *signal* that well-informed managers believe the market has overpriced the stock.[11]**

13.5 The Private Placement

private placement: Sale of securities to a limited number of investors without a public offering.

Whenever a company makes a public offering, it must register the issue with the SEC. It could avoid this costly process by selling the issue privately. There are no hard-and-fast definitions of a **private placement,** but the SEC has insisted that the security should be sold to no more than a dozen or so knowledgeable investors.

[10]See, for example, P. Asquith and D. W. Mullins, "Equity Issues and Offering Dilution," *Journal of Financial Economics* 15 (January–February 1986), pp. 61–90; R. W. Masulis and A. N. Korwar, "Seasoned Equity Offerings: An Empirical Investigation," *Journal of Financial Economics* 15 (January–February 1986), pp. 91–118; W. H. Mikkelson and M. M. Partch, "Valuation Effects of Security Offerings and the Issuance Process," *Journal of Financial Economics* 15 (January–February 1986), pp. 31–60. There appears to be a smaller price decline for utility issues. Also Marsh observed a smaller decline for rights issues in the United Kingdom; see P. R. Marsh, "Equity Rights Issues and the Efficiency of the UK Stock Market," *Journal of Finance* 34 (September 1979), pp. 839–862.

[11]This explanation was developed in S. C. Myers and N. S. Majluf, "Corporate Financing and Investment Decisions When Firms Have Information that Investors Do Not Have," *Journal of Financial Economics* 13 (1984), pp. 187–222.

One disadvantage of a private placement is that the investor cannot easily resell the security.[12] This is less important to institutions such as life insurance companies, which invest huge sums of money in corporate debt for the long haul. Consequently, an active private placement mechanism has evolved for corporate debt. In recent years almost half of all new corporate debt issues were private placements.

As you would expect, it costs less to arrange a private placement than to make a public issue. That might not be so important for the very large issues where costs are less significant, but it is a particular advantage for companies making smaller issues.

Another advantage of the private placement is that the debt contract can be custom-tailored for firms with special problems or opportunities. Also, if the firm wishes later to change the terms of the debt, it is much simpler to do this with a private placement where only a few investors are involved.

Therefore, it is not surprising that private placements occupy a particular niche in the corporate debt market, namely, loans to small and medium-sized firms. These are the firms that face the highest costs in public issues, that require the most detailed investigation, and that may require specialized, flexible loan arrangements.

We do not mean that large, safe, and conventional firms should rule out private placements. Enormous amounts of capital are sometimes raised by this method. For example, AT&T once borrowed $500 million in a single private placement. Nevertheless, the advantages of private placement—avoiding registration costs and establishing a direct relationship with the lender—are generally more important to smaller firms.

Of course these advantages are not free. Lenders in private placements have to be compensated for the risks they face and for the costs of research and negotiation. They also have to be compensated for holding an asset that is not easily resold. All these factors are rolled into the interest rate paid by the firm. It is difficult to generalize about the differences in interest rates between private placements and public issues, but a typical yield differential is on the order of half a percentage point.

Summary

1. Infant companies raise venture capital to carry them through to the point at which they can make their first public issue of stock. More established publicly traded companies can issue additional securities in a general cash offer.
2. Financing choices should be designed to avoid conflicts of interest. This is especially important in the case of a young company that is raising venture capital. If both managers and investors have an important equity stake in the company, they are more likely to pull in the same direction. The willingness to take that stake also *signals* management's confidence in the new company's future.
3. Larger is cheaper. There are always economies of scale in issuing securities. It is cheaper to go to the market once for $100 million than to make two trips for $50 million each. Consequently firms "bunch" security issues. That may mean relying on short-term financing until a large issue is justified. Or it may mean issuing more than is needed at the moment to avoid another issue later.

---

[12]However, in 1990 the SEC relaxed its restrictions on who could buy unregistered securities. The new rule, Rule 144a, allowed large financial institutions (known as *qualified institutional buyers*) to trade unregistered securities among themselves.

4. Firms often sell new issues of securities for less than their market value. This under-pricing is a hidden cost to the existing shareholders. Fortunately, it is usually serious only for companies that are selling stock to the public for the first time.

5. New issues may depress the stock price. The extent of this price decline varies, but for issues of common stocks by industrial firms the fall in the value of the existing stock may amount to a significant proportion of the money raised. The likely explanation for this pressure is the information the market reads into the company's decision to issue stock.

6. Shelf registration often makes sense for debt issues by blue-chip firms. Shelf registration reduces the time taken to arrange a new issue, it increases flexibility, and it may cut underwriting costs. It seems best suited for debt issues by large firms that are happy to switch between investment banks. It seems least suited for issues of unusually risky securities or for issues by small companies who most need a close relationship with an investment bank.

7. Private placements are well-suited for small, risky, or unusual firms. The special advantages of private placement stem from avoiding registration expenses and a more direct relationship with the lender. These are not worth as much to blue-chip borrowers.

Key Terms

venture capital	prospectus	general cash offer
initial public offering (IPO)	underpricing	shelf registration
underwriter	seasoned offering	private placement
spread	rights issue	

Problems

1. **Underwriting.**

   a. Is a rights issue more likely to be used for an initial public offering or for subsequent issues of stock?

   b. Is a private placement more likely to be used for issues of seasoned stock or seasoned bonds by an industrial company?

   c. Is shelf registration more likely to be used for issues of unseasoned stocks or bonds by a large industrial company?

2. **Underwriting.** Each of the following terms is associated with one of the events beneath. Can you match them up?

   a. Red herring
   b. Shelf registration
   c. Firm commitment
   d. Rights issue

   A. The company issues a preliminary prospectus.
   B. The underwriter agrees to buy the issue from the company at a fixed price.
   C. The company offers to sell stock to existing stockholders.
   D. Several issues of the same security may be sold under the same registration.

3. **Underwriting Costs.** State for each of the following pairs of issues which you would expect to involve the lower proportionate underwriting and administrative costs, other things equal:

   a. A large issue/a small issue
   b. A bond issue/a common stock issue
   c. A small private placement of bonds/a small general cash offer of bonds

4. **Venture Capital.** Why do venture capital companies prefer to advance money in stages?

5. **Private Placements.** You need to choose between the following types of issues:

   A public issue of $10 million face value of 10-year debt. The interest rate on the debt would be 8.5 percent and the debt would be issued at face value. The underwriting spread would be 1.5 percent and other expenses would be $80,000.

   A private placement of $10 million face value of 10-year debt. The interest rate on the private placement would be 9 percent but the total issuing expenses would be only $30,000.

   a. What is the difference in the proceeds to the company net of expenses?

   b. Other things equal, which is the better deal?

   c. What other factors beyond the interest rate and issue costs would you wish to consider before deciding between the two offers?

6. **IPOs.** Your broker calls and says that you can get 500 shares of an imminent IPO at the offering price. Should you buy? Are you worried about the fact that your broker called *you*?

7. **IPO Underpricing.** Having heard about IPO underpricing, I put in an order to my broker for 1,000 shares of every IPO he can get for me. After 3 months, my investment record is as follows:

IPO	Shares Allocated to Me	Price per Share	Initial Return
A	500	$10	7%
B	200	20	12
C	1,000	8	−2
D	0	12	23

   a. What is the average underpricing of this sample of IPOs?

   b. What is the average initial return on my "portfolio" of shares purchased from the four IPOs I bid on? Calculate the average initial return weighting by the amount of money invested in each issue.

   c. Why have I performed so poorly relative to the average initial return on the full sample of IPOs? What lessons do you draw from my experience?

8. **IPO Costs.** Moonscape has just completed an initial public offering. The firm sold 3 million shares at an offer price of $8 per share. The underwriting spread was $.50 a share. The price of the stock closed at $11 per share at the end of the first day of trading. The firm incurred $100,000 in legal, administrative, and other costs. What were flotation costs as a fraction of funds raised? Were flotation costs for Moonscape higher or lower than is typical for IPOs of this size (see Table 13.1)?

9. **Flotation Costs.** "For small issues of common stock, the costs of flotation amount to about 15 percent of the proceeds. This means that the opportunity cost of external equity capital is about 15 percentage points higher than that of retained earnings." Does this follow?

10. **Flotation Costs.** When Microsoft went public, the company sold 2 million new shares (the primary issue). In addition, existing shareholders sold .8 million shares (the secondary issue) and kept 21.1 million shares. Suppose that the new shares had been issued to the underwriters at $33 each, rather than $19.69.

    a. How many shares would the company have needed to issue to raise the same amount of money?

    b. How much more would the existing shareholders have made from the sale?

    c. What would have been the change in the value of the shares that they did *not* sell? *Hint:* What was the market value of Microsoft's total outstanding stock? Would that value change if the company had raised the same amount of money from the underwriters?

How many shares of stock would be outstanding if the shares had been issued for $33 each? What would the stock price be?

Ignore in your calculations any legal and administrative expenses.

11. **Flotation Costs.** The market value of the marketing research firm Fax Facts is $600 million. The firm issues an additional $100 million of stock, but as a result the stock price falls by 2 percent. What is the cost of the price drop to existing shareholders as a fraction of the funds raised?

12. **Flotation Costs.** Young Corporation stock currently sells for $30 per share. There are 1 million shares currently outstanding. The company announces plans to raise $3 million by offering shares to the public at a price of $30 per share.

    a. If the underwriting spread is 8 percent, how many shares will the company need to issue in order to be left with net proceeds of $3 million?

    b. If other administrative costs are $60,000 what is the dollar value of the total direct costs of the issue?

    c. If the share price falls by 3 percent at the announcement of the plans to proceed with a seasoned offering, what is the dollar cost of the announcement effect?

13. **Rights.** Consolidated Jewels needs to raise $2 million to pay for its Diamonds in the Rough campaign. It will raise the funds by offering 200,000 rights. The company currently has outstanding 1 million shares priced at $20 each.

    a. What must be the subscription price on the rights the company plans to offer?

    b. What will be the share price after the rights issue?

    c. What is the value of a right to buy one share?

    d. How many rights would be issued to an investor who currently owns 1,000 shares?

    e. Show that the investor who currently holds 1,000 shares is unaffected by the rights issue. Specifically, show that the value of the rights plus the value of the 1,000 shares after the rights issue equals the value of the 1,000 shares before the rights issue.

14. **Rights.** Associated Breweries is planning to market unleaded beer. To finance the venture it proposes to make a rights issue with a subscription price of $10. One new share can be purchased for each two shares held. The company currently has outstanding 100,000 shares priced at $40 a share. Assuming that the new money is invested to earn a fair return, give values for the

    a. number of new shares

    b. amount of new investment

    c. total value of company after issue

    d. total number of shares after issue

    e. share price after the issue

15. **Rights.** In 1997 Pandora, Inc., makes a rights issue at a subscription price of $5 a share. One new share can be purchased for every four shares held. Before the issue there were 10 million shares outstanding and the share price was $6.

    a. What is the total amount of new money raised?

    b. What is the expected stock price after the rights are issued?

16. **Rights.** Problem 15 contains details of a rights offering by Pandora. Suppose that the company had decided to issue the new stock at $4 instead of $5 a share. How many new shares would it have needed to raise the same sum of money? Recalculate the answers to problem 15. Show that Pandora's shareholders are just as well off if it issues the shares at $4 a share rather than the $5 assumed in problem 15.

17. **Venture Capital.** Here is a difficult question. Pickwick Electronics is a new high-tech company financed entirely by 1 million ordinary shares, all of which are owned by George

Pickwick. The firm needs to raise $1 million now for stage 1 and, assuming all goes well, a further $1 million at the end of 5 years for stage 2.

First Cookham Venture Partners is considering two possible financing schemes:

Buying 2 million shares now at their current valuation of $1.
Buying 1 million shares at the current valuation and investing a further $1 million at the end of 5 years at whatever the shares are worth.

The outlook for Pickwick is uncertain, but as long as the company can secure the additional finance for stage 2, it will be worth either $2 million or $12 million after completing stage 2. (The company will be valueless if it cannot raise the funds for stage 2.) Show the possible payoffs for Mr. Pickwick and First Cookham and explain why one scheme might be preferred. Assume an interest rate of zero.

18. **IPO Costs.** Look at the illustrative new issue prospectus in the appendix.

a. Is this issue a primary offering, a secondary offering, or both?
b. What are the direct costs of the issue as a percentage of the total proceeds? Are these more than the average for an issue of this size?
c. Suppose that on the first day of trading the price of Hotch Pot stock is $15 a share. What are the *total* costs of the issue as a percentage of the market price?
d. After paying her share of the expenses, how much will the firm's president, Emma Lucullus, receive from the sale? What will be the value of the shares that she retains in the company?

19. **IPO Costs.** Why are the issue costs for debt issues generally less than those for equity issues?

Solutions to Self-Test Questions

13.1 Unless the firm can secure second-stage financing, it is unlikely to succeed. If the entrepreneur is going to reap any reward on his own investment, he needs to put in enough effort to get further financing. By accepting only part of the necessary venture capital, management increases its own risk and reduces that of the venture capitalist. This decision would be costly and foolish if management lacked confidence that the project would be successful enough to get past the first stage. A credible signal by management is one that only managers who are truly confident can afford to provide. However, words are cheap and there is little to be lost by *saying* that you are confident (although if you are proved wrong, you may find it difficult to raise money a second time).

13.2 If an investor can distinguish between overpriced and underpriced issues, she will bid only on the underpriced ones. In this case she will purchase only issues that provide a 10 percent gain. However, the ability to distinguish these issues requires considerable insight and research. The return to the informed IPO participant may be viewed as a return on the resources expended to become informed.

13.3 Direct expenses:

Underwriting spread = 2.8 million × ($27 − 25)	$ 5.6 million
Other expenses	.5
Total direct expenses	$ 6.1 million
Underpricing = 2.8 million × ($35 − 27)	$22.4 million
Total expenses	$28.5 million
Market value of issue = 2.8 million × $35	$98 million

Expenses as proportion of market value = 28.5/98 = .291 = 29.1%.

13.4 Ten issues of $15 million each will cost about 9 percent of proceeds, or .09 × $150 million = $13.5 million. One issue of $150 million will cost only 4 percent of $150 million, or $6 million.

Minicase

Information Management Resources (IMR) is a Florida corporation founded in 1988 by Satish K. Sunan, who is the CEO and majority shareholder. It is in the business of providing applications software outsourcing solutions for information technology departments at large companies. It has operations in the United States, United Kingdom, and Bangalore, India, that are linked so that the firm can provide 24-hour English-speaking service to its clients.

IMR had its initial public offering in 1996. The offer price was $14.00 and the first day close was $15.50. The IPO sold 3.5 million shares. The underwriter spread was 98 cents per share, so that underwriting fees were $3.43 million. An additional $1 million was paid by the company for legal fees, auditing, printing, and other expenses. The gross proceeds of the IPO were $49 million, with the company and selling shareholders netting $44.57 million. Of the 3.5 million shares offered, 550,000 were from selling shareholders (most preissue shareholders sold a small part of their holdings) and 2,950,000 shares were from the company. All expenses were shared proportionately based on shares sold to the public.

What was the percentage cost of IMR's initial public offering? How do the various costs of its IPO stack up to the average costs detailed in Table 13.1?

An analyst interviewed in the financial pages scoffed at the idea that the initial day's return on the IPO should be considered part of the underwriting costs. He was quoted as follows: "Managers obviously prefer the stock in their firms to be higher rather than lower. Why then would they view an increase in share price as *increasing* the cost of the underwriting? They ought to be happy about a big first-day return. Would they rather have a cheap underwriting and a low stock price?"

Does this analyst have a point? Evaluate his argument.

We are grateful to Professor Jay Ritter for the data used to write this case.

Appendix: Hotch Pot's New Issue Prospectus[13]

Prospectus

800,000 Shares
Hotch Pot. Inc.
Common Stock ($.01 par value)

Of the 800,000 shares of Common Stock offered hereby, 500,000 shares are being sold by the Company and 300,000 shares are being sold by the Selling Stockholders. See "Principal and Selling Stockholders." The Company will not receive any of the proceeds from the sale of shares by the Selling Stockholders.

Before this offering there has been no public market for the Common Stock. **These securities involve a high degree of risk. See "Certain Factors."**

THESE SECURITIES HAVE NOT BEEN APPROVED OR DISAPPROVED BY THE SECURITIES AND EXCHANGE COMMISSION NOR HAS THE COMMISSION PASSED ON THE ACCURACY OR ADEQUACY OF THIS PROSPECTUS. ANY REPRESENTATION TO THE CONTRARY IS A CRIMINAL OFFENSE.

	Price to Public	Underwriting Discount	Proceeds to Company[1]	Proceeds to Selling Shareholders
Per share	$12.00	$1.30	$10.70	$10.70
Total	$9,600,000	$1,040,000	$5,350,000	$3,210,000

[1] Before deducting expenses payable by the Company estimated at $400,000, of which $250,000 will be paid by the Company and $150,000 by the Selling Stockholders.

The Common Stock is offered, subject to prior sale, when, as, and if delivered to and accepted by the Underwriters and subject to approval of certain legal matters by their counsel and by counsel for the Company and the Selling Shareholders. The Underwriters reserve the right to withdraw, cancel, or modify such offer and reject orders in whole or in part.

Silverman Pinch Inc. **April 1, 1997**

No person has been authorized to give any information or to make any representations, other than as contained therein, in connection with the offer contained in this Prospectus, and, if given or made, such information or representations must not be relied upon. This Prospectus does not constitute an offer of any securities other than the registered securities to which it relates or an offer to any person in any jurisdiction where such an offer would be unlawful. The delivery of this Prospectus at any time does not imply that information herein is correct as of any time subsequent to its date.

[13]Most prospectuses have content similar to that of the Hotch Pot prospectus but go into considerably more detail. Also, we have omitted from the Hotch Pot prospectus the company's financial statements.

IN CONNECTION WITH THIS OFFERING, THE UNDERWRITER MAY OVERALLOT OR EFFECT TRANSACTIONS WHICH STABILIZE OR MAINTAIN THE MARKET PRICE OF THE COMMON STOCK OF THE COMPANY AT A LEVEL ABOVE THAT WHICH MIGHT OTHERWISE PREVAIL IN THE OPEN MARKET. SUCH STABILIZING, IF COMMENCED, MAY BE DISCONTINUED AT ANY TIME.

PROSPECTUS SUMMARY

The following summary information is qualified in its entirety by the detailed information and financial statements appearing elsewhere in this Prospectus.

The Company: Hotch Pot, Inc. operates a chain of 140 fast-food outlets in the United States offering unusual combinations of dishes.

The Offering: Common Stock offered by the Company 500,000 shares;
Common Stock offered by the Selling Stockholders 300,000 shares;
Common Stock to be outstanding after this offering 3,500,000 shares.

Use of Proceeds: For the construction of new restaurants and to provide working capital.

The Company

Hotch Pot, Inc. operates a chain of 140 fast-food outlets in Illinois, Pennsylvania, and Ohio. These restaurants specialize in offering an unusual combination of foreign dishes.

The Company was organized in Delaware in 1987.

Use of Proceeds

The Company intends to use the net proceeds from the sale of 500,000 shares of Common Stock offered hereby, estimated at approximately $5 million, to open new outlets in midwest states and to provide additional working capital. It has no immediate plans to use any of the net proceeds of the offering for any other specific investment.

Dividend Policy

The company has not paid cash dividends on its Common Stock and does not anticipate that dividends will be paid on the Common Stock in the foreseeable future.

Certain Factors

Investment in the Common Stock involves a high degree of risk. The following factors should be carefully considered in evaluating the Company:

Substantial Capital Needs. The Company will require additional financing to continue its expansion policy. The Company believes that its relations with its lenders are good, but there can be no assurance that additional financing will be available in the future.

Competition. The Company is in competition with a number of restaurant chains supplying fast food. Many of these companies are substantially larger and better capitalized than the Company.

Capitalization

The following table sets forth the capitalization of the Company as of December 31, 1996, and as adjusted to reflect the sale of 500,000 shares of Common Stock by the Company.

	Actual	As Adjusted
	(in thousands)	
Long-term debt	$ —	$ —
Stockholders' equity	30	35
Common stock –$.01 par value, 3,000,000 shares outstanding, 3,500,000 shares outstanding, as adjusted		
Paid-in capital	1,970	7,315
Retained earnings	3,200	3,200
Total stockholders' equity	5,200	10,550
Total capitalization	$5,200	$10,550

Selected Financial Data

[*The Prospectus typically includes a summary income statement and balance sheet.*]

Management's Analysis of Results of Operations and Financial Condition

Revenue growth for the year ended December 31, 1996, resulted from the opening of ten new restaurants in the Company's existing geographic area and from sales of a new range of desserts, notably crepe suzette with custard. Sales per customer increased by 20% and this contributed to the improvement in margins.

During the year the Company borrowed $600,000 from its banks at an interest rate of 2% above the prime rate.

Business

Hotch Pot, Inc. operates a chain of 140 fast-food outlets in Illinois, Pennsylvania, and Ohio. These restaurants specialize in offering an unusual combination of foreign dishes. 50% of company's revenues derived from sales of two dishes, sushi and sauerkraut and curry bolognese. All dishes are prepared in three regional centers and then frozen and distributed to the individual restaurants.

Management

The following table sets forth information regarding the Company's directors, executive officers, and key employees:

Name	Age	Position
Emma Lucullus	28	President, Chief Executive Officer, & Director
Ed Lucullus	33	Treasurer & Director

Emma Lucullus   Emma Lucullus established the Company in 1987 and has been its Chief Executive Officer since that date.

Ed Lucullus   Ed Lucullus has been employed by the Company since 1987.

Executive Compensation

The following table sets forth the cash compensation paid for services rendered for the year 1996 by the Executive officers

Name	Capacity	Cash Compensation
Emma Lucullus	President and Chief Executive Officer	$130,000
Ed Lucullus	Treasurer	$95,000

Certain Transactions

At various times between 1987 and 1996 First Cookham Venture Partners invested a total of $1.5 million in the Company. In connection with this investment, First Cookham Venture Partners was granted certain rights to registration under the Securities Act of 1933, including the right to have their shares of Common Stock registered at the Company's expense with the Securities and Exchange Commission.

Principal and Selling Stockholders

The following table sets forth certain information regarding the beneficial ownership of the Company's voting Common Stock as of the date of this prospectus by (i) each person known by the Company to be the beneficial owner of more than 5% of its voting Common Stock, and (ii) each director of the Company who beneficially owns voting Common Stock. Unless otherwise indicated, each owner has sole voting and dispositive power over his shares.

Name of Beneficial Owner	Shares Beneficially Owned prior to Offering		Shares to Be Sold	Shares Beneficially Owned after Offering	
	Number	Percent		Number	Percent
Emma Lucullus	400,000	13.3	25,000	375,000	12.9
Ed Lucullus	400,000	13.3	25,000	375,000	12.9
First Cookham Venture Partners	1,700,000	66.7	250,000	1,450,000	50.0
Hermione Kraft	200,000	6.7	—	200,000	6.9

Description of Capital Stock

The Company's authorized capital stock consists of 10,000,000 shares of voting Common Stock.

As of the date of this Prospectus, there are 4 holders of record of the Common Stock.

Under the terms of one of the Company's loan agreements, the Company may not pay cash dividends on Common Stock except from net profits without the written consent of the lender.

Underwriting

Subject to the terms and conditions set forth in the Underwriting Agreement, the Underwriter, Silverman Pinch Inc., has agreed to purchase from the Company and the Selling Stockholders 800,000 shares of Common Stock.

There is no public market for the Common Stock. The price to the public for the Common Stock was determined by negotiation between the Company and the Underwriter and was based on, among other things, the Company's financial and operating history and condition, its prospects, and the prospects for its industry in general, the management of the Company, and the market prices of securities for companies in businesses similar to that of the Company.

Legal Matters

The validity of the shares of Common Stock offered by the Prospectus is being passed on for the Company by Blair, Kohl, and Chirac and for the Underwriter by Chretien Howard.

Legal Proceedings

Hotch Pot was served in January 1997 with a summons and complaint in an action commenced by a customer who alleges that consumption of the Company's products caused severe nausea and loss of feeling in both feet. The Company believes that the complaint is without foundation.

Experts

The consolidated financial statements of the Company have been so included in reliance on the reports of Hooper Firebrand, independent accountants, given on the authority of that firm as experts in auditing and accounting.

Financial Statements

[*Text and tables omitted.*]

Part Five

Capital Structure and Dividend Policy

"Neither a borrower nor a lender be"
So says Polonius in Shakespeare's Hamlet. *Is this sound advice for the modern corporation?*
© Will Gullette/Old Globe Theatre

Chapter 14

Debt Policy

A firm's basic financial resource is the stream of cash flows produced by its assets. When the firm is financed entirely by common stock, all those cash flows belong to the stockholders. When it issues both debt and equity, the firm splits the cash flows into two streams, a relatively safe stream that goes to the debtholders and a more risky one that goes to the stockholders.

The firm's mix of securities is known as its capital structure. Some high-tech firms, such as Merck and Hewlett-Packard, rely almost wholly on equity finance. So do many service companies like Automatic Data Processing and Netscape. At the other extreme, debt accounts for a substantial part of the market value of retailers and utilities.

Capital structure is not immutable. Firms change their capital structure, sometimes almost overnight. Later in the chapter you will read about how Sealed Air Corporation did just that. In this chapter we discuss why some firms have more debt than others and why they sometimes change their capital structure.

Shareholders want management to choose the mix of securities that maximizes firm value. But does this optimal capital structure exist? We must consider the possibility that *no* combination has any greater appeal than any other. Perhaps the really important decisions concern the company's assets, and decisions about capital structure are mere details—matters to be attended to but not worried about.

In the first part of the chapter we will look at the circumstances in which capital structure *doesn't* matter. After that we will put back some of the things that *do* make a difference, such as taxes, bankruptcy, and the signals that your financing decisions may send to investors. At the end of the chapter we will be in a position to draw up a checklist for financial managers who need to decide on the firm's capital structure.

After studying this chapter you should be able to

▶ Analyze the effect of debt finance on the risk and required return of equityholders.

▶ Appreciate the advantages and disadvantages of debt finance.

▶ Cite the various costs of financial distress.

▶ Explain why the debt-equity mix varies across firms and across industries.

14.1 How Borrowing Affects Company Values in a Tax-Free Economy

It is after the ball game and the pizza man is delivering a pizza to Yogi Berra. "Should I cut it into four slices as usual, Yogi?" asks the pizza man. "No," replies Yogi, "Cut it into eight; I'm hungry tonight."

capital structure: Firm's mix of financing.

If you understand why more slices won't sate Yogi's appetite, you will have no difficulty understanding why a company's choice of **capital structure** can't increase the underlying value of the cash flows generated by its real assets and operations. Think of a simple balance sheet:

$$\text{Value of assets} = \frac{\text{Value of liabilities plus}}{\text{shareholders' equity}}$$

$$\frac{\text{Value of cash flows from}}{\text{real assets and operations}} = \frac{\text{Value of debt, common stock, and other}}{\text{securities issued to investors}}$$

The left-hand side determines the size of the pizza; the right-hand side determines how it is sliced. A company can slice its cash flow into as many parts as it likes, but the value of those parts will always sum back to the value of the unsliced cash flow. (Of course, we have to make sure that none of the cash-flow stream is lost in the slicing. We cannot say "The value of a pizza is independent of how it is sliced" if the slicer is also a nibbler.)

The basic idea here (the value of a pizza does not depend on how it is sliced) has various applications. Yogi Berra got friendly chuckles for his misapplication. Franco Modigliani and Merton Miller received Nobel Prizes for applying it to corporate financing. Modigliani and Miller, always referred to as "MM," showed in 1958 that the value of a firm does not depend on how its cash flows are "sliced." More precisely, they demonstrated the following proposition:

> **When there are no taxes and capital markets function well, it makes no difference whether the firm borrows or individual shareholders borrow. Therefore, the market value of a company does not depend on its capital structure. In other words, financial managers cannot increase value by changing the mix of securities used to finance the company.**

The following example retraces MM's original reasoning.

MM's Argument

Cleo, the president of River Cruises, is reviewing the firm's capital structure with Antony, the financial manager. Table 14.1 shows the current position. The company has no debt and all its operating income is paid as dividends to the shareholders. (We assume for now that there are no taxes.) The *expected* earnings and dividends per share are $1.25, but this figure is by no means certain—it could turn out to be more or less than $1.25. For example, earnings could fall to $.75 in a slump or they could jump to $1.75 in a boom.

Table 14.1

River Cruises is entirely equity-financed. Although it expects *to have an income of $125,000 in perpetuity, this income is not certain. This table shows the return to the stockholder under different assumptions about operating income. We assume no taxes.*

Data			
Number of shares	100,000		
Price per share	$10		
Market value of shares	$1 million		

Outcomes	State of the Economy		
	Slump	**Normal**	**Boom**
Operating income	$75,000	125,000	175,000
Earnings per share	$.75	1.25	1.75
Return on shares (%)	7.5%	12.5	17.5
		Expected outcome	

Table 14.2

River Cruises is wondering whether to issue $500,000 of debt at an interest rate of 10 percent and repurchase 50,000 shares. This table shows the return to the shareholder under different assumptions about operating income. Returns to shareholders are increased in normal and boom times but fall more in slumps.

Data			
Number of shares	50,000		
Price per share	$10		
Market value of shares	$500,000		
Market value of debt	$500,000		

Outcomes			
		State of the Economy	
	Slump	**Normal**	**Boom**
Operating income	$75,000	125,000	175,000
Interest	$50,000	50,000	50,000
Equity earnings	$25,000	75,000	125,000
Earnings per share	$.50	1.50	2.50
Return on shares (%)	5	15	25
		Expected outcome	

The price of each share is $10. The firm expects to produce a level stream of earnings and dividends in perpetuity. With no growth forecast, stockholders' expected return is equal to the dividend yield—that is, the expected dividend per share divided by the price, $1.25/$10.00 = .125, or 12.5 percent.

Cleo has come to the conclusion that shareholders would be better off if the company had equal proportions of debt and equity. She therefore proposes to issue $500,000 of debt at an interest rate of 10 percent and to use the proceeds to repurchase 50,000 shares. This is called a **restructuring.** The assets and investment policy of the firm are not affected. Only the financing mix changes.

restructuring: Process of changing the firm's capital structure without changing its assets.

To support her proposal, Cleo has analyzed the situation under different assumptions about operating income. These calculations are shown in Table 14.2.

In order to see more clearly how debt finance would affect earnings per share, Cleo has also produced Figure 14.1. The black line shows how earnings per share would

Figure 14.1

Borrowing increases River Cruises' earnings per share (EPS) when operating income is greater than $100,000 but reduces it when operating income is less than $100,000. Expected EPS rises from $1.25 to $1.50.

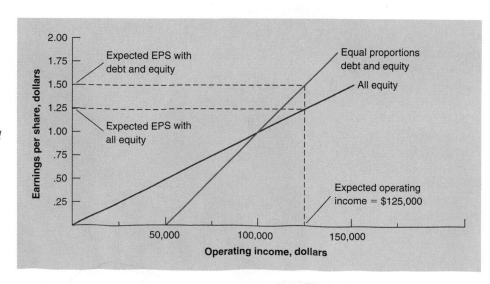

Table 14.3

Individual investors can replicate River Cruises' borrowing by borrowing on their own. In this example we assume that River Cruises has not restructured. However, the investor can put up $10 of her own money, borrow $10 more, and buy two shares at $10 apiece. This generates the same rates of return as in Table 14.2.

	State of the Economy		
	Slump	**Normal**	**Boom**
Earnings on two shares	$1.50	2.50	3.50
Less interest at 10%	$1.00	1.00	1.00
Net earnings on investment	$.50	1.50	2.50
Return on $10 investment (%)	5	15	25
		Expected outcome	

vary with operating income under the firm's current all-equity financing. It is therefore simply a plot of the data in Table 14.1. The blue line shows how earnings per share would vary if the company moves to equal proportions of debt and equity. It is therefore a plot of the data in Table 14.2. The table is identical to Table 14.1 except that now River Cruises is financed partly by debt.

Cleo reasons as follows: "It is clear that debt could either increase or reduce the return to the equityholder. In a slump the return to the equityholder is *reduced* by the use of debt, but otherwise it is *increased*. We could be heading for a recession but it doesn't look likely. So we can probably best help our shareholders by going ahead with the debt issue."

As financial manager, Antony should reply as follows: "I agree that borrowing will help the shareholders as long as we avoid a slump. But your argument ignores the fact that River Cruises' shareholders have the alternative of borrowing on their own account. For example, suppose River Cruises does *not* borrow. In that case an investor could go to the bank, borrow $10, and then invest $20 in two shares. Such an investor would put up only $10 of her own money. Table 14.3 shows how the payoffs on this $10 investment vary with River Cruises' operating income. You can see that these payoffs are exactly the same as the investor would get by buying one share in the company after the restructuring. (Compare the last two lines of Table 14.2 and 14.3.) It makes no difference whether shareholders borrow directly or whether River Cruises borrows on their behalf. Therefore, if River Cruises goes ahead and borrows, it will not allow investors to do anything that they could not do already, and so it cannot increase the value of the firm."

"We can run the same argument in reverse and show that investors also won't be any *worse* off after the restructuring. Imagine an investor who owns two shares in the company before the restructuring. If River Cruises borrows money, there is some chance that the return on the shares will be lower than before. If that possibility is not to our investor's taste, he can buy one share in the restructured company and also invest $10 in the firm's debt. Table 14.4 shows how the payoff on this investment varies with River Cruises' operating income. You can see that these payoffs are exactly the same as the investor got before the restructuring. (Compare the last lines of Table 14.1 and 14.4.) By lending half of his capital (by investing in River Cruises' debt), the investor exactly offsets the effect of the company borrowing. So if River Cruises goes ahead and borrows, it won't *stop* investors from doing anything that they could previously do."

This recreates MM's argument. As long as investors can borrow or lend on their own account on the same terms as the firm, they are not going to pay more for a firm that has borrowed on their behalf. The value of the firm after the restructuring must be the same as before.

Table 14.4
Individual investors can also undo the effects of River Cruises' borrowing. Here the investor buys one share for $10 and lends out $10 more. Compare these rates of return to the original returns of River Cruises in Table 14.1.

	State of the Economy		
	Slump	Normal	Boom
Earnings on one share	$.50	1.50	2.50
Plus interest at 10%	$1.00	1.00	1.00
Net earnings on investment	$1.50	2.50	3.50
Return on $20 investment (%)	7.5	12.5	17.5
		Expected outcome	

MM's proposition I (debt irrelevance proposition): The value of a firm is unaffected by its capital structure.

> **In other words, the value of the firm must be unaffected by its capital structure.**

This conclusion is widely known as **MM's proposition I.** It is also called the **MM debt irrelevance proposition,** because it shows that under ideal conditions the firm's debt policy shouldn't matter to shareholders.

▶ **Self-Test 14.1**

Suppose that River Cruises had issued $750,000 of debt, using the proceeds to buy back stock.

a. What would be the impact of a $50,000 change in operating income on earnings per share?
b. Show how a conservative investor could "undo" the change in River Cruises' capital structure by varying the investment strategy shown in Table 14.4. *Hint:* The investor will have to lend $3 for every dollar invested in River Cruises' stock.

How Borrowing Affects Risk and Return

Cleo's calculations in Table 14.2 showed that issuing debt would increase the shareholder's *expected* return. But what about risk? You can see that the company's operating income is the same after the restructuring. So the debt-equity ratio does not affect the **operating risk,** or equivalently, the **business risk** of the firm. But with less equity outstanding, a change in operating income has a greater impact on earnings per share. Suppose operating income drops from $125,000 to $75,000. Under all-equity financing, there are 100,000 shares; so earnings per share fall by $.50. With 50 percent debt, there are only 50,000 shares outstanding; so the same drop in operating income reduces earnings per share by $1.00.

operating risk, business risk: Risk in firm's operating income.

financial leverage: Increase in the variability of shareholder returns that comes from the use of debt.

You can see now why the use of debt finance is known as **financial leverage** and a firm that has issued debt is described as a *levered firm.* The debt increases the spread of percentage stock returns. If the firm is financed entirely by equity, a decline of $50,000 in operating income reduces the return on the shares by 5 percentage points. If the firm issues debt, then the same decline of $50,000 in operating income reduces the return on the shares by 10 percentage points. (Compare Tables 14.1 and 14.2.) In other words, the effect of leverage is to double the magnitude of the swings in the return on River Cruises' shares. Whatever the beta of the firm's shares before the restructuring, it would be twice as high afterward.

financial risk: Risk to shareholders resulting from the use of debt.

> Debt finance does not affect the operating risk but it does add *financial risk*. With only half the equity to absorb the same amount of operating risk, risk per share must double.[1]

Consider now the implications of MM's proposition I for the expected return on River Cruises' stock. Before the proposed debt issue, the expected stream of earnings and dividends per share is $1.25. Since investment in the shares is risky, the shareholders require a return of 12.5 percent, or 2.5 percent above the interest rate. So the share price (which for a perpetuity is equal to the expected dividends divided by the required return) is $1.25/.125 = $10. The good news is that after the debt issue, expected earnings and dividends rise to $1.50. The bad news is that the risk of the shares has now doubled. So instead of being content with a return of 2.5 percent above the interest rate, shareholders now demand a return of 5 percent more than the interest rate—that is, a required return of 10 + 5 = 15 percent. The benefit from the rise in dividends is exactly canceled out by the rise in the required return. The share price after the debt issue is $1.50/.15 = $10—exactly the same as before.

	Current Structure: All Equity	Proposed Structure: Equal Debt and Equity
Expected earnings per share	$1.25	$1.50
Share price	$10	$10
Expected return on share	12.5%	15.0%

Thus leverage increases the expected return to shareholders but it also increases the risk. The two effects offset each other, leaving shareholder value unchanged.

Debt and the Cost of Capital

In Chapter 10 you learned that the expected return on the firm's bundle of assets is simply a weighted average of the expected returns on the firm's securities. This is termed the *weighted-average cost of capital,* or *WACC*. WACC is the required rate of return for a project with the same risk as the firm's existing business. Firms use WACC as a discount rate for "average risk" projects and as a benchmark for thinking about the discount rate for safer or riskier projects.

The formula for the weighted-average cost of capital is

$$\text{WACC} = \begin{array}{c}\text{expected return} \\ \text{on firm's assets}\end{array} = \begin{array}{c}\text{expected return} \\ \text{on debt}\end{array} \times \begin{array}{c}\text{proportion} \\ \text{in debt}\end{array}$$
$$+ \begin{array}{c}\text{expected return} \\ \text{on equity}\end{array} \times \begin{array}{c}\text{proportion} \\ \text{in equity}\end{array}$$

$$\textbf{WACC} = r_{\text{assets}} = r_{\text{debt}}\left(\frac{D}{D+E}\right) + r_{\text{equity}}\left(\frac{E}{D+E}\right)$$

Note that we are ignoring taxes.[2] Also remember that D and E are the *market* values of the firm's debt and equity.

---

[1] Think back to Section 7.2, where we showed that fixed costs increase the variability in a firm's profits. These fixed costs are said to provide *operating leverage*. It is exactly the same with debt. Debt interest is a fixed cost and therefore debt magnifies the variability of profits after interest. These interest charges provide *financial leverage*.

[2] When taxes are recognized, r_{debt} is multiplied by $(1 - T_c)$, where T_c is the marginal corporate tax rate. See Section 10.2 of Chapter 10.

MM's proposition I states that the firm's choice of capital structure does not affect the firm's operating income or the value of its assets. So r_{assets}, the expected return on the package of debt and equity, is unaffected.

However, we have just seen that leverage does increase the risk of the equity and the return that shareholders demand. To see how the expected return on equity varies with leverage, we simply rearrange the weighted-average cost of capital formula as follows:

$$r_{equity} = r_{assets} + \frac{D}{E}(r_{assets} - r_{debt})$$

which in words says that

$$\begin{array}{ccc} \text{Expected} & \text{expected} & \\ \text{return} = \text{return} + & \left[\begin{array}{c}\text{debt-}\\ \text{equity} \times \\ \text{ratio}\end{array}\left(\begin{array}{cc}\text{expected} & \text{expected}\\ \text{return on} - \text{return on}\\ \text{assets} & \text{debt}\end{array}\right)\right] \\ \text{on equity} & \text{on assets} & \end{array}$$

MM's proposition II: The required rate of return on equity increases as the firm's debt-equity ratio increases.

This is **MM's proposition II.** It states that the expected rate of return on the common stock of a levered firm increases in proportion to the debt-equity ratio (D/E), expressed in market values. Note that $r_{equity} = r_{assets}$ if the firm has no debt.

▶ Example 14.1 *River Cruises' Cost of Equity*

We can check out MM's proposition II for River Cruises. Before the decision to borrow

$$r_{equity} = r_{assets} = \frac{\text{expected operating income}}{\text{market value of all securities}}$$
$$= \frac{125,000}{1,000,000} = .125, \text{ or } 12.5\%$$

If the firm goes ahead with its plan to borrow, the expected return on assets, r_{assets}, is still 12.5 percent. So the expected return on equity is

$$r_{equity} = r_{assets} + \frac{D}{E}(r_{assets} - r_{debt})$$
$$= .125 + \frac{500,000}{500,000}(.125 - .10)$$
$$= .15, \text{ or } 15\%$$

We pointed out in Chapter 10 that you can think of a debt issue as having an explicit cost and an implicit cost. The explicit cost is the rate of interest charged on the firm's debt. When Cleo said that debt would benefit shareholders as long as the firm earned more than the interest rate on its assets, she was focusing only on the explicit cost.

Debt also increases shareholder risk and causes shareholders to demand a higher return on their investment. Once you recognize this implicit cost, debt is no cheaper than equity—the return that investors require on their assets is unaffected by the firm's borrowing decision.

▶ Self-Test 14.2

When the firm issues debt, why does r_{assets}, the weighted-average cost of capital, remain fixed, while the expected return on equity r_{equity}, changes? Why is it not the other way around?

Figure 14.2

MM's proposition II with risk-free debt. The expected return on River Cruises' equity rises in line with the debt-equity ratio. The weighted average of the expected returns on debt and equity is constant, equal to the expected return on assets.

You can now see how MM's theory underlies calculations of the weighted-average cost of capital. When in Chapter 10 we asserted that r_{assets} should not depend on the fractions of debt and equity financing, we were really relying on MM's proposition I; when we calculated r_{equity} for Geothermal, Inc. (in Section 10.1), and Big Oil (in Section 10.5), we were really using MM's proposition II.

The implications of MM's proposition II are shown in Figure 14.2. No matter how much the firm borrows, the expected return on the package of debt and equity, r_{assets}, is unchanged, but the expected rate of return on the separate parts of the package does change. How is this possible? Because the proportions of debt and equity in the package are also changing.

In Figure 14.2 we have drawn the rate of interest on the debt as constant no matter how much the firm borrows. That is not wholly realistic. It is true that most large companies could borrow a little more or less without noticeably affecting the interest rate that they pay. But at extreme debt levels lenders become concerned that they may not get their money back and they demand higher rates of interest to reflect this. Figure 14.3

Figure 14.3

MM's proposition II when debt is not risk-free. As the debt-equity ratio increases, debtholders demand a higher expected rate of return to compensate for the risk of default. The expected return on equity increases more slowly when debt is risky because the debtholders take on part of the risk. The expected return on the package of debt and equity, r_{assets}, remains constant.

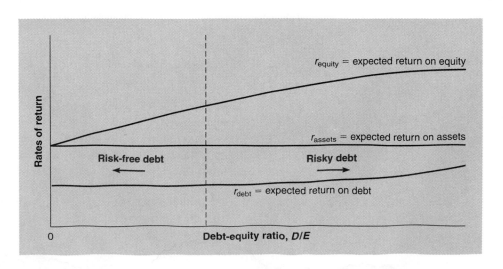

modifies Figure 14.2 to take account of this. You can see that as the firm borrows more, the risk of default increases and the firm has to pay higher rates of interest. Proposition II continues to predict that the expected return on the package of debt and equity does not change. However, the slope of the r_{equity} line now tapers off as D/E increases. Why? Essentially because holders of risky debt begin to bear part of the firm's operating risk. As the firm borrows more, more of that risk is transferred from stockholders to bondholders.

14.2 *How Corporate Taxes Affect Debt Policy*

The MM propositions suggest that debt policy should not matter in well-functioning capital markets. No matter how much the firm borrows, the value of the firm stays the same. So does the weighted-average cost of capital. Yet financial managers do worry about debt policy and for good reasons. Now we are ready to see why.

If debt policy were *completely* irrelevant, actual debt ratios would vary randomly from firm to firm and from industry to industry. Yet almost all airlines, utilities, banks, and real estate development companies rely heavily on debt. And so do many firms in capital-intensive industries like steel, aluminum, chemicals, petroleum, and mining. On the other hand, it is rare to find a drug company or advertising agency that is not predominantly equity-financed. Glamorous "growth" companies seldom use much debt despite rapid expansion and often heavy requirements for capital.

The explanation of these patterns lies partly in the things that we have so far left out of our discussion. We have ignored taxes, bankruptcy, potential conflicts of interest between the firm's security holders, and ways that the firm's financing decisions could affect its investment decisions. Now we will put all these things back in: taxes first, then the costs of bankruptcy and financial distress. This will lead us to conflicts of interest and to those possible interactions between financing and investment decisions. In the end we will see that debt policy *does* matter.

However, we will not throw away the MM theory. The MM propositions tell us when debt policy does *not* matter. As a result they also tell us where to look for reasons why firms *should* care about capital structure. Let's start looking.

Debt and Taxes at River Cruises

Debt financing has one important advantage. The interest that the company pays is a tax-deductible expense but equity income is subject to corporate tax.

To see the advantage of debt finance, let's look once again at River Cruises. Table 14.5 shows how expected income is reduced if profits are taxed at a rate of 35 percent. The left-hand column sets out the position if River Cruises is financed entirely by equity, whereas the right-hand column shows what happens if the firm issues $500,000 of debt at an interest rate of 10 percent.

Notice that the combined income of the debtholders and equityholders is higher by $17,500 when the firm is levered. This is because the interest payments are tax-deductible. Thus every dollar of interest reduces taxes by $.35. The total amount of

Table 14.5

Since debt interest is tax-deductible, River Cruises' debtholders and equityholders expect to receive a higher combined income when the firm is leveraged

	Zero Debt	$500,000 of Debt
Expected operating income	$125,000	$125,000
Debt interest at 10%	0	50,000
Before-tax income	125,000	75,000
Tax at 35%	43,750	26,250
After-tax income	81,250	48,750
Combined debt and equity income (debt interest + after-tax income)	81,250	98,750

interest tax shield: Tax savings resulting from deductibility of interest payments.

tax savings is simply .35 × interest payments. In the case of River Cruises, the **interest tax shield** is .35 × $50,000 = $17,500 each year. Since the debtholders receive no more than the going rate of interest, all the benefit of this interest tax shield is captured by the shareholders.[3]

The interest tax shield is a valuable asset. Suppose that River Cruises plans to replace its bonds when they mature and to keep "rolling over" the debt indefinitely. It therefore looks forward to a permanent stream of tax savings of $17,500 per year. These savings depend only on the corporate tax rate and on the ability of River Cruises to earn enough to cover interest payments. So the risk of the tax shield is likely to be small. Therefore, if we wish to compute the present value of all the future tax savings associated with permanent debt, we should discount the interest tax shields at a relatively low rate.

But what rate? The most common assumption is that the risk of the tax shields is the same as that of the interest payments generating them. Thus we discount at 10 percent, the expected rate of return demanded by investors who are holding the firm's debt. If the debt is permanent, then the firm can look forward to annual savings of $17,500 in perpetuity. Their present value is

$$\text{PV tax shield} = \frac{\$17,500}{.10} = \$175,000$$

This is what the tax savings are worth to River Cruises.

How does company value change? We continue to assume that if the firm is all-equity financed, the shareholders will demand a 12.5 percent return and therefore the company will be valued at $81,250/.125 = $650,000.[4] But if River Cruises issues $500,000 of permanent debt, the package of all the firm's securities increases by the value of the tax shield to $650,000 + $175,000 = $825,000.

Let us generalize. The interest payment each year equals the rate of interest times the amount borrowed, or $r_{\text{debt}} \times D$. The annual tax saving is the corporate tax rate T_c times the interest payment. Therefore,

$$\text{Annual tax shield} = \text{corporate tax rate} \times \text{interest payment}$$
$$= T_c \times (r_{\text{debt}} \times D)$$

[3]Table 14.5 shows that the *expected* combined income of debtholders and equityholders increases by the interest tax shield, $17,500. In fact, we can say more than this: as long as the firm is paying taxes, the value of the tax shield equals $17,500 in all three economic scenarios considered in Tables 14.1 and 14.2. Problem 6 at the end of the chapter asks you to show that tax savings are independent of business conditions.

[4]The firm was worth $1 million when the corporate tax rate was zero (see Table 14.1). It is worth only $650,000 when all-equity financed because 35 percent of income is lost to taxes.

If the tax shield is perpetual, we use the perpetuity formula to calculate its present value:

$$\textbf{PV tax shields} = \frac{\textbf{annual tax shield}}{r_{\text{debt}}} = \frac{T_c \times (r_{\text{debt}} \times D)}{r_{\text{debt}}} = T_c D$$

Of course the present value of the tax shield is less if the firm does not plan to borrow permanently or if it may not be able to use the tax shields in the future.[5]

▶ **Self-Test 14.3**   In 1995 Exxon paid out $571 million as debt interest. How much more tax would Exxon have paid if the firm was entirely equity-financed? What is the present value of Exxon's interest tax shield if (a) Exxon planned to keep its borrowing permanently at the 1995 level, (b) it intended to eliminate all debt after 1 year? Assume an interest rate of 8 percent and a corporate tax rate of 35 percent.

How Interest Tax Shields Contribute to the Value of Stockholders' Equity

MM's proposition I amounts to saying that "the value of the pizza does not depend on how it is sliced." The pizza is the firm's assets, and the slices are the debt and equity claims. If we hold the pizza constant, then a dollar more of debt means a dollar less of equity value.

But there is really a third slice—the government's. MM would still say that the value of the pizza—in this case the company value before taxes—is not changed by slicing. But anything the firm can do to reduce the size of the government's slice obviously leaves more for the others. One way to do this is to borrow money. This reduces the firm's tax bill and increases the cash payments to the investors. The value of their investment goes up by the present value of the tax savings.

In a no-tax world, MM's proposition I states that the value of the firm is unaffected by capital structure. But MM also modified proposition I to recognize corporate taxes:

Value of levered firm = value if all-equity financed + present value of tax shield

In the special case of permanent debt,

Value of levered firm = value if all-equity financed + $T_c D$

This "corrected" formula is illustrated in Figure 14.4. It implies that borrowing increases firm value and shareholders' wealth.

Corporate Taxes and the Weighted-Average Cost of Capital

We have shown that when there are corporate taxes, debt provides the company with a valuable tax shield. Few companies explicitly calculate the present value of

---

[5]The value of the interest tax shield is also reduced if the future level of debt is not fixed, but it is increased when the firm does well and paid down when it does poorly. In this case the future interest tax shields are correlated with the firm's performance and therefore risky.

Figure 14.4

The heavy green line shows how the availability of interest tax shields affects the market value of the firm. Additional borrowing decreases corporate income tax payments and increases the cash flows available to lenders and stockholders. Thus market value increases.

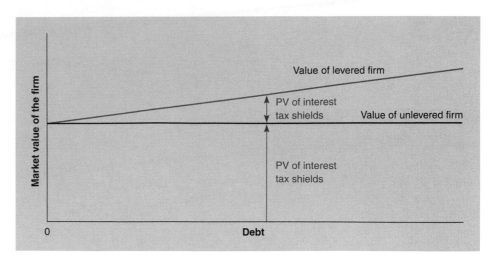

interest tax shields associated with a particular borrowing policy. The tax shields are not forgotten, however, because they show up in the discount rate used to evaluate capital investments.

Since debt interest is tax-deductible, the government in effect pays 35 percent of the interest cost. So to keep its investors happy, the firm has to earn the *after-tax* rate of interest on its debt and the return required by shareholders. Once we recognize the tax benefit of debt, the weighted-average cost of capital formula (see Section 11.2 for a review if you need one) becomes

$$\text{WACC} = (1 - T_c)\, r_{\text{debt}} \left(\frac{D}{D + E} \right) + r_{\text{equity}} \left(\frac{E}{D + E} \right)$$

Notice that when we allow for the tax advantage of debt, the weighted-average cost of capital depends on the *after-tax* rate of interest, $(1 - T_c) \times r_{\text{debt}}$. Of course if the tax rate, T_c, is zero, we are back to our original formula, which ignored taxes.

▶ **Example 14.2**   *WACC and Debt Policy*

We can use the weighted-average cost of capital formula to see how leverage affects River Cruises' cost of capital if the company pays corporate tax. When a company has no debt, the weighted-average cost of capital and the return required by shareholders are identical. In the case of River Cruises the WACC with all-equity financing is 12.5 percent, and the value of the firm is $650,000.

Now let us calculate the weighted-average cost of capital if River Cruises issues $500,000 of permanent debt ($D = \$500,000$). Company value increases by the $175,000 interest tax shield to $825,000 (meaning that $D + E = \$825,000$) and therefore the value of equity must be $825,000 - \$500,000 = \$325,000$ ($E = \$325,000$). Table 14.5 shows that when River Cruises borrows, the expected equity income and dividend is $48,750. So the expected return to shareholders is 48,750/325,000 = 15 percent ($r_{\text{equity}} = .15$). The interest rate is 10 percent ($r_{\text{debt}} = .10$) and the corporate tax rate is 35 percent ($T_c = .35$). This is all the information we need to see how

Figure 14.5

Changes in River Cruises' cost of capital with increased leverage when there are corporate taxes. The after-tax cost of debt is assumed to be constant at $(1 - .35)10 = 6.5$ percent. With increased borrowing the cost of equity rises, but more slowly than in the no-tax case (see Figure 14.2). The weighted-average cost of capital (WACC) declines as the firm borrows more.

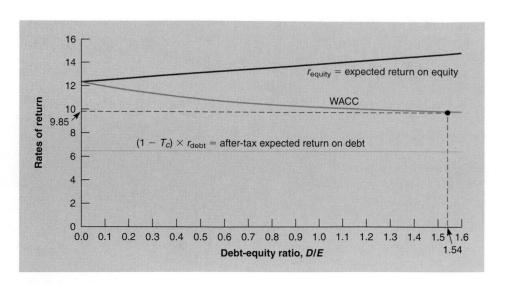

leverage affects River Cruises' weighted-average cost of capital:

$$\text{WACC} = (1 - T_c)r_{\text{debt}}\left(\frac{D}{D + E}\right) + r_{\text{equity}}\left(\frac{E}{D + E}\right)$$

$$= (1 - .35)\ .10\left(\frac{500{,}000}{825{,}000}\right) + .15\left(\frac{325{,}000}{825{,}000}\right) = .0985,\ \text{or } 9.85\%$$

We saw earlier that if there are no corporate taxes, the weighted-average cost of capital is unaffected by borrowing. But when there are corporate taxes, debt provides the company with a new benefit—the interest tax shield. In this case leverage reduces the weighted-average cost of capital (in River Cruises' case from 12.5 percent to 9.85 percent).

Figure 14.5 repeats Figure 14.2 except that now we have allowed for the effect of taxes on River Cruises' cost of capital. You can see that as the company borrows more, the expected return on equity rises, but the rise is less rapid than in the absence of taxes. As a result, the weighted-average cost of capital declines. For example, if the company has debt of $500,000 the equity is worth $325,000 and the debt/equity ratio (D/E) is $500,000/$325,000 = 1.54. Figure 14.5 shows that with this amount of debt the weighted-average cost of capital is 9.85 percent, the same figure that we calculated above.

The Implications of Corporate Taxes for Capital Structure

If borrowing provides an interest tax shield, the implied optimal debt policy appears to be embarrassingly extreme: all firms should borrow to the hilt. This maximizes firm value and minimizes the weighted-average cost of capital.

MM were not that fanatical about it. No one would expect the gains to apply at extreme debt ratios. For example, if a firm borrows heavily, all its operating income may go to pay interest and therefore there are no corporate taxes to be paid. There is no point in such firms borrowing any more.

There may also be some tax *disadvantages* to borrowing, for bondholders have to pay personal income tax on any interest they receive. Stockholders, on the other hand, can get a tax break, because some of their returns come as capital gains. Capital gains are not taxed until the stock is sold and are then taxed at a lower rate.[6]

All this suggests that there may come a point at which the tax savings from debt level off and may even decline. But it doesn't explain why highly profitable companies with large tax bills often thrive with little or no debt. There are clearly factors besides tax to consider.

14.3 *Costs of Financial Distress*

Financial distress occurs when promises to creditors are broken or honored with difficulty. Sometimes financial distress leads to bankruptcy. Sometimes it only means skating on thin ice.

costs of financial distress: Costs arising from bankruptcy or distorted business decisions before bankruptcy.

As we will see, financial distress is costly. Investors know that levered firms may run into financial difficulty, and they worry about the **costs of financial distress.** That worry is reflected in the current market value of the levered firm's securities. Even if the firm is not now in financial distress, investors factor the potential for future distress into their assessment of current value. This means that the overall value of the firm is

$$\begin{array}{c} \text{Overall market} \\ \text{value} \end{array} = \begin{array}{c} \text{value if all-equity} \\ \text{financed} \end{array} + \begin{array}{c} \text{PV tax} \\ \text{shield} \end{array} - \begin{array}{c} \text{PV costs of} \\ \text{financial distress} \end{array}$$

The present value of the costs of financial distress depends both on the probability of distress and on the magnitude of the costs encountered if distress occurs.

Figure 14.6 shows how the trade-off between the tax benefits of debt and the costs of distress determines optimal capital structure. The present value of the tax shield initially increases as the firm borrows more but eventually levels off as the firm runs out of taxable profits.

> **At moderate debt levels the probability of financial distress is trivial and therefore the tax advantages of debt dominate. But at some point the probability of financial distress increases rapidly with additional borrowing and the potential costs of distress begin to take a substantial bite out of firm value. The theoretical optimum is reached when the present value of tax savings due to additional borrowing is just offset by increases in the present value of costs of distress.**

Let us now identify these costs of financial distress.

Bankruptcy Costs

In principle, bankruptcy is merely a legal mechanism for allowing creditors to take over the firm when the decline in the value of its assets triggers a default on outstanding debt. If the company cannot pay its debts, the company is turned over to the creditors, who become the new owners; the old stockholders are left with nothing. Bankruptcy is not the *cause* of the decline in the value of the firm. It is the result.

---

[6]Recall from Chapter 2 that tax rates on ordinary income can reach 39.6 percent. The maximum tax rate on capital gains is only 20 percent.

Figure 14.6

The trade-off theory of capital structure. The curved green line shows how the market value of the firm at first increases as the firm borrows, but finally decreases as the costs of financial distress become more and more important. The optimal capital structure balances the costs of financial distress against the value of the interest tax shields generated by borrowing.

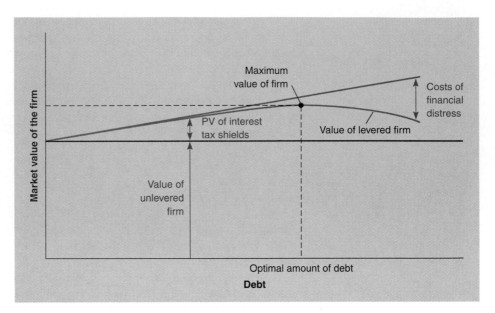

In practice, of course, anything involving courts and lawyers cannot be free. The fees involved in a bankruptcy proceeding are paid out of the remaining value of the firm's assets. Creditors end up with only what is left after paying the lawyers and other court expenses. If there is a possibility of bankruptcy, the current market value of the firm is reduced by the present value of these potential costs.

It is easy to see how increased leverage affects the costs of financial distress. The more the firm owes, the higher the chance of default and therefore the greater the expected value of the associated legal costs. This reduces the current market value of the firm.

Creditors foresee the costs and realize that if default occurs, the lawyers' fees will come out of the value of the firm. For this they demand compensation in advance in the form of a higher promised interest rate. This reduces the possible payoffs to stockholders and reduces the current market value of their shares.

▶ **Self-Test 14.4**

Suppose investors foresee $2 million of legal costs if the firm defaults on its bonds. How does this affect the value of the firm's bonds if bankruptcy occurs? How does it affect the value of the bonds *today*? Their promised yield to maturity?

Evidence on Bankruptcy Costs

Bankruptcy costs can add up fast. Manville, which declared bankruptcy in 1982 because of expected liability for asbestos-related health claims, spent $200 million on bankruptcy fees before it emerged from bankruptcy in 1988.[7] The legal and professional fees of the Braniff International Corporation bankruptcy were reported to be $12 million; legal fees in the Continental Airlines bankruptcy were running $2 million a

---

[7]S. P. Sherman, "Bankruptcy's Spreading Blight," *Fortune*, June 3, 1991, pp. 123–132.

month.[8] Daunting as these numbers may seem, they are not a large fraction of these airlines' asset values. For example, in 1984 it cost about $95 million to buy *one* airplane, a Boeing 747.

This is typical. Researchers have found that the legal and administrative costs of bankruptcies amount to only a small percentage of the total prebankruptcy value of the companies' debt and equity.[9]

Direct versus Indirect Costs of Bankruptcy

Thus far we have discussed only the *direct* (that is, legal and administrative) costs of bankruptcy. There are also indirect costs, which are nearly impossible to measure. But we have circumstantial evidence indicating their importance.

The indirect costs reflect the difficulties of running a company while it is going through bankruptcy. Management's efforts to prevent further deterioration in the firm's business are often undermined by the delays and legal tangles that go with bankruptcy. When Eastern Airlines entered bankruptcy in 1989, it was in severe financial trouble, but it still had some valuable, profit-making routes and readily saleable assets such as planes and terminal facilities. After nearly 2 years under the "protection" of a bankruptcy court, which allowed Eastern to continue loss-making operations, there was hardly anything of value left when it was finally forced to liquidate in 1991. Another illustration of the indirect costs of bankruptcy is provided in the nearby box, which describes the disruption to Penn Central Railroad's business.

 See box p. 412

We don't know how much these indirect costs add to the expenses of bankruptcy. We suspect it is a significant number, particularly in the case of large firms for which bankruptcy proceedings may be prolonged. Perhaps the best evidence is the reluctance of creditors to force a firm into bankruptcy. In principle, they would be better off to end the agony and seize the assets as soon as possible. But instead creditors often overlook defaults in the hope of nursing the firm over a difficult period. They do this in part to avoid the costs of bankruptcy. There is an old financial saying, "Borrow $1,000 and you've got a banker. Borrow $10,000,000 and you've got a partner."

Financial Distress without Bankruptcy

Not every firm that gets into trouble goes bankrupt. As long as the firm can scrape up enough cash to pay the interest on its debt, it may be able to postpone bankruptcy for many years. Eventually the firm may recover, pay off its debt, and escape bankruptcy altogether.

Skating on thin ice can be useful if it makes the skater concentrate. Likewise, some observers believe that managers of highly levered firms are more likely to work harder, run a leaner operation, and think more carefully before they spend money. This was one of the justifications for the increased use of leverage during the 1980s.

See box p. 413

The nearby box tells the story of how Sealed Air Corporation borrowed over $300 million, using the proceeds of the loan to pay a special cash dividend to shareholders. The net effect was to increase debt from a trivial level to fully 65 percent of the total value of the firm. The dramatic increase in debt committed the firm to pay out large sums of money as interest, leaving it with little opportunity to fritter its cash

---

[8]*Aviation Week and Space Technology,* April 23, 1984, p. 35.

[9]J. B. Warner, "Bankruptcy Costs: Some Evidence," *Journal of Finance* 26 (May 1977), pp. 337–348.

Penn Central's Bankruptcy*

The Penn Central Railroad went under in June 1970. It was the largest and most dramatic corporate failure up to that time. Four years later, with bankruptcy proceedings nowhere near completion, *Business Week* published an article called "Why the Penn Central Is Falling Apart." Here are some excerpts.

The article noted that although the railroad needed to invest huge sums of money to rebuild its facilities and continue operations, its creditors were more concerned with getting their own money back, even if that meant shutting down the railroad. In a chicken-and-egg type of problem, the capital necessary to make the railroad viable would not be forthcoming unless Penn Central could convince investors that it could be reorganized as a viable corporation.

Penn Central could have raised money by selling off some of its assets, but its creditors naturally opposed this.

As the *Business Week* article put it:

Agonizingly for everyone on the Penn Central, there is a tremendous source of capital that cannot be touched. For example, just about every abandoned mine branch in the Allegheny Mountains is chock full of old Penn Central cars destined for scrap. With today's scrap prices, they are a potential gold mine. But the creditors will not allow this asset to be turned into cash that will be reinvested in the estate, since that estate is eroding everyday.

Penn Central's problems show that some of the most important costs of bankruptcy are difficult to measure. The disruption of business activity is less visible but can be far more costly than the firm's legal bills.

*Business Week, October 12, 1974.

away in pursuit of a comfortable life. Perhaps not surprisingly, Sealed Air showed great improvements in efficiency after the change in capital structure.

However, there are also drawbacks to extreme amounts of leverage. When a firm is in trouble, suppliers worry that they may not be paid, potential customers fear that the firm will not be able to honor its warranties, and employees start contemplating their next job. The firm's bondholders and stockholders both want it to recover, but in other respects their interests may be in conflict. In times of financial distress the security holders are like many political parties—united on generalities but threatened by squabbling on any specific issue.

> **Financial distress is costly when conflicts get in the way of running the business. Stockholders are tempted to forsake the usual objective of maximizing the overall market value of the firm and to pursue narrower self-interest instead. They are tempted to play games at the expense of their creditors. These games add to the costs of financial distress.**

We can illustrate some financial games with the case of Circular File, which is tottering on the brink of bankruptcy. It has large debts and large losses. As a result, Circular's assets have little value and if the debts were due today, Circular would default, leaving the firm bankrupt. The assets would then be sold off, the debtholders would receive a few cents on the dollar, and the shareholders would be left with nothing.

But suppose the debts are not due to be repaid until the end of the year. That 1-year grace period explains why Circular's shares still have value. The shareholders are betting on a stroke of luck that will rescue the firm and allow it to pay off its debts with something left over. The bet is a long shot—unless firm value increases sharply, the stock will be valueless. But the owners have a secret weapon: they control investment and operating strategy.

How Sealed Air's Change in Capital Structure Acted as a Catalyst to Organizational Change

Sealed Air Corporation manufactures a wide variety of packaging materials such as plastic packing bubbles and Jiffy padded envelopes.

As it entered 1989, Sealed Air was very conservatively financed with $33 million in total debt and over $54 million in cash. Thus, rather than borrowing cash, the company was actually a net lender. However, in June of that year Sealed Air dramatically changed its capital structure by paying a special one-time dividend of $40 a share. With about 8.25 million shares trading, the total cash payout amounted to almost $330 million, or close to 90 percent of the total market value of the firm's common stock. To help finance this special dividend, the company borrowed a total of $307 million. Thus, the company went overnight from being a net lender to being a very heavy borrower. Debt now amounted to 125 percent of the book value of the assets and 65 percent of their market value.

Until the change in capital structure Sealed Air's performance was no better than that of the industry as a whole. But the change was a prelude to a sharp improvement in the company's operating performance. In the following 5 years, operating profit increased by 70 percent while the asset base grew by only 9 percent. This improvement in profitability was more than matched by the company's stock market performance. The initial effect of Sealed Air's announced change in capital structure was a jump of 10 percent in the stock price. Over the next 5 ½ years the stock outperformed the market by 400 percent.

What then motivated the change in capital structure and what role, if any, did this change play in the company's subsequent performance?

Some of the gains from the change in capital structure may have come from the fact that the company was able to offset the interest payments against tax. But this does not appear to have been a primary motive. Instead, the change appears to have been management's response to the realization that life at Sealed Air was in many respects too comfortable. For years patents had insulated the company from competition. Cash was plentiful. So the company never needed to think hard about requests to invest in new projects and there was no sense of urgency in removing inefficiencies. In the management's view it would take nothing less than a "crisis" to shake employees out of their complacency. The change in capital structure was just such a crisis.

The sharp increase in debt levels meant that cash was no longer abundant for it was now needed to pay the debtholders and was literally essential to the company's survival. Thus managers now felt under pressure to make those efficiency gains that previously had not seemed worthwhile. As employees became aware of the need for more effective operations, it was possible to decentralize decision making within the company and to install a more effective system of performance measurement and compensation. The result was a sharp increase in profit margins and a reduction in the working capital and fixed assets employed to generate each dollar of sales. It seemed that the capital structure change had succeeded in kickstarting a remarkable improvement in Sealed Air's performance.

Source: Adapted from K. H. Wruck, "Financial Policy as a Catalyst for Organizational Change: Sealed Air Corporation's Leveraged Special Dividend," *Journal of Applied Corporate Finance* 7 (Winter 1995), pp. 20–37.

The First Game: Bet the Bank's Money. Suppose the company has the opportunity to take a wild, and possibly lousy, gamble. If it does not come off, the shareholders will be no worse off; the company will probably go under anyway. But if the gamble does succeed, there will be more than enough assets to pay off the debt and the surplus will go into the shareholders' pockets. You can see why management might want to take the chance. In taking the gamble, they are essentially betting the bank's money, but if Circular does hit the jackpot, the equityholders get most of the loot.

One owner-manager of a small bankrupt company called KenDavis Industries put the point this way: "Everyone agrees there is no shareholder equity—so *we've* got *nothing* to lose. The *banks* have it all on the line now—not us." In another case, the managers of the failing firm took the incentive to gamble literally. They went to Las Vegas and bet the company's money, hoping to win enough to pay off the creditors. The effects of such distorted incentives to take on risk are usually not this blatant, but the results can be the same. For example, Sambo's Restaurants borrowed against unencumbered assets while in bankruptcy proceedings and used the funds to pay for a risky marketing initiative, changing the name and concept of its restaurants. When the gamble failed, unsecured creditors suffered most of the loss: they received only 11 cents of each dollar owed them.[10]

These kinds of warped strategies for capital budgeting clearly are costly for the bondholders and for the firm as a whole. Why do we say they create costs of financial distress? Because the temptation to follow such strategies is strongest when the odds of default are high. A healthy firm would never invest in Circular File's negative-NPV gamble, since it would be gambling with its own money, not the bondholders'. The healthy firm's creditors would not be vulnerable to this type of game.

The Second Game: Don't Bet Your Own Money. We have just seen how shareholders, acting in their narrow self-interest, may take on unprofitable projects. These are errors of commission. We will now illustrate how conflicts of interest may also lead to errors of omission.

Suppose Circular File uncovers a relatively safe project with a positive NPV. Unfortunately, the project requires a substantial investment and Circular will need to raise the extra cash from its shareholders. Although the project has a positive NPV, the profits may not be sufficient to rescue the company from bankruptcy. If that is so, all the profits from the new project will be used to help pay off the banks, and the shareholders will get no return on the cash they put up. Although it is in the firm's interest to go ahead with the project, it is *not* in the owners' interest, and the project will be passed up.

Again, our example illustrates a general point. The value of any investment opportunity to the firm's *stockholders* is reduced because project benefits must be shared with the bondholders. Thus it may not be in the stockholders' self-interest to contribute fresh equity capital even if that means forgoing positive-NPV opportunities.

> These problems, which theoretically affect all levered firms, are most serious when firms are staring bankruptcy in the face. If the probability of default is high, then stockholders will not put up new money that will be used to pay off the bondholders. They are more concerned with taking money out of the firm than with putting new money in.

▶ **Self-Test 14.5** Suppose that, instead of changing its investment policy, Circular File issues new 1-year debt and uses the cash to buy back part of its stock. What happens to firm value? Who gains or loses? The new bondholders? The old bondholders? The stockholders?

What the Games Cost

The more the firm borrows, the greater the temptation to play such games. The increased odds of poor decisions in the future prompt investors to reduce today's assessment of the market value of the firm. Potential lenders, realizing that games

[10]These cases are cited in Lynn M. LoPucki, "The Trouble with Chapter 11," *Wisconsin Law Review,* 1993, pp. 729–760.

may be played at their expense in the future, protect themselves by demanding better terms on the money they lend today. So the fall in value comes out of stockholders' pockets. This is the reason that it is ultimately in the stockholders' interest to avoid temptation. The easiest way to do this is to limit borrowing to levels at which the firm's debt is safe or close to it.

Here we have the economic rationale for all that fine print in the bond agreement. Debt contracts almost always limit the amount of additional borrowing. Often they also limit dividend payments to stockholders. But lawyers cannot anticipate all eventualities. For example, they can't ensure that the company accepts all positive-NPV projects.

We do not mean to leave the impression that managers and stockholders always succumb to temptation unless restrained. Usually they refrain voluntarily, not only from a sense of fair play, but also on pragmatic grounds: a firm or individual that makes a killing today at the expense of a creditor will be coldly received when the time comes to borrow again. Aggressive game playing is done only by out-and-out crooks and by firms in extreme financial distress. Firms limit borrowing precisely because they don't wish to land in distress and be exposed to the temptation to play.

Costs of Distress Vary with Type of Asset

Suppose your firm's only asset is a large downtown hotel, mortgaged to the hilt. A recession hits, occupancy rates fall, and the mortgage payments cannot be met. The lender takes over and sells the hotel to a new owner and operator. The stock is worthless and you use the firm's stock certificates for wallpaper.

What is the cost of bankruptcy? In this example, probably very little. The value of the hotel is, of course, much less than you hoped, but that is due to the lack of guests, not to bankruptcy. Bankruptcy does not damage the hotel itself. The direct bankruptcy costs are restricted to items such as legal and court fees, real estate commissions, and the time the lender spends sorting things out.

Suppose we repeat the story of Heartbreak Hotel for Fledgling Electronics. Everything is the same, except for the underlying assets. Fledgling is a high-tech going concern and much of its value reflects investors' belief that its research team will come up with profitable ideas. Fledgling is a "people business"; its most important assets go down in the elevator and into the parking lot every night.

If Fledgling gets into trouble, the stockholders may be reluctant to put up money to cash in on those profitable ideas—why should they put up cash which will simply go to pay off the banks? Failure to invest is likely to be much more serious for Fledgling than for a company like Heartbreak Hotel.

If Fledgling finally defaults on its debt, the lender would find it much more difficult to cash in by selling off the assets. In fact, if trouble comes, many of those assets may drive into the sunset and never come back.

Some assets, like good commercial real estate, can pass through bankruptcy and reorganization largely unscathed; the values of other assets are likely to be considerably diminished. The losses are greatest for intangible assets that are linked to the continuing prosperity of the firm. That may be why debt ratios are low in the pharmaceutical industry, where company values depend on continued success in research and development. It may also explain the low debt ratios in many service companies, whose main asset is their skilled labor. The moral of these examples is:

> **Do not think only about whether borrowing is likely to bring trouble. Think also of the value that may be lost if trouble comes.**

14.4 Explaining Financing Choices

The Trade-Off Theory

Financial managers often think of the firm's debt-equity decision as a trade-off between interest tax shields and the costs of financial distress. Of course, there is controversy about how valuable interest tax shields are and what kinds of financial trouble are most threatening, but these disagreements are only variations on a theme. Thus Figure 14.6 illustrates the debt-equity trade-off.

This **trade-off theory** of capital structure recognizes that target debt ratios may vary from firm to firm. Companies with safe, tangible assets and plenty of taxable income to shield ought to have high target ratios. Unprofitable companies with risky, intangible assets ought to rely primarily on equity financing.

All in all, this trade-off theory of capital structure tells a comforting story. Unlike MM's theory, which seemed to say that with corporate taxes firms should take on as much debt as possible, it avoids extreme predictions and rationalizes moderate debt ratios. But what are the facts? Can the trade-off theory of capital structure explain how companies actually behave?

The answer is "yes and no." On the yes side, the trade-off theory successfully explains many industry differences in capital structure. For example, high-tech growth companies, whose assets are risky and mostly intangible, normally use relatively little debt. Utilities or retailers can and do borrow heavily because their assets are tangible and relatively safe.

On the no side, there are other things the trade-off theory cannot explain. It cannot explain why some of the most successful companies thrive with little debt. Consider, for example, the large pharmaceutical company Merck, which is basically all-equity financed. Granted, Merck's most valuable assets are intangible: the fruits of its research and development. We know that intangible assets and conservative capital structures should go together. But Merck also has a very large corporate income tax bill ($1.5 billion in 1995) and the highest possible credit rating. It could borrow enough to save tens of millions of tax dollars without raising a whisker of concern about possible financial distress.

Merck illustrates an odd fact about real-life capital structures: the most profitable companies generally borrow the least. Here the trade-off theory fails, for it predicts exactly the reverse. Under the trade-off theory, high profits should mean more debt-servicing capacity and more taxable income to shield and therefore should give a *higher* debt ratio.

▶ **Self-Test 14.6** Rank these industries in order of predicted debt ratios under the trade-off theory of capital structure (a) bioengineering; (b) auto manufacturing; (c) electric utilities

A Pecking Order Theory

There is an alternative story which could explain why profitable companies borrow less. Financial managers worry about how investors may interpret an equity issue. Remember from Chapter 13 that the announcement of a stock issue drives down the stock price. It seems that investors believe managers are more likely to issue stock when they believe it is overpriced.

Issuing debt, on the other hand, seems to have a trifling effect on stock prices. Presumably this is because there is less scope for debt to be misvalued and therefore a debt issue is a less worrisome signal to investors.

These observations suggest a **pecking order theory** of capital structure. It goes like this:

pecking order theory: Theory stating that firms prefer to issue debt rather than equity if internal finance is insufficient.

1. Firms prefer internal finance, since these funds are raised without sending any adverse signals that may lower the stock price.
2. If external finance is required, firms issue debt first and issue equity only as a last resort. This pecking order arises because an issue of debt is less likely to be interpreted by investors as a bad omen.

In this story, there is no clear target debt-equity mix, because there are two kinds of equity, internal and external. The first is at the top of the pecking order and the second is at the bottom. The pecking order explains why the most profitable firms generally borrow less; it is not because they have low target debt ratios but because they don't need outside money. Less profitable firms issue debt because they do not have sufficient internal funds for their capital investment program and because debt is first in the pecking order for *external* finance.

14.5 Summary

1. The firm's financing decision is a marketing problem. Think of the financial manager as taking all the firm's real assets and selling them to investors as a package of securities. Some financial managers choose the simplest package possible: all-equity financing. Others end up issuing dozens of debt and equity securities. The problem is to find the particular combination that maximizes the market value of the firm.

2. Modigliani and Miller's (MM's) famous proposition I states that no combination of securities is better than any other—the firm's overall market value (the value of all its securities) is independent of capital structure. MM agree that borrowing increases the expected rate of return on shareholders' investment. But it also increases the risk of the firm's shares. MM show that the extra risk offsets the increase in expected return, leaving shareholders no better or worse off.

3. MM's proposition I is important because it exposes logical traps which unwary financial managers are sometimes lured into and it draws attention to the fact that debt has both an explicit cost (the interest rate) and an implicit cost (the increased risk of the equity). It also tells us *where* to look for reasons why capital structure could be important. We discussed two such reasons—tax and financial distress.

4. Debt interest is deductible when computing taxes. So borrowing provides an interest tax shield, which is equal to the marginal corporate tax rate T_c times the interest payment $r_{\text{debt}} \times D$. This tax is usually valued by discounting at the borrowing rate r_{debt}. In the special case of permanent debt

$$\text{PV tax shield} = \frac{T_c \, (r_{\text{debt}} \times D)}{r_{\text{debt}}} = T_c D$$

Of course this tax shield is valuable only for companies that are making profits and therefore paying taxes.

5. The costs of financial distress can be broken down as follows:

  * Bankruptcy costs
    * Direct costs include legal fees and administrative costs.
    * Indirect costs reflect the difficulty of managing a company undergoing reorganization.
  * Costs of financial distress short of bankruptcy
    * Conflicts of interest between bondholders and stockholders of firms in financial distress may lead to poor operating performance and investment decisions.
    * The fine print in debt contracts tries to prevent stockholders playing "games" that reduce the overall value of the firm but it increases the costs of writing, monitoring, and enforcing the debt contract.

6. The capital structure choice involves a trade-off between the tax advantages of borrowing and the costs of financial distress. Firms with safe, tangible assets and plenty of taxable income to shield ought to have high debt targets. Unprofitable companies with risky, intangible assets ought to rely primarily on equity financing.

7. There is an alternative pecking order theory of capital structure, which states that firms use internal finance when available and choose debt over equity when external finance is needed. This pecking order may reflect managers' desire to avoid the adverse signals that seem to be associated with the announcement of an equity issue.

8. There are no simple answers to the capital structure decision. For example, debt may be better than equity in some cases, worse in others. However, there are at least four things that firms need to think about.

  * *Taxes:* If your firm is in a taxpaying position, an increase in leverage reduces the income tax paid by the company, though it may also increase the tax paid by investors. Of course you are not interested just in whether the company is currently paying taxes but in whether it will do so throughout the life of the debt. Firms with high and stable income streams are more likely to remain in a taxpaying position.
  * *Risk:* With or without bankruptcy, financial distress is costly. Other things equal, distress is more likely for firms with high business risk. That is why risky firms generally issue less debt.
  * *Asset Type:* If distress does occur, the costs are likely to be greatest for firms whose value depends on intangible assets. These firms are more likely to forgo profitable investment opportunities and, if default occurs, their assets may erode rapidly. Hence such firms should borrow less than firms that hold tangible and saleable assets.
  * *Financial Slack:* Since investors are likely to interpret an equity issue unfavorably, firms like to keep a certain amount of financial slack. By this we mean that firms try to ensure that they can find the cash for future investment opportunities without needing to issue equity. Firms that do not have financial slack may be caught at the bottom of the pecking order, and they may be forced to choose between passing over a good investment opportunity or damaging the share price by issuing equity.

Key Terms

capital structure	operating risk, business risk	interest tax shield
restructuring	financial leverage	costs of financial distress
MM's proposition I	financial risk	trade-off theory
(debt irrelevance proposition)	MM's proposition II	pecking order theory

Problems

1. **Effects of Leverage.** True or false? Explain briefly.

   a. Stockholders always benefit from an increase in company value.
   b. The reason that borrowing increases equity risk is that it increases the probability of bankruptcy.
   c. As long as the firm is *certain* that the return on assets will be higher than the interest rate, an issue of debt makes the shareholders better off.
   d. MM's proposition I implies that an issue of debt increases expected earnings per share and leads to an offsetting fall in the price-earnings ratio.

2. **Earnings and Leverage.** Suppose that River Cruises, which currently is all-equity financed, issues $250,000 of debt and uses the proceeds to repurchase 25,000 shares. Assume the firm pays no taxes, and that debt finance has no impact on its market value.

   a. Rework Table 14.2 to show how earnings per share and share return now vary with operating income.
   b. If the beta of River Cruises' assets is .8 and its debt is risk-free, what would be the beta of the equity after the increased borrowing?

3. **Leverage and Risk.**

   a. Calculate the rate of return on shares of River Cruises in all three economic scenarios of Table 14.1 for both the all-equity case and the case you worked out in the preceding problem in which debt = $250,000.
   b. Think of the "degree of financial leverage" as analogous to the notion of degree of operating leverage introduced in Chapter 7. Degree of financial leverage can be defined as the ratio of the change in rate of return on shares to the change in return on total assets, that is, operating income as a percentage of assets. What is the degree of financial leverage for River Cruises?
   c. Use your results from problem 2 to show that the beta of River Cruises after it issues the $250,000 of debt equals its unlevered beta times its degree of financial leverage.

4. **Debt Irrelevance.** Suppose an investor is unhappy with River Cruises' decision to borrow $250,000 (see problem 2). What modifications can she make to her own investment portfolio to offset the effects of the firm's additional borrowing?

5. **Leverage and P/E Ratio.** Calculate the ratio of price to expected earnings for River Cruises both before and after it borrows the $250,000. Why does the P/E ratio fall after the increase in leverage?

6. **Tax Shields.** Now suppose that the corporate tax is $T_c = .35$. Demonstrate that when River Cruises borrows the $250,000, the combined after-tax income of its debtholders and equityholders increases (compared to all-equity financing) by 35 percent of the firm's interest expense regardless of the state of the economy.

7. **Tax Shields.** Turn back to Table 14.1, which shows the operating income of River Cruises in various economic scenarios. Suppose now that the firm issues $1.25 million in debt. What would be the firm's taxable income in each of the three economic scenarios? Would the interest tax shield still have an expected value equal to .35 × interest expense? Would the tax shield still be nearly riskless?

8. **Equity Return and Leverage.** The common stock and debt of Northern Sludge are valued at $70 million and $30 million, respectively. Investors currently require a 16 percent return on the common stock and an 8 percent return on the debt.

   a. If Northern Sludge issues an additional $10 million of common stock and uses this money to retire debt, what happens to the expected return on the stock? Assume that the change in capital structure does not affect the risk of the debt and that there are no taxes.

b. If the risk of the debt did change, would your answer underestimate or overestimate the expected return on the stock?

9. **Earnings and Leverage.** Reliable Gearing currently is all-equity financed. It has 10,000 shares of equity outstanding, selling at $100 a share. The firm is considering a capital restructuring. The low-debt plan would entail a debt issue of $200,000 with the proceeds used to buy back stock. The high-debt plan would exchange $400,000 of debt for equity. The debt will pay an interest rate of 10 percent. The firm pays no taxes.

   a. What will be the debt-to-equity ratio after each possible restructuring?
   b. If earnings before interest and tax (EBIT) will be either $90,000 or $130,000, what will be earnings per share for each financing mix for both possible values of EBIT? If both scenarios are equally likely, what is expected EPS under each financing mix? Is the high-debt mix preferable?
   c. Suppose that EBIT is $100,000. What is EPS under each financing mix? Why are they the same in this particular case?

10. **Leverage and Risk Premiums.** Schuldenfrei A.G. is financed entirely by common stock and has a beta of 1.0. The firm pays no taxes. The stock has a price-earnings multiple of 10 and is priced to offer a 10 percent expected return. The company decides to repurchase half the common stock and substitute an equal value of debt. If the debt yields a *risk-free* 5 percent, calculate

   a. the beta of the common stock after the refinancing.
   b. the required return and risk premium on the common stock before the refinancing.
   c. the required return and risk premium on the common stock after the refinancing.
   d. the required return on the debt.
   e. the required return on the company (i.e., stock and debt combined) after the refinancing.

   Assume that the operating profit of the firm is expected to remain constant. Give

   f. the percentage increase in earnings per share.
   g. the new price-earnings multiple. *Hint:* Has anything happened to the stock price?

11. **Leverage and Capital Costs.** Hubbard's Pet Foods is financed 80 percent by common stock and 20 percent by bonds. The expected return on the common stock is 12 percent and the rate of interest on the bonds is 6 percent. Assume that the bonds are default-free and that there are no taxes. Now assume that Hubbard's issues more debt and uses the proceeds to retire equity. The new financing mix is 40 percent equity and 60 percent debt. If the debt is still default-free, what happens to the expected rate of return on equity? What happens to the expected return on the package of common stock and bonds?

12. **Leverage and Capital Costs.** "MM totally ignore the fact that as you borrow more, you have to pay higher rates of interest." Explain carefully whether this is a valid objection.

13. **Debt Irrelevance.** Indicate what's wrong with the following arguments:

   a. As the firm borrows more and debt becomes risky, both stock- and bondholders demand higher rates of return. Thus by *reducing* the debt ratio we can reduce *both* the cost of debt and the cost of equity, making everybody better off.
   b. Moderate borrowing doesn't significantly affect the probability of financial distress or bankruptcy. Consequently, moderate borrowing won't increase the expected rate of return demanded by stockholders.

c. A capital investment opportunity offering a 10 percent internal rate of return is an attractive project if it can be 100 percent debt-financed at an 8 percent interest rate.

d. The more debt the firm issues, the higher the interest rate it must pay. That is one important reason why firms should operate at conservative debt levels.

14. **Leverage and Capital Costs.** A firm currently has a debt-equity ratio of 1/2. The debt, which is virtually riskless, pays an interest rate of 6 percent. The expected rate of return on the equity is 12 percent. What would happen to the expected rate of return on equity if the firm reduced its debt-equity ratio to 1/3? Assume the firm pays no taxes.

15. **Leverage and Capital Costs.** If an increase in the debt-equity ratio makes both debt and equity more risky, how can the cost of capital remain unchanged?

16. **Trade-Off Theory.** Smoke and Mirrors currently has EBIT of $25,000 and is all-equity financed. EBIT is expected to stay at this level indefinitely. The firm pays corporate taxes equal to 35 percent of taxable income. The discount rate for the firm's projects is 10 percent.

a. What is the market value of the firm?

b. Now assume the firm issues $50,000 of debt paying interest of 6 percent per year, using the proceeds to retire equity. The debt is expected to be permanent. What will happen to the total value of the firm (debt plus equity)?

c. Recompute your answer to (b) under the following assumptions. The debt issue raises the possibility of bankruptcy. The firm has a 30 percent chance of going bankrupt after 3 years. If it does go bankrupt, it will incur bankruptcy costs of $200,000. The discount rate is 10 percent. Should the firm issue the debt?

17. **Tax Shields.** Here are book- and market-value balance sheets of the United Frypan Company:

BOOK-VALUE BALANCE SHEET

Net working capital	$ 20	Debt	$ 40
Long-term assets	80	Equity	60
	$100		$100

MARKET-VALUE BALANCE SHEET

Net working capital	$ 20	Debt	$ 40
Long-term assets	140	Equity	120
	$160		$160

Assume that MM's theory holds with taxes. There is no growth and the $40 of debt is expected to be permanent. Assume a 35 percent corporate tax rate.

a. How much of the firm's value is accounted for by the debt-generated tax shield?

b. Now suppose that Congress passes a law that eliminates the deductibility of interest for tax purposes after a grace period of 5 years. What will be the new value of the firm, other things equal? Assume an 8 percent borrowing rate.

18. **Tax Shields.** Look back to Table 2.2 where we provided a summary 1995 income statement for Nike, Inc. If the tax rate is 35 percent, what is Nike's annual interest tax shield? What is the present value of the annual tax shield if the company plans to increase its borrowing and interest payments by 5 percent a year indefinitely? Assume a discount rate of 8 percent.

19. **Costs of Financial Distress.** The Salad Oil Storage Company (SOS) has financed a large part of its facilities with long-term debt. There is a significant risk of default, but the company is not on the ropes yet. Explain

a. why SOS stockholders could lose by investing in a positive-NPV project financed by an equity issue.

    b. why SOS stockholders could gain by investing in a negative-NPV project financed by cash.

    c. why SOS stockholders could gain from paying out a large cash dividend.

20. **Financial Distress.**

    a. Who benefits from the fine print in bond contracts *after* the firm gets into financial trouble?

    b. Who benefits from the fine print when the bonds are issued?

21. **Costs of Financial Distress.** Let's go back to Circular File Company. Suppose that Circular's bonds have a face value of $50. Its current *market-value* balance sheet is

Assets		Liabilities and Equity	
Net working capital	$20	Bonds outstanding	$25
Fixed assets	10	Common stock	5
Total assets	$30	Total liabilities and shareholders' equity	$30

Who would gain or lose from the following maneuvers?

    a. Circular pays a $10 cash dividend.

    b. Circular halts operations, sells its fixed assets for $6, and converts net working capital into $20 cash. It invests its $26 in Treasury bills.

    c. Circular encounters an investment opportunity requiring a $10 initial investment with NPV = $0. It borrows $10 to finance the project by issuing more bonds with the same security, seniority, and so on, as the existing bonds.

    d. Circular finances the investment opportunity in part (c) by issuing more common stock.

22. **Trade-Off Theory.** Ronald Masulis[11] has analyzed the stock price impact of *exchange offers* of debt for equity or vice versa. In an exchange offer, the firm offers to trade freshly issued securities for seasoned securities in the hands of investors. Thus a firm that wanted to move to a higher debt ratio could offer to trade new debt for outstanding shares. A firm that wanted to move to a more conservative capital structure could offer to trade new shares for outstanding debt securities. Masulis found that debt-for-equity exchanges were good news (stock price increased on announcement) and equity-for-debt exchanges were bad news.

    a. Are these results consistent with the trade-off theory of capital structure?

    b. Are the results consistent with the evidence that investors regard announcements of (i) stock issues as bad news, (ii) stock repurchases as good news, and (iii) debt issues as no news, or at most trifling disappointments?

23. **Pecking Order Theory.** Construct a simple example to show that a firm's existing stockholders gain if it can sell overpriced stock to new investors and invest the cash in a zero-NPV project. Who loses from these actions? If investors are aware that managers are likely to issue stock when it is overpriced, what will happen to the stock price when the issue is announced?

24. **Pecking Order Theory.** When companies announce an issue of common stock, the share price typically falls. When they announce an issue of debt, there is typically only a negligible change in the stock price. Explain why.

25. **Bankruptcy.** What are the drawbacks of operating a firm that is close to bankruptcy? Give some examples.

---

[11]R. W. Masulis, "The Effects of Capital Structure Change on Security Prices: A Study of Exchange Offers," *Journal of Financial Economics* 8 (June1980), pp. 139–177, and "The Impact of Capital Structure Change on Firm Value," *Journal of Finance* 38 (March 1983), pp. 107–126.

26. **Taxes.** MM's proposition I suggests that in the absence of taxes it makes no difference whether the firm borrows on behalf of its shareholders or whether they borrow directly. However, if there are corporate taxes, this is no longer the case. Construct a simple example to show that with taxes it is better for the firm to borrow than for the shareholders to do so.

27. **Taxes.** MM's proposition I, when modified to recognize corporate taxes, suggests that there is a tax advantage to firm borrowing. If there is a tax advantage to firm borrowing, there is also a tax *disadvantage* to firm lending. Explain why.

Solutions to Self-Test Questions

14.1 a. Data:

Number of shares	25,000
Price per share	$10
Market value of shares	$250,000
Market value of debt	$750,000

	State of the Economy		
	Slump	Normal	Boom
Operating income, dollars	75,000	125,000	175,000
Interest, dollars	75,000	75,000	75,000
Equity earnings, dollars	0	50,000	100,000
Earnings per share, dollars	0	2.00	4.00
Return on shares, %	0	20	40

Every change of $50,000 in operating income leads to a change in the return to equityholders of 20 percent. This is double the swing in equity returns when debt was only $500,000.

b. The stockholder should lend out $3 for every $1 invested in River Cruises' stock. For example, he could buy one share for $10 and then lend $30. The payoffs are:

	State of the Economy		
	Slump	Normal	Boom
Earnings on one share	$0	2.00	4.00
Plus interest at 10%	$3.00	3.00	3.00
Net earnings	$3.00	5.00	7.00
Return on $40 investment	7.5%	12.5	17.5

14.2 The weighted-average cost of capital reflects the business risk of the firm's projects. That risk is unaffected by capital structure. As the financing mix changes, whatever equity is outstanding must absorb the fixed business risk of the firm. The less equity, the more risk absorbed per share. Therefore, as capital structure changes, r_{assets} is held fixed while r_{equity} adjusts.

14.3 Exxon's borrowing reduced taxable profits by $571 million. With a tax rate of 35 percent, tax was reduced by $.35 \times \$571 = \$200$ million. If the borrowing was permanent, Exxon would save this amount of tax each year. The present value of the tax saving would be $\$200/.08 = \$2,500$ million. If the tax shield lasted only for 1 year, the present value would be $\$200/1.08 = \$185$ million.

14.4 The bondholders will receive $2 million less than they would otherwise. This lowers the expected cash flow from the bond and reduces its present value. Therefore, the bonds will be priced lower and offer a higher *promised* yield to maturity. If the firm wants to issue the bonds at face value, it will need to offer a higher coupon rate and promised yield to maturity.

14.5 As long as the new bonds are issued at a fair price, the new bondholders don't lose and firm value is unaffected. The existing bondholders lose because Circular is more likely to default and the assets in the event of default will be shared with the new bondholders. The old bondholders' loss is the stockholders' gain.

14.6 The electric utility has the most stable cash flow. It also has the highest reliance on tangible assets that would not be impaired by a bankruptcy. It should have the highest debt ratio. The bioengineering firm has the least dependence on tangible assets and the most on assets that have value only if the firm continues as an ongoing concern. It probably also has the most unpredictable cash flows. It should have the lowest debt ratio.

Minicase

In March 2001 the management team of Londonderry Air (LA) met to discuss a proposal to purchase five shorthaul aircraft at a total cost of $25 million. There was general enthusiasm for the investment and the new aircraft were expected to generate an annual cash flow of $4 million for 20 years.

The focus of the meeting was on how to finance the purchase. LA had $20 million in cash and marketable securities (see table), but Ed Johnson, the Chief Financial Officer, pointed out that the company needed at least $10 million in cash to meet normal outflow and as a con-tingency reserve. This meant that there would be a cash deficiency of $15 million, which the firm would need to cover either by the sale of common stock or by additional borrowing. While admitting that the arguments were finely balanced, Johnson recommended an issue of stock. He pointed out that the airline industry was subject to wide swings in profits and the firm should be careful to avoid the risk of excessive borrowing. He estimated that in market value terms the long-term debt ratio was about 62 percent and that a further debt issue would raise the ratio to 64 percent.

Summary financial statements for Londonderry Air, 2000 (figures are book values, in millions of dollars)

Balance Sheet			
Bank debt	$ 50	Cash	$ 20
Other current liabilities	20	Other current assets	20
10% bond, due 2020[1]	100	Fixed assets	250
Stockholders' equity[2,3]	120		
Total liabilities	$290	Total assets	$290

Income Statement	
Gross profit	57.5
Depreciation	20.0
Interest	7.5
Pretax profit	30.0
Tax	10.5
Net profit	19.5
Dividend	6.5

Notes:
1. The yield to maturity on LA debt currently is 5 percent.
2. LA has 10 million shares outstanding, with a market price of $10 a share.
3. LA's equity beta is estimated at 1.25, the market risk premium is 8 percent, and the Treasury bill rate is 4 percent.

Johnson's only doubt about making a stock issue was that investors might jump to the conclusion that management believed the stock was overpriced, in which case the announcement might prompt an unjustified sell-off by investors. He stressed therefore that the company needed to explain carefully the reasons for the issue. Also, he suggested that demand for the issue would be enhanced if at the same time LA increased its dividend payment. This would provide a tangible indication of management's confidence in the future.

These arguments cut little ice with LA's chief executive. "Ed," she said, "I know that you're the expert on all this, but everything you say flies in the face of common sense. Why should we want to sell more equity when our stock has fallen over the past year by nearly a fifth? Our stock is currently offering a dividend yield of 6.5 percent, which makes equity an expensive source of capital. Increasing the dividend would simply make it more expensive. What's more, I don't see the point of paying out more money to the stockholders at the same time that we are asking *them* for cash. If we hike the dividend, we will need to increase the amount of the stock issue; so we will

just be paying the higher dividend out of the shareholders' own pockets. You're also ignoring the question of dilution. Our equity currently has a book value of $12 a share; it's not playing fair by our existing shareholders if we now issue stock for around $10 a share.

"Look at the alternative. We can borrow today at 5 percent. We get a tax break on the interest, so the after-tax cost of borrowing is $.65 \times 5 = 3.25$ percent. That's about half the cost of equity. We expect to earn a return of 15 percent on these new aircraft. If we can raise money at 3.25 percent and invest it at 15 percent, that's a good deal in my book.

"You finance guys are always talking about risk, but as long as we don't go bankrupt, borrowing doesn't add any risk at all. In any case my calculations show that the debt ratio is only 45 percent, which doesn't sound excessive to me.

"Ed, I don't want to push my views on this—after all, you're the expert. We don't need to make a firm recommendation to the board until next month. In the meantime, why don't you get one of your new business graduates to look at the whole issue of how we should finance the deal and what return we need to earn on these planes?"

Robert DeNiro clearly prefers large cash payouts, but can companies increase share value simply by increasing their dividend payout?

© *Warner Brothers/photo, courtesy The Kobal Collection*

Chapter 15

Dividend Policy

*I*n this chapter we explain how companies set their dividend payments and we discuss the controversial question of how dividend policy affects value.

Why should you care about these issues? Of course, if you are responsible for deciding on your company's dividend payment, you will want to know how it affects the value of your stock. But there is a more general reason. When we discussed the company's investment decision, we assumed that it was not affected by financing policy. In that case, a good project is a good project, no matter how it is ultimately financed. If dividend policy does not affect value, this still holds true. But suppose that it *does* affect value. Then the attractiveness of a project would depend on where the money was coming from. For example, if investors prefer companies with high dividend payouts, then these firms might be reluctant to take on new projects that required them to cut back dividends.

We start the chapter with a discussion of how dividends are paid. We then show that in an ideal world, the value of a firm would be independent of its dividend policy. This demonstration is in the same spirit as the Modigliani and Miller debt-irrelevance proposition of the previous chapter.

That leads us to look at the real-world complications that might favor one dividend policy over another. These complications include transaction costs, taxes, and the signals that investors might read into the firm's dividend announcement.

After studying this chapter you should be able to

▶ Describe how dividends are paid and how companies decide on dividend payments.

▶ Explain why dividend policy would not affect firm value in an ideal world.

▶ Explain why dividends may be used by management to signal the prospects of the firm.

▶ Show how differences in the tax treatment of dividends and capital gains might affect dividend policy.

15.1 How Dividends Are Paid

Cash Dividends

cash dividend: Payment of cash by the firm to its shareholders.

In January 1997, Exxon's board of directors met to discuss the company's dividends. The company announced a regular quarterly **cash dividend** of $0.79 per share, making a total payment for the year of $3.16. The term *regular* indicates that Exxon expected to maintain the payment in the future. If it did not want to give that kind of assurance, it could have declared both a regular and an *extra dividend*. Investors realize that extra dividends are less likely to be repeated.[1]

Who receives the Exxon dividend? That may seem an obvious question but, because shares trade constantly, the firm's records of who owns its shares can never be fully

---

[1]Companies also use the term *special dividend* for payments that are unlikely to be repeated.

Figure 15.1

The key dates for Exxon's quarterly dividend.

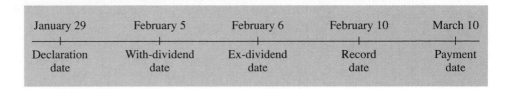

January 29	February 5	February 6	February 10	March 10
Declaration date	With-dividend date	Ex-dividend date	Record date	Payment date

up-to-date. So Exxon announced that it would send a dividend check to all shareholders recorded in its books on Monday, February 10. This is known as the *record date*.

The *payment date* for Exxon's dividend was March 10. On that date the dividend checks were mailed to investors. If Exxon's records were not up-to-date, some of those checks would be sent to the wrong investor. To handle this problem, stock exchanges fix a cutoff date, called the *with-dividend date,* several days prior to the record date. If you owned Exxon stock on the with-dividend date, which in this case was Wednesday, February 5, you were entitled to the dividend. If Exxon mistakenly sent that dividend to someone else, that person was obliged to pass it on to you. If you acquired the stock after February 5, you were not entitled to the dividend. If Exxon sent you that dividend by mistake, you had to send it on to the previous owner.

Through February 5, Exxon stock was said to be trading "with dividend" or "cum dividend." Beginning on February 6, the stock traded "ex dividend." The only difference between buying Exxon before and after the **ex-dividend date** is that in the second case you miss out on the dividend. Other things equal, the stock is worth more when it is with dividend. Thus when the stock "goes ex," we would expect the stock price to drop by the amount of the dividend.

Figure 15.1 illustrates the sequence of the key dividend dates. This sequence is the same whenever companies pay a dividend (though of course the actual dates will differ).

Some of Exxon's shareholders may have desired the cash payment, but others preferred to reinvest the dividend in the company. To help these investors, Exxon had an automatic dividend reinvestment plan. If a shareholder belonged to this plan, his or her dividends were automatically used to buy additional shares.[2]

ex-dividend date:

Date that determines whether a stockholder is entitled to a dividend payment; anyone holding stock before this date is entitled to a dividend.

▶ **Self-Test 15.1**   Mick Milekin buys 100 shares of Junk Bombs, Inc., on Tuesday, June 2. The company has declared a dividend of $1 per share payable on June 30 to shareholders of record as of Friday, June 5. If the ex-dividend date is June 1, is Mick entitled to the dividend? When will the checks go out in the mail?

Some Legal Limitations on Dividends

Suppose that an unscrupulous board decided to sell all the firm's assets and distribute the money as dividends. That would not leave anything in the kitty to pay the company's debts. Therefore, bondholders often guard against this danger by placing limits on dividend payments.

State law also helps to protect the company's creditors against excessive dividend payments. Most states prohibit a company from paying dividends if doing so would

---

[2]Often the new shares in an automatic dividend investment plan are issued at a small discount from the market price; the firm offers this sweetener because it saves the underwriting costs of a regular share issue. Sometimes 10 percent or more of total dividends will be reinvested under such plans.

make the company insolvent.[3] In addition, state law prevents a company from paying a dividend if it cuts into the company's legal capital. Legal capital is generally defined as the par value of all its outstanding shares.[4]

Par value and legal capital rarely have much economic significance. Par value is often arbitrarily set at $1 per share. The laws restricting payment of legal capital probably serve some purpose, however. They give most corporations a large degree of flexibility in deciding what to pay out, but they help prevent unscrupulous managers from gutting the firm by paying out all its assets as dividends and then escaping creditors.

Stock Dividends and Stock Splits

stock dividend: Distribution of additional shares to a firm's stockholders.

stock split: Issue of additional shares to firm's stockholders.

Exxon's dividend was in the form of cash but companies often declare **stock dividends.** For example, Archer Daniels Midland has paid a yearly stock dividend of 5 percent for nearly two decades. That means it sends each shareholder 5 additional shares for every 100 shares that are currently owned.

A stock dividend is very much like a **stock split.** In both cases the shareholder is given a fixed number of new shares for each share held. For example, in a two-for-one split, each investor would receive one additional share for each share already held. The investor ends up with two shares rather than one. A two-for-one stock split is therefore like a 100 percent stock dividend. Both result in a doubling of the number of outstanding shares, but neither changes the total assets held by the firm. In both cases, therefore, we would expect the stock price to fall by half, leaving the total market value of the firm (price per share times shares outstanding) unchanged.[5]

▶ **Example 15.1** *Stock Dividends and Splits*

Amoeba Products has issued 2 million shares currently selling at $15 each. Thus investors place a total market value on Amoeba of $30 million. The company now declares a 50 percent stock dividend. This means that each shareholder will receive one new share for every two shares that are currently held. So the total number of Amoeba shares will increase from 2 million to 3 million. The company's assets are not changed by this paper transaction and are still worth $30 million. The value of each share after the stock dividend is therefore $30/3 = $10.

If Amoeba split its stock three for two, the effect would be the same.[6] In this case two shares would split into three. (Amoeba's motto is "divide and conquer.") So each shareholder has 50 percent more shares with the same total value. Share price must decline by a third.

---

[3] The statutes define insolvency in different ways. In some cases, it just means an inability to meet immediate obligations; in other cases, it means a deficiency of assets compared with all outstanding fixed liabilities.

[4] Where there is no par value, legal capital consists of part or all the receipts from the issue of shares.

[5] One survey of managers indicated that 93.7 percent of splits are motivated by the desire to bring the stock price into an acceptable "trading range." They seem to believe that if the price is too high, investors won't be able to afford to buy a "round lot" of 100 shares. Of course that might be a problem for you or us, but it isn't a worry for the Prudential or GM pension fund. See J. Lakonishok and B. Lev, "Stock Splits and Stock Dividends: Why, Who, and When," *Journal of Finance* 42: (September 1987), pp. 913–932.

[6] The distinction between stock dividends and stock splits is a technical one. A stock dividend is shown on the balance sheet as a transfer from retained earnings to par value and additional paid-in capital, whereas a split is shown as a proportional reduction in the par value of each share. Neither affects the total book value of stockholders' equity.

There are other types of noncash dividends. For example, companies sometimes send shareholders a sample of their product. The British company Dundee Crematorium once offered its more substantial shareholders a discount cremation. Needless to say, you were not *required* to receive this dividend.

Share Repurchase

stock repurchase: Firm buys back stock from its shareholders.

When a firm wants to pay cash to its shareholders, it usually declares a cash dividend. But an alternative and increasingly popular method is for the firm to repurchase its own stock. In a **stock repurchase,** the company pays cash to repurchase shares from its shareholders. These shares are usually kept in the company's treasury and then resold if or when the company needs money.

To see why share repurchase is similar to a dividend, look at panel A of Table 15.1, which shows the market value of Hewlard Pocket's assets and liabilities. Shareholders hold 100,000 shares worth in total $1 million, so price per share equals $1 million/100,000 = $10.

Pocket is proposing to pay a dividend of $1 a share. With 100,000 shares outstanding, that amounts to a total payout of $100,000. Panel B shows the effect of this dividend payment. The cash account is reduced by $100,000 and the market value of the firm's assets falls to $900,000. Since there are still 100,000 shares outstanding, share price falls to $9. Suppose that before the dividend payment you owned 1,000 shares of Pocket worth $10,000. After the payment you would have $1,000 in cash and 1,000 shares worth $9,000.

Rather than paying out $100,000 as a dividend, Pocket could use the cash to buy back 10,000 shares at $10 each. Panel C shows what happens. The firm's assets fall to $900,000 just as in panel B, but only 90,000 shares remain outstanding, so price

Table 15.1

Cash dividend versus share repurchase. Hewlard Pocket's market value balance sheet.

Assets		Liabilities and Shareholders' Equity	
A. Original balance sheet			
Cash	$ 150,000	Debt	$ 0
Other assets	850,000	Equity	1,000,000
Value of firm	$1,000,000	Value of firm	$1,000,000
Shares outstanding = 100,000			
Price per share = $1,000,000/100,000 = $10			
B. After cash dividend			
Cash	$ 50,000	Debt	$ 0
Other assets	850,000	Equity	900,000
Value of firm	$900,000	Value of firm	$900,000
Shares outstanding = 100,000			
Price per share = $900,000/100,000 = $9			
C. After stock repurchase			
Cash	$ 50,000	Debt	$ 0
Other assets	850,000	Equity	900,000
Value of firm	$900,000	Value of firm	$900,000
Shares outstanding = 90,000			
Price per share = $900,000/90,000 = $10			

per share remains at $10. If you owned 1,000 shares before the repurchase, you would own 1 percent of the company. If you then sold 100 of your shares to Pocket, you would still own 1 percent of the company. Your sale would put $1,000 of cash in your pocket and you would keep 900 shares worth $9,000. This is precisely the position that you would have been in if Pocket had paid a dividend of $1 per share.

It is not surprising that a cash dividend and a share repurchase are equivalent transactions. In both cases, the firm pays out some of its cash, which then goes into the shareholders' pockets. The assets that are left in the company are the same regardless of whether that cash was used to pay a dividend or to buy back shares. Later, however, we will see that how the company chooses to pay out cash may affect the tax that the investor is obliged to pay.

Share repurchases are generally used to make major adjustments to the firm's capital, particularly when cash resources have outrun good capital investment opportunities. For example, in October 1997 IBM announced plans to repurchase an additional $3.5 billion of common stock. It had already spent $16 billion over the previous two years buying back its stock.

▶ **Self-Test 15.2**   What would Table 15.1 look like if the dividend changes to $1.50 per share and the share repurchase to $150,000?

15.2 *How Do Companies Decide on Dividend Payments?*

What does the board of directors think about when it sets the dividend? To help answer this question, John Lintner conducted a classic series of interviews with corporate managers about their dividend policies.[7] His description of how dividends are determined can be summarized in four "stylized facts":

dividend payout ratio:
Percentage of earnings paid out as dividends.

1. Firms have long-run target **dividend payout ratios.** This ratio is the fraction of earnings paid out as dividends.
2. Managers focus more on dividend *changes* than on absolute levels. Thus paying a $2.00 dividend is an important financial decision if last year's dividend was $1.00, but it's no big deal if last year's dividend was $2.00.
3. Dividend changes follow shifts in long-run, sustainable levels of earnings rather than short-run changes in earnings. Managers are unlikely to change dividend payouts in response to temporary variation in earnings. Instead, they "smooth" dividends.
4. Managers are reluctant to make dividend changes that might have to be reversed. They are particularly worried about having to rescind a dividend increase.

A firm that always stuck to its target payout ratio would have to change its dividend whenever earnings changed. But the managers in Lintner's survey were loath to do this. They believed that shareholders prefer a steady progression in dividends. Therefore, even if circumstances appeared to warrant a large increase in their company's dividend, they would move only partway toward their target payment.

[7]J. Lintner, "Distribution of Incomes of Corporations among Dividends, Retained Earnings, and Taxes," *American Economic Review* 46 (May 1956), pp. 97–113.

Figure 15.2

Motorola's earnings and dividends per share.

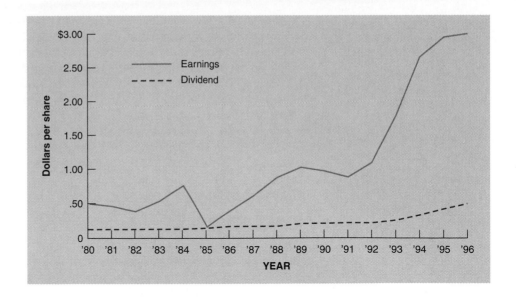

An extensive study by Fama and Babiak confirms Lintner's survey.[8] They found that if the company enjoys a good year, dividends may increase but to a lesser extent than earnings. Managers wait to see that the earnings increase is permanent before the dividend is fully adjusted.

If managers are reluctant to make dividend changes that might have to be reversed, we should also expect them to take *future* prospects into account when setting the payment. And that is what we find. When companies pay unexpectedly low dividends, earnings on the average subsequently decline. When they pay unexpectedly high dividends, earnings subsequently increase.[9] That is why investors pay close attention to the dividend decision.

To see Lintner's model at work, consider Figure 15.2, which plots the dividends and earnings per share of Motorola. While earnings per share fluctuate quite erratically, dividends per share do not. Dividends grow gradually from 12 cents per share in 1980 to 46 cents in 1996. Dividends remained constant between 1981 and 1983, and between 1986 and 1988, as management seemed to cautiously wait for evidence that any dividend increase could be supported over the long run. Moreover, when earnings fell dramatically in 1985, Motorola maintained the annual dividend at $.15.

15.3 Why Dividend Policy Should Not Matter

The first step toward understanding dividend policy is to recognize that the phrase means different things to different people. Therefore, we must start by defining what *we* mean by it.

---

[8]E. F. Fama and H. Babiak, "Dividend Policy: An Empirical Analysis," *Journal of the American Statistical Association* 63 (December 1968), pp. 1132–1161.

[9]See, for example, R. Watts, "The Information Content of Dividends," *Journal of Business* 46 (April 1973), pp. 191–211, for an analysis of the information effects in the United States.

A firm's decisions about dividends are often intertwined with other financing and investment decisions. Some firms pay low dividends because management is optimistic about the firm's future and wishes to retain earnings for expansion. In this case the dividend is a by-product of the firm's capital budgeting decision. Another firm might finance capital expenditures largely by borrowing. This frees up cash for dividends. In this case the firm's dividend is a by-product of the borrowing decision.

We wish to isolate dividend policy from other problems of financial management. The precise question we should ask is: "What is the effect of a change in cash dividends paid, *given the firm's capital budgeting and borrowing decisions?*" Of course the cash used to finance a dividend increase has to come from somewhere. If we fix the firm's investment outlays and borrowing, there is only one possible source—an issue of stock.

> **We define *dividend policy* as the trade-off between retaining earnings on the one hand and paying out cash and issuing shares on the other.**

One nice feature of economics is that it can accommodate not just two, but three opposing points of view. And so it is with dividend policy. On one side there is a group that believes high dividends increase firm value. On the other side there is a group that believes high dividends bring high taxes and therefore reduce firm value. And in the center there is a middle-of-the-road party that believes dividend policy makes no difference.

Dividend Policy Is Irrelevant in Competitive Markets

The middle-of-the-road party was founded in 1961 by Miller and Modigliani (MM)[10]—the same two who showed that in idealized conditions capital structure also is irrelevant.

We can illustrate MM's views about dividend policy by considering the Pickwick Paper Company, which had set aside $100 million in cash to construct a new paper mill. But Pickwick's directors now propose to use the $100 million to increase the dividend payment. If Pickwick is to continue to build its new mill, that cash needs to be replaced. If the borrowing is fixed, there is only one place the money can come from, and that is the sale of new shares. The combination of the dividend payment and the new issue of shares leaves Pickwick and its shareholders in exactly the same position they started from. All that has happened is that Pickwick has put an extra $100 million in investors' pockets (the dividend payment) and then taken it out again (the share issue). In other words, Pickwick is simply recycling cash. To suggest that this makes investors better off is like advising the cook to cool the kitchen by leaving the refrigerator door open.

After Pickwick pays the additional dividend and replaces the cash by selling new shares, the company value is unchanged. The old shareholders now have an extra $100 million of cash in their pockets, but they have given up a stake in the firm to those investors who buy the newly issued shares. The new stockholders are putting up $100 million and therefore will demand to receive shares *worth* $100 million. Since the total value of the company is the same, the value of the old stockholders' stake in the company falls by this $100 million. Thus the extra dividend that the old stockholders receive just offsets the loss in the value of the shares that they hold.

[10]M. H. Miller and F. Modigliani, "Dividend Policy, Growth and the Valuation of Shares," *Journal of Business* 34 (October 1961), pp. 411–433.

Does it make any difference to the old stockholders that they receive an extra dividend payment plus an offsetting capital loss? It might if that were the only way they could get their hands on the cash. But as long as there are efficient capital markets, they can raise cash by selling shares. Thus Pickwick's old shareholders can "cash in" either by persuading the management to pay a higher dividend or by selling some of their shares. In either case there will be the same transfer of value from the old to the new stockholders.

> **Because investors to not need dividends to convert their shares to cash, they will not pay higher prices for firms with higher dividend payouts. In other words, dividend policy will have no impact on the value of the firm.**

MM dividend-irrelevance proposition: Theory that under ideal conditions, the value of the firm is unaffected by dividend policy.

This conclusion is known as the **MM dividend-irrelevance proposition.**

The example of the Pickwick Paper Company showed that the firm cannot make shareholders better off simply by increasing the proportion of earnings paid out as dividends. But what about the reverse? Can a firm increase its value by *reducing* the dividend payout?

In the case of Pickwick, the extra cash paid out as a dividend needed to be replaced by a sale of stock. The same argument works in reverse: If investment and borrowing are held constant, any *reduction* in dividends must be balanced by a *purchase* of stock. For example, suppose that Old Curiosity Shops has $100 million surplus cash which it had been proposing to pay out to shareholders as a dividend. If Old Curiosity now decides not to pay this dividend, then the surplus cash can be used only to buy back some of the company's shares. The shareholders miss out on $100 million of dividend payments but they receive $100 million from the sale to the company of part of their shareholdings. Thus MM's dividend-irrelevance proposition holds both for increases in dividends and for reductions.

> **As these examples illustrate, dividend policy is a trade-off between cash dividends and the issue or repurchase of common stock. In a perfect capital market, dividend choice would have no impact on firm value.**

These examples may seem artificial at first, for we do not observe firms scheduling a stock issue with every dividend payment. But there are many firms that pay dividends and also issue stock from time to time. They could avoid the stock issues by paying lower dividends and retaining more funds in the firm. Many other firms restrict dividends so that they *do not* have to issue shares. They could instead issue stock occasionally and increase the dividend.

Of course our demonstrations of dividend irrelevance have ignored taxes, issue costs, and a variety of other real-world complications. We will turn to these intricacies shortly, but before we do, we note that the crucial assumption in our proof is that the sale or purchase of shares occurs at a fair price. The shares that Pickwick sells to raise $100,000 must actually be worth $100,000; those that Old Curiosity buys for $100,000 must also be worth that figure. In other words, dividend irrelevance assumes efficient capital markets.

▶ **Example 15.2** *Dividend Irrelevance*

Panel A of Table 15.2 shows that Consolidated Pasta is expected to pay annual dividends of $10 a share in perpetuity. Shareholders expect a 10 percent rate of return

Table 15.2
Consolidated Pasta is currently expected to pay a dividend of $10 million in perpetuity. However, the president is proposing to pay a one-time bumper dividend of $20 million in Year 1. To replace the lost cash, the firm will need to issue more shares and the dividends that will need to be diverted to the new shareholders will exactly offset the effect of the higher dividend in Year 1.

	Old Dividend Plan		Revised Dividend Plan	
	Year 1	Year 2 on	Year 1	Year 2 on
Total dividend payments ($ million)	10	10	20	10
Total dividends paid to old shareholders ($ million)	10	10	20	9
Total dividends paid to new shareholders ($ million)	—	—	—	1

Note: New shareholders are putting up $10 million of cash at the end of Year 1. Since they require a return of 10 percent, the total dividends paid to the new shares (starting in Year 2) must be 10 percent of $10 million, or $1 million.

from Consolidated stock and therefore the value of each share is

$$PV = \frac{10}{1.10} + \frac{10}{1.10^2} + \frac{10}{1.10^3} + \ldots = \frac{10}{.10} = \$100$$

Consolidated has issued 1 million shares. So the total forecast dividend payment in each year is 1 million × $10 = $10 million and the total value of Consolidated Pasta equity is 1 million × $100 = $100 million. The president, Al Dente, has read that the value of a share depends on the dividends it pays. That suggests an easy way to keep shareholders happy—increase next year's dividend to $20 per share. That way, he reasons, share price should rise by the present value of the increase in the first-year dividend to a new value of

$$PV = \frac{20}{1.10} + \frac{10}{1.10^2} + \frac{10}{1.10^3} + \ldots = \frac{10}{.10} + \frac{10}{1.10} = \$109.91$$

The president's heart is obviously in the right place. Unfortunately, his head isn't. Let's see why.

Consolidated is proposing to pay out an extra $10 million in dividends. It can't do that *and* earn the same profits in the future, unless it also replaces the lost cash by an issue of shares. The new shareholders who provide this cash will require a return of 10 percent on their investment. So Consolidated will need to pay $1 million a year of dividends to the new shares ($1 million/$10 million = .10, or 10%). This is shown in the last line of Table 15.2.

As long as the company replaces the extra cash it pays out, it will continue to earn the same profits and to pay out $10 million of dividends each year from Year 2. However, $1 million of this total will be needed to satisfy the new shareholders, leaving only $9 million (or $9 a share) for the original shareholders. Now recalculate the value of the original shares under the revised dividend plan.

$$PV = \frac{20}{1.10} + \frac{9}{1.10^2} + \frac{9}{1.10^3} + \ldots = \frac{9}{.10} + \frac{11}{1.10} = \$100$$

The value of the shares is unchanged. The extra cash dividend in Year 1 is exactly offset by the reduction of dividends per share in later years. This reduction is necessary because some of the money paid out as dividends in later years is diverted to the new shareholders.[11]

▶ **Self-Test 15.3** Suppose that Consolidated Pasta had issued $10 million in preferred stock rather than common stock to pay the extra dividend. What would be the stock price?

The Assumptions behind Dividend Irrelevance

Many stockholders and businesspeople find it difficult to accept the suggestion that dividend policy is irrelevant. When faced with MM's argument, they often reply that dividends are cash in hand while capital gains are at best in the bush. It may be true, they say, that the recipient of an extra cash dividend forgoes an equal capital gain, but if the dividend is safe and the capital gain is risky, isn't the stockholder ahead?

It's correct that dividends are more predictable than capital gains. Managers can stabilize dividends but they cannot control stock price. From this it seems a small step to conclude that increased dividends make the firm less risky.[12] But the important point is, once again, that as long as investment policy and borrowing are held constant, a firm's *overall* cash flows are the same regardless of payout policy. The risks borne by *all* the firm's stockholders are likewise fixed by its investment and borrowing policies and unaffected by dividend policy.

If we really believed that old stockholders are better off by trading a risky asset for cash, then we would also have to argue that the new stockholders—those who trade cash for the newly issued shares—are worse off. But this doesn't make sense: the new stockholders are bearing risk, but they are getting paid for it. They are willing to buy because the new shares are priced to offer an expected return adequate to compensate for the risk.

MM's argument for the irrelevance of dividend policy does not assume a world of certainty; it assumes an efficient capital market. Market efficiency means that the transfers of ownership created by shifts in dividend policy are carried out on fair terms. And since the *overall* value of (old and new) stockholders' equity is unaffected, nobody gains or loses.

---

[11]Notice that at the end of Year 1, when the new shareholders purchase their shares, the dividend per share they can look forward to receiving will be $9; since this dividend is expected to be a perpetuity, the share price at that time will be $9/.10 = $90. So the new shareholders will receive $10,000,000/$90 = 111,111 shares. Consistent with Table 15.2, the new shareholders therefore will receive total dividend payments of 111,111 × $9 = $1 million and the old shareholders will receive total dividend payments of 1 million × $9 = $9 million. Notice also that after the extra $10 million dividend is paid in Year 1, the share price falls to $90, and the value of the shares held by the original shareholders falls by exactly $10 million to $90 million.

[12]In that case one might also argue that interest payments are even more predictable, so that a company's risk would be reduced by increasing the proportion of profits paid out as interest. How would you respond to that suggestion?

15.4 Why Dividends May Increase Firm Value

Market Imperfections

Most economists believe that MM's conclusions are correct, given their assumptions of perfect and efficient capital markets. However, nobody claims their model is an exact description of the so-called real world. Thus the impact of dividend policy finally boils down to arguments about imperfections and inefficiencies.

Those who believe that dividends are good argue that some investors have a natural preference for high-payout stocks. For example, some financial institutions are legally restricted from holding stocks lacking established dividend records. Trusts and endowment funds may prefer high-dividend stocks because dividends are regarded as spendable "income," whereas capital gains are "additions to principal," which may not be spent.[13]

In addition, many investors look to their stock portfolios for a steady source of cash to live on. In principle this cash can be generated from stocks paying no dividends at all; the investor can just sell off a small fraction of his or her holdings from time to time. For example, an investor who holds 1,000 shares of AT&T stock can sell 10 shares (1 percent of the total holdings) this year. This "homemade dividend" is equivalent to an increase of one percentage point in AT&T's annual dividend yield.

However, instead of AT&T's stockholders making regular sales, it is simpler and cheaper for the company to send them a dividend check. The costs of trading small numbers of shares can be extremely high. AT&T's regular dividends relieve many of its shareholders of these transaction costs and considerable inconvenience.

All this is undoubtedly true, but it does not follow that you can increase the value of *your* firm by increasing the dividend payout. Smart managers already have recognized that there is a clientele of investors who would be prepared to pay a premium for high-payout stocks. High-payout fans already have a wide variety of stocks to choose from.

> There are natural clienteles for high-payout stocks, but it does not follow that any particular firm can benefit by increasing its dividends. The high-dividend clienteles already have plenty of high-dividend stocks to choose from.

You don't hear businesspeople argue that because there is a clientele of car buyers, their company should manufacture cars. So why should you believe that because there is a clientele of investors who like high payouts, your company can increase value by manufacturing a high payout? That clientele was probably satisfied long ago.

▶ **Self-Test 5.4**   Suppose an investor in AT&T does not need a regular income. What could she do to offset AT&T's "overly generous" payout policy? If there were no trading costs, would she have any reason to care about AT&T's dividend payout policy? What if there is a brokerage fee on the purchase of new shares? What if AT&T has a dividend reinvestment plan that allows the investor to buy shares at a 5 percent discount?

---

[13]Most colleges and universities are legally free to spend capital gains from their endowments, but this is rarely done.

Dividends as Signals

Another line of argument for high payouts does not rely on market imperfections like trading costs. Think of a market in which investors receive very little reliable information about a firm's earnings. Such markets exist in some countries where a passion for secrecy and a tendency to construct many-layered corporate organizations produce earnings figures that are next to meaningless. Some people say that the situation is little better in the United States, thanks to creative accounting.

How might an investor in such a world separate marginally profitable firms from the real money makers? One clue is dividends. A firm that reports good earnings and pays a generous dividend is putting its money where its mouth is. Accounting numbers may lie, but dividends require the firm to come up with hard cash. We can understand why investors would favor firms with established dividend records. We can also see how investors would value the information content of dividends. Investors would refuse to believe a firm's reported earnings announcements unless they were backed up by an appropriate dividend policy.

Of course, firms can cheat in the short run by overstating earnings and scraping up cash to pay a generous dividend. But it is hard to cheat in the long run, for a firm that is not making money will not have the cash flow to pay out. Only the firms with sufficient cash flow will find that it pays to signal their good fortune by choosing a high dividend level. If a firm chooses a high dividend payout without the cash flow to back it up, that firm ultimately will have to cut back on investment or turn to investors for additional debt or equity financing. All of these consequences are costly. Therefore, most managers don't increase dividends until they are confident that sufficient cash will flow in to pay them.

Investors can't read managers' minds, but they learn from managers' actions. When dividends increase, they infer managers' confidence in the firm's cash flow and earnings.

> **Because a high-dividend-payout policy will be costly to firms that do not have the cash flow to support it, dividend increases signal a company's good fortune and its managers' confidence in future cash flow.**

Healy and Palepu report that between 1970 and 1979 companies that made a dividend payment for the first time experienced relatively flat earnings growth until the year before the announcement.[14] In that year earnings grew by an average 43 percent. If managers thought that this was a temporary windfall, they might have been cautious about committing themselves to paying out cash. But it looks as if they had good reason to be confident about prospects, for over the next 4 years earnings grew by a further 164 percent.

information content of dividends: Dividend increases send good news about cash flow and earnings. Dividend cuts send bad news.

Since dividends anticipate future earnings, it is no surprise to find that announcements of dividend cuts are usually taken as bad news (stock price typically falls) and that dividend increases are good news (stock price rises). This is called the **information content of dividends.**

It's important not to jump to the conclusion that investors like higher dividends for their own sake. A dividend initiation or increase may be welcomed *only* as a sign of

[14]P. Healy and K. Palepu, "Earnings Information Conveyed by Dividend Initiations and Omissions," *Journal of Financial Economics* 21 (1988), pp. 149–175.

See box p. 441

higher future earnings. Even investors who prefer low-dividend policies might find that a drop in the dividend is unwelcome news about the firm's prospects.[15]

The nearby box illustrates the signaling power of dividends. When Florida Power & Light cut its dividend, the firm stressed that the cut was not a response to low or uncertain profits but part of a rethinking of its financial strategy for a deregulated world. Despite these reassurances, the stock price fell. The market apparently paid more attention to what the firm did than to what its management said. The stock price recovered only later, as the market became convinced that the prospects of the firm were in fact OK.

▶ **Self-Test 15.5**

In 1974 Consolidated Edison announced that it would omit its regular 45 cents per share cash quarterly dividend. It cited losses due to increased oil prices following the OPEC oil embargo. The stock price fell by about 30 percent in 1 day, from about $18 a share to $12 a share. Why would omission of a $.45 per share dividend result in a stock price drop of $6 a share?

15.5 *Why Dividends May Reduce Firm Value*

The low-dividend creed is simple. Companies can convert dividends into capital gains by shifting their dividend policies. If dividends are taxed more heavily than capital gains, such financial alchemy should be welcomed by any taxpaying investor. Firms should pay the lowest cash dividend they can get away with. Available cash should be retained and reinvested or used to repurchase shares.

Table 15.3 illustrates this. It assumes that dividends are taxed at a combined federal plus state tax rate of 40 percent but that capital gains are taxed at only 20 percent.[16] The stocks of firms A and B are equally risky and investors demand an expected *after-tax* rate of return of 10 percent on each. Investors expect A to be worth $112.50 per share next year. The share price of B is expected to be only $102.50, but a $10 dividend is also forecast, so the total pretax payoff is the same, $112.50.

Both stocks offer the same pretax dollar payoff. Yet B's stock sells for less than A's and therefore offers a high pretax rate of return. The reason is obvious: investors are willing to buy stock A because its return comes in the form of low-taxed capital gains. After tax, each stock offers the same 10 percent return.

Suppose the management of firm B eliminates the $10 dividend and uses the cash to repurchase stock instead. We saw earlier that stock repurchase is equivalent to a cash dividend but it is treated differently by the tax authorities. Stockholders who sell shares back to their firm pay tax only on any capital gains realized in the sale. Therefore, B's new policy would reduce the taxes paid by stockholders and its stock price should rise.

---

[15]For example, in an article in *Fortune* Carol Loomis tells the story of General Public Utilities ("A Case for Dropping Dividends," *Fortune*, June 15, 1968, pp. 181ff.). In 1968 its management decided to reduce its cash dividend to avoid a stock issue. Despite the company's assurances, it encountered considerable opposition. Individual shareholders advised the president to see a psychiatrist, institutional holders threatened to sell their stock, the share price fell nearly 10 percent, and eventually management capitulated.

[16]While the actual federal tax bracket on capital gains income for most stockholders is 20 percent, the effective rate can be even lower because of the ability to defer the realization of gains. More on this later.

The Dividend Cut Heard 'Round the World

On May 9, 1994, FPL Group, the parent company of Florida Power & Light Company, announced a 32 percent reduction in its quarterly dividend payout, from 62 cents per share to 42 cents. This was the first-ever dividend cut by a healthy utility. A number of utilities had reduced their dividends in the past, but only after cash flow problems—often associated with heavy investment in nuclear plants—had given them no other choice.

In its announcement, FPL stressed that it had studied the situation carefully and that, given the prospect of increased competition in the electric utility industry, the company's high dividend payout ratio (which had averaged 90 percent in the past 4 years) was no longer in the stockholders' best interests. The new policy resulted in a dividend payout of about 60 percent of the prior year's earnings. Management also announced that, starting in 1995, the dividend payout would be reviewed in February instead of May to reinforce the linkage between dividends and annual earnings. In doing so, the company wanted to minimize unintended "signaling effects" from any future changes in the dividend.

At the same time it announced this change in dividend policy, FPL Group's board authorized the repurchase of up to 10 million shares of common stock over the next 3 years. FPL's management said that 4 million shares would be repurchased over the next 12 months, depending on market conditions. In adopting this strategy, the company noted that changes in the U.S. tax code since 1990 had made capital gains more attractive than dividends to shareholders.

Besides providing a more tax-efficient means of distributing excess capital to its stockholders, FPL's substitution of stock repurchases for dividends was also designed to increase the company's financial flexibility in preparation for a new era of deregulation and heightened competition among utilities. Although much of the cash savings from the dividend cut would be returned to investors in the form of stock repurchases, the rest would be used to retire debt at Florida Power & Light and so reduce the company's leverage ratio. This deleveraging and strengthening of FPL's financial condition were intended to prepare the company for an increase in business risk and to provide the financial resources to take advantage of future growth opportunities.

The stock market's initial reaction to FPL's announcement was negative. On the day of the announcement, the company's stock price fell from $31.88 to $27.50, a drop of nearly 14 percent. But, as analysts digested the news and considered the reasons for the reduction, they concluded that the action was not a signal of financial distress but rather a strategic decision that would improve the company's long-term financial flexibility and prospects for growth. This view spread throughout the financial community, and FPL's stock began to recover.

On May 31, less than a month after the announcement, FPL's stock closed at $32.17 (adjusted for the quarterly dividend of 42 cents), or about 30 cents higher than the pre-announcement price. By the middle of June, at least 15 major brokerage houses had placed FPL's common stock on their "buy" lists. On May 9, 1995—exactly one year after the announcement of the cut—FPL's stock price closed at $37.75, giving stockholders a one-year post-announcement return (including dividends) of 23.8 percent, more than double the 11.2 percent of the S&P Index and well above the 14.2 percent of the S&P utilities index over the same period.

Source: Modified from D. Soter, E. Brigham, and P. Evanson, "The Dividend Cut 'Heard 'Round the World': The Case of FPL," *Journal of Applied Corporate Finance* 9 (Spring 1996), pp. 4–15.

▶ **Self-Test 15.6**　Look again at Table 15.3. What would happen to the price and pretax rate of return on stock B if the tax on capital gains were eliminated?

Why Pay Any Dividends at All?

If dividends are taxed more heavily than capital gains, why should *any* firm *ever* pay a cash dividend? If cash is to be distributed to stockholders, isn't share repurchase the best channel for doing so?

Table 15.3

Effects of a shift in dividend policy when dividends are taxed more heavily than capital gains. The high-payout stock (firm B) must sell at a lower price in order to provide the same after-tax return.

	Firm A	Firm B
Next year's price	$112.50	$102.50
Dividend	$0	$10.00
Total *pretax* payoff	$112.50	$112.50
Today's stock price	$100	$97.78
Capital gain	$12.50	$4.72
Before-tax rate of return (%)	$\dfrac{12.5}{100} = .125 = 12.5\%$	$\dfrac{14.72}{97.78} = .1505 = 15.05\%$
Tax on dividend at 40%	$0	$.40 \times \$10 = \$4.00$
Tax on capital gain at 20%	$.20 \times \$12.50 = \$2.50$	$.20 \times \$4.72 = \$.94$
Total after-tax income (dividends plus capital gains less taxes)	$(0 + 12.50) - 2.50 =$ $10.00	$(10 + 4.72)$ $- (4.00 + .94) = \$9.78$
After-tax rate of return (%)	$\dfrac{10}{100} = .10 = 10\%$	$\dfrac{9.78}{97.78} = .10 = 10\%$

Few would go quite that far. The Internal Revenue Service has attempted to prevent firms from disguising dividends as repurchases; for example, proportional or regular repurchases are liable to be treated as dividend payments. A firm that eliminates dividends and starts repurchasing stock on a regular basis may find that the IRS would recognize the repurchase program for what it really is and would tax the payments accordingly. That is why financial managers have never announced that they are repurchasing shares to save stockholders taxes; they give some other reason.[17]

Nevertheless, one could argue that firms which pay dividends and as a result have to issue shares from time to time are making a serious mistake. Any such firm is essentially financing its dividends by issuing stock; it should cut its dividends at least to the point at which stock issues are unnecessary. This would not only save taxes for shareholders; it would also avoid the transaction costs of stock issues.

Taxation of Dividends and Capital Gains under Current Tax Law

In the United States the case for low dividends was strongest before 1986. The top rate of tax on dividends was then 50 percent, while realized capital gains were taxed at only 20 percent.

The 1986 Tax Reform Act eliminated much of the tax disadvantage of dividends and thereby undercut the argument for low dividends. But by 1997, tax rates on dividends are again greater than on capital gains. The maximum tax rate on long-term capital gains is 20 percent, while the tax rate on dividends ranges from 31 percent to 39.6 percent for taxable incomes above $58,150.[18]

Tax law is on the side of capital gains in another important respect. Taxes on dividends have to be paid immediately, but taxes on capital gains can be deferred until shares are sold and capital gains are realized. Stockholders can choose when to sell

---

[17]They might say, "Our stock is a good investment," or, "We want to have the shares available to finance acquisitions of other companies." What do you think of these rationales?

[18]See Chapter 2, Table 2.6, for a table of tax rates on ordinary income.

their shares and thus when to pay the capital gains tax.[19] The longer they wait, the less the present value of the capital gains tax liability.[20]

Tax motives are not as important for financial institutions, many of which operate free of all taxes and therefore have no tax reason to prefer capital gains to dividends, or vice versa. Pension funds are untaxed, for example.

Only corporations have a tax reason to *prefer* dividends. They pay corporate income tax on only 30 percent of any dividends received.[21] Thus the effective tax rate on dividends received by large corporations is 30 percent of 35 percent (the marginal corporate tax rate), or 10.5 percent. But they have to pay a 35 percent tax on the full amount of any realized capital gain.

Summary

1. Dividends come in many forms. The most common is the regular cash dividend, but sometimes companies pay an extra cash dividend, and sometimes they pay a dividend in the form of stock. A firm is not free to pay whatever dividends it likes. For example, it may have accepted restrictions on dividends as a condition for borrowing money.

2. Most managers seem to have a target payout rate. But if firms simply applied this target payout rate to each year's earnings, dividends could fluctuate wildly. Managers therefore try to smooth dividends by moving only partway toward the target payout in each year. Also, they don't look just at past earnings: they try to look into the future when they set the payment. Investors are aware of this and they know that a dividend increase is usually a sign of optimism on the part of management.

3. Instead of paying dividends, the company can repurchase its own stock. The Internal Revenue Service taxes shareholders only on the capital gains that they realize as a result of the repurchase.

4. If we hold the company's investment policy and capital structure constant, then dividend policy is a trade-off between cash dividends and the issue or repurchase of common stock. In an ideally simple and perfect world, the choice has no effect on market value. The dividend controversy centers on the effects of dividend policy in our flawed world. A common—though by no means universal—view is that high payout enhances share price. While there are natural clienteles for high-payout stocks, we find it difficult to explain a *general* preference for dividends except as an irrational prejudice.

---

[19]If the stock is willed to your heirs, capital gains escape taxation altogether.

[20]Suppose the discount rate is 8 percent, and an investor in a 20 percent capital gains tax bracket has a $100 capital gain. If the stock is sold today, the capital gains tax will be $20. If sale is deferred 1 year, the tax due on that $100 gain still will be $20, but by virtue of delaying the sale for a year, the present value of the tax falls to $20/1.08 = $18.52. The effective tax rate falls to 18.52 percent. The longer the sale is deferred, the lower the effective tax rate.

[21]Actually, the percentage of dividend income on which tax is paid depends on the firm's ownership share in the company paying the dividend. If the share is less than 20 percent, taxes are paid on 30 percent of dividends received.

5. The most obvious and serious market imperfection has been the different tax treatment of dividends and capital gains. Capital gains are taxed less. If dividend income is seriously tax-disadvantaged, we would expect investors to demand a higher before-tax return on high-payout stocks.

6. It is difficult to take a strong stand on dividend policy. Our recommendations to companies emphasize the following points. First, there is little doubt that sudden shifts in dividend policy can cause abrupt changes in stock price. The principal reason is that dividend changes are liable to be interpreted as signals of a change in the firm's prospects. If a sharp dividend change is necessary, then the company should provide as much forewarning and explanation as possible. Second, a firm should adopt a target payout that is sufficiently low to minimize its reliance on external equity. Why pay out cash to stockholders if that requires issuing new shares to get the cash back? It's better to hold on to the cash in the first place.

Key Terms

cash dividend
ex-dividend date
stock dividend

stock split
stock repurchase
dividend payout ratio

MM dividend-irrelevance proposition
information content of dividends

Problems

1. **Dividend Sequence.** In 1996 Reebok International paid a regular quarterly dividend of $.075 a share.

   a. Connect each of the following dates to the correct term:

May 7, 1996	Record date
June 6, 1996	Payment date
June 7, 1996	Ex-dividend date
June 11, 1996	Last with-dividend date
July 2, 1996	Declaration date

   b. On one of these dates the stock price is likely to fall by about the value of the dividend. Why?

   c. The stock price in early January 1996 was $27. What was the prospective dividend yield?

   d. The earnings per share for 1996 were forecast at around $1.90. What was the percentage payout rate?

   e. Suppose that in 1996 the company paid a 10 percent stock dividend. What would be the expected fall in the stock price?

2. **Institutional Background.** True or false? If false, correct the statement.

   a. A company may not generally pay a dividend out of legal capital.

   b. A company may not generally pay a dividend if it is insolvent.

   c. The *effective* tax rate on capital gains can be less than the stated tax rate on such gains.

   d. Corporations are not taxed on dividends received from other corporations.

3. **Splits and Dividends.** Shares in Raven Products are selling for $40 per share. There are 1 million shares outstanding. What will be the share price in each of the following situations? Ignore taxes.

   a. The stock splits five for four.

   b. The company pays a 25 percent stock dividend.

   c. The company repurchases 100,000 shares.

4. **Dividend Irrelevance.** You own 1,000 shares of Patriot Corporation, which is about to raise its dividend from $.75 to $1.00 per share. The share price is currently $50. You would prefer that the dividend remain at its current level. What would you do to offset the effects of the increase in the dividend?

5. **DRIPs.** A firm considers initiating an aggressive dividend reinvestment plan (DRIP) in which it allows its investors to use dividends to buy shares at a discount of 40 percent from current market value. The firm's financial manager argues that the policy will benefit shareholders by giving them the opportunity to buy additional shares at a deep discount and will benefit the firm by providing a source of cash. Is the manager correct?

6. **Dividends and Repurchases.** While dividend yields in the United States in 1997 were at historically low levels, share repurchases were at historical highs. Was this a coincidence?

7. **Dividends and Taxes.** Suppose that the tax rate on dividends is 28 percent, and the tax rate on capital gains is zero. Eagle Net Resources is about to pay a $2 per share dividend.

   a. By how much will Eagle Net's share price fall when the stock goes ex dividend?
   b. Will anything happen to the share price on the payment date when the dividend checks are sent out?

8. **Cash Dividends.** The stock of Payout Corp. will go ex dividend tomorrow. The dividend will be $1.00 per share, and there are 20,000 shares of stock outstanding. The market-value balance sheet for Payout is shown below.

   a. What price is Payout stock selling for today?
   b. What price will it sell for tomorrow? Ignore taxes.

Assets		Liabilities and Equity	
Cash	$100,000	Equity	$1,000,000
Fixed assets	900,000		

9. **Repurchases.** Now suppose that Payout from question 8 announces its intention to repurchase $20,000 worth of stock instead of paying out the dividend.

   a. What effect will the repurchase have on an investor who currently holds 100 shares and sells 2 of those shares back to the company in the repurchase?
   b. Compare the effects of the repurchase to the effects of the cash dividend that you worked out in problem 8.

10. **Stock Dividend.** Now suppose that Payout again changes its mind and decides to issue a 2 percent stock dividend instead of either issuing the cash dividend or repurchasing 2 percent of the outstanding stock. How would this action affect a shareholder who owns 100 shares of stock? Compare with your answers to problems 8 and 9.

11. **Stock Dividends and Splits.** Suppose that you own 1,000 shares of Nocash Corp. and the company is about to pay a 25 percent stock dividend. The stock currently sells at $50 per share.

   a. What will be the number of shares that you hold and the total value of your equity position after the dividend is paid?
   b. What will happen to the number of shares that you hold and the value of your equity position if the firm splits five for four instead of paying the stock dividend?

12. **Dividend Irrelevance.** Respond to the following comment: "It's all very well saying that I can sell shares to cover cash needs, but that may mean selling at the bottom of the market. If the company pays a regular dividend, investors avoid the risk."

13. **Dividends and Taxes.** Good Values, Inc., is all-equity financed. The total market value of the firm currently is $100,000, and there are 2,000 shares outstanding.

   a. The firm has declared a $5 per share dividend. The stock will go ex dividend tomorrow. At what price will the stock sell today? Ignore taxes.
   b. Now assume that the tax rate on dividend income is 28 percent, and the tax rate on capital gains is zero. At what price will the stock sell today?

14. **Repurchases and Taxes.** Now suppose that instead of paying a dividend Good Values (from problem 13) plans to repurchase $10,000 worth of stock.

   a. What will be the stock price before and after the repurchase?
   b. Suppose an investor who holds 200 shares sells 20 of her shares back to the firm. If there are no taxes on dividends or capital gains, show that she should be indifferent between the repurchase and the dividend.
   c. Show that if dividends are taxed at 28 percent and capital gains are not taxed, the value of the firm is higher if it pursues the share repurchase instead of the dividend.

15. **Dividends and Taxes.** Investors require an after-tax rate of return of 10 percent on their stock investments. Assume that the tax rate on dividends is 28 percent while capital gains escape taxation. A firm will pay a $2 per share dividend 1 year from now, after which it is expected to sell at a price of $20.

   a. Find the current price of the stock.
   b. Find the expected before-tax rate of return for a 1-year holding period.
   c. Now suppose that the dividend will be $3 per share. If the expected after-tax rate of return is still 10 percent, and investors still expect the stock to sell at $20 in 1 year, at what price must the stock now sell?
   d. What is the before-tax rate of return? Why is it now higher than in part (b)?

16. **Dividend Policy.** Here are several assertions about typical corporate dividend policies. Which of them are true? Write out a corrected version of any false statements.

   a. Most companies set a target dividend payout ratio.
   b. They set each year's dividend equal to the target payout ratio times that year's earnings.
   c. Managers and investors seem more concerned with dividend changes than dividend levels.
   d. Managers often increase dividends temporarily when earnings are unexpectedly high for a year or two.

17. **Dividend Policy.** "Risky companies tend to have lower target payout ratios and more gradual adjustment rates." Explain what is meant by this statement. Why do you think it is so?

18. **Signaling.** It is well documented that stock prices tend to rise when firms announce an increase in their dividend payouts. How then can it be said that dividend policy is irrelevant?

19. **Dividends and Taxes.** The expected pretax return on three stocks is divided between dividends and capital gains in the following way:

Stock	Expected Dividend	Expected Capital Gain
A	$ 0	$10
B	5	5
C	10	0

   a. If each stock is priced at $100, what are the expected net returns on each stock to (i) a pension fund that does not pay taxes, (ii) a corporation paying tax at 35 percent, and (iii) an individual paying tax at 36 percent on investment income and 20 percent on capital gains?

b. Suppose that before the 1986 Tax Reform Act stocks A, B, and C were priced to yield an 8 percent *after-tax* return to individual investors paying 50 percent tax on dividends and 20 percent tax on capital gains. What would A, B, and C each sell for?

20. **Dividends and Taxes.** Suppose all investments offered the same expected return *before* tax. Consider two equally risky shares, Hi and Lo. Hi shares pay a generous dividend and offer low expected capital gains. Lo shares pay low dividends and offer high expected capital gains. Which of the following investors would prefer the Lo shares? Which would prefer the Hi shares? Which wouldn't care? Explain. Assume that any stock purchased will be sold after 1 year.

a. A pension fund
b. An individual
c. A corporation

21. **Dividends versus Repurchases.** Big Industries has the following market-value balance sheet. The stock currently sells for $20 a share, and there are 1,000 shares outstanding. The firm will either pay a $1 per share dividend or repurchase $1,000 worth of stock. Ignore taxes.

Assets		Liabilities and Equity	
Cash	$ 2,000	Debt	$10,000
Fixed assets	28,000	Equity	20,000

a. What will be the price per share under each alternative (dividend versus repurchase)?
b. If total earnings of the firm are $2,000 a year, find earnings per share under each alternative.
c. Find the price-earnings ratio under each alternative.
d. Adherents of the "dividends-are-good" school sometimes point to the fact that stocks with high dividend payout ratios tend to sell at above-average price-earnings multiples. Is this evidence convincing? Discuss this argument with regard to your answers to parts (a)–(c).

22. **Dividend Policy.** For each of the following four groups of companies, state whether you would expect them to distribute a relatively high or low proportion of current earnings and whether you would expect them to have a relatively high or low price-earnings ratio.

a. High-risk companies
b. Companies that have recently experienced a temporary decline in profits
c. Companies that expect to experience a decline in profits
d. "Growth" companies with valuable future investment opportunities

23. **Dividend Irrelevance.** Suppose Mr. Dente from Example 15.2 changes his mind and cuts out Consolidated's Year 1 dividend entirely, instead spending $10 million to buy back stock. Are shareholders any better or worse off than if Consolidated had paid out $10 million as cash dividends? *Hints:* How many shares will be repurchased? The purchase price at Year 1 will be $110.

Solutions to Self-Test Questions

15.1 The ex-dividend date is June 1. Therefore, Mick buys the stock ex-dividend and will not receive the dividend. The checks will be mailed on June 30.

15.2.

Assets		Liabilities and Equity	
After cash dividend			
Cash	$ 0	Debt	$ 0
Other assets	850,000	Equity	850,000
Value of firm	$850,000	Value of firm	$850,000

Shares outstanding = 100,000
Price per share = $850,000/100,000 = $8.50

Assets		Liabilities and Equity	
After stock repurchase			
Cash	$ 0	Debt	$ 0
Other assets	850,000	Equity	850,000
Value of firm	$850,000	Value of firm	$850,000

Shares outstanding = 85,000
Price per share = $850,000/85,000 − $10

If a dividend is paid, the stock price falls by the amount of the dividend. If the company instead uses the cash for a share repurchase, the stock price remains unchanged, but with fewer shares left outstanding, the market value of the firm falls by the same amount as if the dividend had been paid. If a shareholder wants to receive the same amount of cash as if the firm had paid a dividend, he or she must sell shares, and the market value of the remaining stock will be the same as if the firm had paid a dividend.

15.3 The total value of the firm remains at $100 million. Since the firm issues $10 million in new preferred stock and the total value of the firm is fixed, the total value of common equity must fall by $10 million, which translates into the same $1 per share price drop as when equity was issued. If the firm starts out all-equity financed, the market-value balance sheet of the firm will be as follows (in millions):

Assets		Liabilities and Equity	
Assets	$100	Preferred stock	$10
		Common equity	90
Value of firm	$100	Value of firm	$100

Shares outstanding = 1 million
Price per share = $90 million/1 million = $90

15.4 An investor who prefers a zero-dividend policy can reinvest any dividends received. This will cause the value of the shares held to be unaffected by payouts. The price drop on the ex-dividend date is offset by the reinvestment of the dividends. However, if the investor had to pay brokerage fees on the newly purchased shares, she would be harmed by a high-payout policy since part of the proceeds of the dividends would go toward paying the broker. On the other hand, if the firm offers a dividend reinvestment plan (DRIP) with a 5 percent discount, she is better with a high-dividend policy. The DRIP is like a "negative trading cost." She can increase the value of her stock by 5 percent of the dividend just by participating in the DRIP.

15.5 The stock price dropped by more than the dividend because investors interpreted the news as a signal that in addition to omitting the current dividend Con Ed would have to reduce future dividends. The omitted dividend conveyed bad news about the future prospects of the firm.

15.6 The price of the stock will equal the after-tax cash flows discounted by the required (after-tax) rate of return:

$$P = \frac{102.5 + 10 \times (1 - .4)}{1.10} = 98.64.$$

Notice that the after-tax proceeds from the stock would increase by the amount that previously went to pay capital gains taxes, $.20 \times \$4.72 = \$.944$. The present value of this tax saving is $\$.944/1.10 = \$.86$. Therefore, the price increases to $\$97.78 + \$.86 = \$98.64$. The pretax rate of return falls to $\dfrac{102.50 - 98.64 + 10}{98.64} = .1405$,

or 14.05 percent, but the after-tax rate of return remains at 10 percent.

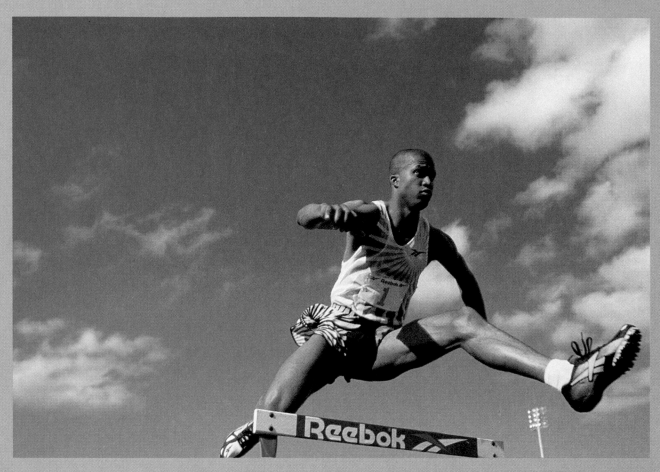

Reebok Corporation

If Reebok Corporation wishes to understand the policies of its competitors, it may start by studying their financial statements. This chapter shows you how to make sense of all that accounting information.

Chapter 16

Financial Statement Analysis

"**D**ivide and conquer" is the only practical strategy for presenting a complex topic like financial management. That is why we have broken down the financial manager's job into separate areas: capital budgeting, dividend policy, equity financing, and debt policy. In the end the financial manager has to consider the combined effects of decisions in each of these areas on the firm as a whole. That is why we devote all of Part Six to financial planning. We begin in this chapter by looking at the analysis of financial statements.

Why do companies provide accounting information? Public companies have a variety of stakeholders, such as shareholders, bondholders, bankers, suppliers, employees, and management. These stakeholders all need to monitor how well their interests are being served. They rely on the company's periodic financial statements to provide the basic information on the profitability of the firm.

In this chapter we look at how you can use these financial statements to analyze a firm's overall performance and assess its current financial standing. You may wish to understand the policies of a competitor or the financial health of a customer. Or you may need to check whether your own firm's financial performance meets standard criteria and, if it doesn't, the dimensions in which it can improve.

We will look at how analysts summarize the large volume of accounting information by calculating some key financial ratios. We will then describe these ratios and look at some interesting relationships among them. Finally, we will show how the ratios are used and note the limitations of the accounting data on which most ratios are based.

After studying this chapter you should be able to

▶ Calculate and interpret measures of a firm's leverage, liquidity, profitability, asset management, and market valuation.

▶ Use the Du Pont formula to understand the determinants of the firm's return on its assets and equity.

▶ Evaluate the potential pitfalls of ratios based on accounting data.

▶ Interpret the company's earnings record.

16.1 Financial Ratios

We have all heard stories of financial whizzes who can take a company's accounts apart in minutes and find its innermost secrets in financial ratios. The truth, however, is that financial ratios are no substitute for a crystal ball. They are just a convenient way to summarize large quantities of financial data and to compare firms' performance. Ratios help you to ask the right questions; they seldom answer them.

We will describe and calculate five types of financial ratios:

• Leverage ratios show how heavily the company is in debt.
• Liquidity ratios measure how easily the firm can lay its hands on cash.
• Efficiency or turnover ratios measure how productively the firm is using its assets.

Table 16.1

INCOME STATEMENT FOR NIKE, INC., 1995 (figures in millions)	
Revenue	$4,761
Cost of goods sold	2,794
Administrative expenses	1,210
Depreciation	71
Other expenses	11
Earnings before interest and taxes (EBIT)	675
Interest expense	24
Income before tax	651
Taxes	250
Net income	400
Preferred stock dividend	0.03
Earnings available for common stock	$ 400
Allocation of net income	
Repurchase of outstanding stock	143
Addition to retained earnings	192
Dividends	65

Note: Numbers may not add because of rounding.
Source: Nike, Inc., 1995 *Annual Report.*

- Profitability ratios are used to measure the firm's return on its investments.
- Market-value ratios show how the firm is valued by investors.

We introduced you to Nike's financial statements in Chapter 2. Now let's analyze them. For convenience, Tables 16.1 and 16.2 present again Nike's income statement and balance sheet.

income statement: Financial statement that shows the revenues, expenses, and net income of a firm over a period of time.

The **income statement** summarizes the firm's revenues and expenses and the difference between the two, which is the firm's profit. You can see that after deducting the cost of goods sold and other expenses, Nike had earnings before interest and taxes (EBIT) of $675 million. Of this sum, $24 million was used to pay debt interest (remember, interest is paid out of pretax income), and $250 million was set aside for taxes. Preferred stock dividends took up a small amount of the after-tax profit, and the balance belonged to the common stockholders. However, Nike did not pay out all its earnings as dividends: $192 million was plowed back into the business and $143 million was used to repurchase common stock.[1]

common-size income statement: Income statement that presents items as a percentage of revenues.

The income statement in Table 16.1 shows the number of dollars that Nike earned in 1995. Sometimes to facilitate comparison between firms, analysts calculate a **common-size income statement.** In this case all items in the income statement are expressed as a percentage of revenues. Table 16.2 is Nike's common-size income statement. You can see for example, that the cost of goods sold consumes over 58 percent of revenues and administrative expenses consume another 25 percent.

balance sheet: Financial statement that shows the value of the firm's assets and liabilities at a particular time.

Whereas the income statement summarizes activity during a period, the **balance sheet** presents a "snapshot" of the firm at a given moment. For example, the balance sheet in Table 16.3 is a snapshot of Nike's assets and liabilities at the end of 1995.

[1] This is in addition to $71 million of cash flow earmarked for depreciation.

Table 16.2

1995 COMMON-SIZE INCOME STATEMENT FOR NIKE, INC. (all items expressed as a percentage of revenues)	
Revenue	100.0
Cost of goods sold	58.7
Administrative expenses	25.4
Depreciation	1.5
Other expenses	0.2
Earnings before interest and taxes (EBIT)	14.2
Interest expense	0.5
Income before tax	13.7
Taxes	5.3
Net income	8.4
Preferred stock dividend	0.0
Earnings available for common stock	8.4
Allocation of net income	
Repurchase of outstanding stock	3.0
Addition to retained earnings	4.0
Dividends	1.4

Note: Numbers may not add because of rounding.

As we pointed out in Chapter 2, the accountant lists first the assets that are most likely to be turned into cash in the near future. They include cash itself, short-term securities, receivables (that is, bills unpaid by the firm's customers), and inventories of raw materials, work-in-process, and finished goods. These assets are all known as *current assets*. The second main group of assets consists of long-term assets such as building, land, machinery, and equipment. Note that the balance sheet does not show the market value of each asset. Instead the accountant records the amount that the asset originally cost and then, in the case of plant and equipment, deducts an annual charge for depreciation. Nike also owns many valuable assets that are *not* shown on the balance sheet—its brand name and skilled labor force, for instance.

Nike's liabilities show the amount of the many claims on the firm's assets. These also are classified as current versus long-term. Current liabilities are bills that the company expects to pay in the near future. They include debts that are due to be repaid within the next year and payables (that is, amounts the company owes to its suppliers). In addition to these short-term debts, Nike has borrowed money that will not be repaid for several years. These are shown as long-term liabilities.

After taking account of all the firm's liabilities and a small issue of preferred stock, the remaining assets belong to the common stockholders. The shareholders' equity is simply the total value of the assets less the current and long-term liabilities and the preferred stock. It is also equal to common stock plus retained earnings, that is, the net amount that the firm has raised from stockholders or reinvested on their behalf.

Table 16.3 also provides some other financial information which is not part of the balance sheet. For example, it shows the market value of Nike's common stock. It is often helpful to compare the *book value* of the equity shown on the company's balance sheet with the *market value* established in the capital markets.

Table 16.3

| BALANCE SHEET FOR NIKE, INC. (figures in millions) | | | | | |
Assets	1995	1994	Liabilities and Shareholders' Equity	1995	1994
Current assets			Current liabilities		
Cash and marketable securities	216	519	Debt due for repayment	429	131
Accounts receivable	1,053	704	Accounts payable	298	211
Inventories	630	470	Other current liabilities	381	220
Other current assets	147	78	Total current liabilities	1,108	562
Total current assets	2,046	1,770			
			Long-term debt and other long-term liabilities	70	71
Fixed assets					
Property, plant, and equipment	891	639	Total liabilities	1,178	633
Less accumulated depreciation	336	233	Preferred stock	0.3	0.3
Net fixed assets	555	406	Shareholders' equity		
Other assets	542	197	Common stock and other paid-in capital	127	96
			Retained earnings	1,838	1,645
Total assets	3,143	2,374	Total shareholders' equity	1,965	1,741
			Total liabilities and shareholders' equity	3,143	2,374

Note: Columns may not add because of rounding.
Other financial information:
Market value of equity	$5,797.3	
Average number of shares	146.8	million
Earnings per share	$ 2.72	
Share price	$ 39.50	

common-size balance sheet: Balance sheet that presents items as a percentage of total assets.

Just as it is sometimes useful to provide a common-size income statement, so we can also calculate a **common-size balance sheet.** In this case all items are reexpressed as a percentage of total assets. Table 16.4 is Nike's common-size balance sheet. The table shows, for example, that cash and marketable securities fell from 21.9 to 6.9 percent of total assets between 1994 and 1995. Nike is somewhat unusual in that the bulk of its assets, about 65 percent, are current. For most firms, fixed assets comprise the majority of total assets. Nike's long-term debt as a fraction of assets, 2.2 percent in 1995, is also unusually low.

Leverage Ratios

When a firm borrows money, it generally promises to make a series of fixed payments. Because the shareholders get only what is left over after the debtholders have been paid, debt is said to create *financial leverage*. Fluctuations in the firm's business have a greater impact on equity returns when firms are levered because the debtholders have first claim on the firm's revenues and assets. Therefore, financial leverage makes the rate of return on equity riskier. In extreme cases, if hard times come, firms with high leverage are liable to find that they cannot pay their debts. So, for example, when a firm wishes to take out a bank loan, it can be sure that the bank will scrutinize several measures of whether the firm is borrowing too much. The bank will also usually insist that the firm *keep* its debt within reasonable bounds. These borrowing limits are usually stated in terms of financial ratios.

Table 16.4

COMMON-SIZE BALANCE SHEET FOR NIKE, INC. (all items expressed as percentage of total assets)					
Assets	**1995**	**1994**	**Liabilities and Shareholders' Equity**	**1995**	**1994**
Current assets			Current liabilities		
Cash and marketable securities	6.9%	21.9%	Debt due for repayment	13.6%	5.5%
Accounts receivable	33.5	29.7	Accounts payable	9.5	8.9
Inventories	20.0	19.8	Other current liabilities	12.1	9.3
Other current assets	4.7	3.3	Total current liabilities	35.3	23.7
Total current assets	65.1	74.6			
			Long-term debt and other long-term liabilities	2.2	3.0
Fixed assets					
Property, plant, and equipment	28.3	26.9			
Less accumulated depreciation	10.7	9.8	Total liabilities	37.5	26.7
Net fixed assets	17.7	17.1	Preferred stock	0.0	0.0
Other assets	17.2	8.3	Shareholders' equity		
			Common stock and other paid-in capital	4.0	4.0
Total assets	100.0	100.0	Retained earnings	58.5	69.3
			Total shareholders' equity	62.5	73.3
			Total liabilities and shareholders' equity	100.0	100.0

Note: Columns may not add because of rounding.

Source: From E. B. Lindberg and S. A. Ross, "Tobin's *q* Ratio and Industrial Organization," *Journal of Business* 54 (January 1981), pp. 1–33. Used by Permission of the Publisher, The University of Chicago Press.

Debt Ratio.   Financial leverage is usually measured by the ratio of long-term debt to total long-term capital. Here "long-term debt" should include not just bonds or other borrowing, but also the value of long-term leases.[2] Total long-term capital, sometimes called *total capitalization,* is the sum of long-term debt and shareholders' equity. Thus for Nike:

$$\text{Long-term debt ratio} = \frac{\text{long-term debt}}{\text{long-term debt} + \text{equity}}$$

$$= \frac{70}{70 + 1{,}965} = .034$$

This means that 3.4 cents of every dollar of long-term capital is in the form of long-term debt. Another way to express leverage is in terms of the company's debt-equity ratio.

$$\text{Debt-equity ratio} = \frac{\text{long-term debt}}{\text{equity}}$$

$$= \frac{70}{1{,}965} = .036$$

[2]A lease is a long-term rental agreement and therefore commits the firm to make regular rental payments. As we emphasized in Chapter 12, leases are quite similar to debt obligations. The value of so-called financial lease commitments is included in "other long-term liabilities." Other lease obligations are described in footnotes to the financial statements.

Notice that both these measures make use of book (that is, accounting) values rather than market values.[3] The market value of the company finally determines whether debtholders get their money back, so you would expect analysts to look at the face amount of the debt as a proportion of the total *market value* of debt and equity. One reason that they don't do this is that market values are often not readily available. Does it matter much? Perhaps not; after all, the market value of the firm includes the value of intangible assets generated by research and development, advertising, staff training, and so on. These assets are not readily saleable and, if the company falls on hard times, the value of these assets may disappear altogether. Thus when banks demand that a borrower keep within a maximum debt ratio, they are usually content to define this debt ratio in terms of book values and to ignore the intangible assets that are not shown in the balance sheet.

Notice also that these measures of leverage take account only of long-term debt obligations. Managers sometimes also define debt to include all liabilities:

$$\text{Total debt ratio} = \frac{\text{total liabilities}}{\text{total assets}} = \frac{1,178}{3,143} = .374$$

Therefore, Nike is financed 37.4 percent with debt, both long-term and short-term, and 62.6 percent with equity. We could also say that its ratio of total debt to equity is 37.4/62.6 = .60.

Managers sometimes refer loosely to a company's debt ratio, but we have just seen that the debt ratio may be measured in several different ways. For example, Nike could be said to have a debt ratio of 3.4 percent (the long-term debt ratio) or 37.4 percent (the total debt ratio). There is a general point here. There are a variety of ways to define most financial ratios and there is no law stating how they *should* be defined. So be warned: Don't accept a ratio at face value without understanding how it has been calculated.

Times Interest Earned Ratio.　Another measure of the financial leverage is the extent to which interest is covered by earnings. Banks prefer to lend to firms whose earnings are far in excess of interest payments. Therefore, analysts often calculate the ratio of earnings before interest and taxes (EBIT) to interest payments. For Nike.[4]

$$\text{Times interest earned} = \frac{\text{EBIT}}{\text{interest payments}} = \frac{675}{24} = 28.1$$

Nike's earnings would need to fall by a factor of 28.1 before they were exceeded by its interest obligations.

The regular interest payment is a hurdle that companies must keep jumping if they are to avoid default. The *times interest earned ratio* (or *interest cover*) measures how much clear air there is between hurdle and hurdler. However, always bear in mind that such summary measures tell only part of the story. For example, it might make

---

[3]In the case of leased assets accountants try to estimate the present value of the lease commitments. In the case of long-term debt they simply show the face value. This can sometimes be very different from present values. For example, the present value of low-coupon debt may be only a fraction of its face value.

[4]The numerator of times interest earned can be defined in several ways. Sometimes it is just net earnings plus interest—that is, earnings before interest *but after tax*. This definition seems inappropriate to us, because the point of times interest earned is to assess the risk that the firm won't have enough money to pay interest. If EBIT falls below interest obligations, taxable income will be negative, and the firm won't pay any income taxes. Interest is paid before the firm pays income taxes.

sense to include in the measure other fixed charges such as regular repayments of existing debt or long-term lease obligations. In 1995, Nike repaid $4 million of long-term debt. That gives

$$\frac{\text{EBIT}}{\text{Interest } + \text{ repayments of long-term debt}} = \frac{675}{24 + 4} = 24.1$$

Cash Coverage Ratio. We have pointed out that depreciation is deducted when calculating the firm's earnings even though no cash goes out the door. Thus, rather than asking whether *earnings* are sufficient to cover interest payments, it might be more interesting to calculate the extent to which interest is covered by the cash flow from the firm's operations. This is measured by the cash coverage ratio. For Nike:

$$\text{Cash coverage ratio} = \frac{\text{EBIT} + \text{depreciation}}{\text{interest payments}} = \frac{675 + 71}{24} = 31.1$$

▶ **Self-Test 16.1**   A firm buys back $10 million par value of outstanding debt and issues $10 million of new debt with a lower rate of interest. What happens to its long-term debt ratio? What happens to its times interest earned and cash coverage ratios?

Liquidity Ratios

liquidity: Ability of an asset to be converted to cash quickly at low cost.

If you are extending credit or lending to a company for a short period, you are interested in more than the company's leverage. You want to know whether it will be able to lay its hands on the cash to repay you. That is why credit analysts and bankers look at several measures of **liquidity.** Liquid assets can be converted into cash quickly and easily.

Think, for example, what you would do to meet a large unexpected bill. You might have some assets that are easily sold, but it would not be so easy to convert old sweaters into cash. Companies also own assets with different degrees of liquidity. For example, accounts receivable and inventories of finished goods are generally quite liquid. As inventories are sold and customers pay their bills, cash flows into the firm. At the other extreme, real estate may be quite *illiquid*. It can be hard to find a buyer, negotiate a fair price, and close a deal at short notice.

Another reason that managers focus on liquid assets is that the accounting figures are more reliable. The book value of a catalytic cracker may be a poor guide to its true value, but at least you know what cash in the bank is worth.

Liquidity ratios also have some *less* desirable characteristics. Because short-term assets and liabilities are easily changed, measures of liquidity can rapidly become outdated. You might not know what the catalytic cracker is worth, but you can be fairly sure that it won't disappear overnight. Also, companies often choose a slack period for the end of their financial year. For example, retailers may end their financial year in January after the Christmas boom. At these times the companies are likely to have more cash and less short-term debt than during busier seasons.

Net Working Capital to Total Assets Ratio. We have seen that current assets are those which the company expects to turn into cash in the near future; current liabilities are liabilities which it expects to meet in the near future. The difference between the current assets and current liabilities is known as *net working capital*. It roughly measures the company's potential reservoir of cash. Managers often express net working capital as a proportion of total assets. For Nike:

$$\frac{\text{Net working capital}}{\text{Total assets}} = \frac{2{,}046 - 1{,}108}{3{,}143} = .30$$

Current Ratio. Another measure which serves a similar purpose is the current ratio:

$$\text{Current ratio} = \frac{\text{current assets}}{\text{current liabilities}} = \frac{2{,}046}{1{,}108} = 1.85$$

So Nike has $1.85 in current assets for every $1 in current liabilities.

Rapid decreases in the current ratio sometimes signify trouble. For example, a firm that drags out its payables to delay paying its bills will suffer an increase in current liabilities and a decrease in the current ratio.

Changes in the current ratio can mislead, however. For example, suppose that a company borrows a large sum from the bank and invests it in marketable securities. Current liabilities rise and so do current assets. Therefore, if nothing else changes, net working capital is unaffected but the current ratio changes. For this reason, it is sometimes preferable to net short-term investments against short-term debt when calculating the current ratio.

Quick (or Acid-Test) Ratio. Some assets are closer to cash than others. If trouble comes, inventory may not sell at anything above fire-sale prices. (Trouble typically comes *because* the firm can't sell its finished-product inventory for more than production cost.) Thus managers often exclude inventories and other relatively less liquid components of current assets (such as prepaid expenses) when comparing current assets to current liabilities. They instead focus on cash, marketable securities, and bills that customers have not yet paid. This results in the quick ratio:

$$\text{Quick ratio} = \frac{\text{cash} + \text{marketable securities} + \text{receivables}}{\text{current liabilities}}$$

$$= \frac{216 + 1{,}053}{1{,}108} = 1.15$$

▶ **Self-Test 16.2**

a. A firm has $1.2 million in current assets and $1.0 million in current liabilities. If it uses $.5 million of cash to pay off some of its accounts payable, what will happen to the current ratio? What happens to the net working capital?

b. A firm uses cash on hand to pay for additional inventories. What will happen to the current ratio? To the quick ratio?

Cash Ratio. A company's most liquid assets are its holdings of cash and marketable securities. That is why financial analysts also look at the cash ratio:

$$\text{Cash ratio} = \frac{\text{cash} + \text{marketable securities}}{\text{current liabilities}} = \frac{216}{1{,}108} = .19$$

Nike has $.19 of cash and securities for every dollar of current liabilities. Of course, lack of cash may not matter if the firm can borrow on short notice. Who cares whether the firm has actually borrowed from the bank or whether it has a guaranteed line of credit that enables it to borrow whenever it chooses? None of the standard liquidity measures takes the firm's "reserve borrowing power" into account.

Interval Measure. Instead of looking at a firm's liquid assets relative to its current liabilities, it may be useful to measure whether liquid assets are large relative to the firm's regular cash outgoings. We ask how long the firm could keep up with its bills using only its cash and other liquid assets. This is the so-called interval measure, which is computed by dividing liquid assets by daily expenditures:

$$\text{Interval measure} = \frac{\text{cash} + \text{marketable securities} + \text{receivables}}{\text{average daily expenditures from operations}}$$

For Nike the cost of goods sold amounted to $2,794 million over the year and there were administrative and other expenses totaling $1,221 million. Therefore,

$$\text{Interval measure} = \frac{216 + 1,053}{(2,794 + 1,221)/365} = 115.4 \text{ days}$$

Nike has sufficient liquid assets to finance operations for 115.4 days even if it sells no more goods.

Efficiency Ratios

Financial analysts employ another set of ratios to judge how efficiently the firm is using its assets.

Asset Turnover Ratio. The sales-to-assets ratio, also known as asset turnover, shows how hard the firm's assets are being put to use. It measures the revenue generated per dollar of assets. For Nike, each dollar of assets resulted in $1.73 in sales:

$$\frac{\text{Sales}}{\text{Average total assets}} = \frac{4,761}{(3,143 + 2,374)/2} = 1.73$$

A high ratio compared to other firms in the industry could indicate that the firm is working close to capacity. It may prove difficult to generate further business without an increase in invested capital.

Notice that since the assets are likely to change over the year, we use the *average* of the assets at the beginning and the end of the year. Averages are usually used whenever a flow figure (in this case, *annual sales*) is compared with a snapshot figure *(total assets)*.

Instead of looking at the ratio of sales to *total* assets, managers sometimes look at how hard particular types of capital are being put to use. For example, they might look at the value of sales per dollar invested in fixed assets. Or they might look at the ratio of sales to net working capital.

Thus for Nike, each dollar of fixed assets supported $9.91 of revenue:

$$\frac{\text{Sales}}{\text{Average fixed assets}} = \frac{4,761}{(555 + 406)/2} = 9.91$$

and each dollar of net working capital (NWC) was associated with $4.44 of sales:

$$\text{NWC turnover} = \frac{\text{sales}}{\text{average net working capital}} = \frac{4,761}{(938 + 1,208)/2} = 4.44$$

Inventory Turnover Ratio. Managers may also monitor the rate at which the company is turning over its inventories. In Nike's case:[5]

$$\text{Inventory turnover} = \frac{\text{cost of goods sold}}{\text{average inventory}} = \frac{2{,}794}{(630 + 470)/2} = 5.08$$

A high inventory turnover ratio compared to other firms in the industry is often regarded as a sign of efficiency. But don't jump to conclusions—it may sometimes indicate that the firm is living from hand to mouth.

Another useful measure of how rapidly inventory turns over is the number of days' sales in inventory. First convert cost of goods sold to a daily basis by dividing by 365. Then express inventories as a multiple of daily sales. The result is the number of days it would take to sell off the firm's current level of inventory:

$$\text{Days' sales in inventories} = \frac{\text{average inventory}}{\text{cost of goods sold}/365}$$

$$= \frac{(630 + 470)/2}{2{,}794/365} = 71.9 \text{ days}$$

Notice that days' sales in inventories is the reciprocal of inventory turnover multiplied by 365.

Average Collection Period. The average collection period measures the speed with which customers pay their bills. It expresses accounts receivable in terms of daily sales:

$$\text{Average collection period} = \frac{\text{average receivables}}{\text{average daily sales}}$$

$$= \frac{(1{,}053 + 704)/2}{4{,}761/365} = 67.3 \text{ days}$$

Therefore, Nike's accounts receivable correspond to 67.3 days' worth of sales. This can be interpreted as the average delay before Nike's customers pay their bills. A comparatively low ratio is often believed to indicate an efficient collection department. Sometimes, however, it is the result of an unduly restrictive credit policy. In such cases, the firm may offer credit only to customers that can be relied on to pay promptly.[6]

▶ **Self-Test 16.3** The average collection period measures the number of days it takes Nike to collect its bills. But Nike also delays *paying* its own bills. Use the information in Tables 16.1 and 16.3 to calculate the average number of days that it takes the company to pay its bills.

Profitability Ratios

Other measures of the efficiency and success of the firm are provided by several profitability measures. These focus on the firm's earnings.

---

[5]The denominator in the inventory turnover ratio is the level of inventories, which is valued at cost. Therefore, we use the cost of goods sold (that is, the value of the goods drawn out of inventory) in the numerator rather than sales.

[6]If possible, it would make more sense to divide average receivables by average daily *credit* sales. Otherwise a low ratio might simply indicate that only a small proportion of sales was made on credit.

Net Profit Margin. If you want to know the proportion of revenue that finds its way into profits, you look at the profit margin. Thus

$$\text{Net profit margin} = \frac{\text{EBIT} - \text{tax}}{\text{sales}} = \frac{675 - 250}{4,761} = .0893, \text{ or } 8.93\%$$

It is common to see the net profit margin calculated using net income rather than EBIT − tax in the numerator. (Remember that net income equals EBIT − tax − interest expense.) This practice strikes us as inappropriate: Why deduct interest on debt in calculating the profit margin? We should not say that a firm is less profitable simply because it relies more heavily on debt finance.

Holding everything else constant, a firm would naturally prefer a high profit margin. But all else cannot be held constant. A high-price and high-margin strategy typically will result in lower sales. So while Bloomingdales might have higher margins than J.C. Penney, it will not necessarily enjoy higher profits. A low-margin but high-volume strategy can be quite successful. We return to this issue later. (See Table 16.5.)

Return on Assets (ROA). Managers often measure the performance of a firm by the ratio of income to total assets. Income is defined as earnings before interest but after taxes. Again, some use net income rather than EBIT − tax to compute ROA. Because net income measures profits net of interest expense, this practice makes the apparent profitability of the firm a function of its capital structure. It is better to use income before interest because we are measuring the return on *all* the firm's assets, not just the equity investment:[7]

$$\text{Return on assets} = \frac{\text{EBIT} - \text{tax}}{\text{average total assets}}$$

$$= \frac{675 - 250}{(3,143 + 2,374)/2} = .154, \text{ or } 15.4\%$$

The assets in a company's books are valued on the basis of their original cost (less any depreciation). A high return on assets does not always mean that you could buy the same assets today and get a high return. Nor does a low return on assets imply that the assets could be better employed elsewhere. But it does suggest that you should ask some searching questions.

In a competitive industry firms can expect to earn only their cost of capital. Therefore, a high return on assets is sometimes cited as an indication that the firm is taking advantage of a monopoly position to charge excessive prices. For example, when

---

[7]This definition of ROA also can be misleading if it is used to compare firms with different capital structures. The reason is that firms that pay more interest pay less taxes. Thus this ratio reflects differences in financial leverage as well as in operating performance. If you want a measure of operating performance alone, we suggest adjusting taxes by adding back interest tax shields (interest payments × marginal tax rate). This gives the taxes the firm would pay if all-equity financed. Thus, using a tax rate of 35 percent for Nike,

$$\text{Return on total assets} = \frac{\text{EBIT} - (\text{tax} + \text{interest tax shields})}{\text{average total assets}}$$

$$= \frac{675 - [250 + (.35 \times 24)]}{(3,143 + 2,374)/2} = .151, \text{ or } 15.1\%$$

We could use this measure to compare the operating performance of two firms even if they had radically different debt ratios.

a public utility commission tries to determine whether a utility is charging a fair price, much of the argument will center on a comparison of the return that the utility is earning on its assets (its ROA) and the cost of capital.

Return on Equity (ROE). Another measure of profitability focuses on the return on shareholders' equity:

$$\text{Return on equity} = \frac{\text{earnings available for common stock}}{\text{average equity}}$$

$$= \frac{400}{(1,965 + 1,741)/2} = .216, \text{ or } 21.6\%$$

Payout Ratio. The payout ratio measures the proportion of earnings that is paid out as dividends. Thus

$$\text{Payout ratio} = \frac{\text{dividends}}{\text{earnings}} = \frac{65}{400} = .16$$

We saw in Section 15.2 that managers don't like to cut dividends because of a shortfall in earnings. Therefore, if a company's earnings are particularly variable, management is likely to play safe by setting a low average payout ratio.

When earnings fall unexpectedly, the payout ratio is likely to rise temporarily. Likewise, if earnings are expected to rise next year, management may feel that it can pay somewhat more generous dividends than it would otherwise have done.

Earnings not paid out as dividends are retained, or plowed back into the business. The proportion of earnings reinvested in the firm is called the *plowback ratio.*

$$\text{Plowback ratio} = 1 - \text{payout ratio} = \frac{\text{earnings} - \text{dividends}}{\text{earnings}}$$

If you multiply this figure by the return on equity, you can see how rapidly shareholders' equity is growing as a result of plowing back part of its earnings each year. Thus for Nike, earnings plowed back into the firm increased the book value of equity by 18.1 percent:

$$\text{Growth in equity from plowback} = \frac{\text{earnings} - \text{dividends}}{\text{equity}}$$

$$= \frac{\text{earnings} - \text{dividends}}{\text{earnings}} \times \frac{\text{earnings}}{\text{equity}}$$

$$= \text{plowback ratio} \times \text{ROE}$$

$$= .84 \times .216 = .181, \text{ or } 18.1\%$$

If Nike can continue to earn 21.6 percent on its book equity and plow back 84 percent of earnings, both earnings and equity will grow at 18.1 percent a year.[8]

Is this a reasonable prospect? We saw in Chapter 4 that such high growth rates are unlikely to persist. While Nike might continue to grow rapidly for a while, as the firm and its industry mature, such rapid growth will inevitably slow.

---

[8]Analysts sometimes refer to this figure as the *sustainable rate of growth.* We discussed the sustainable rate of growth at greater length in Chapter 4.

Market-Value Ratios

There is no law prohibiting the financial manager from introducing data that are not in the company accounts. For example, if you were analyzing a steel company, you might want to look at the cost per ton of steel produced or the sales per employee. Frequently managers also find it helpful to look at ratios that combine accounting and stock market data. Here are four of these market-based ratios.

Price-Earnings Ratio.   The price-earnings, or P/E, ratio is a common measure of the esteem in which the company is held by investors. In the case of Nike the stock market price is $39.50 and earnings per share are $2.72.[9] Therefore,

$$P/E \text{ ratio} = \frac{\text{stock price}}{\text{earnings per share}} = \frac{39.50}{2.72} = 14.5$$

What does it mean when a company's stock sells at a high or low P/E? To answer this question, you might find it helpful to look back to the dividend discount model that we introduced in Chapter 4. If a company's dividends are expected to grow at a steady rate, then the current stock price (P_0) is

$$P_0 = \frac{DIV_1}{r - g}$$

In this formula DIV_1 measures the expected dividend next year, r is the expected return that investors require from similar investments, and g is the expected rate of dividend growth. In order to find the P/E ratio, simply divide through by expected earnings per share:

$$\frac{P_0}{EPS_1} = \frac{DIV_1}{EPS_1} \times \frac{1}{r - g}$$

Thus a high P/E ratio may indicate that (1) investors expect high dividend growth *(g);* or (2) the stock has low risk and therefore investors are content with a low prospective return *(r);* or (3) the company is expected to achieve average dividend growth despite paying out a high proportion of earnings (DIV_1/EPS_1).

Dividend Yield.   The stock's dividend yield is simply the expected dividend as a proportion of the stock price. Thus for Nike dividends per share equal 65/146.8 = $.44, so

$$\text{Dividend yield} = \frac{\text{dividend per share}}{\text{stock price}} = \frac{.44}{39.50} = .011, \text{ or } 1.1\%$$

Again it is helpful to consider a company with a steady expected growth in dividends. In this case

$$\text{Dividend yield} = \frac{DIV_1}{P_0} = r - g$$

Thus a high dividend yield may indicate that investors expect low dividend growth or that they require a high rate of return.

---

[9]We follow common practice when we use 1995 earnings per share and the price at the end of 1995. Since stockholders always look forward, not back, it would be better to use earnings that were forecast for 1996.

Market-to-Book Ratio.   The market-to-book ratio is the ratio of stock price to book value per share:

$$\text{Market-to-book ratio} = \frac{\text{stock price}}{\text{book value per share}} = \frac{39.50}{1,965/146.8} = 2.95$$

Book value per share is just stockholders' book equity divided by the number of shares outstanding. Book equity equals common stock plus retained earnings—the net amount that the firm has received from stockholders plus what it has reinvested on their behalf. Thus Nike's market-to-book ratio of 2.95 means that the market value of the stock is 2.95 times the sum of paid-in capital and retained earnings.

Suppose that you need to estimate the value of a business that is proposing to make an initial sale of its common stock. You would probably wish to make some careful forecasts of its cash flows and discount them to find their present value (see Chapter 4). But it would also make sense to use a few key market-value ratios to check that your estimate of value is in the right ballpark. For example, suppose that you can identify some comparable companies whose values you already know. If the market values of these firms are well in excess of their book values and they truly have similar prospects and accounting policies, then you might reasonably conclude that your business also is worth much more than its book value. Similarly, if the comparable firms are selling at above-average price-earnings multiples, you might judge that the value of your business would be a similarly high multiple of its earnings.

▶ Self-Test 16.4

Show that ROE equals the market-to-book ratio divided by the price-earnings ratio. Are firms with a high ROE necessarily good stock market investments?

Tobin's *q*.   The ratio of the market value of a company's debt and equity to the current replacement cost of its assets is often called *Tobin's q*, after the economist James Tobin:[10]

$$\text{Tobin's } q = \frac{\text{market value of assets}}{\text{estimated replacement cost}}$$

This ratio is similar to the market-to-book ratio, but there are several important differences. The numerator of *q* includes all the firm's debt and equity securities, not just its common stock. The denominator includes all assets, not just the firm's equity. Also, these assets are not entered at original cost, as shown in the firm's books, but at what it would cost to replace them.

Tobin argued that firms have an incentive to invest when *q* is greater than 1 (that is, when capital equipment is worth more than it costs to replace), and that they will stop investing only when *q* is less than 1 (when equipment is worth less than its replacement cost). When *q* is less than 1, it may be cheaper to acquire assets through merger than through purchase of new assets. At these times investors sometimes joke that the cheapest place for a firm to buy assets is on Wall Street.

Of course it is possible to think of cases when the *existing* assets are worth much more than they would cost to replace but there is no scope for *further* profitable

[10]J. Tobin, "A General Equilibrium Approach to Monetary Theory," *Journal of Money, Credit and Banking* 1 (February 1969), pp. 15–29.

investment. Nevertheless, a high market value is usually a sign that investors believe that there are good opportunities in your business.

The reverse is also true. Just because an asset is worth *less* than it would cost to buy today, it does not necessarily mean that it can be better employed elsewhere. But companies whose assets are valued below replacement cost ought to look over their shoulders to see whether predators are threatening to take them over and redeploy the assets.

We should also expect q to be higher for firms with a strong competitive advantage, and this seems to be the case.[11] The companies with the highest values of q tend to be those with very strong brand images or patent protection. Those with the lowest values generally are in highly competitive or shrinking industries.

The Du Pont System

Du Pont system: A breakdown of ROE and ROA into component ratios.

Some profitability or efficiency ratios can be linked in useful ways. These relationships are often referred to as the **Du Pont system,** in recognition of the chemical company that popularized them.

The first relationship links the return on assets (ROA) with the firm's turnover ratio and its profit margin:

$$ROA = \frac{EBIT - taxes}{assets} = \underset{\underset{\text{turnover}}{\underset{\uparrow}{\text{asset}}}}{\frac{sales}{assets}} \times \underset{\underset{\text{margin}}{\underset{\uparrow}{\text{profit}}}}{\frac{EBIT - taxes}{sales}}$$

All firms would like to earn a higher return on assets, but their ability to do so is limited by competition. If the expected return on assets is fixed by competition, firms face a trade-off between the turnover ratio and the profit margin. Thus we find that fast-food chains, which have high turnover, also tend to operate on low profit margins. Hotels have relatively low turnover ratios but tend to compensate for this with higher margins. The example in Table 16.5 illustrates the trade-off. Both the fast-food chain and the hotel have the same return on assets. However, their profit margins and turnover ratios are entirely different.

Firms often seek to improve their profit margins by acquiring a supplier. The idea is to capture the supplier's profit as well as their own. Unfortunately, unless they have some special skill in running the new business, they are likely to find that any gain in profit margin is offset by a decline in the sales-to-assets ratio.

Table 16.5

Fast-food chains and hotels may have a similar return on assets but different asset turnover ratios and profit margins

	Turnover Ratio	×	Profit Margin	=	Return on Assets
Fast-food chains	2.0		5%		10%
Hotels	0.5		20		10

[11]See, for example, E. B. Lindberg and S. A. Ross, "Tobin's q Ratio and Industrial Organization," *Journal of Business* 54 (January 1981), pp 1–33.

Table 16.6

Merging with suppliers or customers will generally increase the profit margin but this will be offset by a reduction in the turnover ratio.

	Millions of Dollars			Asset Turnover	Profit Margin	ROA
	Sales	Profits	Assets			
Admiral Motors	$20	$4	$40	.50	20%	10%
Diana Corp.	8	2	20	.40	25	10
Diana Motors	20	6	60	.33	30	10

A few numbers may help to illustrate this point. Table 16.6 shows the sales, profits, and assets of Admiral Motors and its components supplier Diana Corporation. Both earn a 10 percent return on assets, though Admiral has a lower profit margin (20 percent versus Diana's 25 percent). Since all of Diana's output goes to Admiral, Admiral's management reasons that it would be better to merge the two companies. That way, the merged company could capture the profit margin on both the auto components and the assembled car.

The bottom line of Table 16.6 shows the effect of the merger. The merged firm does indeed earn the combined profits. Total sales remain at $20 million, however, because all of the components produced by Diana are used within the company. With higher profits and unchanged sales, the profit margin increases. Unfortunately, the asset turnover ratio is *reduced* by the merger since the merged firm operates with higher assets. This exactly offsets the benefit of the higher profit margin. The return on assets is unchanged.

It is also useful to break down financial ratios to show how the return on equity (ROE) depends on the return on assets and leverage:

$$\text{ROE} = \frac{\text{earnings available for common stock}}{\text{equity}} = \frac{\text{EBIT} - \text{taxes} - \text{interest}}{\text{equity}}$$

Therefore,

$$\text{ROE} = \underset{\substack{\uparrow \\ \text{leverage} \\ \text{ratio}}}{\frac{\text{assets}}{\text{equity}}} \times \underset{\substack{\uparrow \\ \text{asset} \\ \text{turnover}}}{\frac{\text{sales}}{\text{assets}}} \times \underset{\substack{\uparrow \\ \text{profit} \\ \text{margin}}}{\frac{\text{EBIT} - \text{taxes}}{\text{sales}}} \times \underset{\substack{\uparrow \\ \text{"debt} \\ \text{burden"}}}{\frac{\text{EBIT} - \text{taxes} - \text{interest}}{\text{EBIT} - \text{taxes}}}$$

Notice that the product of the two middle terms is the return on assets. This depends on the firm's production and marketing skills and is unaffected by the firm's financing mix.[12] However, the first and fourth terms do depend on the debt–equity mix. The first term, assets/equity, which we call the leverage ratio, can be expressed as (equity + liabilities)/equity, which equals 1 + total debt-to-equity ratio. The last term, which we call the "debt burden," measures the proportion by which interest expense reduces profits.

Suppose that the firm is financed entirely by equity. In this case both the first and fourth terms are equal to 1.0 and the return on equity is identical to the return on assets. If the firm is leveraged, the first term is greater than 1.0 (assets are greater

[12]There is a complication here because the amount of taxes paid depends on the financing mix. We suggested in footnote 7 that it would be better to add back any interest tax shields when calculating the firm's profit margin.

than equity) and the fourth term is less than 1.0 (part of the profits are absorbed by interest). Thus leverage can either increase or reduce return on equity. In fact we showed in Section 14.1 that leverage increases ROE when the firm earns a return higher than the interest rate on its debt.

▶ **Self-Test 16.5**

a. Sappy Syrup has a profit margin below the industry average, but its ROA equals the industry average. How is this possible?

b. Sappy Syrup's ROA equals the industry average, but its ROE exceeds the industry average. How is this possible?

16.3 *Using Financial Ratios*

Many years ago a British bank chairman observed that not only did the bank's accounts show its true position but the actual situation was a little better still.[13] Since that time accounting standards have been much more carefully defined, but companies still have considerable discretion in calculating profits and deciding what to show on the balance sheet. Thus when you calculate financial ratios, you need to look below the surface and understand some of the potential pitfalls of accounting data.

For example, the 1995 entry for other long-term assets shown in Nike's balance sheet includes a figure of $339 million for "goodwill." This is the difference between the amount that Nike paid when it acquired several companies and the book value of their assets. Nike writes off 2½ percent of this goodwill from each year's profits. We don't want to debate whether goodwill is really an asset, but we should warn you about the dangers of comparing ratios of firms whose balance sheets include a substantial goodwill element with those that do not.

Another pitfall arises because many of the company's liabilities are not shown in the balance sheet at all. For example, the balance sheet entry "other long-term liabilities" includes leases that meet certain tests—for example, leases lasting more than 75 percent of the leased asset's life. But a lease lasting only 74 percent of asset life escapes the net and is shown only in the footnotes to the financial statements. Read the footnotes carefully; if you take the balance sheet uncritically, you may miss important obligations of the company.

Choosing a Benchmark

We have shown you how to calculate the principal financial ratios for Nike. In practice you may not have to calculate all of them, because many measure essentially the same thing. For example, once you know that Nike's EBIT is 28 times interest payments and that long-term debt is only 3.4 percent of total capitalization, the other leverage ratios are of little interest.

---

[13]Speech by the chairman of the London and County Bank at the Annual Meeting, February 1901. Reported in *The Economist,* 1901, p. 204, and cited in C. A. E. Goodhart, *The Business of Banking 1891–1914* (London: Weidenfeld and Nicholson, 1972), p. 15.

Table 16.7

Financial ratios for Nike and Reebok

	Nike		Reebok
	1995	**1994**	**1995**
Leverage ratios			
Long-term debt ratio	.03	.04	.27
Total debt ratio	.37	.27	.46
Times interest earned	28.13	33.09	11.75
Liquidity ratios			
NWC to assets	.30	.51	.55
Current ratio	1.85	3.15	3.11
Quick ratio	1.15	2.18	1.36
Cash ratio	.19	.92	.19
Interval measure (days)	115	139	68
Efficiency ratios			
Asset turnover	1.73	1.66	2.11
NWC turnover	4.44	3.19	4.01
Inventory turnover	5.08	4.21	27.7
Average collection period (days)	67	66	54
Profitability ratios			
Net profit margin (%)	8.9	8.3	5.8
Return on assets (%)	15.4	13.8	12.2
Return on equity (%)	21.6	34.4	17.5
Market-value ratios			
Price-earnings ratio	14.5	14.9	10.7
Dividend yield (%)	1.0	1.4	1.1
Market-to-book ratio	3.0	2.5	2.5

Once you have selected and calculated the important ratios, you still need some way of judging whether they are high or low. A good starting point is to compare them with the equivalent figures for the same company in earlier years. For example, you can see from the first two columns of Table 16.7 that Nike's ROA was a bit higher in 1995 than in 1994. The increase can be traced to an increase in the profit margin, since asset turnover was essentially unchanged.

When making comparisons of this kind remember our earlier warning about the need to dig behind the figures. For example, Nike's increase in ROA stems largely from an increase in profit margin. Was this due to across-the-board aggressive pricing or to a change in the product mix? You can obtain some clues by comparing *segment accounts,* which break down profitability according to product and area of operation. Are there any indications that the reduction in turnover may be temporary? A closer examination of turnover in each segment may help you to decide.

It is also helpful to compare Nike's financial position with that of other firms. However, you would not expect companies in different industries to have similar financial ratios. For example, an athletic shoe manufacturer is unlikely to have the same profit margin as a jeweler or the same leverage as a finance company. It makes sense, therefore, to limit the comparison to other firms in the same industry.

Table 16.8

Financial ratios for major industry groups, first quarter 1996

	All Manufac- turing Corporations	Food and Kindred Products	Printing and Publish- ing	Chemical and Allied Products	Petroleum and Coal Products	Electrical and Electronic Equipment	Retail[a] Trade
Leverage ratios							
Long-term debt ratio[b]	.49	.53	.52	.54	.48	.39	.48
Total debt ratio	.62	.65	.60	.66	.58	.52	.67
Liquidity ratios							
Net working capital to total assets	.10	.05	.08	.03	.01	.14	.17
Current ratio	1.39	1.24	1.42	1.10	1.08	1.51	1.55
Cash ratio	.20	.18	.24	.12	.13	.23	.12
Efficiency and profitability ratios							
Asset turnover	1.05	1.17	.93	.75	.92	1.04	2.28
Profit margin[c] (%)	7.0	7.3	7.9	11.0	6.6	8.4	5.1
Return on assets (%)	1.82	2.12	1.85	2.06	1.52	2.17	2.89
Return on equity[d]	4.00	4.32	3.61	5.53	3.94	4.17	3.00
Payout ratio	.37	.49	.21	.42	.57	.30	.23

[a]Figures are for fourth quarter, 1995.

[b]Long-term debt includes capitalized leases and deferred income taxes.

[c]Reflects operating income only.

[d]Reflects nonoperating as well as operating income.

Source: U.S. Department of Commerce, *Quarterly Financial Report for Manufacturing, Mining and Trade Corporations,* First Quarter 1996, pp. 2–156.

The third column of Table 16.7 shows the financial ratios for Reebok, one of Nike's main competitors.[14] In most respects the two sets of financial ratios are similar. The long-term debt ratios for both firms are relatively low. The liquidity ratios are also similar. Reebok has an edge in terms of generally higher turnover ratios, but Nike has a significantly higher profit margin. The net effect is that Nike's return on assets is higher than Reebok's.

Financial ratios for industries are published by the U.S. Department of Commerce, Dun & Bradstreet, Robert Morris Associates, and others. Table 16.8 shows the principal ratios for major industry groups. This should give you a feel for some of the differences between industries.

▶ **Self-Test 16.6** Look at the financial ratios shown in Table 16.8. The retail trade industry has a higher ratio of net working capital to total assets than manufacturing corporations. It also has a higher asset turnover and a lower profit margin. What do you think accounts for these differences?

[14]Ideally, we would compare Nike's financial statements to average values for the entire industry rather than one competitor. However, there are few firms as concentrated in sports shoes as these two, so we rely on the firm-to-firm comparison.

16.4 *The Earnings Record*

Figure 16.1 summarizes Nike's earnings record over the past 15 years. But Nike is affected by the state of the economy as a whole and by the prosperity of its particular industry. Thus to interpret this record you need to take into account what was happening to other companies.

Figure 16.1 also shows Reebok's earnings performance. Notice that Nike's earnings record closely mirrors that of its competitor. This tells us that if we want to understand Nike's recent growth in profits, we probably need to look at events affecting the whole industry.

Does Nike's growth in earnings bode well for the future? Not necessarily. Statisticians who have studied the time path of firms' reported earnings conclude that earnings behave much as stock prices do—that is, they follow a random walk.[15] There is almost no relationship between a company's earnings growth in one period and that in the next. Therefore, you should never extrapolate growth mechanically. A firm with above-average earnings growth is equally likely to follow up with either below-average or above-average future growth. There is little point in fitting a trend line to past earnings, and such a trend line tells you little about likely future earnings.

Of course there are many sources of information that may help you forecast earnings. For example, when a firm enjoys a high P/E ratio despite disappointing earnings, this suggests that investors expect an earnings rebound. Or suppose a firm announces a significant technological jump ahead of its competitors; you don't need a Ph.D. to figure out the likely impact on earnings.

Figure 16.1

Earnings per share of Nike and Reebok (Source: Value Line Investment Survey, 1996)

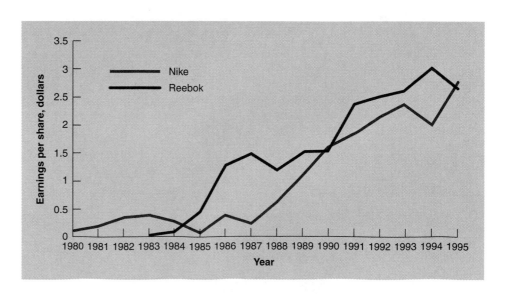

[15]See, for example, R. Ball and R. Watts, "Some Time Series Properties of Accounting Income," *Journal of Finance* 27 (June 1972), pp. 663–682.

Summary

1. If you are analyzing a company's financial statements, there is a danger of being overwhelmed by the sheer volume of data. Managers use a few salient ratios to summarize the firm's leverage, liquidity, efficiency, profitability, and market valuation. You will sometimes find that financial analysts define the same ratio in different ways or use different terms to describe the same ratio.
2. Table 16.9 summarizes the five categories of financial ratios that we have discussed in this chapter.
3. Leverage ratios measure the indebtedness of the firm. Liquidity ratios measure how easily the firm can obtain cash. Efficiency ratios measure how intensively the firm is using its assets. Profitability ratios measure the firm's return on its investments. Market-value ratios measure how the firm is valued by investors. Be selective in your choice of ratios. Different ratios often tell you similar things.
4. The Du Pont system provides a useful way to link ratios to explain the firm's return on assets and equity.
5. Financial ratio analysis will rarely be useful if practiced mechanically. It requires a good dose of good judgment. Financial ratios seldom provide answers but they do help you ask the right questions.
6. You need a benchmark for assessing a company's financial position. It is usual to compare financial ratios with the company's ratios in earlier years and with the ratios of other firms in the same business.

Table 16.9

Summary of financial ratios

Leverage ratios

$$\text{Long-term debt ratio} = \frac{\text{long-term debt}}{\text{long-term debt} + \text{equity}}$$

$$\text{Debt-equity ratio} = \frac{\text{long-term debt}}{\text{equity}}$$

$$\text{Total debt ratio} = \frac{\text{total liabilities}}{\text{total assets}}$$

$$\text{Times interest earned} = \frac{\text{EBIT}}{\text{interest payments}}$$

$$\text{Cash coverage} = \frac{\text{EBIT} + \text{depreciation}}{\text{interest payments}}$$

Liquidity ratios

$$\text{NWC to assets} = \frac{\text{net working capital}}{\text{total assets}}$$

$$\text{Current ratio} = \frac{\text{current assets}}{\text{current liabilities}}$$

$$\text{Quick ratio} = \frac{\text{cash} + \text{marketable securities} + \text{accounts receivable}}{\text{current liabilities}}$$

Table 16.9 *(continued)*
Summary of financial ratios

$$\text{Cash ratio} = \frac{\text{cash} + \text{marketable securities}}{\text{current liabilities}}$$

$$\text{Interval measure} = \frac{\text{cash} + \text{marketable securities} + \text{receivables}}{\text{average daily expenditures from operations}}$$

Efficiency ratios

$$\text{Total asset turnover} = \frac{\text{sales}}{\text{average total assets}}$$

$$\text{NWC turnover} = \frac{\text{sales}}{\text{average net working capital}}$$

$$\text{Inventory turnover} = \frac{\text{cost of goods sold}}{\text{average inventory}}$$

$$\text{Days' sales in inventories} = \frac{\text{average inventory}}{\text{cost of goods sold}/365}$$

$$\text{Average collection period} = \frac{\text{average receivables}}{\text{average daily sales}}$$

Profitability ratios

$$\text{Net profit margin} = \frac{\text{EBIT} - \text{tax}}{\text{sales}}$$

$$\text{Return on assets} = \frac{\text{EBIT} - \text{tax}}{\text{average total assets}}$$

$$\text{Return on equity} = \frac{\text{earnings available for common stock}}{\text{average equity}}$$

$$\text{Payout ratio} = \frac{\text{dividends}}{\text{earnings}}$$

$$\text{Plowback ratio} = 1 - \text{payout ratio}$$

$$\text{Growth in equity from plowback} = \text{plowback ratio} \times \text{ROE}$$

Market-value ratios

$$\text{P/E ratio} = \frac{\text{stock price}}{\text{earnings per share}}$$

$$\text{Dividend yield} = \frac{\text{dividend per share}}{\text{stock price}}$$

$$\text{Market-to-book ratio} = \frac{\text{stock price}}{\text{book value per share}}$$

$$\text{Tobin's } q = \frac{\text{market value of assets}}{\text{estimated replacement cost}}$$

Key Terms

income statement
common-size income statement

balance sheet
common-size balance sheet

liquidity
Du Pont system

Problems

1. **Calculating Ratios.** Here are simplified financial statements of Nynex Corporation from a recent year:

INCOME STATEMENT
(figures in millions of dollars)

Net sales	13,194
Cost of goods sold	4,060
Other expenses	4,049
Depreciation	2,518
Earnings before interest and taxes (EBIT)	2,566
Interest expenses	685
Income before tax	1,882
Taxes	570
Net income	1,311
Dividends	856

BALANCE SHEET
(figures in millions of dollars)

	End of Year	Start of Year
Assets		
Cash and marketable securities	89	158
Receivables	2,382	2,490
Inventories	187	238
Other current assets	867	932
Total current assets	3,524	3,818
Net property, plant, and equipment	19,973	19,915
Other long-term assets	4,216	3,770
Total assets	27,714	27,503
Liabilities and shareholders' equity		
Payables	2,564	3,040
Short-term debt	1,419	1,573
Other current liabilities	811	787
Total current liabilities	4,795	5,400
Long-term debt and leases	7,018	6,833
Other long-term liabilities	6,178	6,149
Shareholders' equity	9,724	9,120
Total liabilities and shareholders' equity	27,714	27,503

Calculate the following financial ratios:

   a. Long-term debt ratio
   b. Total debt ratio
   c. Times interest earned
   d. Cash coverage ratio
   e. Current ratio
   f. Quick ratio
   g. Net profit margin
   h. Inventory turnover
   i. Days in inventory
   j. Average collection period
   k. Return on equity

l. Return on assets

m. Payout ratio

2. **Interval Measure.** Suppose that Nynex shut down operations. For how many days could it pay its bills?

3. **Gross Investment.** What was Nynex's gross investment in plant and other equipment?

4. **Market Value Ratios.** If the market value of Nynex stock was $17.2 billion at the end of the year, what was the market-to-book ratio? If there were 205 million shares outstanding, what were earnings per share? The P/E ratio?

5. **Common-Size Balance Sheet.** Prepare a common-size balance sheet for Nynex using its balance sheet from problem 1.

6. **Du Pont Analysis.** Use the data for Nynex to confirm that ROA = asset turnover × profit margin.

7. **Du Pont Analysis.** Use the data for Nynex from problem 1 to

a. calculate the ROE for Nynex

b. demonstrate that ROE = leverage ratio × asset turnover ratio × profit margin × debt burden.

8. **Asset Turnover.** In each case, choose the firm that you expect to have a higher asset turnover ratio.

a. Economics Consulting Group or Nike

b. Catalog Shopping Network or Neiman Marcus

c. Electric Utility Co. or Standard Supermarkets

9. **Defining Ratios.** There are no universally accepted definitions of financial ratios, but *some* of the following ratios make no sense at all. Substitute the correct definitions.

a. Debt-equity ratio $= \dfrac{\text{long-term debt}}{\text{long-term debt} + \text{equity}}$

b. Return on equity $= \dfrac{\text{EBIT} - \text{tax}}{\text{average equity}}$

c. Profit margin $= \dfrac{\text{EBIT} - \text{tax}}{\text{sales}}$

d. Inventory turnover $= \dfrac{\text{total assets}}{\text{average inventory}}$

e. Current ratio $= \dfrac{\text{current liabilities}}{\text{current assets}}$

f. Interval measure $= \dfrac{\text{current assets} - \text{inventories}}{\text{average daily expenditure from operations}}$

g. Average collection period $= \dfrac{\text{sales}}{\text{average receivables}/365}$

h. Quick ratio $= \dfrac{\text{cash} + \text{marketable securities} + \text{receivables}}{\text{current liabilities}}$

i. Tobin's $q = \dfrac{\text{market value of assets}}{\text{replacement cost of assets}}$

j. Payout ratio $= \dfrac{\text{dividend}}{\text{stock price}}$

10. **Financial Statements.** As you can see, someone has spilled ink over some of the entries in the balance sheet and income statement of Transylvania Railroad. Can you use the following information to work out the missing entries:

Long-term debt ratio	.4
Times interest earned	8.0
Current ratio	1.4
Quick ratio	1.0
Cash ratio	.2
Return on assets	18%
Return on equity	41%
Inventory turnover	5.0
Average collection period	71.2 days

INCOME STATEMENT
(figures in millions of dollars)

Net sales	•••
Cost of goods sold	•••
Selling, general, and administrative expenses	10
Depreciation	20
Earnings before interest and taxes (EBIT)	•••
Interest expense	•••
Income before tax	•••
Tax	•••
Net income	•••

BALANCE SHEET
(figures in millions of dollars)

	This Year	Last Year
Assets		
Cash and marketable securities	•••	20
Receivables	•••	34
Inventories	•••	26
Total current assets	•••	80
Net property, plant, and equipment	•••	25
Total assets	•••	105
Liabilities and shareholders' equity		
Accounts payable	25	20
Notes payable	30	35
Total current liabilities	•••	55
Long-term debt	•••	20
Shareholders' equity	•••	30
Total liabilities and shareholders' equity	115	105

11. **Current Liabilities.** Suppose that at year-end Nike had unused lines of credit which would have allowed it to borrow a further $300 million. Suppose also that it used this line of credit to borrow $300 million and invested the proceeds in marketable securities. Would the company have appeared to be (a) more or less liquid, (b) more or less highly leveraged? Calculate the appropriate ratios.

12. **Current Ratio.** How would the following actions affect a firm's current ratio?

    a. Inventory is sold at cost.
    b. The firm takes out a bank loan to pay its accounts due.
    c. A customer pays its accounts receivable.
    d. The firm uses cash to purchase additional inventories.

13. **Liquidity Ratios.** A firm uses $1 million in cash to purchase inventories. What will happen to its current ratio? Its quick ratio?

14. **Receivables.** Chik's Chickens has average accounts receivable of $6,333. Sales for the year were $9,800. What is its average collection period?

15. **Inventory.** Salad Daze maintains an inventory of produce worth $400. Its total bill for produce over the course of the year was $73,000. How old on average is the lettuce it serves its customers?

16. **Inventory Turnover.** If a firm's inventory level of $10,000 represents 30 days' sales, what is the annual cost of goods sold? What is the inventory turnover ratio?

17. **Leverage Ratios.** Lever Age pays an 8 percent coupon on outstanding debt with face value $10 million. The firm's EBIT was $1 million.

    a. What is times interest earned?
    b. If depreciation is $200,000, what is cash coverage?
    c. If the firm must retire $300,000 of debt for the sinking fund each year, what is its "fixed-payment cash-coverage ratio" (the ratio of cash flow to interest plus other fixed debt payments)?

18. **Du Pont Analysis.** Keller Cosmetics maintains a profit margin of 5 percent and asset turnover ratio of 3.

    a. What is its ROA?
    b. If its debt-equity ratio is 1.0, its interest payments and taxes are each $8,000, and EBIT is $20,000, what is its ROE?

19. **Du Pont Analysis.** Torrid Romance Publishers has total receivables of $3,000, which represents 20 days' sales. Average total assets are $75,000. The firm's profit margin is 5 percent. Find the firm's ROA and asset turnover ratio.

20. **Leverage.** A firm has a long-term debt-equity ratio of .4. Shareholders' equity is $1 million. Current assets are $200,000 and the current ratio is 2.0. The only current liabilities are notes payable. What is the total debt ratio?

21. **Leverage Ratios.** A firm has a debt-to-equity ratio of .5 and a market-to-book ratio of 2.0. What is the ratio of the book value of debt to the market value of equity?

22. **Times Interest Earned.** In the past year, TVG had revenues of $3 million, cost of goods sold of $2.5 million, and depreciation expense of $200,000. The firm has a single issue of debt outstanding with face value of $1 million, market value of $.92 million, and a coupon rate of 8 percent. What is the firm's times interest earned ratio?

23. **Du Pont Analysis.** CFA Corp. has a debt-equity ratio that is lower than the industry average, but its cash coverage ratio is also lower than the industry average. What might explain this seeming contradiction?

24. **Leverage.** Suppose that a firm has both floating rate and fixed rate debt outstanding. What effect will a decline in market interest rates have on the firm's times interest earned ratio? On the market value debt-to-equity ratio? Based on these answers, would you say that leverage has increased or decreased?

25. **Interpreting Ratios.** In each of the following cases, explain briefly which of the two companies is likely to be characterized by the higher ratio:

a. Debt-equity ratio: a shipping company or a computer software company
b. Payout ratio: United Foods Inc. or Computer Graphics Inc.
c. Ratio of sales to assets: an integrated pulp and paper manufacturer or a paper mill
d. Average collection period: Regional Electric Power Company or Z-Mart Discount Outlets
e. Price-earnings multiple: Basic Sludge Company or Fledgling Electronics
f. Tobin's q: an iron foundry or a pharmaceutical company with strong patent protection

26. **Using Financial Ratios.** For each category of financial ratio discussed in this chapter, give some examples of who would be likely to examine these ratios and why.
27. **Market Value Ratios.** Imagine that you could not observe Nike's market value. Use the market value ratios for Reebok to estimate the value of Nike's common stock. How good are your estimates?

Solutions to Self-Test Questions

16.1 Nothing will happen to the long-term debt ratio computed using book values, since the face values of the old and new debt are equal. However, times interest earned and cash coverage will increase since the firm will reduce its interest expense.

16.2. a. The current ratio starts at 1.2/1.0 = 1.2. The transaction will reduce current assets to $.7 million and current liabilities to $.5 million. The current ratio increases to .7/.5 = 1.4. Net working capital is unaffected: current assets and curent liabilities fall by equal amounts.
b. The current ratio is unaffected, since the firm merely exchanges one current asset (cash) for another (inventories). However, the quick ratio will fall since inventories are not included among the most liquid assets.

16.3 Average daily expenses are (2,794 + 1,210 + 11)/365 = $11.0 million. Average accounts payable are (298 + 211)/2 = 254.5 million. The average payment delay is therefore 254.5/11.0 = 23.1 days.

16.4
$$\text{Market-to-book} = \frac{\text{price}}{\text{book value per share}}$$

$$\frac{\text{Market-to-book}}{\text{Price/earnings per share}} = \frac{\text{price/book value per share}}{\text{price/earnings per share}}$$

$$= \frac{\text{earnings per share}}{\text{book value per share}} = \text{ROE}$$

Firms with high ROE are not necessarily good investments. A high ROE will be associated with a high stock price (assuming that investors expect the high ROE to persist). Even though the *firm* earns a good return on its investments, investors in the *firm's stock* might not earn attractive returns on their investments since they buy into the firm at prices that already reflect the attractive ROE. There is a difference between a "good firm" and a "good stock."

16.5 a. The firm must compensate for its below-average profit margin with an above-average turnover ratio. Remember that ROA is the *product* of margin × turnover.
b. If ROA equals the industry average but ROE exceeds the industry average, the firm must have above-average leverage. As long as ROA exceeds the borrowing rate, leverage will increase ROE.

16.6. Retailers maintain large inventories of goods, specifically the products they stock in their stores. This shows up in the high net working capital ratio. Their profit margin on sales is relatively low, but they make up for that low margin by turning over goods rapidly. The high asset turnover allows retailers to earn an adequate return on assets even with a low profit margin, and competition prevents them from increasing prices and margins to a level that would provide a better ROA. In contrast, manufacturing firms have low turnover, and therefore need higher profit margins to remain viable.

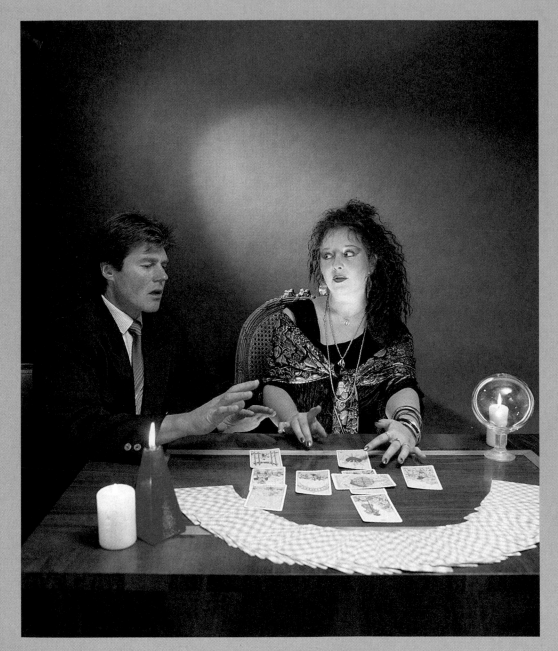

Financial planning?
Financial planners don't guess the future, they prepare for it.
SuperStock

Chapter 17

Financial Planning

*I*t's been said that a camel looks like a horse designed by committee. If a firm made all its financial decisions piecemeal, it would end up with a financial camel. Therefore, smart financial managers consider the overall effect of future investment and financing decisions. This process is called *financial planning,* and the end result is called a *financial plan.*

New investments need to be paid for. So investment and financing decisions cannot be made independently. Financial planning forces managers to think systematically about their goals for growth, investment, and financing. Planning should reveal any inconsistencies in these goals.

Planning also helps managers avoid some surprises and think about how they should react to those surprises that *cannot* be avoided. In Chapter 7 we stressed that good financial managers insist on understanding what makes projects work and what could go wrong with them. The same approach should be taken when investment and financing decisions are considered as a whole.

Finally, financial planning helps establish goals to motivate managers and provide standards for measuring performance.

We start the chapter by summarizing what financial planning involves and we describe the contents of a typical financial plan. We then discuss the use of financial models in the planning process. Finally, we examine the relationship between a firm's growth and its need for new financing.

After studying this chapter you should be able to

▶ Describe the contents and uses of a financial plan.

▶ Construct a simple financial planning model.

▶ Estimate the effect of growth on the need for external financing.

17.1 What Is Financial Planning?

Financial planning is a *process* consisting of:

1. Analyzing the investment and financing choices open to the firm.
2. Projecting the future consequences of current decisions.
3. Deciding which alternatives to undertake.
4. Measuring subsequent performance against the goals set forth in the financial plan.

Notice that financial planning is not designed to minimize risk. Instead it is a process of deciding which risks to take and which are unnecessary or not worth taking.

Firms must plan for both the short-term and the long-term. Short-term planning rarely looks ahead further than the next 12 months. It is largely the process of making sure the firm has enough cash to pay its bills and that short-term borrowing and lending are arranged to the best advantage. We discuss short-term planning in the next chapter.

planning horizon: Time horizon for a financial plan.

Here we are more concerned with long-term planning, where a typical **planning horizon** is 5 years (although some firms look out 10 years or more). For example, it can take at least 10 years for an electric utility to design, obtain approval for, build, and test a major generating plant.

Financial Planning Focuses on the Big Picture

Many of the firm's capital expenditures are proposed by plant managers. But the final budget must also reflect strategic plans made by senior management. Positive-NPV opportunities occur in those businesses where the firm has a real competitive advantage. Strategic plans need to identify such businesses and look to expand them. The plans also seek to identify businesses to sell or liquidate as well as businesses that should be allowed to run down.

Strategic planning involves capital budgeting on a grand scale. In this process, financial planners try to look at the investment by each line of business and avoid getting bogged down in details. Of course, some individual projects are large enough to have significant individual impact. When Ford committed $6 billion to the development of its self-proclaimed world car, the Mondeo, you can bet that this project was explicitly analyzed as part of Ford's long-range financial plan. Normally, however, financial planners do not work on a project-by-project basis. Smaller projects are aggregated into a unit that is treated as a single project.

At the beginning of the planning process the corporate staff might ask each division to submit three alternative business plans covering the next 5 years:

1. A *best case* or aggressive growth plan calling for heavy capital investment and rapid growth of existing markets.
2. A *normal growth* plan in which the division grows with its markets but not significantly at the expense of its competitors.
3. A plan of *retrenchment* if the firm's markets contract. This is planning for lean economic times.

Of course, the planners might also want to look at the opportunities and costs of moving into a wholly new area where the company may be able to exploit some of its existing strengths. Often they may recommend entering a market for "strategic" reasons—that is, not because the *immediate* investment has a positive net present value, but because it establishes the firm in a new market and creates *options* for possibly valuable follow-up investments.

As an example, think of the decision by IBM to acquire Lotus Corporation for $3.3 billion. Lotus added less than $1 billion of revenues, but Lotus with its Notes software has considerable experience in helping computers talk to each other. This know-how gives IBM an option to produce and market new products in the future.

Because the firm's future is likely to depend on the options that it acquires today, we would expect planners to take a particular interest in these options.

In the simplest plans, capital expenditures might be forecast to grow in proportion to sales. In even moderately sophisticated models, however, the need for additional investments will recognize the firm's ability to use its fixed assets at varying levels of intensity by adjusting overtime or by adding additional shifts. Similarly, the plan will alert the firm to needs for additional investments in working capital. For example, if sales are forecast to increase, the firm should plan to increase inventory levels and should expect an increase in accounts receivable.

Most plans also contain a summary of planned financing. This part of the plan should logically include a discussion of dividend policy, because the more the firm pays out, the more capital it will need to find from sources other than retained earnings.

Some firms need to worry much more than others about raising money. A firm with limited investment opportunities, ample operating cash flow, and a moderate dividend payout accumulates considerable "financial slack" in the form of liquid assets and unused borrowing power. Life is relatively easy for the managers of such firms, and their financing plans are routine. Whether that easy life is in the interests of their stockholders is another matter. For example, when we discussed capital structure in Chapter 14, we described how Sealed Air Corporation deliberately reduced its financial slack and increased its leverage in order to encourage its managers to run a tight ship.

Other firms have to raise capital by selling securities. Naturally, they give careful attention to planning the kinds of securities to be sold and the timing of the offerings. The plan might specify bank borrowing, debt issues, equity issues, or other means to raise capital.

> **Financial plans help managers ensure that their financing strategies are consistent with their capital budgets. They highlight the financing decisions necessary to support the firm's production and investment goals.**

Financial Planning Is Not Just Forecasting

Forecasting concentrates on the most likely future outcome. But financial planners are not concerned solely with forecasting. They need to worry about unlikely events as well as likely ones. If you think ahead about what could go wrong, then you are less likely to ignore the danger signals and you can react faster to trouble.

Companies have developed a number of ways of asking "what-if" questions about both their projects and the overall firm. We examined some of these techniques in Chapter 7. Often planners work through the consequences of the plan under the most likely set of circumstances and then use *sensitivity analysis* to vary the assumptions one at a time. For example, they might look at what would happen if a policy of aggressive growth coincided with a recession. Companies using *scenario analysis* might look at the consequences of each business plan under different plausible scenarios in which several assumptions are varied at once. For example, one scenario might envisage high interest rates lending to a slowdown in world economic growth and lower commodity prices. A second scenario might involve a buoyant domestic economy, high inflation, and a weak currency. The nearby box describes how Georgia Power Company used scenario analysis to help develop its business plans.

 See box p. 487

Three Requirements for Effective Planning

Forecasting.   The firm will never have perfectly accurate forecasts. If it did, there would be less need for planning. Still, managers must strive for the best forecasts possible.

> **Forecasting should not be reduced to a mechanical exercise. Naive extrapolation or fitting trends to past data is of limited value. Planning is needed because the future is *not* likely to resemble the past.**

Do not forecast in a vacuum. By this we mean that your forecasts should recognize that your competitors are developing their own plans. For example, your ability

Contingency Planning at Georgia Power Company

The oil price hikes in 1973–1974 and 1979 caused consternation in the planning departments of electric utilities. Planners, who had assumed a steady growth in energy usage and prices, found that assumption could no longer be relied on.

The planning department of the Georgia Power Company responded by developing a number of possible scenarios and exploring their implications for Georgia Power's business over the following 10 years. In planning for the future, the company was not simply interested in the most likely outcome; it also needed to develop contingency plans to cover any unexpected occurrences.

Georgia Power's planning process involved three steps: (1) identify the key factors affecting the company's prospects; (2) determine a range of plausible outcomes for each of these factors; and (3) consider whether a favorable outcome for one factor was likely to be matched by a favorable outcome for the other factors.

This exercise generated three principal scenarios. For example, in the most rosy scenario, the growth in gross national product was expected to exceed 3.2 percent a year. This higher economic growth was likely to be accompanied by high productivity growth and lower real interest rates as the baby boom generation matured. However, high growth was also likely to mean that economic prosperity would be more widely spread, so that the net migration to Georgia and the other sunbelt states was likely to decline. The average price of oil would probably remain below $18 a barrel as the power of OPEC weakened, and this would encourage industry to substitute oil for natural gas. The government was likely to pursue a free-market energy policy, which would tend to keep the growth in electricity prices below the rate of inflation.

Georgia Power's planners explored the implications of each scenario for energy demand and the amount of investment the company needed to make. That in turn allowed the financial managers to think about how the company could meet the possible demands for cash to finance the new investment.

Source: Georgia Power Company's use of scenario analysis is described in D. L. Goldfarb and W. R. Huss, "Building Scenarios for an Electric Utility," *Long Range Planning* 21 (1988), pp. 78–85.

to implement an aggressive growth plan and increase market share depends on what the competition is likely to do. So try putting yourself in the competition's shoes and think how they are likely to behave. Of course, if your competitors are also trying to guess *your* movements, you may need the skills of a good poker player to outguess them. For example, Boeing and Airbus both have schemes to develop a new 600- to 800-seat super-jumbo jet. But since there isn't room for two producers, the companies have been engaging in a game of bluff and counterbluff.

Planners draw on information from many sources. Therefore, inconsistency may be a problem. For example, forecast sales may be the sum of separate forecasts made by many product managers, each of whom may make different assumptions about inflation, growth of the national economy, availability of raw materials, and so on. In such cases, it makes sense to ask individuals for forecasts based on a common set of macroeconomic assumptions.

Choosing the Optimal Financial Plan.   In the end, the financial manager has to choose which plan is best. We would like to tell you exactly how to make this choice. Unfortunately, we can't. There is no model or procedure that encompasses all the complexity and intangibles encountered in financial planning.

You sometimes hear managers state corporate goals in terms of accounting numbers. They might say, "We want a 25 percent return on book equity and a profit margin of 10 percent." On the surface such objectives don't make sense. Shareholders want to be richer, not to have the satisfaction of a 10 percent profit margin. Also, a goal that is stated in terms of accounting ratios is not operational unless it is translated back into what that means for business decisions. For example, a higher profit margin can result from higher prices, lower costs, a move into new, high-margin products, or taking over the firm's suppliers.[1] Setting profit margin as a goal gives no guidance about which of these strategies is best.

So why do managers define objectives in this way? In part such goals may be a mutual exhortation to work harder, like singing the company song before work. But we suspect that managers are often using a code to communicate real concerns. For example, a target profit margin may be a way of saying that in pursuing sales growth the firm has allowed costs to get out of control.

The danger is that everyone may forget the code and the accounting targets may be seen as goals in themselves.

Watching the Plan Unfold.   Financial plans are out of date as soon as they are complete. Often they are out of date even earlier. For example, suppose that profits in the first year turn out to be 10 percent below forecast. What do you do with your plan? Scrap it and start again? Stick to your guns and hope profits will bounce back? Revise down your profit forecasts for later years by 10 percent? A good financial plan should be easy to adapt as events unfold and surprises occur.

Long-term plans can also be used as a benchmark to judge subsequent performance as events unfold. But performance appraisals have little value unless you also take into account the business background against which they were achieved. You are likely to be much less concerned if profits decline in a recession than if they decline when the economy is buoyant and your competitors' sales are booming. If you know how a downturn is likely to throw you off plan, then you have a standard to judge your performance during such a downturn and a better idea of what to do about it.

17.2 *Financial Planning Models*

Financial planners often use a financial planning model to help them explore the consequences of alternative financial strategies. These models range from simple models, such as the one presented later in this chapter, to models that incorporate hundreds of equations.

Financial planning models support the financial planning process by making it easier and cheaper to construct forecast financial statements. The models automate an important part of planning that would otherwise be boring, time-consuming, and labor-intensive.

Programming these financial planning models used to consume large amounts of computer time and high-priced talent. These days standard spreadsheet programs such as Lotus 1-2-3 and Microsoft Excel are regularly used to solve complex financial planning problems.

Components of a Financial Planning Model

A completed financial plan for a large company is a substantial document. A smaller corporation's plan would have the same elements but less detail. For the smallest,

---

[1]If you take over a supplier, total sales are not affected (to the extent that the supplier is selling to you), but you capture both the supplier's and your own profit margin. See Chapter 16, Table 16.6, for an example.

| **Inputs**
Current financial statements.
Forecasts of key variables
such as sales or interest
rates. | → | **Planning Model**
Equations specifying key
relationships. | → | **Outputs**
Projected financial statements
(pro formas).
Financial ratios.
Sources and uses of funds. |

Figure 17.1

The components of a financial plan.

youngest businesses, financial plans may be entirely in the financial managers' heads. The basic elements of the plans will be similar, however, for firms of any size.

Financial plans include three components: inputs, the planning model, and outputs. The relationship among these components is represented in Figure 17.1. Let's look at these components in turn.

Inputs. The inputs to the financial plan consist of the firm's current financial statements and its forecasts about the future. Usually, the principal forecast is the likely growth in sales, since many of the other variables such as labor requirements and inventory levels are tied to sales. These forecasts are only in part the responsibility of the financial manager. Obviously, the marketing department will play a key role in forecasting sales. In addition, because sales will depend on the state of the overall economy, large firms will seek forecasting help from firms that specialize in preparing macroeconomic and industry forecasts.

The Planning Model. The financial planning model calculates the implications of the manager's forecasts for profits, new investment, and financing. The model consists of equations relating output variables to forecasts. For example, the equations can show how a change in sales is likely to affect costs, working capital, fixed assets, and financing requirements. The financial model could specify that the total cost of goods produced may increase by 80 cents for every $1 increase in total sales, that accounts receivable will be a fixed proportion of sales, and that the firm will need to increase fixed assets by 8 percent for every 10 percent increase in sales.

Outputs. The output of the financial model consists of financial statements such as income statements, balance sheets, and statements describing sources and uses of cash. These statements are called **pro formas,** which means that they are forecasts based on the inputs and the assumptions built into the plan. Usually the output of financial models also includes many of the financial ratios we discussed in the last chapter. These ratios indicate whether the firm will be financially fit and healthy at the end of the planning period.

pro formas: Projected or forecasted financial statements.

An Example of a Planning Model

We can illustrate the basic components of a planning model with a very simple example. In the next section we will start to add some complexity.

Suppose that Executive Cheese has prepared the simple balance sheet and income statement shown in Table 17.1. The firm's financial planners forecast that total sales next year will increase by 10 percent from this year's level. They expect that costs will be a fixed proportion of sales, so they too will increase by 10 percent. Almost

Table 17.1

Financial statements of Executive Cheese Company for past year

INCOME STATEMENT	
Sales	$1,200
Costs	1,000
Net income	$ 200

BALANCE SHEET, YEAR-END			
Assets	$2,000	Debt	$ 800
		Equity	1,200
Total	$2,000	Total	$2,000

percentage of sales models: Planning model in which sales forecasts are the driving variables and most other variables are proportional to sales.

all the forecasts for Executive Cheese are proportional to the forecast of sales. Such models are therefore called **percentage of sales models.** The result is the pro forma, or forecast, income statement in Table 17.2, which shows that next year's income will be $200 × 1.10 = $220.

Executive Cheese has no spare capacity, and in order to sustain this higher level of output, it must increase plant and equipment by 10 percent, or $200. Therefore, the left-hand side of the balance sheet, which lists total assets, must increase to $2,200. What about the right-hand side? The firm must decide how it intends to finance its new assets. Suppose that it decides to maintain a fixed debt-equity ratio. Then both debt and equity would grow by 10 percent, as shown in the pro forma balance sheet in Table 17.2. Notice that this implies that the firm must issue $80 in additional debt. On the other hand, no equity needs to be issued. The 10 percent increase in equity can be accomplished by retaining $120 of earnings.

This raises a question, however. If income is forecast at $220, why does equity increase by only $120? The answer is that the firm must be planning to pay a dividend of $220 − $120 = $100. Notice that this dividend payment is not chosen independently but is a *consequence* of the other decisions. Given the company's need for funds and its decision to maintain the debt-equity ratio, dividend policy is completely determined. Any other dividend payment would be inconsistent with the two conditions that (1) the right-hand side of the balance sheet increase by $200, and (2) both debt and equity increase by 10 percent. For this reason we call dividends the **balancing item,** or *plug.* The balancing item is the variable that adjusts to make the sources of funds equal to the uses.

balancing item: Variable that adjusts to maintain the consistency of a financial plan. Also called *plug.*

Table 17.2

Pro forma financial statements of Executive Cheese

INCOME STATEMENT	
Sales	$1,320
Costs	1,100
Net income	$ 220

BALANCE SHEET			
Assets	$2,200	Debt	$ 880
		Equity	1,320
Total	$2,200	Total	$2,200

Table 17.3

Pro forma balance sheet with dividends fixed at $180 and debt used as the balancing item

Assets	$2,200	Debt	$ 960
		Equity	1,240
Total	$2,200	Total	$2,200

Of course, most firms would be reluctant to vary dividends simply because they have a temporary need for cash; instead, they like to maintain a steady progression of dividends. In this case Executive Cheese could commit to some other dividend payment and allow the debt-equity ratio to vary. The amount of debt would therefore become the balancing item.

For example, suppose the firm commits to a dividend level of $180, and raises any extra money it needs by an issue of debt. In this case the amount of debt becomes the balancing item. With the dividend set at $180, retained earnings would be only $40, so the firm would have to issue $160 in new debt to help pay for the additional $200 of assets. Table 17.3 is the new balance sheet.

Is the second plan better than the first? It's hard to give a simple answer. The choice of dividend payment depends partly on how investors will interpret the decision. If last year's dividend was only $50, investors might regard a dividend payment of $100 as a sign of a confident management; if last year's dividend was $150, investors might not be so content with a payment of $100. The alternative of paying $180 in dividends and making up the shortfall by issuing more debt leaves the company with a debt-equity ratio of 77 percent. That is unlikely to make your bankers edgy, but you may worry about how long you can continue to finance expansion predominantly by borrowing.

Our example shows how experiments with a financial model, including changes in the model's balancing item, can raise important financial questions. But the model does not answer these questions.

Financial models ensure consistency between growth assumptions and financing plans, but they do not identify the best financing plan.

▶ **Self-Test 17.1**   Suppose that the firm is prevented by bond covenants from issuing more debt. It is committed to increasing assets by 10 percent to support the forecast increase in sales, and it strongly believes that a dividend payment of $180 is in the best interests of the firm. What must be the balancing item? What is the implication for the firm's financing activities in the next year?

An Improved Model

Now that you have grasped the idea behind financial planning models, we can move on to a more sophisticated example.

Table 17.4 shows current (year-end 1997) financial statements for Executive Fruit Company. Judging by these figures, the company is ordinary in almost all respects. Its earnings before interest and taxes were 10 percent of sales revenue. Net income was $96,000 after payment of taxes and 10 percent interest on $400,000 of long-term debt. The company paid out two-thirds of its net income as dividends.

Table 17.4

Financial statements for Executive Fruit Co., 1997 (figures in thousands)

INCOME STATEMENT		
		Comment
Revenue	$2,000	
Cost of goods sold	1,800	90% of sales
EBIT	200	Difference = 10% of sales
Interest	40	10% of debt at start of year
Earnings before taxes	160	EBIT – interest
State and federal tax	64	40% of (EBIT – interest)
Net income	$ 96	EBIT – interest – taxes
Dividends	$ 64	Payout ratio = ⅔
Retained earnings	$ 32	Net income – dividends
BALANCE SHEET		
Assets		
Net working capital	$ 200	10% of sales
Fixed assets	800	40% of sales
Total assets	$1,000	50% of sales
Liabilities and shareholders' equity		
Long-term debt	$ 400	
Shareholders' equity	600	
Total liabilities and shareholders' equity	$1,000	Equals total assets

Next to each item on the financial statements in Table 17.4 we have entered a comment about the relationship between that variable and sales. In most cases, the comment gives the value of each item as a percentage of sales. This may be useful for forecasting purposes. For example, it would be reasonable to assume that cost of goods sold will remain at 90 percent of sales even if sales grow by 10 percent next year. Similarly, it is reasonable to assume that net working capital will remain at 10 percent of sales.

On the other hand, the fact that long-term debt currently is 20 percent of sales does not mean that we should assume that this ratio will continue to hold next period. Many alternative financing plans with varying combinations of debt issues, equity issues, and dividend payouts may be considered without affecting the firm's operations.

Now suppose that you are asked to prepare pro forma financial statements for Executive Fruit for 1998. You are told to assume that (1) sales and operating costs are expected to be up 10 percent over 1997. You interpret "business as usual" to mean that (2) interest rates will remain at their current level, (3) the firm will stick to its traditional dividend policy of paying out two-thirds of earnings, and (4) fixed assets and net working capital will need to increase by 10 percent to support the larger sales volume.

In Table 17.5 we present the resulting first-stage pro forma calculations for Executive Fruit. These calculations show what would happen if the size of the firm increases along with sales, but at this preliminary stage, the plan does not specify a particular mix of new security issues.

Table 17.5

First-stage pro forma statements for Executive Fruit Co., 1998 (figures in thousands)

INCOME STATEMENT

		Comment
Revenue	$2,200	10% higher
Cost of goods sold	1,980	10% higher
EBIT	220	10% higher
Interest	40	Unchanged
Earnings before taxes	180	EBIT – interest
State and federal tax	72	40% of (EBIT – interest)
Net income	$ 108	EBIT – interest – taxes
Dividends	$ 72	⅔ of net income
Retained earnings	$ 36	Net income – dividends

BALANCE SHEET

Assets		
Net working capital	$ 220	10% higher
Fixed assets	880	10% higher
Total assets	$1,100	10% higher
Liabilities and shareholders' equity		
Long-term debt	$ 400	Temporarily held fixed
Shareholders' equity	636	Increased by retained earnings
Total liabilities and shareholders' equity	$1,036	Sum of debt plus equity
Required external financing	$ 64	Balancing item or plug (= $1,100 − $1,036)

Without any security issues, the balance sheet will not balance: assets will increase to $1,100,000 while debt plus shareholders' equity will amount to only $1,036,000. Somehow the firm will need to raise an extra $64,000 to help pay for the increase in assets. In this first pass, external financing is the balancing item. Given the firm's growth forecasts and its dividend policy, the financial plan calculates how much money the firm needs to raise.

In the second-stage pro forma, the firm must decide on the financing mix that best meets its needs for additional funds. It must choose some combination of new debt or new equity that supports the contemplated acquisition of additional assets. For example, it could issue $64,000 of equity or debt, or it could choose to maintain its long-term debt-equity ratio at two-thirds by issuing both debt and equity.

Table 17.6 shows the second-stage pro forma balance sheet if the required funds are raised by issuing $64,000 of debt. Therefore, in Table 17.6, debt is treated as the balancing item. Notice that while the plan requires the firm to specify a financing plan *consistent* with its growth projections, it does not provide guidance as to the *best* financing mix.

Table 17.7 sets out the firm's sources and uses of funds. It shows that the firm requires an extra investment of $20,000 in working capital and $80,000 in fixed assets. Therefore, it needs $100,000 from retained earnings and new security issues.

Table 17.6

Second-stage pro forma balance sheet for Executive Fruit Co., 1998 (figures in thousands)

		Comment
Assets		
Net working capital	$ 220	10% higher
Fixed assets	880	10% higher
Total assets	$1,100	10% higher
Liabilities and shareholders' equity		
Long-term debt	$ 464	16% higher (new borrowing = $64; this is the balancing item)
Shareholders' equity	$ 636	Increased by retained earnings
Total liabilities and shareholders' equity	$1,100	Again equals total assets

Table 17.7

Pro forma statement of sources and uses of funds for Executive Fruit, 1998 (figures in thousands)

Sources		Uses	
Retained earnings	$ 36	Investment in working capital	$ 20
New borrowing	64	Investment in fixed assets	80
Total sources	$100	Total uses	$100

Retained earnings are $36,000, so $64,000 must be raised from the capital markets. Under the financing plan presented in Table 17.6, the firm borrows the entire $64,000.

We have spared you the trouble of actually calculating the figures necessary for Table 17.5 and 17.7. The calculations do not take more than a few minutes for this simple example, *provided* you set up the calculations correctly and make no arithmetic mistakes. If that time requirement seems trivial, remember that in reality you probably would be asked for four similar sets of statements covering each year from 1998 to 2001. Probably you would be asked for alternative projections under different assumptions (for example, 5 percent instead of 10 percent growth rate of revenue) or different financial strategies (for example, freezing dividends at their 1997 level of $64,000). This would be far more time-consuming. Moreover, actual plans will have many more line items than this simple one. Building a model and letting the computer toil in your place have obvious attractions.

▶ **Self-Test 17.2**

a. Suppose that Executive Fruit is committed to its expansion plans and to its dividend policy. It also wishes to maintain its debt-equity ratio at ⅔. What are the implications for external financing?

b. If the company is prepared to freeze dividends at the 1997 level, how much external financing would be needed?

Planners Beware

Pitfalls in Model Design

The Executive Fruit model is still too simple for practical application. You probably have already noticed several ways to improve it. For example, we ignored depreciation of fixed assets. Depreciation is important because it provides a tax shield. If Executive Fruit deducts depreciation before calculating its tax bill, it could plow back more money into new investments and would need to borrow less. We also ignored the fact that there would probably be some interest to pay in 1998 on the new borrowing, which would cut into the cash for new investment.

You would certainly want to make these obvious improvements. But beware: there is always the temptation to make a model bigger and more detailed. You may end up with an exhaustive model that is too cumbersome for routine use.

Exhaustive detail gets in the way of the intended use of corporate planning models, which is to project the financial consequences of a variety of strategies and assumptions. The fascination of detail, if you give in to it, distracts attention from crucial decisions like stock issues and dividend policy and allocation of capital by business area.

Shortcomings of Percentage of Sales Models

Percentage of sales models are useful first approximations for financial planning. However, in reality, many variables will not be proportional to sales. For example, we will see in Chapter 19 that important components of working capital such as inventories and cash balances will generally rise less than proportionally with sales.

In addition, fixed assets such as plant and equipment are typically not added in small increments as sales increase. Instead, they are added in large or "lumpy" increments. Factories normally operate at less than full capacity. As sales initially increase, the factory utilization rate will increase, so the additional sales can be supported without a major addition to fixed assets. Ultimately, however, if sales continue to increase, the firm will need to add new capacity. Therefore, when the financial plan is prepared, the contemplated addition to fixed assets should not simply track sales growth; it will depend also on the current level of excess capacity. If there is considerable excess capacity, even rapid sales growth may not require big additions to fixed assets. On the other hand, if the firm is already operating near capacity, even small sales growth may call for large investments in plant and equipment.

▶ **Self-Test 17.3**　Carter Tools has $50 million invested in fixed assets and generates sales of $60 million. Currently the company is working at only 80 percent of capacity.

a. How much can sales expand without any further investment in fixed assets?
b. How much investment in fixed assets would be required to support a 50 percent expansion in sales?

There Is No Finance in Financial Planning Models

Why do we say that there is no finance in corporate financial models? The first reason is that most such models incorporate an accountant's view of the world. They are designed to forecast accounting statements. Consequently, the models do not empha-size the tools of financial analysis: incremental cash flow, present value, market risk, and so on.[2]

Second, we emphasize again corporate financial models produce no signposts pointing toward optimal financial decisions. They do not even tell which alternatives are worth examining. All this is left to their users.

For example, we saw that Executive Fruit is planning to grow its sales and earn-ings per share. Is that good news for the shareholders? Well, not necessarily; it depends on the opportunity cost of the additional capital that Executive Fruit needs to invest to achieve its planned growth. In 1998 the company proposes to invest $100 in fixed assets and working capital. This extra investment is expected to generate $12 of additional income, equivalent to a return of 12 percent on the new investment. If the opportunity cost of that capital is less than 12 percent, the new investment will have a positive NPV and will add to shareholder wealth. But suppose that the cost of capital is higher at, say, 15 percent. In this case Executive Fruit's investment makes shareholders *worse off* by $3 a year, even though the company is recording steady growth in earnings per share.[3] Executive Fruit's planning model tells us how much money the firm must raise to fund the planned growth, but it cannot tell us whether that growth contributes to shareholder value.

Notice also that the capital that Executive Fruit needs to raise depends on its deci-sion to pay out two-thirds of its earnings as a dividend. But the financial planning model does not disclose whether this dividend payment makes sense or whether the firm should issue long-term debt, short-term debt, or some other security. While the plan enforces consistency in assumptions, it is silent on the best of the many feasi-ble strategies.

▶ **Self-Test 17.4**   Which of the following questions will a financial plan help to answer?

a. Is the firm's assumption for asset growth consistent with its plans for debt and equity issues and dividend policy?
b. Will accounts receivable increase in direct proportion to sales?
c. Will the contemplated debt-equity mix maximize the value of the firm?

17.4 *External Financing and Growth*

See box p. 497

Financial plans force managers to be consistent in their goals for growth, investments, and financing. The nearby box describes how a weakness in financial planning led one company to underestimate the implications of growth for its future cash needs, with disastrous consequences. Therefore, before leaving the topic of long-term plan-ning, we should look at the relationship between a firm's growth objectives and its requirements for external financing.

---

[2]Of course there is no reason that the manager can't use the output to calculate the present value of the firm (given some assumptions about growth beyond the planning period), and this is sometimes done.

[3]Executive Fruit expects to earn an additional $12 on its new investment, but investors require an expected return of 15 percent of $100, or $15.

The Bankruptcy of W.T. Grant: A Failure in Planning

W.T. Grant was the largest and one of the most successful department store chains in the United States with 1,200 stores, 83,000 employees, and $1.8 billion of sales. Yet in 1975 the company filed for bankruptcy, in what *Business Week* termed "the most significant bankruptcy in U.S. history."

The seeds of Grant's difficulties were sown in the mid-1960s when the company foresaw a shift in shopping habits from inner-city areas to out-of-town centers. The company decided to embark on a rapid expansion policy that involved opening up new stores in suburban areas. In addition to making a substantial investment in new buildings, the company needed to ensure that the new stores were stocked with merchandise and it encouraged customers by extending credit more freely. As a result, the company's investment in inventories and receivables more than doubled between 1967 and 1974.

W.T. Grant's expansion plan led to impressive growth. Sales grew from $900 million in 1967 to $1.8 billion in 1974. For a while profits also boomed, growing from $63 million in 1967 to a peak of $90 million in 1970. Shareholders were delighted. By 1971 the share price had reached a high of $71, up from $20 in 1967.

To achieve the growth in sales, W.T. Grant needed to invest a total of $650 million in fixed assets, inventories, and receivables. However, it takes time for new stores to reach full profitability, so while profits initially increased, the return on capital fell. At the same time, the company decided to increase its dividends in line with earnings. This meant that the bulk of the money to finance the new investment had to be raised from the capital market. W.T. Grant was reluctant to sell more shares and chose instead to raise the money by issuing more than $400 million of new debt.

By 1974 Grant's debt-equity ratio had reached 1.8. This figure was high, but not alarmingly so. The problem was that rapid expansion combined with recession had begun to eat into profits. Almost all the operating cash flows in 1974 were used to service the company's debt. Yet the company insisted on maintaining the dividend on its common stock. Effectively, it was borrowing to pay the dividend. By the next year, W.T. Grant could no longer service its mountain of debt and had to seek postponement of payments on a $600 million bank loan.

W.T. Grant's failure was partly a failure of financial planning. It did not recognize and plan for the huge cash drain involved in its expansion strategy.

Recall that Executive Fruit started with $1,000,000 of fixed assets and working capital. It forecast sales growth of 10 percent. This higher sales volume required a 10 percent addition to its assets. Thus

$$\text{New investment} = \text{growth rate} \times \text{initial assets}$$
$$\$100,000 = .10 \times \$1,000,000$$

Part of the funds to pay for the new assets is provided by retained earnings. The remainder must come from external financing. Therefore,

Required external financing = new investment − retained earnings

$$= \textbf{(growth rate} \times \textbf{assets)} - \textbf{retained earnings}$$

This simple equation highlights that the amount of external financing depends on the firm's projected growth. The faster the firm grows, the more it needs to invest and therefore the more it needs to raise new capital.

In the case of Executive Fruit,

$$\text{Required external financing} = (.10 \times \$1,000,000) - \$36,000$$
$$= \$100,000 - \$36,000$$
$$= \$64,000$$

If Executive Fruit's assets remain a constant percentage of sales, then the company needs to raise $64,000 to produce a 10 percent addition to sales.

The sloping line in Figure 17.2 illustrates how required external financing increases with the growth rate. At low growth rates, the firm generates more funds than necessary for expansion. In this sense, its requirement for further external funds is negative. It may choose to use its surplus to pay off some of its debt or buy back its stock. In fact, the vertical intercept in Figure 17.2, at zero growth, is the negative of retained earnings. When growth is zero, no funds are needed for expansion, so all the retained earnings are surplus.

As the firm's projected growth rate increases, more funds are needed to pay for the necessary investments. Therefore, the plot in Figure 17.2 is upward-sloping. For high rates of growth the firm must issue new securities to pay for new investments.

Where the sloping line crosses the horizontal axis, external financing is zero: the firm is growing as fast as possible without resorting to new security issues. This is called the **internal growth rate.** The growth rate is internal because it can be maintained without resort to additional external sources of capital.

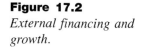

internal growth rate:
Maximum rate of growth without external financing.

Notice that if we set required external financing to zero, we can solve for the internal growth rate as

$$\text{Internal growth rate} = \frac{\text{retained earnings}}{\text{assets}}$$

Thus the firm's rate of growth without additional external sources of capital will equal the ratio of retained earnings to assets. This means that a firm with a high volume of retained earnings relative to its assets can generate a higher growth rate without needing to raise more capital.

We can gain more insight into what determines the internal growth rate by multiplying the top and bottom of the expression for internal growth by *net income* and *equity* as follows:

$$\text{Internal growth rate} = \frac{\text{retained earnings}}{\text{net income}} \times \frac{\text{net income}}{\text{equity}} \times \frac{\text{equity}}{\text{assets}}$$

$$= \text{plowback ratio} \times \text{return on equity} \times \frac{\text{equity}}{\text{assets}}$$

Figure 17.2
External financing and growth.

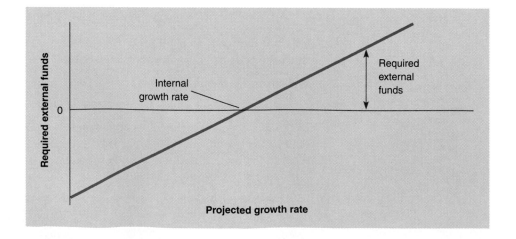

A firm can achieve a higher growth rate without raising external capital if (1) it plows back a high proportion of its earnings, 2) it has a high return on equity (ROE), and (3) it has a low debt-to-asset ratio.

Instead of focusing on the maximum growth rate that can be supported without *any* external financing, firms also may be interested in the growth rate that can be sustained without additional *equity* issues. Of course, if the firm is able to issue enough debt, virtually any growth rate can be financed. It makes more sense to assume that the firm has settled on an optimal capital structure which it will maintain even as equity is augmented by retained earnings. The firm issues only enough debt to keep its debt-equity ratio constant. The **sustainable growth rate** is the highest growth rate the firm can maintain without increasing its financial leverage. It turns out that the sustainable growth rate depends only on the plowback ratio and return on equity:[4]

sustainable growth rate:
Steady rate at which a firm can grow without changing leverage; plowback ratio × return on equity.

$$\text{Sustainable growth rate} = \text{plowback ratio} \times \text{return on equity}$$

You may remember this formula from Chapter 4, where we first used it when we looked at the valuation of the firm and the dividend discount model.

▶ **Example 17.1**   *Internal and Sustainable Growth for Executive Fruit*

Executive Fruit has chosen a plowback ratio of ⅓. Assume that equity outstanding at the start of the year is 600, and that outstanding assets at the start of the year are 1000. Because net income during 1997 is 96, Executive Fruit's return on equity[5] is ROE = 96/600 = .16, and its ratio of equity to assets is 600/1,000 = .60. If it is

---

[4]Here is a proof.

$$\text{Required equity issues} = \text{growth rate} \times \text{assets} - \text{retained earnings} - \text{new debt issues}$$

We find the sustainable growth rate by setting required new equity issues to zero and solving for growth:

$$\text{Sustainable growth rate} = \frac{\text{retained earnings} + \text{new debt issues}}{\text{assets}}$$

$$= \frac{\text{retained earnings} + \text{new debt issues}}{\text{debt} + \text{equity}}$$

However, because both debt and equity are growing at the same rate, new debt issues must equal retained earnings multiplied by the ratio of debt to equity, D/E. Therefore, we can write the sustainable growth as

$$\text{Sustainable growth rate} = \frac{\text{retained earnings} \times (1 + D/E)}{\text{debt} + \text{equity}}$$

$$= \frac{\text{retained earnings} \times (1 + D/E)}{\text{equity} \times (1 + D/E)} = \frac{\text{retained earnings}}{\text{equity}}$$

$$= \frac{\text{retained earnings}}{\text{net income}} \times \frac{\text{net income}}{\text{equity}} = \text{plowback} \times \text{ROE}$$

[5]Note that when we calculate internal or sustainable growth rates, ROE is properly measured by earnings as a proportion of equity at the *start* of the year rather than as a proportion of either end-of-year equity or the *average* of outstanding equity at the start and end of the year.

unwilling to raise new capital, its maximum growth rate is

$$\text{Internal growth rate} = \text{plowback ratio} \times \text{ROE} \times \frac{\text{equity}}{\text{assets}}$$

$$= \frac{1}{3} \times .16 \times .60$$

$$= .032, \text{ or } 3.2\%$$

This is much less than the 10 percent growth it projects, which explains its need for external financing.

If Executive is prepared to maintain its current ratio of equity to total assets, it can issue an additional 40 cents of debt for every 60 cents of retained earnings. In this case, the maximum growth rate would be

$$\text{Sustainable growth rate} = \text{plowback ratio} \times \text{ROE}$$

$$= \frac{1}{3} \times .16$$

$$= .0533, \text{ or } 5.33\%$$

Executive's planned growth rate of 10 percent requires not only new borrowing but an increase in the debt-equity ratio. In the long run the company will need to either issue new equity or cut back its rate of growth.[6]

▶ **Self-Test 17.5** Suppose Executive Fruit reduces the dividend payout ratio to 25 percent. Calculate its growth rate assuming (a) that no new debt or equity will be issued and (b) that the firm maintains its equity-to-asset ratio at .60.

Summary

1. Most firms take financial planning seriously and devote considerable resources to it. The tangible product of the planning process is a financial plan describing the firm's financial strategy and projecting its future consequences by means of pro forma balance sheets, income statements, and statements of sources and uses of funds. The plan establishes financial goals and is a benchmark for evaluating subsequent performance. Usually it also describes why that strategy was chosen and how the plan's financial goals are to be achieved.

2. The plan is the end result. The process that produces the plan is valuable in its own right. Planning forces the financial manager to consider the combined effects of all the firm's investment and financing decisions. This is important because these decisions interact and should not be made independently.

---

[6]As the firm issues more debt, its return on equity also changes. But Executive would need to have a very high debt-equity ratio before it could support a growth rate of 10 percent a year and maintain a constant debt ratio.

3. Planning, if it is done right, forces the financial manager to think about events that could upset the firm's progress and to devise strategies to be held in reserve for counterattack when unfortunate surprises occur. Planning is more than forecasting, because forecasting deals with the most likely outcome. Planners also have to think about events that may occur even though they are unlikely.

4. In long-range, or strategic, planning, the planning horizon is usually 5 years or more. This kind of planning deals with aggregate decisions; for example, the planner would worry about whether the broadax division should go for heavy capital investment and rapid growth, but not whether the division should choose machine tool A versus tool B. In fact, planners must be constantly on guard against the fascination of detail, because giving in to it means slighting crucial issues like investment strategy, debt policy, and the choice of a target dividend payout ratio.

5. There is no theory or model that leads straight to *the* optimal financial strategy. Consequently, financial planning proceeds by trial and error. Many different strategies may be projected under a range of assumptions about the future before one strategy is finally chosen. The dozens of separate projections that may be made during this trial-and-error process generate a heavy load of arithmetic and paperwork. Firms have responded by developing corporate planning models to forecast the financial consequences of specified strategies and assumptions about the future. These models are efficient and widely used. But remember that there is not much finance in them. Their primary purpose is to produce accounting statements. The models do not search for the best financial strategy, but only trace out the consequences of a strategy specified by the model user.

Key Terms

planning horizon	percentage of sales models	internal growth rate
pro formas	balancing item	sustainable growth rate

Problems

1. **Financial Planning.** True or false? Explain.

   a. Financial planning should attempt to minimize risk.
   b. The primary aim of financial planning is to obtain better forecasts of future cash flows and earnings.
   c. Financial planning is necessary because financing and investment decisions interact and should not be made independently.
   d. Firms' planning horizons rarely exceed 3 years.
   e. Individual capital investment projects are not considered in a financial plan unless they are very large.
   f. Financial planning requires accurate and consistent forecasting.
   g. Financial planning models should include as much detail as possible.

2. **Financial Models.** What are the dangers and disadvantages of using a financial model? Discuss.

3. **Using Financial Plans.** Corporate financial plans are often used as a basis for judging subsequent performance. What can be learned from such comparisons? What problems might arise and how might you cope with such problems?

4. **Interpreting Financial Models.** Why do we say that "there is no finance in financial planning models"?

5. **Percentage of Sales Models.** Here are the abbreviated financial statements for Planners Corporation:

INCOME STATEMENT, 1998

Sales	$2,000
Cost	1,500
Net income	$ 500

BALANCE SHEET, YEAR-END

	1997	1998		1997	1998
Assets	$2,500	$3,000	Debt	$ 833	$1,000
			Equity	1,667	2,000
Total	$2,500	$3,000	Total	$2,500	$3,000

If sales increase by 20 percent in 1999, and the company uses a strict percentage of sales planning model (meaning that all items on the income and balance sheet also increase by 20 percent), what must be the balancing item? What will be its value?

6. **Required External Financing.** If the dividend payout ratio in problem 5 is fixed at 50 percent, calculate the required total external financing for growth rates in 1999 of 15 percent, 20 percent, and 25 percent.

7. **Feasible Growth Rates.** What is the maximum possible growth rate for Planners Corporation (see problem 5) if the payout ratio remains at 50 percent and

a. no external debt or equity is to be issued
b. the firm maintains a fixed debt ratio but issues no equity

8. **Building Financial Models.** How would Executive Fruit's financial model change if the dividend payout ratio were cut to ⅓? Use the revised model to generate a new financial plan for 1998 assuming that debt is the balancing item. Show how the financial statements given in Table 17.6 would change. What would be required external financing?

9. **Required External Financing.** Executive Fruit's financial manager believes that sales in 1998 could rise by as much as 20 percent or by as little as 5 percent.

a. Recalculate the first-stage pro forma financial statements (Table 17.5) under these two assumptions. How does the rate of growth in revenues affect the firm's need for external funds?
b. Assume any required external funds will be raised by issuing long-term debt and that any surplus funds will be used to retire such debt. Prepare the completed (second-stage) pro forma balance sheet.

10. **Using Percentage of Sales.** Eagle Sport Supply has the following financial statements. Assume that Eagle's assets are proportional to its sales.

INCOME STATEMENT, 1997

Sales	$950
Costs	250
EBIT	700
Taxes	200
Net income	$500

BALANCE SHEET, YEAR-END

	1996	1997		1996	1997
Assets	$2,700	$3,000	Debt	$ 900	$1,000
			Equity	1,800	2,000
Total	$2,700	$3,000	Total	$2,700	$3,000

a. Find Eagle's required external funds if it maintains a dividend payout ratio of 60 percent and plans a growth rate of 15 percent in 1998.

b. If Eagle chooses not to issue new shares of stock, what variable must be the balancing item? What will its value be?

c. Now suppose that the firm plans instead to increase long-term debt only to $1,100 and does not wish to issue any new shares of stock. Why must the dividend payment now be the balancing item? What will its value be?

11. **Feasible Growth Rates.**

a. What is the internal growth rate of Eagle Sports (see problem 10) if the dividend payout ratio is fixed at 60 percent and the equity-to-asset ratio is fixed at ⅔?

b. What is the sustainable growth rate?

12. **Building Financial Models.** The following tables contain financial statements for Dynastatics Corporation. Although the company has not been growing, it now plans to expand and will increase net fixed assets (that is, assets net of depreciation) by $200 per year for the next 5 years and forecasts that the ratio of revenues to total assets will remain at 1.50. Annual depreciation is 10 percent of net fixed assets at the start of the year. Fixed costs are expected to remain at $56 and variable costs at 80 percent of revenue. The company's policy is to pay out two-thirds of net income as dividends and to maintain a book debt ratio of 25 percent of total capital.

a. Produce a set of financial statements for 1998. Assume that net working capital will equal 50 percent of fixed assets.

b. Now assume that the balancing item is debt, and that no equity is to be issued. Prepare a completed pro forma balance sheet for 1998. What is the projected debt ratio for 1998?

INCOME STATEMENT, 1997
(figures in thousands of dollars)

Revenue	$1,800
Fixed costs	56
Variable costs (80% of revenue)	1,440
Depreciation	80
Interest (8% of beginning-of-year debt)	24
Taxable income	200
Taxes (at 40%)	80
Net income	$ 120
Dividends	$80
Retained earnings	$40

BALANCE SHEET, YEAR-END
(figures in thousands of dollars)

	1996	1997
Assets		
Net working capital	$ 400	$ 400
Fixed assets	800	800
Total assets	$1,200	$1,200
Liabilities and shareholders' equity		
Debt	$ 300	$ 300
Equity	900	900
Total liabilities and shareholders' equity	$1,200	$1,200

13. **Internal Growth.** Go Go Industries is growing at 30 percent per year. It is all-equity financed and has total assets of $1 million. Its return on equity is 20 percent. Its plowback ratio is 40 percent.

    a. What is the internal growth rate?
    b. What is the firm's need for external financing this year?
    c. By how much would the firm increase its internal growth rate if it reduced its payout ratio to zero?
    d. By how much would such a move reduce the need for external financing? What do you conclude about the relationship between dividend policy and requirements for external financing?

14. **Sustainable Growth.** A firm's profit margin is 10 percent and its asset turnover ratio is .5. It has no debt, has net income of $10 per share, and pays dividends of $4 per share. What is the sustainable growth rate?

15. **Internal Growth.** An all-equity–financed firm plans to grow at an annual rate of at least 10 percent. Its return on equity is 15 percent. What is the maximum possible dividend payout rate the firm can maintain without resorting to additional equity issues?

16. **Internal Growth.** Suppose the firm in the previous question has a debt-equity ratio of ⅓. What is the maximum dividend payout ratio it can maintain without resorting to any external financing?

17. **Internal Growth.** A firm has an asset turnover ratio of 2.0. Its plowback ratio is 50 percent, and it is all-equity financed. What must its profit margin be if it wishes to finance 8 percent growth using only internally generated funds?

18. **Internal Growth.** If the profit margin of the firm in the previous problem is 6 percent, what is the maximum payout ratio that will allow it to grow at 8 percent without resorting to external financing?

19. **Internal Growth.** If the profit margin of the firm in problem 17 is 6 percent, what is the maximum possible growth rate that can be sustained without external financing?

20. **Sustainable Growth.** A firm has decided that its optimal capital structure is 100 percent equity financed. It perceives its optimal dividend policy to be a 40 percent payout ratio. Asset turnover is sales/assets = .8, the profit margin is 10 percent, and the firm has a target growth rate of 5 percent.

    a. Is the firm's target growth rate consistent with its other goals?
    b. If not, by how much does it need to increase asset turnover to achieve its goals?
    c. How much would it need to increase the profit margin instead?

21. **Sustainable Growth.** Plank's Plants had net income of $2,000 on sales of $40,000 last year. The firm paid a dividend of $500. Total assets were $100,000, of which $40,000 was financed by debt.

    a. What is the firm's sustainable growth rate?
    b. If the firm grows at its sustainable growth rate, how much debt will be issued next year?
    c. What would be the maximum possible growth rate if the firm did not issue any debt next year?

22. **Using Percentage of Sales.** The 1997 financial statements for Growth Industries are presented below. Sales and costs in 1998 are projected to be 20 percent higher than in 1997. Both current assets and accounts payable are projected to rise in proportion to sales. The firm is currently operating at full capacity, so it plans to increase fixed assets in proportion to sales. What external financing will be required by the firm? Interest expense in 1998

will equal 10 percent of long-term debt outstanding at the start of the year. The firm will maintain a dividend payout ratio of .40.

INCOME STATEMENT, 1997

Sales	$200,000
Costs	150,000
EBIT	50,000
Interest expense	10,000
Taxable income	40,000
Taxes (at 35%)	14,000
Net income	$26,000
Dividends	10,400
Retained earnings	15,600

BALANCE SHEET, YEAR-END, 1997

Assets		Liabilities	
Current assets		Current liabilities	
Cash	$ 3,000	Accounts payable	$ 10,000
Accounts receivable	8,000	Total current liabilities	10,000
Inventories	29,000	Long-term debt	100,000
Total current assets	$ 40,000	Stockholders' equity	
Net plant and equipment	160,000	Common stock plus additional paid-in capital	15,000
		Retained earnings	75,000
Total assets	$200,000	Total liabilities plus stockholders' equity	$200,000

23. **Capacity Use and External Financing.** Now suppose that the fixed assets of Growth Industries (from the previous problem) are operating at only 75 percent of capacity. What is required external financing over the next year?

24. **Capacity Use and External Financing.** If Growth Industries from problem 22 is operating at only 75 percent of capacity, how much can sales grow before the firm will need to raise any external funds? Assume that once fixed assets are operating at capacity, they will need to grow thereafter in direct proportion to sales.

25. **Internal Growth.** We will see in Chapter 19 that for many firms, cash and inventory needs may grow less than proportionally with sales. When we recognize this fact, will the firm's internal growth rate be higher or lower than the level predicted by the formula

$$\text{Internal growth rate} = \frac{\text{retained earnings}}{\text{assets}}$$

26. **Percentage of Sales Models.** Percentage of sales models usually assume that costs, fixed assets, and working capital all increase at the same rate as sales. When do you think that these assumptions do not make sense? Would you feel happier using a percentage of sales model for short-term or long-term planning?

27. **Relationships among Variables.** Comebaq Computers is aiming to increase its market share by slashing the price of its new range of personal computers. Are costs and assets likely to increase or decrease as a proportion of sales? Explain.

28. **Balancing Items.** What are the possible choices of balancing items when using a financial planning model? Discuss whether some are generally preferable to others.

29. **Financial Targets.** Managers sometimes state a target growth rate for sales or earnings per share. Do you think that either makes sense as a corporate goal? If not, why do you think that managers focus on them?

Solutions to Self-Test Questions

17.1 The firm cannot issue debt, and its dividend payment is effectively fixed, which limits retained earnings to $40. Therefore, the balancing item must be new equity issues. The firm must raise $200 − $40 = $160 through equity sales in order to finance its plans for $200 in asset acquisitions.

17.2 a. The *total amount* of external financing is unchanged, since the dividend payout is unchanged. The $100,000 increase in total assets will now be financed by a mixture of debt and equity. If the debt-equity ratio is to remain at ⅔, the firm will need to increase equity by $60,000 and debt by $40,000. Since retained earnings already increase shareholders' equity by $36,000, the firm needs to issue an additional $24,000 of new equity and $40,000 of debt.

  b. If dividends are frozen at $64,000 instead of increasing to $72,000 as envisioned in Table 17.5, then the required external funds fall by $8,000 to $56,000.

17.3 a. The company currently runs at 80 percent of capacity given the current level of fixed assets. Sales can increase until the company is at 100 percent of capacity; therefore, sales can increase to $60 million × (100/80) = $75 million.

  b. If sales were to increase by 50 percent to $90 million, new fixed assets would need to be added. The ratio of assets to sales when the company is operating at 100 percent of capacity (from part a) is $50 million/$75 million = 2/3. Therefore, to support sales of $90 million, the company needs at least $90 million × 2/3 = $60 million of fixed assets. This calls for a $10 million investment in additional fixed assets.

17.4 a. This question is answered by the planning model. Given assumptions for asset growth, the model will show the need for external financing, and this value can be compared to the firm's plans for such financing.

  b. Such a relationship may be *assumed* and built into the model. However, the model does not help to determine whether it is a reasonable assumption.

  c. Financial models do not shed light on the best capital structure. They can tell us only whether contemplated financing decisions are consistent with asset growth.

17.5 a. If the payout ratio were reduced to 25 percent, the maximum growth rate assuming no external financing would be .75 × 16 percent × .6 = 7.2 percent.

  b. If the firm also can issue enough debt to maintain its equity-to-asset ratio unchanged, the sustainable growth rate will be .75 × 16 percent = 12 percent.

A warehouse of finished-goods inventory.
Inventory is a major part of working capital. Investment in working capital has to be planned and managed.
© *John Lund/Tony Stone Images*

Chapter 18

Working Capital Management and Short-Term Planning

509

uch of this book is devoted to long-term financial decisions such as capital budgeting and the choice of capital structure. These decisions are called *long-term* for two reasons. First, they usually involve long-lived assets or liabilities. Second, they are not easily reversed and thus may commit the firm to a particular course of action for several years.

Short-term financial decisions generally involve short-lived assets and liabilities, and usually they are easily reversed. Compare, for example, a 60-day bank loan for $50 million with a $50 million issue of 20-year bonds. The bank loan is clearly a short-term decision. The firm can repay it 2 months later and be right back where it started. A firm might conceivably issue a 20-year bond in January and retire it in March, but it would be extremely inconvenient and expensive to do so. In practice, such a bond issue is a long-term decision, not only because of the bond's 20-year maturity, but because the decision to issue it cannot be reversed on short notice.

A financial manager responsible for short-term financial decisions does not have to look far into the future. The decision to take the 60-day bank loan could properly be based on cash-flow forecasts for the next few months only. The bond issue decision will normally reflect forecast cash requirements 5, 10, or more years into the future.

Short-term financial decisions do not involve many of the difficult conceptual issues encountered elsewhere in this book. In a sense, short-term decisions are easier than long-term decisions—but they are not less important. A firm can identify extremely valuable capital investment opportunities, find the precise optimal debt ratio, follow the perfect dividend policy, and yet founder because no one bothers to raise the cash to pay this year's bills. Hence the need for short-term planning.

In this chapter, we will review the major classes of short-term assets and liabilities, show how long-term financing decisions affect the firm's short-term financial planning problem, and describe how financial managers trace changes in cash and working capital. We will also describe how managers forecast month-by-month cash requirements or surpluses and how they develop short-term investment and financing strategies.

After studying this chapter you should be able to

▶ Understand *why* the firm needs to invest in net working capital.

▶ Show how long-term financing policy affects short-term financing requirements.

▶ Trace a firm's sources and uses of cash and evaluate its need for short-term borrowing.

▶ Develop a short-term financing plan that meets the firm's need for cash.

Working Capital

The Components of Working Capital

Short-term, or *current,* assets and liabilities are collectively known as *working capital.* Table 18.1 gives a breakdown of current assets and liabilities for all manufacturing corporations in the United States in 1996. Total current assets were $1,173 billion and total current liabilities were $842 billion.

Current Assets. One important current asset is *accounts receivable.* Accounts receivable arise because companies do not usually expect customers to pay for their purchases immediately. These unpaid bills are a valuable asset that companies expect to be able to turn into cash in the near future. The bulk of accounts receivable consists of unpaid bills from sales to other companies and are known as *trade credit.* The remainder arises from the sale of goods to the final consumer. These are known as *consumer credit.*

Another important current asset is *inventory.* Inventories may consist of raw materials, work in process, or finished goods awaiting sale and shipment. Table 18.1 shows that firms in the United States have about the same amount invested in inventories as in accounts receivable.

The remaining current assets are cash and marketable securities. The cash consists partly of dollar bills, but most of the cash is in the form of bank deposits. These may be *demand deposits* (money in checking accounts that the firm can pay out immediately) and *time deposits* (money in savings accounts that can be paid out only with a delay). The principal marketable security is *commercial paper* (short-term unsecured debt sold by other firms). Other securities include *Treasury bills,* which are short-term debts sold by the United States government, and state and local government securities.

In managing their cash companies face much the same problem you do. There are always advantages to holding large amount of ready cash—they reduce the risk of running out of cash and having to borrow more on short notice. On the other hand, there is a cost to holding idle cash balances rather than putting the money to work earning interest. In Chapter 19 we will tell you how the financial manager collects and pays out cash and decides on an optimal cash balance.

Current Liabilities. We have seen that a company's principal current asset consists of unpaid bills. One firm's credit must be another's debit. Therefore, it is not

Table 18.1

Current assets and liabilities, U.S. manufacturing corporations, first quarter 1996 (figures in billions)

Current Assets		Current Liabilities	
Cash	$ 85	Short-term loans	$143
Marketable securities	82	Accounts payable	264
Accounts receivable	439	Accrued income taxes	34
Inventories	429	Current payments due on long-term debt	58
Other current assets	139	Other current liabilities	343
Total	1,173	Total	842

Notes: Net working capital (current assets − current liabilities) = $1,173 − $842 = $331 billion. Column sums subject to rounding error.
Source: U.S. Department of Commerce, *Quarterly Financial Report for Manufacturing, Mining and Trade Corporations,* First Quarter 1996, pp. 2–4.

surprising that a company's principal current liability consists of *accounts payable*—that is, outstanding payments due to other companies.

The other major current liability consists of short-term borrowing. We will have more to say about this later in the chapter.

Working Capital and the Cash Conversion Cycle

net working capital: Current assets minus current liabilities. Often called *working capital.*

The difference between current assets and current liabilities is known as **net working capital,** but financial managers often refer to the difference simply (but imprecisely) as *working capital.* Usually current assets exceed current liabilities—that is, firms have positive net working capital. For United States manufacturing companies, current assets are on average nearly 1½ times current liabilities.

To see why firms need net working capital, imagine a small company, Simple Souvenirs, that makes small novelty items for sale at gift shops. It buys raw materials such as leather, beads, and rhinestones for cash, processes them into finished goods like wallets or costume jewelry, and then sells these goods on credit. Figure 18.1 shows the whole cycle of operations.

If you prepare the firm's balance sheet at the beginning of the process, you see cash (a current asset). If you delay a little, you find the cash replaced first by inventories of raw materials and then by inventories of finished goods (also current assets). When the goods are sold, the inventories give way to accounts receivable (another current asset) and finally, when the customers pay their bills, the firm takes out its profit and replenishes the cash balance.

The components of working capital constantly change with the cycle of operations, but the amount of working capital is fixed. This is one reason why net working capital is a useful summary measure of current assets or liabilities.

Figure 18.2 depicts four key dates in the production cycle that influence the firm's investment in working capital. The firm starts the cycle by purchasing raw materials, but it does not pay for them immediately. This delay is the *accounts payable period.* The firm processes the raw material and then sells the finished goods. The delay between the initial investment in inventories and the sale date is the *inventory period.* Some time after the firm has sold the goods its customers pay their bills. The delay between the date of sale and the date at which the firm is paid is the *accounts receivable period.*

The top part of Figure 18.2 shows that the total delay between initial purchase of raw materials and ultimate payments from customers is the sum of the inventory and

Figure 18.1

Simple cycle of operations.

Figure 18.2

Cash conversion cycle

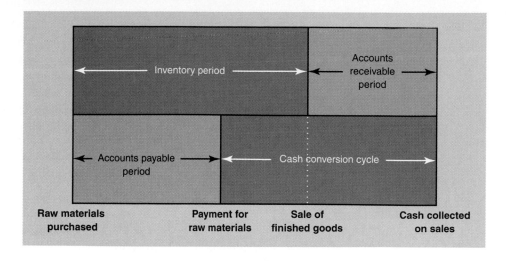

accounts receivable periods: first the raw materials must be purchased, processed, and sold, and then the bills must be collected. However, the *net* time that the company is out of cash is reduced by the time it takes to pay its own bills. The length of time between the firm's payment for its raw materials and the collection of payment from the customer is known as the firm's **cash conversion cycle.** To summarize,

cash conversion cycle: Period between firm's payment for materials and collection on its sales.

$$\text{Cash conversion cycle} = (\textbf{inventory period} + \textbf{receivables period}) - \textbf{accounts payable period}$$

The longer the production process, the more cash the firm must keep tied up in inventories. Similarly, the longer it takes customers to pay their bills, the higher the value of accounts receivable. On the other hand, if a firm can delay paying for its own materials, it may reduce the amount of cash it needs. In other words, accounts payable *reduce* net working capital.

In Chapter 16 we showed you how the firm's financial statements can be used to estimate the inventory period, also called days' sales in inventory:

$$\text{Inventory period} = \frac{\textbf{average inventory}}{\textbf{annual costs of goods sold/365}}$$

The denominator in this equation is the firm's daily output. The ratio of inventory to daily output measures the average number of days from the purchase of the inventories to the final sale.

We can estimate the accounts receivable period and the accounts payable period in a similar way:[1]

$$\text{Accounts receivable period} = \frac{\textbf{average accounts receivable}}{\textbf{annual sales/365}}$$

$$\text{Accounts payable period} = \frac{\textbf{average accounts payable}}{\textbf{annual cost of goods sold/365}}$$

[1]Because inventories are valued at cost, we divide inventory levels by cost of goods sold rather than sales revenue to obtain the inventory period. This way, both numerator and denominator are measured by cost. The same reasoning applies to the accounts payable period. On the other hand, because accounts receivable are valued at product price, we divide average receivables by daily sales revenue to find the receivables period.

▶ **Example 18.1** *Cash Conversion Cycle*

Table 18.2 provides the information necessary to compute the cash conversion cycle for manufacturing firms in the United States in 1996. We can use the table to answer four questions. How long on average does it take United States manufacturing firms to produce and sell their product? How long does it take to collect bills? How long does it take to pay bills? And what is the cash conversion cycle?

The delays in collecting cash are given by the inventory and receivables period. The delay in paying bills is given by the payables period. The net delay in collecting payments is the cash conversion cycle. We calculate these periods as follows:

$$\text{Inventory period} = \frac{\text{average inventories}}{\text{annual cost of goods sold}/365}$$

$$= \frac{(390 + 420)/2}{3{,}257/365} = 45.4 \text{ days}$$

$$\text{Receivables period} = \frac{\text{average accounts receivable}}{\text{annual sales}/365}$$

$$= \frac{(403 + 432)/2}{3{,}635/365} = 41.9 \text{ days}$$

$$\text{Payables period} = \frac{\text{average accounts payable}}{\text{annual cost of goods sold}/365}$$

$$= \frac{(249 + 272)/2}{3{,}257/365} = 29.2 \text{ days}$$

The cash conversion cycle is

Inventory period + receivables period − accounts payable period =
45.4 + 41.9 − 29.2 = 58.1 days

It is taking United States manufacturing companies an average of just under 2 months from the time they lay out money on inventories to collect payment from their customers.

Table 18.2

These data can be used to calculate the cash conversion cycle for U.S. manufacturing firms (figures in billions)

Income Statement Data		Balance Sheet Data		
	1995		**Beginning of 1995**	**End of 1995**
Sales	$3,635	Inventory	$390	$420
Cost of goods sold	3,257	Accounts receivable	403	432
		Accounts payable	249	272

Source: U.S. Department of Commerce, *Quarterly Financial Report for Manufacturing, Mining and Trade Corporations,* Fourth Quarter 1995, pp. 2–4.

▶ **Self-Test 18.1**

a. Suppose United States manufacturers are able to reduce inventory levels to a year-average value of $250 billion and average accounts receivable to $300 billion. By how many days will this reduce the cash conversion cycle?

b. Suppose that with the same level of inventories, accounts receivable, and accounts payable, United States manufacturers can increase production and sales by 10 percent. What will be the effect on the cash conversion cycle?

Managing Working Capital

Of course the cash conversion cycle is not cast in stone. To a large extent it is within management's control. Working capital can be *managed*. For example, accounts receivable are affected by the terms of credit the firm offers to its customers. You can cut the amount of money tied up in receivables by getting tough with customers who are slow in paying their bills. (You may find, however, that in the future they take their business elsewhere.) Similarly, the firm can reduce its investment in inventories of raw materials. (Here the risk is that it may one day run out of inventories and production will grind to a halt.)

carrying costs: Costs of maintaining current assets, including opportunity cost of capital.

These considerations show that investment in working capital has both costs and benefits. For example, the cost of the firm's investment in receivables is the interest that could have been earned if customers had paid their bills earlier. The firm also forgoes interest income when it holds idle cash balances rather than putting the money to work in marketable securities. The cost of holding inventory includes not only the opportunity cost of capital but also storage and insurance costs and the risk of spoilage or obsolescence. All of these **carrying costs** encourage firms to hold current assets to a minimum.

shortage costs: Costs incurred from shortages in current assets.

While carrying costs discourage large investments in current assets, too low a level of current assets makes it more likely that the firm will face **shortage costs.** For example, if the firm runs out of inventory of raw materials, it may have to shut down production. Similarly, a producer holding a small finished goods inventory is more likely to be caught short, unable to fill orders promptly. There are also disadvantages to holding small "inventories" of cash. If the firm runs out of cash, it may have to sell securities and incur unnecessary trading costs. The firm may also maintain too low a level of accounts receivable. If the firm tries to minimize accounts receivable by restricting credit sales, it may lose customers.

> **An important job of the financial manager is to strike a balance between the costs and benefits of current assets, that is, to find the level of current assets that minimizes the sum of carrying costs and shortage costs.**

We will have more to say about these trade-offs in the next two chapters.

▶ **Self-Test 18.2**

How will the following affect the size of the firm's optimal investment in current assets?

a. The interest rate rises from 6 percent to 8 percent.

b. A just-in-time inventory system is introduced that reduces the risk of inventory shortages.

c. Customers pressure the firm for a more lenient credit sales policy.

18.2 Links between Long-Term and Short-Term Financing

Businesses require capital—that is, money invested in plant, machinery, inventories, accounts receivable, and all the other assets it takes to run a company efficiently. Typically, these assets are not purchased all at once but are obtained gradually over time as the firm grows. The total cost of these assets is called the firm's *total capital requirement*.

When we discussed long-term planning in Chapter 17, we showed how the firm needs to develop a sensible strategy that allows it to finance its long-term goals and weather possible setbacks. But the firm's total capital requirement does not grow smoothly and the company must be able to meet temporary demands for cash. This is the focus of short-term financial planning.

Figure 18.3 illustrates the growth in the firm's total capital requirements. The upward-sloping line shows that as the business grows, it is likely to need additional fixed assets and current assets. You can think of this trendline as showing the base level of capital that is required. In addition to this base capital requirement, there may be seasonal fluctuations in the business that require an additional investment in current assets. Thus the wavy line in the illustration shows that the total capital requirement peaks late in each year. In practice, there would also be week-to-week and month-to-month fluctuations in the capital requirement, but these are not shown in Figure 18.3.

The total capital requirement can be met through either long- or short-term financing. When long-term financing does not cover the total capital requirement, the firm must raise short-term capital to make up the difference. When long-term financing *more* than covers the total capital requirement, the firm has surplus cash available for short-term investment. Thus the amount of long-term financing raised, given the total capital requirement, determines whether the firm is a short-term borrower or lender.

The three panels in Figure 18.4 illustrate this. Each depicts a different long-term financing strategy. The "relaxed strategy" in panel *a* always implies a short-term cash surplus. This surplus will be invested in marketable securities. The "restrictive" policy illustrated in panel *c* implies a permanent need for short-term borrowing. Finally,

Figure 18.3

The firm's total capital requirement grows over time. It also exhibits seasonal variation around the trend.

Figure 18.4

Alternative approaches to long- versus short-term financing.
(a) Relaxed strategy, where the firm is always a short-term lender.
(b) Middle-of-the-road policy.
(c) Restrictive policy, where the firm is always a short-term borrower.

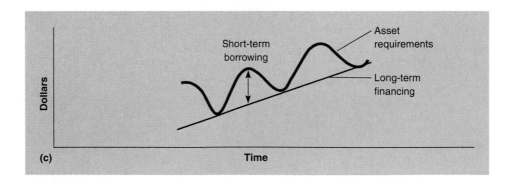

panel *b* illustrates an intermediate strategy: the firm is a short-term lender during the part of the year when total capital requirements are relatively low and a borrower during the rest of the year when capital requirements are relatively high.

What is the *best* level of long-term financing relative to the total capital requirement? It is hard to say. We can make several practical observations, however.

1. *Matching maturities.* Most financial managers attempt to "match maturities" of assets and liabilities. That is, they finance long-lived assets like plant and machinery with long-term borrowing and equity. Short-term assets like inventory and accounts receivable are financed with short-term bank loans or by issuing short-term debt like commercial paper.

2. *Permanent working-capital requirements.* Most firms have a permanent investment in net working capital (current assets less current liabilities). By this we mean that they plan to have at all times a positive amount of working capital. This is financed from long-term sources. This is an extension of the maturity-matching principle. Since the working capital is permanent, it is funded with long-term sources of financing.

3. *The comforts of surplus cash.* Many financial managers would feel more comfortable under the relaxed strategy illustrated in Figure 18.4a than the restrictive strategy in panel c. Consider, for example, General Motors. At the end of 1996 it was sitting on a cash mountain of $16 billion, almost certainly far more than it needed to meet any seasonal fluctuations in its capital requirements. Such firms with a surplus of long-term financing never have to worry about borrowing to pay next month's bills. But is the financial manager paid to be comfortable? Firms usually put surplus cash to work in Treasury bills or other marketable securities. This is *at best* a zero-NPV investment for a tax-paying firm.[2] Thus we think that firms with a *permanent* cash surplus ought to go on a diet, retiring long-term securities to reduce long-term financing to a level at or below the firm's total capital requirement. That is, if the firm is described by panel *a*, it ought to move down to panel *b*, or perhaps even lower.

18.3 Tracing Changes in Cash and Working Capital

Table 18.3 compares 1996 and 1997 year-end balance sheets for Dynamic Mattress Company. Table 18.4 shows the firm's income statement for 1997. Note that Dynamic's cash balance increases from $4 million to $5 million in 1997. What caused this increase? Did the extra cash come from Dynamic Mattress Company's additional

Table 18.3

Year-end balance sheets for Dynamic Mattress Company (figures in millions)

Assets	1996	1997	Liabilities and Shareholders' Equity	1996	1997
Current assets			Current liabilities		
Cash	$ 4	$ 5	Bank loans	$ 5	$ 0
Marketable securities	0	5	Accounts payable	20	27
Inventory	26	25	Total current liabilities	$25	$ 27
Accounts receivable	25	30	Long-term debt	5	12
Total current assets	$55	$ 65	Net worth (equity and	65	76
Fixed assets			retained earnings)		
Gross investment	$56	$ 70			
Less depreciation	16	20	Total liabilities and	$95	$115
Net fixed assets	$40	$ 50	owners' equity		
Total assets	$95	$115			

[2]Why do we say *at best* zero NPV? Not because we worry that the Treasury bills may be overpriced. Instead, we worry that when the firm holds Treasury bills, the interest income is subject to double taxation, first at the corporate level, and then again at the personal level when the income is passed through to investors as dividends. The extra layer of taxation can make corporate holdings of Treasury bills a negative-NPV investment even if the bills would provide a fair rate of interest to an individual investor.

Table 18.4

Income statement for Dynamic Mattress Company, 1997 (figures in millions)

Sales	$350
Operating costs	321
Depreciation	4
EBIT	25
Interest	1
Pretax income	24
Tax at 50 percent	12
Net income	$ 12

Note: Dividend = $1 million; retained earnings = $11 million.

long-term borrowing? From reinvested earnings? From cash released by reducing inventory? Or perhaps it came from extra credit extended by Dynamic's suppliers. (Note the increase in accounts payable.)

The correct answer? All of the above. There is rarely any point in linking a particular source of funds with a particular use. Instead financial analysts list the various sources and uses of cash in a statement like the one shown in Table 18.5. The statement shows that Dynamic *generated* cash from the following sources:

1. It issued $7 million of long-term debt.
2. It reduced inventory, releasing $1 million.
3. It increased its accounts payable, in effect borrowing an additional $7 million from its suppliers.
4. By far the largest source of cash was Dynamic's operations, which generated $16 million. Note that the $12 million net income reported in Table 18.4 understates cash flow because depreciation is deducted in calculating income. Depreciation is *not* a cash outlay. Thus it must be added back in order to obtain operating cash flow.

Table 18.5

Sources and uses of cash for Dynamic Mattress Company (figures in millions)

Sources	
Issued long-term debt	$ 7
Reduced inventories	1
Increased accounts payable	7
Cash from operations	
Net income	12
Depreciation	4
Total sources	$31
Uses	
Repaid short-term bank loan	$ 5
Invested in fixed assets	14
Purchased marketable securities	5
Increased accounts receivable	5
Dividend	1
Total uses	$30
Increase in cash balance	$ 1

Dynamic *used* cash for the following purposes:

1. It paid a $1 million dividend. (*Note:* The $11 million increase in Dynamic's equity is due to retained earnings: $12 million of equity income, less the $1 million dividend.)
2. It repaid a $5 million short-term bank loan.
3. It invested $14 million. This shows up as the increase in gross fixed assets in Table 18.3.
4. It purchased $5 million of marketable securities.
5. It allowed accounts receivable to expand by $5 million. In effect, it lent this additional amount to its customers.

▶ **Self-Test 18.3**   How will the following affect *cash* and *net working capital*?

a. The firm takes out a short-term bank loan and uses the funds to pay off some of its accounts payable.
b. The firm uses cash on hand to buy raw materials.
c. The firm repurchases outstanding shares of stock.
d. The firm sells long-term bonds and puts the proceeds in its bank account.

 Cash Budgeting

The financial manager's task is to forecast *future* sources and uses of cash. These forecasts serve two purposes. First, they alert the financial manager to future cash needs. Second, the cash-flow forecasts provide a standard, or budget, against which subsequent performance can be judged.

There are several ways to produce a quarterly cash budget. Many large firms have developed elaborate "corporate models"; others use a spreadsheet program to plan their cash needs. The procedures of smaller firms may be less formal. But no matter what method is chosen, there are three common steps to preparing a cash budget:

Step 1. Forecast the sources of cash. The largest inflow of cash comes from payments by the firm's customers.
Step 2. Forecast uses of cash.
Step 3. Calculate whether the firm is facing a cash shortage or surplus.

The financial *plan* sets out a strategy for investing cash surpluses or financing any deficit. We will illustrate these issues by continuing the example of Dynamic Mattress.

Forecast Sources of Cash

Most of Dynamic's cash inflow comes from the sale of mattresses. We therefore start with a sales forecast by quarter for 1998:[3]

Quarter:	First	Second	Third	Fourth
Sales, millions of dollars	87.5	78.5	116	131

[3]For simplicity, we present a quarterly forecast. However, most firms would forecast by month instead of by quarter. Sometimes weekly or even daily forecasts are made.

But unless customers pay cash on delivery, sales become accounts receivable before they become cash. Cash flow comes from *collections* on accounts receivable.

Most firms keep track of the average time it takes customers to pay their bills. From this they can forecast what proportion of a quarter's sales is likely to be converted into cash in that quarter and what proportion is likely to be carried over to the next quarter as accounts receivable. This proportion depends on the lags with which customers pay their bills. For example, if customers wait 1 month to pay their bills, then on average one-third of each quarter's bills will not be paid until the following quarter. If the payment delay is 2 months, then two-thirds of quarterly sales will be collected in the following quarter.

Suppose that 80 percent of sales are collected in the immediate quarter and the remaining 20 percent in the next. Table 18.6 shows forecast collections under this assumption.

In the first quarter, for example, collections from current sales are 80 percent of $87.5 million, or $70 million. But the firm also collects 20 percent of the previous quarter's sales, or .20 × $75 million = $15 million. Therefore, total collections are $70 million + $15 million = $85 million.

Dynamic started the first quarter with $30 million of accounts receivable. The quarter's sales of $87.5 million were *added* to accounts receivable, but $85 million of collections was *subtracted*. Therefore, as Table 18.6 shows, Dynamic ended the quarter with accounts receivable of $30 million + $87.5 million − $85 million = $32.5 million. The general formula is

Ending accounts receivable = beginning accounts receivable + sales − collections

The top section of Table 18.7 shows forecast sources of cash for Dynamic Mattress. Collection of receivables is the main source but it is not the only one. Perhaps the firm plans to dispose of some land or expects a tax refund or payment of an insurance claim. All such items are included as "other" sources. It is also possible that you may raise additional capital by borrowing or selling stock, but we don't want to prejudge that question. Therefore, for the moment we just assume that Dynamic will not raise further long-term finance.

Table 18.6

Dynamic Mattress's collections on accounts receivable, 1998 (figures in millions)

	First	Second	Third	Fourth
	Quarter			
	First	**Second**	**Third**	**Fourth**
1. Receivables at start of period	$30.0	$32.5	$ 30.7	$ 38.2
2. Sales	87.5	78.5	116.0	131.0
3. Collections				
Sales in current period (80%)	70.0	62.8	92.8	104.8
Sales in last period (20%)	15.0[a]	17.5	15.7	23.2
Total collections	$85.0	$80.3	$108.5	$128.0
4. Receivables at end of period (4 = 1 + 2 − 3)	$32.5	$30.7	$ 38.2	$ 41.2

[a]Sales in the fourth quarter of the previous year were $75 million.

Table 18.7

Dynamic Mattress's cash budget for 1998 (figures in millions)

	Quarter			
	First	**Second**	**Third**	**Fourth**
Sources of cash				
Collections on accounts receivable	$ 85.0	$80.3	$108.5	$128
Other	1.5	0	12.5	0
Total sources of cash	$ 86.5	$80.3	$121.0	$128
Uses of cash				
Payments of accounts payable	$ 65.0	$60.0	$ 55.0	$ 50
Labor and administrative expenses	30.0	30.0	30.0	30
Capital expenditures	32.5	1.3	5.5	8
Taxes, interest, and dividends	4.0	4.0	4.5	5
Total uses of cash	$131.5	$95.3	$ 95.0	$ 93
Net cash inflow equals sources minus uses	−$ 45.0	−$15.0	+$ 26.0	+$ 35

Forecast Uses of Cash

There always seem to be many more uses for cash than there are sources. The second section of Table 18.7 shows how Dynamic expects to use cash. For simplicity, in Table 18.7 we condense the uses into four categories:

1. *Payments of accounts payable.* Dynamic has to pay its bills for raw materials, parts, electricity, and so on. The cash-flow forecast assumes all these bills are paid on time, although Dynamic could probably delay payment to some extent. Delayed payment is sometimes called *stretching your payables*. Stretching is one source of short-term financing, but for most firms it is an expensive source, because by stretching they lose discounts given to firms that pay promptly. (This is discussed in more detail in Chapter 19.)
2. *Labor, administrative, and other expenses.* This category includes all other regular business expenses.
3. *Capital expenditures.* Note that Dynamic Mattress plans a major outlay of cash in the first quarter to pay for a long-lived asset.
4. *Taxes, interest, and dividend payments.* This includes interest on currently outstanding long-term debt and dividend payments to stockholders.

The Cash Balance

The forecast net inflow of cash (sources minus uses) is shown on the bottom row of Table 18.7. Note the large negative figure for the first quarter: a $45 million forecast *outflow*. There is a smaller forecast outflow in the second quarter, and then substantial cash inflows in the second half of the year.

Table 18.8 calculates how much financing Dynamic will have to raise if its cash-flow forecasts are right. It starts the year with $5 million in cash. There is a $45 million cash outflow in the first quarter, and so Dynamic will have to obtain at least

Table 18.8

Short-term financing requirements for Dynamic Mattress (figures in millions)

Cash at start of period	$ 5 →	−$40 →	−$55 →	−$29
+ Net cash inflow (from Table 18.7)	− 45	− 15	+ 26	+ 35
= Cash at end of period[a]	− 40 ⌐	55 ⌐	− 29 ⌐	+ 6
Minimum operating cash balance	5	5	5	5
Cumulative short-term financing required (minimum cash balance minus cash at end of period)[b]	$45	$60	$34	−$ 1

[a]Of course firms cannot literally hold a negative amount of cash. This line shows the amount of cash the firm will have to raise to pay its bills.

[b]A negative sign indicates that no short-term financing is required. Instead the firm has a cash *surplus*.

$45 million − $5 million = $40 million of additional financing. This would leave the firm with a forecast cash balance of exactly zero at the start of the second quarter.

Most financial managers regard a planned cash balance of zero as driving too close to the edge of the cliff. They establish a *minimum operating cash balance* to absorb unexpected cash inflows and outflows. We will assume that Dynamic's minimum operating cash balance is $5 million. That means it will have to raise $45 million instead of $40 million in the first quarter, and $15 million more in the second quarter. Thus its *cumulative* financing requirement is $60 million in the second quarter. Fortunately, this is the peak; the cumulative requirement declines in the third quarter when its $26 million net cash inflow reduces its cumulative financing requirement to $34 million. (Notice that the change in cumulative short-term financing in Table 18.8 equals the net cash inflow in that quarter from Table 18.7.) In the final quarter Dynamic is out of the woods. Its $35 million net cash inflow is enough to eliminate short-term financing and actually increase cash balances above the $5 million minimum acceptable balance.

Before moving on, we offer two general observations about this example:

1. The large cash outflows in the first two quarters do not necessarily spell trouble for Dynamic Mattress. In part they reflect the capital investment made in the first quarter: Dynamic is spending $32.5 million, but it should be acquiring an asset worth that much or more. The cash outflows also reflect low sales in the first half of the year; sales recover in the second half.[4] If this is a predictable seasonal pattern, the firm should have no trouble borrowing to help it get through the slow months.
2. Table 18.7 is only a best guess about future cash flows. It is a good idea to think about the *uncertainty* in your estimates. For example, you could undertake a sensitivity analysis, in which you inspect how Dynamic's cash requirements would be affected by a shortfall in sales or by a delay in collections.

Our next step will be to develop a short-term financing plan that covers the forecast requirements in the most economical way possible.

▶ **Self-Test 18.4**   Calculate Dynamic Mattress's quarterly cash receipts if customers pay for only 60 percent of purchases in the current quarter and pay the remaining 40 percent in the following quarter.

[4]Maybe people buy more mattresses late in the year when the nights are longer.

18.5 A Short-Term Financing Plan

Options for Short-Term Financing

Suppose that Dynamic can borrow up to $40 million from the bank at an interest cost of 8 percent per year or 2 percent per quarter. Dynamic can also raise capital by putting off paying its bills and thus increasing its accounts payable. In effect, this is taking a loan from its suppliers. The financial manager believes that Dynamic can defer the following amounts in each quarter:

Quarter:	First	Second	Third	Fourth
Amount deferrable, millions of dollars	52	48	44	40

That is, $52 million can be saved in the first quarter by *not* paying bills in that quarter. (Note that Table 18.7 was prepared assuming these bills *are* paid in the first quarter.) If deferred, these payments *must* be made in the second quarter. Similarly, $48 million of the second quarter's bills can be deferred to the third quarter and so on.

Stretching payables is often costly, however, even if no ill will is incurred.[5] This is because many suppliers offer discounts for prompt payment, so that Dynamic loses the discount if it pays late. In this example we assume the lost discount is 5 percent of the amount deferred. In other words, if a $52 million payment is delayed in the first quarter, the firm must pay 5 percent more, or $54.6 million in the next quarter. This is like borrowing at an interest rate of over 20 percent ($1.05^4 - 1 = .216$, or 21.6%).

With these two options, the short-term financing strategy is obvious: use the lower cost bank loan first. Stretch payables only if you can't borrow enough from the bank.

Table 18.9 shows the resulting plan. The first panel (cash requirements) sets out the cash that needs to be raised in each quarter. The second panel (cash raised) describes the various sources of financing the firm plans to use. The third and fourth panels describe how the firm will use net cash inflows when they turn positive.

In the first quarter the plan calls for borrowing the full amount available from the bank ($40 million). In addition, the firm sells the $5 million of marketable securities it held at the end of 1997. Thus under this plan it raises the necessary $45 million in the first quarter.

In the second quarter, an additional $15 million must be raised to cover the net cash outflow predicted in Table 18.7. In addition, $.8 million must be raised to pay interest on the bank loan. Therefore, the plan calls for Dynamic to maintain its bank borrowing and to stretch $15.8 million in payables. Notice that in the first two quarters, when net cash flow from operations is negative, the firm maintains its cash balance at the minimum acceptable level. Additions to cash balances are zero. Similarly, repayments of outstanding debt are zero. In fact outstanding debt rises in each of these quarters.

In the third and fourth quarters, the firm generates a cash-flow surplus, so the plan calls for Dynamic to pay off its debt. First it pays off stretched payables, as it is required to do, and then it uses any remaining cash-flow surplus to pay down its bank loan. In the third quarter, all of the net cash inflow is used to reduce outstanding short-term borrowing. In the fourth quarter, the firm pays off its remaining short-term borrowing and uses the extra $3 million to increase its cash balances.

---

[5]In fact, ill will is likely to be incurred. Firms that stretch payments risk being labeled as credit risks. Since stretching is so expensive, suppliers reason that only customers that cannot obtain credit at reasonable rates elsewhere will resort to it. Suppliers naturally are reluctant to act as the lender of last resort.

Table 18.9

Dynamic Mattress's financing plan (figures in millions)

	Quarter			
	First	**Second**	**Third**	**Fourth**
Cash requirements				
1. Cash required for operations[a]	$45	$15	−$26	−$35
2. Interest on bank loan[b]	0	0.8	0.8	0.6
3. Interest on stretched payables[c]	0	0	0.8	0
4. Total cash required	$45	$15.8	−$24.4	−$34.4
Cash raised				
5. Bank loan	$40	$ 0	$ 0	$ 0
6. Stretched payables	0	15.8	0	0
7. Securities sold	5	0	0	0
8. Total cash raised	$45	$15.8	$ 0	$ 0
Repayments				
9. Of stretched payables	0	0	$15.8	$ 0
10. Of bank loan	0	0	8.6	$31.4
Increase in cash balances				
11. Addition to cash balances	$ 0	$ 0	$ 0	$ 3
Line of credit				
12. Beginning of quarter	$ 0	$40	$40	$31.4
13. End of quarter	40	40	31.4	0

[a]From Table 18.7, bottom line. A negative cash requirement implies positive cash flow from operations
[b]The interest rate on the bank loan is 2 percent per quarter applied to the bank loan outstanding at the start of the quarter. Thus the interest due in the second quarter is .02 × $40 million = $.8 million.
[c]The "interest" cost of the stretched payables is 5 percent of the amount of payment deferred. For example, in the third quarter, 5 percent of the $15.8 million stretched in the second quarter is about $.8 million.

▶ **Self-Test 18.5**   Revise Dynamic Mattress's short-term financial plan assuming it can borrow up to $45 million through its line of credit. Assume that the firm will still sell its $5 million of short-term securities in the first quarter.

Evaluating the Plan

Does the plan shown in Table 18.9 solve Dynamic's short-term financing problem? No—the plan is feasible, but Dynamic can probably do better. The most glaring weakness of this plan is its reliance on stretching payables, an extremely expensive financing device. Remember that it costs Dynamic 5 percent *per quarter* to delay paying bills—20 percent per year at simple interest. This first plan should merely stimulate the financial manager to search for cheaper sources of short-term borrowing.

The financial manager would ask several other questions as well. For example:

1. Does Dynamic need a larger reserve of cash or marketable securities to guard against, say, its customers stretching *their* payables (thus slowing down collections on accounts receivable)?

2. Does the plan yield satisfactory current and quick ratios?[6] Its bankers may be worried if these ratios deteriorate.

3. Are there hidden costs to stretching payables? Will suppliers begin to doubt Dynamic's creditworthiness?

4. Does the plan for 1998 leave Dynamic in good financial shape for 1999? (Here the answer is yes, since Dynamic will have paid off all short-term borrowing by the end of the year.)

5. Should Dynamic try to arrange long-term financing for the major capital expenditure in the first quarter? This seems sensible, following the rule of thumb that long-term assets deserve long-term financing. It would also dramatically reduce the need for short-term borrowing. A counterargument is that Dynamic is financing the capital investment *only temporarily* by short-term borrowing. By year-end, the investment is paid for by cash from operations. Thus Dynamic's initial decision not to seek immediate long-term financing may reflect a preference for ultimately financing the investment with retained earnings.

6. Perhaps the firm's operating and investment plans can be adjusted to make the short-term financing problem easier. Is there any easy way of deferring the first quarter's large cash outflow? For example, suppose that the large capital investment in the first quarter is for new mattress-stuffing machines to be delivered and installed in the first half of the year. The new machines are not scheduled to be ready for full-scale use until August. Perhaps the machine manufacturer could be persuaded to accept 60 percent of the purchase price on delivery and 40 percent when the machines are installed and operating satisfactorily.

> **Short-term financing plans must be developed by trial and error. You lay out one plan, think about it, then try again with different assumptions on financing and investment alternatives. You continue until you can think of no further improvements.**

A Note on Short-Term Financial Planning Models

Working out a consistent short-term plan requires burdensome calculations. Fortunately, much of the arithmetic can be delegated to a computer. Many large firms have built short-term financial planning models to do this. Smaller companies like Dynamic Mattress do not face so much detail and find it easier to work with a spreadsheet program on a personal computer. In either case the financial manager specifies forecast cash requirements or surpluses, interest rates, credit limits, and so forth, and the model grinds out a plan like that shown in Table 18.9. The computer can also be used to produce balance sheets, income statements, and other special reports the financial manager may require.

18.6 Sources of Short-Term Financing

We suggested that Dynamic's manager might want to investigate alternative sources of short-term borrowing. Here are some of the possibilities.

---

[6]These ratios are discussed in Chapter 16.

Bank Loans

The simplest and most common source of short-term finance is an unsecured loan from a bank. For example, Dynamic might have a standing arrangement with its bank allowing it to borrow up to $40 million. The firm can borrow and repay whenever it wants so long as it does not exceed the credit limit. This kind of arrangement is called a **line of credit.**

A close relative of the line of credit is the *revolving credit arrangement.* Revolving credit arrangements usually last for a few years and formally commit the bank to providing loans up to some limit for the term of the agreement. In contrast, a line of credit is typically reviewed annually and it is possible that the bank may seek to cancel it if the firm's creditworthiness deteriorates. The borrowing firm must pay a commitment fee to establish a revolving credit arrangement, in part to compensate the bank for its legal obligation to honor the agreement.

line of credit: Agreement by a bank that a company may borrow at any time up to an established limit.

Commercial Paper

When banks lend money, they provide two services. They match up would-be borrowers and lenders and they check that the borrower is likely to repay the loan. Banks recover the costs of providing these services by charging borrowers on average a higher interest rate than they pay to lenders. These services are less necessary for large, well-known companies that regularly need to raise large amounts of cash. These companies have increasingly found it profitable to bypass the bank and to sell short-term debt, known as **commercial paper,** directly to large investors. Banks have been forced to respond by reducing the interest rates on their loans to blue-chip customers.

commercial paper: Short-term unsecured notes issued by firms.

In the United States commercial paper has a maximum maturity of 9 months, though most paper matures in 60 days or less. Commercial paper is not secured, but companies generally back their issue of paper by arranging a special backup line of credit with a bank. This guarantees that they can find the money to repay the paper, and the risk of default is therefore small.

Some companies regularly sell commercial paper in huge amounts. For example, GE Capital Corporation has about $50 billion of commercial paper in issue.

Secured Loans

Many short-term loans are unsecured, but sometimes the company may offer assets as security. Since the bank is lending on a short-term basis, the security generally consists of liquid assets such as receivables, inventories, or securities. For example, a firm may decide to borrow short-term money secured by its accounts receivable. When its customers pay their bills, it can use the cash collected to repay the loan. Banks will not usually lend the full value of the assets that are used as security. For example, a firm that puts up $100,000 of receivables as security may find that the bank is prepared to lend only $75,000. The safety margin (or *haircut,* as it is called) is likely to be even larger in the case of loans that are secured by inventory.

Accounts Receivable Financing. When a loan is secured by receivables, the firm *assigns* the receivables to the bank. If the firm fails to repay the loan, the bank can collect the receivables from the firm's customers and use the cash to pay off the debt. However, the firm is still responsible for the loan even if the receivables ultimately cannot be collected. The risk of default on the receivables is therefore borne by the firm.

An alternative procedure is to *sell* the receivables at a discount to a financial institution known as a *factor* and let it collect the money. In other words, some companies solve their financing problem by borrowing on the strength of their current assets; others solve it by selling their current assets. Once the firm has sold its receivables, the factor bears all the responsibility for collecting on the accounts. Therefore, the factor plays three roles: it administers collection of receivables, takes responsibility for bad debts, and provides finance.

▶ **Example 18.1**

Factoring

To illustrate factoring, suppose that the firm sells its accounts receivables to a factor at a 2 percent discount. This means that the factor pays 98 cents for each dollar of accounts receivable. If the average collection period is 1 month, then in a month the factor should be able to collect $1 for every 98 cents it paid today. Therefore, the implicit interest rate is 2/98 = 2.04 percent per month, which corresponds to an effective annual interest rate of $(1.0204)^{12} - 1 = .274$, or 27.4 percent. ◀

While factoring would appear from this example to be an expensive source of financing for the firm, part of the apparently steep interest rate represents payment for the assumption of default risk as well as for the cost of running the credit operation.

Inventory Financing. Banks also lend on the security of inventory, but they are choosy about the inventory they will accept. They want to make sure that they can identify and sell it if you default. Automobiles and other standardized nonperishable commodities are good security for a loan; work in progress and ripe strawberries are poor collateral.

Banks need to monitor companies to be sure they don't sell their assets and run off with the money. Consider, for example, the story of the great salad oil swindle. Fifty-one banks and companies made loans for nearly $200 million to the Allied Crude Vegetable Oil Refining Corporation in the belief that these loans were secured on valuable salad oil. Unfortunately, they did not notice that Allied's tanks contained false compartments which were mainly filled with seawater. When the fraud was discovered, the president of Allied went to jail and the 51 lenders stayed out in the cold looking for their $200 million. The nearby box presents a similar story that illustrates the potential pitfalls of secured lending. Here, too, the loans were not as "secured" as they appeared: the supposed collateral did not exist.

 See box p. 529

To protect themselves against this sort of risk, lenders often insist on *field warehousing*. An independent warehouse company hired by the bank supervises the inventory pledged as collateral for the loan. As the firm sells its product and uses the revenue to pay back the loan, the bank directs the warehouse company to release the inventory back to the firm. If the firm defaults on the loan, the bank keeps the inventory and sells it to recover the debt.

18.7 *The Cost of Bank Loans*

Bank loans often extend for several years. Interest payments on these loans are sometimes fixed for the term of the loan but more commonly they are adjusted up or down as the general level of interest rates changes.

The interest rate on bank loans of less than a year is almost invariably fixed for the term of the loan. However, you need to be careful when comparing rates on these shorter term bank loans, for the rates may be calculated in different ways.

The Hazards of Secured Bank Lending

The National Safety Council of Australia's Victoria Division had been a sleepy outfit until John Friedrich took over. Under its new management, NSC members trained like commandos and were prepared to go anywhere and do anything. They saved people from drowning, they fought fires, found lost bushwalkers and went down mines. Their lavish equipment included 22 helicopters, 8 aircraft and a mini-submarine. Soon the NSC began selling its services internationally.

Unfortunately the NSC's paramilitary outfit cost millions of dollars to run—far more than it earned in revenue. Friedrich bridged the gap by borrowing $A236 million of debt. The banks were happy to lend because the NSC's debt appeared well secured. At one point the company showed $A107 million of receivables (that is, money owed by its customers), which it pledged as security for bank loans. Later checks revealed that many of these customers did not owe the NSC a cent. In other cases banks took comfort in the fact that their loans were secured by containers of valuable rescue gear. There were more than 100 containers stacked around the NSC's main base. Only a handful contained any equipment, but these were the ones that the bankers saw when they came to check that their loans were safe. Sometimes a suspicious banker would ask to inspect a particular container. Friedrich would then explain that it was away on exercise, fly the banker across the country in a light plane and point to a container well out in the bush. The container would of course be empty, but the banker had no way to know that.

Six years after Friedrich was appointed CEO, his massive fraud was uncovered. But a few days before a warrant could be issued, Friedrich disappeared. Although he was eventually caught and arrested, he shot himself before he could come to trial. Investigations revealed that Friedrich was operating under an assumed name, having fled from his native Germany, where he was wanted by the police. Many rumors continued to circulate about Friedrich. He was variously alleged to have been a plant of the CIA and the KGB and the NSC was said to have been behind an attempted counter-coup in Fiji. For the banks there was only one hard truth. Their loans to the NSC, which had appeared so well secured, would never be repaid.

Source: Adapted from Chapter 7 of T. Sykes, *The Bold Riders* (St. Leonards, NSW, Australia: Allen & Unwin, 1994).

Simple Interest

The interest rate on bank loans frequently is quoted as simple interest. For example, if the bank quotes an annual rate of 12 percent on a simple interest loan of $100,000 for 1 month, then at the end of the month you would need to repay $100,000 plus 1 month's interest. This interest is calculated as

$$\text{Amount of loan} \times \frac{\text{annual interest rate}}{\text{number of periods in the year}} = \$100,000 \times \frac{.12}{12} = \$1,000$$

Your total payment at the end of the month would be

$$\text{Repayment of face value } plus \text{ interest} = \$100,000 + \$1,000 = \$101,000$$

In Chapter 3 you learned to distinguish between simple interest and compound interest. We have just seen that your 12 percent simple interest bank loan costs 1 percent per month. One percent per month compounded for 1 year cumulates to $1.01^{12} = 1.1268$. Thus the compound, or *effective*, annual interest rate on the bank loan is 12.68 percent, not the quoted rate of 12 percent.

The general formula for the equivalent compound interest rate on a simple interest loan is

$$\text{Effective annual rate} = \left(1 + \frac{\text{quoted annual interest rate}}{n}\right)^n - 1$$

where the annual interest rate is stated as a fraction (.12 in our example) and n is the number of periods in the year (12 in our example).

Discount Interest

The interest rate on a bank loan is often calculated on a discount basis. Similarly, when companies issue commercial paper, they also usually quote the interest rate as a discount. With a discount interest loan, the bank deducts the interest up front. For example, suppose that you borrow $100,000 on a discount basis for 1 year at 12 percent. In this case the bank hands you $100,000 less 12 percent, or $88,000. Then at the end of the year you repay the bank the $100,000 face value of the loan. This is equivalent to paying interest of $12,000 on a loan of $88,000. The effective interest rate on such a loan is therefore $12,000/$88,000 = .1364, or 13.64 percent.

Now suppose that you borrow $100,000 on a discount basis for 1 *month* at 12 percent. In this case the bank deducts 1 percent up-front interest and hands you

$$\text{Face value of loan} \times \left(1 - \frac{\text{quoted annual interest rate}}{\text{number of periods in the year}}\right)$$

$$= \$100,000 \times \left(1 - \frac{.12}{12}\right) = \$99,000$$

At the end of the month you repay the bank the $100,000 face value of the loan, so you are effectively paying interest of $1,000 on a loan of $99,000. The *monthly* interest rate on such a loan is $1,000/$99,000 = 1.01 percent and the compound, or effective, *annual* interest rate on this loan is $1.0101^{12} - 1 = .1282$, or 12.82 percent. The effective interest rate is higher than on the simple interest rate loan because the interest is paid at the beginning of the month rather than the end.

The general formula for the equivalent compound interest rate on a discount interest loan is

$$\begin{matrix}\text{Effective annual rate} \\ \text{on a discount loan}\end{matrix} = \left(\frac{1}{1 - \dfrac{\text{quoted annual interest rate}}{n}}\right)^n - 1$$

where the quoted annual interest rate is stated as a fraction (.12 in our example) and n is the number of periods in the year (12 in our example).

Interest with Compensating Balances

Bank loans often require the firm to maintain some amount of money on balance at the bank. This is called a *compensating balance*. For example, a firm might have to maintain a balance of 20 percent of the amount of the loan. In other words, if the firm borrows $100,000, it gets to use only $80,000, because $20,000 (20 percent of $100,000) must be left on deposit in the bank.

If the compensating balance does not pay interest (or pays a below-market rate of interest), the actual interest rate on the loan is higher than the stated rate. The reason is that the borrower must pay interest on the full amount borrowed but has access to only part of the funds. For example, we calculated above that a firm borrowing $100,000 for 1 month at 12 percent simple interest must pay interest at the end of the month of $1,000. If the firm gets the use of only $80,000, the effective monthly interest rate is $1,000/$80,000 = .0125$, or 1.25 percent. This is equivalent to a compound annual interest rate of $1.0125^{12} - 1 = .1608$, or 16.08 percent.

In general, the compound annual interest rate on a loan with compensating balances is

$$\text{Effective annual rate on a loan with compensating balances} = \left(1 + \frac{\text{actual interest paid}}{\text{borrowed funds available}}\right)^n - 1$$

where n is the number of periods in the year (again 12 in our example).

▶ **Self-Test 18.6**   Suppose that Dynamic Mattress needs to raise $20 million for 6 months. Bank A quotes a simple interest rate of 7 percent but requires the firm to maintain an interest-free compensating balance of 20 percent. Bank B quotes a simple interest rate of 8 percent but does not require any compensating balances. Bank C quotes a discount interest rate of 7.5 percent and also does not require compensating balances. What is the effective (or compound) annual interest rate on each of these loans?

Summary

1. Short-term financial planning is concerned with the management of the firm's short-term, or *current,* assets and liabilities. The most important current assets are cash, marketable securities, inventory, and accounts receivable. The most important current liabilities are bank loans and accounts payable. The difference between current assets and current liabilities is called *net working capital.*

2. Net working capital arises from lags between the time the firm obtains the raw materials for its product and the time it finally collects its bills from customers. The cash conversion cycle is the length of time between the firm's payment for materials and the date that it gets paid by its customers. The cash conversion cycle is partly within management's control. For example, it can choose to have a higher or lower level of inventories. Management needs to trade off the benefits and costs of investing in current assets.

3. The nature of the firm's short-term financial planning problem is determined by the amount of long-term capital it raises. A firm that issues large amounts of long-term debt or common stock, or which retains a large part of its earnings, may find that it has permanent excess cash. Other firms raise relatively little long-term capital and end up as permanent short-term debtors. Most firms attempt to find a golden mean by financing all fixed assets and part of current assets with equity and long-term debt. Such firms may invest cash surpluses during part of the year and borrow during the rest of the year.

4. The starting point for short-term financial planning is an understanding of sources and uses of cash. Firms forecast their net cash requirement by forecasting collections on accounts receivable, adding other cash inflows, and subtracting all forecast cash outlays. If the forecast cash balance is insufficient to cover day-to-day operations and to provide a buffer against contingencies, you will need to find additional finance. For example, you may borrow from a bank on an unsecured line of credit, you may borrow by offering receivables or inventory as security, or you may issue your own short-term notes known as commercial paper.

5. The search for the best short-term financial plan inevitably proceeds by trial and error. The financial manager must explore the consequences of different assumptions about cash requirements, interest rates, limits on financing from particular sources, and so on. Firms are increasingly using computerized financial models to help in this process.

6. Remember the key differences between the various sources of short-term financing—for example, the differences between bank lines of credit and commercial paper. Remember too that firms often raise money on the strength of their current assets, especially accounts receivable and inventories.

Key Terms

net working capital   carrying costs   line of credit
cash conversion cycle   shortage costs   commercial paper

Problems

1. **Working Capital Management.** Indicate how each of the following six different transactions that Dynamic Mattress might make would affect (i) cash and (ii) net working capital:

   a. Paying out a $2 million cash dividend.
   b. A customer paying a $2,500 bill resulting from a previous sale.
   c. Paying $5,000 previously owed to one of its suppliers.
   d. Borrowing $1 million long-term and investing the proceeds in inventory.
   e. Borrowing $1 million short-term and investing the proceeds in inventory.
   f. Selling $5 million of marketable securities for cash.

2. **Forecasting Collections.** Here is a forecast of sales by National Bromide for the first 4 months of 1998 (figures in thousands of dollars):

Month:	1	2	3	4
Cash sales	15	24	18	14
Sales on credit	100	120	90	70

   On average, 50 percent of credit sales are paid for in the current month, 30 percent in the next month, and the remainder in the month after that. What are expected cash collections in months 3 and 4?

3. **Short-Term Financial Plans.** Fill in the blanks in the following statements:

   a. A firm has a cash surplus when its _____ exceeds its _____. The surplus is normally invested in _____.
   b. In developing the short-term financial plan, the financial manager starts with a(n) _____ budget for the next year. This budget shows the _____ generated or absorbed by the firm's operations and also the minimum _____ needed to support these operations. The financial manager may also wish to invest in _____ as a reserve for unexpected cash requirements.

4. **Sources and Uses of Cash.** State how each of the following events would affect the firm's balance sheet. State whether each change is a source or use of cash.

   a. An automobile manufacturer increases production in response to a forecast increase in demand. Unfortunately, the demand does not increase.
   b. Competition forces the firm to give customers more time to pay for their purchases.

c. The firm sells a parcel of land for $100,000. The land was purchased 5 years earlier for $200,000.

d. The firm repurchases its own common stock.

e. The firm pays its quarterly dividend.

f. The firm issues $1 million of long-term debt and uses the proceeds to repay a short-term bank loan.

5. **Managing Working Capital.** A new computer system allows your firm to more accurately monitor inventory and anticipate future inventory shortfalls. As a result, the firm feels more able to pare down its inventory levels. What effect will the new system have on working capital and on the cash conversion cycle?

6. **Cash Conversion Cycle.** What effect will the following events have on the cash conversion cycle?

a. Higher financing rates induce the firm to reduce its level of inventory.

b. The firm obtains a new line of credit that enables it to avoid stretching payables to its suppliers.

c. The firm factors its accounts receivable.

d. A recession occurs, and the firm's customers increasingly stretch their payables.

7. **Sources and Uses of Cash.** The accompanying tables show Dynamic Mattress's year-end 1995 balance sheet and its income statement for 1996. Use these tables (and Table 18.3) to work out a statement of sources and uses of cash for 1996.

YEAR-END BALANCE SHEET FOR 1995
(figures in millions of dollars)

Assets		Liabilities	
Current assets		Current liabilities	
Cash	4	Bank loans	4
Marketable securities	2	Accounts payable	15
Inventory	20	Total current liabilities	19
Accounts receivable	22	Long-term debt	5
Total current assets	48	Net worth (equity and	
Fixed assets		retained earnings)	60
Gross investment	50		
Less depreciation	14	Total liabilities	84
Net fixed assets	36	and net worth	
Total assets	84		

INCOME STATEMENT FOR 1996
(figures in millions of dollars)

Sales	300
Operating costs	−285
	15
Depreciation	− 2
EBIT	13
Interest	− 1
Pretax income	12
Tax at 50 percent	− 6
Net income	6

Note: Dividend = $1 million and retained earnings = $5 million.

8. **Compensating Balances.** Suppose that Dynamic Sofa (a subsidiary of Dynamic Mattress) has a line of credit with a stated interest rate of 10 percent and a compensating balance of 25 percent. The compensating balance earns no interest.

   a. If the firm needs $10,000, how much will it need to borrow?
   b. Suppose that Dynamic's bank offers to forget about the compensating balance requirement if the firm pays interest at a rate of 12 percent. Should the firm accept this offer? Why or why not?
   c. Redo part (b) if the compensating balance pays interest of 4 percent. *Warning:* You cannot use the formula in the chapter for the effective interest rate when the compensating balance pays interest. Think about how to measure the effective interest rate on this loan.

9. **Compensating Balances.** The stated bank loan rate is 8 percent, but the loan requires a compensating balance of 10 percent on which no interest is earned. What is the effective interest rate on the loan? What happens to the effective rate if the compensating balance is doubled to 20 percent?

10. **Factoring.** A firm sells its accounts receivables to a factor at a 1.5 percent discount. The average collection period is 1 month. What is the implicit effective annual interest rate on the factoring arrangement? Suppose the average collection period is 1.5 months. How does this affect the implicit effective annual interest rate?

11. **Discount Loan.** A discount bank loan has a quoted annual rate of 6 percent.

   a. What is the effective rate of interest if the loan is for 1 year and is paid off in one payment at the end of the year?
   b. What is the effective rate of interest if the loan is for 1 month?

12. **Compensating Balances.** A bank loan has a quoted annual rate of 6 percent. However, the borrower must maintain a balance of 25 percent of the amount of the loan, and the balance does not earn any interest.

   a. What is the effective rate of interest if the loan is for 1 year and is paid off in one payment at the end of the year?
   b. What is the effective rate of interest if the loan is for 1 month?

13. **Cash Conversion Cycle.** What effect will the following have on the cash conversion cycle?

   a. Customers are given a larger discount for cash transactions.
   b. The inventory turnover ratio falls from 8 to 6.
   c. New technology streamlines the production process.
   d. The firm adopts a policy of reducing outstanding accounts payable.
   e. The firm starts producing more goods in response to customers' advance orders instead of producing for inventory.
   f. A temporary glut in the commodity market induces the firm to stock up on raw materials while prices are low.

14. **Cash Conversion Cycle.** Calculate the accounts receivable period, accounts payable period, inventory period, and cash conversion cycle for the following firm:

Income statement data:

Sales	5,000
Cost of goods sold	4,200

Balance sheet data:

	Beginning of Year	End of Year
Inventory	500	600
Accounts receivable	100	120
Accounts payable	250	290

15. **Short-Term Plan.** Recalculate Dynamic Mattress's financing plan (Table 18.9) assuming that the firm wishes to maintain a minimum cash balance of $10 million instead of $5 million. Assume the firm can convince the bank to extend its line of credit to $45 million.

 16. **Forecasting Payments.** If a firm pays its bills with a 30-day delay, what fraction of its purchases will be paid for in the current quarter? In the following quarter? What if its payment delay is 60 days?

 17. **Short-Term Planning.** Paymore Products places orders for goods equal to 75 percent of its sales forecast in the next quarter. What will be orders in each quarter of the year if the sales forecasts for the next five quarters are:

	Quarter in Coming Year				Following Year
	First	Second	Third	Fourth	First quarter
Sales forecast	$372	$360	$336	$384	$384

18. **Forecasting Payments.** Calculate Paymore's cash payments to its suppliers under the assumption that the firm pays for its goods with a 1-month delay. Therefore, on average, two-thirds of purchases are paid for in the quarter that they are purchased and one-third are paid in the following quarter.

19. **Forecasting Collections.** Now suppose that Paymore's customers pay *their* bills with a 2-month delay. What is the forecast for Paymore's cash receipts in each quarter of the coming year? Assume that sales in the last quarter of the previous year were $336.

20. **Forecasting Net Cash Flow.** Assuming that Paymore's labor and administrative expenses are $65 per quarter and that interest on long-term debt is $40 per quarter, work out the net cash inflow for Paymore for the coming year using a table like Table 18.7.

21. **Short-Term Financing Requirements.** Suppose that Paymore's cash balance at the start of the first quarter is $40 and its minimum acceptable cash balance is $30. Work out the short-term financing requirements for the firm in the coming year using a table like Table 18.8. The firm pays no dividends.

22. **Short-Term Financing Plan.** Now assume that Paymore can borrow up to $100 from a line of credit at an interest rate of 2 percent per quarter. Prepare a short-term financing plan. Use Table 18.9 to guide your answer.

 23. **Cash Budget.** The following data are from the budget of Ritewell Publishers. Half the company's sales are transacted on a cash basis. The other half are paid for with a 1-month delay. The company pays all of its credit purchases with a 1-month delay. Credit purchases in January were $30 and total sales in January were $180.

	February	March	April
Total sales	200	220	180
Cash purchases	70	80	60
Credit purchases	40	30	40
Labor and administrative expenses	30	30	30
Taxes, interest, and dividends	10	10	10
Capital purchases	100	0	0

Complete the following cash budget:

	February	March	April
Sources of cash			
Collections on current sales			
Collections on accounts receivable			
Total sources of cash			
Uses of cash			
Payments of accounts payable			
Cash purchases			
Labor and administrative expenses			
Capital expenditures			
Taxes, interest, and dividends			
Total uses of cash			
Net cash inflow			
Cash at start of period	100		
+ Net cash inflow			
= Cash at end of period			
+ Minimum operating cash balance	100	100	100
= Cumulative short-term financing required			

Solutions to Self-Test Questions

18.1 a. The new values for the accounts receivable period and inventory period are

$$\text{Days in inventory} = \frac{250}{3,257/365} = 28.0 \text{ days}$$

This is a reduction of 17.4 days from the original value of 45.4 days.

$$\text{Days in receivables} = \frac{300}{3,635/365} = 30.1 \text{ days}$$

This is a reduction of 11.8 days from the original value of 41.9 days
The cash conversion cycle falls by a total of $17.4 + 11.8 = 29.2$ days.

    b. The inventory period, accounts receivable period, and accounts payable period will all fall by a factor of 1.10. (The numerators are unchanged, but the denominators are higher by 10 percent.) Therefore, the conversion cycle will fall from 58.1 days to $58.1/1.10 = 52.8$ days.

18.2 a. An increase in the interest rate will increase the cost of carrying current assets. The effect is to reduce the optimal level of such assets.

    b. The just-in-time system lowers the expected level of shortage costs and reduces the amount of goods the firm ought to be willing to keep in inventory.

    c. If the firm decides that more lenient credit terms are necessary to avoid lost sales, it must then expect customers to pay their bills more slowly. Accounts receivable will increase.

18.3 a. This transaction merely substitutes one current liability (short-term debt) for another (accounts payable). Neither cash nor net working capital is affected.

    b. This transaction will increase inventory at the expense of cash. Cash falls but net working capital is unaffected.

    c. The firm will use cash to buy back the stock. Both cash and net working capital will fall.

    d. The proceeds from the sale will increase both cash and net working capital.

18.4

Quarter:	First	Second	Third	Fourth
Sales	87.5	78.5	116.0	131.0
Collections	52.5	47.1	69.6	78.6
Sales in current period (60%)				
Sales in last period (40%)	30.0^a	35.0	31.4	46.4
Total collections	82.5	82.1	101.0	125.0

^{a}Sales in the fourth quarter of the previous year were $75 million.

18.5 The major change in the plan is the substitution of the extra $5 million of borrowing via the line of credit (bank loan) in the second quarter and the corresponding reduction in the stretched payables. This substitution is advantageous because the bank loan is a cheaper source of funds. Notice that the cash balance at the end of the year is higher under this plan than in the original plan.

Quarter:	First	Second	Third	Fourth
Cash requirements				
1. Cash required for operations	45	15	−26.0	−35
2. Interest on line of credit	0	0.8	0.9	0.6
3. Interest on stretched payables	0	0	0.5	0
4. Total cash required	45	15.8	−24.6	−34.4
Cash raised				
5. Bank loan	40	5	0	0
6. Stretched payables	0	10.8	0	0
7. Securities sold	5	0	0	0
8. Total cash raised	45	15.8	0	0
Repayments				
9. Of stretched payables	0	0	10.8	0
10. Of bank loan	0	0	13.8	31.2
Increase in cash balances				
11. Addition to cash balances	0	0	0	3.2
Bank loan				
12. Beginning of quarter	0	40	45	31.2
13. End of quarter	40	45	31.2	0

18.6 Bank A: The interest paid on the $20 million loan over the 6-month period will be $20 million $\times$ .07/2 = $.7 million. With a 20 percent compensating balance, $16 million is available to the firm. The effective annual interest rate is

$$\frac{\text{Effective annual rate on a}}{\text{loan with compensating balances}} = \left(1 + \frac{\text{actual interest paid}}{\text{borrowed funds available}}\right)^n - 1$$

$$= \left(1 + \frac{\$.7 \text{ million}}{\$16 \text{ million}}\right)^2 - 1 = .0894, \text{ or } 8.94\%$$

Bank B: The compound annual interest rate on the simple loan is

$$\text{Effective annual rate} = \left(1 + \frac{\text{quoted interest rate}}{n}\right)^n - 1$$

$$= \left(1 + \frac{.08}{2}\right)^2 - 1 = 1.04^2 - 1 = .0816, \text{ or } 8.16\%$$

Bank C: The compound annual interest rate is

$$\text{Effective annual rate on a discount loan} = \left(\frac{1}{1 - \dfrac{\text{annual interest rate}}{n}} \right)^{n} - 1$$

$$= \left(\frac{1}{1 - \dfrac{.075}{2}} \right)^{2} - 1 = \left(\frac{1}{.9625} \right)^{2} - 1 = .0794, \text{ or } 7.94\%$$

Minicase

Capstan Autos operated an East Coast dealership for a major Japanese car manufacturer. Capstan's owner, Sidney Capstan, attributed much of the business's success to its no-frills policy of competitive pricing and immediate cash payment. The business was basically a simple one—the firm imported cars at the beginning of each quarter and paid the manufacturer at the end of the quarter. The revenues from the sale of these cars covered the payment to the manufacturer and the expenses of running the business, as well as providing Sidney Capstan with a good return on his equity investment.

By the fourth quarter of 2001 sales were running at 250 cars a quarter. Since the average sale price of each car was about $20,000, this translated into quarterly revenues of 250 × $20,000 = $5 million. The average cost to Capstan of each imported car was $18,000. After paying wages, rent, and other recurring costs of $200,000 per quarter and deducting depreciation of $80,000, the company was left with earnings before interest and taxes (EBIT) of $220,000 a quarter and net profits of $140,000.

The year 2002 was not a happy year for car importers in the United States. Recession led to a general decline in auto sales, while the fall in the value of the dollar shaved profit margins for many dealers in imported cars. Capstan more than most firms foresaw the difficulties ahead and reacted at once by offering 6 months' free credit while holding the sale price of its cars constant. Wages and other costs were pared by 25 percent to $150,000 a quarter and the company effectively eliminated all capital expenditures. The policy appeared successful. Unit sales fell by 20 percent to 200 units a quarter, but the company continued to operate at a satisfactory profit (see table).

The slump in sales lasted for 6 months, but as consumer confidence began to return, auto sales began to recover. The company's new policy of 6 months' free credit was proving sufficiently popular that Sidney Capstan decided to maintain the policy. In the third quarter of 2002 sales had recovered to 225 units; by the fourth quarter they were 250 units; and by the first quarter of the next year they had reached 275 units. It looked as if by the second quarter of 2003 that the company could expect to sell 300 cars. Earnings before interest and tax were already in excess of their previous high and Sidney Capstan was able to congratulate himself on weathering what looked to be a tricky period. Over the 18-month period the firm had earned net profits of over half a million dollars, and the equity had grown from just under $1 million to about $2 million.

Sidney Capstan was first and foremost a superb salesman and always left the financial aspects of the business to his financial manager. However, there was one feature of the financial statements that disturbed Sidney Capstan—the mounting level of debt, which by the end of the first quarter of 2003 had reached $9.7 million. This unease turned to alarm when the financial manager phoned to say that the bank was reluctant to extend further credit and was even questioning its current level of exposure to the company.

Capstan found it impossible to understand how such a successful year could have landed the company in financial difficulties. The company had always had good relationships with its bank, and the interest rate on its bank loans was a reasonable 8 percent a year (or about 2 percent a quarter). Surely, Capstan reasoned, when the bank saw the projected sales growth for the rest of 2003, it would realize that there were plenty of profits to enable the company to start repaying its loans.

SUMMARY INCOME STATEMENT
(all figures except unit sales in thousands of dollars)

Year:	2001	2002					2003
Quarter:	4	1	2	3	4		1
1. Number of cars sold	250	200	200	225	250		275
2. Unit price	20	20	20	20	20		20
3. Unit cost	18	18	18	18	18		18
4. Revenues (1 × 2)	5,000	4,000	4,000	4,500	5,000		5,500
5. Cost of goods sold (1 × 3)	4,500	3,600	3,600	4,050	4,500		4,950
6. Wage and other costs	200	150	150	150	150		150
7. Depreciation	80	80	80	80	80		80
8. EBIT (4 − 5 − 6 − 7)	220	170	170	220	270		320
9. Net interest	4	0	76	153	161		178
10. Pretax profit (8 − 9)	216	170	94	67	109		142
11. Tax (.35 × 10)	76	60	33	23	38		50
12. Net profit (10 − 11)	140	110	61	44	71		92

SUMMARY BALANCE SHEETS
(figures in thousands of dollars)

	End of 3rd Quarter 2001	End of 1st Quarter 2003
Cash	10	10
Receivables	0	10,500
Inventory	4,500	5,400
Total current assets	4,510	15,910
Fixed assets, net	1,760	1,280
Total assets	6,270	17,190
Bank loan	230	9,731
Payables	4,500	5,400
Total current liabilities	4,730	15,131
Shareholders' equity	1,540	2,059
Total liabilities	6,270	17,190

Questions

1. Is Capstan Auto in trouble?
2. Is the bank correct to withhold further credit?
3. Why is Capstan's indebtedness increasing if its profits are higher than ever?

Part Seven

Short-Term Financial Decisions

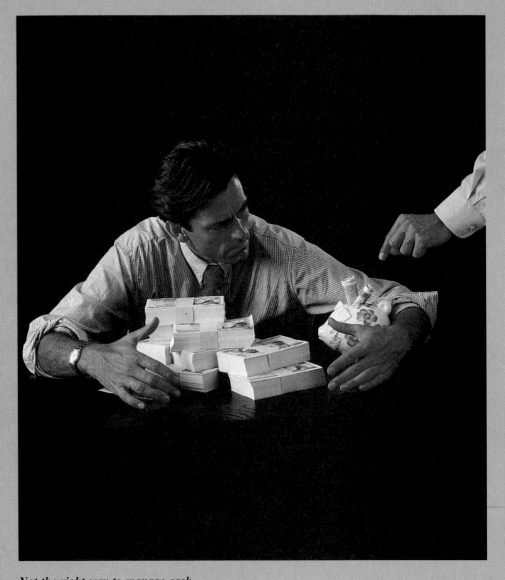

Not the right way to manage cash.
Why hoard cash when you could invest it and earn interest? Still, you need some cash to pay bills. What's the right cash inventory? We will see that managing an inventory of cash is similar to managing an inventory of raw materials or finished goods.
© *Telegraph Colour Library/FPG International Corporation*

Chapter 19

Cash and Inventory Management

*I*n mid-1997 citizens and corporations in the United States held approximately $1,140 billion in cash. This included about $430 billion of currency and $710 billion of demand deposits (checking accounts) with commercial banks. Cash pays no interest. Why, then, do sensible people hold it? Why, for example, don't you take all your cash and invest it in interest-bearing securities? The answer is that cash gives you more *liquidity* than securities. By this we mean that you can use it to buy things. It is hard enough getting New York cab drivers to give you change for a $20 bill, but try asking them to split a Treasury bill.

Of course, rational investors will not hold an asset like cash unless it provides the same benefit on the margin as other assets such as Treasury bills. The benefit from holding Treasury bills is the interest that you receive; the benefit from holding cash is that it gives you a convenient store of liquidity. When you have only a small proportion of your assets in cash, a little extra liquidity can be extremely useful; when you have a substantial holding, any additional liquidity is not worth much. Therefore, as a financial manager you want to hold cash balances up to the point where the value of any additional liquidity is equal to the value of the interest forgone.

Cash is simply a raw material that companies need to carry on production. As we will explain later, the financial manager's decision to stock up on cash is in many ways similar to the production manager's decision to stock up on inventories of raw materials. We will therefore look at the general problem of managing inventories and then show how this helps us to understand how much cash you should hold.

But first you need to learn about the mechanics of cash collection and disbursement. This may seem a rather humdrum topic but you will find that it involves some interesting and important decisions.

After studying this chapter you should be able to

▶ Measure float and explain why it arises and how it can be controlled.

▶ Calculate the value of changes in float.

▶ Understand the costs and benefits of holding inventories.

▶ Cite the costs and benefits of holding cash.

▶ Explain why an understanding of inventory management can be useful for cash management.

19.1 Cash Collection, Disbursement, and Float

Companies don't keep their cash in a little tin box; they keep it in a bank deposit. To understand how they can make best use of that deposit, you need to understand

Figure 19.1
Delays create float. Each heavy arrow represents a source of delay. Recipients try to reduce delay to get available cash sooner. Payers prefer delay so they can use their cash longer.

- The time that it takes to mail a check.
- The time that it takes the company to process the check after it has been received.
- The time that it takes the bank to clear the check and adjust the firm's account.

The total collection time is the sum of these three sources of delay.

> **Delays that help the payer hurt the recipient. Recipients try to speed up collections. Payers try to slow down disbursements. Both attempt to minimize net float.**

You probably have come across attempts by companies to reduce float in your own financial transactions. For example, some stores now encourage you to pay bills with your bank debit card instead of a credit card. The payment is automatically debited from your bank account on the day of the transaction, which eliminates the considerable float you otherwise would enjoy until you were billed by your credit card company and paid your bill. Similarly, many companies now arrange *preauthorized payments* with their customers. For example, if you have a mortgage payment on a house, the lender can arrange to have your bank account debited by the amount of the payment each month. The funds are automatically transferred to the lender. You save the work of paying the bill by hand, and the lender saves the few days of float during which your check would have been processed through the banking system.

Speeding Up Collections

...on banking:
...eby customers
...ts to a
...tion center
...funds to a

One way to speed up collections is by a method known as **concentration banking.** In this case customers in a particular area make payments to a local branch office rather than to company headquarters. The local branch office then deposits the checks into a local bank account. Surplus funds are periodically transferred to a concentration account at one of the company's principal banks.

---

what happens when companies withdraw money from their account or pay money into it.

Float

Suppose that the United Carbon Company has $1 million in a demand deposit (checking account) with its bank. It now pays one of its suppliers by writing and mailing a check for $200,000. The company's records are immediately adjusted to show a cash balance of $800,000. Thus the company is said to have a *ledger balance* of $800,000.

But the company's bank won't learn anything about this check until it has been received by the supplier, deposited at the supplier's bank, and finally presented to United Carbon's bank for payment. During this time United Carbon's bank continues to show in *its* ledger that the company has a balance of $1 million.

payment float: Checks written by a company that have not yet cleared.

While the check is clearing, the company obtains the benefit of an extra $200,000 in the bank. This sum is often called disbursement float, or **payment float.**

Float sounds like a marvelous invention; every time you spend money, it takes the bank a few days to catch on. Unfortunately it can also work in reverse. Suppose that in addition to paying its supplier, United Carbon *receives* a check for $120,000 from a customer. It first processes the check and then deposits it in the bank. At this point both the company and the bank increase the ledger balance by $120,000:

availability float: Checks already deposited that have not yet been cleared.

But this money isn't available to the company immediately. The bank doesn't actually have the money in hand until it has sent the check to the customer's bank and received payment. Since the bank has to wait, it makes United Carbon wait too—usually 1 or 2 business days. In the meantime, the bank will show that United Carbon still has an available balance of only $1 million. The extra $120,000 has been deposited but is not yet available. It is therefore known as **availability float**

Company's ledger balance $920,000	+	Payment float $200,000

equals

Bank's ledger balance $1,120,000

equals

Available balance $1,000,000	+	Availability float $120,000

net float: Difference between payment float and availability float.

Notice that the company gains as a result of the payment float and loses as a result of availability float. The **net float** available to the firm is the difference between payment and availability float:

$$\text{Net float} = \text{payment float} - \text{availability float}$$

In our example, the net float is $80,000. The company's available balance is $80,000 greater than the balance shown in its ledger.

▶ **Self-Test 19.1**

Your bank account currently shows a balance of $940. You now deposit $100 into the account and write a check for $40.

a. What is the ledger balance in your account?
b. What is the availability float?
c. What is payment float?
d. What is the bank's ledger balance?
e. Show that your ledger balance plus payment float equals the bank's ledger balance, which in turn equals the available balance plus availability float.

Valuing Float

Float results from the delay between your writing a check and the reduction in your bank balance. The amount of float will therefore depend on the size of the check and the delay in collection.

▶ **Example 19.1**

Float

Suppose that your firm writes checks worth $6,000 per day. It may take 3 days to mail these checks to your suppliers, who then take a day to process the checks and deposit them with their bank. Finally, it may be a further 3 days before the supplier's bank sends the check to your bank, which then debits your account. The total delay is 7 days and the payment float is $7 \times \$6,000 = \$42,000$. On average, the available balance at the bank will be $42,000 more than is shown in your firm's ledger. ◀

As financial manager your concern is with the available balance, not with the company's ledger balance. If you know that it is going to be a week before some of your checks are presented for payment, you may be able to get by on a smaller cash balance. The smaller you can keep your cash balance, the more funds you can hold in interest-earning accounts or securities. This game is often called *playing the float.*

You can increase your available cash balance by increasing your net float. This means that you want to ensure that checks received from customers are cleared rapidly and those paid to suppliers are cleared slowly. Perhaps this may sound like rather small change, but think what it can mean to a company like Ford. Ford's daily sales average over $250 million. If it could speed up collections by 1 day, and the interest rate is .02 percent per day (about 7.3 percent per year), it would increase earnings by $.0002 \times \$250$ million = $50,000 *per day.*

What would be the present value to Ford if it could *permanently* reduce its collection period by 1 day? That extra interest income would then be a perpetuity, and the present value of the income would be $50,000/.0002 = $250 million, exactly equal to the reduction in float.

Why should this be? Think about the company's cash-flow stream. It receives $2_ million a day. At any time, suppose that 4 days' worth of payments are deposited "in the pipeline." When it speeds up the collection period by a day, the pipeline shrink to 3 days' worth of payments. At that point, Ford receives an extra $25_ lion cash flow: it receives the "usual" payment of $250 million, and it also _ the $250 million for which it ordinarily would have had to wait an extra d_ that day forward, it continues to receives $250 million a day, exactly as _ the net effect of reducing the payment pipeline from 4 days to 3 is that F_ extra up-front payment equal to 1 day of float, or $250 million. We conc_ present value of a permanent reduction in float is simply the amount b_ is reduced.

However, you should be careful not to become overenthusiastic _ float. Writing checks on your account for the sole purpose of creatir_ ing interest is called *check kiting* and is illegal. In 1985 the brokera_ ton pleaded guilty to 2,000 separate counts of mail and wire frau_ that it had created nearly $1 billion of float by shuffling funds _ and through various accounts at different banks.

▶ **Self-Test 19.2**

Suppose Ford's stock price is $60 per share, and there are 4_ outstanding. Assume that daily sales average $250 millio_ nological improvements in the check-clearing process re_ 4 days to 2 days. What would happen to the stock price_ willing to pay for a new computer system that would_ days?

Managing Float

There are several kinds of delay that create fl_ business refer to several kinds of float. Figu_

concentra
System wher_
make paymen_
regional collec_
which transfers_
principal ban_

Concentration banking reduces float in two ways. First, because the branch office is nearer to the customer, mailing time is reduced. Second, because the customers are local, the chances are that they have local bank accounts and therefore the time taken to clear their checks is also reduced. Another advantage is that concentration brings many small balances together in one large, central balance, which then can be invested in interest-paying assets through a single transaction.

Unfortunately, concentration banking also involves additional costs. First, the company is likely to incur additional administrative costs. Second, the company's local bank needs to be paid for its services. Third, there is the cost of transferring the funds to the concentration bank. The fastest but most expensive arrangement is *wire transfer,* in which funds are transferred from one account to another via computer entries in the accounts. A wire transfer might cost $10, but funds become available on the day they are wired. A slower but cheaper method is a *depository transfer check,* or *DTC.* This is a preprinted check used to transfer funds between specified accounts. The funds become available within 2 days.

Wire transfer makes more sense when large funds are being transferred. For example, at a daily interest rate of .02 percent, the daily interest on a $10 million payment would be $2,000. It clearly would pay to spend $10 on a wire transfer to save 2 days' float. On the other hand, it would not be worth using wire transfer for just $5,000. The extra 2 days' interest that you pick up amounts to only $2, not nearly enough to justify the extra expense of the wire transfer.

▶ **Example 19.2**   *Break-Even Wire Transfer Amount*

Suppose the daily interest rate is .02 percent and that a wire transfer saves 2 days of float but costs $10 more than a depository transfer check. How large a transfer is necessary to justify the additional cost of a wire transfer?

The interest savings are .02 percent per day $\times$ 2 days $\times$ funds to be transferred. So the break-even level of funds to be transferred is found by solving

$$.0004 \times \text{size of transfer} = \$10$$

$$\text{Size of transfer} = \frac{\$10}{.0004} = \$25,000$$

The cost of the wire transfer can be justified for any transfer above this amount.

---

lock-box system: System whereby customers send payments to a post office box and a local bank collects and processes checks.

Often concentration banking is combined with a **lock-box system.** In a lock-box system, you pay the local bank to take on the administrative chores. It works as follows. The company rents a locked post office box in each principal region. All customers within a region are instructed to send their payments to the post office box. The local bank empties the box at regular intervals (as often as several times per day) and deposits the checks in your company's local account. Surplus funds are transferred periodically to one of the company's principal banks.

How many collection points do you need if you use a lock-box system or concentration banking? The answer depends on where your customers are and on the speed of the United States mail.

▶ **Example 19.3**

Lock-Box Systems

Suppose that you are thinking of opening a lock box. The local bank shows you a map of mail delivery times. From that and knowledge of your customers' locations, you come up with the following data:

Average number of daily payments to lock box = 150
Average size of payment = $1,200
Rate of interest *per day* = .02 percent
Saving in mailing time = 1.2 days
Saving in processing time = .8 day

On this basis, the lock box would reduce collection float by

150 items per day $\times$ $1,200 per item $\times$ (1.2 + .8) days saved = $360,000

Invested at .02 percent per day, that gives a daily return of

$.0002 \times \$360,000 = \$72$

The bank's charge for operating the lock-box system depends on the number of checks processed. Suppose that the bank charges $.26 per check. That works out to 150 $\times$ $.26 = $39.00 per day. You are ahead by $72.00 − $39.00 = $33.00 per day, plus whatever your firm saves from not having to process the checks itself. ◀

Our example assumes that the company has only two choices. It can do nothing or it can operate the lock box. But maybe there is some other lock-box location, or some mixture of locations, that would be still more effective. Of course, you can always find this out by working through all possible combinations, but many banks have computer programs that find the best locations for lock boxes.[1]

▶ **Self-Test 19.3**

How will the following conditions affect the price that a firm should be willing to pay for a lock-box service?

a. The average size of its payments increases.
b. The number of payments per day increases (with no change in average size of payments).
c. The interest rate increases.
d. The average mail time saved by the lock-box system increases.
e. The processing time saved by the lock-box system increases.

Controlling Disbursements

Speeding up collections is not the only way to increase the net float. You can also do this by slowing down disbursements. One tempting strategy is to increase mail time. For example, United Carbon could pay its New York suppliers with checks mailed from Nome, Alaska, and its Los Angeles suppliers with checks mailed from Vienna, Maine.

But on second thought you will realize that these kinds of post office tricks are unlikely to help you. Suppose you have promised to pay a New York supplier on March 29. Does it matter whether you mail the check from Alaska on the 26th or from New York on the 28th? Such mailing games would buy you time only if your creditor cares more about the date you mailed the check than the day it arrives. This is unlikely: with the notable exception of tax returns sent to the IRS, mailing dates are irrelevant. Of course you could use a remote mailing address as an *excuse* to pay

---

[1]These usually involve linear programming. Linear programming is an efficient method of hunting through the possible solutions to find the optimal one.

late, but that's a trick easily seen through. If you have to pay late, you may as well mail late.

Remote Disbursement.   There are effective ways of increasing payment float, however. For example, suppose that United Carbon pays its suppliers with checks written on a New York City bank. From the time that the check is deposited by the supplier, there will be an average lapse of little more than a day before it is presented to United Carbon's bank for payment. The alternative is for United Carbon to pay its suppliers with checks mailed to *arrive* on time, but written on a bank in Helena, Montana; Midland, Texas; or Wilmington, Delaware. In these cases, it may take 3 or 4 days before each check is presented for payment. United Carbon thus gains several days of additional float. Some firms even maintain disbursement accounts in different parts of the country. The computer looks up each supplier's zip code and automatically produces a check on the most distant bank.

The suppliers won't object to these machinations because the Federal Reserve guarantees a maximum clearing time of 2 days on all checks cleared through the Federal Reserve system. Therefore, the supplier never gives up more than 2 days of float. Instead, the victim of remote disbursement is the Federal Reserve, which loses float if it takes more than 2 days to collect funds. The Fed has been trying to prevent remote disbursement.

Zero-Balance Accounts.   A New York City bank receives several check deliveries each day. Thus if United Carbon uses a New York City bank for paying its suppliers, it will not know at the beginning of the day how many checks will be presented for payment. Either it must keep a large cash balance to cover contingencies, or it must be prepared to borrow.

However, instead of having a disbursement account with, say, Morgan Guaranty Trust in New York, United Carbon could open a **zero-balance account** with Morgan's affiliated bank in Wilmington, Delaware. Because it is *not* in a major banking center, this affiliated bank receives almost all check deliveries in the form of a single, early-morning delivery from the Federal Reserve. Therefore, it can let the cash manager at United Carbon know early in the day exactly how much money will be paid out that day. The cash manager then arranges for this sum to be transferred from the company's concentration account to the disbursement account. Thus by the end of the day (and at the start of the next day), United Carbon has a zero balance in the disbursement account.

United Carbon's Wilmington account has two advantages. First, by choosing a remote location, the company has gained several days of float. Second, because the bank can forecast early in the day how much money will be paid out, United Carbon does not need to keep extra cash in the account to cover contingencies.

zero-balance account:
Regional bank account to which just enough funds are transferred daily to pay each day's bills.

19.3 *Inventories and Cash Balances*

So far we have focused on managing the *flow* of cash efficiently. We have seen how efficient float management can improve a firm's income and its net worth. Now we turn to the management of the *stock* of cash that a firm chooses to keep on hand and ask: How much cash does it make sense for a firm to hold?

Recall that cash management involves a trade-off. If the cash were invested in securities, it would earn interest. On the other hand, you can't use securities to pay the firm's bills. If you had to sell those securities every time you needed to pay a bill, you would incur heavy transactions costs. The art of cash management is to balance these costs and benefits.

If that seems more easily said than done, you may be comforted to know that production managers must make a similar trade-off. Ask yourself why they carry inventories of raw materials, work in progress, and finished goods. They are not obliged to carry these inventories; for example, they could simply buy materials day by day, as needed. But then they would pay higher prices for ordering in small lots, and they would risk production delays if the materials were not delivered on time. That is why they order more than the firm's immediate needs. Similarly, the firm holds inventories of finished goods to avoid the risk of running out of product and losing a sale because it cannot fill an order.

But there are costs to holding inventories: money tied up in inventories does not earn interest; storage and insurance must be paid for; and often there is spoilage and deterioration. Production managers must try to strike a sensible balance between the costs of holding too little inventory and those of holding too much.

In this sense, cash is just another raw material you need for production. There are costs to keeping an excessive inventory of cash (the lost interest) and costs to keeping too small an inventory (the cost of repeated sales of securities).

Managing Inventories

Let us take a look at what economists have had to say about managing inventories and then see whether some of these ideas can help us manage cash balances. Here is a simple inventory problem.

A builders' merchant faces a steady demand for engineering bricks. When the merchant every so often runs out of inventory, it replenishes the supply by placing an order for more bricks from the manufacturer.

There are two costs associated with the merchant's inventory of bricks. First, there is the *order cost*. Each order placed with a supplier involves a fixed handling expense and delivery charge. The second type of cost is the *carrying cost*. This includes the cost of space, insurance, and losses due to spoilage or theft. The opportunity cost of the capital tied up in the inventory is also part of the carrying cost.

Here is the kernel of the inventory problem:

As the firm increases its order size, the number of orders falls and therefore the order costs decline. However, an increase in order size also increases the average amount in inventory, so that the carrying cost of inventory rises. The trick is to strike a balance between these two costs.

Let's insert some numbers to illustrate. Suppose that the merchant plans to buy 1 million bricks over the coming year. Each order that it places costs $90, and the annual carrying cost of the inventory is $.05 per brick. To minimize order costs, the merchant would need to place a single order for the entire 1 million bricks on January 1 and would then work off the inventory over the remainder of the year. *Average* inventory over the year would be 500,000 bricks and therefore carrying costs would be 500,000 × $.05 = $25,000. The first row of Table 19.1 shows that if the firm places

Table 19.1

How inventory costs vary with the number of orders

Order Size = Bricks per Order	Orders per Year = $\dfrac{\text{Annual Purchases}}{\text{Bricks per Order}}$	Average Inventory = $\dfrac{\text{Order Size}}{2}$	Order Costs = $90 per Order	Carrying Costs = $.05 per Brick	Total Costs = Order Costs plus Carrying Costs
1,000,000	1	500,000	$ 90	$25,000	$25,090
500,000	2	250,000	180	12,500	12,680
200,000	5	100,000	450	5,000	5,450
100,000	10	50,000	900	2,500	3,400
60,000	16.7	30,000	1,500	1,500	3,000
50,000	20	25,000	1,800	1,250	3,050
20,000	50	10,000	4,500	500	5,000
10,000	100	5,000	9,000	250	9,250

just this one order, total costs are $25,090:

$$\text{Total costs} = \text{order costs} + \text{carrying costs}$$
$$\$25{,}090 = \$90 \qquad + \qquad \$25{,}000$$

To minimize *carrying* costs, the merchant would need to minimize inventory by placing a large number of very small orders. For example, the bottom row of Table 19.1 shows the costs of placing 100 orders a year for 10,000 bricks each. The average inventory is now only 5,000 bricks and therefore the carrying costs are only 5,000 × $.05 = $250. But the order costs have risen to 100 × $90 = $9,000.

Each row in Table 19.1 illustrates how changes in the order size affect the inventory costs. You can see that as the order size decreases and the number of orders rises, total inventory costs at first decline because carrying costs fall faster than order costs rise. Eventually, however, the curve turns up as order costs rise faster than carrying costs fall. Figure 19.2 illustrates this graphically. The downward-sloping curve charts annual order costs and the upward-sloping straight line charts carrying costs. The U-shaped curve is the sum of these two costs. Total costs are minimized in this example when the order size is 60,000 bricks. About 17 times a year the merchant should place an order for 60,000 bricks and it should work off this inventory over a period of about 3 weeks. Its inventory will therefore follow the sawtoothed pattern in Figure 19.3.

Note that it is worth increasing order size as long as the decrease in total order costs outweighs the increase in carrying costs. The optimal order size is the point at which these two effects offset each other. This order size is called the **economic order quantity.** There is a neat formula for calculating the economic order quantity. The formula is

economic order quantity:
Order size that minimizes total inventory costs.

$$\text{Economic order quantity} = \sqrt{\dfrac{2 \times \text{annual sales} \times \text{cost per order}}{\text{carrying cost}}}$$

Figure 19.2

Determination of optimal order size.

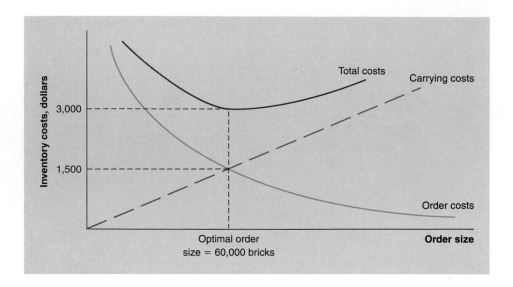

In the present example,

$$\text{Economic order quantity} = \sqrt{\frac{2 \times 1,000,000 \times 90}{.05}} = 60,000 \text{ bricks}$$

You have probably already noticed several unrealistic features in our simple example. First, rather than allowing inventories of bricks to decline to zero, the firm would want to allow for the time it takes to fill an order. If it takes 5 days before the bricks can be delivered and the builders' merchant waits until it runs out of stock before placing an order, it will be out of stock for 5 days. In this case the firm should reorder when its stock of bricks falls to a 5-day supply.

The firm also might want to recognize that the rate at which it sells its goods is subject to uncertainty. Sometimes business may be slack; on other occasions the firm may land a large order. In this case it should maintain a minimum *safety stock* below which it would not want inventories to drop.

Figure 19.3

The builders' merchant minimizes inventory costs by placing about 17 orders a year for 60,000 bricks each. That is, it places orders at about 3-week intervals.

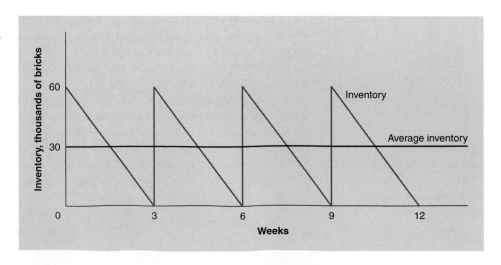

The number of bricks the merchant plans to buy in the course of the year, in this case 1 million, is also a forecast that is subject to uncertainty. The optimal order size is proportional to the square root of the *forecast* of annual sales.

> **These are refinements: the important message of our simple example is that the firm needs to balance carrying costs and order costs. Carrying costs include both the cost of storing the goods and the cost of the capital tied up in inventory. So when storage costs or interest rates are high, inventory levels should be kept low. When the costs of restocking are high, inventories should also be high.**

In recent years a number of firms have used a technique known as *just-in-time inventory management* to make dramatic reductions in inventory levels. Firms that use the just-in-time system receive a nearly continuous flow of deliveries, with no more than 2 or 3 hours' worth of parts inventory on hand at any time. For these firms the extra cost of restocking is completely outweighed by the saving in carrying cost. Just-in-time inventory management requires much greater coordination with suppliers to avoid the costs of stock-outs, however.

Just-in-time inventory management also can reduce costs by allowing suppliers to produce and transport goods on a steadier schedule. However, just-in-time systems rely heavily on predictability of the production process. A firm with shaky labor relations, for example, would adopt a just-in-time system at its peril, for with essentially no inventory on hand, it would be particularly vulnerable to a strike.

▶ **Self-Test 19.4**

The builders' merchant has experienced an increase in demand for engineering bricks. It now expects to sell 1.25 million bricks a year. Unfortunately, interest rates have risen and the annual carrying cost of the inventory has increased to $.09 per brick. Order costs have remained steady at $90 per order.

a. Rework Table 19.1 for each of the eight order sizes shown in the table.
b. Has the optimal inventory level risen or fallen? Explain why.

Managing Inventories of Cash

William Baumol was the first to notice that this simple inventory model can tell us something about the management of cash balances.[2] Suppose that you keep a reservoir of cash that is steadily drawn down to pay bills. When it runs out, you replenish the cash balance by selling short-term securities. In these circumstances your inventory of cash also follows a sawtoothed pattern like the pattern for inventories we saw in Figure 19.3.

In other words, your cash management problem is just like the problem of finding the optimal order size faced by the builders' merchant. You simply need to redefine the variables. Instead of bricks per order, the order size is defined as the value of short-term securities that are sold whenever the cash balance is replenished. Total cash outflow takes the place of the total number of bricks sold. Cost per order becomes the cost per sale of securities, and the carrying cost is just the interest rate. Our formula for the amount of securities to be sold or, equivalently, the initial cash balance is therefore

$$\frac{\text{Initial cash}}{\text{balance}} = \sqrt{\frac{2 \times \text{annual cash outflows} \times \text{cost per sale of securities}}{\text{interest rate}}}$$

[2]See W. J. Baumol, "The Transactions Demand for Cash: An Inventory Theoretic Approach," *Quarterly Journal of Economics* 66 (November 1952), pp. 545–556.

> **The optimal amount of short-term securities sold to raise cash will be higher when annual cash outflows are higher and when the cost per sale of securities is higher. Conversely, the initial cash balance falls when the interest rate is higher.**

▶ **Example 19.4** *The Optimal Cash Balance*

Suppose that you can invest spare cash in U.S. Treasury bills at an interest rate of 8 percent, but every sale of bills costs you $20. Your firm pays out cash at a rate of $105,000 per month, or $1,260,000 per year. Our formula for the initial cash balance tells us that the optimal amount of Treasury bills that you should sell at one time is

$$\sqrt{\frac{2 \times 1,260,000 \times 20}{.08}} = \$25,100$$

Thus your firm would sell approximately $25,000 of Treasury bills four times a month—about once a week. Its average cash balance will be $25,000/2, or $12,500.

In Baumol's model a higher interest rate implies smaller sales of bills. In other words, when interest rates are high, you should hold more of your funds in interest-bearing securities and make small sales of these securities when you need the cash. On the other hand, if you use up cash at a high rate or there are high costs to selling securities, you want to hold large average cash balances. Think about that for a moment. *You can hold too little cash.* Many financial managers point with pride to the extra interest that they have earned. Such benefits are highly visible. The costs are less visible but they can be very large. When you allow for the time that the manager spends in monitoring the cash balance, it may make some sense to forgo some of that extra interest.

▶ **Self-Test 19.5** Suppose now that the interest rate is only 4 percent. How will this affect the optimal initial cash balance derived in Example 19.2? What will be the *average* cash balance? What will be annual trading costs? Explain why the optimal cash position now involves fewer trades.

Uncertain Cash Flows

Baumol's model stresses the essential similarity between the inventory problem and the cash management problem. It also demonstrates the relationship between the optimal cash balance on the one hand and the level of interest rates and the cost of transactions on the other. However, it is clearly too simple for practical use. For example, firms do not pay out cash at a steady rate day after day and week after week. Sometimes the firm may collect a large unpaid bill and therefore receive a net *inflow* of cash. On other occasions it may pay its suppliers and so incur a net *outflow* of cash.

Economists and management scientists have developed a variety of more elaborate and realistic models that allow for the possibility of both cash inflows and outflows. For example, Figure 19.4 illustrates how the firm should manage its cash balance if

Figure 19.4

If cash flows are unpredictable, the cash balance should be allowed to meander until it hits an upper or lower limit. At this point the firm buys or sells securities to restore the balance to the return point, which is the lower limit plus one-third of the spread between the upper and lower limits.

it cannot predict day-to-day cash inflows and outflows. You can see that the cash balance meanders unpredictably until it reaches an upper limit. At this point the firm buys enough securities to return the cash balance to a more normal level. Once again the cash balance is allowed to meander until this time it hits a lower limit. This may be zero, some minimum safety margin above zero, or a balance necessary to keep the bank happy. When the cash balance hits the lower limit, the firm *sells* enough securities to restore the balance to a normal level. Thus the rule is to allow the cash holding to wander freely until it hits an upper or lower limit. When this happens, the firm should buy or sell securities to regain the desired balance.

How far should the firm allow its cash balance to wander? The answer depends on three factors. If the day-to-day variability in cash flows is large or if the cost of buying and selling securities is high, then the firm should set the upper and lower limits far apart. The firm allows wider limits when cash flow volatility is high to keep down the frequency of costly security sales and purchases. Similarly, the firm tolerates wider limits if the cost of security transactions is high. Conversely, if the rate of interest is high and the incentives to manage cash are correspondingly more important, the firm will set the limits close together.[3]

Have you noticed one odd feature about Figure 19.4? The cash balance does not return to a point halfway between the lower and upper limits. It always comes back to a point one-third of the distance from the lower to the upper limit. Always starting at this return point means the firm hits the lower limit more often than the upper limit. This does not minimize the number of transactions—that would require always starting exactly at the middle of the spread. However, always starting at the middle would mean a larger average cash balance and larger interest costs. The lower return point minimizes the sum of transaction costs and interest costs.

Recognizing uncertainty in cash flows adds some extra realism, but few managers would concede that cash inflows and outflows are entirely unpredictable. The manager of Toys 'R' Us knows that there will be substantial cash inflows around Christmas. Financial managers know when dividends will be paid and when taxes will be

[3]See M. H. Miller and D. Orr, "A Model of the Demand for Money by Firms," *Quarterly Journal of Economics* 80 (August 1966), pp. 413–435.

due. In Chapter 18 we described how firms forecast cash inflows and outflows and how they arrange short-term investment and financing decisions to supply cash when needed and put cash to work earning interest when it is not needed.

This kind of short-term financial plan is usually designed to produce a cash balance that is stable at some lower limit. But there are always fluctuations that financial managers cannot plan for, certainly not on a day-to-day basis. You can think of the decision rule depicted in Figure 19.4 as a way to cope with the cash inflows and outflows which cannot be predicted, or which are not *worth* predicting. Trying to predict *all* cash flows would chew up enormous amounts of management time.

You should therefore think of these cash management rules as helping us *understand* the problem of cash management. But they are not generally used for day-to-day management and would probably not yield substantial savings compared with policies based on a manager's judgment, providing of course that the manager understands the trade-offs we have discussed.

▶ Self-Test 19.6

How would you expect the firm's cash balance to respond to the following changes?

a. Interest rates increase.
b. The volatility of daily cash flow decreases.
c. The transaction cost of buying or selling marketable securities goes up.

Cash Management in the Largest Corporations

For very large firms, the transaction costs of buying and selling securities become trivial compared with the opportunity cost of holding idle cash balances. Suppose that the interest rate is 4 percent per year, or roughly $4/365 = .011$ percent per day. Then the daily interest earned on $1 million is $.00011 \times \$1,000,000 = \$110$. Even at a cost of $50 per transaction, which is generous, it pays to buy Treasury bills today and sell them tomorrow rather than to leave $1 million idle overnight.

A corporation with $1 billion of annual sales has an average daily cash flow of $\$1,000,000,000/365$, about $2.7 million. Firms of this size end up buying or selling securities once a day, every day, unless by chance they have only a small positive cash balance at the end of the day.

Why do such firms hold any significant amounts of cash? For two reasons. First, cash may be left in non-interest-bearing accounts to compensate banks for the services they provide. Second, large corporations may have literally hundreds of accounts with dozens of different banks. It is often less expensive to leave idle cash in some of these accounts than to monitor each account daily and make daily transfers between them.

One major reason for the proliferation of bank accounts is decentralized management. You cannot give a subsidiary operating freedom to manage its own affairs without giving it the right to spend and receive cash.

Good cash management nevertheless implies some degree of centralization. You cannot maintain your desired inventory of cash if all the subsidiaries in the group are responsible for their own private pools of cash. And you certainly want to avoid situations in which one subsidiary is investing its spare cash at 8 percent while another is borrowing at 10 percent. It is not surprising, therefore, that even in highly decentralized companies there is generally central control over cash balances and bank relations.

Investing Idle Cash: The Money Market

We have seen that when firms have excess funds, they can invest the surplus in interest-bearing securities. Treasury bills are only one of many securities that might be appropriate for such short-term investments. More generally, firms may invest in a variety of securities in the **money market,** the market for short-term financial assets.

money market: Market for short-term financial assets.

Only fixed-income securities with maturities less than 1 year are considered to be part of the money market. In fact, however, most instruments in the money market have considerably shorter maturity. Limiting maturity has two advantages for the cash manager. First, short-term securities entail little interest-rate risk. Recall from Chapter 4 that price risk due to interest-rate fluctuations increases with maturity. Very-short-term securities, therefore, have almost no interest-rate risk. Second, it is far easier to gauge financial stability over very short horizons. One need not worry as much about deterioration in financial strength over a 90-day horizon as over the 30-year life of a bond. These considerations imply that high-quality money-market securities are a safe "parking spot" to keep idle balances until they are converted back to cash.

Most money-market securities are also highly marketable or *liquid,* meaning that it is easy and cheap to sell the asset for cash. This property, too, is an attractive feature of securities used as temporary investments until cash is needed. Treasury bills are the most liquid asset. Treasury bills are issued by the United States government with original maturities ranging from 90 days to 1 year.

Some of the other important instruments of the money market are

Commercial paper. This is the short-term, usually unsecured, debt of large and well-known companies. While maturities can range up to 270 days, commercial paper usually is issued with maturities of less than 2 months. Because there is no active trading in commercial paper, it has low marketability. Therefore, it would not be an appropriate investment for a firm that could not hold it until maturity. Both Moody's and Standard & Poor's rate commercial paper in terms of the default risk of the issuer.

Certificates of deposit. CDs are time deposits at banks, usually in denominations greater than $100,000. Unlike demand deposits (checking accounts), time deposits cannot be withdrawn from the bank on demand: the bank pays interest and principal only at the maturity of the deposit. However, short-term CDs (with maturities less than 3 months) are actively traded, so a firm can easily sell the security if it needs cash.

Repurchase agreements. Also known as *repos,* repurchase agreements are in effect collateralized loans. A government bond dealer sells Treasury bills to an investor, with an agreement to repurchase them at a later date at a higher price. The increase in price serves as implicit interest, so the investor in effect is lending money to the dealer, first giving money to the dealer and later getting it back with interest. The bills serve as collateral for the loan: if the dealer fails, and cannot buy back the bill, the investor can keep it. Repurchase agreements are usually very short term, with maturities of only a few days.

19.4 Summary

1. The cash shown in the company ledger is not the same as the available balance in its bank account. The difference is the net float. When you write a check, it takes time before your bank balance is adjusted downward. During this time the available balance will be larger than the ledger balance. When you deposit a check, there is again a delay before it gets credited to your bank account. In this case the available balance will be smaller than the ledger balance. If you can predict how long it will take checks to clear, you may be able to play the float and get by on a smaller cash balance.

2. You can also manage the float by speeding up collections and slowing down payments. One way to speed collections is by concentration banking. Customers make payments to a regional office, which then pays the checks into a local bank account. Surplus funds are transferred from the local account to a concentration bank. A related technique is lock-box banking. In this case customers send their payments to a local post office box. A local bank empties the box at regular intervals and clears the checks. Concentration banking and lock-box banking reduce mailing time and the time required to clear checks.

3. Cash provides liquidity, but it doesn't pay interest. Securities pay interest, but you can't use them to buy things. As financial manager you want to hold cash up to the point where the incremental or marginal value of liquidity is equal to the interest that you could earn on securities.

4. Cash is simply a raw material that you need to do business. It is expensive keeping capital tied up in large inventories of any raw material when it could be earning interest. So why do you hold inventories at all? Why not order materials as and when you need them? The answer is that it is also expensive to keep placing many small orders.

5. Try to strike a balance between holding too large an inventory of cash (and losing interest on the money) and making too many small adjustments to your inventory (and incurring additional transaction or administrative costs). If interest rates are high, you want to hold relatively small inventories of cash. If your cash needs are variable and your transaction or administrative costs are high, you want to hold relatively large inventories.

6. Firms can invest idle cash in the money market, the market for short-term financial assets. These assets tend to be short-term, low risk, and highly liquid, making them ideal instruments in which to invest funds for short periods of time before cash is needed.

Key Terms

payment float	concentration banking	economic order quantity
availability float	lock-box system	money market
net float	zero-balance account	

Problems

1. **Float.** On January 25, Coot Company has $250,000 deposited with a local bank. On January 27, the company writes and mails checks of $20,000 and $60,000 to suppliers. At the end of the month, Coot's financial manager deposits a $45,000 check received from a customer in the morning mail and picks up the end-of-month account summary from the bank.

The manager notes that only the $20,000 payment of the 27th has cleared the bank. What are the company's ledger balance and payment float? What is the company's net float?

2. **Float.** A company has the following cash balances:

   Company's ledger balance = $600,000
   Bank's ledger balance = $625,000
   Available balance = $550,000

   a. Calculate the payment float and availability float.
   b. Why does the company gain from the payment float?
   c. Suppose the company adopts a policy of writing checks on a remote bank. How is this likely to affect the three measures of cash balance?

3. **Float.** General Products writes checks that average $20,000 daily. These checks take an average of 6 days to clear. It receives payments that average $22,000 daily. It takes 3 days before these checks are available to the firm.

   a. Calculate payment float, availability float, and net float.
   b. What would be General Products's annual savings if it could reduce availability float to 2 days? The interest rate is 6 percent per year. What would be the present value of these savings?

4. **Lock Boxes.** Anne Teak, the financial manager of a furniture manufacturer, is considering operating a lock-box system. She forecasts that 300 payments a day will be made to lock boxes with an average payment size of $1,500. The bank's charge for operating the lock boxes is $.40 a check. The interest rate is .015 percent per day.

   a. If the lock box saves 2 days in collection float, is it worthwhile to adopt the system?
   b. What minimum reduction in the time to collect and process each check is needed to justify use of the lock-box system?

5. **Lock Boxes.** Sherman's Sherbet currently takes about 6 days to collect and deposit checks from customers. A lock-box system could reduce this time to 4 days. Collections average $10,000 daily. The interest rate is .02 percent per day.

   a. By how much will the lock-box system reduce collection float?
   b. What is the daily interest savings of the system?
   c. Suppose the lock-box service is offered for a fixed monthly fee instead of payment per check. What is the maximum monthly fee that Sherman's should be willing to pay for this service? (Assume a 30-day month.)

6. **Lock Boxes.** The financial manager of JAC Cosmetics is considering opening a lock box in Pittsburgh. Checks cleared through the lock box will amount to $300,000 per month. The lock box will make cash available to the company 3 days earlier.

   a. Suppose that the bank offers to run the lock box for a $20,000 compensating balance. Is the lock box worthwhile?
   b. Suppose that the bank offers to run the lock box for a fee of $.10 per check cleared instead of a compensating balance. What must the average check size be for the fee alternative to be less costly? Assume an interest rate of 6 percent per year.
   c. Why did you need to know the interest rate to answer (b) but not to answer (a)?

7. **Collection Policy.** Major Manufacturing currently has one bank account located in New York to handle all of its collections. The firm keeps a compensating balance of $300,000 to pay for these services (see Section 18.7). It is considering opening a bank account with West Coast National Bank to speed up collections from its many California-based

customers. Major estimates that the West Coast account would reduce collection time by 1 day on the $1 million a day of business that it does with its California-based customers. If it opens the account, it can reduce the compensating balance with its New York bank to $200,000 since it will do less business in New York. However, West Coast also will require a compensating balance of $200,000. Should Major open the new account?

8. **Cash Management.** Complete the following passage by choosing the appropriate term from the following list: *lock-box banking, wire transfer, payment float, concentration banking, availability float, net float, depository transfer check.*

    The firm's available balance is equal to its ledger balance plus the _____ and minus the _____. The difference between the available balance and the ledger balance is often called the _____. Firms can increase their cash resources by speeding up collections. One way to do this is to arrange for payments to be made to regional offices which pay the checks into local banks. This is known as _____. Surplus funds are then transferred from the local bank to one of the company's main banks. Transfer may be by the quick but expensive _____ or by the slightly slower but cheaper _____. Another technique is to arrange for a local bank to collect the checks directly from a post office box. This is known as _____.

9. **Cash Management.** A firm maintains a separate account for cash disbursements. Total disbursements are $100,000 per month spread evenly over the month. Administrative and transaction costs of transferring cash to the disbursement account are $10 per transfer. Marketable securities yield 1 percent per month. Determine the size and number of transfers that will minimize the cost of maintaining the special account.

10. **Economic Order Quantity.** Assume that Everyman's Bookstore uses up cash at a steady rate of $200,000 a year. The interest rate is 2 percent and each sale of securities costs $20.

    a. How many times a year should the store sell securities?
    b. What is its average cash balance?

11. **Cash Management.** If cash flows change unpredictably, the firm should allow the cash balance to move within limits.

    a. What three factors determine how far apart these limits are?
    b. How far should the firm adjust its cash balance when it reaches the upper or lower limit?
    c. Why does it not restore the cash balance to the halfway point?

12. **Float Management.** The Automated Clearinghouse (ACH) system uses electronic communication to provide next-day delivery of payments. The processing cost of making a payment through the ACH system is roughly half the cost of making the same payment by check. Why then do firms often rationally choose to make payments by check?

13. **Cash Management.** Suppose that the rate of interest increases from 4 to 8 percent per year. Would firms' cash balances go up or down relative to sales? Explain.

14. **Float Management.** A parent company settles the collection account balances of its subsidiaries once a week. (That is, each week it transfers any balances in the accounts to a central account.) The cost of a wire transfer is $10. A depository transfer check costs $.80. Cash transferred by wire is available the same day, but the parent must wait 3 days for depository transfer checks to clear. Cash can be invested at 12 percent per year. How much money must be in a collection account before it pays to use a wire transfer?

15. **Float Management.** Knob, Inc., is a nationwide distributor of furniture hardware. The company now uses a central billing system for credit sales of $182.5 million annually. First National, Knob's principal bank, offers to establish a new concentration banking system for a flat fee of $100,000 per year. The bank estimates that mailing and collection time can be reduced by 3 days.

what happens when companies withdraw money from their account or pay money into it.

Float

Suppose that the United Carbon Company has $1 million in a demand deposit (checking account) with its bank. It now pays one of its suppliers by writing and mailing a check for $200,000. The company's records are immediately adjusted to show a cash balance of $800,000. Thus the company is said to have a *ledger balance* of $800,000.

But the company's bank won't learn anything about this check until it has been received by the supplier, deposited at the supplier's bank, and finally presented to United Carbon's bank for payment. During this time United Carbon's bank continues to show in *its* ledger that the company has a balance of $1 million.

While the check is clearing, the company obtains the benefit of an extra $200,000 in the bank. This sum is often called disbursement float, or **payment float.**

payment float: Checks written by a company that have not yet cleared.

Float sounds like a marvelous invention; every time you spend money, it takes the bank a few days to catch on. Unfortunately it can also work in reverse. Suppose that in addition to paying its supplier, United Carbon *receives* a check for $120,000 from a customer. It first processes the check and then deposits it in the bank. At this point both the company and the bank increase the ledger balance by $120,000:

But this money isn't available to the company immediately. The bank doesn't actually have the money in hand until it has sent the check to the customer's bank and received payment. Since the bank has to wait, it makes United Carbon wait too—usually 1 or 2 business days. In the meantime, the bank will show that United Carbon still has an available balance of only $1 million. The extra $120,000 has been deposited but is not yet available. It is therefore known as **availability float.**

availability float: Checks already deposited that have not yet been cleared.

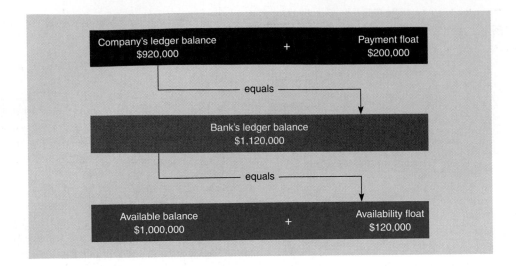

net float: Difference between payment float and availability float.

Notice that the company gains as a result of the payment float and loses as a result of availability float. The **net float** available to the firm is the difference between payment and availability float:

$$\text{Net float} = \text{payment float} - \text{availability float}$$

In our example, the net float is $80,000. The company's available balance is $80,000 greater than the balance shown in its ledger.

▶ **Self-Test 19.1**

Your bank account currently shows a balance of $940. You now deposit $100 into the account and write a check for $40.

a. What is the ledger balance in your account?
b. What is the availability float?
c. What is payment float?
d. What is the bank's ledger balance?
e. Show that your ledger balance plus payment float equals the bank's ledger balance, which in turn equals the available balance plus availability float.

Valuing Float

Float results from the delay between your writing a check and the reduction in your bank balance. The amount of float will therefore depend on the size of the check and the delay in collection.

▶ **Example 19.1**

Float

Suppose that your firm writes checks worth $6,000 per day. It may take 3 days to mail these checks to your suppliers, who then take a day to process the checks and deposit them with their bank. Finally, it may be a further 3 days before the supplier's bank sends the check to your bank, which then debits your account. The total delay is 7 days and the payment float is 7 × $6,000 = $42,000. On average, the available balance at the bank will be $42,000 more than is shown in your firm's ledger. ◀

Figure 19.1

Delays create float. Each heavy arrow represents a source of delay. Recipients try to reduce delay to get available cash sooner. Payers prefer delay so they can use their cash longer.

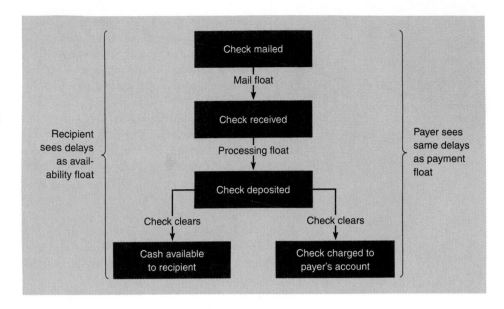

- The time that it takes to mail a check.
- The time that it takes the company to process the check after it has been received.
- The time that it takes the bank to clear the check and adjust the firm's account.

The total collection time is the sum of these three sources of delay.

> **Delays that help the payer hurt the recipient. Recipients try to speed up collections. Payers try to slow down disbursements. Both attempt to minimize net float.**

You probably have come across attempts by companies to reduce float in your own financial transactions. For example, some stores now encourage you to pay bills with your bank debit card instead of a credit card. The payment is automatically debited from your bank account on the day of the transaction, which eliminates the considerable float you otherwise would enjoy until you were billed by your credit card company and paid your bill. Similarly, many companies now arrange *preauthorized payments* with their customers. For example, if you have a mortgage payment on a house, the lender can arrange to have your bank account debited by the amount of the payment each month. The funds are automatically transferred to the lender. You save the work of paying the bill by hand, and the lender saves the few days of float during which your check would have been processed through the banking system.

Speeding Up Collections

concentration banking: System whereby customers make payments to a regional collection center which transfers funds to a principal bank.

One way to speed up collections is by a method known as **concentration banking.** In this case customers in a particular area make payments to a local branch office rather than to company headquarters. The local branch office then deposits the checks into a local bank account. Surplus funds are periodically transferred to a concentration account at one of the company's principal banks.

As financial manager your concern is with the available balance, not with the company's ledger balance. If you know that it is going to be a week before some of your checks are presented for payment, you may be able to get by on a smaller cash balance. The smaller you can keep your cash balance, the more funds you can hold in interest-earning accounts or securities. This game is often called *playing the float*.

You can increase your available cash balance by increasing your net float. This means that you want to ensure that checks received from customers are cleared rapidly and those paid to suppliers are cleared slowly. Perhaps this may sound like rather small change, but think what it can mean to a company like Ford. Ford's daily sales average over $250 million. If it could speed up collections by 1 day, and the interest rate is .02 percent per day (about 7.3 percent per year), it would increase earnings by .0002 × $250 million = $50,000 *per day*.

What would be the present value to Ford if it could *permanently* reduce its collection period by 1 day? That extra interest income would then be a perpetuity, and the present value of the income would be $50,000/.0002 = $250 million, exactly equal to the reduction in float.

Why should this be? Think about the company's cash-flow stream. It receives $250 million a day. At any time, suppose that 4 days' worth of payments are deposited and "in the pipeline." When it speeds up the collection period by a day, the pipeline will shrink to 3 days' worth of payments. At that point, Ford receives an extra $250 million cash flow: it receives the "usual" payment of $250 million, and it also receives the $250 million for which it ordinarily would have had to wait an extra day. From that day forward, it continues to receives $250 million a day, exactly as before. So the net effect of reducing the payment pipeline from 4 days to 3 is that Ford gets an extra up-front payment equal to 1 day of float, or $250 million. We conclude that the present value of a permanent reduction in float is simply the amount by which float is reduced.

However, you should be careful not to become overenthusiastic at managing the float. Writing checks on your account for the sole purpose of creating float and earning interest is called *check kiting* and is illegal. In 1985 the brokerage firm E. F. Hutton pleaded guilty to 2,000 separate counts of mail and wire fraud. Hutton admitted that it had created nearly $1 billion of float by shuffling funds between its branches and through various accounts at different banks.

▶ **Self-Test 19.2** Suppose Ford's stock price is $60 per share, and there are 450 million shares of Ford outstanding. Assume that daily sales average $250 million. Now suppose that technological improvements in the check-clearing process reduce availability float from 4 days to 2 days. What would happen to the stock price? How much should Ford be willing to pay for a new computer system that would reduce availability float by 2 days?

 Managing Float

There are several kinds of delay that create float, so people in the cash management business refer to several kinds of float. Figure 19.1 shows the three sources of float:

a. By how much will Knob's availability float be reduced under the new system?

b. How much extra interest income will the new system generate if the extra funds are used to reduce borrowing under Knob's line of credit with First National? Assume the interest rate is 12 percent.

c. Finally, should Knob accept First National's offer if collection costs under the old system are $40,000 per year?

16. **Float Management.** A few years ago, Merrill Lynch increased its float by mailing checks drawn on West Coast banks to customers in the East and checks drawn on East Coast banks to customers in the West. A subsequent class action suit against Merrill Lynch revealed that in 28 months from September 1976 Merrill Lynch disbursed $1.25 billion in 365,000 checks to New York State customers alone. The plaintiff's lawyer calculated that by using a remote bank Merrill Lynch had increased its average float by 1½ days.[4]

a. How much did Merrill Lynch disburse per day to New York State customers?

b. What was the total gain to Merrill Lynch over the 28 months, assuming an interest rate of 8 percent?

c. What was the present value of the increase in float if the benefits were expected to be permanent?

d. Suppose that the use of remote banks had involved Merrill Lynch in extra expenses. What was the maximum extra cost per check that Merrill Lynch would have been prepared to pay?

17. **Optimal Cash Balances.** Suppose that your weekly cash expenses are $80. Every time you withdraw money from the automated teller at your bank, you are charged 15 cents. Your bank account pays interest of 3 percent annually.

a. How often should you withdraw funds from the bank?

b. What is the optimal-sized withdrawal?

c. What is your average amount of cash on hand?

18. **Economic Order Quantity.** A large consulting firm orders photocopying paper by the carton. The firm pays a $30 delivery charge on each order. The total cost of storing the paper, including forgone interest, storage space, and deterioration, comes to about $1.50 per carton per month. The firm uses about 1,000 cartons of paper per month.

a. Fill in the following table:

	Order Size			
	100	**200**	**250**	**500**
Orders per month	_____	_____	_____	_____
Total order cost	_____	_____	_____	_____
Average inventory	_____	_____	_____	_____
Total carrying costs	_____	_____	_____	_____
Total inventory costs	_____	_____	_____	_____

b. Calculate the economic order quantity. Is your answer consistent with your findings in part (a)?

19. **Economic Order Quantity.** Micro-Encapsulator Corp. (MEC) expects to sell 7,200 miniature home encapsulators this year. The cost of placing an order from its supplier is $250. Each unit costs $50 and carrying costs are 20 percent of the purchase price.

a. What is the economic order quantity?

b. What are total costs—order costs plus carrying costs—of inventory over the course of the year?

[4]See I. Ross, "The Race Is to the Slow Payer," *Fortune,* April 1983, pp. 75–80.

20. **Inventory Management.** Suppose now that the supplier in the previous problem offers a 1 percent discount on orders of 1,800 units or more. Should MEC accept the supplier's offer?

21. **Economic Order Quantity.** Genuine Gems orders a full month's worth of precious stones at the beginning of every month. Over the course of the month, it sells off its stock, at which point it restocks inventory for the following month. It sells 200 gems per month, and the monthly carrying cost is $1 per gem. The fixed order cost is $20 per order. Should the firm adjust its inventory policy? If so, should it order smaller stocks more frequently or larger stocks less frequently?

22. **Economic Order Quantity.** Patty's Pancakes orders pancake mix once a week. The mix is used up by the end of the week, at which point more is reordered. Each time Patty orders pancake mix, she spends about a half hour of her time, which she estimates is worth $20. Patty sells 200 pounds of pancakes each week. The carrying cost of each pound of the mix is 5 cents per week. Should Patty restock more or less frequently? What is the cost-minimizing order size? How many times per month should Patty restock?

23. **Inventory Management.** A just-in-time inventory system reduces the cost of ordering additional inventory by a factor of 100. What is the change in the optimal order size predicted by the economic order quantity model?

24. **Cash and Inventory Management.** According to the economic order quantity inventory model and the Baumol model of cash management, what will happen to cash balances and inventory levels if the firm's production and sales both double? What is the implication of your answer for percentage of sales financial planning models (see Section 17.2)?

Solutions to Self-Test Questions

19.1 a. The ledger balance is $940 + $100 − $40 = $1,000.
 b. Availability float is $100, since you do not yet have access to the funds you have deposited.
 c. Payment float is $40, since the check that you wrote has not yet cleared.
 d. The bank's ledger balance is $940 + $100 = $1,040. The bank is aware of the check you deposited but is not aware of the check you wrote.
 e. Ledger balance plus payment float = $1,000 + $40 = $1,040, which equals the bank's ledger balance. Available balance + availability float = $940 + $100 = $1,040, also equal to the bank's ledger balance.

19.2 The current market value of Ford is $27 billion. The 2-day reduction in float is worth $500 million. This increases the value of Ford to $27.5 billion. The new stock price will be $61.11 per share. Ford should be willing to pay up to $500 million for the system, since the present value of the savings is $500 million.

19.3 The benefit of the lock-box system, and the price the firm should be willing to pay for the system, is higher when:

 a. Payment size is higher (since interest is earned on more funds).
 b. Payments per day are higher (since interest is earned on more funds).
 c. The interest rate is higher (since the cost of float is higher).
 d. Mail time saved is higher (since more float is saved).
 e. Processing time saved is higher (since more float is saved).

19.4 a.

Order Size	Orders per Year	Average Inventory	Order Costs	Carrying Costs	Total Costs
Bricks per Order	$\dfrac{1{,}250{,}000}{\text{Bricks per Order}}$	$\dfrac{\text{Order Size}}{2}$	$90 per Order	$.09 per Brick	Order Costs plus Carrying Costs
1,000,000	1.25	500,000	$ 113	$45,000	$45,113
500,000	2.50	250,000	225	22,500	22,725
200,000	6.25	100,000	563	9,000	9,563
100,000	12.50	50,000	1,125	4,500	5,625
60,000	20.83	30,000	1,875	2,700	4,575
50,000	25.00	25,000	2,250	2,250	4,500
20,000	62.50	10,000	5,625	900	6,525
10,000	125.00	5,000	11,250	450	11,700

b. The optimal order size decreases to 50,000 bricks:

$$Q^* = \sqrt{\frac{2 \times \text{annual sales} \times \text{costs per order}}{\text{carrying cost}}}$$

$$= \sqrt{\frac{2 \times 1{,}250{,}000 \times 90}{.09}} = 50{,}000$$

Therefore, the average inventory level will fall to 25,000 bricks. The effect of the higher carrying costs more than offsets the effect of the higher sales.

19.5 At an interest rate of 4 percent, the optimal initial cash balance is

$$\sqrt{\frac{2 \times 1{,}260{,}000 \times 20}{.04}}$$

= $35,496. The average cash balance will be one-half this amount, or $17,748. The firm will need to sell securities 1,260,000/35,496 = 35.5 times per year. Therefore, annual trading costs will be 35.5 × $20 = $710 per year. Because the interest rate is lower, the firm is willing to hold larger cash balances.

19.6 a. Higher interest rates will lead to lower cash balances.

b. Higher volatility will lead to higher cash balances.

c. Higher transaction costs will lead to higher cash balances.

Consolidated Balance Sheet

(in millions except per share amount)
PepsiCo, Inc. and Subsidiaries
December 28, 1996 and December 30, 1995

	1996	1995
ASSETS		
Current Assets		
Cash and cash equivalents	$ 447	$ 382
Short-term investments, at cost	339	1,116
	786	1,498
Accounts and notes receivable, less allowance: $183 in 1996 and $150 in 1995.	2,516	2,407
Inventories	1,038	1,051
Prepaid expenses, deferred income taxes and other current assets	799	590
Total Current Assets	5,139	5,546
Property, Plant and Equipment, net.	10,191	9,870
Intangible Assets, net.	7,136	7,584
Investments in Unconsolidated Affiliates	1,375	1,635
Other Assets.	671	797
Total Assets	$24,512	$25,432
LIABILITIES AND SHAREHOLDERS' EQUITY		
Current Liabilities		
Accounts payable and other current liabilities	$ 4,626	$ 4,137
Income taxes payable	487	387
Short-term borrowings	26	706
Total Current Liabilities.	5,139	5,230
Long-term Debt	8,439	8,509
Other Liabilities	2,533	2,495
Deferred Income Taxes.	1,778	1,885
Shareholders' Equity		
Capital stock, par value 1 2/3¢ per share: authorized 3,600 shares, issued 1,726 shares	29	29
Capital in excess of par value.	1,201	1,045
Retained earnings	9,184	8,730
Currency translation adjustment and other	(768)	(808)
	9,646	8,996
Less: Treasury stock, at cost: 181 shares and 150 shares in 1996 and 1995, respectively	(3,023)	(1,683)
Total Shareholders' Equity.	6,623	7,313
Total Liabilities and Shareholders' Equity.	$24,512	$25,432

PepsiCo's accounts show that it is owed $2.5 billion by its customers.
How do companies decide on the amount of credit that they give their customers?
Printed with permission of © PepsiCo, Inc. 1996

Credit Management and Bankruptcy

When companies sell their products, they sometimes demand cash on delivery, but in most cases they allow a delay in payment. The customers' promises to pay for their purchases constitute a valuable asset; therefore, the accountant enters these promises in the balance sheet as accounts receivable. If you turn back to the balance sheet in Table 18.1, you can see that accounts receivable constitute on the average more than one-third of a firm's current assets. These receivables include both trade credit to other firms and consumer credit to retail customers. The former is by far the larger and will therefore be the main focus of this chapter. Credit management involves the following steps, which we will discuss in turn.

First, you must establish the *terms of sale* on which you propose to sell your goods. How long are you going to give customers to pay their bills? Are you prepared to offer a cash discount for prompt payment?

Second, you must decide what evidence you need that the customer owes you money. Do you just ask the buyer to sign a receipt, or do you insist on a more formal IOU?

Third, you must consider which customers are likely to pay their bills. This is called *credit analysis*. Do you judge this from the customer's past payment record or past financial statements? Do you also rely on bank references?

Fourth, you must decide on *credit policy*. How much credit are you prepared to extend to each customer? Do you play safe by turning down any doubtful prospects? Or do you accept the risk of a few bad debts as part of the cost of building up a large regular clientele?

Fifth, after you have granted credit, you have the problem of collecting the money when it becomes due. This is called *collection policy*. How do you keep track of payments and pursue slow payers? If all goes well, this is the end of the matter. But sometimes you will find that the customer is bankrupt and cannot pay. In this case you need to understand how bankruptcy works.

After studying the chapter you should be able to

▶ Measure the implicit interest rate on credit.

▶ Understand when it makes sense to ask the customer for a formal IOU.

▶ Explain how firms can assess the probability that a customer will pay.

▶ Decide whether it makes sense to grant credit to that customer.

▶ Summarize the bankruptcy procedures when firms cannot pay their creditors.

Terms of Sale

terms of sale: Credit, discount, and payment terms offered on a sale.

Whenever you sell goods, you need to set the **terms of sale.** For example, if you are supplying goods to a wide variety of irregular customers, you may require cash on delivery (COD). And if you are producing goods to the customer's specification or incurring heavy delivery costs, then it may be sensible to ask for cash before delivery (CBD).

Some contracts provide for *progress payments* as work is carried out. For example, a large consulting contract might call for 30 percent payment after completion of field research, 30 percent more on submission of a draft report, and the remaining 40 percent when the project is finally completed.

In many other cases, payment is not made until after delivery, so the buyer receives *credit*. Each industry seems to have its own typical credit arrangements. These arrangements have a rough logic. For example, the seller will naturally demand earlier payment if its customers are financially less secure, if their accounts are small, or if the goods are perishable or quickly resold.

When you buy goods on credit, the supplier will state a final payment date. To encourage you to pay *before* the final date, it is common to offer a cash discount for prompt settlement. For example, a manufacturer may require payment within 30 days but offer a 5 percent discount to customers who pay within 10 days. These terms would be referred to as 5/10, net 30:

5	/	10,	net 30
↑		↑	↑
percent discount for early payment		number of days that discount is available	number of days before payment is due

Similarly, if a firm sells goods on terms of 2/30, net 60, customers receive a 2 percent discount for payment within 30 days or else must pay in full within 60 days. If the terms are simply net 30, then customers must pay within 30 days of the invoice date, and no discounts are offered for early payment.

▶ **Self-Test 20.1**   Suppose that a firm sells goods on terms of 2/10, net 20. On May 1 you buy goods from the company with an invoice value of $20,000. How much would you need to pay if you took the cash discount? What is the latest date on which the cash discount is available? By what date should you pay for your purchase if you decide not to take the cash discount?

For many items that are bought regularly, it is inconvenient to require separate payment for each delivery. A common solution is to pretend that all sales during the month in fact occur at the end of the month (EOM). Thus goods may be sold on terms of 8/10, *EOM,* net 60. This allows the customer a cash discount of 8 percent if the bill is paid within 10 days of the end of the month; otherwise the full payment is due within 60 days of the invoice date.

When purchases are subject to seasonal fluctuations, manufacturers often encourage customers to take early delivery by allowing them to delay payment until the usual order season. This practice is known as *season dating*. For example, summer products might have terms of 2/10, net 30, but the invoice might be dated May 1 even if the sale takes place in February. The discount is then available until May 10, and the bill is not due until May 30.

> **A firm that buys on credit is in effect borrowing from its supplier. It saves cash today but will have to pay later. This, of course, is an implicit loan from the supplier.**

Of course, a free loan is always worth having. But if you pass up a cash discount, then the loan may prove to be very expensive. For example, a customer who buys on terms of 3/10, net 30 may decide to forgo the cash discount and pay on the thirtieth day. The customer obtains an extra 20 days' credit by deferring payment from 10 to 30 days after the sale but pays about 3 percent more for the goods. This is equivalent to borrowing money at a rate of 74.3 percent a year. To see why, consider an order of $100. If the firm pays within 10 days, it gets a 3 percent discount and pays only $97. If it waits the full 30 days, it pays $100. The extra 20 days of credit increase the payment by the fraction 3/97 = .0309, or 3.09 percent. Therefore, the implicit interest charged to extend the trade credit is 3.09 percent *per 20 days*. There are 365/20 = 18.25 twenty-day periods in a year, so the effective annual rate of interest on the loan is $(1.0309)^{18.25} - 1 = .743$, or 74.3 percent.

The general formula for calculating the implicit annual interest rate for customers who do not take the cash discount is

$$\text{Effective annual rate} = \left(1 + \frac{\text{discount}}{\text{discounted price}}\right)^{365/\text{extra days credit}} - 1$$

The discount divided by the discounted price is the percentage increase in price paid by a customer who forgoes the discount. In our example, with terms of 3/10, net 30, the percentage increase in price is 3/97 = .0309, or 3.09 percent. This is the per-period implicit rate of interest. The period of the loan is the number of extra days of credit that you can obtain by forgoing the discount. In our example, this is 20 days. To annualize this rate, we compound the per-period rate by the number of periods in a year.

Of course any firm that delays payment beyond day 30 gains a cheaper loan but damages its reputation for creditworthiness.

▶ Example 20.1   *Trade Credit Rates*

What is the implied interest rate on the trade credit if the discount for early payment is 5/10, net 60?

The cash discount in this case is 5 percent and customers who choose not to take the discount receive an extra $60 - 10 = 50$ days credit. So the effective annual interest is

$$\text{Effective annual rate} = \left(1 + \frac{\text{discount}}{\text{discounted price}}\right)^{365/\text{extra days credit}} - 1$$

$$= \left(1 + \frac{5}{95}\right)^{365/50} - 1 = .454, \text{ or } 45.4\%$$

In this case the customer who does not take the discount is effectively borrowing money at an annual interest rate of 45.4 percent.

You might wonder why the effective interest rate on trade credit is typically so high. Part of the rate should be viewed as compensation for the costs the firm anticipates in collecting from slow payers. After all, at such steep effective rates, most purchasers will choose to pay early and receive the discount. Therefore, you might interpret the choice to stretch payables as a sign of financial difficulties. It follows that the interest rate you charge to these firms should be high.

▶ **Self-Test 20.2**   What would be the effective annual interest rate in Example 20.1 if the terms of sale were 5/10, net 50? Why is the rate higher?

Credit Agreements

open account: Agreement whereby sales are made with no formal debt contract.

The terms of sale define the amount of any credit but not the nature of the contract. Repetitive sales are almost always made on **open account** and involve only an implicit contract. There is simply a record in the seller's books and a receipt signed by the buyer.

Sometimes you might want a more formal agreement that the customer owes you money. Where the order is very large and there is no complicating cash discount, the customer may be asked to sign a *promissory note*. This is just a straightforward IOU, worded along the following lines:

> New York
> April 1, 1997
>
> Sixty days after date, ABC, Inc., promises to pay to the order of the XYZ Company ten thousand dollars ($10,000) for value received.
>
> Signature

Such an arrangement is not common but it does eliminate the possibility of any subsequent disputes about the amount and existence of the debt; the customer knows that he or she may be sued immediately for failure to pay on the due date.

If you want a clear commitment from the buyer, it is more useful to have it *before* you deliver the goods. In this case the common procedure is to arrange a *commercial draft*.[1] This is simply jargon for an order to pay. It works as follows. The seller prepares a draft ordering payment by the customer and sends this draft to the customer's bank. If immediate payment is required, the draft is termed a *sight draft;* otherwise it is known as a *time draft*. Depending on whether it is a sight or a time draft, the customer either tells the bank to pay up or acknowledges the debt by adding the word *accepted* and a signature. Once accepted, a time draft is like a post-dated check and is called a *trade acceptance*. This trade acceptance is then forwarded to the seller, who holds it until the payment becomes due.

If the customer's credit is for any reason suspect, the seller may ask the customer to arrange for his or her bank to accept the time draft. In this case, the bank guarantees the customer's debt and the draft is called a *banker's acceptance*. Banker's acceptances are often used in overseas trade. They are actively bought and sold in the money market, the market for short-term high-quality debt.

If you sell goods to a customer who proves unable to pay, you cannot get your goods back. You simply become a general creditor of the company, in common with

---

[1] For example, a check is an example of a draft. Whenever you write a check, you are ordering the bank to make a payment.

other unfortunates. You can avoid this situation by making a *conditional sale,* so that ownership of the goods remains with the seller until full payment is made. The conditional sale is common in Europe. In the United States it is used only for goods that are bought on installment. In this case, if the customer fails to make the agreed number of payments, then the equipment can be immediately repossessed by the seller.

Credit Analysis

credit analysis: Procedure to determine the likelihood a customer will pay its bills.

There are a number of ways to find out whether customers are likely to pay their debts, that is, to carry out **credit analysis.** The most obvious indication is whether they have paid promptly in the past. Prompt payment is usually a good omen, but beware of the customer who establishes a high credit limit on the basis of small payments and then disappears, leaving you with a large unpaid bill.

If you are dealing with a new customer, you will probably check with a credit agency. Dun & Bradstreet, which is by far the largest of these agencies, provides credit ratings on several million domestic and foreign firms. In addition to its rating service, Dun & Bradstreet provides on request a full credit report on a potential customer.

Credit agencies usually report the experience that other firms have had with your customer, but you can also get this information by contacting those firms directly or through a credit bureau.

Your bank can also make a credit check. It will contact the customer's bank and ask for information on the customer's average bank balance, access to bank credit, and general reputation.

In addition to checking with your customer's bank, it might make sense to check what everybody else in the financial community thinks about your customer's credit standing. Does that sound expensive? Not if your customer is a public company. You just look at the Moody's or Standard & Poor's rating for the customer's bonds.[2] You can also compare prices of these bonds to the prices of other firms' bonds. (Of course the comparisons should be between bonds of similar maturity, coupon, and so on.) Finally, you can look at how the customer's stock price has been behaving recently. A sharp fall in price doesn't mean that the company is in trouble, but it does suggest that prospects are less bright than formerly.

Financial Ratio Analysis

We have suggested a number of ways to check whether your customer is a good risk. You can ask your collection manager, a specialized credit agency, a credit bureau, a banker, or the financial community at large. But if you don't like relying on the judgment of others, you can do your own homework. Ideally this would involve a detailed analysis of the company's business prospects and financing, but this is usually too expensive. Therefore, credit analysts concentrate on the company's financial statements, using rough rules of thumb to judge whether the firm is a good credit risk. The rules of thumb are based on *financial ratios.* Chapter 16 described how these ratios are calculated and interpreted.

[2]We described bond ratings in Chapter 12, Section 12.3.

Numerical Credit Scoring

Analyzing credit risk is like detective work. You have a lot of clues—some important, some fitting into a neat pattern, others contradictory. You must weigh these clues to come up with an overall judgment.

When the firm has a small, regular clientele, the credit manager can easily handle the process informally and make a judgment about what are often termed the *five Cs of credit:*

1. The customer's *character*
2. The customer's *capacity* to pay
3. The customer's *capital*
4. The *collateral* provided by the customer[3]
5. The *condition* of the customer's business

When the company is dealing directly with consumers or with a large number of small trade accounts, some streamlining is essential. In these cases it may make sense to use a scoring system to prescreen credit applications.

If you apply for a credit card or bank loan, you will be asked various questions about your job, home, and financial position. One medium-sized bank required each loan applicant to answer a standard questionnaire, of which a condensed version is shown in Table 20.1.[4] It found that in total only 1.2 percent of these loans subsequently defaulted. Some categories of borrower, however, proved to be much worse credit risks than others. We have added the actual default rates for each category in the right-hand margin of Table 20.1. For example, you can see that 7.0 percent of the borrowers who had no telephone subsequently defaulted. Similarly, poor credit risks included borrowers who lived in rented rooms, had no bank account, needed the loan to pay medical bills, and so on.

Given this experience, it might make sense for the bank to calculate an overall risk index for each applicant.[5] For example, it could construct a rough-and-ready index simply by adding up all the probabilities in Table 20.1. In this case, the higher the score, the worse the credit rating. The wretch who gave the most unfavorable response to each question would have a risk index of

$$7.0 + 7.3 + 2.6 + \cdots = 51.8$$

As if he (or she) didn't have enough troubles!

▶ **Self-Test 20.3**   How much better would the score be if the person bought a phone? What feature in Table 20.1 is potentially the most important determinant of credit rating?

---

[3]For example, the customer can offer bonds as collateral. These bonds can then be seized by the seller if the customer fails to pay.

[4]See P. F. Smith, "Measuring Risk on Consumer Installment Credit," *Management Science* 11 (November 1964), pp. 327–340.

[5]There are some measures you *cannot* use in calculating this risk index or in any other credit evaluation—the applicant's sex or race, for example. We also should note that this table is designed for evaluating the credit risk of an individual. Obviously, a firm's creditworthiness will entail different considerations.

1.	Do you have:		7.	What is your marital status:	
	1 or more telephones?	(.7)		Single?	(1.6)
	No telephone?	(7.0)		Married?	(1.0)
2.	Do you:			Divorced?	(2.9)
	Own your home?	(.7)	8.	What is your postal zone?	(.1 to 11.4)
	Rent a house?	(2.2)	9.	For how long do you require the loan:	
	Rent an apartment?	(3.3)		12 months or less?	(1.6)
	Rent a room?	(7.3)		More than 12 months?	(1.0)
3.	Do you:		10.	What is your occupation?	(.4 to 3.5)
	Have 1 or more bank accounts?	(.8)	11.	What is your monthly income:	
	No bank account?	(2.6)		$200 or less?	(2.3)
4.	Is the purpose of the loan:			$200 to $1000?	(1.1)
	To buy an automobile?	(.8)		More than $1000?	(.7)
	To buy household goods?	(.6)	12.	What is your age:	
	To pay medical expenses?	(2.5)		25 or under?	(1.5)
	Other?	(1.3)		26 to 30?	(1.8)
5.	How long did you spend in your last residence:			More than 30?	(1.0)
	6 months or less?	(3.1)	13.	How many are there in your family:	
	7 to 60 months?	(1.4)		One?	(1.6)
	More than 60 months?	(1.8)		Two to seven?	(1.1)
6.	How long did you spend in your last job?			Eight or more?	(2.6)
	6 months?	(3.2)			
	7 to 60 months?	(1.5)			
	More than 60 months?	(.9)			

Source: Reprinted by permission from Paul F. Smith, "Measuring Risk on Consumer Installment Credit," *Management Science,* **II:** 327–340 (November 1964). Copyright 1964, The Institute of Management Sciences, Currently (informs), 2 Charles Street, Suite 300, Providence, RI 02904 USA.

Table 20.1

A condensed version of a questionnaire used by a bank for personal loan applicants. We have added in parentheses the percentage of borrowers in each category who subsequently defaulted.

The questionnaire in Table 20.1 is of course dated—not many loan applicants have a monthly income below $200! We wish we could give a real, current example, but they are all top secret: a bank with a superior method for identifying good and bad borrowers has a significant advantage over the competition.

Many users of credit scoring systems employ ad hoc formulas. For example, just adding up the separate probabilities, as in our bank example, ignores the interactions between the different factors. It may be much more alarming when a family of eight rents a single room than when a single applicant does.

Firms use several statistical techniques to separate the creditworthy sheep from the impecunious goats. One common method employs *multiple discriminant analysis* to produce a measure of solvency called a *Z score*. For example, a study by Edward Altman suggested the following relationship between a firm's financial ratios and its creditworthiness (Z):[6]

$$Z = 3.3 \frac{\text{EBIT}}{\text{total assets}} + 1.0 \frac{\text{sales}}{\text{total assets}} + .6 \frac{\text{market value of equity}}{\text{total book debt}}$$

$$+ 1.4 \frac{\text{retained earnings}}{\text{total assets}} + 1.2 \frac{\text{working capital}}{\text{total assets}}$$

[6]EBIT is earnings before interest and taxes. E. I. Altman, "Financial Ratios, Discriminant Analysis and the Prediction of Corporate Bankruptcy," *Journal of Finance* 23 (September 1968), pp. 589–609.

This equation did a good job at distinguishing the bankrupt and nonbankrupt firms. Of the former, 94 percent had *Z* scores *less* than 2.7 before they went bankrupt. In contrast, 97 percent of the nonbankrupt firms had *Z* scores *above* this level.[7]

▶ **Example 20.2** *Credit Scoring*

Consider a firm with the following financial ratios:

$$\frac{\text{EBIT}}{\text{total assets}} = .12 \qquad \frac{\text{sales}}{\text{total assets}} = 1.4 \qquad \frac{\text{market equity}}{\text{book debt}} = .9 \qquad \frac{\text{retained earnings}}{\text{total assets}} = .4$$

$$\frac{\text{working capital}}{\text{total assets}} = .12$$

The firm's *Z* score is thus

$$(3.3 \times .12) + (1.0 \times 1.4) + (.6 \times .9) + (1.4 \times .4) + (1.2 \times .12) = 3.04$$

This score is above the cutoff level for predicting bankruptcy, and thus would be considered favorably in terms of evaluating the firm's creditworthiness.

 See box p. 576

The nearby box describes how statistical scoring systems similar to the *Z* score can provide timely first-cut estimates of creditworthiness. These assessments can streamline the credit decision and free up labor for other, less mechanical tasks. The box notes that these scoring systems can be used in conjunction with large databases on firms, such as that of Dun & Bradstreet, to provide quick credit scores for thousands of firms.

When to Stop Looking for Clues

We told you earlier where to start looking for clues about a customer's creditworthiness, but we never said anything about when to *stop*. A detailed credit analysis costs money, so you need to keep the following basic principle in mind

Credit analysis is worthwhile only if the expected savings exceed the cost.

This simple rule has two immediate implications:

1. *Don't undertake a full credit analysis unless the order is big enough to justify it.* If the maximum profit on an order is $100, it is foolish to spend $200 to check whether the customer is a good prospect. Rely on a less detailed credit check for the smaller orders and save your energy and your money for the big orders.
2. *Undertake a full credit analysis for the doubtful orders only.* If a preliminary check suggests that a customer is almost certainly a good prospect, then the extra gain from a more searching inquiry is unlikely to justify the costs. That is why many firms use a numerical credit scoring system to identify borderline applicants, who are then the subject of a full-blown detailed credit check. Other applicants are either accepted or rejected without further question.

---

[7]This equation was fitted with hindsight. The equation did slightly less well when used to *predict* bankruptcies after 1965.

System Cuts the Risks

Case Study / Hunter Timber

When Hunter Timber, an offshoot of the Wickes Group, appointed a credit director who describes himself as primarily a business analyst it got more than it bargained for. Risk assessment is now undertaken by a powerful credit monitoring system developed in conjunction with Dun & Bradstreet, the business information group. Not only does the program eliminate many of the mundane duties which were executed by credit analysts, it also assists the operations of the marketing department.

The system, called Decision Index, was created for the company after the arrival of John Griffiths as credit director. Mr. Griffiths, who is now merchanting director at the company, found the methods of traditional credit management too labor-intensive. Particularly unsatisfactory, he thought, were the response times, averaging four to five days, to credit requests from Hunter's branches. To speed up such response times and generally streamline the credit analysis operation, Mr. Griffiths wanted a system that would cut the paperwork involved in many credit applications and free credit analysts to meet customers.

Hunter Timber's approach to Dun & Bradstreet to work on the production of a credit monitoring system was a natural one as the company had used D&B's financial information services for a number of years. D&B's business information service had been contemplating the development of such a program. The system took 12 months to complete and Hunter's credit management implemented it last August. Mr. Griffiths believes it has transformed the role of credit analysis. "The response time to branches has been reduced from days to just minutes. Also, we are able to pre-credit customers and give answers to their credit requests far more quickly."

Decision Index functions by tapping into a large database supplied by Dun & Bradstreet and cross-referring to Hunter's own customer information and credit demands. In the databases is filed comprehensive information on several thousand companies which supply their details to D&B. In addition to the detailed information, basic business dossiers are potentially available on 38 thousand companies worldwide and nearly 2 thousand in the UK.

The detailed files in the databases used by Decision Index enables sales data updates and payment records to be accessed. Another important feature of the system, according to Mr. Philip Mellor, senior analyst at D&B, is that the information is dynamically updated. "It is updated overnight with any information that we may receive on a company from a variety of sources such as payment data." However, Mr. Mellor is quick to stress that such a monitoring device is no substitute for human credit management. Rather it is a sophisticated filter after which significant decisions are still the responsibility of the credit analyst. "It doesn't work without people being involved. If a score goes to a certain level then that is fine and it is accepted by the system, but if it doesn't reach the required level then we don't necessarily say we won't deal with the customer. A credit analyst will then look more closely at the proposal," says Mr. Griffiths.

Source: Christine Buckley, "System Cuts the Risks: Case Study/Hunter Timber," *Financial Times Survey of Credit Management,* March 6, 1995.

The Credit Decision

You have taken the first three steps toward an effective credit operation. In other words, you have fixed your terms of sale; you have decided whether to sell on open account or to ask your customers to sign an IOU; and you have established a procedure for estimating the probability that each customer will pay up. Your next step is to decide on **credit policy.**

credit policy: Standards set to determine the amount and nature of credit to extend to customers.

If there is no possibility of repeat orders, the credit decision is relatively simple. Figure 20.1 summarizes your choice. On the one hand, you can refuse credit and pass up the sale. In this case you make neither profit nor loss. The alternative is to offer

Figure 20.1
If you refuse credit, you make neither profit nor loss. If you offer credit, there is a probability p that the customer will pay and you will make REV − COST; there is a probability (1 − p) that the customer will default and you will lose COST.

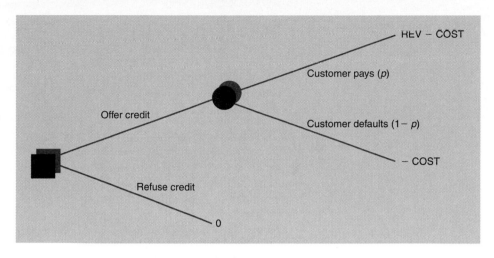

credit. If you offer credit and the customer pays, you benefit by the profit margin on the sale. If the customer defaults, you lose the cost of the goods delivered.

> **The decision to offer credit depends on the probability of payment. You should grant credit if the expected profit from doing so is greater than the profit from refusing.**

Suppose that the probability that the customer will pay up is p. If the customer does pay, you receive additional revenues (REV) and you deliver goods that you incurred costs to produce; your net gain is the present value of REV − COST. Unfortunately, you can't be certain that the customer will pay; there is a probability $(1 − p)$ of default. Default means you receive nothing but still incur the additional costs of the delivered goods. The *expected profit*[8] from the two sources of action is therefore as follows:

> **Refuse credit: 0**
> **Grant credit: $p \times$ PV(REV − COST) − $(1 − p) \times$ PV(COST)**

You should grant credit if the expected profit from doing so is positive.

▶ **Example 20.3** *The Credit Decision*

Consider the case of the Cast Iron Company. On each nondelinquent sale Cast Iron receives revenues with a present value of $1,200 and incurs costs with a present value of $1,000. Therefore, the company's expected profit if it offers credit is

$$p \times \text{PV(REV − COST)} − (1 − p) \times \text{PV(COST)} = p \times 200 − (1 − p) \times 1{,}000$$

---

[8]Notice that we use the present values of costs and revenues. This is because there sometimes are significant lags between costs incurred and revenues generated. Also, while we follow convention in referring to the "expected profit" of the decision, it should be clear that our equation for expected profit is in fact the net present value of the decision to grant credit. As we emphasized in Chapter 1, the manager's task is to add value, not to maximize accounting profits.

If the probability of collection is 5/6, Cast Iron can expect to break even:

$$\text{Expected profit} = 5/6 \times 200 - (1 - 5/6) \times 1,000 = 0$$

Thus Cast Iron's policy should be to grant credit whenever the chances of collection are better than 5 out of 6.

In this last example, the net present value of granting credit is positive if the probability of collection exceeds 5/6. In general, this break-even probability can be found by setting the net present value of granting credit equal to zero and solving for p. It turns out that the formula for the break-even probability is simply the ratio of the present value of costs to revenues:

$$p \times \text{PV(REV} - \text{COST)} - (1 - p) \times \text{PV(COST)} = 0$$

Break-even probability of collection, then, is

$$p = \frac{\text{PV(COST)}}{\text{PV(REV)}}$$

▶ **Self-Test 20.4**   What is the break-even probability of collection if the present value of the revenues from the sale are $1,100 rather than $1,200? Why does the break-even probability increase? Use your answer to decide whether firms that sell high-profit-margin or low-margin goods should be more willing to issue credit.

Credit Decisions with Repeat Orders

What effect does the possibility of repeat orders have on your credit decision? One of the reasons for offering credit today is that you may get yourself a good, regular customer.

Cast Iron has been asked to extend credit to a new customer. You can find little information on the firm and you believe that the probability of payment is no better than .8. If you grant credit, the expected profit on this order is

$$\text{Expected profit on initial order} = p \times \text{PV(REV} - \text{COST)} - (1 - p) \times \text{PV(COST)}$$
$$= (.8 \times 200) - (.2 \times 1,000) = -\$40$$

You decide to refuse credit.

This is the correct decision *if* there is no chance of a repeat order. But now consider future periods. If the customer does pay up, there will be a reorder next year. Having paid once, the customer will seem less of a risk. For this reason, any repeat order is very profitable.

Think back to Chapter 7, and you will recognize that the credit decision bears many similarities to our earlier discussion of real options. By granting credit now, the firm retains the option to grant credit on an entire sequence of potentially profitable repeat sales. This option can be very valuable and can tilt the decision toward granting credit. Even a dubious prospect may warrant some initial credit if there is a chance that it will develop into a profitable steady customer.

h accepting a rel-
customer will grow
card companies are
can point to an estab-
incur more bad debts
yet formed relation-
of building up a good

with Repeat Orders

an extreme case. Suppose that if a customer pays up on the
you will have a regular and completely reliable customer.
uch a customer is not the profit on one order but an entire
at purchases. For example, suppose that the customer will
ear from Cast Iron. If the discount rate is 10 percent and
200 a year, then the present value of an indefinite stream
omer is not $200 but $200/.10 = $2,000. There is a prob-
secure a good customer with a value of $2,000. There is
the customer will default, resulting in a loss of $1,000.
nefits of securing a good and permanent customer, the
credit is

$$= (p \times 2,000) - (1 - p) \times (1,000)$$

ity of collection above .33. Thus the break-even prob-

date. But they don't, and,
gether blame them.
require the firm to spend
he firm to invest more in
eivable are proportional to
receivables):

ollection period

a longer collection period
must establish a **collection**

nces with each customer. In
awing up a schedule of the
ints receivable by the length
Table 20.2. The table shows
no bills outstanding for more
lems, as there are $15,000 in

s.
to send a *statement of account*
ent letters, telephone calls, or
mpanies turn the debt over to

table repeat sales, the firm should be
e initial purchase.

vary with the discount rate? Try a rate of 20 per-
ntuition behind your answer?

nore complex than our simple examples. Cus-
ny pay late consistently; you get your money,
se a few months' interest. And estimating the
is far from an exact science.
edit allocation involves a strong dose of judg-
inders of the issues involved rather than as
ings to remember.

r job is not to minimize the number of bad
i are faced with a trade-off. The best that
iromptly; the worst is default. In the one
revenues from the sale less the additional
nd loses the costs. You must weigh the
the margin of profit is high, you are jus-
, you cannot afford many bad debts.
iu should not expend the same effort on
ion is small or clear-cut, your decision
doubtful, you may do better to move
edit managers don't make credit deci-
y set a credit limit for each customer.
ie order for approval only if the cus-

	More than 3 Months	Total Owed
s	$ 0	$ 10,000
	0	11,000
	•	•
	•	•
	•	•
	15,000	30,000
	$43,000	$298,000

3. *Look beyond the immediate order.* Sometimes it may b
   atively poor risk as long as there is a likelihood that t
   into a regular and reliable buyer. (This is why cred
   eager to sign up college students even though few student
   lished credit history.) New businesses must be prepared t
   than established businesses because they have not
   ships with low-risk customers. This is part of the cost
   customer list.

Collection Policy

It would be nice if all customers paid their bills by the due
since you may also "stretch" your payables, you can't altog

Slow payers impose two costs on the firm. First, they
more resources in collecting payments. They also force t
working capital. Recall from Chapter 16 that accounts rec
the average collection period (also known as days' sales i

$$\text{Accounts receivable} = \text{daily sales} \times \text{average}$$

collection policy: Procedures to collect and monitor receivables.

aging schedule: Classification of accounts receivable by time outstanding.

When your customers stretch payables, you end up with
and a greater investment in accounts receivable. Thus you
policy.

The credit manager keeps a record of payment experie
addition, the manager monitors overdue payments by d
aging of receivables. The **aging schedule** classifies acco
of time they are outstanding. This may look roughly like
that customer A, for example, is fully current: there are
than a month. Customer Z, however, might present prob
bills that have been outstanding for more than 3 month

When a customer is in arrears, the usual procedure is
and to follow this at intervals with increasingly insist
fax messages. If none of these has any effect, most cc
a collection agency or an attorney.

Table 20.2
An aging schedule of receivables

Customer's Name	Less than 1 Month	1–2 Months	2–3 Month
A	$ 10,000	$ 0	$ 0
B	8,000	3,000	0
•	•	•	•
•	•	•	•
•	•	•	•
Z	5,000	4,000	6,00
Total	$200,000	$40,000	$15,00

▶ **Self-Test 20.6**   Suppose a customer who buys goods on terms 1/10, net 45 always forgoes the cash discount and pays on the 45th day after sale. If the firm typically buys $10,000 of goods a month, spread evenly over the month, what will the aging schedule look like?

There is always a potential conflict of interest between the collection department and the sales department. Sales representatives commonly complain that they no sooner win new customers than the collection department frightens them off with threatening letters. The collection manager, on the other hand, bemoans the fact that the sales force is concerned only with winning orders and does not care whether the goods are subsequently paid for. This conflict is another example of the agency problem introduced in Chapter 1.

> **Good collection policy balances conflicting goals. The company wants cordial relations with its customers. It also wants them to pay their bills on time.**

There are instances of cooperation between sales managers and the financial managers who worry about collections. For example, the specialty chemicals division of a major pharmaceutical company actually made a business loan to an important customer that had been suddenly cut off by its bank. The pharmaceutical company bet that it knew its customer better than the customer's bank did—and the pharmaceutical company was right. The customer arranged alternative bank financing, paid back the pharmaceutical company, and became an even more loyal customer. It was a nice example of financial management supporting sales.

Bankruptcy

We have reviewed some of the techniques that firms use to evaluate the creditworthiness of their customers and to decide whether to issue credit. It would be helpful if these techniques were refined to perfectly distinguish among customers that will pay their bills and those that will go belly up, but this is not a realistic goal. In any event, we have seen that granting credit to a financially shaky customer may pay off if there is a chance that the offer will lead to a profitable future relationship. Therefore, it is not uncommon for firms to have to deal with an insolvent customer.

bankruptcy: The reorganization or liquidation of a firm that cannot pay its debts.

Each year about 500,000 individuals and 100,000 businesses file for **bankruptcy.** So it is a rare firm that never has a customer who becomes bankrupt. In this section we outline the procedures involved.

Our focus here is on business bankruptcies. These account for only about 15 percent of the total number of bankruptcies, but because they are larger than individual bankruptcies, they involve about half of all claims by value. There are also more complications when a business declares bankruptcy than when an individual does so.

Bankruptcy Procedures

workout: Agreement between a company and its creditors establishing the steps the company must take to avoid bankruptcy.

A corporation that cannot pay its debts will often try to come to an informal agreement with its creditors. This is known as a **workout.** A workout may take several forms. For example, the firm may negotiate an *extension,* that is, an agreement with its creditors to delay payments. Or the firm may negotiate a *composition,* in which the firm makes partial payments to its creditors in exchange for relief of its debts.

The advantage of a negotiated agreement is that the costs and delays of formal bankruptcy are avoided. However, the larger the firm, and the more complicated its capital structure, the less likely it is that a negotiated settlement can be reached. (For example, Wickes Corp. tried—and failed—to reach a negotiated settlement with its 250,000 creditors.)

If the firm cannot get an agreement, then it may have no alternative but to file for bankruptcy.[9] Under the federal bankruptcy system the firm has a choice of procedures. In about two-thirds of the cases a firm will file for, or be forced into, bankruptcy under Chapter 7 of the 1978 Bankruptcy Reform Act. Then the firm's assets are **liquidated**—that is, sold—and the proceeds are used to pay creditors.

liquidation: Sale of bankrupt firm's assets.

There is a pecking order of unsecured creditors.[10] First come claims for expenses that arise after bankruptcy is filed, such as attorneys' fees or employee compensation earned after the filing. If such postfiling claims did not receive priority, no firm in bankruptcy proceedings could continue to operate. Next come claims for wages and employee benefits earned in the period immediately prior to the filing. Taxes are next in line, together with debts to some government agencies such as the Small Business Administration or the Pension Benefit Guarantee Corporation. Finally come general unsecured claims such as bonds or unsecured trade debt.

reorganization: Restructuring of financial claims on failing firm to allow it to keep operating.

The alternative to a liquidation is to seek a **reorganization,** which keeps the firm as a going concern and usually compensates creditors with new securities in the reorganized firm. Such reorganizations are generally in the shareholders' interests— they have little to lose if things deteriorate further and everything to gain if the firm recovers.

Firms attempting reorganization seek refuge under Chapter 11 of the Bankruptcy Reform Act. Chapter 11 is designed to keep the firm alive and operating and to protect the value of its assets while a plan of reorganization is worked out. During this period, other proceedings against the firm are halted and the company is operated by existing management or by a court-appointed trustee.

The responsibility for developing a plan of reorganization may fall on the debtor firm. If no trustee is appointed, the firm has 120 days to present a plan to creditors. If these deadlines are *not* met, or if a trustee is appointed, anyone can submit a plan— the trustee, for example, or a committee of creditors.

The reorganization plan is basically a statement of who gets what; each class of creditors gives up its claim in exchange for new securities. (Sometimes creditors receive cash as well.) The problem is to design a new capital structure for the firm that will (1) satisfy the creditors and (2) allow the firm to solve the *business* problems that got the firm into trouble in the first place. Sometimes only a plan of baroque complexity can satisfy these two requirements. When the Penn Central Corporation was finally reorganized in 1978 (7 years after it became the largest railroad bankruptcy ever), more than a dozen new securities were created and parceled out among 15 classes of creditors.

[9]Occasionally creditors will allow the firm to petition for bankruptcy after it has reached an agreement with the creditors. This is known as a *prepackaged bankruptcy.* The court simply approves the agreed workout plan.

[10]Secured creditors have the first priority to the collateral pledged for their loans.

The reorganization plan goes into effect if it is accepted by creditors and confirmed by the court. Acceptance requires approval by a majority of each class of creditor. Once a plan is accepted, the court normally approves it, provided that *each* class of creditors has approved it and that the creditors will be better off under the plan than if the firm's assets were liquidated and distributed. The court may, under certain conditions, confirm a plan even if one or more classes of creditors vote against it. This is known as a *cram-down*.

The terms of a cram-down are open to negotiation among all parties. For example, unsecured creditors may threaten to slow the process as a way of extracting concessions from secured creditors. The secured creditors may take less than 100 cents on the dollar and give something to unsecured creditors in order to expedite the process and reach an agreement.

The Choice between Liquidation and Reorganization

Here is an idealized view of the bankruptcy decision. Whenever a payment is due to creditors, management checks the value of the firm. If the firm is worth more than the promised payment, the firm pays up (if necessary, raising the cash by an issue of shares). If not, the equity is worthless, and the firm defaults on its debt and petitions for bankruptcy. If in the court's judgment the assets of the bankrupt firm can be put to better use elsewhere, the firm is liquidated and the proceeds are used to pay off the creditors. Otherwise, the creditors simply become the new owners and the firm continues to operate.

In practice, matters are rarely so simple. For example, we observe that firms often petition for bankruptcy even when the equity has a positive value. And firms are often reorganized even when the assets could be used more efficiently elsewhere. There are several reasons.

First, although the reorganized firm is legally a new entity, it is entitled to any tax-loss carry-forwards belonging to the old firm. If the firm is liquidated rather than reorganized, any tax-loss carry-forwards disappear. Thus there is an incentive to continue in operation even if assets are better used by another firm.

Second, if the firm's assets are sold off, it is easy to determine what is available to pay the creditors. However, when the company is reorganized, it needs to conserve cash as far as possible. Therefore, claimants are generally paid in a mixture of cash and securities. This makes it less easy to judge whether they have received their entitlement. For example, each bondholder may be offered $300 in cash and $700 in a new bond which pays no interest for the first 2 years and a low rate of interest thereafter. A bond of this kind in a company that is struggling to survive may not be worth much, but the bankruptcy court usually looks at the face value of the new bonds and may therefore regard the bondholders as paid in full.

Senior creditors who know they are likely to get a raw deal in a reorganization are likely to press for a liquidation. Shareholders and junior creditors prefer a reorganization. They hope that the court will not interpret the pecking order too strictly and that they will receive some crumbs.

Third, although shareholder and junior creditors are at the bottom of the pecking order, they have a secret weapon: they can play for time. Bankruptcies of large companies often take several years before a plan is presented to the court and agreed to by each class of creditor. (The bankruptcy proceedings of the Missouri Pacific Railroad took a total of 22 years.) When they use delaying tactics, the junior claimants are betting on a turn of fortune that will rescue their investment. On the other hand, the senior creditors know that time is working against them, so they may be prepared to accept a smaller payoff as part of the price for getting a plan accepted. Also, prolonged bankruptcy cases are costly (the Wickes case involved $250 million in legal and administrative costs). Senior claimants may see their money seeping into lawyers' pockets and therefore decide to settle quickly.

Fourth, while a reorganization plan is being drawn up, the company is allowed to buy goods on credit and borrow money. Postpetition creditors (those who extend credit to a firm already in bankruptcy proceedings) have priority over the old creditors and their debt may even be secured by assets that are already mortgaged to existing debtholders. This also gives the prepetition creditors an incentive to settle quickly, before their claim on assets is diluted by the new debt.

Finally, profitable companies may file for Chapter 11 bankruptcy to protect themselves against "burdensome" suits. For example, in 1982 Manville Corporation was threatened by 16,000 damage suits alleging injury from asbestos. Manville filed for bankruptcy under Chapter 11, and the bankruptcy judge agreed to put the damage suits on hold until the company was reorganized. This took 6 years. Of course legislators worry that these actions are contrary to the original intent of the bankruptcy acts.

20.7 Summary

1. The first step in credit management is to set normal terms of sale. This means that you must decide the length of the payment period and the size of any cash discounts. In most industries these conditions are standardized.

2. Your second step is to decide the form of the contract with your customer. Most domestic sales are made on open account. In this case the only evidence that the customer owes you money is the entry in your ledger and a receipt signed by the customer. Sometimes, you may require a more formal commitment before you deliver the goods. For example, the supplier may arrange for the customer to provide a trade acceptance.

3. The third task is to assess each customer's creditworthiness. There are various sources of information: your own experience with the customer, the experience of other creditors, the assessment of a credit agency, a check with the customer's bank, the market value of the customer's securities, and an analysis of the customer's financial statements. Firms that handle a large volume of credit information often use a formal system for combining the various sources into an overall credit score.

4. When you have made an assessment of the customer's credit standing, you can establish sensible credit limits. The job of the credit manager is not to minimize the number of bad debts; it is to maximize profits. This means that you need to weigh the odds that the customer will pay, providing you with a profit, against the odds that the customer will default, resulting in a loss. Remember not to be too shortsighted when reckoning the expected profit. It is often worth accepting the marginal applicant if there is a chance that the applicant may become a regular and reliable customer.

5. The next problem is to collect. This requires tact and judgment. You want to be firm with the truly delinquent customer, but you don't want to offend the good one by writing demanding letters just because a check has been delayed in the mail. You will find it easier to spot troublesome accounts if you keep a careful record of the aging of receivables.

6. Firms that cannot meet their obligations may file for bankruptcy, in which case the business may be liquidated or reorganized. Liquidation means that the firm's assets are sold and the proceeds used to pay creditors. Reorganization means that the firm is maintained as an ongoing concern, and creditors are compensated with securities in the reorganized firm. Ideally, reorganization should be chosen over liquidation when the firm as a going concern is worth more than its liquidation value. However, the conflicting interests of the different parties can result in violations of this principle.

Key Terms

terms of sale	collection policy	workout
open account	aging schedule	liquidation
credit analysis	bankruptcy	reorganization
credit policy		

Problems

1. **Trade Credit Rates.** Company X sells on a 1/20, net 60, basis. Customer Y buys goods with an invoice of $1,000.

   a. How much can Company Y deduct from the bill if it pays on Day 20?
   b. How many extra days of credit can Company Y receive if it passes up the cash discount?
   c. What is the effective annual rate of interest if Y pays on the due date rather than Day 20?

2. **Terms of Sale.** Indicate which firm of each pair you would expect to grant shorter or longer credit periods:

   a. One firm sells hardware; the other sells bread.
   b. One firm's customers have an inventory turnover ratio of 10; the other's customers have turnover of 15.
   c. One firm sells mainly to electric utilities; the other to fashion boutiques.

3. **Payment Lag.** The lag between purchase date and the date at which payment is due is known as the *terms lag*. The lag between the due date and the date on which the buyer actually pays is termed the *due lag,* and the lag between the purchase and actual payment dates is the *pay lag*. Thus

$$\text{Pay lag} = \text{terms lag} + \text{due lag}$$

   State how you would expect the following events to affect each type of lag:

   a. The company imposes a service charge on late payers.
   b. A recession causes customers to be short of cash.
   c. The company changes its terms from net 10 to net 20.

4. **Trade Credit Rates.** A firm currently offers terms of sale of 3/20, net 40. What effect will the following actions have on the implicit interest rate charged to customers that pass up the cash discount? State whether the implicit interest rate will increase or decrease.

   a. The terms are changed to 4/20, net 40.
   b. The terms are changed to 3/30, net 40.
   c. The terms are changed to 3/20, net 30.

5. **Trade Credit and Receivables.** A firm offers terms of 2/15, net 30. Currently, two-thirds of all customers take advantage of the trade discount; the remainder pay bills at the due date.

   a. What will be the firm's typical value for its accounts receivable period? (See Chapter 18, Section 18.1 for a review of the accounts receivable period.)
   b. What is the average investment in accounts receivable if annual sales are $20 million?
   c. What would likely happen to the firm's accounts receivable period if it changed its terms to 3/15, net 30?

6. **Terms of Sale.** Microbiotics currently sells all of its frozen dinners cash on delivery but believes it can increase sales by offering supermarkets 1 month of free credit. The price per carton is $50 and the cost per carton is $40.

   a. If unit sales will increase from 1,000 cartons to 1,060 per month, should the firm offer the credit? The interest rate is 1 percent per month, and all customers will pay their bills.
   b. What if the interest rate is 1.5 percent per month?
   c. What if the interest rate is 1.5 percent per month, but the firm can offer the credit only as a special deal to new customers, while old customers will continue to pay cash on delivery?

7. **Credit Policy.** A firm currently makes only cash sales. It estimates that allowing trade credit on terms of net 30 would increase monthly sales from 200 to 220 units per month. The price per unit is $101 and the cost (in present value terms) is $80. The interest rate is 1 percent per month.

   a. Should the firm change its credit policy?
   b. Would your answer to (a) change if 5 percent of all customers will fail to pay their bills under the new credit policy?
   c. What if 5 percent of only the *new* customers fail to pay their bills? The current customers take advantage of the 30 days of free credit but remain safe credit risks.

8. **Terms of Sale.** Complete the following passage by selecting the appropriate terms from the following list (some terms may be used more than once): *acceptance, open, commercial, trade, the United States, his or her own, note, draft, account, promissory, bank, banker's, the customer's.*
   Most goods are sold on ____ ____. In this case the only evidence of the debt is a record in the seller's books and a signed receipt. When the order is very large, the customer may be asked to sign a(n) ____ ____, which is just a simple IOU. An alternative is for the seller to arrange a(n) ____ ____ ordering payment by the customer. In order to obtain the goods, the customer must acknowledge this order and sign the document. This signed acknowledgment is known as a(n) ____ ____. Sometimes the seller may also ask ____ ____ bank to sign the document. In this case it is known as a(n) ____ ____.

9. **Credit Decision/Repeat Sales.** Locust Software sells computer training packages to its business customers at a price of $101. The cost of production (in present value terms) is $95. Locust sells its packages on terms of net 30 and estimates that about 7 percent of all orders will be uncollectible. An order comes in for 20 units. The interest rate is 1 percent per month.

   a. Should the firm extend credit if this is a one-time order? The sale will not be made unless credit is extended.
   b. What is the break-even probability of collection?
   c. Now suppose that if a customer pays this month's bill, it will place an identical order in each month indefinitely and can be safely assumed to pose no risk of default. Should credit be extended?
   d. What is the break-even probability of collection in the repeat-sales case?

10. **Credit Decision.** The Branding Iron Company sells its irons for $50 apiece wholesale. Production cost is $40 per iron. There is a 25 percent chance that a prospective customer will go bankrupt within the next half year. The customer orders 1,000 irons and asks for 6 months' credit. Should you accept the order? Assume a 10 percent per year discount rate, no chance of a repeat order, and that the customer will pay either in full or not at all.

11. **Credit Decision.** Look back at Example 20.3. Cast Iron's costs have increased from $1,000 to $1,050. Assuming there is no possibility of repeat orders, and that the probability of successful collection from the customer is $p = .9$, answer the following:

    a. Should Cast Iron grant or refuse credit?
    b. What is the break-even probability of collection?

12. **Credit Decision/Repeat Sales.** Surf City sells its network browsing software for $15 per copy to computer software distributors and allows its customers 1 month to pay its bills. The cost of the software is $10 per copy. The industry is very new and unsettled, however, and the probability that a new customer granted credit will go bankrupt within the next month is 25 percent. The firm is considering switching to a cash-on-delivery credit policy to reduce its exposure to defaults on trade credit. The discount rate is 1 percent per month.

    a. Should the firm switch to a cash-on-delivery policy? If it does so, its sales will fall by 40 percent.
    b. How would your answer change if a customer which is granted credit and pays its bills can be expected to generate repeat orders with negligible likelihood of default for each of the next 6 months? Similarly, customers which pay cash also will generate on average 6 months of repeat sales.

13. **Credit Analysis.** This is a bit harder. Use the data in Example 20.3. Now suppose, however, that 10 percent of Cast Iron's customers are slow payers, and that slow payers have a probability of 30 percent of defaulting on their bills. If it costs $5 to determine whether a customer has been a prompt or slow payer in the past, should Cast Iron undertake such a check? *Hint:* What is the expected savings from the credit check? It will depend on both the probability of uncovering a slow payer and the savings from denying these payers credit.

14. **Credit Analysis.** Look back at problem 13, but now suppose that if a customer defaults on a payment, you can eventually collect about half the amount owed to you. Will you be more or less tempted to pay for a credit check once you account for the possibility of partial recovery of debts?

15. **Bankruptcy.** True or false?

    a. It makes sense to evaluate the credit manager's performance by looking at the proportion of bad debts.
    b. When a company becomes bankrupt, it is usually in the interests of the equityholders to seek a liquidation rather than a reorganization.
    c. A reorganization plan must be presented for approval by each class of creditor.
    d. The Internal Revenue Service has first claim on the company's assets in the event of bankruptcy.
    e. In a reorganization, creditors may be paid off with a mixture of cash and securities.
    f. When a company is liquidated, one of the most valuable assets to be sold is often the tax-loss carry-forward.

16. **Credit Policy.** As treasurer of the Universal Bed Corporation, Aristotle Procrustes is worried about his bad debt ratio, which is currently running at 6 percent. He believes that imposing a more stringent credit policy might reduce sales by 5 percent and reduce the bad debt ratio to 4 percent. If the cost of goods sold is 80 percent of the selling price, should Mr. Procrustes adopt the more stringent policy?

17. **Credit Policy.** Jim Khana, the credit manager of Velcro Saddles, is reappraising the company's credit policy. Velcro sells on terms of net 30. Cost of goods sold is 85 percent of sales. Velcro classifies customers on a scale of 1 to 4. During the past 5 years, the collection experience was as follows:

Classification	Defaults as Percentage of Sales	Average Collection Period in Days for Nondefaulting Accounts
1	0	45
2	2	42
3	10	50
4	20	80

The average interest rate was 15 percent. What conclusions (if any) can you draw about Velcro's credit policy? Should the firm deny credit to any of its customers? What other factors should be taken into account before changing this policy?

18. **Credit Analysis.** Financial ratios were described in Chapter 16. If you were the credit manager, to which financial ratios would you pay most attention?

19. **Bankruptcy.** Explain why equity can sometimes have a positive value even when companies petition for bankruptcy.

20. **Credit Analysis.** Galenic, Inc., is a wholesaler for a range of pharmaceutical products. Before deducting any losses from bad debts, Galenic operates on a profit margin of 5 percent. For a long time the firm has employed a numerical credit scoring system based on a small number of key ratios. This has resulted in a bad debt ratio of 1 percent.

Galenic has recently commissioned a detailed statistical study of the payment record of its customers over the past 8 years and, after considerable experimentation, has identified five variables that could form the basis of a new credit scoring system. On the evidence of the past 8 years, Galenic calculates that for every 10,000 accounts it would have experienced the following default rates:

Credit Score under Proposed System	Number of Accounts		
	Defaulting	Paying	Total
Better than 80	60	9,100	9,160
Worse than 80	40	800	840
Total	100	9,900	10,000

By refusing credit to firms with a poor credit score (worse than 80) Galenic calculates that it would reduce its bad debt ratio to 60/9,160, or just under .7 percent. While this may not seem like a big deal, Galenic's credit manager reasons that this is equivalent to a decrease of one-third in the bad debt ratio and would result in a significant improvement in the profit margin.

a. What is Galenic's current profit margin, allowing for bad debts?

b. Assuming that the firm's estimates of default rates are right, how would the new credit scoring system affect profits?

c. Why might you suspect that Galenic's estimates of default rates will not be realized in practice?

d. Suppose that one of the variables in the proposed new scoring system is whether the customer has an existing account with Galenic (new customers are more likely to default). How would this affect your assessment of the proposal? *Hint:* Think about repeat sales.

Solutions to Self-Test Questions

20.1 To get the cash discount, you have to pay the bill within 10 days, that is, by May 11. With the 2 percent discount, the amount that needs to be paid by May 11 is $20,000 × .98 = $19,600. If you forgo the cash discount, you do not have to pay your bill until May 21, but on that date, the amount due is $20,000.

20.2 The cash discount in this case is 5 percent and customers who choose not to take the discount receive an extra $50 - 10 = 40$ days credit. So the effective annual interest is

$$\text{Effective annual rate} = \left(1 + \frac{\text{discount}}{\text{discounted price}}\right)^{365/\text{extra days credit}} - 1$$

$$= \left(1 + \frac{5}{95}\right)^{365/40} - 1 = .597, \text{ or } 59.7\%$$

In this case the customer who does not take the discount is effectively borrowing money at an annual interest rate of 59.7 percent. This is higher than the rate in Example 20.1 because fewer days of credit are obtained by forfeiting the discount.

20.3 The credit score would improve by 6.3, the difference between the score for no telephone (7.0) and one or more telephones (.7). The feature with the potentially greatest impact on credit score is the postal zone.

20.4 The present value of costs is still $1,000. Present value of revenues is now $1,100. The break-even probability is defined by

$$p \times 100 - (1 - p) \times 1,000 = 0$$

which implies that $p = .909$. The break-even probability is higher because the profit margin is now lower. The firm cannot afford as high a bad debt ratio as before since it is not making as much on its successful sales. We conclude that high-margin goods will be offered with more liberal credit terms.

20.5 The higher the discount rate the less important are future sales. Because the value of repeat sales is lower, the break-even probability on the initial sale is higher. For instance, we saw that the break-even probability was 1/3 when the discount rate was 10 percent. When the discount rate is 20 percent, the value of a perpetual flow of repeat sales falls to $200/.20 = $1,000, and the break-even probability increases to 1/2:

$$1/2 \times \$1,000 - 1/2 \times \$1,000 = 0$$

20.6 The customer pays bills 45 days after the invoice date. Because goods are purchased daily, at any time there will be bills outstanding with "ages" ranging from 1 to 45 days. At any time, the customer will have 30 days' worth of purchases, or $10,000, outstanding for a period of up to 1 month, and 15 days' worth of purchases, or $5,000, outstanding for between 1 month and 45 days. The aging schedule will appear as follows:

Age of Account	Amount
< 1 month	$10,000
1–2 months	$ 5,000

Minicase

George Stamper, a credit analyst with Micro-Encapsulators Corp. (MEC), needed to respond to an urgent e-mail request from the South-East sales office. The local sales manager reported that she had an opportunity to clinch an order from Miami Spice (MS) for 50 encapsulators at $10,000 each. She added that she was particularly keen to secure this order since MS was likely to have a continuing need for 50 encapsulators a year and could therefore prove a very valuable customer. However, orders of this size to a new customer generally required head office agreement, and it was therefore George's responsibility to make a rapid assessment of MS's creditworthiness and to approve or disapprove the sale.

George knew that MS was a medium-sized company, with a patchy earnings record. After growing rapidly in the 1980s, MS had encountered strong competition in its principal markets and earnings had fallen sharply. George Stamper was not sure exactly to what extent this

Table 20.3

Miami Spice: summary financial statements (figures in millions of dollars)

	1997	1996
Assets		
Current assets		
Cash and marketable securities	5.0	12.2
Accounts receivable	16.2	15.7
Inventories	27.5	32.5
Total current assets	48.7	60.4
Fixed assets		
Property, plant, and equipment	228.5	228.1
Less accumulated depreciation	129.5	127.6
Net fixed assets	99.0	100.5
Total assets	147.7	160.9
Liabilities and Shareholders' Equity		
Current liabilities		
Debt due for repayment	22.8	28.0
Accounts payable	19.0	16.2
Total current liabilities	41.8	44.2
Long-term debt	40.8	42.3
Shareholders' equity		
Common stock[a]	10.0	10.0
Retained earnings	55.1	64.4
Total shareholders' equity	65.1	74.4
Total liabilities and shareholders' equity	147.7	160.9
Income Statement		
Revenue	149.8	134.4
Cost of goods sold	131.0	124.2
Other expenses	1.7	8.7
Depreciation	8.1	8.6
Earnings before interest and taxes	9.0	− 7.1
Interest expense	5.1	5.6
Income taxes	1.4	− 4.4
Net income	2.5	− 8.3
Allocation of net income		
Addition to retained earnings	1.5	− 9.3
Dividends	1.0	1.0

[a]10 million shares, $1 par value.

was a bad omen. New management had been brought in to cut costs and there were some indications that the worst was over for the company. Investors appeared to agree with this assessment, for the stock price had risen to $5.80 from its low of $4.25 the previous year. George had in front of him MS's latest financial statements, which are summarized in Table 20.3. He rapidly calculated a few key financial ratios and the company's Z score.

George also made a number of other checks on MS. The company had a small issue of bonds outstanding, which were rated B by Moody's. Inquiries through MEC's bank indicated that MS had unused lines of credit totaling $5 million but had entered into discussions with its bank for a renewal of a $15 million bank loan that was due to be repaid at the end of the year. Telephone calls to MS's other suppliers suggested that the company had recently been 30 days late in paying its bills.

George also needed to take into account the profit that the company could make on MS's order. Encapsulators were sold on standard terms of 2/30, net 60. So if MS paid promptly, MEC would receive additional revenues of $50 \times \$9,800 = \$490,000$. However, given MS's cash position, it was more than likely that it would forgo the cash discount and would not pay until sometime after the 60 days. Since interest rates were about 8 percent, any such delays in payment would reduce the present value to MEC of the revenues. George also recognized that there were production and transportation costs in filling MS's order. These worked out at $475,000, or $9,500 a unit. Corporate profits were taxed at 35 percent.

Questions

1. What can you say about Miami Spice's creditworthiness?
2. What is the break-even probability of default? How is it affected by the delay before MS pays its bills?
3. How should George Stamper's decision be affected by the possibility of repeat orders?

Part Eight

Special Topics

A merger is consummated.
These two managers are clearly delighted, but why do companies decide to merge?
Peter Morgan/Reuters/Archive Photos

Mergers, Acquisitions, and Corporate Control

T he pace of merger activity in the United States is sometimes remarkable. You can see from Table 21.1 that the money involved is sometimes even more remarkable. During periods of intense merger activity, financial managers spend significant amounts of time searching for firms to acquire or worrying that some other firm will acquire them.

When one company buys another, it is making an investment, and the basic principles of capital investment decisions apply. You should go ahead with the purchase if it makes a net contribution to shareholders' wealth. But mergers are often awkward transactions to evaluate, and you have to be careful to define benefits and costs properly.

Many mergers are arranged amicably, but in other cases one firm will make a hostile takeover bid for the other. We describe the principal techniques of modern merger warfare, and since the threat of hostile takeovers has stimulated corporate restructurings and leveraged buy-outs (LBOs), we describe them too, and attempt to explain why these deals have generated rewards for investors. We close with a look at who gains and loses from mergers and we discuss whether mergers are beneficial on balance.

After studying this chapter you should be able to

▶ Describe ways that companies change their ownership or management.

▶ Explain why it may make sense for companies to merge.

▶ Estimate the gains and costs of mergers to the acquiring firm.

▶ Describe takeover defenses.

▶ Summarize the evidence on whether mergers increase efficiency and on how the gains from mergers are distributed between shareholders of the acquired and acquiring firms.

21.1 The Market for Corporate Control

The shareholders are the owners of the firm. But most shareholders do not feel like the boss, and with good reason. Try buying a share of General Motors stock and marching into the boardroom for a chat with your employee, the chief executive officer.

The *ownership* and *management* of large corporations are almost always separated. Shareholders do not directly appoint or supervise the firm's managers. They elect the board of directors, who act as their agents in choosing and monitoring the managers of the firm. Shareholders have a direct say in very few matters. Control of the firm is in the hands of the managers, subject to the general oversight of the board of directors.

The separation of ownership and management or control creates potential *agency costs*. Agency costs occur when managers or directors take actions adverse to shareholders' interests.

The temptation to take such actions may be ever-present, but there are many forces and constraints working to keep managers' and shareholders' interests in line. As we pointed out in Chapter 1, managers' paychecks in large corporations are almost always tied to the profitability of the firm and the performance of its shares. Boards of directors take their responsibilities seriously—they may face lawsuits if they don't—and therefore are reluctant to rubber-stamp obviously bad financial decisions.

Table 21.1

Some important recent mergers

Year	Selling Company	Acquiring Company	Payment, Billions of Dollars
1994	McCaw Cellular Communications	AT&T	18.9
1994	Paramount	Viacom	9.6
1994	Blockbuster Entertainment	Viacom	8.0
1994	American Cyanamid	American Home Products	9.6
1995	Capital Cities/ABC	Disney	19.0
1995	Chase Manhattan	Chemical Bank	10.0
1995	Scott Paper	Kimberly-Clark	7.4
1995	Marion Merrell Dow	Hoechst A.G.	7.1
1995	Martin Marietta	Lockheed	10.0
1995	Time Warner	Turner Broadcasting System	7.5
1996	First Interstate Bancorp	Wells Fargo	11.6

Source: Mergers and Acquisitions, various issues.

But what ensures that the board has engaged the most talented managers? What happens if managers are inadequate? What if the board of directors is derelict in monitoring the performance of managers? Or what if the firm's managers are fine, but resources of the firm could be used more efficiently by merging with another firm? Can we count on managers to pursue arrangements that would put them out of jobs?

These are all questions about *the market for corporate control,* the mechanisms by which firms are matched up with management teams and owners who can make the most of the firm's resources. You should not take a firm's current ownership and management for granted. If it is possible for the value of the firm to be enhanced by changing management or by reorganizing under new owners, there will be incentives for someone to make a change.

> **There are four ways to change the management of a firm. These are (1) a successful proxy contest in which a group of stockholders votes in a new group of directors, who then pick a new management team; (2) the purchase of one firm by another in a merger or acquisition; (3) a leveraged buy-out of the firm by a private group of investors; and (4) a divestiture, in which a firm either sells part of its operations to another company or spins it off as an independent firm.**

We will review briefly each of these methods.

Proxy Contests

Shareholders elect the board of directors to keep watch on management and replace unsatisfactory managers. If the board is lax, shareholders are free to elect a different board. In theory this assures that the corporation is run in the best interests of shareholders.

In practice things are not so clear-cut. Ownership in large corporations is widely dispersed. Usually even the largest single shareholder holds only a small fraction of the shares. Most shareholders have little notion who is on the board or what the members stand for. Management, on the other hand, deals directly with the board and has a personal relationship with its members. In most corporations, management sits on the committee that nominates candidates for the board. It is not surprising that some boards seem less than aggressive in forcing managers to run a lean, efficient operation and to act primarily in the interests of shareholders.

proxy contest: Takeover attempt in which outsiders compete with management for shareholders' votes. Also called *proxy fight.*

When a group of investors believes that the board and its management team should be replaced, they can launch a **proxy contest.** A proxy is the right to vote another shareholder's shares. In a proxy contest, the dissident shareholders attempt to obtain enough proxies to elect their own slate to the board of directors. Once the new board is in control, management can be replaced. A proxy fight is therefore a direct contest for control of the corporation.

But most proxy contests fail. Dissidents who engage in such fights must use their own money, while management can use the corporation's funds and lines of communication with shareholders to defend itself. Such fights can cost millions of dollars.[1]

Institutional shareholders such as large pension funds have become more aggressive in pressing for managerial accountability. These funds have been able to gain concessions from firms without initiating proxy contests. For example, firms have agreed to split the jobs of chief executive officer and chairman of the board of directors. This ensures that an outsider is responsible for keeping watch over the company. Also, more firms now bar corporate insiders from serving on the committee that nominates candidates to the board. Perhaps as a result of shareholder pressure, boards also seem to be getting more aggressive. For example, outside directors were widely credited for hastening the recent replacement of top management at AT&T, GM, IBM, American Express, and Westinghouse.

Mergers and Acquisitions

Proxy contests are rare, and successful ones are rarer still. Poorly performing managers face a greater risk from acquisition. If the management of one firm observes another firm underperforming, it can try to acquire the business and replace the poor managers with its own team. In practice, corporate takeovers are the arenas where contests for corporate control are usually fought.

merger: Combination of two firms into one, with the acquirer assuming assets and liabilities of the target firm.

There are three ways for one firm to acquire another. One possibility is to *merge* the two companies into one, in which case the acquiring company assumes *all* the assets and *all* the liabilities of the other. Such a **merger** must have the approval of at least 50 percent of the stockholders of each firm.[2] The acquired firm ceases to exist, and its former shareholders receive cash and/or securities in the acquiring firm. In many mergers there is a clear acquiring company, whose management then runs the enlarged firm. However, a merger is often a combination of two equals with both managements having a major say in the running of the new company. The merger between Chemical Bank and Chase Manhattan was an example of a merger of equals. Table 21.1 lists some recent important mergers.

---

[1]P. Dodd and J. Warner have written a detailed description and analysis of proxy fights. See "On Corporate Governance: A Study of Proxy Contests," *Journal of Financial Economics* 2 (April 1985), pp. 401–438.

[2]Corporate charters and state laws sometimes specify a higher percentage.

tender offer: Takeover attempt in which outsiders directly offer to buy the stock of the firm's shareholders.

A second alternative is for the acquiring firm to buy the target firm's stock in exchange for cash, shares, or other securities. The acquired firm may continue to exist as a separate entity, but it is now owned by the acquirer. The approval and cooperation of the target firm's managers are generally sought, but even if they resist, the acquirer can attempt to purchase a majority of the outstanding shares. By offering to buy shares directly from shareholders, the acquiring firm can bypass the target firm's management altogether. The offer to purchase stock is called a **tender offer.** If the tender offer is successful, the buyer obtains control and can, if it chooses, toss out incumbent management.

The third approach is to buy the target firm's assets. In this case ownership of the assets needs to be transferred, and payment is made to the selling firm rather than directly to its stockholders. Usually, the target firm sells only some of its assets, but occasionally it sells *all* of them. In this case, the selling firm continues to exist as an independent entity, but it becomes an empty shell—a corporation engaged in no business activity.

The terminology of mergers and acquisitions (M&A) can be confusing. These phrases are used loosely to refer to any kind of corporate combination or takeover. But strictly speaking, *merger* means the combination of all the assets and liabilities of two firms. The purchase of the stock or assets of another firm is an **acquisition.**

acquisition: Takeover of a firm by purchase of that firm's common stock or assets.

Leveraged Buy-outs

leveraged buy-out (LBO): Acquisition of the firm by a private group using substantial borrowed funds.

Sometimes a group of investors takes over a firm by means of a **leveraged buy-out,** or **LBO.** The LBO group takes the firm private and its shares no longer trade in the securities markets. Usually a considerable proportion of LBO financing is borrowed, hence the term *leveraged* buy-out.

If the investor group is led by the management of the firm, the takeover is called a **management buy-out,** or **MBO.** In this case, the firm's managers actually buy the firm from the shareholders and continue to run it. They become owner-managers. We will discuss LBOs and MBOs later in the chapter.

management buy-out (MBO): Acquisition of the firm by its own management in a leveraged buy-out.

Divestitures and Spin-offs

Firms not only acquire businesses; they also sell them. *Divestitures* are part of the market for corporate control. In recent years the number of divestitures has been about half the number of mergers.

Instead of selling a business to another firm, companies may *spin off* the business by separating it from the parent firm and distributing stock in the newly independent company to the shareholders of the parent company. For example, in 1996, AT&T was split into four separate firms: AT&T continued to operate telecommunication services, Lucent took responsibility for telecommunication equipment manufacturing, NCR took on the computer business, and AT&T Capital, which handled leasing, was spun off and sold to another firm. Instead of holding shares in one megafirm, AT&T's shareholders were given shares in Lucent and NCR as well as AT&T. Investors clearly welcomed this move: when the announcement of the split was made in 1995, AT&T's shares jumped 11 percent.

Probably the most frequent motive for spin-offs is improved efficiency. Companies sometimes refer to a business as being a "poor fit." By spinning off a poor fit, the management of the parent company can concentrate on its main activity. If each business must stand on its own feet, there is no risk that funds will be siphoned off from one in order to support unprofitable investments in the other. Moreover, if the two parts of the business are independent, it is easy to see the value of each and to reward managers accordingly.

21.2 Sensible Motives for Mergers

Mergers are often categorized as *horizontal, vertical,* or *conglomerate.* A horizontal merger is one that takes place between two firms in the same line of business; the merged firms are former competitors. Most of the mergers around the turn of the century were of this type. Recent examples of horizontal mergers have occurred in banking, such as the merger between Chemical Bank and Chase Manhattan, and in retailing, such as the merger between Staples and Office Depot.

A horizontal merger can be blocked if the U.S. Department of Justice or Federal Trade Commission establishes that it would be anticompetitive or create too much market power. The Staples–Office Depot merger was challenged, but it was finally consummated after the two companies agreed to sell a number of stores to other retailers.

During the 1920s, vertical mergers were predominant. A vertical merger is one in which the buyer expands backward toward the source of raw material or forward in the direction of the ultimate consumer. Thus a soft drink manufacturer might buy a sugar producer (expanding backward) or a fast-food chain as an outlet for its product (expanding forward). Pepsi owns BurgerKing, for example.

A conglomerate merger involves companies in unrelated lines of business. For example, Textron owns Bell Helicopter and Cessna Aircraft, as well as Paul Revere, which is an insurance company, and several companies producing automotive components. Conglomerate mergers were common in the 1960s and 1970s. However, the number of conglomerate mergers declined in the 1980s. In fact much of the action in the 1980s came from breaking up the conglomerates that had been formed 10 to 20 years earlier.

▶ **Self-Test 21.1**   Are the following hypothetical mergers horizontal, vertical, or conglomerate?

a. IBM acquires Apple Computer.
b. Apple Computer acquires Stop & Shop (a supermarket chain).
c. Stop & Shop acquires Campbell Soup.
d. Campbell Soup acquires IBM.

We have already seen that one motive for a merger is to replace the existing management team. If this motive is important, one would expect that poorly performing firms would tend to be targets for acquisition; this seems to be the case.[3] However, firms also acquire other firms for reasons that have nothing to do with inadequate management. Many mergers and acquisitions are motivated by possible gains in efficiency from combining operations. These mergers create *synergies.* By this we mean that the two firms are worth more together than apart.

> A merger adds value only if synergies, better management, or other changes make the two firms worth more together than apart.

---

[3]For example, Palepu found that investors in firms that were subsequently acquired earned relatively low rates of return for several years before the merger. See K. Palepu, "Predicting Takeover Targets: A Methodological and Empirical Analysis,"*Journal of Accounting and Economics* 8 (March 1986), pp. 3–36.

It would be nice if we could say that certain types of mergers are usually successful and other types fail. Unfortunately, there are no such simple generalizations. Many mergers that appear to make sense nevertheless fail because managers cannot handle the complex task of integrating two firms with different production processes, accounting methods, and corporate cultures. Moreover, the value of most businesses depends on *human* assets—managers, skilled workers, scientists, and engineers. If these people are not happy in their new roles in the acquiring firm, the best of them will leave. Beware of paying too much for assets that go down in the elevator and out to the parking lot at the close of each business day.

With this caveat in mind, we will now consider possible sources of synergy.

Economies of Scale

Just as most of us believe that we would be happier if only we were a little richer, so managers always seem to believe their firm would be more competitive if only it were just a little bigger. They hope for *economies of scale,* that is, the opportunity to spread fixed costs across a larger volume of output. The banking industry provides many examples. By the 1970s, it was clear that the United States had too many small, local banks. Some (now very large) banks grew by systematically buying up smaller banks and streamlining their operations. Most of the cost savings came from consolidating "backoffice" operations, such as computer systems for processing checks and credit-card transactions and payments.

These economies of scale are the natural goal of horizontal mergers. But they have been claimed in conglomerate mergers, too. The architects of these mergers have pointed to the economies that come from sharing central services such as accounting, financial control, and top-level management.

Economies of Vertical Integration

Large industrial companies commonly like to gain as much control and coordination as possible over the production process by expanding back toward the output of the raw material and forward to the ultimate consumer. One way to achieve this is to merge with a supplier or a customer. Consider Du Pont's purchase of an oil company, Conoco. This was vertical integration because petroleum is the ultimate raw material for much of Du Pont's chemical production.

Do not assume that more vertical integration is necessarily better than less. Carried to extremes, it is absurdly inefficient. For example, before the Polish economy was restructured, LOT, the Polish state airline, found itself raising pigs to make sure that its employees had fresh meat on their tables. (Of course, in a centrally managed economy it may prove necessary to grow your own meat, since you can't be sure you'll be able to buy it.)

Combining Complementary Resources

Many small firms are acquired by large firms that can provide the missing ingredients necessary for the firm's success. The small firm may have a unique product but lack the engineering and sales organization necessary to produce and market it on a large scale. The firm could develop engineering and sales talent from scratch, but it may be quicker and cheaper to merge with a firm that already has ample talent. The two firms have *complementary resources*—each has what the other needs—so it may make sense for them to merge. Also the merger may open up opportunities that neither firm would pursue otherwise. Federal Express's purchase of Caliber System, a trucking company, is an example. Federal Express specializes in shipping packages by air, mostly for overnight delivery. Caliber's RMS subsidiary moves nonexpress packages by truck. RMS greatly increases Federal Express's capability to move packages on the ground. At the same time, RMS-originated business can move easily on the Federal Express system when rapid or distant delivery is essential.

▶ **Example 21.1**

Complementary Reserves

Of course two large firms may also merge because they have complementary resources. Consider the 1989 merger between two electric utilities, Utah Power & Light and PacifiCorp, which serves customers in California. Utah Power's peak demand comes in the summer, for air conditioning. PacifiCorp's peak comes in the winter, for heating. The savings from combining the two firms' generating systems were estimated at $45 million annually. ◀

Mergers as a Use for Surplus Funds

Suppose that your firm is in a mature industry. It is generating a substantial amount of cash, but it has few profitable investment opportunities. Ideally such a firm should distribute the surplus cash to shareholders by increasing its dividend payment or by repurchasing its shares. Unfortunately, energetic managers are often reluctant to shrink their firm in this way.

If the firm is not willing to purchase its own shares, it can instead purchase someone else's. Thus firms with a surplus of cash and a shortage of good investment opportunities often turn to mergers *financed by cash* as a way of deploying their capital.

Firms that have excess cash and do not pay it out or redeploy it by acquisition often find themselves targets for takeover by other firms that propose to redeploy the cash for them. During the oil price slump of the early 1980s, many cash-rich oil companies found themselves threatened by takeover. This was not because their cash was a unique asset. The acquirers wanted to capture the companies' cash flow to make sure it was not frittered away on negative-NPV oil exploration projects. We return to this *free-cash-flow* motive for takeovers later in this chapter.

21.3 Dubious Reasons for Mergers

The benefits that we have described so far all make economic sense. Other arguments sometimes given for mergers are more dubious. Here are two.

Diversification

We have suggested that the managers of a cash-rich company may prefer to see that cash used for acquisitions. That is why we often see cash-rich firms in stagnant industries merging their way into fresh woods and pastures new.

What about diversification as an end in itself? It is obvious that diversification reduces risk. Isn't that a gain from merging?

The trouble with this argument is that diversification is easier and cheaper for the stockholder than for the corporation. Why should firm A buy firm B to diversify when the shareholders of firm A can buy shares in firm B to diversify their own portfolios?

It is far easier and cheaper for individual investors to diversify than it is for firms to combine operations.

The Bootstrap Game

During the 1960s some conglomerate companies made acquisitions which offered no evident economic gains. Nevertheless, the conglomerates' aggressive strategy produced several years of rising earnings per share. To see how this can happen, let us look at the acquisition of Muck and Slurry by the well-known conglomerate World Enterprises.

▶ **Example 21.2**

The Bootstrap Game

The position before the merger is set out in the first two columns of Table 21.2. Notice that because Muck and Slurry has relatively poor growth prospects, its stock sells at a lower price-earnings ratio than World Enterprises (line 3). The merger, we assume, produces no economic benefits, so the firms should be worth exactly the same together as apart. The value of World Enterprises after the merger is therefore equal to the sum of the separate values of the two firms (line 6).

Since World Enterprises stock is selling for double the price of Muck and Slurry stock (line 2), World Enterprises can acquire the 100,000 Muck and Slurry shares for 50,000 of its own shares. Thus World will have 150,000 shares outstanding after the merger.

World's total earnings double as a result of the acquisition (line 5), but the number of shares increases by only 50 percent. Its earnings *per share* rise from $2.00 to $2.67. We call this a *bootstrap effect* because there is no real gain created by the merger and no increase in the two firms' combined value. Since World's stock price is unchanged by the acquisition of Muck and Slurry, the price-earnings ratio falls (line 3).

Before the merger, $1 invested in World Enterprises bought 5 cents of current earnings and rapid growth prospects. On the other hand, $1 invested in Muck and Slurry bought 10 cents of current earnings but slower growth prospects. If the *total* market value is not altered by the merger, then $1 invested in the merged firm gives World shareholders 6.7 cents of immediate earnings but slower growth than before the merger. Muck and Slurry shareholders get lower immediate earnings but faster growth. Neither side gains or loses provided that everybody understands the deal. ◀

Table 21.2

Impact of merger on market value and earnings per share of World Enterprises

	World Enterprises (before merger)	Muck and Slurry	World Enterprises (after acquiring Muck and Slurry)
1. Earnings per share	$2.00	$2.00	$2.67
2. Price per share	$40.00	$20.00	$40.00
3. Price-earnings ratio	20	10	15
4. Number of shares	100,000	100,000	150,000
5. Total earnings	$200,000	$200,000	$400,000
6. Total market value	$4,000,000	$2,000,000	$6,000,000
7. Current earnings per dollar invested in stock (line 1 divided by line 2)	$.05	$.10	$.067

Note: When World Enterprises purchases Muck and Slurry, there are no gains. Therefore, total earnings and total market value should be unaffected by the merger. But earnings *per share* increase. World Enterprises issues only 50,000 of its shares (priced at $40) to acquire the 100,000 Muck and Slurry shares (priced at $20).

Financial manipulators sometimes try to ensure that the market does *not* understand the deal. Suppose that investors are fooled by the exuberance of the president of World Enterprises and mistake the 33 percent postmerger increase in earnings per share for *sustainable* growth. If they do, the price of World Enterprises stock rises and the shareholders of both companies receive something for nothing.

You should now see how to play the bootstrap game. Suppose that you manage a company enjoying a high price-earnings ratio. The reason it is high is that investors anticipate rapid growth in future earnings. You achieve this growth not by capital investment, product improvement, or increased operating efficiency, but by purchasing slow-growing firms with low price-earnings ratios. The long-run result will be slower growth and a depressed price-earnings ratio, but in the short run earnings per share can increase dramatically. If this fools investors, you may be able to achieve the higher earnings per share without suffering a decline in your price-earnings ratio. But in order to *keep* fooling investors, you must continue to expand by merger *at the same compound rate*. Obviously you cannot do this forever; one day expansion must slow down or stop. Then earnings growth will cease, and your house of cards will fall.

> **Buying a firm with a lower P/E ratio can increase earnings per share. But the increase should not result in a higher share price. The short-term increase in earnings should be offset by lower future earnings growth.**

▶ **Self-Test 21.2**   Suppose that Muck and Slurry has even worse growth prospects than in our example and its share price is only $10. Recalculate the effects of the merger in this case. You should find that earnings per share increase by a greater amount, since World Enterprises can now buy the same *current* earnings for fewer shares.

21.4 *Evaluating Mergers*

If you are given the responsibility for evaluating a proposed merger, you must think hard about the following two questions:

1. Is there an overall economic gain to the merger? In other words, is the merger value-enhancing? Are the two firms worth more together than apart?
2. Do the terms of the merger make my company and its shareholders better off? There is no point in merging if the cost is too high and all the economic gain goes to the other company.

Answering these deceptively simple questions is rarely easy. Some economic gains can be nearly impossible to quantify, and complex merger financing can obscure the true terms of the deal. But the basic principles for evaluating mergers are not too difficult.

Mergers Financed by Cash

We will concentrate on a simple numerical example. Your company, Cislunar Foods, is considering acquisition of a smaller food company, Targetco. Cislunar is proposing to finance the deal by purchasing all of Targetco's outstanding stock for $19 per share.

Some financial information on the two companies is given in the left and center columns of Table 21.3.

Question 1. Why would Cislunar and Targetco be worth more together than apart? Suppose that operating costs can be reduced by combining the companies' marketing, distribution, and administration. Revenues can also be increased in Targetco's region. The rightmost column of Table 21.3 contains projected revenues, costs, and earnings for the two firms operating together: annual operating costs postmerger will be $2 million less than the sum of the separate companies' costs, and revenues will be $2 million more. Therefore, projected earnings increase by $4 million.[4] We will assume that the increased earnings are the only synergy to be generated by the merger.

The economic gain to the merger is the present value of the extra earnings. If the earnings increase is permanent (a level perpetuity), and the cost of capital is 20 percent,

$$\text{Economic gain} = \text{PV (increased earnings)} = \frac{4}{.20} = \$20 \text{ million}$$

This additional value is the basic motivation for the merger.

Question 2. What are the terms of the merger? What is the cost to Cislunar and its shareholders?

Targetco's management and shareholders will not consent to the merger unless they receive at least the stand-alone value of their shares. They can be paid in cash or by new shares issued by Cislunar. In this case we are considering a cash offer of $19 per Targetco share, $3 per share over the prior share price. Targetco has 2.5 million shares outstanding, so Cislunar will have to pay out $47.5 million, a premium of $7.5 million over Targetco's prior market value. On these terms, Targetco stockholders will capture $7.5 million out of the $20 million gain from the merger. That ought to leave $12.5 million for Cislunar.

Table 21.3

Cislunar Foods is considering an acquisition of Targetco. The merger would increase the companies' combined earnings by $4 million.

	Cislunar Foods	Targetco	Combined Companies	
Revenues	$150	$20	$172	(+2)
Operating costs	118	16	132	(−2)
Earnings	$ 32	$ 4	$ 40	(+4)
Cash	$ 55	$ 2.5		
Other assets' book value	185	17.0		
Total assets	$240	$19.5		
Price per share	$ 48	$16		
Number of shares	10.0	2.5		
Market value	$480	$40		

Note: Figures in millions except price per share.

[4]To keep things simple, the example ignores taxes and assumes that both companies are all-equity financed. We also ignore the interest income that could have been earned by investing the cash used to finance the merger.

Table 21.4

Financial forecasts after the Cislunar–Targetco merger. The left column assumes a cash purchase at $19 per Targetco share. The right column assumes Targetco stockholders receive one new Cislunar share for every three Targetco shares.

	Cash Purchase	**Exchange of Shares**
Earnings	$ 40	$ 40
Cash	$ 10	$ 57.5
Other assets' book value	202	202
Total assets	$212	$259.5
Price per share	$ 49.25	$ 49.85
Number of shares	10.0	10.833
Market value	$492.5	$540

Note: Figures in millions except price per share.

This is confirmed in the Cash Purchase column of Table 21.4. Start at the *bottom* of the column, where the total market value of the merged firms is $492.5 million. This is derived as follows:

Cislunar market value prior to merger	$480	million
Targetco market value	40	
Present value of gain to merger	20	
Less Cash paid out to Targetco shareholders	−47.5	
Postmerger market value	$492.5	million

The postmerger share price for Cislunar will be $49.25, an increase of $1.25 per share. There are 10 million shares now outstanding, so the total increase in the value of Cislunar shares is $12.5 million.

Now let's summarize. The merger makes sense for Cislunar for two reasons. First, the merger adds $20 million of overall value. Second, the terms of the merger give only $7.5 million of the $20 million overall gain to Targetco's stockholders, leaving $12.5 million for Cislunar. You could say that the *cost* of acquiring Targetco is $7.5 million, the difference between the cash payment and the value of Targetco as a separate company.

$$\text{Cost} = \text{cash paid out} - \text{Targetco value} = \$47.5 - 40 = \$7.5 \text{ million}$$

Of course the Targetco stockholders are ahead by $7.5 million. *Their gain is your cost.* As we've already seen, Cislunar stockholders come out $12.5 million ahead. This is the merger's NPV:

$$\text{NPV} = \text{economic gain} - \text{cost} = 20 - 7.5 = \$12.5 \text{ million}$$

Writing down the economic gain and cost of a merger in this way separates the motive for the merger (the economic gain, or value added) from the terms of the merger (the *division* of the gain between the two merging companies).

▶ **Self-Test 21.3**   Killer Shark Inc. makes a surprise cash offer of $22 a share for Goldfish Industries. Before the offer, Goldfish was selling for $18 a share. Goldfish has 1 million shares outstanding. What must Killer Shark believe about the present value of the improvement it can bring to Goldfish's operations?

Mergers Financed by Stock

What if Cislunar wants to conserve its cash for other investments, and therefore decides to pay for the Targetco acquisition with new Cislunar shares? The deal calls for Targetco shareholders to receive one Cislunar share in exchange for every three Targetco shares.

It's the same merger, but the financing is different. The right column of Table 21.4 works out the consequences. Again, start at the *bottom* of the column. Note that the market value of Cislunar's shares after the merger is $540 million, $47.5 million higher than in the cash deal, because that cash is kept rather than paid out to Targetco shareholders. On the other hand, there are more shares outstanding, since 833,333 new shares have to be issued in exchange for the 2.5 million Targetco shares (a 1 to 3 ratio). Therefore, the price per share is 540/10.833 = $49.85, which is 60 cents higher than in the cash offer.

Why do Cislunar stockholders do better from the share exchange? The economic gain from the merger is the same, but the Targetco stockholders capture less of it. They get 833,333 shares at $49.85, or $41.5 million, a premium of only $1.5 million over Targetco's prior market value.

$$\text{Cost} = \text{value of shares issued} - \text{Targetco value}$$
$$= \$41.5 - 40 = \$1.5 \text{ million}$$

The merger's NPV to Cislunar's original shareholders is

$$\text{NPV} = \text{economic gain} - \text{cost} = 20 - 1.5 = \$18.5 \text{ million}$$

Note that Cislunar stock rises by $1.85 from its prior value. The total increase in value for Cislunar's original shareholders, who retain 10 million shares, is $18.5 million.

Evaluating the terms of a merger can be tricky when there is an exchange of shares. The target company's shareholders will retain a stake in the merged firms, so you have to figure out what the firm's shares will be worth *after* the merger is announced and its benefits appreciated by investors. Notice that we started with the total market value of Cislunar and Targetco postmerger, took account of the merger terms (833,333 new shares issued), and worked back to the postmerger share price. Only then could we work out the division of the merger gains between the two companies.

There is a key distinction between cash and stock for financing mergers. If cash is offered, the cost of the merger is not affected by the size of the merger gains. If stock is offered, the cost depends on the gains because the gains show up in the post-merger share price, and these shares are used to pay for the acquired firm. The nearby box illustrates how complex a stock offer can be. When Gillette offered to buy Duracell, giving Duracell shareholders about a 20 percent stake in the merged firm, the attractiveness of the deal depended on the stock market's valuation of *both* firms.

 See box p. 608

▶ **Self-Test 21.4**   Suppose Targetco shareholders demand one Cislunar share for every 2.5 Targetco shares. Otherwise they will not accept the merger. Under these revised terms, is the merger still a good deal for Cislunar?

A Warning

The cost of a merger is the premium the acquirer pays for the target firm over its value as a separate company. If the target is a public company, you can measure its

Blades, Batteries and a Fifth of Gillette

Back in 1988, when Kraft Inc. decided to unload its battery subsidiary, Gillette Co. was tempted. But the bidding went up and up and out of Gillette's reach. Kohlberg Kravis Roberts & Co. eventually bought the battery maker—it was Duracell, of course—for a seemingly extravagant $1.8 billion.

After eight years of due diligence, Gillette has finally agreed to fork over stock valued at more than $7 billion for the very same Duracell International Inc. Just as KKR now looks shrewd, rear-view analysts may snicker at Gillette for buying dear what it could have had then for, let us assume, only $2 billion in stock.

In fact, Gillette shareholders should thank their lucky stars the earlier deal didn't happen. In share-for-share acquisitions, what you are getting is only half the picture; what you are giving up is just as important. The standard analysis values such deals according to the dollar value of the target, but that approach is flawed. The key question isn't whether Duracell is worth $7 billion, because Gillette isn't giving up $7 billion. It is giving up a part—in this case 20%—of itself.

Schematically, Gillette is trading razor blades for batteries (not bucks for batteries), and the results can be very different. Since 1988, for instance, the blade business, at least under Gillette's management, has performed much better than batteries. While Duracell's stock has quadrupled, Gillette's has multiplied eight times. Thus if Gillette had in fact made that "cheap" $2 billion acquisition, it would have acquired a jack rabbit but given up a prize thoroughbred. The passed-over purchase back then would have cost Gillette *more than one-third* of its stock; today, it is buying the same business for only a fifth of its stock.

Clearly, taking a pass was the right move. Duracell *was* cheap in 1988, but Gillette was cheaper. And shopping with inexpensive currency, meaning issuing undervalued stock, amounts to selling the company (or a piece of it) on the cheap.

Going forward, the same analysis holds. The imputed dollar value of the deal will forever drift with Gillette's

Gillette's Stock

share price; the one constant is that each shareholder is trading away one-fifth of his interest in the old Gillette. Whether Duracell will be worth it, a subject no analyst has addressed, is what matters.

Such deals are manna for investment bankers (and bound to wind up in B-school texts) because you need to size up two businesses instead of one.

On balance, the blade business is more distinct, and better, than batteries. But how much better? Duracell for one-fifth of Gillette works out to this: For each dollar of Gillette earnings that shareholders are giving up, they are getting roughly $1.30 in cash earnings from batteries.

Blades should trade at a premium, but this one is steep. That premium, of course, reflects the current very high price of Gillette's stock, which in turn reflects a view that Gillette will forever keep profit growing twice as fast as its sales. Gillette's managers wouldn't come out and say that 34 times earnings reflects unwarranted optimism, or even a bull-market joie de vivre, but if that is what they thought, trading part of their company at that price for a cheaper one would be a smart move. And that is what they are doing.

Source: R. Lowenstein, "Intrinsic Value," *The Wall Street Journal,* September 19, 1996, p. C1. Reprinted with permission of The Wall Street Journal. Copyright 1996 Dow Jones & Company. All Rights Reserved Worldwide.

separate value by multiplying its stock price by the number of outstanding shares. Watch out, though: if investors expect the target to be acquired, its stock price may overstate the company's separate value. The target company's stock price may already have risen in anticipation of a premium to be paid by an acquiring firm.

Stock financing also mitigates the effects of over- or undervaluation of either firm. Suppose, for example, that A overestimates B's value as a separate entity, perhaps because it has overlooked some hidden liability. Thus A makes too generous an offer. Other things equal, A's stockholders are better off if it is a stock rather than a cash offer. With a stock offer, the inevitable bad news about B's value will fall partly on B's former stockholders.

Another Warning

Some companies begin their merger analyses with a forecast of the target firm's future cash flows. Any revenue increases or cost reductions attributable to the merger are included in the forecasts, which are then discounted back to the present and compared with the purchase price:

$$\text{Estimated net gain} = \text{DCF valuation of target including merger benefits}$$
$$- \text{cash required for acquisition}$$

This is a dangerous procedure. Even the brightest and best-trained analyst can make large errors in valuing a business. The estimated net gain may come up positive not because the merger makes sense, but simply because the analyst's cash-flow forecasts are too optimistic. On the other hand, a good merger may not be pursued if the analyst fails to recognize the target's potential as a stand-alone business.

A better procedure *starts* with the target's current and stand-alone market value and concentrates instead on the *changes* in cash flow that would result from the merger. Always ask why the two firms should be worth more together than apart. Remember, *you add value only if you can generate additional economic benefits—* some competitive edge that other firms can't match and that the target firm's managers can't achieve on their own.

It makes sense to keep an eye on the value that investors place on the gains from merging. If A's stock price falls when the deal is announced, investors are sending a message that the merger benefits are doubtful *or* that A is paying too much for these benefits.

Merger Tactics

Many mergers are agreed upon by both parties, but in other cases the acquirer will go over the heads of the target firm's management and make a *tender offer* directly to its stockholders. The management of the target firm may advise shareholders to accept the tender, or it may attempt to fight the bid in the hope that the acquirer will either raise its offer or throw in the towel.

The rules of merger warfare are largely set by federal and state laws[5] and the courts act as referee to see that contests are conducted fairly. We will look at one classic contest, which illustrates many of the tactics and weapons employed.

---

[5]The principal federal act regulating takeovers is the Williams Act of 1968.

▶ **Example 21.3**

The Fight for Cities Service[6]

The battle for Cities began in May 1982 when T. Boone Pickens, the chairman of Mesa Petroleum, began buying Cities shares as preparation for a takeover bid. Foreseeing the bid, Cities made an issue of equity that diluted Mesa's holding and followed this up with a retaliatory offer for Mesa.[7] Over the following month Mesa's bid was revised once and Cities's bid was revised twice before both companies agreed to drop their bids for the other. Cities repurchased Mesa's holding—at an $80 million profit to Mesa—and in exchange Mesa agreed not to attempt a hostile takeover of Cities for 5 years.

The principal reason for the cessation of hostilities between Mesa and Cities was the announcement that Cities had found a more congenial partner in Gulf Oil. Also, Gulf was prepared to pay substantially more than Mesa for Cities's stock. Unfortunately, this proposal fell afoul of the Federal Trade Commission (FTC), which is responsible for ensuring that mergers do not reduce competition. The FTC issued a temporary restraining order and shortly thereafter Gulf withdrew its offer.

white knight: Friendly potential acquirer sought by a target company threatened by an unwelcome suitor.

In response, Cities charged Gulf with not attempting to resolve the FTC's objections, and it filed a $3 billion lawsuit against Gulf. At the same time it began to look for another **white knight** to take it over in a friendly acquisition. The only interested suitor was Occidental Petroleum. Occidental's initial offer for Cities was revised twice and finally accepted. The battle for Cities Service had lasted 3 months and involved a total of nine bids from four separate companies.

In several instances the bidders employed both carrot and stick; for example, Occidental followed up its initial friendly offer for Cities with a hostile tender offer before finally reaching a friendly agreement.

The generous Gulf offer would have provided Cities's shareholders with a profit of almost 80 percent, but the collapse of that offer and the shortage of other suitors caused Cities's stock price to lose all its earlier gains. From then on Cities was in a relatively weak bargaining position, and the Occidental offer resulted in a profit of only 12 percent for Cities's stockholders. The merger scarcely affected Occidental's stock price, which suggests that investors believed the merger to be a zero-NPV investment for Occidental. Gulf's stockholders fared worst. Its high-priced offer led to a 14 percent fall in the price of Gulf stock. Even though this offer was subsequently withdrawn, the prospect of a costly lawsuit left Gulf's stock price depressed.

As with many real-life stories, there is an epilogue. One year after losing its battle for Cities, Gulf itself became a takeover target, when Mesa Petroleum proposed to buy Gulf stock in order to break the company up and sell it in pieces. At this point Chevron came to the rescue and acquired Gulf for $13.2 billion, more than double its value of 6 months earlier. Chevron's bid gave Mesa a profit of $760 million on the Gulf shares that it had bought. Asked for his views, Pickens commented, "Shucks, I guess we lost another one." ◀

Takeover Defenses

The Cities Service case illustrates some of the stratagems of modern merger warfare. Firms that are worried about being taken over usually prepare their defenses in

[6]The Cities Service takeover is described in R. S. Ruback, "The Cities Service Takeover: A Case Study," *Journal of Finance* 38 (May 1983), pp. 319–330.

[7]This practice of defending yourself against merger by making a counterbid for the predator's stock is sometimes known as the *Pacman defense.*

shark repellent: Amendments to a company charter made to forestall takeover attempts.

poison pill: Measure taken by a target firm to avoid acquisition; for example, the right for existing shareholders to buy additional shares at an attractive price if a bidder acquires a large holding.

advance. A common first step is to persuade the shareholders to agree to **shark-repellent** changes in the corporate charter to dissuade potential acquirers from attempting a takeover. For example, the charter may be amended to require that any merger must be approved by a *supermajority* of 80 percent of the shares rather than the normal 50 percent.

A firm may also deter potential bidders by devising **poison pills,** which make the company unappetizing. Often the poison pill will give existing shareholders the right to buy the company's shares at half price as soon as a bidder acquires more than 15 percent of the shares. The bidder is not entitled to the discount. Thus the bidder resembles Tantalus—as soon as it has acquired 15 percent of the shares, control is lifted further away from its reach.

If you have to sell out, it is more agreeable to sell to a firm of your own choosing rather than being taken over by a hostile predator. Therefore, firms that are threatened by takeover often look around for a white knight that will be a more congenial partner. We saw, for example, that Cities Service found a white knight in Occidental Petroleum.

Who Gets the Gains?

Is it better to own shares in the acquiring firm or the target? In our example, the stockholders of the target firm (Cities Service) made a profit of 12 percent. Investors in Occidental broke even and Gulf's shareholders lost money.

In general, shareholders of the target firm do best. Franks, Harris, and Titman studied 399 acquisitions by large U.S. firms between 1975 and 1984. They found that shareholders who sold following the announcement of the bid received a healthy gain averaging 28 percent.[8] On the other hand, it appears that investors expected acquiring companies to just about break even. The prices of their shares fell by 1 percent.[9] The value of the *total* package—buyer plus seller—increased by 4 percent. Of course, these are averages; selling shareholders sometimes obtain much higher returns. When IBM took over Lotus, it paid a premium of 100 percent, or about $1.7 billion, for Lotus stock.

Why do sellers earn higher returns? The most important reason is the competition among potential bidders. Once the first bidder puts the target company "in play," one or more additional suitors often jump in, sometimes as white knights at the invitation of the target firm's management. Every time one suitor tops another's bid, more of the merger gain slides toward the target. At the same time the target firm's management may mount various legal and financial counterattacks, ensuring that capitulation, if and when it comes, is at the highest attainable price.

Of course, bidders and targets are not the only possible winners. Unsuccessful bidders often win, too, by selling off their holdings in target companies at substantial profits. Such shares may be sold on the open market or sold back to the target company.[10] Sometimes they are sold to the successful suitor. We saw how Mesa Petroleum earned $80 million by selling its Cities Service shares back to Cities Service and $760 million by selling its Gulf stock to Chevron, the winning bidder.

[8]J. R. Franks, R. S. Harris, and S. Titman, "The Postmerger Share-Price Performance of Acquiring Firms," *Journal of Financial Economics* 29 (March 1991), pp. 81–96.

[9]The small loss to the shareholders of acquiring firms is not statistically significant. Other studies using different samples have observed a small positive return.

[10]When a potential acquirer sells the shares back to the target, the transaction is known as *greenmail*.

Other winners include investment bankers, lawyers, accountants, and in some cases arbitrageurs, or "arbs," who speculate on the likely success of takeover bids.

"Speculate" has a negative ring, but it can be a useful social service. A tender offer may present shareholders with a difficult decision. Should they accept, should they wait to see if someone else produces a better offer, or should they sell their stock in the market? This quandary presents an opportunity for the arbitrageurs. In other words, they buy from the target's shareholders and take on the risk that the deal will not go through.[11]

21.6 Leveraged Buy-outs

Leveraged buy-outs, or *LBOs,* differ from ordinary acquisitions in two ways. First, a large fraction of the purchase price is debt-financed. Some, perhaps all, of this debt is junk, that is, below investment grade. Second, the shares of the LBO no longer trade on the open market. The remaining equity in the LBO is privately held by a small group of (usually institutional) investors. When this group is led by the company's management, the acquisition is called a *management buy-out (MBO).* Many LBOs are in fact MBOs.

In the 1970s and 1980s many management buy-outs were arranged for unwanted divisions of large, diversified companies. Smaller divisions outside the companies' main lines of business often lacked top management's interest and commitment, and divisional management chafed under corporate bureaucracy. Many such divisions flowered when spun off as MBOs. Their managers, pushed by the need to generate cash for debt service and encouraged by a substantial personal stake in the business, found ways to cut costs and compete more effectively.

During the 1980s MBO/LBO activity shifted to buy-outs of entire businesses, including large, mature public corporations. The largest, most dramatic, and best-documented LBO of them all was the $25 billion takeover of RJR Nabisco in 1988 by Kohlberg Kravis Roberts (KKR). The players, tactics, and controversies of LBOs are writ large in this case.

▶ **Example 21.4**

RJR Nabisco[12]

On October 28, 1988, the board of directors of RJR Nabisco revealed that Ross Johnson, the company's chief executive officer, had formed a group of investors prepared to buy all the firm's stock for $75 per share in cash and take the company private. Johnson's group was backed up and advised by Shearson Lehman Hutton, the investment bank subsidiary of American Express.

RJR's share price immediately moved to about $75, handing shareholders a 36 percent gain over the previous day's price of $56. At the same time RJR's bonds fell, since it was clear that existing bondholders would soon have a lot more company.

Johnson's offer lifted RJR onto the auction block. Once the company was in play, its board of directors was obliged to consider other offers, which were not long com-

---

[11]Strictly speaking, an arbitrageur is an investor who makes a riskless profit. Arbitrageurs in merger battles often take very large risks indeed. Their activities are sometimes known as "risk arbitrage."

[12]The story of the RJR Nabisco buy-out is reconstructed by B. Burrough and J. Helyar in *Barbarians at the Gate: The Fall of RJR Nabisco* (New York: Harper & Row, 1990) and is the subject of a movie with the same title.

ing. Four days later, a group of investors led by LBO specialists Kohlberg Kravis Roberts bid $90 per share, $79 in cash plus preferred stock valued at $11.

The bidding finally closed on November 30, some 32 days after the initial offer was revealed. In the end it was Johnson's group against KKR. KKR offered $109 per share, after adding $1 per share (roughly $230 million) at the last hour. The KKR bid was $81 in cash, convertible subordinated debentures valued at about $10, and preferred shares valued at about $18. Johnson's group bid $112 in cash and securities.

But the RJR board chose KKR. True, Johnson's group had offered $3 per share more, but its security valuations were viewed as "softer" and perhaps overstated. Also, KKR's planned asset sales were less drastic; perhaps their plans for managing the business inspired more confidence. Finally, the Johnson group's proposal contained a management compensation package that seemed extremely generous and had generated an avalanche of bad press.

But where did the merger benefits come from? What could justify offering $109 per share, about $25 billion in all, for a company that only 33 days previously had been selling for $56 per share?

KKR and other bidders were betting on two things. First, they expected to generate billions of additional dollars from interest tax shields, reduced capital expenditures, and sales of assets not strictly necessary to RJR's core businesses. Asset sales alone were projected to generate $5 billion. Second, they expected to make those core businesses significantly more profitable, mainly by cutting back on expenses and bureaucracy. Apparently there was plenty to cut, including the RJR "Air Force," which at one point operated 10 corporate jets.

In the year after KKR took over, new management was installed. This group sold assets and cut back operating expenses and capital spending. There were also layoffs. As expected, high interest charges meant a net loss of $976 million for 1989, but pretax operating income actually increased, despite extensive asset sales, including the sale of RJR's European food operations.

While management was cutting costs and selling assets, prices in the junk bond market were rapidly declining, implying much higher future interest charges for RJR and stricter terms on any refinancing. In mid-1990 KKR made an additional equity investment, and later that year the company announced an offer of cash and new shares in exchange for $753 million of junk bonds. By 1993 the burden of debt had been reduced from $26 billion to $14 billion. For RJR, the world's largest LBO, it seemed that high debt was a temporary, not permanent, virtue. ◀

Barbarians at the Gate?

The buy-out of RJR crystallized views on LBOs, the junk bond market, and the takeover business. For many it exemplified all that was wrong with finance in the 1980s, especially the willingness of "raiders" to carve up established companies, leaving them with enormous debt burdens, basically in order to get rich quick.

There was plenty of confusion, stupidity, and greed in the LBO business. Not all the people involved were nice. On the other hand, LBOs generated enormous increases in market value, and most of the gains went to selling stockholders, not raiders. For example, the biggest winners in the RJR Nabisco LBO were the company's stockholders.

We should therefore consider briefly where these gains may have come from before we try to pass judgment on LBOs. There are several possibilities.

The Junk Bond Markets. LBOs and debt-financed takeovers may have been driven by artificially cheap funding from the junk bond markets. With hindsight it seems that investors in junk bonds underestimated the risks of default. Default rates climbed painfully between 1989 and 1991. At the same time the junk bond market became much less liquid after the demise of Drexel Burnham Lambert, the chief market maker. Yields rose dramatically, and new issues dried up. Suddenly junk-financed LBOs seemed to disappear from the scene.[13]

Leverage and Taxes. As we explained in Chapter 14, borrowing money saves taxes. But taxes were not the main driving force behind LBOs. The value of interest tax shields was just not big enough to explain the observed gains in market value.

Of course, if interest tax shields were the main motive for LBOs' high debt, then LBO managers would not be so concerned to pay off debt. We saw that this was one of the first tasks facing RJR Nabisco's new management.

Other Stakeholders. It is possible that the gain to the selling stockholders is just someone else's loss and that no value is generated overall. Therefore, we should look at the total gain to *all* investors in an LBO, not just the selling stockholders.

Bondholders are the obvious losers. The debt they thought was well-secured may turn into junk when the borrower goes through an LBO. We noted how market prices of RJR Nabisco debt fell sharply when Ross Johnson's first LBO offer was announced. But again, the value losses suffered by bondholders in LBOs are not nearly large enough to explain stockholder gains.

Leverage and Incentives. Managers and employees of LBOs work harder and often smarter. They have to generate cash to service the extra debt. Moreover, managers' personal fortunes are riding on the LBO's success. They become owners rather than organization men or women.

It is hard to measure the payoff from better incentives, but there is some evidence of improved operating efficiency in LBOs. Kaplan, who studied 48 management buyouts between 1980 and 1986, found average increases in operating income of 24 percent over the following 3 years. Ratios of operating income and net cash flow to assets and sales increased dramatically. He observed cutbacks in capital expenditures but not in employment. Kaplan suggests that these operating changes "are due to improved incentives rather than layoffs or managerial exploitation of shareholders through inside information."[14]

Free Cash Flow. The free-cash-flow theory of takeovers is basically that mature firms with a surplus of cash will tend to waste it. This contrasts with standard finance theory, which says that firms with more cash than positive-NPV investment opportunities should give the cash back to investors through higher dividends or share repurchases. But we see firms like RJR Nabisco spending on corporate luxuries and questionable capital investments. One benefit of LBOs is to put such companies on a diet and force them to pay out cash to service debt.

[13]There was a sharp revival of junk bond sales in 1992 and 1993 and 1996 was a banner year. But many of these issues simply replaced existing bonds. It remains to be seen whether junk bonds will make a lasting recovery.

[14]S. Kaplan, "The Effects of Management Buyouts on Operating Performance and Value," *Journal of Financial Economics* 24 (October 1989), pp. 217–254.

The free-cash-flow theory predicts that mature, "cash cow" companies will be the most likely targets of LBOs. We can find many examples that fit the theory, including RJR Nabisco. The theory says that the gains in market value generated by LBOs are just the present values of the future cash flows that would otherwise have been frittered away.[15]

We do not endorse the free-cash-flow theory as the sole explanation for LBOs. We have mentioned several other plausible rationales, and we suspect that most LBOs are driven by a mixture of motives. Nor do we say that all LBOs are beneficial. On the contrary, there are many mistakes and even soundly motivated LBOs can be dangerous, as the bankruptcies of Campeau, Revco, National Gypsum, and many other highly leveraged companies prove. However, we do take issue with those who portray LBOs *simply* as Wall Street barbarians breaking up the traditional strengths of corporate America. In many cases LBOs have generated true gains.

In the next section we sum up the long-run impact of mergers and acquisitions, including LBOs, in the United States economy. We warn you, however, that there are no neat answers. Our assessment has to be mixed and tentative.

21.7 *Mergers and the Economy*

Merger Waves

Mergers come in waves. The first episode of intense merger activity occurred at the turn of the century and the second in the 1920s. There was a further boom from 1967 to 1969 and then again in the 1980s and 1990s. Each episode coincided with a period of buoyant stock prices, though in each case there were substantial differences in the types of companies that merged and how they went about it.

We don't really understand why merger activity is so volatile. If mergers are prompted by economic motives, at least one of these motives must be "here today, gone tomorrow," and it must somehow be associated with high stock prices. But none of the economic motives that we review in this chapter has anything to do with the general level of the stock market. None of the motives burst on the scene in 1967, departed in 1970, reappeared for most of the 1980s, and reappeared again in the mid-1990s.

Some mergers may result from mistakes in valuation on the part of the stock market. In other words, the buyer may believe that investors have underestimated the value of the seller or may hope that they *will* overestimate the value of the combined firm. Why don't we see just as many firms hunting for bargain acquisitions when the stock market is low? It is possible that "suckers are born every minute," but it's difficult to believe that they can be harvested only in bull markets.

During the 1980s merger boom, only the very largest companies were immune from attack from a rival management team. For example, in 1985 Pantry Pride, a small supermarket chain recently emerged from bankruptcy, made a bid for the cosmetics company Revlon. Revlon's assets were more than five times those of Pantry Pride. What made the bid possible (and eventually successful) was the ability of

[15]The free-cash-flow theory's chief proponent is Michael Jensen. See M. C. Jensen, "The Eclipse of the Public Corporation," *Harvard Business Review* 67 (September–October 1989), pp. 61–74, and "The Agency Costs of Free Cash Flow, Corporate Finance and Takeovers," *American Economic Review* 76 (May 1986), pp. 323–329.

Pantry Pride to finance the takeover by borrowing $2.1 billion. The growth of leveraged buy-outs during the 1980s depended on the development of a junk bond market that allowed bidders to place low-grade bonds rapidly and in high volume.

By the end of the decade the merger environment had changed. Many of the obvious targets had disappeared, and the battle for RJR Nabisco highlighted the increasing cost of victory. Institutions were reluctant to increase their holdings of junk bonds. Moreover, the market for these bonds had depended to a remarkable extent on one individual, Michael Milken, of the investment bank Drexel Burnham Lambert. By the late 1980s Milken and his employer were in trouble. Milken was indicted by a grand jury on 98 counts and was subsequently sentenced to jail and ordered to pay $600 million. Drexel filed for bankruptcy, but by that time the junk bond market was moribund and the finance for highly leveraged buy-outs had largely dried up.[16] Finally, in reaction to the perceived excess of the merger boom, the state legislatures and the courts began to lean against takeovers.

The decline in merger activity proved temporary; by the mid-1990s stock markets and mergers were booming again. However, LBOs remained out of fashion, and relatively few mergers were intended simply to replace management. Instead, companies began to look once more at the possible benefits from combining two businesses. Cuts in defense spending encouraged defense firms to combine their operations, and new technologies led to mergers in the communications and entertainment industries. Some of the largest mergers in the 1990s have involved one or more foreign firms. For example, two Swiss chemical and pharmaceutical companies, Sandoz and Ciba-Geigy, combined in a $36 billion merger.

Do Mergers Generate Net Benefits?

There are undoubtedly good acquisitions and bad acquisitions, but economists find it hard to agree on whether acquisitions are beneficial *on balance.* We do know that mergers generate substantial gains to stockholders of acquired firms.

Since buyers seem roughly to break even and sellers make substantial gains, it seems that there are positive gains to mergers. But not everybody is convinced. Some believe that investors analyzing mergers pay too much attention to short-term earnings gains and don't notice that these gains are at the expense of long-term prospects.

Since we can't observe how companies would have fared in the absence of a merger, it is difficult to measure the effects on profitability. Studies of recent merger activity suggest that mergers *do* seem to improve real productivity. For example, Healy, Palepu, and Ruback examined 50 large mergers between 1979 and 1983 and found an average increase in the companies' pretax returns of 2.4 percentage points.[17] They argue that this gain came from generating a higher level of sales from the same assets. There was no evidence that the companies were mortgaging their long-term futures by cutting back on long-term investments; expenditures on capital equipment and research and development tracked the industry average.

If you are concerned with public policy toward mergers, you do not want to look only at their impact on the shareholders of the companies concerned. For instance,

---

[16]For a history of the role of Milken in the development of the junk bond market, see C. Bruck, *The Predator's Ball: The Junk Bond Raiders and the Man Who Staked Them* (New York: Simon and Schuster, 1988).

[17]See P. Healy, K. Palepu, and R. Ruback, "Does Corporate Performance Improve after Mergers?" *Journal of Financial Economics* 31 (April 1992), pp. 135–175. The study examined the pretax returns of the merged companies relative to industry averages.

we have already seen that in the case of RJR Nabisco some part of the shareholders' gain was at the expense of the bondholders and the Internal Revenue Service (through the enlarged interest tax shield). The acquirer's shareholders may also gain at the expense of the target firm's employees, who in some cases are laid off or are forced to take pay cuts after takeovers.

Many people believe that the merger wave of the 1980s led to excessive debt levels and left many companies ill-equipped to survive a recession. Also, many savings and loan companies and some large insurance firms invested heavily in junk bonds. Defaults on these bonds threatened, and in some cases extinguished, their solvency.

Perhaps the most important effect of acquisition is felt by the managers of companies that are *not* taken over. For example, one effect of LBOs was that the managers of even the largest corporations could not feel safe from challenge. Perhaps the threat of takeover spurs the whole of corporate America to try harder. Unfortunately, we don't know whether on balance the threat of merger makes for more active days or sleepless nights.

We do know that merger activity is very costly. For example, in the RJR Nabisco buy-out, the total fees paid to the investment banks, lawyers, and accountants amounted to over $1 billion.

Even if the gains to the community exceed these costs, one wonders whether the same benefits could not be achieved more cheaply another way. For example, are leveraged buy-outs necessary to make managers work harder? Perhaps the problem lies in the way that many corporations reward and penalize their managers. Perhaps many of the gains from takeover could be captured by linking management compensation more closely to performance.

21.8 Summary

1. If the board of directors fails to replace an inefficient management, there are four ways to effect a change: (a) shareholders may engage in a proxy fight to replace the board, (b) the firm may be acquired by another, (c) the firm may be purchased by a private group of investors in a leveraged buy-out, or (d) it may sell off part of its operations to another company.

2. A merger may be undertaken in order to replace an inefficient management. But there may also be synergies from combining the operations of two firms. These may stem from economies of scale, economies of vertical integration, the combination of complementary resources, or redeployment of surplus funds. We don't know how common these benefits are, but they do make economic sense. Sometimes mergers are undertaken to diversify risks or artificially increase growth of earnings per share. These motives are dubious.

3. A merger generates an economic gain if the two firms are worth more together than apart. You should go ahead with the merger if the gain exceeds the cost. The cost is the premium that the buyer pays for the selling firm over its value as a separate entity. When payment is in the form of shares, the value of this payment naturally depends on what those shares are worth after the merger is complete.

4. There are three ways for one firm to acquire another. It can merge all the assets and liabilities of the target into those of its own company; it can buy the stock of the target; or it can buy the individual assets of the target. Mergers are often

amicably negotiated between the management and directors of the two companies; but if the seller is reluctant, the would-be buyer can decide to make a tender offer for the stock. We sketched some of the offensive and defensive tactics used in takeover battles. We also observed that when the target firm loses, its shareholders typically win: target firms' shareholders earn abnormally large returns. The bidding firm's shareholders roughly break even. The typical merger appears to generate positive net benefit to investors, but competition among bidders and active defense by target managements push most of the gains toward selling shareholders.

5. In a leveraged buy-out (LBO) or management buy-out (MBO), all public shares are repurchased and the company "goes private." LBOs tend to involve mature businesses with ample cash flow and modest growth opportunities. LBOs and other debt-financed takeovers are driven by a mixture of motives, including (a) the value of interest tax shields; (b) transfers of value from bondholders, who may see the value of their bonds fall as the firm piles up more debt; and (c) the opportunity to create better incentives for managers and employees, who have a personal stake in the company. In addition, many LBOs were designed to force firms with surplus cash to distribute it to shareholders rather than plowing it back. Investors feared such companies would channel free cash flow into negative-NPV investments.

6. Mergers seem to generate economic gains, but they are also costly. Investment bankers, lawyers, and arbitrageurs thrived during the 1980s merger and LBO boom. Many companies were left with heavy debt burdens and had to sell assets or improve performance to stay solvent. By the end of 1990, the new-issue junk bond market had dried up, and the corporate jousting field was strangely quiet. But not for long. As we write this chapter at the end of 1997, stock markets and mergers are once again booming.

Key Terms

proxy contest	leveraged buy-out (LBO)	shark repellent
merger	management buy-out(MBO)	poison pill
tender offer	white knight	
acquisition		

Problems

1. **Merger Gains.** Acquiring Corp. is considering a takeover of Target Inc. Acquiring has 10 million shares outstanding, which sell for $40 each. Target has 5 million shares outstanding, which sell for $20 each. If the merger gains are estimated at $20 million, what is the highest price per share that Acquiring should be willing to pay to Target shareholders?

2. **Mergers and P/E Ratios.** If Acquiring Corp. from problem 1 has a price-earnings ratio of 12, and Target has a P/E ratio of 8, what should be the P/E ratio of the merged firm? Assume in this case that the merger is financed by an issue of new Acquiring Corp. shares. Target will get one Acquiring share for every two Target shares held.

3. **Merger Motives.** Explain why it might make good sense for Northeast Heating and Northeast Air Conditioning to merge into one company.

4. **Merger Gains.** Immense Appetite, Inc., believes that it can acquire Sleepy Industries and improve efficiency to the extent that the market value of Sleepy will increase by $5 million. Sleepy currently sells for $20 a share, and there are 1 million shares outstanding.

   a. Sleepy's management is willing to accept a cash offer of $25 a share. Can the merger be accomplished on a friendly basis?

   b. What will happen if Sleepy's management holds out for an offer of $28 a share?

5. **Merger Gains and Costs.** Velcro Saddles is contemplating the acquisition of Pogo Ski Sticks, Inc. The values of the two companies as separate entities are $20 million and $10 million, respectively. Velcro Saddles estimates that by combining the two companies, it will reduce marketing and administrative costs by $500,000 per year in perpetuity. Velcro Saddles is willing to pay $14 million cash for Pogo. The opportunity cost of capital is 10 percent.

   a. What is the gain from merger?
   b. What is the cost of the cash offer?
   c. What is the NPV of the acquisition under the cash offer?

6. **Stock versus Cash Offers.** Suppose that instead of making a cash offer as in problem 5, Velcro Saddles considers offering Pogo shareholders a 50 percent holding in Velcro Saddles.

   a. What is the value of the stock in the merged company held by the original Pogo shareholders?
   b. What is the cost of the stock alternative?
   c. What is its NPV under the stock offer?

7. **Merger Motives.** Which of the following motives for mergers make economic sense?

   a. Merging to achieve economies of scale.
   b. Merging to reduce risk by diversification.
   c. Merging to redeploy cash generated by a firm with ample profits but limited growth opportunities.
   d. Merging to increase earnings per share.

8. **Empirical Facts.** True or false?

   a. Sellers almost always gain in mergers.
   b. Buyers almost always gain in mergers.
   c. Firms that do unusually well tend to be acquisition targets.
   d. Merger activity in the United States varies dramatically from year to year.
   e. On the average, mergers produce substantial economic gains.
   f. Tender offers require the approval of the selling firm's management.
   g. The cost of a merger is always independent of the economic gain produced by the merger.

9. **Merger Tactics.** Connect each term to its correct definition or description:

A. LBO	1. Attempt to gain control of a firm by winning the votes of its stockholders.
B. Poison pill	
C. Tender offer	2. Changes in corporate charter designed to deter unwelcome takeover.
D. Shark repellent	
E. Proxy contest	3. Friendly potential acquirer sought by a threatened target firm.
F. White knight	4. Shareholders are issued rights to buy shares if bidder acquires large stake in the firm.
	5. Offer to buy shares directly from stockholders.
	6. Company or business bought out by private investors, largely debt-financed.

10. **Empirical Facts.** True or false?

    a. One of the first tasks of an LBO's financial manager is to pay down debt.
    b. Shareholders of bidding companies earn higher abnormal returns when the merger is financed with stock than in cash-financed deals.
    c. Targets for LBOs in the 1980s tended to be profitable companies in mature industries with limited investment opportunities.

11. **Stock versus Cash Offers.** Sweet Cola Corp. (SCC) is bidding to take over Salty Dog Pretzels (SDP). SCC has 3,000 shares outstanding, selling at $50 per share. SDP has 2,000 shares outstanding, selling at $17.50 a share. SCC estimates the economic gain from the merger to be $10,000.

a. If SDP can be acquired for $20 a share, what is the NPV of the merger to SCC?

b. What will SCC sell for when the market learns that it plans to acquire SDP for $20 a share? What will SDP sell for? What are the percentage gains to the shareholders of each firm?

c. Now suppose that the merger takes place through an exchange of stock. Based on the premerger prices of the firms, SCC sells for $50, so instead of paying $20 cash, SCC issues .40 of its shares for every SDP share acquired. What will be the price of the merged firm?

d. What is the NPV of the merger to SCC when it uses an exchange of stock? Why does your answer differ from part (a)?

12. **Mergers and P/E Ratios.** Castles in the Sand currently sells at a price-earnings multiple of 10. The firm has 2 million shares outstanding, and sells at a price per share of $40. Firm Foundation has a P/E multiple of 8, has 1 million shares outstanding, and sells at a price per share of $20.

a. If Castles acquires the other firm by exchanging one of its shares for every two of Firm Foundation's, what will be the earnings per share of the merged firm?

b. What should be the P/E of the new firm if the merger has no economic gains? What will happen to Castles's price per share? Show that shareholders of neither Castles nor Firm Foundation realize any change in wealth.

c. What will happen to Castles's price per share if the market does not realize that the P/E ratio of the merged firm ought to differ from Castles's premerger ratio?

d. How are the gains from the merger split between shareholders of the two firms if the market is fooled as in part (c)?

13. **Bootstrap Game.** The Muck and Slurry merger has fallen through (see Section 21.3). But World Enterprises is determined to report earnings per share of $2.67. It therefore acquires the Wheelrim and Axle Company. You are given the following facts:

	World Enterprises	Wheelrim and Axle	Merged Firm
Earnings per share	$2.00	$2.50	$2.67
Price per share	$40.00	$25.00	____
Price-earnings ratio	20	10	____
Number of shares	100,000	200,000	____
Total earnings	$200,000	$500,000	____
Total market value	$4,000,000	$5,000,000	____

Once again there are no gains from merging. In exchange for Wheelrim and Axle shares, World Enterprises issues just enough of its own shares to ensure its $2.67 earnings per share objective.

a. Complete the above table for the merged firm.

b. How many shares of World Enterprises are exchanged for each share of Wheelrim and Axle?

c. What is the cost of the merger to World Enterprises?

d. What is the change in the total market value of those World Enterprises shares that were outstanding before the merger?

14. **Merger Gains and Costs.** As treasurer of Leisure Products, Inc., you are investigating the possible acquisition of Plastitoys. You have the following basic data:

	Leisure Products	Plastitoys
Forecast earnings per share	$5.00	$1.50
Forecast dividend per share	$3.00	$.80
Number of shares	1,000,000	600,000
Stock price	$90.00	$20.00

You estimate that investors currently expect a steady growth of about 6 percent in Plastitoys' earnings and dividends. You believe that Leisure Products could increase Plastitoys' growth rate to 8 percent per year, without any additional capital investment required.

a. What is the gain from the acquisition?

b. What is the cost of the acquisition if Leisure Products pays $25 in cash for each share of Plastitoys?

c. What is the cost of the acquisition if Leisure Products offers one share of Leisure Products for every three shares of Plastitoys?

d. How would the cost of the cash offer and the share offer alter if the expected growth rate of Plastitoys were not increased by the merger?

Solutions to Self-Test Questions

21.1 a. Horizontal merger. IBM is in the same industry as Apple Computer.

b. Conglomerate merger. Apple Computer and Stop & Shop are in different industries.

c. Vertical merger. Stop & Shop is expanding backward to acquire one of its suppliers, Campbell Soup.

d. Conglomerate merger. Campbell Soup and IBM are in different industries.

21.2 Given current earnings of $2.00 a share, and a share price of $10, Muck and Slurry would have a market value of $1,000,000 and a price-earnings ratio of only 5. It can be acquired for only half as many shares of World Enterprises, 25,000 shares. Therefore, the merged firm will have 125,000 shares outstanding and earnings of $400,000, resulting in earnings per share of $3.20, higher than the $2.67 value in the third column of Table 21.2.

21.3 The cost of the merger is $4 million: the $4 per share premium offered to Goldfish shareholders times 1 million shares. If the merger has positive NPV to Killer Shark, the gain must be greater than $4 million.

21.4 Yes. Look again at Table 21.4. Total market value is still $540, but Cislunar will have to issue 1 million shares to complete the merger. Total shares in the merged firm will be 11 million. The postmerger share price is $49.09, so Cislunar and its shareholders still come out ahead.

Foreign exchange quotes on September 18, 1997.

How does corporate finance change when it is conducted in more than one currency?

Courtesy Reuters

Chapter 22

International Financial Management

*T*hus far we have talked principally about doing business at home. But many companies have substantial overseas interests. Of course the objectives of international financial management are still the same. You want to buy assets that are worth *more* than they cost, and you want to pay for them by issuing liabilities that are worth *less* than the money raised. But when you try to apply these criteria to an international business, you come up against some new wrinkles.

You must, for example, know how to deal with more than one currency. Therefore we open this chapter with a look at foreign exchange markets.

The financial manager must also remember that interest rates differ from country to country. For example, in mid-1997 the short-term rate of interest was about .5 percent in Japan, 5.5 percent in the United States, and 7 percent in Britain. We will discuss the reasons for these differences in interest rates, along with some of the implications for financing overseas operations.

Exchange rate fluctuations can knock companies off course and transform black ink into red. We will therefore discuss how firms can protect themselves against exchange risks.

We will also discuss how international companies decide on capital investments. How do they choose the discount rate? You'll find that the basic principles of capital budgeting are the same as for domestic projects, but there are a few pitfalls to watch for.

After studying this chapter you should be able to

▶ Understand the difference between spot and forward exchange rates.

▶ Understand the basic relationships between spot exchange rates, forward exchange rates, interest rates, and inflation rates.

▶ Formulate simple strategies to protect the firm against exchange rate risk.

▶ Perform an NPV analysis for projects with cash flows in foreign currencies.

22.1 *Foreign Exchange Markets*

An American company that imports goods from Switzerland may need to exchange its dollars for Swiss francs in order to pay for its purchases. An American company exporting to Switzerland may *receive* Swiss francs, which it sells in exchange for dollars. Both firms must make use of the foreign exchange market, where currencies are traded.

The foreign exchange market has no central marketplace. All business is conducted by computer and telephone. The principal dealers are the large commercial banks, and any corporation that wants to buy or sell currency usually does so through a commercial bank.

Turnover in the foreign exchange markets is huge. In London alone about $460 billion of currency changes hands each day (that is, over $100 *trillion* a year). New York and Tokyo between them account for a further $400 billion of turnover a day.

Compare this to trading volume on the New York Stock Exchange, where about $15 billion of stock might change hands on a typical day.

Exchange rates are the amount of one country's currency needed to purchase one unit of another currency. Table 22.1 reproduces a table of exchange rates from *The Wall Street Journal.* The first pair of columns, labeled "U.S. $ equiv," tells you how many dollars it takes to buy one unit of foreign currency. This is called the *direct quote.* For example, it takes .6782 U.S. dollar to buy 1 Swiss franc (SFr). The second pair of columns, labeled "Currency per U.S. $," tells you how many units of foreign currency you can buy for 1 U.S. dollar. This is called the *indirect quote.* You can buy 1.4745 Swiss francs for 1 dollar.

Most exchange rates are expressed as indirect quotes (e.g., ¥119 per dollar), but to make life confusing the British pound (and the Irish punt) are usually shown as direct quotes (e.g., $1.60 per pound). Of course, these two types of quotes give precisely the same information. If ¥119 buys 1 dollar, then ¥1 buys 1/119 = $.0084, and the dollar-yen exchange rate could equally well be expressed using a direct quote as $.0084 per yen. Similarly, since $1.60 buys £1, $1 will buy only £.625, and the indirect quote for the British pound is £.625 per dollar.

Table 22.1

Currency exchange rates on September 11, 1997

CURRENCY TRADING

Thursday, September 11, 1997
EXCHANGE RATES

The New York foreign exchange selling rates below apply to trading among banks in amounts of $1 million and more, as quoted at 4 p.m. Eastern time by Dow Jones and other sources. Retail transactions provide fewer units of foreign currency per dollar.

Country	U.S. $ equiv. Thu	U.S. $ equiv. Wed	Currency per U.S. $ Thu	Currency per U.S. $ Wed
Argentina (Peso)	1.0014	1.0014	.9986	.9986
Australia (Dollar)	.7198	.7293	1.3893	1.3712
Austria (Schilling)	.07931	.07884	12.608	12.684
Bahrain (Dinar)	2.6525	2.6525	.3770	.3770
Belgium (Franc)	.02718	.02695	36.795	37.099
Brazil (Real)	.9160	.9163	1.0918	1.0914
Britain (Pound)	1.5997	1.5866	.6251	.6303
1-month forward	1.5978	1.5846	.6259	.6311
3-months forward	1.5938	1.5807	.6274	.6326
6-months forward	1.5886	1.5755	.6295	.6347
Canada (Dollar)	.7184	.7211	1.3920	1.3867
1-month forward	.7198	.7226	1.3893	1.3839
3-months forward	.7221	.7249	1.3848	1.3795
6-months forward	.7254	.7281	1.3786	1.3734
Chile (Peso)	.002413	.002413	414.35	414.35
China (Renminbi)	.1202	.1202	8.3189	8.3187
Colombia (Peso)	.0008000	.0008076	1250.00	1238.20
Czech. Rep. (Koruna) .				
Commercial rate	.02971	.02933	33.658	34.100
Denmark (Krone)	.1475	.1460	6.7790	6.8480
Ecuador (Sucre)				
Floating rate	.0002436	.0002436	4105.00	4105.00
Finland (Markka)	.1874	.1857	5.3368	5.3836
France (Franc)	.1670	.1654	5.9885	6.0475
1-month forward	.1673	.1657	5.9768	6.0349
3-months forward	.1680	.1663	5.9532	6.0122
6-months forward	.1690	.1673	5.9180	5.9769
Germany (Mark)	.5616	.5560	1.7805	1.7985
1-month forward	.5628	.5571	1.7769	1.7949
3-months forward	.5651	.5594	1.7696	1.7876
6-months forward	.5685	.5628	1.7591	1.7769
Greece (Drachma)	.003567	.003531	280.35	283.18
Hong Kong (Dollar)	.1291	.1291	7.7460	7.7454
Hungary (Forint)	.005103	.005068	195.96	197.33
India (Rupee)	.02736	.02735	36.555	36.560
Indonesia (Rupiah)	.0003396	.0003408	2945.00	2934.00
Ireland (Punt)	1.5085	1.4921	.6629	.6702
Israel (Shekel)	.2861	.2848	3.4958	3.5107
Italy (Lira)	.0005750	.0005698	1739.00	1755.00
Japan (Yen)	.008363	.008393	119.58	119.15
1-month forward	.008398	.008429	119.07	118.64
3-months forward	.008472	.008502	118.04	117.62
6-months forward	.008585	.008616	116.48	116.06
Jordan (Dinar)	1.4094	1.4094	.7095	.7095
Kuwait (Dinar)	3.2808	3.2798	.3048	.3049
Lebanon (Pound)	.0006517	.0006516	1534.50	1534.75
Malaysia (Ringgit)	.3378	.3420	2.9600	2.9243
Malta (Lira)	2.5478	2.5253	.3925	.3960
Mexico (Peso)				
Floating rate	.1286	.1287	7.7780	7.7680
Netherland (Guilder)	.4989	.4935	2.0044	2.0264
New Zealand (Dollar) .	.6336	.6353	1.5783	1.5741
Norway (Krone)	.1366	.1349	7.3233	7.4128
Pakistan (Rupee)	.02496	.02496	40.070	40.070
Peru (new Sol)	.3807	.3801	2.6268	2.6308
Philippines (Peso)	.03086	.03150	32.400	31.750
Poland (Zloty)	.2871	.2867	3.4835	3.4885
Portugal (Escudo)	.005529	.005472	180.88	182.75
Russia (Ruble) (a)	.0001711	.0001712	5843.00	5841.50
Saudi Arabia (Riyal)	.2666	.2666	3.7505	3.7505
Singapore (Dollar)	.6609	.6637	1.5130	1.5068
Slovak Rep. (Koruna) .	.02889	.02909	34.617	34.379
South Africa (Rand)	.2128	.2127	4.6995	4.7025
South Korea (Won)	.001100	.001100	908.75	908.90
Spain (Peseta)	.006659	.006594	150.17	151.66
Sweden (Krona)	.1291	.1282	7.7465	7.8028
Switzerland (Franc)	.6782	.6764	1.4745	1.4785
1-month forward	.6806	.6789	1.4692	1.4729
3-months forward	.6855	.6836	1.4588	1.4629
6-months forward	.6926	.6906	1.4439	1.4480
Taiwan (Dollar)	.03495	.03495	28.613	28.612
Thailand (Baht)	.02865	.02928	34.900	34.150
Turkey (Lira)	.00000589	.00000589	169660.00	169850.00
United Arab (Dirham)	.2723	.2723	3.6725	3.6725
Uruguay (New Peso) ..				
Financial	.1026	.1026	9.7500	9.7500
Venezuela (Bolivar)	.002016	.002018	496.00	495.60
SDR	1.3604	1.3569	.7351	.7370
ECU	1.1022	1.0900		

Special Drawing Rights (SDR) are based on exchange rates for the U.S., German, British, French, and Japanese currencies. Source: International Monetary Fund.

European Currency Unit (ECU) is based on a basket of community currencies.

a-fixing, Moscow Interbank Currency Exchange.

The Wall Street Journal daily foreign exchange data for 1996 and 1997 may be purchased through the Readers' Reference Service (413) 592-3600.

Source: The Wall Street Journal, September 12, 1997. Reprinted with permission of Dow Jones & Company. All Rights Reserved Worldwide.

▶ **Example 22.1** *A Yen for Trade*

How many yen will it cost a Japanese importer to purchase $1,000 worth of oranges from a California farmer? How many dollars will it take for that farmer to buy a Japanese VCR priced in Japan at 30,000 yen (¥)?

The exchange rate is ¥119.58 per dollar. The $1,000 of oranges will require the Japanese importer to come up with 1,000 × 119.58 = ¥119,580. The VCR will require the American importer to come up with 30,000/119.58 = $251, or, using the direct quote, 30,000 × .008363 = $251.

---

spot rate of exchange:
Exchange rate for an immediate transaction.

The exchange rates in the first column next to the country name in Table 22.1 are the prices of currency for immediate delivery. These are known as **spot rates of exchange.** The spot rate of exchange for Swiss francs is SFr1.4745/$.

> **Spot exchange rates fluctuate from day to day, sometimes dramatically. When the dollar increases in value, meaning that one dollar can buy more units of other currencies, it is said to *appreciate*. When it can buy less, it is said to *depreciate*. Similarly, if a foreign currency depreciates with respect to the dollar, one dollar can buy more of that currency or, equivalently, that currency can buy fewer dollars.**

For example, on June 30, 1997, the exchange rate for the Thai baht was 25.79 baht per dollar. Only one week later, the exchange rate was 29.096 baht per dollar. This meant that you could buy about 13 percent more bahts for your dollar than the week before. So the baht was said to have depreciated, or fallen, against the dollar.

These fluctuations in exchange rates can get companies into hot water. For example, suppose you have agreed to buy a shipment of Japanese VCRs for ¥100 million and to make the payment when you take delivery of the VCRs at the end of 12 months. You could wait until the 12 months have passed and then buy 100 million yen at the spot exchange rate. If the spot rate is unchanged at ¥119.58/$, then the VCRs will cost you 100 million/119.58 = $836,260. But you are taking a risk by waiting, for the yen may become more expensive. For example, if the yen appreciates to ¥100/$, then you will have to pay out 100 million/100 = $1 million.

forward exchange rate:
Exchange rate for a forward transaction.

You can avoid exchange rate risk and fix the dollar cost of VCRs by "buying the yen forward," that is, by arranging *now* to buy yen in the future. A foreign exchange *forward contract* is an agreement to exchange at a future date a given amount of currency at an exchange rate agreed to *today*. The **forward exchange rate** is the price of currency for delivery at some time in the future. The rows of figures following the first row for Japan in Table 22.1 show 1-month, 3-month, and 6-month forward exchange rates. For example, the 6-month forward rate for the yen is quoted at 116.48 yen per dollar. If you buy 100 million yen forward, you don't pay anything today; you simply fix today the price which you will pay for your yen in the future. At the end of the 6 months you receive your 100 million yen and hand over 100 million/116.48 = $858,516 in payment.

Notice that if you buy Japanese yen forward, you get fewer yen for your dollar than if you buy spot. In this case, the yen is said to trade at a forward *premium* relative to the dollar. Expressed as a percentage, the 6-month forward premium is

$$\frac{119.58 - 116.48}{116.48} \times 100 = 2.66\%$$

You could also say that the dollar was selling at a *forward discount* of about 5.3 percent per year.

A forward purchase or sale is a made-to-order transaction between you and the bank. It can be for any currency, any amount, and any delivery day. You could buy, say, 99,999 Vietnamese dong or Haitian gourdes for a year and a day forward as long as you can find a bank ready to deal. Most forward transactions are for 6 months or less, but banks are prepared to buy or sell the major currencies for up to 10 years forward.

There is also an organized market for currency for future delivery known as the currency *futures* market. Futures contracts are highly standardized versions of forward contracts—they exist only for the main currencies, they are for specified amounts, and choice of delivery dates is limited. The advantage of this standardization is that there is a very low-cost market in currency futures. Huge numbers of contracts are bought and sold daily on the futures exchanges.

▶ **Self-Test 22.1**   A skiing vacation in Switzerland costs SFr1,500.

a. How many dollars does that represent? Use the exchange rates in Table 22.1.
b. Suppose that the dollar depreciates by 10 percent relative to the Swiss franc, so that each dollar buys 10 percent fewer Swiss francs than before. What will be the new value of the indirect exchange rate?
c. If the Swiss vacation continues to cost the same number of Swiss francs, what will happen to the cost in dollars?
d. If the tour company that is offering the vacation keeps the price fixed in dollars, what will happen to the number of Swiss francs that it will receive?

22.2 *Some Basic Relationships*

The president of VCR Importers has also been looking at the financial pages and has dashed off the following memo to you:

I have been looking at *The Wall Street Journal* and I am not happy with some of our policies.

First, we have been buying yen forward to cover the cost of our imports. You say that this ensures us against the risk that the dollar may depreciate over the next 6 months, but it is incredibly expensive insurance. Each dollar buys only 116.48 yen when we buy forward, compared with the current spot rate of 119.58 yen to the dollar. We could save a fortune by buying yen as and when we need them rather than buying them forward.

Another possibility has occurred to me. If we are worried that the dollar may depreciate, why don't we buy yen today at the low spot rate of ¥119.58/$ and then put them on deposit until we have to pay for the VCRs?

I am also worried that we are missing out on some cheap financing. It is true that the interest rate on our bank loans is much lower than it used to be but Japanese interest rates are even lower. Why don't we repay our dollar loans and borrow yen instead? That would slash our interest payments.

Before you respond to the president's memo, you need some understanding of how exchange rates are determined and why one country may have a lower interest rate than another. These are complex issues, but as a first cut we suggest that you think of spot and forward exchange rates, interest rates, and inflation rates as being linked as in Figure 22.1. Let's explain.

Exchange Rates and Inflation

Consider first the relationship between changes in the exchange rate and inflation rates (the two boxes on the right of Figure 22.1). The idea here is simple: if country X suffers a higher rate of inflation than country Y, then the value of X's currency will decline relative to Y's. The decline in value shows up in the spot exchange rate for X's currency.

But let's slow down and consider why changes in inflation and spot interest rates are linked. Think first about the prices of the *same* good or service in two different countries and currencies.

Suppose you notice that gold can be bought in New York for $400 an ounce and sold in Tokyo for ¥50,000. You think you may be onto a good thing. You buy gold for $400 and put it on the first plane to Tokyo, where you sell it for ¥50,000. Then you exchange your ¥50,000 for 50,000/119.58 = $418. You have made a gross profit of $18 an ounce. Of course you have to pay transportation and insurance costs out of this, but there should still be something left over for you.

At these prices you would have a sure-fire profit. Sure-fire profits don't exist—not for long. As others notice the disparity between the price of gold in Tokyo and the price in New York, the price will be forced down in Tokyo and up in New York until the profit opportunity disappears. This ensures that the dollar price of gold is about the same in the two countries.[1]

Gold is a standard and easily transportable commodity, but to some degree you might expect that the same forces would be acting to equalize the domestic and foreign prices

Figure 22.1

Some simple theories linking spot and forward exchange rates, interest rates, and inflation rates.

[1]Activity of this kind is known as *arbitrage*. The arbitrageur makes a riskless profit by noticing discrepancies in prices.

of other goods. Those goods that can be bought more cheaply abroad will be imported, and that will force down the price of the domestic product. Similarly, those goods that can be bought more cheaply in the United States will be exported, and that will force down the price of the foreign product.

This conclusion is often called the **law of one price.** Just as the price of goods in Safeway must be roughly the same as the price of goods in A&P, so the price of goods in Japan when converted into dollars must be roughly the same as the price in the United States:

law of one price:
Theory that prices of goods in all countries should be equal when translated to a common currency.

$$\text{Dollar price of goods in USA} = \frac{\text{yen price of goods in Japan}}{\text{number of yen per dollar}}$$

$$\$400 = \frac{\text{yen price of gold in Japan}}{119.58}$$

$$\text{Price of gold in Japan} = 400 \times 119.58 = ¥47,832$$

No one who has compared prices in foreign stores with prices at home really believes that the law of one price holds exactly. Look at the first column of Table 22.2, which shows the price of a Big Mac in different countries in 1996. Using the exchange rates at that time (second column), we can convert the local price to dollars (third column). You can see that the price varies considerably across countries. For example, Big Macs were twice as expensive in Switzerland as in the United States and about half the price in China.[2]

Table 22.2

Price of a Big Mac in different countries

	Price in Local Currency	Exchange Rate (currency/dollar)	Local Price Converted to Dollars
Australia	A$2.50	1.27	1.97
Belgium	BFr109	31.2	3.50
Canada	C$2.86	1.36	2.10
China	Yuan9.60	8.35	1.15
Denmark	DKr25.75	5.85	4.40
France	FFr17.5	5.13	3.41
Germany	DM4.90	1.52	3.22
Holland	FL5.45	1.70	3.21
Hong Kong	HK$9.90	7.74	1.28
Italy	Lire4500	1551	2.90
Japan	¥288	107	2.70
Mexico	Peso14.9	7.37	2.02
Poland	Zloty3.80	2.64	1.44
Russia	Ruble9500	4918	1.93
Spain	Pta365	126	2.89
Switzerland	SFr5.90	1.23	4.80
United Kingdom	£1.79	.662	2.70
United States	2.36	—	2.36

Source: "MacCurrencies: Where's the Beef?" *The Economist,* April 27, 1996, p. 110. © *The Economist,* April 1996. © 1996 The Economist Newspaper Group, Inc. Reprinted with permission. Further reproduction prohibited.

[2]Of course, it could also be that Big Macs come with a bigger smile in Switzerland. If the quality of the hamburgers or the service differs, we are not comparing like with like.

Table 22.3

The cost of a hangover in different cities

City	1 Liter of Scotch, Dollars	36 Alka Seltzer, Dollars	Exchange Rate[a]
Copenhagen	48.22	4.63	6.11
Singapore	42.33	5.33	1.63
Frankfurt	21.49	11.46	1.59
London	23.81	4.61	0.66
Paris	20.32	6.85	5.37
New York	22.84	3.85	
Toronto	19.42	3.57	1.27
Moscow	12.95	4.70	250

[a]Exchange rate is the number of units of foreign currency to one dollar in November 1992.

Source: Financial Times, December 16, 1992. Copyright © 1992. Used by permission of the *Financial Times.*

This suggests a possible way to make a quick buck. Why don't you buy a hamburger-to-go in the United States for $2.36 and take it for resale to Switzerland where the price in dollars is $4.80? The answer, of course, is that the gain would not cover the costs. The law of one price works very well for commodities like gold where transportation costs are relatively small; it works far less well for Big Macs and very badly indeed for haircuts and appendectomies, which cannot be transported at all.

▶ **Example 22.2** *The Cost of a Hangover*

Table 22.3 provides another example where the law of one price does not give the whole story. The cost of a hangover appears to differ substantially in different cities. What would the exchange rate need to be to equalize the cost of a liter of scotch in New York and Copenhagen? What would it need to be to equalize the cost of Alka Seltzer in New York and Frankfurt?

Scotch costs $22.84 in New York and $48.22 × 6.11 = DKr294.62 in Copenhagen. The cost of scotch would be the same in the two countries if $22.84 could be exchanged for exactly DKr294.62. That implies that $1 would need to be equal in value to 294.62/22.84 = DKr12.90. This compares with the *actual* exchange rate of $1 = DKr6.11.

Similarly, Alka Seltzer costs $3.85 in New York and $11.46 × 1.59 = DM18.22 in Frankfurt. The cost would be the same in the two countries if $3.85 were equivalent to DM18.22—that is, if $1 were equivalent to DM4.73. The actual exchange rate was $1 = DM1.59.

purchasing power parity (PPP): Theory that the cost of living in different countries is equal, and exchange rates adjust to offset inflation differentials across countries.

A weaker version of the law of one price is known as **purchasing power parity,** or **PPP.** PPP states that although some goods may cost different amounts in different countries, the *general* cost of living should be the same in any two countries.

> **Purchasing power parity implies that the relative costs of living in two countries will not be affected by differences in their inflation rates. Instead, the different inflation rates in local currencies will be offset by changes in the exchange rate between the two currencies.**

For example, by 1995 prices in Brazil were nearly 70,000 times their level in 1990. To put it another way, you could say that the purchasing power of the real (the Brazilian currency) declined by about 99.999 percent relative to other currencies. With Brazilian prices 70,000 times their previous values, Brazilian exporters would have found it impossible to sell their goods if exchange rates had not adjusted. But, of course, exchange rates did adjust. In fact, on average, one real bought 99.999 percent fewer dollars than before. Thus a 99.999 percent relative decline in purchasing power was offset by a 99.999 percent decline in the value of the Brazilian currency.

Brazil is an extreme case, but in Figure 22.2 we have plotted the relative change in purchasing power for a sample of countries against the change in the exchange rate. Brazil is tucked in the bottom left-hand corner; the United States is closer to the top right. You can see that although the relationship is far from exact, large differences in inflation rates are generally accompanied by an offsetting change in the exchange rate. In fact, if you have to make a long-term forecast of the exchange rate, it is very difficult to do much better than to assume that it will offset the effect of any differences in the inflation rates.

Figure 22.2

Countries with high inflation rates tend to see their currencies depreciate.

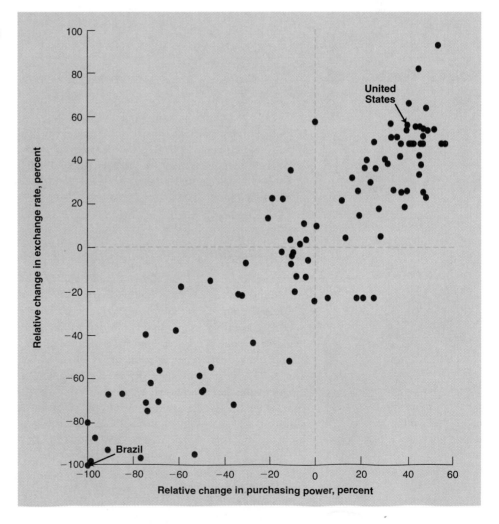

If purchasing power parity holds, then your forecast of the difference in inflation rates is also your best forecast of the change in the spot rate of exchange. Thus the expected difference between inflation rates in Japan and the United States is given by the right-hand boxes in Figure 22.1:

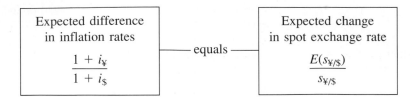

$$\begin{array}{c} \text{Expected difference} \\ \text{in inflation rates} \\ \dfrac{1 + i_¥}{1 + i_\$} \end{array} \quad \text{— equals —} \quad \begin{array}{c} \text{Expected change} \\ \text{in spot exchange rate} \\ \dfrac{E(s_{¥/\$})}{s_{¥/\$}} \end{array}$$

For example, if inflation is 3.0 percent in the United States and .2 percent in Japan, then purchasing power parity implies that the expected spot rate for the yen at the end of the year is ¥116.33/$:

$$\begin{array}{c} \text{Current} \\ \text{spot rate} \end{array} \times \begin{array}{c} \text{expected difference} \\ \text{in inflation rates} \end{array} = \text{expected spot rate}$$

$$119.58 \times \frac{1.002}{1.030} = 116.33$$

▶ **Self-Test 22.2**   Suppose that gold currently costs $390 an ounce in the United States and £260 an ounce in Great Britain.

a. What must be the pound/dollar exchange rate?
b. Suppose that gold prices rise by 2 percent in the United States and by 5 percent in Great Britain. What will be the price of gold in the two currencies at the end of the year? What must be the exchange rate at the end of the year?
c. Show that at the end of the year each dollar buys about 3 percent more pounds, as predicted by PPP.

Inflation and Interest Rates

Interest rates in Turkey at the beginning of 1996 were just over 80 percent. So why didn't you (and a few million other investors) put your cash in a Turkish bank deposit where the return seemed to be so attractive?

The answer lies in the distinction that we made in Chapter 3 between nominal and real rates of interest. Bank deposits usually promise you a fixed nominal rate of interest but they don't promise what that money will buy. If you invested 100 Turkish dinars for a year at an interest rate of 80 percent, you would have 80 percent more dinars at the end of the year than you did at the start. But you wouldn't be 80 percent better off. With an inflation rate in Turkey of almost 80 percent, you would be able to buy only (say) 3 percent more goods than at the beginning of the year. The nominal interest rate was over 80 percent but the real rate was close to zero. Investors in Turkey *needed* that high nominal interest rate to compensate them for Turkey's high rate of inflation.

The nominal rate of interest is much lower in the United States, but then so is the inflation rate. The real rate of interest is likely to be similar in the two countries.

> There is a general law at work here. Just as water always flows downhill, so capital always flows where returns are greatest. But it is the *real* returns that concern investors, not the *nominal* returns. Two countries may have different nominal interest rates but the same expected real interest rate.

international Fisher effect: Theory that real interest rates in all countries should be equal, with differences in nominal rates reflecting differences in expected inflation.

Do you remember from Chapter 3 Irving Fisher's theory that changes in the expected inflation rate are reflected in the nominal interest rate? We have just described here the **international Fisher effect**—international variations in the expected inflation rate are reflected in the nominal interest rates:

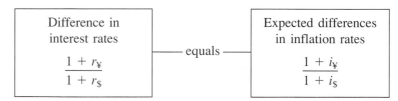

In other words, capital market equilibrium requires that *real* interest rates be the same in any two countries.

▶ **Example 22.3**

International Fisher Effect

If the nominal interest rate in Japan is 1.0 percent and the expected inflation rate is .2 percent, then

$$r_¥(\text{real}) = \frac{1 + r_¥}{E(1 + i_¥)} - 1 = \frac{1.010}{1.002} - 1 = .008, \text{ or } .8\%$$

In the United States, where the nominal interest rate is about 6 percent and the expected inflation rate is about 3.0 percent,

$$r_\$(\text{real}) = \frac{1 + r_\$}{E(1 + i_\$)} - 1 = \frac{1.06}{1.03} - 1 = .029, \text{ or } 2.9\%$$

The real interest rate is higher in the United States than in Japan, but the difference in the real rates is much smaller than the difference in nominal rates. ◀

How similar are real interest rates around the world? It is hard to say, because we cannot directly observe *expected* inflation. In Figure 22.3 we have plotted the average interest rate in each of 29 countries against the inflation that subsequently occurred. You can see that the countries with the highest interest rates generally had the highest inflation rates.

▶ **Self-Test 22.3**

American investors can invest $1,000 at an interest rate of 6.0 percent. Alternatively, they can convert those funds to 125,945 pesetas at the current exchange rate and invest at 8 percent in Spain. If the expected inflation rate in the United States is 3.0 percent, what must be investors' forecast of the inflation rate in Spain?

Interest Rates and Exchange Rates

You are an investor with $1 million to invest for 1 year. The interest rate in Japan is 1.03 percent and in the United States it is 6.03 percent. Is it better to make a yen loan or a dollar loan?

Figure 22.3

Countries with the highest interest rates generally have the highest subsequent inflation rates. In this diagram, each point represents a different country.

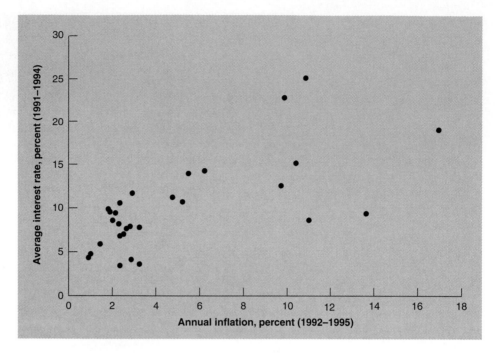

The answer seems obvious: Isn't it better to earn an interest rate of 6.03 percent than 1.03 percent? But appearances may be deceptive. If you lend in Japan, you first need to convert your $1 million into yen. When the loan is repaid at the end of the year, you need to convert your yen back into dollars. Of course you don't know what the exchange rate will be at the end of the year but you can fix the future value of your yen by selling them forward. If the forward rate of exchange is sufficiently attractive, it may compensate you for the lower rate of interest in Japan. The forward exchange rate for 1-year delivery is ¥113.94/$.

Let's use the data from Table 22.1 to check which loan is the better deal:

- *Dollar loan:* The rate of interest on a 1-year dollar loan is 6.03 percent. Therefore, at the end of the year you get 1,000,000 × 1.0603 = $1,060,300.
- *Yen loan:* The current rate of exchange (from Table 22.1) is ¥119.58/$. Therefore, for $1 million, you can buy 1,000,000 × 119.58 = ¥119,580,000. The rate of interest on a 1-year yen loan is 1.03 percent. So at the end of the year, you get ¥119,580,000 × 1.0103 = ¥120,811,674. Of course, you don't know what the exchange rate will be at the end of the year. But that doesn't matter. You can nail down the price at which you can sell your yen. The 1-year forward rate is ¥113.94/$. Therefore, by selling the ¥120,811,674 forward, you make sure that you will get 120,811,674/113.94 = $1,060,310.

Thus the two investments offer almost exactly the same rate of return. They have to—they are both risk-free. If the domestic interest rate were different from the "covered" foreign rate, you would have a money machine: you could borrow in the market with the lower rate and lend in the market with the higher rate.

> **A difference in interest rates must be offset by a difference between spot and forward exchange rates. If the risk-free interest rate in country X is higher than in country Y, then country X's currency will buy less of Y's in a forward transaction than in a spot transaction.**

When you make a yen loan, you lose because you get a lower interest rate. But you gain because you sell the yen forward at a higher price than you have to pay for them today. The interest rate differential is

$$\frac{1 + r_¥}{1 + r_\$} = \frac{1.0103}{1.0603} = .9528$$

and the differential between the forward and spot exchange rates is virtually identical:

$$\frac{f_{¥/\$}}{s_{¥/\$}} = \frac{113.94}{119.58} = .9528$$

interest rate parity:
Theory that forward premium equals interest rate differential.

Interest rate parity theory says that the interest rate differential must equal the differential between the forward and spot exchange rates. Thus

Difference in interest rates $\dfrac{1 + r_¥}{1 + r_\$}$	— equals —	Difference between forward and spot rates $\dfrac{f_{¥/\$}}{s_{¥/\$}}$

▶ Example 22.4 *What Happens if Interest Rate Parity Theory Does Not Hold?*

Suppose that the forward rate on the yen is not ¥113.94/$ but is ¥119.58/$, the same as today's spot rate. Here is what you do. Borrow ¥1 million at an interest rate of 1.03 percent and change these yen into dollars at the spot exchange rate of ¥119.58/$. That gives you $8,362.60, which you invest for a year at 6.03 percent. At the end of the year you will have $8,362.60 × 1.0603 = $8,866.87. Of course, this is not money to spend because you need to repay your yen loan. The amount that you need to repay is 1,000,000 × 1.0103 = ¥1,010,300. If you buy the yen forward, you can fix in advance the number of dollars that you will need to lay out. With a forward rate of ¥119.58/$, you need to set aside 1,010,300/119.58 = $8,448.74. Thus, after paying off your yen loan, you walk away with a risk-free profit of 8,866.87 − 8,448.74 = $418.13. It is a pity that in practice interest rate parity almost always holds and the opportunities for such easy profits are rare.

▶ Self-Test 22.4

Look at the exchange rates in Table 22.1. Does the French franc sell at a forward premium or discount on the dollar? Does this suggest that the interest rate in France is higher or lower than in the United States? Use the interest rate parity relationship to estimate the 6-month interest rate in France.

The Forward Rate and the Expected Spot Rate

If you buy yen forward, you get fewer yen for your dollar than if you buy them spot. So the yen is selling at a forward premium. Now let us think how the forward premium is related to expected changes in spot rates of exchange.

The 1-year yen forward rate is ¥113.94/$. Would you buy yen forward at this rate if you expected the yen to decline in value? Probably not. You would be tempted to wait and get more yen for your dollar in the spot market. If other traders felt the same way, nobody would buy yen forward and the number of yen that you could buy for a dollar in the forward market would rise. Similarly, if traders expected the yen to increase in value, they might be reluctant to *sell* forward and the number of yen that you could buy for a dollar would fall.[3]

expectations theory of exchange rates:
Theory that expected spot exchange rate equals the forward rate.

This is the reasoning behind the **expectations theory of exchange rates,** which predicts that the forward rate equals the expected future spot exchange rate: $f_{¥/\$} = E(S_{¥/\$})$. Equivalently, we can say that the *percentage* difference between the forward rate and today's spot rate is equal to the expected *percentage* change in the spot rate:

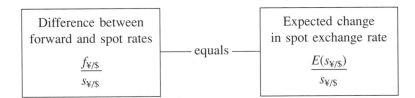

This is the final leg of our quadrilateral in Figure 22.1.

> **The expectations theory of forward rates does not imply that managers are perfect forecasters. Sometimes the *actual* future spot rate will turn out to be above the previous forward rate. Sometimes it will fall below. But if the theory is correct, we should find that *on the average* the forward rate is equal to the future spot rate.**

The theory passes this simple test reasonably well. This is important news for the financial manager; it means that a company which always covers its foreign exchange commitments by buying or selling currency in the forward market does not have to pay a premium to avoid exchange rate risk: *on average,* the forward price at which it agrees to exchange currency will equal the eventual spot exchange rate, no better but no worse.

We should also warn you that the forward rate does not tell you very much about the future spot rate. This does not mean that the forward rate is a poor measure of managers' expectations; it just means that exchange rates are very tough to predict.

Some Implications

Our four simple relationships ignore many of the complexities of interest rates and exchange rates. But they capture the more important features and emphasize that

---

[3]This reasoning ignores risk. If a forward purchase reduces your risk sufficiently, you *might* be prepared to buy forward even if you expected to pay more as a result. Similarly, if a forward sale reduces risk, you *might* be prepared to sell forward even if you expected to receive less as a result.

international capital markets and currency markets function well and offer no free lunches. For example, in the late 1980s, several Australian banks observed that interest rates in Switzerland were about 8 percentage points lower than those in Australia and advised their clients to borrow Swiss francs. Was this advice correct? According to the international Fisher effect, the lower Swiss interest rate indicated that investors were expecting a lower inflation rate in Switzerland than in Australia and this in turn would result in an appreciation of the Swiss franc relative to the Australian dollar. Thus it was likely that the advantage of the low Swiss interest rate would be offset by the fact that it would cost the borrowers more Australian dollars to repay the loan. As it turned out, the Swiss franc appreciated very rapidly, the Australian banks found that they had a number of very irate clients and agreed to compensate them for the losses they had incurred. *Moral:* Don't assume automatically that it is cheaper to borrow in a currency with a low nominal rate of interest.

▶ **Self-Test 22.5**   In 1986 Philip Morris borrowed 100,000 New Zealand dollars at an interest rate of 17.25 percent when the exchange rate between the New Zealand and U.S. dollar was NZ\$1.91/\$. The exchange rate was NZ\$1.69/\$ in 1987 and NZ\$1.52/\$ in 1988. When Philip Morris came to repay its loan in 1989 the exchange rate was about NZ\$1.67/\$. Calculate in U.S. dollars the amount that Philip Morris borrowed and the amounts that it paid in interest and principal (assume annual interest payments). What was the effective *U.S. dollar* interest rate on the loan? You will need the internal rate of return function on your calculator.

Here is another case where our simple relationships can stop you falling into a trap. Managers sometimes talk as if you make money simply by buying currencies that go up in value and selling those that go down. But if investors anticipate the change in the exchange rate, then it will be reflected in the interest rate differential; therefore, what you gain on the currency you will lose in terms of interest income. You make money from currency speculation only if you can predict whether the exchange rate will change by more or less than the interest rate differential. In other words, you must be able to predict whether the exchange rate will change by more or less than the forward premium.

▶ **Example 22.5**   *Measuring Currency Gains*

The financial manager of Universal Waffle is proud of his acumen. Instead of keeping his cash in U.S. dollars, he has for many years invested it in deutschemark deposits. He calculates that between the end of 1977 and 1995, the deutschemark increased in value by nearly 47 percent, or about 2.1 percent a year. But has the manager really gained from investing in foreign currency? Let's check.

The compound rate of interest on dollar deposits during the period was 9.0 percent, while the compound rate of interest on deutschemark deposits was only 6.9 percent. So the 2.1 percent a year appreciation in the value of the deutschemark was almost exactly offset by the lower rate of interest on deutschemark deposits.

The interest rate differential (which by interest rate parity is equal to the forward premium) is a measure of the market's expectation of the change in the value of the currency. The difference between the German and United States interest rates during this period suggests that the market was expecting the deutschemark to appreciate by just over 2 percent a year,[4] and that is almost exactly what happened.

22.3 Hedging Exchange Rate Risk

Firms with international operations are subject to exchange rate risk. As exchange rates fluctuate, the dollar value of the firm's revenues or expenses also fluctuates. It helps to distinguish two types of exchange rate risk: contractual and noncontractual. By *contractual risk,* we mean that the firm is committed either to pay or to receive a known amount of foreign currency. For example, our VCR importer was committed to pay ¥100 million at the end of 12 months. If the value of the yen appreciates rapidly over this period, those VCRs will cost more dollars than the firm expected.

Noncontractual risk arises because exchange rate fluctuations can affect the competitive position of the firm. For example, during 1991 and 1992 the value of the deutschemark appreciated relative to that of other major currencies. As a result, Porsche and other German luxury car manufacturers found it increasingly difficult to compete in the United States. American dealers that had a franchise to sell German luxury cars also took a bath. Thus the German car producers and their dealers in the United States were exposed to exchange rate changes even if they had no fixed obligations to pay or receive dollars.

Exchange rate changes can get companies into *big* trouble and therefore most companies aim to limit at least their contractual exposure to currency fluctuations. Let us look at an example of how this can be done.

In 1989 a British company, Enterprise Oil, bought some oil properties from Texas Eastern for $440 million.[5] Since the payment was delayed a couple of months, Enterprise's plans for financing the purchase could have been thrown out of kilter if the dollar had strengthened during this period.

Enterprise therefore decided to avoid, or *hedge,* this risk. It did so by borrowing pounds, which it converted into dollars at the current spot rate and invested for 2 months. In that way Enterprise guaranteed it would have just enough dollars available to pay for the purchase. Of course it was possible that the dollar would *depreciate* over the 2 months, in which case Enterprise would have regretted that it did not wait and buy the dollars spot. Unfortunately, you cannot have your cake and eat it too. By fixing its dollar cost, Enterprise forfeited the chance of pleasant as well as unpleasant surprises.

Was there any other way that Enterprise could hedge against exchange loss? Of course. It could buy $440 million 2 months forward. No cash would change hands immediately but Enterprise would fix the price at which it buys its dollars at the end of 2 months. It would therefore eliminate all exchange risk on the deal. Interest rate

---

[4]If the interest rate is 9.0 percent on dollar deposits and 6.9 percent on deutschemark deposits, our simple relationship implies that the expected change in the value of the deutschemark was $(1 + r_\$)/(1 + r_{DM}) - 1 = 1.090/1.069 - 1 = .020$, or 2.0 percent per year.

[5]See "Enterprise Oil's Mega Forex Option," *Corporate Finance* 53 (April 1989), p. 13.

parity theory tells us that the difference between buying spot and buying forward is equal to the difference between the rate of interest that you pay at home and the interest that you earn overseas. In other words, the two methods of eliminating risk should be equivalent.

Let us check this. In March 1989 the 2-month interest rate in the United States was about 9.7 percent and the interest rate in the United Kingdom was 13.0 percent. The spot exchange rate was $1.743 to the pound and the 2-month forward rate was $1.730/£. Table 22.4 shows that the cash flows from the two methods of hedging the dollar payment for Texas Eastern were almost identical.[6]

What is the cost of such a hedge? You sometimes hear managers say that it is equal to the difference between the forward rate and *today's* spot rate. This is wrong. If Enterprise did not hedge, it would pay the spot rate for dollars at the time that the payment for Texas Eastern was due. Therefore, the cost of hedging is the difference between the forward rate and the *expected* spot rate when payment is received.

Hedge or speculate? We generally vote for hedging. First, it makes life simpler for the firm and allows it to concentrate on its own business. Second, it does not cost much. (In fact the cost is zero if the forward rate equals the expected spot rate, as our simple relations imply.) Third, the foreign exchange market seems reasonably efficient, at least for the major currencies. Speculation should be a zero-sum game unless financial managers have superior information to the pros who make the market.

Table 22.4

Enterprise Oil could hedge its future dollar payment either by borrowing sterling and lending dollars or by buying dollars forward

	Cash Flow, Millions	
	£	$
Method 1: Borrow sterling, convert proceeds to dollars, and invest dollars until needed		
Now:		
Borrow £248.6m at 13%	+248.6	
Convert to $ at $1.743/£	−248.6	+433.3
Invest $433.3m for 2 months at 9.7%		−433.3
Net cash flow now	0	0
Month 2:		
Repay £ loan with interest	−253.7	
Receive payment on $ loan		+440
Pay for oil properties		−440
Net cash flow, Month 2	−253.7	0
Method 2: Buy dollars forward		
Now:		
Buy $440m forward at $1.73/£	0	0
Month 2:		
Pay for $	−254.3	+440
Payment for oil properties		−440
Net cash flow, Month 2	−254.3	0

[6]We are not sure of Enterprise's borrowing rate but the company is rumored to have hedged at an effective forward rate of $1.73/£.

▶ **Self-Test 22.6**   You should now be in a position to reply to that memo you received from the president of VCR Importers (see page 627). What is the cost to the company of ensuring against exchange rate changes by buying yen forward? Is the president correct to compare the forward rate with the *current* spot rate? What is the disadvantage of buying yen now and leaving them on deposit? Is it better to do this than to buy yen forward? And what do you think of the president's suggestion of borrowing yen at a "low" interest rate of 1 percent?

22.4 *International Capital Budgeting*

Net Present Value Analysis

KW Corporation is an American firm manufacturing flat-packed kit wardrobes. Its export business has risen to the point that it is considering establishing a small manufacturing operation overseas in Narnia. KW's decision to invest overseas should be based on the same criteria as a decision to invest in the United States—that is, the company needs to forecast the incremental cash flows from the project, discount the cash flows at the opportunity cost of capital, and accept those projects with a positive NPV.

Suppose KW's Narnian facility is expected to generate the following cash flows *in Narnian leos:*

Year	0	1	2	3	4	5
Cash flow (millions of leos)	−7.6	2.0	2.5	3.0	3.5	4.0

The interest rate in the United States is 5 percent. KW's financial manager estimates that the company requires an additional expected return of 10 percent to compensate for the risk of the project, so the opportunity cost of capital for the project is $5 + 10 = 15$ percent.

Notice that KW's opportunity cost of capital is stated in terms of the return on a dollar-denominated investment, but the cash flows are given in leos. A project that offers a 15 percent expected return in leos could fall far short of offering the required return in dollars if the value of the leo is expected to decline. Conversely, a project that offers an expected return of less than 15 percent in leos may be worthwhile if the leo is likely to appreciate.

> **You cannot compare the project's return measured in one currency with the return that you require from investing in another currency. If the opportunity cost of capital is measured as a dollar-denominated return, consistency demands that the forecast cash flows should also be stated in dollars.**

To translate the leo cash flows into dollars, KW needs a forecast of the leo/dollar exchange rate. Where does this come from? We suggest using the simple parity relationships in Figure 22.1. These tell us that the expected annual change in the spot rate (the southeast box in Figure 22.1) is equal to the difference between the interest rates in the two countries (the northwest box). For example, suppose that the financial manager looks in the newspaper and finds that the current exchange rate is 2 leos to the dollar ($s_{L/\$} = 2.0$), while the interest rate is 5 percent in the United States ($r_\$ = .05$) and 10 percent in Narnia ($r_L = .10$). Thus the manager sees right away that the leo is likely to depreciate by about 5 percent a year.[7] For example, at the end of one year

$$\begin{array}{c}\text{Expected spot}\\\text{rate in Year 1}\end{array} = \begin{array}{c}\text{spot rate}\\\text{in Year 0}\end{array} \times \begin{array}{c}\text{expected change}\\\text{in spot rate}\end{array}$$

$$= 2.00 \times \frac{1.10}{1.05} = L2.095/\$$$

The forecast exchange rates for each year of the project are calculated in a similar way as follows:

Year	Forecast Exchange Rate
0	Spot exchange rate = L2.00/$
1	$2.00 \times (1.10/1.05) = L2.095/\$$
2	$2.00 \times (1.10/1.05)^2 = L2.195/\$$
3	$2.00 \times (1.10/1.05)^3 = L2.300/\$$
4	$2.00 \times (1.10/1.05)^4 = L2.409/\$$
5	$2.00 \times (1.10/1.05)^5 = L2.524/\$$

The financial manager can use these projected exchange rates to convert the leo cash flows into dollars:[8]

Year	0	1	2	3	4	5
Cash flow ($ millions)	$-\frac{7.6}{2.00}$	$\frac{2.0}{2.095}$	$\frac{2.5}{2.195}$	$\frac{3.0}{2.300}$	$\frac{3.5}{2.409}$	$\frac{4.0}{2.524}$
	= −$3.8	= $.95	= $1.14	= $1.30	= $1.45	= $1.58

Now the manager discounts these *dollar* cash flows at the 15 percent *dollar* cost of capital:

$$NPV = -3.8 + \frac{.95}{1.15} + \frac{1.14}{1.15^2} + \frac{1.30}{1.15^3} + \frac{1.45}{1.15^4} + \frac{1.58}{1.15^5}$$

$$= \$.36 \text{ million, or } \$360,000$$

Notice that the manager discounted cash flows at 15 percent, not the United States risk-free interest rate of 5 percent. The cash flows are risky, so a risk-adjusted interest rate is appropriate. The positive NPV tells the manager that the project is worth undertaking; it increases shareholder wealth by $360,000.

[7]The financial manager could equally well use the forward exchange rate ($f_{L/\$}$) to estimate the expected spot rate. In practice it is usually easier to find interest rates in the financial press than yearly forward rates.

[8]Suppose KW's managers do not go along with what market prices are telling them. For example, perhaps they believe that the leo is likely to appreciate relative to the dollar. Should they plug their own currency forecasts into their present value calculations? We think not. It would be stupid to undertake what might be an unprofitable investment just because management is optimistic about the currency. Given its exchange rate forecast, KW would do better to pass up the investment in wardrobe manufacturing and buy leos instead.

▶ **Self-Test 22.7**   Suppose that the nominal interest rate in Narnia is 3 percent rather than 10 percent. The spot exchange rate is still L2.00/$ and the forecast leo cash flows on KW's project are also the same as before.

a. What do you deduce about the likely difference in the inflation rates in Narnia and the United States?
b. Would you now forecast that the leo will appreciate against the dollar or depreciate?
c. Do you think that the NPV of KW's project will now be higher or lower than the figure we calculated above? Check your answer by calculating NPV under this new assumption.

The Cost of Capital for Foreign Investment

We did not say how KW arrived at a 15 percent dollar discount rate for its Narnian project. That depends on the risk of overseas investment and the reward that investors require for taking this risk. These are issues on which few economists can agree, but we will tell you where we stand.[9]

Remember that the risk of an investment cannot be considered in isolation; it depends on the securities that the investor holds in his or her portfolio. For example, suppose KW's shareholders invest mainly in companies that do business in the United States. They would find that the value of KW's Narnian venture was relatively unaffected by fluctuations in the value of United States shares. So an investment in the Narnian furniture business would appear to be a relatively low-risk project to KW's shareholders. That would not be true of a Narnian company, whose shareholders are already exposed to the fortunes of the Narnian market. To them an investment in the Narnian furniture business might seem a relatively high-risk project. They would therefore demand a higher return *(measured in dollars)* than KW's shareholders.

Avoiding Fudge Factors

We certainly don't pretend that we can put a precise figure on the cost of capital for foreign investment. But you can see that we disagree with the frequent practice of *automatically* increasing the domestic cost of capital when foreign investment is considered. We suspect that managers mark up the required return for foreign investment because it is more costly to manage an operation in a foreign country and to cover the risk of expropriation, foreign exchange restrictions, or unfavorable tax changes. A fudge factor is added to the discount factor to cover these costs.

We think managers should leave the discount rate alone and reduce expected cash flows instead. For example, suppose that KW is expected to earn L2.5 million in the first year *if no penalties are placed on the operations of foreign firms.* Suppose also that there is a 20 percent chance that KW's cash flow may be expropriated without compensation. The *expected* cash flow is not L2.5 million but .8 × 2.5 million = L2.0 million.

The end result may be the same if you pretend that the expected cash flow is L2.5 million but add a fudge factor to the discount rate. Nevertheless, adjusting cash flows brings management's assumptions about "political risks" out in the open for scrutiny and sensitivity analysis.

---

[9]Why don't economists agree? One fundamental reason is that economists have never been able to agree on what makes one country different from another. Is it just that they have different currencies? Or is it that their citizens have different tastes? Or is it that they are subject to different regulations and taxes? The answer affects the relationship between security prices in different countries.

Summary

1. To produce order out of chaos, the international financial manager needs some model of the relationship between exchange rates, interest rates, and inflation rates. Four very simple theories prove useful:
   - In its strict form, purchasing power parity states that $1 must have the same purchasing power in every country. You only need to take a vacation abroad to know that this doesn't square well with the facts. Nevertheless, *on average* changes in exchange rates match differences in inflation rates and, if you need a long-term forecast of the exchange rate, it is difficult to do much better than to assume that the exchange rate will offset the effect of any differences in the inflation rates.
   - In an open world capital market *real* rates of interest would have to be the same. Thus differences in *nominal* interest rates result from differences in expected inflation rates. This suggests that firms should not simply borrow where interest rates are lowest. Those countries are also likely to have the lowest inflation rates and the strongest currencies.
   - Interest rate parity theory states that the interest differential between two countries must be equal to the difference between the forward and spot exchange rates. In the international markets, arbitrage ensures that parity almost always holds.
   - The expectations theory of foreign exchange rates tells us that the forward rate equals the expected spot rate (though it is very far from being a perfect forecaster of the spot rate).

2. Our simple theories about forward rates have two practical implications for the problem of hedging overseas operations. First, the expectations theory suggests that hedging exchange risk is on average costless. Second, there are two ways to hedge against exchange risk—one is to buy or sell currency forward, the other is to lend or borrow abroad. Interest rate parity tells us that the cost of the two methods should be the same.

3. Overseas investment decisions are no different in principle from domestic decisions. You need to forecast the project's cash flows and then discount them at the opportunity cost of capital. But it is important to remember that if the opportunity cost of capital is stated in dollars, the cash flows must also be converted to dollars. This requires a forecast of foreign exchange rates. We suggest that you rely on our simple parity relationships and use the interest rate differential to produce these forecasts.

4. In international capital budgeting the return that shareholders require from foreign investments must be estimated. Adding a premium for the "extra risks" of overseas investment is not a good solution.

Key Terms

exchange rate	law of one price	international Fisher effect
spot rate of exchange	purchasing power parity	interest rate parity
forward exchange rate	(PPP)	expectations theory of exchange rates

Problems

1. **Exchange Rates.** Use Table 22.1 to answer these questions:

   a. How many Italian lire can you buy for $100? How many dollars can you buy for 100 lire?

b. How many British pounds can you buy for $100? How many dollars can you buy for £100?

c. If the lira depreciates with respect to the dollar, will the direct exchange rate quoted in Table 22.1 increase or decrease? What about the indirect exchange rate?

d. Is a United States or an Australian dollar worth more?

2. **Exchange Rate Relationships.** Look at Table 22.1.

a. How many German marks do you get for your dollar?

b. What is the 6-month forward rate for the mark?

c. Is the mark at a forward discount or premium on the dollar?

d. Calculate the annual percentage discount or premium on the mark.

e. If the 6-month interest rate on dollars is 3 percent (per half year), what do you think is the 6-month interest rate on marks?

f. According to the expectations theory, what is the expected spot rate for the mark in 6 months' time?

g. According to purchasing power parity, what then is the expected difference in the rate of price inflation in the United States and Germany?

3. **Exchange Rate Relationships.** Define each of the following theories in a sentence or simple equation:

a. Interest rate parity theory.

b. Expectations theory of forward rates.

c. Law of one price

d. International Fisher effect (relationship between interest rates in different countries).

4. **Interest Rate Parity.** The following table shows interest rates and exchange rates for the U.S. dollar and Greek drachma. The spot exchange rate is 240 drachmas per dollar. Complete the missing entries:

	1 Month	1 Year
Dollar interest rate (annually compounded)	5.5	7.0
Drachma interest rate (annually compounded)	27.9%	____
Forward drachmas per dollar	_____	278.1

Hint: When calculating the 1-month forward rate, remember to translate the annual interest rate into a monthly interest rate.

5. **Hedging Exchange Rate Risk.** An importer in the United States is due to take delivery of silk scarves from Italy in 6 months. The price is fixed in lire. Which of the following transactions could eliminate the importer's exchange risk?

a. Buy lire forward.

b. Sell lire forward.

c. Borrow lire, buy dollars at the spot exchange rate.

d. Sell lire at the spot exchange rate, lend dollars.

6. **Currency Risk.** Sanyo produces audio and video consumer goods and exports a large fraction of its output to the United States under its own name and the Fisher brand name. It prices its products in yen, meaning that it seeks to maintain a fixed price in terms of yen. Suppose the yen moves from ¥108.02/$ to ¥100/$. What currency risk does Sanyo face? How can it reduce its exposure?

7. **Managing Exchange Rate Risk.** A firm in the United States is due to receive payment of DM1 million in 8 years' time. It would like to protect itself against a decline in the value

of the deutschemark but finds it difficult to arrange a forward sale for such a long period. Is there any other way that it can protect itself?

8. **International Capital Budgeting.** Which of the following items do you need if you do all your capital budgeting calculations in your own currency?

   Forecasts of future exchange rates
   Forecasts of the foreign inflation rate
   Forecasts of the domestic inflation rate
   Foreign interest rates
   Domestic interest rates

9. **Expectations Theory.** Table 22.1 shows the 6-month forward rate on the French franc.

   a. Is the franc at a forward discount or a premium on the dollar?
   b. What is the annualized *percentage* discount or premium?
   c. If you have no other information about the two currencies, what is your best guess about the spot rate on the franc 6 months hence?
   d. Suppose that you expect to receive 100,000 French francs in 6 months. How many dollars is this likely to be worth?

10. **Exchange Rate Risk.** An American investor buys 100 shares of London Enterprises at a price of £50 when the exchange rate is $1.60/£. A year later the shares are selling at £52. No dividends have been paid.

    a. What is the rate of return to an American investor if the exchange rate is still $1.60/£?
    b. What if the exchange rate is $1.70/£?
    c. What if the exchange rate is $1.50/£?

11. **Interest Rate Parity.** Look at Table 22.1. If the 3-month interest rate on dollars is 6.0 percent (annualized), what do you think is the 3-month sterling (U.K.) interest rate? Explain what would happen if the rate were substantially above your figure. *Hint:* In your calculations remember to convert the annually compounded interest rate into a rate for 3 months.

12. **Interest Rate Parity.** Suppose the interest rate on 1-year loans in the United States is 5 percent while in the United Kingdom the interest rate is 6 percent. The spot exchange rate is $1.55/£ and the forward rate is $1.54/£. In what country would you choose to borrow? To lend? Can you profit from this situation?

13. **Cross Rates.** Look at Table 22.1. How many French francs can you buy for $1? How many deutschemarks can you buy? What rate do you think a German bank would quote for buying or selling French francs? Explain what would happen if it quoted a rate that was substantially above your figure.

14. **Foreign Currency Management.** Ms. Rosetta Stone, the treasurer of International Reprints, Inc., has noticed that the interest rate in Switzerland is below the rates in most other countries. She is therefore suggesting that the company should make an issue of Swiss franc bonds. What considerations ought she first take into account?

15. **Purchasing Power Parity.** Suppose that the inflation rate in the United States is 4 percent and in Canada it is 5 percent. What would you expect is happening to the exchange rate between the United States and Canadian dollars?

16. **International Capital Budgeting.** An American firm is evaluating an investment in Spain. The project costs 500 million Spanish pesetas and it is expected to produce an income of 250 million pesetas a year in *real* terms for each of the next 3 years. The expected inflation rate in Spain is 6 percent a year and the firm estimates that an appropriate discount rate for the project would be about 8 percent above the risk-free rate of interest. Calculate the net present value of the project in dollars. Exchange rates are given in Table 22.1. The interest rate is about 8.0 percent in Spain and 4 percent in the United States.

17. **International Capital Budgeting.** Suppose that you do use your own views about exchange rates when valuing an overseas investment proposal. Specifically, suppose that you believe that the leo will depreciate by 2 percent per year. Recalculate the NPV of KW's project.

18. **Currency Risk.** You have bid for a possible export order that would provide a cash inflow of DM1 million in 6 months. The spot exchange rate is DM1.7805/$ and the 6-month forward rate is DM1.7591/$. There are two sources of uncertainty: (1) the deutschemark could appreciate or depreciate, and (2) you may or may not receive the export order. Illustrate in each case the profits or losses that you would make if you sell DM1 million forward by filling in the following table. Assume that the exchange rate in 6 months will be either DM1.90/$ or DM1.60/$.

	Profit/Loss	
Spot Rate	**Receive Order**	**Lose Order**
DM1.90/$	_____	_____
DM1.60/$	_____	_____

19. **Managing Currency Risk.** General Gadget corp. (GGC) is a United States–based multinational firm that makes electrical coconut scrapers. These gadgets are made only in the United States using local inputs. The scrapers are sold mainly to Asian and West Indian countries where coconuts are grown.

   a. If GGC sells scrapers in Trinidad, what is the currency risk faced by the firm?
   b. In what currency should GGC borrow funds to pay for its investment in order to mitigate its foreign exchange exposure?
   c. Suppose that GGC begins manufacturing its products in Trinidad using local (Trinidadian) inputs and labor. How does this affect its exchange rate risk?

20. **Currency Risk.** If investors recognize the impacts of inflation and exchange rate changes on a firm's cash flows, changes in exchange rates should be reflected in stock prices. How would the stock price of each of the following Swiss companies be affected by an unanticipated appreciation in the Swiss franc of 10 percent, only 2 percent of which could be justified by comparing Swiss inflation to that in the rest of the world:

   a. *Swiss Air:* More than two-thirds of its employees are Swiss. Most revenues come from international fares set in U.S. dollars.
   b. *Nestlé:* Fewer than 5 percent of its employees are Swiss. Most revenues are derived from sales of consumer goods in a wide range of countries with competition from local producers.
   c. *Union Bank of Switzerland:* Most employees are Swiss. All non–Swiss franc monetary positions are fully hedged.

Solutions to Self-Test Questions

22.1 a. 1,500/1.4745 = $1,017
   b. Indirect exchange rate: $1 = .9 × 1.4745 = 1.3271 francs.
   c. 1,500/1.3271 = $1,130. The dollar price increases.
   d. 1,017 × 1.3271 = 1,350 francs.

22.2 a. £260 = $390. Therefore £1 = 390/260 = $1.50.
   b. In the United States, price = $390 × 1.02 = $397.80. In Great Britain, price = £260 × 1.05 = £273. The new exchange rate = $397.80/£273 = $1.457/£.

c. Initially $1 buys 1/1.50 = £.667. At the end of the year, $1 buys 1/1.457 = £.686, which is about 3 percent higher than the original value of £.667.

22.3 The real interest rate in the United States is 1.06/1.03 − 1 = .029, or 2.9%. If the real rate is the same in Spain, then expected inflation must be (1 + nominal rate)/(1 + real rate) − 1 = 1.08/1.029 − 1 = .050, or 5.0%.

22.4 The franc is at a forward premium (that is, you get fewer francs for $1 in the forward market). This implies that interest rates in France are lower than in the United States. The interest rate in the U.S. is about 3 percent over 6 months. Interest rate parity states

$$\frac{1 + r_{franc}}{1 + r_{\$}} = \frac{f_{franc/\$}}{s_{franc/\$}}$$

Therefore $r_{franc} = 1.03 \times \dfrac{5.9180}{5.9885} - 1 = .018$ or 1.8%

This is equivalent to about 3.6% a year.

22.5 Cash flows in dollars were

$$1986: \quad \frac{+100,000}{1.91} = +\$52,356$$

$$1987: \quad \frac{-17,250}{1.69} = -\$10,207$$

$$1988: \quad \frac{-17,250}{1.52} = -\$11,349$$

$$1989: \quad \frac{-117,250}{1.67} = -\$70,210$$

The internal rate of return on these cash flows is about 24 percent, that is,

$$+52,356 - \frac{10,207}{1.24} - \frac{11,349}{1.24^2} - \frac{70,210}{1.24^3} = 0$$

22.6 The points you should make are

a. When judging the cost of forward cover, the relevant comparison is between the forward rate and the *expected* spot rate. Since the forward rate is *on average* close to the subsequent spot rate, the cost of insurance is low.

b. The firm could buy spot yen today but would then receive the low yen rate of interest for 1 year rather than the higher dollar rate. Interest rate parity states that the two methods of hedging (buying yen forward or buying spot and investing in yen deposits) have similar cost.

c. The yen interest rate is likely to be low because investors expect the yen to appreciate against the dollar. The firm can expect the benefit of borrowing at the low interest rate to be offset by the extra cost of buying yen to pay the interest and principal. Also, borrowing yen would add currency risk and it would be odd to do this at the same time as buying yen and putting them on deposit.

22.7 a. The lower interest rate in Narnia than in the United States suggests that forecast inflation is lower in Narnia. If real interest rates are the same in the two countries, then the difference in inflation rates is about 5 − 3 = 2 percent.

b. The lower interest rate (and lower expected inflation rate) in Narnia suggests that investors are expecting the leo to appreciate against the dollar.

c. Since KW can now expect to change its leo cash flows into more dollars than before, the project's NPV is increased. Forecast exchange rates will be as follows:

Year	Forecast Exchange Rate
0	Spot exchange rate = L2.00/$
1	$2.00 \times (1.03/1.05) = L1.962/\$$
2	$2.00 \times (1.03/1.05)^2 = L1.925/\$$
3	$2.00 \times (1.03/1.05)^3 = L1.888/\$$
4	$2.00 \times (1.03/1.05)^4 = L1.852/\$$
5	$2.00 \times (1.03/1.05)^5 = L1.817/\$$

The expected dollar cash flows from the project are

Year	0	1	2	3	4	5
Cash flow (millions of dollars)	$\dfrac{-7.6}{2.00}$ = −$3.8	$\dfrac{2.0}{1.962}$ = $1.02	$\dfrac{2.5}{1.925}$ = $1.30	$\dfrac{3.0}{1.888}$ = $1.59	$\dfrac{3.5}{1.852}$ = $1.89	$\dfrac{4.0}{1.817}$ = $2.20

Discounting these dollar cash flows at the 15 percent *dollar* cost of capital gives

$$NPV = -3.8 + \frac{1.02}{1.15} + \frac{1.30}{1.15^2} + \frac{1.59}{1.15^3} + \frac{1.89}{1.15^4} + \frac{2.20}{1.15^5}$$

$$= \$1.29 \text{ million, or } \$1,290,000$$

The project is worth more because the reduced interest rate in Narnia suggests that investors expect the leo to appreciate in value. Thus the dollar cash flows from the project are higher than in Section 22.4.

Traders on the floor of the Chicago Board Options Exchange.
These traders clearly need to understand options, but why does the financial manager of an industrial company need to do so?
Courtesy The Chicago Board Options Exchange, Inc.
Note: "This is not a Chicago Board Options Exchange, Inc. ("CBOE") publication or creation and CBOE makes no representations or endorsements with respect to any of the contents hereof."

Chapter 23
Options

The Chicago Board Options Exchange (CBOE) was founded in 1973 and was an almost instant success. Within 5 years, investors were trading options to buy or sell more than 10 million shares of stock daily. Today, average daily volume on the CBOE is nearly 10 times that level. A number of exchanges have since copied the CBOE's example, and in addition to options on individual stocks, you can now trade options on stock indexes, bonds, commodities, and foreign exchange.

You will see that options can be valuable tools for managing the risk characteristics of an investment portfolio. But why should the financial manager of an industrial company read further? There are several reasons. First, most capital budgeting projects have options embedded in them that allow the company to expand at a future date or to bail out. These options allow the company to profit if things go well but give downside protection when they don't.

Second, many of the securities that firms issue include an option. For example, companies often issue convertible bonds. The holder has the option to exchange the bond for common stock. Most corporate bonds also contain a call provision, meaning that the issuer has the option to buy back the bond from the investor.

Finally, managers routinely use currency, commodity, and interest-rate options to protect the firm against a variety of risks. (We will have more to say about this in Chapter 24.)

In one chapter we can provide you with only a brief introduction to options. Our first goal in this chapter is to explain how options work and how option value is determined. Then we will tell you how to recognize some of the options that crop up in capital investment proposals and in company financing.

After studying this chapter you should be able to

▶ Calculate the payoff to buyers and sellers of call and put options.

▶ Understand the determinants of option values.

▶ Recognize options in capital investment proposals.

▶ Identify options that are provided in financial securities.

Calls and Puts

call option: Right to buy an asset at a specified exercise price on or before the exercise date.

A **call option** gives its holder the right to buy stock for a fixed *exercise price* (also called the *strike price*) on or before a specified exercise date.[1] For example, if you buy a call option on IBM with an expiration date in October and an exercise price of $100, you have the right to buy shares of IBM at a price of $100 any time until October.

---

[1]In some cases, the option can be exercised only on one particular day, and it is then conventionally known as a *European call;* in other cases, it can be exercised on or before that day, and it is then known as an *American call.*

You need not exercise a call option; it will be profitable to do so only if the share price exceeds the exercise price. If it does not, the option will be left unexercised and will prove to be valueless. But suppose IBM shares are selling above the $100 exercise price, say at $120, just before the call option expires. You will choose to exercise your option to pay $100 to buy shares worth $120. Your net proceeds upon exercise equal the difference between the $100 paid and the $120 you can realize for the shares. More generally, the proceeds would equal the difference between the stock price and the exercise price.

In summary, the value of the call option at expiration is as follows:

Stock Price at Expiration	Value of Call at Expiration
Greater than exercise price	Stock price − exercise price
Less than exercise price	Zero

Of course, the ultimate value of the option is not all profit: you have to pay for the option. The price of the call is called the option *premium*. Option buyers pay the premium for the right to exercise later. Your profit equals the ultimate payoff to the call option (which may be zero) minus the initial premium.

▶ **Example 23.1**   *Call Options on Compaq*

A January 1998 maturity call option on Compaq with an exercise price of $65 per share sold on September 9, 1997, for $11.375. If you had purchased the call on this date, you would have had the right to purchase shares of Compaq for $65 anytime until the option expired in January. On September 9, Compaq shares sold for $69.50. Immediate exercise of the call would have resulted in net proceeds of $69.50 − $65 = $4.50. Obviously, anyone who paid $11.375 for the call on September 9 had no intention of exercising it immediately. A buyer of the call was betting on an increase in the stock price, which would make the option turn out to be a profitable investment. For example, if Compaq sold in January for $85, the proceeds from exercising the call would have been

$$\text{Proceeds} = \text{stock price} - \text{exercise price} = \$85 - \$65 = \$20$$

and the profit on the call would have been

$$\text{Profits} = \text{proceeds} - \text{original investment} = \$20 - \$11.375 = \$8.625$$

---

put option: Right to sell an asset at a specified exercise price on or before the exercise date.

Whereas a call option gives you the right to buy a share of stock, a **put option** gives you the right to *sell* it for the exercise price. If you hold a put on a share of stock with exercise price $65 and the stock price turns out to be greater than $65, you will not want to exercise your option to sell the shares for the exercise price. The put will be left unexercised and will expire valueless. But if the share price turns out to be less than $65, it will pay to buy the share at the low price and then exercise your option to sell it for $65. The put would then be worth the difference between the exercise price and the stock price.

Table 23.1

Option values on expiration date as a function of stock price on that date (exercise price = $65)

Compaq value	$40	$50	$60	$70	$80	$90
Call value	0	0	0	$5	$15	$25
Put value	$25	$15	$5	0	0	0

▶ **Example 23.2** *Put Options*

Suppose Compaq is selling for $60 just before the put option expires. Then if you hold a put, you can buy a share of stock for $60 and exercise your right to sell it for $65. The put will be worth $65 − $60 = $5. If you paid $3 for the put originally, your profit will be $2. If, however, the stock price is above $65 on the maturity date, you will let the put option expire worthless. Your loss equals the $3 you originally spent to purchase the put.

In general, the value of the put option at expiration is as follows:

Stock Price at Expiration	Value of Put Option at Expiration
Greater than exercise price	Zero
Less than exercise price	Exercise price − stock price

Table 23.1 shows the value on their expiration date of call and put options on Compaq stock with exercise price $65 as a function of Compaq's share price on that date. You can see that once the stock price is above $65, the call value rises dollar for dollar with the stock price, and that once the stock price is below $65, the put value rises $1 for each dollar *decrease* in the stock price. Figure 23.1 plots the values of each option on the expiration date.

Figure 23.2 is an excerpt of listed stock quotations from *The Wall Street Journal* showing options for shares of Compaq. The value 69½ below the company name is the current price of the stock. The first column lists the exercise prices at which various Compaq options trade. The next column contains the expiration month for each option. Following this are two pairs of columns; the first pair reports trading volume[2] and closing price for the call option, and the next pair reports the same data for the put. You can see from the listings that calls are worth more when the exercise price is lower, while puts are worth more when the exercise price is higher. This makes sense: you would rather have the right to buy at a low price and the right to sell at a high price.

▶ **Self-Test 23.1**

a. What will be the proceeds and net profits (i.e., net of the option premium) to an investor who purchases the January maturity Compaq call options with exercise price $65 if the stock price at maturity is $55? What if the stock price at maturity is $75? Use the data in Figure 23.2.

b. Now answer part (a) for an investor who purchases a January maturity Compaq put option with exercise price $65.

---

[2]Volume is reported as the number of option contracts traded. Each contract is for 100 shares of stock. For example, if a call price is reported as $6, you would pay $600 to buy one contract, which would give you the right to buy 100 shares of stock. You would pay the exercise price for each share.

Figure 23.1

Values of call options and put options on Compaq stock on option expiration date (exercise price = $65)

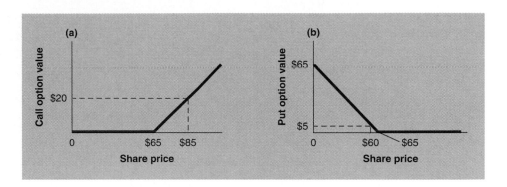

Selling Calls and Puts

The traded options that you see quoted in the financial pages are not sold by the companies themselves but by other investors. If one investor buys an option on Compaq stock, some other investor must be on the other side of the bargain. We will look now at the position of the investor who sells an option.[3]

We have already seen that the January-maturity Compaq calls with exercise price $65 are trading at $11⅜. Thus if you *sell* the January call option on Compaq stock, the buyer pays you $11⅜. However, in return you promise to sell Compaq shares at a price of $65 if the call buyer decides to exercise his option. The option seller's obligation to *sell* Compaq is just the other side of the coin to the option holder's right to *buy* the stock. The buyer *pays* the option premium for the right to exercise advantageously; the seller *receives* the premium but may be required at a later date to deliver the stock for an exercise price that is less than the market price of the stock. If the share price is below the exercise price of $65 when the option expires in January, holders of the call will not exercise their option and you, the seller, will have no further liability. However, if the price of Compaq is greater than $65, the option will be exercised and you must give up your shares for $65 each. You therefore lose the difference between the share price and the $65 that you receive from the buyer.

Suppose that Compaq's stock price turns out to be $85. In this case the buyer will exercise the call option and will pay $65 for stock that can be resold for $85. The buyer therefore has a payoff of $20—not bad on an investment of only $11⅜. Of

Figure 23.2

Options on shares of Compaq. (Source: The Wall Street Journal, *September 8, 1997).*

Option/Strike		Exp.	—Call— Vol.	Last	—Put— Vol.	Last
Compaq	60	Sep	905	9¾	522	¼
69½	60	Oct	668	11⅜	200	1⅜
69½	60	Jan	339	14⅜	30	4
69½	65	Sep	4183	5½	1434	15/16
69½	65	Oct	1150	7½	222	2⁹/16
69½	65	Jan	241	11⅜	25	5⅝
69½	70	Sep	4430	2⁷/16	300	2⅝
69½	70	Oct	1153	4¾	290	5⅛
69½	70	Jan	423	9⅛	17	8⅜
69½	75	Sep	1967	⅞	66	6⅜
69½	75	Oct	836	2¾	41	7⅞
69½	80	Oct	287	1¾	...	...
69½	80	Jan	403	5⅛	...	...

[3]The option seller is known as the *writer.*

Figure 23.3

Payoffs to sellers of call and put options on Compaq stock (exercise price = $65).

course, that positive payoff for the *buyer* means a negative payoff for you the *seller,* for you are obliged to sell Compaq stock worth $85 for only $65.

In general, the seller's loss is the buyer's gain, and vice versa. Figure 23.3*a* shows the payoffs to the call option seller. Note that Figure 23.3*a* is just Figure 23.1*a* drawn upside down.

The position of an investor who sells the Compaq put option can be shown in just the same way by standing Figure 23.1*b* on its head. The put *buyer* has the right to sell a share for $65; so the *seller* of the put has agreed to pay $65 for the share if the put buyer should demand it. Clearly the seller will be safe as long as the share price remains above $65 but will lose money if the share price falls below this figure. The worst thing that can happen to the put seller is for the stock to be worthless. The seller would then be obliged to pay $65 for a worthless stock. The payoff to the seller would be −$65. Note that the advantage always lies with the option buyer, the obligation with the seller. Therefore, the buyer must pay the seller to acquire the option.

> **The purchaser of an option has the right to buy or sell an asset at a fixed and possibly advantageous price. The option seller is obliged to sell or buy at this price if the buyer wants to exercise. The option buyer pays the seller to take on this obligation.**

Table 23.2 summarizes the rights and obligation of buyers and sellers of calls and puts.

▶ **Self-Test 23.2**

a. What will be the proceeds and profits to an investor who sells the January maturity Compaq call options with exercise price $65 if the stock price at maturity is $55? What if the stock price at maturity is $75? Use the data in Figure 23.2.

b. Now answer part (a) for an investor who sells a January maturity Compaq put option with exercise price $65.

Table 23.2

Rights and obligations of various options positions

	Buyer	Seller
Call option	Right to buy asset	Obligation to sell asset
Put option	Right to sell asset	Obligation to buy asset

Figure 23.4

Payoff to protective put strategy. If the ultimate stock price exceeds $65, the put is valueless but you own the stock. If it is less than $65, you can sell the stock for the exercise price.

Financial Alchemy with Options

Now we can see how options can be used to modify the risk characteristics of a portfolio. Suppose, for example, that you are generally optimistic about Compaq's prospects, but you perceive enough risk that a large investment in the stock would cause you sleepless nights. Here is a strategy that might appeal to you: buy the stock, but also buy a put option on the stock with exercise price $65. If the stock price rises, your put turns out to be worthless, but you win on the stock investment. If the stock price falls, your losses are limited, since the put gives you the right to sell the stock for the $65 exercise price. Thus the value of your stock-plus-put position cannot be less than $65.

Here is another way to view your overall position. You hold the stock and the put option. The value of each component of the portfolio will be as follows:

	Stock Price < $65	Stock Price ≥ $65
Value of stock	Stock price	Stock price
Value of put option	$65 − stock price	0
Total value	$65	Stock price

No matter how far the stock price falls, the total value of your portfolio cannot fall below the $65 exercise price.

The value of your position when the options expire is graphed in Figure 23.4. You have downside protection at $65 but still share in potential gains on the stock. This strategy is called a *protective put,* because the put option gives protection against losses. Of course, such protection is not free. Look again at Figure 23.2 and you will find the cost of such protection. "Stock price insurance" at a level of $65 between September 1997 and January 1998 cost $5⅝ per share; this was the price of the put option with exercise price $65 and January expiration.

▶ **Example 23.3** *Profiting from Volatility*

Suppose you believe that Compaq is going to be subject to considerable volatility over the next few months. Perhaps a new product shortly due to come to market will

Figure 23.5
Payoff and profit on a straddle. Call option is drawn in blue, put option in black.

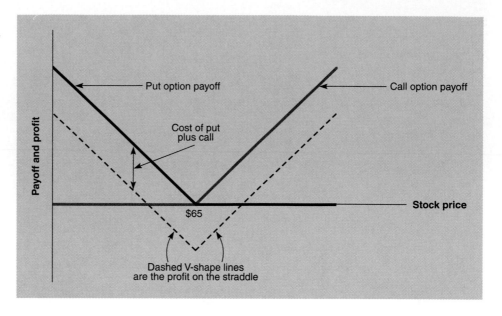

be either a fabulous success or, if technological bugs cannot be overcome, a dismal failure. How can you bet on the expected volatility of the stock?

Try buying one call and one put option, both with exercise price $65. This position—holding a call and a put—is called a *straddle*. If the stock price falls, the put will be profitable; if the stock price rises, the call will be profitable. Figure 23.5 illustrates your position. The blue line is the value of the call. The black line is the value of the put. You hold the call *and* the put, so the total value of your holdings is a V-shaped profile.

Of course, there is no free lunch here. Although the value of the position cannot be negative, remember that you have to pay to establish this position: you pay for both the call and the put. Unless the ultimate payoff exceeds the cost of the two options, you will lose money. Thus the *profit* on this strategy is given by the dashed V-shaped line in Figure 23.5. Unless the stock moves far enough that the profit on either the call or the put covers the initial cost of the two options, your profits will be negative.

Of course there are many other interesting option strategies that one might envision. These instruments give you considerable leeway to tailor the risk features of a portfolio. Try your skill at financial alchemy with Self-Test 23.3.

▶ **Self-Test 23.3** What strategy using a call, a put, and a share of stock can create a payoff that depends on the price of Compaq stock in the manner depicted in Figure 23.6? Why might someone establish this position?

Figure 23.6

This strategy provides a total payoff of $60 if the stock price is below $60, a payoff of $70 if the stock price is above $70, and a payoff equal to the stock price for values between $60 and $70. Can you create this payoff?

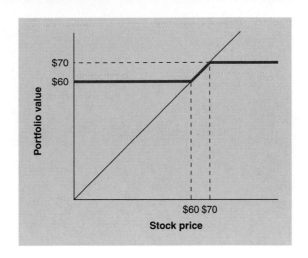

23.2 What Determines Option Values?

We have seen that January-maturity calls on Compaq are trading at $11⅜. But we have said nothing about how the market values of options are determined.

Upper and Lower Limits on Option Values

We know what an option is worth when it expires. Consider, for example, the option to buy stock at $65. If the stock price is below $65 at the expiration date, the call will be worthless; if the stock price is above $65, the call will be worth the value of the stock minus the $65 exercise price. The relationship is depicted by the heavy line in Figure 23.7.

Even before expiration, the price of the option can never remain *below* the heavy blue line in Figure 23.7. For example, if our option were priced at $10 and the stock at $85, it would pay any investor to buy the option, exercise it for an additional $65, and then sell the stock for $85. That would give a "money machine" with a profit of $85 − $75 = $10. The demand for options from investors using this strategy would quickly force the option price up at least to the heavy blue line in the figure. The heavy blue line is therefore a *lower* limit on the market price of the option. Thus

$$\text{Lower limit on value of call option} = \text{the greater of } zero \text{ or } (stock\ price - exercise\ price)$$

The diagonal red line in Figure 23.7, which is the plot of the stock price, is the *upper* limit to the option price. Why? Because the stock itself gives a higher final payoff whatever happens. If when the option expires the stock price ends up above the exercise price, the option is worth the stock price *less* the exercise price. If the stock price ends up below the exercise price, the option is worthless, but the stock's

Figure 23.7

Value of a call before its expiration date (dashed line). The value depends on the stock price. The call is always worth more than its value if exercised now (heavy line). It is never worth more than the stock price itself.

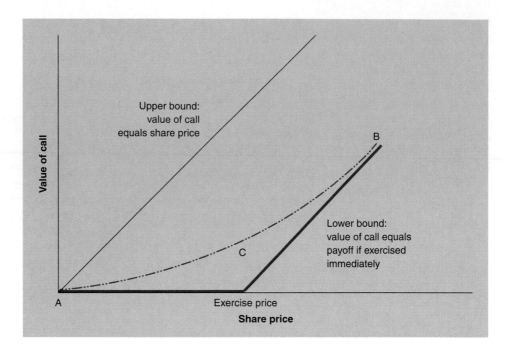

owner still has a valuable security. Thus the extra payoff to holding the stock rather than the option is as follows:

Stock Price at Expiration	Stock Payoff	Option Payoff	Extra Payoff from Holding Stock Rather than Option
Greater than $65	Stock price	Stock price − $65	$65
Less than or equal to $65	Stock price	$0	Stock price

The Determinants of Option Value

The option price must lie between the upper and lower limits in Figure 23.7. In fact, the price will lie on a curved, upward-sloping line like the dashed curve shown in the figure. This line begins its travels where the upper and lower bounds meet (at zero). Then it rises, gradually becoming parallel to the lower bound. This line tells us an important fact about option values: given the exercise price, *the value of a call option increases as the stock price increases.*

That should be no surprise. Owners of call options clearly hope for the stock price to rise and are happy when it does. But let us look more carefully at the shape and location of the dashed line. Three points, *A*, *B*, and *C*, are marked on the dashed line. As we explain each point, you will see why the option price has to behave as the dashed line predicts.

Point *A*. *When the stock is worthless, the option is worthless.* A stock price of zero means that there is no possibility the stock will ever have any future value.[4] If so, the option is sure to expire unexercised and worthless, and it is worthless today.

---

[4] If a stock *can* be worth something in the future, then investors will pay *something* for it today, although possibly a very small amount.

Point B. *When the stock price becomes very high, the option price approaches the stock price less the present value of the exercise price.* Notice that the dashed line representing the option price in Figure 23.7 eventually becomes parallel to the ascending heavy line representing the lower bound on the option price. The reason is as follows. The higher the stock price, the greater the odds that the option will eventually be exercised. If the stock price is high enough, exercise becomes a virtual certainty; the probability that the stock price will fall below the exercise price before the option expires becomes trivial.

If you own an option that you *know* will be exchanged for a share of stock, you effectively own the stock now. The only difference is that you don't have to pay for the stock (by handing over the exercise price) until later, when formal exercise occurs. In these circumstances, buying the call is equivalent to buying the stock now with deferred payment and delivery. The value of the call is therefore equal to the stock price less the present value of the exercise price.[5]

This brings us to another important point about options. Investors who acquire stock by way of a call option are buying on "installment credit." They pay the purchase price of the option today, but they do not pay the exercise price unt'l they actually exercise the option. The delay in payment is particularly valuable if interest rates are high and the option has a long maturity. Thus *the value of a call option increases with both the rate of interest and the time to expiration.*

▶ **Self-Test 23.4**   How would the value of a put option be affected by an increase in the exercise price? Explain. Check your answer by looking at the price of put options in Figure 23.2.

Point C. *The option price always exceeds its minimum value* (except at maturity or when stock price is zero). We have seen that the dashed and heavy lines in Figure 23.7 coincide when stock price is zero (point *A*), but elsewhere the lines diverge; that is, the option price must exceed the minimum value given by the heavy blue line. You can see why by examining point *C*.

At point *C*, the stock price exactly equals the exercise price. The option therefore would be worthless if it expired today. However, suppose that the option will not expire until 3 months hence. Of course we do not know what the stock price will be at the expiration date. There is roughly a 50 percent chance that it will be higher than the exercise price, and a 50 percent chance that it will be lower. The possible payoffs to the option are therefore:

Outcome	Payoff
Stock price rises (50 percent probability)	Stock price − exercise price (option is exercised)
Stock price falls (50 percent probability)	Zero (option expires worthless)

If there is some chance of a positive payoff, and if the worst payoff is zero, then the option must be valuable. That means the option price at point *C* exceeds its lower bound, which at point *C* is zero. In general, the option price will exceed the lower bound as long as there is time left before expiration.

---

[5]We assume here that the stock pays no dividends until after the option matures. If dividends were paid, you *would* care about when you get to own the stock because the option holder misses out on any dividends.

One of the most important determinants of the *height* of the dashed curve (that is, of the difference between actual and lower-bound value) is the likelihood of substantial movements in the stock price. An option on a stock whose price is unlikely to change by more than 1 or 2 percent is not worth much; an option on a stock whose price may halve or double is very valuable.

For example, suppose that a call option has an exercise price of $65 and the stock price will be either $55 or $75 when the option expires. The possible payoffs to the option are as follows:

Stock price at expiration	$55	$75
Call value at expiration	0	$10

Now suppose that the value of the stock when the option expires can be $45 or $85. The *average* of the possible stock prices is the same as before, but the volatility is greater. In this case the payoffs to the call are

Stock price at expiration	$45	$85
Call value at expiration	0	$20

A comparison of the two cases highlights the valuable asymmetry that options offer. If the stock price turns out to be below the exercise price when the option expires, the option is valueless regardless of whether the shortfall is a cent or a dollar. However, the option holder reaps all the benefits of stock price advances. Thus in our example the option is worth only $10 if the stock price reaches $75, but it is worth $20 if the stock price rises to $85. Therefore, volatility helps the option holder.

The probability of large stock price changes during the remaining life of an option depends on two things: (1) the variability of the stock price *per unit of time,* and (2) the length of time until the option expires. Other things equal, you would like to hold an option on a volatile stock. Given volatility, you would like to hold an option with a long life ahead of it, since that longer life means that there is more opportunity for the stock price to change.

> **The value of an option increases with both the variability of the share price and the time to expiration.**

It's a rare person who can keep all these properties straight at first reading. Therefore, we have summed them up in Table 23.3.

▶ **Self-Test 23.5**   Rework our numerical example for a put option with an exercise price of $65. Show that put options also are more valuable when the stock price is more volatile.

Table 23.3

What the price of a call option depends on

If the following variables *increase*, ...	...the value of a call option will
stock price	increase
exercise price	decrease
interest rate	increase
time to expiration	increase
volatility of stock price	increase

Option-Valuation Models

If you want to value an option, you need to go beyond the qualitative statements of Table 23.3; you need an exact option-valuation model—a formula that you can plug numbers into and come up with a figure for option value.

Valuing complex options is a high-tech business and well beyond the scope of this book. Our aim here is not to make you into instant option whizzes, but we can illustrate the basics of option valuation by walking you through a very simple example. It turns out that the trick to option valuation is to find a combination of borrowing and an investment in the stock that exactly replicates the option. The nearby box illustrates a simple version of one of these option-valuation models.

 See box p. 664

This model achieves simplicity by assuming that the share price can take on only two values at the expiration date of the option. This assumption is clearly unrealistic, but it turns out that this approach can be generalized to allow for a large number of possible future share prices rather than just the two values in our example.

In 1973 Fischer Black, Myron Scholes, and Robert Merton came up with a formula which showed that even when share prices are changing continuously, you can still replicate an option by a series of levered investments in the stock. The Black-Scholes formula is regularly used by option traders, investment bankers, and financial managers to value a wide variety of options. Scholes and Merton shared the 1997 Nobel prize in economics for their work on the development of this formula.[6]

Today, there are many ever-more-sophisticated variants on the Black-Scholes formula that can better capture some aspect of real-life markets. As computer power continues to increase, these models can be made more complex and increasingly accurate.

▶ **Self-Test 23.6**

Use the box on page 664 as a model to help you answer this question. Suppose that the price of Disney stock is $40 and could either double to $80 or halve to $20 by April. Show that the following two strategies have exactly the same payoffs regardless of whether the stock price rises or falls: *Strategy A*—Buy three call options with an exercise price of $40; *Strategy B*—Buy two shares and borrow the present value of $40. What is your cash outflow today if you follow Strategy B? What does this tell you about the value of three call options? Continue to assume that the interest rate is 2 percent per 3 months.

23.3 *Spotting the Option*

In our discussion so far we may have given you the impression that financial managers are concerned only with traded options to buy or sell shares. But once you have learned to recognize the different kinds of options, you will find that they are everywhere. Unfortunately, they rarely come with a large label attached. Often the trickiest part of the problem is to identify the option.

We will start by looking briefly at options on real assets and then turn to options on financial assets. You should find that you have already encountered many of these options in earlier chapters.

[6]Fischer Black passed away in 1995.

A Simple Option-Valuation Model

Imagine that it is January and that you are contemplating the purchase of a call option on Compaq stock. The call has an April exercise date and an exercise price of $70. Compaq's stock price is currently $70, so the option will be valueless unless the stock price appreciates over the next 3 months. The outlook for Compaq stock is uncertain and all you know is that at the end of the 3 months it will be either $90 or $60. Finally we assume that the rate of interest on a bank loan is 8 percent a year, or about 2 percent a quarter.

The following figure depicts the outlook for three alternative investments:

Compaq Stock		Call Option		Bank Loan	
January	April	January	April	January	April
$70	$90	?	$20	$100	$102
	$60		$0		$102

The first investment is Compaq stock. Its current price is $70 but the price could rise to $90 or fall to $60. The second investment is the call option. When the call expires in April, the option will be valueless if the stock price falls to $60 and it will be worth $90 − $70 = $20 if the stock price rises to $90. We don't know (yet) how much the call is worth today, so for the time being we put a question mark against the January value. Our third investment is a bank loan at an interest rate of 2 percent a quarter. The payoff on a $100 bank loan is $102 no matter what happens to the price of Compaq stock.

Consider now two investment strategies. The first (Strategy A) is to buy three call options. The second (Strategy B) is to buy two Compaq shares and to borrow the present value of $120 from the bank. Table 23.4 shows the possible payoffs from the two strategies. Notice that when you borrow from the bank, you receive a *positive* cash flow now but have a *negative* flow when the loan is repaid in April.

You can see that *regardless of whether the stock price falls to $60 or rises to $90,* the payoffs from the two strategies are identical. To put it another way, you can exactly *replicate* an investment in call options by a combination of a bank loan and an investment in the stock.[1] If two investments give the same payoffs in all circumstances, then their value must be the same today. In other words, the cost of buying three call options must be exactly the same as borrowing $117.65 from the bank and buying two Compaq shares:

$$\text{Price of 3 calls} = \$140 - \$117.65$$

$$\text{Price of 1 call} = \frac{\$140 - \$117.65}{3} = \$7.45$$

Presto! You have just valued a call option.

Table 23.4

It is possible to replicate the payoffs from Compaq call options by borrowing to invest in Compaq stock

	Cash Flow in January	Payoff in April if Stock Price Equals	
		$60	$90
Strategy A			
Buy three calls	?	$ 0	+$ 60
Strategy B			
Buy two shares	−$140.00	+$120	+$180
Borrow PV($120)	+ 117.65	− 120	− 120
	− $ 22.35	$ 0	+$ 60

Note: PV($120) at an interest rate of 2 percent for 3 months is 120/1.02 = $117.65.

[1] The only tricky part in valuing the Compaq option was to work out the number of shares that were needed to replicate one option. Fortunately, there is a simple formula that says that the number of shares needed is equal to

$$\frac{\text{Spread of possible option prices}}{\text{Spread of possible stock prices}} = \frac{\$20 - \$0}{\$90 - \$60} = \frac{2}{3}$$

To replicate a call option, you need to buy two-thirds of a share of stock. To replicate three calls, you need to buy two shares of stock.

Options on Real Assets

In Chapter 7 we pointed out that the capital investment projects that you accept today may affect the opportunities you have tomorrow.[7] Today's capital budgeting decisions need to recognize these future opportunities. We looked in Chapter 7 at several ways that companies may build future flexibility into a project.

Other things equal, a capital investment project that generates new opportunities is more valuable than one that doesn't. A flexible project—one that doesn't commit management to a fixed operating strategy—is more valuable than an inflexible one. When a project is flexible or generates new opportunities for the firm, it is said to contain **real options.** Here are a few specific examples.

real options: Options embedded in real assets.

The Option to Expand. Many capital investment proposals include an option to buy additional equipment in the future. For instance, a drug company may invest in a patent that allows it to exploit a new technology, an airline may acquire an option to buy a new aircraft, or a retailer may purchase adjoining land that has no immediate value but offers an opportunity to expand at a later date.

▶ Example 23.4

Options

Here is another disguised option that might arise in a capital budgeting analysis. You are considering the purchase of a tract of desert land that is known to contain gold deposits. Unfortunately, the cost of extraction is higher than the current price of gold. Does that mean the land is almost worthless? Not at all. You are not obliged to mine the gold, but ownership of the land gives you the *option* to do so. Of course, if you know that the gold price will remain below the extraction cost, then the option is worthless. But if there is uncertainty about future gold prices, you could be lucky and make a killing.

Buying the mine gives you an option to extract the gold. The exercise price of that option is the cost of extraction. In effect, you have a call option to acquire gold for the extraction cost. If there is a chance that gold prices will increase enough to make extraction profitable, the option will have value and might justify the cost of the option, which is the purchase price of the land. ◀

The Option to Abandon. Suppose that you need a new plant ready to produce turboencabulators in 3 years. You have a choice of designs. If design A is chosen, construction must begin immediately. Design B is more expensive but you can wait a year before breaking ground.

If you know with certainty that the plant will be needed, you should opt for design A. But suppose that there is some possibility that demand for turboencabulators will fall off and that in a year's time you will decide the plant is not required. Then design B may be preferable because it gives you the option to bail out at low cost any time during the next 12 months.

You can think of the option to abandon as a put option. The exercise price of the put is the amount that you could recover if you abandon the project. The abandonment option makes design B more attractive by limiting the downside exposure; the worst outcome is that you receive the project's salvage value. The more uncertain is the need for the new plant, the more valuable is the downside protection offered by the abandonment option. As always, options are more valuable when the value of the underlying asset is more volatile.

[7]See Section 7.3.

It is also possible that, once built, design B can be readily converted to producing retro-chrysalids, while design A has no alternative uses. Again, the extra flexibility provided by design B may tip the balance in its favor.

These are only two examples of options encountered in capital investment decisions. The others could fill (and have filled) entire books. If you look out for real options, you'll find them almost everywhere.

> **Whenever management can decide in the future how best to operate a project—for example, to expand, contract, delay, or abandon it—the project contains a real option.**

▶ **Self-Test 23.7**   A real estate developer buys 70 acres of land in a rural area, planning to build a subdivision on the land if and when the population from the city begins to expand into the area. If population growth is less than anticipated, the developer believes that the land can be sold to a country club that would build a golf course on the property.

a. In what way does the possibility of sale to the country club provide a put option to the developer?
b. What is the exercise price of the option? The asset value?
c. How does the golf course option increase the NPV of the land project to the developer?

Options on Financial Assets

When companies issue securities, they often include an option in the package. Here are a few examples of the options that are associated with new financing.

warrant: Right to buy shares from a company at a stipulated price before a set date.

Warrants.   A **warrant** is a long-term call option on the company's stock. Unlike the Compaq option that we considered earlier, a warrant is issued by the company. The company sells the warrant; the investor buys it.

A company that issues a bond will sometimes add some warrants as a "sweetener." Since these warrants are valuable to investors, they are prepared to pay a higher price for a package of bonds and warrants than for the bond on its own. Managers sometimes look with delight at this higher price, forgetting that in return the company has incurred a liability to sell its shares to the warrant holders at what with hindsight may turn out to be a low price.

Warrants may also be issued when a firm becomes bankrupt; the bankruptcy court offers the firm's bondholders warrants in the reorganized company as part of the settlement. For example, when Federated Department Stores was reorganized, it issued warrants, each of which entitled the owner to buy one share of Federated stock before 2001 at $29.92. Investors who hold these warrants are betting that the stock price will rise above $29.92; if it does not, their warrants will be worthless.

convertible bond: Bond that the holder may exchange for a specified number of shares.

Convertible Bonds.   The **convertible bond** is a close relative of the bond-warrant package. It allows the bondholder to exchange the bond for a given number of shares of common stock. Therefore, it is a package of a straight bond with a call option. The exercise price of the call option is the value of the "straight bond" (that is, a bond that is not convertible). If the value of the stock exceeds the value of the straight bond, it will be profitable to convert.

▶ Example 23.5

Convertible Bonds

In 1994 Boston Chicken issued 10-year convertible bonds. Each bond could be converted at any time before maturity into 35.75 shares of Boston Chicken stock. In other words, the owner had a 10-year option to return the bond to Boston Chicken and receive 35.75 shares in exchange. The number of shares that are received for each bond is called the bond's *conversion ratio*. The conversion ratio of the Boston Chicken bond was 35.75.

In order to receive 35.75 shares of Boston Chicken stock you had to surrender bonds with a face value of $1,000. Therefore, in order to receive *one* share, you had to surrender a face amount of $1,000/35.75 = \$27.97$. This figure is called the *conversion price*. Anybody who bought the bond at $1,000 in order to convert into 35.75 shares paid the equivalent of $27.97 per share. ◀

The owner of a convertible bond owns a bond and a call option on the firm's stock. So does the owner of a package of a bond and a warrant. However, there are differences, the most important being that a convertible bond owner must give up the bond to exercise the option. The owner of a package of bonds and warrants exercises the warrants for cash and keeps the bond.

The value of a convertible bond depends on its *bond value* and its *conversion value*. The bond value is what the bond would sell for if it could *not* be converted into stock. The conversion value is what the bond would be worth if it were converted immediately.

Since the owner of the convertible always has the option *not* to convert, bond value establishes a lower bound, or *floor,* to the price of a convertible. Of course, this floor is not completely flat. If the firm falls on hard times, the bond may not be worth much. In the extreme case where the firm becomes worthless, the bond is also worthless.

Conversion value is the value of the convertible bond if it were converted immediately. For example, the Boston Chicken convertible could be exchanged for 35.75 shares. Thus if the share price is $32, the conversion value is $35.75 \times \$32 = \$1,144$.

A convertible can never sell for *less* than its conversion value. If it did, smart investors would buy the convertible, exchange it for stock, and sell the stock. Their profit would be the difference between the conversion value and the price of the convertible.

This means that there are *two* lower bounds to the price of any convertible: its bond value and its conversion value. When the firm does well, conversion value exceeds bond value; the investor would choose to convert if forced to make an immediate choice. Bond value exceeds conversion value when the firm does poorly. In these circumstances the investor would hold on to the bonds if forced to choose.

Convertible holders do not have to make a now-or-never choice for or against conversion. They can wait and then, with the benefit of hindsight, take whatever course turns out to give them the highest payoff. Thus a convertible is always worth *more* than its bond value or its conversion value (except when time runs out at the bond's maturity).

We stated earlier that it is useful to think of a convertible bond as a package of a straight bond and an option to buy the common stock in exchange for the straight bond. The value of this call option is equal to the difference between the convertible's selling price and its bond value.

Callable Bonds.   Unlike warrants and convertibles, which give the *investor* an option, a **callable bond** gives an option to the *issuer.* A company that issues a callable bond has an option to buy the bond back at the stated exercise or "call" price. Therefore, you can think of a callable bond as a *package* of a straight bond (a bond that is not callable) and a call option held by the issuer.

callable bond: Bond that may be repurchased by the issuer before maturity at specified call price.

The option to call the bond is obviously attractive to the issuer. If interest rates decline and bond prices rise, the company has the opportunity to repurchase the bond at a fixed call price. Therefore, the option to call the bond puts a ceiling on the bond price.

Of course, when the company issues a callable bond, investors are aware of this ceiling on the bond price and will pay less for a callable bond than for a straight bond. The difference between the value of a straight bond and a callable bond with the same coupon rate and maturity is the value of the call option that investors have given to the company:

Value of callable bond = value of straight bond − value of the issuer's call option

---

▶ **Self-Test 23.8**   "Extendable bonds" allow the investor to redeem the bond at par or let the bond remain outstanding until maturity. Suppose a 20-year extendable bond is issued with the investor allowed after 5 years to redeem the bond at par.

a. These bonds are sometimes called put bonds. Why? Who holds an implicit put option?
b. On what asset is the option written? (What asset do the option holders have the right to sell?)
c. What is the exercise price of the option?
d. In what circumstances will the option be exercised?

Summary

1. There are two basic types of options. A call option is the right to buy an asset at a specific exercise price on or before the exercise date. A put is the right to sell an asset at a specific exercise price on or before the exercise date.
2. The value of a call option depends on the following considerations:
   - To exercise the option you must pay the exercise price. Other things equal, the less you are obliged to pay, the better. Therefore, the value of the option is higher when the exercise price is low relative to the stock price.
   - Investors who buy the stock by way of a call option are buying on installment credit. They pay the purchase price of the option today but they do not pay the exercise price until they exercise the option. The higher the rate of interest and the longer the time to expiration, the more this "free credit" is worth.
   - No matter how far the stock price falls, the owner of the call cannot lose more than the price of the call. On the other hand, the more the stock price rises above the exercise price, the greater the profit on the call. Therefore, the option holder does not lose from increased variability if things go wrong, but gains if they go right. The value of the option increases with the variability of stock returns. Of course the longer the time to the final exercise date, the more opportunity there is for the stock price to vary.
3. The importance of building flexibility into investment projects (discussed in Chapter 7) can be reformulated in the language of options. For example, many capital investments provide the flexibility to expand capacity in the future if demand turns

out to be unusually buoyant. They are in effect providing the firm with a call option on the extra capacity. Firms also think about alternative uses for their assets if things go wrong. The option to abandon a project is a put option; the put's exercise price is the value of the project's assets if shifted to an alternative use.

4. Many of the securities that firms issue contain an option. For example, warrants are nothing but a long-term call option issued by the firm. Convertible bonds give the investor the option to buy the firm's stock in exchange for the value of the underlying bond. Unlike warrants and convertibles, which give an option to the investor, callable bonds give the option to the issuing firm. If interest rates decline and the value of the underlying bond rises, the firm can buy the bonds back at a specified exercise price.

Key Terms

| call option | real options | convertible bond |
| put option | warrant | callable bond |

Problems

1. **Option Payoffs.** Turn back to Figure 23.2, which lists prices of various Compaq options. Use the data in the figure to calculate the payoff and the profits for investments in each of the following September maturity options, assuming that the stock price on the expiration date is $70.

   a. Call option with exercise price of $65
   b. Put option with exercise price of $65
   c. Call option with exercise price of $70
   d. Put option with exercise price of $70
   e. Call option with exercise price of $75
   f. Put option with exercise price of $75

2. **Option Payoffs.** Redo the preceding problem assuming the stock price on the expiration date is (a) $80; (b) $60.

3. **Determinants of Option Value.** Look at the data in Figure 23.2.

   a. What is the price of a call option with an exercise price of $65 and expiration in September? What if expiration is in October?
   b. Why do you think the October calls cost more than the September calls?
   c. Is the same true of put options? Why?

4. **Option Contracts.** Fill in the blanks by choosing the appropriate terms from the following list: *call, exercise, put.*
   A(n) _____ option gives its owner the opportunity to buy a stock at a specific price which is generally called the _____ price. A(n) _____ option gives its owner the opportunity to sell stock at a specified _____ price.

5. **Option Payoffs.** Note Figure 23.8a and 23.8b. Match each figure with one of the following positions:

   a. Call buyer
   b. Call seller
   c. Put buyer
   d. Put seller

Figure 23.8
See problem 5.

(a)   (b)

6. **Puts versus Calls.** "The buyer of a call and the seller of a put both hope that the stock price will rise. Therefore the two positions are identical." Is the speaker correct? Illustrate with a simple example.

7. **Hedging with Options.** Suppose that you hold a share of stock and a put option on that share with an exercise price of $100. What is the value of your portfolio when the option expires if

   a. the stock price is below $100?
   b. the stock price is above $100?

8. **Option Portfolios.** Mixing options and securities can often create interesting payoffs. For each of the following combinations show what the payoff would be when the option expires if (i) the stock price is below the exercise price, and (ii) the stock price is above the exercise price. Assume that each option has the same exercise price and date.

   a. Buy a call and invest the present value of the exercise price in a bank deposit.
   b. Buy a share and a put option on the share.
   c. Buy a share, buy a put option on the share, and sell a call option on the share.
   d. Buy a call option and a put option on the share.

9. **Option Values.** What is the lower bound to the price of a call option? What is the upper bound?

10. **Option Values.** What is a call option worth if

    a. the stock price is zero?
    b. the stock price is extremely high relative to the exercise price?

11. **Option Valuation.** Figure 23.2 shows call options on Compaq stock with the same exercise date in January and with exercise prices $60, $65, and $70. Notice that the price of the middle call option (with exercise price $65) is less than halfway between the prices of the other two calls (with exercise prices $60 and $70). Suppose that this were not the case. For example, suppose that the price of the middle call were the average of the prices of the other two calls. Show that if you sell two of the middle calls and use the proceeds to buy one each of the other calls, your proceeds in January may be positive but cannot be negative despite the fact that your net outlay today is zero. What can you deduce from this example about option pricing?

12. **Put Prices.** How does the price of a *put* option respond to the following changes, other things equal? Does the put price go up or down?

    a. Stock price increases.
    b. Exercise price is increased.

    c. Risk-free interest rate increases.

    d. Expiration date of the option is extended.

    e. Volatility of the stock price falls.

    f. Time passes, so the option's expiration date comes closer.

13. **Option Values.** As manager of United Bedstead you own substantial executive stock options. These options entitle you to buy the firm's shares during the next 5 years at a price of $100 a share. The plant manager has just outlined two alternative proposals to reequip the plant. Both proposals have the same net present value but one is substantially riskier than the other. At first you are undecided which to choose but then you remember your stock options. How might these influence your choice?

14. **Option Pricing.** Look again at the Compaq call option that we valued in Section 23.3. Suppose that by the end of April the price of Compaq stock could rise to $100 or fall to $50. Everything else is unchanged from our example.

    a. What would be the value of the Compaq call at the end of April if the stock price is $100? If it is $50?

    b. Show that a strategy of buying 5 calls provides exactly the same payoffs as borrowing the present value of $150 from the bank and buying 3 shares.

    c. What is the net cash flow in July from the policy of borrowing PV($150) and buying 3 shares?

    d. What does this tell you about the value of the call option?

    e. Why is the value of the call option different from the value that we calculated in Section 23.2? What does this tell you about the relationship between the value of a call and the volatility of the share price?

15. **Option Pricing.** Look once more at the Compaq call option that we valued in Section 23.3. Suppose (just suppose) that the interest rate on bank loans is zero. Recalculate the value of the Compaq call option. What does this tell you about the relationship between interest rates and the value of a call?

16. **Real and Financial Options.** Fill in the blanks:

    a. An oil company acquires mining rights to a silver deposit. It is not obliged to mine the silver, however. The company has effectively acquired a _____ option, where the exercise price is the cost of opening the mine and extracting the silver.

    b. Some preferred shareholders have the right to redeem their shares at par value after a specified date. (If they hand over their shares, the firm sends them a check equal to the shares' par value.) These shareholders have a _____ option.

    c. A firm buys a standard machine with a ready secondhand market. The secondhand market gives the firm a _____ option.

17. **Real Options.** What is the option in each of the following cases. Is it a call or a put?

    a. Western Telecom commits to production of digital switching equipment specifically designed for the European market. The project has a negative NPV, but it is justified by the need for a strong market position in the rapidly growing, and potentially very profitable, market.

    b. Western Telecom vetoes a fully integrated automated production line for the new digital switches. It will rely on standard, less expensive equipment even though the automated production line would be more efficient overall using the specialized equipment, according to a discounted-cash-flow calculation.

18. **Real Options.** Describe each of the following situations in the language of options.

    a. Drilling rights to undeveloped heavy crude oil in southern California. Development and production of the oil now is a negative-NPV endeavor. The break-even price is $32 per barrel, versus a spot price of $20. However, the decision to develop can be put off for up to 5 years.

    b. A restaurant producing net cash flows, after all out-of-pocket expenses, of $700,000 per year. There is no upward or downward trend in the cash flows, but they fluctuate. The real estate occupied by the restaurant is owned, and it could be sold for $5 million.

19. **Real Options.** The price support system for various agricultural products allows farmers to sell their crops to the government for a specified "support price." What kind of option has the government given to the farmers? What is the exercise price?

20. **Implicit Options.** Some investment management contracts give the portfolio manager a bonus proportional to the amount by which a portfolio return exceeds a specified threshold.

    a. In what way is this an implicit call option on the portfolio?

    b. Can you think of a way in which such contracts can lead to incentive problems? For example, what happens to the value of the prospective bonus if the manager invests in high-volatility stocks?

21. **Implicit Options.** The Rank and File Company is considering a stock issue to raise $50 million. An underwriter offers to guarantee the success of the issue by buying any unwanted stock at the $25 issue price. The underwriter's fee is $2 million.

    a. What kind of option does Rank and File acquire if it accepts the underwriter's offer?

    b. What determines the value of the option?

22. **Implicit Options.**

    a. Some banks have offered their customers an unusual type of time deposit. The deposit does not pay any interest if the market falls, but instead the depositor receives a proportion of any rise in the Standard & Poor's Index. What implicit option do the investors hold? How should the bank invest the money in order to protect itself against the risk of offering this deposit?

    b. You can also make a deposit with a bank which does not pay interest if the market index rises but which makes an increasingly large payment as the market index falls. How should the bank protect itself against the risk of offering this deposit?

23. **Loan Guarantees.** The FDIC insures bank deposits. If a bank's assets are insufficient to pay off all depositors, the FDIC will contribute enough money to ensure that all depositors can be paid off in full. (We ignore the $100,000 maximum coverage on each account.) In what way is this guarantee of deposits the provision of a put option by the FDIC? *Hint:* Write out the funds the FDIC will have to contribute when bank assets are less than deposits owed to depositors. What is the exercise price of the put option?

24. **Real Options.** After dramatic increases in oil prices in the 1970s, the United States government funded several projects to create synthetic oil or natural gas from abundant United States supplies of coal and oil shale. Although the cost of producing such synthetic fuels at the time was greater than the price of oil, it was argued that the projects still could be justified for their insurance value since the cost of synthetic fuel would be essentially fixed while the price of oil was risky. Evaluate the synthetic fuel program as an option on fuel sources. Is it a call or a put option? What is the exercise price? How would uncertainty in the future price of oil affect the amount the United States should have been willing to spend on such projects?

25. **Arbitrage Opportunities.**

    a. Circular File stock is selling for $25 a share. You see that call options on the stock with exercise price of $20 are selling at $3. What should you do? What will happen to the option price as investors identify this opportunity?

    b. Now you observe that put options on Circular File with exercise price $30 are selling for $4. What should you do?

26. **Implicit Options.** A 10-year maturity convertible bond with a 6 percent coupon on a company with a bond rating of Aaa is selling for $1,050. Each bond can be exchanged for 20 shares, and the stock price currently is $50 per share. Other Aaa-rated bonds with the same maturity would sell at a yield to maturity of 8 percent. What is the value of the implicit call option on the bond? Why is the bond selling for more than the value of the shares it can be converted into?

Solutions to Self-Test Questions

23.1 a. The call with exercise price $65 costs $11⅜. If the stock price at maturity is $55, the call expires valueless and the investor loses the entire $11⅜. If the stock price is $75, the value of the call is $75 − $65 = $10, and the investor's profit is $10 − $11⅜ = −$1⅜. For the investor to earn a positive profit, the stock must rise above $76⅜ by option expiration.

    b. The put costs $5⅝. If the stock price at maturity is $55, the put value at expiration is $65 − $55 = $10 and the investor's profit is $10 − $5⅝ = $4⅜. If the stock price is $75, the value of the put is zero, and the investor's loss is the price paid for the put, $5⅝.

23.2 a. The call seller receives $11⅜ for writing the call. If the stock price at maturity is $55, the call expires valueless and the investor keeps the entire $11⅜ as a profit. If the stock price is $75, the value of the call is $75 − $65 = $10. In other words, the option seller must deliver a stock worth $75 for an exercise price of only $65. The investor's net profit is $11⅜ − $10 = $1⅜. The call seller will profit as long as the stock price remains below $76⅜.

    b. The put seller receives $5⅝ for writing the put. If the stock price at maturity is $55, the put value at expiration is $65 − $55 = $10. In other words, the put option seller must pay an exercise price of $65 to buy a stock worth only $55. The seller's loss is $10 − $5⅝ = $4⅜. If the stock price is $75, the final value of the put is zero, and the investor's profit is the price originally received for the put, $5⅝.

23.3 This payoff can be achieved by buying a share of stock, *buying* a put option on the stock with exercise price $60, and *selling* a call option on the stock with exercise price $70. If the stock price falls below $60, the call will expire valueless, and the put will allow you to sell the share for $60. Therefore, the strategy offers protection against the stock price falling below $60. If the stock price rises above $70, the put will be valueless and the call will be exercised against you; you will have to deliver the stock for an exercise price of $70. Thus the maximum value of the position will be $70.

    Such a strategy might be appropriate for an investor who wishes to take a position in the stock, wants downside protection, and is willing to pay for that protection by selling a call option and thereby forfeiting upside potential beyond a price of $70. The call sold offsets the cost of the put purchased. Extremely poor investment performance is eliminated at the cost of also eliminating the potential for extremely good returns.

23.4 The value of a put option is higher when the exercise price is higher. You would be willing to pay more for the right to sell a stock at a high price than the right to sell it at a low price.

23.5 First consider the payoff to the put holder in the lower volatility scenario:

Stock price	$55	$75
Put value	$10	0

In the higher volatility scenario, the value of the stock can be $45 or $85. Now the payoff to the put is

Stock price	$45	$85
Put value	$20	0

The expected value of the payoff of the put doubles.

23.6 The payoffs are as follows:

	Cash flow in January	Payoff in April if Stock Price Equals	
		$20	**$80**
Strategy A	?	$ 0	+$120
Buy three calls			
Strategy B			
Buy two shares	−$80	+$40	+$160
Borrow PV($40)	− 39.22	− 40	− 40
	−$40.78	$ 0	+$120

Note: PV($40) at an interest rate of 2 percent for 3 months is 40/1.02 = $39.22.

The net cash outflow in January from strategy B is $40.78. Since the three calls offer the same payoffs in the future, they also must be worth $40.78. One call is worth 40.78/3 = $13.59.

23.7 a. The developer has the option to sell the potential housing development to the country club. This abandonment option is like a put that guarantees a minimum payoff from the investment.

  b. The exercise price of the option is the price at which it can be sold to the country club. The asset value is the present value of the project if maintained as a housing development. If this value is less than the value as a golf course, the project will be sold.

  c. The abandonment option increases NPV by placing a lower bound on the possible payoffs from the project.

23.8 a, b. In 5 years, the bond will be a 15-year maturity bond. The bondholder can sell the bond back to the firm at par value. The bondholder therefore has a put option to sell a 15-year bond for par value even if interest rates have risen and the bond would otherwise sell below par.

  c. The exercise price is the par value of the bond.

  d. The bondholder will extend the loan if interest rates decrease.

Risk management does not mean avoiding risk.
It means deciding what risks to take.
© *Steve Vidler/Tony Stone Images*

Chapter 24
Risk Management

We often assume that risk is beyond our control. A business is exposed to unpredictable changes in raw material costs, tax rates, technology, and a long list of other variables. There's nothing the manager can do about it.

This is not wholly true. To some extent a manager can *select* the risks of an asset or business. For example, in the last chapter we saw that companies can consciously affect the risk of an investment by building in flexibility. A company that reduces the cost of bailing out of a project by using standardized equipment is taking less risk than a similar firm that uses specialized equipment with no alternative uses. In this case the option to resell the equipment serves as an insurance policy.

Sometimes, rather than building flexibility into the project, companies accept the risk but then use financial instruments to offset it. This practice of taking offsetting risks is known as *hedging*. In this chapter we will explain how hedging works and we will describe some of the specialized financial instruments that have been devised to help manage risk. These instruments include options, futures, forwards, and swaps. Each of these instruments provides a payoff that depends on the price of some underlying commodity or financial asset. Because their payoffs derive from the prices of other assets, they are often known collectively as *derivative instruments* (or *derivatives* for short).[1]

After reading this chapter you should be able to

▸ Understand why companies hedge to reduce risk.

▸ Use options, futures, and forward contracts to devise simple hedging strategies.

▸ Explain how companies can use swaps to change the risk of securities that they have issued.

Why Hedge?

In this chapter we will explain *how* companies use derivatives to hedge the risks of their business. But first we should give some of the reasons *why* they do it.

Hedging is seldom free. Most businesses hedge to reduce risk, not to make money. Why then bother to hedge? For one thing, reducing the risk makes financial planning easier and reduces the odds of an embarrassing shortfall. A shortfall might mean only an unexpected trip to the bank, but in extreme cases it could trigger bankruptcy. Why not reduce the odds of these awkward outcomes with a hedge?

We saw in our discussion of debt policy in Chapter 14 that financial distress can result in indirect as well as direct costs to a firm. Costs of financial distress arise from disruption to normal business operations as well as from the effect financial distress has on the firm's investment decisions. The better the risk management policies, the less the risk and expected costs of financial distress. As a side benefit, better risk management increases the firm's debt capacity.

---

[1]Derivatives often conjure up an image of wicked speculators. Derivative instruments attract their share of speculators, some of whom may be wicked, but they are also used by sober and prudent businesspeople who simply want to reduce risk.

In some cases hedging also makes it easier to decide whether an operating manager deserves a stern lecture or a pat on the back. Suppose that your export division shows a 50 percent decline in profits when the dollar unexpectedly strengthens against other currencies. How much of that decrease is due to the exchange rate shift and how much to poor management? If the company had protected itself against the effect of exchange rate changes, it's probably bad management. If it wasn't protected, you have to make a judgment with hindsight, probably by asking, "What would profits have been *if* the firm had hedged against exchange rate movements?"

Finally, hedging extraneous events can help focus the operating manager's attention. We know we shouldn't worry about events outside our control, but most of us do anyway. It's naive to expect the manager of the export division not to worry about exchange rate movements if his bottom line and bonus depend on them. The time spent worrying could be better spent if the company hedged itself against such movements.

24.2 *Reducing Risk with Options*

In the last chapter we introduced you to put and call options. Managers regularly buy options on currencies, interest rates, and commodities to limit their downside risk. Many of these options are traded on options exchanges, but often they are simply private deals between the corporation and a bank.

Petrochemical Parfum, Inc., is concerned about potential increases in the price of heavy crude oil, which is one of its major inputs. To protect itself against such increases Petrochemical buys 6-month options to purchase 1,000 barrels of crude oil at an exercise price of $20. These options might cost $.50 per barrel.

If the price of crude is above the $20 exercise price when the options expire, Petrochemical will exercise the options and will receive the difference between the oil price and the exercise price. If the oil price falls below the exercise price, the options will expire worthless. The net cost of oil will therefore be

	Oil Price, Dollars per Barrel		
	$18	**$20**	**$22**
Cost of 1,000 barrels	$18,000	$20,000	$22,000
− Payoff on call option	0	0	2,000
Net cost	$18,000	$20,000	$20,000

You can see that by buying options Petrochemical protects itself against increases in the oil price while continuing to benefit from oil price decreases. If prices fall, it can discard its call option and buy its oil at the market price. If oil prices rise, however, it can exercise its call option to purchase oil for $20 a barrel. Therefore, options create an attractive asymmetry. Of course, this asymmetry comes at a price—the $500 cost of the options.

▶ **Example 24.1** *Hedging with Options*

Consider now the problem of Onnex, Inc., which supplies Petrochemical with crude oil. Its problem is the mirror image of Petrochemical's; it loses when oil prices fall and gains when oil prices rise.

Figure 24.1

Onnex can buy put options to place a floor on its overall revenues.

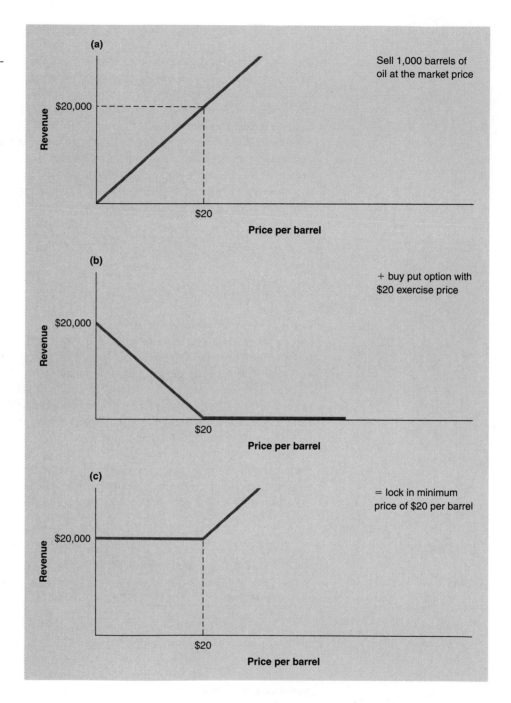

Onnex wants to lock in a minimum price of oil but still benefit from rising oil prices. It can do so by purchasing *put* options that give it the right to *sell* oil at an exercise price of $20 per barrel. If oil prices fall, it will exercise the put. If they rise, it will discard the put and sell oil at the market price:

		Oil Price, Dollars per Barrel		
		$18	**$20**	**$22**
	Revenue from 1,000 barrels	$18,000	$20,000	$22,000
+	Payoff on put option	2,000	0	0
	Net revenues	$20,000	$20,000	$22,000

If oil prices rise, Onnex reaps the benefit. But if oil prices fall below $20 a barrel the payoff of the put option exactly offsets the revenue shortfall. As a result, Onnex realizes net revenues of at least $20 a barrel, which is the exercise price of the put option.

> **Once again you don't get something for nothing. The price that Onnex pays for insurance against a fall in the price of oil is the cost of the put option. Similarly, the price that Petrochemical paid for insurance against a rise in the price of oil was the cost of the call option. Options provide protection against adverse price changes for a fee—the option premium.**

Notice that both Petrochemical and Onnex use options to insure against an adverse move in oil prices. But the options do not remove all uncertainty. For example, Onnex may be able to sell oil for much more than the exercise price of the option.

Figure 24.1 illustrates the nature of Onnex's hedge. Panel *a* shows the total revenue derived from selling the 1,000 barrels of oil. The firm is currently exposed to oil price risk: as prices fall, so will the firm's revenue. But, as panel *b* illustrates, the payoff on a put option to sell 1,000 barrels rises as oil prices fall below $20 a barrel, and therefore can offset the firm's exposure. Panel *c* shows the firm's net revenues after it buys the put option. For prices below $20 per barrel, revenues are $20,000. But revenues rise $1,000 for every dollar that oil prices rise above $20. The profile in panel *c* should be familiar to you: think back to the protective put strategy we first saw in Example 23.1. In both cases, the put provides a floor on the value of the overall position.

▶ **Self-Test 24.1**   Draw three graphs like those in Figure 24.1 to illustrate how Petrochemical hedges its costs by purchasing call options on oil.

24.3 *Futures Contracts*

futures contract:
Exchange-traded promise to buy or sell an asset in the future at a prespecified price.

Suppose you are a wheat farmer. You are optimistic about next year's wheat crop, but still you can't sleep. You are worried that when the time comes to sell the wheat, prices may have fallen through the floor. The cure for insomnia is to sell wheat *futures*. In this case, you agree to deliver so many bushels of wheat in (say) September at a price that is set today. Do not confuse this **futures contract** with an option, where the holder has a *choice* whether or not to make delivery; your futures contract is a firm promise to deliver wheat at a fixed selling price.

A miller is in the opposite position. She needs to *buy* wheat after the harvest. If she would like to fix the price of this wheat ahead of time, she can do so by *buying* wheat futures. In other words, she agrees to take delivery of wheat in the future at a price that is fixed today. The miller also does not have an option; if she still holds the futures contract when it matures, she is obliged to take delivery.

Let's suppose the farmer and the miller strike a deal. They enter a futures contract. What happens? First, no money changes hands when the contract is initiated.[2] The miller agrees to buy wheat at the futures price on a stated *future* date (the contract maturity date). The farmer agrees to sell at the same price and date. Second, the futures contract is a binding obligation, not an option. Options give the right to buy or sell *if* buying or selling turns out to be profitable. The futures contract *requires* the farmer to sell and the miller to buy regardless of who profits and who loses.

> No money changes hands when a futures contract is entered into. The contract is a binding obligation to buy or sell at a fixed price at contract maturity.

The profit on the futures contract is the difference between the initial futures price and the ultimate price of the asset when the contract matures. For example, if the futures price is originally $4.00 and the market price of wheat turns out to be $4.40, the farmer delivers and the miller receives the wheat for a price $.40 below market value. The farmer loses $.40 per bushel and the miller gains $.40 per bushel as a result of the futures transaction. In general, the seller of the contract benefits if the price initially locked in turns out to exceed the price that could have been obtained at contract maturity. Conversely, the buyer of the contract benefits if the ultimate market price of the asset turns out to exceed the initial futures price. Therefore, the profits on the futures contract to each party are:

Profit to seller = initial futures price − ultimate market price

Profit to buyer = ultimate market price − initial futures price

Now it is easy to see how the farmer and the miller can both use the contract to hedge. Consider the farmer's overall cash flows:

	Cash Flow
Sale of wheat	Ultimate price of wheat
Futures profits	Futures price − ultimate price of wheat
Total	Futures price

The profits on the futures contract offset the risk surrounding the sales price of wheat and lock in total revenue equal to the futures price. Similarly, the miller's all-in cost for the wheat also is fixed at the futures price. Any increase in the cost of wheat will be offset by a commensurate increase in the profit realized on the futures contract.

Both the farmer and the miller have less risk than before. The farmer has hedged (that is, offset) risk by selling wheat futures; the miller has hedged risk by buying wheat futures.[3]

---

[2]Actually, each party will be required to set up a margin account to guarantee performance on the contract. Despite this, the futures contract still may be considered as essentially requiring no money down. First, the amount of margin is small. Second, it may be posted in interest-bearing securities, so that the parties to the trade need not suffer opportunity cost from placing assets in the margin account.

[3]Neither has eliminated all risk. For example, the farmer still has quantity risk. He does not know for sure how many bushels of wheat he will produce.

▶ **Example 24.2**   *Hedging with Futures*

Suppose that the farmer originally sold 5,000 bushels of December wheat futures at a price of $4.00 a bushel. In December, when the futures contract matures, the price of wheat is only $3.50 a bushel. The farmer buys back the wheat futures at $3.50 just before maturity, giving him a profit of $.50 a bushel on the sale and subsequent repurchase. At the same time he sells his wheat at the spot price of $3.50 a bushel. His total receipts are therefore $4.00 a bushel:

Profit on sale and repurchase of futures	$ .50
Sale of wheat at the September spot price	$3.50
Total receipts	$4.00

You can see that the futures contract has allowed the farmer to lock in total proceeds of $4.00 a bushel.

Figure 24.2 illustrates how the futures contract enabled the farmer in Example 24.2 to hedge his position. Panel *a* is the value of 5,000 bushels of wheat as a function of the spot price of wheat. The value rises by $5,000 for every dollar increase in wheat prices. Panel *b* is the profit on a futures contract to deliver 5,000 bushels of wheat at a futures price of $4.00 per bushel. The profit will be zero if the ultimate price of wheat equals the original futures price, $4.00. The profit on the contract to deliver at $4.00 rises by $5,000 for every dollar the spot price of wheat *falls* below $4.00. The exposures to the price of wheat depicted in panels *a* and *b* obviously cancel out. Panel *c* shows that the total value of the 5,000 bushels plus the futures position is unaffected by the ultimate price of wheat, and equals $4.00 × 5,000 = $20,000. In other words, the farmer has locked in proceeds per bushel equal to the original futures price.

The Mechanics of Futures Trading

In practice the farmer and miller would not sign the futures contract face to face. Instead each would go to an organized futures exchange. The largest of these futures exchanges is the Chicago Board of Trade, which traded 210 million futures contracts in 1995.

Table 24.1 shows the price of wheat futures at the Chicago Board of Trade in September 1997, when the spot price was about $3.64 a bushel. Notice that there is a choice of possible delivery dates. If, for example, you were to sell wheat for delivery in May before the main harvest, you would get a higher price than by selling July futures.

The miller would not be prepared to buy futures contracts if the farmer were free to deliver half-rotten wheat to a leaky barn at the end of a cart track. Futures trading is possible only because the contracts are highly standardized. For example, in the case of wheat futures, each contract calls for the delivery of 5,000 bushels of wheat of a specified quality at a warehouse in Chicago or Toledo.

When you buy or sell a futures contract, the price is fixed today, but payment is not made until later. However, you will be asked to put up some cash or securities as *margin* to demonstrate that you are able to honor your side of the bargain.

Figure 24.2

The farmer can use wheat futures to hedge the value of the crop. See Example 24.2

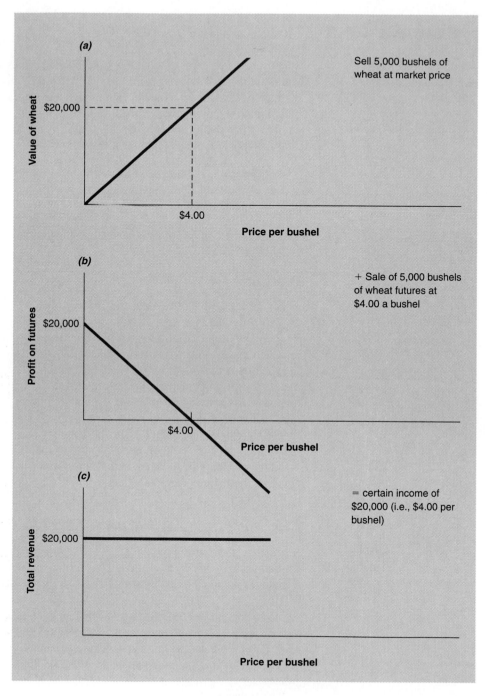

(a)

Value of wheat

$20,000

$4.00

Price per bushel

Sell 5,000 bushels of wheat at market price

(b)

Profit on futures

$20,000

$4.00

Price per bushel

+ Sale of 5,000 bushels of wheat futures at $4.00 a bushel

(c)

Total revenue

$20,000

Price per bushel

= certain income of $20,000 (i.e., $4.00 per bushel)

In addition, futures contracts are *marked to market*. This means that each day any profits or losses on the contract are calculated; you pay the exchange any losses and receive any profits. For example, our farmer agreed to deliver 5,000 bushels of wheat at $4.00 a bushel. Suppose that the next day the price of wheat futures increases to $4.05 a bushel. The farmer now has a loss on his sale of 5,000 × $.05 = $250 and must pay this sum to the exchange. You can think of the farmer as buying back his

Table 24.1

The price of wheat futures at the Chicago Board of Trade on September 11, 1997

Delivery Date	Price per Bushel
September 1997	$3.640
December 1997	3.785
March 1998	3.908
May 1998	3.935
July 1998	3.865
December 1998	4.000

futures position each day and then opening up a new position. Thus after the first day the farmer has realized a loss on his trade of $.05 a bushel and now has an obligation to deliver wheat for $4.05 a bushel.

Of course our miller is in the opposite position. The rise in futures price leaves her with a *profit* of 5 cents a bushel. The exchange will therefore pay her this profit. In effect the miller sells her futures position at a profit and opens a new contract to take delivery at $4.05 a bushel.

The price of wheat for immediate delivery is known as the *spot price*. When the farmer sells wheat futures, the price that he agrees to take for his wheat may be very different from the spot price. But the future eventually becomes the present. As the date for delivery approaches, the futures contract becomes more and more like a spot contract and the price of the futures contract approaches the spot price.

The farmer may decide to wait until the futures contract matures and then deliver wheat to the buyer. But in practice such delivery is rare, for it is more convenient for the farmer to buy back the wheat futures just before maturity.[4]

▶ **Self-Test 24.2**

Suppose that 2 days after taking out the futures contracts the price of September wheat increases to $4.20 a bushel. What additional payments will be made by or to the farmer and the miller? What will be their remaining obligation at the end of this second day?

Commodity and Financial Futures

We have shown how the farmer and the miller can both use wheat futures to hedge their risk. It is also possible to trade futures in a wide variety of other commodities, such as sugar, soybean oil, pork bellies, orange juice, crude oil, and copper.

Commodity prices can bounce up and down like a bungee jumper. For example, raw sugar prices rose from about 4 cents a pound in 1986 to touch 15 cents in 1990 before falling to 8 cents a year later. For a large buyer of sugar, such as Hershey, these price fluctuations could knock the company badly off course. Hershey therefore reduces its exposure to movements in sugar and cocoa prices by hedging with commodity futures.

---

[4]In the case of some of the financial futures described later, you *cannot* deliver the asset. At maturity the buyer simply receives (or pays) the difference between the spot price and the price at which he or she has agreed to purchase the asset.

Figure 24.3

Trading on the Chicago Board of Trade has come to be dominated by financial futures and options

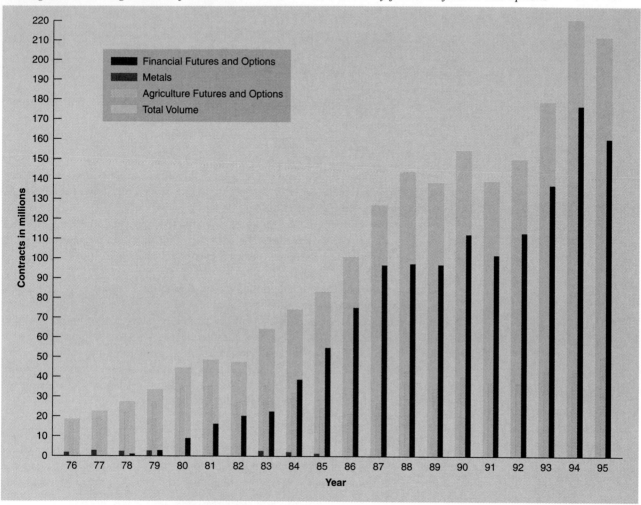

Source: Chicago Board of Trade 1995 Annual Report.

For many firms, the wide fluctuations in interest rates and exchange rates have become at least as important a source of risk as changes in commodity prices. You can use *financial futures* to hedge against these risks.

> **Financial futures are similar to commodity futures but, instead of placing an order to buy or sell a commodity at a future date, you place an order to buy or sell a financial asset at a future date. You can use financial futures to protect yourself against fluctuations in short- and long-term interest rates, exchange rates, and the level of share prices.**

Financial futures have been a remarkable success. They were invented in 1972; within a few years, trading in financial futures significantly exceeded trading in commodity futures. Figure 24.3 shows the explosive growth of trading on the Chicago Board of Trade. The figure shows that while financial futures barely registered in 1976, they now dominate the market. Table 24.2 lists some of the more popular financial futures contracts.

Table 24.2

Some financial futures con-
tracts

Future	Principal Exchange
U.S. Treasury notes	CBT
U.S. Treasury bonds	CBT
Eurodollar deposits	IMM
Standard & Poor's Index	IMM
Deutschemark	IMM
Yen	IMM
Sterling	LIFFE

Key to abbreviations

CBT	Chicago Board of Trade
IMM	International Monetary Market (at the Chicago Mercantile Exchange)
LIFFE	London International Financial Futures Exchange

▶ **Self-Test 24.3**   You plan to issue long-term bonds in 9 months but are worried that interest rates may have increased in the meantime. How could you use financial futures to protect yourself against a general rise in interest rates?

Forward Contracts

forward contract: Agreement to buy or sell an asset in the future at an agreed price.

Each day billions of dollars of futures contracts are bought and sold. We have seen that this liquidity is possible only because futures contracts are standardized. Futures contracts mature on a limited number of dates each year (take another look at the wheat contract in Table 24.1), and the contract size is standardized. For example, a contract may call for delivery of 5,000 bushels of wheat, 100 ounces of gold, or 62,500 British pounds. If the terms of a futures contract do not suit your particular needs, you may be able to buy or sell a **forward contract.**

Forward contracts are custom-tailored futures contracts.[5] You can write a forward contract with any maturity date for delivery of any quantity of goods. For example, suppose that you know that you will need to pay out yen in 3 months time. You can fix today the price that you will pay for the yen by arranging with your bank to buy yen forward. At the end of the 3 months, you pay the agreed sum and take delivery of the yen.

▶ **Example 24.3**   *Forward Contracts*

Computer Parts Inc. has ordered memory chips from its supplier in Japan. The bill for ¥53 million must be paid on July 27. The company can arrange with its bank today to buy this number of yen forward for delivery on July 27 at a forward price

[5]One difference between forward and futures contracts is that forward contracts are not marked to market. Thus with a forward contract you settle up any profits or losses when the contract matures.

of ¥110 per dollar. Therefore, on July 27, Computer Parts pays the bank 54 million/110 = $481,818 and receives ¥53 million, which it can use to pay its Japanese supplier. By committing forward to exchange $481,818 for ¥53 million, its dollar costs are locked in. Notice that if the firm had not used the forward contract to hedge and the dollar had depreciated over this period, the firm would have had to pay a greater amount of dollars. For example, if the exchange rate had fallen to ¥100/dollar, the firm would have had to exchange $540,000 for the ¥53 million necessary to pay its bill. The firm could have used a futures contract to hedge its foreign exchange exposure, but standardization of futures would not allow for delivery of precisely ¥53 million on precisely July 27.

The most active trading in forwards is in foreign currencies, but in recent years companies have increasingly entered into forward rate agreements that allow them to fix in advance the interest rate at which they borrow or lend.

Swaps

Suppose Computer Parts from Example 24.3 decides to produce memory chips instead of purchasing them from outside suppliers. It has issued $100 million in floating-rate bonds to help finance the construction of a new plant. (Recall from Chapter 12 that floating-rate bonds make interest payments that go up and down with the general level of interest rates. The coupon payments on the bonds are tied to a specific short-term interest rate.) But the financial manager is concerned that interest rates are becoming more volatile, and she would like to lock in the firm's interest expenses. One approach would be to buy back the floating-rate bonds and replace them with a new issue of fixed-rate debt. But it is costly to issue new debt to the public; in addition, buying back the outstanding bonds in the market will result in considerable trading costs.

swap: Arrangement by two counterparties to exchange one stream of cash flows for another.

A better approach to hedge out its interest rate exposure is for the firm to enter an interest rate **swap**. The firm will pay or "swap" a fixed payment for another payment that is tied to the level of interest rates. Thus if rates do rise, increasing the firm's interest expense on its floating-rate debt, its cash flow from the swap agreement will rise as well, offsetting its exposure.

Suppose the firm pays the LIBOR rate on its floating-rate bonds. (Recall that LIBOR, or London Interbank Offer Rate, is the interest rate at which banks borrow from each other in the Eurodollar market. It is the most frequently used short-term interest rate in the swap market.) The firm's interest expense each year therefore equals the LIBOR rate times $100 million. It would like to transform this obligation into one that will not fluctuate with interest rates.

Suppose that current rates in the swaps market are LIBOR for 8 percent fixed. This means that Computer Parts can enter into a swap agreement to *pay* 8 percent on "notional principal" of $100 million to a swap dealer and *receive* payment of the LIBOR rate on the same amount of notional principal. The firm pays the dealer .08 × $100 million and receives LIBOR × $100 million. The dealer and the firm are called *counterparties* in the swap. The firm's *net* cash payment to the dealer is therefore (LIBOR − .08) × $100 million. (If LIBOR exceeds 8 percent, the firm receives money from the dealer; if it is less than 8 percent, the firm pays money to the dealer.) Figure 24.4 illustrates the cash flows paid by Computer Parts and the swap dealer.

Figure 24.4

Interest rate swap. Computer Parts currently pays the LIBOR rate on its outstanding bonds (the arrow on the left). If the firm enters a swap to pay a fixed rate of 8 percent and receive a floating rate of LIBOR, its exposure to LIBOR will cancel out, and its net cash outflow will be a fixed rate of 8 percent.

Table 24.3 shows Computer Parts net payments for three possible interest rates. The total payment on the bond-with-swap agreement equals $8,000,000 regardless of the interest rate. The swap has transformed the floating-rate bond into synthetic fixed-rate debt with an effective coupon rate of 8 percent. The firm has thus hedged away its interest rate exposure without actually having to replace its floating-rate bonds with fixed-rate bonds. Swaps offer a much cheaper way to "rearrange the balance sheet."[6]

There are many other applications of interest rate swaps. A portfolio manager who is holding a portfolio of long-term bonds but is worried that interest rates might increase, causing a capital loss on the portfolio, can enter a swap to pay a fixed rate and receive a floating rate, thereby converting the holdings into a synthetic floating-rate portfolio (see Self-Test 24.4). Or a pension fund manager might identify some money market securities that are paying excellent yields compared to other comparable-risk short-term securities. However, the manager might believe that such short-term assets are inappropriate for the portfolio. The fund can hold these securities and enter a swap in which it receives a fixed rate and pays a floating rate. It thus captures the benefit of the advantageous *relative* yields on these securities, but still establishes a portfolio with interest rate-risk characteristics more like those of long-term bonds.

▶ **Self-Test 24.4**

Consider the portfolio manager who is holding a $100 million portfolio of long-term bonds and wishes to reduce price risk by transforming the holdings into a synthetic floating-rate portfolio. Assume the portfolio currently pays an 8 percent fixed rate and that swap dealers currently offer terms of 8 percent fixed for LIBOR. What swap would the manager establish? Show the total income on the fund in a table like Table 24.3, and illustrate the cash flows in a diagram like Figure 24.4.

Table 24.3

An interest rate swap can transform floating-rate bonds into synthetic fixed-rate bonds

	LIBOR Rate		
	7.5%	**8.0%**	**8.5%**
Interest paid on floating-rate bonds (= LIBOR × $100 million)	$7,500,000	$8,000,000	$8,500,000
+ Cash payment on swap [= (.08 − LIBOR) × notional principal of $100 million]	500,000	0	−500,000
Total payment	$8,000,000	$8,000,000	$8,000,000

[6]You might wonder what's in this arrangement for the swap dealer. The dealer will profit by charging a bid-ask spread. Since the dealer pays LIBOR in return for 8 percent in this swap, it might search for another trader who wishes to receive a fixed rate and pay LIBOR. The dealer will pay a 7.9 percent rate to that trader in return for the LIBOR rate. So the dealer pays a fixed rate and receives floating with one trader but pays floating and receives fixed with the other. Its net cash flow is thus riskless and equal to .1 percent of LIBOR times notional principal.

Meltdown at Metallgesellschaft

Metallgesellschaft AG was one of Germany's most respected companies with more than 20,000 employees and revenues of some $10 billion. Its 251 subsidiaries were engaged in engineering, mining, financial services, and commodities trading, and its major shareholders included such blue-chip German companies as Deutsche Bank, Daimler-Benz, and Allianz.

However, in 1993 Metallgesellschaft was nearly brought to its knees by losses of $1.4 billion from trading in oil futures. The problem arose in one of its U.S. subsidiaries, MGRM. MGRM offered its customers firm price guarantees for up to 10 years on any oil that they agreed to buy. These guarantees proved very popular, so that by the end of 1993 the company had entered into long-term contracts to supply 160 million barrels of oil worth more than $3 billion.

There was only one problem. MGRM did not own the oil that it had promised to deliver and would therefore have to buy it from the major oil companies. If the price of oil rose above the price that customers had agreed to pay, MGRM would make a loss on every barrel of oil that it had sold. The apparent solution was for MGRM to hedge its exposure by buying oil futures. This would fix the price at which the company could buy oil when it needed to deliver it. The company would have liked to buy oil futures that matured on the same dates as it was obliged to deliver the oil, but, unfortunately, most futures trading takes place in contracts that mature within a year. MGRM's solution was to buy short-term oil futures and to replace them when they matured.

During the second half of 1993 oil prices fell by 25 percent and MGRM's contracts to deliver oil at a predetermined price looked increasingly attractive. However, at the same time the company started to pile up large losses on its purchases of oil futures. This was not in itself a cause for concern. If MGRM was truly hedged, the profits on the oil contracts should have exactly offset the losses on the futures.

So what went wrong? One view is that management focused on the accumulating losses on the futures positions and failed to recognize the gains on the oil contracts. When the losses became sufficiently large, management's nerve cracked and it sold out of its futures positions at the wrong time. Moreover, because MGRM's futures positions were marked to market, the company had to find the cash each day to cover the losses on these positions. This problem of financing the hedge may have contributed to management's decision to abandon its strategy.

Other commentators are less convinced that all would have come right if only management had not panicked. They argue that the company's strategy of hedging long-term liabilities with short-term futures was fundamentally flawed. The problem was that MGRM could not predict the price at which it would be able to replace each futures contract when it matured. If the price of the new future was *below* that of the maturing one, MGRM would make a profit from the trade. But unfortunately for MGRM, the reverse proved to be the case, so that the company incurred a loss each time it replaced the maturing futures contract with a new one.

While financial experts continued to debate the cause of MGRM's losses, the company's bankers struggled to put together a rescue package. A massive $1.9 billion loan from 150 international banks was needed to keep the company from foundering.

---

have the option to sell it at the current price, then you have effectively insured yourself against loss.

3. Futures contracts are agreements made today to buy or sell an asset in the future. The price is fixed today, but the final payment does not occur until the delivery date. Futures contracts are highly standardized and are traded on organized exchanges. Commodity futures allow firms to fix the future price that they pay for a wide range of agricultural commodities, metals, and oil. Financial futures help firms to protect themselves against unforeseen movements in interest rates, exchange rates, and stock prices.

4. Forward contracts are equivalent to tailor-made futures contracts. For example, firms often enter into forward agreements with a bank to buy or sell foreign exchange or to fix the interest rate on a loan to be made in the future.

5. Swaps allow firms to exchange one series of future payments for another. For example, the firm might agree to make a series of regular payments in one currency in return for receiving a series of payments in another currency.

Key Terms

futures contract   forward contract   swap

Problems

1. **Risk Management.** Large businesses spend millions of dollars annually on insurance. Why? Should they insure against all risks or does insurance make more sense for some risks than others?

2. **Hedging.**

   a. An investor currently holding $1 million in long-term Treasury bonds becomes concerned about increasing volatility in interest rates. She decides to hedge her risk using Treasury bond futures contracts. Should she buy or sell such contracts?

   b. The treasurer of a corporation that will be issuing bonds in 3 months also is concerned about interest rate volatility and wants to lock in the price at which he could sell 8 percent coupon bonds. How would he use Treasury bond futures contracts to hedge his firm's position?

3. **Hedging with Futures versus Puts.** A gold mining firm is concerned about short-term volatility in its revenues. Gold currently sells for $300 an ounce, but the price is extremely volatile and could fall as low as $280 or rise as high as $320 in the next month. The company will bring 1,000 ounces to the market next month.

   a. What will be total revenues if the firm remains unhedged for gold prices of $280, $300, and $320 an ounce?

   b. The futures price of gold for 1-month-ahead delivery is $301. What will be the firm's total revenues at each gold price if the firm enters a 1-month futures contract to deliver 1,000 ounces of gold?

   c. What will total revenues be if the firm buys a 1-month put option to sell gold for $300 an ounce? The puts cost $2 per ounce.

4. **Hedging with Calls.** A large dental lab plans to purchase 1,000 ounces of gold in 1 month. Assume again that gold prices can be $280, $300, or $320 an ounce.

   a. What will total expenses be if the firm purchases call options on 1,000 ounces of gold with an exercise price of $300 an ounce? The options cost $3 per ounce.

   b. What will total expenses be if the firm purchases call options on 1,000 ounces of gold with an exercise price of $295 an ounce? These options cost $7 per ounce.

5. **Swaps.** What is a currency swap? An interest rate swap? Give one example of how each might be used.

6. **Swaps.** Firms A and B face the following borrowing rates for a 5-year fixed-rate debt issue in U.S. dollars or Swiss francs:

	U.S. Dollars	Swiss Francs
Firm A	10%	7%
Firm B	8%	6%

Suppose that A wishes to borrow U.S. dollars and B wishes to borrow Swiss francs. Show how a swap could be used to reduce the borrowing costs of each company. Assume a spot exchange rate of 2 Swiss francs to the dollar.

7. **Forward Contract.** Assume that the 1-year interest rate is 10 percent and the 2-year interest rate is 12 percent. You approach a bank and ask at what rate the bank will promise to make a 1-year loan in 12 months' time. The bank offers to make a forward commitment to lend to you at 15 percent. Would you accept the offer? Can you think of a simple, cheaper alternative?

8. **Hedging Project Risk.** Your firm has just tendered for a contract in Japan. You won't know for 3 months whether you get the contract but if you do, you will receive a payment of ¥10 million 1 year from now. You are worried that if the yen declines in value, the dollar value of this payment will be less than you expect and the project could even show a loss. Discuss the possible ways that you could protect the firm against a decline in the value of the yen. Illustrate the possible outcomes if you do get the contract and if you don't.

9. **Hedging with Futures.** Show how Petrochemical Parfum (see Section 24.2) can also use futures contracts to protect itself against a rise in the price of crude oil. Show how the payoffs would vary if the oil price is $18, $20, or $22 a barrel. What are the advantages and disadvantages for Petrochemical of using futures rather than options to reduce risk? Repeat the exercise for Onnex.

10. **Commodity Futures.** What other commodity futures are traded on futures exchanges? Who do you think could usefully reduce risk by buying each of these contracts? Who do you think might wish to sell each contract?

11. **Hedging.** "The farmer does not avoid risk by selling wheat futures. If wheat prices stay above $3.40 a bushel, then he will actually have lost by selling wheat futures at $3.40." Is this a fair comment?

12. **Marking to Market.** Suppose that in the 5 days following a farmer's sale of September wheat futures at a futures price of $3.83 the futures price is

Day	1	2	3	4	5
Price	$3.83	$3.98	$3.70	$3.50	$3.70

At the end of day 5 the farmer decides to quit wheat farming and buys back his futures contract. What payments are made between the farmer and the exchange on each day? What is the total payment over the 5 days? Would the total payment be any different if the contract was not marked to market?

13. **Futures Contracts.** Look in *The Wall Street Journal* at the prices of gold futures quoted on the COMEX futures exchange. What is the date of the most distant contract? Suppose that you buy 100 ounces of gold futures for this date. When do you receive the gold? When do you pay for it? Is the futures price higher or lower than the current spot price? Can you suggest why?

14. **Hedging Currency Risk.** We saw in Chapter 22 that when the deutschemark strengthened in 1991 and 1992, German luxury car manufacturers found it increasingly difficult to compete in the United States market. How could they have hedged themselves against this risk? Would a company that was hedged have been in a better position to compete? Explain why or why not.

15. **Futures versus Spot Positions.** What do you think are the advantages of holding futures rather than the underlying commodity? What do you think are the disadvantages?

Solutions to Self-Test Questions

24.1 See Figure 24.5 on page 695.

24.2 The farmer has a further loss of 15 cents a bushel ($4.20 − $4.05) and will be required to pay this amount to the exchange. The miller has a further profit of 15 cents per bushel and will receive this from the exchange. The farmer is now committed to delivering wheat in September for $4.20 per bushel and the miller is committed to paying $4.20 per bushel.

Figure 24.5

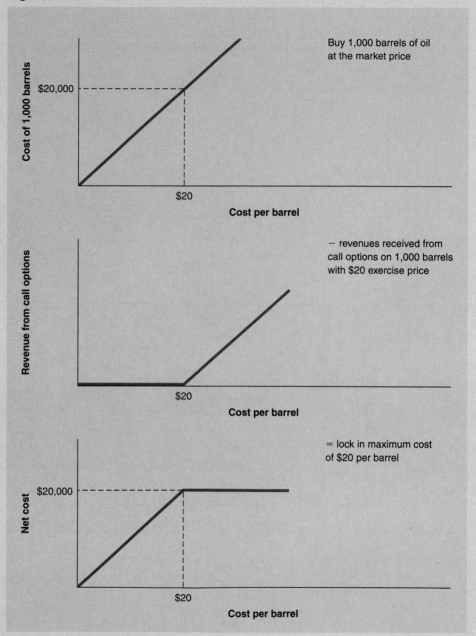

24.3 You sell long-term bond futures with a delivery date of 9 months. Suppose, for example, that you agree to deliver long-term bonds in 9 months at a price of 100. If interest rates fall, the price of the bond futures will rise to (say) 105. (Remember that when interest rates fall, bond prices rise.) In this case the profit that you make on your bond futures offsets the lower price that the firm is likely to receive on the sale of its own bonds. Conversely, if interest rates fall, the company will make a loss on its futures position but will receive a higher price for its own bonds.

24.4 The manager should enter a swap to pay an 8 percent fixed rate and receive LIBOR on notional principal of $100 million. The cash flows will then rise in tandem with the LIBOR rate:

	LIBOR Rate		
	7.5%	**8.0%**	**8.5%**
Interest received on fixed-rate bonds (= .08 × $100 million)	$8,000,000	$8,000,000	$8,000,000
+ Cash flow on swap [= (LIBOR − .08) × notional principal of $100 million]	−500,000	0	+500,000
Total payment	$7,500,000	$8,000,000	$8,500,000

The diagram describing the cash flows is as follows:

The manager nets a cash flow proportional to the LIBOR rate.

24.5 The following table shows revised cash flows from Possum's dollar loan and currency swap (figures in millions):

	Year 0		Years 1–4		Year 5	
	$	**DM**	**$**	**DM**	**$**	**DM**
1. Issue dollar loan	+10		−.5		−10.5	
2. Arrange currency swap						
a. Possum receives $	−10		+.5		+10.5	
b. Possum pays DM		+30		−2.4		−32.4
3. Net cash flow	0	+30	0	−2.4	0	−32.4

Notice that in exchange for $10 million today the bank is now prepared to pay over DM30 million. Since the German interest rate is now 8 percent, the bank will expect to earn .08 × 30 = DM2.4 million interest on its deutschemark outlay.

Part Nine

Conclusion

25

What We Do and Do Not Know about Finance

Why do mergers seem to happen in waves?
Mergers seem so often to happen in waves; for a period of a couple of years, many firms seem to merge while for other periods, very few seem to occur. This is just one phenomenon in finance which we cannot explain.
AP/Wide World, Sergio Perez/ Reuters/Archive Photos, AP Photo/Tom Ewart

Chapter 25

What We Do and Do Not Know about Finance

25.1 What We Do Know: The Six Most Important Ideas in Finance

What would you say if you were asked to name the six most important ideas in finance? Here is our list.

Net Present Value (Chapter 3)

When you wish to know the value of a used car, you look at prices in the second-hand car market. Similarly, when you wish to know the value of a future cash flow, you look at prices quoted in the capital markets, where claims to future cash flows are traded (remember, those highly paid investment bankers are just secondhand cash-flow dealers). If you can buy cash flows for your shareholders at a cheaper price than they would have to pay in the capital market, you have increased the value of their investment.

This is the simple idea behind *net present value* (NPV). When we calculate a project's NPV, we are asking whether the project is worth more than it costs. We are estimating its value by calculating what its cash flows would be worth if a claim on them were offered separately to investors and traded in the capital markets.

This is why we calculate NPV by discounting future cash flows at the opportunity cost of capital—that is, at the expected rate of return offered by securities having the same degree of risk as the project. In well-functioning capital markets, all equivalent-risk assets are priced to offer the same expected return. By discounting at the opportunity cost of capital, we calculate the price at which investors in the project could expect to earn that rate of return.

Like most good ideas, the net present value rule is obvious when you think about it. But notice what an important idea it is. The NPV rule allows thousands of shareholders, who may have vastly different levels of wealth and attitudes toward risk, to participate in the same enterprise and to delegate its operation to a professional manager. They give the manager one simple instruction: "Maximize net present value."

Risk and Return (Chapters 8 and 9)

Some people say that modern finance is all about the capital asset pricing model. That's nonsense. If the capital asset pricing model had never been invented, our advice to financial managers would be essentially the same. The attraction of the model is that it gives us a manageable way of thinking about the required return on a risky investment.

Again, it is an attractively simple idea. There are two kinds of risks—those that you can diversify away and those that you can't. The only risks people care about are the ones that they can't get rid of—the nondiversifiable ones.

You can measure the *nondiversifiable,* or *market,* risk of an investment by the extent to which the value of the investment is affected by a change in the *aggregate* value of all the assets in the economy. This is called the *beta* of the investment. The required return on an asset increases in line with its beta.

Many people are worried by some of the rather strong assumptions behind the capital asset pricing model, or they are concerned about the difficulties of estimating a project's beta. They are right to be worried about these things. In 10 or 20 years' time we will probably have much better theories than we do now, but we are prepared to bet that these more sophisticated theories will retain the two crucial ideas behind the capital asset pricing model:

- Investors don't like risk and require a higher return to compensate.
- The risk that matters is the risk that investors cannot get rid of.

Efficient Capital Markets (Chapter 11)

The third fundamental idea is that security prices accurately reflect available information and respond rapidly to new information as soon as it becomes available. This *efficient-market theory* comes in three flavors, corresponding to different definitions of "available information." The weak form (or random-walk theory) says that prices reflect all the information in past prices, the semistrong form says that prices reflect all publicly available information, and the strong form holds that prices reflect all acquirable information.

Don't misunderstand the efficient-market idea. It doesn't say that there are no taxes or costs; it doesn't say that there aren't some clever people and some stupid ones. It merely implies that competition in capital markets is very tough—there are no money machines, and security prices reflect the true underlying values of assets based on the best information available to investors.

MM's Irrelevance Propositions (Chapters 14 and 15)

The irrelevance propositions of Modigliani and Miller (MM) imply that you can't increase value through financing policies unless these policies also increase the total cash flow available to investors. Financing decisions that simply repackage the same cash flows don't add value.

Financial managers often ask how much their company should borrow. MM's response is that as long as borrowing does not alter the *total* cash flow generated by the firm's assets, it does not affect firm value.

Miller and Modigliani used a similar argument to show that dividend policy does not affect value unless it affects the total cash flow available to present and future shareholders. A firm that pays you an increased dividend and gets the cash back by selling more shares is simply putting cash in one of your pockets and taking it out of another.

The same ideas can be run in reverse. Just as splitting up the cash flows doesn't add value, neither does combining different cash-flow streams. This implies that you can't increase value by putting two whole companies together unless you thereby increase total cash flow. Thus there are no benefits to mergers solely for diversification.

Option Theory (Chapter 23)

In everyday conversation we often use the word *option* as synonymous with *choice* or *alternative;* thus we speak of someone as *having a number of options*. In finance an option refers specifically to the opportunity to trade in the future on terms that are fixed today. Smart managers know that it is often worth paying today for the option to buy or sell an asset tomorrow.

We saw in Chapters 7 and 23 that companies are willing to pay extra for capital projects that give them future flexibility. Also, many securities provide the company or the investor with options. For example, a convertible bond gives the owner an option to exchange the bond for shares.

Managers spend much more time thinking about options than they used to. This is partly because they increasingly use options to help limit risk. Also, managers and economists are more aware that many assets contain disguised real options. For example, the opportunity to abandon a project and recover its salvage value is a put option.

If options are so prevalent, it is important to know how to value them. One of the great finance developments of recent years was the discovery by Black Scholes and Merton of a formula to value options. We reviewed briefly the determinants of option value in Chapter 23.

Agency Theory

A modern corporation is a team effort involving many players, including management, employees, shareholders, and bondholders. The members of this corporate team are bound together by a series of formal and informal contracts to ensure that they pull together.

For a long time economists assumed that all players acted for the common good. But in the last 20 years we have learned a lot about the possible conflicts of interest and how companies try to overcome such conflicts. These ideas are collectively known as *agency theory*.

Although we didn't allocate a separate chapter to agency theory, the theory has helped us to think about such questions as these:

- How can an entrepreneur persuade venture capital investors to join in his or her enterprise? (Chapter 13)
- What are the reasons for all the fine print in bond agreements? (Chapter 14)
- Are mergers, acquisitions, and LBOs simply attempts to "rip off" other players, or do they change management's incentives to maximize company value? (Chapter 21)

Are these six ideas exciting theories or plain common sense? Call them what you will, they are basic to the financial manager's job. If after reading this book you really understand these ideas and know how to apply them, you have learned a great deal.

25.2 What We Do Not Know: Seven Unsolved Problems in Finance

Since the unknown is never exhausted, the list of what we do not know about finance could go on forever. Here are seven unsolved problems that seem ripe for productive research.

How Are Major Financial Decisions Made?

We need to know more about how firms make major financial decisions. What is the process that causes one company to make a major investment and another to reject it? Why does one company decide to issue debt and another to issue equity? If we knew why companies made particular decisions, we would be better able to improve those decisions.

Our ignorance is largest when it comes to major *strategic* decisions. In Chapter 17 we described long-term strategic planning as "capital budgeting on a grand scale." Strategic planning attempts to identify the lines of businesses where the firm has the greatest long-run opportunities and to develop a plan for achieving success in those businesses. But it is hard to calculate the NPV of major strategic decisions. Think, for example, of a firm which makes a major commitment to the design and manufacture of computer memories. It is really embarking on a long-term effort which will require capital outlays over many years. It cannot identify all those future projects, much less evaluate their NPVs. Instead, it decides to go ahead because the computer memory business is growing rapidly, because firms already in that business are doing well, and because it has intangible assets—special technology, perhaps—which it thinks will give it a leg up on the competition.

Strategic planning is a "top-down" approach to capital budgeting: you choose the businesses you want to be in and make the capital outlays necessary for success. It's perfectly sensible and natural for firms to look at capital investments that way *in addition to* looking at them "bottom-up." The trouble is that we understand the bottom-up part of the capital budgeting process better than the top-down part.

Top-down and bottom-up should not be competing approaches to capital budgeting. They should be two aspects of a single integrated procedure. Not all firms integrate the two approaches successfully. No doubt some firms do so, but we don't really know how.

What Determines Project Risk and Present Value?

A good capital investment is one that has a positive NPV. We have talked at some length about how to calculate NPV, but we have given you very little guidance about how to find positive-NPV projects, except to say in Chapter 7 that projects have positive NPVs when the firm can earn "economic rents," above-normal rates of return. But why do some companies earn economic rents while others in the same industry do not? Are the rents merely windfall gains, or can they be anticipated and planned for? What is their source, and how long do they persist before competition destroys them? Very little is known about any of these important questions.

Here is a related question: Why are some real assets risky and others relatively safe? In Chapter 9 we suggested a few reasons for differences in project betas—differences in operating leverage, for example, or in the extent to which a project's cash flows respond to the performance of the national economy. These are useful clues, but we have as yet no general procedure for estimating project betas. Assessing project risk is therefore still largely a seat-of-the-pants matter.

Risk and Return—Have We Missed Something?

In 1848 John Stuart Mill wrote, "Happily there is nothing in the laws of value which remains for the present or any future writer to clear up; the theory is complete." Economists today are not so sure about that. For example, the capital asset pricing model is an enormous step toward understanding the effect of risk on the value of an asset, but there are many puzzles left, some statistical and some theoretical.

The statistical problems arise because the capital asset pricing model is hard to prove or disprove conclusively. It appears that average returns from low-beta stocks are too high (that is, higher than the capital asset pricing model predicts), and those from high-beta stocks are too low. But this could be a problem with the way the tests are conducted and not with the model itself.[1] In addition, some tests indicate that average return has been related to diversifiable risk as well as to beta.[2] This is, of course, inconsistent with the capital asset pricing model, which states that diversifiable risk does not bother investors and therefore does not affect expected or average return.

Of course, these statistical results could be spurious—an accidental result of inadequate testing procedures. But if they are true, they pose a puzzle. If investors are concerned with diversifiable risk, then corporations ought to be able to increase value just by diversifying. Yet there is evidence that investors do *not* pay extra for firms that diversify. It is hard to see why they would do so, because investors can usually diversify more cheaply and effectively than firms can. Maybe diversifiable risk only *appears* to matter because it happens to be correlated with some other variable *x* that, along with beta, truly determines the expected rates of return demanded by investors. That would resolve the puzzle, but we cannot identify variable *x* and prove that it matters.

Meanwhile, work is proceeding on the theoretical front to relax the simple assumptions underlying the capital asset pricing model. Here is one example. Suppose that you love fine wine. It may make sense for you to buy shares in a grand cru chateau, even if that soaks up a large fraction of your personal wealth and leaves you with a relatively undiversified portfolio. However, you are *hedged* against a rise in the price of fine wine: your hobby will cost you more in a bull market for wine, but your stake in the chateau will make you correspondingly richer. Thus you are holding a relatively undiversified portfolio for a good reason. We would not expect you to demand a premium for bearing that portfolio's undiversifiable risk.

In general, if two people have different tastes, it may make sense for them to hold different portfolios. You may hedge your consumption needs with an investment in winemaking, whereas somebody else may do better to invest in Baskin-Robbins. The capital asset pricing model isn't rich enough to deal with such a world. It assumes that all investors have similar tastes; the "hedging motive" does not enter, and therefore they hold the same portfolio of risky assets. Merton has extended the capital asset pricing model to accommodate the hedging motive.[3] If enough investors are attempting to hedge against the same thing, this model implies a more complicated risk-return relationship. However, it is not yet clear who is hedging against what, so the model remains difficult to test.

Are There Important Exceptions to the Efficient-Market Theory?

The efficient-market theory is very persuasive, but no theory is perfect—there must be exceptions. What are the exceptions and how well does the evidence stand up?

We noted some apparent exceptions in Section 11.2. For example, we saw that the stocks of small companies appear to have yielded higher average returns than those of large companies with comparable betas. Thus whatever your target portfolio beta, you can apparently generate superior average returns by investing in small companies.

---

[1]See R. Roll, "A Critique of the Asset Pricing Theory's Tests; Part 1: On Past and Potential Testability of the Theory," *Journal of Financial Economics* 4 (March 1977), pp. 129–176; and for a critique of the critique, D. Mayers and E. M. Rice, "Measuring Portfolio Performance and the Empirical Content of Asset Pricing Models," *Journal of Financial Economics* 7 (March 1979), pp. 3–28.

[2]For example, see I. Friend, R. Westerfeld, and M. Granito, "New Evidence on the Capital Asset Pricing Model," *Journal of Finance* 33 (June 1978), pp. 903–916.

[3]See R. Merton, "An Intertemporal Capital Asset Pricing Model," *Econometrica* 41 (1973), pp. 867–887.

Now this could mean one of several things:

- The stock market is inefficient and consistently underprices stocks of small firms.
- The difference between the stock market performance of small and large firms is just a coincidence. (The more researchers study stock performance, the more strange coincidences they are likely to find.)
- Firm size happens to be correlated with variable x, that mysterious second risk variable that investors may rationally take into account in pricing shares.

In searching for an explanation of the small-firm phenomenon, researchers have uncovered other puzzles. For example, look again at Figure 11.5, which shows the abnormal return on small- and large-company stocks for each month of the year. You can see that almost all the extra return on small-company stocks occurred in January. So the mystery deepens. Does the turn-of-the-year effect provide a clue to the explanation of the small-company effect or is it just a false trail? Sorting out what is really going on in these cases will take considerable work and thought.

If stocks were fairly priced, there would be no easy ways to make superior profits. That is why most tests of market efficiency have analyzed whether there are simple rules that produce superior investment performance. Unfortunately, the converse does *not* hold: stock prices could deviate substantially from fair value, and yet it could be difficult to make superior profits.

For example, suppose that the price of IBM stock is always one-half its fair value. As long as IBM is *consistently* underpriced, the percentage capital gain is the same as it would be if the stock always sold at a fair price. Of course, if IBM stock is underpriced, you get correspondingly more future dividends for your money, but for low-yield stocks that does not make much difference to your total return. So, while the bulk of the evidence shows that it is difficult to earn high returns, we should be cautious about assuming that stocks are *necessarily* fairly priced.

How Can We Explain Capital Structure?

Modigliani and Miller's article about capital structure emphasized that the value of a firm depends on real variables—the goods it produces, the prices it charges, and the costs that it incurs. Financing decisions merely affect the way that the cash flows are packaged for distribution to investors. What goes into the package is more important than the package itself.

Does it really not matter how much your firm borrows? We have come across several reasons why it *may* matter. Tax is one possibility. Debt provides a corporate tax shield, and this tax shield may more than compensate for any extra personal tax that the investor has to pay on debt interest. Perhaps managers are concerned with potential bankruptcy costs. Perhaps differences in capital structure reflect differences in the relative importance of growth opportunities. So far, none of these possibilities has been either proved relevant or definitely excluded.

The upshot of the matter is that we still don't have an accepted, coherent theory of capital structure. It is not for want of argument on the subject.

How Can We Resolve the Dividend Controversy?

We spent all of Chapter 15 on dividend policy without being able to resolve the dividend controversy. Many people believe dividends are good, others believe they are bad, and still others believe they are irrelevant. If pressed, we stand somewhere in the middle, but we can't be dogmatic about it.

We don't mean to disparage existing research; rather, we say that more research is in order. Whether future research will change anybody's mind is another matter. In 1979 Joel Stern wrote an article for the editorial page of *The Wall Street Journal* arguing for low dividends and citing statistical tests in support of his position.[4] The article attracted several strongly worded responses, including one from a manager who wrote, "While Mr. Stern is gamboling from pinnacle to pinnacle in the upper realms of the theoretical, those of us in financial management are down below slogging through the foothills of reality."[5]

How Can We Explain Merger Waves?

There are many plausible reasons why two firms might wish to merge. If you single out a *particular* merger, it is usually possible to think up a reason why that merger could make sense. But that leaves us with a special hypothesis for each merger. What we need is a *general* hypothesis to explain merger waves. For example, everybody seemed to be merging in 1989 and nobody 3 years later. Why?

We can think of other instances of financial fashions. For example, from time to time there are hot new-issue periods when there seems to be an endless supply of speculative new issues and an insatiable demand for them. In recent years economists have been developing new theories of speculative bubbles. Perhaps such theories will help to explain these mystifying financial fashions.

That concludes our list of unsolved problems. We have given you the seven uppermost in our minds. If there are others that you find more interesting and challenging, by all means construct your own list and start thinking about it.

A Final Word

We titled this chapter "What We Do and Do Not Know about Finance." We should perhaps have added a third section, "What We Know about Finance but Haven't Told You." After all, this book is an introduction to finance and there are plenty of topics that we have only skimmed over. Here are some examples:

- Investment decisions always have side effects on financing—every dollar has to be raised somehow. Sometimes these side effects may be important. For instance, if the project allows the company to issue more debt, it may bring with it valuable tax shields. How can companies allow for these financing side effects when evaluating new investment projects? We touched on this issue in Chapter 10 when we showed you how to calculate the weighted-average cost of capital, but there is a huge body of knowledge about how best to allow for financing side effects in project valuation.
- We stressed in Chapter 12 the wide variety of claims that companies can sell to raise money. We described the principal ones, but there are others that we largely ignored. Leasing is an example. Companies lease assets rather than buy

---

[4]J. Stern, "The Dividend Question," *The Wall Street Journal,* July 16, 1979, p. 13.

[5]*The Wall Street Journal,* August 20, 1979, p. 16. The letter was from A. J. Sandblute, senior vice president of Minnesota Light and Power Company.

them because it is convenient and because in some circumstances there can be tax advantages. A lot is now known about how to value leases.

- Treasurers of large corporations worry about fluctuations in exchange rates, interest rates, and commodity prices. Various tools—including options, futures, forwards, and swaps—have been invented to help managers hedge against these risks. Many of the best brains in finance have been applied to devising and valuing these new instruments. We only touched on the problem of option valuation and said nothing at all about valuing futures. It's an exciting area and there is no shortage of books and articles to help you learn more.

 Quiz

If you have reached this far, you deserve a break. So we haven't provided any heavyweight problems at the end of this chapter. Instead we have included a quiz of the "Trivial Pursuit" variety. You don't need to know the answers to be a financial wizard and for the most part they are not to be found in earlier chapters. However, they may help you to impress your friends at smart dinner parties.[6]

1. What do these countries' currencies have in common?

   - Australia
   - Canada
   - Hong Kong
   - New Zealand
   - Singapore
   - Taiwan
   - United States

   [Score 10]

2. Each of these indexes measures stock market performance in a different country. What are the countries?

   - CAC Index
   - DAX Index
   - FTSE Index
   - Hang Seng Index
   - Nikkei Index

   [Score 2 for each correct answer]

3. Where is each of these financial futures markets located?

   - CME
   - DTB
   - LIFFE
   - MATIF
   - SIMEX

   [Score 2 for each correct answer]

---

[6]The answers are given on pages 710–712.

4. Which of the following firms is the "odd one out"?

   - Fidelity
   - Goldman Sachs
   - Merrill Lynch
   - Morgan Stanley
   - Salomon Brothers

   [Score 10]

5. Match the acquiring firms with the acquired.

Acquiring Firms	Acquired Firms
AT&T	Chase Manhattan
Chemical Bank	Lotus Corporation
IBM	McCaw Cellular Communications
Merck	Medco
Paramount	Viacom

   [Score 2 for each correct answer]

6. To which country does each of the following banks belong?

   - ABN-Amro
   - Banesto
   - Barclays Bank
   - Commerzbank
   - Sanwa Bank

   [Score 2 for each correct answer]

7. In which state are the major United States corporations commonly incorporated?

   - Alabama
   - California
   - Delaware
   - Illinois
   - Maryland

   [Score 10]

8. Spot the "odd one out."

   - Butterfly
   - Odd lot
   - Straddle
   - Vertical spread

   [Score 10]

9. What do the following abbreviations stand for?

   - CD
   - LBO
   - MTN

- OTC
- SEC

[Score 2 for each correct answer]

10. Spot the "odd one out."

- Braniff
- Continental Airlines
- Delta
- Eastern Airlines
- Pan Am

[Score 10]

11. Match up the following events and dates:

- 1963   The first financial futures contract was traded in Chicago.
- 1972   The first swap was arranged (between the World Bank and IBM).
- 1973   The first eurobond was issued (by the Italian company Autostrade).
- 1981   The first traded options market was formed in the United States.
- 1997   The United States Treasury first issued indexed bonds.

[Score 2 for each correct answer]

12. Match each of the following Asian countries with its currency:

- China   Baht
- South Korea   Dong
- Mongolia   Tugrik
- Thailand   Won
- Vietnam   Yuan

[Score 2 for each correct answer]

13. In which year did the United States stock market decline by 43 percent?

- 1931
- 1939
- 1987

[Score 10]

14. Brokers on the New York Stock Exchange often refer to stocks by their nicknames. To which stocks do the following nicknames refer?

- Ketchup
- Mickey Mouse
- Timber
- Whiskey

[Score 2½ for each correct answer]

15. Each of the following organizations made large losses from trading. Match each firm with a major cause of the loss.

- Barings   Copper futures
- Metallgesellschaft Nikkei index futures
- Orange County   Oil futures

- Procter & Gamble   Reverse floaters
- Sumitomo Corporation   Swaps

[Score 2 for each correct answer]

16. What do the following professors of finance have in common?

  - Harry Markowitz   • Robert Merton
  - Merton Miller   • Myron Scholes
  - William Sharpe

[Score 10]

17. Match each of the following individuals with one of the quotations.

  - Bernie Cornfeld   a. "Do you sincerely want to be rich?"
  - Gordon Gecko   b. "Where are the customers' yachts?"
  - John Maynard Keynes   c. "Believing that fundamental conditions of the country are sound...my son and I have for some days been purchasing sound common stocks."
  - John D. Rockefeller   d. The stock market "is, so to speak, a game of Snap, of Old Maid, of Musical Chairs—a pastime in which he is a victor who says Snap neither too soon nor too late, who passes the Old Maid to his neighbor before the game is over, who secures a chair for himself when the music stops."
  - Fred Schwed   e. "Greed is good."

[Score 2 for each correct answer]

18. International bond issues are often known by nicknames. For example, an international bond issued in Southeast Asia is known as a "dragon bond." What is the common term for a bond issued by a foreign company in the bond market of each of the following countries?

  - Japan
  - Netherlands
  - Spain
  - United Kingdom
  - United States

[Score 2 for each correct answer]

Answers to Quiz

1. They all use the dollar.
2. CAC Index = France
   DAX Index = Germany
   FTSE Index = United Kingdom
   Hang Seng Index = Hong Kong
   Nikkei Index = Japan
3. CME (Chicago Mercantile Exchange) = Chicago
   DTB (Deutsche Terminbörse) = Frankfurt
   LIFFE (London International Financial Futures and Options Exchange) = London

MATIF (Marché à Terme International de France) = Paris
SIMEX (Singapore International Monetary Exchange) = Singapore

4. Fidelity is an investment management company. The others are investment banks.

5. AT&T: McCaw Cellular Communications
   Chemical Bank: Chase Manhattan
   IBM: Lotus Corporation
   Merck: Medco
   Paramount: Viacom

6. ABN-Amro = Netherlands
   Banesto = Spain
   Barclays Bank = United Kingdom
   Commerzbank = Germany
   Sanwa Bank = Japan

7. Delaware

8. "Odd lot" refers to an order to buy or sell fewer than 100 shares. The other terms all refer to combinations of options.

9. CD = certificate of deposit
   LBO = leveraged buy-out
   MTN = medium-term note
   OTC = over-the-counter
   SEC = Securities and Exchange Commission

10. Delta is the only one of these airlines that has not been through Chapter 11 bankruptcy proceedings.

11. 1963   The first eurobond was issued (by the Italian company Autostrade)
    1972   The first financial futures contract traded in Chicago
    1973   The first traded options market was formed in the United States
    1981   The first swap was arranged (between the World Bank and IBM)
    1997   The United States Treasury first issued indexed bonds

12. China = Yuan
    South Korea = Won
    Mongolia = Tugrik
    Thailand = Baht
    Vietnam = Dong

13. 1931

14. Ketchup = Heinz
    Mickey Mouse = Disney
    Timber = Weyerhaeuser
    Whiskey = Seagram Co.

15. Barings   Nikkei index futures
    Metallgesellschaft   Oil futures
    Orange County   Reverse floaters
    Procter & Gamble   Swaps
    Sumitomo Corporation   Copper futures

16. Each received the Nobel Prize for his contribution to financial economics.

17. 1. Bernie Cornfeld   (head of Investors' Overseas Services in addresses to the fund sales force) = a
    2. Gordon Gecko   (in the movie *Wall Street*) = e
    3. John Maynard Keynes   (writing in *The General Theory of Employment, Interest and Money*, 1936) = d

4. John D. Rockefeller (at the start of the 1929 Great Crash) = c
5. Fred Schwed (in a 1940 book of that title) = b

18. Japan = Samurai bond
Netherlands = Rembrandt bond
Spain = Matador bond
United Kingdom = Bulldog bond
United States = Yankee bond

If you scored

0–40	You weren't trying.
41–70	Not bad.
71–110	You are probably going to be an investment banker.
111–140	You are probably an investment banker *already*.
141–180	You probably cheated.

Appendix A

Present Value Tables

Appendix Table A.1

*Future value of $1 after t years = $ $(1 + r)^t$

Interest Rate per Year

Number of Years	1%	2%	3%	4%	5%	6%	7%	8%	9%	10%	11%	12%	13%	14%	15%
1	1.010	1.020	1.030	1.040	1.050	1.060	1.070	1.080	1.090	1.100	1.110	1.120	1.130	1.140	1.150
2	1.020	1.040	1.061	1.082	1.102	1.124	1.145	1.166	1.188	1.210	1.232	1.254	1.277	1.300	1.323
3	1.030	1.061	1.093	1.125	1.158	1.191	1.225	1.260	1.295	1.331	1.368	1.405	1.443	1.482	1.521
4	1.041	1.082	1.126	1.170	1.216	1.262	1.311	1.360	1.412	1.464	1.518	1.574	1.630	1.689	1.749
5	1.051	1.104	1.159	1.217	1.276	1.338	1.403	1.469	1.539	1.611	1.685	1.762	1.842	1.925	2.011
6	1.062	1.126	1.194	1.265	1.340	1.419	1.501	1.587	1.677	1.772	1.870	1.974	2.082	2.195	2.313
7	1.072	1.149	1.230	1.316	1.407	1.504	1.606	1.714	1.828	1.949	2.076	2.211	2.353	2.502	2.660
8	1.083	1.172	1.267	1.369	1.477	1.594	1.718	1.851	1.993	2.144	2.305	2.476	2.658	2.853	3.059
9	1.094	1.195	1.305	1.423	1.551	1.689	1.838	1.999	2.172	2.358	2.558	2.773	3.004	3.252	3.518
10	1.105	1.219	1.344	1.480	1.629	1.791	1.967	2.159	2.367	2.594	2.839	3.106	3.395	3.707	4.046
11	1.116	1.243	1.384	1.539	1.710	1.898	2.105	2.332	2.580	2.853	3.152	3.479	3.836	4.226	4.652
12	1.127	1.268	1.426	1.601	1.796	2.012	2.252	2.518	2.813	3.138	3.498	3.896	4.335	4.818	5.350
13	1.138	1.294	1.469	1.665	1.886	2.133	2.410	2.720	3.066	3.452	3.883	4.363	4.898	5.492	6.153
14	1.149	1.319	1.513	1.732	1.980	2.261	2.579	2.937	3.342	3.797	4.310	4.887	5.535	6.261	7.076
15	1.161	1.346	1.558	1.801	2.079	2.397	2.759	3.172	3.642	4.177	4.785	5.474	6.254	7.138	8.137
16	1.173	1.373	1.605	1.873	2.183	2.540	2.952	3.426	3.970	4.595	5.311	6.130	7.067	8.137	9.358
17	1.184	1.400	1.653	1.948	2.292	2.693	3.159	3.700	4.328	5.054	5.895	6.866	7.986	9.276	10.76
18	1.196	1.428	1.702	2.026	2.407	2.854	3.380	3.996	4.717	5.560	6.544	7.690	9.024	10.58	12.38
19	1.208	1.457	1.754	2.107	2.527	3.026	3.617	4.316	5.142	6.116	7.263	8.613	10.20	12.06	14.23
20	1.220	1.486	1.806	2.191	2.653	3.207	3.870	4.661	5.604	6.727	8.062	9.646	11.52	13.74	16.37
25	1.282	1.641	2.094	2.666	3.386	4.292	5.427	6.848	8.623	10.83	13.59	17.00	21.23	26.46	32.92
30	1.348	1.811	2.427	3.243	4.322	5.743	7.612	10.06	13.27	17.45	22.89	29.96	39.12	50.95	66.21

Interest Rate per Year

Number of Years	16%	17%	18%	19%	20%	21%	22%	23%	24%	25%	26%	27%	28%	29%	30%
1	1.160	1.170	1.180	1.190	1.200	1.210	1.220	1.230	1.240	1.250	1.260	1.270	1.280	1.290	1.300
2	1.346	1.369	1.392	1.416	1.440	1.464	1.488	1.513	1.538	1.563	1.588	1.613	1.638	1.664	1.690
3	1.561	1.602	1.643	1.685	1.728	1.772	1.816	1.861	1.907	1.953	2.000	2.048	2.097	2.147	2.197
4	1.811	1.874	1.939	2.005	2.074	2.144	2.215	2.289	2.364	2.441	2.520	2.601	2.684	2.769	2.856
5	2.100	2.192	2.288	2.386	2.488	2.594	2.703	2.815	2.932	3.052	3.176	3.304	3.436	3.572	3.713
6	2.436	2.565	2.700	2.840	2.986	3.138	3.297	3.463	3.635	3.815	4.002	4.196	4.398	4.608	4.827
7	2.826	3.001	3.185	3.379	3.583	3.797	4.023	4.259	4.508	4.768	5.042	5.329	5.629	5.945	6.275
8	3.278	3.511	3.759	4.021	4.300	4.595	4.908	5.239	5.590	5.960	6.353	6.768	7.206	7.669	8.157
9	3.803	4.108	4.435	4.785	5.160	5.560	5.987	6.444	6.931	7.451	8.005	8.595	9.223	9.893	10.60
10	4.411	4.807	5.234	5.695	6.192	6.728	7.305	7.926	8.594	9.313	10.09	10.92	11.81	12.76	13.79
11	5.117	5.624	6.176	6.777	7.430	8.140	8.912	9.749	10.66	11.64	12.71	13.86	15.11	16.46	17.92
12	5.936	6.580	7.288	8.064	8.916	9.850	10.87	11.99	13.21	14.55	16.01	17.61	19.34	21.24	23.30
13	6.886	7.699	8.599	9.596	10.70	11.92	13.26	14.75	16.39	18.19	20.18	22.36	24.76	27.39	30.29
14	7.988	9.007	10.15	11.42	12.84	14.42	16.18	18.14	20.32	22.74	25.42	28.40	31.69	35.34	39.37
15	9.266	10.54	11.97	13.59	15.41	17.45	19.74	22.31	25.20	28.42	32.03	36.06	40.56	45.59	51.19
16	10.75	12.33	14.13	16.17	18.49	21.11	24.09	27.45	31.24	35.53	40.36	45.80	51.92	58.81	66.54
17	12.47	14.43	16.67	19.24	22.19	25.55	29.38	33.76	38.74	44.41	50.85	58.17	66.46	75.86	86.50
18	14.46	16.88	19.67	22.90	26.62	30.91	35.85	41.52	48.04	55.51	64.07	73.87	85.07	97.86	112.5
19	16.78	19.75	23.21	27.25	31.95	37.40	43.74	51.07	59.57	69.39	80.73	93.81	108.9	126.2	146.2
20	19.46	23.11	27.39	32.43	38.34	45.26	53.36	62.82	73.86	86.74	101.7	119.1	139.4	162.9	190.0
25	40.87	50.66	62.67	77.39	95.40	117.4	144.2	176.9	216.5	264.7	323.0	393.6	478.9	581.8	705.6
30	85.85	111.1	143.4	184.7	237.4	304.5	389.8	497.9	634.8	807.8	1026	1301	1646	2078	2620

E.g., if the interest rate is 10 percent per year, the investment of $1 today will be worth $1.611 at year 5.

Appendix Table A.2

Discount factors: Present value of $1 to be received after t years = 1/(1 + r)^t

Number of Years	1%	2%	3%	4%	5%	6%	7%	8%	9%	10%	11%	12%	13%	14%	15%
1	.990	.980	.971	.962	.952	.943	.935	.926	.917	.909	.901	.893	.885	.877	.870
2	.980	.961	.943	.925	.907	.890	.873	.857	.842	.826	.812	.797	.783	.769	.756
3	.971	.942	.915	.889	.864	.840	.816	.794	.772	.751	.731	.712	.693	.675	.658
4	.961	.924	.888	.855	.823	.792	.763	.735	.708	.683	.659	.636	.613	.592	.572
5	.951	.906	.863	.822	.784	.747	.713	.681	.650	.621	.593	.567	.543	.519	.497
6	.942	.888	.837	.790	.746	.705	.666	.630	.596	.564	.535	.507	.480	.456	.432
7	.933	.871	.813	.760	.711	.665	.623	.583	.547	.513	.482	.452	.425	.400	.376
8	.923	.853	.789	.731	.677	.627	.582	.540	.502	.467	.434	.404	.376	.351	.327
9	.914	.837	.766	.703	.645	.592	.544	.500	.460	.424	.391	.361	.333	.308	.284
10	.905	.820	.744	.676	.614	.558	.508	.463	.422	.386	.352	.322	.295	.270	.247
11	.896	.804	.722	.650	.585	.527	.475	.429	.388	.350	.317	.287	.261	.237	.215
12	.887	.788	.701	.625	.557	.497	.444	.397	.356	.319	.286	.257	.231	.208	.187
13	.879	.773	.681	.601	.530	.469	.415	.368	.326	.290	.258	.229	.204	.182	.163
14	.870	.758	.661	.577	.505	.442	.388	.340	.299	.263	.232	.205	.181	.160	.141
15	.861	.743	.642	.555	.481	.417	.362	.315	.275	.239	.209	.183	.160	.140	.123
16	.853	.728	.623	.534	.458	.394	.339	.292	.252	.218	.188	.163	.141	.123	.107
17	.844	.714	.605	.513	.436	.371	.317	.270	.231	.198	.170	.146	.125	.108	.093
18	.836	.700	.587	.494	.416	.350	.296	.250	.212	.180	.153	.130	.111	.095	.081
19	.828	.686	.570	.475	.396	.331	.277	.232	.194	.164	.138	.116	.098	.083	.070
20	.820	.673	.554	.456	.377	.312	.258	.215	.178	.149	.124	.104	.087	.073	.061
25	.780	.610	.478	.375	.295	.233	.184	.146	.116	.092	.074	.059	.047	.038	.030
30	.742	.552	.412	.308	.231	.174	.131	.099	.075	.057	.044	.033	.026	.020	.015

Interest Rate per Year

Interest Rate per Year

Number of Years	16%	17%	18%	19%	20%	21%	22%	23%	24%	25%	26%	27%	28%	29%	30%
1	.862	.855	.847	.840	.833	.826	.820	.813	.806	.800	.794	.787	.781	.775	.769
2	.743	.731	.718	.706	.694	.683	.672	.661	.650	.640	.630	.620	.610	.601	.592
3	.641	.624	.609	.593	.579	.564	.551	.537	.524	.512	.500	.488	.477	.466	.455
4	.552	.534	.516	.499	.482	.467	.451	.437	.423	.410	.397	.384	.373	.361	.350
5	.476	.456	.437	.419	.402	.386	.370	.355	.341	.328	.315	.303	.291	.280	.269
6	.410	.390	.370	.352	.335	.319	.303	.289	.275	.262	.250	.238	.227	.217	.207
7	.354	.333	.314	.296	.279	.263	.249	.235	.222	.210	.198	.188	.178	.168	.159
8	.305	.285	.266	.249	.233	.218	.204	.191	.179	.168	.157	.148	.139	.130	.123
9	.263	.243	.225	.209	.194	.180	.167	.155	.144	.134	.125	.116	.108	.101	.094
10	.227	.208	.191	.176	.162	.149	.137	.126	.116	.107	.099	.092	.085	.078	.073
11	.195	.178	.162	.148	.135	.123	.112	.103	.094	.086	.079	.072	.066	.061	.056
12	.168	.152	.137	.124	.112	.102	.092	.083	.076	.069	.062	.057	.052	.047	.043
13	.145	.130	.116	.104	.093	.084	.075	.068	.061	.055	.050	.045	.040	.037	.033
14	.125	.111	.099	.088	.078	.069	.062	.055	.049	.044	.039	.035	.032	.028	.025
15	.108	.095	.084	.074	.065	.057	.051	.045	.040	.035	.031	.028	.025	.022	.020
16	.093	.081	.071	.062	.054	.047	.042	.036	.032	.028	.025	.022	.019	.017	.015
17	.080	.069	.060	.052	.045	.039	.034	.030	.026	.023	.020	.017	.015	.013	.012
18	.069	.059	.051	.044	.038	.032	.028	.024	.021	.018	.016	.014	.012	.010	.009
19	.060	.051	.043	.037	.031	.027	.023	.020	.017	.014	.012	.011	.009	.008	.007
20	.051	.043	.037	.031	.026	.022	.019	.016	.014	.012	.010	.008	.007	.006	.005
25	.024	.020	.016	.013	.010	.009	.007	.006	.005	.004	.003	.003	.002	.002	.001
30	.012	.009	.007	.005	.004	.003	.003	.002	.002	.001	.001	.001	.001	.000	.000

E.g., if the interest rate is 10 percent per year, the present value of $1 received at year 5 is $.621.

Appendix Table A.3

Annuity table: Present value of $1 per year for each of t years = $1/r - 1/[r(1 + r)^t]$

Number of Years	\multicolumn{15}{c}{Interest Rate per Year}

Number of Years	1%	2%	3%	4%	5%	6%	7%	8%	9%	10%	11%	12%	13%	14%	15%
1	.990	.980	.971	.962	.952	.943	.935	.926	.917	.909	.901	.893	.885	.877	.870
2	1.970	1.942	1.913	1.886	1.859	1.833	1.808	1.783	1.759	1.736	1.713	1.690	1.668	1.647	1.626
3	2.941	2.884	2.829	2.775	2.723	2.673	2.624	2.577	2.531	2.487	2.444	2.402	2.361	2.322	2.283
4	3.902	3.808	3.717	3.630	3.546	3.465	3.387	3.312	3.240	3.170	3.102	3.037	2.974	2.914	2.855
5	4.853	4.713	4.580	4.452	4.329	4.212	4.100	3.993	3.890	3.791	3.696	3.605	3.517	3.433	3.352
6	5.795	5.601	5.417	5.242	5.076	4.917	4.767	4.623	4.486	4.355	4.231	4.111	3.998	3.889	3.784
7	6.728	6.472	6.230	6.002	5.786	5.582	5.389	5.206	5.033	4.868	4.712	4.564	4.423	4.288	4.160
8	7.652	7.325	7.020	6.733	6.463	6.210	5.971	5.747	5.535	5.335	5.146	4.968	4.799	4.639	4.487
9	8.566	8.162	7.786	7.435	7.108	6.802	6.515	6.247	5.995	5.759	5.537	5.328	5.132	4.946	4.772
10	9.471	8.983	8.530	8.111	7.722	7.360	7.024	6.710	6.418	6.145	5.889	5.650	5.426	5.216	5.019
11	10.37	9.787	9.253	8.760	8.306	7.887	7.499	7.139	6.805	6.495	6.207	5.938	5.687	5.453	5.234
12	11.26	10.58	9.954	9.385	8.863	8.384	7.943	7.536	7.161	6.814	6.492	6.194	5.918	5.660	5.421
13	12.13	11.35	10.63	9.986	9.394	8.853	8.358	7.904	7.487	7.103	6.750	6.424	6.122	5.842	5.583
14	13.00	12.11	11.30	10.56	9.899	9.295	8.745	8.244	7.786	7.367	6.982	6.628	6.302	6.002	5.724
15	13.87	12.85	11.94	11.12	10.38	9.712	9.108	8.559	8.061	7.606	7.191	6.811	6.462	6.142	5.847
16	14.72	13.58	12.56	11.65	10.84	10.11	9.447	8.851	8.313	7.824	7.379	6.974	6.604	6.265	5.954
17	15.56	14.29	13.17	12.17	11.27	10.48	9.763	9.122	8.544	8.022	7.549	7.120	6.729	6.373	6.047
18	16.40	14.99	13.75	12.66	11.69	10.83	10.06	9.372	8.756	8.201	7.702	7.250	6.840	6.467	6.128
19	17.23	15.68	14.32	13.13	12.09	11.16	10.34	9.604	8.950	8.365	7.839	7.366	6.938	6.550	6.198
20	18.05	16.35	14.88	13.59	12.46	11.47	10.59	9.818	9.129	8.514	7.963	7.469	7.025	6.623	6.259
25	22.02	19.52	17.41	15.62	14.09	12.78	11.65	10.67	9.823	9.077	8.422	7.843	7.330	6.873	6.464
30	25.81	22.40	19.60	17.29	15.37	13.76	12.41	11.26	10.27	9.427	8.694	8.055	7.496	7.003	6.566

Interest Rate per Year

Number of Years	16%	17%	18%	19%	20%	21%	22%	23%	24%	25%	26%	27%	28%	29%	30%
1	.862	.855	.847	.840	.833	.826	.820	.813	.806	.800	.794	.787	.781	.775	.769
2	1.605	1.585	1.566	1.547	1.528	1.509	1.492	1.474	1.457	1.440	1.424	1.407	1.392	1.376	1.361
3	2.246	2.210	2.174	2.140	2.106	2.074	2.042	2.011	1.981	1.952	1.923	1.896	1.868	1.842	1.816
4	2.798	2.743	2.690	2.639	2.589	2.540	2.494	2.448	2.404	2.362	2.320	2.280	2.241	2.203	2.166
5	3.274	3.199	3.127	3.058	2.991	2.926	2.864	2.803	2.745	2.689	2.635	2.583	2.532	2.483	2.436
6	3.685	3.589	3.498	3.410	3.326	3.245	3.167	3.092	3.020	2.951	2.885	2.821	2.759	2.700	2.643
7	4.039	3.922	3.812	3.706	3.605	3.508	3.416	3.327	3.242	3.161	3.083	3.009	2.937	2.868	2.802
8	4.344	4.207	4.078	3.954	3.837	3.726	3.619	3.518	3.421	3.329	3.241	3.156	3.076	2.999	2.925
9	4.607	4.451	4.303	4.163	4.031	3.905	3.786	3.673	3.566	3.463	3.366	3.273	3.184	3.100	3.019
10	4.833	4.659	4.494	4.339	4.192	4.054	3.923	3.799	3.682	3.571	3.465	3.364	3.269	3.178	3.092
11	5.029	4.836	4.656	4.486	4.327	4.177	4.035	3.902	3.776	3.656	3.543	3.437	3.335	3.239	3.147
12	5.197	4.988	4.793	4.611	4.439	4.278	4.127	3.985	3.851	3.725	3.606	3.493	3.387	3.286	3.190
13	5.342	5.118	4.910	4.715	4.533	4.362	4.203	4.053	3.912	3.780	3.656	3.538	3.427	3.322	3.223
14	5.468	5.229	5.008	4.802	4.611	4.432	4.265	4.108	3.962	3.824	3.695	3.573	3.459	3.351	3.249
15	5.575	5.324	5.092	4.876	4.675	4.489	4.315	4.153	4.001	3.859	3.726	3.601	3.483	3.373	3.268
16	5.668	5.405	5.162	4.938	4.730	4.536	4.357	4.189	4.033	3.887	3.751	3.623	3.503	3.390	3.283
17	5.749	5.475	5.222	4.990	4.775	4.576	4.391	4.219	4.059	3.910	3.771	3.640	3.518	3.403	3.295
18	5.818	5.534	5.273	5.033	4.812	4.608	4.419	4.243	4.080	3.928	3.786	3.654	3.529	3.413	3.304
19	5.877	5.584	5.316	5.070	4.843	4.635	4.442	4.263	4.097	3.942	3.799	3.664	3.539	3.421	3.311
20	5.929	5.628	5.353	5.101	4.870	4.657	4.460	4.279	4.110	3.954	3.808	3.673	3.546	3.427	3.316
25	6.097	5.766	5.467	5.195	4.948	4.721	4.514	4.323	4.147	3.985	3.834	3.694	3.564	3.442	3.329
30	6.177	5.829	5.517	5.235	4.979	4.746	4.534	4.339	4.160	3.995	3.842	3.701	3.569	3.447	3.332

E.g., if the interest rate is 10 percent per year, the present value of $1 received in each of the next 5 years is $3.791.

Appendix Table A.4

Annuity table: Future value of $1 per year for each of t years = $[(1 + r)^t - 1]/r$

Number of Years	1%	2%	3%	4%	5%	6%	7%	8%	9%	10%	11%	12%	13%	14%	15%
1	1.000	1.000	1.000	1.000	1.000	1.000	1.000	1.000	1.000	1.000	1.000	1.000	1.000	1.000	1.000
2	2.010	2.020	2.030	2.040	2.050	2.060	2.070	2.080	2.090	2.100	2.110	2.120	2.130	2.140	2.150
3	3.030	3.060	3.091	3.122	3.153	3.184	3.215	3.246	3.278	3.310	3.342	3.374	3.407	3.440	3.473
4	4.060	4.122	4.184	4.246	4.310	4.375	4.440	4.506	4.573	4.641	4.710	4.779	4.850	4.921	4.993
5	5.101	5.204	5.309	5.416	5.526	5.637	5.751	5.867	5.985	6.105	6.228	6.353	6.480	6.610	6.742
6	6.152	6.308	6.468	6.633	6.802	6.975	7.153	7.336	7.523	7.716	7.913	8.115	8.323	8.536	8.754
7	7.214	7.434	7.662	7.898	8.142	8.394	8.654	8.923	9.200	9.487	9.783	10.089	10.405	10.730	11.067
8	8.286	8.583	8.892	9.214	9.549	9.897	10.260	10.637	11.028	11.436	11.859	12.300	12.757	13.233	13.727
9	9.369	9.755	10.159	10.583	11.027	11.491	11.978	12.488	13.021	13.579	14.164	14.776	15.416	16.085	16.786
10	10.462	10.950	11.464	12.006	12.578	13.181	13.816	14.487	15.193	15.937	16.722	17.549	18.420	19.337	20.304
11	11.567	12.169	12.808	13.486	14.207	14.972	15.784	16.645	17.560	18.531	19.561	20.655	21.814	23.045	24.349
12	12.683	13.412	14.192	15.026	15.917	16.870	17.888	18.977	20.141	21.384	22.713	24.133	25.650	27.271	29.002
13	13.809	14.680	15.618	16.627	17.713	18.882	20.141	21.495	22.953	24.523	26.212	28.029	29.985	32.089	34.352
14	14.947	15.974	17.086	18.292	19.599	21.015	22.550	24.215	26.019	27.975	30.095	32.393	34.883	37.581	40.505
15	16.097	17.293	18.599	20.024	21.579	23.276	25.129	27.152	29.361	31.772	34.405	37.280	40.417	43.842	47.580
16	17.258	18.639	20.157	21.825	23.657	25.673	27.888	30.324	33.003	35.950	39.190	42.753	46.672	50.980	55.717
17	18.430	20.012	21.762	23.698	25.840	28.213	30.840	33.750	36.974	40.545	44.501	48.884	53.739	59.118	65.075
18	19.615	21.412	23.414	25.645	28.132	30.906	33.999	37.450	41.301	45.599	50.396	55.750	61.725	68.394	75.836
19	20.811	22.841	25.117	27.671	30.539	33.760	37.379	41.446	46.018	51.159	56.939	63.440	70.749	78.969	88.212
20	22.019	24.297	26.870	29.778	33.066	36.786	40.995	45.762	51.160	57.275	64.203	72.052	80.947	91.025	102.444
25	28.243	32.030	36.459	41.646	47.727	54.865	63.249	73.106	84.701	98.347	114.413	133.334	155.620	181.871	212.793
30	34.785	40.568	47.575	56.085	66.439	79.058	94.461	113.283	136.308	164.494	199.021	241.333	293.199	356.787	434.745

Interest Rate per Year

Interest Rate per Year

Number of Years	16%	17%	18%	19%	20%	21%	22%	23%	24%	25%	26%	27%	28%	29%	30%
1	1.000	1.000	1.000	1.000	1.000	1.000	1.000	1.000	1.000	1.000	1.000	1.000	1.000	1.000	1.000
2	2.160	2.170	2.180	2.190	2.200	2.210	2.220	2.230	2.240	2.250	2.260	2.270	2.280	2.290	2.300
3	3.506	3.539	3.572	3.606	3.640	3.674	3.708	3.743	3.778	3.813	3.848	3.883	3.918	3.954	3.990
4	5.066	5.141	5.215	5.291	5.368	5.446	5.524	5.604	5.684	5.766	5.848	5.931	6.016	6.101	6.187
5	6.877	7.014	7.154	7.297	7.442	7.589	7.740	7.893	8.048	8.207	8.368	8.533	8.700	8.870	9.043
6	8.977	9.207	9.442	9.683	9.930	10.183	10.442	10.708	10.980	11.259	11.544	11.837	12.136	12.442	12.756
7	11.414	11.772	12.142	12.523	12.916	13.321	13.740	14.171	14.615	15.073	15.546	16.032	16.534	17.051	17.583
8	14.240	14.773	15.327	15.902	16.499	17.119	17.762	18.430	19.123	19.842	20.588	21.361	22.163	22.995	23.858
9	17.519	18.285	19.086	19.923	20.799	21.714	22.670	23.669	24.712	25.802	26.940	28.129	29.369	30.664	32.015
10	21.321	22.393	23.521	24.709	25.959	27.274	28.657	30.113	31.643	33.253	34.945	36.723	38.593	40.556	42.619
11	25.733	27.200	28.755	30.404	32.150	34.001	35.962	38.039	40.238	42.566	45.031	47.639	50.398	53.318	56.405
12	30.850	32.824	34.931	37.180	39.581	42.142	44.874	47.788	50.895	54.208	57.739	61.501	65.510	69.780	74.327
13	36.786	39.404	42.219	45.244	48.497	51.991	55.746	59.779	64.110	68.760	73.751	79.107	84.853	91.016	97.625
14	43.672	47.103	50.818	54.841	59.196	63.909	69.010	74.528	80.496	86.949	93.926	101.465	109.612	118.411	127.913
15	51.660	56.110	60.965	66.261	72.035	78.330	85.192	92.669	100.815	109.687	119.347	129.861	141.303	153.750	167.286
16	60.925	66.649	72.939	79.850	87.442	95.780	104.935	114.983	126.011	138.109	151.377	165.924	181.868	199.337	218.472
17	71.673	78.979	87.068	96.022	105.931	116.894	129.020	142.430	157.253	173.636	191.735	211.723	233.791	258.145	285.014
18	84.141	93.406	103.740	115.266	128.117	142.441	158.405	176.188	195.994	218.045	242.585	269.888	300.252	334.007	371.518
19	98.603	110.285	123.414	138.166	154.740	173.354	194.254	217.712	244.033	273.556	306.658	343.758	385.323	431.870	483.973
20	115.380	130.033	146.628	165.418	186.688	210.758	237.989	268.785	303.601	342.945	387.389	437.573	494.213	558.112	630.165
25	249.214	292.105	342.603	402.042	471.98	554.24	650.96	764.61	898.09	1054.79	1238.64	1454.20	1706.80	2002.62	2348.80
30	530.312	647.439	790.948	966.712	1181.88	1445.15	1767.08	2160.49	2640.92	3227.17	3942.03	4812.98	5873.23	7162.82	8729.99

E.g., if the interest rate is 10 percent per year, the future value of $1 received in each of the next 5 years is $6.105.

a. $P_0 =$)
b. DIV 5.52%

a. P/E $3/4 = 8.33$
b. P/E ses to 10.

a. Marl-book ratio $= \$400/\$100 = 4$
b. Marl-book ratio $= \frac{1}{2}$

a. P_0 25
b. Assn place $= \$80$
   PV = \$45

a. (i) invest 0% of earnings
   $_0 = \$33.33$
   (ii) einvest at 40%
   $P_0 = \$33.33$
   (iii) Reinvest at 60%
   $P_0 = \$33.33$

b. (i) Reinvest at 0%
   $P_0 = \$33.33$
   (ii) Reinvest at 40%
   $P_0 = 42.86$
   PVGO $= \$9.53$
   (iii) Reinvest at 60%
   $P_0 = \$66.67$
   PVGO $= \$33.34$

c. In part (a), the return on reinvested earnings was equal to the discount rate.
   In part (b), the return on reinvested earnings was greater than the discount rate.

39. a. $P_0 = \$26.40$
    b. $P_1 = \$28.57$
    c. Return $= 12\%$

41. a. Expected return $= 8\%$
    b. PVGO $= \$16.67$
    c. $P_0 = \$106.22$

Chapter 5

1. Both projects are worth pursuing.

3. NPV$_A = \$11.93$ and NPV$_B = \$12.29$. Choose B.

5. No.

7. Project A has a payback period of 2.5 years. Project B has a payback period of 2 years.

9.

	Year	Book Return
Project A	1	.15
	2	.20
	3	.30
	4	.60
Project B	1	.167
	2	.25
	3	.50

11. a. The equivalent annual cost of Econo-cool is \$252.53. The equivalent annual cost of Luxury Air is \$234.21.
    b. Luxury Air.
    c. Econo-cool equivalent annual cost is \$229.14. Luxury Air equivalent annual cost is \$193.72

13. a. The equivalent cost of owning and operating the new machine is \$4,590. The old machine costs \$5,000 a year to operate. You should replace.
    b. If $r = 10\%$, do not replace.

15. NPV$_{9\%} = \$2,139.28$ and NPV$_{14\%} = -\$1,444.54$. The IRR is 11.81%.

17. a.

Year	Book Rate of Return
1	10%
2	12.5%
3	16.7%
4	25%
5	50%

b. NPV $= \$1,978$

c.

Year	Book Rate of Return
1	−60%
2	50%
3	66.7%
4	100%
5	200%

d. NPV unaffected

19. b. At 5% NPV $= -\$.443$
    c. At 20% NPV $= \$.840$
       At 40% NPV $= -\$.634$

21. IRR$_A = 25.7\%$
    IRR$_B = 20.7\%$

23. NPV $= -\$197.7$. Reject.

25. a. $r = 0$ implies NPV $= \$15,750$.
       $r = 50\%$ implies NPV $= \$4,250$.
       $r = 100\%$ implies NPV $= 0$.
    b. IRR $= 100\%$

27. NPV must be negative.

29. a. If $r = 2\%$, choose A.
    b. If $r = 12\%$, choose B.

31. a.

Project	Payback
A	3
B	2
C	3

b. Only B
c. All three projects

Appendix B

Solutions to Selected End-of-Chapter Problems

Chapter 1

1. real, executive airplanes, brand names, financial, stock, investment, capital budgeting, financing

3. a. financial
   b. financial
   c. real
   d. real
   e. real
   f. financial
   g. real
   h. financial

5. The contingency arrangement aligns the interests of the lawyer and the client.

7. If you know that you will engage in business with another party on a repeated basis, you will be less likely to take advantage of your business partner should the opportunity to do so arise.

13. Managers who are more securely entrenched in their positions are more able to pursue their own interests.

15. Such a plan would burden them with a considerable personal risk tied to the fortunes of the firm.

17. Mutual funds; Pension funds; Venture capital firms

Chapter 2

1.

Assets		Liabilities and Shareholders' Equity	
Cash	$ 10,000	Accounts payable	$ 17,000
Receivables	22,000	Long-term debt	170,000
Inventory	200,000		
Store and property	100,000	Shareholders' equity	145,000
Total assets	$332,000	Liabilities and shareholders' equity	$332,000

3.

Sales	$10,000
Cost of goods sold	6,500
G & A expenses	1,000
Depreciation expense	1,000
EBIT	1,500
Interest expense	500
Taxable income	1,000
Taxes (35%)	350
Net income	$ 650

Cash flow = net income + depreciation = $1,650

5. Total taxes are reduced by $2,955.50.

7. a. Book value = $200,000
   Market value = $50,200,000

b. Price per share = $25.10
   Book value per share = $.10

9. a. Taxes = $3,000
   Marginal and average tax rates are 15%.
   b. Taxes = $10,880
   Average tax rate = 21.76%
   Marginal tax rate = 28%
   c. Taxes = $86,495.50
   Average tax rate = .3204 = 32.04%
   Marginal tax rate = 39.6%
   d. Taxes = $1,167,575.50
   Average tax rate = 38.92%
   Marginal tax rate = 39.6%

11. Cash flow will be $3,000 less than profits.

13. Dividends = $600,000

15. a. 1996: Equity = 890 − 650 = 240
    1997: Equity = 1,040 − 810 = 230
    b. 1996: NWC = 90 − 50 = 40
    1997: NWC = 140 − 60 = 80
    c. Taxable income = 1,950 − 1,030 − 350 − 240 = 330
    Taxes paid = .35 × 330 = 115.50
    d. Cash flow from operations = 174.50
    e. Gross investment = 450
    f. Other current liabilities increased by 45.

17. Net working capital decreased by 50.

19. Earnings per share in 1996 = $1.70
    Earnings per share in 1997 = $1.52

23. Price per share = $6,650,000/500,000 = $13.30

Chapter 3

1. a. 38.55
   b. 14.86
   c. 61.39
   d. 37.69

3. $100 \times (1.05)^{113} = \$24,797$
   $100 \times (1.10)^{113} = \$4,757,441$

5. PV = $523

7. a. $t = 23.36$
   b. $t = 11.91$
   c. $t = 6.17$

8. Effective annual rate
   a. 12.68%
   b. 8.24%
   c. 10.25%

9. EAR = 67.77%

11.

Discount Rate	PV of 10-Year, $1,000 Annuity	PV of 15-Year, $800 Annuity
a. 5%	$7,722	$8,304
b. 20%	4,192	3,740

13. $n = 9.01$ years

15. PV = 812.44

17. The PV for the quarterback is $10.81 million. The PV for the receiver is $7.21 million.

19. APR = 15.58%

21. a. EAR = 6.80%
    b. PMT = 573.14

23. a. $r = 11.11\%$
    b. $r = 1/(1 - d) - 1$

25. $ 61,796.71

27. The present value of your payments is $671. The present value of your receipts is $579. This is a bad deal.

29. $r = 8\%$

31. a. The present value of the payoff is $1,228. This is a good deal.
    b. PV is $771. This is a bad deal.

33. 18 years

35. The value of the lease payments is $40,801. It is cheaper to buy the truck.

37. Installment plan: PV = 91.83% of stated price
    Pay in full: Payment net of discount is only 90% of stated price

39. a. PMT = 277.41
    b. PMT = 247.69

41. $4,139

43. $4,126.57

45. $83,862

47. $.8418

49. $3,947.90

51. $100 \times e^{.10 \times 6} = \$182.21$
    $100 \times e^{.06 \times 10} = \$182.21$

53. $n = 44.74$ months

55. a. Nominal rate = 4%
    b. Nominal rate = 8.16%
    c. Nominal rate = 10.24%

57. a. $79.38
    b. $91.51
    c. Real interest rate = 4.854%
    d. $91.51/(1.04854)^3 = 79.38$

59. a. $228,107
    b. $13,950

61. Inflation = 1,099% per year

Chapter 4

1. a. Coupon rate remains unchanged.
   b. Price will fall.
   c. Yield to maturity increases.
   d. Current yield increases.

3. Bond price = $1,066.67

5. Rate of return on both bonds = 10%

7. Coupon rate = 8.0%
   Current yield = 8.42%
   Yield to maturity = 9.12%

9. a. Bondholder receives $80 per year.
   b. Price = $940.05
   c. The bond will sell for $1,065.15.

11. a. Price will be $1,000.
    b. Rate of return = 2.86%
    c. Real return = −.14%

13. a. Price = $721.67
    b. $r = 11.97\%$

15. a. Yield to maturity = 7.23%
    b. Rate of return = 15.31%

17. Initial price = $967.19
    New price = $948.20

19. a. 14%
    b. $P_0 = \$20$

21. a. $DIV_1 = \$1.04$
    $DIV_2 = \$1.0816$
    $DIV_3 = \$1.1249$
    b. $P_0 = \$13$
    c. $P_3 = \$14.62$
    d. Your payments are:

	Year 1	Year 2	Year
DIV	1.04	1.0816	1.
Sales price			14.
Total cash flow	1.04	1.0816	15.
PV of cash flow	0.9286	0.8622	11.

Sum of PV = $13.00

23. a. $P_0 = \$21$
    b. $P_0 = \$30$

25. $r = 5\%$

27. $P_0 = \$33.33$

29.

31.

33.

35.

37

Appendix B

Solutions to Selected End-of-Chapter Problems

Chapter 1

1. real, executive airplanes, brand names, financial, stock, investment, capital budgeting, financing

3. a. financial
   b. financial
   c. real
   d. real
   e. real
   f. financial
   g. real
   h. financial

5. The contingency arrangement aligns the interests of the lawyer and the client.

7. If you know that you will engage in business with another party on a repeated basis, you will be less likely to take advantage of your business partner should the opportunity to do so arise.

13. Managers who are more securely entrenched in their positions are more able to pursue their own interests.

15. Such a plan would burden them with a considerable personal risk tied to the fortunes of the firm.

17. Mutual funds; Pension funds; Venture capital firms

Chapter 2

1.

Assets		Liabilities and Shareholders' Equity	
Cash	$ 10,000	Accounts payable	$ 17,000
Receivables	22,000	Long-term debt	170,000
Inventory	200,000		
Store and property	100,000	Shareholders' equity	145,000
Total assets	$332,000	Liabilities and shareholders' equity	$332,000

3.

Sales	$10,000
Cost of goods sold	6,500
G & A expenses	1,000
Depreciation expense	1,000
EBIT	1,500
Interest expense	500
Taxable income	1,000
Taxes (35%)	350
Net income	$ 650

Cash flow = net income + depreciation = $1,650

5. Total taxes are reduced by $2,955.50.

7. a. Book value = $200,000
   Market value = $50,200,000

   b. Price per share = $25.10
   Book value per share = $.10

9. a. Taxes = $3,000
   Marginal and average tax rates are 15%.
   b. Taxes = $10,880
   Average tax rate = 21.76%
   Marginal tax rate = 28%
   c. Taxes = $86,495.50
   Average tax rate = .3204 = 32.04%
   Marginal tax rate = 39.6%
   d. Taxes = $1,167,575.50
   Average tax rate = 38.92%
   Marginal tax rate = 39.6%

11. Cash flow will be $3,000 less than profits.

13. Dividends = $600,000

15. a. 1996: Equity = 890 − 650 = 240
   1997: Equity = 1,040 − 810 = 230
   b. 1996: NWC = 90 − 50 = 40
   1997: NWC = 140 − 60 = 80
   c. Taxable income = 1,950 − 1,030 − 350 − 240 = 330
   Taxes paid = .35 × 330 = 115.50
   d. Cash flow from operations = 174.50
   e. Gross investment = 450
   f. Other current liabilities increased by 45.

17. Net working capital decreased by 50.

19. Earnings per share in 1996 = $1.70
   Earnings per share in 1997 = $1.52

23. Price per share = $6,650,000/500,000 = $13.30

Chapter 3

1. a. 38.55
   b. 14.86
   c. 61.39
   d. 37.69

3. $100 \times (1.05)^{113} = \$24,797$
   $100 \times (1.10)^{113} = \$4,757,441$

5. PV = $523

7. a. $t = 23.36$
   b. $t = 11.91$
   c. $t = 6.17$

8. Effective annual rate
   a. 12.68%
   b. 8.24%
   c. 10.25%

9. EAR = 67.77%

11.	Discount Rate	PV of 10-Year, $1,000 Annuity	PV of 15-Year, $800 Annuity
a.	5%	$7,722	$8,304
b.	20%	4,192	3,740

13. $n = 9.01$ years

15. $PV = 812.44$

17. The PV for the quarterback is $10.81 million. The PV for the receiver is $7.21 million.

19. APR = 15.58%

21. a. EAR = 6.80%
    b. PMT = 573.14

23. a. $r = 11.11\%$
    b. $r = 1/(1 - d) - 1$

25. $ 61,796.71

27. The present value of your payments is $671. The present value of your receipts is $579. This is a bad deal.

29. $r = 8\%$

31. a. The present value of the payoff is $1,228. This is a good deal.
    b. PV is $771. This is a bad deal.

33. 18 years

35. The value of the lease payments is $40,801. It is cheaper to buy the truck.

37. Installment plan: PV = 91.83% of stated price
    Pay in full: Payment net of discount is only 90% of stated price

39. a. PMT = 277.41
    b. PMT = 247.69

41. $4,139

43. $4,126.57

45. $83,862

47. $.8418

49. $3,947.90

51. $100 \times e^{.10 \times 6} = \$182.21$
    $100 \times e^{.06 \times 10} = \$182.21$

53. $n = 44.74$ months

55. a. Nominal rate = 4%
    b. Nominal rate = 8.16%
    c. Nominal rate = 10.24%

57. a. $79.38
    b. $91.51
    c. Real interest rate = 4.854%
    d. $91.51/(1.04854)^3 = 79.38$

59. a. $228,107
    b. $13,950

61. Inflation = 1,099% per year

Chapter 4

1. a. Coupon rate remains unchanged.
   b. Price will fall.
   c. Yield to maturity increases.
   d. Current yield increases.

3. Bond price = $1,066.67

5. Rate of return on both bonds = 10%

7. Coupon rate = 8.0%
   Current yield = 8.42%
   Yield to maturity = 9.12%

9. a. Bondholder receives $80 per year.
   b. Price = $940.05
   c. The bond will sell for $1,065.15.

11. a. Price will be $1,000.
    b. Rate of return = 2.86%
    c. Real return = −.14%

13. a. Price = $721.67
    b. $r = 11.97\%$

15. a. Yield to maturity = 7.23%
    b. Rate of return = 15.31%

17. Initial price = $967.19
    New price = $948.20

19. a. 14%
    b. $P_0 = \$20$

21. a. $DIV_1 = \$1.04$
       $DIV_2 = \$1.0816$
       $DIV_3 = \$1.1249$

    b. $P_0 = \$13$

    c. $P_3 = \$14.62$

    d. Your payments are:

	Year 1	Year 2	Year 3
DIV	1.04	1.0816	1.1249
Sales price			14.6232
Total cash flow	1.04	1.0816	15.7481
PV of cash flow	0.9286	0.8622	11.2092

Sum of PV = $13.00

23. a. $P_0 = \$21$
    b. $P_0 = \$30$

25. $r = 5\%$

27. $P_0 = \$33.33$

29. a. $P_0 = \$18.10$
    b. $DIV_1/P_0 = 5.52\%$

31. a. $P/E = 33.33/4 = 8.33$
    b. P/E increases to 10.

33. a. Market-to-book ratio $= \$400/\$100 = 4$
    b. Market-to-book ratio $= \frac{1}{2}$

35. a. $P_0 = \$125$
    b. Assets in place $= \$80$
       PVGO $= \$45$

37. a. (i) Reinvest 0% of earnings
          $P_0 = \$33.33$
       (ii) Reinvest at 40%
          $P_0 = \$33.33$
       (iii) Reinvest at 60%
          $P_0 = \$33.33$
    b. (i) Reinvest at 0%
          $P_0 = \$33.33$
       (ii) Reinvest at 40%
          $P_0 = 42.86$
          PVGO $= \$9.53$
       (iii) Reinvest at 60%
          $P_0 = \$66.67$
          PVGO $= \$33.34$
    c. In part (a), the return on reinvested earnings was equal to the discount rate.
       In part (b), the return on reinvested earnings was greater than the discount rate.

39. a. $P_0 = \$26.40$
    b. $P_1 = \$28.57$
    c. Return $= 12\%$

41. a. Expected return $= 8\%$
    b. PVGO $= \$16.67$
    c. $P_0 = \$106.22$

Chapter 5

1. Both projects are worth pursuing.
3. $NPV_A = \$11.93$ and $NPV_B = \$12.29$. Choose B.
5. No.
7. Project A has a payback period of 2.5 years. Project B has a payback period of 2 years.

9.
	Year	Book Return
Project A	1	.15
	2	.20
	3	.30
	4	.60
Project B	1	.167
	2	.25
	3	.50

11. a. The equivalent annual cost of Econo-cool is $252.53. The equivalent annual cost of Luxury Air is $234.21.
    b. Luxury Air.
    c. Econo-cool equivalent annual cost is $229.14. Luxury Air equivalent annual cost is $193.72

13. a. The equivalent cost of owning and operating the new machine is $4,590. The old machine costs $5,000 a year to operate. You should replace.
    b. If $r = 10\%$, do not replace.

15. $NPV_{9\%} = \$2,139.28$ and $NPV_{14\%} = -\$1,444.54$. The IRR is 11.81%.

17. a.
Year	Book Rate of Return
1	10%
2	12.5%
3	16.7%
4	25%
5	50%

    b. NPV $= \$1,978$
    c.
Year	Book Rate of Return
1	−60%
2	50%
3	66.7%
4	100%
5	200%

    d. NPV unaffected

19. b. At 5% NPV $= -\$.443$
    c. At 20% NPV $= \$.840$
       At 40% NPV $= -\$.634$

21. $IRR_A = 25.7\%$
    $IRR_B = 20.7\%$

23. NPV $= -\$197.7$. Reject.

25. a. $r = 0$ implies NPV $= \$15,750$.
       $r = 50\%$ implies NPV $= \$4,250$.
       $r = 100\%$ implies NPV $= 0$.
    b. IRR $= 100\%$

27. NPV must be negative.

29. a. If $r = 2\%$, choose A.
    b. If $r = 12\%$, choose B.

31. a.
Project	Payback
A	3
B	2
C	3

    b. Only B
    c. All three projects

d.

Project	NPV
A	−1,011
B	3,378
C	2,405

e. False

Chapter 6

3. Increase in net cash flow = $106 million

5. Cash flow = $3.38085 million

7.

Revenue	$160,000
Rental costs	35,000
Variable costs	45,000
Depreciation	10,000
Pretax profit	$ 70,000
Taxes (35%)	24,500
Net income	$ 45,500

9. Cash flow = $3,300

11. Cash flow = $56,250

13. a.

Year	Depreciation	Book Value (end of year)
1	8,000	32,000
2	12,800	19,200
3	7,680	11,520
4	4,608	6,912
5	4,608	2,304
6	2,304	0

b. After-tax proceeds are $17,032.

15. a. Incremental operating CF = $1,300 in years 1–6
Net cash flow at time 0 = −$4,000
b. NPV = −4,000 + 1,300 × annuity factor (15%, 6 years) = $919.83
c. NPV = $1,062.43

17. a. Initial investment = $58,000

b.

Year	Cash Flow ($000)
1	21.4
2	17.8
3	14.2
4	10.6

c. NPV = −$5,926
d. IRR = 4.59%

19. Equivalent annual (net-of-tax) capital costs:
Quick and Dirty: $2.075 million
Do-It-Right: $1.891 million
Choose Do-It-Right.

21. NPV = −$408,435

23. Net present value = −$.182

Chapter 7

1. Variable costs = $.50 per burger
Fixed costs = $1.25 million

3. a. 4,286 diamonds annually
b. 5,978 diamonds per year

5. Accounting breakeven is unaffected. NPV breakeven increases.

7. CF breakeven is less than zero-profit break-even sales level.

9. a. Accounting break-even sales level is $6,400 per year. NPV break-even sales level is $7,166.
b. Accounting breakeven is unchanged. NPV breakeven is $7,676.

11. DOL = 1

13. a. $1.836 million
$3.673 million
b. $544,588
c. $1.95 million

15. a. Accounting breakeven increases.
b. NPV breakeven falls.
c. ACRS makes the project more attractive.

19. a. NPV = $5.1 million
b. NPV = $2.5 million
c. NPV = $6.2 million
d. Price = $1.61 per jar

21. NPV will be negative.

23. a. Average CF = 0
b. Average CF = $15,000

25. a. Expected NPV = −$681,728. The firm will reject the project.
b. Expected NPV = $69,855. The project is now worth pursuing.

Chapter 8

1. Return = 15%
Dividend yield = 5%
Capital gains yield = 10%

3. a. Rate of return = 0
Real rate = −4.76%
b. Rate of return = 5%
Real rate = 0
c. Rate of return = 10%
Real rate = 4.76%

5.

Asset Class	Real Rate
Treasury bills	0.96%
Treasury bonds	1.63
Common stock	9.50

7.

Week	Average Price of Stock in Market	Index Using DJIA Method	Index Using S&P Method
1	85.90	100.00	100.00
2	85.00	98.95	96.77
3	84.80	98.72	94.56
4	85.70	99.77	93.96
5	88.60	103.14	96.61
6	86.00	100.12	96.65
7	85.20	99.19	96.94
8	83.60	97.32	96.04
9	78.60	91.50	89.44

9. a.

Year	Risk Premium
1992	4.17
1993	6.90
1994	−2.62
1995	32.13
1996	17.80
Average	11.68

b. Average risk premium $= 11.68\%$

c. Standard deviation $= 12.16\%$

13. $P_0 = \$45.53$

15. The bankruptcy lawyer

17. b. $r_{stock} = 13\%$
$r_{bonds} = 8.4\%$
Standard deviation (stocks) $= 9.8\%$
Standard deviation (bonds) $= 3.2\%$

19. Our estimate of "normal" risk premiums will fall.

21. a. General Steel
b. Club Med

23. Sassafras is *not* a risky investment to a diversified investor. Its return is better when the economy enters a recession. In contrast, the Leaning Tower of Pita has returns that are positively correlated with the rest of the economy.

Chapter 9

1. a. False
b. False
c. False
d. True
e. True

5. Required return $= r_f + \beta(r_m - r_f) = 16\%$
Expected return $= 16\%$
The security is neither under- nor overpriced.

7. a. $\beta_A = 1.2$
$\beta_D = .75$

b. $r_m = 12\%$
$r_A = 14\%$
$r_D = 9\%$
c. $r = r_f + \beta(r_m - r_f)$
$r_A = 13.6\%$
$r_D = 10\%$
d. Stock A

9. a. Nike, which has a beta of 1.20.
b. Nike, with standard deviation of 31%.
c. $\beta = .807$
d. The portfolio beta $= .69$
Portfolio standard deviation $= 13.8\%$
e. Exxon: $r = 9.52\%$
Polaroid: $r = 8.24\%$
Nike: $r = 13.60\%$

11. It is not well diversified.

13. NPV $= -\$34.92$

15. $P_1 = \$53$

17. $\$400,000$

19.

Company	Cost of Capital
Bristol-Myers Squibb	14.8%
Digital Equipment	12.5
General Mills	11.1
McGraw-Hill	13.0
Microsoft	12.1

21. a. False
b. True
c. False
d. True
e. False

23. $r = r_f + \beta(r_m - r_f) = 13\%$
The 12% expected return is too low relative to its risk.

27. $\beta = .5$

Chapter 10

1. 5.50%

3. 13.75%

5. a. 10.55%
b. 6.86%

7. $D/V = .3125$ and $E/V = .6875$

9. The cost of equity capital is 10.4%.
WACC $= 8.78\%$

11. WACC $= 12.4\%$

13.

	Dollars	Percent
Bonds	$ 9.36 million	30.3%
Preferred stock	1.50 million	4.9
Common stock	20.00 million	64.8
Total	$30.86 million	100.0%

15. The IRR is less than the WACC of firms in the computer industry. Reject the project.

17. a. $r = 19\%$
    b. Weighted-average beta = .9
    c. WACC = 12.36%
    d. Discount rate = 12.36%
    e. $r = 16\%$

Chapter 11

1. weak, semistrong, strong, fundamental, strong, technical, weak

7. Investments in financial markets such as stocks or bonds are available to all participants in the marketplace. Prices of these investments are bid up to "fair" levels. In contrast, investments in product markets are made by firms with various forms of protection from full competition.

9. diversification, tax planning and management, risk management

11. If the price of the firm already reflects this fact, the stock may not be a bargain.

13. The market has no memory. Just because long-term interest rates are high relative to past levels doesn't mean they won't go higher still.

15. a. No
    b. No
    c. Earnings per share will fall by half.
    d. The firm's stock price will fall by half.
    e. Shareholders' wealth is unaffected.

17. A downward-sloping yield curve might indicate that investors anticipate future short-term rates lower than today's.

Chapter 12

1. a. 60,000 shares issued
   b. Outstanding shares = 58,000
   c. 40,000

3. Par value of common shares = $300,000
   Additional paid-in capital = $1,700,000
   Retained earnings = $500,000

5. a. 90 votes
   b. 900 votes

7. a. funded
   b. Eurobond
   c. subordinated
   d. sinking fund
   e. call
   f. prime rate
   g. floating rate
   h. private placement, public issue
   i. lease
   j. convertible
   k. warrant

9. a. Common shares ($2.00 par value per share) $ 911
      Additional paid-in capital   2,548
      Retained earnings   19,108
      Currency translation adjustment   (73)
      Treasury shares at cost   (2,643)
      Net common equity $19,851
   b. Common shares ($2.00 par value per share) $ 911
      Additional paid-in capital   2,548
      Retained earnings   19,108
      Currency translation adjustment   (73)
      Treasury shares at cost   (2,703)
      Net common equity $19,791

11. Similarity: the firm promises to make specified payments. Advantage of income bonds: interest payments are tax-deductible expenses.

Chapter 13

1. a. Subsequent issue
   b. Bond issue
   c. Bond issue

3. a. A large issue
   b. A bond issue
   c. Private placements

5. a. Net proceeds of public issue = $9,770,000
      Net proceeds of private placement = $9,970,000
   b. The public issue
   c. The private placement can be custom-tailored and its terms can be more easily renegotiated.

7. a. 10%
   b. Average return = 3.94%
   c. I have suffered the winner's curse.

9. No

11. 12% of the value of funds raised.

13. a. $10
    b. $18.333
    c. $8.333
    d. 200 rights

15. a. $12.5 million
    b. $5.80 per share

19. Less underwriter risk; less signaling effect from debt; easier to value

Chapter 14

1. a. True
   b. False
   c. False
   d. True

3. a.

	Slump	Normal	Boom
Return on shares (no debt)	7.50%	12.50%	17.50%
Return on shares (debt = $250,000)	6.67%	13.33%	20.00%

   b. DFL (unleveraged) = 1.0
      DFL (leveraged) = 1.333
   c. Leveraged beta = unleveraged beta × DFL
      1.067 = .8 × 1.333

5. P/E = 10/1.25 = 8 (no leverage)
   P/E = 10/1.33 = 7.5 (leveraged)

7. Income assuming $1,250,000 of debt financing

	Slump	Normal	Boom
Before-tax income	−50,000	0	50,000

   The firm has positive taxable income only in a boom. The tax shield is lost in moderate to poor economic conditions, and therefore is risky.

9. a. Low-debt plan: $D/E = .25$
      High-debt plan: $D/E = .67$
   b.

	Low-Debt Plan		High-Debt Plan	
EPS	8.75	13.75	8.33	15.00
Expected EPS	$11.25		$11.67	

   c.

	Low-Debt	High-Debt
EPS	10	10

11. r_{equity} = 18%

17. a. PV tax shield = $14
    b. PV tax shield = $4.47

21. a. Stockholders gain; bondholders lose.
    b. Bondholders gain; stockholders lose.
    c. Bondholders lose; stockholders gain.
    d. Original stockholders lose; bondholders gain.

25. Distorted investment decisions, impeded relations with other firms and creditors

Chapter 15

1. a.

May 7:	Declaration date
June 6:	Last with-dividend date
June 7:	Ex-dividend date
June 11:	Record date
July 2:	Payment date

   b. The ex-dividend date, June 7
   c. Dividend yield = 1.1%
   d. Payout ratio = 15.8%
   e. New stock price = $24.55

3. a. Price = $32
   b. Price = $32
   c. Price = $40, unchanged

7. a. The after-tax dividend, $1.44
   b. No

9. a. No effect on total wealth
   b. Identical to position after the stock repurchase

11. a. 1,250 shares. Value of equity remains at $50,000.
    b. Same effect as the stock dividend.

13. a. $50
    b. $48.60

15. a. Price = $19.49
    b. Before-tax return = 12.9%
    c. Price = $20.15
    d. Before-tax return = 14.1%

19. a.

Stock	Pension	Corporation	Individual
A	10.00%	6.50%	8.00%
B	10.00	7.73	7.20
C	10.00	8.95	6.40

    b.

Stock	Price
A	$100
B	$81.25
C	$62.50

21. a. $20 per share
    b. If the firm pays a dividend, EPS = $2. If the firm does the repurchase, EPS = $2.105.
    c. If the dividend is paid, the P/E ratio = 9.5. If the stock is repurchased, the P/E ratio = 9.5.

23. No impact on wealth.

Chapter 16

1. a. Long-term debt ratio = .42
   b. Total debt ratio = .65
   c. Times interest earned = 3.75

d. Cash coverage ratio = 7.42

e. Current ratio = .73

f. Quick ratio = .52

g. Net profit margin = .15

h. Inventory turnover = 19.11

i. Days sales in inventory = 19.10

j. Average collection period = 67.39 days

k. ROE = .14

l. ROA = .072

m. Payout ratio = .65

3. Gross investment = 2,576

5. Balance sheet for Nynex:

	Common Size (% amounts)	
	End of Year	Start of Year
Assets		
Cash and marketable securities	0.32%	0.57%
Receivables	8.59	9.05
Inventories	0.67	0.87
Other current assets	3.13	3.39
Total current assets	12.72%	13.88%
Net property, plant, and equipment	72.07	72.41
Other long-term assets	15.21	13.71
Total assets	100.00%	100.00%
Liabilities and Shareholders' Equity		
Payables	9.25%	11.05%
Short-term debt	5.12	5.72
Other current liabilities	2.93	2.86
Total current liabilities	17.30%	19.63%
Long-term debt and leases	25.32	24.84
Other long-term liabilities	22.29	22.36
Shareholders' equity	35.09	33.16
Total liabilities and shareholders' equity	100.00%	100.00%

7. a. ROE = 13.9%

b. $\dfrac{\text{assets}}{\text{equity}} \times \dfrac{\text{sales}}{\text{assets}} \times \dfrac{\text{EBIT} - \text{taxes}}{\text{sales}}$

$\times \dfrac{\text{EBIT} - \text{taxes} - \text{interest}}{\text{EBIT} - \text{taxes}}$

$\dfrac{27,608.5}{9,422} \times \dfrac{13,194}{27,608.5} \times \dfrac{2,566 - 570}{13,194}$

$\times \dfrac{2,566 - 570 - 685}{2,566 - 570} = .139$

9. a. Debt-equity ratio = $\dfrac{\text{long-term debt}}{\text{equity}}$

b. Return on equity

$= \dfrac{\text{earnings available for common stock}}{\text{average equity}}$

c. Profit margin = $\dfrac{\text{EBIT} - \text{tax}}{\text{sales}}$

d. Inventory turnover = $\dfrac{\text{cost of goods sold}}{\text{average inventory}}$

e. Current ratio = $\dfrac{\text{current assets}}{\text{current liabilities}}$

f. Interval measure

$= \dfrac{\text{cash} + \text{marketable securities} + \text{receivables}}{\text{average daily expenditures from operations}}$

g. Average collection period = $\dfrac{\text{average receivables}}{\text{average daily sales}}$

h. Quick ratio

$= \dfrac{\text{cash} + \text{marketable securities} + \text{accounts receivable}}{\text{current liabilities}}$

i. Tobin's q = $\dfrac{\text{market value of assets}}{\text{estimated replacement cost of assets}}$

j. Payout ratio = $\dfrac{\text{dividends}}{\text{earnings}}$

11. a. Liquidity ratios:

Current ratio = 1.67 (decreases)

Quick ratio = 1.11 (decreases)

Cash ratio = .37 (increases)

b. Leverage ratios:

$\dfrac{\text{Total liabilities}}{\text{Total assets}} = .43$

13. The current ratio is unaffected. The quick ratio falls.

15. Days sales in inventory = 2

17. a. Times interest earned = 1.25

b. Cash coverage ratio = 1.5

c. Fixed-payment coverage = 1.09

19. Total sales = $54,750

Asset turnover = .73

ROA = 3.65%

21. $\dfrac{\text{Book debt}}{\text{Book equity}} = .5$

$\dfrac{\text{Market equity}}{\text{Book equity}} = 2$

$\dfrac{\text{Book debt}}{\text{Market equity}} = \dfrac{.5}{2} = .25$

23. Perhaps the firm has a lower ROA than its competitors; perhaps it pays a higher interest rate on its debt.

25. a. The shipping company

b. United Foods

c. The paper mill

d. The power company

e. Fledgling Electronics

f. The pharmaceutical company

Chapter 17

1. a. False
   b. False
   c. True
   d. False
   e. True
   f. True
   g. False

5. The balancing item is dividends. Dividends must be $200.

7. a. Internal growth rate = 10%
   b. Sustainable growth rate = 15%

9. a.

INCOME STATEMENT	20% GROWTH
Revenue	2,400
Cost of goods sold	2,160
EBIT	240
Interest expense	40
Earnings before taxes	200
State and federal taxes	80
Net income	120
Dividends	80
Retained earnings	40

BALANCE SHEET

Assets

Net working capital	240
Fixed assets	960
Net assets	1,200

Liabilities and Shareholders' Equity

Long-term debt	400
Shareholders' equity	640
Total liabilities and shareholders' equity	1,040
Required external financing	160

b. SECOND-STAGE PRO FORMA

BALANCE SHEET

Assets

Net working capital	240
Fixed assets	960
Net assets	1,200

Liabilities and Shareholders' Equity

Long-term debt	560
Shareholders' equity	640
Total liabilities and shareholders' equity	1,200

11. a. Internal growth rate = 7.4%
    b. Sustainable growth rate = 11.1%

13. a. Internal growth rate = 8%
    b. External financing = $220,000
    c. Internal growth rate = 20%
    d. External financing = $100,000

15. Payout ratio can be at most 1/3.

17. Profit margin = 8%

19. g = 12%

21. a. g = .025
    b. Issue $1,000 in new debt.
    c. 1.5%

23. Required external financing is zero.

25. Higher

27. Sales revenue will increase less than proportionally to output; costs and assets will increase roughly in proportion to output. Costs and assets will increase as a proportion of sales.

Chapter 18

1.

	Cash	Net Working Capital
a.	$2 million decline	$2 million decline
b.	$2,500 increase	Unchanged
c.	$5,000 decline	Unchanged
d.	Unchanged	$1 million increase
e.	Unchanged	Unchanged
f.	$5 million increase	Unchanged

3. a. Long-term financing, total capital requirement, marketable securities
   b. Cash, cash, cash balance, marketable securities

5. Lower inventory period and cash conversion cycle; reduce net working capital.

7. **Sources of Cash**

Sale of marketable securities	2
Increase in bank loans	1
Increase in accounts payable	5
Cash from operations:	
Net income	6
Depreciation	2
Total	16

Uses of Cash

Increase in inventories	6
Increase in accounts receivable	3
Investment in fixed assets	6
Dividend paid	1
Total	16
Change in cash balance	0

9. Effective rate = 8.89% if the compensating balance is 20%, the effective rate is 10%.

11. a. 6.38%
    b. 6.20%

13. a. Cash conversion cycle falls.
    b. Cash conversion cycle increases.
    c. Cash conversion cycle falls.
    d. Cash conversion cycle increases.
    e. Cash conversion cycle falls.
    f. Cash conversion cycle increases.

15.

| | Quarter | | | |
	First	Second	Third	Fourth
Cash requirements				
1. Cash required for operations	$45	$15	−$26	−$35
2. Interest on line of credit	0	0.9	0.9	0.6
3. Interest on stretched payables	0	0	0.8	0
4. Total cash required	$45	$15.9	−$24.3	−$34.4
Cash raised				
5. Line of credit (bank loan)	$45	$ 0	$0	$0
6. Stretched payables	0	15.9	0	0
7. Securities sold	5	0	0	0
8. Total cash raised	$50	$15.9	$0	$0
Repayments				
9. Of stretched payables	0	0	$15.9	0
10. Of line of credit (bank loan)	0	0	8.4	34.4
Increase in cash balances				
11. Addition to cash balances	$5	$0	$0	$0
Line of credit (bank loan)				
12. Beginning of quarter	$0	$45	$45	$36.6
13. End of quarter	45	45	36.6	2.2

17. The order is .75 times the following quarter's sales forecast:

Quarter	Order
1	270
2	252
3	288
4	288

19.

Quarter	Collections
1	348
2	368
3	276
4	288

21.

| | Quarter | | | |
	First	Second	Third	Fourth
Cash at start of period	$40	$10	$15	−$14
+ Net cash inflow (from problem 20)	−30	+5	−29	−41
= Cash at end of period	10	15	−14	−55
Minimum operating cash balance	30	30	30	30
Cumulative short-term financing required (minimum cash balance minus cash at end of period)	$20	$15	$44	$85

23.

	February	March	April
Sources of cash			
Collections on current sales	$100	$110	$ 90
Collections on accounts receivable	90	100	110
Total sources of cash	$190	$210	$200
Uses of cash			
Payments of accounts payable	$ 30	$ 40	$ 30
Cash purchases	70	80	60
Labor and administrative expenses	30	30	30
Capital expenditures	100	0	0
Taxes, interest, and dividends	10	10	10
Total uses of cash	$240	$160	$130
Net cash inflow (sources − uses)	−$50	+$50	+$70
Cash at start of period	$100	$50	$100
+ Net cash inflow	−50	+50	+70
= Cash at end of period	$ 50	$100	$170
Minimum operating cash balance	$100	$100	$100
Cumulative short-term financing required (minimum cash balance minus cash at end of period)	$50	$0	−$70

Chapter 19

1. Ledger balance = $215,000
   Net float = $15,000

3. a. Payment float   = $120,000
      Availability float = 66,000
      Net float   = 54,000
   b. Annual interest earnings = $1,320
      Present value of earnings = $22,000

5. a. $20,000
   b. $4
   c. $120

7. Yes

9. Cash balance = $14,142
   Transfers per month = 7.07

11. a. The interest rate, the cost of each transaction, and the variability of each cash flow.
    b. It should restore it to one-third of the distance from the lower to the upper limit.

13. Cash balances fall relative to sales.

15. a. $1.5 million
    b. $180,000
    c. Yes

17. a. Once every 2½ weeks
    b. $204
    c. $102

19. a. Economic order quantity = 600
    b. Total costs = $6,000

21. The economic order quantity = 90 gems. The firm should place smaller but more frequent orders.

23. Economic order quantity falls by a factor of 10.

Chapter 20

1. a. $10
   b. 40 days
   c. 9.6%

3. a. Due lag and pay lag fall.
   b. Due lag and pay lag increase.
   c. Terms lag and pay lag increase.

5. a. 20 days
   b. $1.096 million
   c. Average days in receivables will fall.

7. a. Yes
   b. Credit should not be advanced.
   c. Net benefit from advancing credit = $100

9. a. The expected profit from a sale is –2. Do not extend credit.
   b. $p = .95$
   c. The present value of a sale, net of default, is positive, $458.35
   d. $p = 16\%$

11. a. The expected profit of a sale is positive, $30.
    b. $p = .875$

13. PV (REV) = $1,200
    PV (COST) = $1,000

Slow payers have a 70% probability of paying their bills. The expected profit of a sale to a slow payer is therefore .70 ($1,200 − $1,000) − .30 ($1,000) = −$160.

Expected savings = $16. The credit check costs $5, so it is cost effective.

15. a. False
    b. False
    c. True
    d. False
    e. True
    f. False

17. Sell only to groups 1, 2, and 3.

Chapter 21

1. $24 per share

3. By merging, the firms can even out the work load over the year.

5. a. $5 million
   b. $4 million
   c. NPV = $1 million

7. a. Economies of scale is a valid reason.
   b. Diversification is not a valid reason.
   c. Possibly a valid reason.
   d. The bootstrap strategy is not a valid reason.

9. LBO: 6
   Poison pill: 4
   Tender offer: 5
   Shark repellent: 2
   Proxy contest: 1
   White knight: 3

11. a. NPV = $5,000
    b. SCC will sell for $51.67; SDP will sell for $20.
    c. Price = $51.32
    d. NPV = $3,960

13. a. Total market value = $4,000,000 + 5,000,000 = $9,000,000
       Total earnings = $200,000 + 500,000 = $700,000
       Number of shares = 262,172
       Price per share = $9,000,000/262,172 = $34.33
       Price-earnings ratio = 34.33/2.67 = 12.9
    b. .81 share
    c. $567,365
    d. $567,365

Chapter 22

1. a. 173,900 lira; $.0575
   b. 62.51 pounds = 159.97 dollars

c. Direct exchange rate will decrease and indirect exchange rate will decrease.

d. U.S. dollar is worth more.

3. a. $\dfrac{1 + r_x}{1 + r_\$} = \dfrac{f_{x/\$}}{s_{x/\$}}$

   b. $\dfrac{f_{x/\$}}{s_{x/\$}} = \dfrac{E(s_{x/\$})}{s_{x/\$}}$

   c. $\dfrac{E(1 + i_x)}{E(1 + i_\$)} = \dfrac{E(s_{x/\$})}{s_{x/\$}}$

   d. $\dfrac{1 + r_x}{1 + r_\$} = \dfrac{E(1 + i_x)}{E(1 + i_\$)}$

5. a

7. Borrow the present value of DM1 million, sell the marks for dollars in the spot market, and invest the proceeds in an 8-year dollar loan. In 8 years, it can repay the deutschemark loan with the anticipated deutschemark payment.

9. a. Forward premium
   b. 2.4% annualized premium
   c. $1 = Ffr5.9180
   d. $16,898

11. 7.57%

13. Ffr5.9885
    DM1.7805
    DM1 = Ffr3.363

15. Canadian dollar should be depreciating relative to the U.S. dollar.

17. Net present value = $.72 million

19. a. Depreciation of Trinidadian dollars
    b. Borrow in Trinidad.
    c. Its exposure is mitigated.

Chapter 23

1.

	Payoff	Profit
a. Call option, $X = 65$	5	$-\frac{1}{2}$
b. Put option, $X = 65$	0	$-\frac{15}{16}$
c. Call option, $X = 70$	0	$-2\frac{7}{16}$
d. Put option, $X = 70$	0	$-2\frac{5}{8}$
e. Call option, $X = 75$	0	$-\frac{7}{8}$
f. Put option, $X = 75$	5	$+1\frac{3}{8}$

3. a. The September call costs 5½. The October call costs 7½.
   b. More uncertainty about the stock price in October.
   c. This is true of puts as well.

5. Figure 23.8a represents a call seller; Figure 23.8b represents a call buyer.

7. a. The exercise price of the put option.
   b. The value of the stock.

9. Lower bound is either zero or the stock price minus the exercise price, whichever is greater. The upper bound is the stock price.

11.

Payoff of Option Position at Expiration

	$S<60$	$60<S<65$	$65<S<70$	$S\geq70$
Buy call ($X = 60$)	0	$S - 60$	$S - 60$	$S - 60$
Sell 2 calls ($X = 65$)	0	0	$-2(S - 65)$	$-2(S - 65)$
Buy call ($X = 70$)	0	0	0	$S - 70$
Total	0	$S - 60$	$70 - S$	0

13. You will be more tempted to choose the high-risk proposal.

15. Call price = $6.67

17. a. Call option to pursue a project.
    b. Put option to sell the equipment.

19. Put option with exercise price equal to support price.

21. a. Option to put (sell) the stock to the underwriter.
    b. Volatility of the stock value; the length of the period for which the underwriter guarantees the issue; the interest rate; the price at which the underwriter is obligated to buy the stock; and the market value of the stock.

23. Put option on the bank assets with exercise price equal to the deposits owed to bank customers.

25. a. Buy a call option for $3. Exercise the call to purchase stock. Pay the $20 exercise price. Sell the share for $25.
    b. Buy a share and put option. Exercise the put. Riskless profit equals $1.

Chapter 24

1. Both activities eliminate the firm's exposure to a particular source of risk.

3.

	Gold Price		
	$280	$300	$320
a. Revenues	$280,000	$300,000	$320,000
Futures contract	21,000	1,000	-19,000
b. Total	$301,000	$301,000	$301,000
c. Revenues	$280,000	$300,000	$320,000
+ Put option payoff	20,000	0	0
- Put option cost	2,000	2,000	2,000
Net revenue	$298,000	$298,000	$298,000

5. A currency swap is an agreement to exchange a series of payments in one currency for a given series of payments in another currency. An interest rate swap is an exchange

of a series of fixed payments for a series of payments that are linked to market interest rates.

7. Reject its offer.

9. Assume that the futures price for oil is $20 per barrel. Petrochemical will take a long position to hedge its cost of buying oil. Onnex will take a short position to hedge its revenue from selling oil.

	Oil Price ($ per barrel)		
	$18	$20	$22
Cost for Petrochemical:			
Cash flow on purchase of oil	−18,000	−20,000	−22,000
+ Cash flow on long futures position	− 2,000	0	+ 2,000
Total cash flow	−20,000	−20,000	−20,000
Revenue for Onnex:			
Revenue from 1,000 barrels	$18,000	$20,000	$22,000
+ Payoff on short futures position	2,000	0	(2,000)
Net revenue	$20,000	$20,000	$20,000

The benefit of futures is the ability to lock in a riskless position without paying any money. The benefit of the option hedge is that you benefit if prices move in one direction without losing if they move in the other direction. However, this asymmetry comes at a price: the cost of the option.

11. No

13. The futures price is greater than the spot price for gold. This reflects the fact that the futures contract ensures your receipt of the gold without tying up your money now. The difference between the spot price and the futures price reflects compensation for the time value of money. Another way to put it is that the spot price must be lower than the futures price to compensate investors who buy and store gold for the opportunity cost of their funds until the futures maturity date.

15. Advantages: liquidity, no storage costs, no spoilage. Disadvantages: no income or benefits that could accrue from holding asset in portfolio.

Glossary

Accelerated Cost Recovery System (ACRS): Depreciation method that allows higher tax deductions in early years and lower deductions later.

acquisition: Takeover of a firm by purchase of that firm's common stock or assets.

additional paid-in capital: Difference between issue price and par value of stock. Also called *capital surplus*.

agency problems: Conflict of interest between the firm's owners and managers.

aging schedule: Classification of accounts receivable by time outstanding.

annual percentage rate (APR): Interest rate that is annualized using simple interest.

annuity: Equally spaced level stream of cash flows.

annuity due: Level stream of cash flows starting immediately.

annuity factor: Present value of a $1 annuity.

authorized share capital: Maximum number of shares that the company is permitted to issue, as specified in the firm's articles of incorporation.

availability float: Checks already deposited that have not yet been cleared.

average tax rate: Total taxes owed divided by total income.

balance sheet: Financial statement that shows the value of the firm's assets and liabilities at a particular time.

balancing item: Variable that adjusts to maintain the consistency of a financial plan. Also called *plug*.

bankruptcy: The reorganization or liquidation of a firm that cannot pay its debts.

beta: Sensitivity of a stock's return to the return on the market portfolio.

bond: Security that obligates the issuer to make specified payments to the bondholder.

book rate of return: Accounting income divided by book value. Also called *accounting rate of return*.

book value: Net worth of the firm's assets or liabilities according to the balance sheet.

break-even analysis: Analysis of the level of sales at which the company breaks even.

call option: Right to buy an asset at a specified exercise price on or before the exercise date.

callable bond: Bond that may be repurchased by the issuer before maturity at specified call price.

capital asset pricing model (CAPM): Theory of the relationship between risk and return which states that the expected risk premium on any security equals its beta times the market risk premium.

capital budget: List of planned investment projects.

capital budgeting decision: Decision as to which real assets the firm should acquire.

capital markets: Markets for long-term financing.

capital rationing: Limit set on the amount of funds available for investment.

capital structure: Firm's mix of long-term financing.

carrying costs: Costs of maintaining current assets, including opportunity cost of capital.

cash conversion cycle: Period between firm's payment for materials and collection on its sales.

cash dividend: Payment of cash by the firm to its shareholders.

chief financial officer (CFO): Officer who oversees the treasurer and controller and sets overall financial strategy.

collection policy: Procedures to collect and monitor receivables.

commercial paper: Short-term unsecured notes issued by firms.

common-size balance sheet: Balance sheet that presents items as a percentage of total assets.

common stock: Ownership shares in a publicly held corporation.

common-size income statement: Income statement that presents items as a percentage of revenues.

company cost of capital: Expected rate of return demanded by investors in a company, determined by the average risk of the company's assets and operations.

compound interest: Interest earned on interest.

concentration banking: System whereby customers make payments to a regional collection center which transfers funds to a principal bank.

constant-growth dividend discount model: Version of the dividend discount model in which dividends grow at a constant rate.

controller: Officer responsible for budgeting, accounting, and auditing.

convertible bond: Bond that the holder may exchange for a specified number of shares.

corporation: Business owned by stockholders who are not personally liable for the business's liabilities.

costs of financial distress: Costs arising from bankruptcy or distorted business decisions before bankruptcy.

coupon: The interest payments paid to the bondholder.

coupon rate: Annual interest payment as a percentage of face value.

credit analysis: Procedure to determine the likelihood a customer will pay its bills.

credit policy: Standards set to determine the amount and nature of credit to extend to customers.

cumulative voting: Voting system in which all the votes one shareholder is allowed to cast can be cast for one candidate for the board of directors.

current yield: Annual coupon payments divided by bond price.

decision tree: Diagram of sequential decisions and possible outcomes.

default premium: Difference in promised yields between a default-free bond and a riskier bond.

degree of operating leverage (DOL): Percentage change in profits given a 1 percent change in sales.

depreciation tax shield: Reduction in taxes attributable to the depreciation allowance.

discount factor: Present value of a $1 future payment.

discount rate: Interest rate used to compute present values of future cash flows.

diversification: Strategy designed to reduce risk by spreading the portfolio across many investments.

dividend: Periodic cash distribution from the firm to its shareholders.

dividend discount model: Computation of today's stock price which states that share value equals the present value of all expected future dividends.

dividend payout ratio: Percentage of earnings paid out as dividends.

Dow Jones Industrial Average: Index of the investment performance of a portfolio of 30 "blue-chip" stocks.

Du Pont system: A breakdown of ROE and ROA into component ratios.

economic order quantity: Order size that minimizes total inventory costs.

effective annual interest rate: Interest rate that is annualized using compound interest.

efficient capital markets: Financial markets in which security prices rapidly reflect all relevant information about asset values.

equivalent annual cost: The cost per period with the same present value as the cost of buying and operating a machine.

eurobond: Bond that is marketed internationally.

eurodollars: Dollars held on deposit in a bank outside the United States.

exchange rate: Amount of one currency needed to purchase one unit of another.

ex-dividend date: Date that determines whether a stockholder is entitled to a dividend payment; anyone holding stock before this date is entitled to a dividend.

expectations theory of exchange rates: Theory that expected spot exchange rate equals the forward rate.

face value: Payment at the maturity of the bond. Also called *par value* or *maturity value*.

financial assets: Claims to the income generated by real assets. Also called *securities*.

financial intermediary: Firm that raises money from many small investors and provides financing to businesses or other organizations by investing in their securities.

financial leverage: Increase in the variability of shareholder returns that comes from the use of debt.

financial markets: Markets in which financial assets are traded.

financial risk: Risk to shareholders resulting from the use of debt.

financing decision: Decision as to how to raise the money to pay for investments in real assets.

fixed costs: Costs that do not depend on the level of output.

floating-rate security: Security paying dividends or interest that vary with short-term interest rates.

forward contract: Agreement to buy or sell an asset in the future at an agreed price.

forward exchange rate: Exchange rate for a forward transaction.

fundamental analysts: Analysts who attempt to find under- or overvalued securities by analyzing fundamental information, such as earnings, asset values, and business prospects.

funded debt: Debt with more than 1 year remaining to maturity.

future value: Amount to which an investment will grow after earning interest.

futures contract: Exchange-traded promise to buy or sell an asset in the future at a prespecified price.

general cash offer: Sale of securities open to all investors by an already-public company.

generally accepted accounting principles (GAAP): Procedures for preparing financial statements.

income statement: Financial statement that shows the revenues, expenses, and net income of a firm over a period of time.

inflation: Rate at which prices as a whole are increasing.

information content of dividends: Dividend increases send good news about cash flow and earnings. Dividend cuts send bad news.

initial public offering (IPO): First offering of stock to the general public.

interest rate parity: Theory that forward premium equals interest rate differential.

interest tax shield: Tax savings resulting from deductibility of interest payments.

internal growth rate: Maximum rate of growth without external financing.

internal rate of return (IRR): Discount rate at which project NPV = 0.

internally generated funds: Cash reinvested in the firm; depreciation plus earnings not paid out as dividends.

international Fisher effect: Theory that real interest rates in all countries should be equal, with differences in nominal rates reflecting differences in expected inflation.

investment grade: Bonds rated Baa or above by Moody's or BBB or above by Standard & Poor's.

issued shares: Shares that have been issued by the company.

junk bond: Bond with a rating below Baa or BBB.

law of one price: Theory that prices of goods in all countries should be equal when translated to a common currency.

lease: Long-term rental agreement.

leveraged buy-out (LBO): Acquisition of the firm by a private group using substantial borrowed funds.

limited liability: The owners of the corporation are not personally responsible for its obligations.

line of credit: Agreement by a bank that a company may borrow at any time up to an established limit.

liquidation: Sale of bankrupt firm's assets.

liquidation value: Net proceeds that would be realized by selling the firm's assets and paying off its creditors.

liquidity: Ability of an asset to be converted to cash quickly at low cost.

lock-box system: System whereby customers send payments to a post office box and a local bank collects and processes checks.

majority voting: Voting system in which each director is voted on separately.

management buy-out (MBO): Acquisition of the firm by its own management in a leveraged buy-out.

marginal tax rate: Additional taxes owed per dollar of additional income.

market index: Measure of the investment performance of the overall market.

market portfolio: Portfolio of all assets in the economy. In practice a broad stock market index, such as the Standard & Poor's Composite, is used to represent the market.

market risk: Economy-wide (macroeconomic) sources of risk that affect the overall stock market. Also called *systematic risk.*

market risk premium: Risk premium of market portfolio. Difference between market return and return on risk-free Treasury bills.

market-value balance sheet: Financial statement that uses the market value of all assets and liabilities.

maturity premium: Extra average return from investing in long- versus short-term Treasury securities.

merger: Combination of two firms into one, with the acquirer assuming assets and liabilities of the target firm.

MM dividend-irrelevance proposition: Theory that under ideal conditions, the value of the firm is unaffected by dividend policy.

MM's proposition I (debt irrelevance proposition): The value of a firm is unaffected by its capital structure.

MM's proposition II: The required rate of return on equity increases as the firm's debt-equity ratio increases

money market: Market for short-term financial assets.

mutually exclusive projects: Two or more projects that cannot be pursued simultaneously.

net float: Difference between payment float and availability float.

net present value (NPV): Present value of cash flows minus initial investment.

net working capital: Current assets minus current liabilities.

net worth: Book value of common stockholders' equity plus preferred stock.

nominal interest rate: Rate at which money invested grows.

open account: Agreement whereby sales are made with no formal debt contract.

operating leverage: Degree to which costs are fixed.

operating risk, business risk: Risk in firm's operating income.

opportunity cost of capital: Expected rate of return given up by investing in a project.

opportunity cost: Benefit or cash flow forgone as a result of an action.

outstanding shares: Shares that have been issued by the company and are held by investors.

par value: Value of security shown on certificate.

partnership: Business owned by two or more persons who are personally responsible for all its liabilities.

payback period: Time until cash flows recover the initial investment of the project.

payment float: Checks written by a company that have not yet cleared.

payout ratio: Fraction of earnings paid out as dividends.

pecking order theory: Theory stating that firms prefer to issue debt rather than equity if internal finance is insufficient.

percentage of sales models: Planning model in which sales forecasts are the driving variables and most other variables are proportional to sales.

perpetuity: Stream of level cash payments that never ends.

planning horizon: Time horizon for a financial plan.

plowback ratio: Fraction of earnings retained by the firm.

poison pill: Measure taken by a target firm to avoid acquisition; for example, the right for existing shareholders to buy additional shares at an attractive price if a bidder acquires a large holding.

preferred stock: Stock that takes priority over common stock in regard to dividends.

present value (PV): Value today of a future cash flow.

present value of growth opportunities (PVGO): Net present value of a firm's future investments.

price-earnings (P/E) multiple: Ratio of stock price to earnings per share.

primary market: Market for the sale of new securities by corporations.

prime rate: Benchmark interest rate charged by banks.

private placement: Sale of securities to a limited number of investors without a public offering.

pro formas: Projected or forecasted financial statements.

profitability index: Ratio of net present value to initial investment.

project cost of capital: Minimum acceptable expected rate of return on a project given its risk.

prospectus: Formal summary that provides information on an issue of securities.

protective covenant: Restriction on a firm to protect bondholders.

proxy contest: Takeover attempt in which outsiders compete with management for shareholders' votes. Also called *proxy fight.*

purchasing power parity (PPP): Theory that the cost of living in different countries is equal, and exchange rates adjust to offset inflation differentials across countries.

put option: Right to sell an asset at a specified exercise price on or before the exercise date.

random walk: Security prices change randomly, with no predictable trends or patterns.

rate of return: Total income per period per dollar invested.

real assets: Assets used to produce goods and services.

real interest rate: Rate at which the purchasing power of an investment increases.

real options: Options embedded in real assets.

real value of $1: Purchasing power-adjusted value of a dollar.

reorganization: Restructuring of financial claims on failing firm to allow it to keep operating.

restructuring: Process of changing the firm's capital structure without changing its assets.

retained earnings: Earnings not paid out as dividends.

rights issue: Issue of securities offered only to current stockholders.

risk premium: Expected return in excess of risk-free return as compensation for risk.

scenario analysis: Project analysis given a particular combination of assumptions.

seasoned offering: Sale of securities by a firm that is already publicly traded.

secondary market: Market in which already issued securities are traded among investors.

secured debt: Debt that has first claim on specified collateral in the event of default.

security market line: Relationship between expected return and beta.

semi-strong-form efficiency: Market prices reflect all publicly available information.

sensitivity analysis: Analysis of the effects of changes in sales, costs, and so on, on project profitability.

shark repellent: Amendments to a company charter made to forestall takeover attempts.

shelf registration: A procedure that allows firms to file one registration statement for several issues of the same security.

shortage costs: Costs incurred from shortages in current assets.

simple interest: Interest earned only on the original investment; no interest is earned on interest.

simulation analysis: Estimation of the probabilities of different possible outcomes, e.g., from an investment project.

sinking fund: Fund established to retire debt before maturity.

sole proprietor: Sole owner of a business which has no partners and no shareholders. The proprietor is personally liable for all the firm's obligations.

spot rate of exchange: Exchange rate for an immediate transaction.

spread: Difference between public offer price and price paid by underwriter.

stakeholder: Anyone with a financial interest in the firm.

Standard & Poor's Composite Index: Index of the investment performance of a portfolio of 500 large stocks. Also called the *S&P 500.*

standard deviation: Square root of variance. Another measure of volatility.

statement of cash flows: Financial statement that shows the firm's cash receipts and cash payments over a period of time.

stock dividend: Distribution of additional shares to a firm's stockholders.

stock repurchase: Firm buys back stock from its shareholders.

stock split: Issue of additional shares to firm's stockholders.

straight-line depreciation: Constant depreciation for each year of the asset's accounting life.

strong-form efficiency: Market prices rapidly reflect all information that could in principle be used to determine true value.

subordinated debt: Debt that may be repaid in bankruptcy only after senior debt is paid.

sustainable growth rate: Steady rate at which a firm can grow without changing leverage; plowback ratio $\times$ return on equity.

swap: Arrangement by two counterparties to exchange one stream of cash flows for another.

technical analysts: Investors who attempt to identify over- or undervalued stocks by searching for patterns in past prices.

tender offer: Takeover attempt in which outsiders directly offer to buy the stock of the firm's shareholders.

terms of sale: Credit, discount, and payment terms offered on a sale.

trade-off theory: Theory that capital structure is based on a trade-off between tax savings and distress costs of debt.

treasurer: Manager responsible for financing, cash management, and relationships with financial markets and institutions.

treasury stock: Stock that has been repurchased by the company and held in its treasury.

underpricing: Issuing securities at an offering price set below the true value of the security.

underwriter: Firm that buys an issue of securities from a company and resells it to the public.

unique risk: Risk factors affecting only that firm. Also called *diversifiable risk.*

variable costs: Costs that change as the level of output changes.

variance: Average value of squared deviations from mean. A measure of volatility.

venture capital: Money invested to finance a new firm.

warrant: Right to buy shares from a company at a stipulated price before a set date.

weak-form efficiency: Market prices rapidly reflect all information contained in the history of past prices.

weighted-average cost of capital (WACC): Expected rate of return on a portfolio of all the firm's securities.

white knight: Friendly potential acquirer sought by a target company threatened by an unwelcome suitor.

workout: Agreement between a company and its creditors establishing the steps the company must take to avoid bankruptcy.

yield curve: Graph of the relationship between time to maturity and yield to maturity.

yield to maturity: Interest rate for which the present value of the bond's payments equals the price.

zero-balance account: Regional bank account to which just enough funds are transferred daily to pay each day's bills.

Index